READINGS IN

Multimedia Computing
and Networking

THE MORGAN KAUFMANN SERIES IN

Multimedia Information and Systems

SERIES EDITOR:

Edward A. Fox
Virginia Polytechnic University

READINGS IN
Multimedia Computing
and Networking

Kevin Jeffay
University of North Carolina - Chapel Hill

HongJiang Zhang
Microsoft Research, China

MORGAN KAUFMANN PUBLISHERS

AN IMPRINT OF ACADEMIC PRESS
A Harcourt Science and Technology Company
SAN FRANCISCO   SAN DIEGO   NEW YORK   BOSTON
LONDON   SYDNEY   TOKYO

Senior Editor Rick Adams
Publishing Services Manager Scott Norton
Assistant Acquisitions Editor Karyn P. Johnson
Assistant Development Editor Marilyn Alan
Production Coordinator Mei Levenson
Cover Design Ross Carron Design
Cover Image Kent A. Hall/Modern Bovary
Text Design/Technical Illustration/Composition Susan M. Sheldrake/ShelDragon Graphic Design
Copyeditor Erin Milnes
Proofreader Mei Levenson
Printer Victor Graphics

Designations used by companies to distinguish their products are often claimed as trademarks or registered trademarks. In all instances in which Morgan Kaufmann Publishers is aware of a claim, the product names appear in initial capital or all capital letters. Readers, however, should contact the appropriate companies for more complete information regarding trademarks and registration.

Morgan Kaufmann Publishers
340 Pine Street, Sixth Floor, San Francisco, CA 94104-3205, USA

ACADEMIC PRESS
A Harcourt Science and Technology Company
525 B Street, Suite 1900, San Diego, CA 92101-4495, USA
http://www.academicpress.com

Academic Press
Harcourt Place, 32 Jamestown Road, London, NW1 7BY, United Kingdom
http://www.academicpress.com

Library of Congress Control Number: 2001090720
ISBN 1-55860-651-3

This book is printed on acid-free paper.

Contents

CHAPTER 3   AUDIO RETRIEVAL AND NAVIGATION INTERFACES   199
Philippe Aigrain

CHAPTER 4   CONTENT-BASED IMAGE INDEXING AND RETRIEVAL   247
HongJiang Zhang

Part II: Systems, Networking and Tools

Foreword

Edward A. Fox

Virginia Polytechnical University

I AM pleased to introduce *Readings in Multimedia Computing and Networking*, which has been a goal of the Multimedia Information and Systems Series at Morgan Kaufmann for a number of years. Many have encouraged and assisted in this work. I am grateful to all of those who have contributed to bringing this important project to fruition, especially the editors.

The editors have added substantial value to this volume. It was a pleasure to work with the contributing editors who introduce each group of papers. I learned a good deal, gaining a clearer perspective on where the field has been and where it is going. I am grateful for their extra work done in response to some of my questions and suggestions regarding early drafts. Having a group of the top researchers in the field—who help set the tone for future inventions and discoveries—discuss the seminal papers and suggest the best sources for additional study helped bring me up-to-date across the board in this rapidly developing area. I know of no other place where so much important information about multimedia can be found.

This book helps demonstrate the progress, and the importance of the multimedia field. It makes clear that there is a substantial body of scholarly literature, significant research results, and agreement on what is at the core of the field. *Readings in Multimedia Computing and Networking* marks a significant milestone in the maturity of the discipline.

This book makes it easy for instructors of courses on multimedia to refer to seminal papers. It also simplifies for instructors the task of discussing the research literature in seminars by enabling them to build upon both the papers and the chapter introductions. Graduate students embarking on advanced studies in the field can refer to become broadly grounded in the fundamental work on which they may build new systems and results. It can provide the basis for graduate-level qualifying or comprehensive examinations that assess the knowledge of candidates wishing to add new research results to the area. For practitioners, it is a handy reference volume. For scholars it also serves as an excellent annotated bibliography. Indeed, while the contents come from key journals, conferences, and workshops, the references cover most of the broad range of relevant publications, drawing together and elucidating a very large body of literature.

The volume editors and the contributing editors, as well as the authors of the papers, constitute a representative cross-section of the community of multimedia researchers and developers. They are drawn from corporate, academic, and government settings and come from many different countries around the globe. They include theoreticians, experimentalists, designers, and implementers. They have interest in multimedia itself and also may have interest in one or more of a number of diverse yet related fields, including but not limited to the following:

- Algorithms
- Database management
- High-performance computing
- Human-computer interaction
- Information retrieval
- Internet
- Operating systems
- Networking
- Probability
- Real-time systems
- Security
- Signal processing
- Speech
- Storage
- WWW

This book is important in part because of the impact of multimedia on a broad range of activities in the information age. Everywhere we see efforts to digitize content across the various media types. We are surrounded by consumer products, which depend upon the advances chronicled in this book. Supporting entertainment for the young (at heart), MP3 is a very popular way to manage audio, while multimedia interactive games are ubiquitous. For videophiles, DVD and high-quality TV are viewed as the first serious consumer-oriented advance in decades. For photographers, digital cameras are growing in popularity, while digital camcorders are making serious inroads into the world of videography. New audio recordings, soundtracks, and motion pictures all benefit from multimedia technology and tools. Already, some of our requirements for travel and education are met by videoconferencing and video streaming.

The fruits of the multimedia field are evident in the equipment (*e.g.*, hardware, networking) and software (*e.g.*, tools, programs) that have emerged. These have supported many investigations and studies that have led to refinements and improvements, in many cases yielding standards, which in turn have facilitated the emergence of important industries. But in this field, successes are just interim steps on the path to even higher quality. Solid work on serious problems like synchronization and jitter have yielded useful models and helpful techniques. These techniques and models facilitate efforts to achieve engineering compromises and solutions, in lieu of constraints of space and bandwidth, and have led to solutions in spite of the costs for processing and storage, and the inevitable congestion faced on networks, regardless of their speed. And these have been shown to apply across a broad range of variations among users and applications. They allow adjustments to requirements regarding quality, accounting for constraints on loss that depend on a developing understanding of human perception (*e.g.*, as studied in fields like psychoacoustics).

This work also covers the many techniques that have evolved in the last decade. Handling multimedia requires compression, which in turn depends on coding. At the heart of multimedia is content, which must be processed; this may require analysis, indexing, and summarization to support activities like browsing and querying. Other important techniques include modeling and simulation, and the identification and validation of suitable architectures. Since multimedia involves people using computers, human-computer interfaces play an important role. Multimedia in turn can liberate such interfaces from the keyboard and mouse, allowing people to gesture, hum, or work in three or higher dimensional spaces (*e.g.*, 3D with motion and sonification). We still face challenges in authoring for these rich environments, and in better understanding not only color but also shape, texture, and the many manifestations of structure.

We hope that *Readings in Multimedia Computing and Networking* convinces you of the importance of multimedia as an integrative home for exciting work in computing, whether you investigate this field further or apply some of its concepts and exciting applications to increase interest in fields like those listed above. Please share with us your perspective on this volume, and let us know what novel uses you make of it!

Acknowledgments

E. Zwicker and U. Tilmann Zwicker, "Audio engineering and psychoacoustics: Matching signals to the final receiver, the human auditory system," *Journal Audio Engineering Society* 39, no. 3, (March 1991): 115–26. Copyright © 1996 Audio Engineering Society. Reprinted with permission.

A. Gersho, "Advances in speech and audio compression," in *Proceedings of the IEEE* 82, no. 6 (June 1994): 900–18. Copyright © 1994 IEEE. Reprinted with permission.

D. Pan, "A tutorial on MPEG/Audio compression," *IEEE Multimedia* 2, no. 2 (Summer 1995): 60–74. Copyright © 1995 IEEE. Reprinted with permission.

E. D. Scheirer, "Structured audio and effects processing in the MPEG-4 multimedia standard," *Multimedia Systems Journal* 7, no. 1 (1999): 11–22. Copyright © 1999 Springer-Verlag. Reprinted with permission.

C. Kyriakakis, "Fundamental and technological limitation of immersive audio system," in *Proceedings of the IEEE* 86, no. 5 (May 1998): 941–51. Copyright © 1998 IEEE. Reprinted with permission.

B. G. Haskell, P. G. Howard, Y. A. LeCun, A. Puri, J. Ostermann, M. R. Civanlar, L. Raminer, L. Bottou, and P. Haffner, "Image and video coding—Emerging standards and beyond," *IEEE Transactions on Circuits and Systems for Video Technology* 8, no. 7 (Nov. 1998): 814–837. Copyright © 1998 IEEE. Reprinted with permission.

R. B. Arps and T. K. Truong, "Comparison of international standards for lossless still image compression," in *Proceedings of the IEEE* 82, no. 6 (June 1994): 889–99. Copyright © 1994 IEEE. Reprinted with permission.

J. M. Shapiro, "Embedded image coding using zerotrees of wavelets coefficients," *IEEE Transactions on Signal Processing* 41 (Dec. 1993): 3445–62. Copyright © 1993 IEEE. Reprinted with permission.

T. Sikora, "The MPEG-4 video standard verification model," *IEEE Transactions on Circuits and Systems for Video Technology* 7, no. 1 (1997): 19–31. Copyright © 1997 IEEE. Reprinted with permission.

M. D. Swanson, M. Kobayashi, and A. H. Tewfik, "Multimedia data-embedding and watermarking technologies," in *Proceedings of the IEEE* 86, no. 6 (June 1998): 1064–83. Copyright © 1998 IEEE. Reprinted with permission.

B. C. Smith and L. A. Rowe, "Algorithms for manipulating compressed images," *IEEE Computer Graphics and Applications* 13, no. 5 (1993): 34–42. Copyright © 1993 IEEE. Reprinted with permission.

S.-F. Chang and D. G. Messerschmitt, "Manipulation and compositing of MC-DCT compressed video," *IEEE Journal of Selected Areas in Communications: Special Issue on Intelligent Signal Processing* 13, no. 1 (Jan. 1995): 1–11. Copyright © 1995 IEEE. Reprinted with permission.

P. Aigrain, P. Joly, P. Lepain, and V. Longueville, "Representation-based user interfaces for the Audiovisual Library of Year 2000," in *Proceedings of IS&T/SPIE 95 Multimedia Computing and Networking Conference,* SPIE 2417 (1995): 35–45. Copyright © 1995 SPIE—The International Society for Optical Engineering. Reprinted with permission.

A. Ghias, J. Logan, D. Chamberlain, B. C. Smith, "Query by humming: Music information retrieval in an audio database," in *Proceedings of ACM Multimedia 95,* 231–36. Copyright ©

1999, Association for Computing Machinery, Inc. Reprinted with permission.

E. Wold, T. Blum, D. Keisler, and J. Wheaton, "Audio databases with content-based retrieval," *IEEE MultiMedia* 3, no. 3 (Fall 1996): 27–36. Copyright © 1996 IEEE. Reprinted with permission.

L. Wyse and S. W. Smoliar, "Toward content-based audio indexing and retrieval and a new speaker discrimination technique," in *Computational Auditory Scene Analysis: Proceedings of the IJCAI 95 Workshop*, D. F. Rosenthal and H. G. Okuno, eds., (1995): 351–60. Copyright © 1998 Lawrence Erlbaum. Reprinted with permission.

M. G. Brown, J. T. Foote, G.J.F. Jones, K. Sparck Jones, and S. J. Young, "Open-vocabulary speech indexing for voice and video mail retrieval," in *Proceedings of ACM Multimedia 96* (1996): 307-316. Best paper award at the conference. Copyright © 1996, Association for Computing Machinery, Inc. Reprinted with permission.

M. Flickner, H. Sawhney, W. Niblack, J. Ashley, Q. Huang, B. Dom, M. Gorkani, J. Hafner, D. Lee, D. Petkovic, D. Steele, and P. Yanker, "Query by image and video content: The QBIC system," *IEEE Computer Magazine* 28, no. 9 (Sept. 1995): 23–32. Copyright © 1995 IEEE. Reprinted with permission.

M. J. Swain and D. H. Ballard, "Color indexing," *International Journal of Computer Vision* 7, no. 1 (1991): 11–32. Copyright © 1995 Kluwer Academic Publishers. Reprinted with permission.

H.J. Zhang and D. Zhong, "A scheme for visual feature based image indexing," in *Proceedings of SPIE Conference on Storage and Retrieval for Image and Video Database* (1995): 36–46. Copyright © 1995 SPIE—The International Society for Optical Engineering. Reprinted with permission.

T. P. Minka and R. W. Picard, "Interactive learning with a 'society of models,'" *Pattern Recognition* 30, no. 4 (1997): 447–52. Copyright © 1997 Elsevier Science. Reprinted with permission.

I. J. Cox, M. L. Miller, T. P. Minka, T. V. Papathomas, P. N. Yianilos, "The Bayesian image retrieval system, *PicHunter*: Theory, implementation and psychophysical experiments," *IEEE Transactions on Image Processing* 9, no. 1 (2000): 20–37. Copyright © 2000 IEEE. Reprinted with permission.

H.J. Zhang, A. Kankanhali, and S. W. Smoliar, "Automatic partitioning of full-motion video," *Multimedia Systems Journal* 1, no. 1 (July 1993): 10–28. Copyright © 1993 Springer-Verlag. Reprinted with permission.

Y. Tonomura, A. Akutsu, Y. Taniguchi, and G. Suzuki, "Structured video computing," *IEEE Multimedia Magazine* 1, no. 3 (Fall 1994): 34–43. Copyright © 1994 IEEE. Reprinted with permission.

H.J. Zhang, C. Y. Low, S. W. Smoliar, and D. Zhong, "Video parsing, retrieval and browsing: An integrated and content-based solution," in *Proceedings of ACM Multimedia* (1995): 15–24. Also in *Intelligent Multimedia Information Retrieval*, M. T. Maybury, ed., AAAI Press and MIT Press. Copyright © 1999, Association for Computing Machinery, Inc. Reprinted with permission.

M. Yeung, B.-L. Yeo, and B. Liu, "Extracting story units from long programs for video browsing and navigation," in *Proceedings of the IEEE International Conference on Multimedia Computing and Systems* (1996): 509–16. Copyright © 1996 IEEE. Reprinted with permission.

M. A. Smith and T. Kanade, "Video skimming and characterization through the combination of image and language understanding techniques," in *Proceedings of CVPR 97: Computer Vision and Pattern Recognition* (1997): 775–81. Copyright © 1997 IEEE. Reprinted with permission.

J. D. N. Dionisio and A. F. Cárdenas, "A unified data model for representing multi-media, timeline, and simulation data," *IEEE Transactions on Knowledge and Data Engineering* 10, no. 5 (Sept./Oct. 1998): 746–67. Copyright © 1998 IEEE. Reprinted with permission.

T. Lee, L. Sheng, T. Bozkaya, N. H. Balkir, Z. M. Özsoyoglu, and G. Özsoyoglu, "Querying multimedia presentations based on content," *IEEE Transactions on Knowledge and Data*

Engineering 11, no. 3 (May/June 1999): 361–85. Copyright © 1999 IEEE. Reprinted with permission.

A. Zhang, W. Chang, G. Sheikholeslami, and T. F. Syeda-Mahmood, "NetView: A framework for integration of large-scale distributed visual databases," *IEEE Multimedia* 5, no. 3 (July–Sept. 1998): 47–59. Copyright © 1998 IEEE. Reprinted with permission.

S. Berchtold, D. A. Keim, and H.-P. Kriegel, "The X-tree: An index Structure for high-dimensional data," in *Proceedings of the 22nd International Conference on Very Large Databases (VLDB 96)* (1996): 28–39. Copyright © 1996 VLDB Endowment. Reprinted with permission.

M. B. Jones, J. S. Barrera III, A. Forin, P. J. Leach, D. Rosu, and M. C. Rosu, "An overview of the Rialto real-time architecture," *ACM SIGOPS European Workshop* (1996): 249–56. Copyright © 1996, Association for Computing Machinery, Inc. Reprinted with permission.

R. Rajkumar, K. Juvva, A. Molano, and S. Oikawa, "Resource kernels: A resource-centric approach to real-time and multimedia systems," in *Proceedings of the SPIE/ACM Conference on Multimedia Computing and Networking* 3310 (1997): 150–65. Copyright © 1998 SPIE—The International Society for Optical Engineering. Reprinted with permission.

P. Goyal, X. Guo, and H. M. Vin, "A hierarchical CPU scheduler for multimedia operating systems," in *Proceedings of the IEEE International Conference On Multimedia Computing and Systems* (1996): 1–15. Copyright © 1996 IEEE. Reprinted with permission.

J. Nieh and M. S. Lam, "The design, implementation and evaluation of SMART: A scheduler for multimedia applications," *ACM Symposium on Operating Systems Principles* (1997): 1–14. Copyright © 1997, Association for Computing Machinery, Inc. Reprinted with permission.

D. L. Stone and K. Jeffay, "An empirical study of delay jitter management policies," *Multimedia Systems Journal* 2, no. 6 (Jan.
1995): 267–79. Copyright © 1995 Springer-Verlag. Reprinted with permission.

L. Delgrossi, C. Halstrick, D. Hehmann, R. G. Herrtwich, O. Krone, J. Sandvoss, and C. Vogt, "Media scaling for audiovisual communication with the Heidelberg transport system," in *Proceedings of ACM Multimedia 93* (1993): 99–104. Copyright © 1993, Association for Computing Machinery, Inc. Reprinted with permission.

I. Rhee, "Retransmission-based error control for interactive video applications over the Internet," in *Proceedings of the IEEE International Conference On Multimedia Computing and Systems* (1998): 118–27. Copyright © 1998 IEEE. Reprinted with permission.

E. A. Isaacs and J. C. Tang, "What video can and cannot do for collaboration: A case study," *Multimedia Systems Journal* 2 (1994): 63–73. Copyright © 1994 Springer-Verlag. Reprinted with permission.

S. McCanne and V. Jacobson, "vic: A flexible framework for packet video," in *Proceedings of ACM Multimedia* (1995): 511–22. Copyright © 1995, Association for Computing Machinery, Inc. Reprinted with permission.

P. Nee, K. Jeffay, and G. Danneels, "The performance of two-dimensional media scaling for Internet video conferencing," *NOSSDAV 97: Proceedings of the International Workshop on Network and Operating System Support for Digital Audio and Video* (1997): 223–34. Copyright © 1997 IEEE. Reprinted with permission.

S. McCanne, V. Jacobson, and M. Vetterli, "Receiver-driven layered multicast," *ACM SIGCOMM 96* (1996): 117–30. Copyright © 1996, Association for Computing Machinery, Inc. Reprinted with permission.

C. Perkins, O. Hodson, and V. Hardman, "A survey of packet-loss recovery techniques for streaming audio," *IEEE Network Magazine* (September/October 1998): 40–8. Copyright © 1998 IEEE. Reprinted with permission.

J.-C. Bolot, S. Fosse-Parisis, and D. Towsley, "Adaptive FEC-based error control for Internet telephony," in *Proceedings of Infocom 99* (1999): 1453–60. Copyright © 1999 IEEE.

Reprinted with permission.

L. Zhang, S. Deering, D. Estrin, S. Shenker, and D. Zappala, "RSVP: A new resource ReSerVation protocol," *IEEE Network* 5, no. 5 (September 1993): 8–18. Copyright © 1993 IEEE. Reprinted with permission.

H. Schulzrinne and J. Rosenberg, "Internet Telephony: Architecture and protocols—an IETF perspective," *Computer Networks* 31 (1999): 237–55. Copyright © 1999 Elsevier Science. Reprinted with permission.

D. J. Gemmell, H. M. Vin, D. D. Kandlur, P. V. Rangan, and L A. Rowe, "Multimedia storage servers: A tutorial," *IEEE Computer* (May 1995): 40–49. Copyright © 1995 IEEE. Reprinted with permission.

Y. Birk, "Random RAIDs with selective exploitation of redundancy for high performance video servers," *NOSSDAV'97: Proceedings of the 7th International Workshop on Network and Operating System Support for Digital Audio and Video* (1997): 13–24. Copyright © 1997 IEEE. Reprinted with permission.

A. L. Narasimha Reddy and J. Wyllie, "Disk scheduling in a multimedia I/O system," in *Proceedings of ACM Multimedia 93* (1993): 225–34. Copyright © 1993, Association for Computing Machinery, Inc. Reprinted with permission.

H. M. Vin, P. Goyal, A. Goyal, and A. Goyal, "A statistical admission control algorithm for multimedia servers," in *Proceedings of ACM Multimedia 94* (1994): 33–40. Copyright © 1994, Association for Computing Machinery, Inc. Reprinted with permission.

A. Dan and D. Sitaram, "A generalized interval caching policy for mixed interactive and long video workloads," in *Proceedings of IS&T SPIE Multimedia Computing and Networking Conference 96* (1996): 344–51. Copyright © 1996 SPIE—The International Society for Optical Engineering. Reprinted with permission.

C. Aggarwal, J. Wolf, and P. S. Yu, "On optimal piggyback merging policies for video-on-demand systems," in *Proceedings of ACM SIGMETRICS 96* (1996): 200–09. Copyright © 1996, Association for Computing Machinery, Inc. Reprinted with permission.

M. J. J. Pérez-Luque and T.D.C. Little, "A temporal reference framework for multimedia synchronization," *IEEE Journal on Selected Areas in Communication* 14, no. 1 (Jan. 1996): 5–35. Copyright © 1996 IEEE. Reprinted with permission.

R. Steinmetz and C. Engler, "Human perception of media synchronization," Technical Report #43.9310, IBM European Networking Center, Heidelberg, Germany, (Aug. 1993): 1-31. Copyright © 1993 IBM Germany. Reprinted with permission.

D. L. Mills, "Improved algorithms for synchronizing computer network clocks," *IEEE/ACM Transactions on Networking* 3, no. 3 (June 1995): 245–54. Copyright © 1995 IEEE. Reprinted with permission.

B. Bailey, J. A. Konstan, R. Cooley, and M. Dejong, "Nsync—A toolkit for building intractive multimedia presentations," in *Proceedings of ACM Multimmedia 98* (1998): 257–66. Copyright © 1998, Association for Computing Machinery, Inc. Reprinted with permission.

B. K. Schmidt, J. D. Northcutt, and M. S. Lam, "A method and apparatus for measuring media synchronization," *NOSSDAV 95: Proceedings of the International Workshop on Network and Operating System Support for Digital Audio and Video* (1995): 203–14. Copyright © 1995 IEEE. Reprinted with permission.

L. Hardman, D.C.A. Bulterman, and G. van Rossum, "The Amsterdam hypermedia model," *Communications of the ACM* 37, no. 2 (Feb. 1994): 50–62. Copyright © 1994, Association for Computing Machinery, Inc. Reprinted with permission.

F. Garzotto, P. Paolini, and D. Schwabe, "HDM—A model-based approach to hypertext application design," *ACM Transactions on Information Systems* 11, no. 1 (Jan. 1993): 1–26. Copyright © 1993, Association for Computing Machinery, Inc. Reprinted with permission.

M. C. Buchanan and P. T. Zellweger, "Automatic temporal layout mechanisms," in *Proceedings of ACM Multimedia 93* (1993): 341–50. Copyright © 1993, Association for Computing Machinery, Inc. Reprinted with permission.

D.C.A. Bulterman, L. Hardman, J. Jansen, K. S. Mullender, and L. Rutledge, "GRiNS: A GRaphical INterface for creating and playing SMIL documents," *Computer Networks and ISDN Systems* 30 (Sept. 1998): 519–29. Copyright © 1998 Elsevier Science. Reprinted with permission.

M. Jourdan, C. Roisin, and L. Tardif, "Multiviews interfaces for multimedia authoring environments," in *Proceedings of Multimedia Modeling 98* (1998): 72–9. Copyright © 1998 IEEE. Reprinted with permission.

R. Baecker, A. J. Rosenthal, N. Friedlander, E. Smith, and A. Cohen, "A multimedia system for authoring motion pictures," in *Proceedings of ACM Multimedia 96* (1996) 31–42. Copyright © 1996, Association for Computing Machinery, Inc. Reprinted with permission.

Introduction

Kevin Jeffay
University of North Carolina - Chapel Hill

HongJiang Zhang
Microsoft Research, China

READINGS in Multimedia Computing is a collection of seminal research papers culled from the literature of the last ten years. Although the origins of multimedia computing and networking can be traced back to the development of systems such as the AT&T Picturephone in the late 1960s, it wasn't until the 1990s that the field came into its own. The development and mass marketing of the "cheap" personal computer with a CD-ROM drive and a processor powerful enough to process and display multimedia streams enabled the widespread development of multimedia applications for education and training, as well as entertainment and gaming. The privatization and the accessibility of the Internet motivated the use of personal computers as communication devices that could integrate applications such as audio and video conferencing into your desktop computing environment to create a computer-supported collaborative system. And then came the World Wide Web! The text and command-line oriented applications such as *ftp* and *gopher* were replaced overnight by Web browsers, and shared files were largely replaced by multimedia Web pages and streaming media.

These developments fueled a boom in multimedia research. Indeed, virtually every subdiscipline of computer science research has considered the problem of supporting or processing multimedia data types. As a result, the field of multimedia computing is spread out across such diverse fields as image and signal processing, user interface design, operating systems, computer-supported cooperative work, networking, databases, and programming languages. To gain an overall perspective on the field you would have to search numerous proceedings and journals and follow the threads of research across several communities.

The goal of this text is to provide a roadmap through the field of multimedia computing and networking. We have assembled a dozen of the leading multimedia researchers and charged them with selecting the most important papers in their area of expertise. Each set of papers is presented as a chapter in the readings with an introduction to the field and the selected papers written by the chapter editor. By reading a given chapter you will learn about the fundamental problems, solutions, and research trends in a specific area of importance in multimedia computing. Given the chapter introductions, the papers are accessible to most professional computer scientists as well as graduate students and advanced undergraduates.

This book is divided into two parts. Part I considers the general area of multimedia processing and retrieval and includes the following chapters:

- *Digital audio*: edited by Hao Jiang and HongJiang Zhang, Microsoft Research, China.
- *Digital image and video compression and processing*: edited by Bing Zeng, The Hong Kong University of Science and Technology, Hong Kong.
- *Audio retrieval and navigation interfaces*: edited by Philippe Aigrain, European Commission, Belgium.
- *Content-based image indexing and retrieval*: edited by HongJiang Zhang, Microsoft Research, China.
- *Content-based video browsing and retrieval*: edited by HongJiang Zhang, Microsoft Research, China.

Part II considers the general area of network and computer system support for multimedia and includes the following chapters:

- *Multimedia database systems*: edited by Aidong Zhang, State University of New York - Buffalo.
- *Multimedia operating systems*: edited by Klara Nahrstedt, University of Illinois - Urbana-Champaign.
- *Videoconferencing*: edited by Kevin Jeffay, University of North Carolina at Chapel Hill.
- *Networking and media streaming*: edited by Ketan Mayer-Patel, University of North Carolina - Chapel Hill.
- *Multimedia servers*: edited by Prashant J. Shenoy, University of Massachusetts - Amherst, and Harrick M. Vin, University of Texas at Austin.
- *Multimedia synchronization*: edited by Lawrence A. Rowe, University of California - Berkeley.
- *Authoring systems*: edited by Dick C. A. Bulterman, Oratrix Development BV, Amsterdam.

Together, these chapters cover the "core" of multimedia computing and networking and provide an excellent starting point for the reader interested in multimedia research, engineering, and applications. For further reference, each chapter also includes suggestions for additional and more in-depth readings in the subject area. Many new research papers can also be found in the journals and conferences of the field. The principal journals are the following:

- *IEEE Transactions on Multimedia*
- ACM/Springer-Verlag journal *Multimedia Systems*
- *IEEE Transactions on Circuits and Systems for Video Technology*
- *IEEE Transactions on Image Processing*

The primary annual conferences focused on multimedia computing are the following:

- ACM International Conference on Multimedia
- IEEE International Conference on Multimedia and Expo
- ACM/SPIE Conference on Multimedia Computing and Networking (MMCN)

In addition to these publications, the professional magazine *IEEE Multimedia* provides good, timely survey articles on emerging technologies and applications.

In developing this text we received help from numerous individuals to whom we are greatly indebted. Brian Smith was one of the early contributors to this project and was instrumental in designing the overall structure of the this book and in selecting many of the papers that appear herein. It was Ed Fox who initiated the proposal of this project. We would also like to thank the following reviewers of this book's initial proposal for their suggestions that have helped significantly in shaping up this reader:

Meera Blattner; Wolfgang Effelsberg, University of Mannheim; Ed Fox, Virgina Tech; Stephan Fischer, Mobile Video Communication AG; Wu-chi Feng, Oregon Graduate Institute; Nicolas D. Georganas, University of Ottawa; Thomas D. C. Little, Boston University; Roy Rada, University of Maryland, Baltimore County; Douglas Reeves, North Carolina State University; David Slattner, Hewlett-Packard, U.K.; Michael Vernick, Lucent/Bell Labs; and Boon-Lock Yeo.

We are extraordinarily grateful for the patience and perseverance of, Jennifer Mann, Marilyn Alan, and Karyn Johnson, our editors at Morgan Kaufmann Publishers. Without their professional expertise and calm demeanor this project, which involved coordinating ten editors spread out across three continents, could never have been possible.

PART I
MULTIMEDIA PROCESSING AND RETRIEVAL

Introduction

HongJiang Zhang
Microsoft Research, China

THE RAPID advances in multimedia computing in recent years have been driven by the needs of Internet and other applications to efficiently store, process, and communicate multimedia data. In Part I of this book, we consider that audio, image, video, and their combinations are the major types of multimedia data. The key tasks involved in handling multimedia data include processing, compression, and retrieval of audio, image, and video data. In the last few decades, enormous research efforts have been devoted to these areas of multimedia computing and significant scientific and technological advancements have resulted. However, many challenging problems and issues in these areas remain that continue to attract significant research efforts and make these areas a center of today's multimedia computing field. The papers selected for this part of the collection present the landscape, recent progress, and major remaining research topics in the areas of processing, and more specifically, compressing and retrieving multimedia data. It should be noted, however, that it is impossible in the space allowed to offer a complete survey of the numerous new algorithms and contributions made in recent years and inevitably, we were forced to omit some important papers and works. (However, we have included pointers to these works in "Additional Readings" section of each chapter.)

By processing, we refer to multimedia data enhancement and manipulation to improve or transform the representation of multimedia in different applications, such as immersive audio and multimedia compression and content analysis.

Processing is essential to both compression and retrieval of multimedia. Multimedia processing has been researched extensively in the signal processing community, and thousands of papers have been published. For this same reason, multimedia data processing technologies are not covered extensively in this book; rather, only a few papers have been selected to provide some background for immersive audio in Chapter 1 and for image and video compression and watermarking in Chapter 2.

Because audio, image, and video content usually require a vast amount of data for their representation, compression is necessary in order to store, playback, transfer, and stream multimedia data. Therefore, the first part of the book focuses significantly on compression algorithms and standards for multimedia data. Developing algorithms and systems for multimedia data compression or coding has been a key theme in signal processing for the last three decades and significant progress has been made. There are now many effective coding algorithms and, more importantly, international coding standards, such as JPEG and MPEG. Such technological developments also have led to rapid advancements in multimedia industries involving communications, broadcasting, and the Internet. These industrial successes, in return, have stimulated more research and investment in the aspects of multimedia coding and streaming germane to the Internet. For this reason, multimedia compression remains an active but mature research area. We have devoted two chapters (Chapters 1 and 2), consisting of mainly overview papers by leading experts in this area, to providing the readers with fundamental knowledge of the major research topics of the field. Unlike the other chapters of the books, these two include papers more centered on established or emerging international standards. The reason for this decision is twofold: First, the existing and emerging multimedia coding standards have covered almost all aspects of compression algorithms developed so far, and second, a unique phenomenon in this field is that most researchers from either industrial or academic research institutions have been pushing their research results as standards. To enhance the utility of these overviews, a large number of references to detailed descriptions of most important technologies and research contributions in the multimedia coding field have been given in Chapters 1 and 2. Therefore, these two chapters also provide good pointers for in-depth research on multimedia compression. A research topic in media computing closely related to media compression is media streaming, which is discussed in more detail in Chapter 9 of the second part of this book.

As computer networks improve and digital libraries become more readily available to homes and offices via the Internet, multimedia data have increased explosively. As a result, the issue of rapidly accessing relevant information from the ocean of multimedia data becomes more pressing. This issue has to be resolved before we can take full advantage of multimedia information, though the most important investments have been targeted at the information infrastructure, including networks, servers, coding and compression, and systems architecture, as described in other chapters of this book. To address this need, research on multimedia data indexing, retrieval, and browsing technologies have become a major and active area in the multimedia computing field. We have devoted three chapters (Chapters 3–5) in Part I of the book to cover content-based indexing of audio, image, and video content, respectively. The papers chosen in these three chapters not only present the landscape of this research field, but also give detailed descriptions of the most significant contributions and milestones on algorithms and systems for multimedia indexing and retrieval in the last decade.

Algorithms and schemes for indexing and retrieval of multimedia data have been studied extensively in the last two decades by researchers in the database and multimedia applications fields. However, the early efforts before the last decade had all taken a keyword or text-based approach for indexing and retrieval of multimedia data. As discussed in Chapters 3–5, there are several limitations inherent in multimedia systems and databases that are indexed exclusively using text descriptors. The papers we have chosen in this book are focused most on a new indexing and retrieval approach: content- or feature-based indexing and retrieval of multimedia data. That is, instead of describing the content of multimedia data by text descriptors only, content features, either audio or visual, extracted automatically from the media data are used for indexing. For many applications, such indexing schemes may be either supplemental or preferable to text, and in some other cases they may be necessary. Furthermore, queries may simply be easier to formulate in native media form.

With the content-based indexing approach, formulating a query for a search may not involve typing in a keyword, but rather selecting or creating one or more representative examples and then searching through a database or Web site to find those instances that resemble the query examples. In other words, with a feature-based indexing scheme, the search is driven by first establishing one or more media samples, then identifying specific features of those samples, and finally using these features to match media objects in the database. Furthermore, as content features are automatically extracted from media data, it is possible that the indexing of multimedia data will become fully automated, thus eliminating the limitations and problems of manual indexing of multimedia data.

The papers chosen in Chapters 3–5 cover all main research topics in content-based indexing and retrieval of multimedia data: content feature definition and extraction, content-based similarity, indexing schemes, video structure parsing, retrieval algorithms, and browsing schemes. Although the content features for representing audio, image, and video content are often different, the indexing and search schemes and ideas developed for one type of media also can be used for the other two types of media data. More importantly, efficient and effective indexing of video, and often images as well, requires the integration of content information from multimedia sources. Another major issue in indexing and retrieval of multimedia is database management systems that support content-based indexing and retrieval of multimedia data. This issue is addressed in detail in Chapter 6 of Part II of the book.

The research in processing, compression, and retrieval of multimedia also involves many other areas of computer science, signal processing, and communication systems, which cannot be covered in this book. However, we believe the collection of papers in Part I of this book presents the most significant and most often referenced works, covering recent progress and important research topics in the areas of media processing, coding, and retrieval. We hope these papers can serve as good references for researchers, engineers, and students in the areas of multimedia computing research and applications.

CHAPTER ONE

Digital Audio

HongJiang Zhang
Microsoft Research, China

Hao Jiang
Microsoft Research, China

AS A BASIC component of multimedia computing, digital audio signal processing and compression have advanced rapidly in recent years, spurred on by the new generation of technologies for cost-effective digital signal processing and by diverse commercial applications centered around wired and wireless telecommunications, voice storage, and both consumer and professional digital audio products. As a research field, digital audio has been researched extensively in the signal processing community, and thousands of papers have been published. However, we look at this area more from the perspective of the multimedia computing community and the applications of audio in multimedia systems. We make no attempt to offer a complete survey of the numerous new algorithms developed and contributions made in recent years, and, inevitably, we have overlooked some important papers and works. Because of space limitation, we have decided to focus on digital audio coding, while briefly touching on immersive audio systems in multimedia systems.

Based on our objective, we have chosen five papers for this chapter. The three papers on audio coding (Gersho; Pan; and Scheirer) present excellent overviews on the state of the art in speech and audio coding, a brief history of this field, current research directions, and standards activities. We also have chosen a paper on psychoacoustics foundations (Zwicker and Zwicker), including audio perception, masking, and perceptual coding, and a paper on immersive audio systems (Kyriakakis), which

have wide applications in virtual reality systems and the Internet. In the rest of this introduction, we briefly describe the most important and prevailing technologies and algorithms of audio coding and standards activities covered in the selected papers. We do give some additional references, without attempting to give a historical overview of the evolution of audio coding.

SPEECH CODING

Speech coding has been an active research area for several decades. However, in the last decade, there has been an explosion of interest and research activity in this area with numerous applications in telecommunications and storage. The explosive growth of digital cellular communication systems and IP phone systems are among the most important driving forces. As a result of this rapid technology development, high-quality speech coding can now be achieved at a bit rate as low as 4 Kbps, and speech coded at 2.4 Kbps can be reproduced with fairly good naturalness. Also, several national and international standards have been adopted.

Speech coding assumes that the input is the human voice and other sounds are treated as background noise, a reasonable assumption for speech coding in voice telecommunications. In general, speech coders can be classified into two categories: waveform coder and parametric coder or vocoder. The term *vocoder* originated as a contraction of voice coder. Waveform speech coders try to encode the original speech waveform in the time domain or frequency domain at a given bit rate. That is, the reproduced audio signal will approximate the original waveform such that it will produce an approximate re-creation of the original sound. In contrast, vocoders try to make the coded voice sound like the original but the decoded speech waveform may be very different from the original. That is, parameters that characterize individual sound segments are specified and used in the decoder to reconstruct a new and often different waveform that will have a similar sound. This is the reason that vocoders are also called parametric coders. Vocoders operate at lower bit rates than waveform coders, but the reproduced speech quality usually suffers from a loss of naturalness and the characteristics of an individual speaker. Such distortions are caused by modeling inaccuracy and often are very difficult to remove.

Vocoders widely use speech production models by which speech can be modeled as the output of a time-variant filter. In a short time interval, such as 20 to 30 ms, a speech signal can be approximated as a stationary and ergodic random process, and a time-invariant system can be used. That is the reason that most speech coders use block-wise analysis and synthesis. The earliest vocoder is a channel coder, which is still used in many applications for its robust performance in noisy environments. The LPC (line predictive coding) vocoder, one of the most important parametric speech coders, has formed the basis for a large family of speech coders [1, 2]. In recent years much progress has been made to achieve high-quality and low bit rate parametric speech coding. These speech coders will eventually replace higher bit rate speech coders in telecommunication networks. Such modern speech coders can be classified into three classes: mixed excitation LPC or MELP [3]; harmonic speech coders such as STC (sinusoidal transform coding) [4] and MBE (multiband excitation) [5, 6]; and interpolation speech coders such as WI [7, 8] and TFI [9]. These speech coders adopt more complex models. One of the common features in these coders is that they all use multimodal excitation.

Many classic speech coders can be classified into waveform coders, such as ADPCM (adaptive differential pulse code modulation) [10], subband speech coders [11], and transform speech coders [12, 13]. Most developments in recent years have focused on modifications and enhancements of a few generic methods and, more notably, on hybrid speech coders that borrow some features of vocoders, though they basically belong to the family of waveform coders. The well-known hybrid coders are CELP (code-excited linear predication), MPE-LPC [14], and RPE-LPC (regular pulse excitation LPC) [15]. Recent activity in speech coding is dominated by research and development regarding the CELP family of coding techniques. These algorithms exploit models of speech production and auditory perception. They use the LPC model but base the excitation optimization on the best waveform fit with the perceptive weighting. These algorithms offer a quality versus bit rate tradeoff that significantly exceeds most prior compression techniques for rates in the range of 4 to 16 Kbps. Techniques also have been emerging in recent years that offer enhanced quality in the neighborhood of 2.4 Kbps over traditional vocoder methods.

The second paper that appears in this chapter, "Advances in speech and audio compression" by A. Gersho is one of the best survey papers on the state of the art of speech and audio coding. It highlights the most important and prevailing algorithms, approaches, and activities of current interest in speech coding researches. Detailed description of algorithms of a number of vocoders, LPAS (linear-predication based analysis-by-synthesis) coders, VBR (variable bit rate) coders, and, most importantly, the family of coders, as well as their late development and applications, can be found in this paper. More detailed discussions on other speech coding technologies can be found in the book by Kleijn [16].

WIDE-BAND AUDIO CODING

Wideband high-fidelity audio coding has advanced rapidly in the last decade, accelerated by the commercial success of consumer and professional digital audio applications. Wideband audio coding refers to the compression of audio signals with 15–20 kHz bandwidth and is generally aimed at a quality that is nearly indistinguishable from consumer compact disc audio. Applications of wideband audio coding are mainly in consumer hi-fi, professional audio including motion picture and HDTV audio, various multimedia PCs and systems, and, lately, audio/music streaming over the Internet. Wideband audio sometimes also refers to wideband speech signals for video conferencing and for ISDN voice communication, where higher quality speech is feasible and desirable. Sub-band and transform coding methods combined with sophisticated perceptual coding techniques dominate in this arena with nearly transparent quality achieved at bit rates in the neighborhood of 128 Kbps per channel. Virtually all the current work in hi-fi audio coding relies on either sub-band or transform coding to achieve a spectral decomposition of the signal. The paper by Gersho presents an excellent overview on wideband audio. Speech coding algorithms as well as their late development and applications can also be found in this paper.

AUDIO CODING STANDARDS

Given the divers applications of different audio and speech coding methods and algorithms, audio coding standards for compatibility of voice and audio communication and storage systems are essential. The ITU plays a very important role in the process of speech coding standardization. In the 1970s, the CCITT (now combined into the ITU) published the 64 Kkbps PCM international standard. The 32 Kbps ADPCM and 16 Kbps LD-CELP (low-delay CELP) were published afterward. Some organizations and government departments also presented speech coding standards, such as the 13 Kbps RPE-LPC, which has been used in Western European digital mobile communications, and the 8 Kbps VSELP [17], which has been adopted as the North American standard for mobile phones. In 1995, the ITU presented G.723.1 [18], which includes 6.3 Kbps MP-MLQ and 5.3 Kbps ACELP. G.723.1 was developed for multimedia communications. After one year, another high-quality speech coding standard, 8 Kbps CS-ACELP (G.729) [19] was published. Low bit rate speech coding with a bit rate from 1.2 to 4 Kbps has gained much interest in recent years. The 2.4 Kbps MB-LPC (multiband LPC) has been adopted as the federal standard in the United States for secure communications. Its quality is comparable to the 4.8 Kbps CELP (FS1016) [20] for clean speech and has better performance than FS1016 in noisy background. Sinusoidal speech coding algorithms such as STC and MBE are also very popular in low bit rate speech coding. The ITU also has a standard for 7 kHz bandwidth wideband speech coding: G.722.

MPEG has played a key role in standardizing wideband audio coding techniques just as it has in video coding standardization (as presented in the next chapter). MPEG-1/2 Audio is a generic audio coding standard and it achieves its compression without making assumptions about the nature of the audio source. Instead, like wideband audio coders, the MPEG/Audio coder exploits the perceptual limitations of the human auditory system. The paper entitled "A tutorial on MPEG/Audio compression," by D. Pan, summarizes the fundamentals of MPEG/Audio, including all functional features, and provides a detailed description of the coding algorithms.

MPEG-1/2 Audio offers a divers set of compression modes and features such as random access and fast-forwarding. Also the MPEG/Audio coder has been evolving through several phases. MPEG-1 (ISO/IEC 11172-3) [21, 22] provides single-channel and two-channel coding at 32, 44.1, and 48 kHz sampling rates. MPEG-1/Audio also provides a choice of three compression layers. Each higher layer is more complex and more efficient than lower layers. Such a layered coding scheme gives scalability to MPEG/Audio and makes it especially useful in audio streaming over IP. The predefined bit rates range from 32 to 448 Kbps for Layer I, from 32 to 384 Kbps for Layer II, and from 32 to 320 Kbps for Layer III. MPEG-2 BC (ISO/IEC 13818-3) provides a backward compatible multichannel extension to MPEG-1: up to five main channels plus a low frequency enhancement channel can be coded. The bit rate range is extended up to about 1 Mbps. Another extension is toward lower sampling rates, 16, 22.05, and 24 kHz for bit rates from 32 to 256 Kbps (Layer I) and from 8 to 160 Kbps (Layers II and III). MPEG-2 AAC (ISO/IEC 13818-7) [23] provides a very high quality audio coding standard for 1 to 48 channels at sampling rates of 8 to 96 kHz, with multichannel, multilingual, and multiprogram capabilities.

Although previous generations of the MPEG multimedia standard have focused primarily on coding and transmission of content digitally sampled from the real world, MPEG-4 contains extensive support for structured, synthetic, and synthetic/natural hybrid coding methods. The synthetic audio coding part of MPEG-4 is composed of tools for the realization of symbolically defined music and speech. This includes MIDI and text-to-speech systems. Furthermore, tools for the 3-D localization of sound are included, allowing the creation of artificial sound environments using artificial and natural sources. MPEG-4 also standardizes natural audio coding at bit rates ranging from 2 Kbps up to 64 Kbps. In order to achieve the highest audio quality within the full range of bit rates, three types of codecs have been defined: a parametric codec for the lower bit rates in the range; a CELP codec for the medium bit rates in the range; and time to frequency (TF) codecs, including an MPEG-2 AAC and a vector-quantization based coder, for the higher bit rates in the range. In addition, MPEG-4 audio also provides functionality such as speed control, pitch change, error resilience, and scalability. MPEG-4 addresses several types of scalability such as bit-rate, bandwidth, and complexity scalability.

An important difference between MPEG-4/Audio and other audio coding standards is the introduction of the concept of structured audio and audio objects, which allows coding and transmitting of sound using ultra-low bit rates. In MPEG-4/Audio an algorithmic sound language and several related tools for the structured coding of audio objects are standardized. MPEG-4/Audio also adopts structured audio (SA) as a new type of audio coding tool. In the SA format, a sound bit stream contains one or more algorithms written in SAOL (Structured Audio Orchestra Language), whereas the streaming data consists of access units containing parametric events written in SASL (Structured Audio Score Language). In the sound synthesis phase, a re-configurable engine interprets the SAOL programs and configures itself for sound manipulation accordingly. SA enables MPEG-4 audio to use multiple models, divide a single soundtrack into components, and code each component with a different model.

The paper entitled "Structured audio and effects processing in the MPEG-4 multimedia standard," by E. D. Scheirer, presents an overview of objectives, main features, and targeted applications of the MPEG-4/Audio standard. In particular, it provides a detailed description of *structured audio* and *AudioBIFS* components of MPEG-4. The paper also discusses the separation of functionality between the systems layer and the audio toolset of MPEG-4 and prospects for efficient DSP-based implementations.

AUDIO PERCEPTION

As with other data compressions, the basic processing in audio coding is to remove redundant data

from an original audio. Audio coding uses psychoacoustical properties, such as audio masking, of audio signals as well as statistical properties to reduce redundancy and irrelevant data. That is, because of the characteristics of the human auditory system, much irrelevant data can be removed without compromising the audio quality perceived by humans. Psychoacoustic modeling is widely used in MPEG-1/2 Audio coders to facilitate the coding procedure.

The primary psychoacoustic effect is auditory masking, where parts of a signal are not audible because of the masking effect of the human auditory system. Audio masking exists not only in the frequency domain but also in the time domain. In its quantization and coding stage, the MPEG-2/Audio coder tries to allocate the available number of data bits in a way that meets both the bit rate and masking requirements. Because of the importance of audio perception and psychoacoustic theories in audio processing and audio coding, we have chosen the paper entitled "Audio engineering and psychoacoustics: Matching signals to the final receiver," by E. Zwicker and U. T. Zwicker, for this chapter.

IMMERSIVE AUDIO

Numerous multimedia and Internet applications are currently envisioned for immersive audio systems. These applications include teleconferencing and telepresence; augmented and virtual reality for manufacturing and entertainment; air-traffic control, pilot warning, and guidance systems; displays for the visually or aurally impaired; home entertainment; distance learning; and professional sound and picture editing for television and film in an immersive audio system. The principal function of immersive audio systems is, in real time, to synthesize, manipulate, and render 3-D sound fields that do not exist in the current physical environment, thus immersing users in a seamless blend of visual and aural information. Accurate spatial reproduction of sound can significantly enhance the visualization of 3-D information for applications in which it is important to achieve sound localization relative to visual images. Unfortunately, compared to image and video processing, audio signal processing for immersive systems has been largely neglected.

To cover this important area in multimedia system applications, we have chosen the paper entitled "Fundamental and technological limitation of immersive audio systems," by C. Kyriakakis. This paper presents a brief historical overview to outline the development of immersive audio technologies and discusses the performance and future research directions of immersive audio systems. Also, it examines several fundamental and technological limitations that impede the development of seamless immersive audio systems. Finally, the paper presents a novel desktop audio system with integrated listener-tracking capability that circumvents several of the technological limitations faced by today's digital audio workstations. More discussions on immersive audio systems and the signal processing issues that pertain to the acquisition and subsequent rendering of 3-D sound fields over loudspeakers can be found by another paper from the same author and colleagues [24].

In summary, audio processing is still a fast progressing research field. New algorithms and standards for audio coding are being developed quickly to meet the growing needs of diverse applications. As the research focus moves toward rates of 2.4 Kbps and below, waveform coding with the best CELP algorithms will face difficulties in meeting the ever-higher quality objectives. Consequently, interest in vocoder studies is resurging as researchers focus on lower bit rates. On the other hand, wideband audio coding activities have been dominated by the work developed for the MPEG/Audio standards. New research in wideband audio coding at lower rates is now in progress, mostly stimulated by plans for MPEG standards and by demand of new technologies for audio streaming over the Internet. As more and more audio data become available in databases and over the Internet, locating a particular audio clip may not be an easy job. Chapter 3 presents technologies to address issues related to management and retrieval in audio databases.

REFERENCES

[1] J. Makhout, "Linear prediction: A tutorial review," *Proceedings of the IEEE* 63, no. 4 (April 1975): 561–79.

[2] T. E. Tremain, "The government standard linear predictive coding algorithm: LPC-10," *Speech Technology* (April 1982): 44–9.

[3] A. V. McCree and T. P. Barnwell, "Mixed excitation LPC vocoder model for low bit rate speech coding," *IEEE Transactions on Speech and Audio Processing* 3, no. 4 (July 1995): 242–50.

[4] R. J. McAulay and T. F. Quatieri, "Speech analysis/synthesis based on a sinusoidal representation," *IEEE Transactions on ASSP* ASSP-34 (1986): 744–54.

[5] D. W. Griffin and J. S. Lim, "Multi-band excitation vocoder," *IEEE Transactions on ASSP* 36, no. 8 (Aug. 1988): 1223–35.

[6] D. W. Griffin, "Multi-band excitation vocoder," Ph.D. thesis, EECS Department, MIT, 1988.

[7] W. B. Kleijn, "Continuous representation in linear predictive coding," *ICASSP* (Toronto: IEEE, 1991), 501–04.

[8] W. B. Kleijn, "Encoding speech using prototype waveforms," *IEEE Transactions on Speech and Audio Processing* I, no. 4 (Oct 1993): 386–399

[9] Y. Shoham, "High-quality speech coding at 2.4 to 4.0 Kbps based on time frequency interpolation," ICASSP (Minneapolis: IEEE, 1993), 167–68

[10] T. Nishitani, et al., "A toll quality ADPCM coded," in *Proceedings of ICASSP 82* (Paris: IEEE, 1982).

[11] J. Princen, A. Johnson, and A. Bradley, "Subband/transform coding using filter band designs based on time-domain aliasing cancellation," in *Proceedings of ICASSP 87* (Dallas: IEEE,1987), 2161–64.

[12] K. Brandenburg, "OCF—A new coding algorithm for high-quality sound signals," in *Proceedings of ICASSP 92* (Dallas: IEEE,1992), 141–45.

[13] J. Johnston, "Transform coding of audio signals using perceptual noise criteria," *IEEE Journal on Selected Areas in Communication* 6, no. 2 (Feb. 1998): 314–23.

[14] B. S. Atal and J. R. Remde, "A new nodel of LPC excitation for producing natural sounding speech at low bit rates," in *Proceedings of ICASSP 82* (Paris: IEEE, 1982), 614–17.

[15] E. F. Peprettere and P. Kroon, "Regular excitation for effective and efficient LP-coding

of speech," in *Proceedings of ICASSP 85* (Tampa: IEEE, 1985), 965–68.

[16] W. B. Kleijn and K. K. Paliwal, *Speech coding and synthesis* (New York/Amsterdam: Elsevier Science, 1995).

[17] I. A. Gerson and M. A. Jasiuk, "Vector sum excited linear prediction (VSELP)," in *Advances in Speech Coding*, C. B. Atal, V. Cuperman, and A.Gersho, eds. (Boston: Kluwer Academic Publishers, 1991), 69–79

[18] Draft Recommendation G.723.

[19] Draft Recommendation G.729.

[20] J. P.Campbell, Jr., T. E.Tremain, and V. C. Welch, "The DOD 4.8 KBIT/S standard (proposed federal standard 1016)," in *Advances in Speech Coding*, B. S. Atal, V. Cuperman, and A. Gersho, eds. (Boston: Kluwer Academic Publishers, 1991), 121–33.

[21] MPEG-Audio draft, description as of Dec. 10, 1990, ISO/IEC JTC1/SC2/WG11.

[22] P. Noll, "MPEG digital audio coding," *IEEE Signal Processing Magazine* 14, no. 5 (Sept, 1997): 59–81.

[23] A. Bosiet, "ISO/IEC MPEG-2 advanced audio coding," *Journal of AES* (Oct. 1997): 789–814.

[24] C. Kyriakakis, P. Tsakalides, and T. Holman, "Surrounded by sounds," *IEEE Signal Processing Magazine* (Jan. 1999): 55–66.

Audio Engineering and Psychoacoustics: Matching Signals to the Final Receiver, the Human Auditory System*

EBERHARD ZWICKER AND U. TILMANN ZWICKER

Institute of Electroacoustics, Technical University Munich, D-8000 München 2, Germany

The consequences of the fact that the human auditory system is the final receiver in almost all cases of sound recording, transmission, and reproduction are discussed. The strategies of processing and transmitting sound as effectively as possible on one hand, and also as "undistorted" as possible on the other need adaption to the perception characteristics of the auditory system. The transformation of frequency to critical-band rate as well as the transformation of level to specific loudness are the tools used for this adaption. Examples for practical applications of the basic idea are illustrated.

0 INTRODUCTION

During the last few years, digital sound processing and storage have been adopted widely in audio, and are providing excellent sound quality. However, converting an audio stereo signal to a 16-bit digital format with appropriate redundancy for error correction and with a minimum sampling rate around 44 kHz requires extremely extended bandwidth for signal transmission and storage, the latter coupled with huge mass-storage necessities. The large bandwidth results in problems for radio transmission in particular, so there is considerable interest in avoiding any redundancy in the signal other than for error-correction purposes. To achieve sound transmission or reproduction that is not only very good but also efficient, all equipment has to be adapted to the characteristics of the final receiver, in this case the human ear. Any part of the transmitted signal that is not recognized by the auditory system shows bad matching to the receiver and provides unnecessary redundancy. Considerable progress has been made to implement methods of reduction of unnecessary data derived from findings in the field of psychoacoustics. Most of these efforts concern the future digital audio broadcasting (DAB), for example [1]–[3], but

digital storage can profit from the possible information reduction as well.

In fields other than audio, such as the transmission of electrical power, the adaption to the final receivers is very well established and generally applied for transmission from power plant to power plant as well as from power plant to factories and even to individual households. In the field of transmitting information, the same rule holds as for power transmission. Therefore, all of our efforts in improving electroacoustic information transmission—including recording—have to be seen from the perspective of the final receiver, the human auditory system. This perspective has many more advantages in audio engineering, such as in instrumentation and with public-address applications, as discussed in this paper.

1 THE FINAL RECEIVER: THE HUMAN AUDITORY SYSTEM AND PERCEPTION

Eventually important is the *perception* of sound. We do not perceive frequency, we rather perceive pitch; we do not perceive level, but loudness. We do not perceive spectral shape, modulation depth, or frequency of modulation; instead we perceive "sharpness," "fluctuation strength," or "roughness." We also do not perceive time directly; our perception is the subjective duration, often quite different from the physical du-

---

* Manuscript received 1990 July 18; revised 1990 December 12.

ration. In all of the hearing sensations mentioned, which are described in detail elsewhere [4]–[6], masking plays an important role in the frequency, as well as in the time domain. Consequently Sec. 2 deals with masking effects and the transformation from frequency scale to critical-band-rate scale and from level scale to specific-loudness scale. The information received by our auditory system can be described most effectively in the three dimensions of specific loudness, critical-band rate, and time. The resulting three-dimensional pattern is the measure from which the assessment of sound quality can be achieved. Some applications of this pattern, which is reproduced in a modern loudness meter, for example, are discussed especially in view of modern electroacoustic transmission and reproduction.

In this paper, the main emphasis is on practical applications of psychoacoustics in the field of perception and reproduction of sound, and many scientific details are therefore omitted. Rather, the basic, important facts are enhanced. Further information is available from books on psychoacoustics and electroacoustics [4]–[8].

2 PSYCHOACOUSTICAL PRINCIPLES APPLICABLE IN AUDIO ENGINEERING PRACTICE

2.1 Transformation from Frequency to Critical-Band Rate

The effect of masking plays a very important role in hearing, and is differentiated into simultaneous and nonsimultaneous masking. An example for the simultaneous condition would be the case where we have a conversation with our neighbor while a loud truck passes by. In this case our conversation is severely disturbed. To continue our conversation successfully we have to raise our voice to produce more speech power and greater loudness. In music, similar effects take place. The different instruments can mask each other, and softer instruments become audible only when the loud instrument pauses. Such simultaneous masking is outlined here for quantitatively easily describable conditions, while nonsimultaneous masking is discussed in Sec. 2.3. Simultaneous masking can be understood more easily if instead of the frequency scale a hearing

equivalent scale, that is, the critical-band-rate scale, is used.

Masking usually is described as the sound-pressure level of a test sound (a pure tone in most cases) necessary to be barely audible in the presence of a masker. For narrow-band noises used as maskers and pure tones used as test sounds, masking patterns can be produced for different center frequencies of the narrow-band noise maskers, as shown in Fig. 1. The same information is given in Fig. 1(a) and (b). However, in Fig. 1(a) the level of the barely audible pure tone is plotted as a function of frequency on a linear scale, in contrast to the logarithmic scale used in Fig. 1(b). In order to make the masking patterns directly comparable through having the same peak values, the so-called masking index, a value of 2–6 dB (for details see the literature mentioned), is added to the sound-pressure level of the barely audible test tone, and the resulting level, called excitation level, is shown as ordinate. The level of the narrow-band maskers is 60 dB for all curves. Comparing the results produced from different center frequencies of the masker, we find the form of the curves to be rather dissimilar, no matter what frequency scaling we use. It seems as if the shape of the curves is similar for center frequencies up to about 500 Hz on linear frequency scale, while for center frequencies above 500 Hz there is a similarity on a logarithmic frequency scale. This intuitive result is quite accurate since the hearing-equivalent critical-band-rate scale mentioned follows a linear frequency scale up to about 500 Hz and then a logarithmic frequency scale above 500 Hz. This relation is illustrated in Fig. 2 by two different frequency scales, one divided linearly, the other logarithmically. Approximations, which sometimes may be useful within certain frequency ranges, are also indicated. Fig. 2(a) shows the uncoiled inner ear, including the basilar membrane. It indicates that the critical-band-rate scale is directly related to the place along the basilar membrane where all the sensory cells are located in a very equidistant configuration (one row of inner hair cells and three rows of outer hair cells). Thus the critical-band-rate scale is closely related to our physiology, too.

The critical-band concept is based on the well-proven

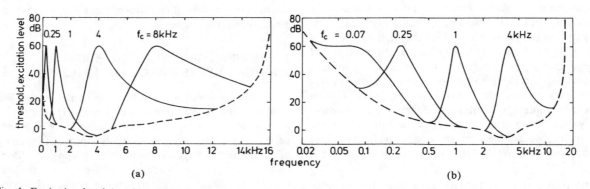

Fig. 1. Excitation level (masking level with added masking index) of narrow-band noises of given center frequency as a function of frequency. Broken lines—threshold is quiet. (a) Linear scale. (b) Logarithmic scale.

assumption that our auditory system analyzes a broad spectrum in parts that correspond to critical bands. Adding one critical band to the next, so that the upper limit of the lower critical band corresponds to the lower limit of the next higher critical band, produces the scale of the critical-band rate. Since critical bands have a 100-Hz width up to 500 Hz and above 500 Hz take a relative width of 20%, it becomes clear why the critical-band rate is dependent on frequency as illustrated. This can also be seen in Fig. 2(c), where the critical-band rate is plotted as a function of frequency on the logarithmic scale, a scale more appropriate for approximating the critical-band rate. The latter fact is especially advantageous for problems dealing with speech transmission, where important spectral features are located in the spectral region between 300 and 5000 Hz. However, it is also necessary to realize that the linear relation between frequency and critical-band rate plays an important role in music based on harmony.

Because the critical-band concept is used in so many models and hypotheses, a unit for the critical-band rate was defined, which is one critical band wide. It is the *bark*, in memory of Barkhausen, a scientist from Dresden, Germany, who introduced the phon, a unit describing the loudness level for which the critical band plays an important role.

When frequency is transferred into critical-band rate, the masking patterns outlined in Fig. 1 change to those seen in Fig. 3. There the level of the barely audible pure tone (again expressed as excitation level, that is, including the masking index) is plotted as a function of the critical-band rate for the same narrow-band maskers as shown in Fig. 1. The effectiveness of the natural frequency scale, that is, the critical-band-rate scale, is obvious. The shapes of the curves for different center frequencies are very similar. Only at very low frequencies, below about 100 Hz, where special masking effects (such as the masking-period patterns) lower the amount of masking, the upper slope is somewhat steeper.

It is not only the masking effect that can be described more simply and become more easily understandable in terms of this natural scale corresponding to location

along the basilar membrane, but also many other effects, such as pitch, frequency differences barely noticeable, or the growth of loudness as a function of bandwidth. Therefore when dealing with hearing sensations, it is very effective to transfer first the frequency scale into the critical-band-rate scale.

The effect of masking produced by narrow-band maskers is level dependent and, therefore, a nonlinear effect. As shown in Fig. 4(a), all masked thresholds show a steep rise from low to higher frequencies up to the maximum of masking. Beyond this maximum, the masked threshold decreases quite rapidly toward higher frequencies for low and medium masker levels. At higher masker levels, however, the slope toward high frequencies, that is, larger critical-band rate, becomes increasingly shallow. This nonlinear rise of the upper slope of the masked threshold with the masker level is an effect that is assumed to be produced in the inner ear already. The outer hair cell rows form a feedback system which, through saturation, is effective at low levels only. At higher levels the feedback automatically disappears. This leads to a shape of the masking curve corresponding to the amplitude of the traveling wave along the basilar membrane, as seen for higher levels. Recent data of this traveling wave measured at very low levels have proven that feedback takes place in

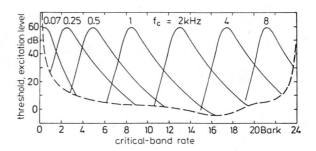

Fig. 3. Excitation level versus critical-band rate for narrow-band noises of given center frequency and 60-dB sound pressure level. Broken lines—threshold in quiet. Adopted from [5].

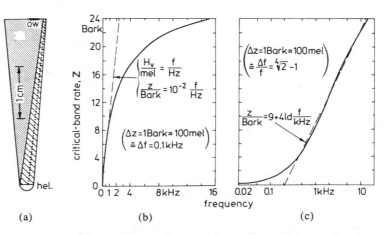

(a)   (b)   (c)

Fig. 2. (a) Scale of uncoiled cochlea. (b), (c) Critical-band rate (ordinate, linear scale) as a function of frequency. (b) Linear scale. (c) Logarithmic scale. Useful approximations are indicated by broken lines and related equations. Adopted from [5].

the inner ear already, producing a narrower amplitude distribution of the traveling wave and consequently a narrower masking pattern at low masker levels. This is also seen in data for masking patterns produced by a model reproducing peripheral preprocessing in the inner ear, including nonlinear feedback with lateral coupling. The real masking data [Fig. 4(a)] and the model data [Fig. 4(b)] compare very nicely. Therefore, and in accordance with physiological data from animals, it can be assumed that simultaneous masking is already produced in the peripheral preprocessing of the inner ear, that is, before the information is transferred to the neural level.

Another possibility to measure masking is psychoacoustical tuning curves. In this case the level of the test tone is fixed, while the level of the masker, in most cases also a tone, is increased so that the test tone just becomes inaudible. Plotting this masker level as a function of critical-band rate results in the so-called psychoacoustical tuning curves. Such a curve is outlined in Fig. 4(c); it has a shape that correlates quite strongly with the data seen in Fig. 4(d), as described in the following.

The assumption that frequency selectivity takes place in the peripheral part of the auditory system (the inner ear) and produces the critical-band-rate scale can also be supported by experiments on the suppression of so-

called spontaneous otoacoustic emissions [9], which appear in half of all ears at levels around 0 dB SPL. These tonal emissions, which are proven to be produced in the inner ear, can be suppressed by adding a suppressor tone, the level of which is given in the related suppression tuning curves as a function of the critical-band rate. The curve given belongs to the criterion of 6-dB amplitude reduction of the spontaneous otoacoustic emission. These are objective data because they do not depend on a subject's response at all. By comparing Fig. 4(c) and (d), one can easily see that the psycho-acoustically measured tuning curves, which involve the highest possible signal processing level in the brain, show the same frequency selectivity as the suppression tuning curves resulting from purely peripheral processing. Therefore the frequency-selective and nonlinear effect of simultaneous masking produced in our auditory system can be assumed as being produced already in the peripheral part of the inner ear and still in the analog domain, that is, installed before the signal information is transferred into neural information using spike rates. Since the arrangement of the hair cells is equidistant and the form of the traveling wave in the inner ear, besides the shift along the basilar membrane, does not change much as a function of frequency, it becomes understandable why the natural scale of the critical-band rate, which corresponds to the location along the

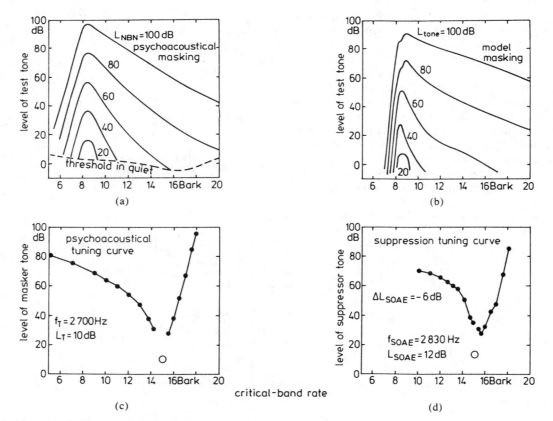

Fig. 4. (a) Level of test tone barely masked by narrow-band noise of given level. (b) Test-tone level needed in model to produce 1-dB increment anywhere along basilar membrane. (c) Psychoacoustical and (d) suppression tuning curve; each as a function of critical-bank rate.

basilar membrane, is the adequate scale to describe frequency and frequency-selective effects in hearing.

2.2 Transformation from Level to Specific Loudness

When we talk about loudness in view of quantitative relations, we often think of the loudness function of a 1-kHz tone. This function is established by answering the question of how much louder a sound is heard relative to a standard sound. The standard sound in electro-acoustics is a 1-kHz tone, and the reference level in this case is 40 dB. Many measurements of different laboratories have produced similar results so that eventually the loudness function of a 1-kHz-tone in the free-field was standardized. It is given in Fig. 5 as a solid curve. With the definition that a 1-kHz tone of 40-dB SPL has the loudness of 1 sone, the curve indicates that doubling the loudness from 1 to 2 sone is equivalent to increasing the sound-pressure level from 40 to 50 dB. The same holds for larger levels: a doubling in loudness is achieved with each increment of 10 dB of the 1-kHz tone. This means that 50 dB corresponds to 2 sone, while 100 dB corresponds to 64 sone. The loudness function of the 1-kHz tone above 40 dB corresponds to a power law if loudness is related to sound intensity. Its exponent can be extracted easily by the fact that a 10-dB increment produces an increment in loudness of a factor of 2, which in logarithmic values is equivalent to an increment of 3 dB. Therefore the exponent of the power law connecting loudness with the sound intensity of the 1-kHz tone for sound pressure levels above 40 dB is 0.3. At sound pressure levels below 40 dB, the loudness function becomes steeper and steeper toward threshold in quiet, which per definition corresponds to a loudness of 0 sone. On the logarithmic loudness scale this zero corresponds to a value of minus infinity.

From the masking pattern outlined in Fig. 4(a) and the corresponding excitation pattern, we already know that a 1-kHz tone, although it has an infinitely small spectral width, does not lead to an infinitesimally narrow excitation in our auditory system—the final receiver—and thus on the critical-band-rate scale. Instead, it results in an excitation over a range increasing with larger SPL values of the 1-kHz tone. Although easily describable in purely physical terms, the 1-kHz tone produces a complex pattern of excitation, which from this point of view does not seem directly useful for answering the question we are interested in, namely, transferring the excitation into an equivalent psychoacoustic value.

When we talk about loudness, we mean total loudness, knowing that this loudness is comprised of very many partial loudnesses which are located along the critical-band-rate scale. The physiological equivalent of this assumption would be that all the neural activity of the sensory cells along the basilar membrane is summed up into a value that finally leads to the total loudness. Many experiments dealing with the loudness of sounds of different spectral widths have shown that the instruments our auditory system uses are the critical bands that shape and weigh the many partial loudnesses to be summed up. If the summation or integral mentioned leads to the loudness that is given in units of sones, the value we are looking for has to have the dimension of sones per bark. This value is called specific loudness and is denoted by N'. The total loudness N is thus the integral of specific loudness over the critical-band rate, which can be expressed mathematically as follows [10]:

$$N = \int_{z=0}^{24 \text{ bark}} N'(z) \, dz \; . \tag{1}$$

Since the 1-kHz tone produces a complicated excitation pattern and therefore also a complicated specific-loudness pattern, we have to search for a sound that produces more homogeneous excitation versus the critical-band-rate pattern. This sound is the uniform exciting noise, which fills up the entire auditory range in such a way that the same sound intensity falls into each of the 24 abutting critical bands (meaning that all critical bands are positioned adjacent without space between them). The loudness of such a uniform exciting noise was measured. It was found that the loudness of 1 sone is reached at a level of about 30 dB for uniform exciting noise. The entire loudness function of uniform exciting noise is shown by the dotted line in Fig. 5. The curve rises somewhat more steeply with level than the loudness of the 1-kHz tone, at least for levels of uniform exciting noise to about 50 dB. Above 60 dB, the dotted line can also be approximated by a straight line, which is shown dotted-dashed in Fig. 5. This straight line again means that a power law holds for the relation between the loudness of uniform exciting noise and the sound intensity of that noise. The exponent of this dotted-dashed line is smaller, however, than that for the loudness function of the 1-kHz tone (dashed straight line). It has a value of only 0.23, and thus the two loudness functions shown in Fig. 5 come closer together at higher

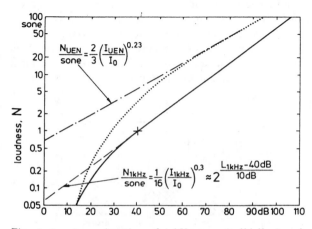

Fig. 5. Loudness function of 1-kHz tone (solid line) and uniform exciting noise (dotted line). Loudness is given as a function of sound pressure level. Approximations using power laws are indicated as broken and dashed-dotted lines together with the corresponding equations. Adopted from [5].

levels. Besides the different exponents of the two loudness functions at higher levels it is also interesting to see that the loudness of uniform exciting noise is much larger than the loudness of the 1-kHz tone in almost the entire level range indicated. For example, the loudness of a 60-dB uniform exciting noise is about 3.5 times larger than the loudness of the 1-kHz tone with the same level. This difference is a very distinct effect, which plays an important role in judging and measuring the loudness of noises. It indicates very clearly that an overall sound-pressure level of broad-band noises is an extremely inadequate value if loudness is to be approximated. Unfortunately most noises producing annoyance to people are broad-band noises, and the A-weighted sound-pressure level is a measure of the total level, which creates misleading values when used as an indication for loudness. Almost all sounds occurring in audio broadcasting and recording not only have a large bandwidth but also differ in spectral shape. Therefore meters based merely on total level (such as VU or peak-level meters) usually give readings quite unrelated to loudness, although these readings should correspond to loudness sensation as closely as possible from the view of the listener as the final receiver. This is referred to later.

Because uniform exciting noise produces the same excitation along the whole critical-band-rate scale, it can be used very nicely to calculate the value we are searching for (the specific loudness) out of its total loudness. Fig. 6 shows the procedure schematically. In Fig. 6(a) the excitation levels of uniform exciting noise (dashed) and of narrow-band noise, one critical band wide and centered at 1 kHz (solid), are shown. The two distributions are given for the condition that both the uniform exciting noise and the narrow-band noise have the same sound-pressure level of 64 dB. This value was chosen because the level in each of the 24 abutting critical bands produced by the uniform exciting noise is 50 dB, leading to an overall sound-pressure level of 50 dB + (10 × log 24) dB = 64 dB. For the narrow-band noise, the entire intensity is concentrated around 1 kHz, corresponding to a critical-band rate of 8.5 bark. The distribution of the excitation level as a function of critical-band rate reaches a peak value of 64 dB for the narrow-band noise, while it remains constant for the uniform exciting noise at 50 dB.

Using our assumption that total loudness is the integral over specific loudness along the critical-band-rate scale (as discussed), we can calculate the specific loudness corresponding to an excitation level of 50 dB from the total loudness of uniform exciting noise. According to Fig. 5, uniform exciting noise with a level of 64 dB produces a total loudness of 20 sone. Dividing this value by 24 bark, the entire width of the critical-band-rate scale, leads to the value for the specific loudness caused by an excitation level of 50 dB, that is, 20 sone divided by 24 bark leads to about 0.85 sone/bark. The same procedure can be used to calculate the relation between specific loudness and the excitation level for different values of the excitation level, that is, different values of the total level and total loudness of uniform exciting noise. The results show that specific loudness is related to the excitation in a similar way as the total loudness of uniform exciting noise is related to the sound intensity of the noise at high levels, namely, through a power law with an exponent of 0.23. The effect of threshold, which influences the relation between specific loudness and excitation level for levels ranging between threshold and about 40 dB above threshold, is ignored here for reasons of simplicity and accessibility. For practical applications, the exponent of 0.23 is often approximated with 0.25, as it then corresponds to the factor 0.5 of the sound pressure, and this square root is easily available technically.

The distribution of specific loudness as a function of critical-band rate for the 1-kHz narrow-band noise with the same level of 64 dB is shown in Fig. 6(b) by a solid line. It is obvious that the loudness of the two noises, the uniform exciting noise and the narrow-band noise, that is, the integral of specific loudness over critical-band rate, is quite different for the two noises. For the narrow-band noise, the area below the curve corresponding to the integral is only about one quarter of that of the rectangularly shaped area of the uniform exciting noise. The same relation can be seen in Fig. 5 for a level of 64 dB, where the two curves indicate a loudness of 20 sone for the uniform exciting noise, but only 5 sone for the 1-kHz tone, which is as loud as the narrow-band noise centered at 1 kHz.

The distributions of specific loudness as a function of critical-band rate shown in Fig. 6(b) are the most extreme cases. The one produced by uniform exciting

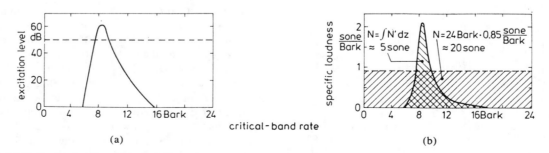

(a)   (b)

Fig. 6. (a) Excitation level and (b) specific loudness of narrow-band noise (solid lines) and uniform exciting noise (broken lines) of equal sound-pressure levels (64 dB) as a function of critical-bank rate.

noise is completely flat. However, even this noise produces a flat shape only if the frequency response between the free-field condition and the sound pressure at the ear drum is not accounted for. In our discussion we ignore this for didactical reasons, but for precise loudness measurements all these effects naturally have to be included [4], [6]. The distribution of specific loudness over the critical-band rate is often called the loudness pattern. This pattern varies for different kinds of noises, tones, or complex tones quite drastically. However, this loudness pattern is the pattern that is most interesting for the assessment of sound quality in the case of steady-state conditions because it shows on both coordinates the adequate hearing values: frequency is expressed via critical-band rate and level is expressed via specific loudness. If temporal effects are taken into account as well, then the time-varying specific-loudness versus critical-band-rate pattern contains all the information that eventually is evaluated by our auditory system.

2.3 Pattern of Specific Loudness versus Critical-Band Rate versus Time

From the many temporal effects included in the masking mechanisms only that of postmasking is discussed here, because it has the biggest impact on efficient coding for digital audio broadcasting (DAB) [2]. Postmasking results from the gradual release of the effect of a masker, that is, masking does not immediately stop with switching off the masker but still lasts while there is actually no masker present. Postmasking depends on the duration of the masker. Fig. 7 shows a typical result for a 2-kHz test-tone burst of 5-ms duration. The delay time at which the test-tone burst is presented after the end of the masker is plotted as the abscissa. The level of the test-tone burst necessary for audibility is the ordinate. For a long masker duration of at least 200 ms, the solid curve indicates postmasking.

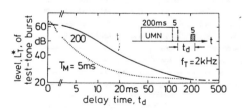

Fig. 7. Dependence of postmasking on masker duration: Level of barely audible test-tone burst as a function of its delay time (time between end of masker and end of test tone). Duration of maskers 200 and 5 ms; level of masker (uniform masking noise) 60 dB; duration of 2-kHz test tone 5 ms. Adopted from [5].

It decreases from the value for simultaneous masking (plotted on the left, outside the logarithmic scale) as a function of the delay time. However, postmasking produced by a very short masker burst (such as 5 ms) behaves quite differently. Postmasking in this case (as indicated by the dotted line in Fig. 7) decays much faster so that already after about a 50-ms threshold in quiet is reached. This implies that postmasking strongly depends on the duration of the masker and therefore is another highly nonlinear effect.

Specific loudness as calculated from excitation in the steady-state condition can also be considered as being a time-dependent value. Simultaneous masking and postmasking can be used to approximate the time functions of the specific loudness. Using this complete transformation, the specific loudness for a tone burst of 200 ms and that for a tone burst of 5 ms is plotted over time in Fig. 8. The tone bursts are located on the linear time scale in such a way that both bursts end at the same instant (200 ms). For the 200-ms tone burst, the specific loudness shows a very steep rise and stays at the peak value for almost 200 ms. The subsequent decay does not seem to have only one time constant. The specific loudness of the 5-ms tone burst rises just as quickly as for the 200-ms tone burst; the decay, however, is quite different and much faster, as can be expected from the postmasking pattern shown in Fig. 7. The different behavior of the specific loudness after the end of the tone bursts is shown by a dotted and a solid line. The two different decays can be approximated very roughly by single time constants of about 30 ms for a tone-burst duration of 200 ms and about 8 ms for a duration of 5 ms. Actually, in both cases the slope is much steeper during the early decay and less steep during the later decay (compared to the approximation using only one time constant).

These functions of specific loudness versus critical-band rate versus time illustrate best the information flow in the human auditory system. As three-dimensional patterns, they contain all the information that is subsequently processed and leads to the different hearing sensations. An example for such a complete pattern is shown in Fig. 9 for the spoken word "electroacoustics" fed into the auditory system. The specific loudness produced by this sound is plotted for 22 places with a 1-bark spacing along the critical-band-rate scale. For speech transmission, the spectral resolution in about 20 abutting channels is sufficient; for the transmission of music, additional information on pitch is necessary. However, the most important information, especially in music with strong temporal effects, can already be

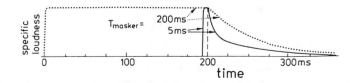

Fig. 8. Specific loudness produced by masker bursts of 200 ms (dotted line) and 5 ms (solid line) as a function of time.

seen nicely in patterns showing the specific loudness as a function of critical-band rate and of time. The pattern in Fig. 9 clearly shows the formants of the vowels and the spectral centers of the consonants, and also indicates the relatively quick rise following the stimulus, as well as a longer decay corresponding to postmasking. .

Total loudness can be derived from the 24 specific-loudness channels by summing up all 24 channels and feeding this function through a special low pass which in useful approximation reproduces the behavior of our auditory system in regard to temporal effects in loudness perception. Through this special low pass, the time function of the perceived loudness is strongly smoothed, but shows single syllables with clear separation. It is then evident that peak loudness, normally assumed to be the perceived loudness, is produced by the vowels in speech. Consonants and plosives are very important for the understanding of speech and are also very clearly visible in the specific-loudness versus critical-band-rate versus time pattern; their contribution to the total loudness, however, is almost negligible.

3 APPLICATIONS

3.1 Loudness

Loudness is a sensation of great interest in many problems related to audio engineering. For example, it is of interest how the loudness of a piece of music is perceived where the level changes drastically as a function of time. Often engineers are interested in a single number that is comparable with other data. Fig.

10(a) shows the loudness versus time function of pieces of broadcast music interrupted by a commercial. In order to get an estimate of the loudness perceived by the listener, the so-called cumulative loudness distribution is calculated for the different parts of the broadcast, as indicated by the numbers and the dashed vertical dividing lines. The cumulative loudness distribution supplies information about the probability that a given loudness is exceeded. This probability is shown in Fig. 10(b) for the three different temporal parts indicated by the numbers in Fig. 10(a). At the start of the specific sequence, around (0) a jingle is presented.

Comparisons of the loudnesses perceived by many subjects have indicated that the average loudness corresponding to N_{50} (the loudness exceeded in 50% of the time) gives an inadequate number, whereas N_5 to N_{10} give adequate readings of what the subjects really perceive. It becomes very clear from Fig. 10(b) that the commercial ② is perceived far louder than the adjacent pieces of music ③.

Sometimes in broadcasting different voices follow each other in the program, with the level being monitored on a volume meter. Adjustment for equal level of the voices often leads to strongly unequal loudness perceived by the listener (the final receiver), who can be rather annoyed by this. In accordance with the basic idea introduced at the beginning of this paper, it would be much better to control the broadcasting level utilizing a loudness level meter [11], [12] rather than a volume meter, the reading of which is only of importance for preventing equipment overload but not for the listener.

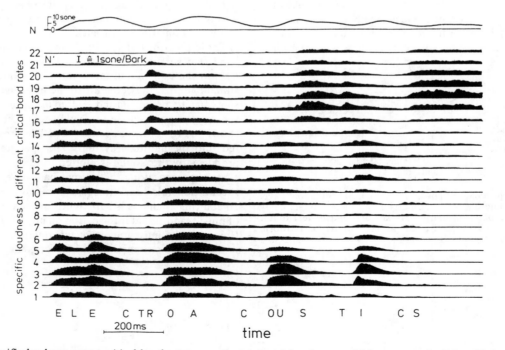

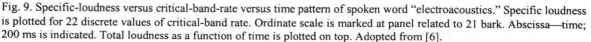

Fig. 9. Specific-loudness versus critical-band-rate versus time pattern of spoken word "electroacoustics." Specific loudness is plotted for 22 discrete values of critical-band rate. Ordinate scale is marked at panel related to 21 bark. Abscissa—time; 200 ms is indicated. Total loudness as a function of time is plotted on top. Adopted from [6].

3.2 Sharpness

Sharpness is an important concept correlated with the color of sound, and can also be calculated from the specific-loudness versus critical-band-rate pattern. It was found that the sharpness of narrow-band noises increases proportionally with the critical-band rate for center frequencies below about 3 kHz. At higher frequencies, however, sharpness increases more strongly, an effect that has to be taken into account when the sharpness S is calculated using a formula that gives the weighted first momentum of the critical-band-rate distribution of specific loudness,

$$S = 0.11 \frac{\int_0^{24 \text{ bark}} N' \cdot g(z)z \, dz}{\int_0^{24 \text{ bark}} N' \, dz} \text{ acum.} \quad (2)$$

In Eq. (2) the denominator gives the total loudness, while the upper integral is the weighted momentum mentioned. The weighting factor $g(z)$ takes into account the fact that spectral components above 3 kHz contribute more to sharpness than components below that frequency. An example of the calculation of sharpness is given in Fig. 11 for uniform exciting noise and for a high-pass noise above 3 kHz. The weighted specific loudnesses are shown as a function of the critical-band rate together with the location of their first momentum (center of gravity) marked by arrows. When the cutoff frequency of the high-pass noise is shifted toward lower values and the noise is finally transformed into a uniform exciting noise, loudness increases quite strongly; however, sharpness decreases markedly, in agreement with psychoacoustical results.

3.3 Fluctuation Strength

Fluctuation strength is a sensation correlated to the temporal variation of sounds. It was examined quite extensively by Fastl [13] during the last decade. It is important for the transmission of music as well as for the transmission of speech. Interestingly, the fluctuation strength measured as a function of the modulation fre-

quency shows a maximum near 4 Hz, a value for which the frequency of syllables in running speech has a maximum as well.

Fluctuation strength can also be calculated using the temporal dependence of the specific-loudness versus critical-band-rate pattern. The period of the modulation (or its frequency) as well the ratio between maximum specific loudness and minimum specific loudness are of importance. Without going into detail, the influence of room acoustics on the fluctuation strength may be illustrated by using a 100% amplitude-modulated 1-kHz tone. Such a tone, recorded under free-field conditions, is played back in a room. The 100% amplitude modulation is decreased quite strongly to a nonsinusoidal amplitude modulation (Fig. 12). The specific loudness corresponding to the frequency range around 1 kHz is shown as a function of time in Fig. 12(a) for the recorded sound and in Fig. 12(b) for the sound picked up by a microphone in the room. The difference between the two time functions is remarkable, indicating that room acoustics influence the fluctuation strength quite strongly and thus the quality of sound reproduction. Actual values in the example illustrated lead to a 75% reduction of fluctuation strength.

3.4 Room Acoustics

Room acoustics, however, produce positive effects, too. For example, reverberation increases the loudness of a speaker in a room because of the many reflections

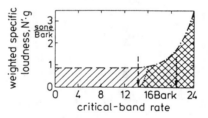

Fig. 11. Sharpness of uniform exciting noise (broken line, area hatched lower left to upper right), and high-pass noise (dotted line, hatched upper left to lower right). Weighted specific loudness is shown as a function of critical-band rate. Calculated sharpness is indicated by vertical arrows. Adopted from [5].

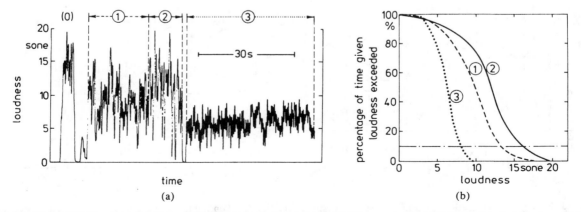

Fig. 10. (a) Loudness—time function of broadcast including a jingle at (0), preparation for a commercial ①, commercial ②, and music ③. (b) Cumulative loudness distributions.

that finally lead to a more diffuse field rather than to a free field. As an example, a speaker is approximated as a source of constant volume velocity, and Fig. 13 indicates the effect of increasing reverberation in a room when the same speech source produces loudness versus time functions under three different conditions. Curves (a) give the free-field condition, curves (b) the condition for a room with a reverberation time of 0.6 s, and curves (c) give the same for a room with a reverberation time of 2.5 s. Short periods from a 10-min speech are shown in the left part of Fig. 13. The right part indicates the corresponding cumulative distributions resulting from the loudness versus time functions for the three conditions. Using the loudness exceeded in 10% of the time as an indication of the perceived loudness, it can be expected that the speech is 1.2 times louder in the room with 0.6-s reverberation time and about two times louder in the room with 2.5-s reverberation compared with the loudness produced in the free-field condition. This increment in loudness is often very helpful for the intelligibility of speech in rooms as long as the reverberation time does not produce temporal masking, which reduces the audibility of faint consonants appearing in sequence to loud vowels.

3.5 Digital Transmission and Reproduction of Audio Signals at Reduced Bit Rate

Transmission and reproduction at reduced bit rate (especially in light of the proposed realizations for DAB) as a new and important area in electroacoustics and audio engineering were a major motivation for writing this paper. The pattern of specific loudness versus critical-band rate versus time can be used as a 'yardstick' that we have to follow in order to reduce information without introducing audible distortion of the sound. This holds for music as well as for speech. The systems realized in this area are strictly following this basic idea and, so far, mostly masking effects have been taken into account. Since this particular area is well covered by other publications and this paper deals with the fundamental ideas behind DAB, there is no need to go into the technical details here. It should be mentioned, though, that in music the physical equivalent of spectral pitch percepts—which can be extracted by a hearing-equivalent spectral analysis—can also be used as a tool to reduce the information flow drastically without making this reduction audible [14].

The specific-loudness versus critical-band-rate versus

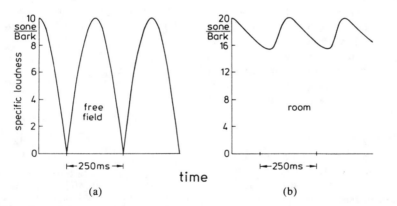

(a) (b)

Fig. 12. Specific-loudness versus time function of tone with 100% amplitude modulation. (a) in free-field condition. (b) played back in room.

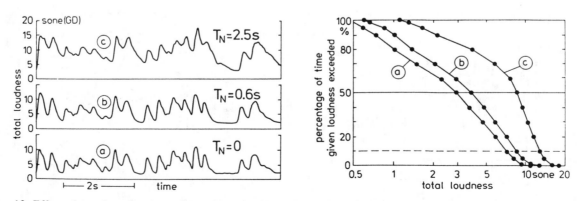

Fig. 13. Effect of reverberation time on loudness–time functions (left) and on loudness distributions (right). Data obtained (a) in free-field condition and in rooms with reverberation times of (b) 0.6 s and (c) 2.5 s indicate increase of loudness with increasing reverberation time. Adopted from [6].

time pattern produced by music or speech can be seen on the screen incorporated in modern loudness meters. It is very interesting and impressive to listen to music or speech and at the same time look at this information flow indicated by the movement of this pattern. It illustrates very strongly what we have tried to convey to the reader as the basic idea behind the data reduction necessary for efficient DAB.

4 CONCLUSIONS

The specific-loudness versus critical-band-rate versus time pattern contains all the information that is used by our auditory system in order to produce the different hearing sensations. We propose not to transfer less information than contained in this pattern; however, we also do not need to transfer more than this information. A reproduction accuracy of 1 dB in excitation level, corresponding to a relative value of 7% in specific loudness, is sufficient for practical applications.

A Personal Comment of E. Z.

In 1950 I had to solve the problem of why tape-recorded music was accepted differently if recorded and played back by different apparatus. The barely noticeable amplitude and frequency modulation as a function of modulation frequency and level, as characteristics of the final receiver (our auditory system), have led to the solution. Today, after having published more than 200 papers related to the field, I am propagating the same approach for a solution of the problems in modern electroacoustics and audio engineering, although at a somewhat higher level. It is obvious that we have learned quite a bit during the last 40 years, and I would like to thank all those who have contributed to that very much.

5 REFERENCES

[1] D. Krahé, "Ein Verfahren zur Datenreduktion bei digitalen Audio-Signalen unter Ausnutzung psychoakustischer Phänomene," *Rundfunktech. Mitt.*, vol. 30, no. 3, pp. 117–123 (1986).

[2] G. Stoll, M. Link, and G. Theile, Masking-Pattern Adapted Subband Coding: Use of the Dynamic Bit-Rate Margin," presented at the 84th Convention of the Audio Engineering Society, *J. Audio Eng. Soc. (Abstracts)*, vol. 36, p. 382 (1988 May), preprint 2585.

[3] G. Stoll and Y. Dehery, "High Quality Audio Bit-Rate Reduction System Family for Different Applications," in *Proc. IEEE ITC '90* (1990), pp. 937–941.

[4] E. Zwicker and R. Feldtkeller, *Das Ohr als Nachrichtenempfänger* (Hirzel, Stuttgart, 1967).

[5] E. Zwicker, *Psychoakustik* (Springer, Berlin, 1982).

[6] E. Zwicker and H. Fastl, *Psychoacoustics: Facts and Models* (Springer, Berlin, 1990).

[7] E. Zwicker and M. Zollner, *Elektroakustik* (Springer, Berlin, 1987).

[8] H. Fastl, "Dynamic Hearing Sensations: Facts and Models," Trans. Comm. on Hearing Research H-84-13, Acoust. Society of Japan, 1984.

[9] E. Zwicker, "The Inner Ear, a Sound Processing and a Sound Emitting System," *J. Acoust. Soc. Jpn* (E), vol. 9, pp. 59–74 (1988).

[10] ISO 532, "Acoustics—Method for Calculating Loudness Level," International Organization for Standardization, Geneva, Switzerland, 1975.

[11] B. Bauer and E. L. Torick, "Researches in Loudness Measurements," *IEEE Trans. Audio Electroacoust.*, vol. Au-14, no. 3, 1966.

[12] B. L. Jones and E. L. Torick, "A New Loudness Indicator for Use in Broadcasting," *SMPTE* (1981 Sept.).

[13] H. Fastl, "Fluctuation Strength of Modulated Tones and Broadband Noise," in: R. Klinke and R. Hartmann Eds., *Hearing—Physiological Bases and Psychophysics* (Springer, Berlin, 1989).

[14] W. Heinbach, "Aurally Adequate Signal Representation: The Part-Tone-Time-Pattern," *Acustica*, vol. 67, pp. 113–121 (1988).

THE AUTHORS

E. Zwicker

U. T. Zwicker

Eberhard Zwicker was born in Öhringen, Germany, in 1924. He studied physics at the University Tübingen (1945/46), and electrical engineering (communications) Dr. R. Feldtkeller at the Technical University Stuttgart (TUS), he began a career of teaching and research. He spent one year as a researcher at the Harvard University Psychoacoustics Laboratories, Cambridge, MA (1956/57), as associate professor at the TUS (1957/61), lecturing with Dr. J. Zwislocki at Syracuse University Bio-Acoustic-Laboratory, Syracuse, NY, with visits to numerous colleges in the USA at the invitation of the American Institute of Physics (1961/62); extraordinary professor at TUS (1962/67); research at Bell Telephone Labs, Murray Hill, NJ (1964); and as Professor and Director of the Institute of Electroacoustics, Technical University Munich (1967/90).

During those years, Professor Zwicker was also a member of the Kuratorium der Technisch-Physikalischen Bundesanstalt (1970/76), Speaker of the special research group Cybernetics sponsored by the Deutsche Forschungsgemeinschaft (1971/77), Dean of the Faculty of Electrical Engineering at the Technical University of Munich (1977/79), Speaker of the special research group Hearing sponsored by the Deutsche Forschungsgemeinschaft (1983/90), and did research and lecturing throughout the world including the USA, Great Britain, Japan, France, Switzerland, The Netherlands, Belgium, Spain, Poland, Czechoslovakia, Hungary, Italy, Austria, and Argentina.

Professor Zwicker's committee activity in the field of acoustics started in 1955 as a member of the German DIN standardization committees on Acoustic Measurements, Loudness and Noise Measurements, and Electronic Filters. In 1958 he became a member of ISO TC 43/working group Loudness From Objective Analysis, and was the German delegate to ISO meetings in Stockholm (1958), Rapallo (1960), Helsinki (1961), and Baden-Baden (1962). In 1959 he was secretary of the 3rd Congress of the International Commission on Acoustics in Stuttgart. He became international correspondent of the Committee of Hearing and Bioacoustics (CHABA) in 1963, a member of the International Commission on Acoustics from 1966 to 1972, and in 1984 was corresponding member of the Institute of Noise Control Engineering.

In 1956, Professor Zwicker was awarded the venia legendi in electroacoustics by the Nachrichtentechnische Gesellschaft. He received a Fellowship from the Acoustical Society of America in 1962, and, in 1987, he was awarded that society's Silver Medal. In 1982 he was made an Honorary Member of the Audio Engineering Society, and in 1988 he received the following

at the Technical University Stuttgart from 1946 to 1950. He received a doctor-engineer degree in electroacoustics in 1952. That year, as scientific assistant with Professor awards, Bundesverdienstkreuz am Bande des Verdienstordens der Bundesrepublik Deutschland, the Karl-Küpfmüller-Ehrenring from the Technical University Darmstadt, and the Preis der Hörgeräte-Akustiker.

In 1990 October Professor Zwicker retired from his duties as Director of the Institute of Electroacoustics at the Technical University Munich. A little more than a month later, on November 22, he died of cancer at his home in Icking, Germany. In 1991 February, the AES Gold Medal was awarded to him posthumously.

Professor Zwicker's obituary appears in *In Memoriam* in the 1991 March issue of the AES Journal.

●

Ulrich Tilmann Zwicker was born in Stuttgart, Germany, in 1955. He studied physics and electrical engineering at the Technical University Munich (TUM) from which he received a bachelor's degree specializing in communications engineering, electroacoustics, and psychoacoustics in 1978, and a master's degree in 1981.

After graduating, Dr. Zwicker became a research associate at the Institute of Electroacoustics (TUM) in the area of acoustics, electroacoustics, psychoacoustics, acoustical measurements, and audio. In 1983 he became assistant professor at the Institute of Instrumentation (TUM) where his research moved into the field of high-frequency/solid-state acoustics, instrumentation, and control. In addition to administrative tasks, his work included teaching instrumentation with associated laboratory courses, and cooperative projects with Siemens AG, Mercedes-Benz AG, and the 1st Institute of Metrology, Beijing, China. In 1988 he received the Dr.-Ing. degree with a dissertation in instrumentation.

In 1989, Dr. Zwicker continued his research in the area of psychoacoustics and acoustics as visiting research associate to the Department of Audiology and Department of Electrical and Computer Engineering at Northeastern University, Boston, MA; the Physics/Astronomy Department of Michigan State University, East Lansing, MI; and the Department of Neurophysiology of the University of Wisconsin Medical School, Madison, WI. He became an associate professor at the Institute of Electroacoustics (TUM) in 1990 doing research in binaural hearing. In 1990 September, he joined the European Patent Office, in Munich, as a patent examiner doing substantive examination.

Dr. Zwicker has published extensively and has given numerous invited and contributed lectures in his field of interest. He is a member of the AES.

Advances in Speech and Audio Compression

ALLEN GERSHO, FELLOW, IEEE

Invited Paper

Speech and audio compression has advanced rapidly in recent years spurred on by cost-effective digital technology and diverse commercial applications. Recent activity in speech compression is dominated by research and development of a family of techniques commonly described as code-excited linear prediction (CELP) coding. These algorithms exploit models of speech production and auditory perception and offer a quality versus bit rate tradeoff that significantly exceeds most prior compression techniques for rates in the range of 4 to 16 kb/s. Techniques have also been emerging in recent years that offer enhanced quality in the neighborhood of 2.4 kb/s over traditional vocoder methods. Wideband audio compression is generally aimed at a quality that is nearly indistinguishable from consumer compact-disc audio. Subband and transform coding methods combined with sophisticated perceptual coding techniques dominate in this arena with nearly transparent quality achieved at bit rates in the neighborhood of 128 kb/s per channel.

I. INTRODUCTION

Compression of telephone-bandwidth speech has been an ongoing area of research for several decades. Nevertheless, in the last several years, there has been an explosion of interest and activity in this area with numerous applications in telecommunications and storage, and several national and international standards have been adopted. High-fidelity audio compression has also advanced rapidly in recent years, accelerated by the commercial success of consumer and professional digital audio products. The surprising growth of activity in the relatively old subject of speech compression is driven by the insatiable demand for voice communication, by the new generation of technology for cost-effective implementation of digital signal processing algorithms, by the need to conserve bandwidth in both wired and wireless telecommunication networks, and the need to conserve disk space in voice storage systems. Most of this effort is focused on the usual telephone bandwidth of roughly 3.2 kHz (200 Hz to 3.4 kHz). There has also

Manuscript received November 1, 1993; revised January 15, 1994. This work was supported in part by the National Science Foundation, Fujitsu Laboratories, Ltd., the UC Micro program, Rockwell International Corporation, Hughes Aircraft Company, Echo Speech Corporation, Signal Technology, Inc., and Qualcomm, Inc.

The author is with the Center for Information Processing Research, Department of Electrical and Computer Engineering, University of California, Santa Barbara, CA 93106, USA.

IEEE Log Number 9401177.

been a very large increase in research and development in the coding of audio signals, particularly, wideband audio (typically 20-kHz bandwidth) for transmission and storage of CD-quality music. Interest in wideband (7-kHz) speech for audio in video teleconferencing has also increased in recent years.

Since standards are essential for compatibility of terminals in voice and audio communication systems, standardization of speech and audio coding algorithms has lately become a major activity of central importance to industry and government. As a result, the driving force for much of the research in speech and audio coding has been the challenge of meeting the objectives of standards committees. The most important organization involved in speech coding standardization is the Telecommunication Standardization Sector of the International Telecommunications Union, referred to by the acronym ITU-T (the successor of the International Telephone and Telegraph Consultative Committee, CCITT). Other standards organizations will be mentioned later in this paper.

This paper highlights the state of the art for digital compression of speech and audio signals. The scope is limited to surveying the most important and prevailing methods, approaches, and activities of current interest without attempting to give a tutorial presentation of specific algorithms or a historical perspective of the evolution of speech coding methods. No attempt is made to offer a complete review of the numerous contributions that have been made in recent years, and inevitably some important papers and methods will be overlooked. Nevertheless, the major ideas and trends are covered here and attention is focused on those contributions which have had the most impact on the current state of the art. Many algorithms that are no longer of current importance are not covered at all or only briefly mentioned here, even though they may have been widely studied in the past. We do not attempt to describe the quantitative performance of different coding algorithms as determined from the many subjective evaluations that have taken place in recent years.

For reviews, tutorials, or collections of papers on earlier work in speech compression, see [205], [83], [204], [110],

[67], [115], [85], [46], [79], [253]. A recent survey of audio compression is given in [77]. For a cross section of recent work in speech compression, see [8], [9]. A general perspective of issues, techniques, targets, and standards in signal compression is given in [112]. A comprehensive review of the methods and procedures involved in speech standardization and some recent activity in this area is given in [65].

Virtually all work in speech and audio compression involves *lossy compression* where the numerical representation of the signal samples is never recovered exactly after decoding (decompression). There is a wide range of tradeoffs between bit rate and recovered speech quality that are of practical interest in the coding of telephone speech, where users are accustomed to tolerating various degrees of degradation. On the other hand, for wideband audio compression, consumers have higher expectations today, and quality close to that of the compact disc (CD) is generally needed. Thus research in speech compression includes concurrent studies for different distortion-rate tradeoffs motivated by various applications with different quality objectives. For wideband audio compression, most research aims at the same or similar standard of quality as offered by the CD.

Although the term *compression* is commonly used in the lay press and in the computer science literature, researchers working in speech or audio generally prefer the term *coding*. This avoids ambiguity with the alternative use of *speech compression* that refers to time-scale modification of speech, as in the speeding-up of the speech signal, e.g., in learning aids for the blind. Information theorists refer to signal compression as *source coding*. Henceforth, we shall use the term *coding*.

The ease of real-time implementation of speech-coding algorithms with single-chip digital signal processors has led to widespread implementations of speech algorithms in the laboratory as well as an extension of applications to communication and voice storage systems. The largest potential market for speech coding is in the emerging area of personal communication systems (PCS) where volumes of hundreds of millions are expected in the U.S. alone, and comparable numbers in Western Europe and Japan. In the next decade or so, a significant number (perhaps more than 50%) of telephones are expected to become wireless. Another new area of application is multimedia in personal computing where voice storage is becoming a standard feature. With so many applications already emerging or expected to emerge in the next few years, it is not surprising that speech coding has become such an active field of research in recent years.

Wideband audio coding for high-fidelity reproduction of voice and music has emerged as an important activity in the past decade. Applications of audio coding lie largely with the broadcasting industry, motion picture industry, and consumer audio and multimedia products. A key international standard developed by the Motion Picture Experts Group (MPEG) of the International Standards Organization (ISO) includes an audio coding algorithm [21].

Speech-coding algorithms can be divided into two main categories *waveform coders* and *vocoders*. The term vocoder historically originated as a contraction of *voice coder*. In waveform coders, the data transmitted from encoder to decoder specify a representation of the original speech as a waveform of amplitude versus time, so that the reproduced signal approximates the original waveform and, consequently, provides an approximate recreation of the original sound. In contrast, vocoders do not reproduce an approximation to the original waveform; instead, parameters that characterize individual sound segments are specified and transmitted to the decoder, which then reconstructs a new and different waveform that will have a similar sound. Vocoders are sometimes called *parametric coders* for obvious reasons. Often these parameters characterize the short-term spectrum of a sound. Alternatively, the parameters specify a mathematical model of human speech production suited to a particular sound. In either case, the parameters do not provide sufficient information to regenerate a close approximation to the original waveform but the information is sufficient for the decoder to synthesize a perceptually similar speech sound. Vocoders operate at lower bit rates than waveform coders but the reproduced speech quality, while intelligible, usually suffers from a loss of naturalness and some of the unique characteristics of an individual speaker are often lost.

Most work on speech coding today is based on telephone-bandwidth speech, nominally limited to about 3.2 kHz and sampled at the rate of 8 kHz. Wideband speech coding is of increasing interest today and is intended for speech or audio signals of 7 kHz, sampled at 16 kHz. High-fidelity audio signals of bandwidth 20 kHz are generally sampled at rates of 44.1 or 48 kHz although there is also some interest in 15-kHz bandwidth signals with a 32-kHz sampling rate. Audio coding schemes of interest today include joint coding of multiple audio channels.

Much of the work in waveform speech coding, is dominated by a handful of different algorithmic approaches and most of the developments in recent years have focused on modifications and enhancements of these generic methods. Most notable and most popular for speech coding is *code-excited linear prediction* (CELP). Other methods in commercial use today that continue to receive some attention include *adaptive delta modulation* (ADM), *adaptive differential pulse code modulation* (ADPCM), *adaptive predictive coding* (APC), *multipulse linear predictive coding* (MP-LPC), and *regular pulse excitation* (RPE). MP-LPC, RPE, and CELP belong to a common family of analysis-by-synthesis algorithms to be described later. These algorithms are sometimes viewed as "hybrid" algorithms because they borrow some features of vocoders, but they basically belong to the class of waveform coders.

Although many vocoders were studied several decades ago, the most important survivor is the *linear predictive coding* (LPC) vocoder, which is extensively used in secure voice telephony today and is the starting point of some current vocoder research. Another vocoding approach that has emerged as an effective new direction in the past decade is *sinusoidal coding*. In particular, *sinusoidal transform coding* (STC) and *multiband excitation* (MBE) coding are both very actively studied versions of sinusoidal coding.

Many waveform coders with other names are closely related to those listed here. Of diminishing interest are RPE, MP-LPC, ADPCM, and ADM although versions of these have become standardized for specific application areas. Perhaps the oldest algorithm to be used in practice is ADM, one well-known version of which is *continuously variable slope delta modulation* (CVSD). Although the performance of ADPCM at 32 kb/s can today be achieved at much lower rates by more "modern" algorithms, ADPCM remains of interest for some commercial applications because of its relatively low complexity.

Subband and transform coding methods have been extensively studied for speech coding a decade ago. Today, they serve as the basis for most wideband audio-coding algorithms and for many image- and video-coding schemes but they are generally not regarded today as competitive techniques for speech coding. Nevertheless, many researchers continue to study subband and transform techniques for speech coding and a few very interesting and effective coding schemes of current interest make use of filter banks or some form of linear transformation. These techniques generally function as building blocks that contribute to an overall algorithm for some effective coding schemes such as IMBE and CELP. One ITU-T standard, Recommendation G.722, for wideband (7-kHz) speech at 64, 56, and 48 kb/s, uses a two-band subband coder [225], [174].

Compression algorithms of current interest for wideband audio are based on signal decompositions via linear transformations or subband filter banks (including wavelet methods) which allow explicit and separate control of the coding of different frequency regions in the auditory spectrum. Efficient coding is achieved with the aid of sophisticated perceptual masking models for dynamically allocating bits to different frequency bands. The quality objectives for audio coding are generally much more demanding than for speech coding. The usual goal is to attain a quality that is nearly indistinguishable from that of the compact disc (CD). In contrast, most speech coding is applied to signals already limited by the telephone bandwidth so that users are not accustomed to high-fidelity reproduction.

This paper is organized as follows. In Section II, we give a brief overview of the most important family of speech coding algorithms that includes CELP and in Section III we review the recent activity in CELP coding, the most widely studied algorithmic approach of current interest. Section IV examines the advances in low-delay speech coding and Section V reviews the area of variable-rate speech coding. In Section VI, we examine recent developments in vocoders. Section VII looks at wideband speech and audio coding. Section VIII summarized the current performance achievable today in speech and audio coding at various bit rates. Finally, in Section IX, some concluding remarks are offered.

II. LPAS SPEECH CODING

The approach to speech coding most widely studied and implemented today is *linear-prediction-based analysis-by-synthesis* (LPAS) coding. An LPAS coder has three basic features:

- Basic decoder structure: The decoder receives data which specify an excitation signal and a synthesis filter; the reproduced speech is generated as the response of the synthesis filter to the excitation signal.
- Synthesis filter: The time-varying linear-prediction-based synthesis filter is periodically updated and is determined by *linear prediction* (LP) analysis of the current segment or *frame* of the speech waveform; the filter functions as a shaping filter which maps a relatively flat spectral-magnitude signal into a signal with an autocorrelation and spectral envelope that are similar to those of the original speech.
- Analysis-by-synthesis excitation coding: The encoder determines the excitation signal one segment at a time, by feeding candidate excitation segments into a replica of the synthesis filter and selecting the one that minimizes a perceptually weighted measure of distortion between the original and reproduced speech segments.

The earliest proposals for LPAS coder configurations appeared in 1981. Schroeder and Atal described a tree-code excitation generator [206] and Stewart proposed a codebook excitation source [222]. The first effective and practical form of LPAS coder to be introduced was *multipulse LPC* (MP-LPC) due to Atal and Remde [11] where in each frame of speech, a *multipulse* excitation is computed as a sparse sequence of amplitudes (pulses) separated by zeros. The locations and amplitudes of the pulses in the frame are transmitted to the decoder. An MP-LPC algorithm at 9.6 kb/s was recently adopted as a standard for aviation satellite communications by the Airlines Electronic Engineering Committee (AEEC).

In 1986 *regular pulse excitation* (RPE) coding was introduced by Kroon, Deprettere, and Sluyter [145]. Also an LPAS technique, RPE uses regularly spaced pulse patterns for the excitation with the position of the first pulse and the pulse amplitudes determined in the encoding process. Although inspired by MP-LPC, it is also close in spirit to CELP. A modified version of RPE, called *regular pulse excitation with long-term prediction* (RPE-LTP), was selected as part of the first standard for time-division multiple-access (TDMA) digital cellular telephony by the global system for mobile telecommunications (GSM) subcommittee of the European Telecommunications Standards Institute (ETSI) [93].

Most early LPAS methods were based on a synthesis filter which is a cascade of a short-term or *formant* filter and a long-term or *pitch* filter. The short-delay filter is typically a 10th-order all-pole filter with parameters obtained by conventional LP analysis The long-term filter is typically based on a single-tap or three-tap pitch·prediction. The properties of these pitch filters were extensively studied by Ramachandran and Kabal [193], [194].

A key element of LPAS coding is the use of *perceptual weighting* of the error signal for selecting the best excitation via analysis-by-synthesis. The error between original and synthesized speech is passed through a time-varying perceptual weighting filter which emphasizes the error in frequency bands where the input speech has valleys and de-emphasizes the error near spectral peaks. The effect is to reduce the resulting quantization noise in the valleys and increase it near the peaks. This is generally done by an all-pole filter obtained from the LP synthesis filter by scaling down the magnitude of the poles by a constant factor. This technique exploits the masking feature of the human hearing system to reduce the audibility of the noise. It is based on the classic work of Atal and Schroeder in 1979 on subjective error criteria [12].

The most important form of LPAS coding today is commonly known as *code-excited linear prediction* (CELP) coding, but has also been called *stochastic coding*, *vector excitation coding* (VXC), or *stochastically excited linear prediction* (SELP). CELP improves on MP-LPC by using vector quantization (VQ) [76], where a predesigned set of excitation vectors is stored in a *codebook*, and for each time segment the encoder searches for that code vector whose set of samples best serves as the excitation signal for the current time segment. The address of the selected code vector is transmitted to the receiver, which has a copy of the codebook, so that the receiver can regenerate the selected excitation segment. For example, a codebook containing 1024 code vectors each of dimension 40 would require a 10-b word to specify each successive 40 samples of the excitation signal. The superior performance capability of CELP compared to MP-LPC and earlier coding methods for bit rates ranging from 4.8 to 16 kb/s has become generally recognized. Today, the terminology "CELP" refers to a family of coding algorithms rather than to one specific technique; all algorithms in this family are based on LPAS with VQ for coding the excitation.

The invention of CELP is generally attributed to Atal and Schroeder [13], [207]. A somewhat similar coding technique was also introduced by Copperi and Sereno [42]. At least one earlier research study contained the key element of CELP, namely, LPAS coding with VQ [222]. In fact, MP-LPC is sometimes viewed as a special form of CELP, in which a multistage VQ structure with a particular set of deterministic codebooks are used [135]. RPE can even more easily be seen as a form of CELP coding. Another coding method, *vector-adaptive predictive coding* (VAPC) has many features of CELP including the use of VQ and analysis-by-synthesis but differs in the encoder search structure and in the ordering of short-term and long-term synthesis filtering [36], [37]. Rose and Barnwell introduced the *self-excited coder* [196], which used prior excitation segments as code vectors for the current excitation. Although MP-LPC perhaps represents a conceptually more fundamental advance in speech coding,

CELP has had a much greater impact in the field. While newer coding techniques have since been developed, none clearly overtakes CELP in the range of bit rates 4–16 kb/s.

III. CELP ALGORITHMS

A. History

Initially viewed as an algorithm of extraordinary complexity, CELP served only as an existence proof (with the help of supercomputers) that it is possible to get very high speech quality at bit rates far below what was previously considered feasible. The first papers on CELP coding by Atal and Schroeder [13], [207] attracted great attention, intrigued researchers, and continue to be widely cited today. In 1986, soon after CELP's introduction, several reduced complexity methods for implementation of the basic CELP algorithm were reported [239], [52], [94], [157]. By circumventing the initial complexity barrier of CELP, these papers indicated that CELP is more than a theoretical curiousity, but rather an algorithm of potential practical importance. It was quickly recognized that real-time implementation of CELP was indeed feasible. The number of studies of CELP coding algorithms has grown steadily since 1986. Numerous techniques for reducing complexity and enhancing the performance of CELP coders emerged in the next seven years, and CELP has found its way into national and international standards for speech coding. Some current speech coding algorithms are hybrids of CELP and other coding approaches. Our definition of CELP encompasses any coding algorithm that combines the features of LPAS with some form of VQ for representing the excitation signal.

Significant landmarks in the history of CELP are the adoptions of several telecommunications standards for speech coding based on the CELP approach. The first of these was the development and adoption of the U.S. Federal Standard 1016, a CELP algorithm operating at 4.8 kb/s, intended primarily for secure voice transmission and incorporating various modifications and refinements of the initial CELP concept. For a description of this standard, see Campbell *et al.* [26]. Another important landmark is the development of a particular CELP algorithm called *vector-sum excited linear prediction* (VSELP) by Gerson and Jasiuk [81] which has been adopted as a standard for North American TDMA digital cellular telephony and, in a modified form, for the Japanese Digital Cellular (JDC) TDMA standard. Very recently, the JDC has adopted a half-rate standard for the Japanese TDMA digital cellular system called *pitch synchronous innovation* CELP (PSI-CELP) [176]. In 1992, the CCITT (now ITU-T) adopted the *low-delay CELP* (LD-CELP) algorithm, developed by Chen *et al.*, [30], [34] as an international standard for 16-kb/s speech coding. Currently, the GSM is establishing a standard for half-rate TDMA digital cellular systems in Europe and the two remaining candidates for the speech-coding component are both CELP algorithms. Also, the Telephone Industry Association (TIA) is now evaluating eight candidate algorithms for a North American half-rate TDMA digital cellular standard, and most of the candidates are CELP algorithms.

Numerous advances to CELP coding have been developed, to reduce complexity, increase robustness-to-channel errors, and improve quality. Much of this effort is oriented to improving the excitation signal while controlling or reducing the excitation search complexity. Some advances have been made to improve the modeling of the short-term synthesis filter or the quantization of the linear predictor parameters. Below we highlight some of the more important improvements to CELP coding.

B. Closed-Loop Search

In the initial description of CELP [13], [207] only the basic conceptual idea was reported without regard to a practical mechanism for performing the encoder's search operation. Subsequently, some essential details were reported in 1986 for efficiently handling the search operation. In particular, it is efficient to separately compute the *zero-input response* (the ringing) of the synthesis filter after the previously selected optimal excitation vector has passed through it. After accounting for the effect of this ringing, the search for the next excitation vector can be conducted based on a zero initial condition assumption; thus the *zero-state response* of the synthesis filter is computed for each candidate code vector [239], [52]. This use of superposition greatly simplifies the codebook search process.

In [13], the gain scaling factor of the excitation vector was determined from the energy of the original speech prediction error signal, (called the *residual*). The residual is obtained after both short-term prediction and pitch prediction are performed. Subsequently, it was recognized that a *closed-loop gain computation* is easily done so that, in effect, the selection of both gain and code vector is jointly optimized in the analysis-by-synthesis process [7]. This leads to an important quality improvement.

C. Excitation Codebooks

In the *stochastic* excitation codebook initially proposed for CELP, each element of each code vector was an independently generated Gaussian random number. The resulting unstructured character of the codebook is not amenable to efficient search methods, and exhaustive search requires a very high complexity. A variety of structural constraints on the excitation codebook have been introduced to achieve one or more of the following features: reduced search complexity, reduced storage space, reduced sensitivity to channel errors, and increased speech quality. Some of the key innovations are summarized here.

An *overlapped* codebook technique, due to Lin, substantially reduces computation as well as codebook storage [157]. In this method, each code vector of the excitation codebook is a block of samples taken from a larger sequence of random samples by performing a cyclical shift of one or more samples on the sequence. Thus if a one-sample shift is used, a sequence of 1024 Gaussian samples can generate 1024 distinct code vectors of dimension 40. The effect of filtering each such excitation vector through the synthesis filter is achieved by a single convolution operation on the sequence. The search for the optimal code vector in an overlapped codebook is further accelerated by the use of a modified error weighting criterion introduced by Kleijn *et al.*, allowing a fast recursive computation [136].

A widely used approach to reduce search complexity and storage space is the use of *sparse* excitation codebooks where most of the code vector elements have the value zero. This is usually done in combination with other constraints on the magnitude or location of the nonzero elements. Sparse codebooks for CELP were proposed by Davidson and Gersho [52] and Lin [157]. Sparse codebooks can also be combined with overlapped codebooks. In *ternary* codebooks, proposed by Lin [157], and later Xydeas [254], the nonzero entries of a sparse codebook are forced to be $+1$ or -1. This can be achieved by hard-limiting the nonzero values of a stochastic codebook or by directly designing specific ternary codebook structures. Salami [200] proposed fixed regularly spaced positions for the nonzero entries so that a short binary word can directly specify the nonzero polarities, eliminating the need for a stored excitation codebook. This technique, called BCELP (for binary CELP), reduces complexity and sensitivity to channel errors while reportedly maintaining good quality. Sparse excitation signals were, of course, central to the technique of MP-LPC and preceded CELP. Attempts to improve MP-LPC by using a codebook of sparse excitation vectors may also be viewed as complexity-reduction methods for CELP. (See in particular Kroon *at al.* [145] and Hernandez-Gomez [71].) Many other sparse codebook schemes have been proposed, for example, Kipper *et al.* [128] and Akamini and Miseki [3].

Another family of excitation codebook methods are based on *lattices*, regularly spaced arrays of points in multiple dimensions. Lattice VQ was proposed in [74] and [75] and extensively studied by various researchers. (See in particular, Gibson and Sayood [84] and Jeong and Gibson [116].) Codebook storage is eliminated since lattices are easily generated and suitable mappings between lattice points (code vectors) and binary words are known. The use of lattice structures for excitation codebooks in CELP has been proposed by Adoul *et al.* who coined the phrase *algebraic codebooks* [1]. In their work, lattice codebooks with all code vectors having the same energy are generated from standard error-correcting codes by replacing the binary symbols 1 and 0 with $+1$ and -1, respectively. For additional examples of algebraic codebooks for CELP, see [150], [104], [148], and [63]. Le Guyader *et al.* [155] use binary-valued code vectors of unit magnitude so that binary words directly map into excitations without any codebook storage.

An alternative way of generating excitation codebooks is by designing them directly from actual speech files with a suitable *training* algorithm. This is the standard approach to codebook generation in vector quantization (VQ) [76]. However, a closed-loop design method is needed for CELP, which takes into account the role of the synthesis filter in order to optimize the codebook. A closed-loop design method for vector-predictive coding was reported in [47] and a closed-loop gain-adaptive codebook design was reported in [38]. A similar design specifically applied to CELP coding algorithms was described in [54]. Several codebook design algorithms for CELP were studied by LeBlanc and Mahmoud [152]. Closed-loop codebook design from training data has been used effectively in the LD-CELP algorithm by Chen *et al.* [34] and also in a CELP candidate for the current TIA half-rate standardization due to Serizawa *et al.* [210].

A number of excitation coding methods are based on the use of multistage excitation codebooks, where the excitation is generated as a sum of code vectors, one from each codebook, and the codebooks are sequentially searched. Multistage VQ was introduced by Juang and Gray [121] in 1980 and its application to CELP coding began in 1988. Davidson and Gersho proposed the general use of multiple excitation codebooks with sequential search and separate gain factors for each selected code vector [53]. Kroon and Atal briefly mentioned the idea of multistage excitation codebooks in [141]. Kleijn *et al.* proposed the use of two codebooks, one a stochastic codebook and the other an adaptive codebook [135], [134]. The adaptive codebook, which handles the pitch periodicity, and eliminates the need for a long-term synthesis filter, is now a standard part of most CELP coders and is discussed separately below. Subsequently, many authors have found effective ways to benefit from multiple excitation codebooks for the so-called stochastic (or nonperiodic) excitation component [177], [80], [66], [117], [233], [118], [92], [179], [178], [210]. Multiple codebooks offer reduced search and storage complexity as well as greater robustness to channel errors.

The usual sequential search of multiple codebooks in multistage VQ is suboptimal in comparison with a joint search which, however, would typically have excessive complexity. To approach or attain, with manageable complexity, the jointly optimal excitation as a sum of code vectors with one from each codebook, some form of orthogonalization is needed. Orthogonalization for searching multiple CELP excitation codebooks was proposed by Moreau and Dymarski [177], Gerson and Jasuik [80], and Johnson and Taniguchi [117]. See also [66] and [179]. Orthogonalization is also used in the PSI-CELP coder [176].

An important and effective CELP coder, the 8-kb/s VSELP coding algorithm of Gerson and Jasiuk, has a multiple codebook structure with two stochastic codebooks and two gain values, and each codebook is itself structured in a manner that can be viewed as a multistage technique [80]. An excitation in VSELP is formed by taking a binary linear combination of N *basis* vectors, so that each of N codebooks contains two code vectors, a basis vector, and the negative of that vector. With only a small number of basis vectors that need to be passed through the synthesis filter, the excitation search complexity is quite small. With this method, the binary word sent to the receiver directly specifies the polarities of the linear combination of the basis vectors. Thus a single channel bit error can alter only one term in this sum, causing only a moderate change in the decoded excitation vector. This simple relation between excitation vector and the corresponding binary codeword is very similar to the earlier work of LeGuyader *et al.* [155] and Salami [200].

A number of other complexity-reducing techniques have been proposed which do not fall into the above indicated categories for structuring the excitation codebooks. One interesting example is *CELP with base-band coding* (CELP-BB), due to Kondoz and Evans [139], [140], [14]. In this scheme, the short-term linear-prediction residual after low-pass filtering and downsampling is CELP-coded using only long-term (pitch) synthesis. The reduced sampling rate provides a large complexity reduction.

Another approach to reducing search complexity is the *preselection* method, where a simplified but suboptimal search procedure first selects a small subset of candidate code vectors from a codebook and then a second stage search is performed under the desired performance measure to select from the surviving candidates the optimal or near-optimal code vector. Preselection methods were introduced in [52], [94], [43], and have subsequently been applied to other coders, for example [176].

One novel technique for stochastic excitation coding is *pitch synchronous innovation* (PSI) reported by Miki *et al.* as part of their PSI-CELP coder [176]. In this technique, the adaptive codebook is searched in the usual way. If the resulting lag (loosely called the "pitch period") is less than the subframe length, the stochastic codebook is made to have vectors with periodicity based on this lag. This is done by taking the first part of each stored stochastic vector with a number of samples equal to the lag and repeating it till the entire subframe dimension is filled. This technique reportedly gives better performance than the comb filter method in [245] and with lower complexity.

D. Representation of Pitch Periodicity

An important advance in CELP coding came with the introduction of the so-called *adaptive codebook* for representing the periodicity of voiced speech in the excitation signal. In this method, after a search for the optimal time lag, a time-shifted and amplitude-scaled block of prior excitation samples is used as the current excitation; a stochastic codebook is then searched to provide a second vector which is scaled and added to the current excitation. With this technique, only the short-term synthesis filter representing the spectral envelope of the speech is needed—the long-term synthesis filter is eliminated. This method of achieving the needed periodicity in the synthesized speech was introduced by Singhal and Atal for MP-LPC [217] and applied to CELP coding by Kleijn *et al.* who introduced the term *adaptive codebook* [135]. When the pitch period is less than the dimension of the excitation vectors, a modified *virtual search* procedure, proposed in [135] and [122], is generally used. The adaptive codebook has become a standard feature of CELP coders. A somewhat similar concept to the adaptive codebook was the basis for the *self-excited* coder, introduced by Rose and Barnwell [196], in which no fixed excitation codebook is used but a new excitation segment is obtained (after an initialization) from delayed replicas of the past excitation.

The importance of an accurate reproduction of the periodicity in voiced speech led to the use of high-resolution or *fractional-pitch* methods proposed independently in 1989 by Marques *et al.* [169], [168], and by Kroon and Atal [142]–[144]. In this technique, improved speech quality is achieved by refining the resolution of the pitch period search to a fraction of a sample by means of interpolation. This method increases the size of the adaptive codebook and correspondingly the bit rate for pitch. This leads to more accurate prediction of the current subframe of speech from the filtered past excitation.

With the adaptive codebook, a pitch value is needed for each subframe, leading to a rather high bit rate for pitch information. This can be reduced by differential coding of the pitch within a frame: an average pitch for the frame is first determined, and incremental differences for each subframe are then specified. (See, for example, [265].) A version of this method is used in the FS 1016 CELP coder [26].

An interesting technique called *generalized analysis-by-synthesis* reported by Kleijn *et al.* allows piecewise-linear segments to track the pitch, substantially reducing the bit rate for pitch and eliminating the need for fractional pitch [137].

Further improvements to voiced speech coding were offered by the introduction of the *constrained-excitation* method by Shoham [213]. In this method some of the "gravelly" character of voiced speech in CELP is suppressed, by constraining the gain of the stochastic excitation, based on how good an approximation to the current speech segment is offered by the adaptive codebook. A modified version of constrained excitation, called *pitch sharpening* was proposed by Taniguchi *et al.* [229]. More recently, a smoothing method was proposed by Kleijn which explains the basic impediment to attaining high-pitch periodicity and does not significantly suppress the SNR as do the previous methods [113].

E. Coding of LP Spectral Parameters

In CELP and many other speech coders, the linear prediction parameters are used in modeling the signal and are quantized and transmitted every 20 to 30 ms. These parameters consume a large fraction of the total bit rate for low-rate coders. Hence considerable efforts have been invested in finding efficient ways to represent these parameters, most of them based on the use of VQ. The first application of VQ to quantization of LP parameters is due to Buzo *et al.* [25] in 1980. Most of the recent work on this topic is based on the quantization of *line spectral pairs* (LSP) also known as *line spectral frequencies* (LSF) originally introduced by Itakura in 1979 and first reported by Sugamura and Itakura in [223]. Perhaps the most important study of quantization of the LSF parameters

was presented in the comprehensive report of Kang and Fransen [124] and summarized in their paper [125]. This was the first application of VQ to LSF quantization. They were aiming for an 800-b/s LPC vocoder and designed a 12-b VQ scheme with a weighted distortion measure based on several considerations including auditory perception. Interframe coding of LSF parameters with vector prediction and VQ was later reported in [267] and [248].

Of the various efforts in applying VQ to high-resolution quantization of LSF parameters, the work that is often used as a benchmark for comparing other results is due to Paliwal and Atal [189]. Many authors have studied various alternatives and improvements. Some high-quality work on attaining "transparent" perceptual quality coding of LP parameters at low rates using multistage VQ while controlling complexity was reported by Bhattacharya *et al.* [16]. A multistage VQ technique including a partially adaptive codebook was introduced by Tanaka and Tanichuchi [226]. A computationally efficient algorithm for finding LSP parameters was reported by Kabal and Ramachandran [123]. Other computational methods have also been reported. See, for example, [219] and [203]. Examples of the use of product-code VQ for LSF quantization includes Paksoy *et al.* [187], Chan and Law, [28], Wang *et al.* [248], and Laroia *et al.* [151]. An LSF coding method which adapts to the long-term history of the speech spectral parameters was introduced by Xydeas [255]. Finally, some interesting methods for LSP quantization take into account the effect of channel errors. (See, for example, Secker and Perkis [208] and Hagen and Hedelin [87].) The latter method, based on a linear mapping of codewords in a block code into code vectors, is similar in concept but more general than the prior work of LeGuyader *et al.* [155], Salami [200], and Gerson and Jasuik [80].

F. Multimode Coding and Phonetic Classification

An important advance in CELP algorithms is the use of *multimode* coding or *dynamic bit allocation*, where the bits in each frame are dynamically allocated among the code components (e.g., excitation, pitch, and LP parameters) to adaptively match the local character of the speech. Multimode coding was proposed for low-rate ADPCM coding by Taniguchi *et al.* [236] and subsequently examined for CELP coding by Taniguchi *et al.* [227], [234], [235], Yong and Gersho [264], Kroon and Atal [141], and Jayant and Chen [114]. In one approach to multimode coding, one of several coding modes is selected in each frame by comparing an objective measure of performance offered by each mode. Other criteria have also been used for controlling the mode switching.

Phonetic classification of speech frames in CELP was subsequently introduced as an alternative and more sophisticated means for mode selection. Speech is a highly heterogeneous signal with a time-varying statistical character, ranging from highly predictable quasi-periodic to the almost completely random. The best coding strategies for such extremely diverse classes should adapt to these variations in the waveform and consider both the acoustic features and the phonetic content of the frame to be coded. With this approach, pattern-classification methods are used to identify each of a small set of phonetically distinct categories, which are defined so that each class is well-suited to a particular coding strategy. Identifying the voiced or unvoiced character of subframes is usually the starting point of such methods. Frames containing *onsets* having a transition from an unvoiced region to a voiced region or from a voiced stop into another voiced phoneme are usually given special attention [244], [246], [247], [188].

G. Interpolative Coding Methods

So much of the effort in CELP coding is devoted to accurately handling the reproduction of periodicity in speech. One promising approach to substantially reduce the rate needed for representing quasi-periodic speech segments is *prototype waveform interpolation* (PWI) introduced by Kleijn [130] and further developed by Kleijn and Granzow [132]. They represent and code a single prototype pitch cycle every 20 to 30 ms and reconstruct the signal by interpolating the sequence of pitch cycles between prototypes either in the time or spectral (i.e. discrete Fourier transform) domain. Linear interpolation of the pitch between prototypes and differential coding of the prototypes in the frequency domain are proposed. For lower rate coding, only the magnitudes of the spectral samples are coded. PWI is used to model the voiced excitation of speech so that synthesis is achieved by passing the reconstructed excitation through an LP synthesis filter. This is combined with conventional CELP coding for unvoiced speech.

By transmitting the coefficients of a Fourier series representation of the prototypes, the coder is in effect specifying a set of harmonic sinusoids which (with the aid of interpolation) could be used to synthesize speech. Although the synthesis does not proceed in this manner, it suggests a strong relation to sinusoidal coding, a parametric coding method to be discussed in the section on vocoders. The PWI approach lies somewhere in a gray region between vocoding and waveform coding.

An effective implementation of a coder based on PWI, called *time-frequency interpolative* (TFI) coding was reported by Shoham [215], [216]. The differential frequency-domain prototype parameters are coded here with a hierarchical VQ technique to obtain a low bit rate while maintaining an accurate representation. Subjective tests indicated an impressive quality at 2.4 and 4 kb/s compared to corresponding conventional schemes for these rates.

H. Postfiltering and Pitch Prefiltering

CELP coders tend to introduce some roughness (a noisy quality or hoarseness) to the reproduced speech. However, it is possible to enhance the speech by a postprocessing operation on the decoder output. Adaptive postfiltering based on the short-term prediction parameters has been proposed earlier to reduce perceived noise in ADPCM speech [195], [111]. This approach was extended to exploit long-term (pitch) prediction parameters in [259]. For LPAS

coders, a particular form of adaptive postfiltering which eliminates most of the muffling effect previously associated with postfiltering methods was introduced for both short-term [29], [37] and long-term postfiltering [29]. By avoiding the spectral tilt that postfiltering tends to introduce in the frequency response, this method has been found effective in enhancing performance for a variety of CELP coders [39]. With minor variations this method has been included in the TIA IS-54 VSELP standard, the JDC digital cellular standard, the U.S. Federal Standard 1016, and the ITU-T G.728 standard.

In the VSELP algorithm [80], the long-term (pitch) postfilter is relocated prior to the short-term synthesis filter, while the short-term postfilter remains after the synthesis filter. This variation, called *pitch prefiltering*, reportedly reduces artifacts sometimes introduced by pitch postfiltering. In another technique, called *adaptive comb filtering*, the pitch filtering is introduced in the encoder search loop as a prefiltering operation prior to the short-term synthesis filter [245]. The idea is to remove some of the annoying noise components from the excitation signal while retaining the various pitch harmonics. To reduce the influence of a random code vectors in one frame on the selection of the code vector in the adaptive codebook for subsequent frames, the comb filter is included in the pitch loop.

I. Other CELP Techniques

The techniques reviewed above constitute only a selected subset of a large variety of techniques and indicate the extensive effort that many researchers and engineers have undertaken to advance the family of CELP coders. Our coverage here represents primarily those methods that have found their way into standards or commercial products or those that have been frequently cited by subsequent papers. It is generally difficult to assess the quality of many individual methods for enhancing coder performance. Reported SNR improvements do not necessarily indicate perceptual quality improvements and self-reported quality assessments of researchers are difficult to calibrate. Thus many other clever or effective contributions may well be overlooked. Some additional examples of contributions to CELP coding are [156], [66], [70], [58], [6], [41], [2], [232], [228], [166].

IV. Low-Delay Speech Coding

For many applications, the time delay introduced by speech coding into the communications link is a critical factor in overall system performance. While the classical ADPCM algorithm introduces negligible delay, most contemporary coding algorithms must buffer a large block of input speech samples for linear prediction analysis prior to further signal processing. In addition to this buffering delay there is also computational delay in both encoder and decoder as well as delay in unpacking groups of data bits in the decoder. One-way end-to-end coder/decoder (codec) delays of 60 to 100 ms and occasionally even higher are common in speech coders. Algorithms which include error correcting codes and bit interleaving to combat high channel error rates can incur a substantial additional delay. In 1988, the CCITT (now ITU-T) established a maximum delay requirement of 5 ms with a desired objective of only 2 ms for a 16-kb/s standard algorithm. This culminated in the adoption of the LD-CELP algorithm as CCITT standard G.728 in 1992. The 16-kb/s G.728 algorithm was developed by Chen et al. [30]–[32], [34] as an international standard for 16-kb/s speech coding.

Several important ideas for modifying the CELP algorithm to achieve very low coding delay with high quality for both 16- and 8-kb/s rates emerged in a sequence of papers from 1987 to 1992. The key idea of gradient-based backward adaptation of the LP synthesis was well known prior to its application to LPAS (see Gibson [83]). Its application to LPAS coding was reported by Taniguchi et al. [230] and by Watts and Cuperman [250]. A high-quality low-delay tree coder with lattice-structured backward prediction filters and backward pitch prediction was reported by Iyengar and Kabal [109]. Backward adaptation of the pitch predictor in a CELP coder was reported by Pettigrew and Cuperman [191]. The use of lattice predictors for backward adaptation of the LP synthesis filter in a CELP configuration was studied by Peng and Cuperman [190]. A low-delay CELP coder called *low-delay vector excitation coding* (LD-VXC) for 16 kb/s was reported in [49].

The LD-CELP algorithm of Chen et al. [30]–[34] has the unusual feature of using a 50th-order LP block backward-adaptive synthesis filter, whereas prior CELP coders were almost invariably of 10th order or thereabouts. Furthermore, no pitch predictor or adaptive codebook is used at all. This coder also includes backward gain-adaptive VQ [38], pseudo-Gray coding [268], [61], [269], a novel hybrid of block and recursive windowing for LP analysis, white-noise correction, bandwidth expansion, and spectral smoothing, resulting in excellent robustness to channel errors.

Several studies of low-delay 8-ms coders have shown that in spite of the severe constraint on coding delay (e.g., a 5-ms buffering constraint), a fairly high quality is achievable [49], [40], [256], [258], [102], [266], [103], and [218]. However, these coders did not attain the quality of the G.728 LD-CELP coder at 16 kb/s.

Recently, the ITU-T has been conducting a standardization study of *medium-delay* coders where the delay requirement allows a frame size of up to 16 ms and total codec delay of at most 32 ms [90]. A medium-delay 8-kb/s coder with a 12-ms frame size was recently developed by Adoul et al., and was submitted to the ITU-T as a candidate [154], [202]. A technique for combining forward and backward pitch prediction for medium-delay coding at 8 kb/s was introduced by Kataoka and Moriya at NTT in Japan [126]. More recently, a high-quality medium-delay coder with a 10-ms frame length was reported by Kataoka et al. [127]; this is also a candidate for the ITU-T 8-kb/s standardization program. Their method makes use of the conjugate VQ technique [178].

A general review of the principal methods and techniques for low-delay coding is given in [48]. Finally, we note that an excellent historical review of the development of the G.728 LD-CELP algorithm is given by Chen and Cox in [33]. This fascinating paper offers a unique insider's perspective on speech coding by describing the four-year effort that led to the final algorithm.

V. VARIABLE-RATE SPEECH CODING

For digital transmission, a constant bit-rate data stream at the output of a speech encoder is usually needed. However, for digital storage and for some applications in telecommunications a variable bit-rate output is advantageous. *Variable bit-rate* (VBR) speech coders can exploit the pauses and silent intervals which occur in conversational speech and may also be designed to take advantage of the fact that different speech segments may be encoded at different rates while maintaining a given reproduction quality. Consequently, the *average* bit rate for a given reproduced speech quality can be substantially reduced if the rate is allowed to vary with time. Typically, VBR coders switch from one rate to another at intervals as short as 10 ms. The rate may be controlled *internally* by the statistical character of the incoming speech signal and/or *externally* by the current traffic level in a multi-user communication network. For a recent review of variable rate coding, see [78].

Traditional applications that have motivated the study of variable-rate speech coding include speech storage, packetized voice, and digital speech interpolation (DSI) for digital circuit multiplication equipment (DCME). Multiple-access schemes for wireless communication, particularly code-division multiple access (CDMA) systems have lately become an important application for VBR coding. Recently, the TIA has adopted a CDMA digital cellular telephony standard, known as IS-95, as an alternative to the earlier time-division multiple-access (TDMA) standard IS-54. A variable rate coding algorithm known as QCELP has been evaluated by the TIA as a speech-coding standard for use with IS-95. For a description of the QCELP algorithm, see [73], [60].

Most of the literature in VBR coding report on older methods such as ADPCM [260], [182] or subband coding [252], [162]. Recently, several interesting studies on variable-rate coding based on CELP have been reported [62], [64], [243], [251], [59], [188], [27].

An important component in variable rate speech coding is *voice activity detection* (VAD) which is needed to distinguish active speech segments from pauses, when the speaker is silent and only background acoustical noise is present. An effective VAD algorithm is critical for achieving low average rate without degrading speech quality in variable rate coders. An example of a good VAD scheme for asynchronous transfer mode (ATM) digital transmission is the work of Nakada and Sato (Japan) [182]. The design of a VAD algorithm is particularly challenging for mobile or portable telephones due to vehicle noise or other environmental noise. An important contribution in this category is due to Freeman et al. [68] whose VAD technique has been adopted as a part of the ETSI/GSM digital mobile telephony standard [220], [24]. More recently, a new VAD algorithm was reported which improves on the GSM algorithm in high-background-noise environments considering both vehicle and babble noise [221].

VI.   VOCODERS

Speech quality obtained by waveform coding methods including CELP coding is generally found to degrade rapidly as the bit rate drops below 4 kb/s. This is usually explained by the fact that the sparsity of bits (less than 1 b for every two amplitude samples of speech) makes it impossible to adequately approximate the original waveform. Even though LPAS coders attempt to pay more attention to accuracy in reproducing the short-term spectral magnitude in the perceptually important regions, they still devote precious bits to reproducing the general shape of the waveform. Vocoders, on the other hand, make no attempt to reproduce a waveform similar to the original. They generally abandon any attempt to encode the phase of the short-term spectrum and provide only information about the spectral magnitude for the decoder to synthesize speech. Thus vocoders have greater potential for reproducing a signal perceptually similar to the original, while operating at bit rates in the region of 2 kb/s and below, where effective waveform reproduction is virtually impossible.

A. LPC Vocoders

Among the various vocoders, the most widely studied in the past was the classical *linear-prediction coding* (LPC) vocoder due to Itakura and Saito [106] and Atal and Hanauer [10]. A version of the LPC vocoder has been used for many years as a U.S. Government standard, Federal Standard 1015, for secure voice communication. This particular coder, known informally as *LPC-10* because it uses 10th-order linear prediction, is based on a simple model of speech production [241]. The decoder synthesizes speech by passing an excitation signal through an LP synthesis filter. However, unlike LPAS coders, the excitation is generated in the receiver only from a relatively crude specification of the general character of the current speech frame and without actually sending bits that specify the excitation waveform. Each frame is characterized as *voiced* or *unvoiced* and for voiced frames the pitch period is specified. The gain (or, equivalently, the energy) of the excitation is coded and transmitted. The receiver generates a random-noise excitation for unvoiced frames and a train of impulses with the given periodicity for voiced frames.

While vocoders have been studied for many years [205], most of the classical methods are of little current interest because of their poor quality. Often the reproduced speech sounds artificial or "unnatural" with a "buzzy" character and the identity of the speaker is hard to recognize. These coders tend to degrade even further if the original speech contains acoustical background noise of various kinds. Recently, several new vocoder algorithms have emerged which appear

to be competitive with CELP coders at 4 kb/s and superior to CELP at 2.4 kb/s.

McCree and Barnwell have developed a very effective vocoder called the *mixed-excitation vocoder*, based on a number of substantive enhancements to the LPC vocoder concept [172], [173]. A mixed pulse and noise excitation signal is generated and applied to a synthesis filter. The excitation provides a frequency-dependent voicing strength which removes much of the buzzy quality of the standard LPC-10. Separate voicing decisions for different subbands of the speech band are made, similar to that of the MBE coder [86] discussed below. An adaptive spectral enhancement technique, similar to the adaptive postfiltering method of [37], is included as the first (rather than last) stage of the synthesis filter. Subjective test results reported in [173] indicate that the quality at 2.4-kb/s approaches that of the 4.8-kb/s Federal Standard 1016 CELP at 4.8 kb/s under clean speech conditions, and exceeds the 4.8-kb/s standard for noisy speech.

B. Sinusoidal Coders

An important class of vocoders, generically called *sinusoidal coders*, has emerged in recent years as a viable alternative to CELP, particularly for rates of 2–4 kb/s. These coders characterize the evolving short-term spectra of the speech by extracting and quantizing certain parameters which specify the spectra, giving particular attention to the pitch harmonics present in voiced speech. The key feature of sinusoidal coders is that voiced speech is synthesized in the decoder by generating a sum of sinusoids whose frequencies and phases are carefully modified in successive frames to represent and track the evolving short-term spectral character of the original speech. Three main variants of sinusoidal coding have been studied: harmonic coding, sinusoidal transform coding (STC), and multiband excitation coding (MBE). In some versions, the phase information (as well as magnitude) of the sinusoids is obtained from the input speech spectrum and transmitted to the receiver. Other versions, operating at lower rates, do not transmit phase information.

The conceptual introduction of this approach is due to Hedelin [91]. Later Almeida and Tribolet [5] developed *harmonic coding* algorithms and in subsequent papers reported very high quality at 6 to 8 kb/s. (See for example, [167].) More recently, Marques, Almeida, and Tribolet studied critical issues needed to achieve high quality with harmonic coding at lower rates and they presented a 4.8-kb/s version of the algorithm [167].

Another version of sinusoidal coding, called *sinusoidal transform coding* (STC) was developed and extensively refined by McAuley and Quatieri [170], [171]. A third version of sinusoidal coding called *multiband excitation coding* (MBE) was developed by Griffin and Lim [86] and one version called *improved MBE* (IMBE), [23], was subsequently adopted by Inmarsat as a standard for satellite voice communications. A coder based on MBE is currently one of the finalists for the TIA half-rate TDMA digital cellular standardization [183].

Both STC and MBE identify spectral peaks in successive frame of speech and encode and transmit the amplitude (and in some cases the phase) of these peaks. The receiver synthesizes speech with similar time-varying spectra by controlling the magnitude and phase of a set of sine waves. In MBE, the selected spectral samples are harmonics of the pitch.

Several studies have shown that more efficient quantization can allow the MBE coder to operate with little drop in quality at rates of 2.4 kb/s or below. Brandstein [22], Yeldener et al. [197], [261]–[263], Garcia-Mateo et al. [72], and Rowe and Secker [198], have shown that the bit rate may be substantially reduced by replacing the spectral modeling with an LP modeling technique. Vector quantization of the spectral magnitudes without the use of LP models has been reported in [175] for 2.4 kb/s and in [183] for 3 kb/s. A different approach was taken by Hassenein et al. [89] for 2.4 kb/s, where the MBE analysis is followed by a postprocessor which selects three fixed bandwidth windows and sends spectral information only for these regions. They report comparable quality with full-band MBE for noise-free speech. Recently, a high-quality variable rate was reported, which combines MBE with phonetic classification and a novel spectral VQ technique [270].

Although the amount of work on sinusoidal coders has been very small compared to CELP, indications are that this is a promising approach and will lead to more efforts in future. The sinusoidal coders still retain some remnants of the traditional vocoder type of imperfections in the reproduced speech but generally give a cleaner, crisper reproduction than is available with CELP coders at comparable rates, i.e., 2.4–4 kb/s. An interesting comparison between CELP and sinusoidal coding by Trancoso et al. [240] suggests that these techniques are complementary and future work might lead to some merging of these two approaches. In fact, the PWI approach described earlier already performs a similar merger.

VII. Audio and Wideband Speech Compression

Audio coding usually refers to the compression of high-fidelity audio signals, i.e., with 15- or 20-kHz bandwidth for consumer hi-fi, professional audio including motion picture and HDTV audio, and various multimedia systems. Sometimes the term audio coding is also used to refer to wideband speech coding, the compression of 7-kHz bandwidth speech audio for videoteleconferencing and for future integrated subscriber digital network (ISDN) voice communication, where higher quality speech is feasible and desirable.

Digital coding of audio probably began in the early 1970's. Initial efforts simply used uniform or nonuniform (e.g., logarithmic) quantization of audio samples for digital transmission and storage. The British Broadcasting Corporation developed an audio compression scheme called *nearly instantaneous companding audio multiplex* (NICAM) for digital audio transmission. NICAM uses a block adaptive-gain amplitude scale, where one of five scale factors is specified for every block of 32 samples represented with 10 b/ sample. Including overhead bits, the NICAM standard carries a stereo audio signal of 15-kHz bandwidth at a rate of 728 kb/s. For an overview of NICAM and its application to digital transmission, see, for example, [199].

Virtually all the current work in hi-fi audio coding relies on either subband or transform coding to achieve a spectral decomposition of the signal. A transform coding technique with fully overlapping windows called *time-domain alias cancellation* (TDAC) was introduced by Princen and Bradley in 1986 [192] and combines features of both subband and transform coding. Scalar quantization and entropy coding are generally performed on the transformed signal components. Perceptual masking models determine adaptive bit allocations across the spectral components. Important contributions to transform-based audio coding with perceptual masking techniques include Brandenburg [18], Johnston [119], [120], Brandenburg et al. [19], [20], and the AC-2 coder of Davidson et al. [50], [51]. A collaborative effort led to the ASPEC (adaptive spectral perceptual entropy coding) of high-quality music signals, a transform coding scheme [20].

Recently, a transform coding scheme called AC-3, developed by Todd et al. [238] at Dolby Laboratories, was adopted for the multichannel audio portion of the forthcoming high-definition television (HDTV) terrestrial broadcasting standard of the U.S. Federal Communications Commission (FCC). The algorithm operates at a range of bit rates as low as 32 kb/s per channel with up to 5.1 channels. (The 0.1 channel is a low-frequency effects (subwoofer) channel.) The coder uses TDAC filter banks and perceptual masking. Other features include the transmission of a variable-frequency resolution spectral envelope and hybrid backward/forward adaptive bit allocation.

Subband coding has also been the basis of effective audio coding methods. An early example of subband coding is the ITU-T G.722 standard for 7-kHz audio which employs ADPCM to code each of two subbands. For wideband audio compression, a subband coding scheme called *masking pattern adapted subband coding and multiplexing* (MASCAM) was developed by Theile et al. [237]. Subsequently, a closely related algorithm called *masking pattern adapted universal subband integrated coding and multiplexing* (MUSICAM) was adopted in Europe for use in digital audio broadcasting. See Dehery et al. [56].

Most of the current international interest in audio compression algorithms is centered around the recently completed ISO/MPEG audio standardization. For an outline of the MPEG audio algorithm, see Brandenburg and Stoll [21] or Noll [77]. The standard supports sampling rates of 32, 44.1, and 48 kHz and bit rates ranging from 32 to 448 kb/s per monophonic or stereo channel. The ISO/MPEG audio algorithm has three layers of coding, each of increasing complexity and quality, which offer different versions suited to distinct application needs. A polyphase filter bank of 32 equal-size bands is used. Layer 1 has the lowest complexity: it performs a relatively simple perceptual weighting for bit allocation and is less adaptive to transitory material. Layer 2 is more flexible in sending gains for blocks of samples in one band or shared for two or more adjacent bands. Layer 2 is based on MUSICAM and layer 1 is a simplified version of layer 2. Block companding is used in each subband to quantize blocks of 12 samples each. Quantization resolution is determined by a masking model. Layer 2 differs from Layer 1 only in the joint quantization and coding of each triplet of scaling factors from three consecutive companding blocks in each subband. Layer 3 has the highest complexity and best quality versus rate tradeoff and consists of a combination of the ASPEC transform coding algorithm and the MUSICAM filterbank: an overlap-DCT transform is performed in each subband to provide increased frequency resolution. An adaptive block size for transform coding, inspired by the work of Sugiyama *et al.* [224], [108], mitigates "pre-echos." the audible noise preceding the onset of a sound. Thus both temporal masking as well as the usual frequency-domain masking give an improved performance in Layer 3. Each layer of the MPEG standard also includes a technique for joint coding of two stereo channels. For examples of interesting recent research in stereo coding see [120] and [95].

Two new consumer hi-fi audio products both use audio coding. They are the DCC (digital compact cassette) and the MiniDisc. Both use compression based on perceptual masking methods. The DCC scheme is called *precision adaptive subband coding* or PASC, the MiniDisc system is called *adaptive transform acoustic coding* (ATRAC). The PASC algorithm is essentially the same as the ISO/MPEG Layer 1 algorithm. The ATRAC coder is reported by Tsutsui *et al.* [242] and PASC is described by Lockhoff [161].

There has been considerable interest in wideband coding of speech for ISDN and teleconferencing applications. Effective coding methods here are often based on CELP. (See for example, Laflamme *et al.* [149]. Salami *et al.* [201], Ordentlich and Shoham [184], Fuldseth *et al.* [69], and Paulus *et al.* [186].) In some cases, the perceptual weighting used in CELP is modified and low-delay constraints are imposed. Much of this work is quite similar in methodology to the coding of telephone speech.

VIII. State of the Art

The current state of speech and audio coding from the users perspective is best summarized by describing the performance achievable with established algorithms. We give here only a qualitative description of quality.

The quality of a good connection in a normal wired network telephone call, i.e., *wireline* or *toll* quality, is achievable at 16 kb/s with the LD-CELP G.728 algorithm. The performance at this rate offers low delay and is suited to a large variety of applications. The coder is robust to moderate bit errors, moderate background acoustical noise, a reasonable range of input power levels, and to tandemed network connections where up to three separate encoding/decoding stages may arise.

Speech coding at 8 kb/s with medium delay is now under study for ITU-T standardization. Based on the reported results obtained by two candidate algorithms [127], [154], it is likely that the emerging standard will achieve wireline quality for most operating conditions.

At 4–6 kb/s, with the best current CELP algorithms, the speech exhibits noticeable coding noise, but the features of intelligibility, naturalness, and identifiability of the speaker's voice are retained. This quality is sometimes described as *digital cellular* quality since it is typical of the performance of current standards for digital cellular telephony. Sinusoidal vocoders at this rate region have a different type of distortion but still belong to the same general category of quality. These coders generally suffer from a lack of robustness to nonspeech sounds, such as the noise in a moving vehicle or babble noise. They also introduce a codec delay in the region of 60 to 100 ms.

At 2–3 kb/s, the quality of CELP is further degraded with noisy "hoarse" speech quality and the new generation of vocoders (sinusoidal and mixed-excitation), and PWI or TFI coders appear to offer better quality. The quality at this rate, described as *communications* quality, is intelligible with speaker intonation and identity preserved, but there is a slight loss of naturalness with some slight degree of buzziness in most coders. These coders generally have poor robustness to nonspeech sounds and they also introduce a relatively large coding delay.

At rates below 1 kb/s, the available speech coders are generally vocoders that operate on large segments of speech. They range from barely intelligible to reasonably intelligible but distortion is substantial and speaker identity and naturalness are lost. The coders introduce a delay of hundreds of milliseconds.

Wideband speech coding with 7 kHz based on CELP algorithms can achieve at 32 kb/s the same quality as the ITU-T G.722 algorithm at 64 kb/s. This provides roughly the quality of an FM radio announcer, with a richness notably greater than telephone bandwidth speech and with very high intelligibility, naturalness, and free from any noticeable distortion.

Wideband audio coding in the range of 96 to 128 kb/s per channel for 15- to 20-kHz bandwidth music achieves nearly transparent quality. In other words, most casual listeners will find the music indistinguishable from the original CD audio output for most source materials. Some particularly difficult music segments can reveal an audible distortion when coded at rates of 128 kb/s at least with a more discriminating than average listener. The ISO/MPEG standard with its choice of bit rates represents the current state of the art in audio coding.

IX. Concluding Remarks

Speech coding in the last decade has been dominated by the extensive studies and advances in the LPAS approach and more specifically with CELP algorithms. As the research frontier moves towards 2.4 kb/s and below, waveform coding with the best CELP techniques available today appears to be inadequate to meet the increasing quality objectives. Consequently, vocoder studies are experiencing a resurgence today as the focus of research on speech compression is gradually moving to lower bit rates. Sinusoidal and mixed-excitation coders appear to offer the potential for meeting the needs of future standards for 2.4-kb/s coding of speech.

Nevertheless, there are considerable difficulties to surmount before these low-rate coders can become telecommunication standards. In particular, adequate robustness of these coders in the presence of background noise and nonspeech sounds or transmission errors is not easy to achieve. For wireless schemes, a very large increase in bit rate is essential to handle the high error rates that arise. Mobile environments also have high levels of background noise and sophisticated adaptive noise cancellation schemes may be needed to achieve adequate performance. There are indeed many challenges ahead for researchers in speech coding.

Since ADPCM was standardized in 1984 (ITU-T G.721 standard), research at 32 kb/s diminished rapidly. With the new 16-kb/s ITU-T G.728 standard, there is relatively little remaining research interest at this bit rate. The recently developed first generation of standards for TDMA digital cellular telephony concentrated on rates ranging from a high of 13 kb/s for the ETSI/GSM RPE-LTP standard, to the (North American) Telephone Industry Association (TIA) IS-54 standard with VSELP at 8 kb/s, and the JDC standard at 6.7 kb/s. All of these cellular applications also provide channel error protection that add to the data rates needed for transmission, but which are not included in above bit-rate specifications. Most of the mobile applications of speech coding currently focus on the second-generation "half-rate" digital speech compression, where the rate is half of the first generation rates. In Japan, the JDC has already adopted a half-rate standard. The U.S. CDMA standard, IS-95, provides for alternative service options and a new variable-rate coding option is currently under study. Following the imminent "half-rate" standards for speech coding in Europe and in the U.S., future efforts in the next five years are likely to concentrate on coding algorithms for 2.4 kb/s with some continued activity at 4.8 and 8 kb/s for some specialized applications.

Audio coding activities have been dominated by the work developed for the MPEG audio standardization. New research in wideband audio coding at lower rates is now in progress, stimulated by plans for future MPEG standards.

There are many topics of importance in speech coding that have not been discussed in this paper due to length limitations. Progress in pitch and voicing detection (e.g., [98]), very-low bit-rate coding at 200 to 600 b/s (see, for example, [100]), coding for robustness to channel errors (e.g., [268] [35], [82] [44], [138]), improved perceptual error criteria for codebook searching (e.g., [249], [209]), objective measures of perceptual quality for evaluating coding algorithms [146], [129], [105] [185], [88], [45], [96], [55], [249], and the development of effective subjective testing methods are some of the additional topics actively being pursued but not covered here.

Speech and audio compression is indeed a very active area of research and development and generally requires a high level of specialization which combines strength in digital signal processing with a good understanding of human psychophysics and modern quantization methods.

ACKNOWLEDGMENT

Several colleagues have offered very helpful corrections and suggestions based on an early draft of this manuscript. In particular, the author wishes to thank S. Dimolitsas, J.-H. Chen, V. Cuperman, B. Kleijn, P. Kroon, M. Iwadare, E. Paksoy, A. Sekey, E. Shlomot, and T. Taniguchi.

REFERENCES

[1] J.-P. Adoul, P. Mabilleau, M. Delprat, and S. Morissette, "Fast CELP coding based on algebraic codes," in *Proc. Int. Conf. on Acoustics, Speech, and Signal Processing*, pp. 1957–1960, Apr. 1987.

[2] M. Akamine and K. Miseki, "CELP coding with an adaptive density pulse excitation model," in *Proc. IEEE Int. Conf. on Acoustics, Speech, and Signal Processing*, pp. 29–32, vol. 1, 1990.

[3] ——, "Efficient excitation model for low bit rate speech coding," in *Proc. 1991 IEEE Int. Symp. on Circuits and Systems*, vol. 1, pp. 586–589, 1991.

[4] ——, "Adaptive bit–allocation between the pole-zero synthesis filter and excitation in CELP," in *Proc. IEEE Int. Conf. on Acoustics, Speech, and Signal Processing* (Glasgow, Scotland, 1991), vol. 1, pp. 229–232.

[5] L. B. Almeida and J. M. Tribolet, "Harmonic coding: a low bit-rate good-quality speech coding technique," in *Proc. Int. Conf. on Acoustics, Speech, and Signal Processing* (Paris, France, 1982), pp. 1664–1667.

[6] F. G. Andreotti, V. Maiorano, and L. Vetrano, "A 6.3 kb/s CELP codec suitable for half-rate system," *Proc. IEEE Int. Conf. on Acoustics, Speech, and Signal Processing* (Toronto, Ont., Canada, 1991), vol. 1, pp. 621–624.

[7] B. S. Atal, "High-quality speech at low bit rates: multi-pulse and stochastically excited linear predictive coders," in *Proc. Int. Conf. on Acoustics, Speech, and Signal Processing* (Tokyo, Japan, 1986), pp. 1681–1684.

[8] B. S. Atal, V. Cuperman, and A. Gersho, *Advances in Speech Coding*. Norwell, MA: Kluwer, 1991.

[9] ——, *Speech and Audio coding for Wireless and Network Applications*. Norwell, MA: Kluwer, 1993.

[10] B. S. Atal and S. L. Hanauer, "Speech analysis and synthesis by linear prediction of the speech wave," *J. Acoust. Soc. Amer.*, vol. 50, pp. 637–655, 1971.

[11] B. S. Atal and J. R. Remde, "A new model of LPC excitation for producing natural-sounding speech at low bit rates," in *Proc. IEEE Int. Conf. on Acoustics, Speech, and Signal Processing* (Paris, France, May 1982), vol. 1, pp. 614–617.

[12] B. S. Atal and M. R. Schroeder, "Predictive coding of speech signals and subjective error criteria," *IEEE Trans. Acoust., Speech, Signal Process.*, vol. ASSP-27, no. 3, pp. 247–254, 1979.

[13] ——, "Stochastic coding of speech signals at very low bit rates," in *Proc. Int. Conf. on Communications*, pp. 1610–1613, May 1984.

[14] S. A. Atungsiri, A. M. Kondoz, and B. G. Evans, "Robust 4.8 kbit/s CELB-BB speech coder for satellite-land mobile communications," *Space Commun.*, vol. 7, no. 4–6, pp. 589–595, Nov. 1990.

[15] T. P. Barnwell, III, "Recursive windowing for generating autocorrelation coefficients for LPC analysis," *IEEE Trans. Acoust., Speech., Signal Process.*, vol. ASSP-29, pp. 1062–1066, Oct. 1981.

[16] B. Bhattacharya, W. LeBlanc, S. Mahmoud, and V. Cuperman, "Tree searched multi-stage vector quantization of LPC parameters for b/s speech coding," in *Proc. IEEE Int. Conf. on Acoustics, Speech, and Signal Processing* (San Francisco, CA, Mar. 1992), vol. 1, pp. 105–108.

[17] R. Boite, H. Leich, and G. Yang, "Simplification and improvement of the binary coded excited linear prediction (BCELP) for speech coding," in *Signal Processing V. Theories and Applications. (Proc. 5th European Signal Processing Conf.)*, vol. 2, pp. 1211–1214, 1990.

[18] K. Brandenburg, "OCF—A new coding algorithm for high quality sound signals," in *Proc. IEEE Int. Conf. on Acoustics, Speech, and Signal Processing* (Dallas, TX, Mar. 1992), vol. 1, pp. 141–145.

[19] K. Brandenburg, H. Gerhauser, D. Seitzer, and T. Sporer, "Transform coding of high quality digital audio at low bit rates-algorithms and implementations," in *Proc. IEEE Int. Conf. on Communications*, vol. 3, pp. 932–936, 1990.

[20] K. Brandenburg, J. Herre, J. D. Johnston, Y. Mahieux, and E. F. Schroeder, "ASPEC: Adaptive spectral perceptual entropy coding of high quality music signals," presented at the 90th Audio Engineering Soc. Conv., Paris, France, 1991, Reprint 3011.

[21] K. Brandenburg and G. Stoll, "The ISO/MPEG-audio codec: A generic standard for coding of high quality digital audio," presented at the 92nd Audio Engineering Soc. Conv., Vienna, Austria, Mar. 1992, Preprint 3336.

[22] M. S. Brandstein, "A 1.5 kbps multi-band excitation speech coder," S.M. thesis, EECS Dept., Mass. Inst. Technol., 1990.

[23] M. S. Brandstein, P. A. Monta, J. C. Hardwick, and J. S. Lim, "A real-time implementation of the improved MBE speech coder," in *Proc. IEEE Int. Conf. on Acoustics, Speech, and Signal Processing* (Albuquerque, NM, Apr. 1990), vol. 1, pp. 5–8.

[24] H. J. Braun, G. Cosier, D. Freeman, A. Gilloire, D. Sereno, C. B. Southcott, and A. Van der Krogt, "Voice control of the pan-European digital mobile radio system," *CSELT Tech. Reps.*, vol. 18, no. 3, pp. 183–187, June 1990.

[25] A. Buzo, A. H. Gray, Jr., R. M. Gray, and J. D. Markel, "Speech coding based upon vector quantization," *IEEE Trans. Acoust., Speech, Signal Process.*, vol. ASSP-28, no. 5, pp. 562–574, Oct. 1980.

[26] J. P. Campbell, Jr., T. E. Tremain, and V. C. Welch, "The DOD 4.8 KBPS Standard (Proposed Federal Standard 1016)," in *Advances in Speech Coding*, B. S. Atal, V. Cuperman, and A. Gersho, Eds. Norwell, MA: Kluwer, 1991, pp. 121–133.

[27] L. Cellario and D. Sereno, "Variable rate speech coding for UMTS," in *Proc. IEEE Workshop on Speech Coding for Telecommunications* (Ste. Adele, Que., Canada, 1993), pp. 1–2.

[28] C.-F. Chan and K.-W. Law, "New multistage scheme for vector quantization of PARCOR coefficients," *Electron. Lett.*, vol. 28, pp. 1267–1268, June 18,1992.

[29] J.-H. Chen, "Low-bit-rate predictive coding of speech waveforms based on vector quantization," Ph.D. dissertation, Univ. of Calif., Santa Barbara, Mar. 1987.

[30] ____, "A robust low-delay CELP speech coder at 16 kbits/s," in *Conf. Rec. IEEE Global Telecomm. Conf.* (Dallas, TX, Nov. 1989), vol. 2, pp. 1237–1241.

[31] "A robust low-delay CELP speech coder at 16 kb/s," in *Advances in Speech Coding*, B. S. Atal, V. Cuperman, and A. Gersho, Eds. Dordrecht, The Netherlands: Kluwer, 1991, pp. 25–36.

[32] "LD-CELP: A high quality 16 kb/s speech coder with low delay," in *Conf. Rec. IEEE Global Telecomm. Conf.* (San Diego, CA, Dec. 1990), vol. 1, pp. 528–532.

[33] J.-H. Chen, "The creation and evolution of 16 kbit/s LD-CELP: From concept to standard," *Speech Commun.*, vol. 12, no. 2, pp. 103–111, June 1993.

[34] J.-H. Chen, R. V. Cox, Y.-C. Lin, N. Jayant, and M. J. Melchner, "A low delay CELP coder for the CCITT 16 kb/s speech coding standard," *IEEE J. Sel. Areas Commun.*, vol. 10, pp. 830–849, June 1992.

[35] J.-H. Chen, G. Davidson, A. Gersho, and K. Zeger, "Speech coding for the mobile satellite experiment," in *Proc. IEEE Int. Conf. on Communications*, pp. 756–763, 1987.

[36] J.-H. Chen and A. Gersho, "Vector adaptive predictive coding of speech at 9.6 kb/s," in *Proc. Int. Conf. on Acoustics, Speech, and Signal Processing* (Tokyo, Japan, Apr. 1986), vol. 3, pp. 1693–1696.

[37] ____, "Real-time vector APC speech coding at 4800 bps with adaptive postfiltering," in *Proc. Int. Conf. on Acoustics, Speech, and Signal Processing*, pp. 2185–2188, Apr. 1987.

[38] ____, "Gain-adaptive vector quantization with application to speech coding," *IEEE Trans. on Commun.*, vol. COM-35, no. 9, pp. 918–930, Sept. 1987.

[39] ____, "Adaptive postfiltering for quality enhancement of coded speech," submitted for publication, 1994.

[40] J.-H. Chen and M. S. Rauchwerk, "An 8 kb/s low-delay CELP speech coder," in *Conf. Rec. IEEE Global Telecommunications Conf.* (Phoenix, AZ, Dec. 1991), vol. 3, pp. 1894–1898.

[41] M. Copperi, "Efficient excitation modeling in a low bit-rate CELP coder," in *Proc. IEEE Int. Conf. on Acoustics, Speech, and Signal Processing*, vol. 1, pp. 233–236, May 1991.

[42] M. Copperi and D. Sereno, "Improved LPC excitation based on pattern classification and perceptual criteria," in *Proc. 7th Int. Conf. on Pattern Recognition* (Montreal, Que., Canada, 1984), pp. 860–862.

[43] ____, "CELP coding for high-quality speech at 8 kbit/s," in *Proc. Int. Conf. on Acoustics, Speech, and Signal Processing* (Tokyo, Japan, Apr. 1986), vol. 3, pp. 1685–1689.

[44] R. V. Cox, W. B. Kleijn, and P. Kroon, "Robust CELP coders for noisy backgrounds and noisy channels," in *Proc. Int. Conf. on Acoustics, Speech, and Signal Processing* (Glasgow, Scotland, May 1989), pp. 739–742.

[45] D. P. Crowe, "Objective quality assessment," in *Dig. IEE Coll. on Speech Coding-Techniques and Applications* (London, England, Apr. 1992), pp. 5/1–5/4.

[46] V. Cuperman, "Speech coding," *Adv. Electron. Electron Phys.*, vol. 82, pp. 97–196, 1991.

[47] V. Cuperman and A. Gersho, "Vector predictive coding of speech at 16 kb/s," *IEEE Trans. Commun.*, vol. COM-33, pp. 685–696, July 1985.

[48] ____, "Low delay speech coding," *Speech Commun.*, vol. 12, no. 2, pp. 193–204, June 1993.

[49] V. Cuperman, A. Gersho, R. Pettigrew, J. S. Shynk, and J.-H. Yao, "Backward adaptation techniques for low delay vector excitation coding of speech," in *Conf. Rec. IEEE Global Telecomm. Conf.*, pp. 1242–1246, Nov. 1989.

[50] G. Davidson, W. Anderson and A. Lovrich, "A low cost adaptive transform decoder implementation for high-quality audio," in *Proc. IEEE Int. Conf. on Acoustics, Speech, and Signal Processing* (San Francisco, CA, Mar. 1992), vol. 2, pp. 193–196.

[51] G. Davidson, L. Fielder, and M. Antill, "High-quality audio transform coding at 128 kbit/s," in *Proc. IEEE Int. Conf. on Acoustics, Speech, and Signal Processing* (Albuquerque, NM, Apr. 1990), vol. 2, pp. 1117–1120.

[52] G. Davidson and A. Gersho, "Complexity reduction methods for vector excitation coding," in *Proc. IEEE Int. Conf. on Acoustics, Speech, and Signal Processing* (Tokyo, Japan, 1986), pp. 3055–2058.

[53] ____, "Multiple-stage vector excitation coding of speech waveforms," in *Proc. IEEE Int. Conf. on Acoustics, Speech, and Signal Processing* (New York, Apr. 1988), pp. 163–166.

[54] G. Davidson, M. Yong, and A. Gersho, "Real-time vector excitation coding of speech at 4800 bps," in *Proc. Int. Conf. on Acoustics, Speech, and Signal Processing* (Dallas, TX, Apr. 1987), pp. 2189–2192.

[55] A. De and P. Kabal, "Rate-distortion function for speech coding based on perceptual distortion measure," in *Conf. Rec., IEEE Global Telecomm. Conf.*, pp. 452–456, 1992.

[56] Y. F. Dehery, M. Lever, and P. Urcun, "A MUSICAM source codec for digital audio broadcasting and storage," in *Proc. IEEE Int. Conf. on Acoustics, Speech, and Signal Processing* vol. 1, pp. 3605–3609, 1991.

[57] R. Drogo de Jacovo, R. Montagna, F. Perosino, and D. Sereno, "Some experiments of 7 kHz audio coding at 16 kbit/s," in *Proc. IEEE Int. Conf. on Acoustics, Speech, and Signal Processing* (Glasgow, Scotland, May 1989), vol. 1, pp. 192–195.

[58] R. Drogo de Iacovo and D. Sereno, "6.55 kbit/s speech coding for application in the pan-European digital mobile radio cellular system," in *Proc. 5th European Signal Processing Conf.*, vol. 2, pp. 1231–1234, 1990.

[59] ____, "Embedded CELP coding for variable bit-rate between 6.4 and 9.6 kb/s," in *Proc. IEEE Int. Conf. on Acoustics, Speech, and Signal Processing* (Toronto, Ont., Canada, May 1991), pp. 681–683.

[60] A. DeJaco, W. Gardner, P. Jacobs, and C. Lee, "QCELP: The North American CDMA digital cellular variable rate speech coding standard," in *Proc. IEEE Workshop on Speech Coding*

for Telecommunications (Ste. Adele, Que., Canada, 1993), pp. 5–6.

[61] J. R. B. De Marca and N. S. Jayant, "An algorithm for assigning binary indices to the codevectors of a multi-dimensional quantizer," in *Proc. IEEE Int. Conf. on Communications* (Seattle, WA, June 1987), vol. 2, pp. 1128–1132.

[62] R. J. Di Francesco, "Real-time speech segmentation using pitch and convexity jump models: application to variable rate speech coding," *IEEE Trans. Acoust. Speech. Signal Process.*, vol. 38, no. 5, pp. 741–748, May 1990.

[63] ——, "Algebraic speech coding: ternary code excited linear prediction," *Annal. Telecommun.*, vol. 47, no. 5–6, pp. 214–226, May–June 1992.

[64] R. Di Francesco, C. Lamblin, A. Leguyader, and D. Massaloux, "Variable rate speech coding with online segmentation and fast algebraic codes," in *Proc. IEEE Int. Conf. on Acoustics, Speech, and Signal Processing*, vol. 1, pp. 233–236, 1990.

[65] S. Dimolitsas, "Standardizing speech-coding technology for network applications," *IEEE Commun. Mag.*, vol. 31, no. 11, pp. 26–33, Nov. 1993.

[66] P. Dymarski, N. Moreau and A. Vigier, "Optimal and sub-optimal algorithms for selecting the excitation in linear predictive coders," in *Proc. Int. Conf. on Acoustics, Speech, and Signal Processing* (Albuquerque, NM, April 1990), pp. 485–488.

[67] J. L. Flanagan, M. R. Schroeder, B. S. Atal, R. E. Crochiere, N. S. Jayant, and J. M. Tribolet, "Speech coding," *IEEE Trans. Commun.*, vol. COM-27, no. 4, pp. 710–737, Apr. 1979.

[68] D. K. Freeman, G. Cosier, C. B. Southcott, and I. Boyd, "The voice activity detector for the pan-European digital cellular mobile telephone service," in *Proc. IEEE Int. Conf. on Acoustics, Speech, and Signal Processing* (Glasgow, Scotland, May 1989), vol. 1, pp. 369–372.

[69] A. Fuldseth, E. Harborg, F. T. Johansen, and J. E. Knudsen, "Wideband speech coding at 16 kbit/s for a videophone application," *Speech Commun.*, vol. 11, no. 2–3, pp. 139–148, June 1992.

[70] C. Galand, J. Menez, and M. Rosso, "Adaptive code excited predictive coding," *IEEE Trans. Signal Process.*, vol. 40, no. 6, pp. 1317–1327, June 1992.

[71] R. Garcia-Gomez, F. J. Casajus-Quiros, and L. Hernandez-Gomez, "Vector quantized multipulse LPC," in *Proc. IEEE Int. Conf. on Acoustics, Speech, and Signal Processing* (Paris, France, Apr. 1987), vol. 4, pp. 2197–2200.

[72] C. Garcia Mateo, E. Rodriguez Banga, J. L. Alba, and L. A. Hernandez Gomez, "Analysis, synthesis and quantization procedures for a 2.5 kbps voice coder obtained by combining LP and harmonic coding," in *Proc. European Signal Processing Conf.* (Brussels, Belgium, Aug. 1992), vol. 1, pp. 471–474.

[73] W. Gardner, P. Jacobs, and C. Lee, "QCELP: A variable rate speech coder for CDMA digital cellular," in *Speech and Audio Coding for Wireless and Network Applications*, B. S. Atal, V. Cuperman, and A. Gersho, Eds. Norwell, MA: Kluwer, 1993, pp. 77–84.

[74] A. Gersho, "Asymptotically optimal block quantization," *IEEE Trans. Informat. Theory*, vol. IT-25, no. 4, pp. 373–380, July 1979.

[75] ——, "On the structure of vector quantizers," *IEEE Trans. Informat. Theory*, vol. IT-28, no. 2, pp. 157–166, Mar. 1982.

[76] A. Gersho and R. M. Gray, *Vector Quantization and Signal Compression*. Norwell, MA: Kluwer 1991.

[77] P. Noll, "Wideband speech and audio coding," *IEEE Commun. Mag.*, vol. 31, no. 11, pp. 34–44, Nov. 1993.

[78] A. Gersho and E. Paksoy, "Variable rate speech coding for cellular networks," in *Speech and Audio Coding for Wireless and Network Applications*, B. S. Atal, V. Cuperman, and A. Gersho, Eds. Norwell, MA: Kluwer, 1993, pp. 77–84.

[79] A. Gersho and S. Wang, "Recent trends and techniques in speech coding," in *Conf. Rec. 24th Asilomar Conf. on Signals, Systems, Computers* (Pacific Grove, CA, Nov. 1990), vol. 2, pp. 634–638.

[80] I. Gerson and M. Jasiuk, "Vector sum excited linear prediction (VSELP) speech coding at 8 kb/s," in *Proc. Int. Conf. on Acoustics, Speech, and Signal Processing* (Albuquerque, NM, Apr. 1990), vol. 1, pp. 461–464.

[81] ——, "Vector sum excited linear prediction (VSELP)," in *Advances in Speech Coding*, B. S. Atal, V. Cuperman, and A. Gersho, Eds. Norwell, MA: Kluwer, 1991, pp. 69–79.

[82] I. A. Gerson, M. A. Jasiuk, M. J. McLaughlin, and E. H. Winter, "Combined speech and channel coding at 11.2 kbps," in *European Signal Processing Conf.* (Barcelona, Spain, Sept. 1990), vol. 2, pp. 1339–1342.

[83] J. D. Gibson, "Adaptive prediction for speech differential encoding systems," *Proc. IEEE*, vol. 68, pp. 1789–1797, Nov. 1974.

[84] J. Gibson and K. Sayood, "Lattice quantization," *Adv. Electron. Electron Phys.*, vol. 72, pp. 259–330, 1988.

[85] N. Gouvianakis and C. Xydeas, "Advances in analysis by synthesis LPC speech coders," *J. Inst. ERE*, vol. 57, no. 6 (suppl.), pp. S272–S286, Nov./Dec. 1987.

[86] D. W. Griffin and J. S. Lim, "Multi-band excitation vocoder," *IEEE Trans. Acoust., Speech, Signal Process.*, vol. 36, no. 8, pp. 1223–1235, Aug. 1988.

[87] R. Hagen and P. Hedelin, "Robust vector quantization in spectral coding," in *Proc. IEEE Int. Conf. on Acoustics, Speech, and Signal Processing*, vol. 2, pp. 13–16, 1993.

[88] U. Halka and U. Heute, "A new approach to objective quality-measures based on attribute-matching," *Speech Commun.*, vol. 11, no. 1, pp. 15–30, Mar. 1992.

[89] H. Hassanein, A. Brind'Amour, and K. Bryden, "A hybrid multiband excitation coder for low bit rates," in *Proc. IEEE Int. Conf. on Wireless Communications* (Vancouver, BC, Canada, 1992), pp. 184–187.

[90] S. Hayashi and M. Taka, "Standardization activities on 8 -kbit/s speech coding in CCITT SGXV," in *Proc. IEEE Int. Conf. on Wireless Communication* (Vancouver, BC, Canada, June 1992), pp. 188–191.

[91] P. Hedelin, "A tone-oriented voice-excited vocoder," in *Proc. Int. Conf. on Acoustics, Speech, and Signal Processing*, pp. 205–208, 1981.

[92] P. Hedelin and A. Bergstrom, "Amplitude quantization for CELP excitation signals," in *Proc. Int. Conf. on Acoustics, Speech, and Signal Processing* (Toronto, Ont., Canada, 1991), pp. 225–228.

[93] K. Hellwig, P. Vary, D. Massaloux, and J. P. Petit, "Speech codec for the European mobile radio system," in *Conf. Rec., IEEE Global Telecomm. Conf.* (Dallas, TX, Nov. 1989), vol. 2, pp. 1065–1069.

[94] L. A. Hernandez-Gomez, F. Casajus-Quiros, A. R. Figueiras-Vidal, and R. Garcia-Gomez, "On the behavior of reduced complexity code-excited linear prediction (CELP)," in *Proc. Int. Conf. on Acoustics, Speech, and Signal Processing* (Tokyo, Japan, 1986), pp. 469–472.

[95] J. Herre, E. Eberlein, and K. Brandenburg, "Combined stereo coding," presented at the 93nd Audio Engineering Society Conv., San Francisco, CA, Oct. 1992, Preprint 3369.

[96] J. Herre, E. Eberlein, H. Schott, and K. Brandenburg, "Advanced audio measurement system using psychoacoustic properties," presented at the 92nd Audio Engineering Society Conv., Vienna, Austria, Mar. 1992, Preprint 3321.

[97] W. Hess, *Pitch Determination of Speech Signals: Algorithms and Devices*. New York: Springer-Verlag, 1983.

[98] W. Hess, "Pitch and Voicing Determination," in *Advances in Speech Signal Processing*, S. Furui and M. M. Sondhi, Eds. New York, Basel, Hong Kong: Marcel Dekker, 1992, pp. 3–48.

[99] M. Honda, "Speech coding using waveform matching based on LPC residual phase equalization," in *Proc. IEEE Int. Conf. on Acoustics, Speech, and Signal Processing* (Albuquerque, NM, Apr. 1990), vol. 2, pp. 213–216.

[100] M. Honda and Y. Shiraki, "Very low-bit-rate speech coding," in *Speech Signal Processing*, S. Furui and M. M. Sondhi, Eds. New York, Basel, Hong Kong: Marcel Dekker, 1992, pp. 209–230.

[101] G. Hult, "Some remarks on a halting criterion for iterative low-pass filtering in a recently proposed pitch detection algorithm," *Speech Commun.*, vol. 10, no. 3, pp. 223–226, Aug. 1991.

[102] A. Husain and V. Cuperman, "Low delay vector excitation speech coding at 8 kbits/s," in *1992 IEEE Int. Workshop on Intelligent Signal Processing Communication Systems* (Taipei, Taiwan, ROC, Mar. 1992), pp. 148–155.

[103] ——, "Lattice low delay vector excitation for 8 kb/s speech coding," in *Speech and Audio Coding for Wireless and Network Applications*, B. S. Atal, V. Cuperman, and A. Gersho, Eds. Norwell, MA: Kluwer, 1993.

[104] M. A. Ireton and C. S. Xydeas, "On improving vector excitation coders through the use of spherical lattice codebooks

(SLCs)," in *Proc. IEEE Int. Conf.on Acoustics, Speech, and Signal Processing*, pp. 57–60, May 1989.

[105] H. Irii, K. Kurashima, N. Kitawaki, and K. Itoh, "Objective measurement method for estimating speech quality of low-bit-rate speech coding," *NTT Rev.*, vol. 3, no. 5, pp. 79–87, Sept. 1991.

[106] F. I. Itakura and S. Saito, "Analysis-synthesis telephony based on the maximum likelihood method," in *Proc. 6th Int. Congr. on Acoustics* (Tokyo, Japan, 1968), pp. C17–20.

[107] K. Itoh and N. Kitawaki, "Real and artificial speech signals for objective quality evaluation of speech coding systems," *Electron. Commun. in Japan*, pt. 3 (*Fund. Electron. Sci.*), vol. 72, no. 11, pp. 1–9, Nov. 1989.

[108] M. Iwadare, A. Sugiyama, F. Hazu, A. Hirano, and T. Nishitani, "A 128 kb/ hi-fi audio codec based on adaptive transform coding with adaptive block size MDDCT," *J. Selected Areas Commun.*, vol. 10, no. 1, pp. 138–144, 1992.

[109] V. Iyengar and P. Kabal, "A low delay 16 kb/s speech coder," in *Proc. IEEE Int. Conf. on Acoustics, Speech, and Signal Processing*, pp. 243–246, 1988.

[110] N. S. Jayant, Ed., *Waveform Quantization and Coding*. New York: IEEE Press, 1976.

[111] N. S. Jayant and V. Ramamoorthy, "Adaptive postfiltering of 16 kb/s-ADPCM speech," in *Proc. IEEE Int. Conf. on Acoustics, Speech, and Signal Processing* (Tokyo, Japan, Apr. 1986), pp. 829–832.

[112] N. S. Jayant, "Signal compression: technology targets and research directions," *IEEE Trans. Selected Areas Commun.*, vol. 10, no. 5, pp. 795–818, June 1992.

[113] N. S. Jayant, J. Johnston, and R. Sofranek, "Signal compression based on models of human perception," *Proc. IEEE*, vol. 81, no. 10, pp. 1385–1422, Oct. 1993.

[114] N. S. Jayant and J. H. Chen, "Speech coding with time-varying bit allocations to excitation and LPC parameters," in *Proc. Int. Conf. on Acoustics, Speech, and Signal Processing* (Glasgow, Scotland, May 1989), vol. 1, pp. 65–69.

[115] N. S. Jayant and P. Noll, *Digital Coding of Waveforms*. Englewood Cliffs, NJ: Prentice-Hall, 1984.

[116] D. G. Jeong and J. D. Gibson, "Uniform and piecewise uniform lattice vector quantization for memoryless Gaussian and Laplacian sources," *IEEE Trans. Informat. Theory*, vol. 39, no. 3, pp. 786–804, May 1993.

[117] M. Johnson and T. Taniguchi, "Pitch-orthogonal code-excited LPC," in *Conf. Rec. IEEE Global Telecomm. Conf.*, vol. 1, pp. 542–546, Dec. 1990.

[118] ——, "Low-complexity multi-mode VXC using multi-stage optimization and mode selection," in *Proc. Int. Conf. on Acoustics, Speech, and Signal Processing* (Toronto, Ont., Canada, May 1991), vol. 1, pp. 221–224.

[119] J. D. Johnston, "Transform coding of audio signals using perceptual noise criteria," *IEEE J. Selected Areas Commun.*, vol. 6, pp. 314–323, Feb. 1988.

[120] J. D. Johnston and A. J. Ferreira, "Sum-difference stereo transform coding," in *Proc. IEEE Int. Conf. on Acoustics, Speech, and Signal Processing* (San Francisco, CA, Apr. 1992), vol. 2, pp. 569–572.

[121] B.-H. Juang and A. H. Gray, Jr., "Multiple stage vector quantization for speech coding," in *Proc. IEEE Int. Conf. on Acoustics, Speech, and Signal Processing* (Paris, France, Apr. 1982), vol. 1, pp. 597–600.

[122] P. Kabal, J. L. Moncet, and C. C. Chu, "Synthesis filter optimization and coding: applications to CELP," in *Proc. IEEE Int. Conf. on Acoustics, Speech, and Signal Processing* (New York, Apr. 1988), vol. 2, pp. 569–572.

[123] P. Kabal and R. P. Ramachandran, "The computation of line spectral frequencies using Chebyshev polynomials," *IEEE Trans. Acoust., Speech, Signal Process.*, vol. ASSP-34, no. 6, pp. 1419–1426, Dec. 1986.

[124] G. S. Kang and L. J. Fransen, "Low-bit-rate speech encoders based on line-spectrum frequencies (LSFs)," Naval Res. Lab., Rep. 8857, Nov. 1984.

[125] ——, "Application of line-spectrum pairs to low-bit-rate speech encoders," in *Proc. IEEE Int. Conf. on Acoustics, Speech, and Signal Processing* (Tampa, FL, Mar. 1985), pp. 244–247.

[126] A. Kataoka and T. Moriya, "A backward adaptive 8 kb/s speech coder using conditional pitch prediction," in *Conf. Rec. IEEE Global Telecommunication Conf.*, pp. 1889–1893, Dec. 1991.

[127] A. Kataoka, T. Moriya, and S. Hayashi, "An 8-kbit/s speech coder based on conjugate structure CELP," in *Proc. IEEE Int. Conf. on Acoustics, Speech, and Signal Processing* (Minneapolis, MN, 1993), vol. 2, pp. 592–595.

[128] U. Kipper, H. Reininger, and D. Wolf, "Improved CELP coding using adaptive excitation codebooks," in *Proc. IEEE Int. Conf. on Acoustics, Speech, and Signal Processing* (Toronto, Ont., Canada, May 1991), vol. 1, pp. 237–240.

[129] N. Kitawaki, "Research of objective speech quality assessment," *NTT Rev.*, vol. 3, no. 5, pp. 65–70, Sept. 1991.

[130] W. B. Kleijn, "Continuous representations in linear predictive coding," in *Proc. IEEE Int. Conf. on Acoustics, Speech, and Signal Processing* (Toronto, Ont., Canada, May 1991), vol. 1, pp. 201–204.

[131] ——, "Improved pitch prediction," in *Proc. IEEE Workshop on Speech Coding for Telecommunications* (Ste. Adele, Que., Canada, 1993), pp. 19–20.

[132] W. B. Kleijn and W. Granzow, "Methods for waveform interpolation in speech coding," *Dig. Signal Process.*, vol. 1, no. 4, pp. 215–230, Oct. 1991.

[133] W. B. Kleijn, "Encoding speech using prototype waveforms," *Proc. IEE Trans. Acoust., Speech, Signal Process.*, vol. 1, no. 4, pp. 386–399, Oct. 1993.

[134] W. B. Kleijn, D. J. Krasinski, and R. H. Ketchum, "An efficient stochastically excited linear predictive coding algorithm for high quality low bit rate transmission of speech," *Speech Commun.*, vol. 7, no. 3, pp. 305–316, Oct. 1988,

[135] W. B. Kleijn, D. J. Krasinski, and R. H. Ketchum, "Improved speech quality and efficient vector quantization in SELP," in *Proc. Int. Conf. on Acoustics, Speech, and Signal Processing* (New York, 1988), pp. 155–158.

[136] ——, "Fast methods for the CELP speech coding algorithm," *IEEE Trans. Acoust., Speech. Signal Process.*, vol. 38, no. 8, pp. 1330–1342, Aug. 1990.

[137] W. B. Kleijn, R. P. Ramachandran, and P. Kroon, "Generalized analysis-by-synthesis coding and its application to pitch prediction," in *Proc. Int. Conf. on Acoustics, Speech, and Signal Processing* (San Francisco, CA, Mar. 1992), vol. 1, pp. 337–40.

[138] W. B. Kleijn and R. A. Sukkar, "Efficient channel coding for CELP using source information," *Speech Commun.*, vol. 11, pp. 547–566, 1992.

[139] A. M. Kondoz and B. G. Evans, "CELP base-band coder for high quality speech coding at 9.6 to 2.4 kbps," in *Proc. Int. Conf. on Acoustics, Speech, and Signal Processing*, pp. 159–162, 1988.

[140] A. M. Kondoz, K. Y. Lee, and B. G. Evans, "Improved quality CELP base-band coding of speech at low-bit rates," in *Proc. IEEE Int. Conf. on Acoustics, Speech, and Signal Processing* (Glasgow, Scotland, May 1989), vol. 1, pp. 128–131.

[141] P. Kroon and B. S. Atal, "Strategies for improving the performance of CELP coders at low bit rates," in *Proc. IEEE Int. Conf. on Acoustics, Speech, and Signal Processing* (New York, 1988), vol. 1, pp. 151–154.

[142] ——, "On improving the performance of pitch predictors in speech coding systems," in *Proc. IEEE Workshop on Speech Coding for Telecommunications* (Vancouver, BC, Canada, Sept. 1989), pp. 49–50.

[143] ——, "Pitch predictors with high temporal resolution," in *Proc. IEEE Int. Conf. on Acoustics, Speech, and Signal Processing* (Albuquerque, NM, Apr. 1990), vol. 2, pp. 661–664.

[144] ——, "On the use of pitch predictors with high temporal resolution," *IEEE Trans. Signal Process.*, vol. 39, no. 3, pp. 733–735, 1991.

[145] P. Kroon, E. F. Deprettere, and R. J. Sluyter, "Regular-pulse excitation: A novel approach to effective and efficient multi-pulse coding of speech," *IEEE Trans. Acoust., Speech, Signal Process.*, vol. ASSP-34, pp. 1054–1063, Oct. 1986.

[146] R. F. Kubichek, E. A. Qunicy, and K. L. Kiser, "Speech quality assessment using expert pattern recognition techniques," in *Proc. IEEE Pacific Rim Conf. on Computers, Communications, and Signal Processing*, Jun. 1989.

[147] G. Kubin, B. S. Atal, and W. B. Kleijn, "Performance of noise excitation for unvoiced speech," in *Proc. IEEE Workshop on Speech Coding for Telecommunications* (Ste. Adele, Que., Canada), pp. 1–2.

[148] C. Laflamme, J.-P. Adoul, H. Y. Su, and S. Morissette, "On reducing computational complexity of codebook search in CELP coders through the use of algebraic codes," *Proc. Int. Conf.*

on Acoustics, Speech, and Signal Processing, pp. 177–180, Apr. 1990.

[149] C. Laflamme, J.-P. Adoul, R. Salami, S. Morissette, and P. Mabileau. "16 kbps wideband speech coding technique based on algebraic CELP," *Proc. IEEE Int. Conf. on Acoustics, Speech, and Signal Processing* (Toronto, Ont., Canada, 1991), pp. 13–16.

[150] C. Lamblin, J. P. Adoul, D. Massaloux, and S. Morissette. "Fast CELP coding based on the Barnes-Wall lattice in 16 dimensions," *Proc. IEEE Int. Conf. on Acoustics, Speech, and Signal Processing* (Glasgow, Scotland, 1989), vol. 1, pp. 61–64.

[151] R. Laroia, N. Phamdo, and N. Farvardin. "Robust and efficient quantization of speech LSP parameters using structured vector quantizers," *Proc. IEEE Int. Conf. on Acoustics, Speech, and Signal Processing* (Toronto, Ont., Canada, May 1991), vol. 5, pp. 641–644.

[152] W. P. LeBlanc and S. A. Mahmoud. "Structured codebook design in CELP," in *Proc. 2nd Int. Mobile Satellite Conf.* (Ottawa, Ont., Canada, June 1990), pp. 667–672.

[153] J. I. Lee and C. K. Un, "Multistage self-excited linear predictive speech coder," *Electron. Lett.*, vol. 25, no. 18, pp. 1249–1251, Aug. 1989.

[154] R. Lefebvre, R. Salami, C. Laflamme, and J.-P. Adoul. "8 kbit/s coding of speech with 6 ms frame-length," in *Proc. IEEE Int. Conf. on Acoustics, Speech, and Signal Processing* (Minneapolis, MN, Apr. 1993), vol. 2, pp. 612–615.

[155] A. Le Guyader, D. Massaloux, and F. Zurcher. "A robust and fast CELP coder at 16 kbit/s," *Speech Commun.*, vol. 7, no. 2, pp. 217–226, July 1988.

[156] A. Le Guyader, D. Massaloux, and J. P. Petit, "Robust and fast code-excited linear predictive coding of speech signals," in *Proc. IEEE Int. Conf. on Acoustics, Speech, and Signal Processing* (Glasgow, Scotland, May 1989), vol. 1, pp. 120–123.

[157] D. Lin. "New approaches to stochastic coding of speech sources at very low bit rates," in *Signal Processing III: Theories and Applications*, I. T. Young et al., Eds. Amsterdam, The Netherlands: Elsevier, North-Holland, 1986 pp. 445–447.

[158] ———, "Speech coding using efficient pseudo-stochastic block codes," in *Proc. IEEE Int. Conf. on Acoustics, Speech, and Signal Processing* (Dallas, TX, Apr. 1987), pp. 1354–1357.

[159] X. Lin, R. A. Salami, and R. Steele, "High quality audio coding using analysis-by-synthesis technique," in *Proc. IEEE Int. Conf. on Acoustics, Speech, and Signal Processing* (Toronto, Ont., Canada, May 1991), vol. 5, pp. 3617–2620.

[160] T. M. Liu and H. Hoege "Phonetically-based LPC vector quantization of high quality speech," in *Proc. European Conf. on Speech Communication and Technology* (Paris, France, Sept. 1989), vol. 2, pp. 356–359.

[161] G. C. P. Lokhoff, "Precision adaptive sub-band coding (PASC) for the digital compact cassette (DCC)," *IEEE Trans. Consumer Electron.*, vol. 38, no. 4, pp 784–789, Nov. 1992.

[162] L. M. Lundheim and T. A. Ramstad. "Variable rate coding for speech storage." in *Proc. IEEE Int. Conf. on Acoustics, Speech, and Signal Processing* (Tokyo, Japan, Apr. 1986), vol. 4, pp. 3079–3082.

[163] J. Makhoul and M. Berouti. "Adaptive noise spectral shaping and entropy coding in predictive coding of speech," *IEEE Trans. Acoust., Speech, Signal Process.*, pp. 63–73, Feb. 1979.

[164] J. Makhoul, S. Roucos and Gish. "Vector quantization in speech coding," *Proc. IEEE*, vol. 73, no. 11, pp. 1551–1588, Nov. 1985.

[165] K. Mano and T. Moriya. "4.8 kbit/s delayed decision CELP coder using tree coding," in *Proc. IEEE Int. Conf. on Acoustics, Speech, and Signal Processing*, vol. 1, pp. 21–24, 1990.

[166] ———. "Delay decision CELP coding using tree coding," *Trans. Inst. Electron., Informat. Commun. Eng.—A*, vol. J74A, no. 4, pp. 619–627, Apr. 1991.

[167] J. S. Marques, L. B. Almeida, and J. M. Tribolet. "Harmonic coding at 4.8 kb/s," in *Proc. IEEE Int. Conf. on Acoustics, Speech, and Signal Processing*, vol. 1, pp. 17–20, 1990.

[168] J. S. Marques, J. M. Tribolet, I. M. Trancoso, and L. B. Almeida, "Pitch prediction with fractional delays in CELP coding," in *European Conf. on Speech Communication and Technology* (Paris, France, Sept. 1989), vol. 2, pp. 509–512.

[169] ———. "Pitch prediction with fractional delays in CELP coding." in *European Conf. on Speech Communication and Technology* (Paris, France, Sept. 1989), vol. 2, pp. 509–512.

[170] R. J. McAulay and T. F. Quatieri, "Speech analysis/synthesis based on a a sinusoidal representation," *IEEE Trans. Acoust., Speech Signal Processing*, vol. ASSP-34, pp. 744–754, 1986.

[171] ———, "Low-rate speech coding based on the sinusoidal model," in *Advances in Acoustics and Speech Processing*, M. Sondhi and S. Furui, Eds. New York: Marcel Deckker, 1992, pp. 165–207.

[172] A. V. McCree and T. P. Barnwell, III. "Improving the performance of a mixed excitation LPC vocoder in acoustic noise," in *Proc. IEEE Int. Conf. on Acoustics, Speech, and Signal Processing* (San Francisco, CA, Mar. 1992), vol. 2, pp. 163–166.

[173] ———, "Implementation and evaluation of a 2400 bps mixed excitation LPC vocoder," in *Proc. IEEE Int. Conf. on Acoustics, Speech, and Signal Processing* (Minneapolis, MN, Apr. 1993), vol. 2, pp. 159–162.

[174] P. Mermelstein "G. 722, A new CCITT coding standard for digital transmission of wideband audio signals," *IEEE Comm. Mag.*, vol. 26, no. 1, pp 8–15, Jan. 1988.

[175] P. C. Meuse. "A 2400 bps multi-band excitation vocoder," in *Proc. IEEE Int. Conf. on Acoustics, Speech, and Signal Processing* (Albuquerque, NM, Apr. 1990), vol. 1, pp. 9–12.

[176] S. Miki, K. Mano, H. Ohmuro, and T. Moriya. "Pitch synchronous innovation CELP (PSI-CELP)," in *Proc. European Conf. on Speech Communication and Technology* (Berlin, Germay, Sept. 1993), pp. 261–264.

[177] N. Moreau and P. Dymarksi, "Mixed excitation CELP coder," in *Proc. European Conf. on Speech Communication and Technology* (Paris, France, Sept. 1989), pp. 322–325.

[178] T. Moriya, "Two-channel conjugate vector quantizer for noisy channel speech coding," *IEEE J. Selected Areas Commun.*, vol. 10, no. 5, pp. 866–874, June 1992.

[179] T. J. Moulsley and P. W. Elliot, "Fast vector quantisation using orthogonal codebooks," in *6th Int. Conf. on Digital Processing of Signals in Communications* (Loughborough, England, Sept. 1991), pp. 294–299.

[180] T. J. Moulsley and P. R. Holmes. "An adaptive voiced/unvoiced speech classifier," in *European Conf. on Speech Communication and Technology* (Paris, France, Sept. 1989), vol. 1, pp. 466–469.

[181] J.-M. Muller, "Improving performance of code-excited LPC-coders by joint optimization," *Speech Commun.*, vol. 8, no. 4, pp. 363–369, Dec. 1989.

[182] H. Nakada and K.-I. Sato, "Variable rate speech coding for asynchronous transfer mode," *IEEE Trans. Commun.*, vol. 38, pp. 277–284, Mar. 1990.

[183] M. Nishiguchi, J. Matsumoto, R. Wakatsuki, and S. Ono "Vector quantized MBE with simplified V/UV division at 3.0 kbps," in *Proc. IEEE Int. Conf. on Acoustics, Speech, and Signal Processing* (Minneapolis, MN, Apr. 1993), vol. 2, pp. 151–154.

[184] E. Ordentlich and Y. Shoham, "Low-delay code-excited linear predictive coding of wideband speech at 32 kbps," in *Proc. IEEE Int. Conf. on Acoustics, Speech, and Signal Processing* (Toronto, Ont., Canada, May 1991), pp. 9–12.

[185] B. Paillard, P. Mabilleau, S. Morissette, and J. Soumagne. "PERCEVAL: Perceptual evaluation of the quality of audio signals," *J. Audio Eng. Soc.*, vol. 40, no. 1–2 pp. 21–31, Jan.–Feb. 1992.

[186] J. Paulus, C. Antweiler, and C. Gerlach. "High quality coding of wideband speech at 24 kbit/s," in *Proc. European Conf. on Speech Communication and Technology* (Berlin, Germany, Sept. 1993), vol. 2, pp. 1107–1110.

[187] E. Paksoy, W.-Y. Chan, and A. Gersho, "Vector quantization of speech LSF parameters with generalized product codes," in *Proc. Int. Conf. Spoken Language Processing* (Banff, Alta, Canada, Nov. 1992), pp. 33–36.

[188] E. Paksoy, K. Srinivasan, and A. Gersho, "Variable rate speech coding with phonetic segmentation," in *Proc. IEEE Int. Conf. on Acoustics, Speech, and Signal Processin* (Minneapolis, MN, Apr. 1993), vol. 2, pp. 155–158.

[189] K. K. Paliwal and B. S. Atal, "Efficient vector quantization of LPC parameters at 24 bits/frame," in *Proc. IEEE Int. Conf. on Acoustics, Speech, and Signal Processing* (Toronto, Ont., Canada, May 1991), pp. 661–664.

[190] R. Peng and V. Cuperman, "Variable-rate low-delay analysis-by-synthesis speech coding at 8–16 kbit/s," in *Proc. IEEE Int. Conf. on Acoustics, Speech, and Signal Processing*, pp. 29–32 1991.

[191] R. Pettigrew and V. Cuperman, "Backward pitch prediction for low-delay speech coding," in *Conf. Rec., IEEE Global Telecommunications Conf.*, pp. 34.3.1–34.3.6, Nov. 1989

[192] J. Princen and A. Bradley, "Analysis/synthesis filter bank design based on time-domain aliasing cancellation," *IEEE Trans.*

Acoust., Speech, Signal Process., vol. ASSP-34, no. 5, pp. 1153–1161, 1986.

[193] R. P. Ramachandran and P. Kabal, "Stability and performance analysis of pitch filters in speech coders" *IEEE Trans. Acoust., Speech, Signal Process.*, vol. ASSP-35, no. 7, pp. 937–946, 1987.

[194] ____, "Pitch prediction filters in speech coding," *IEEE Trans. Acoust., Speech, Signal Process.*, vol. 37, no. 4, pp. 467–477, 1989.

[195] V. Ramamoorthy and N. S. Jayant, "Enhancement of ADPCM speech by adaptive postfiltering," *Bell Syst. Tech. J.*, vol. 63, no. 8, pp. 1465–1475, Oct. 1984.

[196] R. C. Rose and T. P. Barnwell III, "The self-excited vocoder–an alternative approach to toll quality at 4.8 kbs." in *Proc. IEEE Int. Conf. on Acoustics, Speech, and Signal Processing* (Tokyo, Japan, Apr. 1986), vol. 1, pp. 453–456.

[197] D. Rowe, W. Cowley, and P. Secker, "A multiband excitation linear predictive hybrid speech coder," in *Proc. European Conf. on Speech Communication and Technology (Eurospeech 91)* (Genova, Italy, Sept. 1991), vol. 1, pp. 239–242.

[198] D. Rowe and P. Secker, "A robust 2400 bit/s MBE-LPC speech coder incorporating joint source and channel coding," in *Proc. IEEE Int. Conf. on Acoustics, Speech, and Signal Processing* (San Francisco, CA, Mar. 1992), vol. 2, pp. 141–144.

[199] F. Rumsey, "Hearing both sides-stereo sound for TV in the UK," *IEE Rev.*, vol. 36, no. 5, pp. 173–176, May 10, 1990.

[200] R. A. Salami, "Binary code excited linear prediction (BCELP): new approach to CELP coding of speech without codebooks," *Electron. Lett.*, vol. 25, no. 6, pp. 401–403, Mar. 1989.

[201] R. Salami, C. LaFlamme, and J.-P. Adoul, "Real-time implementation of a 9.6 kbit/s ACELP wideband speech coder," in *Conf. Rec., IEEE Global Telecomm. Conf.*, pp. 447–451, 1992.

[202] ____, "ACELP speech coding at 8 kbit/s with a 10 ms frame: a candidate for CCITT standardization," presented at the IEEE Workshop on Speech Coding for Telecommunications, Oct. 1993.

[203] S. Saoudi, J. M. Boucher and A. Le Guyader, "A new efficient algorithm to compute the LSP parameters for speech coding," *Signal Process.*, vol. 28, pp. 201–212, 1992.

[204] R. W. Schafer and L. R. Rabiner, "Digital representation of speech signals," *Proc. IEEE*, vol. 63, pp. 662–677, Apr. 1975.

[205] M. R. Schroeder, "Vocoders: Analysis and synthesis of speech," *Proc. IEEE*, vol. 54, no. 3, pp. 720–734, May 1966.

[206] M. Schroeder and B. S. Atal, "Rate distortion theory and predictive coding," in *Proc. Int. Conf. on Acoustics, Speech, and Signal Processing* (Atlanta, GA, Mar. 1981), vol. 1, pp. 201–204.

[207] ____, "Code-excited linear prediction (CELP) high quality speech at very low bit rates," in *Proc. IEEE Int. Conf. on Acoustics, Speech, and Signal Processing*, pp. 937–940, Mar. 1985.

[208] P. Secker and A. Perkis, "Joint source and channel trellis coding of line spectrum pair parameters," *Speech Commun.*, vol. 11, pp. 149–158, 1992.

[209] D. Sen, D. H. Irving, and W. H. Holmes, "Use of an auditory model to improve speech coders," in *Proc. IEEE Int. Conf. on Acoustics, Speech, and Signal Processing*, vol. 2, pp. 411–414, 1993.

[210] M. Serizawa, K. Ozawa, T. Miyano, and T. Nomura, "M-LPCELP speech coding at bit-rates below 4 kbps," in *Proc. IEEE Workshop on Speech Coding for Telecommunications*, pp. 45–46, 1993.

[211] Y. Shiraki and M. Honda, "LPC speech coding based on variable-length segment quantization," *IEEE Trans. Acoust., Speech, Signal Processing*, vol. 36, no. 9, pp. 1437–1444, Sept. 1988.

[212] Y. Shoham, "Constrained excitation coding of speech at 4.8 kb/s," in *Proc. IEEE Workshop on Speech Coding for Telecommunications* (Vancouver, BC, Canada, Sept. 1989), p. 65.

[213] ____, "Constrained-stochastic excitation coding of speech at 4.8 kb/s," in *Proc. Int. Conf. on Spoken Language Process* (Kobe, Japan, Nov. 1990).

[214] ____, "Constrained-excitation coding of speech at 4.8 kb/s," in *Advances in Speech Coding.* B. S. Atal, V. Cuperman, and A. Gersho, Eds.   Dordrecht, The Netherlands: Kluwer, 1991, pp. 339–348.

[215] ____, "High-quality speech coding at 2.4 to 4.0 kbsp based on time-frequency interpolation," in *Proc. IEEE Int. Conf. on*

Acoustics, Speech, and Signal Processing (Minneapolis, MN, Apr. 1993), vol. 2, pp. 167–170.

[216] ____, "High-quality speech coding at 2.4 kbps based on time-frequency interpolation," in *Proc. European Conf. on Speech Communication and Technology* (Berlin, Germany, Sept. 1993), vol. 2, pp. 741–744.

[217] Y. Shoham, S. Singhal, and B. S. Atal, "Improving performance of multi-pulse LPC coders at low bit rates," in *Proc. Int. Conf. on Acoustics, Speech, and Signal Processing*, pp. 1.3.1–1.3.4, 1984

[218] R. Soheili, A. M. Kondoz, and B. G. Evans, "An 8 kb/s LD-CELP with improved excitation and perceptual modelling," in *Proc. IEEE Int. Conf. on Acoustics, Speech, and Signal Processing* (Minneapolis, MN, 1993), vol. 2, pp. 616–619.

[219] F. K. Soong and B.-H. Juang, "Optimal quantization of LSP parameters," *IEEE Trans. Speech Audio Process.*, vol. 1, no. 1, pp. 15–24, Jan. 1993.

[220] C. B. Southcott, D. Freeman, G. Cosier, D. Sereno, A. van der Krogt, A. Gilloire, and H. J. Braun, "Voice control of the pan-European digital mobile radio system," in *Conf. Rec. IEEE Global Telecomm. Conf.*, vol. 2, pp. 1070–1074, Nov. 1989.

[221] K. Srinivasan and A. Gersho, "Voice activity detection for digital cellular networks," in *Proc. IEEE Workshop on Speech Coding for Telecommunications*, pp. 85–86, Oct. 1993.

[222] L. C. Stewart, "Trellis data compression," Information Systems Lab., Tech. Rep. L905-1, Stanford Univ., July 1981. See also L. C. Stewart, R. M. Gray, and Y. Linde, "The design of trellis waveform coders," *IEEE Trans. Commun.*, vol. 30, pp. 702–710, Apr. 1982.

[223] N. Sugamura and F. Itakura, "Line spectrum representation of linear predictor coefficients of speech signal and its statistical properties," *Trans. Inst. Electron., Commun. Eng. Japan*, vol. J64-A, pp. 323–340, 1981.

[224] A. Sugiyama, F. Hazu, M. Iwadare, and T. Nishitani, "Adaptive transform coding with an adaptive block size (ATC-ABS)," in *Proc. IEEE Int. Conf. on Acoustics, Speech, and Signal Processing* (Albuquerque, NM, Apr. 1990), vol. 2, pp. 1093–1096.

[225] M. Taka, P. Combescure, P. Mermelstein, and F. Westall, "Overview of the 64 kb/s (7 kHz) audio coding standard," in *Conf. Rec. IEEE Global Telecomm. Conf.* (Houston, TX, 1986), pp. 17.1.1–17.1.6.

[226] Y. Tanaka and T. Taniguchi, "Efficient coding of LPC parameters using adaptive prefiltering and MSVQ with partially adaptive codebook," in *Proc. IEEE Int. Conf. on Acoustics, Speech, and Signal Processing*, vol. 2, pp. 5–8, 1993.

[227] T. Taniguchi, S. Unagami, and R. M. Gray, "Multimode coding: a novel approach to narrow- and medium-band coding," *J. Acoust. Soc. Amer.*, suppl. 1, vol. 84, p. S12, Nov. 1988.

[228] T. Taniguchi, F. Amano, and M. Johnson, "Improving the performance of CELP-based speech coding at low bit rates," in *Proc. IEEE Int. Symp. on Circuits and Systems* (Singapore, June 1991), vol. 1, pp. 590–593.

[229] T. Taniguchi, M. Johnson, and Y. Ohta, "Pitch sharpening for perceptually improved CELP, and the sparse-delta codebook for reduced computation," in *Proc. IEEE Int. Conf. on Acoustics, Speech, and Signal Processing*, pp. 241–244, May 1991.

[230] T. Taniguchi, K. Okazaki, F. Amano, and S. Unagami, "4.8 kbps CELP coding with backward prediction," in *IEIC-Nat. Conv. Rec.* (in Japanese), p. 1346, Mar. 1987.

[231] T. Taniguchi, Y. Tanaka, and Y. Ohta, "Tree-structured delta codebook for an efficient implementation of CELP," in *Proc. IEEE Int. Conf. on Acoustics, Speech, and Signal Processing* (San Francisco, CA, Mar. 1992), vol. 1, pp. 325–328.

[232] T. Taniguchi, Y. Tanaka, Y. Ohta, and F. Amano, "Improved CELP speech coding at 4 kb/s and below," in *Proc. Int. Conf. on Spoken Language Processing* (Banff, Alta, Canada, Nov. 1992), pp. 41–44.

[233] T. Taniguchi, Y. Tanaka, A. Sasama and Y. Ohta, "Principal axis extracting vector excitation coding: high quality speech at 8 kb/s," in *Proc. IEEE Int. Conf. on Acoustics, Speech, and Signal Processing* (Albuquerque, NM, Apr. 1990), vol. 1, pp. 241–244.

[234] T. Taniguchi, S. Unagami, and R. M. Gray, "Multimode coding: application to CELP," in *Proc. IEEE Int. Conf. on Acoustics, Speech, and Signal Processing* (Glasgow, Scotland, May 1989), vol. 1, pp. 156–159.

[235] T. Taniguchi, Y. Tanaka, and R. M. Gray, "Speech coding with dynamic bit allocation (multimode coding)," in *Advances in*

Speech Coding, B. S. Atal, V. Cuperman, and A. Gersho, Eds. Dordrecht, The Netherlands: Kluwer, 1991.

[236] T. Taniguchi, S. Unagami, K. Iseda, and S. Tominaga, "ADPCM with a multiquantizer for speech coding," *IEEE J. Select. Areas Commun.*, vol. 6, pp. 410–424, Feb. 1988.

[237] G. Theile, G. Stoll, and M. Link, "Low bit-rate coding of high-quality audio signals. An introduction to the MASCAM system," *EBU Rev.-Tech.*, no. 230, pp. 158–181, Aug. 1988.

[238] C. Todd, G. Davidson, M. Davis, L. Fielder, B. Link, and S. Vernon, "AC-3: Flexible perceptual coding for audio transmission and storage," presented at the 96th Audio Eng. Soc. Conv., Amsterdam, The Netherlands, Feb. 26–Mar. 1 1994, Preprint 3796.

[239] I. M. Trancoso and B. S. Atal, "Efficient procedures for finding the optimum innovation in stochastic coders," in *Proc. IEEE Int. Conf. on Acoustics, Speech, and Signal Processing* (Tokyo, Japan, 1986), pp. 2379–2382.

[240] I. M. Trancoso, J. S. Marques, C. M. Ribeiro, "CELP and sinusoidal coders: two solutions for speech coding at 4.8–9.6 kbps," *Speech Commun.*, vol. 9, no. 5–6, pp. 389–400, Dec. 1990.

[241] T. E. Tremain, "The government standard linear predictive coding algorithm: LPC-10," *Speech Technol.*, pp. 40–49, Apr. 1982.

[242] K. Tsutsui, H. Suzuki, O. Shimoyoshi, M. Sonohara, K. Agagiri, and R. M. Heddle, "ATRAC: Adaptive transform acoustic coding for MiniDisc," in *Conf. Rec., Audio Eng. Soc. Conv.* (San Francisco, CA, Oct. 1992).

[243] S. V. Vaseghi, "Finite state CELP for variable rate speech coding," in *Proc. IEEE Int. Conf. on Acoustics, Speech, and Signal Processing* (Albuquerque, NM, Apr. 1990), pp. 37–40.

[244] S. Wang and A. Gersho, "Phonetically-based vector excitation coding of speech at 3.6 kbps," in *Proc. IEEE Int. Conf. on Acoustics, Speech, and Signal Processing*, pp. 49–52, May 1989.

[245] ——, "Improving the excitation for phonetically-segmented VXC speech coding below 4 KBPS," in *Conf. Rec., IEEE Global Telecomm. Conf.* (San Diego, CA, 1990), vol. 2, pp. 946–950.

[246] ——, "Phonetic segmentation for low rate speech coding," in *Advances in Speech Coding*, B. S. Atal, V. Cuperman, and A. Gersho, Eds. Dordrecht, The Netherlands: Kluwer, 1991, pp. 225–234.

[247] ——, "Improved phonetically-segmented vector excitation coding at 3.4 kb/s," in *Proc. IEEE Int. Conf. on Acoustics, Speech, and Signal Processing* (San Francisco, CA, Mar. 1992), vol. 1, pp. 349–352.

[248] S. Wang, E. Paksoy, and A. Gersho, "Product code vector quantization of LPC parameters," in *Speech and Audio Coding for Wireless and Network Applications*, B. S. Atal, V. Cuperman, and A. Gersho, Eds. Dordrecht, The Netherlands: Kluwer, 1993, pp. 251–258.

[249] S. Wang, A. Sekey, and A. Gersho, "An objective measure for predicting subjective quality of speech coders," *IEEE J. Selected Areas Commun.*, vol. 10, pp. 819–829, June 1992.

[250] L. Watts and V. Cuperman, "A vector ADPCM analysis-by-synthesis configuration for 16 kb/s speech coding," in *Conf. Rec. IEEE Global Telecomm. Conf.*, pp. 275–279, 1988.

[251] D. Y. K. Wong, "Issues on speech storage," in *IEE Coll. on Speech Coding–Techniques and Applications* (London, England, Apr. 1992), pp. 711–714.

[252] G. Wu and J. W. Mark, "Multiuser rate subband coding incorporating DSI and buffer control," *IEEE Trans. Commun.*, vol. 38, no. 12, pp. 2159–2165, Dec. 1990.

[253] C. Xydeas, "An overview of speech coding techniques," in *Dig. IEE Colloq. Speech Coding—Techniques and Applications* (London, Apr. 1992), pp. 111–125.

[254] C. S. Xydeas, M. A. Ireton, and D. K. Baghbadrani, "Theory and real time implementation of a CELP coder at 4.8 and 6.0 Kbit/sec using ternary code excitation," in *Proc. IERE 4th Int. Conf. on Digital Processing of Signals in Communications* (Univ of Loughborough, Sept. 20–23, 1988), pp. 167–174.

[255] C. S. Xydeas and K. K. M. So, "A long history quantization approach to scalar and vector quantization of LSP coefficients," in *Proc. IEEE Int. Conf. on Acoustics, Speech, and Signal Processing*, vol. 2, pp. 1–4, 1993.

[256] J.-H. Yao, J. J. Shynk, and A. Gersho, "Low delay vector excitation coding of speech at 8 kbit/sec," in *Conf. Rec., IEEE Global Telecomm. Conf.* (Phoenix, AZ, Dec. 1991), vol. 3, pp. 695–699.

[257] ——, "Low-delay VXC at 8 Kb/s with interframe coding," in *Proc. IEEE Int. Conf. on Acoustics, Speech, and Signal Processing* vol. 1, (San Francisco, CA, Mar. 1992), pp. 45–48.

[258] ——, "Low-delay speech coding with adaptive interframe pitch tracking," in *Proc. IEEE Int. Conf. on Communication* (Geneva, Switzerland, May 1993).

[259] Y. Yatsuzuka, S. Iizuka, and A. T. Yamazaki, "A variable rate coding by APC with maximum likelihood quantization from 4.8 kbit/s to 16 kbit/s," in *Proc. IEEE Int. Conf. on Acoustics, Speech, and Signal Processing* (Tokyo, Japan, Apr. 1986), pp. 3071–3074.

[260] Y. Yatsuzuka, "Highly sensitive speech detector and high-speed voiceband data discriminator in DSI-ADPCM systems," *IEEE Trans Commun.*, vol. COM-30, pp. 739–750, Apr. 1982.

[261] S. Yeldener, A. M. Kondoz, and B. G. Evans, "High quality multiband LPC coding of speech at 2.4 kb/s," *Electron. Lett.*, vol. 27, no. 14, pp. 1287–1289, July 4, 1991.

[262] ——, "Natural sounding speech coder operation at 2.4 kb/s and below," in *Proc. IEEE Inter. Conf. Wireless Communication* (Vancouver, BC, Canada, 1992), pp. 176–179.

[263] S. Yeldener, W. Ma, A. M. Kondoz, and B. G. Evans, "Low bit rate speech coding at 1.2 and 2.4 kb/s," in *IEE Coll. on Speech Coding—Techniques and Applications* (London, England, Apr. 1992), pp. 611–614.

[264] M. Yong and A. Gersho, "Vector excitation coding with dynamic bit allocation," in *Conf. Rec. IEEE Global Telecomm. Conf.* (Phoenix, AZ, Dec. 1991), vol. 3, pp. 695–699.

[265] "Efficient encoding of the long-term predictor in vector excitation coders," in *Advances in Speech Coding*, B. S. Atal, V. Cuperman, and A. Gersho, Eds. Dordrecht, The Netherlands: Kluwer, 1991, pp. 29–338.

[266] J.-H. Yao, J. J. Shynk, and A. Gersho, "Low-delay VXC at 8 Kb/s with interframe coding," in *Proc. IEEE Int. Conf. on Acoustics, Speech, and Signal Processing* (San Francisco, CA, Nov. 1988), vol. 1, pp. 290–294.

[267] M. Yong, G. Davidson, and A. Gersho, "Encoding of LPC spectral parameters using switched-adaptive interframe vector prediction," in *Proc. IEEE Int. Conf. on Acoustics, Speech, and Signal Processing* (New York, Apr. 1988), pp. 402–405.

[268] K. Zeger and A. Gersho, "Zero redundancy channel coding in vector quantisation," *Electron. Lett.*, vol. 23, no. 12, pp. 654–656, 1987.

[269] ——, "Pseudo-Gray coding," *IEEE Trans. Commun.*, vol. 38, no. 12, pp. 2147–2158, Dec. 1990.

[270] A. Das and A. Gersho, "A variable rate natural quality parametric coder at 1.5 kb/s," in *IEEE Int. Conf. on Communications*, vol. 1, pp. 216–220, May 1994.

Allen Gersho (Fellow, IEEE) received the B.S. degree from the Massachusetts Institute of Technology, Cambridge, in 1960, and the Ph.D. degree from Cornell University, Ithaca, NY, in 1963.

He was at Bell Laboratories from 1963 to 1980. He is now Professor of Electrical and Computer Engineering at the University of California, Santa Barbara (UCSB). His current research activities are in signal compression methodologies and algorithm development for speech, audio, image, and video coding. He holds patents on speech coding quantization, adaptive equalization, digital filtering, and modulation and coding for voiceband data modems. He is co-author with R. M. Gray of the book *Vector Quantization and Signal Compression* (Dordrecht, The Netherlands: Kluwer Academic Publishers, 1992), and co-editor of two books on speech coding. He received NASA "Tech Brief" awards for technical innovation in 1987, 1988, and 1992. In 1980, he was co-recipieeent of the Guillemin-Cauer Prize Paper Award from the IEEE Circuits and Systems Society. He received the Donald McClennan Meritorious Service Award from the IEEE Communications Society in 1983, and in 1984 he was awarded the IEEE Centennial Medal. In 1992, he was co-recipient of the 1992 Video Technology Transactions Best Paper Award from the IEEE Circuits and Systems Society.

He served as a member of the Board of Governors of the IEEE Communications Society from 1982 to 1985, and is a member of various IEEE technical, award, and conference management committees. He has served as Editor of the IEEE COMMUNICATIONS MAGAZINE and Associate Editor of the IEEE TRANSACTIONS ON COMMUNICATIONS.

A Tutorial on MPEG/Audio Compression

Davis Pan
Motorola

This tutorial covers the theory behind MPEG/audio compression. While lossy, the algorithm often can provide "transparent," perceptually lossless compression even with factors of 6-to-1 or more. It exploits the perceptual properties of the human auditory system. The article also covers the basics of psychoacoustic modeling and the methods the algorithm uses to compress audio data with the least perceptible degradation.

This tutorial covers the theory behind MPEG/audio compression. It is written for people with a modest background in digital signal processing and does not assume prior experience in audio compression or psychoacoustics. The goal is to give a broad, preliminary understanding of MPEG/audio compression, so I omitted many of the details. Wherever possible, figures and illustrative examples present the intricacies of the algorithm.

The MPEG/audio compression algorithm is the first international standard[1,2] for the digital compression of high-fidelity audio. Other audio compression algorithms address speech-only applications or provide only medium-fidelity audio compression performance.[3]

The MPEG/audio standard results from more than three years of collaborative work by an international committee of high-fidelity audio compression experts within the Moving Picture Experts Group (MPEG/audio). The International Organization for Standards and the International Electrotechnical Commission (ISO/IEC) adopted this standard at the end of 1992.

Although perfectly suitable for audio-only applications, MPEG/audio is actually one part of a three-part compression standard that also includes video and systems. The MPEG standard addresses the compression of synchronized video and audio at a total bit rate of about 1.5 megabits per second (Mbps).

The MPEG standard is rigid only where necessary to ensure interoperability. It mandates the syntax of the coded bitstream, defines the decoding process, and provides compliance tests for assessing the accuracy of the decoder.[4] This guarantees that, regardless of origin, any fully compliant MPEG/audio decoder will be able to decode any MPEG/audio bitstream with a predictable result. Designers are free to try new and different implementations of the encoder or decoder within the bounds of the standard. The encoder especially offers good potential for diversity. Wide acceptance of this standard will permit manufacturers to produce and sell, at reasonable cost, large numbers of MPEG/audio codecs.

Features and applications

MPEG/audio is a generic audio compression standard. Unlike vocal-tract-model coders specially tuned for speech signals, the MPEG/audio coder gets its compression without making assumptions about the nature of the audio source. Instead, the coder exploits the perceptual limitations of the human auditory system. Much of the compression results from the removal of perceptually irrelevant parts of the audio signal. Since removal of such parts results in inaudible distortions, MPEG/audio can compress any signal meant to be heard by the human ear.

In keeping with its generic nature, MPEG/audio offers a diverse assortment of compression modes, as follows. In addition, the MPEG/audio bitstream makes features such as random access, audio fast-forwarding, and audio reverse possible.

Sampling rate. The audio sampling rate can be 32, 44.1, or 48 kHz.

Audio channel support. The compressed bitstream can support one or two audio channels in one of four possible modes:

1. a monophonic mode for a single audio channel,

2. a dual-monophonic mode for two independent audio channels (functionally identical to the stereo mode),

3. a stereo mode for stereo channels that share bits but do not use joint-stereo coding, and

4. a joint-stereo mode that takes advantage of either the correlations between the stereo channels or the irrelevancy of the phase difference between channels, or both.

Predefined bit rates. The compressed bitstream can have one of several predefined fixed bit rates ranging from 32 to 224 kilobits per second

(Kbps) per channel. Depending on the audio sampling rate, this translates to compression factors ranging from 2.7 to 24. In addition, the standard provides a "free" bit rate mode to support fixed bit rates other than the predefined rates.

Compression layers. MPEG/audio offers a choice of three independent layers of compression. This provides a wide range of trade-offs between codec complexity and compressed audio quality.

Layer I, the simplest, best suits bit rates above 128 Kbps per channel. For example, Philips' Digital Compact Cassette (DCC)[5] uses Layer I compression at 192 Kbps per channel.

Layer II has an intermediate complexity and targets bit rates around 128 Kbps per channel. Possible applications for this layer include the coding of audio for digital audio broadcasting (DAB),[6] the storage of synchronized video-and-audio sequences on CD-ROM, and the full-motion extension of CD-interactive, Video CD.

Layer III is the most complex but offers the best audio quality, particularly for bit rates around 64 Kbps per channel. This layer suits audio transmission over ISDN.

All three layers are simple enough to allow single-chip, real-time decoder implementations.

Error detection. The coded bitstream supports an optional cyclic redundancy check (CRC) error-detection code.

Ancillary data. MPEG/audio provides a means of including ancillary data within the bitstream.

Overview

The key to MPEG/audio compression—quantization—is lossy. Nonetheless, this algorithm can give "transparent," perceptually lossless compression. The MPEG/audio committee conducted extensive subjective listening tests during development of the standard. The tests showed that even with a 6-to-1 compression ratio (stereo, 16 bits per sample, audio sampled at 48 kHz compressed to 256 Kbps) and under optimal listening conditions, expert listeners could not distinguish between coded and original audio clips with statistical significance. Furthermore, these clips were specially chosen as difficult to compress. Grewin and Ryden[7] gave the details of the setup, procedures, and results of these tests.

Figure 1 shows block diagrams of the MPEG/audio encoder and decoder. The input audio stream passes through a filter bank that divides

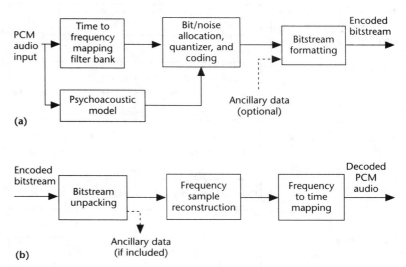

Figure 1. MPEG/audio compression and decompression. (a) MPEG/audio encoder. (b) MPEG/audio decoder.

the input into multiple subbands of frequency. The input audio stream simultaneously passes through a psychoacoustic model that determines the ratio of the signal energy to the masking threshold for each subband. The bit- or noise-allocation block uses the signal-to-mask ratios to decide how to apportion the total number of code bits available for the quantization of the subband signals to minimize the audibility of the quantization noise. Finally, the last block takes the representation of the quantized subband samples and formats this data and side information into a coded bitstream. Ancillary data not necessarily related to the audio stream can be inserted within the coded bitstream. The decoder deciphers this bitstream, restores the quantized subband values, and reconstructs the audio signal from the subband values.

First we'll look at the time to frequency mapping of the polyphase filter bank, then implementations of the psychoacoustic model and more detailed descriptions of the three layers of MPEG/audio compression. That gives enough background to cover a brief summary of the different bit (or noise) allocation processes used by the three layers and the joint stereo coding methods.

The polyphase filter bank

The polyphase filter bank is common to all layers of MPEG/audio compression. This filter bank divides the audio signal into 32 equal-width frequency subbands. Relatively simple, the filters

Figure 2. Flow diagram of the MPEG/audio encoder filter bank.

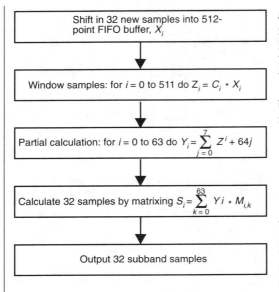

provide good time resolution with reasonable frequency resolution. The design has three notable concessions.

First, the equal widths of the subbands do not accurately reflect the human auditory system's frequency-dependent behavior. Instead, the width of a "critical band" as a function of frequency is a good indicator of this behavior. Many psycho-acoustic effects are consistent with a critical-band frequency scaling. For example, both the perceived loudness of a signal and its audibility in the presence of a masking signal differ for signals within one critical band versus signals that extend over more than one critical band. At lower frequencies a single subband covers several critical bands. In this circumstance the number of quantizer bits cannot be specifically tuned for the noise masking available for individual critical bands. Instead, the critical band with the least noise masking dictates the number of quantization bits needed for the entire subband.

Second, the filter bank and its inverse are not lossless transformations. Even without quantization, the inverse transformation cannot perfectly recover the original signal. However, by design the error introduced by the filter bank is small and inaudible.

Third, adjacent filter bands have a major frequency overlap. A signal at a single frequency can affect two adjacent filter-bank outputs.

To understand the polyphase filter bank, it helps to examine its origin. The ISO MPEG/audio standard describes a procedure for computing the

analysis polyphase filter outputs that closely resembles a method described by Rothweiler.[8] Figure 2 shows the flow diagram from the ISO MPEG/audio standard for the MPEG-encoder filter bank based on Rothweiler's proposal.

By combining the equations and steps shown by Figure 2, we can derive the following equation for the filter bank outputs:

$$s_t[i] = \sum_{k=0}^{63} \sum_{j=0}^{7} M[i][k] \times \left(C[k+64j] \times x[k+64j] \right) \quad (1)$$

where i is the subband index and ranges from 0 to 31; $s_t[i]$ is the filter output sample for subband i at time t, where t is an integer multiple of 32 audio sample intervals; $C[n]$ is one of 512 coefficients of the analysis window defined in the standard; $x[n]$ is an audio input sample read from a 512-sample buffer; and

$$M[i][k] = \cos\left[\frac{(2\times i+1)\times(k-16)\times\pi}{64}\right]$$

are the analysis matrix coefficients.

Equation 1 is partially optimized to reduce the number of computations. Because the function within the parentheses is independent of the value of i, and $M[i][k]$ is independent of j, the 32 filter outputs need only $512 + 32 \times 64 = 2,560$ multiplies and $64 \times 7 + 32 \times 63 = 2,464$ additions, or roughly 80 multiplies and additions per output. Substantially further reductions in multiplies and adds are possible with, for example, a fast discrete cosine transform[3] or a fast Fourier transform implementation.[9]

Note this filter bank implementation is critically sampled: For every 32 input samples, the filter bank produces 32 output samples. In effect, each of the 32 subband filters subsamples its output by 32 to produce only one output sample for every 32 new audio samples.

We can manipulate Equation 1 into a familiar filter convolution equation:

$$s_t[i] = \sum_{n=0}^{511} x[t-n] \times H_i[n] \quad (2)$$

where $x[t]$ is an audio sample at time t, and

$$H_i[n] = h[n] \times \cos\left[\frac{(2\times i+1)\times(n-16)\times\pi}{64}\right]$$

with $h[n] = -C[n]$ if the integer part of $(n/64)$ is odd and $h[n] = C[n]$ otherwise, for $n = 0$ to 511.

In this form, each subband of the filter bank has its own band-pass filter response, $H_i[n]$. Although this form is more convenient for analysis, it is clearly not an efficient solution: A direct implementation of this equation requires $32 \times 512 = 16,384$ multiplies and $32 \times 511 = 16,352$ additions to compute the 32 filter outputs.

The coefficients, $h[n]$, correspond to the prototype low-pass filter response for the polyphase filter bank. Figure 3 compares a plot of $h[n]$ with $C[n]$. The $C[n]$ used in the partially optimized Equation 1 has every odd-numbered group of 64 coefficients of $h[n]$ negated to compensate for $M[i][k]$. The cosine term of $M[i][k]$ only ranges from $k = 0$ to 63 and covers an odd number of half cycles, whereas the cosine terms of $H_i[n]$ range from $n = 0$ to 511 and cover eight times the number of half cycles.

The equation for $H_i[n]$ clearly shows that each is a modulation of the prototype response with a cosine term to shift the low pass response to the appropriate frequency band. Hence, these are called polyphase filters. These filters have center frequencies at odd multiples of $\pi/(64T)$ where T is the audio sampling period and each has a nominal bandwidth of $\pi/(32T)$.

As Figure 4 shows, the prototype filter response does not have a sharp cutoff at its nominal bandwidth. So when the filter outputs are subsampled by 32, a considerable amount of aliasing occurs. The design of the prototype filter, and the inclusion of appropriate phase shifts in the cosine terms, results in a complete alias cancellation at the output of the decoder's synthesis filter bank.[8,10]

Another consequence of using a filter with a wider-than-nominal bandwidth is an overlap in the frequency coverage of adjacent polyphase filters. This effect can be detrimental to efficient audio compression because signal energy near nominal subband edges will appear in two adjacent polyphase filter outputs. Figure 5, next page,

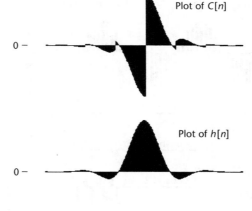

Figure 3. Comparison of **h[n]** *with* **C[n].**

Plot of C[n]

Plot of h[n]

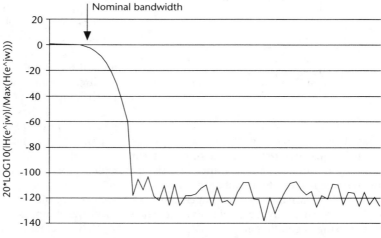

Figure 4. Frequency response of prototype filter, **h[n].**

Nominal bandwidth

Frequencies from 0 to Pi/8

shows how a pure sinusoid tone, which has energy at only one frequency, appears at the output of two polyphase filters.

Although the polyphase filter bank is not lossless, any consequent errors are small. Assuming you do not quantize the subband samples, the composite frequency response combining the response of the encoder's analysis filter bank with that of the decoder's synthesis bank has a ripple of less than 0.07 dB.

Psychoacoustics

The MPEG/audio algorithm compresses the audio data in large part by removing the acoustically irrelevant parts of the audio signal. That is, it takes advantage of the human auditory system's inability to hear quantization noise under condi-

Input audio: 1,500-Hz sine wave sampled at 32 kHz, 64 of 256 samples shown

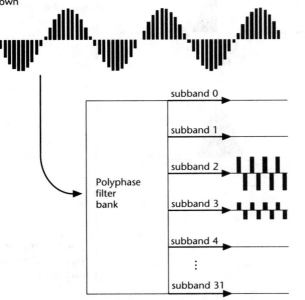

Subband outputs:
8x32 samples; both subbands 3 and 4 have significant output values

Figure 5. Aliasing: Pure sinusoid input can produce nonzero output for two subbands.

tions of auditory masking. This masking is a perceptual property of the human auditory system that occurs whenever the presence of a strong audio signal makes a temporal or spectral neighborhood of weaker audio signals imperceptible. A variety of psychoacoustic experiments corroborate this masking phenomenon.[11]

Empirical results also show that the human auditory system has a limited, frequency-dependent resolution. This dependency can be expressed in terms of critical-band widths that are less than 100 Hz for the lowest audible frequencies and more than 4 kHz at the highest. The human auditory system blurs the various signal components within a critical band, although this system's frequency selectivity is much finer than a critical band.

Because of the human auditory system's frequency-dependent resolving power, the noise-masking threshold at any given frequency depends solely on the signal energy within a limited bandwidth neighborhood of that frequency. Figure 6 illustrates this property.

MPEG/audio works by dividing the audio signal into frequency subbands that approximate critical bands, then quantizing each subband according to the audibility of quantization noise within that band. For the most efficient compres-

sion, each band should be quantized with no more levels than necessary to make the quantization noise inaudible.

The psychoacoustic model

The psychoacoustic model analyzes the audio signal and computes the amount of noise masking available as a function of frequency.[12,13] The masking ability of a given signal component depends on its frequency position and its loudness. The encoder uses this information to decide how best to represent the input audio signal with its limited number of code bits.

The MPEG/audio standard provides two example implementations of the psychoacoustic model. Psychoacoustic model 1 is less complex than psychoacoustic model 2 and makes more compromises to simplify the calculations. Either model works for any of the layers of compression. However, only model 2 includes specific modifications to accommodate Layer III.

There is considerable freedom in the implementation of the psychoacoustic model. The required accuracy of the model depends on the target compression factor and the intended application. For low levels of compression, where a generous supply of code bits exists, a complete bypass of the psychoacoustic model might be adequate for consumer use. In this case, the bit allocation process can iteratively assign bits to the subband with the lowest signal-to-noise ratio. For archiving music, the psychoacoustic model can be made much more stringent.[14]

Now let's look at a general outline of the basic steps involved in the psychoacoustic calculations for either model. Differences between the two models will be highlighted.

Time-align audio data. There is one psychoacoustic evaluation per frame. The audio data sent to the psychoacoustic model must be concurrent with the audio data to be coded. The psychoacoustic model must account for both the delay of the audio data through the filter bank and a data offset so that the relevant data is centered within the psychoacoustic analysis window.

For example, when using psychoacoustic model 1 for Layer I, the delay through the filter bank is 256 samples and the offset required to center the 384 samples of a Layer I frame in the 512-point analysis window is $(512 - 384)/2 = 64$ points. The net offset is 320 points to time-align the psychoacoustic model data with the filter bank outputs.

Convert audio to a frequency domain representation. The psychoacoustic model should use a separate, independent, time-to-frequency mapping instead of the polyphase filter bank because it needs finer frequency resolution for an accurate calculation of the masking thresholds. Both psychoacoustic models use a Fourier transform for this mapping. A standard Hann weighting, applied to the audio data before Fourier transformation, conditions the data to reduce the edge effects of the transform window.

Psychoacoustic model 1 uses a 512-sample analysis window for Layer I and a 1,024-sample window for Layers II and III. Because there are only 384 samples in a Layer I frame, a 512-sample window provides adequate coverage. Here the smaller window size reduces the computational load. Layers II and III use a 1,152-sample frame size, so the 1,024-sample window does not provide complete coverage. While ideally the analysis window should completely cover the samples to be coded, a 1,024-sample window is a reasonable compromise. Samples falling outside the analysis window generally will not have a major impact on the psychoacoustic evaluation.

Psychoacoustic model 2 uses a 1,024-sample window for all layers. For Layer I, the model centers a frame's 384 audio samples in the psychoacoustic window as previously discussed. For Layers II and III, the model computes two 1,024-point psychoacoustic calculations for each frame. The first calculation centers the first half of the 1,152 samples in the analysis window, and the second calculation centers the second half. The model combines the results of the two calculations by using the higher of the two signal-to-mask ratios for each subband. This in effect selects the lower of the two noise-masking thresholds for each subband.

Process spectral values into groupings related to critical-band widths. To simplify the psychoacoustic calculations, both models process the frequency values in perceptual quanta.

Separate spectral values into tonal and nontonal components. Both models identify and separate the tonal and noise-like components of the audio signal because the masking abilities of the two types of signal differ.

Psychoacoustic model 1 identifies tonal components based on the local peaks of the audio power spectrum. After processing the tonal components, model 1 sums the remaining spectral values into a single nontonal component per critical

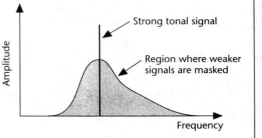

Figure 6. Audio noise masking.

band. The frequency index of each concentrated nontonal component is the value closest to the geometric mean of the enclosing critical band.

Psychoacoustic model 2 never actually separates tonal and nontonal components. Instead, it computes a tonality index as a function of frequency. This index gives a measure of whether the component is more tone-like or noise-like. Model 2 uses this index to interpolate between pure tone-masking-noise and noise-masking-tone values. The tonality index is based on a measure of predictability. Model 2 uses data from the previous two analysis windows to predict, via linear extrapolation, the component values for the current window. Tonal components are more predictable and thus will have higher tonality indices. Because this process relies on more data, it probably discriminates better between tonal and nontonal components than the model 1 method.

Apply a spreading function. The masking ability of a given signal spreads across its surrounding critical band. The model determines the noise-masking thresholds by first applying an empirically determined masking function (model 1) or spreading function (model 2) to the signal components.

Set a lower bound for the threshold values. Both models include an empirically determined absolute masking threshold, the threshold in quiet. This threshold is the lower bound on the audibility of sound.

Find the masking threshold for each subband. Both psychoacoustic models calculate the masking thresholds with a higher frequency resolution than that provided by the polyphase filter bank. Both models must derive a subband threshold value from possibly a multitude of masking thresholds computed for frequencies within that subband.

Model 1 selects the minimum masking thresh-

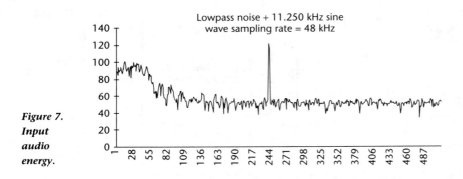

Figure 7. Input audio energy.

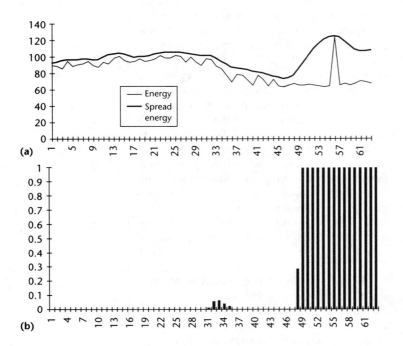

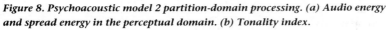

Figure 8. Psychoacoustic model 2 partition-domain processing. (a) Audio energy and spread energy in the perceptual domain. (b) Tonality index.

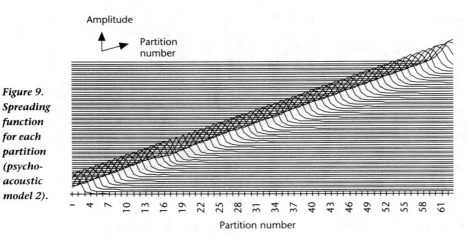

Figure 9. Spreading function for each partition (psycho-acoustic model 2).

old within each subband. While this approach works well for the lower frequency subbands where the subband is narrow relative to a critical band, it might be inaccurate for the higher frequency subbands because critical bands for that frequency range span several subbands. These inaccuracies arise because model 1 concentrates all the nontonal components within each critical band into a single value at a single frequency. In effect, model 1 converts nontonal components into a form of tonal component. A subband within a wide critical band but far from the concentrated nontonal component will not get an accurate nontonal masking assessment. This approach is a compromise to reduce the computational loads.

Model 2 selects the minimum of the masking thresholds covered by the subband only where the band is wide relative to the critical band in that frequency region. It uses the average of the masking thresholds covered by the subband where the band is narrow relative to the critical band. Model 2 has the same accuracy for the higher frequency subbands as for lower frequency subbands because it does not concentrate the nontonal components.

Calculate the signal-to-mask ratio. The psychoacoustic model computes the signal-to-mask ratio as the ratio of the signal energy within the subband (or, for Layer III, a group of bands) to the minimum masking threshold for that subband. The model passes this value to the bit- (or noise-) allocation section of the encoder.

Example of psychoacoustic model analysis

Figure 7 shows a spectral plot of the example audio signal to be psychoacoustically analyzed and compressed. This signal consists of a combination of a strong, 11,250-Hz, sinusoidal tone with low-pass noise.

Because the processes used by psychoacoustic model 2 are somewhat easier to visualize, we will cover this model first. Figure 8a shows the result, according to psychoacoustic model 2, of transforming the audio signal to the perceptual domain (63, one-third critical band, partitions) and then applying the spreading function. Figure 8b shows the tonali-

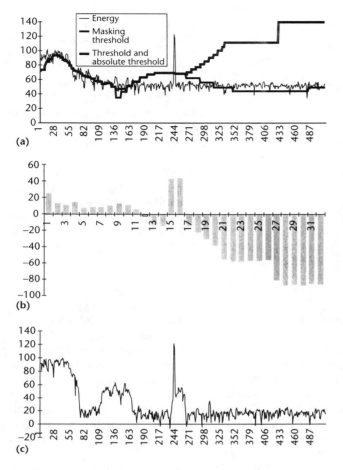

(a)

(b)

(c)

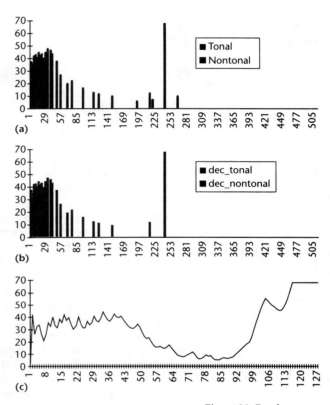

Figure 10. Psychoacoustic model 2 processing. (a) Original signal energy and computed masking thresholds. (b) Signal-to-mask ratios. (c) Coded audio energy (64 Kbps).

ty index for the audio signal as computed by psychoacoustic model 2. Note the shift of the sinusoid peak and the expansion of the low-pass noise distribution. The perceptual transformation expands the low-frequency region and compresses the higher frequency region. Because the spreading function is applied in a perceptual domain, the shape of the spreading function is relatively uniform as a function of partition. Figure 9 shows a plot of the spreading functions.

Figure 10a shows a plot of the masking threshold as computed by the model based on the spread energy and the tonality index. This figure has plots of the masking threshold both before and after the incorporation of the threshold in quiet to illustrate its impact. Note the threshold in quiet significantly increases the noise-masking threshold for the higher frequencies. The human auditory system is much less sensitive in this region. Also note how the sinusoid signal increases the masking threshold for the neighboring frequencies.

The masking threshold is computed in the uniform frequency domain instead of the perceptual domain in preparation for the final step of the psychoacoustic model, the calculation of the signal-to-mask ratios (SMR) for each subband. Figure 10b is a plot of these results, and Figure 10c is a frequency plot of a processed audio signal using these SMRs. In this example the audio compression was severe (768 to 64 Kbps), so the coder cannot necessarily mask all the quantization noise.

For psychoacoustic model 1, we use the same example audio signal as above. Figure 11a shows how the psychoacoustic model 1 identifies the local spectral peaks as tonal and nontonal components. Figure 11b shows the remaining tonal and nontonal components after the decimation

*Figure 11. Psychoacoustic model 1 processing.
(a) Identified tonal and nontonal components.
(b) Decimated tonal and nontonal components. (c) Global masking thresholds.*

Figure 12.
Psycho-
acoustic
model 1
processing
results.
(a) Signal-
to-mask
ratios.
(b) Coded
audio
energy (64
Kbps).

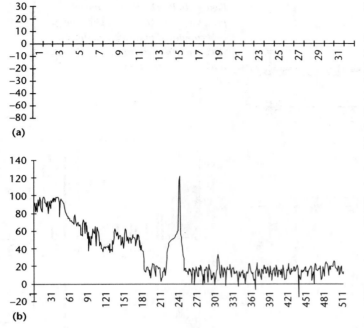

process. This process both removes components that would fall below the threshold in quiet and removes the weaker tonal components within roughly half a critical-band width (0.5 Bark) of a stronger tonal component.

Psychoacoustic model 1 uses the decimated tonal and nontonal components to determine the global masking threshold in a subsampled frequency domain. This subsampled domain corresponds approximately to a perceptual domain.

Figure 11c shows the global masking threshold calculated for the example audio signal. Psychoacoustic model 1 selects the minimum global masking threshold within each subband to compute the SMRs. Figure 12a shows the resulting signal-to-mask ratio, and Figure 12b is a frequency plot of the processed audio signal using these SMRs.

Layer coding options

The MPEG/audio standard has three distinct layers for compression. Layer I forms the most basic algorithm, while Layer II and Layer III are enhancements that use some elements found in Layer I. Each successive layer improves the compression performance—at the cost of greater encoder and decoder complexity.

Every MPEG/audio bitstream contains periodically spaced frame headers to identify the bitstream. Figure 13 gives a pictorial representation of the header syntax. A 2-bit field in the MPEG header identifies the layer in use.

Layer I

The Layer I algorithm codes audio in frames of 384 audio samples. It does so by grouping 12 samples from each of the 32 subbands, as shown in Figure 14. Besides the code for audio data, each frame contains a header, an optional cyclic-redundancy-code (CRC) error-check word, and possibly ancillary data.

Figure 15a shows the arrangement of this data in a Layer I bitstream. The numbers within parentheses give the number of bits possible to encode each field. Each group of 12 samples gets a bit allocation and, if the bit allocation is not zero, a scale factor. The bit allocation tells the decoder the number of bits used to represent each sample. For Layer I this allocation can be 0 to 15 bits per subband.

The scale factor is a multiplier that sizes the samples to fully use the range of the quantizer. Each scale factor has a 6-bit representation. The decoder multiplies the decoded quantizer output with the scale factor to recover the quantized subband value. The dynamic range of the scale factors alone exceeds 120 dB. The combination of the bit allocation and the scale factor provide the potential for representing the samples with a dynamic range well over 120 dB. Joint stereo coding slightly alters the representation of left- and right-channel audio samples and will be covered later.

Layer II

The Layer II algorithm is a straightforward enhancement of Layer I. It codes the audio data in

Figure 13.
MPEG
header
syntax.

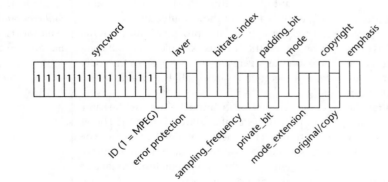

larger groups and imposes some restrictions on the possible bit allocations for values from the middle and higher subbands. It also represents the bit allocation, the scale-factor values, and the quantized samples with more compact code. Layer II gets better audio quality by saving bits in these areas, so more code bits are available to represent the quantized subband values.

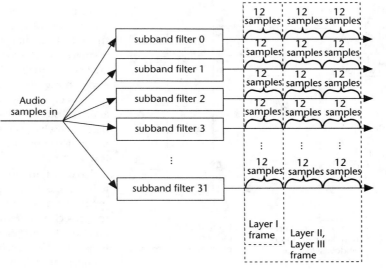

The Layer II encoder forms frames of 1,152 samples per audio channel. Whereas Layer I codes data in single groups of 12 samples for each subband, Layer II codes data in three groups of 12 samples for each subband. Figure 14 shows this grouping. Again discounting stereo redundancy coding, each trio of 12 samples has one bit allocation and up to three scale factors.

The encoder uses a different scale factor for each group of 12 samples only if necessary to avoid audible distortion. The encoder shares scale-factor values among two or all three groups in two other cases: one, when the values of the scale factors are sufficiently close; two, when the encoder anticipates that temporal noise masking by the human auditory system will hide any distortion caused by using only one scale factor instead of two or three. The scale-factor selection information (SCFSI) field in the Layer II bitstream informs the decoder if and how to share the scale-factor values. Figure 15b shows the arrangement of the various data fields in a Layer II bitstream.

Another enhancement covers the occasion when the Layer II encoder allocates three, five, or nine levels for subband quantization. In these circumstances, the Layer II encoder represents three consecutive quantized values with a single, more compact code word.

Layer III

The Layer III algorithm is a much more refined approach derived from ASPEC (audio spectral perceptual entropy coding) and OCF (optimal coding in the frequency domain) algorithms.[12,15,16]

Header (32)	CRC (0,16)	Bit allocation (128-256)	Scale factors (0-384)	Samples	Ancillary data

(a)

Header (32)	CRC (0,16)	Bit allocation (26-188)	SCFSI (0-60)	Scale factors (0-1080)	Samples	Ancillary data

(b)

Header (32)	CRC (0,16)	Side information (136, 256)	Main data; not necessarily linked to this frame. See Figure 18.

(c)

Figure 15. Frame formats of the three MPEG/audio layers' bitstreams: (a) Layer I, (b) Layer II, and (c) Layer III.

Although based on the same filter bank found in Layer I and Layer II, Layer III compensates for some filter-bank deficiencies by processing the filter outputs with a modified discrete cosine transform (MDCT).[17]

Figure 16 on the next page shows a block diagram of this processing for the encoder. Unlike the polyphase filter bank, without quantization the MDCT transformation is lossless. The MDCTs further subdivide the subband outputs in frequency to provide better spectral resolution. Furthermore, once the subband components are subdivided in frequency, the Layer III encoder can partially cancel some aliasing caused by the polyphase filter bank. Of course, the Layer III decoder has to undo the alias cancellation so that the inverse MDCT

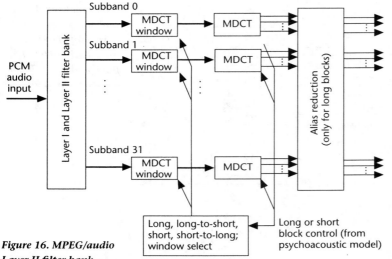

Figure 16. MPEG/audio Layer II filter bank processing (encoder side).

can reconstruct subband samples in their original, aliased, form for the synthesis filter bank.

Layer III specifies two different MDCT block lengths: a long block of 18 samples or a short block of 6. There is a 50-percent overlap between successive transform windows, so the window size is 36 and 12, respectively. The long block length allows greater frequency resolution for audio signals with stationary characteristics, while the short block length provides better time resolution for transients.[18]

Note the short block length is one third that of a long block. In the short block mode, three short blocks replace a long block so that the number of MDCT samples for a frame of audio samples remains unchanged regardless of the block size selection. For a given frame of audio samples, the MDCTs can all have the same block length (long or short) or a mixed-block mode. In the mixed-block mode the MDCTs for the two lower frequency subbands have long blocks, and the MDCTs for the 30 upper subbands have short blocks. This mode provides better frequency resolution for the lower frequencies, where it is needed the most, without sacrificing time resolution for the higher frequencies.

The switch between long and short blocks is not instantaneous. A long block with a specialized long-to-short or short-to-long data window serves to transition between long and short block types. Figure 17 shows how the MDCT windows transition between long and short block modes.

Because MDCT processing of a subband signal provides better frequency resolution, it conse-quently has poorer time resolution. The MDCT operates on 12 or 36 polyphase filter samples, so the effective time window of audio samples involved in this processing is 12 or 36 times larger. The quantization of MDCT values will cause errors spread over this larger time window, so it is more likely that this quantization will produce audible distortions. Such distortions usually manifest themselves as pre-echo because the temporal masking of noise occurring before a given signal is weaker than the masking of noise after.

Layer III incorporates several measures to reduce pre-echo. First, the Layer III psychoacoustic model has modifications to detect the conditions for pre-echo. Second, Layer III can borrow code bits from the bit reservoir to reduce quantization noise when pre-echo conditions exist. Finally, the encoder can switch to a smaller MDCT block size to reduce the effective time window.

Besides the MDCT processing, other enhancements over the Layer I and Layer II algorithms include the following.

Alias reduction. Layer III specifies a method of processing the MDCT values to remove some artifacts caused by the overlapping bands of the polyphase filter bank.

Nonuniform quantization. The Layer III quantizer raises its input to the 3/4 power before quantization to provide a more consistent signal-to-noise ratio over the range of quantizer values. The requantizer in the MPEG/audio decoder relinearizes the values by raising its output to the 4/3 power.

Scale-factor bands. Unlike Layers I and II, where each subband can have a different scale factor, Layer III uses scale-factor bands. These bands cover several MDCT coefficients and have approximately critical-band widths. In Layer III scale factors serve to color the quantization noise to fit the varying frequency contours of the masking threshold. Values for these scale factors are adjusted as part of the noise-allocation process.

Entropy coding of data values. To get better data compression, Layer III uses variable-length Huffman codes to encode the quantized samples. After quantization, the encoder orders the 576 (32 subbands × 18 MDCT coefficients/subband) quantized MDCT coefficients in a predetermined order. The order is by increasing frequency except for the short MDCT block mode. For short blocks there are

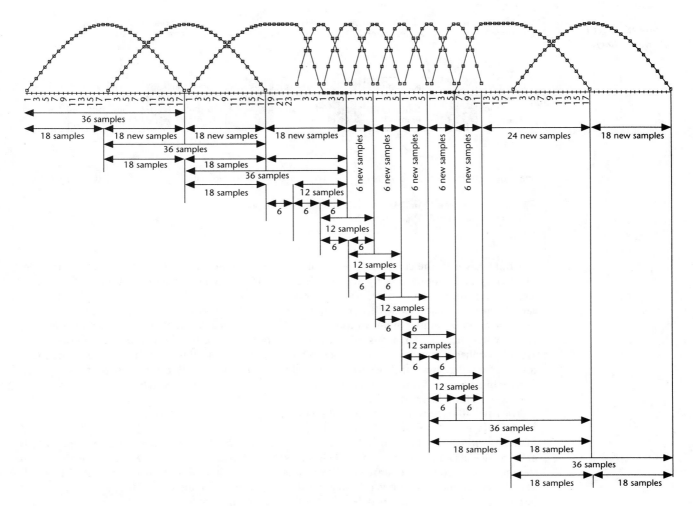

three sets of window values for a given frequency, so the ordering is by frequency, then by window, within each scale-factor band. Ordering is advantageous because large values tend to fall at the lower frequencies and long runs of zero or near-zero values tend to occupy the higher frequencies.

The encoder delimits the ordered coefficients into three distinct regions. This enables the encoder to code each region with a different set of Huffman tables specifically tuned for the statistics of that region. Starting at the highest frequency, the encoder identifies the continuous run of all-zero values as one region. This region does not have to be coded because its size can be deduced from the size of the other two regions. However, it must contain an even number of zeroes because the other regions code their values in even-numbered groupings.

The second region, the "count1" region, consists of a continuous run of values made up only of −1, 0, or 1. The Huffman table for this region codes four values at a time, so the number of values in this region must be a multiple of four.

The third region, the "big values" region, covers all remaining values. The Huffman tables for this region code the values in pairs. The "big values" region is further subdivided into three subregions, each having its own specific Huffman table.

Besides improving coding efficiency, partitioning the MDCT coefficients into regions and subregions helps control error propagation. Within the bitstream, the Huffman codes for the values are ordered from low to high frequency.

Use of a "bit reservoir." The design of the Layer III bitstream better fits the encoder's time-varying demand on code bits. As with Layer II, Layer III processes the audio data in frames of 1,152 samples. Figure 15c shows the arrangement of the various bit fields in a Layer III bitstream.

Figure 17. The arrangement of overlapping MDCT windows.

Figure 18. Layer III bitstream diagram.

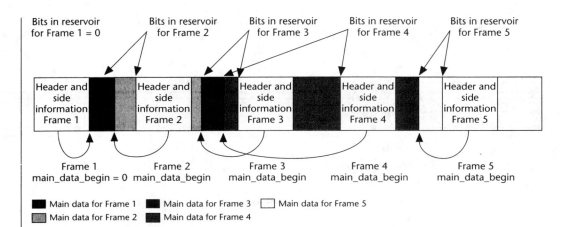

Unlike Layer II, the coded data representing these samples do not necessarily fit into a fixed-length frame in the code bitstream. The encoder can donate bits to a reservoir when it needs fewer than the average number of bits to code a frame. Later, when the encoder needs more than the average number of bits to code a frame, it can borrow bits from the reservoir. The encoder can only borrow bits donated from past frames; it cannot borrow from future frames.

The Layer III bitstream includes a 9-bit pointer, "main_data_begin," with each frame's side information pointing to the location of the starting byte of the audio data for that frame. Figure 18 illustrates the implementation of the bit reservoir within a fixed-length frame structure via the main_data_begin pointer. Although main_data_begin limits the maximum variation of the audio data to 29 bytes (header and side information are not counted because for a given mode they are of fixed length and occur at regular intervals in the bit stream), the actual maximum allowed variation will often be much less. For practical considerations, the standard stipulates that this variation cannot exceed what would be possible for an encoder with a code buffer limited to 7,680 bits. Because compression to 320 Kbps with an audio sampling rate of 48 kHz requires an average number of code bits per frame of 1,152 (samples/frame) × 320,000 (bits/second) / 48,000 (samples/second) = 7,680 bits/frame, absolutely no variation is allowed for this coding mode.

Despite the conceptually complex enhancements to Layer III, a Layer III decoder has only a modest increase in computation requirements over a Layer II decoder. For example, even a direct matrix-multiply implementation of the inverse MDCT requires only about 19 multiplies and additions per subband value. The enhancements mainly increase the complexity of the encoder and the memory requirements of the decoder.

Bit allocation

The bit allocation process determines the number of code bits allocated to each subband based on information from the psychoacoustic model. For Layers I and II, this process starts by computing the mask-to-noise ratio:

$$MNR_{dB} = SNR_{dB} - SMR_{dB}$$

where MNR_{dB} is the mask-to-noise ratio, SNR_{dB} is the signal-to-noise ratio, and SMR_{dB} is the signal-to-mask ratio from the psychoacoustic model.

The MPEG/audio standard provides tables that give estimates for the signal-to-noise ratio resulting from quantizing to a given number of quantizer levels. In addition, designers can try other methods of getting the signal-to-noise ratios.

Once the bit allocation unit has mask-to-noise ratios for all the subbands, it searches for the subband with the lowest mask-to-noise ratio and allocates code bits to that subband. When a subband gets allocated more code bits, the bit allocation unit looks up the new estimate for the signal-to-noise ratio and recomputes that subband's mask-to-noise ratio. The process repeats until no more code bits can be allocated.

The Layer III encoder uses noise allocation. The encoder iteratively varies the quantizers in an orderly way, quantizes the spectral values, counts the number of Huffman code bits required to code the audio data, and actually calculates the resulting noise. If, after quantization, some scale-factor bands still have more than the allowed distortion, the encoder amplifies the values in those scale-factor bands and effectively decreases the quantizer step size for those bands. Then the process repeats. The process stops if any of the following three conditions is true:

1. None of the scale-factor bands have more than the allowed distortion.

2. The next iteration would cause the amplification for any of the bands to exceed the maximum allowed value.

3. The next iteration would require all the scale-factor bands to be amplified.

Real-time encoders also can include a time-limit exit condition for this process.

Stereo redundancy coding

The MPEG/audio compression algorithm supports two types of stereo redundancy coding: intensity stereo coding and middle/side (MS) stereo coding. All layers support intensity stereo coding. Layer III also supports MS stereo coding.

Both forms of redundancy coding exploit another perceptual property of the human auditory system. Psychoacoustic results show that above about 2 kHz and within each critical band, the human auditory system bases its perception of stereo imaging more on the temporal envelope of the audio signal than on its temporal fine structure.

In intensity stereo mode the encoder codes some upper-frequency subband outputs with a single summed signal instead of sending independent left- and right-channel codes for each of the 32 subband outputs. The intensity stereo decoder reconstructs the left and right channels based only on a single summed signal and independent left- and right-channel scale factors. With intensity stereo coding, the spectral shape of the left and right channels is the same within each intensity-coded subband, but the magnitude differs.

The MS stereo mode encodes the left- and right-channel signals in certain frequency ranges as middle (sum of left and right) and side (difference of left and right) channels. In this mode, the encoder uses specially tuned threshold values to compress the side-channel signal further.

Future MPEG/audio standards: Phase 2

The second phase of the MPEG/audio compression standard, MPEG-2 audio, has just been completed. This new standard became an international standard in November 1994. It further extends the first MPEG standard in the following ways:

- Multichannel audio support. The enhanced standard supports up to five high-fidelity audio channels, plus a low-frequency enhancement channel (also known as 5.1 channels). Thus, it will handle audio compression for high-definition television (HDTV) or digital movies.

- Multilingual audio support. It supports up to seven additional commentary channels.

- Lower, compressed audio bit rates. The standard supports additional lower, compressed bit rates down to 8 Kbps.

- Lower audio sampling rates. Besides 32, 44.1, and 48 kHz, the new standard accommodates 16-, 22.05-, and 24-kHz sampling rates. The commentary channels can have a sampling rate that is half the high-fidelity channel sampling rate.

In many ways this new standard is compatible with the first MPEG/audio standard (MPEG-1). MPEG-2/audio decoders can decode MPEG-1/audio bitstreams. In addition, MPEG-1/audio decoders can decode two main channels of MPEG-2/audio bitstreams. This backward compatibility is achieved by combining suitably weighted versions of each of the up to 5.1 channels into a "down-mixed" left and right channel. These two channels fit into the audio data framework of an MPEG-1/audio bitstream. Information needed to recover the original left, right, and remaining channels fits into the ancillary data portion of an MPEG-1/audio bitstream or in a separate auxiliary bitstream.

Results of subjective tests conducted in 1994 indicate that, in some cases, the backward compatibility requirement compromises the audio compression performance of the multichannel coder. Consequently, the ISO MPEG group is currently working on an addendum to the MPEG-2 standard that specifies a non-backward-compatible multichannel coding mode that offers better coding performance. **MM**

Acknowledgments

I wrote most of this article while employed at Digital Equipment Corporation. I am grateful for the funding and support this company provided for my work in the MPEG standards. I also appreciate the many helpful editorial comments given by the many reviewers, especially Karlheinz Brandenburg, Bob Dyas, Jim Fiocca, Leon van de Kerkhof, and Peter Noll.

References

1. ISO/IEC Int'l Standard IS 11172-3 "Information Technology—Coding of Moving Pictures and Associated Audio for Digital Storage Media at up to about 1.5 Mbits/s—Part 3: Audio."

2. K. Brandenburg et al., "The ISO/MPEG-Audio Codec: A Generic Standard for Coding of High Quality Digital Audio," 92nd AES Convention, preprint 3336, Audio Engineering Society, New York, 1992.

3. D. Pan, "Digital Audio Compression", *Digital Technical J.*, Vol.5, No.2, 1993.

4. ISO/IEC International Standard IS 11172-4 "Information Technology—Coding of Moving Pictures and Associated Audio for Digital Storage Media at up to about 1.5 Mbits/s—Part 4: Conformance."

5. G.C. Wirtz, "Digital Compact Cassette: Audio Coding Technique," 91st AES Convention, preprint 3216, Audio Engineering Society, New York, 1991.

6. G. Plenge, "A Versatile High Quality Radio System for the Future Embracing Audio and Other Applications," 94th AES Convention, Audio Engineering Society, New York, 1994.

7. C. Grewin and T. Ryden, "Subjective Assessments on Low Bit-rate Audio Codecs," *Proc. 10th Int'l AES Conf.*, Audio Engineering Society, 1991, pp. 91-102.

8. J.H. Rothweiler, "Polyphase Quadrature Filters—A New Subband Coding Technique," *Proc. Int'l Conf. IEEE ASSP*, 27.2, IEEE Press, Piscataway, N.J., 1983, pp. 1280-1283.

9. H.J. Nussbaumer and M. Vetterli, "Computationally Efficient QMF Filter Banks," *Proc. Int'l Conf. IEEE ASSP*, IEEE Press, Piscataway, N.J., 1984, pp. 11.3.1-11.3.4.

10. P. Chu, "Quadrature Mirror Filter Design for an Arbitrary Number of Equal Bandwidth Channels," *IEEE Trans. on ASSP*, Vol. ASSP-33, No. 1, pp. 203-218, Feb. 1985.

11. B. Scharf, "Critical Bands," in *Foundations of Modern Auditory Theory*, J. Tobias, ed., Academic Press, New York and London, 1970, pp. 159-202.

12. J.D. Johnston, "Transform Coding of Audio Signals Using Perceptual Noise Criteria," *IEEE J. on Selected Areas in Comm.*, Vol. 6, Feb. 1988, pp. 314-323.

13. D. Wiese and G. Stoll, "Bitrate Reduction of High Quality Audio Signals by Modeling the Ears' Masking Thresholds," 89th AES Convention, preprint 2970, Audio Engineering Society, New York, 1990.

14. K. Brandenburg and J. Herre, "Digital Audio Compression for Professional Applications," 92nd AES Convention, preprint 3330, Audio Engineering Society, New York, 1992.

15. K. Brandenburg and J.D. Johnston, "Second Generation Perceptual Audio Coding: The Hybrid Coder," 88th AES Convention, preprint 2937, Audio Engineering Society, New York, 1990.

16. K. Brandenburg et al., "ASPEC: Adaptive Spectral Perceptual Entropy Coding of High Quality Music Signals," 90th AES Convention, preprint 3011, Audio Engineering Society, New York, 1991.

17. J. Princen, A. Johnson, and A. Bradley, "Subband/Transform Coding Technique Based on Time Domain Aliasing Cancellation," *Proc. Int'l Conf. IEEE ASSP*, IEEE Press, Piscataway, N.J., 1987, pp. 2161-2164.

18. B. Elder, "Coding of Audio Signals with Overlapping Block Transform and Adaptive Window Functions," *Frequenz*, Vol. 43, 1989, pp. 252-256 (in German).

Davis Pan is a principal staff engineer in Motorola's Chicago Corporate Research Labs, where he heads a team working on audio compression and audio processing algorithms. He received both a bachelor's and a master's degree in electrical engineering from the Massachusetts Institute of Technology in 1981, and a PhD in electrical engineering from the same institute in 1986.

Pan has worked in the MPEG/audio compression standards since 1990 and led the development of the ISO software simulations for the MPEG/audio algorithm.

Readers may contact the author at Motorola, Inc., 1301 E. Algonquin Rd., Schaumberg, IL 60196, e-mail pan@ukraine.corp.mot.com.

Structured audio and effects processing in the MPEG-4 multimedia standard

Eric D. Scheirer

Machine Listening Group, Room E15-401D, MIT Media Laboratory, Cambridge, MA 02139, USA; e-mail: eds@media.mit.edu

Abstract. While previous generations of the MPEG multimedia standard have focused primarily on coding and transmission of content digitally sampled from the real world, MPEG-4 contains extensive support for structured, synthetic and synthetic/natural hybrid coding methods. An overview is presented of the "Structured Audio" and "AudioBIFS" components of MPEG-4, which enable the description of synthetic soundtracks, musical scores, and effects algorithms and the compositing, manipulation, and synchronization of real and synthetic audio sources. A discussion of the separation of functionality between the systems layer and the audio toolset of MPEG-4 is presented, and prospects for efficient DSP-based implementations are discussed.

Key words: Structured audio – Audio coding – Audio synthesis – MPEG-4 – Multimedia standards

1 Introduction

There has been great progress made recently in the development of efficient coding methods for digital audio. By using techniques for eliminating "perceptually irrelevant" audio components, a wide-band sound such as music may be compressed for transmission by as much as a factor of 10, and a narrow-band sound such as speech by as much as a factor of 50, with little perceptual loss of quality (Noll 1993; Gersho 1994). Concomitantly, there has been a broadening of the scenarios in which delivery of acceptable-quality audio is possible. Internet telephony (Hardman et al. 1995) and radio broadcasts (Progressive Networks 1997) are now becoming commonplace.

The MPEG-1 and MPEG-2 multimedia standards (Brandenburg and Stoll 1994; Brandenburg and Bosi 1995) developed in the International Organisation for Standardisation (ISO) by the Moving Pictures Experts Group (MPEG) made use of compression techniques for coding and transmission of sound. Many consumer products have been based upon inexpensive hardware implementations of these decoders.

Such sound-coding tools, often called *perceptual coders* (since they use psychoacoustic principles to guide lossy compression) only seek to eliminate redundancy at a particular level, that of the audio waveform and its perception. In contrast to this, *structured* coding methods can exploit structure and redundancy at many different levels of a sound scene, and in many cases result in representations which are several orders of magnitude more compressed than the equivalent perceptually coded representation (Vercoe et al. 1998).

A structured representation of multimedia information is one which makes model-based assumptions about the origin and nature of its content. For example, a structured video representation for teleconferencing might use only lip, tongue, and eyebrow positions as a parameter set; rather than receiving frames of video data, an application using this representation would use this *model-based* parametrization to create synthetic facial images from a greatly reduced data stream. Thus, the facial parameter space is a representation particularly appropriate and efficient for coding content within a particular domain (images of talking heads), at the cost of being unable to effectively represent content outside that domain.

An analogous representation for audio might assume that a sound to be coded is a stream of English words. According to this model, symbols corresponding to English phonemes would be transmitted, perhaps in conjunction with other parametric information about vocal timbre or prosody, and synthesized back into sound upon receipt. As in the previous example, this representation is efficient and flexible for transmission within the specific domain (English speech), but less effective for domains slightly disjoint (for example, speech in other languages). It is an unusable model for very different domains, such as symphonic music.

In these examples, the structured transmission is based on a single, fixed model of the content. A more powerful form (Vercoe et al. 1998) of structured audio delivery is to transmit, first, a description of the model to be used for the content, and to follow that with the parameters for using the model. With a sufficiently broad description framework for the model delivery, this *algorithmic* structured audio can encapsulate other forms of model-based coding. It does not suffer from the limited applicability of fixed-model coding schemes, as long as there is a model for the particular content being delivered can be determined.

The new MPEG-4 standard (ISO/IEC 1998) contains extensive support for structured multimedia content in both the audio and visual modalities, as well as system-level support for synchronization with "natural" (waveform-coded) content, and the transmission of synthetic/natural hybrid multimedia scenes. Using this new standard, it will be possible to author representations of video and sound which can be transmitted at extremely low bit rates, but nonetheless render at high fidelity.

In this paper, an overview of the tools provided for structured audio representation in MPEG-4 and their supported functionalities is presented in Sect. 2. In Sect. 3, the various signal paths for audio decoding and rendering in MPEG-4 which make use of structured audio capabilities are discussed, and the scene description format for synthetic/natural hybrid sound scenes detailed. In Sect. 4, implementation issues such as efficiency, conformance, and quality control are considered, and Sect. 5 concludes with remarks on new developments for Version 2 of MPEG-4 audio and on the relationship between MPEG-4 and MPEG-7.

2 Structured audio tools in MPEG-4

The MPEG-4 audio standard (Scheirer 1998a; Quackenbush 1998) is built from a "toolbox" approach: several different tools for decoding natural and synthetic sounds are standardized, and different MPEG receiving systems or "terminals" choose to implement a subset of them appropriate to the application target. One of these tools is called Structured Audio, used for representing synthetic music and sound effects; however, structured audio concepts are also present in the CELP and parametric low-bit-rate speech decoders, and in the phonemic text-to-speech decoder. Each of these will be described briefly, then a more in-depth discussion of the Structured Audio tool presented.

2.1 CELP and parametric low-bit-rate speech tools

There are four "natural" audio-decoding tools in the MPEG-4 standard. Two of them, the *advanced audio coding* and *time-windowed vector quantization* decoders, utilize state-of-the-art versions of standard channel coding techniques and, as such, do not represent structured coding schemes. However, the other two, the *CELP* and *parametric* decoding tools, are somewhat structured; they can be used to represent speech and other harmonic signals over a scalable range of bit rates with proportionate loss of perceptual quality.

The CELP (code-excited linear prediction) tool decodes a sound modeled with linear predictive coding (Makhoul 1975); that is, as a quasi-periodic or noise excitation source filtered with an all-pole spectrum shaping filter. The excitation signal (the glottal pulse signal for speech coding) is compressed using codebook techniques (Gersho 1994). The CELP coder is appropriate for transmission of speech and certain, especially monophonic, musical signals, and operates in the range 6–24 kbps.

The Parametric tool decodes a sound modeled with a hybrid set of techniques, including sinusoidal synthesis, codebook methods for noisy excitations and residuals, and spectrum shaping using LPC. It is appropriate for other sorts of

harmonic musical signals and telephone-quality speech in the range 2–12 kbps. This technique is similar to the Spectral Modeling Synthesis sound model developed by Serra and his collaborators (Serra 1997).

2.2 Text-to-speech

Text-to-speech (TTS) coding is a powerful ultra-low-bit-rate (as low as a few dozen bits per second) method for transmission of speech when the precise timbre and diction of the speaker's voice are not important. MPEG-4 standardizes an interface to TTS synthesis systems so that a single bitstream format can be synthesized with a plug-in TTS module. This interface allows transmission of language-independent phoneme representations, prosody information in the form of pitch and timing, and certain aspects of control over vocal timbre. The particular method of speech synthesis is not standardized; only the parameter stream and its meaning is standardized in MPEG-4. Any desired method for mapping from parameters to audio may be used.

The TTS interface in MPEG-4 can also be used to automatically derive parameters for the Face Animation visual tool. By using this functionality, an audiovisually synchronized "talking head" can be created at very low bandwidth.

2.3 Structured audio

2.3.1 Overview

The MPEG-4 Structured Audio tool allows the efficient description and transmission of synthetic sound. While the previous two model-based coding schemes make use of fixed, standard models, Structured Audio allows for the algorithmic description of new models and their immediate use in content. The Structured Audio standard is built around a sophisticated language, called *SAOL*[1] for "Structured Audio Orchestra Language", which allows the description of parametric signal-processing algorithms (Scheirer 1998b). Algorithms in SAOL are transmitted as part of the bitstream; an MPEG-4-compliant decoding terminal must contain a subsystem capable of understanding this language and synthesizing sound as required by the content stream. The sound synthesis algorithms can be controlled in a number of different ways: through event lists written in a simpler language called SASL, also part of the MPEG-4 specification; through MIDI controls and real-time MIDI interaction; and through dynamic instructions generated by the scene description and interaction facility. The first two of these cases are described in this section, while the last is described in Sect. 3.

For systems and content which can make use of a more restricted fixed synthesis model, a structured audio sample bank format (SASBF) is also standardized in MPEG-4 (Scheirer and Ray 1998). This is a description syntax for banks of wavetable samples and simple processing (such as envelope shaping and reverberation) to apply to them. In the "full profile" of MPEG-4 Structured Audio, sample bank format data may be used for synthesis in conjunction with

---

[1] SAOL is pronounced like the English word "sail".

SAOL programs; there are also profiles of MPEG-4 Structured Audio which disallow the use of SAOL, and synthesis is only performed using SASBF (see below). The SASBF format was developed in technical collaboration between MPEG and the MIDI Manufacturers Association (MMA); it provides certain aspects of compatibility with MMA standards.

2.3.2 Concepts

The idea behind MPEG-4 Structured Audio is that there is a certain kind of high-level redundancy present in waveform recordings of music and other structured sound, which can be termed *timbral redundancy*. For example, in a piece of piano music, each note played has certain attributes of *control*, such as pitch and loudness, and also attributes of *timbre*, which are the "qualities" of the notes orthogonal to pitch and loudness. For many instruments, both acoustic and synthetic, the timbre will be relatively invariant from note to note; a pianist, for example, has little control over the timbre of a note. Thus, since a waveform-based encoding of a piece of piano music repeats the description of "what a piano sounds like" with every note, there is a great deal of timbral redundancy in this encoding method. This sort of redundancy is not removed by perceptual or information-theoretic (lossless) coding of sound.

The MPEG-4 Structured Audio tool allows the control parameters for a piece of music to be transmitted independently from the timbral descriptions. The control parameters are encoded as a list of instructions, called a *score*, and the timbral descriptions are encoded using an algorithmic signal-processing description, called an *orchestra*. The MPEG terminal receives the score and orchestra for a piece of music, compiles the orchestra description into a running digital-signal-processing network, and then feeds the control parameters into the DSP network to activate synthesis. The sound quality depends only upon the quality of *algorithms* specified in the orchestra, not on the channel capacity of the link. Since there are often very few control parameters which must be transmitted, the continuous bit rate of a Structured Audio bitstream is typically extremely low, perhaps less than 100 bits per second.

Figure 1 shows a schematic overview of the processing and decoding flow in a typical Structured Audio terminal (although only the processing results are standardized, not this particular signal flow). The overall process is controlled by the *scheduler*, which has normative (standardized) capabilities specified in the standard.

The same sound algorithm tools are used for *effects processing* in MPEG-4. This is because the kinds of algorithms useful for performing reverberation, equalization, mixing, and other post-production effects are very similar to the kinds of algorithms useful for sound synthesis. By unifying the techniques which allow structured audio transmission with those which allow parametric post-production, a more powerful and concise standard is produced.

Figure 1 integrates elements of operation for occasions when the structured audio tools are used as a bitstream decoder, and for those when they are used as an effects processor. When used as an effects processor, there is no real-time

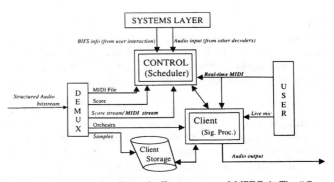

Fig. 1. The structured audio and effects system of MPEG-4. The "*Control*" and "*Client*" boxes together make up the structured audio processing. The incoming bitstream data is only present when the system is used as a decoder. *Labels in italics* represent data streams which continue during real-time operation; *labels in roman* represent data which is only in the bitstream header. See text for details

bitstream delivery, as shown at the left of Fig. 1. The subsequent discussion focuses on use of the Structured Audio system as an audio decoder; use as an effects-processing system will be discussed in Sect. 3.

The Structured Audio bitstream contains several components which are demultiplexed as they are received. The bitstream *header* is transmitted at the beginning of a session and contains the orchestra description, a MIDI and/or SASL score file, and perhaps some sound samples. The *scheduler* in the decoding terminal receives the orchestra and compiles it into a form suitable for use by the signal-processing system. The *signal-processing system* is a reconfigurable synthesis engine capable of executing algorithms written in SAOL; it may be actually running on the same processor or a different one from the scheduler.

During the *streaming*, or run-time, part of the session, the scheduler may receive any or all of the following sorts of data: score or MIDI data, new sample data, audio input from other decoders (when it is used for effects processing), and live MIDI and audio provided by the user with a microphone or MIDI controller. In some implementations, the live microphone or MIDI input might be routed directly to the signal-processing system to reduce latency.

The scheduler acts as a control system for the client signal-processing system during orchestra execution. The two systems maintain communication, and the scheduler tells the client when to create new notes, turn off existing ones, route a particular sound to a particular post-processing algorithm, and so on. The audio output created by the signal processor is the sound output from the Structured Audio decoder.

This process is similar in some ways to Internet-based sound delivery based on the General MIDI standard (MMA 1996), in which a MIDI file is transmitted via the WWW and then synthesized into sound upon receipt, with an important exception. In General MIDI, the control of sound quality and instrument timbre is under the control of the terminal manufacturer (the implementor of the hardware/software synthesizers used for the sound rendering process). In MPEG-4, by contrast, the sound descriptions are also part of the bitstream, and so the composer/sound designer has precise control over the final sound. Related to this, in a simple General

MIDI framework the composer has no ability to create new sounds for a particular composition; he/she is limited to the particular sounds built into the rendering engine. MPEG-4 Structured Audio is openly extensible by the sound designer based upon the needs of a particular composition or application.

These limitations stem from the fact that MIDI, during its design, was never intended as an interchange format for structured audio, but rather as a communications protocol for control of hardware synthesizers (Smith 1991). It serves this task well; its low-level instructions are sufficiently general that any synthesizer can interpret them and create sound. However, this generality means that the stream of commands has little specificity of meaning. The MIDI stream does not represent a "sound", but a set of controls. MPEG-4 Structured Audio is designed to represent sounds.

2.3.3 History

The design of MPEG-4 Structured Audio and its component languages originates with "NetSound", a previous in-house project at the MIT Media Laboratory (Casey and Smaragdis 1996). NetSound was intended to serve the application of providing low-bandwidth, high-quality audio accompaniment for WWW pages ("a Web page with a sound-track"). In NetSound, an orchestra and score in the "Csound" language (see below) are encapsulated, along with any necessary sound samples, in a simple transport wrapper. In this way, Csound programs could be used for structured transmission of synthetic music and sound effects.

NetSound was generally successful in its goals and serves as a useful demonstration platform for structured audio ideas, since highly efficient real-time implementations of Csound are available (Vercoe 1996b). Based on lessons learned in that project, the languages SAOL and SASL were designed and submitted to MPEG (Scheirer and Vercoe 1997a) in response to an MPEG Call for Proposals regarding audio synthesis techniques. SAOL and SASL have evolved in the MPEG working process somewhat since the original proposal, although the basic concepts are unchanged; the MIDI semantics, AudioBIFS capability (Scheirer and Vercoe 1997b; Scheirer et al. 1998) and SASBF formats have since been added to the Structured Audio toolset.

In parallel to the evolution of the textual documentation, the MIT Media Laboratory also developed an interpreted implementation of SAOL for use in evaluation of the draft standard, and to serve as "reference software" for the standard. This implementation is in the public domain and available via the WWW at <http://sound.media.mit.edu/mpeg4>.

2.3.4 SAOL synthesizer description language

The SAOL synthesizer language (Scheirer 1998b) has its roots in the computer music field, where it is similar to previous languages called "Music-V" languages. Matthews developed the original Music V in the early days of computer music (Matthews 1969); since then, many derivative languages have been developed, including Music 11, Csound, and Cmusic (Roads (1996) has an overview of these sorts

of languages). The synthesis concepts underlying Music-V languages are simple. Waveforms are created, through functional construction or dynamically reading from a sampled sound, and stored in *wavetables*, also called *stored function tables*. *Unit generators* cycle over and generate audio signals from wavetables; these streams of samples can be output as sound or themselves used to control reading and oscillating other wavetables. With careful organization of the control flow, nearly any signal-processing network or sound synthesis method can be implemented as the interaction of several banked and cascaded unit generators which refer to appropriate wavetables. Most Music-V languages also contain facilities for filtering, scaling, decimating, and performing other common signal-processing operations on audio signals.

An orchestra in Music V is made of a group of *instruments*, which are encapsulated groupings of these wavetable oscillators and related instructions. Each instrument typically has several parameters, which are the degrees of freedom over which it may be varied (pitch, loudness, etc.). A main advantage of using a sophisticated music-processing language is that the relationship between the parameter settings and the resulting sound may be very complex and non-linear. That is, a "loudness" parameter may control not just the amplitude of an instrument, but its spectral qualities as well, to simulate the brightening of acoustic musical instruments as they are played louder. In addition, there is no fixed set of control parameters (as in MIDI); rather, parameters for each instrument are chosen and designed as appropriate.

To synthesize a musical performance, the instructions in the score specify the particular timings and parameter settings for each *note* in the composition. It is important to realize, that because of the generality of the signal processing model, the concept of "note" is much broader than in typical music usage (a note may represent anything from a parametric sound effect to a continuously evolving vocal sample used for atmosphere).

The most widely ported and popular Music-V language is Vercoe's language Csound (Vercoe 1996a), which updates Music-V concepts to include modern synthesis features such as FOF, phase vocoder, and granular synthesis (Rodet 1979; Dolson 1986; Roads 1991), and support for real-time control and MIDI-based playback. Csound has been embedded in devices from interactive karaoke machines to "synthetic accompanist" systems (Vercoe 1984). Csound also introduced an important abstraction called the *control-rate* signal. Control signals are used for features of a sound which evolve over time, but relatively slowly compared to the sound sampling rate. For example, vibrato pitch and amplitude envelope shapes are typically implemented as control rate signals in Csound instruments.

This control rate/audio rate distinction is important from an implementation perspective, since it allows the use of highly efficient block-processing algorithms in the interpreter or run-time environment. See Sect. 4 for more details on implementation issues.

SAOL can be viewed as an extension to Csound along several dimensions. Most obvious is an update to the language style. While Music-V languages have traditionally been "assembly-like", with implicit variable typing and little support for modular code or sophisticated flow control, SAOL's syntax is C-like, with a complete functional abstraction and explicit, specified semantics for all constructs. The ability to create re-usable instrument components and processing algorithms will aid acceptance of the language.

In addition to the syntactic revisions, there have been several new features added to the language model according to the requirements of the MPEG-4 standard. An "effects bus" metaphor has been created to aid the control of audio post-processing and mixing algorithms (about which see Sect. 3). Arrays of variables and of processing primitives can be used to simplify the construction of highly parallel algorithms. A "template" syntax allows the description of multiple similar instruments concisely. Instruments can spawn and control one another, which allows simple creation of "layering" and granular synthesis instruments. Dynamic control of the signal-processing algorithms is possible not only through MIDI, but also can be specified in SASL streams or scores, which allows more precision and flexibility. Many more details of SAOL, SASL, and the MIDI functionality in MPEG-4 are given elsewhere (Scheirer 1998b).

2.3.5 MIDI support

An important stage in the evolution of structured representations for music transmission has been the emergence of MIDI (Musical Instrument Digital Interface) as an industry standard for musical score exchange. MIDI was originally conceived as a method for communication between musical instrument devices and computers that control them, rather like a network protocol. However, as the MIDI standard has been augmented with file-based descriptions (MMA 1996) and, recently, downloadable sample specifications (MMA 1997), MIDI has become a useful way to transmit and exchange musical content.

Using MIDI, musicians can design musical compositions using powerful, user-friendly tools that interact with their home studio equipment. They then package the compositions into "MIDI files" which contain the score and control information for driving synthesizers. This file is suitable for low-bandwidth transmission as it is very small compared to an equivalent audio waveform; the recipient uses his/her own home studio equipment to resynthesize and listen to the composition.

There are a few obvious limitations in applying this method to high-quality music and sound effects synthesis. MIDI originated as a method for communications between previously incompatible synthesizers; thus, although any MIDI-capable synthesizer can produce sound based on the instructions in a MIDI file, there is no guarantee that this sound will be very much like the sound that the composer heard when writing the music. The "General MIDI" specification (MMA 1996) alleviates this problem somewhat by assigning a specific set of "instrument numbers" to a standard set of instruments. That is, in a General MIDI synthesizer, instrument #1 is always an "Acoustic Grand Piano" and #53 always "Choir Aaahs". However, the composer in this case is limited to the fixed set of instruments and control methods provided by General MIDI, and in any case, the sound of a "Choir Aaahs" may be very different on two different synthesizers.

In certain application domains, karaoke systems being the primary example, there have arisen de facto standards regarding the *brand of synthesizer* to be used for MIDI file re-creation, thus avoiding the problems that arise when different synthesizers have different sounds. However, this standardization restricts even further the creative options of the composer, as he is left with a very narrow and specific range of sounds to use for composition.

The MIDI "downloadable samples" (DLS) specification (MMA 1997) extends the General MIDI concept to allow MIDI files to incorporate specific sound samples for use in resynthesis. Using DLS in conjunction with MIDI moves closer to a true "structured audio" specification; however, the DLS specification is still limited in the kinds of manipulations it can perform on samples. There is additionally no standard for non-sample-based synthesis (most MIDI-capable synthesizers today use wavetable or "sampling" synthesis to generate sound). The DLS standard also allows broad latitude to implementation designers over how to generate sound from the provided samples. The MPEG-4 Structured Audio tools provide tighter control, as required by content providers delivering serious content, over the final quality of the synthetic sound.

Regardless of its shortcomings, there is no question that MIDI is a valuable and important tool for music content representation. There are a wide range of authoring tools (often called "sequencers", for they allow a composer to organize "sequences" of notes) available, and a great deal of content coded in this format, both proprietary and in the public domain. MPEG-4 Structured Audio supports MIDI as an alternative score format, allowing sound designers to design orchestras specifically for use with MIDI files. The particular semantics which MIDI commands take when applied to a SAOL orchestra are normatively described in the standard.

2.3.6 Sample bank format

The structured audio sample bank format (SASBF) allows the transmission of banks of wavetable data to be used in sampling synthesis. The MPEG-4 SASBF is an extension to the DLS wavetable format, and has been standardized in collaborative technical effort with the MIDI Manufacturer's Association. The SASBF specification synthesis model comprises a wavetable oscillator, a dynamic lowpass filter, an enveloping amplifier, and programmable sends to pan, reverb, and chorus effects units. An underlying modulation engine comprises two low-frequency oscillators (LFOs) and two envelope generators with appropriate routing amplifiers.

When SASBF synthesis is used in a "full profile" MPEG-4 Structured Audio system (see Sect. 2.3.7), the audio streams created by the wavetable synthesis process are not turned directly into sound, but integrated into the SAOL framework. Thus, advanced effects (such as custom filters or reverberators) may be written in SAOL and applied to the result of performing SASBF synthesis. See Scheirer and Ray (1998) for more discussion on hybrid wavetable/algorithmic synthesis.

2.3.7 Profiles

Since MPEG-2, the MPEG consortium has utilized a concept called "profiling", which allows reduced, but still standardized, functionality to be included in lower-cost, lower-complexity devices. The MPEG-4 audio standard defines three profiles for Structured Audio. These profiles differ in the functionality they require to be present in a decoding terminal, and in the applications for which they are intended.

The "full profile" allows the use of all the tools (SAOL, SASL, SASBF, and the MIDI semantics) discussed above to perform algorithmic and sample-based synthesis, and to apply software post-production algorithms (see Sect. 3) to natural audio content. The "full profile" is the default profile for MPEG-4 and most implementations will provide this functionality. The two restricted profiles below are targeted only at narrowly focused applications for which the full profile does not meet the requirements.

The "sample-based synthesis" profile allows the delivery of SASBF data and MIDI control, but not SAOL or SASL code. It is thus the MPEG-4 parallel to the current MIDI DLS standard, and is intended for applications similar to those which DLS is targeting today: karaoke systems and simple multimedia presentations. The primary advantage of using MPEG-4 rather than MIDI DLS in these applications comes from the other functionalities provided by MPEG-4; an MPEG-4 sample-based synthesis stream may be automatically mixed with voice tracks or other recorded sound, and synchronized with digital images or computer graphics. A terminal which implements this profile is simpler than one implementing the full profile, because the SASBF implementation is more easily implemented in fixed hardware than a SAOL implementation is.

Finally, a "score-based synthesis" profile is provided for applications which require only minimal control over synthetic sound. This profile provides equivalent synthesis functionality to General MIDI; it simply wraps the General MIDI standard into a format suitable for synchronizing with other media types in MPEG-4. Systems complying with the score-based synthesis profile need implement only minimal score-file-parsing syntax and semantics. They may perform real-time synthesis in software, or pass the score information to an offboard wavetable card or hardware synthesizer for playback. Such systems will have no capability for interpreting customized sound controls, producing a wide variety of novel sounds, or performing software post-production and mixing (see Sect. 3). However, since they can leverage existing hardware and content, the development and deployment cycle is likely to be much shorter than for fully functional structured audio implementations.

2.3.8 Bitstreams and encoders

An important aspect of the MPEG standards has always been that the encoder technology is left unstandardized. This helps to create an active marketplace among companies developing encoders, authoring content, and building terminal systems. For the Structured Audio tool, the bitstream is very simple; the encoding process is in some respects simple, and in other respects beyond the state-of-the-art today.

The Structured Audio bitstream is simply a compressed concatenation of the various syntactic components required to drive the synthesis: the orchestra and score files, any MIDI files used, plus sample files or other data tables which the synthesis algorithms utilize. Any of these may be encapsulated in the bitstream header, which is received and processed before sound playback begins; in addition, score events, MIDI events, sound samples, and wavetable definitions may be transmitted as part of the continuous bitstream. To "encode" in this format is simply to tokenize the orchestra and score, and paste together the relevant files in the proper order with the correct bitstream syntax.

On the other hand, arriving at score and orchestra description files is not yet a task that can be automated. The so-called *automated transcription* or "MIDI encoder" problem (Martin 1996) is a very difficult one, and there are not yet systems that can accomplish it in anything close to generality. In the near future, composers and sound designers will author content specifically for MPEG-4 playback, much as they do now for MIDI playback. Tools for authoring MPEG-4 bitstreams, such as sequencers and visual interfaces for orchestra design, will undoubtedly be developed to aid this process. Perhaps in the future, technology will be available to recode acoustic waveforms containing expressive polyphonic music into structured formats, but at the present, this is not a realistic scenario for MPEG-4.

3 Structured scene descriptions in MPEG-4

As well as standardizing tools for structured audio bitstream decoding. MPEG-4 standardizes the syntax and semantics of a scene description format. In the video and image-processing domain, scene descriptions have a fairly in-depth research history (Bove 1995; ISO 1997), but the use of scene descriptions and general audio transformations in an audio standard is an idea new to MPEG-4. This section presents an overview of the audio scene description and software mixing concept, then discusses the particular implementation of these ideas in the MPEG-4 standard.

3.1 Structured scene descriptions

To understand the functioning of an audio scene description, consider the steps involved in producing the soundtrack for a motion picture. The dialogue is recorded in a sound studio and synchronized with the images of the actors on the video. "Foley artists" produce sound effects by manipulating special sound-effects tools; these effects are recorded on another track of the multitrack recording. In addition, in the modern era, computer methods may be used to generate synthetic sound effects, or to manipulate those recorded in Foley. Musical backgrounds and interludes are composed and recorded, either with a live orchestra or (more commonly today) a MIDI studio.

The component tracks (dialogue, effects, and music) are manipulated and processed depending on the needs of the scene. For example, a scene which takes place in a large hall will have artificial reverberation added to the sound effects, somewhat less reverberation added to the dialogue, and likely no special reverberation added to the music (since the music is not "really in the hall"). Sounds coming from "off-stage", outside the scene, may be filtered in certain ways to emphasize their distance.

Once each track has been processed according to the director's and sound editor's specifications, the multiple tracks are "mixed down" into several formats for presentation - DTS or Lucasfilm THX formats for modern high-end cinemas, Dolby AC-3 "5+1" surround sound for laserdisc playback in home theater systems, and stereo for the VHS videotape format.

It is clear that, until the last mixing step, a structured audio description of the audio scene is being maintained, as each audio source is represented separately and processed differently. Only to fit into the format of current delivery systems (videotapes, film reels, cable TV systems) is the scene description lost from the sound mix.

The MPEG-4 system standardizes a scene description format called AudioBIFS (Scheirer et al. 1998) to allow the distribution of content like that described above in component "objects", and the composition of these sound objects into a scene for presentation. There are several major advantages to this method of coding scenes over the standard perceptual-coding methods: efficiency, flexibility, and ease of manipulation and indexing.

A structured scene description is a more efficient representation for audio scenes than a perceptually coded one, because the component parts may be coded in formats that are maximally efficient piece by piece. Using the soundtrack example above, the dialogue track might be encoded using a narrow-band speech coder, the sound effects as a set of short wide-band samples to be triggered by a score, and the music track as a MIDI file and SAOL orchestra. In this representation, the continuous bitstream bandwidth will be dominated by the narrow-band speech track, with sporadic increases when new sound effects samples are presented. By transmitting this scene in three parallel pieces and compositing the pieces upon receipt, a wide-band soundtrack containing music and sound effects may be transmitted for little more than the cost of a narrow-band speech track. If synthetic speech provided suitable quality to be used for the dialogue, the bandwidth cost would drop dramatically further.

This representation is also more flexible than the wide-band channel encoding; it is easy to build software at the rendering side of the transmission channel which allows for soundtrack customization based on user interaction. For example, the user might choose to attenuate the volume of the soundtrack relative to the dialogue, or to eliminate the sound effects algorithm. These are simple modifications to a structured soundtrack-rendering process, but impossible for a waveform encoding of the soundtrack. Further, it is easy to add augmented information, multiple languages in the soundtrack, for example. These "extra" pieces can be sent as additional sound objects, for only their own marginal cost; the whole musical score need not be retransmitted with the German dubbing track.

Another flexibility advantage provided by the separation of "source sound" and "mixing effect" is that modifications can be more easily made to a soundtrack while preserving quality. To use a dubbing example again, it is often the case that a foreign-language soundtrack will be produced in a

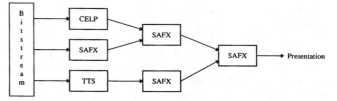

Fig. 2. Several audio streams are composited together for presentation. The leftmost "SAFX" unit is a decoder, and the others are mixers and effects processors (although their internal functioning is identical). Each *arrow* may represent a multichannel audio stream

separate studio from the original-language soundtrack; the dubbing process is typically a lower budget operation than the original mixing. If the soundtrack effects and scene composition are represented separately from the sound sources to which they are applied, it is easy to replace the sound sources with new ones; that is, the effects and mixdown parameters from the original French soundtrack are automatically applied to the new English dub. The resulting English soundtrack is of similar quality to the original (except, perhaps, for the voice acting), with much less effort than remixing.

Soundtracks stored in such a structured format are also more easily searched and indexed. Although automatic source separation is still a technology in its infancy, automatic voice recognition and keyword-spotting systems are becoming robust enough for everyday use. Thus, to search for a particular line of dialogue in a film soundtrack is comparatively easy in a structured format, since the "hard work" of separating the voice from the music and sound effects is unnecessary.

Finally, in this scenario, the burden of making mixes for unusual multichannel sound setups is removed from the sound designer and placed upon the implementor of the terminal. For today's soundtracks, only a few formats are available for each piece of content – THX, 5+1, stereo. In an MPEG-4 representation of the same soundtrack, there is no representation at all of "output format"; the presentation system is responsible for interpreting the scene description and producing waveforms appropriate to the speaker geometry at hand. This is an advantage in some cases, since certain presentation systems may be able to do special things with the sound, such as produce spatialized or "3D" audio which depends on the listener position (Gardner 1997). These types of effects cannot be "mixed into" the sound at the studio. On the other hand, for "optimized" presentations using a fixed presentation system, the skills and creativity of a skilled producer will always sound better than an algorithmic presentation method.

3.2 Effects processing and composition in MPEG-4

The MPEG-4 Structured Audio tool is also sometimes called a "structured audio and effects" tool, because it is used to perform full-functionality mixing, effects processing, post-production, and compositing, as well as to generate synthetic sound. In this section, dataflow paths in the MPEG-4 terminal which make this functionality possible will be described.

Figure 2 shows a conceptual diagram of the run-time structure of a scene composition. Three audio streams are multiplexed in the MPEG-4 bitstream, one each to be decoded with the CELP, TTS, and Structured Audio tools.

In this diagram, the leftmost "SAFX" node is a decoder, converting a bitstream of data into sound; the other "SAFX" nodes are *compositing*[2] nodes, which combine multiple audio streams together into new audio streams. This combination may be as simple as additive mixing, or as complex as desired through the use of SAOL code. No fixed set of algorithms is standardized; novel effects and mixing algorithms may be specified in SAOL and run as "instruments". The multiple inputs to the mixing node are passed as digital waveforms to the SAOL orchestra, where they can be manipulated using code written in SAOL specifically for that purpose.

There are important conceptual and functional advantages to this view of a very full-featured mixing/compositing system. In the modern sound studio, especially with regard to popular music, the distinction between "composition" (in the music-writing sense) and "production" has been blurring in recent years. Using digital technology, techniques previously used as part of the final "mixdown" stage in the authoring process, such as reverberation, flanging, and filtering, are now commonly used by composers to manipulate the materiel of composition itself. Conversely, unusual synthesis-style techniques (phase-vocoder analysis/resynthesis, chorusing, pitch shifting) are useful in post-production of entire audio tracks for mixdown. It is quite natural to encapsulate the worlds of both "composition" and "post-production" using a single digital sound manipulation language.

To specify the compositing and mixing process for a particular audiovisual scene in MPEG-4, the scene is described in terms of a *scene graph*. The scene graph, which represents the relationship between various decoders and compositing processes, is specified using a language called *BIFS*, or "binary format for scene description". BIFS is based on, but not exactly the same as, the VRML language for virtual environment modeling. VRML, which stands for "virtual-reality markup language", is a standard for the creation and transmission of virtual worlds and interactive experiences at "Internet bit rates", which means in practice 28 kbps. In particular, a major change from VRML scenes to MPEG-4 scenes is the inclusion of the AudioBIFS nodes (Scheirer et al. 1998) which allow high-quality sound post-production.

There are several levels of audio-mixing capability in the MPEG-4 audio (and systems, see below) specification from which implementors choose when building a terminal system. Among these, the simplest, the "switching" or "selection" level, only allows gating of signals. That is, if multiple audio sources are provided to a "switch" node, the output of the node will be the same as one of the inputs. The second level, called "mixing", allows the application of a mixing matrix to the input audio sources. Any relationship that can be expressed as a $M \times N$ matrix connecting M inputs to N outputs may be specified. In addition, spatial scene information (source location and position) is contained in the mixing node, and may be used to artificially spatialize the input sounds, although this aspect is non-normative. The

---

[2] The graphics community uses the term "composition" for this process, but in audio contexts, "compositing" is preferred to avoid confusion with the term for the process of creating musical art.

Systems Implementation		Configurable Synthesis Engine (SAOL Compiler/Runtime)			Non-configurable Synthesis Engine	Implementation
Scene Description	Audio Effects	Synthesis Description	Musical Content	Sound Material	Musical Content	Semantics
BIFS nodes		SAOL code	Score data (also MIDI)	Sound samples	Score data	Syntax
Systems Bitstream		Structured Audio Bitstream				Bitstream

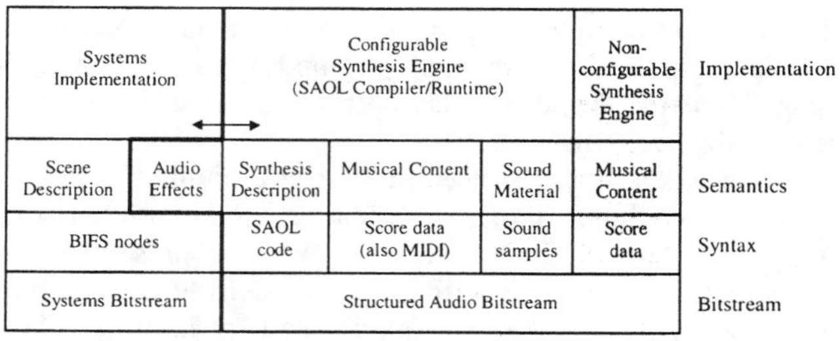

Fig. 3. The relationship of the systems and structured audio tools, showing a "layered" view of MPEG-4. *Items to the left of the dark line* are implemented within the systems implementation; *items to the right*, within the structured audio implementation. The vertical layering shows the various components of the bitstreams and the purposes they serve. The grayed-in section at the right contains the components required for the score-based synthesis profile. The systems layer and the runtime SAOL engine interact to perform synchronization and advanced effects/compositing

third level, called "audio-compositing and advanced effects", allows the inclusion of SAOL code in the BIFS node to perform arbitrary manipulations of the input signals. Facilities for handling these input signals are built into the core capability of the SAOL language. To enable the advanced effects capabilities, the "full" or "algorithmic synthesis" profile of structured audio must also be present in the terminal.

The AudioBIFS scene description is part of the *systems bitstream* in MPEG-4. The systems layer is the MPEG-4 tool which allows for the multiplexing, synchronization, and compositing of multiple MPEG-4 core decoders. That is, by providing a scene graph to the systems component of an MPEG terminal, the terminal is then able to pass on the other core bitstreams to the relevant audiovisual decoders, and synchronize and composite their outputs in complex ways. Even though a certain kind of "audio-processing" (the mixing SAOL code) is being handed to the terminal as part of the systems layer, it will still likely be implemented in the audio subsystem. Figure 3, taken from an earlier draft of the Structured Audio standard, illustrates the relationship between the systems layer and the Structured Audio decoder.

3.3 Comparison with VRML scene compositing

There is another common view of sound mixing, which might be termed the "VRML approach". Many ideas from VRML were examined during the MPEG-4 standardization process, since there is some overlap between the domains of interest of the two toolsets. VRML's approach for both graphics and sound is through *physical modeling* of a virtual scene. That is, a computer model of a scene is constructed, including its appearance and any sounds produced in it. While the "user" or "viewer" is interacting with the scene, the systems continuously attempts to render the scene using audio and video presentation techniques in such a way that the illusion of reality is maximized.

For sound environments, a VRML approach leads to a method of scene composition wherein the surroundings are described in terms of distances, directionalities, reverberation times, room filters, and so forth. This information is used when rendering the audio scene by filtering, reverberating, Doppler shifting, etc. the sound according to the "hear-point" of the virtual listener. Different implementations of VRML may take different approaches to this process (which is part of the standardization difference between MPEG and VRML), but all are attempting to physically reconstruct the scene.

This is a valuable type of presentation for some contexts, such as video gaming and virtual-environment synthesis. However, within the domain of delivery of pre-composed "artistic content", such as films and radio programs, it falls short of the requirements. This is because, in many cases, the sound designer of an artistic sound scene does not *wish* for the content to be physically approximated – a fact which has little to do with the technical abilities of a modern sound studio, and more to do with artistic concerns.

These issues are exemplified both by simple sounds produced in the Foley process ("handgun" sounds are, acoustically, more like cannon shots in many films), and by the mixing and editing of whole scenes. For example, consider a film scene taking place in a large ballroom; a string quartet plays in one corner and couples waltz in the center of the room. The camera position is at the entrance, giving an overview of the visual scene, but the audio mix lets us hear the string quartet clearly (not acoustically likely) and the conversation of the protagonists (which would be drowned out by the rest of the auditory scene). The camera then zooms and dollies in to frame the characters of interest; the visual scene is in motion, but no Doppler shift is applied to the music or dialogue.

The advantage of an *abstract effects* system like MPEG-4 for content delivery over a physical modeling approach is that it gives the content provider finer control over what sorts of effects are applied at what time. Certainly, it is possible to design and deliver a physical-modeling effects system when MPEG-4 is used for virtual-environment transmission (this may even be the default case), but in other scenarios, other mixing and production models may be used.

3.4 User interaction and dynamic Foley

A final capability of the integrated AudioBIFS/Structured Audio system in MPEG-4 is the creation of audio content which adapts to and interacts with the user. Many parameters from the environmental model are exposed to every Structured Audio decoder, such as source directions and locations; not only the "effects processors", but the decoders themselves, may make decisions and generate sound based on this information.

For example, in a virtual-environment application, a Structured Audio bitstream might contain information on the floor covering (rug, gravel, wood, etc.) in various regions of the world. Then, as the user moved through the world, his footstep sounds would be automatically synthesized using parametric descriptions of the various sound textures. As more advanced methods for sound effects and Foley synthesis (Casey 1998) become available, the use of model-based audio rather than sample-based audio for expressive, dynamic control of interactive sound effects will become more common.

Moving outside of a strictly normative MPEG-4 framework, SAOL is also a useful platform for interactive sound

for video games and other interactive media. Modern high-production video games often invest a great amount of time and effort in creating high-quality sound; as a result, the content authors are not willing to trust resynthesis of the sound to today's low-function sound cards. The typical solution is simply to stream audio from CD-ROM, but this greatly limits the interaction capability available to the author. Especially when embedded, robust MPEG-4 plug-in boards become available for multimedia PCs, expressing sound in MPEG-4 formats will allow more interactive possibilities, while still preserving quality.

4 Implementation issues

In this section, aspects of the implementation of the MPEG-4 audio standard which related to the Structured Audio and Effects tool will be discussed. There are two sides to this presentation: first, a discussion of prospects for efficient real-time implementations based on embedded DSP chips; and second, an exploration of verification and conformance issues for structured coding methods.

4.1 Building efficient implementations

One of the keys to acceptance of the standard is the realistic possibility of building real-time and efficient implementations. Complexity considerations, especially in light of the fact that audio is often only part of a multimodal presentation, are an important aspect of the MPEG standardization process. While a real-time system has not yet been built (the author has built a non-real-time interpreted system during the MPEG working process and released it into the public domain), the language has been designed to make efficient compilers for SAOL, and their associated run-time systems, possible on modern DSPs.

Most useful implementations will make use of DSP chips and SAOL compilation in order to push the speed of SAOL execution into real-time for complex scores and orchestras. Although real-time implementations of certain signal-processing languages exist today, they are typically either tailored to a specific platform, like "SuperCollider" (McCartney 1996) or have a relatively simple syntactic basis, like Csound. In addition, the audience for these languages is the computer music community, who are often happy to utilize the full CPU power of a host computer for audio processing alone; this situation will likely not commonly hold for MPEG-4. However, as the development of MPEG-2, Dolby AC-3, and ITU speech codec decoder cards and the rise in sales of 3D video processor cards for PCs demonstrates, the need for sideboard processors is not in itself a barrier to acceptance.

The SAOL language, like its predecessor Csound, uses a multirate processing metaphor to aid efficiency. The distinction between the control rate and the audio rate enables us to build *block-buffering* implementations that will run very efficiently on pipelined DSPs. In a non-block-buffered, or *sample-by-sample* implementation, a sequence of operations is processed on a single audio sample, followed by the same operations on the next sample, and so forth. In a block-buffering system, however, the same operation is repeated

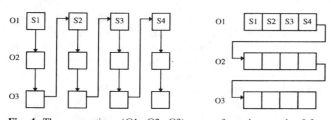

Fig. 4. Three operations (*O1, O2, O3*) are performed on each of four samples (*S1–S4*), in a sample-by-sample manner (*left*) and in a block-buffered manner (*right*). As long as the results of an operation on a sample do not depend on the results of a future operation on the previous sample, the block-buffered method may be used, and will be more efficient on most processors

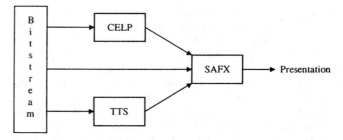

Fig. 5. The "flattened structure" corresponding to the scene graph in Fig. 2. This transformation may be done statically for any scene, without affecting the resulting rendered sound, and will execute more efficiently on most platforms. The SAOL code in the SAFX unit is the union of the code in all SAFX units in Fig. 2

many times on an entire "sample frame" of data before passing results onto the next processing stage (see Fig. 4). The control rate concept makes block-buffering possible by allowing the Csound/SAOL programmer to specify that certain variables change values more slowly than others.

However, unlike Csound, the language semantics of SAOL are defined sample by sample. That is, a SAOL programmer can write code with the assumption that the results of a previous sample's calculations are available for the calculation of the current sample. This is an advantage for the SAOL programmer, since it can be difficult to design implementations of some signal-processing algorithms in a block-buffered language like Csound; however, it is a disadvantage for the system implementor, because it means that efficient compilers must detect when block-buffering is possible and optimize accordingly. The "default" case for a compiler must always be to process sample by sample, because that is the only way that the normative language semantics may be met. The detection of these block-bufferable cases is similar to the detection of vectorizable loops by compilers for vector supercomputers; thus, it is reasonable to believe they will be developed by companies implementing MPEG-4 terminals.

Some algorithms (those containing feedback delays shorter than the block size) are inherently impossible to block-process in this manner. Good SAOL programming practice will still involve an understanding by the programmer/sound designer of the limitations of fast implementations. However, the inefficient cases are those which were simply prohibited in Csound (except by making the control rate equal to the audio rate, thus eliminating the efficiency advantage of the block-buffering method). A sound designer working in SAOL with an optimizing compiler has the ability to construct hybrid algorithms which block-buffer most of the time, and drop to single-sample mode in isolated, exceptional processing stages.

Also, the possibility of constructing multiprocessor implementations has been considered in the design of SAOL. Restrictions are placed on the speed with which multiple notes can communicate with one another, and with which instruments may be spawned and controlled by the scheduler (these functions may only be executed at the control rate). This speed limiting allows adequate time for communication between processors in a SIMD or MIMD architecture. In a parallelized implementation of SAOL, each instrument might be assigned a processor, and only notes for that instrument are executed there; or each processor might be able to

compute all of the instrument code, and new notes assigned to whichever processor is least loaded. Using the principles for block-based processing described above, the individual sample computations within a single note may even be allocated to different processors when appropriate. There are many possibilities for advanced SAOL implementations.

A final aspect of the structured audio system which leads to efficiency is the ability to statically manipulate scene structures, to streamline their processing. That is, since the internal-node effects-processing units in an audio-scene graph are small programs in the same language as the leaf-node Structured Audio decoder units, the SAOL code may be rearranged to combine all of these units together into one. Thus, the scene graph shown in Fig. 2 can be statically flattened into the one shown in Fig. 5 (Scheirer and Vercoe 1997b).

Doing this has several advantages. For one, it is a clear advantage to minimize the number of SAOL processes running, as they will often be the most computationally complex part of an audio system. If there are to be multiple Structured Audio processes (whether for decoding or for effects processing) in a terminal, they will each require a run-time package, and therefore either a multiple-DSP system or a multithreaded scheduler (on the DSP) must be used. Neither of these alternatives is practical today. Also, even if there were multiple DSPs in a terminal, each running a compiled SAOL application, there is a bottleneck in the host CPU (in Fig. 2, the host CPU of the terminal is responsible for managing dataflow along each arrow). Thus, multiple channels of audio data must be shuttled in and out of the SAFX components, causing processor loading on the host CPU. By "flattening" the scene graph as shown in Fig. 5, these problems may be avoided.

4.2 Conformance testing

An important aspect of MPEG, as with other ISO standards, is the conformance model. That is, along with the standard, MPEG publishes a clear set of guidelines outlining the *normative* aspects of the specification, those which are required to be implemented in order for a system to be MPEG-compliant. The scene-compositing and synthetic capability of MPEG-4 pose special challenges to this framework, as it is not always clear what "conformance" means in this context.

Previous MPEG standards have taken a "decode-only" stance towards conformance; that is, a decoder is not required to present output, only to decode legal bitstreams without crashing. However, even this level of conformance might be difficult to reach in MPEG-4, as SAOL programs, like programs in any other computationally complete language, may become arbitrarily complex in a manner that is not statically detectable. To state this another way, in less powerful bitstream syntaxes than the Structured Audio tool bitstream, an implementation can always determine the run-time complexity required for decoding by statically examining the bitstream. However, when SAOL programs are transmitted, this is an incomputable problem which is provably impossible to solve. There is no way to tell statically what resources a particular bitstream might require. A similar problem holds for the processing of complex scene structures represented in BIFS.

Further, the inclusion of testing and branching capability in SAOL (necessary in order to make a computationally complete language) means that bitstreams can be designed to take advantage of any computational differences between implementations. Even though the specification is written to a particular level of numerical precision (32-bit floating point), the precision differences beyond the standardization level can still be exploited. That is, if a SAOL sound designer knows that a particular implementation rounds off a particular computation in the positive direction rather than the negative direction (even though the roundoff error is within the precision level of the standard), he can design instruments which explicitly test for this condition and produce "bad sound" when it is detected.

It is not yet clear what the final solution or stance toward these issues will be within MPEG. On the one hand, content providers require guarantees that compliant MPEG-4 terminals will produce high-quality output when given carefully created bitstreams; on the other, perhaps the benefits of robust standards for synthetic content outweigh the need to constrain the standard to what is easily conformance-tested. This situation is, of course, very similar to that which arises in standards for general-purpose computer languages such as ANSI C.

4.3 MPEG-4 version 2

Work has just begun on a second version of MPEG-4, which will provide advanced features while maintaining backward compability with Version 1. All of the features discussed to this point in the present paper are part of Version 1. Functions currently being discussed or considered for Version 2 include:

- "advanced environmental" effects processing,. These capabilities would augment the VRML-model physical sound description paradigm by allowing reverberations, surface reflection properties, and other such parameters to be delivered for virtual environments (Scheirer et al. 1998)
- advanced interaction systems using Java. MPEG-4 Version 2 will be based on a Java-enabled terminal model; by specifying an Java API for control of the Structured

Audio synthesizer, very sophisticated interactive-music systems could be delivered as content.
- simpler abstract-effects compositing. In Version 1 of MPEG-4, a full Structured Audio system must be available if any reverberation or multi-band equalization is required. For some applications, this may prove too large a constraint, and so a simpler solution to provide a restricted profile, where individual effects are broken out into individual AudioBIFS nodes, is under consideration.

5 Conclusion

This paper has described the Structured Audio tool in the MPEG-4 standard and the capabilities it provides for flexible sound synthesis, effects processing, and software post-production.

Work has also begun on the next generation of the MPEG standard, MPEG-7, which will standardize representations optimized for search and retrieval of multimedia content. Already, textual descriptors are included in the scene description of MPEG-4 to facilitate interaction between these two standards. Parties with interest and expertise in search and retrieval aspects of multimedia databases are encouraged to contact their national standards body and participate in the MPEG-7 process.

Finally, it is important to note that the MPEG-4 standards process is ongoing. The work in progress is vitally dependent on participation. As a necessary caveat, this paper represents the view of one individual involved in the MPEG-4 process, but does not represent a completed standard nor the official positions of the host organization for standardization, which is ISO/IEC JTC1/SC29/WG11.

Acknowledgements. The author wishes to thank Prof. Barry Vercoe and the members of the Machine Listening Group at the MIT Media Laboratory, especially Bill Gardner, for their discussions involving this work. Paris Smaragdis, also from the Machine Listening Group, and two reviewers provided valuable comments during the revision process. This research has been partly supported by a fellowship from Interval Research Corporation.

References

1. Bove VM (1995) Object-Oriented Television. SMPTE J 104:803–807
2. Brandenburg K, Bosi M (1995) Overview of MPEG-Audio: Current and future standards for low bit-rate audio coding. Presented at the 89th Convention of the Audio Engineering Society, October 1995, New York, Aud. Eng. Soc., New York, Preprint #4130
3. Brandenburg K, Stoll G (1994) ISO-MPEG-1 Audio: a generic standard for coding of high quality digital audio. J Audio Eng Soc 42(10):780-794
4. Casey M (1998) Auditory Group Theory with Application to Structured Audio. Ph.D. dissertation, MIT Media Laboratory, Cambridge, Mass.
5. Casey M, Smaragdis P (1996) NetSound. In: Rossiter D (ed) Proc. Int. Computer Music Conf., 1996, Hong Kong. International Comp, Music Assoc., San Francisco, p 143
6. Dolson M (1986) The phase vocoder: a tutorial. Comput Music J 10(4):14-27
7. Gardner WG (1997) 3-D Audio Using Loudspeakers. Ph.D. dissertation, MIT Media Laboratory, Cambridge, Mass.
8. Gersho A (1994) Advances in speech and audio compression. Proc. IEEE 82(6):900–917

9. Hardman V, Sasse MA, Handley M, Watson A (1995) Reliable audio for use over the Internet. In: Chen K (ed) Proceedings Inet '95, June 1995, Honolulu, Hawaii. Internet Society, Reston VA, pp 171–178

10. ISO (1997) Virtual Reality Modeling Language (VRML). ISO 14772-1: 1997. International Organisation for Standardisation, Geneva, Switzerland

11. ISO/IEC (1998) Low-bit-rate coding of moving pictures and associated audio (MPEG-4). ISO/IEC 14496. International Organisation for Standardisation, Geneva, Switzerland

12. Makhoul J (1975) Linear prediction: a tutorial review. Proc. IEEE 63:561–580

13. Matthews M (1969) The Technology of Computer Music. MIT Press, Cambridge, Mass.

14. Martin KD (1996) Automatic transcription of simple polyphonic music: robust front end processing. Media Lab Perceptual Computing Technical Report #399. M.I.T., Cambridge, Mass.; presented at the Third Joint Meeting of the Acoustical Societies of America and Japan, December 1996

15. McCartney J (1996) SuperCollider: A new real-time sound synthesis language. In: Rossiter D (ed) Proc. Intl. Computer Music Conf., 1996, Hong Kong, International Comp. Music Assoc., San Francisco, pp 257–258

16. MIDI Manufacturers Association (MMA) (1996) The Complete MIDI 1.0 Detailed Specification. v. 96.1. MIDI Manufacturers Association, La Habra, CA, USA

17. MIDI Manufacturers Association (MMA) (1997) The Downloadable Sounds Level 1 (DLS-1) Specification. MIDI Manufacturers Association, La Habra, CA, USA

18. Noll P (1993) Wideband speech and audio coding. IEEE Commun Mag 33–44

19. Progressive Networks, Inc. (1996) White Paper on RealAudio Client-Server Architecture. WWW document: <http://brinkley.prognet.com/prognet/openarch/index.html>

20. Quackenbush S (1998) Coding of natural audio in MPEG-4. In: Proc. IEEE ICASSP, 1998, Seattle, Wash. IEEE / Causal Productions, Rundle Mall, S. Australia, pp 3797–3800

21. Roads C (1991) Asynchronous granular synthesis, In: Poli G de, Piccialli A, Road C (eds) Representations of Musical Signals. MIT Press, Cambridge, Mass., pp 143–186

22. Roads C (1996) The Computer Music Tutorial. MIT Press, Cambridge, Mass.

23. Rodet X (1985) Time-Domain Formant-Wave-Functions Synthesis. Computer Music J 8(3):9–14

24. Scheirer E (1998a) The MPEG-4 Structured Audio standard. In: Proc. IEEE ICASSP, 1998, Seattle, Wash. IEEE / Causal Productions, Rundle Mall, S. Australia, pp 3801–3804

25. Scheirer E (1998b) The MPEG-4 Structured Audio Orchestra Language. To appear in Proc. Int. Computer Music Conf., 1998, Ann Arbor, Mich., Int. Comp. Music Assoc., San Francisco

26. Scheirer E, Ray L (1998) Algorithmic and Wavetable Synthesis in the MPEG-4 Multimedia Standard. Presented at the 105th Convention of the Audio Engineering Society, 1998, San Francisco, Calif., Aud. Eng. Soc., New York, Preprint #4811

27. Scheirer E, Vercoe B (1997a) Synthetic Audio Specification Language Proposal for SNHC Audio. ISO/IEC JTC1/SC29/WG11 (MPEG) Document M1788. ISO, Seville, Spain

28. Scheirer E, Vercoe B (1997b) Audio BIFS nodes for Audio Composition using SNHC Audio. ISO/IEC JTC1/SC29/WG11 (MPEG) Document M2044. ISO, Bristol, UK

29. Scheirer E, Huopaniemi J, Väänänen R (1998) AudioBIFS: The MPEG-4 standard for effects processing. To appear in Proc. 1st Cost-G6 Workshop on Digital Audio Effects (DAFX), Barcelona, Spain

30. Serra, X (1997) Musical sound modeling with sinusoids plus noise. In: Roads C, Pope S, Picialli A, Poli G de (eds) Musical Signal Processing. Swets & Zeitlinger, Amsterdam, The Netherlands, pp 91–122

31. Smith, JO (1991) Viewpoints on the history of digital synthesis. In: Alphonce B, Pennycook B (eds) Proc. Int. Computer Music Conf., 1991, Montreal, Canada, Int. Comp. Music Assoc., San Francisco, pp 1–10

32. Vercoe, B (1984) The synthetic performer in the context of live performance. In: Buxton W (ed) Proc. Int. Computer Music Conf, 1984, San Francisco, Calif., Int. Comp. Music Assoc., San Francisco, pp 199–200

33. Vercoe B (1996a) Csound: A Manual for the Audio Processing System. MIT Media Lab, Cambridge, Mass.

34. Vercoe B (1996b) Extended Csound. In: Rossiter D (ed) Proc. Int. Computer Music Conf., 1996, Hong Kong, Int. Comp. Music Assoc., San Francisco, pp 141–142

35. Vercoe B, Gardner W, Scheirer E (1998) Structured audio: creation, transmission, and rendering of parametric sound representations. Proc. IEEE 86:922–940

ERIC D. SCHEIRER is a Ph.D. candidate in the Machine Listening Group at the MIT Media Laboratory, where his research focuses on the construction of music-understanding computer systems. He is an Editor of the MPEG-4 Audio standard, chair of the MPEG Structured Audio ad-hoc group, and the primary technical contributor to the Structured Audio subpart of the standard. He is also an accomplished and award-winning jazz trombonist.

Fundamental and Technological Limitations of Immersive Audio Systems

CHRIS KYRIAKAKIS, MEMBER, IEEE

Numerous applications are currently envisioned for immersive audio systems. The principal function of such systems is to synthesize, manipulate, and render sound fields in real time. In this paper, we examine several fundamental and technological limitations that impede the development of seamless immersive audio systems. Such limitations stem from signal-processing requirements, acoustical considerations, human listening characteristics, and listener movement. We present a brief historical overview to outline the development of immersive audio technologies and discuss the performance and future research directions of immersive audio systems with respect to such limits. Last, we present a novel desktop audio system with integrated listener-tracking capability that circumvents several of the technological limitations faced by today's digital audio workstations.

***Keywords**—Acoustic signal processing, audio systems, auditory system, multimedia systems, signal processing.*

I. INTRODUCTION

Emerging integrated media systems seamlessly combine digital video, digital audio, computer animation, text, and graphics into common displays that allow for mixed media creation, dissemination, and interactive access in *real time*. Immersive audio and video environments based on such systems can be envisioned for applications that include teleconferencing and telepresence; augmented and virtual reality for manufacturing and entertainment; air-traffic control, pilot warning, and guidance systems; displays for the visually or aurally impaired; home entertainment; distance learning; and professional sound and picture editing for television and film. The principal function of immersive systems is to synthesize multimodal perceptions that do not exist in the current physical environment, thus immersing users in a seamless blend of visual and aural information. Significant resources have been allocated over the past 20 years to promote research in the area of image and video processing, resulting in important advances in these fields.

Manuscript received September 8, 1997; revised December 4, 1997. The Guest Editor coordinating the review of this paper and approving it for publication was T. Chen.

The author is with the Integrated Media Systems Center, University of Southern California, Los Angeles, CA 90089-2564 USA (e-mail: ckyriak@imsc.usc.edu).

Publisher Item Identifier S 0018-9219(98)03283-6.

On the other hand, audio signal processing, and particularly immersive audio, have been largely neglected.

Accurate spatial reproduction of sound can significantly enhance the visualization of three-dimensional (3-D) information for applications in which it is important to achieve sound localization relative to visual images. The human ear–brain interface is uniquely capable of localizing and identifying sounds in a 3-D environment with remarkable accuracy. For example, human listeners can detect time-of-arrival differences of about 7 μs. Sound perception is based on a multiplicity of cues that include level and time differences and direction-dependent frequency-response effects caused by sound reflection in the outer ear, head, and torso, cumulatively referred to as the head-related transfer function (HRTF). In addition to such directional cues, human listeners use a multiplicity of other cues in the perception of timbre, frequency response, and dynamic range. Furthermore, there are numerous subjective sound qualities that vary from listener to listener but are equally important in achieving the "suspension of disbelief" desired in an immersive audio system. These include attributes such as the apparent source width, listener envelopment, clarity, and warmth [1], [2]. Vision also plays an important role in localization and can overwhelm the aural impression. In fact, a mismatch between the aurally perceived and visually observed positions of a particular sound causes a cognitive dissonance that can seriously limit the visualization enhancement provided by immersive sound. The amount of mismatch required to cause such a dissonance is subjective and can vary in both the level of perception and annoyance. For professional sound designers, a mere 4° offset in the horizontal plane between the visual and aural image is perceptible, whereas it takes a 15° offset before the average layperson will notice [3].

In this paper, we discuss several issues that pertain to immersive audio system requirements that arise from fundamental physical limitations as well as current technological drawbacks. We will address these issues from three complementary perspectives: identification of fundamental physical limitations that affect the performance of immersive audio systems, evaluation of the current status of immersive audio system development with respect to such fundamental limits, and delineation of technological considerations that affect present and future system design and development. In the final sections, we will present a novel sound-reproduction system that addresses several of the current technological limitations that currently affect the quality of audio at the desktop. This system incorporates a video-based tracking method that allows real-time processing of the audio signal in response to listener movement.

II. THE NATURE OF LIMITATIONS IN IMMERSIVE AUDIO SYSTEMS

There are two classes of limitations that impede the implementation of immersive audio systems. The first class encompasses fundamental limitations that arise from physical laws, and its understanding is essential for determining the feasibility of a particular technology with respect to the absolute physical limits. Many such fundamental limitations are not directly dependent on the choice of systems but instead pertain to the actual process of sound propagation and attenuation in irregularly shaped rooms. The physical properties of the acoustic environment are *encoded* in the sound field and must be *decoded* by an immersive audio system in order to accurately simulate the original environment. The influence of the local acoustic environment is reflected in the perception of spatial attributes such as direction and distance, as well as in the perception of room spaciousness and source size [1], [2]. The situation is further complicated by the fact that the decoding process must include the transformations associated with human hearing. These include the conversion of spatial sound cues into level and time differences and direction-dependent frequency-response effects caused by the pinna, head, and torso through a set of amplitude and phase transformations known as the HRTF's. The *seamless* incorporation of such cues in immersive audio systems is a very active area of research that, if successful, will give rise to systems that begin to approach performance near the fundamental limits.

The second class of limitations consists of constraints that arise purely from technological considerations. These are equally useful in understanding the potential applications of a given system and are imposed by the particular technology chosen for system implementation. For example, the process of encoding parameters associated with room acoustics into sound fields can be modeled using numerical methods. In theory, this would involve the solution of the wave equation for sound subject to the boundary conditions dictated by the complex (absorptive, reflective, and diffractive) room surfaces. The computational complexity of this problem is very high and involves the calculation of estimated 10^{10} normal modes that fall within the range of human hearing (20 Hz–20 kHz) for a large hall [4]. More recent methods have been developed for rendering sound fields through a process called auralization. Such methods utilize a combination of scaled models, digital filtering, and special-purpose hardware for real-time convolution to predict and render the sound field [5]. As the processing power of digital signal processing (DSP) hardware increases, the capability of auralization systems to render complex sound fields will increase proportionally.

III. BRIEF HISTORICAL OVERVIEW

A. Two-Channel Stereo

Although many of the principles of stereophonic sound were developed through research efforts in the early 1930's, there still remains a misconception as to the meaning of the word "stereo" itself. While it is generally associated with sound reproduction from two loudspeakers, the word originates from the Greek *stereos*, meaning solid or three-dimensional. The two-channel association came about in the 1950's because of technological limitations imposed by the phonograph record that had only two groove walls for encoding information.

Stereophony started with the work of Blumlein [6] in the United Kingdom, who recognized early on that it was possible to locate a sound within a range of azimuth angles by using an appropriate combination of delay and level differences. His work focused on accurate reproduction of the sound field at each ear of the listener and on the development of microphone techniques that would allow the recording of the amplitude and phase differences necessary for stereo reproduction. Fletcher, Steinberg, and Snow at Bell Laboratories in the United States [7]–[9] took a different approach. They considered a "wall of sound" in which an infinite number of microphones is used to reproduce a sound field through an infinite number of loudspeakers, similar to the Huygens principle of secondary wavelets. While this made for an interesting theoretical result, the Bell Labs researchers realized that practical implementations would require a significantly smaller number of channels. They showed that a three-channel system consisting of left, center, and right channels in the azimuth plane could represent the lateralization and depth of the desired sound field with acceptable accuracy [Fig. 1(a)]. The first such stereophonic three-channel system was demonstrated in 1934 with the Philadelphia Orchestra performing remotely for an audience in Washington, DC, over wide-band telephone lines.

B. Four-Channel Matrixed Quadraphonic System

While stereophonic methods can be a powerful tool in the reproduction of the spatial attributes of a sound field, they fall short of true three-dimensional reproduction. The quadraphonic system attempted to circumvent such limitations by capturing and transmitting information about the direct sound and the reverberant sound field [10], [11]. To deliver the four channels required by quadraphonic recordings over a two-channel medium (e.g., the phonograph record), it was necessary to develop an appropriate encoding and decoding scheme. Several such schemes were proposed based on 4:2:4 matrix encoding/decoding that relied on phase manipulation of the original stereo signals [12]. Quadraphonic systems were capable of reproducing sound images fairly accurately in the front and rear sectors

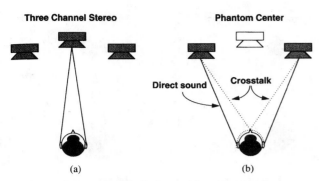

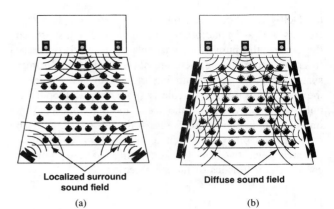

Fig. 1. (a) Stereo was originally invented based on three loudspeakers. Sound images in the center are rendered by a real loudspeaker that delivers the same direct sound to both ears. (b) In the two-loudspeaker stereo configuration with a phantom center, the cross-talk terms give rise to a less stable center image as well as a loss of clarity.

Fig. 2. (a) In early surround-sound systems with a mono surround channel, listeners seated off-center perceived the sound as if it originated from the effects loudspeaker that was closest to them, thus destroying the desired sense of envelopment. (b) Current systems use stereo surrounds reproduced over an array of loudspeakers along the sides of the theater to create a more diffuse sound field.

of the azimuthal plane, but they exhibited serious limitations when attempting to reproduce sound images to the side of the listener. Experiments showed [13], [14] that this was a limitation associated as much with sound-field synthesis using only four channels as with human psychoacoustic mechanisms. These technical limitations and the presence of two competing formats in the consumer marketplace contributed to the early demise of quadraphonic systems.

C. Multichannel Surround Sound

In the early 1950's, the first multichannel sound format was developed by 20th Century Fox. The combination of wide-screen formats such as CinemaScope (35 mm) and six-track Todd-AO (70 mm) with multichannel sound was the film industry's response to the growing threat of television. Stereophonic film sound was typically reproduced over three front loudspeakers, but these new formats included an additional monophonic channel that was reproduced over two loudspeakers behind the audience and was known as the effects channel. This channel increased the sense of space for the audience, but it also suffered from a serious technological limitation. Listeners seated on-center with respect to the rear loudspeakers perceived "inside-the-head" localization similar to the effect of stereo images reproduced over headphones. Listeners seated off-center localized the channel to the effects loudspeaker that was closest to them as dictated by the law of the first-arriving wavefront, thus destroying the sense of envelopment desired [14] [Fig. 2(a)]. The solution to these problems was found by introducing a second channel reproduced over an array of loudspeakers along the sides of the theater to create a more diffuse sound field [Fig. 2(b)].

In the mid-1970's, a new sound technology was introduced by Dolby Laboratories called Dolby Stereo. It was based on the optical technology that had been used for sound on film since the 1930's, and it circumvented the problems associated with magnetic multitrack recording. Dolby developed a matrix method for encoding four channels (left, center, right, and mono surround) into two channels using a technique derived from the matrix methods

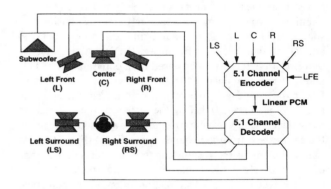

Fig. 3. Current commercial multichannel systems encode the LFE, three front, and two surround channels into a bit stream that is decoded at the user's end. With proper loudspeaker selection and placement, it is possible to simulate the experience of a movie theater. Dipole surround loudspeakers that do not radiate sound directly in the direction of the listener's ears produce the best envelopment.

used in quadraphonic systems but also ensured mono and stereo backward compatibility. In 1992, further enhancements by Dolby were introduced through a new format called Dolby Stereo Digital (SR•D). This format eliminated matrix-based encoding and decoding and provided five discrete channels (left, center, right, and independent left and right surround) in a configuration known as stereo surround. A sixth, low-frequency-enhancement (LFE) channel was introduced to add more head room and prevent the main speakers from overloading at low frequencies. The bandwidth of the LFE channel is limited between 0 and 120 Hz, a frequency regime that is outside the localization range for human listeners in a reverberant room, thus simplifying the placement requirements for the subwoofer used for LFE reproduction (Fig. 3).

Recent advances in digital audio compression and optical storage have made it possible to deliver up to six discrete audio channels in a consumer format centered around the Dolby AC-3 compression scheme.[1] With exciting new formats such as an audio-only digital video disc just around the corner, the number of channels could easily increase to ten or more. While there are several million consumer systems capable of reproducing more than two channels, the majority of users (particularly those with desktop computer systems) would find the use of multiple loudspeakers impractical. In the sections that follow, we examine the requirements of systems that allow delivery of multiple channels over two loudspeakers using DSP to simulate certain characteristics of human listening.

IV. Spatial (3-D) Audio

A. Physiological Signal Processing

The human hearing process is based on the analysis of input signals to the two ears for differences in intensity, time of arrival, and directional filtering by the outer ear. Several theories were proposed as early as 1882 [15] that identified two basic mechanisms as being responsible for source localization: 1) interaural time differences (ITD's) and 2) interaural level differences (ILD's). A later theory by Lord Rayleigh [16] was based on a combination of ITD and ILD cues that operated in different wavelength regimes. For short wavelengths (corresponding to frequencies in the range of about 4–20 kHz), the listener's head casts an acoustical shadow giving rise to a lower sound level at the ear farthest from the sound source (ILD) [Fig. 4(b)]. At long wavelengths (corresponding to frequencies in the range of about 20 Hz–1 kHz), the head is very small compared to the wavelength, and localization is based on perceived differences in the time of arrival of sound at the two ears (ITD) [Fig. 4(a)]. The two mechanisms of interaural time and level differences formed the basis of what became known as the *duplex* theory of sound localization. In the frequency range between approximately 1 and 4 kHz, both of these mechanisms are active, which results in several conflicting cues that tend to cause localization errors.

While time or intensity differences provide source direction information in the horizontal (azimuthal) plane, in the median plane, time differences are constant and localization is based on *spectral filtering*. The reflection and diffraction of sound waves from the head, torso, shoulders, and pinnae, combined with resonances caused by the ear canal, form the physical basis for the HRTF. The outer ear can be modeled (in the static case) as a linear time-invariant system that is fully characterized by the HRTF in the frequency domain. As Blauert [17] describes it, the role of the outer ear is to superimpose angle- and distance-specific linear distortions on the incident sound signal. Spatial information is thus encoded onto the signals received by the eardrums through a combination of direction-dependent and direction-independent filters [18], [19]. The magnitude and phase of these head-related transfer functions vary significantly for each sound direction but also from person to person.

[1] See Dolby Laboratories at http://www.dolby.com.

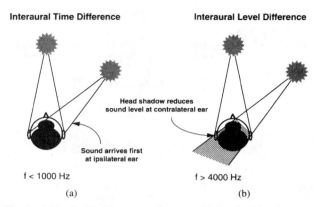

Fig. 4. (a) In the low-frequency regime, sound is localized based on differences in the time of arrival at each ear. (b) At higher frequencies, the wavelength of sound is short relative to the size of the head, and localization is based on perceived level differences caused by head shadowing. In the intermediate-frequency region, both mechanisms are active, and this can give rise to conflicting cues.

The emerging field of 3-D audio is based on digital implementations of such HRTF's. In principle, it is possible to achieve excellent reproduction of three-dimensional sound fields using such methods; however, it has been demonstrated that this requires precise measurement of each listener's individual HRTF's [20]. This seemingly fundamental requirement that derives from inherent physiological and cognitive characteristics of the human ear–brain interface has rendered such systems impractical for widespread use. Current research in this area is focused on achieving good localization performance while using synthetic (nonindividualized) HRTF's derived through averaging or modeling or based on the HRTF's of subjects that have been determined to be "good localizers" [21], [22]. In his review of the challenges in 3-D audio implementations, Begault [23] points out that there are currently three major barriers to successful implementation of such systems: 1) psychoacoustic errors such as front–back reversals typical in headphone-based systems, 2) large amounts of data required to represent measured HRTF's accurately, and 3) frequency- and phase-response errors that arise from mismatches between nonindividualized and measured HRTF's. It should be noted that front–back reversals can be reduced if the listener is allowed to move his head and that the lack of externalization experienced with headphone listening can be alleviated with appropriate use of reverberation.

A fourth challenge arises from technological limitations of current computing systems. One capability that we envision for immersive audio systems is the simulation of room acoustics and listener characteristics for interactive, virtual-, and augmented-reality applications. In addition to the computational requirements for photorealistic rendering of visual images, the synthesis of such acoustical environments requires computation of the binaural room response and subsequent convolution with the HRTF's of the listener *in real time* as the listener moves around the room. Typical impulse response duration is 3 s, which, when sampled at 48 kHz, requires a processor capable of operating at more than 13 Gflops/channel [24]. This problem can be circumvented using special-purpose hardware or hybrid block fast Fourier transform/direct convolution methods [25].[2] The main goal is to reduce the number of operations for such computations, thus making them suitable for real-time interactive applications.

B. Spatial Audio Rendering

A critical issue in the implementation of immersive audio is the reproduction of 3-D sound fields that preserve the desired spatial location, frequency response, and dynamic range. There are two general methods for 3-D audio rendering that can be categorized as "head related" based on headphone reproduction and "nonhead related" based on loudspeaker reproduction [19]. A hybrid category, called transaural stereo, also exists that allows loudspeaker rendering of head-related signals. It should be noted that there are other methods for three-dimensional sound-field capture and synthesis such as ambisonics [26] and wave-field synthesis [27], [28], but these will not be examined in this paper.

Nonheadroom-related methods typically use multiple loudspeakers to reproduce multiple matrixed or discrete channels. Such systems can convey precisely localized sound images that are primarily confined to the horizontal plane and diffuse (ambient) sound to the sides of and behind the listener. In addition to the left and right loudspeakers, they make use of a center loudspeaker that helps create a solidly anchored center-stage sound image, as well as two loudspeakers for the ambient surround sound field. The most prevalent systems currently available to consumers are based on the formats developed by Dolby for film sound, including Pro Logic (four-channel matrixed encoded on two channels) and Dolby Digital (5.1-channel discrete based on the AC-3 compression scheme).[1] Other 5.1-channel schemes include DTS Digital Surround[3] and MPEG-2. Multichannel systems were designed primarily for authentic reproduction of sound associated with movies but have recently started to be used for music recordings and games on CD-ROM. The 5.1-channel Dolby Digital system was adopted in the U.S. standard of the upcoming advanced (high-definition) television system [29]. The design requirements for such loudspeaker-based systems include uniform audience coverage, accurate localization relative to visual images on the screen, diffuse rendering of ambient sounds, and capability for reproduction of the wide (up to 105 dB) dynamic range present in film soundtracks.

Head-related binaural recording, or dummy-head stereophony, methods attempt to accurately reproduce at each eardrum of the listener the sound pressure generated by a set of sources and their interactions with the acoustic environment [30]. Such recordings can be made with specially designed probe microphones that are inserted in the listener's ear canal or by using a dummy-head microphone system that is based on average human

characteristics. Sound recorded using binaural methods is then reproduced through headphones that deliver the desired sound to each ear. It was concluded from early experiments that in order to achieve the desired degree of realism using binaural methods, the required frequency-response accuracy of the transfer function was ±1 dB [31]. Other related work [32] compared direct listening and binaural recordings for the same subject and concluded that directional hearing was accurately preserved using binaural recording.

While there are several commercially available dummy-head systems, binaural recordings are not widely used primarily due to limitations that are associated with headphone listening [20], [33], [34]. These drawbacks can be summarized as follows.

1) Individualized HRTF information does not exist for each listener and the averaged HRTF's that are used make it impossible to match each individual's perception of sound.

2) There are large errors in sound position perception associated with headphones, especially for the most important visual direction, out in front.

3) Headphones are uncomfortable for extended periods of time.

4) It is very difficult to externalize sounds and avoid the "inside-the-head" sensation.

In many applications, however, such as in aircraft cockpits or multiuser environments, the use of headphones is required for practical reasons.

The use of loudspeakers for reproduction can circumvent the limitations associated with headphone reproduction of binaural recordings. To deliver the appropriate binaural sound field to each ear, however, it is necessary to eliminate the cross talk that is inherent in all loudspeaker-based systems. This is a technological limitation of *all* loudspeaker systems, and it arises from the fact that while each ear receives the desired sound from the same-side (ipsilateral) loudspeaker, it also receives undesired sound from the opposite-side (contralateral) loudspeaker.

Several schemes have been proposed to address cross-talk cancellation. The basic principle of such schemes relies on preconditioning the signal into each loudspeaker such that the output sound generates the desired binaural sound pressure at each ear. If we denote the sound pressures that must be delivered to each ear as $P_L(\text{ear})$ and $P_R(\text{ear})$ and the transfer functions from each loudspeaker to each ear as H_{LL}, H_{LR}, H_{RL}, and H_{RR}, then we can write (Fig. 5)

$$P_L(\text{speaker}) = H_{LL}S_L + H_{RL}S_R$$
$$P_R(\text{speaker}) = H_{LR}S_L + H_{RR}S_R \quad (1)$$

in which we denote by S_L and S_R the input signals to each loudspeaker and $P_{L,R}(\text{speaker})$ the sound pressure delivered by each loudspeaker. To accurately reproduce the desired binaural signal at each ear, the input signals S_L and

---

[2] See Lake DSP at http://www.lakedsp.com.
[3] See http://www.dtstech.com/.

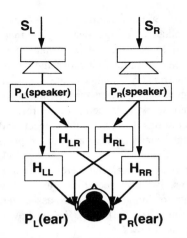

Fig. 5. Transfer functions associated with a loudspeaker sound-rendering system. To deliver the correct binaural sound, it is necessary to prefilter the signal to the loudspeakers so that the cross-talk terms H_{LR} and H_{RL} are cancelled during reproduction.

S_R must be chosen such that

$$P_L(\text{ear}) = P_L(\text{speaker})$$
$$P_R(\text{ear}) = P_R(\text{speaker}). \qquad (2)$$

The desired loudspeaker input signals are then found from

$$S_L = \frac{H_{RR}P_L(\text{ear}) - H_{RL}P_R(\text{ear})}{H_{LL}H_{RR} - H_{LR}H_{RL}}$$
$$S_R = \frac{H_{LL}P_R(\text{ear}) - H_{LR}P_L(\text{ear})}{H_{LL}H_{RR} - H_{LR}H_{RL}}. \qquad (3)$$

The only requirement is that S_L and S_R must be realizable filter responses. The first such cross-talk cancellation scheme was proposed by Bauer [35], later by Atal and Schroeder [4], and by Damaske and Mellert [36], [37] using a system called "True Reproduction of All Directional Information by Stereophony" (TRADIS). The main limitation of these early systems was the fact that any listener movement that exceeded 75–100 mm completely destroyed the spatial effect. Cooper and Bauck [38], [39] showed that under the assumption of left–right symmetry, a much simpler shuffler filter can be used to implement cross-talk cancellation as well as synthesize virtual loudspeakers in arbitrary positions. They went on to use results from Mehrgard and Mellert [40], who showed that the head-related transfer function is minimum phase to within a frequency-independent delay that is a function of the angle of incidence. This new "transaural" system significantly reduced the computational requirements by allowing implementations that use simple finite-duration impulse response filters.

The functionality and practical use of immersive audio systems based on such transaural cross-talk cancellation methods can be greatly enhanced by eliminating the requirement that the user remain stationary with a fixed head position. This increased functionality requires the capability to implement the requisite filters (and associated algorithms) in real time. A further requirement is precise information about the location of the listener's ears relative to the loudspeakers. This is achieved, with reasonable accuracy, in desktop-based audio systems in which the listener is seated at the keyboard at a fixed distance from the loudspeakers. Ultimately, the listener's head (and ear) location must be tracked in order to allow for head rotation and translation. Several issues related to both the desktop and the tracking implementations are discussed below.

V. IMMERSIVE AUDIO RENDERING FOR DESKTOP APPLICATIONS

For desktop applications, in addition to the user-imposed limitation of (typically) two loudspeakers, there exists an entirely different set of design requirements specific to applications such as professional sound editing for film and television, teleconferencing and telepresence, augmented and virtual reality, and home personal-computer (PC) entertainment. Such applications require *high-quality* audio for a single listener in a desktop environment. Issues that must be addressed include the optimization of the frequency response over a given frequency range, the dynamic range, and stereo imaging subject to constraints imposed by room acoustics and human listening characteristics. Several problems are particular to the desktop environment, including frequency-response anomalies that arise due to the local acoustical environment, the proximity of the listener to the loudspeakers, and the acoustics associated with small rooms.

A. Acoustical Limitations

In a typical desktop sound-monitoring environment, delivery of stereophonic sound is achieved through two loudspeakers that are placed on either side of a video or computer monitor. This environment, combined with the acoustical problems of small rooms, causes severe problems that contribute to audible distortion of the reproduced sound. Among these problems, one of the most important is the effect of discrete early reflections [41]–[43]. It has been shown [43] that these reflections are the dominant source of monitoring nonuniformities. These nonuniformities appear in the form of frequency-response anomalies in rooms where the difference between the direct and reflected sound level for the first 15 ms is less than 15 dB [44], [45] (Fig. 6). High levels of reflected sound cause comb filtering in the frequency domain, which in turn gives rise to severe changes in timbre. The perceived effects of such distortions were quantified with psychoacoustic experiments [41], [46] that demonstrated their importance.

A solution that has been proposed to alleviate the problems of early reflections is near-field monitoring. In theory, the direct sound is dominant when the listener is very close to the loudspeakers, thus reducing the room effects to below audibility. In practice, however, there are several issues that must be addressed in order to provide high-quality sound [47]. One such issue relates to the large reflecting surfaces that are typically present near the loudspeakers. Strong reflections from a console or a video/computer monitor act as baffle extensions for the loudspeaker, resulting in a boost of

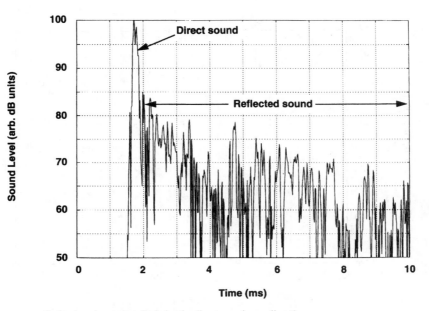

Fig. 6. The time-domain response of a loudspeaker system includes the direct sound as well as the sound due to multiple reflections from the local acoustical environment. Psychoacoustic evidence indicates that in order for these reflections not to be perceived, their spectrum level should be 15 dB below the level of the direct sound.

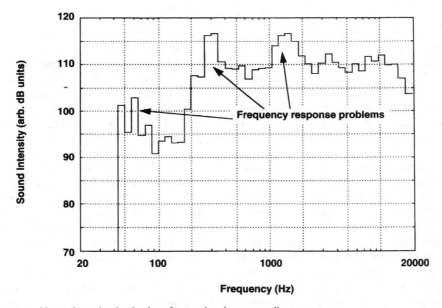

Fig. 7. Frequency-response problems that arise in the low frequencies due to standing-wave buildup in small rooms and in higher frequencies due to interactions with elements in the local acoustical environment (e.g., CRT screen, table top, untreated walls).

midbass frequencies. Furthermore, even if it were possible to place the loudspeakers far away from large reflecting surfaces, this would only solve the problem for middle and high frequencies. Low-frequency room modes do not depend on surfaces in the local acoustical environment but rather on the physical size of the room. These modes produce standing waves that give rise to large variations in frequency response (Fig. 7). Such amplitude and phase distortions can completely destroy carefully designed 3-D audio reproduction that relies on the transaural techniques described above.

B. Design Requirements

To circumvent these limitations, a set of solutions has been developed for single-listener desktop reproduction that delivers sound quality equivalent to a calibrated dubbing stage [43]. These solutions include direct-path dominant design and correct low-frequency response.

Based on our current understanding of psychoacoustic principles, it is possible to combine such cues to place the listener in a direct sound field that is dominant over the reflected and reverberant sound. The design considerations

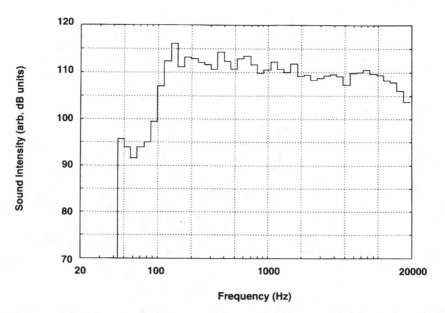

Fig. 8. A properly designed direct-path dominant system that compensates for frequency anomalies produces a much flatter frequency response. Frequencies below 100 Hz are reproduced with a separate subwoofer (response not shown) that is placed at a known distance from the listener to alleviate anomalies from standing waves.

for this direct-path dominant design include compensation of the physical (reflection and diffraction) effects of the video/computer monitor that extends the loudspeaker baffle as well as the large reflecting surface on which the computer keyboard typically rests. The distortions that arise from amplitude and phase anomalies are eliminated, and this results in a listening experience that is dramatically different than what is achievable through traditional near-field monitoring methods (Fig. 8).

Standing waves associated with the acoustics of small rooms give rise to fundamental limitations in the quality of reproduced sound, particularly in the uniformity of low-frequency response. Variations in this frequency regime can be as large as ±15 dB for different listening locations in a typical room. The advantage of immersive audio rendering on desktop systems lies in the fact that the position of the loudspeakers and the listener are known *a priori*. It is therefore possible to use signal processing (equalization) to correct the low-frequency response. This smooth response, however, can only be achieved for a relatively small region around the listener. To correct over a larger region and compensate for listener movement, it is necessary to track the listener's position and use adaptive signal-processing methods that allow real-time correction of spatial as well as frequency-response attributes.

C. Listener-Location Considerations

In large rooms, multichannel sound systems are used to convey sound images that are primarily confined to the horizontal plane and are uniformly distributed over the audience area. Typical systems used for cinema reproduction use three front channels (left, center, right), two surround channels (left and right surround), and a separate

low-frequency channel. Such 5.1-channel systems (a term coined by Holman to represent five full-spectrum channels and a low-frequency-only channel) are designed to provide accurate sound localization relative to visual images in front of the listener and diffuse (ambient) sound to the sides and behind the listener. The use of a center loudspeaker helps create a solid sound image between the left and right loudspeakers and anchors the sound to the center of the stage.

For desktop applications, in which a single user is located in front of a CRT display, we no longer have the luxury of a center loudspeaker because that position is occupied by the display. Size limitations prevent the front loudspeakers from being capable of reproducing the entire spectrum; thus, a separate subwoofer loudspeaker is used to reproduce the low frequencies. The two front loudspeakers can create a virtual (phantom) image that appears to originate from the exact center of the display provided that the listener is seated symmetrically with respect to the loudspeakers. With proper head and loudspeaker placement, it is possible to recreate a spatially accurate sound field with the correct frequency response in *one* exact position, the sweet spot. Even in this static case, however, the sound originating from each loudspeaker arrives at each ear at different times (about 200 μs apart), thereby giving rise to acoustic cross talk [Fig. 1(b)]. These time differences, combined with reflection and diffraction effects caused by the head, lead to frequency-response anomalies that are perceived as a lack of clarity [48].

This problem can be solved by adding a cross-talk cancellation filter (as described above in the description of transaural methods) to the signal of each loudspeaker. While this solution may be satisfactory for the static case, as soon as the listener moves even slightly, the conditions

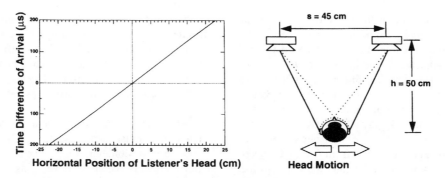

Fig. 9. Desktop sound system with vision-based head tracking. In this early prototype, the time difference of arrival at the two ears is adjusted in real time as the listener moves in the plane parallel to the loudspeakers. Current research is focused on tracking, pose estimation (for head rotations), and pinna shape recognition for real-time cross-talk cancellation and individualized HRTF synthesis.

for cancellation are no longer met, and the phantom image moves toward the closest loudspeaker because of the precedence effect. In order, therefore, to achieve the highest possible quality of sound for a nonstationary listener and preserve the spatial information in the original material, it is necessary to know the precise location of the listener relative to the loudspeakers [47], [49], [50]. In the section below, we describe an experimental system that incorporates a novel listener-tracking method in order to overcome the difficulties associated with two-ear listening as well as the technological limitations imposed by loudspeaker-based desktop audio systems.

VI. Future Research Directions

A. Vision-Based Methods for Listener Tracking

Computer vision has historically been considered problematic, particularly for tasks that require object recognition. Up to now, the complexity of vision-based approaches has prevented their being incorporated into desktop-based integrated media systems. Recently, however, von der Malsburg's Laboratory of Computational and Biological Vision at the University of Southern California (USC) has developed a vision architecture that is capable of recognizing the identity, spatial position (pose), facial expression, gesture identification, and movement of a human subject in *real time*.

This highly versatile architecture integrates a broad variety of visual cues in order to identify the location of a person's head within the image. Object recognition is achieved through pattern-based analysis that identifies convex regions with skin color that are usually associated with the human face and through a stereo algorithm that determines the disparities among pixels that have been moving [51]. This pattern-recognition approach is based on the elastic graph matching method that places graph nodes at appropriate fiducial points of the pattern [52]. A set of features is extracted at each graph node corresponding to the amplitudes of complex Gabor wavelets. The key advantage of this method is that a new pattern (face or ear) can be recognized on the basis of a small number of example images (10–100). For audio applications, in which

the system must remember the last position of a listener that may have stopped moving, a hysteresis mechanism is used to estimate the current position and velocity of the head with a linear predictive filter.

While there are several alternative methods for tracking humans (e.g., magnetic, ultrasound, infrared, laser), they typically are based on tethered operations or require artificial fiducial markings (e.g., colored dots, earrings) to be worn by the user. Furthermore, these methods do not offer any additional functionality to match what can be achieved with vision-based methods (e.g., face and expression recognition, ear classification).

B. Desktop Audio System with Head Tracking

A novel multichannel desktop audio system that meets all the design requirements and acoustical considerations described above has been developed by Holman of TMH Corporation[4] in collaboration with the Immersive Audio Laboratory at USC's Integrated Media Systems Center (IMSC).[5] This system uses two loudspeakers that are positioned on the sides of a video monitor at a distance of 45 cm from each other and 50 cm from the listener's ears (Fig. 9). The seating position height is adjusted so that the listener's ears are at the tweeter level of the loudspeakers (117 cm from the floor), thus eliminating any colorations in the sound due to off-axis lobing. We have also incorporated the vision-based tracking algorithm described above using a standard video camera connected to an SGI Indy workstation. This tracking system provides us with the coordinates of the center of the listener's head relative to the loudspeakers and is currently capable of operating at 10 frames/s with a 3% accuracy.

In this single-camera system, it is possible to track listener movement that is confined in a plane parallel to loudspeakers and at a fixed distance from them. When the listener is located at the exact center position (the sweet spot), sound from each loudspeaker arrives at the corresponding ear at the exact same time (i.e., with zero ipsilateral time delay). At any other position of the listener

[4] See http://www.tmhlabs.com.
[5] See http://imsc.usc.edu.

in this plane, there is a relative time difference of arrival between the sound signals from each loudspeaker. To maintain proper stereophonic perspective, the ipsilateral time delay must be adjusted as the listener moves relative to the loudspeakers. The head coordinates provided from the tracking algorithm are used to determine the necessary time-delay adjustment. This information is processed by a 32-b DSP processor board (ADSP-2106x SHARC) resident in a Pentium-II PC. In this early version of our system, the DSP board is used to delay the sound from the loudspeaker that is closest to the listener so that sound arrives with the same time difference as if the listener were positioned in the exact center between the loudspeakers. In other words, we have demonstrated stereophonic reproduction with an adaptively optimized sweet spot.

We are currently in the process of identifying the bottle-necks of both the tracking and the audio signal-processing algorithms and integrating both into a single, PC-based platform for real-time operation. Furthermore, we are expanding the capability of the current single-camera system to include a second camera in a stereoscopic configuration that will provide distance (depth) information.

C. Pinna Classification for Enhanced Sound Localization

Immersive audio systems based on averaged HRTF's suffer from serious drawbacks. To map the entire three-dimensional auditory space requires a large number of tedious and time-consuming measurements, which is very difficult to do with human subjects. A further, and perhaps insurmountable, complication arises from the fact that this process must be repeated *for every* listener in order to produce accurate results. Last, discrete point measurements represent a quantization of 3-D space that is inherently continuous, thus requiring sophisticated interpolation algorithms that are computationally intensive and can give rise to errors [53]. Several methods have been proposed to overcome such limitations. Functional HRTF representations that make use of models to represent HRTF's have been proposed [54]–[56]; however, most are not suitable for real-time applications because they require significant computational resources.

There is significant evidence to suggest that the identification and incorporation of pinna physical characteristics may be a key factor limiting the development of seamless immersive audio systems. The human pinna is a rather complicated structure that for many years was considered to be a degenerate remain from past evolutionary forms. It was assumed to be a sound-collecting horn whose purpose was to direct sound into the ear canal. If this were true, then its physical dimensions would limit its role to a collector of high frequencies (short wavelengths). Experimental results, however, have shown that the pinna is a much more sophisticated instrument [17], [54], [57], [58]. The pinna folds act as miniature reflectors that create small time delays, which in turn give rise to comb-filtering effects in the frequency domain [59]. Also, the pinna is asymmetric relative to the opening of the ear canal. These ridges are arranged in such a way as to optimally translate a change

in angle of the incident sound into a change in the pattern of reflections. It has been demonstrated [57] that the human ear–brain interface can detect delay differences as short as 7 μs. Furthermore, as the sound source is moved toward 180° in azimuth (directly behind the listener), the pinna also acts as a low-pass filter, thus providing additional localization cues.

To understand the fundamental limitations imposed by such pinna transformations, the IMSC Immersive Audio Laboratory, in collaboration with the USC Laboratory for Computational Vision, is developing a novel method for classification and cross comparison of pinna characteristics. We are currently in the process of implementing a data base of pinna images and associated measured directional characteristics (HRTF's). A picture of the pinna from every new listener allows us to select the HRTF from this data base that corresponds to the ear whose pinna shape is closest to the new ear. The algorithm that will be used for this identification is a modified version of the face-recognition algorithm described above. Initial results have shown successful matching of ears from unknown listeners to those already in our data base, including two artificial ears from the KEMAR dummy-head system. A planned extension of this matching method will select characteristics from several stored ears that best match the corresponding characteristics of the new pinna. An appropriate set of weighting factors will then be determined to form a synthetic HRTF that closely resembles that of the new listener. It is important to note that this method offers significant advantages over previous model-based attempts because it can be performed very fast and with minimum computational overhead.   -

ACKNOWLEDGMENT

The author wishes to thank Prof. T. Holman of the USC IMSC and TMH Corporation for his continued guidance and support, as well as Prof. C. von der Malsburg and Dr. H. Neven from the USC Laboratory for Computational Vision for the development and integration of the vision-based head-tracking and pinna classification algorithms.

REFERENCES

[1] Y. Ando, *Concert Hall Acoustics.*   Berlin, Germany: Springer-Verlag, 1985.
[2] L. Beranek, *Concert and Opera Halls: How They Sound.* Woodbury, NY: Acoustical Society of America, 1996.
[3] S. Komiyama, "Subjective evaluation of angular displacement between picture and sound directions for HDTV sound systems," *J. Audio Eng. Soc.,* vol. 37, pp. 210–214, 1989.
[4] M. R. Schroeder and B. S. Atal, "Computer simulation of sound transmission in rooms," in *IEEE Int. Conv. Rec.,* 1963, vol. 7.
[5] M. Kleiner, B.-I. Dalenback, and P. Svensson, "Auralization—An overview," *J. Audio Eng. Soc.,* vol. 41, pp. 861–945, 1993.
[6] A. D. Blumlein, "Improvements in and relating to sound-transmission, sound-recording and sound-reproducing systems," U.K. Patent 394 325, 1931.
[7] H. Fletcher, "Auditory perspective—Basic requirements," *Elect. Eng.,* vol. 53, pp. 9–11, 1934.
[8] W. B. Snow, "Basic principles of stereophonic sound," *SMPTE J.,* vol. 61, pp. 567–589, 1953.
[9] J. C. Steinberg and W. B. Snow, "Physical factors," *Bell Syst. Tech. J.,* vol. 13, pp. 245–258, 1934.

[10] P. Scheiber, "Quadrasonic sound system," U.S. Patent 3 632 886, 1973.

[11] ——, "Multidirectional sound system," U.S. Patent 3 746 792, 1973.

[12] D. H. Cooper and T. Shiga, "Discrete-matrix multichannel stereo," *J. Audio Eng. Soc.,* vol. 20, pp. 346–360, 1972.

[13] G. Theile and G. Plenge, "Localization of lateral phantom sources," *J. Audio Eng. Soc.,* vol. 25, pp. 196–199, 1977.

[14] T. Holman, "Channel crossing," *Studio Sound,* pp. 40–42, 1996.

[15] S. P. Thompson, "On the function of the two ears in the perception of space," *Philos. Mag.,* vol. 13, pp. 406–416, 1882.

[16] J. W. Strutt and L. Rayleigh, "On the perception of sound direction," *Philos. Mag.,* vol. 13, pp. 214–232, 1907.

[17] J. Blauert, *Spatial Hearing: The Psychophysics of Human Sound Localization,* revised ed. Cambridge, MA: MIT Press, 1997.

[18] K. Genuit, "Ein modell zur beschreibung von außenohrübertragungseigenschaften," Ph.D. dissertation, RWTH Aachen, Germany, 1984.

[19] H. W. Gierlich, "The application of binaural technology," *Appl. Acoust.,* vol. 36, pp. 219–243, 1992.

[20] F. L. Wightman and D. J. Kistler, "Headphone simulation of free-field listening: Psychophysical validation," *J. Acoust. Soc. Amer.,* vol. 85, pp. 868–878, 1989.

[21] E. M. Wenzel, M. Arruda, and D. J. Kistler, "Localization using nonindividualized head-related transfer functions," *J. Acoust. Soc. Amer.,* vol. 94, pp. 111–123, 1993.

[22] D. R. Begault and E. M. Wenzel, "Headphone localization of speech," *Human Factors,* vol. 35, pp. 361–376, 1993.

[23] ——, "Challenges to the successful implementation of 3-D sound," *J. Audio Eng. Soc.,* vol. 39, pp. 864–870, 1991.

[24] H. Lehnert and J. Blauert, "Principles of binaural room simulation," *Appl. Acoust.,* vol. 36, pp. 259–291, 1992.

[25] W. G. Gardner, "Efficient convolution without input–output delay," *J. Audio Eng. Soc.,* vol. 43, pp. 127–136, 1995.

[26] M. A. Gerzon, "Ambisonics in multichannel broadcasting and video," *J. Audio Eng. Soc.,* vol. 33, pp. 859–871, 1985.

[27] A. J. Berkhout, D. de Vries, and P. Vogel, "Acoustics control by wavefield synthesis," *J. Acoust. Soc. Amer.,* vol. 93, p. 2764, 1993.

[28] M. M. Boone, E. N. G. Verheijen, and P. F. von Tol, "Spatial sound-field reproduction by wavefield synthesis," *J. Audio Eng. Soc.,* vol. 43, p. 1003, 1995.

[29] D. J. Meares, "Multichannel sound systems for HDTV," *Appl. Acoust.,* vol. 36, pp. 245–257, 1992.

[30] H. Moller, "Fundamentals of binaural technology," *Appl. Acoust.,* vol. 36, pp. 171–218, 1992.

[31] J. Blauert and P. Laws, "Group delay distortions in electroacoustical systems," *J. Acoust. Soc. Amer.,* vol. 63, pp. 1478–1483, 1978.

[32] H.-J. Platte, P. Laws, and H. v. Hövel, "Apparatus for the exact reproduction of ear input signals (in German)," *Fortschritte der Akustik,* vol. DAGA'75, pp. 361–364, 1975.

[33] F. L. Wightman and D. J. Kistler, "Headphone simulation of free-field listening: stimulus synthesis," *J. Acoust. Soc. Amer.,* vol. 85, pp. 858–867, 1989.

[34] H. Moller, C. B. Jensen, and D. Hammershoi, "Design criteria for headphones," *J. Audio Eng. Soc.,* vol. 43, pp. 218–232, 1995.

[35] B. B. Bauer, "Stereophonic earphones and binaural loudspeakers," *J. Audio Eng. Soc.,* vol. 9, pp. 148–151, 1961.

[36] P. Damaske and V. Mellert, "A procedure for generating directionally accurate sound images in the upper half-space using two loudspeakers," *Acustica,* vol. 22, pp. 154–162, 1969.

[37] P. Damaske, "Head related two channel stereophony with loudspeaker reproduction," *J. Acoust. Soc. Amer.,* vol. 50, pp. 1109–1115, 1971.

[38] D. H. Cooper and J. L. Bauck, "Prospects for transaural recording," *J. Audio Eng. Soc.,* vol. 37, pp. 3–19, 1989.

[39] J. Bauck and D. H. Cooper, "Generalized transaural stereo and applications," *J. Audio Eng. Soc.,* vol. 44, pp. 683–705, 1996.

[40] S. Mehrgard and V. Mellert, "Transformation characteristics of the external human ear," *J. Acoust. Soc. Amer.,* vol. 51, pp. 1567–1576, 1977.

[41] F. E. Toole, "Loudspeaker measurements and their relationship to listener preferences," *J. Audio Eng. Soc.,* vol. 34, pp. 227–235, 1986.

[42] S. Bech, "Perception of timbre of reproduced sound in small rooms: Influence of room and loudspeaker position," *J. Audio Eng. Soc.,* vol. 42, pp. 999–1007, 1994.

[43] T. Holman, "Monitoring sound in the one-person environment," *SMPTE J.,* vol. 106, pp. 673–680, 1997.

[44] R. Walker, "Room modes and low-frequency responses in small enclosures," *Audio Eng. Soc.,* preprint no. 4194, 1994.

[45] T. Holman, "Report on mixing studios sound quality," *J. Jpn. Audio Soc.,* 1994.

[46] F. E. Toole, "Subjective measurements of loudspeaker sound quality and listener performance," *J. Audio Eng. Soc.,* vol. 33, pp. 2–32, 1985.

[47] C. Kyriakakis and T. Holman, "High quality audio for the desktop," *J. Visual Commun. Image Representation,* to be published.

[48] T. Holman, "New factors in sound for cinema and television," *J. Audio Eng. Soc.,* vol. 39, pp. 529–539, 1991.

[49] T. Holman and C. Kyriakakis, "Acoustics and psychoacoustics of desktop sound systems," in *Proc. Ann. Meeting Acoustical Society of America,* San Diego, CA, 1997, p. 3092.

[50] W. G. Gardner, "Head-tracked 3-D audio using loudspeakers," in *Proc. WASPAA,* New Paltz, NY, 1997.

[51] O. Groetenherdt, "Video-based detection of heads using motion and stereo vision (in German)," in *Institute for Neuroinformatics.* Bochum, Germany: Univ. of Bochum, 1997.

[52] L. Wiskott, J. M. Fellous, N. Krueger, and C. von der Malsburg, "Face recognition by elastic bunch graph matching," Institute for Neuroinformatics, Tech. Rep. no. 8, 1996.

[53] F. L. Wightman, D. J. Kistler, and M. Arruda, "Perceptual consequences of engineering compromises in synthesis of virtual auditory objects," *J. Acoust. Soc. Amer.,* vol. 101, pp. 1050–1063, 1992.

[54] D. W. Batteau, "The role of the pinna in human localization," *Proc. Royal Soc. London,* vol. B168, pp. 158–180, 1967.

[55] A. J. Watkins, "The monaural perception of azimuth: A synthesis approach," in *Localization of Sound: Theory and Applications,* R. W. Gatehouse, Ed. Groton, CT: Amphora, 1979.

[56] J. Chen, B. D. Van Veen, and K. E. Hecox, "A spatial feature extraction and regularization model for the head-related transfer function," *J. Acoust. Soc. Amer.,* vol. 97, pp. 439–452, 1995.

[57] J. Hebrank and D. Wright, "Spectral cues used in the localization of sound sources in the median plane," *J. Acoust. Soc. Amer.,* vol. 56, pp. 1829–1834, 1974.

[58] S. S. Stevens and E. B. Newman, "The localization of actual sources of sound," *Amer. J. Physiology,* vol. 48, pp. 297–306, 1936.

[59] C. A. P. Rodgers, "Pinna transformations and sound reproduction," *J. Audio Eng. Soc.,* vol. 29, pp. 226–234, 1981.

Chris Kyriakakis (Member, IEEE) was born in Thessaloniki, Greece, in 1963. He received the B.S. degree in electrical engineering from the California Institute of Technology, Pasadena, in 1985 and the M.S. and Ph.D. degrees in electrical engineering from the University of Southern California (USC), Los Angeles, in 1987 and 1993, respectively.

He currently is an Assistant Professor in the Electrical Engineering Department, USC, and an Investigator in the Integrated Media Systems Center (IMSC), a National Science Foundation Engineering Research Center at USC. He is the head of the IMSC Immersive Audio Laboratory and is currently involved in the development of algorithms, systems, and architectures for immersive audio. These efforts include audio signal processing for accurate spatial rendering of sound at the desktop environment as well as experimental investigation of human listening characteristics. He is involved in several collaborative efforts within the IMSC, including the incorporation of a vision-based system to track a listener's head for precise, spatially accurate rendering of sound in a three-dimensional immersive audio environment as well as implementation of microphone arrays for robust speaker identification and tracking.

CHAPTER TWO

Digital Image and Video Compression and Processing

Bing Zeng

The Hong Kong University of Science and Technology

DIGITAL image and video data undoubtedly form the trunk of the digital multimedia world. As raw data, they often require a huge amount of bits. For instance, typical digital TV images have spatial resolution of approximately 512×512 pixels per frame. At 8 bits per pixel per color component and 30 frames per second, this translates into a rate of nearly 180×10^6 bps. Obviously, transmitting such TV images with the currently available transmission capacity requires some sort of compression. Image and video compression is also needed in many other applications, such as digital facsimiles, image and video storage, multimedia databases/libraries, video streaming over the Internet, geographic image transmission via satellites, video phone and video conferencing, and so on.

By means of image/video compression or coding, we can try to eliminate the observable redundancy (both statistical and subjective) as much as possible from raw image or video data. This research topic has general wide interest in both industry and academic research communities for more than 30 years. As a result, many efficient compression schemes have developed and matured in various applications, including DPCM-based predictive methods, various vector quantizations, transform coding, and wavelet decompositions [1–7]. In the meantime, several international standards have been established, such

as MH, MR/MMR, JBIG, JPEG, H.261/263, and MPEG-1/2 Audio [8–16], [21–27], or are emerging, such as JPEG-2000 [17], MPEG-4 [31–35], and MPEG-7 [36–38]. In this introduction, I have decided to pursue my presentation around the established or emerging international standards. The reason this focus is twofold: First, these existing and emerging coding standards have almost covered all aspects of the image and video compression algorithms developed so far, and second, most researchers are very much willing to submit their newly developed algorithms to standards committees for consideration of possible inclusion into the standards. Because of the space limit of this chapter, I selected primarily overview papers, written by leading experts in this area, so as to show the reader the landscape of this field.

Every image compression method falls into one of the following two categories: *lossless* and *lossy*. Lossless coding refers to compression algorithms that yield images after decompression that are numerically identical with the images that were originally compressed. The international standards addressing lossless coding include MH (modified Huffman), MR (modified READ [Relative Element Address Designate]), MMR (modified MR), JBIG (Joint Bi-level Image Experts Group), and JPEG (Joint Photographic Experts Group)—lossless mode. The basic technique used in all of these algorithms is some form of modeling/prediction over a nearby neighbor, followed by an efficient entropy coding (Huffman or arithmetic). For bi-level (fax) images, these algorithms can achieve about 20–30:1 compression ratios. In particular, JBIG works extremely well for binary halftone images. For multilevel (grayscale) images, JBIG and lossless JPEG can offer about 2.5-to-1 compression.

The international standards for lossy coding of grayscale images include the widely used JPEG and the emerging JPEG-2000. An image to be coded using JPEG is first partitioned into blocks of 8×8 pixels. Each such 8×8 block is mapped into the frequency domain by using the discrete cosine transform (DCT), whereas the resulting DCT coefficients are quantized based on a predetermined quantization table. Then, each 8×8 block is scanned in zig-zag order. Finally, an entropy encoder performs the run-length coding on the resulting sequence of quantized DCT coefficients, with the DC coefficients being coded in a DPCM format (between adjacent blocks). Besides the baseline mode described above, JPEG also offers the progressive mode to provide a layering or progressive encoding capability. That is, the capability to transmit an image first at a low rate (or a low quality) and then progressively improve it with subsequent transmissions. This capability is especially important in browsing applications where a low-quality or low-resolution image is highly desirable for the pre-scanning purpose. JPEG has been demonstrated in many applications to offer excellent compression quality in middle and high bit rates (rates above 0.5 bits/pixel). In particular, at high bit rates (those above 2 bits/pixel), JPEG can offer visually lossless quality for most natural images.

However, at low bit rates (those below 0.25 bits/pixel), the coding quality of JPEG, especially for highly detailed images, is unacceptable to many applications when judged subjectively. Accordingly, JPEG-2000 has started a new round of efforts to define a new state-of-the-art standard [17]. On the basis of keeping some fundamental features of JPEG, JPEG-2000 offers a number of new features, including the processing of large images without tiling, high robustness to bit errors, content-based description, and image security (watermarking, labeling, stamping, encryption, etc.). In addition, the most revolutionary change in JPEG-2000 is that it uses the wavelet/sub-band based coding approach.

Compared with DCT-based JPEG, this new approach not only can achieve better coding quality at low bit rates, but at the same time offers a fully scalable coding capability, which is very important in Web applications.

The international standards that have been established so far for video coding include H.261/263 and MPEG-1/2 Audio. The applications supported by these standards range from video conferencing over POTS/ISDN to video storage on CD-ROM to digital video broadcasting and HDTV. The core technique shared in all these standards is the motion-compensated DCT (MC-DCT). Video frames are divided into intraframes and interframes. Each intraframe is coded using a JPEG-like scheme, whereas every interframe must undergo a motion compensation before the DCT is applied. The majority of the compression comes from the interframe coding. We first partition each interframe into macro-blocks (MBs) (of size 16×16), and then, for each MB, we search for one (or more) motion vector(s) by comparing the MB with a search area in some previously coded reference frames. After motion compensation, the remaining steps are basically the same as those used in JPEG. For transmission or broadcasting, however, how to allocate a given bit-budget (*e.g.*, 1.5 Mbps) over frames and onto MBs online is a critical issue. This rate-control problem has been addressed in several research works [28–30]. For instance, H.263 allows frame skipping/MB dropping and also builds a sophisticated scheme for adjusting the quantization factor for different MBs [28].

All aforementioned schemes are frame based. Their capabilities in terms of the access, manipulation, and identification of individual objects (of arbitrary shapes) are very limited. To overcome this, the ISO/IEC MPEG group is currently working on two important object-based standards: MPEG-4 [31–35] and MPEG-7 [36–38]. The MPEG-4 standard uses an object-based composition approach, supports 2-D, arbitrarily shaped, "natural" video objects as well as synthetic data (such as text, generic 2-D/3-D graphics, and animated faces and bodies), and enables content-based interaction and manipulation. The integration of various objects is taken care of by the powerful MPEG-4 systems layer. In the meantime, MPEG-7 is aiming at the standardization of a set of multimedia content description schemes and descriptors, as well as ways of specifying new description schemes and descriptors. It will also address the coding of these description schemes and descriptors. It is anticipated that MPEG-7 will find its greatest application on the Internet.

One very important step within MPEG-4 is the motion estimation. The optimal motion estimation method is the so-called full (or exhaustive) search within the search area [39]. However, this method requires huge computational resources, which can amount to as much as 70% of the total computation power of a codec system. Consequently, a large number of fast search methods have been proposed to provide near-optimal solutions [40–45].

The first paper selected for this chapter, "Image and video coding—Emerging standards and beyond," by B. G. Haskell, et al., presents a good overview of the existing image and video coding standards. These coding standards include Group 3, Group 4, and JBIG for bi-level fax images; JPEG for still color images; and H.261, H.263, MPEG-1, and MPEG-2 for motion videos; as well as the emerging standards, including JPEG-2000 for still color images, H.263+ and MPEG-4 for motion videos, and MPEG-7 for multimedia metadata.

The second and third papers selected focus on several compression standards or algorithms for still images. The paper by R. Arps and T. Truong, "Comparison of international standards for lossless still image compression," specifically addresses lossless compression for still images through an in-depth comparison between the various existing lossless coding standards, including MH, MR, MMR, JBIG, and JPEG. The results of these comparisons can serve as important benchmarks for people pursuing further studies or choosing technologies for product development.

To enhance this chapter's reference value to academia, I selected the paper by J. M. Shapiro entitled, "Embedded image coding using zerotrees of wavelet coefficients," in the still image coding algorithm category. Another reason for this paper's selection is that the wavelet/sub-band theory has now been fully adopted in JPEG-2000 to provide significantly improved coding performance at low bit rates. Shapiro's embedded zerotree wavelet (EZW) algorithm was the first one to incorporate the zerotree coding concept into the wavelet decomposed hierarchical data structure. Since then, a number of further improved algorithms

have been developed, including Said and Pearlman's set partitioning in hierarchical trees (SPIHT) algorithm [18], Xiong et al.'s space-frequency quantization (SFQ) algorithm [19], Servetto et al.'s morphological representation algorithm [20], and many more. Another advantage of these wavelet-based algorithms over the DCT-based algorithms is that the wavelet-based coding can be made fully scalable.

For the video coding category, I selected only one paper, addressing MPEG-4, "The MPEG-4 video standard verification model," by T. Sikora, to reflect the most recent activities in the MPEG group. This paper first presents a brief introduction of MPEG-4's key features, such as content-based interactivity, hybrid natural and synthetic object coding, coding efficiency, universal access, content-based scalability, and system layers. Then, it provides an overview of the MPEG-4 Video Verification Model process and the structure of the Verification Model algorithm. The issues addressed in this overview include (1) video formats supported by MPEG-4, (2) coding of multiple "video object planes" (VOPs), (3) coding of shape and transparency information of each VOP, (4) temporal and spatial scalability for arbitrarily shaped VOPs, (5) error resilience and resynchronization in error prone environments, and (6) backward compatibility with other standards (H.261/3 or MPEG-1/2 Audio). Finally, the paper gives a short description of MPEG-4's "core experiment" process, including details about the techniques used to address the six issues just described, as well as some related issues (such as motion prediction, rate control, segmentation, etc.).

COMPRESSION DOMAIN IMAGE AND VIDEO PROCESSING

With the rapid deployment of the existing and emerging image and video compression standards, it is reasonable to expect that the future information world will be largely digitized. Audio, images, video, text, graphics, and many other media will be stored, recorded, transmitted, exchanged, and manipulated in the digital format. Usually, these media have been compressed when transmitted over networks or stored in databases. If the manipulation and processing of a compressed image or video data could be done directly in the compression domain, it would largely reduce the computational complexity of the procedure and provide the flexibility necessary for accommodating dynamic resources and heterogeneous quality of service (QoS) requirements [46–50]. Typical image and video manipulations include translation (block-wise or pixel-wise), scalar addition/ multiplication, pixel addition/multiplication, linear filtering, rotation, overlapping (opaque or semitransparent), subtitle, and so forth. I selected two papers for this topic. The first, "Algorithms for manipulating compressed images," by B. C. Smith and L. A. Rowe, presents some algorithms for performing a subset of the manipulation operations describes above for compressed still images and reports a speed-up ratio of 50 to 100 as compared to the algorithms that decompress images before application and re-compress the manipulated results. The second paper, "Manipulation and compositing of MC-DCT compressed video," by S. F. Chang and D. G. Messerschmitt, studies the direct manipulation of compressed motion video in the compression domain. Specifically, this paper proposes a set of algorithms for performing all the manipulation operations in the compressed DCT domain. It then considers the manipulation of MC compressed and MC-DCT compressed video. The general conclusion is that, for these latter two cases, direct compression domain manipulation is impossible. For the MC compressed video, the authors propose effective approaches for simplifying the MC data recalculation by reducing the number of image blocks that require the MC recalculation and using the principle of inferring new motion vectors from the old ones. For the MC-DCT compressed video, the authors propose a modified framework to partially decode the MC-DCT video to the DCT domain first and then perform the desired manipulations in the DCT domain.

MULTIMEDIA DATA-EMBEDDING AND WATERMARKING

The last topic I address in this chapter is multimedia data-embedding and watermarking technology [51–56]. This topic seems to be more and more important as online publishing, e-commerce, digital libraries, and the like become a part of our daily life. The foremost application of digital data embedding is passive and active copyright/IP protection, in which digital watermarking can be used as a means to identify the owner or distributor of digital data. Digital data embedding also provides a mechanism

for embedding important control, descriptive, or reference information in a given signal. Another important application of data embedding is to provide different access levels to the data. For example, we can control the amount of detail that can be seen in a given image, which means that a person with a high access level will be able to view details in an image that person with a lower access level will not.

I have selected one paper, "Multimedia data-embedding and watermarking technologies," by M. D. Swanson, M. Kobayashi, and A. H. Tewfik, to address this subject. Again, this is an overview paper, that presents a very comprehensive summary of the challenges and issues that must be addressed for successful watermarking and data-embedding techniques as well as the current state of the art. Its focus is on perceptually undetectable or transparent data-embedding and watermarking techniques. During the recovery of embedded data, the algorithm can assume access or no access to the original signal. Design of robust data-embedding procedures is also important. That is, the data-embedding procedure should be robust to possible malicious or incidental host signal modifications (including additive noise, linear and nonlinear filtering, compression, quantization, scaling, etc.). The fundamental principle relied upon in this paper is *masking*—the ability to make a component in a given audio or visual signal imperceptible in the presence of another signal (called the masker) because the human auditory and visual systems are imperfect detectors.

I believe the seven representative papers selected for this chapter cover all the important issues of digital image and video compression and processing. Of course, this is still an active research area and many challenging problems remain to be resolved. I foresee that the activity around the standardization of image and video coding will continue, and the manipulation and processing of compressed image and video data in the compression domain will draw more attention and interest. I also believe that some of the unresolved issues in digital data-embedding and watermarking (*e.g.*, unambiguously determining the rightful ownership of a given multimedia signal when multiple ownership claims are made) will reach a satisfactory solution in the near future.

REFERENCES

[1] A. N. Netravali and J. O. Limb, "Picture coding: A review," *Proceedings of the IEEE* 68 (March 1980): 366–406.

[2] A. K. Jain, "Image data compression: A review," *Proceedings of the IEEE* 69 (March 1981): 349–89.

[3] H. G. Musmann, P. Pirsh, and H. J. Grallert, "Advances in picture coding," *Proceedings of the IEEE* 73 (April 1985): 523–48.

[4] M. Kunt, A. Ikonmopoulos, and M. Kocher, "Second-generation image coding techniques," *Proceedings of the IEEE* 73 (April 1985): 549–74.

[5] A. Gersho and R. M. Gray, *Vector Quantization and Signal Compression*, (Boston: Kluwer Academic Press, 1992).

[6] P. P. Vaidyanathan, *Multirate Systems and Filter Banks*, (Englewood Cliffs, NJ: Prentice-Hall, 1993).

[7] M. Vetterli and J. Kovacevic, *Wavelets and Subband Coding*, (Englewood Cliffs, NJ: Prentice-Hall, 1995).

[8] International Telegraph and Telephone Consultative Committee (CCITT), "Standardization of Group 3 facsimile apparatus for document transmission," Recommendation T.4, 1980.

[9] International Telegraph and Telephone Consultative Committee (CCITT), "Facsimile coding schemes and coding control functions for group 4 facsimile apparatus," Recommendation T.6, 1984.

[10] R. Hunter and A. H. Robinson, "International digital facsimile coding standards," *Proceedings of the IEEE* 68, no. 7 (July 1980): 854–67.

[11] International Telegraph and Telephone Consultative Committee (CCITT), "Progressive bi-level image compression," Recommendation T.82, 1993; also appears as International Organization for Standards/International Electrotechnical Commission (ISO/IEC), "Progressive bi-level image compression," International Standard 11544: 1993.

[12] H. Hampel, R. B. Arps, et al., "Technical features of the JBIG standard for progressive bi-level image compression," *Signal Processing: Image Communication* 4, no. 2, (April 1992): 103–11.

[13] K. R. McConnell, D. Bodson, and R. Schaphorst, *Fax, Digital Facsimile Technology and Applications* (Boston: Artech House, 1992).

[14] International Telegraph and Telephone Consultative Committee (CCITT), "Digital compression and coding of continuous-tone still images," Recommendation T.81, 1992, also appears as International Organization for Standards/International Electrotechnical Commission (ISO/IEC), "Digital compression and coding of continuous-tone still images," International Standard 10918-1: 1993.

[15] G. Wallace, "Overview of the JPEG (ISO/IEC) still image compression standard," *Proceedings of SPIE (Image Processing Algorithms and Techniques)* 1244 (1990): 220–33.

[16] W. B. Pennebaker and J. L. Mitchell, *JPEG Still Image Data Compression Standard* (New York: Van Nostrand Reinhold, 1993).

[17] ISO/IEC JTC1/SC29/WG1 N1646, JPEG2000 Part I Final Committee Draft version 1.0, Tokyo, Japan, March 2000.

[18] A. Said and W. Pearlman, "A new, fast, and efficient image codec based on set partitioning in hierarchical trees," *IEEE Transactions on Circuits and Systems for Video Technology* 6 (June 1996): 243–50.

[19] Z. Xiong, K. Ramchandran, and M. T. Orchard, "Space frequency quantization for wavelet image coding," *IEEE Transactions on Image Processing* 6 (May 1997): 677–93.

[20] S. D. Servetto, K. Ramchandran, and M. T. Orchard, "Image coding based on a morphological representation of wavelet data," *IEEE Transactions on Circuits and Systems for Video Technology* 8 (Sept. 1999): 1161–74.

[21] ITU-T, "Video codec for audiovisual services at p*64 kbits/sec." Recommendation H.261.

[22] ITU-T, "Video coding for low bit rate communication." Recommendation H.263.

[23] M. L. Liou, "Overview of the p*64 kbits/s video coding standard," *Communications of the ACM* 34, no. 4 (April 1991).

[24] ISO/IEC, "Information technology—Coding of moving pictures and associated audio for digital storage media up to about 1.5 Mbits/s: Video," 11172-2 (MPEG-1), Aug. 1993.

[25] ISO/IEC "Information technology—Generic coding of moving pictures and associated audio information: Video," 13818-2 MPEG-2 Video Coding Standard, March 1995.

[26] J. L. Mitchell, W. B. Pennebaker, C. E. Fogg, and D. J. LeGall, *MPEG Video Compression Standard* (New York: Chapman & Hall, 1997).

[27] B. G. Haskell, A. Puri, and A. N. Netravali, *Digital Video: An Introduction to MPEG-2* (New York: Chapman & Hall, 1997).

[28] J. Ribas-Corbera and S. Lei, "Rate control in DCT video coding for low-delay communications," *IEEE Transactions on Circuits and Systems for Video Technology* 9, no. 1 (Feb. 1999): 172–85.

[29] W. Ding and B. Liu, "Rate control of MPEG video coding and recording by rate-quantization modeling," *IEEE Transactions on Circuits and Systems for Video Technology* 6 (Feb. 1996): 12–9.

[30] A. Vetro, H. Sun, and Y. Wang, "MPEG-4 rate control for multiple video objects," *IEEE Transactions on Circuits and Systems for Video Technology* 9, no. 1 (Feb. 1999): 186–99.

[31] International Organization for Standardization, Final Committee Draft ISO/IEC, "Coding of audio-visual objects: Systems," 14496-2.

[32] International Organization for Standardization, Final Committee Draft ISO/IEC, "Coding of audio-visual objects: Visual," 14496-2.

[33] N. Brady, "MPEG-4 standardized methods for the compression of arbitrarily shaped video objects," *IEEE Transactions on Circuits and Systems for Video Technology* 9, no. 8 (Dec. 1999): 1170–1189.

[34] Special Issue on MPEG-4, *IEEE Transactions on Circuits and Systems for Video Technology* 7, no. 1 (Feb. 1997).

[35] Special Issue on MPEG-4, *Signal Processing: Image Communication* 9 (May 1997) and 10 (July 1997).

[36] ISO/IEC, MPEG-7 overview v.1.0, MPEG-7 N3158, Maui, Dec. 1999.

[37] ISO/IEC, Working draft of MPEG-7 visual descriptors, MPEG-7 N3069, Maui, Dec. 1999.

[38] MPEG Requirements Group, "MPEG-7: Context and objectives," Doc. ISO/MPEG N1733; also, "Applications for MPEG-7," Doc. ISO/MPEG N1735, MPEG Stockholm Meeting, July 1997.

[39] J. R. Jain and A. K. Jain, "Displacement measurement and its application in interframe image coding," *IEEE Transactions on Communications* 29 (Dec. 1981): 1799–1808.

[40] T. Koga, K. Iinuma, A. Hirano, Y. Iijima, and T. Ishiguro, "Motion-compensated interframe coding for video conferencing," *Proceedings of the National Telecommunications Conference* (New Orleans: 1981), G5.3.1–5.3.5.

[41] R. Srinivasan and K. R. Rao, "Predictive coding based on efficient motion estimation," *IEEE Transactions on Communications* 33 (Sept. 1985): 1011–14.

[42] F. Dufaux and F. Moscheni, "Motion estimation techniques for digital TV: A review and a new contribution," *Proceedings of the IEEE* 83 (June 1995): 858–76.

[43] B. Liu and A. Zaccarin, "New fast algorithms for the estimation of block motion vectors," *IEEE Transactions on Circuits and Systems for Video Technology* 3 (Apr. 1993): 148–57.

[44] R. Li, B. Zeng and M. L. Liou, "A new three-step search algorithm for block motion estimation," *IEEE Transactions on Circuits and Systems for Video Technology* 4 (Aug. 1994): 438–42.

[45] B. Zeng, R. Li, and M. L. Liou, "Optimization of fast block motion estimation algorithms," *IEEE Transactions on Circuits and Systems for Video Technology* 7 (Dec. 1997): 833–44.

[46] B. Chiptrasert and K. R. Rao, "Discrete cosine transform filtering," *Signal Processing* 19, no. 3 (March 1990): 233–45.

[47] J. B. Lee and J. W. Lee, "Transform domain filtering based on pipelining structure," *IEEE Transactions on Signal Processing* 40 (Aug. 1992): 2061–64.

[48] Y. Y. Lee and J. W. Woods, "Video post-production with compressed images," *SMPTE J.* 103 (Feb. 1994): 76–84.

[49] T. Porter and T. Duff, "Compositing digital images," *Computer Graphics* 18 (1984): 253–59.

[50] S.-F. Chang, "Compositing and manipulation of video signals for multimedia network video services," Ph.D. dissertation, Univ. of California - Berkeley, Aug. 1993.

[51] R. Anderson, Ed., "Information hiding," in *Lecture Notes in Computer Science* (Tokyo, Japan: Springer, 1996).

[52] W. Bender, D. Gruhl, N. Morimoto, and A. Lu, "Techniques for data hiding," *IBM Systems Journal* 35, nos. 3 & 4 (1996): 313–36.

[53] I. Cox, J. Kilian , T. Leighton, and T. Shamoon, "Secure spread spectrum water-marking for multimedia," *IEEE Transactions on Image Processing* 6, no. 12 (1997): 1673–87.

[54] *Proceedings of the IEEE International Conference on Image Processing* (1996 and 1997).

[55] *Proceedings of the 4th International Multimedia Conference* (1996).

[56] C. Podilchuk and W. Zeng, "Image-adaptive watermarking using visual models," *IEEE Journal on Selected Areas of Communication,* Special Issue on Copyright and Privacy Protection 16 (May 1998): 525–39.

Image and Video Coding—Emerging Standards and Beyond

Barry G. Haskell, *Fellow, IEEE*, Paul G. Howard, Yann A. LeCun, *Member, IEEE*,
Atul Puri, *Member, IEEE*, Jöern Ostermann, *Member, IEEE*, M. Reha Civanlar, *Member, IEEE*,
Lawrence Rabiner, *Fellow, IEEE*, Leon Bottou, and Patrick Haffner

Abstract— In this paper, we make a short foray through coding standards for still images and motion video. We first briefly discuss standards already in use, including: Group 3 and Group 4 for bilevel fax images; JPEG for still color images; and H.261, H.263, MPEG-1, and MPEG-2 for motion video. We then cover newly emerging standards such as JBIG1 and JBIG2 for bilevel fax images, JPEG-2000 for still color images, and H.263+ and MPEG-4 for motion video. Finally, we describe some directions currently beyond the standards such as hybrid coding of graphics/photo images, MPEG-7 for multimedia metadata, and possible new technologies.

Index Terms— Image, standards, video.

I. INTRODUCTION

IT is by now well agreed that among the necessary ingredients for the widespread deployment of image and video communication services are standards for the coding, compression, representation, and transport of the visual information. Without standards, real-time services suffer because encoders and decoders may not be able to communicate with each other. Nonreal-time services using stored bit streams may also be disadvantaged because of either service providers' unwillingness to encode their content in a variety of formats to match customer capabilities, or the reluctance of customers themselves to install a large number of decoder types to be able to handle a plethora of data formats.

As new technologies offer ever greater functionality and performance, the need for standards to reduce the enormous number of possible permutations and combinations becomes increasingly important. In this paper, we summarize recent activities and possible future needs in establishing image and video coding standards. Some of the material was exerpted (with permission) from a larger companion paper [1], which is a broad tutorial on multimedia.

II. COMPRESSION AND CODING OF IMAGE[1] SIGNALS

Image coding generally involves compressing and coding a wide range of still images, including so-called bilevel or fax images, photographs (continuous tone color or monochrome

Manuscript received July 30, 1998. This paper was recommended by Associate Editor T. Sikora.

The authors are with the Speech and Image Processing Services Research Laboratory, AT&T Laboratories, Red Bank, NJ 07701 USA.

Publisher Item Identifier S 1051-8215(98)08400-6.

[1] We, along with others, use the term *image* for still pictures and *video* for motion pictures.

TABLE I
CHARACTERISTICS AND UNCOMPRESSED BIT RATES OF IMAGE SIGNALS

Image Type	Pixels per Frame	Bits/Pixel	Uncompressed Size
FAX (200 dpi)	1700×2200	1	3.74 Mb
VGA	640×480	8	2.46 Mb
XVGA	1024×768	24	18.87 Mb

images), and document images containing text, handwriting, graphics, and photographs. In order to appreciate the need for compression and coding, Table I shows the uncompressed size needed for bilevel (fax) and color still images.

Unlike speech signals, which can take advantage of a well-understood and highly accurate physiological model of signal production, image signals have no such model to rely on. As such, in order to compress and code image signals [2], it is essential to take advantage of any observable redundancy in the signal. The two most important forms of signal redundancy in image signals are *statistical redundancy* and *subjective redundancy*, also known as irrelevance.

Statistical redundancy takes a variety of different forms in an image, including correlations in the background (e.g., a repeated pattern in a background wallpaper of a scene), correlations across an image (e.g., repeated occurrences of base shapes, colors, patterns, etc.), and spatial correlations that occur between nearby pixels.

Subjective redundancy takes advantage of the human visual system that is used to view the decompressed and decoded images. Through various psychophysical testing experiments, we have learned a great deal about the perception of images, and have learned several ways to exploit the human's inability to see various types of image distortion as a function of image intensity, texture, edges, etc.

A. Coding of Bilevel (Fax) Images [3]

The concepts behind fax coding of bilevel images have been well understood for more than 100 years. However, until a set of standards was created and became well established, fax machines were primarily an office curiosity that were restricted to a few environments that could afford the costs of proprietary methods that could only communicate with like proprietary machines. Eventually, the industry realized that standards-based fax machines were the only way in which widespread acceptance and use of fax would occur, and a set of analog (Group 1 and Group 2) and digital standards (Group 3 and Group 4) were created and widely used. In this section, we briefly consider the characteristics of digital fax [4], along with the more recent JBIG1 standard and the newly proposed JBIG2 standard.

To appreciate the need for compression of fax documents, consider the uncompressed bit rate of a scanned page (8.5 by 11 in) at both 100 and 200 dots/in. At 100 dots/in, the single page requires 935 000 bits for transmission, and at 200 dots/in, the single page requires 3 740 000 bits for transmission. Since most of the information on the scanned page is highly correlated across scan lines (as well as between scan lines), and since the scanning process generally proceeds sequentially from top to bottom (a line at a time), the digital fax coding standards process the document image line by line (or pairs of lines at a time) in a left to right fashion. For MH[2] fax coding, the algorithm emphasizes speed and simplicity, namely, performing a one-dimensional run length coding of the 1728 pixels on each line, with the expedient of providing clever codes for EOL (end-of-line), EOP (end-of-page), and for regular synchronization between the encoder and decoder. The resulting MH algorithm provides, on average, a 20-to-1 compression on simple text documents.

The MREAD[3] fax algorithm provides an improvement over MH fax by using a two-dimensional coding scheme to take advantage of vertical spatial redundancy as well as the horizontal spatial redundancy. In particular, the MREAD algorithm uses the previous scan line as a reference when coding the current scan line. When the vertical correlation falls below a threshold, MREAD encoding becomes identical to MH encoding. Otherwise, the MREAD encoding codes the scan line in either a vertical mode (coding based on the previous scan line), a horizontal mode (locally along the scan line), or a pass mode (which essentially defers the encoding decision until more of the scan line is examined). The simple expedient of allowing the encoding to be based on the previous scan line increases the average compression that is obtained on simple text documents to 25-to-1, a 25% improvement over MH encoding.

MREAD fax coding has proven adequate for text-based documents, but does not provide good compression or quality for documents with handwritten text or continuous tone images. As a consequence, a new set of fax standards was created in the late 1980's, including the JBIG1 (Joint Bilevel Image Experts Group) standard [5], and work began on the more recent JBIG2 standard. The key idea here is that for binary halftone images (i.e., continuous-tone images that are converted to dot patterns, as in newspapers), neither MR nor MREAD fax coding is adequate since each image pixel needs a significantly larger region of support for prediction than that needed for text images. The JBIG1 standard provides this larger region and, moreover, uses an arithmetic coder that dynamically adapts to the statistics for each pixel context. There are two prediction modes that can be used for encoding. The first is a sequential mode in which the pixel to be coded is predicted based on

---

[2] Modified Huffman.

[3] Modified relative address. A modified MREAD algorithm (MMR) is also sometimes used. MMR increases compression somewhat, but at the expense of less resiliency to errors.

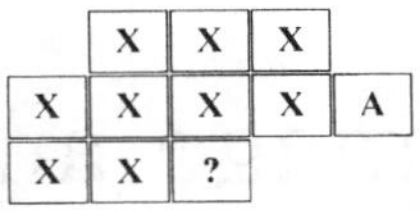

Fig. 1.   JBIG1 sequential template where the "?" marks the pixel to be coded based on the previously coded pixels marked X, plus an adaptively located pixel marked A, which for each page can be moved to a different location.

nine adjacent and previously coded pixels plus one adaptive pixel that can be spatially separated from the others, as shown in Fig. 1. Since each previously encoded pixel is a single bit, the previous pixels used in the sequential coding mode form a 10-bit context index that is used to arithmetically encode the current pixel.

The second coding mode of JBIG1 is a progressive mode that provides for successive resolution increases in successive encodings. This could be useful in browsing applications where a low-resolution image can be received fairly quickly, with higher resolution arriving later if the user wishes to wait. However, so far, it has not been widely used.

The key behind JBIG1 coding is that binary halftone images have statistical properties that are very different from binary text, and therefore need a significantly different coding algorithm to provide high-quality encoding at significant compression rates. The JBIG1 standard provides compression rates that are slightly better than MREAD fax coding for text sequences, and an improvement in compression by a factor of up to 8-to-1 for binary halftone images.

Although JBIG1 compression works quite well, it has become clear over the past few years that there exists a need to provide optimal compression capabilities for both lossless and lossy compression of arbitrary scanned images (containing both text and halftone images) with scanning rates of from 100 to 800 dots/in. This need was the basis for the JBIG2 method, which is being proposed as a standard for bilevel document coding. The key to the JBIG2 compression method is *soft pattern matching* [6], [7], which is a method for making use of the information in previously encountered characters without risking the introduction of character substitution errors that is inherent in the use of optical character recognition (OCR) methods [8].

The basic ideas of the JBIG2 standard are as follows [9].

- The basic image is first segmented into individual marks (connected components of black pixels).
- The resulting set of marks is partitioned into equivalence classes, with each class ideally containing all occurrences of a single letter, digit, or punctuation symbol.
- The image is then coded by coding a representative *token* mark from each class, the position of each mark (relative to the position of the previous mark), the index of the matching class, and finally the resulting error signal between each mark and its class token.
- The classes and the representative tokens are adaptively updated as the marks in the image are determined and coded.
- Each class token is compressed using a statistically based, arithmetic coding model that can code classes independently of each other

The key novelty with JBIG2 coding is the solution to the problem of substitution errors in which an imperfectly scanned symbol (due to noise, irregularities in scanning, etc.) is improperly matched and treated as a totally different symbol. Typical examples of this type occur frequently in OCR representations of scanned documents where symbols like "o" are often represented as "c" when a complete loop is not obtained in the scanned document, or a "t" is changed to an "l" when the upper cross in the "t" is not detected properly. By coding the bitmap of each mark, rather than simply sending the matched class index, the JBIG2 method is robust to small errors in the matching of the marks to class tokens. Furthermore, in the case when a good match is not found for the current mark, that mark becomes a token for a new class. This new token is then coded using JBIG1 with a fixed template of previous pixels around the current mark. By doing a small amount of preprocessing, such as elimination of very small marks that represent noise introduced in the scanning process, or smoothing of marks before compression, the JBIG2 method can be made highly robust to small distortions of the scanning process used to create the bilevel input image.

The JBIG2 method has proven itself to be about 20% more efficient that the JBIG1 standard for lossless compression of bilevel images. By running the algorithm in a controlled lossy mode (by preprocessing and decreasing the threshold for an acceptable match to an existing mark), the JBIG2 method provides compression ratios about two–four times that of the JBIG1 method for a wide range of documents with various combinations of text and continuous-tone images with imperceptible loss in image quality.

B. Coding of Continuous Images—JPEG Methods [10]

In this section, we discuss standards that have been created for compressing and coding continuous-tone still images—both gray scale (monochrome) and color images, of any size and any sampling rate. We assume that the uncompressed images are available in a digital format, with a known pixel count in each dimension (e.g., the rates shown in Table I), and an assumed quantization of 8 bits/pixel for gray-scale images and 24 bits/pixel for color images.

The most widely used standard algorithm for compression of still images is called the JPEG (Joint Photographic Experts Group) algorithm [11], and it has the properties that it is of reasonably low computational complexity, is capable of producing compressed images of high quality, and can provide both lossless and lossy compression of arbitrary sized gray-scale and color images [12]. A block diagram of the JPEG encoder and decoder is shown in Fig. 2. The image to be compressed is first converted into a series of 8 (pixel) × 8 (pixel) blocks which are then processed in a raster scan sequence, from left to right, and from top to bottom. Each such 8 × 8 block of pixels is first spectrally analyzed using a forward discrete cosine transform (FDCT) algorithm, and the resulting DCT coefficients are scalar quantized based on a psychophysically based table of quantization levels. Separate quantization tables are used for the luminance component

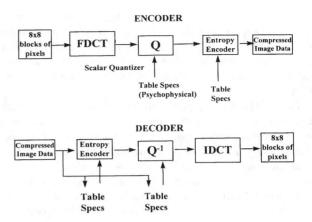

Fig. 2.   Block diagram of JPEG encoder and decoder.

(the image intensity) and the chrominance component (the color). The entries in the quantization tables are based on eye-masking experiments, and are essentially an approximation to the best estimate of levels which provide just-noticeable distortion in the image. The 8 × 8 blocks are then processed in a zig-zag order following quantization. An entropy encoder performs run-length coding on the resulting DCT sequences of coefficients (based on a Huffman coder), with the dc coefficients being represented in terms of their difference between adjacent blocks. Finally, the compressed image data are transmitted over the channel to the image receiver. The decoder performs the inverse operations of the encoder.

1) Progressive Encoding: Progressive encoding modes are provided within the JPEG syntax in order to provide a layering or progressive encoding capability to be applied to an image, i.e., to provide for an image to be transmitted at a low rate (and a low quality) and then progressively improved by subsequent transmissions. This capability is convenient for browsing applications where a low-quality or low-resolution image is more than adequate for things like scanning through the pages of a catalog.

Progressive encoding depends on being able to store the quantized DCT coefficients for an entire image. There are two forms of progressive encoding for JPEG, namely, spectral selection and successive approximation. For spectral selection, the initial transmission sends low-frequency DCT coefficients, followed progressively by the higher frequency coefficients, according to the zig-zag scan used to order the DCT coefficients. Thus, the first transmission might send the lowest three DCT coefficients for all of the 8 × 8 blocks of the image, followed by the next higher three DCT coefficients, and so forth until all of the DCT coefficients have been transmitted. The resulting scheme is simple to implement, but each image lacks the high-frequency components until the end layers are transmitted; hence, the reconstructed images from the early scans are blurred.

With the successive approximation method,[4] all of the DCT coefficients for each 8 × 8 block are sent in each scan. However, instead of sending them at full resolution, only the

---
[4]Sometimes called SNR scalability.

most significant bits of each coefficient are sent in the first scan, followed by the next most significant bits, and so on until all of the bits are sent. The resulting reconstructed images are of reasonably good quality, even for the very early scans, since the high-frequency components of the image are preserved in all scans.

The JPEG algorithm also supports a hierarchical or pyramid mode in which the image can be sent in one of several resolution modes to accommodate different types of displays. The way this is achieved is by filtering and downsampling the image, in multiples of two in each dimension. The resulting decoded image is upsampled and subtracted from the next level, which is then coded and transmitted as the next layer. This process is repeated until all layers have been coded and transmitted.

The lossless mode of JPEG coding is different from the lossy mode shown in Fig. 2. Fundamentally, the image pixels are handled separately (i.e., the 8×8 block structure is not used), and each pixel is predicted based on three adjacent pixels using one of eight possible predictor modes. An entropy encoder is then used to losslessly encode the predicted pixels.

2) JPEG Performance: If we assume that the pixels of an arbitrary color image are digitized to 8 bits for luminance, and 16 bits for chrominance (where the chrominance signals are sampled at one-half the rate[5] of the luminance signal), then effectively there are 16 bits/pixel that are used to represent an arbitrary color image. Using JPEG compression on a wide variety of such color images, the following image qualities have been measured subjectively:

Bits/Pixel	Quality	Compression Ratio
≥ 2	Indistinguishable	8-to-1
1.5	Excellent	10.7-to-1
0.75	Very Good	21.4-to-1
0.50	Good	32-to-1
0.25	Fair	64-to-1

The bottom line is that, for many images, good quality can be obtained with about 0.5 bits/pixel with JPEG providing a 32-to-1 compression.

3) JPEG-2000 Color Still Image Coding [13]: Much research has been undertaken on still image coding since the JPEG standards were established in the early 1990's. JPEG-2000 is an attempt to focus these research efforts into a new standard for coding still color images.

The scope of JPEG-2000 includes not only potential new compression algorithms, but also flexible compression architectures and formats. It is anticipated that an architecturally based standard has the potential of allowing the JPEG-2000 standard to integrate new algorithm components through downloaded software without requiring yet another new standards definition.

Some examples of the application areas for JPEG-2000 include the following.

Document imaging	Medical imagery
Facsimile	Security cameras
Internet/WWW imagery	Client–server
Remote sensing	Scanner/digital copiers
Video component frames	Prepress
Photo and art digital libraries	Electronic photography

JPEG-2000 is intended to provide low bit-rate operation with subjective image quality performance superior to existing standards, without sacrificing performance at higher bit rates. It should be completed by the year 2000, and offer state-of-the-art compression for many years beyond.

JPEG-2000 will serve still image compression needs that are currently not served. It will also provide access to markets that currently do not consider compression as useful for their applications. Specifically, it will address areas where current standards fail to produce the best quality or performance including the following.

- *Low bit-rate compression performance:* Current JPEG offers excellent compression performance in the mid- and high bit rates above about 0.5 bits/pixel. However, at low bit rates (e.g., below 0.25 bits/pixel for highly detailed images), the distortion, especially when judged subjectively, becomes unacceptable compared with more modern algorithms such as wavelet subband coding [14].
- *Large images:* Currently, the JPEG image compression algorithm does not allow for images greater then 64K × 64K without tiling (i.e., processing the image in sections).
- *Continuous-tone and bilevel compression:* JPEG-2000 should be capable of compressing images containing both continuous-tone and bilevel images. It should also compress and decompress images with various dynamic ranges (e.g., 1–16 bits) for each color component. Applications using these features include: compound documents with images and text, medical images with annotation overlays, graphic and computer-generated images with binary and near to binary regions, alpha and transparency planes, and of course bilevel facsimile.
- *Lossless and lossy compression:* It is desired to provide lossless compression naturally in the course of progressive decoding (difference image encoding, or any other technique, which allows for the lossless reconstruction is valid). Applications that can use this feature include medical images, image archival applications where the highest quality is vital for preservation but not necessary for display, network applications that supply devices with different capabilities and resources, and prepress imagery.
- *Progressive transmission by pixel accuracy and resolution:* Progressive transmission that allows images to be reconstructed with increasing pixel accuracy or spatial resolution as more bits are received is essential for many applications. This feature allows the reconstruction of images with different resolutions and pixel accuracy, as needed or desired, for different target devices. Examples of applications include the World Wide Web, image archival applications, printers, etc.

---

[5] The so-called $4:2:2$ color sampling.

- *Robustness to bit errors:* JPEG-2000 must be robust to bit errors. One application where this is important is wireless communication channels. Some portions of the bit stream may be more important than others in determining decoded image quality. Proper design of the bit stream can aid subsequent error-correction systems in alleviating catastrophic decoding failures. Usage of error confinement, error concealment, restart capabilities, or source-channel coding schemes can help minimize the effects of bit errors.

- *Open architecture:* It is desirable to allow open architecture to optimize the system for different image types and applications. This may be done either by the development of a highly flexible coding tool or adoption of a syntactic description language which should allow the dissemination and integration of new compression tools. Work being done in MPEG-4 (see Section V) on the development of downloadable software capability may be of use. With this capability, the user can select tools appropriate to the application and provide for future growth. With this feature, the decoder is only required to implement the core tool set plus a parser that understands and executes downloadable software in the bit stream. If necessary, unknown tools are requested by the decoder and sent from the source.

- *Sequential one-pass decoding capability (real-time coding):* JPEG-2000 should be capable of compressing and decompressing images with a single sequential pass. It should also be capable of processing an image using either component interleaved order or noninterleaved order. However, there is no requirement of optimal compression performance during sequential one-pass operation.

- *Content-based description:* Finding an image in a large database of images is an important problem in image processing. This could have major application in medicine, law enforcement, environment, and for image archival applications. A content-based description of images might be available as a part of the compression system. JPEG-2000 should strive to provide the opportunity for solutions to this problem. (However, see Section VI on MPEG-7.)

- *Image security:* Protection of the property rights of a digital image can be achieved by means of watermarking, labeling, stamping, encryption, etc. Watermarking is an invisible mark inside the image content. Labeling is already implemented in SPIFF,[6] and must be easy to transfer back and forth to JPEG-2000 image files. Stamping is a very visible and annoying mark overlayed onto a displayed image that can only be removed by a specific process. Encryption can be applied on the whole image file or limited to part of it (header, directory, image data) in order to avoid unauthorized use of the image.

- *Side channel spatial information (transparency):* Side channel spatial information, such as alpha planes and transparency planes, are useful for transmitting information for processing the image for display, print, or editing, etc. An example of this is the transparency plane used in World Wide Web applications.

For JPEG-2000, a prime candidate for the base signal processing is wavelet subband coding [15]. Compared with the discrete cosine transform (DCT) as used in JPEG coding, wavelet coding is able to achieve the advantages of low bit-rate coding with large block size, while at the same time providing progressive transmission and scalability features. However, the low-pass wavelet filter may not be optimum in terms of picture quality versus bandwidth. Thus, another candidate might be MPEG intra coding with the pyramid style progressive transmission found in JPEG. With pyramid coding, the filtering can be optimized since it is independent of the coding.

C. Hybrid Coding of Bilevel/Continuous Document Images—DJVU

In this section, we describe the DJVU [16] format (pronounced "Déjà vu") for compressing high-quality document images in color. Traditional color image compression standards such as JPEG are inappropriate for document images. JPEG's usage of local cosine transforms relies on the assumption that the high spatial frequency components in images can be essentially removed (or heavily quantized) without too much quality degradation. While this assumption holds for most pictures of natural scenes, it does not hold for document images. The sharp edges of character images require a special coding technique so as to maximize readability.

It is clear that different elements in the color image of a typical page have different perceptual characteristics. First, the text with sharp edges is usually highly distinct from the background. The text must be rendered at high resolution, 300 dpi in bilevel or 100 dpi in color, if reading the page is to be a pleasant experience. The second type of element in a document image is natural pictures. Rendering natural pictures at 50–100 dpi is typically sufficient for acceptable quality. The third element is the background color and paper texture. Background colors can usually be presented with resolutions less than 25 dpi for adequate quality.

The main idea of DJVU is to decompose the document image into three constituent images [17] from which the original document image can be reconstructed. The constituent images are: the background image, the foreground image, and the mask image. The first two are low-resolution (100 and 25 dpi, respectively) color images, and the latter is a high-resolution bilevel image (300 dpi). A pixel in the decoded document image is constructed as follows.

> If the corresponding pixel in the mask image is 0, the output pixel takes the value of the background image.

> If the mask pixel is 1, the pixel color is taken from the foreground image. The foreground and background images can be encoded with any suitable means, such as JPEG. The mask image can be encoded using JBIG2.

Consider the color histogram of a bicolor document image such as the old text image in Fig. 3. Both the foreground and background colors are represented by peaks in this histogram. There may also be a small ridge between the peaks representing the intermediate colors of the pixels located

[6] Still Picture Interchange File Format, formally known as ITU-T Recommendation T.84|ISO/IEC 10918-4.

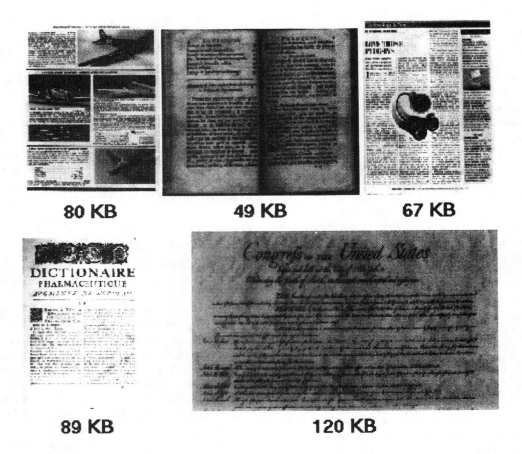

Fig. 3.   Document images with file sizes after compression in the DJVU format at 300 dots/in.

near the character boundaries. Extracting uniform foreground and background colors is achieved by running a clustering algorithm on the colors of all of the pixels.

1) Multiscale Block Bicolor Clustering: Typical document images are seldom limited to two colors. The document design and the lighting conditions induce changes in both the background and foreground colors over the image regions.

An obvious extension of bicolor image clustering consists of dividing the document image using a regular grid to delimit small rectangular blocks of pixels. Running the bicolor clustering algorithm within each block produces a pair of colors for each block. We can therefore build two low-resolution images whose pixels correspond to the cells of the grid. The pixels of the first image (or the second image) are painted with the foreground (or background) color of the corresponding block.

This block bicolor clustering algorithm is affected by several factors involving the choice of a block size, and the selection of which peak of each block color histogram represents the background (or foreground) color. Blocks should be small enough to capture the foreground color change, for instance, of a red word in a line of otherwise black text. However, such a small block size increases the number of blocks located outside the text area. Such blocks contain only background pixels. Blocks may also be entirely located inside the ink of a big character. Such blocks contain only foreground pixels. In both cases, the clustering algorithm fails to determine a pair of well-contrasted foreground and background colors.

Therefore, instead of considering a single block size, we consider now several grids of increasing resolution. Each successive grid employs blocks whose size is a fraction of the size of the blocks in the previous grid. By applying the bicolor clustering algorithm on the blocks of the first grid (the grid with the largest block size), we obtain a foreground and background color for each block in this grid. The blocks of the next smaller grid are then processed with a slightly modified color clustering algorithm.

This modification biases the clustering algorithm toward choosing foreground and background colors for the small blocks that are close to the foreground and background colors found for the larger block at the same location.

This operation alleviates the small block size problem discussed above. If the current block contains only background pixels, for instance, the foreground and background colors of the larger block will play a significant role. The resulting background color will be the average color of the pixels of the block. The resulting foreground color will be the foreground color of the larger block. If, however, the current block contains pixels representing two nicely contrasted colors, the colors identified for the larger block will have a negligible impact on the resulting clusters.

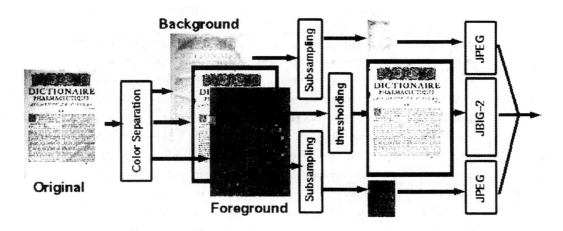

Fig. 4. DJVU compression algorithm first runs the foreground/background separation. Both the foreground and background images are compressed using a sparse wavelet encoding dubbed IW44, while the binarized text and drawings are compressed using AT&T's proposal to the JBIG2 standards committee.

2) Implementation: A fast version of this multiscale foreground–background color identification, as shown in Fig. 4, has been implemented and tested on a variety of high-resolution color images scanned at 24 bits/pixel and 300 pixels/in. The sequence of grids of decreasing block sizes is built by first constructing the smallest grid using a block size of 12×12 pixels. This block size generates foreground and background images at 100 and 25 pixels/in, respectively. Successive grids with increasing block size are built by multiplying the block width and height by four until either the block width or height exceeds the page size.

This coding implementation runs in about 20 s on a 175 MHz Mips R10000 CPU for a 3200×2200 pixel image representing a typical magazine page scanned at 300 pixels/in. Decoding time is a few seconds, most of which is taken up by I/O. When viewing less than the full document, decoding is usually fast enough to keep up with scrolling.

Once the foreground and background colors have been identified with the above algorithm, a gray-level image with the same resolution as the original is computed as follows. The gray level assigned to a pixel is computed from the position of the projection of the original pixel color onto a line in RGB space that joins the corresponding foreground and background colors. If the projection is near the foreground, the pixel is assigned to black, if it is near the background, the pixel is white. This gray-level image will contain the text and all of the areas with sharp local contrast, such as line art and drawings. This gray-level image is transformed into a bilevel mask image by an appropriate thresholding.

The document is now represented by three elements. The first two elements are the 25 dpi color images that represent the foreground and background color for each 12×12 pixel block. Those images contain a large number of neighboring pixels with almost identical colors. The third element is the 300 dpi bilevel mask image whose pixels indicate if the corresponding pixel in the document image should take the foreground or the background color. This mask image acts as a "switch" or stencil for the other two images.

3) Results and Comparison with Other Methods: Table II gives a full comparison of JPEG and the DJVU method on various documents. Compressing 300 dpi documents using JPEG with a quality[7] comparable to DJVU yields compressed images that are typically five–ten times larger. For the sake of comparison, we subsampled the document images to 100 dpi (with local averaging) and applied JPEG compression with a moderate quality[8] so as to produce files with similar sizes as with the DJVU format. It can be seen in Fig. 5 that JPEG causes many "ringing" artifacts that impede the readability.

III. Compression and Coding of Video Signals [18], [19]

In order to appreciate the need for compression and coding of the video signals that constitute the multimedia experience, Table III shows the necessary bitrates for several video types. For standard television, including the North American NTSC standard and the European PAL standard, the uncompressed bit rates are 111.2 (NTSC) and 132.7 Mbits/s (PAL). For videoconferencing and videophone applications, smaller format pictures with lower frame rates are standard, leading to the CIF (Common Intermediate Format) and QCIF (Quarter CIF) standards, which have uncompressed bit rates of 18.2 and 3.0 Mbits/s, respectively. Finally, the digital standard for HDTV (in two standard formats) has requirements for an uncompressed bitrate of between 662.9 and 745.7 Mbits/s. We will see that modern signal compression technology leads to compression rates of over 100-to-1.

There have been several major initiatives in video coding that have led to a range of video standards.

- Video coding for video teleconferencing, which has led to the ITU standards called H.261 for ISDN videoconferencing [20], H.263 for POTS[9] videoconferencing [21], and H.262 for ATM/broadband videoconferencing.[10]

---

[7] Quality factor 25% using the independent JPEG Group's JPEG implementation.

[8] Quality factor 30% using the independent JPEG Group's JPEG implementation.

[9] Plain Old telephone Service, i.e., analog phone line.

[10] H.262 is the same as MPEG-2.

TABLE II
COMPRESSION RESULTS FOR TEN SELECTED IMAGES

File	Description	Raw	DJVU	Ratio	JPEG-300/100	
metric.tif	(Text on various backgrounds)	20,000	56	350	496	89
hobby002.tif	(Mail order catalog page)	24,000	80	300	412	82
plugin.tif	(Weekly magazine page)	21,000	66	318	527	102
pharm1.tif	(XVIIe century book page)	6,000	88	181	630	85
encyc2347.tif	(Dictionary page)	23,000	98	234	950	150
amend.tif	(US first amendment)	61,000	212	287	456	78
carte.tif	(XVIIIe century map)	32,000	146	220	586	100
wpost2.tif	(Newspaper page section)	21,000	96	218	435	64
curry239.tif	(Book page with picture)	13,000	76	171	490	53
curry242.tif	(Book page without picture)	14,000	40	350	410	73

Column "Raw" reports the size in kbytes of an uncompressed TIFF file at 24 bits/pixel and 300 pixels/in. Column "DJVU" reports the total size in kbytes of the DJVU-encoded file. Column "JPEG-300" reports the size in kbytes of 300 pixel/in images JPEG-encoded with quality comparable to DJVU. For the sake of comparison, column "JPEG-100" reports the size in kbytes of 100 pixel/in images JPEG encoded with medium quality. However, the quality of those images is unacceptable for most applications.

- Video coding for storing movies on CD-ROM, with on the order of 1.2 Mbits/s allocated to video coding and 256 kbits/s allocated to audio coding, which led to the initial ISO MPEG-1 (Moving Picture Experts Group) standard.
- Video coding for broadcast and for storing video on DVD (digital video disks), with on the order of 2–15 Mbits/s allocated to video and audio coding, which led to the ISO MPEG-2 standard [22].
- Video coding for low-bit-rate video telephony over POTS networks, with as little as 10 kbits/s allocated to video and as little as 5.3 kbits/s allocated to voice coding, which led to the H.324 standard [23].
- Coding of separate audio–visual objects, both natural and synthetic, which will lead to the ISO MPEG-4 standard.
- Coding of multimedia *Metadata*, i.e., data describing the features of the multimedia data, which will ultimately lead to the MPEG-7 standard.
- Video coding using MPEG-2 for advanced HDTV (high definition TV) with from 15 to 400 Mbits/s allocated to the video coding.

In the following sections, we provide brief summaries of each of these video coders, with the goal of describing the basic coding algorithm as well as the features that support use of the video coding in multimedia applications.

A. H.26X

The ITU-T H-series of video codecs has evolved for a variety of applications. The H.261 video codec, initially intended for ISDN teleconferencing, is the baseline video mode for most multimedia conferencing systems. The H.262 video codec is essentially the high-bit-rate MPEG-2 standard, and will be described later in this paper. The H.263 low-bit-rate video codec is intended for use in POTS teleconferencing at modem rates of from 14.4 to 56 kbits/s, where the modem rate

includes video coding, speech coding, control information, and other logical channels for data.

1) H.261: The H.261 codec codes video frames using a discrete cosine transform (DCT) on blocks of size 8 × 8 pixels, much the same as used for the JPEG coder described previously. An initial frame (called an intra frame) is coded and transmitted as an independent frame. Subsequent frames, which are modeled as changing slowly due to small motions of objects in the scene, are coded efficiently in the inter mode using motion compensation (MC) in which the displacement of groups of pixels from their position in the previous frame (as represented by motion vectors) are transmitted together with the DCT-coded difference between the predicted and original images [24].

Since H.261 is intended for conferencing applications with only small, controlled amounts of motion in a scene, and with rather limited views consisting mainly of head-and-shoulders views of people along with the background, the video formats that are supported include both the CIF and the QCIF format. All H.261 video is noninterlaced, using a simple progressive scanning pattern.

A unique feature of H.261 is that it specifies a standard coded video syntax and decoding procedure, but most choices in the encoding methods, such as allocation of bits to different parts of the picture, are left open and can be changed by the encoder at will. The result is that the quality of H.261 video, even at a given bit rate, depends greatly on the encoder implementation. This explains why some H.261 systems appear to work better than others.

Since motion compensation is a key element in most video coders, it is worthwhile understanding the basic concepts in this processing step. Fig. 6 shows a block diagram of a motion-compensated image coder. The key idea is to combine transform coding (in the form of the DCT of 8 × 8 pixel blocks) with predictive coding (in the form of differential PCM) in

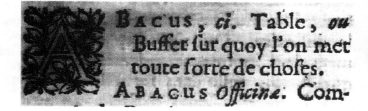

Fig. 5. Comparison of DJVU at 300 dpi (top three pictures) and JPEG at 100 dpi (bottom). The pictures are cut from encyc2347.tif (top), pharm1.tif (bottom), and hobby002.tif (right). The file sizes are given in Table II. The two methods give files of similar sizes, but very different qualities.

TABLE III
CHARACTERISTICS AND UNCOMPRESSED BIT RATES OF VIDEO SIGNALS

Video Type	Pixels per Frame	Image Aspect Ratio	Frames per Second	Bits/Pixel	Uncompressed Bitrate
NTSC	480 × 483	4:3	29.97	16*	111.2 Mb/s
PAL	576 × 576	4:3	25	16	132.7 Mb/s
CIF	352 × 288	4:3	14.98	12†	18.2 Mb/s
QCIF	176 × 144	4:3	9.99	12	3.0 Mb/s
HDTV	1280 × 720	16:9	59.94	12	622.9 Mb/s
HDTV	1920 × 1080	16:9	29.97	12	745.7 Mb/s

*Based on the so-called 4:2:2 color subsampling format with two chrominance samples C_b and C_r for every four luminance samples.

†Based on the so-called 4:1:1 c color subsampling format with one chrominance sample C_b and C_r for every four luminance samples.

order to give a high degree of compression. Since motion compensation is difficult to perform in the transform domain, the first step in the interframe coder is to create a motion-compensated prediction error. This computation requires only a single frame store in the receiver. The resulting error signal is transformed using a DCT, quantized by an adaptive quantizer, entropy encoded using a variable-length coder (VLC) and buffered for transmission over a fixed rate channel. Motion compensation uses 16 × 16 pixel macroblocks with integer pixel displacement.

2) H.263 Coding: The H.263 video codec is based on the same DCT and motion compensation techniques as used in H.261. Several incremental improvements in video coding were added to the H.263 standard for use in POTS conferencing. These included the following.

- Half-pixel motion compensation in order to reduce the roughness in measuring best matching blocks with coarse time quantization. This feature significantly improves the prediction capability of the motion compensation algorithm in cases where there is object motion that needs fine spatial resolution for accurate modeling.
- Improved variable-length coding.
- Reduced overhead.
- Optional modes including unrestricted motion vectors that are allowed to point outside the picture.

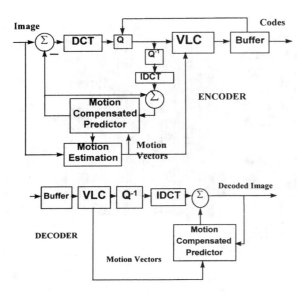

Fig. 6. Motion compensated codec for interframe coding.

- Arithmetic coding in place of the variable length (Huffman) coding.
- Advanced motion prediction mode including overlapped block motion compensation.
- A mode that combines a bidirectionally predicted picture with a normal forward predicted picture.

In addition, H.263 supports a wider range of picture formats including 4CIF (704 × 576 pixels) and 16CIF (1408 × 1152 pixels) to provide a high resolution mode picture capability. Comparisons have shown that H.263 coders can achieve the same quality as H.261 coders at about half the bit rate.

3) Summary of New "H.263+" Extension Features: These revisions add optional features to Recommendation H.263 in order to broaden its range of useful application and to improve its compression performance. The additional optional feature set can be summarized in terms of the new types of pictures it can use, the new coding modes which can be applied to those pictures, and the definition of backward-compatible supplemental enhancement information which can be added into the video bit stream.

a) New types of pictures:

Scalability pictures: Scalable video coding has the potential for improving the delivery of video in error-prone, packet-loss-ridden, and heterogenous networks. It allows the video bit stream to be separated into multiple logical channels, so that some data can be lost or discarded without irreparable harm to the video representation. Three types of scalability pictures were added in this revision, one which provides temporal scalability (B) and two which provide SNR or spatial scalability (EI and EP):

1) B: a picture having two reference pictures, one of which temporally precedes the B picture and one of which is temporally subsequent to the B picture (this is taken from MPEG);
2) EI: a picture having a temporally simultaneous reference picture; and

3) EP: a picture having two reference pictures, one of which temporally precedes the EP picture and one of which is temporally simultaneous.

Improved PB frames: The existing Recommendation H.263 contains a special frame type called a "PB frame," which enables an increase in perceived frame rate with only a moderate increase in bit rate. However, recent investigations have indicated that the Improved PB-frame as it exists is not sufficiently robust for continual use. Encoders wishing to use PB frames are limited in the types of prediction that a PB frame can use, which results in a lack of usefulness for PB frames in some situations. An improved, more robust type of PB frame has been added to enable heavier, higher performance use of the PB frame design. It is a small modification of the existing PB frames mode.

Custom source formats: The existing Recommendation H.263 is very limited in the types of video input to which it can be applied. It allows only five video source formats defining the picture size, picture shape, and picture clock frequency. The new H.263+ feature set allows a wide range of optional custom source formats in order to make the standard apply to a much wider class of video scenes. These modifications help make the standard respond to the new world of resizable computer window-based displays, high refresh rates, and wide format viewing screens.

b) New coding modes: This set of optional extensions of the H.263 video coding syntax also includes nine new coding modes that can be applied to the pictures in the bit stream.

1) Advanced INTRA coding (AIC): A mode which improves the compression efficiency for INTRA macroblock encoding by using spatial prediction of DCT coefficient values.
2) Deblocking filter (DF): A mode which reduces the amount of block artifacts in the final image by filtering across block boundaries using an adaptive filter.
3) Slice structured (SS): A mode which allows a functional grouping of a number of macroblocks in the picture, enabling improved error resilience, improved transport over packet networks, and reduced delay.
4) Reference picture selection (RPS): A mode which improves error resilience by allowing a temporally previous reference picture to be selected which is not the most recent encoded picture that can be syntactically referenced.
5) Reference picture resampling (RPR): A mode which allows a resampling of a temporally previous reference picture prior to its use as a reference for encoding, enabling global motion compensation, predictive dynamic resolution conversion, predictive picture area alteration and registration, and special-effect warping.
6) Reduced-resolution update (RRU): A mode which allows an encoder to maintain a high frame rate during heavy motion by encoding a low-resolution update to a higher resolution picture while maintaining high resolution in stationary areas.
7) Independent segment decoding (ISD): A mode which enhances error resilience by ensuring that corrupted

data from some region of the picture cannot cause propagation of error into other regions.

8) Alternative inter VLC (AIV): A mode which reduces the number of bits needed for encoding predictively coded blocks when there are many large coefficients the block.

9) Modified quantization (MQ): A mode which improves the control of the bit rate by changing the method for controlling the quantizer step size on a macroblock basis, reduces the prevalence of chrominance artifacts by reducing the step size for chrominance quantization, increases the range of representable coefficient values for use with small quantizer step sizes, and increases error detection performance and reduces decoding complexity by prohibiting certain unreasonable coefficient representations.

c) Supplemental enhancement information: This revision also allows the addition of supplemental enhancement information to the video bit stream. Although this information does not affect the semantics for decoding the bit stream, it can enable enhanced features for systems which understand the optional additional information (while being discarded harmlessly by systems that do not understand it). This allows a variety of picture freeze and release commands, as well as tagging information associated synchronously with the pictures in the bit stream for external use.

It also allows for video transparency by the use of *chroma key* information [25]. More specifically, a certain color is assigned to represent transparent pixels, and that color value is sent to the decoder. The motion video can then, for example, be superimposed onto a still image background by overlaying only the nontransparent pixels onto the still image.

B. MPEG-1 Video Coding

The MPEG-1 standard is a true multimedia standard with specifications for coding, compression, and transmission of audio, video, and data streams in a series of synchronized, multiplexed packets. The driving focus of the standard was storage of multimedia content on a standard CDROM, which supported data transfer rates of 1.4 Mbits/s and a total storage capability of about 600 Mbytes. The picture format that was chosen was the SIF format (352×288 at 25 noninterlaced frames/s or 352×240 pixels at 30 noninterlaced frames/s) which was intended to provide VHS VCR-like video and audio quality, along with VCR-like controls.

The video coding in MPEG-1 is very similar to the video coding of the H.26X series described above, namely, spatial coding by taking the DCT of 8×8 pixel blocks, quantizing the DCT coefficients based on perceptual weighting criteria, storing the DCT coefficients for each block in a zig-zag scan, and doing a variable run-length coding of the resulting DCT coefficient stream. Temporal coding was achieved by using the ideas of uni- and bidirectional motion-compensated prediction, with three types of pictures resulting, namely,

- *I* or intra pictures which were coded independently of all previous or future pictures;
- *P* or predictive pictures which were coded based on previous *I* or previous *P* pictures;

- *B* or bidirectionally predictive pictures which were coded based on either the next and/or the previous pictures.

High-quality audio coding also is an implicit part of the MPEG-1 standard, and therefore it included sampling rates of 32, 44.1, and 48 kHz, thereby providing provision for near-CD audio quality.

C. MPEG-2 Coding

The MPEG-2 standard was designed to provide the capability for compressing, coding, and transmitting high-quality, multichannel, multimedia signals over terrestrial broadcast, satellite distribution, and broad-band networks, for example, using ATM (asynchronous transmission mode) protocols. The MPEG-2 standard specifies the requirements for video coding, audio coding, systems coding for combining coded audio and video with user-defined private data streams, conformance testing to verify that bit streams and decoders meet the requirements, and software simulation for encoding and decoding of both the program and the transport streams. Because MPEG-2 was designed as a transmission standard, it supports a variety of packet formats (including long and variable-length packets of from 1 up to 64 kbits), and provides error correction capability that is suitable for transmission over cable TV and satellite links.

1) MPEG-2 Systems: The MPEG-2 systems level defines two types of streams: the program stream and the transport stream. The program stream is similar to that used in MPEG-1, but with a modified syntax and new functions to support advanced functionalities. Program stream decoders typically use long and variable-length packets, which are well suited for software-based processing and error-free environments. The transport streams offer the robustness necessary for noisy channels, and also provide the ability to include multiple programs in a single stream. The transport stream uses fixed-length packets of size 188 bytes, and is well suited for delivering compressed video and audio over error-prone channels such as CATV networks and satellite transponders.

The basic data structure that is used for both the program stream and the transport stream data is called the packetized elementary stream (PES) packet. PES packets are generated by packetizing the compressed video and audio data, and a program stream is generated by interleaving PES packets from the various encoders with other data packets to generate a single bitstream. A transport stream consists of packets of fixed length, consisting of 4 bytes of header followed by 184 bytes of data obtained by chopping up the data in the PES packets. The key difference in the streams is that the program streams are intended for error-free environments, whereas the transport streams are intended for noisier environments where some type of error protection is required.

2) MPEG-2 Video: MPEG-2 video was originally designed for high-quality encoding of interlaced video from standard TV with bit rates on the order of 4–9 Mbits/s. As it evolved, however, MPEG-2 video was expanded to include high-resolution video, such as HDTV, as well as hierarchical or scalable video coding for a range of applications. Since MPEG-2 video does not standardize the encoding method,

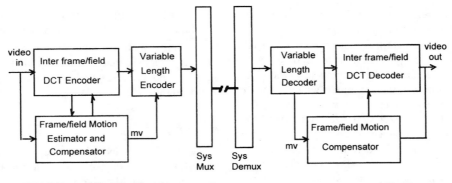

MPEG-2 Nonscalable Video Encoder   MPEG-2 Nonscalable Video Decoder

Fig. 7. Generalized codec for MPEG-2 nonscalable video coding.

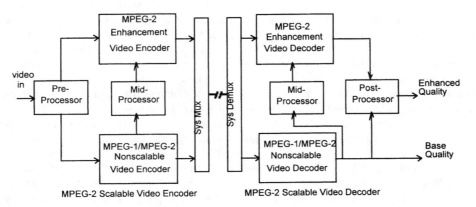

MPEG-2 Scalable Video Encoder   MPEG-2 Scalable Video Decoder

Fig. 8. Generalized codec for MPEG-2 scalable video coding.

but only the video bit stream syntax and decoding semantics, there have evolved two generalized video codecs, one for nonscalable video coding and one for scalable video coding. Fig. 7 shows a block diagram of the MPEG-2 nonscalable video coding algorithm. The video encoder consists of an interframe/field DCT encoder, a frame/field motion estimator and compensator, and a variable-length encoder (VLE). The frame/field DCT encoder exploits spatial redundancies in the video, and the frame/field motion compensator exploits temporal redundancies in the video signal. The coded video bit stream is sent to a systems multiplexer, Sys Mux, which outputs either a transport or a program stream.

The MPEG-2 decoder of Fig. 7 consists of a variable-length decoder (VLD), interframe/field DCT decoder, and the frame/field motion compensator. Sys Demux performs the complementary function of Sys Mux and presents the video bit stream to VLD for decoding of motion vectors and DCT coefficients. The frame/field motion compensator uses a motion vector decoded by VLD to generate motion-compensated prediction that is added back to a decoded prediction error signal to generate decoded video out. This type of coding produces nonscalable video bit streams since, normally, the full spatial and temporal resolution coded is the one that is expected to be decoded.

A block diagram of a generalized codec for MPEG-2 scalable video coding is shown in Fig. 8. Scalability is the property that allows decoders of various complexities to be

able to decode video of resolution/quality commensurate with their complexity from the same bit stream. The generalized structure of Fig. 8 provides capability for both spatial and temporal resolution scalability in the following manner. The input video goes through a preprocessor that produces two video signals, one of which (called the base layer) is input to a standard MPEG-1 or MPEG-2 nonscalable video encoder, and the other (called the enhancement layer) is input to an MPEG-2 enhancement video encoder. The two bit streams, one from each encoder, are multiplexed in Sys Mux (along with coded audio and user data). In this manner, it becomes possible for two types of decoders to be able to decode a video signal of quality commensurate with their complexity from the same encoded bit stream.

D. HDTV—The Ultimate TV Experience

High-definition television is designed to be the ultimate television viewing experience providing, in a cost-effective manner, a high-resolution and wide-screen television system with a more panoramic image aspect ratio (16:9 versus the conventional 4:3 ratio for NTSC or PAL), producing much better quality pictures and sound. HDTV systems will be one of the first systems that will not be backward compatible with NTSC or PAL. The key enablers of HDTV systems are the advanced video and audio compression capability, the availability of inexpensive and powerful VLSI chips to realize the system, and the availability of large displays.

The primary driving force behind HDTV is the high level of picture and sound quality that can be received by consumers in their homes. This is achieved by increasing the spatial resolution by about a factor of 2 in both the horizontal and vertical dimensions, providing a picture with about 1000 scan lines and with more than 1000 pixels per scan line. In addition, HDTV allows the use of progressive (noninterlaced) scanning at about 60 frames/s to allow better fast-action sports and far better interoperability with computers, while eliminating the artifacts associated with interlaced pictures.

Unfortunately, increasing the spatial and temporal resolution of the HDTV signal and adding multichannel sound greatly increases its analog bandwidth. Such an analog signal cannot be accommodated in a single channel of the currently allocated broadcast spectrum. Moreover, even if bandwidth were available, such an analog signal would suffer interference both to and from the existing TV transmissions. In fact, much of the available broadcast spectrum can be characterized as a fragile transmission channel. Many of the 6 MHz TV channels are kept unused because of interference considerations, and are designated as *taboo* channels.

Therefore, all of the current HDTV proposals employ digital compression, which reduces the bit rate from approximately 1 Gbit/s to about 20 Mbits/s which can be accommodated in a 6 MHz channel either in a terrestrial broadcast spectrum or a cable television channel. This digital signal is incompatible with the current television system, and therefore can be decoded only by a special decoder.

The result of all of these improvements is that the number of active pixels in an HDTV signal increases by about a factor of 5 (over NTSC signals), with a corresponding increase in the analog bandwidth or digital rate required to represent the uncompressed video signal. The quality of the audio associated with HDTV is also improved by means of multichannel, CD-quality, surround sound in which each channel is independently transmitted.

Since HDTV will be digital, different components of the information can be simply multiplexed in time, instead of frequency multiplexed on different carriers as in the case of analog TV. For example, each audio channel is independently compressed, and these compressed bits are multiplexed with compressed bits from video, as well as bits for closed captioning, teletext, encryption, addressing, program identification, and other data services in a layered fashion.

The U.S. HDTV standard [26] specifies MPEG-2 for the video coding. It uses hierarchical, subpixel motion compensation, with perceptual coding of interframe differences, a fast response to scene and channel changes, and graceful handling of transmission errors. Early versions of the system provide digital transmission of the video signal at 17 Mbits/s with five-channel surround sound CD-quality audio at 0.5 Mbits/s.

In summary, the basic features of the HDTV system that will be implemented are as follows:

- higher spatial resolution, with an increase in spatial resolution by at least a factor of 2 in both the horizontal and vertical directions;
- higher temporal resolution with an increase in temporal resolution by use of a progressive 60 Hz temporal rate;

- higher aspect ratio with an increase in the aspect ratio to 16 : 9 from 4 : 3 for standard TV providing a wider image;
- multichannel CD-quality surround sound with at least four–six channels of surround sound;
- reduced artifacts as compared to analog TV by removing the composite format artifacts as well as the interlace artifacts;
- bandwidth compression and channel coding to make better use of terrestrial spectrum using digital processing for efficient spectrum usage;
- interoperability with the evolving telecommunications and computing infrastructure through the use of digital compression and processing for ease of interworking.

IV. Techniques for Improved Video Delivery over the Internet

Delivery of play-on-demand video over the Internet involves many problems that simple file transfers do not encounter. These include packet loss, variable delay, congestion, and many others. TCP/IP (transmission control protocol) avoids packet loss by retransmitting lost packets. However, this causes delay that in some cases may become excessive. UDP/IP (universal datagram packets) has no such delay because it does not retransmit packets. However, in that case, the receiving decoder must provide some error recovery mechanism to deal with lost packets.

A. Streaming Issues for Video

The increases in the computing power and the network access bandwidth available to the general public on their desktop and home computers have resulted in a proliferation of applications using multimedia data delivery over the Internet. Early applications that were based on a first-download-then-play approach have been replaced by "*streaming*" applications [27], which start the playback after a short, initial segment of the multimedia data gets buffered at the user's computer. The success of these applications, however, is self limiting. As they get better, more people try to use them, thereby increasing the congestion on the Internet which, in turn, degrades the performance of such real-time applications in the form of lost and delayed packets.

Although several mechanisms, such as smart buffer management and the use of error-resilient coding techniques, can be employed at the end points to reduce the effects of these packet losses in a streaming application, these can only be effective below a certain packet loss level. For example, generally, the amount of data to be buffered at the beginning of the playback and, hence, the start-up delay is determined in real time based on the reception rate and the rate used to encode the particular material being played. If the congestion level is too high, the amount of data to be buffered initially can be as large as the entire material, effectively converting the streaming application into a download-and-play application. In addition, the time needed to download the material can become so long that users lose interest while waiting for the playback to begin.

The four elements of a streaming system are:

- the compressed (coded) information content, e.g., audio, video, multimedia data, etc.;
- the server;
- the clients;
- the data network (e.g., the Internet) and the connections of the server and the clients to the data network.

A successful streaming application requires a well-designed system that takes into account all of these elements.

Currently, streaming in data networks is implemented as part of the application layer protocols of the transmission, i.e., it uses UDP and TCP at the transport layer. Because of the known shortcomings of TCP, most streaming implementations are based on the inherently unreliable UDP protocol. Thus, whenever there is network congestion, packets are dropped. Also, since delay can be large (order of seconds) and often unpredictable on the Internet, some packets may arrive after their nominal presentation time, effectively turning them into lost packets. The extent of the losses is a function of the network congestion, which is highly correlated with the time of the day and the distance (in terms of the number of routers) between the client and the multimedia source. Thus, streaming itself does not inherently guarantee high quality or low delay playback of real-time mulitmedia material.

The practical techniques that have evolved for improving the performance of streaming-based real-time signal delivery can be classified into four broad areas, namely, the following.

- Client side buffer management—determining how much data needs to be buffered both prior to the start of the streaming playback as well as during the playback, and determining a strategy for changing the buffer size as a function of the network congestion and delay and the load on the media server.
- Error-resilient transmission techniques—increasing client-side resilience to packet losses through intelligent transport techniques, such as using higher priority for transmitting more important parts (headers, etc.) of a stream and/or establishing appropriate retransmission mechanisms (where possible).
- Error-resilient coding techniques—using source (and perhaps combined source and channel) coding techniques that have built-in resilience to packet losses.
- Media control mechanisms—using efficient implementations of VCR-type controls when serving multiple clients.

None of these techniques is sufficient to guarantee high-quality streaming, but in combination, they serve to reduce the problems to manageable levels for most practical systems.

B. Quality-of-Service (QOS) Considerations

The ultimate test of any multimedia system is whether it can deliver the quality of service that is required by the user of the system. The ability to guarantee the QOS of any signal transmitted over the POTS network is one of the key strengths of that network. For reasons discussed throughout this paper, the packet network does not yet have the structure to guarantee QOS for real-time signals transmitted over the packet network. Using the standard data protocol of TCP/IP, the packet network can provide guaranteed eventual delivery for data (through the use of the retransmission protocol in TCP). However, for high-quality real-time signals, there is less possibility of retransmission. Using the of UDP/IP protocol, the packet network delivers most of the packets in a timely fashion. However, some packets may be lost. Using the new real time protocol [28] (RTP), a receiver can feed back to the transmitter the state and quality of the transmission, after which the transmitter can adjust its bit rate and/or error resilience to accommodate.

The ultimate solution to this problem lies in one of three directions, namely, the following.

- Significantly increased bandwidth connections between all data servers and all clients, thereby making the issues involved with traffic on the network irrelevant. This solution is highly impractical and somewhat opposed to the entire spirit of sharing the packet network across a range of traffic sites so that it is efficiently and statistically multiplexed by a wide range of traffic. However, such overengineering is often done.
- Provide *virtual circuit* capability for different grades of traffic on the packet network. If real-time signals were able to specify a virtual circuit between the server and the client so that all subsequent packets of a specified type could use the virtual circuit without having to determine a new path for each packet, the time to determine the packet routing path would be reduced to essentially a table lookup instead of a complex calculation. This would reduce the routing delay significantly.
- Provide *grades of service* for different types of packets, so that real-time packets would have a higher grade of service than a data packet. This would enable the highest grade of service packets (hopefully reserved for real-time traffic) to bypass the queue at each router and be moved with essentially no delay through routers and switches in the data network.

Guaranteed, high-quality delivery of real-time information over the Internet requires some form of resource reservations. Although there is ongoing work to bring such functionality to the Internet (via RSVP [29] and IPv6 [30]), its global implementation is still a few years down the line. This is due to the fact that the network bandwidth is bound to stay as a limited resource needed by many in the foreseeable future and, therefore, a value structure must be imposed on data exchanges with any defined QOS. Establishing such a structure may be easy for a corporate intranet; however, a nationwide implementation requires new laws, and a global implementation requires international agreements!

A key problem in the delivery of "on-demand" multimedia communications over the Internet is that the Internet today cannot guarantee the quality of real-time signals such as speech, audio, and video because of lost and delayed packets due to congestion and traffic on the Internet. An alternative to this, which can be implemented immediately, is to use the existing POTS telephone network, in particular the ISDN, together with the Internet to provide a high QOS connection when needed.

The FusionNet [31] service overcomes this problem by using the Internet only to browse (in order to find the multimedia material that is desired), to request the video and audio, and to control the signal delivery (e.g., via VCR-like controls). FusionNet uses either POTS or ISDN to actually deliver guaranteed quality of service (QOS) for real-time transmission of audio and video.

FusionNet service can be provided over a single ISDN B channel. This is possible because the ISP (Internet service provider) provides ISDN access equipment that seamlessly merges the guaranteed QOS audio/video signal with normal Internet traffic to and from the user via PPP (point-to-point protocol) over dialed-up ISDN connections. Unless the traffic at the local ISP is very high, this method provides high-quality FusionNet service with a single ISDN B channel. Of course, additional B channels can always be ganged together for higher quality service.

V. MPEG-4

Most recently, the focus of video coding has shifted to *object-based coding* at rates as low as 8 kbits/s or lower and as high as 1 Mbit/s or higher. Key aspects of this newly proposed MPEG standard [32] include independent coding of objects in a picture; the ability to interactively composite these objects into a scene at the display; the ability to combine graphics, animated objects, and natural objects in the scene; and finally, the ability to transmit scenes in higher dimension formats (e.g., 3-D). Also inherent in the MPEG-4 standard is the concept of video scalability, both in the temporal and spatial domains, in order to effectively control the video bit rate at the transmitter, in the network, and at the receiver so as to match the available transmission and processing resources. MPEG-4 is scheduled to be finished essentially in 1998.

MPEG-4 builds on and combines elements from three fields: digital television, interactive graphics, and the World Wide Web. It aims to provide a merging of the production, distribution, and display elements of these three fields. In particular, it is expected that MPEG-4 will provide:

- multimedia content in a form that is reusable, with the capability and flexibility of incorporating on-the-fly piece parts from anywhere and at any time the application desires;
- protection mechanisms for intellectual property rights associated with that content;
- content transportation with a quality of service (QOS) custom tailored to each component;
- high levels of user interaction, with some control features being provided by the multimedia itself and others available locally at the receiving terminal.

The design of MPEG-4 is centered around a basic unit of content called the *audio-visual object* (AVO). Examples of AVO's are a musician (in motion) in an orchestra, the sound generated by that musician, the chair she is sitting on, the (possibly moving) background behind the orchestra, explanatory text for the current passage, etc. In MPEG-4, each AVO is represented separately, and becomes the basis for an independent stream.

In order for a viewer to receive a selection that can be seen on a display and heard through loudspeakers, the AVO's must be transmitted from a storage (or live) site. Since some AVO's may have an extremely long duration, it is usually undesirable to send each one separately in its entirety one after the other. Instead, some AVO's are *multiplexed* together and sent simultaneously so that replay can commence shortly after transmission begins. Other AVO's needing a different QOS can be multiplexed and sent on another transmission path that is able to provide that QOS.

Upon arrival of the AVO's, they must be assembled or *composed* into an audio-visual *scene*. In general, the scene may be three dimensional. Since some of the AVO's, such as moving persons or music, involve real-time portrayal, proper time synchronization must also be provided.

AVO's can be arbitrarily composed. For example, the musicians could be moved around to achieve special effects, e.g., one could choose to see and hear only the trumpet section. Alternatively, it would be possible to delete the drummer (and the resulting drum audio component), leaving the rest of the band so that the viewer could play along on his own drums. Fig. 9 illustrates scene composition in MPEG-4.

Following composition of a 3-D scene, the visual AVO's must be projected onto a viewer plane for display, and the audio AVO's must be combined for playing through loudspeakers or headphones. This process is called *rendering*. In principle, rendering does not require standardization. All that is needed is a view point and a window size.

A. MPEG-4 Multiplex [33]

The transmission of coded real-time AVO's from one or more sources to a destination is accomplished through the two-layer multiplex shown in Fig. 10. Each coded *elementary* AVO is assigned to an *elementary stream*. The FlexMux layer then groups together elementary streams (ES's) having similar QOS requirements to form *FlexMux streams*. The TransMux layer then provides transport services matched to the required QOS of each FlexMux stream. TransMux can be any of the existing transport protocols such as (UDP)/IP, (AAL5)/ATM, MPEG-2 Transport Stream, etc. It is not standardized by MPEG-4 (as yet).

B. MPEG-4 Systems

The systems part of MPEG-4 specifies the overall architecture of a general receiving terminal. Fig. 11 shows the major elements. FlexMux streams coming from the network are passed to appropriate FlexMux demultiplexers that produce elementary streams (ES). The ES's are then syntactically decoded into intermediate data such as motion vectors and DCT coefficients and then passed to appropriate decompressors that produce the final AVO's, which are composed and rendered into the final display.

To place the AVO's into a scene (composition), their spatial and temporal relationships (the scene structure) must be known. For example, the scene structure may be defined by a multimedia author or interactively by the end viewer. Alternatively, it could be defined by one or more network elements

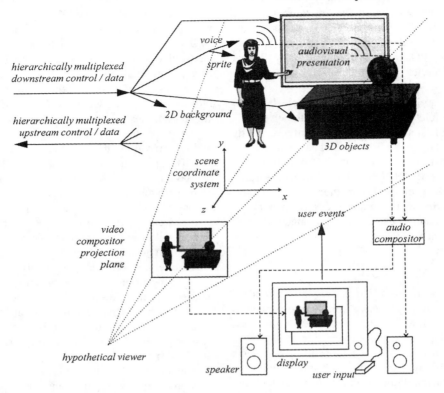

Fig. 9.   Example of an MPEG-4 scene (courtesy of MPEG Systems Group).

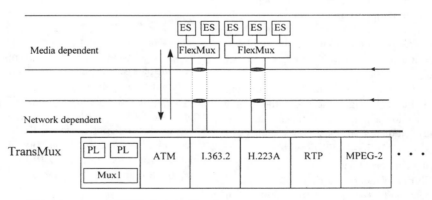

Fig. 10.   MPEG-4 two-layer multiplex (courtesy of MPEG Systems Group).

that manage multiple sources and multipoint communication between them. In any event, the composition part of MPEG-4 systems specifies the methodology for defining this structure.

Temporally, all AVO's have a single time dimension. For real-time, high-quality operation, end-to-end delay from the encoder input to the decoder output should be constant. However, at low bit rates or operation over lossy networks, the ideal of constant delay may have to be sacrificed. This delay is the sum of encoding (including video frame dropping), encoder buffering, multiplexing, communication or storage, demultiplexing, decoder buffering, decoding (including frame repeating), and presentation delays.

The transmitted data streams must contain either implicit or explicit timing information. As in MPEG-1 and MPEG-2, there

are two kinds of timing information. One indicates periodic values of the encoder clock, while the other tells the desired presentation timing for each AVO. Either one is optional, and if missing, must be provided by the receiver compositor.

Spatially, each AVO has its own *local coordinate system*, which serves to describe local behavior independent of the scene or any other AVO's. AVO's are placed in a scene by specifying (possibly dynamic) coordinate transformations from the local coordinate systems into a common *scene coordinate system*, as shown in Fig. 9. Note that the coordinate transformations, which position AVO's in a scene, are part of the scene structure, not the AVO. Thus, object motion in the scene is the motion specified locally by the AVO plus the motion specified by the dynamic coordinate transformations.

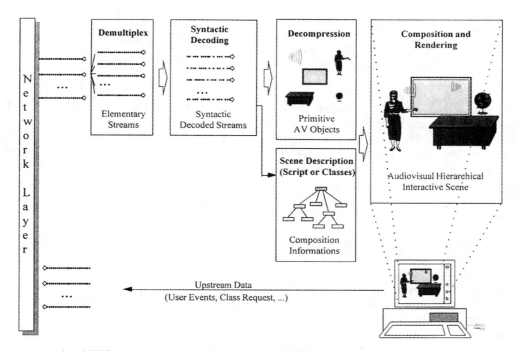

Fig. 11. Major components of an MPEG-4 terminal (receiver side) (courtesy of MPEG Systems Group).

The scene description is sent as a separate elementary stream. This allows for relatively simple bit-stream editing, one of the central functionalities in MPEG-4. In bit-stream editing, we want to be able to change the composition and scene structure without decoding the AVO bit streams and changing their content.

In order to increase the power of editing and scene manipulation even further, the MPEG-4 scene structure may be defined hierarchically and represented as a tree. Each node of the tree is an AVO, as illustrated in Fig. 12. Nodes at the leaves of the tree are *primitive nodes*. Nodes that are parents of one or more other nodes are *compound nodes*. Primitive nodes may have elementary streams assigned to them, whereas compound nodes are of use mainly in editing and compositing.

In the tree, each AVO is positioned in the local coordinate system of its parent AVO. The tree structure may be dynamic, i.e., the positions can change with time, and nodes may be added or deleted. The information describing the relationships between parent nodes and children nodes is sent in the elementary stream assigned to the scene description.

C. Natural 2-D Motion Video [34]

MPEG-4 coding for natural video will, of course, perform efficient compression of traditional video camera signals for storage and transmission in multimedia environments. However, it will also provide tools that enable a number of other functionalities such as object scalability, spatial and temporal scalability, sprite overlays, error resilience, etc. MPEG-4 video will be capable of coding both conventional rectangular video as well as well as arbitrarily shaped 2-D objects in a video scene. The MPEG-4 video standard will be able to code video ranging from very low spatial and temporal resolutions in progressive scanning format up to very high spatial and temporal resolutions for professional studio applications, including

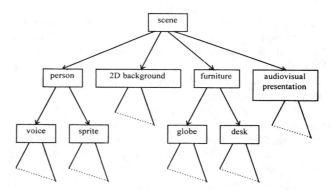

Fig. 12. Logical structure of the scene (courtesy of MPEG Systems Group).

interlaced video. The input frame rate can be nonuniform, including single picture input, which is considered as a special case.

The basic video AVO is called a *video object* (VO). If the VO is *scalable*, it may be split up, coded, and sent in two or more *video object layers* (VOL). One of these VOL's is called the *base layer*, which all terminals must receive in order to display any kind of video. The remaining VOL's are called *enhancement layers*, which may be expendable in case of transmission errors or restricted transmission capacity. For example, in a broadcast application transmitting to a variety of terminals having different processing capabilities or whose connections to the network are at different bit rates, some of the receiving terminals might receive all of the VOL's, while others may receive only a few, while still others may receive only the base layer VOL.

In a scalable video object, the VO is a compound AVO that is the parent of two or more child VOL's. Each VOL is a primitive AVO, and is carried by a separate elementary stream.

A snapshot in time of a video object layer is called a *video object plane* (VOP). For rectangular video, this corresponds to a *picture* in MPEG-1 and MPEG-2 or a *frame* in other standards. However, in general, the VOP can have an arbitrary shape.

The VOP is the basic unit of coding, and is made up of luminance (Y), and chrominance (Cb, Cr) components plus shape information. The shape and location of VOP's may vary from one VOP to the next. The shape may be conveyed either implicitly or explicitly. With implicit shape coding, the irregularly shaped object is simply placed in front of a (say, blue–green) colored background known to the receiver, and a rectangular VOP containing both object and background is coded and transmitted. The decoder retrieves the object by simple chroma keying, as in H.263+.

Explicit shape is represented by a rectangular *alpha plane* that covers the object to be coded [35]. An alpha plane may be *binary* (0 for transparent, 1 for object) if only the shape is of interest, or it may be *gray level* (up to 8 bits/pixel) to indicate various levels of partial transparency for the object. If the alpha plane has a constant gray value inside the object area, that value can be sent separately and the alpha plane coded as a binary alpha plane. Blending the alpha map near the object boundary is not supported by the video decoder since this is a composition issue.

Binary alpha planes are coded as a bitmap one macroblock at a time using a context-based arithmetic encoder with motion compensation. In the case of arbitrary gray-level alpha planes, the outline of the object is coded as a binary shape as above, while the gray levels are coded using DCT and motion compensation.

Coding of texture for an arbitrarily shaped region whose shape is described with an alpha map is different from traditional methods. Techniques are borrowed from both H.263 and earlier MPEG standards. For example, intraframe coding, forward prediction motion compensation, and bidirectional motion compensation are used. This gives rise to the definitions of I-VOP's, P-VOP's, and B-VOP's for VOP's that are intra coded, forward predicted, or bidirectionally predicted, respectively. For boundary blocks, i.e., blocks that are only partially covered by the arbitrarily shaped VOP, the texture of the object is extrapolated to cover the background part of the block. This process is called *padding*, and is used for efficient temporal prediction from boundary blocks in temporally adjacent pictures.

Fig. 13 shows the block diagram of this object-based video coder. In contrast to the block diagram shown in the MPEG-4 standard, this diagram focuses on the object-based mode in order to allow a better understanding of how shape coding influences the encoder and decoder. Image analysis creates the bounding box for the current VOP S_k and estimates texture and shape motion of S_k with respect to the reference VOP S'_{k-1}. Shape motion vectors of transparent macroblocks are set to 0. Parameter coding encodes the parameters predictively. The parameters are transmitted, decoded, and the new reference VOP is stored in the VOP memory and also handed to the compositor of the receiver for display.

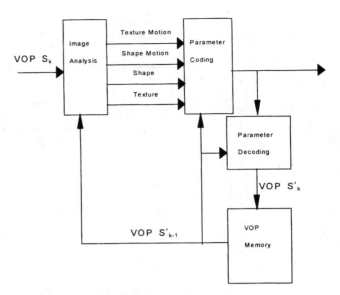

Fig. 13.   Block diagram of MPEG-4 object-based coder for arbitrary-shaped video objects.

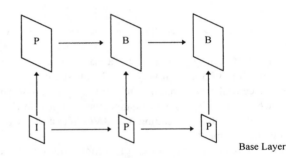

Base Layer

Fig. 14.   Spatial scalability with two layers (courtesy MPEG Video Group).

The parameter coder encodes first the shape of the boundary blocks using shape and texture motion vectors for prediction. Then shape motion vectors are coded. The shape motion coder knows which motion vectors to code by analyzing the possibly lossily encoded shape parameters. For texture prediction, the reference VOP is padded as described above. The prediction error is then padded using the original shape parameters to determine the area to be padded. Using the original shape as a reference for padding is again an encoder choice. Finally, the texture of each macroblock is encoded using DCT.

1) Multifunctional Coding Tools and Algorithms: Multifunctional coding refers to features other than coding efficiency. For example, object based spatial and temporal scalabilities are provided to enable broad-based access over a variety of networks and facilities. This can be useful for Internet and database applications. Also, for mobile multimedia applications, spatial and temporal scalabilities are extremely useful for channel bandwidth scaling for robust delivery. Spatial scalability with two layers is shown in Fig. 14. Temporal scalability with two layers is shown in Fig. 15.

Multifunctional coding also addresses multiview and stereoscopic applications, as well as representations that enable simultaneous coding and tracking of objects for surveillance

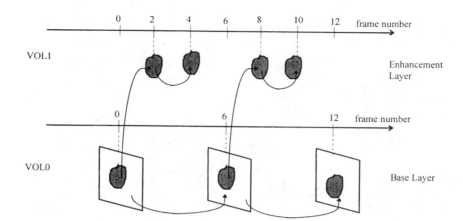

Fig. 15.   Temporal scalability with two layers (courtesy MPEG Video Group).

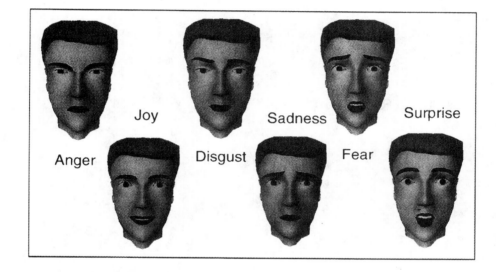

Fig. 16.   Examples of facial expressions as defined by MPEG-4.

and other applications. Besides the aforementioned applications, a number of tools are being developed for segmentation of a video scene into objects and for coding noise suppression.

2) Error Resilience: Error resilience is needed, to some extent, in all transmission media. In particular, due to the rapid growth of mobile communications, it is extremely important that audio and video information is sent successfully via wireless networks. These networks are typically error prone and usually operate at relatively low bit rates., e.g., less than 64 kbits/s. Both MPEG and the ITU-T are working on error resilience methods, including forward error correction (FEC), automatic request for retransmission (ARQ), scalable coding, slice-based bit-stream partitioning, and motion-compensated error correction [36].

D. Synthetic Images

Several efforts are underway to provide synthetic image capabilities in MPEG-4. There is no wish to reinvent existing graphics standards. Thus, MPEG-4 uses the Virtual Reality Modeling Language (VRML) as a starting point for its synthetic image specification. MPEG-4 will add a number of additional capabilities plus predictable performance at the receiving terminal.

The first addition is a synthetic *face and body* (FAB) animation capability, which is a model-independent definition of artificial face and body animation parameters. With these parameters, one can represent facial expressions, body positions, mouth shapes, etc. Fig. 16 shows examples of facial expressions defined by MPEG-4, and Fig. 17 shows the feature points of a face that can be animated using MPEG-4 face animation parameters. The FAB model to be animated can be either resident in the receiver or a model that is completely downloaded by the transmitting application.

Capabilities include 3-D feature point positions, 3-D head and body control meshes for animation, texture mapping of face and body, and personal characteristics. MPEG-4 employs a text-driven mouth animation combined with a text-to-speech synthesizer for a complete text-to-talking-head implementation.

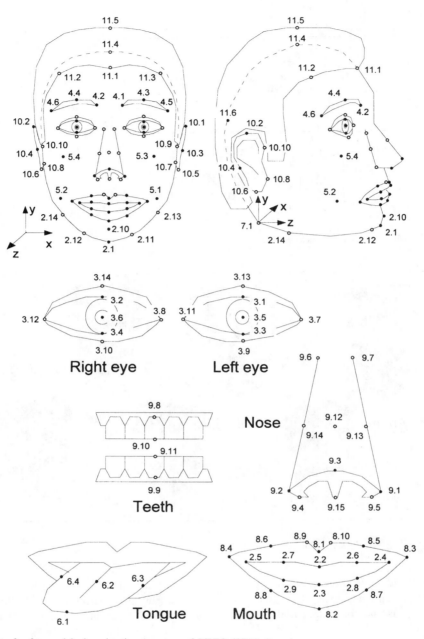

Fig. 17.   Head control points for face and body animation (courtesy of MPEG SNHC Group).

Another capability is for texture mapping of real image information onto artificial models such as the FAB model. For this, wavelet-based texture coding is provided. An advantage of wavelet based coding is the relative ease of adjusting the resolution of the visual information to match the requirements of the rendering. For example, if an object is being composed at a distance far from the viewer, then it is not necessary to send the object with high resolution.

Associated with this is a triangular mesh-modeling capability to handle any type of 2-D or 3-D synthetic or natural shape. This also facilitates integration of text and graphics onto synthetic and natural imagery. For example, putting text onto a moving natural object requires a tracking of features on the natural object, which is made easier by a mesh-based representation of the object.

VI. Conclusion of MPEG-4 and Launching of MPEG-7

In summary, MPEG-4 will integrate most of the capabilities and features of multimedia into one standard, including live audio/video, synthetic objects, and text, all of which can be combined on-the-fly. Multipoint conversations can be facilitated by displays tailored to each viewer of group of viewers. Multimedia presentations can be sent to auditoriums, offices, homes, and mobiles with delivery scaled to the capabilities of the various receivers.

However, MPEG-4 is not the end. Plans are now underway to begin MPEG-7, which is aimed at the definition of audiovisual (AV) multimedia features for purposes such as searching large databases, identification, authentication, cataloging, etc. This phase of MPEG [37] is scheduled for completion essentially in 2000.

MPEG-7 is aiming at the description of content. Some of the ideas and applications are still a little vague, but at its simplest, the content will be described simply by text. For example, "dozens of trees," "six horses," "two cowboys," or "the Queen of England." This would allow classification and searching either by category or by specific naming.

A little more complicated could be the notes of a musical selection. For example, B flat, G sharp, or, in fact, the audio waveform itself. Then you could search for a song you wanted to purchase by singing a few notes. Or businesses could search for copyright infringements by comparing parts of songs with each other.

Now, with a lot more computational complexity comes the hope to be able to specify pictorial features in some parametric way. For example, much work has gone into describing human faces by the positions of eyes, nostrils, chins, cheeks, ears, etc. And for purposes of recognition, at least, we need a representation that is independent of hair color, beards, and mustaches. For children, we would like a representation that is useful even as the child grows.

For marketing applications, we would like to be able find the dress that has a collar that is "sort of shaped like this" and shoulders that "sort of look like this." I would like to be able to stand in front of a camera, and request a necktie that goes with the shirt and sweater I am wearing. I could show a picture of my house. Then I could ask for some flower seeds that would grow into flowers with just the right shape and just the right color.

We also expect MPEG-7 to make it much easier to create multimedia content. For example, if you need a video clip of a talking bird, we want it to be easy to find. Then you simply type or speak the words you want the bird to say, and the talking bird will be instantly added to your program. The possibilities for this technology are limited only by our imagination.

A. MPEG-7 Requirements and Terminology

MPEG-7 aims to standardize a set of multimedia description schemes and descriptors, as well as ways of specifying new description schemes and descriptors. MPEG-7 will also address the coding of these descriptors and description schemes. Some of the terminology (not finalized) needed by MPEG-7 includes the following.

Data—AV information that will be described using MPEG-7, regardless of the storage, coding, display, transmission, medium, or technology. This definition is intended to be sufficiently broad to encompass text, film, and any other medium. For example, an MPEG-4 stream, a videotape, or a paper book.

Feature—A feature is a distinctive part or characteristic of the data which stands for something to somebody in some respect or capacity. Examples might be the color of an image, but also its style, or the author.

Descriptor—A descriptor is a formal semantic for associating a representation value to one or more features. Note: it is possible to have multiple representations for a single feature. Examples might be a time code for representing duration, or both color moments and histograms for representing color.

Description Scheme—The description scheme defines a structure of descriptors and their relationships.

Description—A description is the entity describing the AV data that consist of description schemes and descriptors.

Coded description—Coded description is a compressed description allowing easy indexing, efficient storage, and transmission.

MPEG-7 aims to support a number of audio and visual descriptions, including free text, N-dimensional spatiotemporal structure, statistical information, objective attributes, subjective attributes, production attributes, and composition information. For visual information, descriptions will include color, visual objects, texture, sketch, shape, volume, spatial relations, motion, and deformation.

MPEG-7 also aims to support a means to describe multimedia material hierarchically according to abstraction levels of information in order to efficiently represent a user's information need at different levels. It should allow queries based on visual descriptions to retrieve audio data and vice versa. It should support the prioritization of features in order that queries may be processed more efficiently. The priorities may denote a level of confidence, reliability, etc. MPEG-7 intends to support the association of descriptors to different temporal ranges, both hierarchically as well as sequentially.

MPEG-7 aims to be effective (you get what you are looking for and not other stuff) and efficient (you get what you are looking for, quickly) retrieval of multimedia data based on their contents, whatever the semantic involved.

B. New Technology for Multimedia (MM)

In order to achieve to grand goals of MPEG-7, an enormous amount of new technology needs to be invented. For example, a quantum leap in image understanding algorithms will have to take place, including motion analysis, zoom and pan compensation, foreground–background segmentation, texture modeling, etc.

Some of this technology may be useful for compression coding as well. For example, corresponding to preprocessing and analysis at the transmitter is "synthesis" and "postprocessing" at the receiver.

We need to keep in mind that in our assumed applications, the viewer cannot see the original (MM) information. If a viewer can tell the difference between image information and noise, then so should a very smart postprocessor. For example, many objects have known shape and color. No picture should ever be displayed that has the wrong shape for known objects.

MPEG-7 will find its greatest use on the Internet. On the Internet itself, browsers have become a very popular human interface to deal with the intricacies of database searching.

Bulletin boards of many types offer a huge variety of material, most of it at no additional charge. Multimedia will soon follow.

One of the favorite applications for the global information infrastructure (GII) is home shopping. And from this, we can expect such benefits as virtual stores, search agents, automated reservations, complex services being turned into commodities, specialized services tailored to the individual, and so on, and so on. Commercials ought to be tuned to the user, not the other way around.

Being able to connect to everyone means we will have the usual crowd of (let us say) entrepreneurs trying to get your money. There is no way to tell what is true and what is false just by reading it. Security tools are available if users choose to use them. Anonymity ought to be possible. Impersonation ought to be impossible.

If all of this come to pass, there will be a frightening overload of MM information. We will all be inundated. Today's MM information handling is rather primitive, involving many manual operations for creation and assimilation.

We need automated ways to identify and describe the content of audio, video, text, graphics, numerical data, software, etc. This should involve as little human interaction as possible. Algorithms for MM understanding should disect the MM objects into their constituent parts, identify them, and provide labels. Required technologies include audio speech recognition, video scene analysis, text concept identification, software capability detection, automatic closed captioning, etc.

Given descriptions of MM objects, we want to create databases and catalogs with index information, automatically search for relationships between MM objects and include these in catalog, distribute catalog index information, check for obsolescence, and delete old objects.

We want to automatically determine the quality, technical level, timeliness, and relevance of each MM object. Authenticity should also be checked at this stage. We would like to produce metrics for novelty, utility, redundancy, boredom, etc., tailored to the individual user. We should give feedback to author/creators of an MM object as a straw poll of usefulness.

Database search engines should discover nonredundant, high-quality MM objects of a technical level matched appropriately to the user. These should be combined, using hyperwhatever "glue," into a meaningful, enjoyable, and exciting program.

We want machine-assisted or automatic authoring/creation of MM objects, including database search for MM piece parts useful for current creation, interaction with a quality checker to maintain utility and nonredundancy. Then check that all technical levels are covered.

We would like edutainment capabilities for motivation building customized to the user. This is especially needed for children. We have to compete with MM games and entertainment. We need interactive measures of attention. We need reward mechanisms for cooperation and success.

We would like tools for audio/video speed up or slow down, along with audio gap removal. This can turn a one hour slow talk into a half hour fast-paced talk.

There will be problems of intellectual property rights. The problem of copyrights and patents might be solved by downloadable software that can only be executed or watched once. After that, it self destructs or times out. Another solution is to uniquely label each piece of software so that if a violation is detected, you will know who made the original purchase. This is all reminiscent of the advent of the copying machine. In the early days, lots of copying was illegal, but you could only catch the blatant violators. The motto may be (as in many parts of life), "if you won't get caught, go ahead and do it."

Which brings us to our final topic, virtuous virtuosos. It may turn out that we will see some "unvirtuous" behavior on the GII. Now, should there be any limits on MM GII traffic? Well, the liberals will say no, it is just like a bookstore. The conservatives will say yes, it is like broadcast television. It is clearly a hard question. Violence has been in movies for a long time, the objective being to scare the daylights out of you. Some of the recent computer games are pretty violent too, and I guess the appeal there is to your aggressions... or hostility... or maybe even hatreds?? We can see the day when hate groups use MM games to spread their propaganda. Even now, such messages as, "your grandfather committed genocide" can be found.

Some networks today have censors, both unofficial and unofficial. On some networks, anyone can censor. If you see a message you do not like, you can delete it. Or you can issue a "cancelbot" that looks for a message from a certain individual or organization, and cancels all of them. This might be considered antisocial, but the current paradigm seems to allow it as long as you announce to everyone that you have done it. If there are only a few objections, then it seems to be okay.

Well, what of the future? It is not hard to predict the technical possibilities. Just read Jules Verne. But it is extremely hard to predict exactly when, and at what cost. Herein lies our problem and our opportunity. However, we *are* sure of one thing, and that is that communication standards will make the new technology happen sooner and at a lower cost.

ACKNOWLEDGMENT

The original work described in this paper was done by a number of individuals at AT&T Laboratories as well as outside of AT&T. The authors would like to acknowledge both the strong contributions to the literature, as well as the fine work done by the following individuals, as reported on in this paper: video coding: T. Chen, A. Reibman, R. Schmidt; streaming: D. Gibbon; FusionNet: G. Cash; DJVU: P. Simard.

REFERENCES

[1] R. Cox, B. Haskell, Y. LeCun, B. Shahraray, and L. Rabiner, "On the applications of multimedia processing to communications," *Proc. IEEE*, vol. 86, pp. 755–824, May 1998.
[2] A. N. Netravali and B. G. Haskell, *Digital Pictures-Representation, Compression, and Standards*, 2nd ed. New York: Plenum, 1995.
[3] K. R. McConnell, D. Bodson, and R. Schaphorst, *Fax, Digital Facsimile Technology and Applications.* Boston, MA: Artech House, 1992.
[4] W. B. Pennebaker and J. L. Mitchell, "Other image compression standards," in *JPEG Still Image Data Compression Standard.* New York: Van Nostrand Reinhold, 1993, ch. 20.
[5] ISO/IEC International Standard 11544, "Progressive bi-level image compression," 1993.

[6] K. Mohiudin, J. J. Rissanan, and R. Arps, "Lossless binary image compression based on pattern matching," in *Proc. Int. Conf. Comput., Syst., Signal Processing*, Bangalore, India, 1984.

[7] P. G. Howard, "Lossy and lossless compression of text images by soft pattern matching," in *Proc. Data Compression Conf.*, J. A. Storer and M. Cohn, Eds., Snowbird, UT, IEEE Press, 1996, pp. 210–219.

[8] R. N. Ascher and G. Nagy, "A means for achieving a high degree of compaction on scan-digitized printed text," *IEEE Trans. Comput.*, pp. 1174–1179, Nov. 1974.

[9] P. G. Howard, "Text image compression using soft pattern matching," *Comput. J.*, 1997.

[10] G. K. Wallace, "The JPEG still picture compression standard," *IEEE Trans. Consumer Electron.*, Dec. 1991.

[11] ISO/IEC International Standard 10918-1, "Digital compression and coding of continuous-tone still images," 1991.

[12] W. B. Pennebaker and J. L. Mitchell, *JPEG Still Image Data Compression Standard*. New York: Van Nostrand Reinhold, 1993.

[13] ISO/IEC JTC1/SC29/WG1 N505, "Call for contributions for JPEG-2000," 1997.

[14] A. Said and W. Pearlman, "A new, fast, and efficient image codec based on set partitioning in hierarchical trees," *IEEE Trans. Circuits Syst. Video Technol.*, vol. 6, June 3, 1996.

[15] M. Vetterli and J. Kovacevic, *Wavelets and Subband Coding*. Englewood Cliffs, NJ: Prentice-Hall, 1995.

[16] P. Haffner, L. Bottou, P. G. Howard, P. Simard, Y. Bengio, and Y. L. Cun, "Browsing through high quality document images with DJVU," presented at the Advances in Digital Libraries Conf., IEEE ADL '98, U.C. Santa Barbara, Apr. 21–24, 1998.

[17] ITU-T Recommendation T.44, "Mixed raster content (MRC) colour mode."

[18] J. L. Mitchell, W. B. Pennebaker, C. E. Fogg, and D. J. LeGall, *MPEG Video Compression Standard*. New York: Chapman & Hall, 1997.

[19] H.-M. Hang and J. W. Woods, *Handbook of Visual Communications*. New York: Academic, 1995.

[20] ITU-T Recommendation H.261, "Video codec for audiovisual services at p*64 kbits/sec."

[21] ITU-T Recommendation H.263, "Video coding for low bit rate communication."

[22] B. G. Haskell, A. Puri, and A. N. Netravali, *Digital Video: An Introduction to MPEG-2*. New York: Chapman & Hall, 1997.

[23] ITU-T Recommendation H.324, "Line transmissions of non-telephone signals—Terminal for low bit rate multimedia communication."

[24] A. Puri, R. Aravind, and B. G. Haskell, "Adaptive frame/field motion compensated video coding," *Signal Processing Image Commun.*, vol. 1–5, pp. 39–58, Feb. 1993.

[25] V. G. Devereux, "Digital chroma-key," in *IBC 84, Int. Broadcasting Conv. (Proc. 240)*, Brighton, U.K., Sept. 21–25, 1984, pp. 148–152.

[26] U.S. Advanced Television Systems Committee, "Digital television standard for HDTV transmission," ATSC Standard Doc. A/53, Apr. 1995.

[27] H. Schulzrinne, A. Rao, and R. Lanphier, "Real-time streaming protocol (RTSP)," Internet Draft, draft-ietf-mmusic-rtsp-01.txt, Feb. 1997.

[28] H. Schulzeinne, S. Casner, R. Frederick, and V. Jacobson, "RTP: A transport protocol for real-time applications," IETF RFC 1889, Jan. 1996.

[29] "Resource reservation protocol (RSVP)—Version 1, Functional specification," R. Braden, Ed., L. Zhang, S. Berson, S. Herzog, and S. Jamin, Internet Draft, draft-ietf-rsvp-spec-14.txt, Nov. 1996.

[30] 30. C. Huitema, *IPv6: The New Internet Protocol*. Englewood Cliffs, NJ: Prentice-Hall, 1996.

[31] M. R. Civanlar, G. L. Cash, and B. G. Haskell, "FusionNet: Joining the internet and phone networks for multimedia applications," in *ACM Multimedia Proc.*, Boston, MA, Nov. 1996.

[32] Special Issue on MPEG-4, *Signal Processing: Image Commun.*, vol. 9, May 1997 and vol. 10, July 1997.

[33] International Organization for Standardization, Final Committee Draft ISO/IEC 14496-2, "Coding of audio-visual objects: Systems."

[34] International Organization for Standardization, Final Committee Draft ISO/IEC 14496-2, "Coding of audio-visual objects: Visual."

[35] G. Privat and I. Le-Hin, "Hardware support for shape decoding from 2D-region-based image representations," in *Multimedia Hardware Architectures 1997, Proc. SPIE*, San Jose, CA, vol. 3021, 1997, pp. 149–159.

[36] S.-L. Wee, M. R. Pickering, M. R. Frater, and J. F. Arnold, "Error resilience in video and multiplexing layers for very low bit-rate video coding systems," *IEEE J. Select. Areas Commun.*, vol. 15, pp. 1764–1774, Dec. 1997.

[37] MPEG Requirements Group, "MPEG-7: Context and objectives," Doc. ISO/MPEG N1733; also, "Applications for MPEG-7," Doc. ISO/MPEG N1735, MPEG Stockholm Meeting, July 1997.

Barry G. Haskell (S'65–M'68–SM'76–F'87) received the B.S., M.S., and Ph.D. degrees in electrical engineering from the University of California, Berkeley in 1964, 1965, and 1968, respectively.

From 1964 to 1968 he was a Research Assistant in the University of California Electronics Research Laboratory, with one summer being spent at the Lawrence Livermore Laboratory. From 1968 to 1996 he was at AT&T Bell Laboratories, Holmdel, NJ. Since 1996 he has been at AT&T Labs, Middletown, NJ, where he is presently Division Manager of the Image Processing and Software Technology Research Department. He has also served as Adjunct Professor of Electrical Engineering at Rutgers University, City College of New York and Columbia University.

Since 1984, Dr. Haskell has been very active in the establishment of International Video Communications Standards. These include International Telecommunications Union—Telecommunications Sector (ITU-T) for Video Conferencing Standards (H-series), ISO Joint Photographic Experts Group (JPEG) for still images, ISO Joint Bilevel Image Group (JBIG) for documents and ISO Moving Picture Experts Group (MPEG) for Digital Television. His research interests include digital transmission and coding of images, videotelephone, satellite television transmission, medical imaging as well as most other applications of digital image processing. He has published over 60 papers on these subjects and has over 40 patents either granted or pending. He is also coauthor of the books: *Image Transmission Techniques*, Academic Press, 1979; *Digital Pictures—Representation and Compression*, Plenum Press, 1988; *Digital Pictures—Representation, Compression and Standards*, Plenum Press 1995 and *Digital Video—An Introduction to MPEG-2*, Chapman and Hall, 1997.

In 1997 Dr. Haskell won (with Arun Netravali) Japan's prestigious C&C (Computer & Communications) Prize for his research in video data compression. In 1998 he received the Outstanding Alumnus Award from the University of California, Berkeley Department of Electrical Engineering and Computer Science. He is a member of Phi Beta Kappa and Sigma Xi.

Paul G. Howard received the B.S. degree in computer science from M.I.T. in 1977, and the M.S. and Ph.D. degrees from Brown University in 1989 and 1993, respectively.

He was briefly a Research Associate at Duke University before joining AT&T Labs (then known as AT&T Bell Laboratories) in 1993. He is a Principal Technical Staff Member at AT&T Labs-Research. He is a member of JBIG, the ISO Joint Bi-level Image Experts Group, and an editor of the emerging JBIG2 standard. His research interests are in data compression, including coding, still image modeling, and text modeling.

Yann A. LeCun (S'87–M'87) received the Diplome d'Ingenieur from the Ecole Superieure d'Ingenieur en Electrotechnique et Electronique, Paris in 1983, and the Ph.D. degree in computer science from the Université Pierre et Marie Curie, Paris, in 1987.

He then joined the Department of Computer Science at the University of Toronto as a Research Associate. In 1988, he joined the Adaptive Systems Research Department at AT&T Bell Laboratories in Holmdel, NJ, where he worked among other things on neural networks, machine learning, and handwriting recognition. In 1996, he became head of the Image Processing Services Research Department at AT&T Labs-Research. He has published over 70 technical papers and book chapters on neural networks, machine learning, pattern recognition, handwriting recognition, document understanding, image processing, image compression, VLSI design, and information theory. In addition to the above topics, his current interests include video-based user interfaces, document image compression, and content-based indexing of multimedia material.

Dr. LeCun is serving on the board of the *Machine Learning Journal*, and has served as Associate Editor of the IEEE TRANSACTIONS ON NEURAL NETWORKS. He is general chair of the "Machines that Learn" workshop. He has served as program co-chair of IJCNN 89, INNC 90, NIPS 90, 94, and 95. He is a member of the IEEE Neural Network for Signal Processing Technical Committee.

Atul Puri (S'87–M'85) received the B.S. degree in electrical engineering in 1980, the M.S. degree in electrical engineering from the City College of New York in 1982, and the Ph.D. degree, also in electrical engineering, from the City University of New York in 1988.

While working on his dissertation, he was a Consultant in Visual Communications Research Department of Bell labs and gained experience in developing algorithms, software and hardware for video communications. In 1988 he joined the same department at Bell labs as a Member of Technical staff. Since 1996, he has been a Principal Member of Technical Staff in Image Processing Research Department of AT&T Labs, Red Bank, NJ. He has represented AT&T at the Moving Pictures Experts Group Standard for past ten years and has actively contributed toward development of the MPEG-1, the MPEG-2, and the MPEG-4 audio–visual coding standards. Currently, he is participating in Video and Systems part of the MPEG-4 standard and is one of its technical editors. He has been involved in research in video coding algorithms for a number of diverse applications such as videoconferencing, video on Digital Storage Media, HDTV, and 3D-TV. His current research interests are in the area of flexible multimedia systems and services for web/internet. He holds over 14 patents and has applied for another 8 patents. He has published over 30 technical papers in conferences and journals, including several invited papers. He is a coauthor of a book entitled *Digital Video: An Introduction to MPEG-2*. He is currently coediting a book on multimedia systems.

Dr. Puri has been the recipient of exceptional contribution and individual performance merit awards of AT&T. Furthermore, he has also received awards from the AT&T Communications Services and AT&T Technical Journal. He is a member of the IEEE Communication and Signal Processing societies and was recently appointed as an Associate Editor of IEEE TRANSACTIONS ON CIRCUITS AND SYSTEMS FOR VIDEO TECHNOLOGY.

Lawrence Rabiner (S'62–M'67–SM'75–F'76) was born in Brooklyn, NY, on September 28, 1943. He received the S.B. and S.M. degrees simultaneously in June 1964 and the Ph.D. degree in electrical engineering in June 1967, all from the Massachusetts Institute of Technology, Cambridge.

From 1962 through 1964, he participated in the cooperative program in Electrical Engineering at AT&T Bell Laboratories, Whippany and Murray Hill, NJ. During this period he worked on digital circuitry, military communications problems, and problems in binaural hearing. He joined AT&T Bell Labs in 1967 as a Member of the Technical Staff. He was promoted to Supervisor in 1972, Department Head in 1985, Director in 1990, and Functional Vice President in 1995. His research focused primarily on problems in speech processing and digital signal processing. Presently he is Speech and Image Processing Services Research Vice President at AT&T Labs, and is engaged in managing research on speech and image processing, and the associated hardware and software systems which support services based on these technologies. He is coauthor of the books *Theory and Application of Digital Signal Processing* (Prentice-Hall, 1975), *Digital Processing of Speech Signals* (Prentice-Hall, 1978), *Multirate Digital Signal Processing* (Prentice-Hall, 1983), and *Fundamentals of Speech Recognition* (Prentice-Hall, 1993).

Dr. Rabiner is a member of Eta Kappa Nu, Sigma Xi, Tau Beta Pi, the National Academy of Engineering, the National Academy of Sciences, and a Fellow of the Acoustical Society of America, Bell Laboratories, and AT&T. He is a former President of the IEEE Acoustics, Speech, and Signal Processing Society, a former Vice-President of the Acoustical Society of America, a former editor of the ASSP Transactions, and a former member of the IEEE Proceedings Editorial Board.

Jörn Ostermann (S'86–M'88) studied electrical engineering and communications engineering at the University of Hannover and Imperial College London, respectively. He received the Dipl.-Ing. and Dr.-Ing. degrees from the University of Hannover in 1988 and 1994, respectively. From 1988 till 1994, he worked as a Research Assistant at the Institut für Theoretische Nachrichtentechnik conducting research in low bit-rate and object-based analysis-synthesis video coding. 1994 and 1995 he worked in the Visual Communications Research Department at Bell Labs. Since 1996, he is with Image Processing and Technology Research within AT&T Labs-Research.

From 1993 to 1994, he chaired the European COST 211 sim group coordinating research in low bitrate video coding. Within MPEG-4, he organized the evaluation of video tools to start defining the standard. Currently, he chairs the Adhoc Group on Coding of Arbitrarily-shaped Objects in MPEG-4 Video.

His current research interests are video coding, computer vision, 3D modeling, face animation, coarticulation of acoustic and visual speech.

Leon Bottou received the Diplome degree from Ecole Polytechnique, Paris in 1987, the Magistére en Mathematiques Fondamentales et Appliquees et Informatiques degree from Ecole Normale Superieure, Paris in 1988, and the Ph.D. degree in computer science from Universite de Paris-Sud in 1991, during which he worked on speech recognition and proposed a framework for stochastic gradient learning and global training.

He then joined the Adaptive Systems Research Department at AT&T Bell Laboratories where he worked on neural networks, statistical learning theory, and local learning algorithms. He returned to France in 1992 as a Research Engineer at ONERA. He then became Chairman of Neuristique S.A. He returned to AT&T Bell Laboratories in 1995 where he worked on graph transformer networks for optical character recognition. He is now a member of the Image Processing Services Research Department at AT&T Labs-Research. Besides learning algorithms, his current interests include arithmetic coding, image compression and indexing.

M. Reha Civanlar (S'84–M'84) received the B.S. and M.S. degrees from Middle East Technical University, Turkey, and the Ph.D. degree from North Carolina State University, all in electrical engineering, in 1979, 1981, and 1984, respectively.

From 1984 to 1987, he was a Researcher in the Center for Communications and Signal Processing in NCSU where he worked on image processing, particularly restoration and reconstruction, image coding for low bit rate transmission, and data communications systems. In 1988, He joined Pixel Machines Department of AT&T Bell Laboratories, where he worked on parallel architectures and algorithms for image and volume processing and scientific visualization. Since 1991, he is a Member of Visual Communications Research Department of AT&T Bell Laboratories (renamed AT&T Laboratories-Research in 1996) working on various aspects of video communications. His current research interests include packet video systems, networked video and multimedia applications, video coding and digital data transmissions.

Dr. Civanlar is a Fulbright scholar and a member of Sigma Xi. He is an Editor for IEEE TRANSACTIONS ON COMMUNICATIONS and a member of IMDSP and MMSP technical committees of the Signal Processing Society of IEEE. He has numerous publications and 16 patents either granted or pending. He is a recipient of the 1985 Senior Award of the ASSP Society of IEEE.

Patrick Haffner graduated from Ecole Polytechnique, Paris, France in 1987 and from Ecole Nationale Superieure des Telecommunications (ENST), Paris, France in 1989. He received the Ph.D. degree in speech and signal processing from ENST in 1994.

From 1989 to 1995, as a Research Scientist for CNET/France-Telecom in Lannion, France, he developed connectionist learning algorithms for telephone speech recognition. In 1995, he joined AT&T Bell Laboratories. Since 1997, he has been with the Image processing Services Research Department at AT&T Labs-Research. His research interests include statistical and connectionist models for sequence recognition, machine learning, speech and image recognition, and information theory.

Comparison of International Standards for Lossless Still Image Compression

RONALD B. ARPS, MEMBER, IEEE, AND THOMAS K. TRUONG

Invited Paper

This overview focuses on a comparison of lossless compression capabilities of the international standard algorithms for still image compression known as MH, MR, MMR, JBIG, and JPEG. Where the algorithms have parameters to select, these parameters have been carefully set to achieve maximal compression. Compression variations due to differences in data are illustrated and scaling of these compression results with spatial resolution or amplitude precision are explored. These algorithms are also summarized in terms of the compression technology they utilize, with further references given for precise technical details and the specific international standards involved.

I. BACKGROUND

Image compression and its standardization has become a topic of increasing importance as image processing systems and applications come of age. Continuing cost improvements in computing power, storage and communications are making more and more such systems practical, with compression almost always included in order to achieve cost-effective solutions. With the increasing emphasis on "open" systems, standards come into play where image interchange is desired—not only between systems, but between the components within systems.

For example, the field of facsimile image transmission exploded after decades of prototypes and false starts, spurred by the advent of effective compression algorithms and their international standardization along with simultaneous technology cost reductions. Achieving standardized compressed image interchange between competing facsimile products was a critical factor in creating an extensive international market, which in turn generated the high volumes necessary for significant decreases in facsimile hardware costs.

The international standards to be compared here include the compression algorithms commonly called "Group 3"

Manuscript received November 1, 1993; revised January 15, 1994.

R. B. Arps is with Information Systems Laboratory, Department of Electrical Engineering, Stanford University, Stanford, CA, on sabbatical leave from IBM Research Division, Almaden Research Center, San Jose, CA 95120-6099 USA.

T. K. Truong is with IBM Research Division, Almaden Research Center, San Jose, CA 95120-6099 USA.

IEEE Log Number 9400878.

MH and MR [1], "Group 4" MMR [2], JBIG [3], and Lossless JPEG [4] (to be precisely defined below). They are all aimed at the subset of "still" image processing problems that require strictly *lossless* compression. By strictly lossless we mean compression algorithms that yield images after decompression that are identical, down to the last bit, with the digital images that were originally compressed.

Such algorithms contrast with another subset of image compression algorithms that are *lossy* (e.g. "Baseline JPEG"), which usually capitalize on the *a priori* assumption that their decompressed images will only be presented to the human eye. The lossless compression constraint may arise in applications where preserving exact fidelity is a technical or legal requirement (e.g., in satellite or medical image processing), or where some form of lossy compression has already occurred (e.g., the black/white thresholding done in digitizing facsimile images) and further loss may not be desirable.

Figure 1 illustrates lossless compression for a black/white business letter (JBIG "Stockholm" Test Image "s01" shown at 1/8 its actual size) when using four different international standard algorithms (MH, MR, MMR, and JBIG—defined below). The results for each algorithm are illustrated by organizing their compressed bits into pseudo-images, generated by representing these bits as black/white picture elements ("pel's"), filling an empty frame of the original image's dimensions with these pels at the top and reducing these to 1/8 actual size. The white, empty, lower part of each pseudo-image represents the compression saving achieved and a corresponding "compression ratio" R can be visualized as the ratio between the surface area occupied by the compressed pels S versus the total area of the original image.

II. DATA TYPES

Lossless algorithms rely solely on predictable characteristics of the *data* to be compressed (the data "source") in the design of their compression methods. This is in contrast

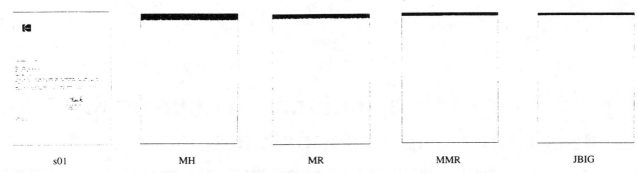

s01	MH	MR	MMR	JBIG

Fig. 1. Visualizing compression of business document (JBIG test image "s01" at 200 pels/in). s01: Rotated 180°. MH: $S = 4.93\%$ $(R = 20.28)$. MR: $S = 3.42\%$ $(R = 29.24)$. MMR: $S = 2.04\%$ $(R = 48.97)$. JBIG: $S = 1.60\%$ $(R = 62.52)$.

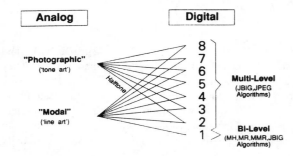

Fig. 2. Still image data types.

to lossy algorithms which also capitalize on predictable characteristics of projected *users* of the data (the data "sink") in their design. The analog data used to design the algorithms discussed here can be divided into two major types:

1) "photographic" data: analog data that predominantly yield *continuous* intensities (e.g., images of natural scenes) categorized in photography as "tone art," and
2) "modal" data: analog data that predominantly yield *discontinuous* intensities (e.g., images of man-made documents) categorized in photography as "line art."

The latter are typically analog images of documents printed or drawn using "information" of one intensity, superimposed on a "background" of another intensity. When the amplitudes of such images are histogrammed they can be characterized as having multimodal distributions (hence the name "modal" data).

The above analog data types are digitized with various amounts of amplitude precision, depending on system or application requirements (Fig. 2). The resulting digital image data can also be divided into two major categories, namely:

1) "multilevel" data: image data that have been digitized using more than two amplitude levels (2+ b/pel), and
2) "bi-level" data: image data that have been digitized using only two amplitude levels (1 b/pel).

Photographic data are sometimes quantized into only bi-level image data, using a digital "halftoning" process. This is generally done to prepare the data for output as hardcopy, typically produced using a printing process constrained to be bi-level. This is represented in Fig. 2 as photographic

data being digitized at only 1 b/pel. Figure 2 also indicates where the MH, MR, MMR, JBIG, and JPEG compression algorithms, to be discussed here, are applicable.

III. INTERNATIONAL STANDARDS

The international standards for lossless still image compression that we are aware of, have all been prepared by two organizations—the International Telegraph and Telephone Consultative Committee (CCITT)[1] and the International Organization for Standardization/International Electrotechnical Commission (ISO/IEC). The MH, MR, and MMR algorithms were prepared solely by the CCITT, whereas the JBIG and Lossless JPEG algorithms were prepared as joint efforts between the CCITT and the ISO/IEC. As such, the latter two algorithms have been issued official names and numbers by, and are available from, both organizations. The official designations for each algorithm are listed, along with their informal acronyms, in Table 1. Note that an official standards document issued by the CCITT is called a *Recommendation*, whereas such a document issued by the ISO/IEC is called an *International Standard*. These documents are available in the U.S. from the American National Standards Institute (ANSI).[2]

IV. ALGORITHM CHARACTERISTICS

The compression technology used in all of the algorithms discussed here is fixed-to-variable-length *coding*, preceded by some form of nearby-neighbor *modeling* [5]. The algorithm models will be discussed in terms of whether they are used for *bi-level* or *multilevel* image data and categorized in terms of whether they are *static, custom,* or *adaptive.* In addition, the bi-level models will be categorized in terms of whether they utilize one or two spatial dimensions (1D or 2D); and the multilevel models in terms of whether they utilize 1D, 2D, or exploit the amplitude dimension as well (3D).

---

[1] The CCITT was recently renamed to be the ITU-T (International Telecommunication Union, Telecommunication standardization sector).

[2] American National Standards Institute, 11 West 42 Street, New York, NY 10036. (212) 642-4900.

Table 1 Overview of Algorithm Characteristics

Algorithm Acronym	CCITT Recommendation	ISO/IEC International Standard	Compression Technology		Error Detection
			Model	Coder	
MH	T.4	—	static, 1D	static Huffman	yes
MR	T.4	—	static, 2D	static Huffman	yes
MMR	T.6	—	static, 2D	static Huffman	maybe
JPEG	T.81	10918-1	custom, 3D	custom Huffman or adaptive arithmetic	maybe
JBIG	T.82	11544	adaptive, 3D	adaptive arithmetic	maybe

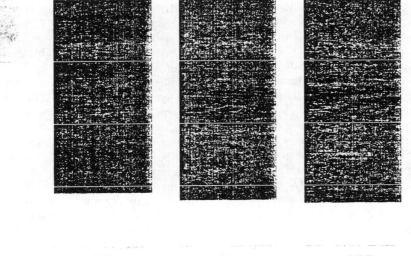

s04a   MH   MR   MMR   JBIG

Fig. 3. Visualizing compression of halftone document (JBIG test image "s04a" at 200 pels/in).
MH: $S = 310\%$ ($R = 0.32$). MR: $S = 323\%$ ($R = 0.31$). MMR: $S = 328\%$ ($R = 0.30$).
JBIG: $S = 15\%$ ($R = 6.84$).

A. Bi-Level Algorithms

The bi-level image compression algorithms used in to-day's digital facsimile systems became published standards in the early 1980's [1], [2], [6]. The technology they use for compression [5] is variable-to-fixed-length (run-length) coding *models*, followed by static Huffman *coding*. The names "Group 3" and "Group 4," sometimes used to refer to them, come from facsimile machine protocols that were standardized in the CCITT. These protocols actually contain multiple compression algorithms and are still adding more as they expand to define color facsimile systems. It is more precise to call out their compression algorithms in terms of the informal acronyms MH, MR, and MMR, or by the CCITT *Recommendations* T.4 or T.6 in which they are defined.

A new generation of lossless image compression algorithm, JBIG, has recently become a published standard [3], [7]. It uses 2D *custom* [8] or *adaptive* modeling [9] and *adaptive* arithmetic coding [10], [11], rather than *static* models and coders. It performs well over a wide range of bi-level images including difficult, digital halftones [12].

The superior ability of adaptive algorithms to encode digital halftones is illustrated in Fig. 3, again using pseudo-images of compressed data. Note that the MH, MR, and MMR algorithms actually expand the sample halftone document (JBIG Test Image "s04a"), requiring multiple times the original image size to record their compressed data. In contrast, the adaptive JBIG algorithm compresses the image, although with more difficulty than in the earlier business letter example of Fig. 1.

These standardized algorithms for *bi-level* image compression can be defined, along with the parameter settings we used to maximize their compression, as follows:

- **MH: Modified Huffman coding.** An algorithm defined in CCITT Recommendation T.4 [1], using a 1D run-length coding model followed by static Huffman coder.
  It also contains redundant end-of-line codewords to provide error detection.
- **MR: Modified READ (Relative Element Address Desig-nate) coding.** An algorithm defined in CCITT Recommendation T.4 [1], which uses a 2D reference and run-length coding model [5], followed by a static Huffman coder.
  It also contains redundant end-of-line codewords to provide error detection and periodically inserts 1D,

MH-coded raster lines to minimize possible error propagation. This periodicity is specified using a parameter, "K".[3]

To maximize compression we uniformly parameterized the periodicity to four lines, "$K = 4$".[4]

- **MMR: Modified Modified READ (Relative Element Address Designate) coding.** An algorithm defined in CCITT Recommendation T.6 [2], which is based on the 2D MR algorithm, modified to maximize compression by removing the MR provisions for error protection.

- **JBIG: Joint Bi-level Image experts Group coding.** An algorithm defined in CCITT Recommendation T.82 [3], which for bi-level compression uses an adaptive, 2D coding model, followed by an adaptive arithmetic coder.

  It utilizes progressive spatial resolution buildup, and can specify the number of different spatial resolution "layers" used with its parameter, "D". Its 2D model utilizes either two or three lines of the image ("$2L$" or "$3L$"). Its model adaptivity is selectable with a switch ("AT") and can be constrained to one preselected "custom" value by specifying a fixed parameter.

  To maximize compression, we parameterized it to use no progressive spatial resolution buildup, "$D = 0$"; use three lines of image ("$3L$"); and use the adaptive model ("AT").[5] For bi-level data we also set "$P = 1$" (defined below).

B. Multilevel Algorithms

Two algorithms for lossless, multilevel image compression have recently become international standards. They are specific cases of the parameterizable JBIG [3], [7] and JPEG [4], [13], [14] standards, respectively. Their being parameterized cases of a larger standard, reflects a trend towards combining sets of closely related algorithms into what can be thought of as *toolkits* of standards. Such toolkits of algorithms are regarded as "generic," requiring further "application-specific" standards to encapsulate them for a particular application.

JBIG scales to multilevel grey or color images, by breaking them down into their constituent "bit-planes" and compressing these bit-planes with its bi-level algorithms. The number of bit-planes to be compressed is specified by a parameter "P", which in the multilevel case is 2 or more: "$P = 2+$". To maximize compression Gray coding ("G") is used, rather than weighted-binary coding, to represent pixel amplitudes when breaking an image into bit-planes.

JPEG has a strictly lossless mode, which does not require use of the Discrete Cosine Transform (DCT) coding [15] that most of its better known modes use. Instead, it utilizes a customizable form of Differential Pulse Code Modulation (DPCM) coding [16] plus a variable-length representation of the DPCM errors [17] as its 3D *model*.[6] The model is followed by either a custom Huffman or adaptive arithmetic *coder*.[7] We use "custom" to indicate the use of *image-specific* tables or parameter settings.

These standardized algorithms for *multilevel* image compression can be defined, along with the parameter settings we used to maximize their compression, as follows:

- **JBIG: Joint Bi-level Image experts Group coding.** An algorithm defined in CCITT Recommendation T.82 [3], which for multilevel coding uses an adaptive 3D coding model, followed by an adaptive arithmetic coder.

  It utilizes progressive spatial resolution buildup, and can specify the number of different spatial resolution "layers" used with its parameter ("D"). Its 3D model utilizes either two or three lines of the image ("$2L$" or "$3L$"), while operating on image bit-planes that have first been Gray-coded ("G"). Its model being adaptive is selectable with a switch ("AT").

  To maximize compression, we parameterized it to use no progressive spatial resolution buildup, "$D = 0$"; three lines of image in the model ("$3L$"); Gray coding of the bit-planes ("G"); and chose not to use the model's adaptivity.

- **JPEG: Joint Photographic (image) Experts Group coding.** An algorithm defined in CCITT Recommendation T.81 [4], which for lossless coding uses a static 3D coding model, followed by a custom Huffman or adaptive arithmetic coder ("H" or "A").

  The model is parameterized, with a choice of seven DPCM predictors ("T"), plus sixteen upper ("U") and lower ("L") thresholds on the coding of DPCM errors. To maximize compression, we parameterized it to use DPCM prediction from the pel value immediately above, "$T = 2$"; used the default settings for the error thresholds, "$U = 1$" and "$L = 0$"[8]; and selected arithmetic coding ("A").

---

[3]Notation: We will define *explicit* algorithm parameters in the text by enclosing them in quote marks. We will define *implicit* parameters (or sometimes modes) by enclosing them in quote marks within parentheses. For conciseness, explicit numerical parameter settings like "$K = 4$" will be abbreviated as "$K4$".

[4]One 1D line followed by three 2D lines. When using a uniform periodicity, maximizing the number of 2D coded scan lines generally maximizes the compression.

[5]The three-line template generally maximizes compression, as does choosing not to use spatial resolution progressive buildup. For ease of verification, we report results with AT using a "custom" parameter value (the difference versus using AT adaptivity is negligible).

[6]JPEG also has a mode, that encodes in its lossy manner using a DCT, followed with extra coded information to arrive at a "lossless" encoding. This combination is not strictly lossless unless compressors and decompressors use matching inverse DCT transforms. It also does not compress as well as the DPCM-based, Lossless JPEG mode. For these reasons, the DPCM-based mode was used for our testing. (The "hierarchical" variation of Lossless JPEG was not tested).

[7]Note that the *optional* "QM" adaptive arithmetic coder used in JPEG is identical to the "QM" coder *always* required in JBIG. It is a modified derivative of the "Q" adaptive arithmetic coder [18]. For Lossless JPEG we always selected the adaptive arithmetic coder, since it generally compresses much better than the custom Huffman coder.

[8]We did 87 696 simulations over all the JPEG test images, their color components and amplitude precisions; to *tune* the most likely 406 possible combinations to one setting of T, U, and L for all the data (since settings of L from 0 through 3 are the most likely with 2- to 8-b/pel data, only these four choices were used in our simulations).

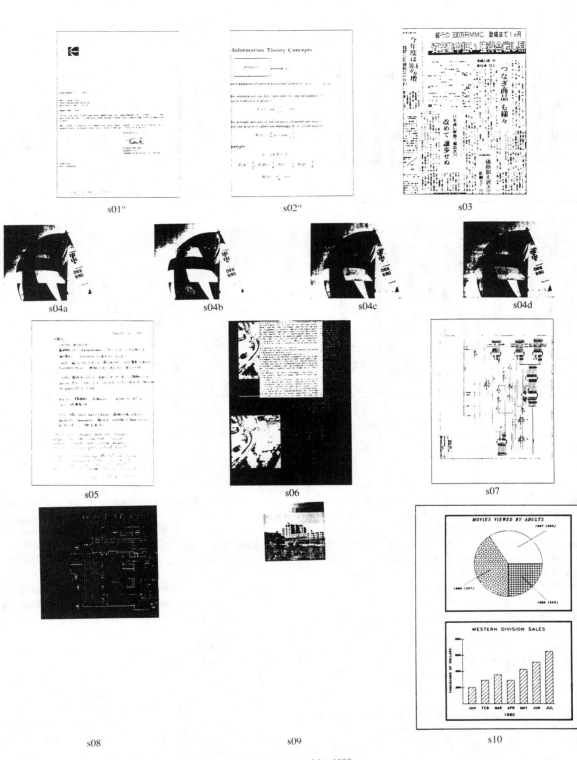

Fig. 4. JBIG Test Image Set. (1/6 actual size) ([a] Actual test image data rotated by 180°.)

An overview of the major algorithm characteristics (acronyms, compression technology, and error detection capability) is also presented in Table 1.

V. Algorithm Compression Comparisons

Lossless image compression varies significantly depending on many factors including the specific image and its type ("photographic" or "modal"), as well as how it was digitized (its spatial resolution and amplitude precision). We will examine and graph how compression varies with these factors for all of the above standard algorithms. Two sets of test images, used in the recent past to design the JBIG and JPEG compression standard algorithms, will be used.

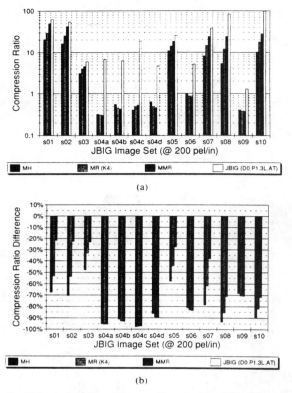

(a)

(b)

Fig. 5. Bi-level data dependence. (a) Compression. (MH, MR, MMR, JBIG algorithms.) (b) Compression differences. (MH, MR, MMR, JBIG: % difference from JBIG.)

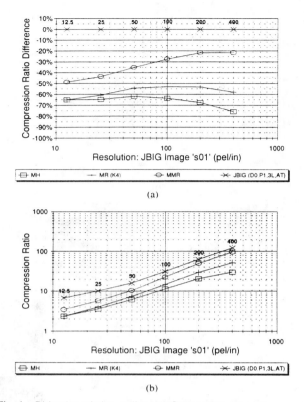

(a)

(b)

Fig. 6. Bi-level resolution scaling. (a) Compression versus resolution. (MH, MR, MMR, JBIG: % difference from JBIG.) (b) Compression differences versus resolution. (MH, MR, MMR, JBIG algorithms.)

Compression will be measured in terms of "compression ratio," the ratio between uncompressed and compressed bits used to represent a given image. For each such experiment we will also measure the compression results in a normalized form, which we call "compression difference"; indicating the difference in compression ratio between each algorithm in an experiment, versus one selected "reference" algorithm in that experiment.[9]

To facilitate cross-comparisons, we have also constrained the vertical axes to be identical in all graphs using the same one of these two measurements. Where the same horizontal axes are used in different graphs, we have also constrained all such axes to be identical.

A. Bi-Level Algorithms

The images used to test bi-level algorithms are shown in Fig. 4, at 1/6 of their actual size. They are the "Stockholm" test images from the JBIG standards committee, which were digitized at 400 pels/in and 1 b/pel. To measure algorithm performance across a wide variety of data these images include scanned business documents ("s01, 2, 3, 5"), generated digital halftones ("s04a, 4b, 4c, 4d, 9"), and generated graphic images ("s07, 8, 10") as well as a mixed

document ("s06"). These images we call here the "JBIG Test Set."

These images were also reduced to spatial resolutions of 200, 100, 50, 25, and 12.5 pels/in in order to provide data for testing how bi-level algorithm performances scale with resolution. The above factor-of-two resolution scalings were done by digitally reducing the images with the "PRES" algorithm suggested in the JBIG standard [3]. Since 200 pels/in appears to be the most commonly used resolution for bi-level images among those above, we chose to use the JBIG Test Set reduced to this resolution for the data difference testing that follows.

1) Data Dependence: Figure 5(a) illustrates how bi-level image compression ratios vary for the MH, MR, MMR, and JBIG algorithms applied to the JBIG Test Set reduced to 200 pels/in. Because of the significant variations in compression ratios, these are plotted with a logarithmic scale.

Note that ratios less than 1 indicate data expansion by the lossless algorithm. This occurs here only on the digital halftone images ("s04a, 4b, 4c, 4d, 9") plus the image which contains a halftone ("s06")—and only when compressed using the nonadaptive MH, MR, and MMR algorithms. For the images without halftones, the compression ratio results are better; and improve monotonically for the algorithms ordered in the sequence: MH, MR, MMR, JBIG.

---

[9] Note that this compression difference percentage is identical to another very useful comparison one can make. It is equal to the percentage *further* difference in compressed file size one obtains with the reference algorithm. when compared to the compressed file sizes *already* achieved with one of the other algorithms.

Table 2 Bi-Level Data Dependence

JBIG TEST IMAGE	IMAGE DIMEN. AT 200 pels/in (pels)	COMPRESSED SIZE (Bytes)				COMPRESSION RATIO				COMPRESSION DIFFERENCE (%)			
		MH	MR^a	MMR	$JBIG^b$	MH	MR^a	MMR	$JBIG^b$	MH	MR^a	MMR	$JBIG^b$
s01	4352×3072	20605	14290	8531	6682	20.28	29.24	48.97	62.52	−67.57	−53.24	−21.67	0.00
s02	4352×3072	26155	16676	9956	7696	15.97	25.05	41.96	54.29	−70.58	−53.85	−22.70	0.00
s03	4352×3072	135705	105684	92100	70703	3.08	3.95	4.54	5.91	−47.90	−33.10	−23.23	0.00
s04a^c	2048×3072	634509	634509	645018	28763	0.32	0.31	0.30	6.84	−95.29	−95.47	−95.54	0.00
s04b^d	2048×3072	357017	435646	460282	31312	0.55	0.45	0.43	6.28	−91.23	−92.81	−93.20	0.00
s04c^c	2048×3072	487279	400809	370268	10530	0.40	0.49	0.53	18.67	−97.84	−97.37	−97.16	0.00
s04d^e	2048×3072	309599	400514	429342	42445	0.64	0.49	0.46	4.63	−86.29	−89.40	−90.11	0.00
s05	4352×3072	39263	29763	22913	16584	10.64	14.04	18.23	25.19	−57.76	−44.28	−27.62	0.00
s06^f	4352×3072	431682	479083	494667	81055	0.97	0.87	0.84	5.15	−81.22	−83.08	−83.61	0.00
s07	4352×3072	51731	28944	17779	11031	8.08	14.43	23.50	37.87	−78.68	−61.89	−37.95	0.00
s08	3040×3072	54477	24636	12235	3519	5.36	11.85	23.85	82.93	−93.54	−85.72	−71.24	0.00
s09	1024×1024	80202	85715	86778	25293	0.41	0.38	0.38	1.30	−68.46	−70.49	−70.85	0.00
s10	5856×4096	74182	42609	27063	7636	10.10	17.59	27.70	98.16	−89.71	−82.08	−71.78	0.00

^{a} MR $(K4)$. ^{b} JBIG $(D0.P1.3L.AT)$, ^{c} JBIG $(AT4)$, ^{d} JBIG $(AT5)$, ^{e} JBIG $(AT6)$, ^{f} JBIG $(AT8)$

Table 3 Bi-Level Resolution Scaling

JBIG IMAGE "s01" RES. (pels/in)	SCALED IMAGE "s01" DIMEN. (pels)	COMPRESSED SIZE (Bytes)				COMPRESSION RATIO				COMPRESSION DIFFERENCE (%)			
		MH	MR^a	MMR	$JBIG^b$	MH	MR^a	MMR	$JBIG^b$	MH	MR^a	MMR	$JBIG^b$
12.5	272×192	697	702	476	244	2.34	2.32	3.43	6.69	−64.99	−65.24	−48.74	0.00
25	544×384	1835	1658	1149	648	3.56	3.94	5.68	10.07	−64.99	−60.92	−43.60	0.00
50	1088×768	4306	3595	2526	1639	6.06	7.26	10.34	15.93	−61.94	−54.41	−35.11	0.00
100	2176×1536	9240	7154	4639	3366	11.30	14.60	22.52	31.03	−63.57	−52.95	−27.44	0.00
200	4352×3072	20605	14290	8531	6682	20.28	29.24	48.97	62.52	−67.57	−53.24	−21.67	0.00
400	8704×6144	56221	32577	17416	13656	29.72	51.30	95.96	122.38	−75.71	−58.08	−21.59	0.00

^{a}MR $(K4)$. ^{b}JBIG $(D0.P1.3L.AT)$

In Fig. 5(b) these data are graphed in terms of compression differences. One can see how much less the compression ratio is for the MH, MR, and MMR algorithms, when compared to that achieved with the reference JBIG algorithm.[10] As mentioned earlier,[9] these differences are also identical to the further differences in compressed file size one would get if MH, MR, or MMR compressed files were recompressed using JBIG.

The numerical data used to generate both Fig. 5(a) and (b) are shown in Table 2. Settings selected for the algorithm parameters, as defined earlier, are shown in accompanying table footnotes.

2) Scaling with Spatial Resolution: We found that the way algorithm compression ratios scale with resolution, varied widely with the kind of bi-level image. It appeared to be the most well-behaved for the scanned business documents ("s01, 2, 3, 5"). In light of this, we selected image "s01" to present here. Figure 6(a) graphs compression ratio versus spatial resolution in an "xy" plot, for all four bi-level algorithms tested. They all show roughly linear increases in compression ratios with spatial resolution (straight lines in a log-log plot).

In Fig. 6(b) these data were graphed in terms of compression differences. One can see that compression ratio differences for the MH and MR algorithms, compared to ratios with the JBIG algorithm, are fairly constant across spatial resolutions. For the MMR algorithm, however, the negative compression differences decrease somewhat with higher resolutions.

The numerical data used to generate both Fig. 6(a) and (b) are shown in Table 3.

B. Multilevel Algorithms

The images used to test multilevel algorithms are shown in Fig. 7 at the size they would be if printed at 400 pels/in. What is shown is the luminance "Y" component of "YUV" color test images from the JPEG standards committee, which were digitized at 8 b/cmp. The Y component was sampled into 720×576 pels, whereas the U and V com-

[10]JBIG was used as the reference algorithm in our bi-level and multilevel studies, since it was the only algorithm common to both.

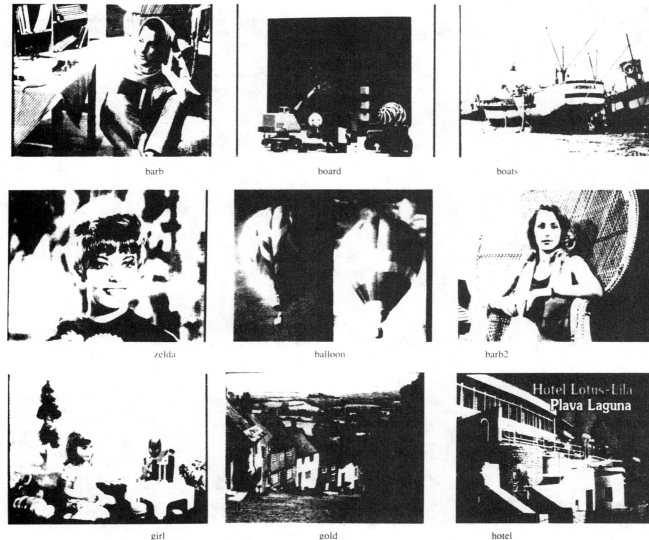

barb   board   boats

zelda   balloon   barb2

girl   gold   hotel

Fig. 7.   JPEG Test Image Set (1/2 actual size at 200 pels/in).

ponents were further down-sampled to 360×576 pels. All compression ratios reported below represent the combined results from compressing all three image components.

These images were also reduced to amplitude precisions of 7, 6, 5, 4, 3. and 2 b/cmp, in order to provide data for testing how multilevel algorithm performances scale with precision. The precision reductions were done by recursively truncating the next "least significant" bit in the test images.[11]

Since 8 b/cmp appears to be the most commonly used multilevel image precision among those above, we chose to use it for the data dependence testing that follows.

1) Data Dependence: Fig. 8(a) illustrates how multilevel image compression ratios vary for the JBIG and JPEG algorithms when applied to the JPEG Test Set at 8 b/cmp. These ratios are plotted on a logarithmic scale. as before.

[11]JPEG precision reduction was done using its "point transform."

for ease of comparison with the bi-level image compression results.

Note that the compression ratio variation produced across the multilevel images is much less than that produced across the bi-level images, and that the compression ratio values are roughly around 2. With the exception of the rightmost image "hotel," the compression ratio results improve monotonically for the algorithms ordered in the sequence: JBIG, JPEG.

In Fig. 8(b) these data are graphed in terms of compression differences. One can see how much more the compression ratio is for the JPEG algorithm. when compared to that achieved with the reference JBIG algorithm.[10] As previously mentioned,[9] these differences are identical to the further differences in compressed file size one would get if JPEG compressed files were recompressed using JBIG. Note that these differences range from about $+7\%$ to -1%

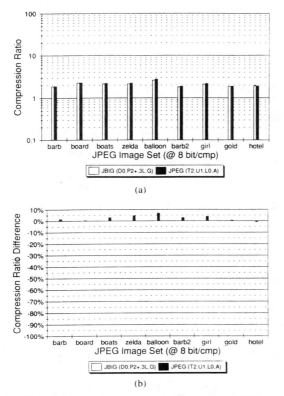

(a)

(b)

Fig. 8. Multilevel data dependence. (a) Compression. (JBIG, JPEG algorithms.) (b) Compression differences. (JBIG, JPEG: % difference from JBIG.)

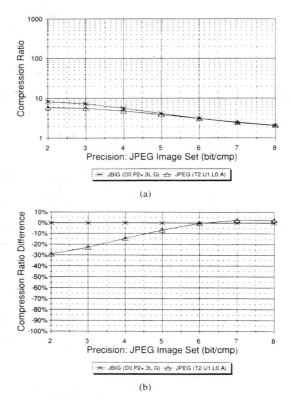

(a)

(b)

Fig. 9. Multilevel precision scaling. (a) Compression versus precision. (JBIG, JPEG algorithms.) (b) Compression differences versus precision. (JBIG, JPEG: % difference from JBIG.)

at this precision (see Table 4), with the better results from the algorithm that could be finely tuned to the data .[8, 12]

The numerical data used to generate both Fig. 8(a) and (b) are shown in Table 4. Settings selected for the algorithm parameters, as defined earlier, are shown in accompanying table footnotes.

2) Scaling with Amplitude Precision: We found that the way algorithm compression ratios scale with resolution was fairly uniform for the kinds of multilevel images in the JPEG Test Set. Therefore, we chose to present the combined results for all the JPEG Test Set images. Figure 9(a) graphs compression ratio versus amplitude precision in an "xy" plot, for the two multilevel algorithms tested. They both show systematic decreases in compression ratio with increasing amplitude precision.

In Fig. 9(b) these data are graphed in terms of compression differences. One can see that compression ratio differences for the JPEG algorithm, when compared to ratios with the JBIG algorithm, are more negative at lower amplitude precisions. These negative differences decrease with higher precisions, crossing over at 6 b/pel to small positive values (shown individually in Fig. 8(b) for the entire test set at 8 b/pel).

The numerical data used to generate both Fig. 9(a) and 9(b) are shown in Table 5.

[12]JPEG optimized *only* for this precision, yields parameter settings *T7, U3, L2* and differences that range from about +8 to +2%.

VI. Future Work[13]

This comparison has been limited to the compression performance of these standards. Further comparisons could compare their relative complexities, ranging from software through firmware, to hardware. We have data on how other image types in the JBIG Test Set scaled with resolution, but their variations could still be generalized. Our experiments on parameterization of the Lossless JPEG algorithm yielded different optimal settings for the individual images, the separate color components, or the different amplitude precisions; which might also be summarized. The ISO/IEC and CCITT (ITU-T) international standards committees continue to study improvements to JBIG and Lossless JPEG, as well as investigate new algorithms for lossless still image compression.[14] The hierarchical form of Lossless JPEG is being explored to see if it may yield better compression than the nonhierarchical form.

VII. Summary

The MH, MR, MMR standards for lossless, bi-level image compression have been available and very successful

[13]Some of this future work, plus the figures in this paper, may become part of a forthcoming Van Nostrand–Reinhold book being prepared by R. Arps, together with W. Pennebaker, entitled *Facsimile Compression Standards*.

[14]In the U.S., contributions are made by participating in the ANSI accredited "X3L3" standards committee. Contact: X3 Secretariat, CBEMA, 1250 Eye Street N.W., Suite 200, Washington, DC 20005.

Table 4　Multilevel Data Dependence

JPEG TEST IMAGE	IMAGE SIZE AT 8 b/cmp (Bytes)	COMPRESSED SIZE (Bytes)		COMPRESSION RATIO		COMPRESSION DIFFERENCE (%)	
		JBIG[a]	JPEG[b]	JBIG[a]	JPEG[b]	JBIG[a]	JPEG[b]
barb	829440	446916	439449	1.86	1.89	0.00	1.70
board	829440	367742	365882	2.26	2.27	0.00	0.51
boats	829440	389692	378499	2.13	2.19	0.00	2.96
zelda	829440	389164	371792	2.13	2.23	0.00	4.67
balloon	829440	322459	301760	2.57	2.75	0.00	6.86
barb2	829440	462789	450273	1.79	1.84	0.00	2.78
girl	829440	400878	386037	2.07	2.15	0.00	3.84
gold	829440	447348	444288	1.85	1.87	0.00	0.69
hotel	829440	435551	439400	1.90	1.89	0.00	−0.88

[a]JBIG $(D0. P2+. 3L. G)$,　[b]JPEG $(T2. U1. L0. A)$

Table 5　Multilevel Precision Scaling

JPEG TEST SET PRECISION (b/pel)	SCALED TEST SET SIZE (Bytes)	COMPRESSED SIZE (Bytes)		COMPRESSION RATIO		COMPRESSION DIFFERENCE (%)	
		JBIG[a]	JPEG[b]	JBIG[a]	JPEG[b]	JBIG[a]	JPEG[b]
2	1866240	227638	321092	8.20	5.81	0.00	−29.11
3	2799360	385057	498798	7.27	5.61	0.00	−22.80
4	3732480	661461	774147	5.64	4.82	0.00	−14.56
5	4665600	1118803	1199295	4.17	3.89	0.00	−6.71
6	5598720	1807233	1814288	3.10	3.09	0.00	−0.39
7	6531840	2696126	2628369	2.42	2.49	0.00	2.58
8	7464960	3662539	3577380	2.04	2.09	0.00	2.38

[a]JBIG $(D0. P2+. 3L. G)$,　[b]JPEG $(T2. U1. L0. A)$

since the early 1980's. Only now has a standard, JBIG, been introduced with significant improvements in compression or function. In particular, JBIG addresses the vexing problem of compressing digital halftones, by demonstrating compression results here ranging from 1.3 to 18.7 at 200 pels/in. These ratios for halftones are an order of magnitude better than those of the previous standard algorithms.

For business documents, these algorithm compression results were monotonically ordered in performance from MH, MR, MMR to JBIG. On the varied JBIG Test Set at 200 pels/in. we saw compression ratios ranging from 0.3 to 98.2. Over a range from 12.5 to 400 pels/in for the typical business image "s01," JBIG was from 22 to 49% better than its closest alternative, MMR. We also found that all of the bi-level algorithms had compression ratios that scale linearly with resolution on image "s01" between 50 and 400 pels/in. for the resolution reduction algorithm that we used.

As some of the new international standard "toolkits," JBIG and JPEG also offer new functions such as "progressive buildup" in spatial resolution or amplitude precision. They both can be parameterized to cover lossless multilevel image compression at various precisions and offer international compression standards for this type of data where none appear to have existed before.

The actual compression ratios achieved on multilevel images were modest. They were within roughly 10% of a compression ratio of 2, for both algorithms at 8 b/pel over the JPEG color test images used. Over varied amplitude precisions, the combined compression ratios ranged from 2.1 at 8 b/pel up to 8.2 at 2 b/pel. The comparative results between JBIG and JPEG over all the JPEG Test Images were mixed. Optimally parameterized JPEG was 2.4–2.6% better at 7 and 8 b/pel, JBIG and JPEG were similar at 6 b/pel, and from 5 down to 2 b/pel JBIG was increasingly better up to a maximum of 29%.[15]

With the continued spread of the popular MH, MR, and MMR algorithms plus the new capabilities introduced with JBIG and JPEG, we foresee significant expansion in the number of new applications enabled by international image compression standards.

ACKNOWLEDGMENT

The authors wish to thank W. Equitz, B. Pennebaker, M. Cooper, K. Anderson, J. Mitchell, R. Pasco, J. Morgan, and many others, who contributed to the IBM software used to implement the compression algorithms in our comparisons. We also wish to thank Eastman Kodak Company and the Independent Broadcasting Authority in the United Kingdom for their efforts in preparing and distributing the JBIG

[15]JPEG optimized *individually* for each precision yielded 3.6–4.5% at 7 and 8 b/pel, with the 6 b/pel. crossover and other numbers remaining the same.

and JPEG test images, respectively, for the international compression standardization community.

REFERENCES

[1] International Telegraph and Telephone Consultative Committee (CCITT), "Standardization of Group 3 Facsimile Apparatus for Document Transmission," *Recommendation* T.4, 1980.

[2] International Telegraph and Telephone Consultative Committee (CCITT), "Facsimile Coding Schemes and Coding Control Functions for Group 4 Facsimile Apparatus," *Recommendation* T.6, 1984.

[3] International Telegraph and Telephone Consultative Committee (CCITT), "Progressive Bi-level Image Compression," *Recommendation* T.82, 1993; also appears as, International Organization for Standards / International Electrotechnical Commission (ISO/IEC), "Progressive Bi-level Image Compression," International Standard 11544: 1993.

[4] International Telegraph and Telephone Consultative Committee (CCITT), "Digital Compression and Coding of Continuous-tone Still Images," *Recommendation* T.81, 1992; also appears as, International Organization for Standards / International Electrotechnical Commission (ISO/IEC), "Digital Compression and Coding of Continuous-tone Still Images," International Standard 10918-1:1993.

[5] R. B. Arps, "Binary image compression," in *Image Transmission Techniques*, W. K. Pratt, Ed. New York: Academic Press, 1979, ch 7.

[6] R. Hunter and A. H. Robinson, "International digital facsimile coding standards," *Proc. IEEE*, vol. 68, no. 7, pp. 854–867, July 1980.

[7] H. Hampel, R. B. Arps, *et al.*, "Technical features of the JBIG standard for progressive bi-level image compression," *Signal Process.: Image Commun.*, vol. 4, no. 2, pp. 103–111, Apr. 1992.

[8] K. Toyokawa, "System for compressing bi-level data," U.S. Patent 4 901 363, Feb. 13, 1990.

[9] C. Chamzas and D. Duttweiler, "Entropy encoder/decoder including context extractor," U.S. Patent 5 023 611, June 11, 1991.

[10] J. J. Rissanen, "Generalized Kraft inequality and arithmetic coding," *IBM J. Res. Devel.*, vol. 20, no. 3, pp. 198–203, 1976.

[11] G. G. Langdon and J. J. Rissanen, "Compression of black-white images with arithmetic coding," *IEEE Trans. Commun.*, vol. COM-29, no. 6, pp. 858–867, June 1981.

[12] R. B. Arps, T. K. Truong, D. J. Lu, R. C. Pasco, and T. D. Friedman, "A multi-purpose VLSI chip for adaptive data compression of bilevel images," *IBM J. Res. Devel.*, vol. 32, no. 6, pp. 775–795, Nov. 1988.

[13] G. Wallace, "Overview of the JPEG (ISO/CCITT) still image compression standard," *Proc. SPIE (Image Processing Algorithms and Techniques)*, vol. 1244, pp. 220–233, 1990.

[14] W. B. Pennebaker and J. L. Mitchell, *JPEG Still Image Data Compression Standard* New York: Van Nostrand Reinhold, 1993.

[15] A. G. Tescher, "Transform image coding," in *Image Transmission Techniques*, W. K. Pratt, Ed. New York: Academic Press, 1979, ch. 4.

[16] H. G. Musmann, "Predictive image coding," in *Image Transmission Techniques*, W. K. Pratt, Ed. New York: Academic Press, 1979, ch. 3.

[17] G. G. Langdon, "Sunset: A hardware-oriented algorithm for lossless compression of grey-scale images," *Proc. SPIE (Medical Imaging V: Image Capture, Formatting, and Display)*, vol. 1444, pp. 272–282, Mar. 1991.

[18] W. B. Pennebaker, J. L. Mitchell, G. G. Langdon, and R. B. Arps, "An overview of the basic principles of the Q-coder adaptive binary arithmetic coder," *IBM J. Res. Develop.*, vol. 32, no. 6, pp. 717–726, Nov. 1988.

Ronald B. Arps (Member, IEEE) received the B.S. degree from the California Institute of Technology, Pasadena, CA, in 1960, the M.S. degree from Oregon State University, Corvallis, OR, in 1963, and the Ph.D. degree from Stanford University, Stanford, CA, in 1969, all in electrical engineering.

From 1960 to 1962 he was with the Electrodata Division of Burroughs in Pasadena, CA. Since 1963 he has been with IBM in San Jose, CA; first in its Advanced Systems Development Division, Los Gatos Laboratory, and subsequently in its Research Division, Almaden Research Center. His assignments have included exploratory studies on processing and compressing binary images, advanced development of computer peripherals and systems, research into hardware-optimized adaptive compression, and implementation of algorithms in VLSI microsystems. He is currently manager of the Data Compression and Scientific Modeling Project at the IBM Almaden Research Center. His research interests include adaptive data compression algorithms as well as image processing, office automation, and computer-aided design of VLSI. IBM recognition has included a Resident Study Award to Stanford University during 1967–1969 and teaching as an IBM visiting scientist at the Swiss Federal Institute of Technology, Zurich, during 1970–1971. During 1977–1978 he was on leave as a visiting associate professor at Linkoping University in Sweden. In 1979, he published a chapter entitled "Binary Image Compression" in *Image Transmission Techniques* (New York: Academic Press). During 1992–1993 he was on sabbatical at Stanford University as IBM's Industrial Visitor to their Center for Integrated Systems.

Dr. Arps is IBM's technical representative to the ISO/IEC and CCITT(ITU-T) Joint Bi-level Image experts Group (JBIG) international standards committee.

Thomas K. Truong received the B.S. degree (*magna cum laude*) in electrical engineering and computer science from the University of California at Berkeley in 1983, and the M.S. degree in electrical engineering from Stanford University, Stanford, CA, in 1987, through the IBM Honors Co–Operative program.

He is an advisory engineeer/scientist at the IBM Almaden Research Center, San Jose, CA, where he has been working in the Data Compression and Scientific Modeling project since 1983. He is the co-designer of the IBM ABIC chip and is also responsible for the design and implementation of various adaptive data compression systems. His assignments have included hardware and software prototyping, technology transfer, as well as commercialization of compression hardware/software. His research interests range from algorithms to implementation of data compression and high-level synthesis systems. He has been involved in both board-level and ASIC VLSI chip designs, and has written many application programs on a wide range of platforms, including AIX/UNIX, DOS, OS/2, and Windows. He received an IBM Resident Study Award to continue his study and research in high-level synthesis at Stanford University from 1988 to 1991. He also received an IBM Outstanding Technical Achievement Award for his contributions to the IBM's data compression technology, and many IBM Informal Awards.

Mr. Truong is a member of Eta Kappa Nu and Tau Beta Pi.

Embedded Image Coding Using Zerotrees of Wavelet Coefficients

Jerome M. Shapiro

Abstract—The embedded zerotree wavelet algorithm (EZW) is a simple, yet remarkably effective, image compression algorithm, having the property that the bits in the bit stream are generated in order of importance, yielding a fully embedded code. The embedded code represents a sequence of binary decisions that distinguish an image from the "null" image. Using an embedded coding algorithm, an encoder can terminate the encoding at any point thereby allowing a target rate or target distortion metric to be met exactly. Also, given a bit stream, the decoder can cease decoding at any point in the bit stream and still produce exactly the same image that would have been encoded at the bit rate corresponding to the truncated bit stream. In addition to producing a fully embedded bit stream, EZW consistently produces compression results that are competitive with virtually all known compression algorithms on standard test images. Yet this performance is achieved with a technique that requires absolutely no training, no pre-stored tables or codebooks, and requires no prior knowledge of the image source.

The EZW algorithm is based on four key concepts: 1) a discrete wavelet transform or hierarchical subband decomposition, 2) prediction of the absence of significant information across scales by exploiting the self-similarity inherent in images, 3) entropy-coded successive-approximation quantization, and 4) universal lossless data compression which is achieved via adaptive arithmetic coding.

I. INTRODUCTION AND PROBLEM STATEMENT

THIS paper addresses the two-fold problem of 1) obtaining the best image quality for a given bit rate, and 2) accomplishing this task in an embedded fashion, i.e., in such a way that all encodings of the same image at lower bit rates are embedded in the beginning of the bit stream for the target bit rate.

The problem is important in many applications, particularly for progressive transmission, image browsing [25], multimedia applications, and compatible transcoding in a digital hierarchy of multiple bit rates. It is also applicable to transmission over a noisy channel in the sense that the ordering of the bits in order of importance leads naturally to prioritization for the purpose of layered protection schemes.

Manuscript received April 28, 1992; revised June 13, 1993. The guest editor coordinating the review of this paper and approving it for publication was Prof. Martin Vetterli.

The author is with the David Sarnoff Research Center, Princeton, NJ 08543.

IEEE Log Number 9212175.

A. Embedded Coding

An embedded code represents a sequence of binary decisions that distinguish an image from the "null," or all gray, image. Since, the embedded code contains all lower rate codes "embedded" at the beginning of the bit stream, effectively, the bits are "ordered in importance." Using an embedded code, an encoder can terminate the encoding at any point thereby allowing a target rate or distortion metric to be met exactly. Typically, some target parameter, such as bit count, is monitored in the encoding process. When the target is met, the encoding simply stops. Similarly, given a bit stream, the decoder can cease decoding at any point and can produce reconstructions corresponding to all lower-rate encodings.

Embedded coding is similar in spirit to binary finite-precision representations of real numbers. All real numbers can be represented by a string of binary digits. For each digit added to the right, more precision is added. Yet, the "encoding" can cease at any time and provide the "best" representation of the real number achievable within the framework of the binary digit representation. Similarly, the embedded coder can cease at any time and provide the "best" representation of an image achievable within its framework.

The embedded coding scheme presented here was motivated in part by universal coding schemes that have been used for lossless data compression in which the coder attempts to optimally encode a source using no prior knowledge of the source. An excellent review of universal coding can be found in [3]. In universal coders, the encoder must *learn* the source statistics as it progresses. In other words, the source model is incorporated into the actual bit stream. For lossy compression, there has been little work in universal coding. Typical image coders require extensive training for both quantization (both scalar and vector) and generation of nonadaptive entropy codes, such as Huffman codes. The embedded coder described in this paper attempts to be universal by incorporating all learning into the bit stream itself. This is accomplished by the exclusive use of adaptive arithmetic coding.

Intuitively, for a given rate or distortion, a nonembedded code should be more efficient than an embedded code, since it is free from the constraints imposed by embedding. In their theoretical work [9], Equitz and Cover proved that a successively refinable description can only be optimal if the source possesses certain Markovian properties. Although optimality is never claimed, a method of generating an embedded bit stream with no apparent sacrifice in image quality has been developed.

B. Features of the Embedded Coder

The EZW algorithm contains the following features

- A discrete wavelet transform which provides a compact multiresolution representation of the image.
- Zerotree coding which provides a compact multiresolution representation of *significance maps*, which are binary maps indicating the positions of the significant coefficients. Zerotrees allow the successful prediction of insignificant coefficients across scales to be efficiently represented as part of exponentially growing trees.
- Successive Approximation which provides a compact *multiprecision* representation of the significant coefficients and facilitates the embedding algorithm.
- A prioritization protocol whereby the ordering of importance is determined, in order, by the precision, magnitude, scale, and spatial location of the wavelet coefficients. Note in particular, that larger coefficients are deemed more important than smaller coefficients regardless of their scale.
- Adaptive multilevel arithmetic coding which provides a fast and efficient method for entropy coding strings of symbols, and requires no training or prestored tables. The arithmetic coder used in the experiments is a customized version of that in [31].
- The algorithm runs sequentially and stops whenever a target bit rate or a target distortion is met. A target bit rate can be met *exactly*, and an operational rate-vs.-distortion function (RDF) can be computed point-by-point.

C. Paper Organization

Section II discusses how wavelet theory and multiresolution analysis provide an elegant methodology for representing "trends" and "anomalies" on a statistically equal footing. This is important in image processing because edges, which can be thought of as anomalies in the spatial domain, represent extremely important information despite that fact that they are represented in only a tiny fraction of the image samples. Section III introduces the concept of a *zerotree* and shows how zerotree coding can efficiently encode a significance map of wavelet coefficients by predicting the absence of significant information across scales. Section IV discusses how successive approximation quantization is used in conjunction with zerotree coding, and arithmetic coding to achieve efficient embedded coding. A discussion follows on the protocol by which EZW attempts to order the bits in order of importance. A key point there is that the definition of importance for the purpose of ordering information is based on the magnitudes of the uncertainty intervals as seen from the viewpoint of what the decoder can figure out. Thus,

there is no additional overhead to transmit this ordering information. Section V consists of a simple 8×8 example illustrating the various points of the EZW algorithm. Section VI discusses experimental results for various rates and for various standard test images. A surprising result is that using the EZW algorithm, terminating the encoding at an arbitrary point in the encoding process does not produce any artifacts that would indicate where in the picture the termination occurs. The paper concludes with Section VII.

II. WAVELET THEORY AND MULTIRESOLUTION ANALYSIS

A. Trends and Anomalies

One of the oldest problems in statistics and signal processing is how to choose the size of an analysis window, block size, or record length of data so that statistics computed within that window provide good models of the signal behavior within that window. The choice of an analysis window involves trading the ability to analyze "anomalies," or signal behavior that is more localized in the time or space domain and tends to be wide band in the frequency domain, from "trends," or signal behavior that is more localized in frequency but persists over a large number of lags in the time domain. To model data as being generated by random processes so that computed statistics become meaningful, stationary and ergodic assumptions are usually required which tend to obscure the contribution of anomalies.

The main contribution of wavelet theory and multiresolution analysis is that it provides an elegant framework in which both anomalies and trends can be analyzed on an equal footing. Wavelets provide a signal representation in which some of the coefficients represent long data lags corresponding to a narrow band, low frequency range, and some of the coefficients represent short data lags corresponding to a wide band, high frequency range. Using the concept of *scale*, data representing a continuous tradeoff between time (or space in the case of images) and frequency is available.

For an introduction to the theory behind wavelets and multiresolution analysis, the reader is referred to several excellent tutorials on the subject [6], [7], [17], [18], [20], [26], [27].

B. Relevance to Image Coding

In image processing, most of the image area typically represents spatial "trends," or areas of high statistical spatial correlation. However "anomalies," such as edges or object boundaries, take on a perceptual significance that is far greater than their numerical energy contribution to an image. Traditional transform coders, such as those using the DCT, decompose images into a representation in which each coefficient corresponds to a fixed size spatial area and a fixed frequency bandwidth, where the bandwidth and spatial area are effectively the same for all coefficients in the representation. Edge information tends to disperse so that many non-zero coefficients are required to represent edges with good fidelity. However, since the edges represent relatively insignificant energy with respect to the entire image, traditional transform coders, such as those using the DCT, have been fairly successful at medium and high bit rates. At extremely low bit rates, however, traditional transform coding techniques, such as JPEG [30], tend to allocate too many bits to the ''trends,'' and have few bits left over to represent ''anomalies.'' As a result, blocking artifacts often result.

Wavelet techniques show promise at extremely low bit rates because trends, anomalies, and information at all ''scales'' in between are available. A major difficulty is that fine detail coefficients representing possible anomalies constitute the largest number of coefficients, and therefore, to make effective use of the multiresolution representation, much of the information is contained in representing the *position* of those few coefficients corresponding to significant anomalies.

The techniques of this paper allow coders to effectively use the power of multiresolution representations by efficiently representing the positions of the wavelet coefficients representing significant anomalies.

C. A Discrete Wavelet Transform

The discrete wavelet transform used in this paper is identical to a hierarchical subband system, where the subbands are logarithmically spaced in frequency and represent an octave-band decomposition. To begin the decomposition, the image is divided into four subbands and critically subsampled as shown in Fig. 1. Each coefficient represents a spatial area corresponding to approximately a 2 × 2 area of the original image. The low frequencies represent a bandwidth approximately corresponding to $0 < |\omega| < \pi/2$, whereas the high frequencies represent the band from $\pi/2 < |\omega| < \pi$. The four subbands arise from separable application of vertical and horizontal filters. The subbands labeled LH_1, HL_1, and HH_1 represent the finest scale wavelet coefficients. To obtain the next coarser scale of wavelet coefficients, the subband LL_1 is further decomposed and critically sampled as shown in Fig. 2. The process continues until some final scale is reached. Note that for each coarser scale, the coefficients represent a larger spatial area of the image but a narrower band of frequencies. At each scale, there are three subbands; the remaining lowest frequency subband is a representation of the information at all coarser scales. The issues involved in the design of the filters for the type of subband decomposition described above have been discussed by many authors and are not treated in this paper. Interested readers should consult [1], [6], [32], [35], in addition to references found in the bibliographies of the tutorial papers cited above.

It is a matter of terminology to distinguish between a transform and a subband system as they are two ways of describing the same set of numerical operations from differing points of view. Let x be a column vector whose elements represent a scanning of the image pixels, let X

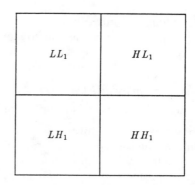

Fig. 1. First stage of a discrete wavelet transform: The image is divided into four subbands using separable filters. Each coefficient represents a spatial area corresponding to approximately a 2 × 2 area of the original picture. The low frequencies represent a bandwidth approximately corresponding to $0 < |\omega| < \pi/2$, whereas the high frequencies represent the band from $\pi/2 < |\omega| < \pi$. The four subbands arise from separable application of vertical and horizontal filters.

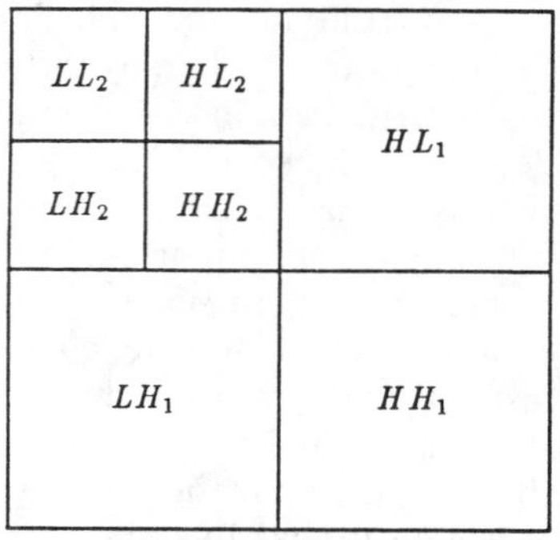

Fig. 2. A two-scale wavelet decomposition: The image is divided into four subbands using separable filters. Each coefficient in the subbands LL_2, LH_2, HL_2 and HH_2 represents a spatial area corresponding to approximately a 4 × 4 area of the original picture. The low frequencies at this scale represent a bandwidth approximately corresponding to $0 < |\omega| < \pi/4$, whereas the high frequencies represent the band from $\pi/4 < |\omega| < \pi/2$.

be a column vector whose elements are the array of coefficients resulting from the wavelet transform or subband decomposition applied to x. From the transform point of view, X represents a linear transformation of x represented by the matrix W, i.e.,

$$X = Wx. \qquad (1)$$

Although not actually computed this way, the effective filters that generate the subband signals from the original signal form basis functions for the transformation, i.e., the rows of W. Different coefficients in the same subband represent the projection of the entire image onto translates of a prototype subband filter, since from the subband point of view, they are simply regularly spaced different outputs of a convolution between the image and a subband filter. Thus, the basis functions for each coefficient in a given subband are simply translates of one another.

In subband coding systems [32], the coefficients from a given subband are usually grouped together for the purposes of designing quantizers and coders. Such a grouping suggests that statistics computed from a subband are in some sense representative of the samples in that subband. However this statistical grouping once again implicitly de-emphasizes the outliers, which tend to represent the most significant anomalies or edges. In this paper, the term "wavelet transform" is used because each wavelet coefficient is individually and deterministically compared to the same set of thresholds for the purpose of measuring significance. Thus, each coefficient is treated as a distinct, potentially important piece of data regardless of its scale, and no statistics for a whole subband are used in any form. The result is that the small number of "deterministically" significant fine scale coefficients are not obscured because of their "statistical" insignificance.

The filters used to compute the discrete wavelet transform in the coding experiments described in this paper are based on the 9-tap symmetric quadrature mirror filters (QMF) whose coefficients are given in [1]. This transformation has also been called a QMF-pyramid. These filters were chosen because in addition to their good localization properties, their symmetry allows for simple edge treatments, and they produce good results empirically. Additionally, using properly scaled coefficients, the transformation matrix for a discrete wavelet transform obtained using these filters is so close to unitary that it can be treated as unitary for the purpose of lossy compression. Since unitary transforms preserve L_2 norms, it makes sense from a numerical standpoint to compare all of the resulting transform coefficients to the same thresholds to assess significance.

III. Zerotrees of Wavelet Coefficients

In this section, an important aspect of low bit rate image coding is discussed: the coding of the positions of those coefficients that will be transmitted as nonzero values. Using scalar quantization followed by entropy coding, in order to achieve very low bit rates, i.e., less than 1 bit/pel, the probability of the most likely symbol after quantization—the zero symbol—must be extremely high. Typically, a large fraction of the bit budget must be spent on encoding the *significance map*, or the binary decision as to whether a sample, in this case a coefficient of a 2-D discrete wavelet transform, has a zero or nonzero quantized value. It follows that a significant improvement in encoding the significance map translates into a corresponding gain in compression efficiency.

A. Significance Map Encoding

To appreciate the importance of significance map encoding, consider a typical transform coding system where a decorrelating transformation is followed by an entropy-coded scalar quantizer. The following discussion is not intended to be a rigorous justification for significance map encoding, but merely to provide the reader with a sense of the relative coding costs of the position information contained in the significance map relative to amplitude and sign information.

A typical low-bit rate image coder has three basic components: a transformation, a quantizer and data compres-

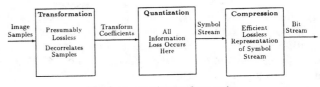

Fig. 3. A generic transform coder.

sion, as shown in Fig. 3. The original image is passed through some transformation to produce transform coefficients. This transformation is considered to be lossless, although in practice this may not be the case exactly. The transform coefficients are then quantized to produce a stream of symbols, each of which corresponds to an index of a particular quantization bin. Note that virtually all of the information loss occurs in the quantization stage. The data compression stage takes the stream of symbols and attempts to losslessly represent the data stream as efficiently as possible.

The goal of the transformation is to produce coefficients that are decorrelated. If we could, we would ideally like a transformation to remove all dependencies between samples. Assume for the moment that the transformation is doing its job so well that the resulting transform coefficients are not merely uncorrelated, but statistically independent. Also, assume that we have removed the mean and coded it separately so that the transform coefficients can be modeled as zero-mean, independent, although perhaps not identically distributed random variables. Furthermore, we might additionally constrain the model so that the probability density functions (PDF) for the coefficients are symmetric.

The goal is to quantize the transform coefficients so that the entropy of the resulting distribution of bin indexes is small enough so that the symbols can be entropy-coded at some target low bit rate, say for example 0.5 bits per pixel (bpp.). Assume that the quantizers will be symmetric midtread, perhaps nonuniform, quantizers, although different symmetric midtread quantizers may be used for different groups of transform coefficients. Letting the central bin be index 0, note that because of the symmetry, for a bin with a nonzero index magnitude, a positive or negative index is equally likely. In other words, for each nonzero index encoded, the entropy code is going to require at least one-bit for the sign. An entropy code can be designed based on modeling probabilities of bin indices as the fraction of coefficients in which the absolute value of a particular bin index occurs. Using this simple model, and assuming that the resulting symbols are independent, the entropy of the symbols H can be expressed as

$$H = -p \log_2 p - (1 - p) \log_2 (1 - p)$$
$$+ (1 - p)[1 + H_{NZ}], \qquad (2)$$

where p is the probability that a transform coefficient is quantized to zero, and H_{NZ} represents the conditional entropy of the absolute values of the quantized coefficients conditioned on them being nonzero. The first two terms in the sum represent the first-order binary entropy of the significance map, whereas the third term represents the conditional entropy of the distribution of nonzero values multiplied by the probability of them being nonzero. Thus, we can express the true cost of encoding the actual symbols as follows:

$$\text{Total Cost} = \text{Cost of Significance Map}$$
$$+ \text{Cost of Nonzero Values.} \quad (3)$$

Returning to the model, suppose that the target is $H = 0.5$. What is the minimum probability of zero achievable? Consider the case where we only use a 3-level quantizer, i.e. $H_{NZ} = 0$. Solving for p provides a lower bound on the probability of zero given the independence assumption

$$p_{\min}(H_{NZ} = 0, H = 0.5) = 0.916. \quad (4)$$

In this case, under the most ideal conditions, 91.6% of the coefficients must be quantized to zero. Furthermore, 83% of the bit budget is used in encoding the significance map. Consider a more typical example where $H_{NZ} = 4$, the minimum probability of zero is

$$p_{\min}(H_{NZ} = 4, H = 0.5) = 0.954. \quad (5)$$

In this case, the probability of zero must increase, while the cost of encoding the significance map is still 54% of the cost.

As the target rate decreases, the probability of zero increases, and the fraction of the encoding cost attributed to the significance map increases. Of course, the independence assumption is unrealistic and in practice, there are often additional dependencies between coefficients that can be exploited to further reduce the cost of encoding the significance map. Nevertheless, the conclusion is that no matter how optimal the transform, quantizer or entropy coder, under very typical conditions, the cost of determining the positions of the few significant coefficients represents a significant portion of the bit budget at low rates, and is likely to become an increasing fraction of the total cost as the rate decreases. As will be seen, by employing an image model based on an extremely simple and easy to satisfy hypothesis, we can efficiently encode significance maps of wavelet coefficients.

B. Compression of Significance Maps using Zerotrees of Wavelet Coefficients

To improve the compression of significance maps of wavelet coefficients, a new data structure called a *zerotree* is defined. A wavelet coefficient x is said to be *insignificant* with respect to a given threshold T if $|x| < T$. The zerotree is based on the hypothesis that if a wavelet coefficient at a coarse scale is insignificant with respect to a given threshold T, then *all* wavelet coefficients of the same orientation in the same spatial location at finer scales are likely to be insignificant with respect to T. Empirical evidence suggests that this hypothesis is often true.

More specifically, in a hierarchical subband system, with the exception of the highest frequency subbands, every coefficient at a given scale can be related to a set of coefficients at the next finer scale of similar orientation. The coefficient at the coarse scale is called the *parent*, and all coefficients corresponding to the same spatial location at the next finer scale of similar orientation are called *children*. For a given parent, the set of all coefficients at all finer scales of similar orientation corresponding to the same location are called *descendants*. Similarly, for a given child, the set of coefficients at all coarser scales of similar orientation corresponding to the same location are called *ancestors*. For a QMF-pyramid subband decomposition, the parent–child dependencies are shown in Fig. 4. A wavelet tree descending from a coefficient in subband $HH3$ is also seen in Fig. 4. With the exception of the lowest frequency subband, all parents have four children. For the lowest frequency subband, the parent–child relationship is defined such that each parent node has three children.

A scanning of the coefficients is performed in such a way that no child node is scanned before its parent. For an N-scale transform, the scan begins at the lowest frequency subband, denoted as LL_N, and scans subbands HL_N, LH_N, and HH_N, at which point it moves on to scale $N - 1$, etc. The scanning pattern for a 3-scale QMF-pyramid can be seen in Fig. 5. Note that each coefficient within a given subband is scanned before any coefficient in the next subband.

Given a threshold level T to determine whether or not a coefficient is significant, a coefficient x is said to be an element of a *zerotree* for threshold T if itself and *all* of its descendents are insignificant with respect to T. An element of a zerotree for threshold T is a *zerotree root* if it is not the descendant of a previously found zerotree root for threshold T, i.e., it is not *predictably insignificant* from the discovery of a zerotree root at a coarser scale at the same threshold. A zerotree root is encoded with a special symbol indicating that the insignificance of the coefficients at finer scales is completely predictable. The significance map can be efficiently represented as a string of symbols from a 3-symbol alphabet which is then entropy-coded. The three symbols used are 1) zerotree root, 2) isolated zero, which means that the coefficient is insignificant but has some significant descendant, and 3) significant. When encoding the finest scale coefficients, since coefficients have no children, the symbols in the string come from a 2-symbol alphabet, whereby the zerotree symbol is not used.

As will be seen in Section IV, in addition to encoding the significance map, it is useful to encode the sign of significant coefficients along with the significance map. Thus, in practice, four symbols are used: 1) zerotree root, 2) isolated zero, 3) positive significant, and 4) negative significant. This minor addition will be useful for embedding. The flow chart for the decisions made at each coefficient are shown in Fig. 6.

Note that it is also possible to include two additional symbols such as "positive/negative significant, but descendants are zerotrees" etc. In practice, it was found that

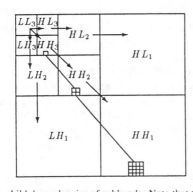

Fig. 4. Parent–child dependencies of subbands: Note that the arrow points from the subband of the parents to the subband of the children. The lowest frequency subband is the top left, and the highest frequency subband is at the bottom right. Also shown is a wavelet tree consisting of all of the descendents of a single coefficient in subband *HH*3. The coefficient in *HH*3 is a zerotree root if it is insignificant and *all* of its descendants are insignificant.

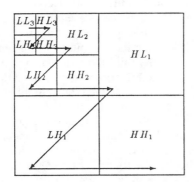

Fig. 5. Scanning order of the subbands for encoding a significance map: Note that parents must be scanned before children. Also note that all positions in a given subband are scanned before the scan moves to the next subband.

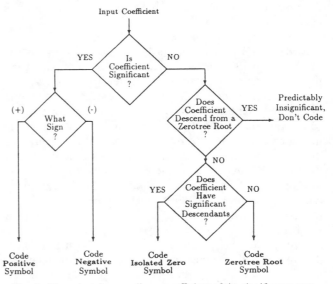

Fig. 6. Flow chart for encoding a coefficient of the significance map.

at low bit rates, this addition often increases the cost of coding the significance map. To see why this may occur, consider that there is a cost associated with partitioning the set of positive (or negative) significant samples into those whose descendents are zerotrees and those with significant descendants. If the cost of this decision is C bits, but the cost of encoding a zerotree is less than $C/4$ bits, then it is more efficient to code four zerotree symbols separately than to use additional symbols.

Zerotree coding reduces the cost of encoding the significance map using self-similarity. Even though the image has been transformed using a decorrelating transform the *occurrences* of insignificant coefficients are not independent events. More traditional techniques employing transform coding typically encode the binary map via some form of run-length encoding [30]. Unlike the zerotree symbol, which is a single "terminating" symbol and applies to all tree-depths, run-length encoding requires a symbol for each run-length which much be encoded. A technique that is closer in spirit to the zerotrees is the end-of-block (EOB) symbol used in JPEG [30], which is also a "terminating" symbol indicating that all remaining DCT coefficients in the block are quantized to zero. To

see why zerotrees may provide an advantage over EOB symbols, consider that a zerotree represents the insignificance information in a given orientation over an approximately square spatial area at all finer scales up to and including the scale of the zerotree root. Because the wavelet transform is a hierarchical representation, varying the scale in which a zerotree root occurs automatically adapts the spatial area over which insignificance is represented. The EOB symbol, however, always represents insignificance over the same spatial area, although the number of frequency bands within that spatial area varies. Given a fixed block size, such as 8 × 8, there is exactly one scale in the wavelet transform in which if a zerotree root is found at that scale, it corresponds to the same spatial area as a block of the DCT. If a zerotree root can be identified at a coarser scale, then the insignificance pertaining to that orientation can be predicted over a larger area. Similarly, if the zerotree root does not occur at this scale, then looking for zerotrees at finer scales represents a hierarchical divide and conquer approach to searching for one or more smaller areas of insignificance over the same spatial regions as the DCT block size. Thus, many more coefficients can be predicted in smooth areas where a root typically occurs at a coarse scale. Furthermore, the zerotree approach can isolate interesting non-zero details by immediately eliminating large insignificant regions from consideration.

Note that this technique is quite different from previous attempts to exploit self-similarity in image coding [19] in that it is far easier to predict insignificance than to predict significant detail across scales. The zerotree approach was developed in recognition of the difficulty in achieving meaningful bit rate reductions for significant coefficients via additional prediction. Instead, the focus here is on reducing the cost of encoding the significance map so that, for a given bit budget, more bits are available to encode expensive significant coefficients. In practice, a large fraction of the insignificant coefficients are efficiently encoded as part of a zerotree.

A similar technique has been used by Lewis and Knowles (LK) [15], [16]. In that work, a "tree" is said to be zero if its energy is less than a perceptually based threshold. Also, the "zero flag" used to encode the tree is not entropy-coded. The present work represents an improvement that allows for embedded coding for two reasons. Applying a deterministic threshold to determine significance results in a zerotree symbol which guarantees that no descendant of the root has a magnitude larger than the threshold. As a result, there is no possibility of a significant coefficient being obscured by a statistical energy measure. Furthermore, the zerotree symbol developed in this paper is part of an alphabet for entropy coding the significance map which further improves its compression. As will be discussed subsequently, it is the first property that makes this method of encoding a significance map useful in conjunction with successive-approximation. Recently, a promising technique representing a compromise between the EZW algorithm and the LK coder has been presented in [34].

C. Interpretation as a Simple Image Model

The basic hypothesis—if a coefficient at a coarse scale is insignificant with respect to a threshold then all of its descendants, as defined above, are also insignificant—can be interpreted as an extremely general image model. One of the aspects that seems to be common to most models used to describe images is that of a "decaying spectrum." For example, this property exists for both stationary autoregressive models, and non-stationary fractal, or "nearly-1/f" models, as implied by the name which refers to a generalized spectrum [33]. The model for the zerotree hypothesis is even more general than "decaying spectrum" in that it allows for some deviations to "decaying spectrum" because it is linked to a specific threshold. Consider an example where the threshold is 50, and we are considering a coefficient of magnitude 30, and whose largest descendant has a magnitude of 40. Although a higher frequency descendant has a larger magnitude (40) than the coefficient under consideration (30), i.e., the "decaying spectrum" hypothesis is violated, the coefficient under consideration can still be represented using a zerotree root since the whole tree is still insignificant (magnitude less than 50). Thus, assuming the more common image models have some validity, the zerotree hypothesis should be satisfied easily and extremely often. For those instances where the hypothesis is violated, it is safe to say that an *informative*, i.e., unexpected, event has occurred, and we should expect the cost of representing this event to be commensurate with its self-information.

It should also be pointed out that the improvement in encoding significance maps provided by zerotrees is specifically *not* the result of exploiting any linear dependencies between coefficients of different scales that were not removed in the transform stage. In practice, the linear correlation between the values of parent and child wavelet coefficients has been found to be extremely small, implying that the wavelet transform is doing an excellent job of producing nearly uncorrelated coefficients. However, there is likely additional dependency between the *squares* (or magnitudes) of parents and children. Experiments run on about 30 images of all different types, show that the correlation coefficient between the square of a child and the square of its parent tends to be between 0.2 and 0.6 with a string concentration around 0.35. Although this dependency is difficult to characterize in general for most images, even without access to specific statistics, it is reasonable to *expect* the magnitude of a child to be smaller than the magnitude of its parent. In other words, it can be reasonably conjectured based on experience with real-world images, that had we known the details of the statistical dependencies, and computed an "optimal" estimate, such as the conditional expectation of the child's magnitude given the parent's magnitude, that the "optimal" estimator would, with very high probability, predict that the child's magnitude would be the smaller of the two. Using only this mild assumption, based on an inexact statistical characterization, given a fixed threshold, and conditioned on the knowledge that a parent is insignificant with respect to the threshold, the "optimal" estimate of the significance of the rest of the descending wavelet tree is that it is entirely insignificant with respect to the same threshold, i.e., a zerotree. On the other hand, if the parent is significant, the "optimal" estimate of the significance of descendants is highly dependent on the details of the estimator whose knowledge would require more detailed information about the statistical nature of the image. Thus, under this mild assumption, using zerotrees to predict the insignificance of wavelet coefficients at fine scales given the insignificance of a root at a coarse scale is more likely to be successful in the absence of additional information than attempting to predict significant detail across scales.

This argument can be made more concrete. Let x be a child of y, where x and y are zero-mean random variables, whose probability density functions (PDF) are related as

$$p_x(x) = ap_y(ax), \qquad a > 1. \qquad (6)$$

This states that random variables x and y have the same PDF shape, and that

$$\sigma_y^2 = a^2\sigma_x^2. \qquad (7)$$

Assume further that x and y are uncorrelated, i.e.,

$$E[xy] = 0. \qquad (8)$$

Note that nothing has been said about treating the subbands as a group, or as stationary random processes, only that there is a similarity relationship between random variables of parents and children. It is also reasonable because for intermediate subbands a coefficient that is a child with respect to one coefficient is a parent with respect to others; the PDF of that coefficient should be the same in either case. Let $u = x^2$ and $v = y^2$. Suppose that u and

v are correlated with correlation coefficient ρ. We have the following relationships:

$$E[u] = \sigma_x^2 \qquad (9)$$

$$E[v] = \sigma_y^2 \qquad (10)$$

$$\sigma_u^2 = E[x^4] - \sigma_x^4 \qquad (11)$$

$$\sigma_v^2 = E[y^4] - \sigma_y^4. \qquad (12)$$

Notice in particular that

$$\sigma_v^2 = a^4 \sigma_u^2. \qquad (13)$$

Using a well known result, the expression for the best linear unbiased estimator (BLUE) of u given v to minimize error variance is given by

$$\hat{u}_{\text{BLUE}}(v) = E[u] - \rho \frac{\sigma_u}{\sigma_v}(E[v] - v) \qquad (14)$$

$$= \frac{1 - \rho}{a^2} \sigma_y^2 + \rho \frac{v}{a^2}. \qquad (15)$$

If it is observed that the magnitude of the parent is below the threshold T, i.e., $v = y^2 < T^2$, then the BLUE can be upper bounded by

$$\hat{u}_{\text{BLUE}}(v|v < T^2) < \frac{1 - \rho}{a^2} \sigma_y^2 + \rho \frac{T^2}{a^2}. \qquad (16)$$

Consider two cases a) $T \geq \sigma_y$ and b) $T < \sigma_y$. In case (a), we have

$$\hat{u}_{\text{BLUE}}(v|v < T^2) \leq \frac{T^2}{a^2} < T^2, \qquad (17)$$

which implies that the BLUE of x^2 given $|y| < T$ is less than T^2, for *any* ρ, including $\rho = 0$. In case (b), we can only upper bound the right hand side of (16) by T^2 if ρ exceeds the lower bound

$$\rho \geq \frac{1 - \dfrac{a^2 T^2}{\sigma_y^2}}{1 - \dfrac{T^2}{\sigma_y^2}} \triangleq \rho_0. \qquad (18)$$

Of course, a better nonlinear estimate might yield different results, but the above analysis suggests that for threshold exceeding the standard deviation of the parent, which by (6) exceeds the standard deviation of all descendants, if it is observed that a parent is insignificant with respect to the threshold, then, using the above BLUE, the estimates for the magnitudes of all descendants is that they are less than the threshold, and a zerotree is expected regardless of the correlation between squares of parents and squares of children. As the threshold decreases, more correlation is required to justify *expecting* a zerotree to occur. Finally, since the lower bound $\rho_0 \rightarrow 1$ as $T \rightarrow 0$, as the threshold is reduced, it becomes increasingly difficult to expect zerotrees to occur, and more knowledge of the particular statistics are required to make inferences. The implication of this analysis is that at very low bit

rates, where the probability of an insignificant sample must be high and thus, the significance threshold T must also be large, expecting the occurrence of zerotrees and encoding significance maps using zerotree coding is reasonable without even knowing the statistics. However, letting T decrease, there is some point below which the advantage of zerotree coding diminishes, and this point is dependent on the specific nature of higher order dependencies between parents and children. In particular, the stronger this dependence, the more T can be decreased while still retaining an advantage using zerotree coding. Once again, this argument is not intended to "prove" the optimality of zerotree coding, only to suggest a rationale for its demonstrable success.

D. Zerotree-Like Structures in Other Subband Configurations

The concept of predicting the insignificance of coefficients from low frequency to high frequency information corresponding to the same spatial localization is a fairly general concept and not specific to the wavelet transform configuration shown in Fig. 4. Zerotrees are equally applicable to quincunx wavelets [2], [13], [23], [29], in which case each parent would have two children instead of four, except for the lowest frequency, where parents have a single child.

Also, a similar approach can be applied to linearly spaced subband decompositions, such as the DCT, and to other more general subband decompositions, such as wavelet packets [5] and Laplacian pyramids [4]. For example, one of many possible parent–child relationship for linearly spaced subbands can be seen in Fig. 7. Of course, with the use of linearly spaced subbands, zerotree-like coding loses its ability to adapt the spatial extent of the insignificance prediction. Nevertheless, it is possible for zerotree-like coding to outperform EOB-coding since more coefficients can be predicted from the subbands along the diagonal. For the case of wavelet packets, the situation is a bit more complicated, because a wider range of tilings of the "space-frequency" domain are possible. In that case, it may not always be possible to define similar parent-child relationships because a high-frequency coefficient may in fact correspond to a larger spatial area than a co-located lower frequency coefficient. On the other hand, in a coding scheme such as the "best-basis" approach of Coifman *et al.* [5], had the image-dependent best basis resulted in such a situation, one wonders if the underlying hypothesis—that magnitudes of coefficients tend to decay with frequency—would be reasonable anyway. These zerotree-like extensions represent interesting areas for further research.

IV. SUCCESSIVE-APPROXIMATION

The previous section describes a method of encoding significance maps of wavelet coefficients that, at least empirically, seems to consistently produce a code with a lower bit rate than either the empirical first-order entropy,

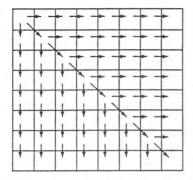

Fig. 7. Parent–child dependencies for linearly spaced subbands systems, such as the DCT. Note that the arrow points from the subband of the parents to the subband of the children. The lowest frequency subband is the top left, and the highest frequency subband is at the bottom right.

or a run-length code of the significance map. The original motivation for employing successive-approximation in conjunction with zerotree coding was that since zerotree coding was performing so well encoding the significance map of the wavelet coefficients, it was hoped that more efficient coding could be achieved by zerotree coding more significance maps.

Another motivation for successive-approximation derives directly from the goal of developing an embedded code analogous to the binary-representation of an approximation to a real number. Consider the wavelet transform of an image as a mapping whereby an amplitude exists for each coordinate in scale-space. The scale-space coordinate system represents a coarse-to-fine "logarithmic" representation of the domain of the function. Taking the coarse-to-fine philosophy one-step further, successive-approximation provides a coarse-to-fine, multiprecision "logarithmic" representation of amplitude information, which can be thought of as the range of the image function when viewed in the scale-space coordinate system defined by the wavelet transform. Thus, in a very real sense, the EZW coder generates a representation of the image that is coarse-to-fine in both the domain and range simultaneously.

A. Successive-Approximation Entropy-Coded Quantization

To perform the embedded coding, successive-approximation quantization (SAQ) is applied. As will be seen, SAQ is related to bit-plane encoding of the magnitudes. The SAQ sequentially applies a sequence of thresholds $T_0, \cdots, T_{N-1}$ to determine significance, where the thresholds are chosen so that $T_i = T_{i-1}/2$. The initial threshold T_0 is chosen so that $|X_j| < 2T_0$ for all transform coefficients x_j.

During the encoding (and decoding), two separate lists of wavelet coefficients are maintained. At any point in the process, the *dominant* list contains the *coordinates* of those coefficients that have not yet been found to be significant in the same relative order as the initial scan. This scan is such that the subbands are ordered, and within each subband, the set of coefficients are ordered. Thus,

using the ordering of the subbands shown in Fig. 5, all coefficients in a given subband appear on the initial dominant list prior to coefficients in the next subband. The *subordinate* list contains the *magnitudes* of those coefficients that have been found to be significant. For each threshold, each list is scanned once.

During a *dominant pass*, coefficients with coordinates on the dominant list, i.e., those that have not yet been found to be significant, are compared to the threshold T_i to determine their significance, and if significant, their sign. This significance map is then zerotree coded using the method outlined in Section III. Each time a coefficient is encoded as significant, (positive or negative), its magnitude is appended to the subordinate list, and the coefficient in the wavelet transform array is set to zero so that the significant coefficient does not prevent the occurrence of a zerotree on future dominant passes at smaller thresholds.

A dominant pass is followed by a *subordinate pass* in which all coefficients on the subordinate list are scanned and the specifications of the magnitudes available to the decoder are refined to an additional bit of precision. More specifically, during a subordinate pass, the *width* of the effective quantizer step size, which defines an uncertainty interval for the true magnitude of the coefficient, is cut in half. For each magnitude on the subordinate list, this refinement can be encoded using a binary alphabet with a "1" symbol indicating that the true value falls in the upper half of the old uncertainty interval and a "0" symbol indicating the lower half. The string of symbols from this binary alphabet that is generated during a subordinate pass is then entropy coded. Note that prior to this refinement, the width of the uncertainty region is exactly equal to the current threshold. After the completion of a subordinate pass the magnitudes on the subordinate list are sorted in decreasing magnitude, to the extent that the decoder has the information to perform the same sort.

The process continues to alternate between dominant passes and subordinate passes where the threshold is halved before each dominant pass. (In principle one could divide by other factors than 2. This factor of 2 was chosen here because it has nice interpretations in terms of bit plane encoding and numerical precision in a familiar base 2, and good coding results were obtained).

In the decoding operation, each decoded symbol, both during a dominant and a subordinate pass, refines and reduces the width of the uncertainty interval in which the true value of the coefficient (or coefficients, in the case of a zerotree root) may occur. The reconstruction value used can be anywhere in that uncertainty interval. For minimum mean-square error distortion, one could use the centroid of the uncertainty region using some model for the PDF of the coefficients. However, a practical approach, which is used in the experiments, and is also MINMAX optimal, is to simply use the center of the uncertainty interval as the reconstruction value.

The encoding stops when some target stopping condition is met, such as when the bit budget is exhausted. The encoding can cease at any time and the resulting bit stream contains all lower rate encodings. Note, that if the bit stream is truncated at an arbitrary point, there may be bits at the end of the code that do not decode to a valid symbol since a codeword has bene truncated. In that case, these bits do not reduce the width of an uncertainty interval or any distortion function. In fact, it is very likely that the first L bits of the bit stream will produce exactly the same image as the first $L + 1$ bits which occurs if the additional bit is insufficient to complete the decoding of another symbol. Nevertheless, terminating the decoding of an embedded bit stream at a specific point in the bit stream produces exactly the same image that would have resulted had that point been the initial target rate. This ability to cease encoding or decoding anywhere is extremely useful in systems that are either rate-constrained or distortion-constrained. A side benefit of the technique is that an operational rate vs. distortion plot for the algorithm can be computed on-line.

B. Relationship to Bit Plane Encoding

Although the embedded coding system described here is considerably more general and more sophisticated than simple bit-plane encoding, consideration of the relationship with bit-plane encoding provides insight into the success of embedded coding.

Consider the successive-approximation quantizer for the case when all thresholds are powers of two, and all wavelet coefficients are integers. In this case, for each coefficient that eventually gets coded as significant, the sign and *bit position* of the most-significant binary digit (MSBD) are measured and encoded during a dominant pass. For example, consider the 10-bit representation of the number 41 as 0000101001. Also, consider the binary digits as a sequence of binary decisions in a binary tree. Proceeding from left to right, if we have not yet encountered a ''1,'' we expect the probability distribution for the next digit to be strongly biased toward ''0.'' The digits to the left and including the MSBD are called the *dominant bits*, and are measured during dominant passes. After the MSBD has been encountered, we expect a more random and much less biased distribution between a ''0'' and a ''1,'' although we might still expect $P(0) > P(1)$ because most PDF models for transform coefficients decay with amplitude. Those binary digits to the right of the MSBD are called the *subordinate bits* and are measured and encoded during the subordinate pass. A zeroth-order approximation suggests that we should expect to pay close to one bit per ''binary digit'' for subordinate bits, while dominant bits should be far less expensive.

By using successive-approximation beginning with the largest possible threshold, where the probability of zero is extremely close to one, and by using zerotree coding, whose efficiency increases as the probability of zero increases, we should be able to code dominant bits with very few bits, since they are most often part of a zerotree.

In general, the thresholds need not be powers of two.

However, by factoring out a constant mantissa, M, the starting threshold T_0 can be expressed in terms of a threshold that is a power of two

$$T_0 = M2^E, \qquad (19)$$

where the exponent E is an integer, in which case, the dominant and subordinate bits of appropriately scaled wavelet coefficients are coded during dominant and subordinate passes, respectively.

C. Advantage of Small Alphabets for Adaptive Arithmetic Coding

Note that the particular encoder alphabet used by the arithmetic coder at any given time contains either 2, 3, or 4 symbols depending whether the encoding is for a subordinate pass, a dominant pass with no zerotree root symbol, or a dominant pass with the zerotree root symbol. This is a real advantage for adapting the arithmetic coder. Since there are never more than four symbols, all of the possibilities typically occur with a reasonably measurable frequency. This allows an adaptation algorithm with a short memory to learn quickly and constantly track changing symbol probabilities. This adaptivity accounts for some of the effectiveness of the overall algorithm. Contrast this with the case of a large alphabet, as is the case in algorithms that do not use successive approximation. In that case, it takes many events before an adaptive entropy coder can reliably estimate the probabilities of unlikely symbols (see the discussion of the zero-frequency problem in [3]). Furthermore, these estimates are fairly unreliable because images are typically statistically nonstationary and local symbol probabilities change from region to region.

In the practical coder used in the experiments, the arithmetic coder is based on [31]. In arithmetic coding, the encoder is separate from the model, which in [31], is basically a histogram. During the dominant passes, simple Markov conditioning is used whereby one of four histograms is chosen depending on 1) whether the previous coefficient in the scan is known to be significant, and 2) whether the parent is known to be significant. During the subordinate passes, a single histogram is used. Each histogram entry is initialized to a count of one. After encoding each symbol, the corresponding histogram entry is incremented. When the sum of all the counts in a histogram reaches the maximum count, each entry is incremented and integer divided by two, as described in [31]. It should be mentioned, that for practical purposes, the coding gains provided by using this simple Markov conditioning may not justify the added complexity and using a single histogram strategy for the dominant pass performs almost as well (0.12 dB worse for Lena at 0.25 bpp.). The choice of maximum histogram count is probably more critical, since that controls the learning rate for the adaptation. For the experimental results presented, a maximum count of 256 was used, which provides an intermediate tradeoff between the smallest possible probability, which is the reciprocal of the maximum count, and the learning rate, which is faster with a smaller maximum histogram count.

D. Order of Importance of the Bits

Although importance is a subjective term, the order of processing used in EZW implicitly defines a precise ordering of importance that is tied to, in order, *precision*, *magnitude*, *scale*, and *spatial location* as determined by the initial dominant list.

The primary determination of ordering importance is the numerical *precision* of the coefficients. This can be seen in the fact that the uncertainty intervals for the magnitude of all coefficients are refined to the same precision before the uncertainty interval for any coefficient is refined further.

The second factor in the determination of importance is *magnitude*. Importance by magnitude manifests itself during a dominant pass because prior to the pass, all coefficients are insignificant and presumed to be zero. When they are found to be significant, they are all assumed to have the same magnitude, which is greater than the magnitudes of those coefficients that remain insignificant. Importance by magnitude manifests itself during a subordinate pass by the fact that magnitudes are refined in descending order of the center of the uncertainty intervals, i.e., the decoder's interpretation of the magnitude.

The third factor, *scale*, manifests itself in the *a priori* ordering of the subbands on the initial dominant list. Until the significance of the magnitude of a coefficient is discovered during a dominant pass, coefficients in coarse scales are tested for significance before coefficients in fine scales. This is consistent with prioritization by the decoder's version of magnitude since for all coefficients not yet found to be significant, the magnitude is presumed to be zero.

The final factor, *spatial location*, merely implies that two coefficients that cannot yet be distinguished by the decoder in terms of either precision, magnitude, or scale, have their relative importance determined arbitrarily by the initial scanning order of the subband containing the two coefficients.

In one sense, this embedding strategy has a strictly nonincreasing operational distortion-rate function for the distortion metric defined to be the sum of the widths of the uncertainty intervals of all of the wavelet coefficients. Since a discrete wavelet transform is an invertible representation of an image, a distortion function defined in the wavelet transform domain is also a distortion function defined on the image. This distortion function is also not without a rational foundation for low-bit rate coding, where noticeable artifacts must be tolerated, and perceptual metrics based on just-noticeable differences (JND's) do not always predict which artifacts human viewers will prefer. Since minimizing the widths of uncertainty intervals minimizes the largest possible errors, artifacts, which result from numerical errors large enough to exceed perceptible thresholds, are minimized. Even using this distortion function, the proposed embedding strategy is not

optimal, because truncation of the bit stream in the middle of a pass causes some uncertainty intervals to be twice as large as others.

Actually, as it has been described thus far, EZW is unlikely to be optimal for *any* distortion function. Notice that in (19), dividing the thresholds by two simply decrements E leaving M unchanged. While there must exist an optimal starting M which minimizes a given distortion function, how to find this optimum is still an open question and seems highly image dependent. Without knowledge of the optimal M and being forced to choose it based on some other consideration, with probability one, either increasing or decreasing M would have produced an embedded code which has a lower distortion for the same rate. Despite the fact that without trial and error optimization for M, EZW is probably suboptimal, it is nevertheless quite effective in practice.

Note also that using the width of the uncertainty interval as a distance metric is exactly the same metric used in finite-precision fixed-point approximations of real numbers. Thus, the embedded code can be seen as an ''image'' generalization of finite-precision fixed-point approximations of real numbers.

E. Relationship to Priority-Position Coding

In a technique based on a very similar philosophy, Huang *et al.* discusses a related approach to embedding, or ordering the information in importance, called priority-position coding (PPC) [10]. They prove very elegantly that the entropy of a source is equal to the average entropy of a particular ordering of that source plus the average entropy of the position information necessary to reconstruct the source. Applying a sequence of decreasing thresholds, they attempt to sort by amplitude all of the DCT coefficients for the entire image based on a partition of the range of amplitudes. For each coding pass, they transmit the significance map which is arithmetically encoded. Additionally, when a significant coefficient is found they transmit its value to its full precision. Like the EZW algorithm, PPC implicitly defines importance with respect to the magnitudes of the transform coefficients. In one sense, PPC is a generalization of the successive-approximation method presented in this paper, because PPC allows more general partitions of the amplitude range of the transform coefficients. On the other hand, since PPC sends the value of a significant coefficient to full precision, its protocol assigns a greater importance to the least significant bit of a significant coefficient than to the identification of new significant coefficients on next PPC pass. In contrast, as a top priority, EZW tries to reduce the width of the largest uncertainty interval in all coefficients before increasing the precision further. Additionally, PPC makes no attempt to predict insignificance from low frequency to high frequency, relying solely on the arithmetic coding to encode the significance map. Also unlike EZW, the probability estimates needed for the arithmetic coder were derived via training on an image database instead of adapting to the image itself. It would be interesting to experiment with variations which combine advantages of EZW (wavelet transforms, zerotree coding, importance defined by a decreasing sequence of uncertainty intervals, and adaptive arithmetic coding using small alphabets) with the more general approach to partitioning the range of amplitudes found in PPC. In practice, however, it is unclear whether the finest grain partitioning of the amplitude range provides any coding gain, and there is certainly a much higher computational cost associated with more passes. Additionally, with the exception of the last few low-amplitude passes, the coding results reported in [10] did use power-of-two amplitudes to define the partition suggesting that, in practice, using finer partitioning buys little coding gain.

63	-34	49	10	7	13	-12	7
-31	23	14	-13	3	4	6	-1
15	14	3	-12	5	-7	3	9
-9	-7	-14	8	4	-2	3	2
-5	9	-1	47	4	6	-2	2
3	0	-3	2	3	-2	0	4
2	-3	6	-4	3	6	3	6
5	11	5	6	0	3	-4	4

Fig. 8. Example of 3-scale wavelet transform of an 8 × 8 image.

V. A SIMPLE EXAMPLE

In this section, a simple example will be used to highlight the order of operations used in the EZW algorithm. Only the string of symbols will be shown. The reader interested in the details of adaptive arithmetic coding is referred to [31]. Consider the simple 3-scale wavelet transform of an 8 × 8 image. The array of values is shown in Fig. 8. Since the largest coefficient magnitude is 63, we can choose our initial threshold to be anywhere in (31.5, 63]. Let $T_0 = 32$. Table I shows the processing on the first dominant pass. The following comments refer to Table I:

1) The coefficient has magnitude 63 which is greater than the threshold 32, and is positive so a positive symbol is generated. After decoding this symbol, the decoder knows the coefficient in the interval [32, 64) whose center is 48.

2) Even though the coefficient 31 is insignificant with respect to the threshold 32, it has a significant descendant two generations down in subband $LH1$ with magnitude 47. Thus, the symbol for an isolated zero is generated.

3) The magnitude 23 is less than 32 and all descendants which include (3, -12, -14, 8) in subband $HH2$ and all coefficients in subband $HH1$ are insignificant. A zerotree symbol is generated, and no symbol will be generated for any coefficient in subbands $HH2$ and $HH1$ during the current dominant pass.

4) The magnitude 10 is less than 32 and all descendants (-12, 7, 6, -1) also have magnitudes less than 32. Thus a zerotree symbol is generated. Notice that this tree has a violation of the ''decaying spectrum'' hypothesis since a coefficient (-12) in subband $HL1$ has a magnitude greater than its parent (10). Nevertheless, the entire tree has magnitude less than the threshold 32 so it is still a zerotree.

5) The magnitude 14 is insignificant with respect to 32. Its children are (-1, 47, -3, 2). Since its child with magnitude 47 is significant, an isolated zero symbol is generated.

6) Note that no symbols were generated from subband $HH2$ which would ordinarily precede subband $HL1$ in the scan. Also note that since subband $HL1$ has no descendants, the entropy coding can resume using a 3-symbol

TABLE I
PROCESSING OF FIRST DOMINANT PASS AT THRESHOLD $T = 32$. SYMBOLS ARE POS FOR POSITIVE SIGNIFICANT, NEG FOR NEGATIVE SIGNIFICANT, IZ FOR ISOLATED ZERO, ZTR FOR ZEROTREE ROOT, AND Z FOR A ZERO WHEN THERE ARE NO CHILDREN. THE RECONSTRUCTION MAGNITUDES ARE TAKEN AS THE CENTER OF THE UNCERTAINTY INTERVAL

Comment	Subband	Coefficient Value	Symbol	Reconstruction Value
(1)	LL3	63	POS	48
	HL3	-34	NEG	-48
(2)	LH3	-31	IZ	0
(3)	HH3	23	ZTR	0
	HL2	49	POS	48
(4)	HL2	10	ZTR	0
	HL2	14	ZTR	0
	HL2	-13	ZTR	0
	LH2	15	ZTR	0
(5)	LH2	14	IZ	0
	LH2	-9	ZTR	0
	LH2	-7	ZTR	0
(6)	HL1	7	Z	0
	HL1	13	Z	0
	HL1	3	Z	0
	HL1	4	Z	0
	LH1	-1	Z	0
(7)	LH1	47	POS	48
	LH1	-3	Z	0
	LH1	-2	Z	0

alphabet where the IZ and ZTR symbols are merged into the Z (zero) symbol.

7) The magnitude 47 is significant with respect to 32. Note that for the future dominant passes, this position will be replaced with the value 0, so that for the next dominant pass at threshold 16, the parent of this coefficient, which has magnitude 14, can be coded using a zerotree root symbol.

During the first dominant pass, which used a threshold of 32, four significant coefficients were identified. These coefficients will be refined during the first subordinate pass. Prior to the first subordinate pass, the uncertainty interval for the magnitudes of all of the significant coefficients is the interval [32, 64). The first subordinate pass will refine these magnitudes and identify them as being either in interval [32, 48), which will be encoded with the symbol ''0,'' or in the interval [48, 64), which will be encoded with the symbol ''1.'' Thus, the decision boundary is the magnitude 48. It is no coincidence that these symbols are exactly the first bit to the right of the MSBD in the binary representation of the magnitudes. The order

TABLE II
PROCESSING OF THE FIRST SUBORDINATE PASS. MAGNITUDES ARE
PARTITIONED INTO THE UNCERTAINTY INTERVALS [32,48) AND
[48,64), WITH SYMBOLS "0" AND "1" RESPECTIVELY

Coefficient Magnitude	Symbol	Reconstruction Magnitude
63	1	56
34	0	40
49	1	56
47	0	40

of operations in the first subordinate pass is illustrated in Table II.

The first entry has magnitude 63 and is placed in the upper interval whose center is 56. The next entry has magnitude 34, which places it in the lower interval. The third entry 49 is in the upper interval, and the fourth entry 47 is in the lower interval. Note that in the case of 47, using the center of the uncertainty interval as the reconstruction value, when the reconstruction value is changed from 48 to 40, the reconstruction error actually increases from 1 to 7. Nevertheless, the uncertainty interval for this coefficient decreases from width 32 to width 16. At the conclusion of the processing of the entries on the subordinate list corresponding to the uncertainty interval [32, 64), these magnitudes are reordered for future subordinate passes in the order (63, 49, 34, 47). Note that 49 is moved ahead of 34 because from the decoder's point of view, the reconstruction values 56 and 40 are distinguishable. However, the magnitude 34 remains ahead of magnitude 47 because as far as the decoder can tell, both have magnitude 40, and the initial order, which is based first on importance by scale, has 34 prior to 47.

The process continues on to the second dominant pass at the new threshold of 16. During this pass, only those coefficients not yet found to be significant are scanned. Additionally, those coefficients previously found to be significant are treated as zero for the purpose of determining if a zerotree exists. Thus, the second dominant pass consists of encoding the coefficient -31 in subband $LH3$ as negative significant, the coefficient 23 in subband $HH3$ as positive significant, the three coefficients in subband $HL2$ that have not been previously found to be significant (10, 14, -13) are each encoded as zerotree roots, as are all four coefficients in subband $LH2$ and all four coefficients in subband $HH2$. The second dominant pass terminates at this point since all other coefficients are predictably insignificant.

The subordinate list now contains, in order, the magnitudes (63, 49, 34, 47, 31, 23) which, prior to this subordinate pass, represent the three uncertainty intervals [48, 64), [32, 48) and [16, 31), each having equal width 16. The processing will refine each magnitude by creating two new uncertainty intervals for each of the three current uncertainty intervals. At the end of the second subordinate pass, the order of the magnitudes is (63, 49, 47, 34, 31, 23), since at this point, the decoder could have identified 34 and 47 as being in different intervals. Using the center of the uncertainty interval as the reconstruction value, the decoder lists the magnitudes as (60, 52, 44, 36, 28, 20).

The processing continues alternating between dominant and subordinate passes and can stop at any time.

VI. EXPERIMENTAL RESULTS

All experiments were performed by encoding and decoding an actual bit stream to verify the correctness of the algorithm. After a 12-byte header, the entire bit stream is arithmetically encoded using a single arithmetic coder with an adaptive model [31]. The model is initialized at each new threshold for each of the dominant and subordinate passes. From that point, the encoder is fully adaptive. Note in particular that there is no training of any kind, and no ensemble statistics of images are used in any way (unless one calls the zerotree hypothesis an ensemble statistic). The 12-byte header contains 1) the number of wavelet scales, 2) the dimensions of the image, 3) the maximum histogram count for the models in the arithmetic coder, 4) the image mean and 5) the initial threshold. Note that after the header, there is no overhead except for an extra symbol for end-of-bit-stream, which is always maintained at minimum probability. This extra symbol is not needed for storage on computer medium if the end of a file can be detected.

The EZW coder was applied to the standard black and white 8 bpp. test images, 512×512 "Lena" and the 512×512 "Barbara," which are shown in Figs. 9(a) and 11(a). Coding results for "Lena" are summarized in Table III and Fig. 9. Six scales of the QMF-pyramid were used. Similar results are shown for "Barbara" in Table IV and Fig. 10. Additional results for the 256×256 "Lena" are given in [22].

Quotes of PSNR for the 512×512 "Lena" image are so abundant throughout the image coding literature that it is difficult to definitively compare these results with other coding results.[1] However, a literature search has only found two published results where authors generate an actual bit stream that claims higher PSNR performance at rates between 0.25 and 1 bit/pixel [12] and [21], the latter of which is a variation of the EZW algorithm. For the "Barbara" image, which is far more difficult than "Lena," the performance using EZW is substantially better, at least numerically, than the 27.82 dB for 0.534 bpp. reported in [28].

The performance of the EZW coder was also compared to a widely available version of JPEG [14]. JPEG does not allow the user to select a target bit rate but instead allows the user to choose a "Quality Factor." In the experiments shown in Fig. 11, "Barbara" is encoded first using JPEG to a file size of 12 866 bytes, or a bit rate of 0.39 bpp. The PSNR in this case is 26.99 dB. The EZW encoder was then applied to "Barbara" with a target file

---

[1]Actually there are multiple versions of the luminance only "Lena" floating around, and the one used in [22] is darker and slightly more difficult than the "official" one obtained by this author from RPI after [22] was published. Also note that this should not be confused with results using only the green component of an RGB version which are also commonly cited.

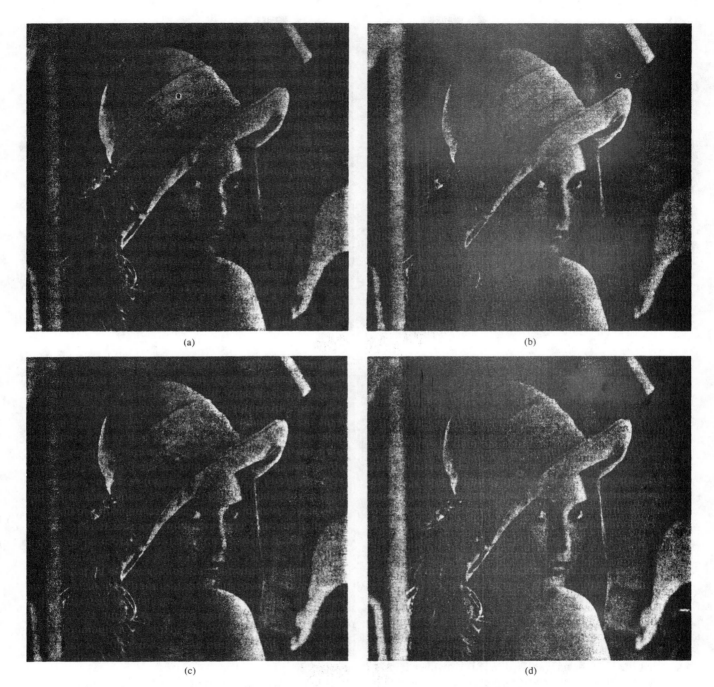

Fig. 9. Performance of EZW Coder operating on "Lena." (a) Original 512 × 512 "Lena" image at 8 bits/pixel (b) 1.0 bits/pixel, 8:1 Compression, PSNR = 39.55 dB, (c) 0.5 bits/pixel 16:1 Compression, PSNR = 36.28, (d) 0.25 bits/pixel, 32:1 Compression, PSNR = 33.17 dB, (e) 0.0625 bits/pixel, 128:1 Compression, PSNR = 27.54 dB, (f) 0.015625 bits/pixel, 512:1 Compression, PSNR = 23.63 dB.

size of exactly 12 866 bytes. The resulting PSNR is 29.39 dB, significantly higher than for JPEG. The EZW encoder was then applied to "Barbara" using a target PSNR to obtain exactly the same PSNR of 26.99. The resulting file size is 8820 bytes, or 0.27 bpp. Visually, the 0.39 bpp. EZW version looks better than the 0.39 bpp. JPEG version. While there is some loss of resolution in both, there

are noticeable blocking artifacts in the JPEG version. For the comparison at the same PSNR, one could probably argue in favor of the JPEG.

Another interesting figure of merit is the number of significant coefficients retained. DeVore *et al.* used wavelet transform coding to progressively encode the same image [8]. Using 68 272 bits, (8534 bytes, 0.26 bpp.), they re-

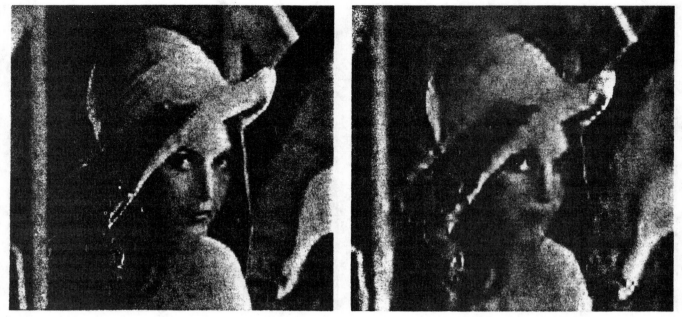

(e)   (f)

Fig. 9. (*Continued.*)

TABLE III
CODING RESULTS FOR 512 × 512 LENA SHOWING PEAK-SIGNAL-TO-NOISE
(PSNR) AND THE NUMBER OF WAVELET COEFFICIENTS THAT WERE
CODED AS NONZERO

# bytes	R	Compression	MSE	PSNR (dB)	signif. coef
32768	1.0	8:1	7.21	39.55	39446
16384	0.5	16:1	15.32	36.28	19385
8192	0.25	32:1	31.33	33.17	9774
4096	0.125	64:1	61.67	30.23	4950
2048	0.0625	128:1	114.5	27.54	2433
1024	0.03125	256:1	188.2.7	25.38	1253
512	0.015625	512:1	281.7	23.63	616
256	0.0078125	1024:1	440.2	21.69	265

TABLE IV
CODING RESULTS FOR 512 × 512 BARBARA SHOWING PEAK-SIGNAL-TO-
NOISE (PSNR) AND THE NUMBER OF WAVELET COEFFICIENTS THAT WERE
CODED AS NONZERO

# bytes	R	Compression	MSE	PSNR (dB)	signif. coef
32768	1.0	8:1	19.92	35.14	40766
16384	0.5	16:1	57.57	30.53	20554
8192	0.25	32:1	136.8	26.77	10167
4096	0.125	64:1	257.1	24.03	4522
2048	0.0625	128:1	318.5	23.10	2353
1024	0.03125	256:1	416.2	21.94	1259
512	0.015625	512:1	546.8	20.75	630
256	0.0078125	1024:1	772.5	19.54	291

tained 2019 coefficients and achieved a RMS error of 15.30 (MSE = 234, 24.42 dB), whereas using the embedded coding scheme, 9774 coefficients are retained, using only 8192 bytes. The PSNR for these two examples differs by over 8 dB. Part of the difference can be attributed to fact that the Haar basis was used in [8]. However, closer examination shows that the zerotree coding provides a much better way of encoding the positions of the significant coefficients than was used in [8].

An interesting and perhaps surprising property of embedded coding is that when the encoding or decoding is terminated during the middle of a pass, or in the middle of the scanning of a subband, there are no artifacts produced that would indicate where the termination occurs. In other words, some coefficients in the same subband are represented with twice the precision of the others. A possible explanation of this phenomena is that at low rates, there are so few significant coefficients that any one does not make a perceptible difference. Thus, if the last pass is a dominant pass, setting some coefficient that might be

significant to zero may be imperceptible. Similarly, the fact that some have more precision than others is also imperceptible. By the time the number of significant coefficients becomes large, the picture quality is usually so good that adjacent coefficients with different precisions are imperceptible.

Another interesting property of the embedded coding is that because of the implicit global bit allocation, even at extremely high compression ratios, the performance scales. At a compression ratio of 512 : 1, the image quality of ''Lena'' is poor, but still recognizable. This is not the case with conventional block coding schemes, where at such high compression ratios, there would be insufficient bits to even encode the DC coefficients of each block.

The unavoidable artifacts produced at low bit rates using this method are typical of wavelet coding schemes coded to the same PSNR's. However, subjectively, they are not nearly as objectionable as the blocking effects typical of block transform coding schemes.

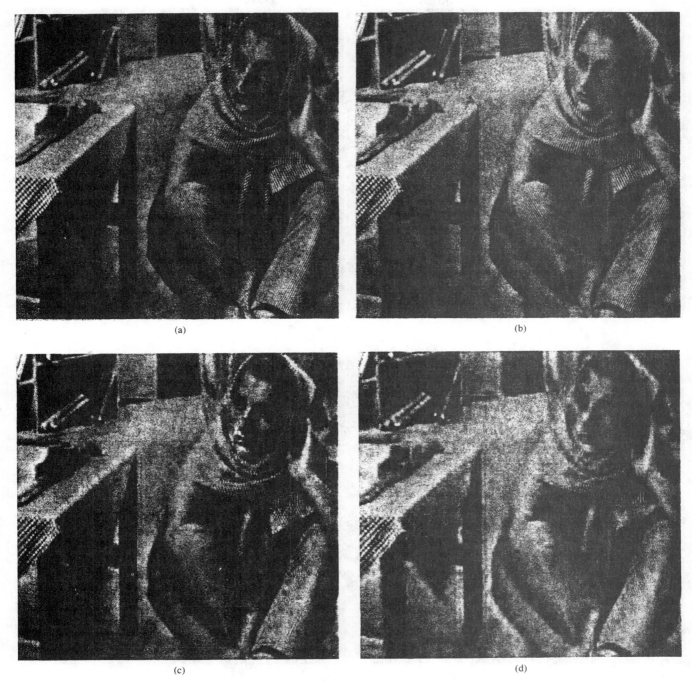

Fig. 10. Performance of EZW Coder operating on ''Barbara'' at (a) 1.0 bits/pixel, 8:1 Compression, PSNR = 35.14 dB (b) 0.5 bits/pixel, 16:1 Compression, PSNR = 30.53 dB, (c) 0.125 bits/pixel, 64:1 Compression, PSNR = 24.03 dB, (d) 0.0625 bits/pixel, 128:1 Compression, PSNR = 23.10 dB.

VII. Conclusion

A new technique for image coding has been presented that produces a fully embedded bit stream. Furthermore, the compression performance of this algorithm is competitive with virtually all known techniques. The remarkable performance can be attributed to the use of the following four features:

- a discrete wavelet transform, which decorrelates most sources fairly well, and allows the more significant bits of precision of most coefficients to be efficiently encoded as part of exponentially growing zerotrees,

- zerotree coding, which by predicting insignificance across scales using an image model that is easy for

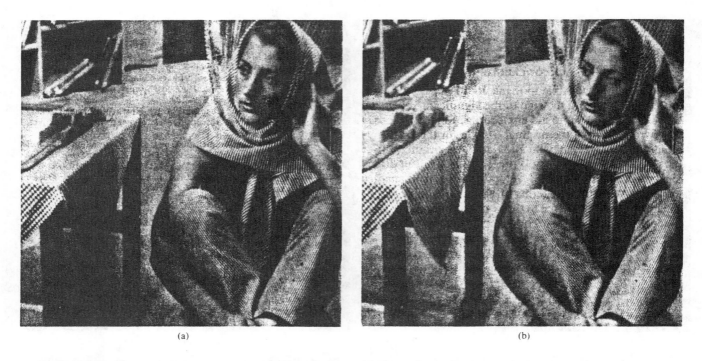

Fig. 11. Comparison of EZW and JPEG operating on ''Barbara'' (a) Original 512 × 512 (b) EZW at 12 866 bytes, 0.39 bits/pixel, 29.39 dB, (c) EZW at 8820 bytes, 0.27 bits/pixel, 26.99 dB, (d) JPEG at 12 866 bytes, 0.39 bits/pixel, 26.99 dB.

most images to satisfy, provides substantial coding gains over the first-order entropy for significance maps,

- successive-approximation, which allows the coding of multiple significance maps using zerotrees, and allows the encoding or decoding to stop at any point,
- adaptive arithmetic coding, which allows the entropy

coder to incorporate learning into the bit stream itself.

The precise rate control that is achieved with this algorithm is a distinct advantage. The user can choose a bit rate and encode the image to *exactly* the desired bit rate. Furthermore, since no training of any kind is required, the algorithm is fairly general and performs remarkably well with most types of images.

ACKNOWLEDGMENT

The author would like to thank Joel Zdepski who suggested incorporating the sign of the significant values into the significance map to aid embedding, Rajesh Hingorani who wrote much of the original C code for the QMF-pyramids, Allen Gersho who provided the original "Barbara" image, and Gregory Wornell whose fruitful discussions convinced me to develop a more mathematical analysis of zerotrees in terms of bounding an optimal estimator. I would also like to thank the editor and the anonymous reviewers whose comments led to a greatly improved manuscript.

REFERENCES

[1] E. H. Adelson, E. Simoncelli, and R. Hingorani, "Orthogonal pyramid transforms for image coding," *Proc. SPIE*, vol. 845, Cambridge, MA, Oct. 1987, pp. 50–58.

[2] R. Ansari, H. Gaggioni, and D. J. LeGall, "HDTV coding using a nonrectangular subband decomposition," in *Proc. SPIE Conf. Visual Commun. Image Processing.* Cambridge, MA, Nov. 1988, pp. 821–824.

[3] T. C. Bell, J. G. Cleary, and I. H. Witten, *Text Compression.* Englewood Cliffs, NJ: Prentice-Hall, 1990.

[4] P. J. Burt and E. H. Adelson, "The Laplacian pyramid as a compact image code," *IEEE Trans. Commun.*, vol. 31, pp. 532–540, 1983.

[5] R.R. Coifman and M. V. Wickerhauser, "Entropy-based algorithms for best basis selection," *IEEE Trans. Informat. Theory*, vol. 38, pp. 713–718, Mar. 1992.

[6] I. Daubechies, "Orthonormal bases of compactly supported wavelets," *Commun. Pure Appl. Math.*, vol. 41, pp. 909–996, 1988.

[7] ——, "The wavelet transform, time-frequency localization and signal analysis," *IEEE Trans. Informat. Theory*, vol. 36, pp. 961–1005, Sept. 1990.

[8] R. A. DeVore, B. Jawerth, and B. J. Lucier, "Image compression through wavelet transform coding," *IEEE Trans. Informat. Theory*, vol. 38, pp. 719–746, Mar. 1992.

[9] W. Equitz and T. Cover, "Successive refinement of information," *IEEE Trans. Informat. Theory*, vol. 37, pp. 269–275, Mar. 1991.

[10] Y. Huang, H. M. Driezen, and N. P. Galatsanos, "Prioritized DCT for Compression and Progressive Transmission of Images," *IEEE Trans. Image Processing*, vol. 1, pp. 477–487, Oct. 1992.

[11] N. S. Jayant and P. Noll, *Digital Coding of Waveforms.* Englewood Cliffs, NJ: Prentice-Hall, 1984.

[12] Y. H. Kim and J. W. Modestino, "Adaptive entropy coded subband coding of images," *IEEE Trans. Image Processing*, vol. 1, pp. 31–48, Jan. 1992.

[13] J. Kovačević and M. Vetterli, "Nonseparable multidimensional perfect reconstruction filter banks and wavelet bases for ℜ," *IEEE Trans. Informat. Theory*, vol. 38, pp. 533–555, Mar. 1992.

[14] T. Lane, Independent JPEG Group's free JPEG software, 1991.

[15] A. S. Lewis and G. Knowles, "A 64 kB/s video Codec using the 2-D wavelet transform," in *Proc. Data Compression Conf.*, Snowbird, Utah, IEEE Computer Society Press, 1991.

[16] ——, "Image compression using the 2-D wavelet transform," *IEEE Trans. Image Processing*, vol. 1, pp. 244–250, Apr. 1992.

[17] S. Mallat, "A theory for multiresolution signal decomposition: The wavelet representation," *IEEE Trans. Pattern Anal. Mach. Intell.*, vol. 11, pp. 674–693, July 1989.

[18] ——, "Multifrequency channel decompositions of images and wavelet models," *IEEE Trans. Acoust. Speech and Signal Processing.*, vol. 37, pp. 2091–2110, Dec. 1990.

[19] A Pentland and B. Horowitz, "A practical approach to fractal-based image compression," in *Proc. Data Compression Conf.*, Snowbird, Utah, IEEE Computer Society Press, 1991.

[20] O. Rioul and M. Vetterli, "Wavelets and signal processing," *IEEE Signal Processing Mag.*, vol. 8, pp. 14–38, Oct. 1991.

[21] A. Said and W. A. Pearlman, "Image Compression using the Spatial-Orientation Tree," in *Proc. IEEE Int. Symp. Circuits and Syst.*, Chicago, IL, May 1993, pp. 279–282.

[22] J. M. Shapiro, "An Embedded Wavelet Hierarchical Image Coder," *Proc. IEEE Int. Conf. Acoust., Speech, Signal Processing*, San Francisco, CA, Mar. 1992.

[23] ——, "Adaptive multidimensional perfect reconstruction filter banks using McClellan transformations," *Proc. IEEE Int. Symp. Circuits Syst.*, San Diego, CA, May 1992.

[24] ——, "An embedded hierarchical image coder using zerotrees of wavelet coefficients," in *Proc. Data Compression Conf.*, Snowbird, Utah, IEEE Computer Society Press, 1993.

[25] ——, "Application of the embedded wavelet hierarchical image coder to very low bit rate image coding," *Proc. IEEE Int. Conf. Acoust., Speech, Signal Processing*, Minneapolis, MN, Apr. 1993.

[26] Special issue of *IEEE Trans. Informat. Theory*, Mar. 1992.

[27] G. Strang, "Wavelets and dilation equations: A brief introduction," *SIAM Rev.*, vol. 4, pp. 614–627, Dec. 1989.

[28] J. Vaisey and A. Gersho, "Image compression with variable block size segmentation," *IEEE Trans. Signal Processing.*, vol. 40, pp. 2040–2060, Aug. 1992.

[29] M. Vetterli, J. Kovačević, and D. J. LeGall, "Perfect reconstruction filter banks for HDTV representation and coding," *Image Commun.*, vol. 2, pp. 349–364, Oct. 1990.

[30] G. K. Wallace, "The JPEG Still Picture Compression Standard," *Commun. ACM*, vol. 34, pp. 30–44, Apr. 1991.

[31] I. H. Witten, R. Neal, and J. G. Cleary, "Arithmetic coding for data compression," *Comm. ACM*, vol. 30, pp. 520–540, June 1987.

[32] J. W. Woods, Ed., *Subband Image Coding.* Boston, MA: Kluwer, 1991.

[33] G. W. Wornell, "A Karhunen-Loéve expansion for $1/f$ processes via wavelets," *IEEE Trans. Informat. Theory*, vol. 36, pp. 859–861, July 1990.

[34] Z. Xiong, N. Galatsanos, and M. Orchard, "Marginal analysis prioritization for image compression based on a hierarchical wavelet decomposition," in *Proc. IEEE Int. Conf. Acoust., Speech, Signal Processing*, Minneapolis, MN, Apr. 1993.

[35] W. Zettler, J. Huffman, and D. C. P. Linden, "Applications of compactly supported wavelets to image compression," *SPIE Image Processing Algorithms*, Santa Clara, CA 1990.

**Jerome M. Shapiro** (S'85–M'90) was born April 29, 1962 in New York City. He received the B.S., M.S., and Ph.D. degrees in electrical engineering from the Massachusetts Institute of Technology, Cambridge, MA, in 1985, 1985, and 1990, respectively.

From 1982 to 1984, he was at GenRad, Concord, MA, as part of the VI-A Cooperative Program, where he did his Master's thesis on phase-locked loop frequency synthesis. From 1985 to 1987, he was a Research Assistant in the Video Image Processing Group of the MIT Research Laboratory of Electronics. From 1988 to 1990, while pursuing his doctoral studies, he was a Research Assistant in the Sensor Processor Technology Group of MIT Lincoln Laboratory, Lexington, MA. In 1990, he joined the Digital HDTV Research Group of the David Sarnoff Research Center, a Subsidiary of SRI International, Princeton, NJ. His research interests are in the areas of video and image data compression, digital signal processing, adaptive filtering and systolic array algorithms.

The MPEG-4 Video Standard Verification Model

Thomas Sikora, *Senior Member, IEEE*

Abstract— The MPEG-4 standardization phase has the mandate to develop algorithms for audio-visual coding allowing for interactivity, high compression, and/or universal accessibility and portability of audio and video content. In addition to the conventional "frame"-based functionalities of the MPEG-1 and MPEG-2 standards, the MPEG-4 video coding algorithm will also support access and manipulation of "objects" within video scenes.

The January 1996 MPEG Video group meeting witnessed the definition of the first version of the MPEG-4 Video Verification Model—a milestone in the development of the MPEG-4 standard. The primary intent of the Video Verification Model is to provide a fully defined core video coding algorithm platform for the development of the standard. As such, the structure of the MPEG-4 Video Verification Model already gives some indication about the tools and algorithms that will be provided by the final MPEG-4 standard. The purpose of this paper is to describe the scope of the MPEG-4 Video standard and to outline the structure of the MPEG-4 Video Verification Model under development.

Index Terms— Coding efficiency, compression, error robustness, flexible coding, functional coding, manipulation, MPEG, MPEG-4, multimedia, natural video, object-based coding, SNHC, standardization, synthetic video, universal accessibility, verification model, video coding.

I. INTRODUCTION

THE ISO SC29 WG11 "Moving Picture Experts Group" (MPEG), within ISO SG 29 responsible for "coding of moving pictures and audio," was established in 1988 [1]. In August 1993, the MPEG group released the so-called MPEG-1 standard for "coding of moving pictures and associated audio at up to about 1.5 Mb/s" [2], [3]. In 1990, MPEG started the so-called MPEG-2 standardization phase [3]. While the MPEG-1 standard was mainly targeted for CD-ROM applications, the MPEG-2 standard addresses substantially higher quality for audio and video with video bit rates between 2 Mb/s and 30 Mb/s, primarily focusing on requirements for digital TV and HDTV applications.

Anticipating the rapid convergence of telecommunications industries, computer, and TV/film industries, the MPEG group officially initiated a new MPEG-4 standardization phase in 1994—with the mandate to standardize algorithms for audio-visual coding in multimedia applications, allowing for interactivity, high compression, and/or universal accessibility and portability of audio and video content. Bit rates targeted for the video standard are between 5–64 kb/s for mobile applications and up to 2 Mb/s for TV/film applications. Seven new (with respect to existing or emerging standards) key video coding

Manuscript received May 10, 1996; revised October 25, 1996. This paper was recommended by Guest Editors Y.-Q. Zhang, F. Pereira, T. Sikora, and C. Reader.

The author is with the Heinrich-Hertz-Institute (HHI) for Communication Technology, 10587 Berlin, Germany.

Publisher Item Identifier S 1051-8215(97)00937-3.

functionalities have been defined which support the MPEG-4 focus and which provide the main requirements for the work in the MPEG Video group. The requirements are summarized in Table I and cover the main topics related to "content-based interactivity," "compression," and "universal access." The release of the MPEG-4 International Standard is targeted for November 1998 [3], [4].

1) Content-Based Interactivity: In addition to provisions for efficient coding of conventional image sequences, MPEG-4 will enable an efficient coded representation of the audio and video data that can be "content-based"—to allow the access and manipulation of audio-visual objects in the compressed domain at the coded data level with the aim to use and present them in a highly flexible way. In particular, future multimedia applications as well as computer games and related applications are seen to benefit from the increased interactivity with the audio-visual content.

The concept of the envisioned MPEG-4 "content-based" video functionality is outlined in Fig. 1 for a simple example of an image scene containing a number of video objects. The attempt is to encode the sequence in a way that will allow the separate decoding and reconstruction of the objects and to allow the manipulation of the original scene by simple operations on the bit stream. The bit stream will be "object layered" and the shape and transparency of each object—as well as the spatial coordinates and additional parameters describing object scaling, rotation, or related parameters—are described in the bit stream of each object layer. The receiver can either reconstruct the original sequence in its entirety, by decoding all "object layers" and by displaying the objects at original size and at the original location, as shown in Fig. 1(a), or alternatively, it is possible to manipulate the video by simple operations. For example, in Fig. 1(b), some objects were not decoded and used for reconstruction, while others were decoded and displayed using subsequent scaling or rotation. In addition, new objects were included which did not belong to the original scene. Since the bit stream of the sequence is organized in an "object layered" form, the manipulation is performed on the bit stream level—without the need for further transcoding. It is targeted to provide these capabilities for both natural and synthetic audio-visual objects as well as for hybrid representations of natural and synthetic objects. Notice that MPEG-4 images as well as image sequences are, in general, considered to be arbitrarily shaped—in contrast to the standard MPEG-1 and MPEG-2 definitions.

2) Coding Efficiency and Universal Access: Provisions for improved coding efficiency, in particular at very low bit rates below 64 kb/s, continues to be an important functionality to be supported by the standard. Other important requirements for the emerging MPEG-4 standard address the heterogeneous

TABLE I
REQUIREMENTS FOR THE MPEG-4 VIDEO STANDARD

Functionality	MPEG-4 Video-Requirements
Content-Based Interactivity	
Content-Based Manipulation and Bitstream Editing	Support for content-based manipulation and bitstream editing without the need for transcoding.
Hybrid Natural and Synthetic Data Coding	Support for combining synthetic scenes or objects with natural scenes or objects. The ability for compositing synthetic data with ordinary video, allowing for interactivity.
Improved Temporal Random Access	Provisions for efficient methods to randomly access, within a limited time and with fine resolution, parts, e.g. video frames or arbitrarily shaped image content from a video sequence. This includes 'conventional' random access at very low bit rates.
Compression	
Improved Coding Efficiency	MPEG-4 Video shall provide subjectively better visual quality at comparable bit rates compared to existing or emerging standards.
Coding of Multiple Concurrent Data Streams	Provisions to code multiple views of a scene efficiently. For stereoscopic video applications, MPEG-4 shall allow the ability to exploit redundancy in multiple viewing points of the same scene, permitting joint coding solutions that allow compatibility with normal video as well as the ones without compatibility constraints.
Universal Access	
Robustness in Error-Prone Environments	Provisions for error robustness capabilities to allow access to applications over a variety of wireless and wired networks and storage media. Sufficient error robustness shall be provided for low bit rate applications under severe error conditions (e.g. long error bursts).
Content-Based Scalability	MPEG-4 shall provide the ability to achieve scalability with fine granularity in content, quality (e.g. spatial and temporal resolution), and complexity. In MPEG-4, these scalabilities are especially intended to result in content-based scaling of visual information.

network environments that can be foreseen for many emerging MPEG-4 multimedia applications, in particular for wireless communications and database access. This introduces the requirements for tolerance of the audio and video compression algorithms with respect to noisy environments, varying bandwidths, and varying degrees of decoder resources and battery power. MPEG-4 will address this problem of error prone environments and provide content-based scalability for constrained bit rate and decoder resources.

The January 1996 MPEG meeting witnessed the release of the first version of the MPEG-4 Video Verification Model. Similar to the MPEG-2 Test Model, the MPEG-4 Video Verification Model defines a first "common core" video coding algorithm for the collaborative work within the MPEG-4 Video Group. Based on this core algorithm, a number of "Core Experiments" are defined with the aim to collaboratively

improve the efficiency and functionality of the first Verification Model—and to iteratively converge through several versions of the Verification Model toward the final MPEG-4 Video coding standard by the end of 1998. To this reason, the MPEG-4 Video Verification Model provides an important platform for collaborative experimentation within the Video Group and should already give some indication about the structure of the final MPEG-4 Video coding standard.

The purpose of this paper is to provide an overview of the MPEG-4 Video Verification Model process and to outline the structure of the Verification Model algorithm. To this end, Section II discusses the role and integration of the MPEG-4 Video coding standard within the MPEG-4 framework. In Section III, the Verification Model methodology is described, and Section IV details the basic algorithm defined in the September 1996 version of the MPEG-4 Video Verification

(a)

(b)

Fig. 1.   The "content-based" approach taken by the MPEG-4 Video coding standard will allow the flexible decoding, representation, and manipulation of video objects in a scene. (a) Original. (b) Manipulated.

Model. Section V discusses the role of the Core Experiment process, and Section VI finally summarizes and concludes the paper.

II. THE MPEG-4 VIDEO "TOOLBOX" APPROACH

The overall MPEG-4 applications scenario envisions the standardization of "tools" and "algorithms" for natural audio and video as well as for synthetic two-dimensional (2-D) or three-dimensional (3-D) audio and video to allow the hybrid coding of these components [4]. The MPEG-4 group has taken further steps toward an open, flexible, and extensible MPEG-4 standard by anticipating the foreseen rapid developments in the area of programmable general purpose DSP technology—and the obvious advantages with respect to software implementations of the standard. In this respect, it is foreseen to provide an open MPEG-4 standard by enabling mechanisms to

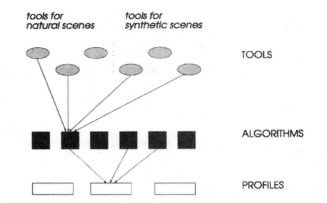

Fig. 2.   Scenario of "tools," "algorithms," and profiles for the MPEG-4 Video coding standard. For the MPEG-4 standard mainly video coding tools (i.e., DCT, motion compensation, etc.) will be standardized. By means of the MSDL, a selection of tools can be flexibly combined to form an algorithm. Profiles define subsets of tools or algorithms suitable for specific applications requirements (i.e., low complexity, low delay, etc.).

download missing software decoder tools at the receiver. As a consequence, the MPEG-4 Video group will not follow the conventional approach taken by the successful MPEG-1 and MPEG-2 standards, which defined only complete algorithms for the audio, video, and systems aspects. In contrast, for MPEG-4 the attempt is to standardize video "tools"—a video "tool" being, for example, a fully defined algorithm, or only a shape coding module, a motion compensation module, a texture coding module, or related techniques. The "glue" that will bind independent coding tools together is the foreseen MPEG-4 Systems Description Language (MSDL) which will comprise several key components. First, a definition of the interfaces between the coding tools; second, a mechanism to combine coding tools and to construct algorithms and profiles; and third, a mechanism to download new tools. While some applications call for very high compression efficiency, others require high robustness in error-prone environments or a very high degree of interaction with audio or video content. No single efficient algorithm exists to cover this broad range of applications requirements. The MSDL will transmit with the bitstream the structure and rules for the decoder—thus the way the tools have to be used at the decoder in order to decode and reconstruct audio and video. At a more advanced stage, MSDL will allow the downloading of tools which are not available at the decoder. Thus, the MPEG-4 MSDL, together with the audio and video toolbox approach, will provide a very flexible framework to tackle this problem by allowing a wealth of different algorithms to be supported by the standard.

The envisioned MPEG-4 scenario in terms of standardized components for coding of visual data is summarized in Fig. 2. Note that the MPEG-4 "visual" part of the "toolbox" contains tools (including fully defined algorithms) for coding both natural (pixel based video) and synthetic visual input (i.e., 2-D or 3-D computer model data sets). The tools can be flexibly combined at the encoder and decoder to enable efficient hybrid natural and synthetic coding of visual data. The same will be the case for natural and synthetic audio data.

TABLE II
TIME SCHEDULE FOR THE MPEG-4 VIDEO STANDARD

Nov. 1995	• Subjective tests of proposals submitted to MPEG-4 Video
Jan. 1996	• Definition of 1st MPEG-4 Video Verification Model (VM)
Jan. 1996 - Nov. 1996	• Iterative improvement of the MPEG-4 Video VM • 1st Version of the MPEG-4 Video Standard Working Draft (WD)
Nov. 1996 - Nov. 1997	• Iterative improvement of the MPEG-4 Video VM and WD
Nov. 1997	• Major technical work on video algorithms finished • MPEG-4 Video Standard Committee Draft (CD)
Jan. 1998	• MPEG-4 Video Draft International Standard (DIS)
July 1998	• MPEG-4 Video Draft International Standard (DIS)

III. DEVELOPMENT OF VIDEO TOOLS AND ALGORITHMS FOR MPEG-4—THE VERIFICATION MODEL METHODOLOGY

Starting from the January 1996 Munich meeting, the work in the MPEG Video group continued in a collaborative phase with respect to the development of the MPEG-4 Video coding standard. To collaboratively develop video tools and algorithms for the final MPEG-4 standard, the MPEG-4 Video group adopted the Verification Model methodology which already proved successful in the course of the development of the MPEG-1 and MPEG-2 standards [5]. The purpose of a Verification Model (VM) within MPEG-4 is to describe completely defined encoding and decoding "common core" algorithms, such that collaborative experiments performed by multiple independent parties can produce identical results and will allow the conduction of "Core Experiments" under controlled conditions in a common environment. A VM specifies the input and output formats for the uncoded data and the format of the bitstream containing the coded data. It specifies the algorithm for encoding and decoding, including the support for one or more functionalities.

Based on the Proposal Package Description [4] for the MPEG-4 standardization phase, which identifies the preliminary requirements for the envisioned MPEG-4 Video standard (see also Table I), a variety of algorithms were developed by companies worldwide in a competitive manner. In November 1994, a "Call for Proposals" was issued by the MPEG-4 group where laboratories were asked to submit results for their video coding algorithm, tools, and proposals to be compared in formal subjective viewing tests [6]. The "Call for Proposals" specified detailed functionalities that needed to be addressed by the proposers and defined test sequences and coding conditions to be used. The functionalities addressed were: coding efficiency, content-based scalability, content-based spatial and temporal scalability, and error robustness and resilience. The subjective viewing tests were carried out in November 1995 and resulted in a ranking of the proposals with respect to the subjective image quality achieved for the diverse functionalities [7], [8]. In addition, laboratories were asked to submit proposals for video tools and algorithms for MPEG-4 which were not subject to formal subjective viewing tests—but were evaluated purely for their technical merit by MPEG Video group experts [9], [10].

As a result, a wealth of promising video coding techniques addressing diverse functionalities were identified. The reader is referred to the references in [11] for an excellent summary of a selection of the techniques submitted to the subjective viewing test and to the informal video group evaluation. Based on the proposals submitted, the first version of the MPEG-4 Video Verification Model was defined in January 1996. This event marked the end of the MPEG-4 competitive phase and the beginning of the collaborative effort in the MPEG Video group.

Anticipating that the final MPEG-4 Video coding standard is intended to be generic by supporting a broad range of applications with varying applications requirements, the MPEG Video group adapted an approach for defining the VM which is functionality driven. The aim was to cover a maximum set of the functionalities in Table I by one VM algorithm to support a maximum of applications requirements. Based on the ranking in the subjective viewing test, and based on the technical merit of the algorithms, it was possible to identify a small number of techniques which performed most promising in the tests and which used similar technology to cover a range of functionalities. These algorithms formed the substance for the first version of the MPEG-4 Video Verification Model algorithm.

Based on the remaining proposals submitted, a list of "Core Experiments" was defined to foster the improvement of the VM between the meetings in the collaboration phase. In subsequent meetings, new tools can be brought to MPEG-4 and these will be evaluated inside the VM process following a Core Experiment procedure if a minimum of two independent companies agree to perform the same experiments. In the final standard, if two tools accomplish the same functionality under the same conditions, only the best will be chosen.

The Core Experiment process will continue until November 1997 when the Committee Draft of the MPEG-4 Video standard will be released. Table II summarizes the foreseen time schedule for the development of the standard.

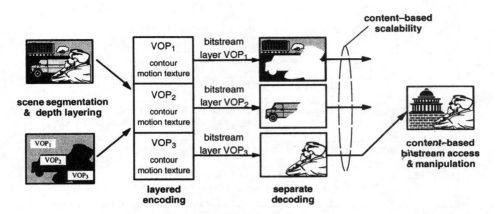

Fig. 3. The coding of image sequences using MPEG-4 VOP's enables basic content-based functionalities at the decoder. Each VOP specifies particular image sequence content and is coded into a separate VOL-layer (by coding contour, motion, and texture information). Decoding of all VOP-layers reconstructs the original image sequence. Content can be reconstructed by separately decoding a single or a set of VOL-layers (content-based scalability/access in the compressed domain). This allows content-based manipulation at the decoder without the need for transcoding.

IV. THE MPEG-4 VIDEO VERIFICATION MODEL

In the January 1996 MPEG Video group meeting in Munich, Germany, the first version of the official MPEG-4 Video Verification Model was defined. The VM has since then, by means of the Core Experiment process, iteratively progressed in each subsequent meeting and has been optimized with respect to coding efficiency and the provisions for new content-based functionalities and error robustness. At the current stage, the MPEG-4 Video Verification Model supports the features summarized below [12].

- Standard $Y : U : V$ luminance and chrominance intensity representation of regularly sampled pixels in $4 : 2 : 0$ format. The intensity of each Y, U, or V pixel is quantized into 8 b. The image size and shape depends on the application.
- Coding of multiple "video object planes" (VOP's) as images of arbitrary shape to support many of the content-based functionalities. Thus, the image sequence input for the MPEG-4 Video VM is, in general, considered to be of arbitrary shape—and the shape and location of a VOP within a reference window may vary over time. The coding of standard rectangular image input sequences is supported as a special case of the more general VOP approach.
- Coding of shape and transparency information of each VOP by coding binary or gray scale alpha plane image sequences.
- Support of intra (I) coded VOP's as well as temporally predicted (P) and bidirectionally (B) predicted VOP's. Standard MPEG and H.263 I, P, and B frames are supported as special case.
- Support of fixed and variable frame rates of the input VOP sequences of arbitrary or rectangular shape. The frame rate depends on the application.
- 8×8 pel block-based and 16×16 pel macroblock-based motion estimation and compensation of the pixel values within VOP's, including provisions for block-overlapping motion compensation.

- Texture coding in I, P, and B-VOP's using a discrete cosine transform (DCT) adopted to regions of arbitrary shape, followed by MPEG-1/2 or H.261/3 like quantization and run-length coding.
- Efficient prediction of dc- and ac-coefficients of the DCT in intra coded VOP's.
- Temporal and spatial scalability for arbitrarily shaped VOP's.
- Adaptive macroblock slices for resynchronization in error prone environments.
- Backward compatibility with standard H.261/3 or MPEG-1/2 coding algorithms if the input image sequences are coded in a single layer using a single rectangular VOP structure.

The reader is referred to the references in [2], [3], and [15] for details related to the H.261/3 and MPEG-1/2 standards video compression algorithms.

A. Provisions for Content Based Functionalities—Decomposition into "Video Object Planes"

The MPEG-4 Video coding algorithm will eventually support all functionalities already provided by MPEG-1 and MPEG-2, including the provision to efficiently compress standard rectangular sized image sequences at varying levels of input formats, frame rates, and bit rates.

Furthermore, at the heart of the so-called "content"-based MPEG-4 Video functionalities is the support for the separate encoding and decoding of content (i.e., physical objects in a scene). Within the context of MPEG-4, this functionality—the ability to identify and selectively decode and reconstruct video content of interest—is referred to as "content-based scalability." This MPEG-4 feature provides the most elementary mechanism for interactivity and manipulation with/of content of images or video in the compressed domain without the need for further segmentation or transcoding at the receiver.

To enable the content-based interactive functionalities envisioned, the MPEG-4 Video Verification Model introduces the concept of VOP's. It is assumed that each frame of

(a)

(b)

Fig. 4. Description of the shape of a VOP by means of an alpha plane mask (binary segmentation mask in this case). (a) Image of the original sequence Akiyo. (b) Binary segmentation mask specifying the location of the foreground content VOP (person Akiyo).

an input video sequence is segmented into a number of arbitrarily shaped image regions (video object planes)—each of the regions may possibly cover particular image or video content of interest, i.e., describing physical objects or content within scenes. In contrast to the video source format used for the MPEG-1 and MPEG-2 standards, the video input to be coded by the MPEG-4 Verification Model is thus no longer considered a rectangular region. This concept is illustrated in Fig. 3. The input to be coded can be a VOP image region of arbitrary shape and the shape and location of the region can vary from frame to frame. Successive VOP's belonging to the same physical object in a scene are referred to as video objects (VO's)—a sequence of VOP's of possibly arbitrary shape and position. The shape, motion, and texture information of the VOP's belonging to the same VO is encoded and transmitted or coded into a separate video object layer (VOL). In addition, relevant information needed to identify each of the VOL's—and how the various VOL's are composed at the receiver to reconstruct the

entire original sequence is also included in the bitstream. This allows the separate decoding of each VOP and the required flexible manipulation of the video sequence as indicated in Fig. 3—similar to the example already discussed in Fig. 1. Notice that the video source input assumed for the VOL structure either already exists in terms of separate entities (i.e., is generated with chroma-key technology) or is generated by means of on-line or off-line segmentation algorithms.

To illustrate the concept, the MPEG-4 Video source input test sequence AKIYO in Fig. 4(a), which as an example consists of a foreground person and of textured stationary background content, is here decomposed into a background VOP_1 and a foreground VOP_2. A binary alpha plane image sequence as depicted in Fig. 4(b) is coded in this example to indicate to the decoder the shape and location of the foreground object VOP_2 with respect to the background VOP_1. In general, the MPEG-4 Video Verification Model also supports the coding of gray scale alpha planes to allow at the receiver the composition of VOP's with various levels of transparency.

Fig. 5(a) and (b) depict an example of the content of the two VOP's to be coded in two separate VOL-layers in Fig. 3. Note that the image regions covered by the two VOP's are nonoverlapping, and that the sum of the pels covered by the two VOP's is identical to the pels contained in the original source sequence in Fig. 4(a). Both VOP's are of arbitrary shape and the shape and the location of the VOP's change over time. The receiver can either decode and display each VOP separately (i.e., the foreground person in VOP_2 only) or reconstruct the original sequence by decoding and appropriate compositing of both VOP's based on the decoded alpha channel information.

The MPEG-4 Video Verification Model also supports the coding of overlapping VOP's as indicated in Fig. 6(a) and (b). Here, the foreground VOP_2 in Fig. 6(b) is identical to the one in Fig. 5(b). However, the background VOP_1 is of rectangular shape with the size of the original input images, and the shape of the background VOP remains the same for the entire sequence. Again, both VOP's are encoded separately and the original is reconstructed at the receiver by decoding each VOP and pasting the foreground VOP content at the appropriate location on top of the background layer content based on the decoded alpha channel information. If the background VOP content is stationary (as is the case in the AKIYO test sequence—meaning that the background content does not change over time), only one frame needs to be coded for the background VOP. Thus the foreground and background VOP's may have different display repetition rates at the receiver.

Notice that, if the original input image sequences are not decomposed into several VOL's of arbitrary shape, the coding structure simply degenerates into a single layer representation which supports conventional image sequences of rectangular shape. The MPEG-4 content-based approach can thus be seen as a logical extension of the conventional MPEG-1 and MPEG-2 coding approach toward image input sequences of arbitrary shape.

(a)

(a)

(b)

(b)

Fig. 5.   Image content of VOP$_1$ [(a) background VOP] and VOP $_2$ [(b) foreground VOP] according to the alpha plane mask in Fig. 4(b). Contour, motion, and texture information for each VOP is coded in a separate VOP-layer. Notice that the two VOP's are nonoverlapping and the image sequence input for each VOP-layer is of arbitrary shape, with the location and shape varying between VOP images depending on the movement of the person Akiyo.

Fig. 6.   An example of the decomposition of the original image sequence AKIYO in Fig. 4 into overlapping VOP's (i.e., if the entire background is known prior to coding). (a) The background VOP$_1$ in this case is a possibly stationary rectangular image. (b) The foreground VOP$_2$ remains the same than the one depicted in Fig. 5(b).

B. Coding of Shape, Motion, and Texture Information for each VOP

As indicated in Fig. 3, the information related to the shape, motion, and texture information for each VO is coded into a separate VOL-layer in order to support separate decoding of VO's. The MPEG-4 Video VM uses an identical algorithm to code the shape, motion, and texture information in each of the layers. The shape information is, however, not transmitted if the input image sequence to be coded contains only standard images of rectangular size. In this case, the MPEG-4 Video coding algorithm has a structure similar to the successful MPEG-1/2 or H.261 coding algorithms—suitable for applications which require high coding efficiency without the need for extended content based functionalities.

The MPEG-4 VM compression algorithm employed for coding each VOP image sequence (rectangular size or not) is based on the successful block-based hybrid DPCM/transform coding technique already employed in the MPEG coding standards [3]. As outlined in Fig. 7(a) for the example of a VOP of rectangular shape, the MPEG-4 coding algorithm encodes the first VOP in intraframe VOP coding mode (*I*-VOP). Each subsequent frame is coded using interframe VOP prediction (*P*-VOP's)—only data from the nearest previously coded VOP frame is used for prediction. In addition, the coding of bidirectionally predicted VOP's (*B*-VOP's) is also supported.

Similar to the MPEG baseline coders, the MPEG-4 VM algorithm processes the successive images of a VOP sequence block-based. Taking the example of arbitrarily shaped VOP's, after coding the VOP shape information, each color input VOP image in a VOP sequence is partitioned into nonoverlapping "macroblocks" as depicted in Figs. 7–9. Each macroblock contains blocks of data from both luminance and cosited chrominance bands—four luminance blocks (Y_1, Y_2, Y_3, Y_4) and two

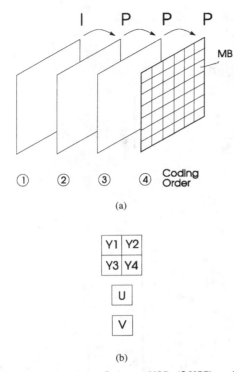

(a)

Y1 Y2
Y3 Y4

U

V

(b)

Fig. 7. (a) Illustration of an *I*-picture VOP (*I*-VOP) and *P*-picture VOP's (*P*-VOP's) in a video sequence. *P*-VOP's are coded using motion-compensated prediction based on the nearest previous VOP frame. Each frame is divided into disjoint "macroblocks" (MB). (b) With each MB, information related to four luminance blocks (Y_1, Y_2, Y_3, Y_4) and two chrominance blocks (U, V) is coded. Each block contains 8×8 pels.

chrominance blocks (U, V), each with size 8×8 pels. The basic diagram of the MPEG-4 VM hybrid DPCM/Transform encoder and decoder structure for processing single Y, U, or V blocks and macroblocks is depicted in Fig. 8. The previously coded VOP frame $N - 1$ is stored in a VOP frame store in both encoder and decoder. Motion compensation is performed on a block or macroblock basis—only one motion vector is estimated between VOP frame N and VOP frame $N - 1$ for a particular block or macroblock to be encoded. The motion-compensated prediction error is calculated by subtracting each pel in a block or macroblock belonging to the VOP frame N with its motion shifted counterpart in the previous VOP frame $N - 1$. An 8×8 DCT is then applied to each of the 8×8 blocks contained in the block or macroblock followed by quantization (Q) of the DCT coefficients with subsequent run-length coding and entropy coding (VLC). A video buffer is needed to ensure that a constant target bit rate output is produced by the encoder. The quantization stepsize for the DCT-coefficients can be adjusted for each macroblock in a VOP frame to achieve a given target bit rate and to avoid buffer overflow and underflow.

The decoder uses the reverse process to reproduce a macroblock of VOP frame N at the receiver. After decoding the variable length words contained in the video decoder buffer, the pixel values of the prediction error are reconstructed. The motion-compensated pixels from the previous VOP frame $N - 1$ contained in the VOP frame store are added to the

prediction error to recover the particular macroblock of frame N.

In general, the input images to be coded in each VOP layer are of arbitrary shape and the shape and location of the images vary over time with respect to a reference window. For coding shape, motion, and texture information in arbitrarily shaped VOP's, the MPEG-4 Video VM introduces the concept of a "VOP image window" together with a "shape-adaptive" macroblock grid. All VOL layers to be coded for a given input video sequence are defined with reference to the reference window of constant size. An example of a VOP image window within a reference window and an example of a macroblock grid for a particular VOP image are depicted in Fig. 9. The shape information of a VOP is coded prior to coding motion vectors based on the VOP image window macroblock grid and is available to both encoder and decoder. In subsequent processing steps, only the motion and texture information for the macroblocks belonging to the VOP image are coded (which includes the standard macroblocks as well as the contour macroblocks in Fig. 9).

1) Shape Coding: Essentially, two coding methods are supported by the MPEG-4 Video VM for binary and gray scale shape information. The shape information is referred to as "alpha planes" in the context of the MPEG-4 VM. The techniques to be adopted for the standard will provide lossless coding of alpha-planes as well as the provision for lossy coding of shapes and transparency information, allowing the tradeoff between bit rate and the accuracy of shape representation. Furthermore, it is foreseen to support both intra shape coding as well as inter shape coding functionalities employing motion-compensated shape prediction—to allow both efficient random access operations as well as an efficient compression of shape and transparency information for diverse applications.

2) Motion Estimation and Compensation: The MPEG-4 VM employs block-based motion estimation and compensation techniques to efficiently explore temporal redundancies of the video content in the separate VOP layers. In general, the motion estimation and compensation techniques used can be seen as an extension of the standard MPEG-1/2 or H.261/3 block matching techniques toward image sequences of arbitrary shape [2], [3]. However, a wealth of different motion prediction methods is also being investigated in the Core Experiment process (see Section V).

To perform block-based motion estimation and compensation between VOP's of varying location, size, and shape, the shape-adaptive macroblock (MB) grid approach for each VOP image as discussed in Fig. 9 is employed. A block-matching procedure shown in Fig. 10 is used for standard macroblocks. The prediction error is coded together with the macroblock motion vectors used for prediction. An advanced motion compensation mode is defined which supports block-overlapping motion compensation as with the ITU H.263 standard as well as the coding of motion vectors for 8×8 blocks [13].

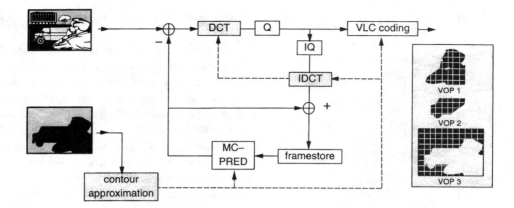

Fig. 8. Block diagram of the basic MPEG-4 VM hybrid DPCM/transform encoder and decoder structure.

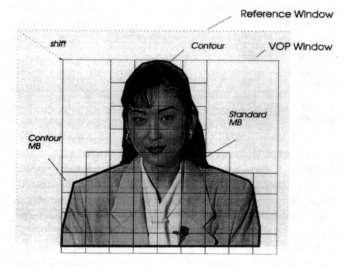

Fig. 9. Example of an MPEG-4 VM macroblock grid for the AKIYO foreground VOP$_2$ image. This macroblock grid is used for alpha plane coding, motion estimation, and compensation as well as for block-based texture coding. A VOP window with a size of multiples of 16 pels in each image direction surrounds the foreground VOP$_2$ of arbitrary shape and specifies the location of the macroblocks, each of size 16 × 16 pels. This window is adjusted to collocate with the top-most and left-most border of the VOP. A shift parameter is coded to indicate the location of the VOP window with respect to the borders of a reference window (original image borders).

The definition of the motion estimation and compensation techniques are, however, modified at the borders of a VOP. An image padding technique is used for the reference VOP frame $N - 1$, which is available to both encoder and decoder, to perform motion estimation and compensation. The VOP padding method can be seen as an extrapolation of pels outside of the VOP based on pels inside of the VOP. After padding the reference VOP in frame $N - 1$ (as shown in Fig. 11 for our example in Fig. 9), a "polygon" matching technique is employed for motion estimation and compensation. A polygon defines the part of the contour macroblock (or the 8 × 8 block for advanced motion compensation, respectively) which belongs to the active area inside of the VOP frame N to be coded and excludes the pels outside of this area. Thus, the pels not belonging to the active area in the VOP to be coded are essentially excluded from the motion estimation process.

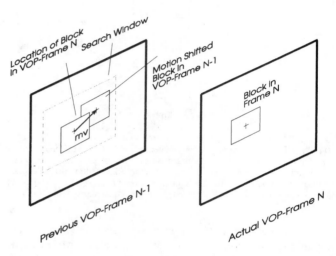

Fig. 10. Block matching approach for motion compensation: One motion vector (MV) is estimated for each block in the actual VOP frame N to be coded. The motion vector points to a reference block of same size in the previously coded VOP frame $N - 1$. The motion-compensated prediction error is calculated by subtracting each pel in a block with its motion-shifted counterpart in the reference block of the previous VOP frame.

The MPEG-4 Video VM supports the coding of both forward-predicted (P) as well as bidirectionally (B) predicted VOP's (P-VOP and B-VOP). Motion vectors are predictively coded using standard MPEG-1/2 and H.263 VLC code tables including the provision for extended vector ranges. Notice that the coding of standard MPEG I-frames, P-frames, and B-frames is still supported by the VM—for the special case of image input sequences (VOP's) of rectangular shape (standard MPEG or H.261/3 definition of frames).

3) Texture Coding: The intra VOP's as well as the residual errors after motion-compensated prediction are coded using a DCT on 8 × 8 blocks similar to the standard MPEG and H.263 standards. Again, the adaptive VOP window macroblock grid specified in Fig. 9 is employed for this purpose. For each macroblock, a maximum of four 8 × 8 luminance blocks and two 8 × 8 chrominance blocks are coded. Particular adaptation is required for the 8 × 8 blocks straddling the VOP borders. The image padding technique in Fig. 11 is used to fill the

Padded Background

(a)

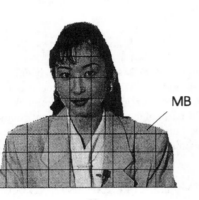

MB

(b)

Fig. 11. An image padding technique is employed for the purpose of contour block motion estimation and compensation as well as for the contour block texture coding. The aim of the padding procedure is to allow separate decoding and reconstruction of VOP's by extrapolating texture inside the VOP to regions outside the VOP (here shown for the foreground VOP₂ of AKIYO). This allows block-based DCT coding of texture across a VOP border as well. Furthermore, the block-based motion vector range for search and motion compensation in a VOP in frame N can be specified covering regions outside the VOP in frame $N - 1$. (a) Previous frame. (b) Actual frame.

macroblock content outside of a VOP prior to applying the DCT in intra-VOP's. For the coding of motion-compensated prediction error P-VOP's, the content of the pels outside of the active VOP area are set to 128. Scanning of the DCT coefficients followed by quantization and run-length coding of the coefficients is performed using techniques and VLC tables defined with the MPEG-1/2 and H.263 standards, including the provision for quantization matrices. An efficient prediction of the dc- and ac-coefficients of the DCT is performed for intra coded VOP's.

In the Core Experiment process, a considerable effort is dedicated to explore alternative techniques for texture coding, such as shape adaptive DCT's and wavelet transforms.

4) Multiplexing of Shape, Motion, and Texture Information: Basically all "tools" (DCT, motion estimation, and compensation, etc.) defined in the H.263 and MPEG-1 standards (and most of the ones defined for MPEG-2 Main Profile) are currently supported by the MPEG-4 Video VM. The compressed alpha plane, motion vector, and DCT bit words are multiplexed into a VOL layer bitstream by coding the shape information first, followed by motion and texture coding based on the H.263 and MPEG definitions.

The VM defines two separate modes for multiplexing texture and motion information: A joint motion vector and DCT-coefficient coding procedure based on standard H.263-like macroblock type definitions is supported to achieve a high compression efficiency at very low bit rates. This guarantees that the performance of the VM at very low bit rates is at least identical to the H.263 standard. Alternatively, the separate coding of motion vectors and DCT-coefficients is also possible—to eventually incorporate new and more efficient motion or texture coding techniques separately into the VM.

C. Coding Efficiency

Besides the provision for new content-based functionalities and error resilience and robustness, the coding of video with very high coding efficiency over a range of bit rates continues to be supported for the MPEG-4 standard. As indicated above, the MPEG-4 Video VM allows the single object-layer (single VOP) coding approach as a special case. In this coding mode, the single VOP input image sequence format may be rectangular as depicted in Fig. 7 (thus not segmented into several VOP's), and the MPEG-4 Video VM coding algorithm can be made almost compatible to the ITU-H.263 or ISO-MPEG-1 standards. Most of the coding techniques used by the MPEG-2 standard at Main Profile are also supported. A number of motion compensation and texture coding techniques are being investigated in the Core Experiment process to further improve coding efficiency for a range of bit rates, including bit rates below 64 kb/s.

D. Spatial and Temporal Scalability

An important goal of scaleable coding of video is to flexibly support receivers with different bandwidth or display capabilities or display requests to allow video database browsing and multiresolution playback of video content in multimedia environments. Another important purpose of scaleable coding is to provide a layered video bit stream which is amenable for prioritized transmission. The techniques adopted for the MPEG-4 Video VM allow the "content-based" access or transmission of arbitrarily-shaped VOP's at various temporal or spatial resolutions—in contrast to the frame-based scalability approaches introduced for MPEG-2. Receivers either not capable or willing to reconstruct the full resolution arbitrarily shaped VOP's can decode subsets of the layered bit stream to display the arbitrarily shaped VOP's content/objects at lower spatial or temporal resolution or with lower quality.

1) Spatial Scalability: Fig. 12 depicts the MPEG-4 general philosophy of a content-based VOP multiscale video coding scheme. Here, three layers are provided, each layer supporting a VOP at different spatial resolution scales, i.e., a multiresolution representation can be achieved by downscaling the input video signal into a lower resolution video (downsampling

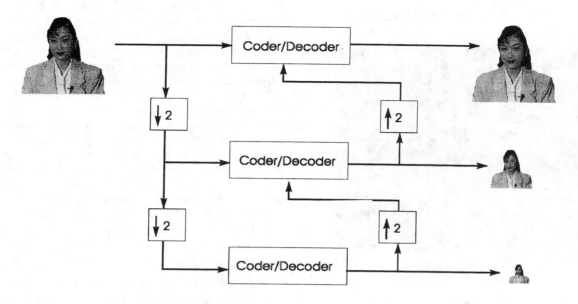

Fig. 12. Spatial scalability approach for arbitrarily shaped VOP's.

spatially in our example). The downscaled version is encoded into a base layer bit stream with reduced bit rate. The upscaled reconstructed base layer video (upsampled spatially in our example) is used as a prediction for the coding of the original input video signal. The prediction error is encoded into an enhancement layer bit stream. If a receiver is either not capable or willing to display the full quality VOP's, downscaled VOP signals can be reconstructed by only decoding the lower layer bit streams. It is important to notice, however, that the display of the VOP at highest resolution with reduced quality is also possible by only decoding the lower bit rate base layer(s). Thus, scaleable coding can be used to encode content-based video with a suitable bit rate allocated to each layer in order to meet specific bandwidth requirements of transmission channels or storage media. Browsing through video data bases and transmission of video over heterogeneous networks are applications expected to benefit from this functionality.

2) Temporal Scalability: This technique was developed with an aim similar to spatial scalability. Different frame rates can be supported with a layered bit stream. Layering is achieved by providing a temporal prediction for the enhancement layer based on coded video from the lower layers. Using the MPEG-4 "content-based" VOP temporal scalability approach, it is possible to provide different display rates for different VOL's within the same video sequence (i.e., a foreground person of interest may be displayed with a higher frame rate compared to the remaining background or other objects).

E. Error Resilience—Error Robustness

A considerable effort has been made to investigate the robust storage and transmission of MPEG-4 Video in error prone environments. To this end, an adaptive macroblock slice technique similar to the one already provided with the MPEG-1 and MPEG-2 standards has been introduced into the MPEG-4 Video VM. The technique provides resynchronization bit words for groups of macroblocks and has been optimized in particular to achieve efficient robustness for low bit rate video under a variety of severe error conditions, i.e., for the transmission over mobile channels.

V. THE CORE EXPERIMENT PROCESS

Based on the "Core Experiment" process, the MPEG-4 Video VM algorithm is being refined with the aim to *collaboratively* improve the efficiency and functionality of the VM—and to iteratively converge through several versions of the VM toward the final MPEG-4 Video coding standard by the end of 1998.

At the current stage, the MPEG-4 Video VM supports functionalities such as high coding efficiency, random access, error robustness, content-based scalability, and content-based random access features. The MPEG Video group has established a number of Core Experiments to improve the efficiency of the MPEG-4 VM between meetings with respect to the functionalities already supported—and to identify new coding techniques that allow provisions for functionalities not yet supported by the VM. Table III details a selection of the diverse Core Experiment techniques.

A Core Experiment is defined with respect to the VM, which is considered as the common core algorithm. A Core Experiment proposal describes a potential algorithmic improvement to the VM, i.e., a motion compensation technique different from the one defined by the VM. Furthermore, the full description of encoder and decoder implementation of the algorithm and the specification of experimental conditions (bit rates, test sequences, etc.) to compare the proposed Core Experiment technique against the performance of the VM are provided. A Core Experiment is being established by the

TABLE III
CORE EXPERIMENTS

Subject	Techniques compared in Core Experiments
Motion Prediction	Global motion compensation, Block partitioning, Short-term/long-term frame memory, Variable block size motion compensation, 2D Triangular mesh prediction, Sub-pel prediction.
Frame Texture Coding	Wavelet transforms, Matching pursuits, 3D-DCT, Lapped transforms, Improved Intra coding, Variable block-size DCT.
Shape and Alpha Channel Coding	Gray scale shape coding, Geometrical transforms, Shape-adaptive region partitioning, Variable block-size segmentation.
Arbitrary-Shaped Region Texture Coding	Padding DCT, Mean-replacement DCT, Shape-adaptive DCT, Extension/interpolation DCT, Wavelet/subband coding.
Error Resilience/Robustness	Resynchronization techniques, Hierarchical structures, Back channel signaling, Error concealment.
Bandwidth and Complexity Scaling	Generalized temporal-spatial coding, content-based temporal scalability.
Misc.	Rate control, Mismatch corrected stereo/multiview coding, 2D triangular mesh for object and content manipulation, Noise removal, Automatic segmentation, Generation of sprites.

MPEG Video group if two independent parties are committed to perform the experiment. If a Core Experiment is successful in improving on techniques described in the VM—i.e., in terms of coding efficiency, provisions for functionalities not supported by the VM, and implementation complexity—the successful technique will be incorporated into the newest version of the VM. The technique will either replace an existing technique or supplement the algorithms supported by the VM. Core Experiments are being performed between two MPEG Video group meetings. At each MPEG Video group meeting, the results of the Core Experiments are being reviewed and the VM is updated depending on the outcome of the experiment and a new version of the VM is being released.

VI. SUMMARY AND CONCLUSION

In this paper, the aim and methodologies of the MPEG-4 Video standardization process has been outlined. Starting from algorithms and tools submitted to the MPEG-4 Video group, and which have been tested by formal subjective viewing tests by the MPEG Test group, a VM methodology is used to develop the envisioned MPEG-4 Video coding standard.

The MPEG-4 Video VM defines a video coding algorithm including a firm definition of the video coder and decoder structure. The primary intent of the MPEG-4 VM methodology is to provide a fully defined core video coding algorithm platform for core experimental purposes. This core algorithm is used to verify the performance of proposed algorithms and tools submitted to the MPEG Video group—and to iteratively converge in a collaborative effort toward the final MPEG-4 Video coding standard by July 1998.

The MPEG-4 Video VM introduces the concept of VOP's to support content-based functionalities at the decoder. The primary intent is to support the coding of image sequences which are presegmented based on image content—and to allow the flexible and separate reconstruction and manipulation of content at the decoder in the compressed domain. To this end, the image input sequences in each VOP to be coded are, in general, considered to be entries of arbitrary shape. The VM encodes shape, motion, and texture information for each VOP to allow a large degree of flexibility for the Core Experiment process. The coding of image sequences using a single layer VOP—thus the coding of standard rectangular size image sequences—is supported as a special case, i.e., if coding efficiency is of primary interest. A number of Core Experiments intended to improve the VM with respect to coding efficiency, error robustness, and content-based functionalities are being investigated. It is targeted to release the Committee Draft of the MPEG-4 Video standard in November 1997 and to promote this draft to the final International Standard by July 1998.

It is envisioned that the final MPEG-4 Video standard will define "tools" and "algorithms" resulting in a toolbox of relevant video tools and algorithms available to both encoder and decoder. These tools and algorithms will be defined based on the MPEG-4 Video VM algorithm. It is likely that, similar to the approach taken by the MPEG-2 standard [3], [13], [14], profiles will be defined for tools and algorithms which include subsets of the MPEG-4 Video tools and algorithms.

The MPEG-4 MSDL will provide sufficient means to flexibly glue video tools and algorithms at the encoder and decoder to suit the particular needs of diverse and specific applications. While some applications may require a high degree of flexibility with respect to random access and interaction with image content (i.e., the provision to separately access, decode, and display VOP's and to further flexibly access shape, motion, and texture information associated with each VOP separately), others call for very high coding efficiency and/or very high error robustness. The MPEG-4 MSDL will allow the flexible definition of a bitstream syntax which multiplexes shape, motion, and texture information in each VOP. It is foreseen to provide a bitstream which is in part or entirely compatible to the H.261, H.263, or MPEG-1 and MPEG-2 standards (i.e., by degenerating the VOP structure into one rectangular VOP and coding and multiplexing the motion and texture information accordingly). Furthermore it may become feasible to achieve an error robustness much more sophisticated than currently provided by these standards, by flexibly redefining standard MPEG or ITU syntax definitions and synchronization bit words tailored for error patterns encountered in specific transmission or storage media.

REFERENCES

[1] L. Chiariglione, "The development of an integrated audiovisual coding standard: MPEG," *Proc. IEEE,* vol. 83, pp. 151–157, Feb. 1995.

[2] D. J. Le Gall, "The MPEG video compression algorithm," *Signal Processing: Image Commun.,* 1992, vol. 4, no. 4, pp. 129–140.

[3] R. Schäfer and T. Sikora, "Digital video coding standards and their role in video communications," *Proc. IEEE,* vol. 83, pp. 907–924, June 1995.

[4] MPEG AOE Group, "Proposal package description (PPD)—Revision 3," Tokyo meeting, document ISO/IEC/JTC1/SC29/WG11 N998, July 1995.

[5] S. Okubo, "Reference model methodology—A tool for collaborative creation of video coding standards," *Proc. IEEE,* vol. 83, pp. 139–150, Feb. 1995.

[6] MPEG AOE Group, "Call for proposals," Tokyo meeting, July 1995.

[7] F. Pereira and T. Alpert, "MPEG-4 video subjective test procedures," *IEEE Trans. Circuits Syst. Video Technol.,* this issue, pp. 32–51.

[8] H. Peterson, "Report of ad-hoc group on MPEG-4 video testing logistics," ISO/IEC/JTC1/SC29/WG11 N1056, Nov. 1995.

[9] MPEG Video Group, "Report of ad-hoc group on the evaluation of tools for nontested functionalities of video submissions to MPEG-4," Dallas meeting, document ISO/IEC/JTC1/SC29/WG11 N1064, Nov. 1995.

[10] MPEG Video Group, "Report of ad-hoc group on the evaluation of tools for nontested functionalities of video submissions to MPEG-4," Munich meeting, document ISO/IEC/JTC1/SC29/WG11 N0679, Jan. 1996.

[11] *IEEE Trans. Circuits Syst. Video Technol.,* special issue on MPEG-4, this issue.

[12] MPEG Video Group, "MPEG-4 video verification model—Version 2.1," ISO/IEC JTC1/SC29/WG11, May 1996, draft in progress.

[13] ISO/IEC 13818-2 MPEG-2 Video Coding Standard, "Information technology—Generic coding of moving pictures and associated audio information: Video," Mar. 1995.

[14] S. Okubo, K. McCann, and A. Lippmann, "MPEG-2 requirements, profiles and performance verification—Framework for developing a generic video coding standard," *Signal Processing: Image Commun.,* vol. 7, pp. 201–209, 1995.

[15] ITU-T Group for Line Transmission of Non-Telephone Signals, "Draft recommendation H.263—Video coding for low bitrate communication," Dec. 1995.

Thomas Sikora (M'93–SM'96), for photograph and biography, see this issue, p. 4.

Multimedia Data-Embedding and Watermarking Technologies

MITCHELL D. SWANSON, MEMBER, IEEE, MEI KOBAYASHI, AND
AHMED H. TEWFIK, FELLOW, IEEE

Invited Paper

In this paper, we review recent developments in transparent data embedding and watermarking for audio, image, and video. Data-embedding and watermarking algorithms embed text, binary streams, audio, image, or video in a host audio, image, or video signal. The embedded data are perceptually inaudible or invisible to maintain the quality of the source data. The embedded data can add features to the host multimedia signal, e.g., multilingual soundtracks in a movie, or provide copyright protection. We discuss the reliability of data-embedding procedures and their ability to deliver new services such as viewing a movie in a given rated version from a single multicast stream. We also discuss the issues and problems associated with copy and copyright protections and assess the viability of current watermarking algorithms as a means for protecting copyrighted data.

Keywords*—Copyright protection, data embedding, steganography, watermarking.*

I. INTRODUCTION

The past few years have seen an explosion in the use of digital media. Industry is making significant investments to deliver digital audio, image, and video information to consumers and customers. A new infrastructure of digital audio, image, and video recorders and players, on-line services, and electronic commerce is rapidly being deployed. At the same time, major corporations are converting their audio, image, and video archives to an electronic form.

Manuscript received July 15, 1997; revised January 15, 1998. The Guest Editor coordinating the review of this paper and approving it for publication was A. M. Tekalp. This work was supported in part by the Air Force Office of Scientific Research under Grant AF/F49620-94-1-0461 and in part by the Advanced Research Project Agency under Grant AF/F49620-93-1-0558.

M. D. Swanson is with Cognicity, Inc., Minneapolis, MN 55344 USA (e-mail: swanson@cognicity.com).

M. Kobayashi is with the Graduate School of Mathematical Sciences, University of Tokyo and IBM Tokyo Research Laboratory, Yamato-shi, Kanagawa-ken 242 Japan (e-mail: mei@trl.ibm.co.jp).

A. H. Tewfik is with Cognicity, Inc., Minneapolis, MN 55344 USA (e-mail: tewfik@cognicity.com) and the Department of Electrical and Computer Engineering, University of Minnesota, Minneapolis, MN 55455 USA (e-mail: tewfik@ece.umn.edu).

Publisher Item Identifier S 0018-9219(98)03519-1.

Digital media offer several distinct advantages over analog media: the quality of digital audio, image, and video signals is higher than that of their analog counterparts. Editing is easy because one can access the exact discrete locations that should be changed. Copying is simple with no loss of fidelity. A copy of a digital media is identical to the original. Digital audio, image, and videos are easily transmitted over networked information systems.

These advantages have opened up many new possibilities. In particular, it is possible to hide data (information) within digital audio, image, and video files. The information is hidden in the sense that it is perceptually and statistically undetectable. With many schemes, the hidden information can still be recovered if the host signal is compressed, edited, or converted from digital to analog format and back.

As we shall see in Section II, pure analog data-hiding techniques had been developed in the past. However, these techniques are not as robust as most of the digital data hiding techniques that we review in this paper. Furthermore, they cannot embed as much data in a host signal as the digital approaches.

Digital data embedding has many applications. Foremost is passive and active copyright protection. Many of the inherent advantages of digital signals increase problems associated with copyright enforcement. For this reason, creators and distributors of digital data are hesitant to provide access to their intellectual property. Digital watermarking has been proposed as a means to identify the owner or distributor of digital data.

Data embedding also provides a mechanism for embedding important control, descriptive, or reference information in a given signal. This information can be used for tracking the use of a particular clip, e.g., for pay-per-use applications, including billing for commercials and video and audio broadcast, as well as Internet electronic commerce of digital media. It can be used to track audio or visual object creation, manipulation, and modification history within a given signal without the overhead associated with creating a separate header or history file. It can also be used to track access to a given signal. This information is important in rights-management applications.

Data embedding is also ideally suited for covert communications. Data embedding can securely hide large amounts of potentially encrypted information in audio, image, and video data.

A most interesting application of data embedding is providing different access levels to the data. For example, the amount of detail that can be seen in a given image can be controlled. A person with a high access level can see details that another person with a lower access level would not see. Similarly, data embedding allows users to tailor a video to their needs, e.g., by watching a movie broadcast over a single channel in a particular rating or in a given language. In this case, data embedding is used to embed extra scenes and multilingual tracks in a given version of the movie that is broadcast [84]. In a sense, data embedding then provides some of the capability of digital video disc (DVD) in a broadcast environment with no extra bandwidth or storage requirements.

Most data-embedding algorithms can extract the hidden data from the host signal with no reference to the original signal. In some scenarios, an original is available to the detection algorithm. Typically, data-embedding algorithms that use the original signal during detection are robust to a larger assortment of distortions. The detection algorithm may "subtract off" the original signal from the received signal prior to data detection. Registration may also be used by receivers to compare the received signal with the original to correct scaling, rotation, and other distortions prior to data detection. Some data-embedding algorithms require access to the original data to derive parameters, e.g., hash values, that are required during detection. As different data-embedding applications have different requirements, we distinguish between these cases in this review.

Note also that most data-embedding algorithms assume that it is desirable to have secure data-embedding and extraction procedures. Specifically, a secret key typically determines how the data are embedded in the host signal. A user needs to know that key to extract the data. Knowledge of that key and the embedding algorithm would also allow the user to overwrite or erase the embedded information. In some applications, e.g., copy control in DVD or fraud detection by a recipient of the signal, it is desirable to give all users access to the embedded data *without* enabling them to change or remove that data. This problem has been addressed in cryptography. However, the solutions developed in cryptography cannot be applied directly in the watermarking or data-hiding context. In fact, to date, no satisfactory solution to that problem has been proposed within the data-embedding or watermarking literature. Some pioneering work in that area is described in [33].

The goal of this paper is to present an overview of the challenges and issues that need to be addressed by successful watermarking and data-embedding techniques and the current state of the art. Data-embedding and water-marking research builds on ideas and concepts developed in cryptography, communications theory, algorithm design, and signal processing. The data-embedding problem is inherently more difficult than any of the problems that have traditionally been addressed in these fields. All data-embedding algorithms combine and extend in a sense many of the solutions developed in these areas. Most of the published work on data embedding that has appeared in technical journals and conferences focuses on image and video data. On the other hand, most of the published work on audio data embedding has appeared in the patent literature. The coverage of this review in the audio, image, and video areas is basically proportional to the existing journal and conference literature in these three fields.

In the next section, a brief historical overview of the field is given. In particular, we relate some of the techniques that have been proposed recently in the areas of data embedding and watermarking to older steganographical techniques. In Section III, the basic requirements of data embedding and watermarking are addressed. We discuss the different security and robustness requirements of data-embedding applications. We also review the deadlock problem that arises in ownership identification and describe two solutions. Data embedding and watermarking in digital media are possible because of the limitations of the human auditory and visual systems. We review some properties of human auditory and visual perception in Section IV. Following this review, we describe the principles that underlie current data-embedding approaches. We provide examples to illustrate the capability of today's technology. Sections V–VII present image, audio, and video data-embedding techniques, respectively. We conclude the paper with a brief overview of visible watermarking approaches.

II. HISTORY

Data-embedding and watermarking techniques are particular embodiments of steganography (from the Greek words $\sigma\tau\epsilon\gamma\alpha\nu\omega$ or *stegano* for "covered" and *graphos*, "to write"). In contrast to cryptography, which focuses on rendering messages unintelligible to any unauthorized persons who might intercept them, the heart of steganography lies in devising astute and undetectable methods of concealing the messages themselves.

Marking of documents may have evolved alongside human writing during the dawn of Western civilization. Since knowledge of writing was often restricted to a privileged and powerful class, the need to conceal messages from traitors and enemies within these circles appears to have been a serious concern. In a historical text on coding [43], Kahn traces the roots of secret writing back 4000 years to the banks of the Nile, where hieroglyphic symbol substitutions were used to inscribe information in the tomb of a nobleman, Khnumhotep II. The intent of the substitutions is ambiguous. The earliest allusion to secret writing in the West with concrete evidence of intent appears in Homer's *Iliad* [35]. Steganographic methods per se made their recorded debut a few centuries later in several tales by Herodotus [34], although the term *steganography* does not come into use until many centuries later, in the 1500's, after the appearance of Trithemius' book on the subject, *Steganographia*. Ancient references to secret writing and steganography also appear in Asia. Indian literature is replete with references as well as explicit formulas for secret writing. Kautilya's *Artha-śāstra* which dates back to 321–300 B.C., the *Lalita-Vistara*, and Vātsāyana's *Kāma-sūtra* are a few of the more famous examples. In fact, the study of many different types or cryptography, not just steganography, flourished in ancient India. In ancient China, military and diplomatic rulers wrote important messages on thin sheets of silk or paper. For secure transport, the sheets were rolled into balls, covered with wax, and swallowed by or placed in the rectum of messengers. Less sensitive, routine messages were usually memorized, then transmitted orally by a messenger.

It is interesting to note that many of the steganographical techniques that had been devised in the past have recently reappeared in the data-embedding and watermarking literature. For example, a class of steganographic techniques relies on using semagrams (*sema* for "sign" and *gramma* for "something written or drawn"), i.e., very slight physical differences in appearance such as special fonts, punctuation marks, or very fine dots. A well-known semagram approach consists of marking text using barely visible pin pricks, small dots, and dashes. The technique was suggested by Aenas the Tactician and used during the Renaissance and up through the twentieth century. (A modern adaptation of the technique is used in WitnesSoft by Aliroo,[1] which marks electronic documents during printout with barely visible dots, which can only be picked up by high-resolution scanners.) Embedding of messages by lowering specified letters and varying spacing between words appears time and again throughout history. Recently, the technique has been revisited in a digital context by scientists who are investigating digital watermarking of text files [6], [49], [56], [93], [98]. Examples of nontextual semagrams are equally replete. Spies have embedded messages in Morse code in drawings, e.g., landscapes with short and tall leaves of grass representing dots and dashes. Graphs have been disguised in mazes in a puzzle book, as have images in autostereograms. A modern extension of these techniques is the embedding of marks, such as "VOID," in an image or document that appear only when photocopied [58]. An early example of copyright or authorship information in musical scores was practiced by Bach. Bach embedded his name in many of his pieces (e.g., his organ chorale *Vor deinem Thron*) using null cipher coding by spelling out *B-A-C-H* in notes (where B-flat represents *B,* and B represents *H*) or by counting the number of occurrences of a note (one occurrence for *A,* two for *B,* three for *C,* and eight for *H*).

III. REQUIREMENTS

As mentioned in the introduction, data embedding can be used in many different applications. Obviously, differ-

[1] See http://www.aliroo.com.

ent applications will have different requirements. Therefore, there is no unique set of requirements that all data-embedding techniques must satisfy. Nevertheless, certain requirements must be satisfied in several application areas. In this section, we shall review some of these requirements and indicate when they are important.

A. Perceptual Transparency

The focus of this paper is on perceptually undetectable or transparent data-embedding and watermarking techniques. In many applications, such as copyright and usage tracking, embedding metadata or additional information, the algorithms must embed data without affecting the perceptual quality of the underlying host signal. In some applications, such as low-quality browsing of signals prior to purchasing, perceptually detectable watermarks have been used. We shall have more to say about such watermarks in Section VIII.

A data-embedding procedure is truly imperceptible if humans cannot differentiate between the original host signal and a host signal with inserted data. Typically, blind tests are used to assess the perceptual transparency of data-embedding procedures. In such tests, subjects are presented randomly with signals with and without embedded data and asked to determine which signal has a perceptually higher quality. A probability of selecting the signal with no embedded data that is roughly equal to 50% is indicative of perceptual transparency. Note that the blind tests must assess also the effect of several of the typical modifications that the signal may undergo. For example, digital pictures typically undergo a sharpening or high-pass filtering operations. Data embedding should not produce artifacts that are perceptually dissimilar from those that may be seen in an untampered image.

B. Recovery of Data with or Without Access to Original Signal

In some applications, such as copy tracking and copyright protection, the data-extraction algorithms may use the original signal to decode the embedded data. However, in most applications, data-embedding algorithms do not have access to the original audio, image, or video signal while extracting the embedded signal. This inability to access the original signal limits the amount of data that can be embedded in a given host signal. It also renders data extraction more difficult.

Specifically, the embedded data may be considered as information transmitted on a communication channel and corrupted by strong interference and channel effects. The strong interference consists of the host signal. Channel effects correspond to postprocessing operations. Most data-extraction procedures are inherently projection techniques on a given direction. Ideally, a larger projection value will indicate the presence of one type of data, e.g., a binary symbol or a watermark that represents an author. A segment of the host signal that is highly correlated with the projection direction will provide a false detection. Furthermore, it may be impossible to modify that segment to reduce its correlation with the projection direction without affecting the perceptual quality of the host signal. Hence, the algorithm may be unable to embed useful data into that segment.

Note that the projection direction cannot be easily changed since the decoder does not have access to the original host signal. Any change in that direction must be accomplished through an algorithm that uses the received modified host signal. Note also that the probability of getting a high correlation between an arbitrary segment of the host signal and the projection direction decreases as the size of the segment increases. However, as that size increases, the amount of data that can be embedded in the host signal decreases.

Postprocessing effects can complicate the detection process. For example, synchronization problems may arise as a consequence of temporal and spatial rescaling, cropping, resampling, rotation, etc. Many modifications lead to new signals, which have a different number of samples than the original signal with embedded data. To extract the embedded information, the extraction algorithm must adapt to the new signal with fewer samples automatically or access the original to register the signal. Note, however, that loss of synchronization does not imply that the embedded data have been erased. If complexity is not an issue, the data can still be recovered.

C. Bit Rate of Data-Embedding Algorithm

Some applications of data embedding, e.g., insertion of a serial number or author identification or fraud detection, require that relatively small amounts of information be incorporated repeatedly in the signal. On the other hand, many envisioned applications of data embedding, e.g., embedding a smaller image into a larger image or embedding multiple speech signals into a video, require a lot of bandwidth. In these cases, the algorithms must be able to embed an amount of data that is a significant fraction of the amount of data in the host signal. As mentioned above, the ability to embed large quantities of data in a host signal will depend critically on how the embedding algorithm can adapt its insertion strategy to the underlying host signal.

D. Robustness

Some data-embedding applications may take place in an error-free or lossless environment. For example, the embedded data may provide digital object identifiers for use in clean signals residing in a controlled data base. In these situations, robustness to signal degradations is not important. In many cases, however, lossy signal-processing operations may be present in the system. For example, in most applications involving storage or transmission of an image, a lossy coding operation is performed on the image to reduce bit rates and increase efficiency. Digital data are readily modified and manipulated using computers and widely available software packages, e.g., Adobe Photoshop or Premiere. Operations that damage the host signal also

damage the embedded data. Furthermore, third parties may attempt to modify the host signal to thwart detection of the embedded data.

Designers of robust data-embedding procedures have focused on several types of malicious or incidental host signal modifications. These modifications include:

- additive Gaussian or non-Gaussian noise;
- linear filtering, e.g., low-pass and high-pass filtering;
- nonlinear filtering, e.g., median filtering;
- compression, e.g., Joint Photographic Experts Group (JPEG), Moving Picture Experts Group (MPEG), wavelet;
- local exchange of samples, e.g., permutations;
- quantization of sample values;
- rotation;
- spatial or temporal scaling;
- removal or insertion of samples, pixels, or video frames;
- temporal averaging, e.g., averaging of successive video frames;
- swapping of data, e.g., swapping of successive video frames;
- averaging multiple watermarked copies of a signal;
- digital–analog (D/A) and analog–digital (A/D) conversions, e.g., printing and scanning or tape recording and redigitization.

Note that software to test robustness and remove data embedded from images is widely available on the Internet. In particular, the UnZign[2] and StirMark [45] programs have shown remarkable success in removing data embedded by commercially available programs. The algorithms generally apply minor geometric distortions, e.g., slight stretching, shearing, shifting, and/or rotations, to the image and then resample the image using bilinear interpolation. The resulting image looks perceptually similar to the original signal with embedded data.

E. Security

In many applications, the embedding procedure must be secure in that an unauthorized user must not be able to detect the presence of embedded data, let alone remove the embedded data. Security requirements vary with application. The most stringent requirements arise in covert communication scenarios. The security of data-embedding procedures is interpreted in the same way as the security of encryption techniques. A secure data-embedding procedure cannot be broken unless the unauthorized user has access to a secret key that controls the insertion of the data in the host signal. Hence, a data-embedding scheme is truly secure if knowing the exact algorithm for embedding the data does not help an unauthorized party to detect the presence of embedded data. An unauthorized user should also be unable to extract the data in a reasonable amount of time even if

---

[2] See http://altern.org/watermark.

he knows that the host signal contains data and is familiar with the exact algorithm for embedding the data. Note that in some applications, e.g., covert communications, the data may also be encrypted prior to insertion in a host signal.

F. Copyright Protection and Ownership Deadlock

Data-embedding algorithms may be used to establish ownership and distribution of data. In fact, this is the application of data embedding or watermarking that has received most attention in the literature. Unfortunately, most current watermarking schemes are unable to resolve rightful ownership of digital data when multiple ownership claims are made, i.e., when a deadlock problem arises. The inability of many data-embedding algorithms to deal with deadlock, first described by Craver et al. [15], is independent of how the watermark is inserted in the multimedia data or how robust it is to various types of modifications.

Today, no scheme can unambiguously determine ownership of a given multimedia signal if it does not use an original or other copy in the detection process to at least construct the watermark to be detected. A pirate can simply add his watermark to the watermarked data or counterfeit a watermark that correlates well or is detected in the contested signal. Current data-embedding schemes used as copyright-protection algorithms are unable to establish who watermarked the data first. Furthermore, none of the current data-embedding schemes has been proven to be immune to counterfeiting watermarks that will correlate well with a given signal as long as the watermark is not restricted to depend partially in a noninvertible manner on the signal.

If the detection scheme can make use of the original to construct the watermark, then it may be possible to establish unambiguous ownership of the data regardless of whether the detection scheme subtracts the original from the signal under consideration prior to watermark detection or not. Specifically, [16] derives a set of sufficient conditions that watermarks and watermarking schemes must satisfy to provide unambiguous proof of ownership. For example, one can use watermarks derived from pseudorandom sequences that depend on the signal and the author. Reference [16] establishes that this will work for all watermarking procedures regardless of whether they subtract the original from the signal under consideration prior to watermark detection or not. Reference [85] independently derived a similar result for a restricted class of watermarking techniques that rely on subtracting a signal derived from the original from the signal under consideration prior to watermark detection. The signal-dependent key also helps to thwart the "mix-and-match" attack described in [16].

An author can construct a watermark that depends on the signal and the author and provides unambiguous proof of ownership as follows. The author has two random keys x_1 and x_2 (i.e., seeds) from which a pseudorandom sequence y can be generated using a suitable pseudorandom sequence generator [76]. Popular generators include RSA, Rabin, Blum/Micali, and Blum/Blum/Shub [25]. With the two proper keys, the watermark may be extracted. Without the two keys, the data hidden in the signal are statistically undetectable and impossible to recover. Note that classical maximal length pseudonoise sequences (i.e., m-sequence) generated by linear feedback shift registers are not used to generate a watermark. Sequences generated by shift registers are cryptographically insecure: one can solve for the feedback pattern (i.e., the keys) given a small number of output bits y.

The noise-like sequence y may be used to derive the actual watermark hidden into the signal or to control the operation of the watermarking algorithm, e.g., to determine the location of pixels that may be modified. The key x_1 is author dependent. The key x_2 is signal dependent. The key x_1 is the secret key assigned to (or chosen by) the author. The key x_2 is computed from the signal that the author wishes to watermark. It is computed from the signal using a one-way hash function. For example, the tolerable error levels supplied by masking models (see Section IV) are hashed in [85] to a key x_2. Any one of a number of well-known secure one-way hash functions may be used to compute x_2, including RSA, MD4 [77], and SHA [60]. For example, the Blum/Blum/Shub pseudorandom generator uses the one-way function $y = g_n(x) = x^2 \bmod n$, where $n = pq$ for primes p and q so that $p = q = 3 \bmod 4$. It can be shown that generating x or y from partial knowledge of y is computationally infeasible for the Blum/Blum/Shub generator.

The signal-dependent key x_2 makes counterfeiting very difficult. The pirate can only provide key x_1 to the arbitrator. Key x_2 is automatically computed by the watermarking algorithm from the original signal. As it is computationally infeasible to invert the one-way hash function, the pirate is unable to fabricate a counterfeit original that generates a desired or predetermined watermark.

Deadlock may also be resolved using the dual watermarking scheme of [85]. That scheme employs a pair of watermarks. One watermarking procedure requires the original data set for watermark detection. The second watermarking procedure does not require the original data set. A data-embedding technique that satisfies the restrictions outlined in [16] can be used to insert the second watermark.

The above discussion clearly highlights the limitation of watermarking as an unambiguous mean of establishing ownership. Future clever attacks may show that the schemes described in [16] or [85] are still vulnerable to deadlock. Furthermore, all parties would need to use watermarking techniques that have been proven or certified to be immune to deadlock to establish ownership of media. Note also that contentions of ownership can occur in too many different forms. Copyright protection will probably not be resolved exclusively by one group or even the entire technical community since it involves too many legal issues, including the very definition of similarity and derived works. Many multidisciplinary efforts are currently investigating standards and rules for national and international copyright protection and enforcement in the digital age.

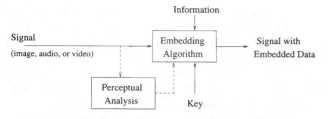

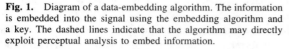

Fig. 1. Diagram of a data-embedding algorithm. The information is embedded into the signal using the embedding algorithm and a key. The dashed lines indicate that the algorithm may directly exploit perceptual analysis to embed information.

IV. Signal Insertion: The Role of Masking

The first problem that all data-embedding and watermarking schemes need to address is that of inserting data in the digital signal without deteriorating its perceptual quality. Of course, we must be able to retrieve the data from the edited host signal, i.e., the insertion method must also be invertible. Since the data-insertion and data-recovery procedures are intimately related, the insertion scheme must take into account the requirement of the data-embedding application. In many applications, we will need to be able to retrieve the data even when the host signal has undergone modifications, such as compression, editing, or translation between formats, including A/D and D/A conversions.

Data insertion is possible because the digital medium is ultimately consumed by a human. The human hearing and visual systems are imperfect detectors. Audio and visual signals must have a minimum intensity or contrast level before they can be detected by a human. These minimum levels depend on the spatial, temporal, and frequency characteristics of the human auditory and visual systems. Further, the human hearing and visual systems are characterized by an important phenomenon called masking. Masking refers to the fact that a component in a given audio or visual signal may become imperceptible in the presence of another signal called the masker. Most signal-coding techniques (e.g., [41]) exploit the characteristics of the human auditory and visual systems directly or indirectly. Likewise, all data-embedding techniques exploit the characteristics of the human auditory and visual systems implicitly or explicitly (see Fig. 1). In fact, embedding data would not be possible without the limitations of the human visual and auditory systems. For example, it is not possible to modify a binary stream that represents programs or numbers that will be interpreted by a computer. The modification would directly and adversely affect the output of the computer.

A. The Human Auditory System (HAS)

Audio masking is the effect by which a faint but audible sound becomes inaudible in the presence of another louder audible sound, i.e., the masker [42]. The masking effect depends on the spectral and temporal characteristics of both the masked signal and the masker.

Frequency masking refers to masking between frequency components in the audio signal. If two signals that occur simultaneously are close together in frequency, the stronger masking signal may make the weaker signal inaudible. The masking threshold of a masker depends on the frequency, sound pressure level, and tone-like or noise-like characteristics of both the masker and the masked signal [61]. It is easier for a broad-band noise to mask a tonal signal than for a tonal signal to mask out a broad-band noise. Moreover, higher frequency signals are more easily masked.

The human ear acts as a frequency analyzer and can detect sounds with frequencies that vary from 10 to 20 000 Hz. The HAS can be modeled by a set of bandpass filters with bandwidths that increase with increasing frequency. The bands are known as the critical bands. The critical bands are defined around a center frequency in which the noise bandwidth is increased until there is a just noticeable difference in the tone at the center frequency. Thus, if a faint tone lies in the critical band of a louder tone, the faint tone will not be perceptible.

Frequency-masking models are readily obtained from the current generation of high-quality audio codecs, e.g., the masking model defined in the International Standards Organization (ISO)-MPEG Audio Psychoacoustic Model 1 for Layer I [40]. The Layer I masking method is summarized as follows for a 32-kHz sampling rate. The MPEG model also supports sampling rates of 44.1 and 48 kHz.

The frequency mask is computed on localized segments (or windows) of the audio signal. The first step consists of computing the power spectrum of a short window (512 or 1024 samples) of the audio signal. Tonal (sinusoidal) and nontonal (noisy) components in the spectrum are identified because their masking models are different. A tonal component is a local maximum of the spectrum. The auditory system behaves as a bank of bandpass filters, with continuously overlapping center frequencies. These "auditory filters" can be approximated by rectangular filters with critical bandwidth increasing with frequency. In this model, the audible band is therefore divided into 24 nonregular critical bands.

Next, components below the absolute hearing threshold and tonal components separated by less than 0.5 Barks are removed. The final step consists of computing individual and global masking thresholds. The frequency axis is discretized according to hearing sensitivity and express frequencies in Barks. Note that hearing sensitivity is higher at low frequencies. The resulting masking curves are almost linear and depend on a masking index different for tonal and nontonal components. They are characterized by different lower and upper slopes depending on the distance between the masked and the masking component. We use f_1 to denote the set of frequencies present in the test signal. The global masking threshold for each frequency f_2 takes into account the absolute hearing threshold S_a and the masking curves P_2 of the N_t tonal components and N_n nontonal components

$$S_m(f_2) = 10 * \log_{10}\left[10^{S_a(f_2)/10} + \sum_{j=1}^{N_t} 10^{P_2(f_2, f_1, P_1)/10}\right.$$
$$\left. + \sum_{j=1}^{N_n} 10^{P_2(f_2, f_1, P_1)/10}\right]. \quad (1)$$

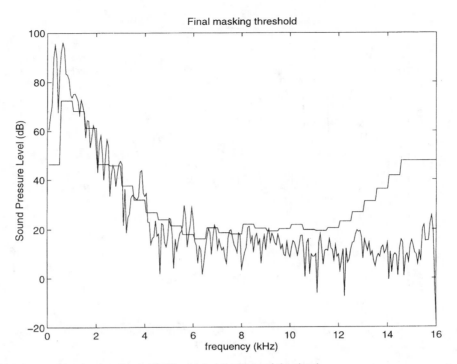

Fig. 2. Example of frequency masking in an audio signal. The original spectrum of the signal, along with the corresponding masking threshold, is shown in the plot.

The masking threshold is then the minimum of the local masking threshold and the absolute hearing threshold in each of the 32 equal-width subbands of the spectrum. Any signal that falls below the masking threshold is inaudible. An example plot of an original spectrum, along with the masking threshold, is shown in Fig. 2.

Temporal masking refers to both pre- and post-masking. Pre-masking effects render weaker signals inaudible before the stronger masker is turned on, and post-masking effects render weaker signals inaudible after the stronger masker is turned off. Pre-masking occurs 5–20 ms before the masker is turned on while post-masking occurs from 50–200 ms after the masker is turned off [61]. Note that temporal and frequency masking effects have dual localization properties. Specifically, frequency-masking effects are localized in the frequency domain, while temporal-masking effects are localized in the time domain.

Temporal-masking effects may be estimated using the envelope of the host audio. The envelope is modeled as a decaying exponential. In particular, the estimated envelope $t(i)$ of signal $s(i)$ increases with $s(i)$ and decays as $e^{-\alpha}$. A 32-kHz audio signal, along with its estimated envelope, is shown in Fig. 3.

B. The Human Visual System (HVS)

Visual masking, which works in a fashion similar to audio masking, refers to a situation where a signal raises the visual threshold for other signals around it. As in audio, a spatial sinusoidal pattern will lower the detectability of other sinusoidal patterns whose frequencies are close to that of the sinusoidal pattern [48]. This is referred to as frequency masking. Similarly, spatial patterns can affect the visibility of other features that are spatially close to them. For example, luminance edges and fine details reduce the visibility of other signals around them.

In our work, we have used a model for frequency masking that is directly based on measurements of the amounts by which the visual threshold for signal gratings around a masking frequency are raised due to a masking grating at that frequency [48]. In particular, a model we use [99], based on the discrete cosine transform (DCT), expresses the contrast threshold at frequency f as a function of f, the masking frequency f_m, and the masking contrast c_m

$$c(f, f_m) = c_0(f) \cdot \text{Max}\{1, [k(f/f_m)c_m]^\alpha\} \quad (2)$$

where $c_0(f)$ is the detection threshold at frequency f. The weighting function $k(f/f_m)$ centered about $f/f_m = 1$ is shown in Fig. 4.

To find the contrast threshold $c(f)$ at a frequency f in an image, we first use the DCT to transform the image into the frequency domain and find the contrast at each frequency. Then, we use a summation rule of the form $c(f) = [\sum_{f_m} c(f, f_m)^\beta]^{1/\beta}$. If the contrast error at f is less than $c(f)$, the model predicts that the error is invisible to human eyes.

A spatial masking model based on the threshold vision model is proposed by Girod [22]. The model accurately predicts the masking effects near edges and in uniform background. Assuming that the modifications to the image are small, the upper channel of Girod's model can be linearized [99] to obtain the tolerable error level for each

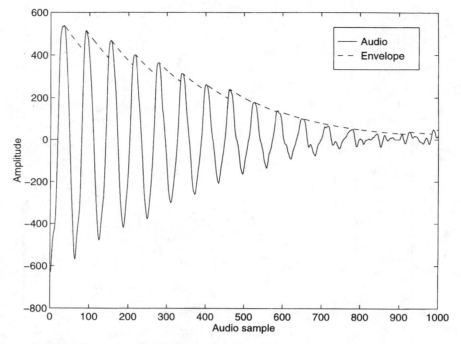

Fig. 3. Example of temporal masking in an audio signal. The original signal and the estimated envelope are plotted in the temporal domain.

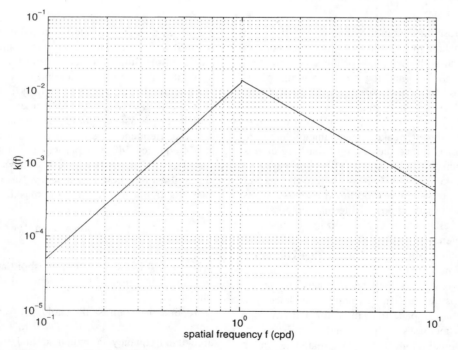

Fig. 4. Normalized image frequency-masking function.

coefficient. This is a reasonable assumption for transparent watermarking.

Under certain simplifying assumptions, the tolerable error level for a pixel $p(x, y)$ can be obtained by first computing the contrast saturation at (x, y)

$$dc_{\text{sat}}(x, y) = dc_{\text{sat}} = \sqrt{\frac{T}{\sum_{x', y'} w_4(0, 0, x', y')}} \quad (3)$$

where the weight $w_4(x, y, x', y')$ is a Gaussian centered at the point (x, y) and T is a visual test-based threshold. Once $dc_{\text{sat}}(x, y)$ is computed, the luminance on the retina l_{ret} is obtained from

$$dc_{\text{sat}}(x, y) = w_2(x, y) \cdot dl_{\text{ret}}(x, y). \quad (4)$$

From dl_{ret}, the tolerable error level $ds(x, y)$ for the pixel

$p(x, y)$ is computed from

$$dl_{\text{ret}}(x, y) = w_1(x, y) \cdot ds(x, y). \qquad (5)$$

The weights $w_1(x, y)$ and $w_2(x, y)$ are based on Girod's model. The masking model predicts that changes to pixel $p(x, y)$ less than $ds(x, y)$ introduce no perceptible distortion.

V.   Image Data-Embedding Approaches

We begin with a review of image data-embedding techniques since they are the most common in the literature. Audio and video data-embedding algorithms are reviewed in the following sections. The data-embedding algorithms are classified into those that *implicitly* use masking and those that *explicitly* employ masking to embed the data. As described in Section IV, all data-embedding algorithms implicitly employ limitations of the HAS and HVS to embed data. However, some use advanced perceptual models to determine the best way to embed data.

A. Image Data Embedding Implicitly Based on Masking

One of the simplest methods for inserting data into digital signals in noise-free environments is least significant bit (LSB) coding. The coding process begins with all of the LSB's of the host image set to zero (or all to one); zeroes and ones are then used to embed information in the LSB plane, e.g., a pattern or image in which "0" represents black and "1" represents white, or words coded in binary form. An analogous procedure can be used for color images, which are represented by three matrices for the intensities of the colors (e.g., red, green, and blue) in the image. LSB coding introduces noise of at most one unit, which, in practice, is imperceptible, so long as the host signal is not extremely low or weak.

LSB coding can be used to tag office memos onto digital data. For example, it has been used for the placement of markers to detect enlargements or reductions of an image that may have taken place during photo editing and to recover the associated dilation factor. Transparent cross marks are embedded in the LSB plane at fixed intervals in both the horizontal and vertical directions prior to editing. Changes in the dimensions made during editing can be detected and quantitatively measured by comparing the distances between the cross marks before and after the edit [27]. If cropping of an image is also expected, horizontal and vertical line numbers can be embedded at fixed intervals in the LSB plane to keep track of the pixel indexes from which a crop is made. The pixel index information will remain with the cropped image and can be recovered without a copy of the original, full-size image.

LSB coding has been practiced for decades; however, proposed use of the method for intellectual property-rights management is relatively new. The concept of a digital signature for authentication of electronic messages was introduced by Diffie and Hellman [19] and has since become a major area of research. More than a decade later, Matsui and Tanaka introduced the notion of video steganography

Table 1   Example of Cipher Key Table

Δ_i	...	-4	-3	-2	-1	0	1	2	3	4	...
c_i	...	0	1	1	0	1	0	0	1	0	...

in a series of conference papers that are surveyed in [54] and [55]. Embedding methods are proposed for grayscale, dithered binary, facsimile, and color still images and video.

The first embedding scheme is for digitized grayscale image data, which consists of a set of integers between 0 and 255, representing the gray levels of an image at sampled points. The digitized image data $\{x_i\}$; $i \in N$ is converted to a sequence in which the first element is x_1 and subsequent elements are the differences between successive points, i.e., $\Delta_i = x_i - x_{i-1}$. Next, the person(s) embedding and extracting the message agree on the use of a particular cipher key table, which assigns a value c_i, either zero or one, to each Δ_i (see Table 1). To embed a binary sequence $B = \{b_i : b_i = 0 \text{ or } 1\}$; $i \in N$, look up the value of c_i corresponding to Δ_i in the table. If $c_i = b_i$, then keep Δ_i as is. If $c_i \neq b_i$, go to the nearest Δ_j such that $c_j = b_i$ and substitute Δ_j in place of Δ_i. The error introduced into the image data during the ith step is $\text{error}_i = \Delta_j - \Delta_i$, which is usually on the same order as noise, i.e., negligible. The hidden message can be retrieved by looking up the value for c_i corresponding to Δ_i.

In a second scheme, which uses ordered dithering, an image is divided into 4-by-4 pixel blocks and brightness thresholds $\{x_i\}$; $i = 0, 1, \cdots, 15$ for each of the 16 pixels in the block are assigned from top to bottom, left to right. Next, define sets

$$S_k = \{(x_i, x_j)_k : x_j - x_i = k\}, \qquad i, j = 0, 1, \cdots, 15;$$
$$i \neq j. \qquad (6)$$

Let $(y_i, y_j)_k$ be a pair of output signals that pass through $(x_i, x_j)_k$. Then $(y_i, y_j)_k$ is either $(0, 0)$, $(1, 0)$, $(0, 1)$, or $(1, 1)$, where 0 indicates that the pixel will be turned "off" and 1 indicates "on." Only the pairs $(1, 0)$ or $(0, 1)$ will be used to embed a sequence of bits $B = \{b_n : b_n = 0 \text{ or } 1\}$; $n \in N$. To embed $b_n = 0$, set $(y_i, y_j)_k = (0, 1)$. To embed $b_n = 1$, set $(y_i, y_j)_k = (1, 0)$. To decode, disregard the $(0, 0)$ and $(1, 1)$ outputs and simply reverse the procedure described above.

Facsimile document signals serve as the host medium for a third message-embedding scheme. Documents are digitized following the international standard facsimile scanning rate of 8.23 pixels/mm in the horizontal direction [12].[3] The scanned data indicate whether a pixel is black or white, the two options. The message-embedding scheme is based on the fact that the data will be compressed using *run-length coding* (RLC) and modified *Huffman* coding schemes. RLC reduces data by replacing repeated characters with three characters: a *flag* character to signal that compression follows, the repeated character, and the number of repetitions. A binary message $B = \{b_n : b_n = 0 \text{ or } 1\}$; $n \in Z$ is embedded by shortening or lengthening runs by one pixel at the boundaries of the runs. In a simple illustrative example,

---

[3] See http://www.infomedia.net/scan/.

runs are set to be even number length when $b_i = 0$ (by leaving it as is if it is already of even length and lengthening it by one if it is odd) and to an odd length when $b_i = 1$ (by leaving it as is if it is already of odd length and by shortening it by one if it is even). Runs used for coding must have a length greater than two.

Van Schydel et al. [90] also propose LSB coding methods that rely on m-sequences for transparently embedding messages with greater security than straightforward LSB coding. A binary sequence is mapped from $\{0, 1\}$ to $\{-1, 1\}$. In one method, the message is embedded in the LSB plane using m-sequences. The second is based on LSB addition. Some disadvantages of the method are: hostile parties will know that all pixels are changed by either ± 1; knowledge of a string of repeating consecutive bits enables the recovery of the data; and embedding is performed without regard to the DCT coefficients, so there is no guarantee of robustness with respect to JPEG.

Wolfgang and Delp [96], [97] extend van Schyndel et al.'s work to two dimensions. Localization, i.e., detection of the presence of the data, is improved under the new scheme. Localization relies on use of the cross-correlation function R_{XY} of two images X and Y, defined as

$$R_{XY}(\alpha, \beta) = \sum_i \sum_j X(i, y) Y(i - \alpha, j - \beta). \quad (7)$$

Let X be the original image, W the watermark, Y the watermarked image, and Z a possible forgery. The test statistic defined as

$$\delta = R_{YW}(0, 0) - R_{ZW}(0, 0) \quad (8)$$

can often detect whether or not Z is a forgery. If Z and Y are identical, then $\delta = 0$. In one implementation of their method, Wolfgang and Delp embed data consisting of changes by $\{0, 1\}$. In another, the changes are bipolar, i.e., $\{-1, 1\}$. The bipolar data are easier to detect using the test statistic δ. Both types of marking are robust with respect to the test statistic under JPEG compression. Information regarding the preservation of the data is not given.

LSB coding can and should be used in contexts that do not require more sophisticated approaches; however, it is not robust enough for general distribution because binary sequences are embedded in a manner that requires perfect preservation of the signal for successful extraction of the hidden message; noisy transmission, filtering, cropping, color space conversion, or resampling would destroy the message. A more serious concern with LSB coding is the possibility of extraction of a binary message by hostile parties.

To alert the user to contamination or tampering of LSB-coded data, Walton [95] suggests using check sums [78]. To circumvent interception of an embedded message by hostile parties, Walton [95] and Matsui and Tanaka [55] recommend controlling the embedding locations through the use of keys, e.g., the use of a pseudorandom number generator to determine a pseudorandom walk on the image pixel plane [44], [53]. After a user-specified number of steps, say, N, a check digit for the pixel values at the N

preceding positions is embedded in the $(N+1)$st pixel along the random walk. This procedure is repeated many times. Users should double-check that the path of the random walk does not cross over itself during the embedding of the check sums since it could lead to false alarms of tampering. If the possible discovery of the pseudorandom sequence-generation mechanism by a hostile party is a consideration, variations that disguise the locations of the check sums can be developed to prevent tampering with the check sums themselves.

For color images, the basic check-sum scheme can be applied, straightforwardly, three times to the three color planes. More interesting variations that take advantage of the three dimensions from the three color planes can be developed. The basis set for representing the images, for example, can be changed from red-green-blue (RGB) to hue-lightness-saturation; the check sum is then calculated in the new coordinate system, and the check-sum digit is encoded in the original coordinate system. (For further details on standard bases for color-image representation and conversion factors, see [79].) Matsui and Tanaka's embedding methods, with and without check sums, are not robust with respect to cropping. In concluding our discussion on LSB coding, we remark that steganographic freeware for image marking is widely available over the Internet.

In Ohnishi and Matsui's Haar wavelet transform-based method, messages are embedded by adding or subtracting one from the transform coefficients of the image [64]. Like LSB coding, the technique is very fragile with respect to simple tampering, e.g., cropping.

Sanford et al. developed software (BMPEMBED, ver. 1.51 in the C programming language) for embedding data information into and extracting the information from color images in bitmap format [80]. The principles of the method are outlined in the algorithm for grayscale images. Embedding consists of two main steps. First, an image is analyzed to identify pairs of elements (i.e., pixel values) d_i and d_j, which are within a "noise range" N

$$|d_i - d_j| = \epsilon \leq N \quad (9)$$

and such that $f(d_i)$ and $f(d_j)$, the frequency of occurrence of d_i and d_j, are fairly large and within a tolerance δ

$$|f(d_i) - f(d_j)| < \delta. \quad (10)$$

Binary information will be embedded by using the value d_i to represent a zero and d_j to represent a one (or vice versa). The main principles used in marking grayscale images are extended to mark color images. Identification of pairs of pixels within acceptable noise ranges is a more complicated process for color-image data. Embedding in JPEG and wavelet transform compressed images is accomplished through the use of the same technique in the DCT and wavelet transform domains. In the experiments described in the report, robustness with respect to (further) JPEG compression and restoration is not considered or tested. This embedding method suffers from other drawbacks, e.g., fragility with respect to cropping and multiple embeddings and (depending on the image) limited available space for embedding. Since a fairly substantial amount of work is required to analyze images to determine suitable embedding locations, real-time image retrieval may only be possible if the locations are determined ahead of time; use of predetermined, fixed embedding locations for a given image increases the ease in tampering and extraction of embedded information by hostile parties.

Bender *et al.* propose *texture block coding,* in which a block from a region with a random texture is copied and placed in a region with similar texture [2]. Extraction of the hidden block is easy. Slides of the original image and its opposite (in which each pixel x_i is replaced by $256 - x_i$) are overlayed. As one slide is moved across the other, a solid black region will appear when the embedded block and the original region, from which it was taken, overlap. The method cannot be applied to all images and is not amenable to automatic embedding since images must be examined one by one by a human to determine whether suitable textured regions exist. The method is not robust to cropping. Although regular, two-dimensional shapes (e.g., solid circles, rectangles) can be readily embedded, the technique is not well suited for handling intricate designs and textual information. Furthermore, texture block coding is easy to detect since anyone can make slides of the original image and its opposite and extract the embedded block or region.

The same scientists also proposed *patchwork,* a statistical approach, in which a subset of the pixels in an image is divided into two distinct sets. The brightness of one set of pixels is shifted by a positive number, and those from the other set are shifted by the corresponding negative number [2]. Only a limited amount of information can be embedded in an image using this approach, even if the image is divided into several regions and a different number is embedded into each (i.e., one number per region). The inventors provide data that the recovery rate is 85% after JPEG compression, with quality parameter 75%, which would likely not stand up as credible evidence beyond a reasonable doubt in a court of law.

Pitas and Kaskalis use shifting in an approach that allows slightly more information to be embedded [69], [70]. A binary signature that consists of equal numbers of "zeros" and "ones" is embedded in an image by assigning pixels into one of two sets. The intensity levels of the pixels in one of the sets are altered. The intensity levels are not changed in the pixels in the other set. The method is limited to signature embedding and cannot be used for embedding text messages. According to the inventors, the degree of certainty can be as low as 84% and as high as 92%, which would likely not stand up as evidence in a court of law for copyright protection. In [94], toral automorphisms are used to chaotically mix binary logos or signatures, which are added to a secret region in the image.

In a similar method by Dautzenberg and Boland, images are partitioned into blocks, and the mean is shifted by one or zero to embed binary code [17]. The code does not necessarily have to consist of equal numbers of zeros and ones. The authors claim robustness to lossy image compression, photocopying, color scanning, and dithering. The method suffers from at least two major drawbacks. The amount of information that can be embedded depends on the number of blocks in the image. The method cannot be used to mark images that will be widely distributed using different marks for each intended recipient because comparison of large numbers of differently marked images will allow hostile parties to recover the original image.

Bruyndonckx *et al.* also use a block partitioning based method but use the change in the mean values of the luminance in blocks for embedding [9]. After an image is divided into blocks, the embedding order and locations can be found using a key. The blocks are classified into one of three types of luminance: hard, progressive, and noise contrast. The pixels are then assigned to zones, which add an extra level of security for embedding. Two categories A and B are created in each zone. Each pixel is assigned to a category based on its block and zone assignment. Embedding of a bit b in a block is carried out by changing the differences in the mean in the luminance values of pixels in categories A and B and zones 1 and 2

$$\begin{aligned} \text{if } b = 0: \quad & m_{1B}^* - m_{1A}^* = L \\ & m_{2B}^* - m_{2A}^* = L \\ \text{if } b = 1: \quad & m_{1A}^* - m_{1B}^* = L \\ & m_{2A}^* - m_{2B}^* = L \end{aligned}$$

where m_{1A}^*, m_{1B}^*, m_{2A}^*, and m_{2B}^* are the mean values after embedding and L is the embedding level. To render the embedding as transparent as possible, the inventors require that the mean value in each zone be left unchanged. This requirement uniquely determines the values of m_{1A}^*, m_{1B}^*, m_{2A}^*, and m_{2B}^* after embedding. To summarize, six parameters are used to embed information: the embedding level L, the categories grid size, the block size, the number of bits to be embedded, the location of the blocks, and the level of redundancies (with the option of error-detection codes if the message is short enough to allow a high level of redundant embedding). Robustness to JPEG depends strongly on the compression ratio, embedding level, and grid sizes. Redundant embedding with error-correcting codes is very effective in reducing the error in extracted messages. Depending on the amount of information to be embedded (which, in turn, determines if redundant embedding can be accommodated), the scheme may or may not be robust to cropping.

Langelaar *et al.* propose a block-based method in which embedding is carried out in the luminance-hue-saturation (YUV) domain [46]. The pixel values from 8×8 JPEG blocks of an image (or multiples of them) are converted to the YUV domain. After embedding binary information, the blocks are converted back to the RGB domain. If an edge-enhancement filter is applied to the luminance pixel values, the error rate for bit extraction after JPEG filtering is reduced significantly (from over 10% for JPEG quality factor 90% to well under 5%). The error rate is under 5%

for JPEG quality factor 100–60% in experiments described in the paper by Langelaar *et al.*

Koch and Zhao's data-embedding method, used in the product SysCop, is similar to direct sequence and frequency hopping spread-spectrum communications [20], [68], [92] and is compatible with JPEG compression quality parameter 50% [51]. An image is partitioned into 8-by-8 blocks, and eight coefficients in the block are used for marking. The blocks are pseudorandomly selected to minimize detection. Since the locations of the eight coefficients have been published, hostile parties can use the information to corrupt or destroy a message. Decoding by unauthorized parties is more difficult because of the pseudorandom sequence used for embedding. Cropping of images may lead to difficulties in extracting messages that were pseudorandomly embedded. And cropping along lines that cut through, rather than along, the 8-by-8 JPEG blocks may lead to an image that is not robust to JPEG compression. Langelaar *et al.* report that image degradation is visible in their implementation studies to assess Koch and Zhao's method, and results are shown in a paper [46]. A variation on Koch and Zhao's method for image authentication is presented by Schneider and Chang [11]. The technique alters transform coefficients to enforce a relationship between the coefficients.

Spread-spectrum embedding spreads the watermark over a larger number of frequency ranges, the idea being that the energy in any given frequency range will be undetectable. The watermark can still be checked since the spreading pattern is known. Another spread-spectrum noise technique is described by Smith and Comiskey [82], where the authors hide data by adding a fixed-amplitude pseudonoise sequence to the image.

Kutter *et al.* use amplitude modulation and a secret key to embed a signature in color images [52]. The signature bits are repeatedly embedded in the blue channel to ensure robustness. The blue channel is used because the HVS is relatively less sensitive in this color domain. A single bit s is embedded in a pseudorandomly selected pixel $p = (i, j)$ in an image $I = \{R, G, B\}$ by modifying the blue channel B by a fraction of the luminance L, i.e.,

$$B_{i,j} \leftarrow B_{i,j} + q(2s - 1)L_{i,j}. \tag{11}$$

Here, $L = 0.299R + 0.587G + 0.114B$ and q is a constant that represents the strength of the signature. q is selected to optimize robustness and invisibility. The embedded message is retrieved using prediction of the original value of the pixel $p = (i, j)$ based on a linear combination of its neighboring pixel values. More precisely, the prediction $\hat{B}_{i,j}$ is

$$\hat{B}_{i,j} = \frac{1}{4c} \left(\sum_{k=-c}^{c} B_{i+k,j} + \sum_{k=-c}^{c} B_{i,j+k} - 2B_{i,j} \right) \tag{12}$$

where c is the size of the cross-shaped neighborhood. The embedded bit is computed to be the difference δ of the predicted and coded bit

$$\delta_{i,j} = B_{i,j} - \hat{B}_{i,j}. \tag{13}$$

To reduce the possibility of incorrect retrieval, the bit is embedded many times, and the computed differences are averaged. Extension to an m-bit signature is straightforward. The inventors claim and discuss the extent to which the algorithm is robust to translation, rotations, slight blurring, JPEG attack, and composition with other images.

Puate and Jordan use fractal compression analysis to embed a signature in an image [74]. In fractal analysis, similar patterns are identified in an image. Domain blocks D_b, which represent patterns that appear frequently, are noted. The intent is to identify a set of domain blocks that can be transformed (i.e., contracted, isometrically transformed, luminance scaled, and luminance shifted) to approximate blocks within an image. The goal is to cover the entire image (as much as possible) with the transformed domain blocks. In fractal compression, the reduced information consists of domain blocks, appropriate transformations on the blocks, and pointers to locations where the transformed blocks should be mapped. A binary signature, consisting of the set of bits $\{s_i\}$, is embedded in an image by varying the regions in which pattern-matching searches are performed. For a bit s_i, range blocks are pseudorandomly chosen to be somewhere in region A if $s = 1$ and in region B if $s = 0$. The inventors present data that show that their method is robust with respect to JPEG compression. If the image is blurred before JPEG compression, the results are not as good. The binary message can be encoded to increase protection from interception by unauthorized parties. Only a limited amount of binary code can be embedded using this method. Since fractal analysis is computationally expensive, and some images do not have many large, self-similar patterns, the technique may not be suitable for general use.

Davern and Scott also propose a fractal-based steganographic method to embed binary messages, either plain or encrypted [18]. Fractal image analysis is used to identify similar blocks. Then transformations are constructed so that one similar block is transformed into an approximation for another. These transformations enable visibly imperceptible substitution of blocks. The set of blocks that can be used as substitutes is divided in two. To embed a zero, substitute blocks from the first set are used, and to embed a one, blocks from the second set are used. Davern and Scott's embedding method suffers from two of the same problems as that of Puate and Jordan. It is very slow, since fractal analysis is computationally expensive, and only a limited amount of information can be embedded. Additionally, Davern and Scott's method appears to be less robust to JPEG compression.

O'Ruanaidh *et al.* [65] describe a technique where image blocks are transformed using the DCT, Walsh transform, or wavelet transform. The data are embedded by incrementing a selected coefficient to encode a "1" and decrementing it to encode a "0." Coefficients are selected according to a criterion based on energy content. The watermark survived $20:1$ JPEG image compression on the standard 256×256 Lena image. In a second approach [66], the authors describe a technique to embed information in the discrete Fourier transform phase.

Data-embedding techniques that require the original signal during detection are now reviewed. Some early algorithms for transparent marking, such as that by Cox et al. [14], require both the original and marked images for recovering an embedded message. The differences in the images is encrypted code. In the algorithm of Cox et al. [14], watermarks are embedded in the largest magnitude DCT coefficients to provide greater robustness to compression algorithms than LSB-type methods. Embedding in the highest coefficients corresponds to placing marks in the most perceptually significant portions of the image, regions that will remain relatively intact when subjected to compression. The marking algorithm consists of four steps.

- Compute the DCT and identify perceptually significant regions of the image suitable for watermark embedding.
- Construct the watermark $X = x_i, x_2, \cdots, x_n$, where each x_i is chosen according to $N(0,1)$, where $N(\mu, \sigma^2)$ denotes a normal distribution with mean μ and variance σ^2.
- Insert the watermark in the DCT domain of the image by setting the frequency component ν_i in the original image to

$$\nu_i \leftarrow \nu_i(1 + x_i\alpha_i) \qquad (14)$$

where α_i is a scalar factor.

- Compute the inverse DCT of the sum from the previous step to recover a transparently marked image.

Note that n, the number of DCT coefficients affected by the watermark, indicates the extent to which the watermark will be spread out among the components of the image. The authors choose α_i to be 0.1 in their experiments. A better approach would be to set α_i adaptively to different values for different frequencies. A Gaussian type of watermark is used for watermarking because it is much more robust to tampering than uniform embedding, particularly when n is large. More specifically, the authors claim that $\Omega(\sqrt{n/\ln n})$ similar types of watermarks would have to be embedded to have "any chance" of destroying the image. The larger the n, the greater the protection provided by the watermark.

Extraction of the watermark by Cox et al. consists of four steps.

- Compute the DCT of a (possibly) watermarked image.
- Compute the DCT of the original image.
- Compute the difference in the results from the previous two steps to a watermark X^*.
- Compare the extracted mark X^* with the original watermark X.

Comparison of the marks is conducted using a similarity measure defined by

$$\text{sim}(X, X^*) = \frac{X^* \cdot X}{\sqrt{X^* \cdot X^*}}. \qquad (15)$$

Studies on the robustness of the watermarks by Cox et al. show that when $n > 1000$ (i.e., 1000 perceptually significant frequency components of the image spectrum are altered), the watermark is reliable after JPEG encoding (quality factor 5%), dithering, clipping, clipping with JPEG encoding (quality factor 10%), and the combination of printing, photocopying, subsequent rescanning, and rescaling. When five watermarks were embedded in an image, all were successfully identified. Successful identification is also reported in averaging five separately watermarked images. Stone has published a report in which he shows how the strength of the technique proposed by Cox et al. can be diminished [83] when multiple watermarked copies are available to a pirate.

Ragusa et al. [75] devised and implemented a modification of the algorithm by Cox et al. in which regions of interest (ROI's) are identified from the DCT components. Ragusa et al. assume that for most images, ROI's that need to be watermarked for protection will have prominent edges. This assumption reduces the regions that will be marked so that only 200 or so ROI's need to be marked, as opposed to the 1000 recommended by Cox et al. The primary advantage of the modified scheme is the reduced time required for embedding and extraction and a decrease in the likelihood of noticeable perceptual differences. The disadvantage is that solid regions and regions without prominent edges will not be marked.

Another algorithm that requires the original image is that by Hsu and Wu [36]. The signature is an image of a seal with Chinese characters. Permutations of the middle-band coefficients of the is DCT are used for encoding. The difference between the original and marked image is used to retrieve the signature. Pseudorandom number generators can be used to increase the security. They can serve several roles, such as designating the permutation and the embedding location. The inventors claim that the signed images are robust to general image-enhancement techniques and JPEG lossy compression.

In Fridrich [21], a low-frequency-based scheme similar to that of Cox et al. is introduced. In the scheme, a random black-and-white pattern is processed by a cellular automaton with the voting rule through several stages and smoothed with a low-pass kernel. The resulting pattern is added to the image. The robustness of the technique is reportedly slightly better than [14].

In an approach, called *tagging*, by Caronni [10], images are partitioned into blocks, and the mean values of the brightness of pseudorandomly selected blocks are altered to embed code. (When very high security is required, better random position-selection mechanisms should be used.) The inventor claims that the tags can be recovered after JPEG compression with quality parameter 30%. And when a modulation strength of 2% and tag size of 16×16 pixels are used, 75% of the tags from enlarged, color-printed, and rescanned images can be recovered. In most cases, tags with a modulation strength of 2% are imperceptible. Let $b_0(x, y)$ and $b_m(x, y)$ represent the brightness of the original and tagged images and m_0 and m_m represent their mean. Then the covariance ν_{0m} between and variances ν_0, ν_m of the

original and marked image are

$$\nu_{0m} = c \sum_{x=1}^{X} \sum_{y=1}^{Y} (b_0(x,y) - m_0)(b_m(x,y) - m_m)$$

$$\nu_0^2 = c \sum_{x=1}^{X} \sum_{y=1}^{Y} (b_0(x,y) - m_0) \qquad (16)$$

$$\nu_m^2 = c \sum_{x=1}^{X} \sum_{y=1}^{Y} (b_m(x,y) - m_m)$$

where $c = 1/(X * Y - 1)$. If two images are identical, then the correlation coefficient between the two images $\|R\| = \nu_{0m}/\sqrt{\nu_0 \nu_m} = 1$. As the images become more dissimilar from tagging, $\|R\| \to 0$. Note that only images of the same size can be compared using this method of measurement. The tag is recovered by comparing the original and marked image and the key for determining the order and positions of the tagged blocks.

Many commercial image data-embedding algorithms are available. Digimarc's PictureMarc[4] uses a spread-spectrum technique. Using a 32-bit binary signature, the least significant bit of the 32 is aligned with the first pixel of the image. If the bit is a "1," the first random number is added to the first pixel; if the bit is a "0," then it is subtracted. The same process is applied to the second pixel using the second bit of the signature number to choose whether to add or subtract the second random number. This is continued until all 32 bits have been used. The process is then repeated by starting over at bit 0 while continuing across the image. The algorithm is terminated when all pixels have been marked. If the original is available during detection, it is subtracted from the signed image, resulting in a difference signal. The sign of each pixel in the difference image is compared with the corresponding code pattern sign. If they match, then the identification signal bit is a one; otherwise, it is a zero. This process is repeated over the entire image, and the individual bits are summed. The sum of each bit is divided by the number of repetitions of the signature. The result is the identification number. In the cases where there is no original image or changes have occurred to the signed image, small-signal detection methods are used to read the signature.

Other commercial software include DICE's Argent technology[5] and Aliroo's ScarLet algorithm.[1]

B. Image Data Embedding Explicitly Based on Masking

A technique based on spatial and frequency masking is presented in [84]. The data embedding works by breaking an image into small (e.g., 8×8) blocks. Each block is then represented as a vector v in an n-dimensional space (e.g., $n = 8^2$) and projected onto a normalized pseudorandom (author-defined) direction z weighted by the masking values for the particular block. With z normalized, the projection of the image block onto the user-defined direction is simply the inner product $p = \langle v, z \rangle = \sum_i v(i)z(i)$.

[4] See http://www.digimarc.com.
[5] See http://www.digital-watermark.com:80/.

Fig. 5. Original 512×512 grayscale image.

The scalar projection value p is then quantized with respect to the masking levels of that block T, creating the value p^*. The quantized value is perturbed by $\pm \frac{1}{4}T$ to embed the data, i.e., $p' = p^* \pm \frac{1}{4}T$. The new projection p' contains the hidden data. To extract the hidden data, each recovered block is projected onto the appropriate pseudorandom direction, and a simple remainder operation is applied

$$b = \begin{cases} 1, & \text{if } (\langle v', z \rangle - [\langle v', z \rangle]) > 0; \\ 0, & \text{otherwise} \end{cases} \qquad (17)$$

where $[\cdot]$ is the rounding operation and b is the bit embedded in the block. The technique easily accommodates the insertion of multiple bits per block. Figs. 5 and 6 provide an example of the algorithm. The image in Fig. 6 was obtained by embedding an 8192-bit text file inside the original image shown in Fig. 5. Note that the two images are perceptually identical. The bit error rate for the embedded data after different levels of JPEG coding is shown in Fig. 7. Using error correction codes and bit repetition, the data are able to survive low JPEG qualities. For example, one may use $15:1$ bit repetition (reducing the effective embedded bit rate to about 500 bits) for environments with a lot of distortion.

Several masking-based image data-embedding algorithms that require the original during detection have been proposed. Cox *et al.* [14] propose to set α_i (14) adaptively according to masking values for different frequencies.

A block-based version of [14] that employs visual models has been developed by Podilchuk and Zeng [71]. The algorithm employs the just noticeable difference paradigm employed by perceptual coders. The watermarked DCT coefficients $X^*(u, v, b)$ are generated by (18), as shown at the bottom of the next page, where $X(u, v, b)$ refers to the DCT coefficients at location (u, v) in block b of the image, $w(u, v, b)$ is the sequence of real valued watermark values,

Fig. 6. Image with embedded information.

and $J(u, v, b)$ is the computed just noticeable difference calculated from the visual models. The detection is performed in the same manner as that of Cox *et al.* The authors claim that the watermark survives uniform noise, cropping, and JPEG compression with a quality factor of 20, as well as printing, photocopying, rescanning, and rescaling of the image. The results were slightly better than the original Cox *et al.* algorithm, indicating some of the advantages of employing masking for data embedding. Another efficient image data-hiding algorithm based on perceptual masking is presented in [24].

In [88], the authors present a technique that exploits HVS to guarantee that the embedded watermark is imperceptible and robust. The watermark is generated by filtering a pseudorandom sequence [owner identification (id)] with a filter that approximates the frequency and spatial masking characteristics of the HVS. The watermark is generated by segmenting the image into blocks $B_{i,j}$ of size $n \times m$, e.g., 8×8. For each block $B_{i,j}$, there are the following steps.

1) Compute the DCT $D_{i,j}$ of the image block $B_{i,j}$.
2) Compute the frequency mask $M_{i,j}$ of the DCT image block $D_{i,j}$.
3) Use the mask $M_{i,j}$ to weight the noise-like author id for that image block, creating the shaped author signature $P_{i,j}$.
4) Create the watermark block $W_{i,j}$ by computing the inverse DCT of $P_{i,j}$ and weighting the result with the corresponding spatial mask $S_{i,j}$.

5) Add the watermark $W_{i,j}$ to the block $B_{i,j}$, creating the watermarked block $B'_{i,j}$.

Detection of the watermark is accomplished via hypothesis testing [91] using the similarity measure defined by (15).

To illustrate the algorithm, the technique was applied to the original image shown in Fig. 8(a). The resulting watermarked image is shown in Fig. 8(b), along with the watermark shown in Fig. 8(c). The watermark has been rescaled to gray levels for display. The watermark values corresponding to smoother background regions are generally smaller than watermark values near edge regions. This is to be expected, as edge regions have more favorable masking characteristics. The absolute values of the watermark range from 2 (smooth regions) to 48 (edge regions).

The robustness of the algorithm to JPEG coding is shown in Fig. 9. The plot indicates the similarity values of the "Peppers" test image with and without a watermark at several bit rates corresponding to JPEG qualities from 5 to 95%. To simulate additional attacks on the watermark, colored noise was added to the test image *prior* to JPEG coding. Each coding quality was tested 100 times, with a different colored noise sequence used during each test. The error bars at each quality correspond to the maximum and minimum similarity values at each bit rate. Even at very low image quality, the similarity values are separated, allowing the existence of a watermark to be easily determined.

VI. Audio Data-Embedding Approaches

A. Audio Data Embedding Implicitly Based on Masking

Several techniques have been proposed in [2] and [28]. Using a phase-coding approach, data are embedded by modifying the phase values of Fourier transform coefficients of audio segments. The authors also proposed embedding data as spread-spectrum noise. A third technique, echo coding, employs multiple decaying echoes to place a peak in the cepstrum at a known location.

Another audio data-embedding technique is proposed in [89], where Fourier transform coefficients over the middle frequency bands, 2.4–6.4 kHz, are replaced with spectral components from a signature. The middle frequency band was selected so that the data remain outside of the more sensitive low-frequency range. The signature is of short time duration and has a low amplitude relative to the local audio signal. The technique is described as robust to noise and the wow and flutter of analog tapes.

Pruess *et al.* [73] embed data into audio by shaping a pseudonoise sequence according to the shape of the original signal. The data are embedded within a preselected band of the audio spectrum after proportionally shaping it by the corresponding audio-signal frequency components. In

$$X^*(u,v,b) = \begin{cases} X(u,v,b) + J(u,v,b)w(u,v,b), & \text{if } X(u,v,b) > J(u,v,b); \\ X(u,v,b), & \text{otherwise} \end{cases} \qquad (18)$$

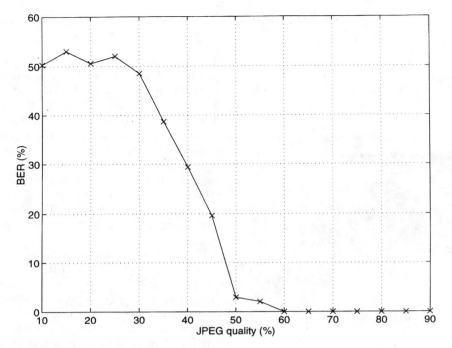

Fig. 7. Bit error rate versus JPEG quality factor for image shown in Fig. 6.

particular, the frequency component ν_i in the original audio signal is modified to

$$\nu_i \leftarrow \nu_i(1 + x_i\alpha_i) \qquad (19)$$

where x_i is a sample of the spread data and α_i is a scalar factor. The inventors claim the composite audio signal is not readily distinguishable from the original audio signal. The data may be recovered by essentially reversing the embedding operation using a whitening filter. As described above, a very similar embedding technique was later employed by Cox *et al.* for image watermarking.

Some commercial products are also available. The Identification Code Embedded system from Central Research Laboratories inserts a pair of very short tone sequences into an audio track.

Solana Technology Development Corporation [47] embeds data into subbands of the audio signal. The data to be embedded modulate a pseudonoise spread-spectrum signal, each subband of which has a bandwidth corresponding to those of the digital audio signal. The modulated data carrier sequence is combined with the audio subband samples to form a combined signal in which the embedded data are carried. The combined signal is then combined into the audio signal. At the decoder, the combined signal is demodulated to recover the auxiliary data signal. The recovered auxiliary data signal is inaudible in the audio signal and is spectrally shaped according to the audio signal to enhance concealment. Solana has an audio marking product called Electronic DNA (E-DNA) and ScarLet by Aliroo.

Patents for audio data embedding have been filed by Radio Audit Systems, Inc., for a radio-broadcast signal-processing system with an information encoder [26] and the

DICE Company for an apparatus and method for encoding information into digital multimedia data [13].

Very few audio data-embedding algorithms that use the original audio signal during detection have been proposed. A few image watermarking schemes, e.g., [14], have been described as generic and applicable to audio, although no results have been reported. This is due to the fact that most audio embedding algorithms are designed for broadcast environments. As a result, most audio embedding algorithms are required to retrieve the embedded information without access to the original.

B. Audio Data Embedding Explicitly Based on Masking

An audio data-embedding technique based on temporal and frequency masking is presented in [84]. The data embedding works by extracting length 512 blocks of the audio. Sequential blocks of length 512 are extracted from the audio signal and projected onto a pseudorandom (author-defined) direction weighted by the masking values for the particular block. The scalar projection value is then quantized with respect to the masking levels of that block. To embed data, the quantized projection value is perturbed to a new value. To extract the hidden data, each recovered block is projected onto the appropriate pseudorandom direction and a simple remainder operation is applied [see (17)].

Moses [57] proposes a technique to embed data by encoding it as one or more whitened direct sequence spread-spectrum signals and/or a narrow-band frequency-shift-keying data signal and transmitted at the time, frequency, and level determined by a neural network (NN) such that the signal is masked by the audio signal. The NN monitors the audio channel to determine opportunities to insert the data signal such that the inserted signals are masked.

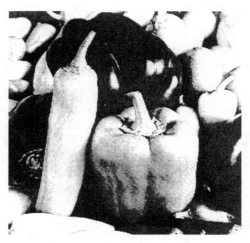

(a)

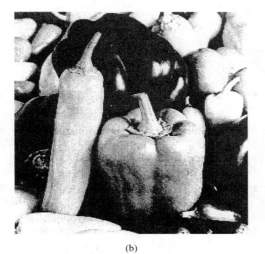

(b)

(c)

Fig. 8. An image (a) original and (b) watermarked. (c) Watermark rescaled to gray levels for display.

In [4] and [87], the authors present an audio watermarking algorithm that exploits temporal and frequency masking (see Section IV-A) to embed robust and inaudible data.

The watermark is constructed by breaking each audio clip into smaller segments and adding a perceptually shaped pseudorandom sequence.

An example showing the robustness of the watermarking technique to MPEG coding is shown in Fig. 10. The audio signal is the beginning of the third movement of the sonata in B flat major D 960 of Schubert (piano, duration 12.8 s), interpreted by Ashkenazy. The coding/decoding was performed using a software implementation of the ISO/MPEG-1 Audio Layer II coder with several different bit rates: 64, 96, and 128 kbits/s. The plot shows the similarity measure of the audio piece with and without the watermark. The increments on the x-axis correspond to 1.16-s segments of audio. For example, the similarity values for block number 2 are measured over the piano signal from $t = 1.16$ s to $t = 2.32$ s. As expected, the similarity values vary over time as the power of the watermark varies temporally with the power of the host signal. Observe that the upper similarity curve for the audio piece is widely separated from the lower curve over the entire duration of the signal.

VII. VIDEO DATA-EMBEDDING APPROACHES

A. Video Data Embedding Implicitly Based on Masking

Fewer documents describing video data embedding are available in the public domain relative to image embedding. Most works are statements in papers to the effect that straightforward extension of a proposed still-image marking technique would be effective, e.g., [18] and [51]. For copyright protection, video data embedding must meet several requirements in addition to those for still images because the volume of data is of a much higher order and real-time embedding may be required in some applications, such as video-on-demand systems. The remainder of this section will focus on works that exploit the three-dimensional character of video data (i.e., two-dimensional images in the temporal domain) and characteristics associated with MPEG compression. Approaches that involve explicit computation of upper and lower bounds for masking by the HVS will then be described.

Video data embedding for copy protection has become a very pertinent issue. The Data Hiding Subgroup of the Copy Protection Technical Working Group is currently evaluating proposals for DVD protection. A data-embedding system is required to mark video content for the purposes of identifying marked material and preventing unauthorized recording/playback. The goal of the technologies is to allow content providers to mark all copyrighted digital video material (NTSC, PAL, and SECAM) with the watermark. Video recorders/players would respond appropriately by refusing to record or play improperly marked material.

One of the earliest examples of video data embedding was proposed by Matsui and Tanaka [55]. First, a frame from the video is divided into 8×8 blocks, and the

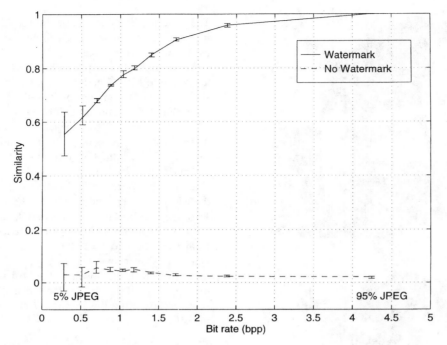

Fig. 9. Detection of watermark in Peppers image after JPEG coding, with qualities from 5 to 95%.

two-dimensional DCT is computed using the formula

$$p_{ij} = \frac{2K(i)}{\sqrt{N}} \cos \frac{(2j+1)i\pi}{2N} \qquad (20)$$

where $i, j = 0, 1, 2, \cdots, 7$, $N = 8$ and

$$K(i) = \begin{cases} 1/\sqrt{2}, & i = 0, \\ 1, & i = 1, 2, \cdots, 7. \end{cases} \qquad (21)$$

The coefficient matrix A for the DCT is

$$\begin{aligned} A &= [a_{ij}] \\ &= [p_{ij}] \cdot [s_{ij}] \cdot [p_{ij}]^T \end{aligned} \qquad (22)$$

where $i, j = 0, 1, 2, \cdots, 7$ and s_{ij} is the pixel value of the (i, j)th element in the block. The matrix A is quantized by

$$b_{ij} = \frac{a_{ij}}{\alpha \cdot t_{ij}} \qquad (23)$$

where $i, j = 0, 1, 2, \cdots, 7$, t_{ij} is the threshold factor, α is specified by a user to control the bit rate per pixel, and the values of b_{ij} are rounded to the nearest integer. Information M_k is embedded by converting it into a binary sequence $\{m_{kn}\}$, where $n = 1, 2, \cdots$ and $m_{kn} = 0$ or 1. If $m_{kn} = 0$, then $a_{ij}/(\alpha \cdot t_{ij})$ is set to be the nearest odd integer b_{ij}, and if $m_{kn} = 1$, then $a_{ij}/(\alpha \cdot t_{ij})$ is set to be the nearest even integer. We denote the operation by $f(b_{ij})$, the modified b_{ij} by $b_{ij}^{(n)}$, where

$$b_{ij}^{(n)} = f(b_{ij}, m_{kn}) \qquad (24)$$

and the matrix of $b(n)_{ij}$ as

$$B' = \left[b_{ij}^{(n)} \right]. \qquad (25)$$

This data-embedding method is very fragile with respect to noise, cropping, and repeatedly embedding data, since values are only changed incrementally up or down. Furthermore, if many copies of the same video frame with different embedded marks are available, hostile parties could compare them and might be able to determine the original, unmarked video frame. Embedded messages might be extracted by hostile parties unless supplementary precautions (e.g., message encryption prior to embedding, pseudorandom embedding locations) are used. Since robustness with respect to MPEG video compression was not a consideration during the design and test phase of the method, no data on the subject are given. It is unlikely that the embedded messages would be preserved after substantial MPEG video compression, but the level of fragility is not known.

Kinoshita et al. [50] have developed a method to embed information transparently in the MPEG motion vector in video. North Carolina State University's SHANG Group has developed software called "Secure MPEG," which is available for free over the Internet.[6] Sanford et al. are currently investigating extensions of their data-embedding method for still images to video data [80].

In extensive studies to extend concepts from still-image marking by Cox et al. [14], Hartung and Girod [23], [29]–[32] propose a spread-spectrum data-embedding method for raw (or uncompressed) video data and a second for MPEG bitstream data. The marking of raw video data v_i to produce a modified signal $\hat{v}_i$ is described by

$$\hat{v}_i = v_i + \alpha \cdot b_i \cdot p_i \qquad (26)$$

---

[6] See http://shang.csc.ncsu.edu/smpeg.html.

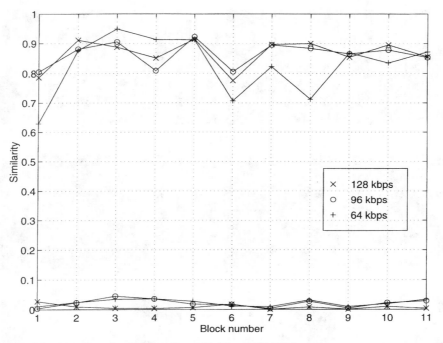

Fig. 10. Detection of watermark in piano piece after MPEG coding at 64, 96, and 128 kbits/s.

where p_i is the pseudonoise sequence, b_i is the embedded bit, and α is a scaling factor. The information is recovered using a matched filter. Use of a variable scaling factor (i.e., use of a sequence α_i rather than a constant α) would improve the level of security and robustness. Similar to Cox *et al.*, the authors remark that α can be varied according to local properties of the video frame or to spatial and temporal masking properties associated with the HVS. A better receiver, which employs a prefilter before decorrelation, is presented in [32].

Hartung and Girod also have a data-embedding method for MPEG compressed video. The approach indirectly exploits masking characteristics, as it is based on the MPEG stream. One of its explicit goals is to avoid an increase in the bit rate. The embedding procedure consists of seven steps.

1) Compute the DCT of the data. Rescan the DCT coefficients using a zigzag scan to obtain a 1×64 vector. Let W_0 denote the zero-frequency (DC) coefficient and W_{63} the highest frequency (AC) component.

2) Let $\hat{V}_n$ and V_n denote the DCT coefficient of unmarked and marked signals and let $\hat{V}_0 = V_0 + W_0$.

3) Find the next variable-length coder (VLC) in the bitstream and identify the run-level pair (r_m, l_m) belonging to the code word and the position and amplitude of the AC DCT coefficient V_m represented by the VLC code word.

4) Let $\tilde{V}_m = V_m + W_m$ denote the candidate for new DCT coefficient. Check that the use of $\tilde{V}_m$ will not increase the bit rate.

5) Let R and $\tilde{R}$ be the number of bits used for transmitting (r_m, l_m) and $(r_m, \tilde{l}_m)$, respectively.

6) If $R \geq \tilde{R}$, then transmit $\tilde{R}$. Else transmit (r_m, l_m).

7) Repeat steps 3)–6) until an end-of-block code word is encountered.

Hartung and Girod discuss the robustness of their method with respect to several types of attacks discussed in Section III-D. They remark that their data are robust to compression, filtering, and modest rotations. A detection and correction mechanism is needed for larger rotations. Removal and insertion of data lead to loss of synchronicity of the pseudonoise sequence between the sender and receiver so that a mechanism for detecting the loss and for resynchronizing the pseudonoise sequence is needed to thwart the attacks.

Similar to the situation with audio data-embedding algorithms, almost no video data-embedding algorithms that use the original have been proposed. Again, a few image watermarking algorithms, e.g., [14], have been described as generic and applicable to video.

B. Video Data Embedding Explicitly Based on Masking

In [84], the authors present a projection-based video watermarking algorithm from an extension of their image data-embedding algorithm (see Section V). An example of the technique is shown in Fig. 11. In the example, a 311 frame, 120×160 grayscale video of a Madonna video is embedded in an equal-length sequence from the movie *Broadcast News*. The Madonna video is embedded for *real-time playback* along with the host video, i.e., 30 frames per second. The Madonna video is encoded using MPEG at a bit rate of 294 bytes per frame (8820 bytes per second). The frames of the *Broadcast News* video are of size 240×360. Sample frames from each of the videos are shown in Fig. 11.

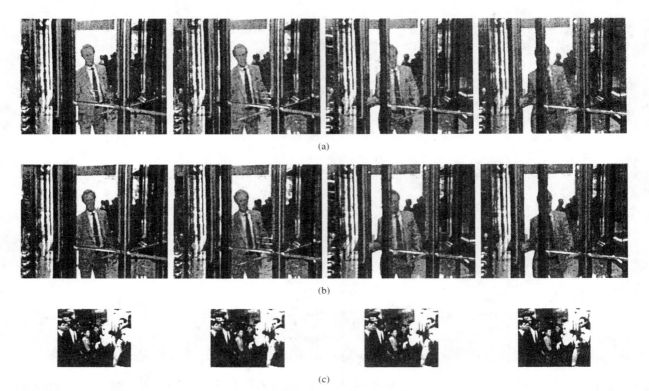

Fig. 11. Video-in-video application. (a) Original *Broadcast News* video. (b) *Broadcast News* video with embedded (c) Madonna video. The Madonna video is embedded in real time.

In [86], the authors propose an object-based video watermarking technique. To address issues associated with video motion and redundancy, individual watermarks are created for objects within the video. Similar strategies were discussed at the July 1997 MPEG-4 meeting. Each object from the video is embedded with a unique watermark according its perceptual characteristics. As the object experiences translations and transformations over time, the watermark remains embedded with it. Objects defined in the video are collected into an object data base. As a result, the detection algorithm does not require information regarding the location (i.e., index) of the test frames in the video. The detection algorithm simply identifies the objects in the test frames. Once objects are identified, their watermarks may be retrieved from the data base and used to determine ownership.

Robustness to MPEG-1 coding at very high compression ratios (CR's) was tested on a 32-frame football video. The frame size of the sequence is 240 × 352. The MPEG quantization tables were set to the coarsest possible level to maximize compression. To simulate additional attacks on the watermark, colored noise was added to the test video prior to MPEG coding. The test video was tested 100 times, with a different colored noise sequence used during each run. The minimum, maximum, and mean frame-by-frame similarity values over the 100 runs are shown in Fig. 12. Even at very low coding quality, the similarity values are widely separated, allowing the existence of a watermark to be easily ascertained.

In a second approach [85], the authors employ a watermark that consists of fixed and varying components. A wavelet transform is applied along the temporal axis of the video to generate a multiresolution temporal representation of the video. The low-pass frames consist of the static components in the video scene. The high-pass frames capture the motion components and changing nature of the video sequence. The watermark is designed and embedded in each of these components. The watermarks embedded in the low-pass frames exist throughout the entire video scene due to wavelet localization properties. The watermarks embedded in the motion frames are highly localized in time and change rapidly from frame to frame. The resulting watermark is a composite of static and dynamic components.

For example, the plot in Fig. 13 shows the robustness of the technique to frame dropping and averaging. In the test, the odd index frames, i.e., $1, 3, \cdots$, were dropped from the test sequence. The missing frames were replaced with the average of the two neighboring frames, $F_{2n+1} = (F_{2n} + F_{2n+2})/2$. Colored noise of similar power to the watermark was added to the result. The resulting detection curves in the figure are shown to be widely separated. The error bars indicate the maximum and minimum similarity values over 100 runs with different colored noise sequences.

VIII. Visible Marking of Images

Sophisticated, attractive, and robust visible watermarking methods for enhancing digital documents have been developed and patented [7] by Braudway *et al.* By robust,

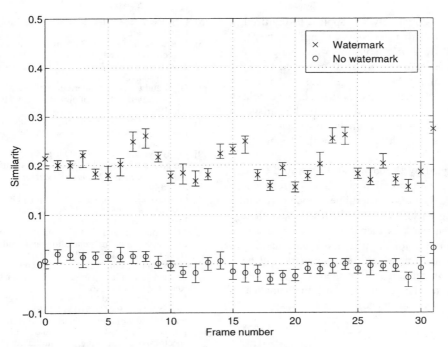

Fig. 12. Frame-by-frame robustness of a football video to MPEG coding at (0.46 Mbits/s, CR 44 : 1). The error bars around each similarity value indicate the maximum and minimum similarity values over the 100 runs.

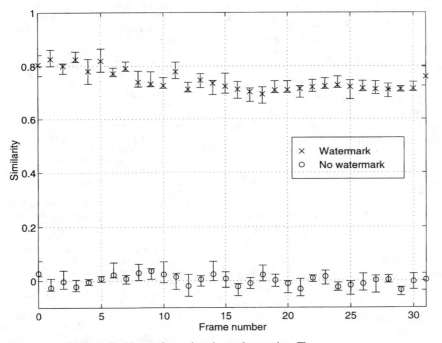

Fig. 13. Frame-by-frame robustness of a football video to frame dropping and averaging. The error bars around each similarity value indicate the maximum and minimum similarity values over the 100 runs.

we mean that the marks are difficult to remove without leaving a trace. The method of Braudway *et al.* for altering pixel values in a still image was used to mark digitized pages of manuscripts from the Vatican's archive and the British Library with a logo, in part for use in authenticating the images and in part for deterring any parties seeking to

"purloin or misappropriate" the documents [8]; samples of marked images can be found at IBM.[7]

[7] See the IBM Digital Library home page, marked images from the Vatican Library Project http://www.software.ibm.com/is/dig-lib/vatican.html and marked images from British Library project http://www.rennard.demon. co.uk/tech/tewamk.htm.

To be attractive and effective when applied to digitized still-image data representing works with artistic merit, according to Braudway *et al.*, a visible watermark must be obvious to any person with normal or corrected vision (including the color blind), be flexible enough that it can be made as obtrusive or unobtrusive as desired, have bold features that (by themselves) form a recognizable image, allow all features of the unmarked image to appear in the marked image, and be very difficult, if not impossible, to remove.

The method designed by Braudway *et al.* to fulfill these criteria begins with the construction of a mask corresponding to the watermark. The mask determines which pixels in an image will remain unchanged and which will have their intensity altered. The mask is then resized, if necessary, to dimensions appropriate for the image size and marking purpose, and the location at which the watermark will be placed is chosen. Last, the intensity in the pixels specified by the mask is altered. The scientists used a mathematical model of the intensity in an image

$$\tilde{Y}_{m,n} = Y_{m,n} + C \times \Delta L^* \tag{27}$$

where $Y_{m,n}$ and $\tilde{Y}_{m,n}$ represent the intensity of the (m,n)th pixel in the original and marked images, respectively, the constant C is a function that reflects various properties of the specific image and watermark mask, and L^* is the intensity (i.e., the amount of light received by the eye, regardless of color [81]). The appearance (or obtrusiveness) of the watermark is controlled by varying the intensity L^*. If the same value of ΔL^* were used to alter all the pixels that fall under the mask, then the watermark could be easily removed by a hostile party. To render robustness to the mark, randomness is introduced by using $2R_{m,n}\Delta L^*$ in place of ΔL^*, where $R_{m,n} \in [0,1]$ is a discrete random variable that (if truly randomly distributed) satisfies

$$\lim_{M \to \infty} \lim_{N \to \infty} \frac{2}{MN} \sum_{m=1}^{M} \sum_{n=1}^{N} R_{m,n}\Delta L^* = \Delta L^*. \tag{28}$$

A watermark needs to have bold features because the introduction of the random variable $R_{m,n}$, depending on its values, can make fine details of the mark less discernible. As an addendum to their method, Braudway *et al.* remark that additional robustness can be achieved by introducing small random variations in the size as well as in the horizontal and vertical placement of the watermark, as suggested by Pickerell and Child [67].

REFERENCES

[1] R. Anderson, Ed., "Information hiding," in *Lecture Notes in Computer Science*. Tokyo, Japan: Springer, 1996.

[2] W. Bender, D. Gruhl, N. Morimoto, and A. Lu, "Techniques for data hiding," *IBM Syst. J.*, vol. 35, nos. 3 and 4, pp. 313–336, 1996.

[3] H. Berghel and L. O'Gorman, "Protecting ownership rights through digital watermarking," *IEEE Computer Mag.*, pp. 101–103, July 1996.

[4] L. Boney, A. Tewfik, and K. Hamdy, "Digital watermarks for audio signals," in *Proceedings of Multimedia'96*. Piscataway, NJ: IEEE Press, 1996, pp. 473–480.

[5] L. Boney, A. Tewfik, K. Hamdy, and M. Swanson, submitted for U.S. patent.

[6] J. Brassil, S. Low, N. Maxemchuk, and L. O'Gorman, "Electronic marking and identification techniques to discourage document copying," *IEEE J. Select. Areas Commun.*, vol. 13, pp. 1495–1504, Oct. 1995.

[7] G. Braudway, K. Magerlein, and F. Mintzer, "Color correct digital watermarking of images," U.S. Patent 5 530 759, June 25, 1996.

[8] ——, "Protecting publically-available images with a visible image watermark," IBM Research Rep. TC-20336(89918), Jan. 15, 1996.

[9] O. Bruyndonckx, J. J. Quisquater, and B. Macq, "Spatial method for copyright labeling of digital images," in *Proc. IEEE Nonlinear Signal Processing Workshop*, 1995, pp. 456–459.

[10] G. Caronni, "Assuring ownership rights for digital images," in *Reliable IT Systems*, H. H. Brüggemann and W. Gerhardt-Häckl, Eds. Vieweg, Germany, 1995.

[11] M. Schneider and S.-F. Chang, "A content-based approach to image signature generation and authentication," in *Proc. ICIP'96*, vol. III, pp. 227–230.

[12] "Facsimile coding schemes and coding control functions for group 4 facsimile apparatus for document transmission," CCITT Recommendation T.6, 1984.

[13] M. Cooperman and S. Moskowitz, "Steganographic method and device," U.S. Patent 5 613 004, Mar. 1997. (Available WWW: http://www.digital-watermark.com/patents.htm.)

[14] I. Cox, J. Kilian, T. Leighton, and T. Shamoon, "Secure spread spectrum watermarking for multimedia," *IEEE Trans. Image Processing*, vol. 6, no. 12, pp. 1673–1687, 1997; see also *Proc. ICIP'96*, vol. III, pp. 243–246.

[15] S. Craver, N. Memon, B.-L. Yeo, and M. Yeung, "Can invisible watermarks resolve rightful ownership?" IBM Research Rep. RC20509, July 1996. (Available WWW: http://www.research.ibm.com:8080.) See also *Proc. SPIE Storage and Retrieval for Image and Video Databases V*, Feb. 1997, vol. 3022, pp. 310–321.

[16] ——, "Resolving rightful ownerships with invisible watermarking techniques: Limitations, attacks, and implications," IBM Research Rep. RC 20755, Mar. 1997.

[17] C. Dautzenberg and F. Boland, "Watermarking images," Dept. of Electrical Engineering, Trinity College, Dublin, Tech. Rep., 1994.

[18] P. Davern and M. Scott, "Fractal based image steganography," in R. Anderson, Ed., *Lecture Notes in Computer Science*. Tokyo, Japan: Springer, 1996, pp. 279–294.

[19] W. Diffie and M. Hellman, "New directions in cryptography," *IEEE Trans. Inform. Theory*, vol. IT-22, pp. 644–654, 1976.

[20] P. Flikkema, "Spread-spectrum techniques for wireless communications," *IEEE Trans. Signal Processing*, vol. 14, pp. 26–36, May 1997.

[21] J. Fridrich, "Methods for data hiding," Center for Intelligent Systems & Dept. of Systems Science and Industrial Engineering, State Univ. of New York-Binghamton, preprint. (Available: http://ssie.binghamton.edu/jirif/.)

[22] B. Girod, "The information theoretical significance of spatial and temporal masking in video signals," in *Proc. SPIE Human Vision, Visual Processing, and Digital Display*, 1989, vol. 1077, pp. 178–187.

[23] B. Girod and F. Hartung, submitted for U.S. patent.

[24] F. Goffin, J.-F. Delaigle, C. D. Vleeschouwer, B. Macq, and J.-J. Quisquater, "Low-cost perceptive digital picture watermarking method," in *Proc. SPIE Storage and Retrieval for Image and Video Databases*, Jan. 1997, vol. 3022, pp. 264–277.

[25] S. Goldwasser and M. Bellare. (July 1996). Lecture notes on cryptography. [Online]. Available WWW: http://www-cse.ucsd.edu/users/mihir/papers/crypto-papers.html.

[26] B. Greenberg, "Method and apparatus for the processing of encoded data in conjunction with an audio broadcast," U.S. Patent 5 379 345, Jan. 1995.

[27] D. Gruhl. (1996). Examples of affine embedding. [Online]. Available WWW: http://nif.www.media.mit.edu/ DataHiding/affine/affine.html.

[28] D. Gruhl, A. Lu, and W. Bender, "Techniques for data hiding," *IBM Syst. J.*, vol. 35, nos. 3 and 4, pp. 313–336, 1996.

[29] F. Hartung and B. Girod, "Digital watermarking of raw and compressed video," in *Proc. SPIE Digital Compression Tech-*

nologies and Systems for Video Communication, Oct. 1996, vol. 2945, pp. 205–213.

[30] ——, "Copyright protection in video delivery networks by watermarking of pre-compressed video," in *Multimedia Applications, Services and Techniques—ECMAST'97, Lecture Notes in Computer Science*, S. Fdida and M. Morganti, Eds. Tokyo, Japan: Springer, 1997, vol. 1242, pp. 423–436.

[31] ——, "Digital watermarking of MPEG-2 coded video in the bitstream domain," in *Proceedings of the International Conference on Acoustics, Speech and Signal Processing 1997*. Piscataway, NJ: IEEE Press, 1997, pp. 2621–2624.

[32] ——, "Digital watermarking of uncompressed and compressed video," *Signal Processing*, to appear in 1997.

[33] ——, "Fast public-key watermarking of compressed video," in *Proceedings of the IEEE International Conference on Image Processing 1997*. Piscataway, NJ: 1997., vol. I, pp. 528–531.

[34] Herodotus, *The Histories (trans. A. de Selincourt)*. Middlesex, England: Penguin, 1972.

[35] Homer, *The Iliad (trans. R. Fagels)*. Middlesex, England: Penguin, 1990.

[36] C.-T. Hsu and J.-L. Wu, "Hidden signatures in images," in *Proceedings of the IEEE International Conference on Image Processing 1996*. Piscataway, NJ: IEEE Press, 1996, pp. 223–226.

[37] *Proceedings of the International Conference on Acoustics, Speech and Signal Processing 1997*. Piscataway, NJ: IEEE Press, 1997.

[38] *Proceedings of the IEEE International Conference on Image Processing 1996*. Piscataway, NJ: IEEE Press, 1996.

[39] *Proceedings of the IEEE International Conference on Image Processing 1997*. Piscataway, NJ: 1997.

[40] "Information technology—Coding of moving pictures and associated audio for digital storage up to about 1.5 Mbits/s," ISO/IEC IS 11172, 1993.

[41] N. Jayant, J. Johnston, and R. Safranek, "Signal compression based on models of human perception," *Proc. IEEE*, vol. 81, pp. 1385–1422, Oct. 1993.

[42] J. Johnston and K. Brandenburg, "Wideband coding—Perceptual considerations for speech and music," in *Advances in Speech Signal Processing*, S. Furui and M. Sondhi, Eds. New York: Marcel Dekker, 1992.

[43] D. Kahn, *The Codebreakers*. New York: MacMillan, 1967.

[44] D. Knuth, *The Art of Computer Programming*, vol. 2, 2nd ed. Menlo Park, CA: Addison-Wesley, 1981.

[45] M. Kuhn. (1997). StirMark, [Online]. Available WWW: http://www.cl.cam.ac.uk/~fapp2/watermarking/image_watermarking/stirmark.

[46] G. Langelaar, J. van der Lubbe, and J. Biemond. (1996). Copy protection for multimedia based on labeling techniques. Available WWW: http://www-it.et.tudelft.nl/pda/smash/public/benelux_cr.html.

[47] C. Lee, K. Moallemi, and J. Hinderling, "Post-compression hidden data transport," U.S. Patent 5 687 191, 1997.

[48] G. Legge and J. Foley, "Contrast masking in human vision," *J. Opt. Soc. Amer.*, vol. 70, no. 12, pp. 1458–1471, Dec. 1990.

[49] S. Low, N. Maxemchuk, J. Brassil, and L. O'Gorman, "Document marking and identification using both line and word shifting," in *Proc. Infocom'95*, Boston, MA, Apr. 1995. (Available WWW: http://www.research.att.com:80/lateinfo/projects/ecom.html.)

[50] Kinoshita, Inaba, and Kasahara, "Digital watermarking of video," in *Proc. 1997 Symp. Cryptography and Information Security*, Jan. 1997, SCIS97-31F (in Japanese).

[51] E. Koch and J. Zhao, "Embedding robust labels into images for copyright protection," in *Proc. Int. Congress Intellectual Property Rights for Specialized Information, Knowledge, and New Technologies*, Vienna, Austria, Aug. 1995, pp. 242–251.

[52] M. Kutter, F. Jordan, and F. Bossen, "Digital signature of color images using amplitude modulation," in *Proc. SPIE-EI97*, 1997, pp. 518–526.

[53] M. Luby, *Pseudorandomness and Cryptographic Applications*. Princeton, NJ: Princeton Univ. Press, 1996.

[54] K. Matsui and K. Tanaka, *Gazo Shinso Ango*. Morikita, 1993 (in Japanese).

[55] ——, "Video-steganography: How to embed a signature in a picture," in *Proc. IMA Intellectual Property*, Jan. 1994, vol. 1, no. 1, pp. 187–206.

[56] N. Maxemchuk, "Electronic document distribution," *AT&T Tech. J.*, pp. 73–80, Sept. 1994.

[57] D. Moses, "Simultaneous transmission of data and audio signals by means of perceptual coding," U.S. Patent 5 473 631, 1995.

[58] W. Mowry, Jr., M. McElligott, V. Tkalenko, J. Baran, and C Ingalls, "Protected document bearing watermark and method of making," U.S. Patent 4 210 346, July 1, 1980.

[59] *Proceedings of Multimedia'96*. Piscataway, NJ: IEEE Press, 1996.

[60] National Institute of Standards and Technology (NIST), *Secure Hash Standard*, NIST FIPS Pub. 180-1, Apr. 1995.

[61] P. Noll, "Wideband speech and audio coding," *IEEE Commun. Mag.*, pp. 34–44, Nov. 1993.

[62] R. Ohbuchi, H. Masuda, and M. Aono, "Embedding data in three-dimensional models," in *Proc. Eur. Workshop Interactive Distributed Multimedia Systems and Telecommunication Services, Darmstadt, Germany, Lecture Notes in Computer Science*, no. 1309. Tokyo, Japan: Springer, 1997.

[63] ——, "Watermarking three-dimensional models," in *Proc. 5th ACM Int. Multimedia Conf.*, Seattle, WA, Nov. 9–13, 1997, pp. 261–272.

[64] J. Ohnishi and K. Matsui, "Embedding a seal into a picture under orthogonal wavelet transform," in *Proceedings of Multimedia'96*. Piscataway, NJ: IEEE Press, 1996., pp. 514–521.

[65] J. O'Ruanaidh, C. Dautzenberg, and F. Boland, "Watermarking digital images for copyright protection," *Proc. Inst. Elect. Eng. Vis. Image Signal Processing*, Aug. 1996, vol. 143, no. 4, pp. 250–256.

[66] ——, "Phase watermarking of digital images," in *Proceedings of the IEEE International Conference on Image Processing 1996*. Piscataway, NJ: IEEE Press, 1996. pp. 239–242.

[67] J. Pickerell and A. Child, "Marketing photography in the digital environment," DiSC, Rockville, MD, 1994.

[68] R. Pickholz, D. Schilling, and L. Milstein, "Theory of spread spectrum communications," *IEEE Trans. Commun.*, vol. COM-30, pp. 855–884, May 1982.

[69] I. Pitas, "A method for signature casting on digital images," in *Proceedings of the IEEE International Conference on Image Processing 1996*. Piscataway, NJ: IEEE Press, 1996., vol. III, pp. 215–218.

[70] I. Pitas and T. Kaskalis, "Applying signatures on digital images," in *Proc. 1995 IEEE Nonlinear Signal Processing Workshop*, 1995, pp. 460–463.

[71] C. Podilchuk and W. Zeng, "Digital image watermarking using visual models," Multimedia Communication Lab, Lucent Technologies, Bell Labs, Tech. Memo, Sept. 1996. See also *Proc. SPIE/IS&T Electronic Imaging'97: Human Vision and Electronic Imaging*, Feb. 1997, vol. 3022, pp. 310–321.

[72] ——, "Perceptual watermarking of still images," in *Proc. IEEE Workshop Multimedia Signal Processing*, June 1997, pp. 363–368.

[73] R. Preuss, S. Roukos, A. Huggins, H. Gish, M. Bergamo, and P. Peterson, "Embedded signalling," U.S. Patent 5 319 735, 1994.

[74] J. Puate and F. Jordan. (1996). Using fractal compression scheme to embed a digital signature into an image. [Online]. Available: http://lswww.epfl.ch/ jordan/watermarking.html.

[75] J. Ragusa, V. Badari, and J. Machuca. (1997). An adaptive spread spectrum approach. [Online]. Available WWW: http://www.csuglab.cornell.edu/Info/People/vbadari/cs631/wmrkproj/proposal.html.

[76] R. Rivest, "Cryptography," in *Handbook of Theoretical Computer Science*, vol. 1, J. van Leeuwen, Ed. Cambridge, MA: MIT Press, 1990, ch. 13, pp. 717–755.

[77] ——, "The MD4 message digest algorithm," in *Advances in Cryptology, CRYPTO'92*. Tokyo, Japan: Springer, 1991, pp. 303–311.

[78] K. Rosen, *Elementary Number Theory and Its Applications*, 3rd ed. Tokyo, Japan: Addison-Wesley, 1992.

[79] J. Russ, *The Image Processing Handbook*, 2nd ed. Tokyo, Japan: CRC Press, 1995.

[80] M. Sanford, J. Bradley, and T. Handel, "The data embedding method," Los Alamos National Laboratory Rep. 9LA-95-2246UR, Sept. 25, 1995. (Available WWW: http://www.lanl.gov/users/u078743/embed1.htm.)

[81] M. Sid-Ahmed, *Image Processing*. Tokyo, Japan: McGraw-Hill, 1995.

[82] J. Smith and B. Comiskey, "Modulation and information hiding in images," in R. Anderson, Ed., "Information hiding," in *Lecture Notes in Computer Science*. Tokyo, Japan: Springer, 1996, pp. 207–226.

[83] H. Stone, "Analysis of attacks on image watermarks with randomized coefficients," NEC Research Institute, Princeton, NJ, Tech. Rep., May 17, 1996. (Available WWW: http://www.neci.nj.nec.com.)

[84] M. Swanson, B. Zhu, and A. Tewfik, "Data hiding for video in video," in *Proceedings of the IEEE International Conference on Image Processing 1997.* Piscataway, NJ: 1997, vol. II, pp. 676–679.

[85] M. Swanson, B. Zhu, and A. Tewfik, "Multiresolution video watermarking using perceptual models and scene segmentation," *IEEE J. Select. Areas Commun.*, to be published. See also *Proceedings of the IEEE International Conference on Image Processing 1997.* Piscataway, NJ: 1997, vol. II, pp. 558–561.

[86] M. Swanson, B. Zhu, and A. Tewfik, "Object-based transparent video watermarking," in *Proc. 1997 IEEE Multimedia Signal Processing Workshop*, 1997, pp. 369–374.

[87] M. Swanson, B. Zhu, A. Tewfik, and L. Boney, "Robust audio watermarking using perceptual masking," *Signal Process.*, to be published.

[88] M. Swanson, B. Zhu, and A. Tewfik, "Transparent robust image watermarking," in *Proceedings of the IEEE International Conference on Image Processing 1996.* Piscataway, NJ: IEEE Press, 1996, vol. III, pp. 211–214.

[89] J. Tilki and A. Beex, "Encoding a hidden digital signature onto an audio signal using psychoacoustic masking," in *Proc. 1996 7th Int. Conf. Sig. Proc. Appls. Tech.*, 1996, pp. 476–480.

[90] R. van Schyndel, A. Tirkel, and C. Osborne, "A digital watermark," in *Proceedings of ICASSP.* Piscataway, NJ: IEEE Press, 1994, vol. II, pp. 86–90.

[91] H. van Trees, *Detection, Estimation, and Modulation Theory*, vol. I. New York: Wiley, 1968.

[92] A. Viterbi, *CDMA Principles of Spread Spectrum Communication.* Tokyo, Japan: Addison-Wesley, 1995.

[93] P. Vogel, "System for altering elements of a text file to mark documents," U.S. Patent 5 388 194, Feb. 7, 1995.

[94] G. Voyatzis and I. Pitas, "Applications of toral automorphisms in image watermarking," in *Proceedings of the IEEE International Conference on Image Processing 1996.* Piscataway, NJ: IEEE Press, 1996, vol. II, pp. 237–240.

[95] S. Walton, "Image authentication for a slippery new age," *Dr. Dobb's J.*, pp. 18–26 and 82–87, Apr. 1995.

[96] R. Wolfgang and E. Delp, "A watermark for digital images," in *Proceedings of the IEEE International Conference on Image Processing 1996.* Piscataway, NJ: IEEE Press, 1996, pp. 219–222.

[97] ——, "A watermarking technique for digital imagery: Further studies," in *Proc. Int. Conf. Imaging Science, Systems and Technology*, Las Vegas, NV, June 30–July 3, 1997.

[98] J. Zhao and Fraunhofer Inst. for Computer Graphics. (1996). [Online]. Available WWW: http://www.igd.fhg.de/~zhao/zhao.html.

[99] B. Zhu, A. Tewfik, and O. Gerek, "Low bit rate near-transparent image coding," in *Proc. SPIE Int. Conf. Wavelet Appls. for Dual Use*, 1995, vol. 2491, pp. 173–184.

Mei Kobayashi received the A.B. degree in chemistry from Princeton University, Princeton, NJ, in 1981 and the M.A. and Ph.D. degrees in pure and applied mathematics from the University of California at Berkeley in 1984 and 1988, respectively.

During her undergraduate and graduate years, she was an Intern in the Chemistry and Physics Divisions at Lawrence Berkeley Laboratories. She has been with the IBM Tokyo Research Laboratory, Japan, since April 1988. From April 1996 to March 1999, she will be a Visiting Associate Professor in the Graduate School of Mathematical Sciences at the University of Tokyo, Tokyo, Japan.

Ahmed H. Tewfik (Fellow, IEEE) was born in Cairo, Egypt, on October 21, 1960. He received the B.Sc. degree from Cairo University in 1982 and the M.Sc., E.E., and Sc.D. degrees from the Massachusetts Institute of Technology, Cambridge, in 1984, 1985, and 1987, respectively.

He was with Alphatech, Inc., Burlington, MA, in 1987. He currently is the E. F. Johnson Professor of Electronic Communications with the Department of Electrical Engineering at the University of Minnesota, Minneapolis. He was a Consultant to MTS Systems, Inc., Eden Prairie, MN, and is a regular Consultant to Rosemount, Inc., Eden Prairie. His current research interests are in signal processing for multimedia (in particular watermarking, data hiding, and content-based retrieval), low-power multimedia communications, adaptive search and data-acquisition strategies for World Wide Web applications, radar and dental/medical imaging, monitoring of machinery using acoustic emissions, and industrial measurements.

Dr. Tewfik is a Distinguished Lecturer of the IEEE Signal Processing Society for July 1997–July 1999. He was a Principal Lecturer at the 1995 IEEE EMBS summer school. He received a Taylor Faculty Development Award from the Taylor Foundation in 1992 and a National Science Foundation Research Initiation Award in 1990. He gave a plenary lecture at the 1994 IEEE International Conference on Acoustics, Speech, and Signal Processing and an invited tutorial on wavelets at the 1994 IEEE Workshop on Time-Frequency and Time-Scale Analysis. He became the first Editor-in-Chief of IEEE SIGNAL PROCESSING LETTERS in 1993. He is a past Associate Editor of IEEE TRANSACTIONS ON SIGNAL PROCESSING and was a Guest Editor of two special issues on wavelets and their applications.

Mitchell D. Swanson (Member, IEEE) received the B.S. (*summa cum laude*), M.S., and Ph.D. degrees in electrical engineering from the University of Minnesota, Minneapolis, in 1992, 1995, and 1997, respectively.

He was with Honeywell, Inc., and Medtronic, Inc., Minneapolis. He currently is with Cognicity, Inc., Minneapolis, and is a Visiting Assistant Professor with the Department of Electrical Engineering at the University of Minnesota. His research interests include multiscale signal processing, image and video coding for interactive retrieval, data hiding, and digital watermarking.

Algorithms for Manipulating Compressed Images

Brian C. Smith and Lawrence A. Rowe
University of California at Berkeley

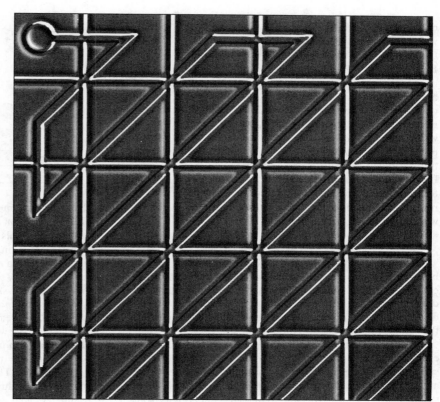

A new technique implements operations directly on compressed JPEG data, yielding performance 50 to 100 times faster than algorithms that must decompress images before application and compress the result.

Multimedia applications that operate on audio and video data will enable many new uses for computers. For example, collaborative work systems can include video conferencing windows, and hypermedia training systems can include audio and video instructional material.

While most research on multimedia applications has focused on compression standards,[1,2] synchronization issues,[3,4] storage representations,[4] and software architectures,[3,5] little work has been reported on techniques for manipulating digital video data in real time, such as implementing special effects and image composition. For instance, suppose you implemented a brute-force algorithm to brighten a compressed image by decompressing the image, modifying each pixel value, and compressing the resulting image. The problems you would encounter implementing this approach on current workstations would stem from two sources: the volume of data to be manipulated (26.3 Mbytes per second for uncompressed 640×480 24-bit video at 30 frames per second) and the computational complexity of image compression and decompression.

This article describes a family of algorithms that implement operations on compressed digital images. These algorithms allow many traditional image manipulation operations to be performed 50 to 100 times faster than their brute-force counterparts. This speedup results from performing the operations directly on the compressed data, since compression reduces the volume of data significantly, typically by factors of 25 or more. Along with the speedup resulting from the smaller data volume, most of the computation associated with compression and decompression is eliminated, and the traffic to and from memory is reduced.

We describe how to apply this technique and evaluate the performance of some representative algorithms. First we describe the compression model. Then we show how the algebraic operations of pixel-wise and scalar addition and multiplication, which are the basis for many image transformations, can be implemented on compressed images. We use these operations to implement two common video transformations: dissolving one video sequence into another and subtitling. We have implemented the operations and here compare their performance with the brute-force approach. Finally we discuss the limitations of the technique, extensions to other compression standards, and the relationship of this research to other work in the area.

Compression model

This section describes the compression model used in transform-based coding, beginning with a general review of transform

Figure 1. Definition of $y[i,j]$.

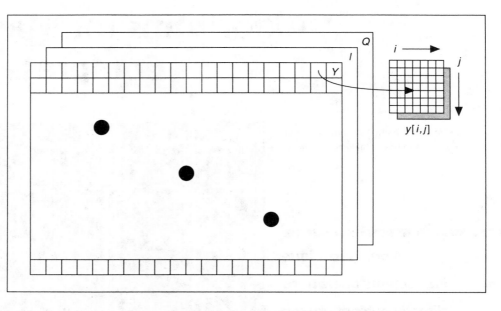

coders and then continuing with a brief description of the CCITT Joint Photographic Expert Group (JPEG) standard for transform-based image coding. A detailed description of the JPEG algorithm is available elsewhere.[1,6] Foley and Van Dam presented a detailed description of image formats,[7] and Lim discussed other transform coding techniques.[8] All results in this section appear in Lim's book, and we state them without proof.

Transform-based coding

A common technique for image compression is transform-based coding. A typical transform coder treats the image's pixels as a matrix of numbers. A linear transform, such as the discrete cosine transform,[9] is applied to this matrix to create a new matrix of coefficients. To recover the original image, apply the inverse linear transformation.

The transformation has two effects. First, it concentrates the energy of the image so that many of the transformed coefficients are nearly zero. Second, it spectrally decomposes the image into high and low frequencies. Since the human visual system is less receptive to some frequencies than others, some coefficients can be more crudely approximated than others without significant image degradation.

A common way to exploit the latter property is to quantize the coefficients. A simple way to quantize coefficients is to truncate low-order bits from an integer (for example, by right arithmetic shifting). A method that provides more control over data loss than arithmetic shifting is to divide the value by a constant, the quantization value, and round the result to the nearest integer. You can recover an approximation of the original value by multiplying the result by the quantization value. Larger quantization values lead to cruder approximations, but fewer significant bits.

When transformed coefficients are quantized in this way, most coefficients are typically zero. For example, with 24:1 compression, measurements indicate that about 90 percent of the coefficients in the transformed image will be zero.

The JPEG algorithm

One standard for transform coding of still images is the JPEG standard. The remainder of this section briefly describes relevant features of JPEG and introduces associated terminology.

Suppose the source image is a 24-bit image, 640 pixels wide by 480 pixels high, and composed of three components: one luminance (Y) and two chrominance (I and Q). That is, for each pixel in the source image, we associate a triplet of 8-bit values (Y, I, Q). Since each component is treated similarly, we de-scribe the algorithm for only the Y component.

The Y component is broken up into contiguous squares 8 pixels wide and 8 pixels high, called *blocks*. Each block is an 8×8 matrix of integers in the range 0...255. The first step of the algorithm, called the *normalization* step, brings all values into the range $-128...127$ by subtracting 128 from each element in the matrix (this step is skipped on the I and Q components, since they are already in the range $-128...127$). Let the resulting matrix be $y[i, j]$, where $i, j \in 0...7$. Figure 1 illustrates the relationship of $y[i, j]$ to the whole image.

The second step in the algorithm—the DCT step—applies the discrete cosine transform to this 8×8 matrix, producing a new 8×8 matrix. The DCT resembles the fast fourier transform in that the values in the resulting 8×8 matrix are related to frequency. That is, the lowest frequency components are in the upper left and the highest frequency components, in the lower right. If we call the new matrix $Y[u, v]$, with $u, v \in 0...7$, by definition of the DCT we have

$$Y[u, v] = \frac{1}{4} \sum_i \sum_j C(i, u)\, C(j, v)\, y[i, j]$$

where

$$C(i, u) = A(u) \cos \frac{(2i + 1)u\pi}{16}$$

$$A(u) = \begin{cases} \dfrac{1}{\sqrt{2}} & \text{for } u = 0 \\ 1 & \text{for } u \neq 0 \end{cases}$$

(1)

The third step in the algorithm quantizes each element of $Y[u, v]$ by a value dependent on the frequency, called $q[u, v]$. This *quantization* step is defined by

$$Y_Q[u, v] = \text{IntegerRound}\left(\frac{Y[u, v]}{q[u, v]} \right) \quad u, v \in 0...$$

(2)

The matrix of integer quantization values is called the *quantization table,* or QT. Different QTs are typically used for the luminance and chrominance components. The choice of the QT

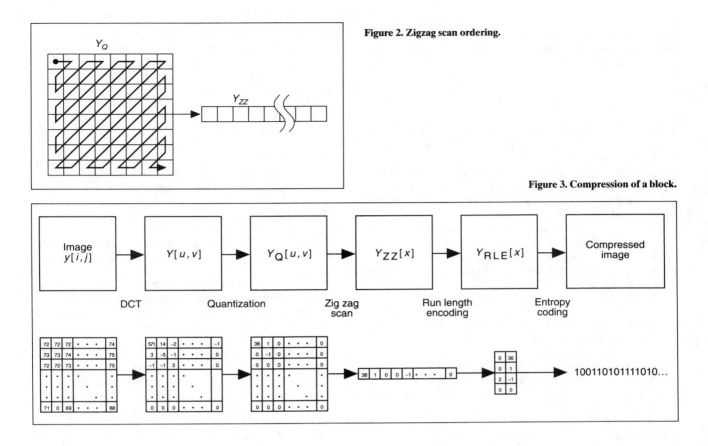

Figure 2. Zigzag scan ordering.

Figure 3. Compression of a block.

determines both the amount of compression and the quality of the decompressed image.[6] The JPEG standard includes recommended luminance and chrominance QTs resulting from human factors studies. A common practice is to scale the values of these default QTs to obtain different image qualities. Specifically, given two images with QTs $q_1[u, v]$ and $q_2[u, v]$, then for all u, v and some constant gamma, often

$$\frac{q_1[u, v]}{q_2[u, v]} = \gamma \tag{3}$$

We will use this fact later.

Step four of the algorithm converts the 8×8 matrix from Equation 2 into a 64-element vector using the "zigzag" ordering shown in Figure 2. This ordering is a heuristic to cluster low-frequency components near the beginning of the vector and high-frequency components near the end. We call the vector the *zig-zag vector* and this step the *zigzag scan* step.

In most images, the vector Y_{zz} will contain a large number of sequential zeros, so the next step in the algorithm, the *run-length encoding* step, encodes the vector into (*skip, value*) pairs. *Skip* indicates how many indices in the Y_{zz} vector to skip to reach the next nonzero value, which is stored in *value*. By convention, the pair (0, 0) indicates that the remaining values in Y_{zz} are all zero. We call the block at this point a *run-length-encoded* (RLE) block, and each (*skip, value*) pair is called an *RLE value*. The RLE block is denoted $Y_{RLE}[x]$, with $Y_{RLE}[x].skip$ and $Y_{RLE}[x].value$ denoting the *skip* and *value* of the xth element in the array. Our algorithms operate on RLE blocks.

In the final step, a conventional entropy coding method such as arithmetic compression or Huffman coding compresses the RLE blocks. Figure 3 graphically displays all the steps in the processing of one block.

Tracing Figure 3 backwards (that is, right to left) illustrates how to decompress the data. The first step of decompression recovers an RLE block from the entropy coded bit stream. By making a single pass through the RLE block $Y_{RLE}[x]$, we recover the zigzag vector $Y_{zz}[x]$. From $Y_{zz}[x]$, we recover $Y_Q[u, v]$ by inverting the zigzag scan. Then we multiply each element of $Y_Q[u, v]$ by $q[u, v]$ from the appropriate QT to recover an approximation of $Y[u, v]$. In the final step, we obtain the image block $y[i, j]$ from $Y[u, v]$ using the inverse DCT (IDCT):

$$y[i, j] = \frac{1}{4} \sum_u \sum_v C(i, u) C(j, v) Y[u, v] \tag{4}$$

Note that Equation 4 closely resembles Equation 1, but the summation is over u and v rather than i and j.

Using this method, we can adjust the compression ratio by altering the QT values. Experience indicates that we can achieve a compression ratio of about 24:1 (that is, one bit per pixel) without serious loss of image quality. At a compression ratio of 10:1, the decompressed image is usually indistinguishable from the original. The entropy coding reduces the data size by about 2.5:1, so the data size of the RLE blocks is typically 10 times smaller than that of the original image if we assume 25:1 overall compression.

Algebraic operations

This section shows how to perform the four algebraic operations of scalar addition, scalar multiplication, pixel-wise addition, and pixel-wise multiplication of two images on RLE blocks.

In the calculations that follow, we derive equations of the form

$$H_{RLE} = \phi (F_{RLE}, G_{RLE})$$

where F_{RLE} and G_{RLE} are the RLE representations of the input images, H_{RLE} is the RLE representation of the output image, and ϕ is a real-valued function. In an implementation, the values stored in the H_{RLE} data structure would be integers, so the value returned by the function ϕ must be rounded to the nearest integer. To simplify the notation in the calculations that follow, this rounding will be implicit.

To further simplify the notation, we perform all calculations on the quantized arrays $F_Q[u, v]$, $G_Q[u, v]$, and $H_Q[u, v]$. Since an RLE block is a data structure that represents these arrays, the derived equations will be valid on RLE blocks provided we perform the appropriate index conversion.

Other notational conventions are

1. Capital letters such as F, G, and H indexed by u, v, and w represent compressed images.
2. Lowercase letters such as f, g, and h indexed by i, j, and k represent uncompressed images.
3. Greek letters such as α and β represent scalars.
4. QTs are represented as arrays, with subscripts indicating the image. For example, $q_H[u, v]$ stands for the QT of the compressed image H.
5. The letters x, y, and z represent zigzag ordered indices.

Often we will index QTs by a single zigzag index (such as x). In such cases the conversion to indices such as $[u, v]$ is implied and will be clear from context.

Scalar multiplication

Consider the operation of scalar multiplication of pixel values. In this operation, if the value of a pixel in the original image is $f[i, j]$, the value of the corresponding pixel in the output image $h[i, j]$ is given by

$$h[i, j] = \alpha f[i, j] \tag{5}$$

Using the linearity of the JPEG compression algorithm and Equation 5, we can easily show that the quantized coefficients of the output image, $H_Q[u, v]$, are just scaled copies of $F_Q[u, v]$. Specifically, using Equations 1 through 5, we can show that

$$H_Q[u, v] = \frac{\alpha q_F(u, v)}{q_H(u, v)} F_Q[u, v] \tag{6a}$$

where $q_F(u, v)$ and $q_H(u, v)$ are the QTs of the input and output images, respectively. The final integer rounding of the right-

hand side is implicit. In other words, to perform the operation of scalar multiplication on a compressed image, we can perform it directly on the quantized coefficients, as long as we take the QTs of the images into account. Note that if the QTs of both images are proportional (as in Equation 3), the equation simplifies to

$$H_Q[u, v] = \alpha \gamma F_Q[u, v] \tag{6b}$$

If the quality of the input and output images are the same, we have the special case where $\gamma = 1$. Note also that if a value in the input, $F_Q[u, v]$, is zero, the corresponding value in the output, $H_Q[u, v]$, is also zero. Thus, we can implement this operation on an RLE block by simply scaling the values in the data structure—we need not reconstruct the quantized array or even the zigzag vector. When implemented this way, the operation avoids useless multiplies where $F_Q[u, v]$ is zero, making it very fast.

Scalar addition

Now consider the scalar addition operation. If the value of a pixel in the original image is $f[i, j]$, the value of the corresponding pixel in the output image $h[i, j]$ is given by

$$h[i, j] = f[i, j] + \beta \tag{7}$$

Now, adding a constant to each pixel changes the mean (that is, the DC component) value, which the DCT stores at the [0,0] entry. Thus, we expect only this coefficient to be affected. We can easily prove this using Equations 1 through 4 and Equation 7, and the properties of the DCT.[8] The result of such a calculation is

$$H_Q[u, v] = \frac{\alpha q_F(u, v)}{q_H(u, v)} F_Q[u, v] + \frac{8\beta}{q_H(u, v)} \delta(u)\delta(v)$$

where

$$\delta(u) = \begin{cases} 1 & u = 0 \\ 0 & u \neq 0 \end{cases} \tag{8a}$$

If the QTs of both images are proportional (as in Equation 3), this equation assumes a particularly simple form, expressed in the equations

$$H_Q[0, 0] = \gamma F_Q(0, 0) + \frac{8\beta}{q_H(0, 0)} \tag{8b}$$

$$H_Q[u, v] = \gamma F_Q[u, v] \qquad (u, v) \neq (0, 0) \tag{8c}$$

Again we see that the operation of scalar addition can be performed directly on the quantized coefficients. More importantly, in the common case where $\gamma = 1$ (that is, when the quality of the

```
ConvolveInit (alpha, fQT, gQT, hQT)
  float alpha, *fQT, *gQT, *hQT
{
  int u1, u2, v1, v2, w1, w2;
  int x, y, z;
  float t1, t2;

  for (u1=0; u1 <8; u1++)
    for (v1=0; v1<8; v1++)
      for (w1=0; w1<8; w1++)
        if ((t1 = W[u1][v1][w1]) != 0.0)
          for (u2=0; u2<8; u2++)
            for (v2=0; v2<8; v2++)
              for (w2=0; w2<8; w2++)
                if ((t2 = W[u2][v2][w2]) != 0.0) {
                  x = ZigZag(u1, u2);
                  y = ZigZag(v1, v2);
                  z = ZigZag(w1, w2);
                  W=t1*t2*alpha*fQT[x]
                    *gQT[y]/hQT[z];
                  comb[x,y] =
                    AddCombElt (z,W,comb[x,y]);
                }
}
```

Figure 4. Initialization of the combination array.

output image is the same as the quality of the input image), this operation involves much less computation than the corresponding operation on uncompressed images, since only the $(0, 0)$ coefficient of the quantized matrix is affected.

Pixel addition

The operation of pixel addition is described by the equation

$$h[i, j] = f[i, j] + g[i, j] \tag{9}$$

As in the case of scalar multiplication, the operation we wish to perform is linear. Since the JPEG compression algorithm is also linear, the quantized coefficients of the output image $H_Q[u, v]$ are summed, scaled copies of $F_Q[u, v]$ and $G_Q[u, v]$. Specifically, we can show, using Equations 1 through 4 and Equation 8, that

$$H_Q[u, v] = \frac{q_F(u, v)}{q_H(u, v)} F_Q[u, v] + \frac{q_G(u, v)}{q_H(u, v)} G_Q[u, v] \tag{10a}$$

Once again we see that if we account for the QTs of the images, the operation can be performed directly on the quantized coefficients. Also, if the QTs for all the images are proportional (with proportionality constants γ_F and γ_G), the equation simplifies to

$$H_Q[u, v] = \gamma_F F_Q[u, v] + \gamma_G G_Q[u, v] \tag{10b}$$

Pixel multiplication

Finally, the operation of pixel multiplication is expressed in the equation

$$h[i, j] = \alpha f[i, j] g[i, j] \tag{11}$$

where α is a scalar value. The scalar α, although mathematically superfluous, is convenient to scale pixel values as they are multiplied. For example, we use this formulation when the image g contains pixel values in the range $[0..255]$ and we want to interpret them as the range $[0..1]$, as is the case when g is a mask. This operation is realized by setting α to $1/256$.

Let $F(v_1, v_2)$, $G(w_1, w_2)$, and $H(u_1, u_2)$ be the quantized values of the compressed images for f, g, and h, respectively. Then using Equations 1, 2, and 11, we can compute the value of $H(u_1, u_2)$ as follows:

$$
\begin{aligned}
&H(u_1, u_2) \\
&= \frac{1}{4q_H[u_1, u_2]} \sum_i \sum_j C(i, u_1) C(j, u_2) h(i, j) \\
&= \frac{\alpha}{4q_H[u_1, u_2]} \sum_i \sum_j C(i, u_1) C(j, u_2) f(i, j) g(i, j) \\
&= \frac{\alpha}{4q_H[u_1, u_2]} \sum_i \sum_j C(i, u_1) C(j, u_2) \\
&\quad \left(\frac{1}{4} \sum_{v_1} \sum_{v_2} C(i, v_1) C(j, v_2) q_F(v_1, v_2) F(v_1, v_2) \right) \\
&\quad \left(\frac{1}{4} \sum_{w_1} \sum_{w_2} C(i, w_1) C(j, w_2) q_G(w_1, w_2) G(w_1, w_2) \right) \\
&= \sum_{v_1, v_2, w_1, w_2} F(v_1, v_2) G(w_1, w_2) W_Q(v_1, v_2, w_1, w_2, u_1, u_2) \tag{12a}
\end{aligned}
$$

where

$$
\begin{aligned}
&W_Q(v_1, v_2, w_1, w_2, u_1, u_2) \\
&= \frac{\alpha q_F[v_1, v_2] q_G[w_1, w_2]}{64 q_H[u_1, u_2]} W(u_1, v_1, w_1) W(u_2, v_2, w_2) \tag{12b}
\end{aligned}
$$

with

$$W(u, v, w) = \sum_i C(i, u) C(i, v) C(i, w) \tag{12c}$$

We can compute this rather lengthy sum efficiently by noticing two facts:

1. For typical compressed images, $G(w_1, w_2)$ and $F(v_1, v_2)$ are zero for most values of (v_1, v_2) and (w_1, w_2).
2. Of the 256K elements in the function $W_Q(v_1, v_2, w_1, w_2, u_1, u_2)$, only about 4 percent of the terms are nonzero. In other words, the matrix W_Q is very sparse.

When implementing this method, we must take care to evaluate only those terms that might contribute to the sum. We take advantage of the first fact when we implement this method on RLE blocks, since the zeros are easily skipped. To take advantage of the second fact, we use the data structure described in

```
Convolve (f, g, hzz)
  RLE_Block *f, *g;   /* The input images */
  float *hzz; /* Array of 64 elements */
(
  int x, y, z;
  float W, tmp;
  RLE_BLOCK *gtmp;
  COMB_LIST *c1

  for (x=0; f != NULL; f = f->next) {
    x += f->skip;
    for (y=0, gtmp = g; gtmp != NULL; gtmp = gtmp->next){
      y += gtmp->skip;
      tmp = f->val*gtmp->val;
      for (c1 = comb[x,y]; c1 != NULL; c1 = c1->next){
        z = c1->z;
        W = c1->W;
        hzz[z] += tmp*W;
      }
    }
  }
}
```

Figure 5. Implementation of the Convolve function.

the following paragraphs. Since the algorithm operates on RLE blocks, the zigzag-ordered indices are used to reference data elements. By convention, we let x, y, and z represent the zigzag-ordered indices of the pairs (v_1, v_2), (w_1, w_2), and (u_1, u_2), respectively. With this substitution, we can write Equations 12a to 12c as

$$H(z) = \sum_{x,y} F(x) G(y) W_Q(x, y, z) \qquad (13)$$

with the summation over x and y running from 0 to 63.

To compute Equation 13 efficiently, we introduce the following data structure: A *combination element* is a pair of numbers z and W, where z is an integer and W is a floating-point value. A *combination list* is a list of combination elements. A *combination array* is a 64×64 array of combination lists. The C code shown in Figure 4 initializes the combination array comb[x, y]. The array contains empty lists when the code is entered. The function ZigZag($u1$, $u2$) returns the zigzag index associated with the element (u_1, u_2). The function AddCombElt(z, W, comb[x, y]) inserts the combination element (z, W) in the combination list stored in the global combination array comb[x, y] (the place of insertion is unimportant) and returns the modified combination list. The array $W[8][8][8]$ is assumed to be initialized with the values of the W function of Equation 12c.

Using the initialized combination array, the C code shown in Figure 5 efficiently implements Equation 13 on two RLE blocks f and g. We call this algorithm the *convolution algorithm*. Notice that comb[] is a constant in the code; once computed for the given QTs, it can be applied to an unlimited number of images.

The code operates as follows: The array hzz, which represents a zigzag vector, is assumed to be all zero. For each pair of RLE values in the two input images f and g, we compute the zigzag indices x and y, and the product of their data values,

Table 1. Mapping of operations.

Operation	Image space definition for $h[i,j]$	RLE definition for $H_{zz}[x]$
Scalar multiplication	$\alpha f[i,j]$	$\alpha \gamma_{F,H}(x) F_{zz}[x]$
Scalar addition	$f[i,j]+\beta$	$\gamma_{F,H}(x) F_{zz}[x] + \dfrac{8\beta\delta(x))}{q_H[0]}$
Pixel addition	$f[i,j]+g[i,j]$	$\gamma_{F,H}(x) F_{zz}[x] + \gamma_{G,H}(x) G_{zz}[x]$
Pixel multiplication	$f[i,j] \ g[i,j]$	Convolve $(F, G, \alpha, q_F, q_G, q_H)$

which is stored in tmp. We then use the z value of each combination element in the combination list stored in comb[x, y] to determine which elements in the output array hzz are affected and accumulate the product W*tmp into each element. In this way, only the multiplies that result in nonzero products accumulate in hzz. When this algorithm is used in a program, a final pass is needed to run-length encode the zeros, perform integer rounding, and construct the resulting RLE block. (Of course, using integer arithmetic might provide an increase in performance, but we chose to describe the floating-point implementation for clarity.)

Summary of operations

We have shown how pixel addition, pixel multiplication, scalar addition, and scalar multiplication can be implemented on quantized matrices. As noted earlier, these transformations can operate directly on RLE blocks. Table 1 summarizes the mapping of image operations into operations on RLE blocks. In the table, the symbol $\gamma_{F,H}(x)$ is defined as

$$\gamma_{F,H}(x) \equiv \frac{q_F[x]}{q_H[x]} \equiv \frac{q_F[u,v]}{q_H[u,v]}$$

The function Convolve(F, G, α, q_F, q_G, q_H) is defined in Equation 13 and implemented in Figures 4 and 5.

Applications

Video data is typically transmitted as a sequence of compressed images. While the entropy encoded data cannot be directly manipulated, we showed how several operations can be performed on RLE blocks. Referring to Figure 3, if we entropy decode the images, perform the operation on the RLE blocks, and entropy encode the result, we can shortcut most of the image decoding and encoding, resulting in a faster algorithm.

We can combine the primitive operations in Table 1 to form more powerful operations such as Dissolve (the simultaneous fade out and fade in of two sequences of images) and Subtitle. The implementation of these operations typically involves computing an output image that is an algebraic combination of one or more input images. Porter and Duff discussed many examples of such operations.[10] One way to perform the combination on a pair of RLE blocks is to use zigzag vectors as the intermediate representation to compute the expression. For example, to multiply two RLE blocks and add a third, we would call the Convolve function of Figure 5 on the first two RLE blocks, add

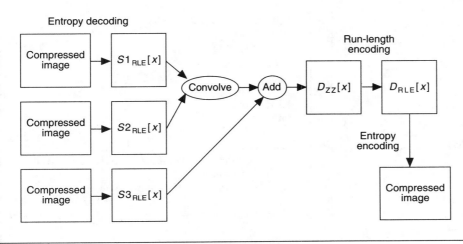

Figure 6. Strategy for manipulating images.

the third RLE block to the zigzag vector, then perform the run-length encoding and entropy coding steps. Figure 6 graphically depicts our strategy.

Two examples illustrate this strategy and compare the performance of these new algorithms with the brute-force algorithm.

The Dissolve operation

We omit the entropy encoding and decoding steps to simplify the presentation. Suppose we want to dissolve a sequence of images $S1[t]$ into a sequence of images $S2[t]$ in a time Δt (typically 0.25 seconds). In other words, at $t = 0$ we should display $S1[0]$, at $t = \Delta t$ we should display $S2[\Delta t]$, and in between we want to display the linear combination of the images:

$$D[t] = \alpha(t)S1[t] + \{1 - \alpha(t)\}S2[t] \qquad (14)$$

where $\alpha(t)$ is a linear function that is 1 at $t = 0$ and 0 at $t = \Delta t$.

Using Table 1, we can map this operation into the corresponding operation on RLE blocks as follows. From the table, we know that the scalar multiplies can be performed directly on the RLE blocks if the coefficient α is changed to $\alpha \gamma_{S1,D}(x)$ in the first half of the expression and a similar substitution is performed for the multiplication by $\{1 - \alpha\}$. Also from the table, we know we can add the coefficients together directly to get the desired result, since the QTs of these two new RLE blocks are the same, namely $q_D(x)$. Thus, we can implement the expression in Equation 13 as

$$D_{ZZ}[x] = \alpha \gamma_{S1,D}(x)S1_{ZZ}[x] + \{1 - \alpha\}\gamma_{S2,D}(x)S2_{ZZ}[x]$$

We can implement this equation efficiently by noticing that the RLE format of the data will skip over zero terms. The C code to implement this operation on an RLE block appears in Figure 7. The function Zero zeros the array passed to it, and the function RunLengthEncode performs the run-length encoding of h. The arrays gamma1 and gamma2 have the precomputed values defined by

gamma1$[x] = \alpha \gamma_{S1,D}(x)$
gamma2$[x] = (1 - \alpha)\gamma_{S2,D}(x)$

These values can be precomputed once for each image or se-

Table 2. Performance measurements of Dissolve operation.		
Algorithm	**Time (seconds)**	
	Mean	**Std Dev**
Brute force	36.86	0.01
RLE	0.34	0.00

quence of images with the same QTs, whereas the Dissolve function is called for each RLE block in an image.

To test this implementation's performance, we wrote programs that executed both the brute-force and the RLE algorithm on images resident in main memory and compared them. Both algorithms were executed on 25 separate pairs of images on a Sparcstation 1+ with 28 Mbytes of memory. The test images were 640×480 and 24 bits per pixel. We compressed the images to approximately one bit per pixel (24:1 compression). Table 2 summarizes the results. As you can seen from the table, the speedup is more than 100 to 1 over the brute-force algorithm.

The Subtitle operation

The second example operation, Subtitle, overlays a subtitle on a compressed image f. Although a workstation could support this operation in many ways (such as displaying the text of the subtitle in a separate window), we chose this operation for two reasons. Fist, it is a common operation that most people understand. And second, it serves as a specific example of the common operation of image masking, which is used when you want to combine a portion of one image with another.

We assume the subtitle to be a compressed image of white letters on a black background denoted S, with white and black represented by pixel values 127 and -128, respectively. We can construct the output image by adding together S and an image obtained by multiplying f by a mask that will blacken the areas on f where the text should go. The output image with subtitling, h, is then given by

$$h[i, j] = s[i, j] + \frac{1}{255}\left(127 - s[i, j]\right)f[i, j] \qquad (15)$$

```
Dissolve (f, g, h, gamm1, gamm2)
   RLE_Block *f, *g, *h;
   float *gamma1, *gamma2;

{
   float hzz[64];
   int x;

   Zero (hzz);
   for (x=0; f != NULL; f = f->next) {
      x += f->skip;
      hzz[x] += gamma1[x]*f->value;
   }
   for (x=0; g != NULL; g = g->next) {
      x += g->skip;
      hzz[x] += gamma2[x]*g->value;
   }
   RunLengthEncode (hzz, h);
}
```

Figure 7. C implementation of the Dissolve operation.

Using Table 1, we see that the corresponding operation on an RLE block is

$$H = \gamma_{s,h} S + \text{Convolve}\left(M, F, \frac{1}{255}, q_F, q_S, q_H \right)$$

with

$$M[x] = -S[x] + \frac{1,016\delta(x)}{q_S[0]}$$

The C code in Figures 8a and 8b implement this operation. The code is divided into two phases, the SubtitleInit function, which is called once when the QTs are defined for the image or sequence of images, and the Subtitle function, which is called for each RLE block in the image. Like the Dissolve operation, the Subtitle function uses a zigzag vector hzz to store the intermediate results. As with the Dissolve operation, we compared the performance of programs implementing the brute-force algorithm and the RLE algorithm on images stored in main memory. The test parameters were the same as with the Dissolve operation. Table 3 summarizes the results, showing a speedup of nearly 50 to 1 over the brute-force algorithm.

Discussion

Next we discuss related work and suggest areas for further research.

Related work

Duff and Porter[10] described an algebra for image composition based on the introduction of an α channel. In their method, the source image and a real-valued image, the α channel, are pixel-wise multiplied before being composited. We have shown how two compressed images can be pixel-wise multiplied and composited, which provides a basis for using α channel techniques on compressed images.

In the area of DCT domain image processing, Chitprasert and Rao[11] presented a convolution algorithm for the DCT and

```
Subtitle (s, f, h, fQT, sQT, hQT)
   RLE_Block *s, *f, *h;
   float *fQT, *sQT, *hQT;

{
   float hzz[64];
   RLE_Block *tmp;
   int x;

   Zero (hzz);
   for (x=0, tmp=s; tmp != NULL; tmp = tmp->next) {
      x += tmp->skip;
      hzz[x] += gammaSH[x]*tmp->value;
                                     /* hzz =gamma * s */
      tmp->value = -tmp->value;      /* set s = -s */
   }
   /* Convert S into mask. . . */
   if (s->skip) {                    /* No (0,0) value! */
      s = NewRLE_Block(s->next);     /* Insert a 0 value */
      s->skip = 0;
      s->value = 0;
   }
   s->value += Round(1016.0/sQT[0]);
                                     /* s is now the mask */
   Convolve (f, s, hzz);
   RunLengthEncode (hzz, h);
}
```

a: Subtitle function

```
static gammaSH[64];

SubtitleInit (fQT, sQT, hQT)
   float *fQT, *sQT, *hQT;
{
   int x;

   ConvolveInit (1/255.0, fQT, sQT, hQT);
   for (x=0; x<64; x++)
      gammaSH[x] = sQT[x]/hQT[x];
}
```

b: SubtitleInit function

Figure 8. (a) C code implementation of the Subtitle function. (b) C code implementation of the SubtitleInit function.

Table 3. Performance measurements of Subtitle operation.

Algorithm	Time (seconds)	
	Mean	Std Dev
Brute force	33.84	0.64
RLE	0.68	0.13

showed how it could be used for image processing in certain special cases. Their technique is applicable to high and low pass filtering, but does not adapt well to the block by block encoding nature of most compression technologies.

Chang et al.[12] independently discovered a technique similar to the one presented here for compositing images in the DCT domain. Their work is a special case of our results in the section "Algebraic operations" and does not contain experimental results. However, they present the solution to a related problem. When two images to be composited are not correctly aligned, one image might require translation. They showed how such a translation operation can be performed in the DCT domain.

Further research

Two areas demand further research. First, we are extending the domain of operations to include more general image operations such as geometric transformations (scaling, rotation, translation, shearing, and perspective transformations) and filtering (smoothing, noise reduction, and image enhancement). Second, we want to derive similar results for other compression techniques, including those that use interframe coding (for example, H.261 or MPEG).

Finally, there is the possibility of designing a coding scheme that would make transformations easier. The area of image coding and compression is an active, current topic of interest in the research community. Many schemes for image coding have been proposed, including vector quantization, transform coding, and sub-band coding. Many practical algorithms, such as JPEG and MPEG, are hybrid solutions, drawing ideas from several techniques. Another area for future research would be to design a coding scheme that offered compression ratios competitive with current algorithms, but simplified manipulation of the compressed data.   ❏

References

1. International Standards Committee International Standard 10918, "Digital Compression and Coding of Continuous Tone Still Images," American National Standards Institute, New York, 1990.

2. International Standards Committee International Standard 11172-2, "Coded Representation of Picture, Audio, and Multimedia/Hypermedia Information," American National Standards Institute, New York, 1990.

3. C. Nicolaou, "An Architecture for Real-Time Multimedia Communication Systems," *IEEE J. on Selected Areas in Communications*, Vol. 8, No. 3, April 1990, IEEE Press, New York, pp. 391-400.

4. T.D.C. Little and A. Ghafoor, "Synchronization and Storage Models for Multimedia Objects," *IEEE J. on Selected Areas in Communications*, Vol. 8, No. 3, April 1990, IEEE Press, New York, pp. 413-427.

5. A. Hopper, "Pandora—An Experimental System for Multimedia Applications," tech. report, Olivetti Research Laboratory, Trumpington St., Cambridge, UK, CB21QA, June 1990.

6. G.K. Wallace, "The JPEG Still Picture Compression Standard," *CACM*, Vol. 34, No. 4, April 1991, pp. 30-44.

7. J.D. Foley et al., *Fundamentals of Interactive Computer Graphics*, 2nd Ed., Addison-Wesley, Reading, Mass., 1990.

8. J.S. Lim, *Two-dimensional Signal and Image Processing*, Prentice Hall, Englewood Cliffs, N.J., 1990.

9. K.R. Rao and P. Kip, *Discrete Cosine Transform—Algorithms, Advantages, Applications*, Academic Press, London, 1990.

10. T. Porter and T. Duff, "Compositing Digital Images," *Computer Graphics* (Proc. Siggraph 84), Vol. 18, No. 3, July 1984, pp. 253-259.

11. B. Chitprasert and K.R. Rao, "Discrete Cosine Transform Filtering," *Signal Processing*, Vol. 19, No. 3, March 1990, pp. 233-245.

12. S.-F. Chang, W.-L. Chen, and D.G. Messerschmitt, "Video Compositing in the DCT Domain," *Proc. IEEE Workshop on Visual Signal Processing and Communications*, IEEE Press, New York, Sept. 1992, pp. 138-143.

Brian C. Smith is currently working towards a PhD degree in computer science at the University of California at Berkeley. He received an AB in physics and MS in computer science from the University of California at Berkeley in 1986 and 1990, respectively. He designed and implemented the Picasso graphical user interface development system and the Sun Access Computer System, used by the city of San Francisco. His research interests include graphical user interfaces, computer graphics, image processing, and multimedia systems.

Lawrence A. Rowe is a professor of electrical engineering and computer science at the University of California at Berkeley. His research interests include multimedia applications and development tools, computer-integrated manufacturing, and programming environments for database systems. He designed and implemented several fourth-generation languages and interface development systems for database applications, process specification languages for the semiconductor industry, hypermedia applications, and video databases and browsers. Rowe received a BA in mathematics and a PhD in information and computer science from the University of California at Irvine in 1970 and 1976, respectively.

Readers may contact Rowe at University of California at Berkeley, College of Engineering, Dept. of Electrical Engineering and Computer Sciences, Computer Science Division, Berkeley, CA 94720. His e-mail address is larry@postgres.berkeley.edu.

Manipulation and Compositing of MC–DCT Compressed Video

Shih-Fu Chang, *Member, IEEE,* and David G. Messerschmitt, *Fellow, IEEE*

Abstract—Many advanced video applications require manipulations of compressed video signals. Popular video manipulation functions include overlap (opaque or semitransparent), translation, scaling, linear filtering, rotation, and pixel multiplication. In this paper, we propose algorithms to manipulate compressed video in the compressed domain. Specifically, we focus on compression algorithms using the discrete cosine transform (DCT) with or without motion compensation (MC). Compression systems of such kind include JPEG, motion JPEG, MPEG, and H.261. We derive a complete set of algorithms for all aforementioned manipulation functions in the transform domain, in which video signals are represented by quantized transform coefficients. Due to a much lower data rate and the elimination of decompression/compression conversion, the transform-domain approach has great potential in reducing the computational complexity. The actual computational speedup depends on the specific manipulation functions and the compression characteristics of the input video, such as the compression rate and the nonzero motion vector percentage. The proposed techniques can be applied to general orthogonal transforms, such as discrete trigonometric transform. For compression systems incorporating MC (such as MPEG), we propose a new decoding algorithm to reconstruct the video in the transform domain and then perform the desired manipulations in the transform domain. The same technique can be applied to efficient video transcoding (e.g., from MPEG to JPEG) with minimal decoding.

I. INTRODUCTION

ADVANCED video services have emerged as a focus of interest as the technologies of digital signal processing, VLSI, and broadband networks advance. Examples of such services include multipoint video conferencing, interactive networked video, video editing/publishing, and advanced multimedia workstations. Usually, video signals are compressed when transmitted over networks or stored in databases. After video signals are compressed, there are still many situations where further manipulations of such compressed video are needed. For example, in a multipoint video conferencing, multiple compressed video sources may need to be manipulated and composited within the network at the so-called *video bridge* [26]. Fig. 1 shows a typical video conferencing scene, in which input video signals are arbitrarily manipulated (e.g., scaled to arbitrary size, translated to arbitrary locations) and composited into a single output video sequence. Typical

Manuscript received September 19, 1993; revised June 19, 1994. This paper was presented in part at IEEE ICASSP, Minneapolis, MN, 1993.

S.-F. Chang is with the Department of Electrical Engineering and the Center for Telecommunications Research, Columbia University, New York, NY 10027 USA.

D. G. Messerschmitt is with the Department of EECS, University of California at Berkeley, Berkeley, CA 94720 USA.

IEEE Log Number 9406079.

Fig. 1. A typical composited scene in the multi-point video conferencing application. (Scene 1).

video manipulation functions include translation (block-wise or pixel-wise), scaling, linear filtering, rotation, overlapping (opaque or semi-transparent),[1] and pixel multiplication. Many applications require only a subset of these features.

There are two possible ways to manipulate compressed video. The first approach fully decodes each compressed input video and then manipulates them in the spatial domain [26]. The output video needs to be reencoded again if the compressed format is required. Alternatively, we can derive equivalent manipulation algorithms in the compressed domain and manipulate compressed video directly in the compressed domain [4]–[6], [32]. Due to a much lower data rate and the removal of the unnecessary decoding/coding pair, the compressed-domain approach has great potential in reducing the computational complexity. In addition, manipulation in the compressed domain provides the flexibility to accommodate dynamic resources and heterogeneous Quality of Service (QoS) requirements. Users with low-end computing/communication resources can process the signal components with the highest significance only (e.g., lower order DCT coefficients, or lower bands in subband coding) to maintain as high video quality as possible within the resource limit. This prioritized significance of signal components is not available in the uncompressed domain.

This paper shows that many video manipulation functions can be performed in the compressed domain more efficiently (i.e., with less computations) than in the uncompressed domain. This statement is particularly true when both input and output video signals need to be compressed, as in the

---

[1] By semitransparent overlapping, we mean that the background image pixels are partly seen through the foreground image pixels (e.g., fade-in and fade-out special effects).

case of network video compositing. We focus on the motion compensated discrete cosine transform (MC–DCT) format, which is widely used in many image/video compression standards (e.g., H.261, MPEG, HDTV [2], [13], [16], [35]). In specific, we derive one set of algorithms to perform all above mentioned manipulations in the transform domain, in which video signals are represented by transform coefficients (such as quantized DCT coefficients) [5]. Our derivations are based on the linearity of the manipulation functions and the orthogonality of the transform algorithms. The proposed techniques can be applied to general orthogonal transform coding algorithms, such as discrete sine transform (DST) and DFT.

For the case where MC is incorporated (such as MPEG and H.261), we will discuss the obstacles preventing the MC-domain manipulation [4]. To avoid these difficulties, we propose a new decoding technique to convert the MC-DCT video to the DCT domain and then perform desired manipulation functions in the DCT domain. The same approach can be applied to efficient video transcoding (e.g., from MPEG to JPEG) with minimal decoding.

There is some independent related work. Smith and Rowe studied a subset of manipulation functions in the DCT domain [32], such as linear combination and pixel multiplication. However, they used a coefficient mapping approach without deriving underlying mathematical formulae. Based on a little different derivations, Lee and Lee derived the transform-domain filtering algorithms and proposed a pipelined hardware architecture [21]. Martucci derived the symmetrical convolution routines for the discrete trigonometric transform [36]. The concept of compressed-domain manipulation can also be applied to other compression algorithms, such as subband coding. Lee and Woods proposed some subband-domain algorithms for simple operations such as picture in picture and text overlay [22]. However, border boxes are used along the overlap boundary to cover some artifacts.

This paper is organized as follows. Section II includes review of MC-DCT compression systems and some terminology definitions. We derive the proposed DCT-domain manipulation algorithms in Section III. We explain the difficulties for video manipulation in the MC domain and propose some techniques to reduce computations of MC recalculation in Section IV. Manipulation of MC-DCT compressed video in the transform domain is proposed in Section V. Performance analysis is presented in Section VI.

II. BACKGROUND AND DOMAIN DEFINITIONS

Fig. 2 shows the block diagram for hybrid compression systems based on the MC–DCT algorithm. Input images are segmented into small blocks, each of which is motion compensated and transformed into DCT coefficients. The *motion estimation* (ME) procedure finds the *optimal reference block* from the previous frame and also outputs the motion vector. The DCT coefficients are quantized and then run-length coded (RLC) to remove redundancy in long sequences of zeroes. In addition, the statistically-based variable-length code (VLC), such as the Huffman code or arithmetic code

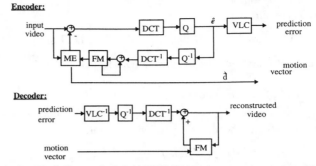

Fig. 2. Block diagram for hybrid MC-DCT based compression systems. ME: Motion Estimation, FM: Frame Memory, VLC: Variable Length Code.

[24], is applied to exploit any remaining data redundancy. For compression systems using intra-frame coding only, the ME block is not needed.

In this paper, we use the *spatial* domain to refer to the raw pixel data format before encoding or after decoding. Sometimes for the purpose of contrast, we also refer to it as the *uncompressed* domain. The *DCT* or *DCT-compressed* domain refers to the quantized DCT coefficients,[2] which can be obtained after the inverse quantizer in the decoder of Fig. 2. Note that a video signal can be transformed into the DCT domain either by applying the DCT on raw image data or by partially decoding the interframe MC–DCT encoded video, as will be described later. Through the context, we will also use the "*transform*" domain to refer to the frequency domain of general orthogonal transforms, such as DST, DFT, and DCT.

The *MC* or *MC-compressed* domain refers to the encoded data format after the MC algorithm. Basic components in the MC domain include the motion vectors ($\vec{d}$) and the prediction errors ($\hat{e}$), as shown in Fig. 2. The *MC-DCT-compressed* or *MC–DCT* domain refers to the hybrid interframe encoded format shown in Fig. 2. It contains the motion vectors and the DCT coefficients of the prediction errors.

III. VIDEO MANIPULATION IN THE DCT DOMAIN

We describe one set of video manipulation primitives—overlap, scaling, translation, linear filtering, rotation, and pixel-multiplication, and their DCT-domain equivalents in this section. Most video services require only a subset of these primitives.

A. Overlap

Opaque overlapping of two video objects requires substituting pixels of the foreground video object for those of the background object. *Semitransparent overlapping* requires a linear combination of the foreground and background pixels, i.e.,

$$P_{\text{new}}(i, j) = \alpha \cdot P_a(i, j) + (1 - \alpha) \cdot P_b(i, j) \qquad (1)$$

where P_{new}, P_a, P_b, and α are new pixels, foreground pixels, background pixels, and the transparency factor [30]. Since it's

---

[2]Without otherwise specified, we assume the transform coefficients are by default quantized, so that we can take advantage of the fact that many coefficients are truncated to zero after quantization.

a linear operation, we can apply the same technique in the DCT domain, i.e.,

$$\text{DCT}(P_{\text{new}}) = \alpha \cdot \text{DCT}(P_a) + (1 - \alpha) \cdot \text{DCT}(P_b) \quad (2)$$

where P represents the blockwise data format in DCT.

B. Pixel Multiplication

If the α coefficients vary from pixel to pixel, semitransparent overlapping becomes a pixelwise operation, i.e.,

$$P_{\text{new}}(i, j) = \alpha(i, j) \cdot P_a(i, j) + (1 - \alpha(i, j)) \cdot P_b(i, j). \quad (3)$$

This operation involves a basic operation called *pixel-multiplication*, i.e.,

$$P_{\text{new}}(i, j) = P_a(i, j) \cdot P_b(i, j). \quad (4)$$

Pixel-multiplication is also required in situations like *subtitling* (adding text on top of an image), *anti-aliasing* (removing the jagged artifacts along the boundaries of irregularly-shaped video objects), and special-effect *masking* (for special graphic patterns). To compute the pixel-wise multiplication in the DCT domain, we derive a multiplication-convolution relationship for the DCT similar to that for the DFT, except that the order for the convolution is increased to $2 \cdot N$ points. We leave the proof in [7] and present the final result here. Similar symmetric convolution routines were studied in [36] independently.

Suppose X_c is the DCT of image block X. First, we form an extended symmetrical version of the DCT coefficients as shown at the bottom of the page. Then, the 2-D *multiplication-convolution theorem* can be described as follows.

If

$$y(i, j) = x(i, j) \cdot h(i, j), \quad i, j = 0, \cdots, N - 1$$

then

$$\begin{aligned} \hat{Y}_c(k_1, k_2) = \frac{1}{2N} \cdot \sum_{l_1, l_2 \in [-N, N-1]} \sum & [\hat{X}_c(l_1, l_2) \\ & \cdot \hat{H}_c(((k_1 - l_1))_{2N}, ((k_2 - l_2))_{2N})] \\ & \cdot \alpha(k_1 - l_1)\alpha(k_2 - l_2) \\ k_1, k_2 = -N, \cdots, N - 1 \\ \alpha(k) = \begin{pmatrix} 1 & k \in [-N, N-1] \\ -1 & \text{otherwise} \end{pmatrix}. \quad (5) \end{aligned}$$

For convenience we use the notation $((n))_{2N}$ to denote (n modulo $2N$). If we ignore the α term, the above equation is equivalent to a 2-D $2N$−point circular convolution. In other words, we expand the $N \times N$ DCT coefficients of an

image block to an extended symmetric $2N \times 2N$ block. The pixel-wise multiplication of two image blocks in the spatial domain corresponds to the two-dimensional $2N$−point circular convolution-like operation of the extended blocks in the DCT domain.

C. Translation (Blockwise and Pixelwise)

In a video scene containing multiple video objects, as in the case of multi-source video conferencing, users may want to move each video object around flexibly. We refer to this general position control operation as *translation*. Two types of translation should be considered separately—blockwise (i.e., fixed block boundary positions) and *pixelwise* (i.e., arbitrary positions). If we restrict both the horizontal and vertical translation distance to be an integral multiple of the block width, then the DCT coefficients are always aligned with the same block structure. (By *block structure*, we refer to the grid lines used to segment the images into small bocks.) Moving a video object around requires updating the origin point of the video object only. Aforementioned manipulation functions such as overlapping and pixel multiplication can be performed in the DCT domain as described if the block structures of input video objects are aligned.

However, if we allow translation by an arbitrary number of pixels, the block structures of the input video objects could be mismatched. Fig. 3 illustrates mismatched block structures of objects A and B. In the spatial domain, this mismatch problem is easy to solve. In the transform domain, due to the rigid block structure, it is no longer a trivial issue. Suppose we want to composite object A and object B as shown in Fig. 3 and we choose the block structure of object A as the final reference block structure. Therefore, we need to resegment object B with respect to the block structure of object A. A new image block of object B, say B′, contains contributions from four original neighboring blocks ($B_1 - B_4$), namely the lower-left corner (B_{13}) of block B_1, the lower-right corner (B_{24}) of block B_2, the upper-right corner (B_{31}) of block B_3, and the upper-left corner (B_{42}) of block B_4. We supplement these four contributions with zeroes as illustrated in Fig. 3 to form N pixels by N pixels image blocks. Then, the new block can be calculated as

$$B' = B_{13} + B_{24} + B_{31} + B_{42}. \quad (6)$$

The same method cannot be applied in the DCT domain. We cannot simply assemble four subblocks from the original DCT

$$\hat{X}_c(k_1, k_2) = \begin{cases} X_c(k_1, k_2)/C(k_1, k_2) & k_1, k_2 = 0, \cdots, N - 1 \\ X_c(-k_1, k_2)/C(-k_1, k_2) & k_1 = -N + 1, \cdots, -1, k_2 = 0, \cdots, N - 1 \\ X_c(k_1, -k_2)/C(k_1, -k_2) & k_1 = 0, \cdots, N - 1, k_2 = -N + 1, \cdots, -1 \\ X_c(-k_1, -k_2)/C(-k_1, -k_2) & k_1, k_2 = -N + 1, \cdots, -1 \\ 0 & k_1 = N, \text{or} k_2 = N \end{cases}$$

where

$$C(k_1, k_2) = \begin{cases} \frac{1}{2} & k_1 = k_2 = 0 \\ 1 & \text{otherwise} \end{cases}$$

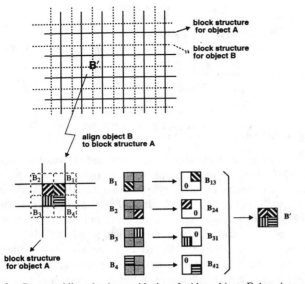

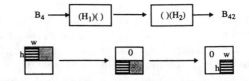

Fig. 4. Using matrix multiplication to extract a subblock and translate it to the opposite corner.

It can be shown that all unitary orthogonal transforms such as the DCT are distributive to matrix multiplication [15], i.e.,

$$\text{DCT(AB)=DCT(A)DCT(B)}. \qquad (9)$$

Using this property, we can compute the DCT of B_{42} directly from the DCT of B_4, i.e.,

$$\text{DCT}(B_{42}) = \text{DCT}(H_1)\text{DCT}(B_4)\text{DCT}(H_2). \qquad (10)$$

Summing all contributions from four corners, we can obtain the DCT coefficients of the new block B' directly from the DCT of old blocks B_1B_4. In other words,

$$\text{DCT}(B') = \sum_{i=1}^{4}\text{DCT}(H_{i1})\text{DCT}(B_i)\text{DCT}(H_{i2}). \qquad (11)$$

The DCT of H_{i1} and H_{i2} can be precomputed and stored in memory. With a block width equal to N, only $2 \cdot N - 2$ matrices need to be stored. Given DCT of B_i and H_{ij}, (11) can be implemented by matrix multiplications. The required computation can be reduced by using sparse matrix multiplication techniques since many DCT coefficients are zeroes. Detailed complexity analysis will be presented in Section VI-A.

D. Linear Filtering

Two-dimensional separable *linear filtering* can also be done in the DCT domain [5], [9], [21], [29]. Linear filtering of images in the horizontal direction can be achieved by multiplications with postmatrices

$$Y = \sum_{i} X_i H_i \qquad (12)$$

where X_i is the input image block, H_i is the filter coefficients represented in the block form, and Y is the output image block. Each output image block has contributions from several input blocks. The number of contributing input blocks depends on the length of the filter kernel. Since the DCT algorithm is distributive to matrix multiplication, we can calculate $\text{DCT}(Y)$ in the following way:

$$\text{DCT}(Y) = \sum_{i}\text{DCT}(X_i)\text{DCT}(H_i). \qquad (13)$$

Similarly, image filtering in the vertical direction can be achieved by multiplication with prematrices. Detailed derivation of the transform-domain filtering algorithm can be found in [7], [21].

Fig. 3. Re-assembling the image blocks of video object B based on a new block structure, which mismatches object B's original block structure. After re-alignment, a new image block, B', consists of contributions $(B_{13}, B_{24}, B_{31},$ and $B_{42})$ from four original neighboring blocks $(B1B4)$.

blocks to form the DCT of the new block. Instead, it should be calculated as

$$\text{DCT}(B') = \text{DCT}(B_{13}) + \text{DCT}(B_{24})$$
$$+ \text{DCT}(B_{31}) + \text{DCT}(B_{42}). \qquad (7)$$

Therefore, if we can find the relationship between the DCT of subblocks $(B_{13}B_{42})$ and the DCT of the original blocks (B_1B_4), then we can calculate the DCT of the new block directly from the DCT of the original blocks. In other words, the conversion processes back and forth between the DCT domain and the spatial domain can be eliminated. Kou and Fjallbrant [18], proposed an algorithm to compute the DCT of a signal block from two original adjacent blocks when the overlap length is one half of the block size. However, the complexity becomes quite high for an arbitrary overlap length. Here, we propose a direct computation method applicable to any arbitrary overlapping length.

Fig. 4 shows a mathematical model for obtaining a subblock from an original block (e.g., B_{42} from B_4) in the spatial domain. Note that the upper-left corner of B_4 is extracted, supplemented by zeroes, and moved to the lower-right corner, as required in Fig. 3. A matrix-form equation for this subblock extraction procedure is

$$B_{42} = H_1 B_4 H_2, \quad \text{where } H_1 = \begin{bmatrix} 0 & 0 \\ I_h & 0 \end{bmatrix} H_2 = \begin{bmatrix} 0 & I_w \\ 0 & 0 \end{bmatrix} \qquad (8)$$

where I_h and I_w are identity matrices with size $h \times h$ and $w \times w$, respectively; h and w are the number of rows and columns extracted. As shown in Fig. 4, multiplying B_4 with a prematrix H_1 extracts the first h rows and translates them to the bottom; multiplying B_4 with a postmatrix H_2 extracts the first w columns and translates them to the right.

E. Scaling

Another important image manipulation technique is *scaling*. Each pixel in the final scaled image is a linear combination of several neighboring pixels in the original image [12]. Thus, it can be treated in a way similar to linear filtering. For example, if we use the simple box area averaging method to implement the $1/2 \times 1/2$ down scaling operation [34], a new block can be computed as $H_1 B_{11} W_1 + H_2 B_{21} W_1 + H_1 B_{12} W_2 + H_2 B_{22} W_2$ where B_i are the original neighboring blocks, H_i are the vertical scaling matrices, and W_i are the horizontal scaling matrices. For example,

$$H_1 = (W_1)' = \begin{bmatrix} 0.5 & 0.5 & 0 & 0 \\ 0 & 0 & 0.5 & 0.5 \\ 0 & 0 & 0 & 0 \\ 0 & 0 & 0 & 0 \end{bmatrix}$$

$$H_2 = (W_2)' = \begin{bmatrix} 0 & 0 & 0 & 0 \\ 0 & 0 & 0 & 0 \\ 0.5 & 0.5 & 0 & 0 \\ 0 & 0 & 0.5 & 0.5 \end{bmatrix} \tag{14}$$

for a block width of 4 pixels. The same linear operations can be performed in the DCT domain as described above.

F. Other Manipulation Functions

In addition to the above operations, *rotation* and *shearing* are also useful in creating visual special effects. Strictly speaking, both these two operations are linear geometrical transformations and should have equivalent counterparts in the transform domain. For example, the horizontal shearing can be implemented as

$$Y = \sum_i W_i X S_i \tag{15}$$

where X is the input image block, W_i extracts the ith row and supplements the remaining rows with zeros, and S_i performs the horizontal 1-D shifting and interpolation [12], [38]. Again, applying the distributive property of DCT, we can derive the shearing algorithm in the DCT domain. For rotation, a typical implementation is based on a column-reserving shearing and a row-reserving shearing, plus some appropriate scaling [12]. Thus, based on the derived DCT-domain scaling and DCT-domain shearing, the DCT-domain rotation algorithm can be derived as well. However, for such complicated operations as rotation, the matrix structure in the DCT domain could become too cumbersome and thus their DCT-domain algorithms may not be attractive, compared to the conventional spatial-domain approach.

IV. MANIPULATION OF MC-COMPRESSED VIDEO

Video signals in the MC-compressed domain consist of two components: motion vector (d), and prediction error (e), denoted as the *MC data*. Given the MC data of input video streams, it would be desirable to compute the MC data of the output video of the manipulation functions directly in the MC domain without any decoding. Unfortunately, the MC algorithm does not have the same linear and orthogonal property as

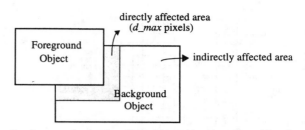

Fig. 5.   An example showing the problem with video compositing directly in the MC domain. d_max is the maximum search distance.

that for the transform algorithms discussed above, thus making the MC-domain video manipulation impossible. In this section, we illustrate this obstacle by using two examples: overlapping and scaling. Given the MC data of the input video streams, we need to convert them back to the uncompressed domain before any manipulations. Recalculation of the MC data is required if the output video needs to be encoded in the MC format again. In order to avoid the intensive computations involved in the *MC data recalculation* process, we propose an *inference principle* to calculate the new motion vector with minimal computations.

A. Obstacles for Video Manipulation in the MC Domain

Fig. 5 shows *overlapping* of two video objects. Assume both the foreground and background objects are MC-encoded and their block structures are aligned. The MC data of the foreground object can be kept in the composited video since it is not affected by the background object. However, part of the background object is obscured by the foreground object. We need to consider two different areas of the background object separately—the *directly affected area* (DAA) and the *indirectly affected area* (IAA). The difference has to do with the *search area*[3] in the MC algorithm. In the DAA, part of its search area is replaced by the foreground object. If the motion vector is from the obscured area, the original prediction block is destroyed. The MC data thus becomes invalid and needs to be recalculated. In the IAA, though the search area is not overlapped by the foreground object, the MC data may still need to be recalculated since its prediction block could be modified through *error propagation*. In other words, the MC data of the composited video cannot be directly obtained from the MC data of the input video streams. Both the foreground and background video need to be fully decoded so that new MC data can be calculated.

Another example is *down scaling*. Suppose every four original image blocks are scaled down to one new image block. The motion vectors of these four original blocks in general are different. Although the new motion vector can be inferred from the original four motion vectors, decoded images still need to be reconstructed so that the correct prediction errors can be recalculated.

B. Simplification of MC Data Recalculation

As discussed above, all MC-encoded video needs to be decoded first so that the new MC data of the composited video

---

[3]The search area is the area in the previous frame where the optimal prediction block is searched.

can be calculated. But the MC process is very computation-intensive. In order to keep low-cost manipulations of MC-coded video feasible, we propose some techniques here to simplify the indispensable MC recalculation. The first approach is to reduce the frequency of MC recalculation. The second approach is to minimize the computations associated with the ME process, by inferring the new motion vectors from the original input motion vectors. We will use the overlap example in Fig. 5 to verify the effectiveness of these two approaches. The underlying concept can be applied to other situations as well. For example, new motion vectors can be interpolated from old motion vectors in the down scaling scenario mentioned above.

Approach I—Reducing the Frequency of Recalculation: The first principle for simplifying the MC recalculation process is to reduce the number of image blocks requiring MC recalculation. For example, in the opaque overlapping situation in Fig. 5, we can assume that only image blocks in the DAA may need recalculation of the motion vector. If the motion vector comes from the foreground area, then the original prediction block is obscured and a new motion vector is needed. Our experiments of some test sequences show that only 5–15% of the directly affected blocks require MC recalculation [4]. Compared to blind recalculation of every block in the background object, the frequency of MC recalculation is greatly reduced. Of course, this number varies with video sequences and depends on the specific manipulation scenario as well.

Approach II—Obtaining New Motion Vectors by Inference: To further reduce the computation cost associated with the MC recalculation, we apply the second principle—*inferring new motion vectors from the old ones.* Our objective is to simplify the ME procedure, which is the most computation-demanding process in the MC algorithm.

To reduce the computational complexity of ME, Jain and Jain [14] have proposed a two-dimensional binary search approach by assuming that the block distortion function is monotonically increasing along the horizontal or vertical direction when the search position moves away from the optimal prediction point. For the overlap scenario considered, if we adopt the same assumption, we can reduce the number of search positions to two only. Fig. 6 shows the spatial relations of these search positions where B represents the current block, D the optimal prediction point, and D_1, D_2 the crossing points when the search position moves away from D horizontally and vertically respectively. Jain and Jain's assumption assures that any search position to the right of D_1 has a larger distortion than D_1, and any search position lower than D_2 has a larger distortion than D_2. So, if we assume that the new optimal prediction location is still from the background object, then either D_1 or D_2 should have the minimal distortion and should be the new optimal prediction. Compared to the full-search ME (which needs $(2 \cdot d\_max + 1)^2$ search positions), the computational complexity is much lower.

Impact on Video Quality: Whenever MC recalculation (including quantization) is performed, video quality will be further degraded even the full-search ME is used. This issue is very similar to the error accumulation issue in repetitive coding of video signals [37]. In the overlap scenario of Fig. 5,

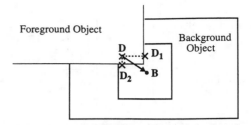

Fig. 6.   Reducing the number of search positions to two by using Jain and Jain's assumption. B is the location of the current image block. D is the optimal reference location. The shaded area represents the search area.

the average SNR among the directly affected blocks which require MC recalculation is decreased by 2.88–5.45 dB if the full-search ME is used. This quality loss depends on the image content and the distribution of the distortion function. The additional SNR loss due to our proposed two-point ME procedure is usually small (within 1 dB). Significant loss occurs in very few frames, where the assumption about the monotonic distribution of the distortion function does not seem to hold.

It is worth mentioning that there is also quality degradation for background pixels outside the directly affected area. For these pixels, we can reasonably assume their motion vectors are unchanged. But their prediction errors may need to be updated because their prediction blocks in the previous frame may be located inside the DAA and need to be recalculated. The change of prediction values will propagate to more outside area as the video sequence proceeds. Our simulations show the average SNR loss among pixels affected by the error propagation effect ranges from 2.38 to 6.19 dB. The percentage of background pixels affected by this error propagation effect remains low in our test, though in reality it could vary with different video streams. Some sparse spots with significant SNR loss are visually noticeable. We have proposed techniques to partially rectify the error propagation problem by updating the prediction errors only, without recalculating the motion vectors [4]. These techniques are proved to be effective in removing abrupt severe quality loss in many frames.

V. MANIPULATION OF MC–DCT COMPRESSED VIDEO

The obstacles preventing the MC-domain video manipulation also exist for the MC–DCT encoded video. In order to keep the benefits of the compressed-domain video manipulation, we propose to keep the video signals as much in the compressed form as possible. In specific, we propose to partially decode the MC–DCT video to the DCT domain first, and then perform desired manipulations in the DCT domain. One potential problem with this approach is that conventional MC-DCT decoding first decodes the DCT part and then the MC part. The nonlinear MC is at the bottom of the compression stack. Our solution is to swap the order of the decoding stack, namely, inverse MC first, then inverse DCT. Note that the encoding stack doesn't have to change, meaning that regular MC-DCT encoders can be used. Fig. 7 illustrates the proposed transform-domain manipulation system.

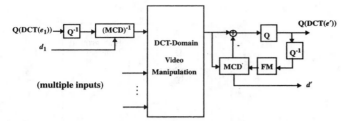

Fig. 7. Manipulation of MC-DCT compressed video in the DCT domain. The output video is MC-DCT encoded as well.

As shown in Fig. 2, the decoding process for MC-DCT video can be described as

$$P_{\text{rec}}(t, x, y) = \text{DCT}^{-1} \left(\text{DCT} \left(e(t, x, y) \right) \right)$$
$$+ P_{\text{rec}}(t - 1, x - d_x, y - d_y) \quad (16)$$

where P_{rec} is the reconstructed image, e is the prediction error, and d is the motion vector. We ship quantization of $\text{DCT}(e)$ for simplicity here. With simple reordering, we can rewrite it as

$$\text{DCT} \left(P_{\text{rec}}(t, x, y) \right)$$
$$= \text{DCT} \left(e(t, x, y) \right)$$
$$+ \text{DCT} \left(P_{\text{rec}}(t - 1, x - d_x, y - d_y) \right). \quad (17)$$

Now, the inverse MC is performed before the inverse DCT. In other words, the inverse MC is performed in the DCT domain, denoted as $(MCD)^{-1}$ in Fig. 7. The $(MCD)^{-1}$ procedure first locates the optimal reference block in the previous frame (by using the received motion vector) and then adds the DCT of the reconstructed optimal reference block to the DCT of the prediction errors. By doing so, the received video is reconstructed in the DCT domain.

However, the DCT of the optimal reference block may not be immediately available. In general, the motion vector of each block is an arbitrary number of pixels. Therefore, the optimal reference block generally overlaps with four blocks, whose DCT coefficients are already available. The situation is the same as that for the pixelwise translation discussed in Section III-C. In both places, we need to calculate the DCT of a new arbitrary-position block from the DCT of four original neighboring blocks. Therefore, the same formula in (11) can be used here to obtain the DCT of the optimal prediction block, i.e., $\text{DCT}(P_{rec}(t - 1, x - d_x, y - d_y))$.

The same approach can be used in the forward MC as well when the manipulation output needs to be MC encoded again. The DCT of the prediction error can be calculated as

$$\text{DCT} \left(e(t, x, y) \right) = \text{DCT} \left(P_{\text{rec}}(t, x, y) \right)$$
$$- \text{DCT} \left(P_{\text{rec}}(t - 1, x - d'_x, y - d'_y) \right)$$
$$(18)$$

where d' is the new motion vector for the output video sequence.

If the motion vectors are zero (as in DPCM interframe coding) or integral multiples of the block width, the block structure alignment procedure is not needed, and motion compensation in the DCT domain requires simple additions only, as in the spatial domain. If only one motion vector component (d_x or d_y) is zero or integral multiples of the block width, the DCT coefficients of the new block can be computed from the DCT coefficients of two original overlapping blocks, instead of four.

VI. PERFORMANCE ANALYSES

We analyze performance of the proposed transform-domain video manipulation techniques both analytically and numerically in this section. Two major performance factors considered are *computational complexity* and *video quality*. Other considerations such as hardware implementation are also briefly discussed. Numerical simulations are done by non-real-time software prototyping. Three different test scenarios are considered. Scene 1 is the scenario with multiple small inputs and a large output display, as shown in Fig. 1. Input videos are down scaled, translated, and then composited together. Scene 2 has multiple input videos and an output display of the same size as the input. Every input video object needs to be scaled down in this case. Scene 3 represents the picture-in-picture scenario. One input video is scaled down and overlapped on top of another video stream, which does not require any scale change. Video sequences used are head-and-shoulder images. We consider the case where both input and output are MC–DCT encoded. Different quantization tables are tested, including those listed in the JPEG and MPEG standards.

A. Computational Complexity

The computational complexity of the transform-domain video manipulation techniques strongly depends on the number of zero DCT coefficients, which in turn depends on the compression rate of the input video. When the MC algorithm is included, the complexity also significantly depends on the motion vector distribution. As far as manipulation functions are concerned, in general, blockwise operations benefit more from the transform-domain approach, compared to the pixel-wise operations. But since the decoding/coding conversion is avoided, the DCT-domain approach may still provide a net efficiency gain for many cases involving pixel-wise operations.

In Table I, we list the number of multiplications and additions required in each major operation, such as the DCT, DCT^{-1}, MCD, MCD^{-1}, pixelwise translation, scaling, quantization, and inverse quantization. Interested readers are referred to [7] for detailed derivations. An important property we assume in deriving the complexity is that the run-length-code (RLC) of the quantized DCT coefficients can indicate the locations of the non-zero DCT coefficients so that the redundant operations associated with zero coefficients can be skipped. In addition, we exploit optimization in spare matrix multiplication, which is the basic computation module in various transform-domain manipulation functions, such as linear filtering and translation. A straightforward implementation of matrix multiplication, $A \cdot P \cdot B$ (where A and B are $N \times N$ matrices, and P represents an N pixels by N pixels image block), requires $2 \cdot N^3$ multiplications and $2 \cdot (N - 1) \cdot N^2$ additions. Based on some assumptions of the nonzero DCT coefficient distribution and optimization techniques for sparse matrix multiplication, the same operation needs $(1/\beta + 1/\sqrt{\beta}) \cdot$

TABLE I
COMPUTATIONAL COMPLEXITY OF MAJOR VIDEO MANIPULATION FUNCTIONS[a]

	operation	# of multi. / pixel	# of add. / pixel
DCT Domain:	MCD, MCD^{-1}	$(4/\beta + 2/\sqrt{\beta}) \cdot N \cdot \alpha_2 + (2/\beta) \cdot N \cdot \alpha_1$	$[(4/\beta + 2/\sqrt{\beta}) \cdot N + 3] \cdot \alpha_2 + [(2/\beta) \cdot N + 1] \cdot \alpha_1 + 1$
	pixel-wise translation	$(2/\beta + 2/\sqrt{\beta}) \cdot N$	$(2/\beta + 2/\sqrt{\beta}) \cdot N + 3$
	scale 1/2×1/2	$(1/\beta + 1/(2\sqrt{\beta})) \cdot N$	$(1/\beta + 1/(2\sqrt{\beta})) \cdot N + 3/4$
	scale 1/3×1/3	$(1/\beta + 1/(3\sqrt{\beta})) \cdot N$	$(1/\beta + 1/(3\sqrt{\beta})) \cdot N + 8/9$
	pixel multiplication	$N^2/(\beta_1 \cdot \beta_2)$	$N^2/(\beta_1 \cdot \beta_2)$
	semi-transparent block-wise overlapping	$< (1/\beta_1 + 1/\beta_2)$	$< 2 \cdot (1/\beta_1 + 1/\beta_2)$
Spatial Domain:	FDCT, FDCT^{-1} [b]	$2 \cdot \log_2 N - 3 + 8/N$	$3 \cdot (\log_2 N - 1) + 4/N$
	MC, MC^{-1}	0	1
	scale 1/2×1/2	1/4	3/4
	scale 1/3×1/3	1/9	8/9
	pixel multiplication	1	0
	semi-transparent block-wise overlapping	1	2
Common:	opaque block-wise overlapping	0	0
	Inverse Quantization	$1/\beta$	0
	Quantization	1	0

a. Notations:
  α_2: the percentage of image blocks which need block boundary adjustment in both directions, i.e., both d_x and d_y are not integral multiples of the block size.
  α_1: the percentage of image blocks which need block boundary adjustment in only one direction, i.e., only one of d_x and d_y is an integral multiple of the block size.
  N: the block width (8 in our experiments).

b. We use the fast DCT algorithm of Chen & Smith [8]. If we use the 2N-point FFT approach, the computational complexity will be doubled.

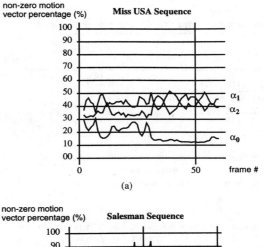
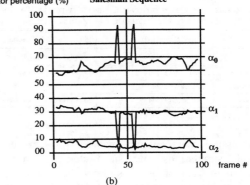

Fig. 8. Experimental results of nonzero motion vectors, α_2, α_1 are defined in Table I, $\alpha_0 = 1 - \alpha_2 - \alpha_1$.

N^3 multiplications and $(1/\beta + 1/\sqrt{\beta}) \cdot N^3$ additions only where β is the *compression rate*[4] of the input image. Since matrix multiplication is the basic building block in many DCT-domain operations, many complexity figures in Table I are closely related to the above formula.

Table I shows that the MCD (MCD^{-1}) operation has the highest computational complexity. This is due to the need of block structure alignment in both directions. If one of the motion vector components is an integral multiple of the block width, then the associated computation can be reduced, as discussed in Section V. The overall computations required for MCD depends on the non-zero motion vector percentage, α_1 and α_2 (defined in Table I). Typical values of (α_2, α_1) are shown in Fig. 8. The composited scenes usually have lower (α_2, α_1) values than input video signals due to the involved down-scaling operations. The compression ratio (β) is about 7–8 for the salesman sequence, 20 for the Miss USA sequence (high-compression ratio due to its flat background), and 7–9 for the composited sequence.

Pixelwise translation in the DCT domain also requires block structure adjustment in both directions. But since some matrix multiplications can be shared, its complexity is lower than that of MCD. The scaling operation, like linear filtering, can be implemented by multiplications with a prematrix and a postmatrix in the DCT domain. In general, the DCT-domain scaling operation has a lower computational complexity than MCD and pixelwise translation. Also, the 1/3×1/3 down

---

[4]Strictly speaking, β defined here is the ratio between the total number of the DCT coefficients and the number of nonzero DCT coefficients. It's more or less proportional to the commonly used *compression ratio*. We use them interchangeably in the context, except in the detailed calculation of computational complexity.

scaling in the DCT domain requires a little bit less computation than 1/2×1/2 down scaling because more image blocks share the same matrix multiplication.

For the spatial-domain operations, the major computations are from the coding/decoding conversion, i.e., the DCT and its inverse. Chen's fast algorithm [8] has a complexity of $2 \cdot \log_2 N - 3 + 8/N$ multiplications per pixel, which is about one half of that using the $2N$–point FFT [10]. There have been many new fast DCT computation methods reported in the literature [3], [27], [20], but all have a similar complexity order. The spatial-domain 1/2×1/2 down scaling operation needs 1/4 multiplication per pixel. (i.e., $P_{new}=(P_{11} + P_{12} + P_{21}+P_{22})/4$ by using the simple box area averaging algorithm described in [34]). It becomes 1/9 multiplication per pixel for 1/3×1/3 down scaling.

One interesting note is that the major component for the transform-domain operations increases linearly with the block width N while it increases with the order of $\log_2 N$ for the spatial-domain approach (although when the block size increases, the image compression ratios may change as well.) Therefore, the transform-domain approach is more suitable for cases using a small block size, which is usually true in image compression.

Simulation Results: Comparison of computational complexity for three test scenarios are shown in Table II. Manipulation features demonstrated here include overlapping, scaling with various factors, and block-wise translation.

TABLE II

COMPARISON OF COMPUTATIONAL COMPLEXITY FOR MC–DCT CODED VIDEO
MANIPULATIONS (THE DCT DOMAIN VERSUS THE SPATIAL DOMAIN)

	Spatial Domain		DCT Domain	
	# op/pixel	CPU time[a]	# op/pixel	CPU time
Scene 1	33.28 mul. 57.57 add	40.72 sec.	26.63 mul. (*1.25*[b]) 38.96 add. (*1.48*)	31.46 sec. (*1.29*)
Scene 2	17.99 mul. 32.53 add	22.53 sec.	16.10 mul. (*1.12*) 23.89 add. (*1.41*)	20.29 sec. (*1.11*)
Scene 3	13.41 mul. 23.39 add	16.57 sec.	13.76 mul. (*0.97*) 20.39 add. (*1.15*)	14.69 sec. (*1.13*)

a. CPU time on a SPARC I machine.

b. Each highlighted score in the parenthesis represents the ratio between the DCT-domain result and the corresponding spatial-domain result. A score greater than one means that the DCT-domain implementation is more efficient than the spatial-domain approach.

TABLE III

COMPARISON OF COMPUTATIONAL COMPLEXITY FOR DCT-CODED VIDEO
MANIPULATIONS (*WITHOUT MC*) (THE DCT DOMAIN VERSUS THE SPATIAL DOMAIN)

	Spatial Domain	DCT Domain
	# op/pixel	# op./pixel
Scene 1	33.28 mul, 50.35 add	9.66 mul (*3.45*), 11.23 add (*4.48*)
Scene 2	17.99 mul, 28.53 add	7.36 mul (*2.44*), 8.01 add (*3.56*)
Scene 3	13.41 mul, 20.39 add	3.3 mul (*4.06*), 2.89 add (*7.06*)

Compression characteristics such as β, α_2, α_1 are collected through simulations and substituted into the analytical formulae in Table I. Results show that for these scenarios (with both input and output MC–DCT compressed), the DCT-domain approach is faster than the spatial-domain approach by about 10% to 30%. We also compare the speed of the software implementations. The CPU time reported in Table II approximately confirms the above speedup by using the DCT-domain approach. However, note that we assume translations in these scenarios are all blockwise. If pixelwise translation is allowed, then the DCT-domain approach will suffer from the overhead of block structure alignment. One trick to minimize the overhead of pixelwise translations is to perform downscaling before translation, if size reduction is needed. Thus, the relative complexity contribution from pixelwise translation can be reduced.

If the original input videos are compressed without the MC algorithm, namely DCT-encoded only as in the JPEG or Motion JPEG standards, the computational speedup by using the DCT-domain approach will increase significantly since the complicated MCD process is not required. Table III shows computational complexity for the case where only DCT coding (without MC) is used. The net computational speedup factor ranges from 3 to 6.

B. Image Quality

One would think that since the DCT-domain approach does not need a second coding pass after manipulation, the video quality should be better than that of the spatial-domain approach. However, this is not true in general. The DCT-domain manipulation algorithms are mathematically equivalent to their counterparts in the spatial domain. Even we keep all operations in the DCT domain, the final DCT coefficients still need to be

TABLE IV

IMPACT OF VIDEO MANIPULATION ON VIDEO QUALITY (THE
DCT-DOMAIN APPROACH VERSUS THE SPATIAL DOMAIN)[a]

	After Manipulation (before the 2nd coding)	After the 2nd coding	
		Spatial-domain Compositing	DCT-Domain Compositing
Scene 1	31.5 dB	28.8 dB (*-2.7*[b] dB)	28.5 dB (*-3.0* dB)
Scene 2	34.7 dB	27.0 dB (*-7.7* dB)	26.3 dB (*-8.4* dB)
Scene 3	30.7 dB	29.5 dB (*-1.2* dB)	29.5 dB (*-1.2* dB)

a. all input video streams are MC-DCT encoded.

b. these highlighted scores show the extra quality degradation introduced in the 2nd coding pass.

quantized. Therefore, the quality degradation suffered in the second quantization still applies to the DCT-domain approach.

The second quantization will introduce quality degradation whenever the image content is modified (e.g., scaled or filtered) in the intermediate operations between two coding passes. This problem is described as the *error accumulation* problem in multipass image coding [37]. Table IV shows the SNR values of reconstructed videos before and after the second coding process. The extent of quality degradation depends on the manipulation functions between two coding passes. For example, modification of image content in Scene 2 is more dramatic than that in Scene 3. Therefore, the SNR loss caused by re-coding is much larger in Scene 2 (7.7 dB) than in Scene 3 (1.2 dB).

In our implementations, the DCT-domain approach suffers an additional minor quality degradation due to the need of thresholding DCT coefficients after each intermediate manipulation. The thresholding process is used to reconstruct the RLC structure of the DCT coefficients, which would be destroyed in each intermediate manipulation. The RLC structure is important because it can indicate the positions of the nonzero DCT coefficients so that redundant computations can be skipped. From Table IV, we can see that this additional quality degradation is very minor, about 0–0.7 dB. Our simulations show that images obtained both by the DCT-domain approach and by the spatial-domain approach suffer some subjective quality degradation due to lossy quantization twice. But there is no noticeable quality difference between images reconstructed from these two approaches.

C. Other Considerations

1) Worst Case Throughput: The DCT-domain operations produce variable throughput, as opposed to the constant throughput of the spatial-domain approach. The higher the compression ratios and the lower the nonzero motion vector percentages the input videos have, the faster the manipulation functions can be executed in the DCT domain. For real-time implementations which need to consider the worst case situation, this variable throughput may be a shortcoming. But in the DCT domain, we have the flexibility to skip high-order DCT coefficients whenever the maximal processing delay bound is exceeded. The image quality degradation can thus be minimized since the high-order coefficients are usually less subjectively important. In essence, the amount of nontrivial DCT coefficients requiring processing is determined based on the hardware processing capability, as opposed to the rate-based criterion used in the constant-rate video encoders. The relationship between the compression rates and computational complexity shown in Table I can assist in allocation of required computing capacity when we design real-time video manipulations.

2) Techniques for Computation Reduction: As we can see in Table I, the most complex operation in the transform domain is the MCD (MCD^{-1}) algorithm. This is mainly due to its need of block structure realignment. We also notice that the computational complexity of the MCD algorithm strongly depends on the nonzero motion vector percentages, i.e., α_2 and α_1. If α_2 and α_1 are both equal to zero, the MCD algorithm can be easily implemented by simple additions. However, with the regular MC algorithm, these percentages vary with different video sequences, as shown in Fig. 8. One way to reduce the nonzero motion vector percentages is to modify the MC encoder to give some preference to zero motion vectors. For example, we can add a fractional weighting factor to the distortion associated with the zero motion vector. We refer to this algorithm as the *weighted MC algorithm.* Our simulations show that if we set the weighting factor associated the zero motion vector to 80%, the non-zero motion vector percentages (α_2, α_1) can be greatly reduced (from (52%, 38%) to (30%, 19%) for "Miss USA" video, and from (8%, 19%) to (6%, 7%) for the "salesman" video). The SNR values of reconstructed images using the weighted MC algorithm are very close to those using the regular MC algorithm. In terms of the computational efficiency, the weighted MC can raise the computational speedup by 10% to 20%, compared to the regular MC.

Another possible technique to reduce the computational complexity in the DCT domain is to combine a sequence of operations into a single operation. For example, for MC–DCT compressed videos, we may need to perform $F(\text{DCT}(e) + G(\text{DCT}(P_{ref})))$, where G represents the MCD^{-1} operation and F represents the scaling operation. Since scaling is a linear operation, we can apply the distributive law to change the above formula to $F(\text{DCT}(e))+H(\text{DCT}(P_{ref}))$, where H represent the composite function $F \cdot G$. The computations associated with function F can thus be reduced since it can operate on a much more sparse matrix now ($\text{DCT}(e)$ versus ($\text{DCT}(e) + G(\text{DCT}(P_{ref}))$)).

VII. CONCLUSION

Many advanced video applications require manipulations of compressed video. We have explored the freedom of performing video manipulation in the compressed domain. In specific, we have derived efficient algorithms in the transform domain for many useful video manipulation functions such as overlapping, translation, scaling, pixel multiplication, rotation, and linear filtering. These algorithms can be applied to general orthogonal transforms, like DCT, DFT, and DST. Compared to the spatial-domain approach which converts compressed video back to the spatial domain and manipulates video data in the spatial domain, the proposed transform-domain approach can increase the computation efficiency, with a factor depending on the compression characteristics of the input videos. For hybrid

MC–DCT encoded video, we have proposed a new decoding algorithm to convert the encoded video to the DCT domain and perform manipulation functions in the DCT domain. This new decoding algorithm can also be applied to efficient transcoding from MPEG to JPEG.

We have derived the formulae for estimating the computational complexity of major DCT-domain manipulation algorithms. We have also evaluated the efficiency of the DCT-domain techniques by software simulations. The DCT-domain compositing approach can reduce the required computations by 60%–75% for DCT-compressed images (without MC), 10%–23% for MC–DCT-compressed images in various simulated scenarios without complicated pixel-wise operations (such as pixel-wise translation). If pixel-wise manipulations are incorporated, the efficiency of DCT-domain operations will drop by some extent, depending on the specific manipulation scenarios. Considerations of the recovered video quality and some real-time implementation issues have been discussed as well.

As shown in this study, compression algorithms have significant impact on the efficiency of the video manipulation techniques. Orthogonal transforms provide great flexibility for pursuing manipulation techniques in the transform domain, but nonlinear coding algorithms such as MC do not. The close interplay between the compression algorithms and the manipulation techniques strongly motivates a joint approach to optimal algorithm designs for video compression and manipulation. For example, we may want to compromise some compression performance in order to provide greater flexibility in video compositing and manipulation in the compressed domain. Currently, we are actively working in this area.

REFERENCES

[1] N. Ahmed, T. Natarajan, and K. R. Rao, "Discrete cosine transform," *IEEE Trans. Comput.*, vol. C-23, pp. 90–93, Jan. 1974.
[2] J. A. Bellisio and K.-H. Tzou, "HDTV and the emerging broadband ISDN network," in *SPIE, Visual Commun. Image Processing '88*, vol. 1001, pp. 772–86.
[3] S. C. Chan and K. L. Ho, "A new two-dimensional fast cosine transform algorithms," *IEEE Trans. Signal Processing*, vol. 39, pp. 481–485, Feb. 1991.
[4] S.-F. Chang and D. G. Messerschmitt, "Compositing motion-compensated video within the network," in *IEEE 4th Workshop Multimedia Commun.*, Monterey, CA, Apr. 1992.
[5] S.-F. Chang, W.-L. Chen, and D. G. Messerschmitt, "Video compositing in the DCT domain," in *IEEE Workshop Visual Signal Processing Commun.*, Raleigh, NC, Sept. 1992, pp. 138–143.
[6] S.-F. Chang and D. G. Messerschmitt, "A new approach to decoding and compositing motion compensated DCT-based images," in *IEEE ICASSP*, Minneapolis, MN, Apr. 1993.
[7] S.-F. Chang, "Compositing and manipulation of video signals for multimedia network video services," Ph.D. dissertation, Univ. California at Berkeley, Aug. 1993.
[8] W.-H. Chen, C. H. Smith, and S. C. Fralick, "A fast algorithm for the discrete cosine transform," *IEEE Trans. Commun.*, vol. COM-25, pp. 1004–1009, Sept. 1977.
[9] B. Chiptrasert and K. R. Rao, "Discrete cosine transform filtering," *Signal Processing*, vol. 19, no. 3, pp. 233–245, Mar. 1990.
[10] R. J. Clarke, *Transform Coding of Images.* New York: Academic, 1985.
[11] T. Duff, "Compositing 3-D rendered images," *Siggraph*, vol. 19, Nov. 1985, pp. 41–44.
[12] J. D. Foley, A. V. Dam, S. K. Feiner, and J. F. Hughes, *Computer Graphics: Principles and Practice.* Reading, PA: Addison-Wesley, 1990, 2nd ed.
[13] CCITT Recommendation H.261, "Video codec for audiovisual services at $p \times 64$ kbits/s," 1990.

[14] J. R. Jain and A. K. Jain, "Displacement measurement and its application in interframe image coding," *IEEE Trans. Commun.*, vol. COM-29, pp. 1799–1808, Dec. 1981.

[15] A. Jain, *Fundamentals of Digital Image Processing.* Englewood Cliffs, NJ: Prentice-Hall Inc., 1989.

[16] Standard Draft, JPEG-9-R7, Feb. 1991.

[17] R. K. Jurgen, "The challenges of digital HDTV," *IEEE Spectrum,* pp. 28–30, Apr. 1991.

[18] W. Kou and T. Fjallbrant, "A direct computation of DCT coefficients for a signal block from two adjacent blocks," *IEEE Trans. Signal Processing,* vol. 39, pp. 1692–1695, July 1991.

[19] M. Kunt, A. Ikonmopoulos, and M. Kocher, "Second-generation image coding techniques," *Proc. IEEE,* vol. 73, pp. 549–574, Apr. 1985.

[20] B. G. Lee, "FCT—A fast cosine transform," in *IEEE ICASSP,* San Diego, CA, Mar. 1984, pp. 28A.3.1–28A.3.4.

[21] J. B. Lee and B. G. Lee, "Transform domain filtering based on pipelining structure," *IEEE Trans. Signal Processing,* pp. 2061–2064, vol. 40, Aug. 1992.

[22] Y. Y. Lee and J. W. Woods, "Video post-production with compressed images," *SMPTE J.,* vol. 103, pp. 76–84, Feb. 1994.

[23] D. Le Gall, "MPEG: A video compression standard for multimedia applications," *Commun. ACM,* vol. 34, no. 4, Apr. 1991.

[24] G. G. Langdon and J. Rissanen, "Compression of black-white images with arithmetic coding," *IEEE Trans. Commun.,* June 1981, pp. 858–867.

[25] M. Liou, "Overview of the $p \times 64$ kbits/s video coding standard," *Commun. ACM,* vol. 34, no. 4, Apr. 1991.

[26] M. Lukacs, "An advanced digital network video bridge for multipoint with individual customer control," Bell Commun. Res., NJ, May 1992, private communication.

[27] M. Narasimha and A. Peterson, "On the computation of the discrete cosine transform," *IEEE Trans. Commun.,* vol. COM-26, pp. 934–936, June 1978.

[28] A. N. Netravali and J. D. Robbins, "Motion-compensated television coding: Part I," *Bell Syst. Tech. J.,* vol. 58, no. 3, pp. 631–670, Mar. 1979.

[29] K. N. Ngan and R. J. Clarks, "Lowpass filtering in the cosine transform domain," in *Int. Conf. Commun.,* Seattle, WA, June 1980, pp. 31.7.1–31.7.5.

[30] T. Porter and T. Duff, "Compositing digital images," *Comput. Graph.,* vol. 18, pp. 253–259, 1984.

[31] P. V. Rangan, H. M. Vin, and S. Ramanathan, "Communication architectures and algorithms for media mixing in multimedia Conferences," *IEEE/ACM Trans. Networking,* vol. 1, Feb. 1993.

[32] B. C. Smith and L. Rowe, "Algorithms for manipulating compressed images," *IEEE Comput. Graph. Appl.,* pp. 34–42, Sept. 1993.

[33] G. K. Wallace, "The JPEG still picture compression standard," *Commun. ACM,* vol. 34, no. 4, Apr. 1991.

[34] C. F. R. Weiman, "Continuous anti-allseed rotation and zoom of raster images," in *SIGGRAPH '80,* pp. 286–293.

[35] Standard Draft, MPEG Video Committee Draft, MPEG 90/176 Rev. 2, Dec. 1990.

[36] S. A. Martucci, "Symmetric convolution and the discrete sine and cosine transforms," *IEEE Trans. Signal Processing,* vol. 42, pp. 1038–1051, May, 1994.

[37] S.-F. Chang and A. Eleftheriadis, "Error accumulation in repetitive image coding," in *IEEE Int. Conf. Circuits Syst.,* London, England, May, 1994.

[38] S.-F. Chang, "Some new algorithms for processing images in the transform compressed domain," Tech. Rep. 390-94-37, Columbia University, New York, NY.

Shih-Fu Chang (S'89–M'93) received the B.S.E.E. degree from National Taiwan University in 1985, and the M.S. and Ph.D. degree in electrical engineering and computer sciences from the University of California at Berkeley in 1991 and 1993, respectively.

From 1985 to 1987, he served in the computer center of the Chinese Air Force. In 1988, he was a full-time teaching assistant in the Department of Electrical Engineering, National Taiwan University, where he taught a communication systems laboratory. He worked in Bell Communications Research, Morristown, NJ, in the summer of 1990. In 1993, he joined Department of Electrical Engineering and Center for Telecommunications Research in Columbia University, where he is currently an Assistant Professor. His current research interests include image/video signal processing, multimedia systems and applications, and high-speed VLSI for signal processing. Since he joined Columbia, he has also started working on image databases and video servers in a video on demand testbed.

Dr. Chang was the recipient of the best student paper award of the ACM Multimedia Conference 1993. He serves on the program committees of several international conferences..

David G. Messerschmitt (S'65–M'68–SM'78–F'83) received the B.S. degree from the University of Colorado in 1967, and the M.S. and Ph.D. degrees from the University of Michigan in 1968 and 1971, respectively.

He is a Professor and Chairman of the Department of Electrical Engineering and Computer Sciences at the University of California at Berkeley. Prior to 1977 he was at Bell Laboratories in Holmdel, NJ. Current research interests include signal processing and transport in broadband networks, advanced video services, and computer aided design of communications and signal processing systems using object-oriented programming methodologies. He has served as a consultant to a number of companies.

Dr. Messerschmitt is a Member of the National Academy of Engineering of the United States. He has served as Editor for Transmission of the IEEE TRANSACTIONS ON COMMUNICATIONS, and as a member of the Board of Governors of the Communications Society. He has also organized and participated in a number of short courses and seminars devoted to continuing engineering education.

CHAPTER THREE

Audio Retrieval and Navigation Interfaces

Philippe Aigrain

European Commission[1] INFSO/E2

SELECTING and presenting the essential readings in multimedia cannot be done without some working definition of multimedia research. This requirement is even more obvious when introducing a chapter on audio retrieval and navigation interfaces. For 30 years, some very fine researchers have developed and matured the technologies of speech and music processing; have studied and modeled auditory perception; and have invented ways of analyzing, representing, and synthesizing sound signals. Without these advances, and without more general work on information retrieval and human-computer interaction, none of the papers presented in this chapter could have been written, and their authors would not have even imagined attempting what they have set as a goal. The recent developments of audio retrieval and navigation interfaces, of which this chapter presents highlights, is the history of the meeting between multimedia research and music and speech technology research. In multimedia, we have witnessed the application-driven integration and redefinition of processing technologies with interaction and retrieval techniques. In parallel, in each of the individual fields, researchers have tried to find ways to eliminate the barriers that prevent their techniques from delivering full benefits. For each of the papers reproduced in this chapter, there are important counterparts in specialized speech, music, human-computer interaction, or information

retrieval literature. One of the purposes of this introduction is do pay justice to the preexisting specialized work that has made mutimedia content processing technology possible. The introduction also refers to several papers, in particular in emerging domains, that would have been included in this collection if size limitations had not prevented it. A recent survey of audio retrieval technology, more specifically focused on speech-based processing, can be found in the work of J. Foote [1]. A specific survey of technology and applications of content-based retrieval of music can be found in my paper of 1999 [2].

A SHORT HISTORY

Multimedia research was initially slow to tackle audio retrieval and representation. Part of the reason lies with the privilege of video in the general social imagination of our societies. Whatever measure you use, audio and, in particular, music are no less important than video in terms of business revenues, entertainment and culture, employment, or communication. But attention was focused on video and television. Even within multimedia applied to video and television, the importance of audio soundtrack processing and representation was only very slowly recognized. Nonetheless, if we look back at the initial developments of multimedia, in particular in the context of hypertext, some of the challenges were clearly identified

---

[1]*Views presented in this paper are only the author's and do not necessarily represent the official position of the European Commission.*

early on. Christodoulakis and Graham [3] tried to tackle in a pioneering paper the difficult issue of how to represent sequences of time-based media contents in hypertext navigation interfaces. This line of research has been very fruitful in the moving image domain, in which it led to the mosaic image and video icon techniques for representing a video shot statically. But in the audio world, this remains largely an unsolved problem, and as we will see, recent work seems to point at playback in sound space as a possible alternative to static image representation of a sound sequence.

The next stage of identification of problems was the progressive recognition that the general audio retrieval and navigation category actually covered a number of quite different areas:

- retrieval of and navigation between segments of a sound document
- indexing and retrieval of short individual sounds in sound databases
- retrieval of sound documents in a relatively consistent set of documents (for instance, songs)
- retrieval of and navigation between segments of a video document using audio, speech, or music information
- retrieval by word spotting in speech databases or video databases with speech indexing

The more general problem of unrestricted audio retrieval (for example, "here is a sound extract, find me all similar ones") is still largely unexplored. It is also ill defined, because retrieval can occur only when it is possible to specify the nature and scale of components that are searched for. One of the reasons for multimedia research's success in delivering new technology and finding overlooked potential of existing technology is that it has worked within precisely defined paradigms of usage. This chapter provides the reader with essential references on a variety of these domains.

In recent months (following the selection for papers in this chapter), the main trend has been toward strengthening technique and evaluating them in a more systematic manner. The MPEG-7 standardization effort is playing an important role in that matter, in particular because it has reached the "core experiments" stage. Researchers in this rapidly growing research community are

experimenting with techniques for spoken content retrieval, timbre classification, sound effects classification, and segmentation.

GENERAL SEGMENTATION AND LABELING TECHNIQUES

Hawley [4] was the first to clearly set out a research program for automatically producing structured representations of audio documents that are fit for summarization, indexing, and retrieval. He also suggested some techniques for making first steps in the direction of speech/music discrimination and developed several music indexing features. In line with Hawley's work, the fourth paper in this chapter, "Toward content-based audio indexing and retrieval and a new speaker descrimination technique," by L. Wyse and S. W. Smoliar, originally presented in 1995, describes a number of techniques for segmenting a sound stream or document and associates content-based labels (such as speech/music discrimination and locutor discrimination) with the segments. The notion of a global processing chain for segmenting and labeling audio content has been pursued more recently in work conducted at IRCAM [5].

BROWSING AND NAVIGATING WITHIN A MUSIC DOCUMENT

Video browsing is a well-established domain of multimedia research and is covered in Chapter 5 of this book. What makes video browsers useful is that they provide a structured access and navigation interface for dealing with the opacity of video documents and for coping with their temporal nature. This opacity is even more problematic in the case of audio documents for reasons that can be illustrated by considering the impossibility of stopping on sound[2] while keeping any meaningful hindsight on the contents. The general privilege of visual human-computer interaction also contributes to the problem. As early as in the 19th century, researchers have tried to develop static visual representations of sound productions. This line of work has been particularly active within ethnomusicology [6], and spectrographical imaging [7] and has brought about new developments, including its association with user annotation [8]. When audio content can be associated with a pre-

---

[2]*You can loop on short stationary sound extracts, and this feature can be useful for analyzing some very low-level features, but certainly is not for representing a more general context.*

scriptive representation, whether a musical score or a speech transcript, they can be used as a representation upon which a browsing interface can be based. But this approach faces the extreme difficulty of automatic transcription and also suffers from the fact that the representation hides some important features of the content (for instance, voices for speech or performance for music). Static representations of audio content take all their value when they can be presented at different scales and levels of abstraction and directly associated with sound production.

The first paper in this chapter, "Representation-based user interfaces for the Audiovisual Library of Year 2000,"by myself, P. Joly, P. Lepain, and V. Longueville, proposed a framework for defining music browsers, using a detailed comparison with a similar approach on video. At the time of its writing (1995) some aspects of the paper were still "works in progress," but they were further evolved into a complete piece of software [9], that was experimentally used by music specialists [10]. One key challenge for establishing a realistic parallel between video and music browsing and indexing is the ability to define significant segments in music, which can then be used as units for representation, interaction (for instance, selection and gravity), navigation, and matching.

MELODY RETRIEVAL AND THE KARAOKE PROBLEM

Querying for a given melodic *motif* is a problem that has attracted many researchers, for reasons that arise from the privilege that Western music gives to pitch and melody. The Karaoke situation has provided a simplified context in which this problem could be explored. In this context a singer hums a melody (or starts singing it) and the system is supposed to answer by recognizing which song is being sung and by then providing the corresponding musical accompaniment. Japanese research laboratories started work on this problem in the early 1990s, and an example of such work was reported in by Kageyama and colleagues [11]. A query-by-humming system consists of a pitch tracker (including segmentation in notes) and a matching algorithm in a database of melodies. Approximate matching has to be used, to deal with deletions or

insertions of notes resulting from ornamentation or simply from errors of either the singer or the pitch-tracking algorithm. The representation of the melody to be matched is also an essential aspect. The melody is always represented as a sequence of relative intervals to make it independent of key changes. Kageyama et al. used intervals expressed in semi-tones and computed a matching distance using the number of matches with one semi-tone difference. The second paper in this chapter "Query by humming: Music information retrieval in an audio database," by A. Ghias and colleagues, describes a technique using melodic contour (that is, a succession of up and down or zero intervals that ignores the size of the up and down intervals). Researchers in auditory perception have pointed out that melodic contour is indeed an essential representation for the human matching of melodies [12]. Ghias and colleagues also proposed a simple evaluation framework. In these simplified contexts, the melody database is monophonic. Of course the next challenge is to be able to match against polyphonic content. Assuming that polyphonic pitch detection is available[3], querying for melodies—from an example or humming—calls for extracting some salient melody either by voice segregation, such as that proposed by Uitdenbogerd and Zobel [13] or by harmonic analysis. Matching in the presence of ornamentation and other modifications to the searched motif, or matching using rules that fit whose structure and tonality varies greatly from that of Western music are difficult challenges. Melodic matching in large databases of musical recordings is still very much unexplored, and we presently lack a clear idea of the scalability of the existing methods. Most recent approaches aim at matching multiple features rather than melodic information only.

RETRIEVAL IN SOUND DATABASES

Content-based retrieval in large audio databases is an easier problem for databases of short sounds, such as the Foley sounds that are used for soundtracks in video or film. The third paper in this chapter, "Content-based classification, search, and retrieval of audio," by E. Wold and colleagues, reports work conducted within the company Muscle Fish. Wold and colleagues use

---

[3] *See the* Journal of New Music Research *special issue,* Content Processing of Music for Multimedia Application 27, *no. 4 (1999), for a review and a number of state-of-the-art papers on the subject.*

multiple features to index short sounds. The choice of features is based on psychoacoustical knowledge, and classification/retrieval is based on classical data analysis techniques. The paper discusses integration with browsers and databases and contains a short discussion of the extension of the proposed methods to retrieval of longer sounds (phrases, video soundtracks, raw audio). A preliminary version of the paper appeared as a communication at the IJCAI '95 Workshop on Intelligent Multimedia Information Retrieval and was also published in 1997 [14]. Multifeature indexing is being extended in recent work to enable the identification of pre-indexed musical recordings from a short extract. For an example, see the RAA project Web site [15]. This process has applications in intellectual property rights management, online music sales, and musical archives.

INDEXING AND NAVIGATING VIDEO SOUNDTRACKS

Researchers long recognized that the audio soundtrack of video contains essential information for retrieval of relevant sequences. In the first paper in the chapter: Aigrain and colleagues proposed the representation of the audio track in a video browser based on classification of music, speech, and noise segments. Shahraray and Gibbon [16] and Maybury and colleagues [17] demonstrated the potential of speech transcripts such as closed captions for browsing, retrieval ,and summarization. But it was through work initiated in 1995 within the Informedia project at Carnegie-Mellon [18], through research on video browsers at FX-PAL [19], and through the Virage Audio logger™ [20] (using technologies from IBM and Muscle Fish) that audio soundtrack information truly became integrated in video indexing and browsing.

RETRIEVAL IN SPEECH DATABASES

Retrieval in speech databases was first explored on real-scale databases for single-speaker databases, using speaker-dependent training of Hidden Markov Models. The fifth paper in this chapter, "Open-vocabulary speech indexing for voice and video mail retrieval," by M.G. Brown and colleagues, generalized these techniques to obtain speaker-independent word spotting capabilities on open-vocabulary databases. In the case of this paper, these techniques are used for indexing and retrieval in voice and video mail systems. Similar techniques

were developed by Meteer and colleagues [21] at BBN/GTE and integrated in applications such as broadcast news soundtrack retrieval.

BROWSING IN SOUND SPACE AND SONIC BROWSING

Sound spatialization techniques open new dimensions to listening. The first obvious application is to allow the listener to explore sound space itself, for instance, by moving closer to some sound sources. Pachet and Delerue [22] have developed an intriguing interactive listening system based on constrained control of a sound spatialization system. The constraints express, for instance, the need to maintain some balance between sound sources. Browsing musical spaces can also be used for sound information retrieval. Fernstrom and Bannon [23] have proposed an approach to sonic browsing with a clear generic potential, though its range of applicability remains to be explored. Sound documents (for instance musical recordings) are analyzed and the features extracted are projected in 3-D space. A document becomes a point in this space, which is assumed to be absorbent for sound. The user can then browse through this space, using a sound spatializer, hearing each document with intensity according to its distance. The quality of such browsing interfaces rests on the relevance of the extracted features and on the ability of the user to navigate meaningfully in the projected feature space.

CONCLUSION

Despite recent developments, content-based retrieval of audio still faces major challenges. Efficient indexing and retrieval for large databases of music and for speech databases with many different locutors has still to be demonstrated. An approach combining navigation techniques and query/retrieval techniques is still in its infancy. Nevertheless, a core set of techniques has been developed, from which more systematic work can proceed.

REFERENCES

[1] J. Foote, "An overview of audio retrieval," *Multimedia Systems* 7, no. 1 (1999): 2–10.

[2] P. Aigrain, "New applications of content processing of music," *Journal of New Music*

Research 28, no. 4 (1999): 271–80.

[3] S. Christodoulakis and S. Graham, "Browsing within time-driven multimedia documents," *ACM SIG-OIS* 9, nos. 2–3 (1988): 219–27.

[4] M. Hawley, "Structure out of sound," Ph. D. dissertation Cambridge: MIT Media Lab, 1993.

[5] S. Rossignol, X. Rodet, J. Soumagne, J-L. Colette, and P. Depalle, "Automatic characterization of musical signals: Feature extraction and temporal segmentation," *Journal of New Music Research* 28, no. 4 (1999): 281-295.

[6] T. Ellington, "Transcription," in H. Myers, ed., *Ethno-Musicology: An Introduction* (London: W.W. Norton, 1992), 110–52.

[7] R. Cogan, *New Images of Musical Sounds* (Cambridge: Harvard University Press, 1984).

[8] D. Besson, "La transcription des musiques électro-acoustiques: Que noter, comment et pourquoi," *Analyse Musicale* 24 (1991): 37–41.

[9] P. Lepain, "SATIE: An interactive software for listening to musical recordings," in *Proceedings of the 4th ACM International Multimedia Conference* (ACM, 1996): 413–14.

[10] P. Aigrain, and P. Lepain, "Le groupe Ecoute Interactive de la Musique de la Bibliothèque Nationale de France," *Actes des Journées d'Informatique Musicale*, (May 1996): 128–38).

[11] T. Kageyama, K. Mochisuki, and Y. Takashima, "Melody retrieval by humming," in *Proceedings of the International Computer Music Conference 1993* (San Francisco: International Computer Music Association, 1993), 349–51.

[12] S. Handel, *Listening: An introduction to the perception of auditory events* (Cambridge: MIT Press, 1989).

[13] A. Uitdenbogerd and J. Zobel "Manipulation of music for melody matching," in *Proceedings of the 6th ACM International Multimedia Conference* (ACM, 1998), 235–40.

[14] T. Blum, D. Keislar, J. Wheaton, and E. Wold, "Audio databases with content-based retrieval," in Mark Maybury, ed., *Intelligent Multimedia Information Retrieval* (AAAI Press/MIT Press, 1997), 113–35.

[15] RAA, http://raa.joanneum.ac.at, 2000.

[16] B. Shahraray and D. C. Gibbon "Automatic generation of pictorial transcripts of video programs," in *Proceedings of the IS&T/SPIE 95—Digital Video Compression: Algorithms and Technologies*, SPIE proceedings 2419, 512–19.

[17] M. Maybury, A. Merlino, and D. Morey, "Broadcast news navigation using story segments," in *Proceedings of the 5th ACM International Multimedia Conference* (ACM, 1997), 381–91.

[18] A. G. Hauptmann and M. J. Witbrock, *Informedia News-On-Demand: Using Speech Recognition to Create a Digital Video Library*, http://www.informedia.cs.cmu.edu/pubs/aaai-info-haupt.pdf, 1997.

[19] J. Foote, J. Borecsky, A.Girgensohn, and L. Wilcox, "An intelligent media browser using multimodal analysis," in *Proceedings of the 6th ACM International Multimedia Conference* (1998), 375–80.

[20] Virage, http://www.virage.com/products/audi-ologger.html, 1999.[23] M. Fernstrom, and L. Bannon, "Explorations in sonic browsing," *Proceedings of HCI 97* (1997). http://www.ul.ie/~idc/library/papersreports/MikaelFernstrom/hciuk97/sonicbrowse.html.

[21] M. Meteer, H. Gish, F. Kubala, R. Schwartz, and R. Weischedel, "Gisting gets the most out of your speech in the least amount of time," *Speech Technology Magazine* 13 (June–July 1998): http://www.speechtechmag.com/st13/justfact.htm

[22] F. Pachet and O. Delerue, "MidiSpace: A constraint-based music spatializer," in *Proceedings of the 6th ACM International Multimedia Conference* (ACM, 1998), 351–60.

Representation-based user interfaces for the audiovisual library of year 2000

Philippe Aigrain *   Philippe Joly   Philippe Lepain
Véronique Longueville

Institut de Recherche en Informatique de Toulouse
Université Paul Sabatier
118, route de Narbonne
31062 Toulouse Cedex, France
e-mail: aigrain@irit.fr

ABSTRACT

The audiovisual library of the future will be based on computerized access to digitized documents. In this communication, we address the user interface issues which will arise from this new situation. One cannot simply transfer an user interface designed for the piece by piece production of some audiovisual presentation and make it a tool for accessing full-length movies in an electronic library. One cannot take a digital sound editing tool and propose it as a means to listen to a musical recording. In our opinion, when computers are used as mediations to existing contents, document representation-based user interfaces are needed. With such user interfaces, a structured visual representation of the document contents is presented to the user, who can then manipulate it to control perception and analysis of these contents. In order to build such manipulable visual representations of audiovisual documents, one needs to automatically extract structural information from the documents contents. In this communication, we describe possible visual interfaces for various temporal media, and we propose methods for the economically feasible large scale processing of documents. The work presented is sponsored by the Bibliothèque Nationale de France: it is part of the program aiming at developing for image and sound documents an experimental counterpart to the digitized text reading workstation of this library.[21]

Keywords: digital library, human-computer interface, document representation, motion picture, music, speech, multi-media, segmentation, digital signal processing, editing

---

*This research was conducted under support from the french Ministère de la Culture et de la Francophonie.

1   RATIONALE FOR A DISCRETE-REPRESENTATION-BASED HUMAN COMPUTER INTERFACE

1.1   An example of discrete manipulable audiovisual document representation interface

Let us start with one example. Figure 1 is a screen copy from a prototype user interface for interactive listening to musical documents which is currently being designed and implemented in our research team. The first and third author have given more complete presentations of some aspects of this work.[1,12] Section 3 summarizes the present state of our developments for various media.

The visual interface is organized in horizontal strips. In each strip the horizontal direction represents a time-line (left to right): the lower strip is indeed the time-line itself. The upper strip is what we call a frequential view of the musical recording because it is primarily organized by studying the evolution of frequential components of the musical recording. The lower strip is what we call a dynamical view of the musical recording because it is primarily organized by analyzing the evolution of the sound dynamics. At first, one may think this to be classical: waveform or amplitude representations of musical signals, as well as sonographical or spectrographical representations are found in many sound editors, and are even part of the basic software of present-day workstations. Let us give a closer look at our visual interface. In both the dynamical and frequential strips, the vertical dimension uses a logarithmical scale, which is better adapted to the corresponding perceptive phenomena than linear scale, and this is still quite usual. But what is displayed? Instead of the classical semi-continuous representation of a function, we find discrete objects: temporal chunks.

The delimitation of these objects is the result of an automatical analysis performed on the document, and may be adjusted by the user. Each of these objects can be selected, "played", the user can control how its representation is displayed, or can define a temporal program for the controlled playback of several objects in succession or alternance. Moreover, in the dynamical strip, elementary objects are aggregated into larger objects in time: there is a hierarchy of objects ranging from what we call *strokes* (elementary objets at the scale of one musical note or chord or of a section of a musical note for sustained sound, and lasting from 100 ms to a few seconds) to what we call *patterns* (temporal objects containing one to maybe 100 strokes, and whose duration is in the range of 1 to 15 seconds) and up to large *sections* of 5 seconds to several minutes, delimited by silences and/or scansions. The entry level for user selection is the pattern: a single mouse click will select the pattern, a double-click will select the whole section of which the pattern is a part. Strokes are not directly accessible: there are used to build the visual representation of a pattern, or when the user modifies its temporal limits.

Temporal chunks are also defined in the frequential line. What is represented is not the presence of energy at a given frequency but an explanation of the humanly perceived frequencies by fundamental frequencies. The third author[12] has showed how such an explanation can be achieved while preserving the correct display of inharmonic or diffuse sounds.

There is a wide range of user parametrization of the visual representation. In particular, the user may choose the degree of detail vs abstraction of this representation. This possibility, in association with the multi-scale nature of the interface is particularly useful in order to switch from a panoramical view of several minutes of a recording to the detailed analysis of a small extract. Colour is used in the dynamical strip to illustrate the fundamental frequencies of dynamical objects: the visible light spectrum is associated to sound frequencies with blue = bass, green = medium, yellow-red = treble. This use of colour is optional and the user can also choose at which temporal scale it is applied (individual colouring of pixels, of strokes or of patterns).

We are also working on other possible strips, such as meter strip, which would provide an assistance for the positionning of bar limits for metered music or timbre strip showing the entry and exit of instruments. As we will see below, there have been many precursors to such discrete manipulable representations of audiovisual documents, most notably in the video virtual editing world. The focus of this communication is to illustrate what is needed to systematize this approach, and what can be gained from doing so.

1.2 "Classical" user interfaces

Let us consider a scholar using a multi-media workstation connected to an electronic library. He or she can access thousands of sound or image documents stored in the library computerized archives (as well as textual documents, of course). But what does "access" mean? As of today, in most cases it means selecting documents from an on-line public access catalog (OPAC), and viewing them or listening to them one by one. While our scholar is accessing one document, in most cases he or she is presently provided with a virtual tape player interface: on the screen a panel of buttons of the virtual tape player is represented, and the user navigates through the document contents by selecting (with a mouse or touchscreen) the virtual buttons for "play"/"pause", "fast forward" or "fast reverse". With little extra-sophistication a scrollbar with a cursor indicating the "present" position in the document can be provided, and one can directly access some relative position in the document duration by positioning this cursor. When the document can be seen as a function of time, as it is the case for audio, it is also easy to associate with it the display of a graph of this function, generally undersampled. The user can then select parts of the document by selecting parts of this graph.

In hypermedia systems and toolkits such as Intermedia,[22,8] some form of visual selection of documents is possible apart from the use of the catalog. Image and sound documents are then represented by icons: the first image of a moving image document, for instance, or an icon representing lips with the short name of the document for a speech document.

For computer assisted learning and multimedia "presentation" in general, the document can often be seen as elementary audiovisual components connected by a directed graph representing their semantic and temporal dependencies. Stavros Christodoulakis and Stephen Graham[6] proposed in their paper "Browsing within time-driven multimedia documents" to represent such documents using one icon for each component, and time-lines and "icon parades" for representation and navigation in the document. This has become usual for "presentation" software. This type of work is limited in two ways: it adresses only the case of contents constituted of small time-driven "bricks" semantically connected and not the case of real length existing time-driven documents such as a feature film or the recording of an opera, and it adresses the representation of moving image documents much better than the representation of sound documents. This last point is easy to account for: the visual representation of a visual medium is easier than the visual representation of an auditory medium. These are the limitations we are trying to overcome.

1.3 Discrete manipulable audiovisual document representation user interfaces

Alan Parkes[16] introduced the idea of manipulable inter-medium encodings, i.e. representation of an audiovisual document in some other medium, providing the user with the ability to manipulate (for instance control the display) the contents of the document by ways of manipulating its representation in the other medium. Generally the representation medium is more static and thus graphical or still image based. This idea generalizes the icon representation of manipulable objects introduced by the Xerox® Star™ user interface[17] and popularized by the Apple® Macintosh™. Not only is the object represented globally by one icon, but the structure of its contents is "translated", "abstracted": a part to part bijection exists between components of the representation and components of the contents. We will mention pioneering work for each medium (often prior to Parkes' explicitation) in the corresponding parts of section 2. Let us try here to characterize the necessary properties of a manipulable representation of a time-based document by 7 words: discrete, objective, informative, multi-scale, multi-angle, affordable, consistent.

1. *Discrete:* We call discrete representation a representation organized in "chunks", corresponding to segments of the contents which can be selected as a whole by a single action and which are at the scale of human perception. A waveform, for instance, is not discrete in our meaning, even if the waveform of a digital recording is a discrete collection of samples, because a single sample cannot be perceived: it is not at the scale of human perception. Remark that the discrete objects composing the representation may segment the contents in several dimensions (for instance time, image space, colour space, frequency space, or any conceivible semantic dimension as long as it relates clearly to perception of contents). The superiority of discrete representations over continuous representation lies in manipulability. Of course it is always possible to ask the user to delimitate himself on some "continuous" representation a segment which will then become manipulable. But the fine tuning of these limits for a time-driven document is a tedious process, and it is much better if the representation can be pre-organized in selectable objects, provided of course that these objects are significant.

2. *Objective:* What kind of components should we try to recognize in the contents of an audiovisual document? It is critical here to remind the reader that the structural representation we are trying to build is a mediation with the contents and not an interpretation or a substitute to the contents. It is for the user to analyze, assign meaning. Moreover we want the representation to be appliable for all types of documents in a given medium, and we do not want to convey the particular conventions or biases of a given school of thought. For instance, for musical documents we want the representation to be adequate for all types of music (or at least to specify clearly to which types of music it can be applied) and we do not want it to be specific of a particular school of musicology. Such generality and objectivity is probably impossible to attain, but there is a good strategy for approaching it, namely to use concepts borrowed essentially from the analysis of elementary structures of perception and from the "production" mechanism of documents (production being used here in the general meaning of "all activities and physical phenomena having lead to the obtention of the existing document").

3. *Informative:* A discrete representation is in some way an abstraction of the contents: the segmentation itself reduces the contents to a limited number of higher level objects. But this abstraction must not hide the significant properties of each object. On the contrary it must ensure that they become more lisible. This will be the case only if the graphical representation of the object is detailed enough to display these properties. There is a necessary trade-off between the quality of the overall structural representation, calling for simplicity in the representation of each component, and the detail allowable for each component. Moreover, the level of detail of information to be displayed for a given object cannot be uniquely defined. Depending on his or her interests at a given moment a user might prefer to see a "smoothe" representation making visible only the general "shape" of an object or on the contrary insist on the full detail insight. User parametrization is thus essential to this issue.

4. *Multi-scale:* While accessing the contents of an audiovisual document, one focuses on objects lying at a very different scale. For instance, one will try to locate some scene in a movie, and then view it repetitively, focus on some short passage, try to analyze how the director designed it, think of another passage with a similar character and try to locate it in the movie (remembering only that it is much earlier in the movie), view it, and so on. The visual representation needed in order to locate a scene in the whole movie, and the visual representation used while analyzing precisely a passage made of 2 or 3 shots must adapt to this change of scale of the focus of attention. Thus, it is necessary not only to recognize elementary components, but also to be able to aggregate them in larger components or to recognize these larger components directly by some other method. Whether small scale (large scope) representations and large scale (focus on a small part) representations should be displayed simultaneously or not is a user interface design choice resulting into difficult compromises between the limitations of screen space and the ergonomy of the interface. The other meaning of the word scale, i.e. the choice of a graduation for a coordinate also raises difficult issues: should it be linear, logarithmic, symbolic? Once more, going back to the characteristics of the perception of the related variable will often provide the answer.

5. *Multi-angle:*Screen space is essentially 2D-space, even if one can use conventions for the representation of 3D-space on a 2D-surface. To these spatial dimensions luminosity or colour of pixels adds a third dimension, but with a lower discrimination ability for the user. As stated above, the contents of audiovisual documents is multi-dimensionnal. For instance, music can be represented in the time / frequency / energy domain, which is 3D. A movie is 3D at least for the image part (2D for each image and one for time), but the soundtrack adds a number of other dimensions. There is a great number of possible semantic dimensions. The multidimensional character of multimedia has been recognized and taken in account in the dimension concept of Muse,[8,14] for instance. As shown in the example of section 1.1, our approach to the visual representation of audiovisual documents is to use for each document a number of strips in the representation. Each strip defines a particular angle of view on the contents by projecting it in a 2D-space, with a limited use of luminance or colour for the representation of a 3rd coordinate. A special treatment of time is sometimes necessary, for instance for the image component of video. The coexistence of various angles on the same contents provides the user with interesting clues.

6. *Affordable:* This is maybe the key issue. One can make wonderful prototypes by spending 6 months to build the visual representation of some movie or the transcription of some musical recording. But this type of representation will never make it in the library world, where one is faced with thousands of documents. When putting together an electronic library, transferring documents to machine accessible form, cataloguing and indexing them can account for as much as 90

The relation between compression and content analysis is complex: most compression techniques use some kind of content analysis the results of which may prove to be useful for building a visual representation (for instance motion estimation in MPEG or frequency band analysis in the MPEG I and II audio codecs). But most often this information is not readily accessible in the compressed document (because of coding) and is not complete enough. Even more, it can become more difficult to do some type of content analysis on a compressed document: for instance timbre analysis becomes more difficult on a document compressed by a psycho-acoustic masking based method such as MPEG-audio.

7. *Consistent (for one document, one medium, various media):* The library user is at the same time a novice and an expert. He or she must be able to get hold of the user interface which is often new to him within a short learning time. He or she is often familiar with many ways of representing documents, both before their making (prescritive representations such as musical scores, scenarios or storyboards) and after their making (descriptive representations). This familiarity can be used for the building of metaphors in the interface, but can also lead to confusions. Consistency is necessary to ensure ease of learning. Consistency in the representation of a single document seems to be a prerequisite, but is not always so easy to attain when one wants to optimize the scope of the representation by adapting for instance the time-scale to changes in the density of significant objects. Consistency in the representation of various documents of the same medium is essential for the sake of comparative perception, which will maybe be the major benefit resulting from computerized access to temporal documents. It can be difficult to obtain when scales which are relative to one document are used (for pitch or for time-scales for instance). Consistency in the representation of various media can only be obtained at an abstract level, of which this communication is trying to set the basis.

2   DISCRETE MANIPULABLE REPRESENTATIONS FOR TEMPORAL MEDIA

2.1   Moving image documents

Building a manipulable representation for a moving image document is in some way a reverse editing process. Virtual video editing software provides the answer to some of the key questions concerning the choice of units for the representation. For the image part of moving image documents, the choice of the lower level temporal units is simple: the image is clearly the smaller independently perceptible temporal unit, and the shot or sequence shot (seemingly continuous filming from one camera) and transitions effects between shots are clearly the good choices for the just higher level aggregates. Many researchers have proposed algorithms for the recognition of shot change, first only for cut transitions[15,20,19] and later for recognition of shot change even through smooth transitions effects,[24,2] the full editing analysis including transition effects recognition being done by our method in real-time on present-day multimedia workstations.[2]

The building of one icon for the representation of a shot raises some difficult issues: how must one choose a representative image in the shot? Can we associate graphical signs to the icon to indicate the type of shot (camera motion and optical changes) and/or motion of objects, or should we modify the shape of the representant image like was proposed by A. Akutsu et el.[4]? The full optical flow analysis being too complex, Akihiro Akutsu et Yoshinobu Tonomura[3] and our own research team[10,9] have proposed methods based on tomography techniques for the efficient analysis of camera work and related fine grain time segmentation of a shot. Should we represent the time-length of a shot by the depth of a pseudo-3D icon built around the representative image or by the distance separating representative images?

In Figure 2, one will find an example of visual interface for interactive viewing of moving image documents developed in our research team. We have chosen to represent each shot by the second image of the shot, to associate with it a 3D-icon whose depth represents the time-length of the shot, to create a separate strip for the transition effects icons. We have not implemented optical flow analysis in the basic representation: the user will have to explicitly request analysis on a segment of the document to obtained a detailed representation of camera effects and object motion. These choices result from a compromise between simplicity of the analysis and quality of the user interface.

Since there can be 800 to 1500 shots in a full-length feature film, we clearly need to build higher level aggregates for user navigation in the document. Sequences (contiguous shots sharing the same environment and narrative setting) or scenes (not necessarily contiguous shots sharing the same environement and narrative setting) would be the ideal macroscopic units. Our own experiments have shown that it is a long process to manually aggregate shots (represented by one image) into sequences. Our approach is to automatically create a high-level segmentation into sequences and have the user modify it if necessary. Unlike some researchers who have developed specific models for some types of documents such as TV news,[23] we propose a general technique for the segmentation in sequences based on the combination of 5 methods:

- Recognition of repetition of similar shots in a limited window of 4 shots. Recognition of repetitions of shots was described by Oliver Koechlin [11] with a different purpose: the elimination of redundant shots in the visual abstract of a movie. In our approach, recognition of shot repetition is achieved by comparing representant images - which is efficient mostly for repetition of still shots, for instance in shot / reverse shot filming - as well as by comparing the last image of one shot with the first image of the next shot.

- Analysis of parameters, such as hue distribution for colour documents, which when constant over consecutive shots are likely to indicate that they belong to the same sequence.

- Recognition of transitions effects which are likely to indicate sequence change (a single cross-dissolve or wipe in the middle of a sequence of cut transitions either indicates sequence change or a particularly important shot in a sequence) or on the contrary indicate continuity in one sequence (several - more than 2 - cross-dissolves or wipes in the middle of a sequence of cut transitions).

- Analysis of editing rhythm: one builds a model predicting the duration of the next shot as a linear combination of the duration of the two preceding shots. A rupture in the parameters of this model is taken as indicating the likeliness of a sequence change.

- Analysis of soundtrack: apparition of music after a section without music is considered as an indication of probable sequence change.

The results of these 5 analysis can be combined to compute the likeliness of scene change between any two consecutive shots. A broad segmentation in sequences can thus be obtained. It remains then to elect one or two representative shots in each sequence: when shot repetition occurs in a sequence, the representative shots should be taken as the most frequently repeated shots, otherwise possible strategies include election of the longest and the shortest shot, or of the middle shot. Using these representative shots, one can build a storyboard-type presentation of the complete movie. Direct positionning in the more detailed representation of the document is then possible simply by selecting one of these sequence images. Ideally, one would like to be able to display all sequence images simultaneously on the screen, but some feature films include 100 sequences which calls for several screen pages. In our present software (cf Figure 2), sequences are represented by a single image in the "sequence window".

Soundtrack analysis and representation is very important for access interfaces to moving image documents: as illustrated in Figure 2, we wish to address it by performing a simple segmentation into blocks classified as "speech", "music", or "intense natural noise". In our present software, labelling of blocks as speech, music or noise (or several of these at the same time) is done "manually". We are conducting research on an automatic labelling program: speech/music discrimination in the absence of noise can be done efficiently, but when some coloured noise is present it can become difficult.

2.2   Musical recordings

A detailed presentation of a possible manipulable representation for musical recordings has been made in section 1.1. In this section, we will focus on the underlying analysis process. Apart from "harmonic grouping", already discussed in section 1.1, the essential task is temporal segmentation. Specialists of music perception have extensively discussed temporal segmentation or grouping.[7,13,18] An important work has been necessary in order to extract from these theories some methods for automatic segmentation which are not specific of tonal music, and which are computationally feasible. Our approach is to construct independant segmentations for each of our strips, each of them using a common initial micro-segmentation.

The segmentation process starts by performing a micro-segmentation and labelling of micro-segments: two different types of analysis are combined to reach these result. A micro-segmentation is performed by detecting ruptures in an autoregressive model of the signal,[5] and labelling is performed by studying the micro-segment durations and by comparison with the dynamics, using the smoothed sum of absolute values of amplitudes in successive 20 milli-seconds windows. Much more sophisticated labelling could be used, based for instance on spectral analysis.

For time segments in the dynamical strip, limits of strokes are recognized as local minima in this smoothed amplitude. Limits of patterns are detected using Lerdahl-like rules adapted in order to constitute numerical decision procedures using the micro-segments labels and durations as data. We will be conducting experiments in order to evaluate the semantic quality of the segments built by this procedure. Segmentation in macroscopic sections is an independant process based on adaptative detection of silences or scansions.

For the frequntial strip, we first perform harmonic grouping on micro-segments labelled as likely to present the characteristics of stationarity which will permit a correct functioning of the detection of fundamentals algorithm used for harmonic grouping. Temporal segmentation is then performed by detecting ruptures in the fundamental components which are present: a time limit is detected when a relatively stable composition on several dynamical strokes is followed by sudden change. At a further stage, we are planning to try to perform some kind of stream segregation and motive repetition detection in order to define more musically valuable time segments in the frequential line.

Segmentation for other representation strips such as timbre strip, meter strip, or what we call spatial strip (a representation of stereo, surround or echo effects) can be conducted at each time in reference to the evolution of significant parameters for this view angle. We are only at the beginning of a long-term research program concerning segmentation of musical recordings along specific angles of study. This program is conducted in collaboration with the Acoustic Research Commission of the Austrian Academy of Sciences in Vienna. Section 3 summarizes the present state of our work.

2.3   Speech documents

We will describe manipulable representations for speech documents only briefly, since our own research work does not concern speech, except for moving image soundtracks. Nonetheless, we would like to outline possible levels of representation, ranging from the simple segmentation in unlabelled speech blocks by silence detection, such as it is performed in Audiotool 3.0 from Sun Microsystems® to the ideal but unpracticable full speech recognition.

One interesting intermediate level would be locutor labelled speech blocks, based on locutor recognition by example. The user would identify some speech blocks as produced by some locutor and the system would try to recognize other blocks produced by the same locutor. The classical multi-locutor identification techniques have to be adapted to function when no standard sentences are available for calibration. The quality of results that can be achieved is still unclear, but it should be noted that performances which would be inacceptable in a locutor identification task (80 % correct identification for instance) would still be very useful for user navigation in a spoken document.

3   SUMMARY OF AUTOMATIC ANALYSIS WORK FOR DISCRETE MANIPULATION INTERFACES

.sequence-shot and shot detection including transition effects recognition	.performed in our integrated software
.camera work-based micro-segmentation and representative image choice	.actually performed in our software
.macro-segmentation in sequences	.automatical methods have been proposed (including in this paper) but our present software requires user grouping of shots
.detection of speech and music	.patented methods exist, a method has been tested in our team which is efficient in the absence of noise
.other feature detections	.automated detection for features such as shot types (wide, head shot, etc), dominant textures (grass, roads, face skin) have been proposed or seem achievable

Table 1: Status of our auto-segmentation work for moving image documents

Tables 1 and 2 summarize the present state of our work in automatic content analysis and related segmentations. It should be noted that we are aware of the fact that full automatic structural data acquisition is still some way off, but we claim that even the present state of automatic segmentation make discrete manipulation user interfaces viable.

.micro-segmentation and labelling	.performed in our software
.dynamical segmentation	.performed in our software
.harmonic grouping	.performed in our software
.frequential segmentation	.only simple frequential segmentation has been tested in our team, stream segregation and motive repetition-based segmentation is planned
.timbre segmentation	.detection of entry and exit of broad classes of instruments seems achievable
.meter analysis for metered music	.assisted segmentation in bars planned and highly desirable but not performed in our present software

Table 2: Status of our auto-segmentation work for musical recordings

4 CONCLUSION: IMPLEMENTING MANIPULABLE DOCUMENT-REPRESENTATION USER INTERFACE

We have presented possible choices for the construction of manipulable visual representation for various temporal media. Our objective is to automatically generate the corresponding user interfaces from data describing the objects in the representation. We are implementing manipulable representation user interfaces in the X / O.S.F. Motif environment on 2 types of platforms: Sun® SparcStations™ with Parallax Graphics® X-Video™, and Silicon Graphics® Indy™ workstations. These implementations do not use one-to-one correspondance between representation objects and interface objects: interface objects are associated to views on the representation and manage data concerning visible representation objects. Finally, let us remark that the type of multi-hierarchical segmentation which we are promoting fits very well in the SGML-based standards for encoding of audiovisual media documents (SMDL, Hytime).

5 REFERENCES

[1] Philippe Aigrain. Segmentation de documents musicaux en vue de leur consultation et de leur analyse. In *Actes du séminaire Musique et Informatique Marseille*. MIM, 1994.

[2] Philippe Aigrain and Philippe Joly. The automatic real-time analysis of film editing and transition effects and its applications. *Computers & Graphics*, 18(1):93–103, January-February 1994.

[3] Akihito Akutsu and Yoshinobu Tonomura. Video tomography: An efficient method for camerawork extraction and motion analysis. In *Proc. A.C.M. Multimedia Conference*, San Francisco, October 1994. A.C.M.

[4] Akihito Akutsu, Yoshinobu Tonomura, Hideo Hashimoto, and Yuji Ohba. Video indexing using motion vectors. In *Proc. Visual Communication and Image Processing*, volume 1818 of *SPIE*, pages 1522–1530, Amsterdam, 1992. SPIE.

[5] Régine André-Obrecht. A new statistical approach for the automatic segmentation of continuous speech signals. *IEEE Trans. On Acoustic Signals and Signal Processing*, 36(1):29–40, January 1988.

[6] Stavros Christodoulakis and Stephen Graham. Browsing within time-driven multimedia documents. *ACM SIG-OIS*, 9(2–3):219–227, 1988.

[7] Stephen Handel. *Listening: An Introduction to the Perception of Auditory Events*. MIT Press, 1989.

[8] Matthew E. Hodges, Russell M. Sassnett, and Mark S. Ackerman. A construction set for multimedia applications. *IEEE Software*, pages 37–43, January 1989.

[9] Philippe Joly and Hae-Kwang Kim. Efficient automatic analysis of camera work and micro-segmentation of video using spatio-temporal images. Technical report, submitted to Image Communication special issue on Image and Video Semantics: Processing, Analysis and Application, 1995.

[10] Hae-Kwang Kim. Analyse et représentation des mouvements de caméra dans un document en image animée numérique. rapport de recherche 94-33R, IRIT, Université Paul Sabatier, Toulouse, France, Septembre 1994.

[11] Olivier Koechlin. L'analyse automatique de l'image: Vers un traitement du contenu. *Dossiers de l'Audiovisuel*, 45:76–82, 1992.

[12] Philippe Lepain. Extraction de fréquences fondamentales d'un document musical pour sa représentation dans un système de consultation interactif. In *Actes des Journées d'Informatique Musicale*, LaBRI, Bordeaux, Mars 1994.

[13] F. Lerdahl and R. Jackendoff. *A Generative Theory of Tonal Music*. MIT Press, 1983.

[14] Wendy E. Mackay and Glorianna Davenport. Virtual video editing in interactive multimedia applications. *Communciations of the A.C.M.*, 32(9), July 1989.

[15] A. Nagasaka and Y. Tanaka. Automatic scene-change detection method for video works. In E. Knuth and I.M. Wegener, editors, *Proc. 40th National Con. Information Processing Sciety of Japan*, 1990.

[16] Alan P. Parkes. Manipulable inter-medium encodings for information retrieval. In *Proc. RIAO'91 Conference*, Barcelona, Spain, April 1991. CID.

[17] D. C. Smith, E. Harslem, C. Irby, R. Kimball, and B. Verplank. Designing the star user interface. *Byte*, pages 242–280, April 1982.

[18] Lasse Thoresen. Un modèle d'analyse auditive. *Analyse Musicale*, 1:44–60, 1985.

[19] Yoshinobu Tonomura. Video handling based on structure information for hypermedia systems. In *Proc. Int. Conf. Multimedia Information Systems*, pages 333–344, Singapore, 1991.

[20] H. Ueda, T. Miyatake, and S. Yoshisawa. Impact: An interactive natural-motion-picture dedicated multimedia authoring system. In *Proc. CHI'91*, pages 343–350. ACM, 1991.

[21] Jacques Virbel. Reading and managing texts on the bibliothèque de france station. In G. Landow and P. Delany, editors, *The Digital World: Text-Based Computing in the Humanities*, pages 31–52. M.I.T. Press, 1993.

[22] Nicole Yankelovich, Bernard J. Haan, and Norman K. Meyrowitz abd Steven Drucker. Intermedia: The concept and the construction of a seamless information environment. *IEEE Computer*, 211, January 1988.

[23] HongJiang Zhang, Yihong Gong, and Stephen Smoliar. Automatic parsing of news video. In *Proc. IEEE Conference on Multimedia Computing and Systems*, Boston, May 1994.

[24] HongJiang Zhang, Atreyi Kankanhalli, and Stephen W.Smoliar. Automatic partitioning of full-motion video. *Multimedia Systems*, 1(1):10–28, 1993.

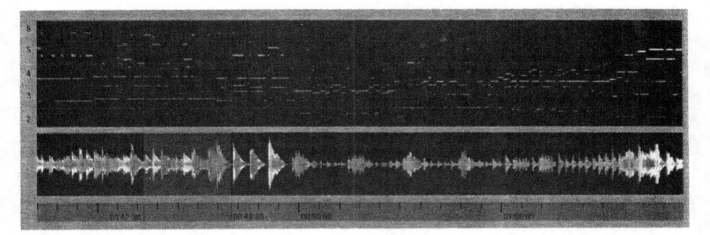

Figure 1: Discrete visual representation of a musical recording: here view on 32 seconds of an interpretation by Michel Dalberto (piano) of Sonata in a minor, Op. 42, D. 845, of Franz Schubert, CD Denon CO-73787

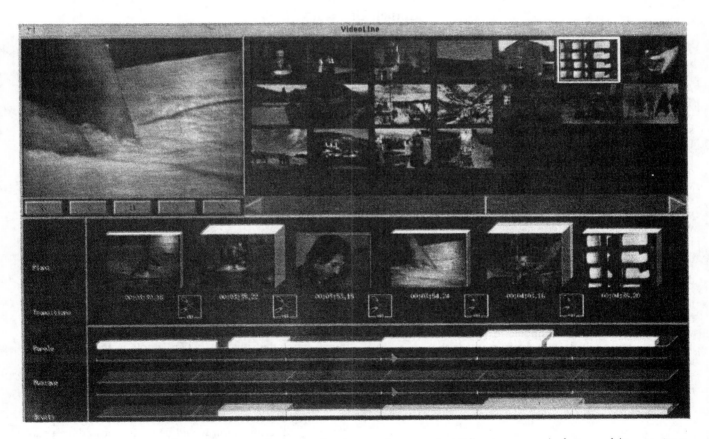

Figure 2: Discrete visual representation for a moving image document, with sequence window, and image, transition effects and sound component strips

Query By Humming
Musical Information Retrieval in
An Audio Database

Asif Ghias   Jonathan Logan   David Chamberlin
Brian C. Smith

Cornell University
{ghias,bsmith}@cs.cornell.edu, logan@ghs.com, chamber@engr.sgi.com

ABSTRACT

The emergence of audio and video data types in databases
will require new information retrieval methods adapted to the
specific characteristics and needs of these data types. An effective and natural way of querying a musical audio database
is by humming the tune of a song. In this paper, a system for
querying an audio database by humming is described along
with a scheme for representing the melodic information in a
song as relative pitch changes. Relevant difficulties involved
with tracking pitch are enumerated, along with the approach
we followed, and the performance results of system indicating its effectiveness are presented.

KEYWORDS: Musical information retrieval, multimedia
databases, pitch tracking

Introduction

Next generation databases will include image, audio and
video data in addition to traditional text and numerical data.
These data types will require query methods that are more
appropriate and natural to the type of respective data. For instance, a natural way to query an image database is to retrieve
images based on operations on images or sketches supplied as
input. Similarly a natural way of querying an audio database
(of songs) is to hum the tune of a song.

Such a system would be useful in any multimedia database
containing musical data by providing an alternative and natural way of querying. One can also imagine a widespread use
of such a system in commercial music industry, music radio
and TV stations, music stores and even for one's personal
use.

In this paper, we address the issue of how to specify a hummed
query and report on an efficient query execution implementation using approximate pattern matching. Our approach
hinges upon the observation that melodic contour, defined as
the sequence of relative differences in pitch between successive notes, can be used to discriminate between melodies.
Handel[3] indicates that melodic contour is one of the most
important methods that listeners use to determine similarities
between melodies. We currently use an alphabet of three
possible relationships between pitches ('U', 'D', and 'S'),
representing the situations where a note is above, below or
the same as the previous note, which can be pitch-tracked
quite robustly. With the current implementation of our system we are successfully able to retrieve most songs within 12
notes. Our database currently comprises a collection of all
parts (melody and otherwise) from 183 songs, suggesting that
three-way discrimination would be useful for finding a particular song among a private music collection, but that higher
resolutions will probably be necessary for larger databases.

This paper is organized as follows. The first section describes
the architecture of the current system. The second section describes what pitch is, why it is important in representing the
melodic contents of songs, several techniques for tracking

pitch we tried and discarded, and the method we settled on. Next we discuss pattern matching as it is used in the current implementation of the database. The last two sections describe our evaluation of the current system and specifie some future extensions that we are considering incorporating in the existing system.

System Architecture

There are three main components to the our system: a pitch-tracking module, a melody database, and a query engine. The architecture is illustrated in Figure . Operation of the system is straight-forward. Queries are hummed into a microphone, digitized, and fed into a pitch-tracking module. The result, a contour representation of the hummed melody, is fed into the query engine, which produces a ranked list of matching melodies.

Figure 1: System Architecture

The database of melodies was acquired by processing public domain MIDI songs, and is stored as a flat-file database. Pitch tracking is performed in Matlab, chosen for its built-in audio processing capabilities and the ease of testing a number of algorithms within it. Hummed queries may be recorded in a variety of formats, depending upon the platform-specific audio input capabilities of Matlab. We have experimented with 16-bit, 44Khz WAV format on a Pentium system, and 8-bit, 8Khz AU format on a Sun Sparcstation. The query engine uses an approximate pattern matching algorithm[1], described in section , in order to tolerate humming errors.

Tracking Pitch in Hummed Queries

This section describes how user input to the system (humming) is converted into a sequence of relative pitch transitions. A note in the input is classified in one of three ways: a note is either the same as the previous note (S), higher than previous note (U), or lower than the previous note (D). Thus, the input is converted into a string with a three letter alphabet (U,D,S). For example, the introductory theme Beethoven's 5th Symphony would be converted into the sequence: - S S D U S S D (the first note is ignored as it has no previous pitch).

To accomplish this conversion, a sequence of pitches in the melody must be isolated and tracked. This is not as straightforward as it sounds, however, as there is still considerable

controversy over exactly what pitch is. The general concept of pitch is clear: given a note, the pitch is the frequency that most closely matches what we hear. Performing this conversion in a computer can become troublesome because some intricacies of human hearing are still not understood. For instance, if we play the 4th, 5th, and 6th harmonics of some fundamental frequency, we actually hear the fundamental frequency, not the harmonics even though the fundamental frequency is not present. This phenomenon was first discovered by Schouten in some pioneer investigations carried out from 1938 to 1940. Schouten studied the pitch of periodic sound waves produced by an optical siren in which the fundamental of 200Hz was canceled completely. The pitch of the complex tone, however, was the same as that prior to the elimination of the fundamental. [12]

Since we were interested in tracking pitch in humming, we examined methods for automatically tracking pitch in a human voice. Before we can estimate the pitch of an acoustic signal, we must first understand how this signal is created, which requires forming a model of sound production at the source. The vibrations of the vocal cords in voiced sounds are caused as a consequence of forces that are exerted on the laryngeal walls when air flows through the glottis (the gap between the vocal cords[1]). Hess [5] describes a model of the vocal cords as proposed by Hirano [6]. For the purposes of this paper though, it is sufficient to know that the glottis repeatedly opens and closes thus providing bursts of air through the vocal tract.

The vocal tract can be modeled as a linear passive transmission system with a transfer function $H(z)$. If we add an additional transfer function $R(z)$ which takes into account the radiation, the output impedance of the vocal tract can approximately be set to zero. In the neutral position where the vocal tract can be regarded as a uniform tube, the resonances of the vocal tract occur at sound wavelengths of

$$\lambda = \frac{4L}{(2k-1)c}; \qquad k = 1, 2, 3, \ldots \qquad (1)$$

With $L = 17$cm (average value of vocal-tract length) and a sound propagation speed of $c = 340\frac{m}{s}$, the frequencies of these resonances will be:

$$F_k = (2k-1) \cdot 500Hz; \qquad k = 1, 2, 3, \ldots \qquad (2)$$

The frequencies F_k are called formant frequencies.

The resulting sound that we hear is considered to be the convolution of the excitation pulse created by the glottis and the formant frequencies. Therefore, if we want to model a speech signal, we start with a train of excitation pulses as shown in figure 2. For the formant frequencies, use equation (2) with $k \in \{1, 2, 3\}$. This gives formant frequencies: $F_1 = 500Hz$, $F_2 = 1500Hz$, and $F_3 = 2500Hz$. Combining these frequencies and adding an exponential envelope produces the formant structure shown in figure 3. By convolving the train of excitation pulses with the formant structure, we get a synthesized pitch as shown in figure 4.

---

[1]The terms vocal folds and vocal chords are more or less used as synonyms in the literature

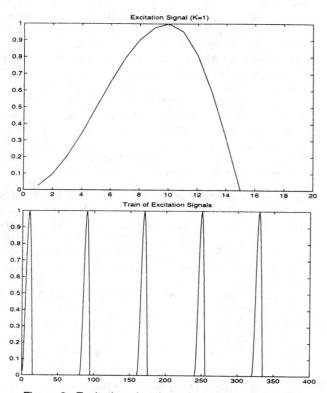

Figure 2: Excitation signal used to create the synthesized pitch. The period in the train of excitations is $T_0 = 0.01$s making the pitch 100Hz.

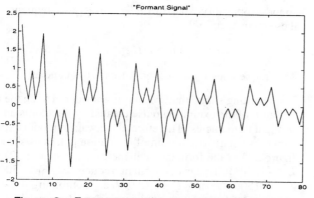

Figure 3: Formant structure created using 500Hz, 1500Hz and 2500MHz as the formant frequencies

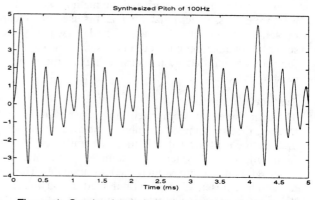

Figure 4: Synthesized pitch of 100Hz created by convolving the train of excitation pulses (spaced by 0.01s) and the formant structure

Now that we have a model of the human voice, how can it be converted to pitch? The most prevalent view on pitch is that what we hear as pitch is actually the frequency at which the bursts of air occur. So if we can track those bursts of air we can find the pitch of the segment.

Tracking pitch

We tried three methods for tracking pitch: Autocorrelation, Maximum Likelihood, Cepstrum Analysis.

- Autocorrelation

Autocorrelation is one of the oldest of the classical pitch trackers[7]. Autocorrelation isolates and tracks the peak energy levels of the signal which is a measure of the pitch. Referring back to figure 3, we see that the signal $s(n)$ peaks where the impulses occur. Therefore, tracking the frequency of this peaks should give us the pitch of the signal. In order to get the frequency of these peaks we can employ autocorrelation as defined by:

$$R(l) = \sum_{k=-\infty}^{\infty} h(k)h(l+k) \qquad (3)$$

Unfortunately autocorrelation is subject to aliasing (picking an integer multiple of the actual pitch) and is computationally complex. We found our implementation of autocorrelation to require approximately 45 seconds for 10 seconds of 44KHz, 16-bit audio on a 90MHz pentium workstation.

- Maximum Likelihood

Maximum Likelihood[14] is a modification of Autocorrelation that increases the accuracy of the pitch and decreases the chances of aliasing.

Unfortunately, the computational complexity of this method makes autocorrelation look blindingly fast. A straight-forward implementation in Matlab takes approximately one hour to evaluate 10 seconds of audio on a 90MHz Pentium workstation. With some optimizations, we improved the performance to approximately 15 minutes per 10 seconds of audio, but this is still far too slow for our purposes. Therefore, we discarded this method. For a detailed explanation of this method, the reader may refer to [14].

• Cepstrum Analysis

Cepstrum analysis is the definitive classical method of pitch extraction. For an explanation, the reader is directed to Oppenheim and Schafer's original work in [10] or in a more compact form in [11]. We found that this method did not give very accurate results for humming.

The output of these methods can be construed as a sequence of frequency estimations for successive pitches in the input. We convert these estimates into a three-step contour representation by comparing each estimated pitch with the previous one. In our system adjacent pitches are considered the same if they are within a quarter-step of each other (on an equal-tempered musical scale), but this parameter is adjustable.

After analyzing the costs and benefits of these methods, we decided to use a modified form of autocorrelation for our implementation.

Searching the database

Having described how the user input (a hummed tune) is converted into a string in a 3 letter alphabet, we now discuss our method for searching an audio database. Our method of searching the database is simple. Songs in the database are preprocessed to convert the melody into a stream of U,D,S characters, and the converted user input (the *key*) is compared with all the songs. The pattern-matching uses a 'fuzzy' search to allow for errors within the matches. These errors reflect the inaccuracies in the way people hum as well as errors in the representation of the songs themselves.

For performing the key-search within the database we need an efficient approximate pattern matching algorithm. By "approximate" we mean that the algorithm should be able to take into account various forms of errors.

Figure summarizes the various forms of errors anticipated in a typical pattern matching scheme. The algorithm that we adopted for this purpose is described by Baesa-Yates and Perleberg [1]. This algorithm addresses the problem of string matching with k mismatches. The problem consists of finding all instances of a pattern string $P = p_1 p_2 p_3 ... p_m$ in a text string $T = t_1 t_2 t_3 .. t_n$ such that there are at most k mismatches (characters that are not the same) for each instance of P in

T. When $k = 0$ (no mismatches) we have the simple string matching problem, solvable in $O(n)$ time. When $k = m$, every substring of T of length m qualifies as a match, since every character of P can be mismatched. Each of the errors in the figure above corresponds to k=1.

It is worth mentioning that several algorithms have been developed that address the problem of approximate string matching. Running times have ranged from $O(mn)$ for the brute force algorithm to $O(kn)$ [9] or $O(n \log(m))$ [2]. The algorithm that we adopted offers better performance for average cases than most other algorithms.

The worst case for this algorithm occurs when P (the key) consists of m occurrences of a single distinct character, and T (contour representation of song) consists of n instances of that character. In this case the running time is $O(mn)$. However this is neither a common nor useful situation for our purposes. In the average case of an alphabet in which each character is equally likely to occur, the running time is $O(n(1 + \frac{m}{|\Gamma|})$ where $|\Gamma|$ is the size of the alphabet.

The database incorporates the key-searching scheme (using pattern matching techniques explained above). We envisioned the following design goals for the database. For a given query, the database returns a list of songs ranked by how well they matched the query, not just one best match. The number of matches that the database should retrieve depends upon the error-tolerance used during the key-search. This error-tolerance could be set in one of two possible ways: either it can be a user-definable parameter or the database can itself determine this parameter based on, for example by heuristics that depends on the length of the key. This design gives the user an opportunity to perform queries even if the user is not sure of some notes within the tune.·

From the results of the query the user can identify the song of interest. If the list is too large, the user can perform a new query on a restricted search list consisting of songs just retrieved. A consequence of this scheme is that the user can identify sets of songs that contain similar melodies.

Evaluation

This section describes the results of an experimental evaluation of the system. Our evaluation tested the tolerance of the system with respect to input errors, whether from mistakes in the user's humming or from problems with the pitch-tracking.

Robustness

The effectiveness of this method is directly related to the accuracy with which pitches that are hummed can be tracked and the accuracy of the melodic information within the database. Under ideal circumstances, we can achieve close to 100% accuracy tracking humming, where ideal circumstances mean the user places a small amount of space between each note and hits each note strongly. For this purpose, humming short notes is encouraged. Even more ideal is for the user to aspirate the notes as much as possible, perhaps going so far as to voice a vowel, as in "haaa haaa haaa". We have currently only experimented with male voices.

The evaluation database currently contains a total of 183

Text:	casablanca	casablanca	casablanca
Pattern:	sbbla	s bla	saabla
	Transposition error	Dropout error	Duplication error

Figure 5: Three forms of anticipated errors with one mismatch

songs. Each song was converted from public domain General MIDI sources. Melodies from different musical genres were included, including both classical and popular music. A few simple heuristics were used to cut down on the amount of irrelevant information from the data, e.g. MIDI channel 10 was ignored as this is reserved for percussion in the General MIDI standard. However the database still contains a great deal of information unrelated to the main theme of the melody. Even with this limitation, we discovered that sequences of 10-12 pitch transitions were sufficient to discriminate 90% of the songs.

As a consequence of using a fast approximate string matching algorithm, search keys can be matched with any portion of the melody, rather than just the beginning. As the size of the database grows larger, however, this may not prove to be an advantage.

Performance
The version of the pitch-tracker using a modified form of autocorrelation[2] takes between 20 and 45 seconds on a Sparc10 workstation to process typical sequences of hummed notes. A brute-force search of the database unsurprisingly shows linear growth with the size of the database, but remains below 4 seconds for 100 songs on a Sparc2. Therefore the search time is currently effectively limited by the efficiency of the pitch-tracker.

Contour representations for each song are currently stored in separate files, so opening and closing files becomes a significant overhead. Performance could be improved by packing all the songs into one file, or by using a database manager. We plan to modularize our code to make it independent of any particular database schema.

Future directions and Related Work
We plan to improve the performance and speed and robustness of the pitch-tracking algorithm by using a cubic-spline wavelet. The cubic spline wavelet peaks at discontinuities in the signal (i.e. the air impulses). One of the most significant features of the wavelet analysis is that it can be computed in $O(n)$ time. Currently, the pitch tracker is the slowest link in our system, so using wavelets for this purpose has obvious advantages.

The pattern matching algorithm in its present form does not discriminate the various forms of pattern matching errors discussed earlier, but only accounts for them collectively. Some forms of errors may be more common than others depending upon the way people casually hum different tunes. For example drop-out errors reflected as dropped notes in tunes are more common than transposition or duplication errors. Tuning the key-search so that it is more tolerant to drop-out errors, for example, may yield better results.

The melodic contours of the source songs are currently generated automatically from MIDI data, which is convenient but not optimal. More accuracy and less redundant information could be obtained by entering the melodic themes for

---

[2]The modifications include low-pass filtering and center-clipping (as described in Sondhi's paper [13]) which help eliminate the formant structure that generally causes difficulty for autocorrelation based pitch detectors.

particular songs by hand. From a research standpoint, an interesting question is how to extract melodies from complex audio signals[4].

Finally, we would like to characterize the improvement gained by increasing the resolution of the relative pitch differences by considering query alphabets of three, five and more possible relationships between adjacent pitches. Early experiments using an alphabet of five relative pitch differences (same, higher, much higher, lower, much lower) verified that changes of this sort are promising. One drawback of introducing more resolution is that the user must be somewhat more accurate in the intervals they actually hum. We will explore the various tradeoffs involved. An important issue is precisely where to draw the line between notes that are a little higher from the previous note and those that are much higher.

Previous work on efficiently searching a database of melodies by humming seems to be limited. Mike Hawley [4] briefly discusses a method of querying a collection of melodic themes by searching for exact matches of sequences of relative pitches input by a MIDI keyboard. We have incorporated approximate pattern matching, implementing an actual audio database (of MIDI songs) and most significantly by allowing queries to be hummed. Kageyama and Takashima [8] published a paper on retrieving melodies using a hummed melody in a Japanese journal, but we were unable to locate a translated version.

REFERENCES
1. Ricardo A. Baesa-Yates and Chris H. Perleberg. Fast and practical approximate string matching. *Combinatorial Pattern Matching, Third Annual Symposium*, pages 185–192, 1992.

2. Ricardo Baeza-Yates and G.H. Gonnet. Fast string matching with mismatches. *Information and Computation*, 1992.

3. Stephen Handel. *Listening: An Introduction to the Perception of Auditory Events*. The MIT Press, 1989.

4. Michael Jerome Hawley. *Structure out of Sound*. PhD thesis, MIT, September 1993.

5. Wolfgang Hess. *Pitch Determination of Speech Signals*. Springer-Verlag, Berlin Heidelberg, 1983.

6. M. Hirano. Structure and vibratory behavior of the vocal folds. In M. Sawashima and F.S. Cooper, editors, *Dynamic aspects of speech production*, pages 13–27. University of Tokyo Press, 1976.

7. L.R. Rabiner J.J. Dubnowski and R.W. Schafer. Real-time digital hardware pitch detector. *IEEE Transactions on Acoustics, Speech and Signal Processing*, ASSP-24(1):2–8, Feb 1976.

8. T. Kageyama and Y. Takashima. A melody retrieval method with hummed melody (language: Japanese). *Transactions of the Institute of Electronics, Information and Communication Engineers D-II*, J77D-II(8):1543–1551, August 1994.

9. G. Landau and U. Vishkin. Efficient string matching with k mismatches. *Theoretical Computer Science*, 43:239–249, 1986.

10. A. V. Oppenheim. A speech analysis-synthesis system based on homomorphic filtering. *J. Acoustical Society of America*, 45:458–465, February 1969.

11. Alan V. Oppenheim and Ronald W. Schafer. *Discrete-time Signal Processing*. Prentice Hall, Englewood Cliffs, NJ, 1989.

12. R. Plomp. *Aspects of tone sensation*. Academic Press, London, 1976.

13. M. M. Sondhi. New methods of pitch extraction. *IEEE Trans. Audio Electroacoust. (Special Issue on Speech Communication and Processing—PartII*, AU-16:262–266, June 1968.

14. James D. Wise, James R. Caprio, and Thomas W. Parks. Maximum likelihood pitch estimation. *IEEE Trans. Acoust., Speech, Signal Processing*, 24(5):418–423, October 1976.

Content-Based Classification, Search, and Retrieval of Audio

**Erling Wold, Thom Blum, Douglas Keislar,
and James Wheaton**
Muscle Fish

Many audio and multimedia applications would benefit from the ability to classify and search for audio based on its characteristics. The audio analysis, search, and classification engine described here reduces sounds to perceptual and acoustical features. This lets users search or retrieve sounds by any one feature or a combination of them, by specifying previously learned classes based on these features, or by selecting or entering reference sounds and asking the engine to retrieve similar or dissimilar sounds.

The rapid increase in speed and capacity of computers and networks has allowed the inclusion of audio as a data type in many modern computer applications. However, the audio is usually treated as an opaque collection of bytes with only the most primitive fields attached: name, file format, sampling rate, and so on. Users accustomed to searching, scanning, and retrieving text data can be frustrated by the inability to look inside the audio objects.

Multimedia databases or file systems, for example, can easily have thousands of audio recordings. These could be anything from a library of sound effects to the soundtrack portion of a news footage archive. Such libraries are often poorly indexed or named to begin with. Even if a previous user has assigned keywords or indices to the data, these are often highly subjective and may be useless to another person. Searching for a particular sound or class of sound (such as applause, music, or the speech of a particular speaker) can be a daunting task.

How might people want to access sounds? We believe there are several useful methods, all of which we have attempted to incorporate into our system.

■ *Simile*: saying one sound is like another sound or a group of sounds in terms of some characteristics. For example, "like the sound of a herd of elephants." A simpler example would be to say that it belongs to the class of speech sounds or the class of applause sounds, where the system has previously been trained on other sounds in this class.

■ *Acoustical/perceptual features*: describing the sounds in terms of commonly understood physical characteristics such as brightness, pitch, and loudness.

■ *Subjective features*: describing the sounds using personal descriptive language. This requires training the system (in our case, by example) to understand the meaning of these descriptive terms. For example, a user might be looking for a "shimmering" sound.

■ *Onomatopoeia*: making a sound similar in some quality to the sound you are looking for. For example, the user could making a buzzing sound to find bees or electrical hum.

In a retrieval application, all of the above could be used in combination with traditional keyword and text queries.

To accomplish any of the above methods, we first reduce the sound to a small set of parameters using various analysis techniques. Second, we use statistical techniques over the parameter space to accomplish the classification and retrieval.

Previous research

Sounds are traditionally described by their pitch, loudness, duration, and timbre. The first three of these psychological percepts are well understood and can be accurately modeled by measurable acoustic features. Timbre, on the other hand, is an ill-defined attribute that encompasses all the distinctive qualities of a sound other than its pitch, loudness, and duration. The effort to discover the components of timbre underlies much of the previous psychoacoustic research that is relevant to content-based audio retrieval.[1]

Salient components of timbre include the amplitude envelope, harmonicity, and spectral envelope. The attack portions of a tone are often essential for identifying the timbre. Timbres with similar spectral energy distributions (as measured by the centroid of the spectrum) tend to be judged as perceptually similar. However, research has shown that the time-varying spectrum of a single musical instrument tone cannot generally be treated as a "fingerprint" identifying the instrument, because there is too much variation across the instrument's range of pitches and across its range of dynamic levels.

Various researchers have discussed or prototyped algorithms capable of extracting audio structure from a sound.[2] The goal was to allow queries such as "find the first occurrence of the note G-sharp." These algorithms were tuned to specific musical constructs and were not appropriate for all sounds.

Other researchers have focused on indexing audio databases using neural nets.[3] Although they have had some success with their method, there are several problems from our point of view. For example, while the neural nets report similarities between sounds, it is very hard to "look inside" a net after it is trained or while it is in operation to determine how well the training worked or what aspects of the sounds are similar to each other. This makes it difficult for the user to specify which features of the sound are important and which to ignore.

Analysis and retrieval engine

Here we present a general paradigm and specific techniques for analyzing audio signals in a way that facilitates content-based retrieval. Content-based retrieval of audio can mean a variety of things. At the lowest level, a user could retrieve a sound by specifying the exact numbers in an excerpt of the sound's sampled data. This is analogous to an exact text search and is just as simple to implement in the audio domain.

At the next higher level of abstraction, the retrieval would match any sound containing the given excerpt, regardless of the data's sample rate, quantization, compression, and so on. This is analogous to a fuzzy text search and can be implemented using correlation techniques. At the next level, the query might involve acoustic features that can be directly measured and perceptual (subjective) properties of the sound.[4,5] Above this, one can ask for speech content or musical content.

It is the "sound" level—acoustic and perceptual properties—with which we are most concerned here. Some of the aural (perceptual) properties of a sound, such as pitch, loudness, and brightness, correspond closely to measurable features of the audio signal, making it logical to provide fields for these properties in the audio database record. However, other aural properties ("scratchiness," for instance) are more indirectly related to easily measured acoustical features of the sound. Some of these properties may even have different meanings for different users.

We first measure a variety of acoustical features of each sound. This set of N features is represented as an N-vector. In text databases, the resolution of queries typically requires matching and comparing strings. In an audio database, we would like to match and compare the aural properties as described above. For example, we would like to ask for all the sounds similar to a given sound or that have more or less of a given property. To guarantee that this is possible, sounds that differ in the aural property should map to different regions of the N-space. If this were not satisfied, the database could not distinguish between sounds with different values for this property. Note that this approach is similar to the "feature-vector" approach currently used in content-based retrieval of images, although the actual features used are very different.[6]

Since we cannot know the complete list of aural properties that users might wish to specify, it is impossible to guarantee that our choice of acoustical features will meet these constraints. However, we can make sure that we meet these constraints for many useful aural properties.

Acoustical features

We can currently analyze the following aspects of sound: loudness, pitch, brightness, bandwidth, and harmonicity.

Loudness is approximated by the signal's root-mean-square (RMS) level in decibels, which is calculated by taking a series of windowed frames of the sound and computing the square root of the sum of the squares of the windowed sample values. (This method does not account for the frequency response of the human ear; if desired, the necessary equalization can be added by applying the Fletcher-Munson equal-loudness contours.) The human ear can hear over a 120-decibel range. Our software produces estimates over a 100-decibel range from 16-bit audio recordings.

Pitch is estimated by taking a series of short-time Fourier spectra. For each of these frames, the frequencies and amplitudes of the peaks are measured and an approximate greatest common divisor algorithm is used to calculate an estimate of the pitch. We store the pitch as a log frequency. The pitch algorithm also returns a pitch confidence value that can be used to weight the pitch in later calculations. A perfect young human ear can hear frequencies in the 20-Hz to 20-kHz range. Our software can measure pitches in the range of 50 Hz to about 10 kHz.

Brightness is computed as the centroid of the

short-time Fourier magnitude spectra, again stored as a log frequency. It is a measure of the higher frequency content of the signal. As an example, putting your hand over your mouth as you speak reduces the brightness of the speech sound as well as the loudness. This feature varies over the same range as the pitch, although it can't be less than the pitch estimate at any given instant.

Bandwidth is computed as the magnitude-weighted average of the differences between the spectral components and the centroid. As examples, a single sine wave has a bandwidth of zero and ideal white noise has an infinite bandwidth.

Harmonicity distinguishes between harmonic spectra (such as vowels and most musical sounds), inharmonic spectra (such as metallic sounds), and noise (spectra that vary randomly in frequency and time). It is computed by measuring the deviation of the sound's line spectrum from a perfectly harmonic spectrum. This is currently an optional feature and is not used in the examples that follow. It is normalized to lie in a range from zero to one.

All of these aspects of sound vary over time. The trajectory in time is computed during the analysis but not stored as such in the database. However, for each of these trajectories, several features are computed and stored. These include the average value, the variance of the value over the trajectory, and the autocorrelation of the trajectory at a small lag. Autocorrelation is a measure of the smoothness of the trajectory. It can distinguish between a pitch glissando and a wildly varying pitch (for example), which the simple variance measure cannot.

The average, variance, and autocorrelation computations are weighted by the amplitude trajectory to emphasize the perceptually important sections of the sound. In addition to the above features, the duration of the sound is stored. The feature vector thus consists of the duration plus the parameters just mentioned (average, variance, and autocorrelation) for each of the aspects of sound given above. Figure 1 shows a plot of the raw trajectories of loudness, brightness, bandwidth, and pitch for a recording of male laughter.

After the statistical analyses, the resulting analysis record (shown in Table 1) contains the computed values. These numbers are the only information used in the content-based classification and retrieval of these sounds. It is possible to

see some of the essential characteristics of the sound. Most notably, we see the rapidly time-varying nature of the laughter.

Training the system

It is possible to specify a sound directly by submitting constraints on the values of the *N*-vector described above directly to the system. For example, the user can ask for sounds in a certain range of pitch or brightness, However, it is also possible to train the system by example. In this case, the user selects examples of sounds that demonstrate the property the user wishes to train, such as "scratchiness."

For each sound entered into the database, the *N*-vector, which we represent as *a*, is computed. When the user supplies a set of example sounds for training, the mean vector μ and the covariance matrix *R* for the *a* vectors in each class are calculated. The mean and covariance are given by

$$\mu = (1/M) \sum_j a[j]$$

$$R = (1/M) \sum_j (a[j] - \mu)(a[j] - \mu)^T$$

where *M* is the number of sounds in the summation. In practice, one can ignore the off-diagonal elements of *R* if the feature vector elements are reasonably independent of each other. This simplification can yield significant savings in computation time. The mean and covariance together become the system's model of the perceptual property being trained by the user.

Classifying sounds

When a new sound needs to be classified, a distance measure is calculated from the new sound's *a* vector and the model above. We use a weighted

Property	Mean	Variance	Autocorrelation
Loudness	−54.4112	221.451	0.938929
Pitch	4.21221	0.151228	0.524042
Brightness	5.78007	0.0817046	0.690073
Bandwidth	0.272099	0.0169697	0.519198

Table 1. Male laughter. Duration: 2.12571.

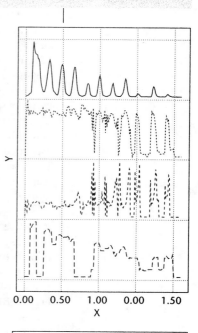

——	LaughterYoungMale.amp
·····	LaughterYoungMale.bright
- - -	LaughterYoungMale.bandwidth
·-· -	LaughterYoungMale.pitch

Figure 1. Male laughter.

L_2 or Euclidean distance:

$$D = ((a - \mu)^T R^{-1} (a - \mu))^{1/2}$$

Again, the off-diagonal elements of R can be ignored for faster computation. Also, simpler measures such as an L_1 or Manhattan distance can be used. The distance is compared to a threshold to determine whether the sound is "in" or "out" of the class. If there are several mutually exclusive classes, the sound is placed in the class to which it is closest, that is, for which it has the smallest value of D.

If it is known a priori that some acoustic features are unimportant for the class, these can be ignored or given a lower weight in the computation of D. For example, if the class models some timbral aspect of the sounds, the duration and average pitch of the sounds can usually be ignored.

We also define a likelihood value L based on the normal distribution and given by

$$L = exp(-D^2/2)$$

This value can be interpreted as "how much" of the defining property for the class the new sound has.

Retrieving sounds

It is now possible to select, sort, or classify sounds from the database using the distance measure. Some example queries are

- Retrieve the "scratchy" sounds. That is, retrieve all the sounds that have a high likelihood of being in the "scratchy" class.

- Retrieve the top 20 "scratchy" sounds.

- Retrieve all the sounds that are less "scratchy" than a given sound.

- Sort the given set of sounds by how "scratchy" they are.

- Classify a given set of sounds into the following set of classes.

For small databases, it is easiest to compute the distance measure(s) for all the sounds in the database and then to choose the sounds that match the desired result. For large databases, this can be too expensive. To speed up the search, we index (sort) the sounds in the database by all the acoustic features. This allows us to quickly retrieve any desired hyper-rectangle of sounds in the database by requesting all sounds whose feature values fall in a set of desired ranges. Requesting such hyper-rectangles allows a much more efficient search. This technique has the advantage that it can be implemented on top of the very efficient index-based search algorithms in existing commercial databases.

As an example, consider a query to retrieve the top M sounds in a class. If the database has M_0 sounds total, we first ask for all the sounds in a hyper-rectangle centered around the mean μ with volume V such that

$$V/V_0 = M/M_0$$

where V_0 is the volume of the hyper-rectangle surrounding the entire database. The extent of the hyper-rectangle in each dimension is proportional to the standard deviation of the class in that dimension.

We then compute the distance measure for all the sounds returned and return the closest M sounds. If we didn't retrieve enough sounds that matched the query from this first attempt, we increase the hyper-rectangle volume by the ratio of the number requested to the number found and try again.

Note that the above discussion is a simplification of our current algorithm, which asks for bigger volumes to begin with to correct for two factors. First, for our distance measure, we really want a hypersphere of volume V, which means we want the hyper-rectangle that circumscribes this sphere. Second, the distribution of sounds in the feature space is not perfectly regular. If we assume some reasonable distribution of the sounds in the database, we can easily compute how much larger V has to be to achieve some desired confidence level that the search will succeed.

Quality measures

The magnitude of the covariance matrix R is a measure of the compactness of the class. This can be reported to the user as a quality measure of the classification. For example, if the dimensions of R are similar to the dimensions of the database, this class would not be useful as a discriminator, since all the sounds would fall into it. Similarly, the system can detect other irregularities in the training set, such as outliers or bimodality.

The size of the covariance matrix in each dimension is a measure of the particular dimension's importance to the class. From this, the user can see if a particular feature is too important or not important enough. For example, if all the sounds in the training set happen to have a very similar duration, the classification process will rank this feature highly, even though it may be irrelevant. If this is the case, the user can tell the system to ignore duration or weight it differently, or the user can try to improve the training set. Similarly, the system can report to the user the components of the computed distance measure. Again, this is an indication to the user of possible problems in the class description.

Note that all of these measures would be difficult to derive from a non-statistical model such as a neural network.

Segmentation

The discussion above deals with the case where each sound is a single gestalt. Some examples of this would be single short sounds, such as a door slam, or longer sounds of uniform texture, such as a recording of rain on cement. Recordings that contain many different events need to be segmented before using the features above. Segmentation is accomplished by applying the acoustic analyses discussed to the signal and looking for transitions (sudden changes in the measured features). The transitions define segments of the signal, which can then be treated like individual sounds. For example, a recording of a concert could be scanned automatically for applause sounds to determine the boundaries between musical pieces. Similarly, after training the system to recognize a certain speaker, a recording could be segmented and scanned for all the sections where that speaker was talking.

Performance

We have used the above algorithms at Muscle Fish on a test sound database that contains about 400 sound files. These sound files were culled from various sound effects and musical instrument sample libraries. A wide variety of sounds are represented from animals, machines, musical instruments, speech, and nature. The sounds vary in duration from less than a second to about 15 seconds.

A number of classes were made by running the classification algorithm on some perceptually similar sets of sounds. These classes were then used to reorder the sounds in the database by their likelihood of membership in the class. The following discussion shows the results of this process for several sound sets. These examples illustrate the character of the process and the fuzzy nature of the retrieval. (For more information, and to duplicate these examples, see the "Interactive Web Demo" sidebar.)

Example 1: Laughter. For this example, all the recordings of laughter except two were used in creating the class. Figure 2 shows a plot of the class membership likelihood values (the *Y*-axis) for all of the sound files in the test database. Each vertical strip along the *X*-axis is a user-defined category (the directory in which the sound resides). See the "Class Model" sidebar on p. 32 for details on how our system computed this model.

The highest returned likelihoods are for the laughing sounds, including the two that were not included in the original training set, as well as one of the animal recordings. This animal recording is of a chicken coop and has strong similarities in sound to the laughter recordings, consisting of a number of strong sound bursts.

Example 2: Female speech. Our test database contains a number of very short recordings of a

Interactive Web Demo

The Muscle Fish World Wide Web site, http://www.musclefish.com, contains an interactive demo of our content-based retrieval algorithms. The interface lets the user see and select any of the sound files in our small demo database. The database is the same as that used for the examples in this article. The user can audition the selected sounds or can reorder the sounds in the database by closeness to the group of sounds selected. The associated Web pages include some suggested groupings that are good starting points for browsing.

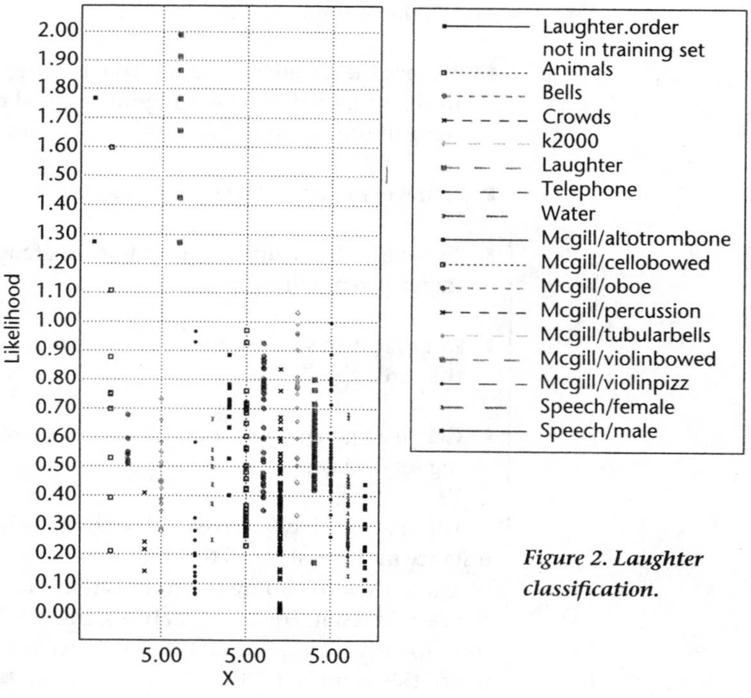
2.00
1.90
1.80
1.70
1.60
1.50
1.40
1.30
1.20
1.10
1.00
0.90
0.80
0.70
0.60
0.50
0.40
0.30
0.20
0.10
0.00
Likelihood
5.00
5.00
5.00
X
Laughter.order
not in training set
Animals
Bells
Crowds
k2000
Laughter
Telephone
Water
Mcgill/altotrombone
Mcgill/cellobowed
Mcgill/oboe
Mcgill/percussion
Mcgill/tubularbells
Mcgill/violinbowed
Mcgill/violinpizz
Speech/female
Speech/male

Figure 2. Laughter classification.

Class Model

The model computed by our system for the laughter example is detailed in Table A. The "importance" is computed as the absolute value of the mean divided by the standard deviation. This is a normalized measure of how similar this feature is among all the members of the training set, and thus how important this feature is to the definition of the class. That is, sounds that have features close to the class's mean values for the important parameters will end up with a high likelihood of being in the class. For this class, the rapidly changing loudness is the most distinctive feature.

Table A. Class model for laughter example.

Feature		Mean	Variance	Importance
Duration		2.71982	0.191312	6.21826
Loudness:	Mean	−45.0014	18.9212	10.3455
	Variance	200.109	1334.99	5.47681
	Autocorrelation	0.955071	7.71106e-05	108.762
Brightness:	Mean	6.16071	0.0204748	43.0547
	Variance	0.0288125	0.000113187	2.70821
	Autocorrelation	0.715438	0.0108014	6.88386
Bandwidth:	Mean	0.363269	0.000434929	17.4188
	Variance	0.00759914	3.57604e-05	1.27076
	Autocorrelation	0.664325	0.0122108	6.01186
Pitch:	Mean	4.48992	0.39131	7.17758
	Variance	0.207667	0.0443153	0.986485
	Autocorrelation	0.562178	0.00857394	6.07133

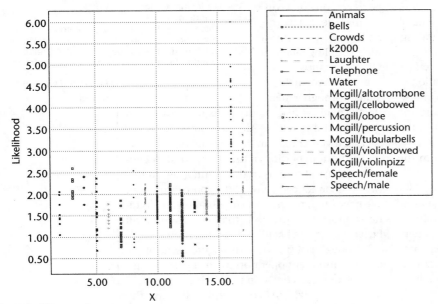

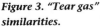

Figure 3. "Tear gas" similarities.

group of female and male speakers. For this example, the female-spoken phrase "tear gas" was used. Figure 3 shows a plot of the similarity (likelihood) of each of the sound files in the test database to this sound using a default value for the covariance matrix *R*. The highest likelihoods are for the other female speech recordings, with the male speech recordings following close behind.

Example 3: Touchtones. A set of telephone touchtones was used to generate the class in Figure 4. Again, the touchtone likelihoods are clearly separated from those of other categories. One of the touchtone recordings that was left out of the training set also has a high likelihood, but notice that the other one, as well as one of those included in the training set, returned very low likelihoods. Upon investigation, we found that the two low-likelihood touchtone recordings were of entire seven-digit phone numbers, whereas all the high-likelihood touchtone recordings were of single-digit tones. In this case, the automatic classification detected an aural difference that was not represented in the user-supplied categorization.

Applications

The above technology is relevant to a number of application areas. The examples in this section will show the power this capability can bring to a user working in these areas.

Audio databases and file systems

Any audio database or, equivalently, a file system designed to work with large numbers of audio files, would benefit from content-based capabilities. Both of these require that the audio data be represented or supplemented by a data record or object that points to the sound and adds the necessary analysis data.

When a new sound is added to the database, the analyses presented in the previous section are run on the sound and a new database record or object is formed with this supplemental information. Typically, the database would allow the user to add his or her own information to this record. In a multiuser system, users could have their own copies of the database records that they could modify for their particular requirements.

Figure 5 shows the record used in our sound browser, described in the next section. Fields in this record include features such as the sound file's name and properties, the acoustic features as computed by system analysis routines, and user-defined keywords and comments.

Any user of the database can form an audio class by presenting a set of sounds to the classification algorithm of the last section. The object returned by the algorithm contains a list of the sounds and the resulting statistical information. This class can be private to the user or made available to all database users. The kinds of classes that would be useful depend on the application area. For example, a user doing automatic segmentation of sports and news footage might develop classes that allow the recognition of various audience sounds such as applause and cheers, referees' whistles, close-miked speech, and so forth.

The database should support the queries described in the last section as well as more standard queries on the keywords, sampling rate, and so on.

An audio database browser

In this section, we present a front-end database application named SoundFisher that lets the user search for sounds using queries that can be content based. In addition, it permits general maintenance of the database's entries by adding, deleting, and describing sounds.

Figure 6 shows the graphical user interface (GUI) for the application during the formation of a query. The upper window is the Query window. The Search button initiates a search using the query and the results are then displayed in the Current Sounds window. Initially, the Results window shows a listing of all the sounds in the database.

A query is formed using a combination of constraints on the various fields in the database schema and a set of sounds that form a training set for a class. The example in Figure 6 is a query to find recent high-fidelity sounds in the database containing the "animal" or "barn" keywords that are similar to goose sounds, ignoring sound duration and average loudness.

The top portion of the Query window consists of a set of rows, each of which is a component of the total query. Each component includes the name of the field, a constraint operator appropriate for the data type of that field, and the value to which the operator is applied. Pressing one of the

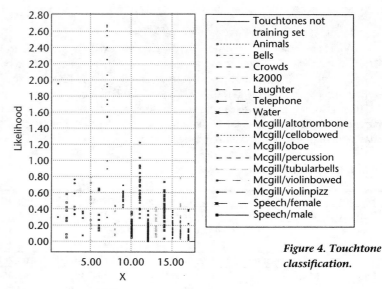

Figure 4. Touchtone classification.

buttons in the row pops up a menu of possibilities or a slider and entry window combination for floating-point values. In Figure 6, there is one component that constrains the date to be recent, one that constrains the keywords, and one that specifies a high sampling rate. The OR subcomponent on the keyword field is added through a menu item. There are also menu items for adding and deleting components. All the components are ANDed together to form the final query.

The bottom portion of the Query window consists of a list of sounds in the training set. In this case, the sounds consist of all the goose recordings. We have brought up sliders for duration and loudness and set them to zero so that these features will be ignored in the likelihood computation.

Although not shown in this figure, some of the query component operators are fuzzy. For example, the user can constrain the pitch to be approximately 100 Hz. This constraint will cause the system to compute a likelihood for each sound equal to the inverse of the distance between that sound's pitch feature and 100 Hz. This likelihood is used as a multiplier against the likelihood computed from the similarity calculation or other parts of the query that yield fuzzy results. Note

Sound file attributes
  File name
  Sample rate
  Sample size
  Sound file format
  Number of channels
  Creation date
  Analysis date
User attributes
  Keywords
  Comments
Analysis feature vector
  Duration
  Pitch   [mean, variance, autocorrelation]
  Amplitude   [mean, variance, autocorrelation]
  Brightness   [mean, variance, autocorrelation]
  Bandwidth   [mean, variance, autocorrelation]

Figure 5. Database record.

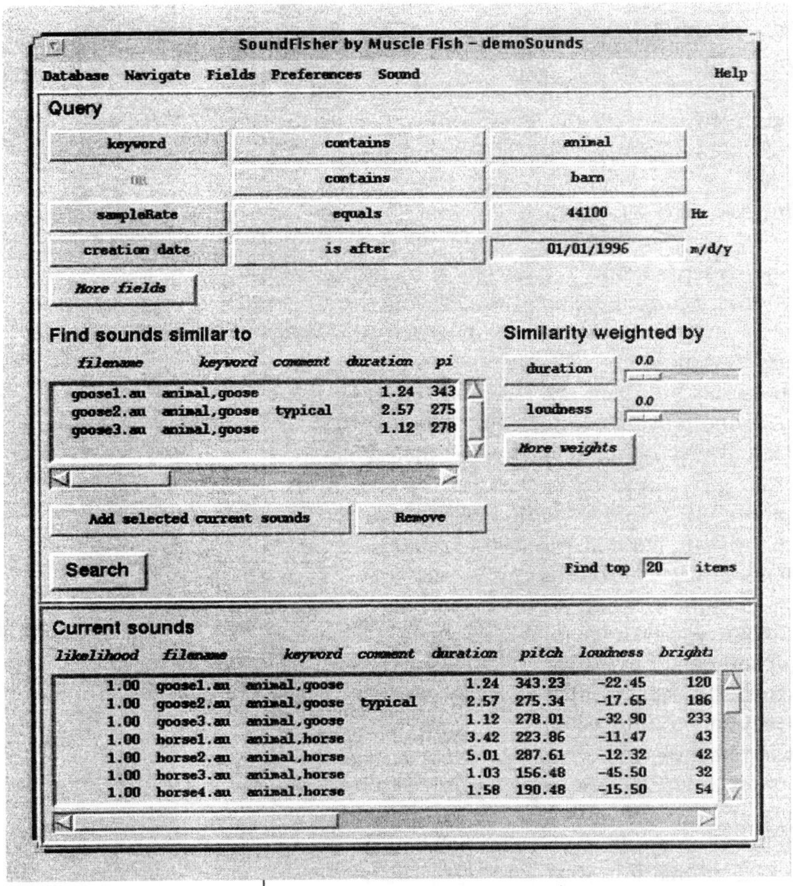

Figure 6. SoundFisher browser.

as "scratchiness," save that model under a name, then reuse that concept in future queries.

Audio editors

Current audio editors operate directly on the samples of the audio waveform. The user can specify locations and values numerically or graphically, but the editor has no knowledge of the audio content. The audio content is only accessible by auditioning the sound, which is tedious when editing long recordings.

A more useful editor would include knowledge of the audio content. Using the techniques presented in this article, a variety of sound classes appropriate for the particular application domain could be developed. For example, editing a concert recording would be aided by classes for audience applause, solo instruments, loud and soft ensemble playing, and other typical sound features of concerts. Using the classes, the editor could have the entire concert recording initially segmented into regions and indexed, allowing quick access to each musical piece and subsections thereof. During the editing process, all the types of queries presented in the preceding sections could be used to navigate through the recording. For example, the editor could ask the system to highlight the first C-sharp in the oboe solo section for pitch correction.

A graphical editor with these capabilities would have Search or Find commands that functioned like the query command of the SoundFisher audio browser. Since it would often be necessary to build new classes on the fly, there should be commands for classification and analysis or tight integration with a database application such as the SoundFisher audio browser.

Surveillance

The application of content-based retrieval in surveillance is identical to that of the audio editor except that the identification and classification would be done in real time. Many offices are already equipped with computers that have built-in audio input devices. These could be used to listen for the sounds of people, glass breaking, and so on. There are also a number of police jurisdictions using microphones and video cameras to continuously survey areas having a high incidence of criminal activity or a low tolerance of such activity. Again, such surveillance could be made more efficient and easier to monitor with the ability to detect sounds associated with criminal activity.

that ANDing two fuzzy searches is accomplished by multiplying the likelihoods and ORing two fuzzy searches by adding the likelihoods.

There are a number of ways to refine searches through this interface, and all queries can be saved under a name given by the user. These queries can be recalled and modified. The Navigate menu contains these commands as well as a history mechanism that remembers all the queries on the current query path. The Back and Forward commands allow navigation along this path. An entry is made in the path each time the Search button is pressed. It is, of course, possible to start over from scratch. There is also an option to apply the query to the current sounds or to the entire database of sounds.

Any saved query can be used as part of a new query. One of the fields available for constructing query components is "query," meaning "saved query." This lets the user perform complex searches that combine previous queries in Boolean expressions. It also lets the user train the system with a class of sounds embodying a concept such

Automatic segmentation of audio and video

In large archives of raw audio and video, it is useful to have some automatic indexing and segmentation of the raw recordings. There has been quite a bit of work on the video side of the segmentation problem using scene changes and camera movement.[7] The audio soundtrack of video as well as audio-only recordings can be automatically indexed and segmented using the analysis methods discussed previously.

This is accomplished by analyzing the recording and extracting the trajectories for loudness, pitch, brightness, and other features. Some segmentation can be done at this level by looking at transitions and sudden changes in the analysis data. We used this technique to develop the Audio-to-MIDI conversion system that is part of the Studio Vision Pro 3.0 product from Opcode Systems. In this product, the raw trajectories are segmented by amplitude and pitch and converted into musical score information in the form of MIDI data. This is a convenient representation for understanding and manipulating the musical content of the audio recording. This product assumes musical instrument recordings, so pitch is very important. In a more general context, it might be more appropriate to segment the sound by amplitude or spectral changes.

You could treat these segments as individual sounds that can then be analyzed for their statistical features, as we have described above. Alternately, you could arbitrarily look at overlapping windows of the raw analysis data as the individual sounds. Once this is done, each of these sounds can be classified and thus indexed.

Future directions

In our current work, we are focusing on several areas to improve and refine the performance of our search, analysis, and retrieval engine.

Additional analytic features

An analysis engine for content-based audio classification and retrieval works by analyzing the acoustic features of the audio and reducing these to a few statistical values. The analyzed features are fairly straightforward but suffice to describe a relatively large universe of sounds. More analyses could be added to handle specific problem domains.

General phrase-level content-based retrieval

Our current set of acoustic features is targeted toward short or single-gestalt sounds. Matching sets of our features as trajectories in time or matching segmented sequences of single-gestalt sounds would allow phrase-level audio content to be stored and retrieved. For example, the Audio-to-MIDI system referenced above could be used to do matching of musical melodies. As with all media search, a fuzzy match is what is desired.

Source separation

In our current system, simultaneously sounding sources are treated as a single ensemble. We make no attempt to separate them, as source separation is a difficult task. Approaches to separating simultaneous sounds typically involve either Gestalt psychology[8] or non-perceptual signal-processing techniques.[9,10] For musical applications, polyphonic pitch-tracking has been studied for many years, but might well be an intractable problem in the general case.

Sound synthesis

Sound synthesis could assist a user in making content-based queries to an audio database. When the user was unsure what values to use, the synthesis feature would create sound prototypes that matched the current set of values as they were manipulated. The user could then refine the synthesized example until it bore enough similarity to the desired sort of sound.

Our examples show the efficacy and useful fuzzy nature of the search. The results of searches are sometimes surprising in that they cross semantic boundaries, but aurally the results are reasonable. This is work in progress. Further implementation and testing of the system will reveal whether the chosen acoustical features are sufficient or excessive for usefully analyzing and classifying most sounds. We believe, however, that the basic approach presented here works well for a wide variety of audio database applications. **MM**

Acknowledgments

We would like to thank Dragutin Petkovic at IBM Almaden for encouraging us to write this article. We have had helpful discussions with Stephen Smoliar and Hong Zhang at the Institute for Systems Science in Singapore and with Mike Olson and Chuck O'Neill at Illustra Information Technologies. We also thank the anonymous referees for their helpful comments and suggestions.

References

1. R. Plomp, *Aspects of Tone Sensation: A Psychophysical Study*, Academic Press, London, 1976.

2. S. Foster, W. Schloss, and A.J. Rockmore, "Towards an Intelligent Editor of Digital Audio: Signal Processing Methods," *Computer Music J.*, Vol. 6, No. 1, 1982, pp. 42-51.

3. B. Feiten and S. Gunzel, "Automatic Indexing of a Sound Database Using Self-Organizing Neural Nets," *Computer Music J.*, Vol. 18, No. 3, Summer 1994, pp. 53-65.

4. T. Blum et al., "Audio Databases with Content-Based Retrieval," workshop on Intelligent Multimedia Information Retrieval, 1995 Int'l Joint Conf. on Artificial Intelligence, available at http://www.musclefish.com.

5. D. Keislar et al., "Audio Databases with Content-Based Retrieval," *Proc. Int'l Computer Music Conference 1995*, International Computer Music Association, San Francisco, 1995, pp. 199-202.

6. H. Zhang, B. Furht, and S. Smoliar, *Video and Image Processing in Multimedia Systems*, Kluwer Academic Publishers, Boston, 1995.

7. H. Zhang, A. Kankanhalli, and S. Smoliar, "Automatic Partitioning of Full-Motion Video," *Multimedia Systems*, Vol. 1, No. 1, 1993, pp. 10-28.

8. S. McAdams, "Recognition of Sound Sources and Events," *Thinking in Sound: The Cognitive Psychology of Human Audition*, Clarendon Press, Oxford, 1993.

9. J. Moorer, "On the Transcription of Musical Sound by Computer," *Computer Music J.*, Vol. 1, No. 4, 1977, pp. 32-38.

10. E. Wold, *Nonlinear Parameter Estimation of Acoustic Models*, PhD Thesis, University of California at Berkeley, Berkeley, Calif., 1987.

Erling Wold earned a PhD in EECS at the University of California, Berkeley in 1987 where he did research in source separation, FFT computer architectures, and stochastic sampling. Since that time, he has concentrated on signal processing and software architectures for music applications. He is a prolific composer and has written music for a variety of ensembles as well as for several feature films and theatrical works, including two operas. With the co-authors, he founded Muscle Fish, a software engineering firm specializing in audio and music.

Thomas Blum received a BA in Computer Applications to Music Synthesis from Ohio State in 1978. He creates software to help manage complex data, like sound, and creative tasks, like music composition. In 1978, he cofounded the Computer Music Association and served for roughly 10 years as an associate editor of *Computer Music Journal* (MIT Press).

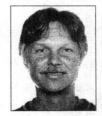

Douglas Keislar received a PhD in Music from Stanford University, where he conducted psycho-acoustical research at the Center for Computer Research in Music and Acoustics (CCRMA). He is an associate editor of *Computer Music Journal* (MIT Press).

James A. Wheaton is president of Harmonic Systems, Inc. He received his BS in Philosophy from MIT in 1980. His research interests include new musical instruments, interactive music, and Internet audio applications.

Readers may contact Erling Wold at Muscle Fish LLC, 2550 Ninth Street, Suite 207B, Berkeley, CA 94710, e-mail erling@musclefish.com.

23

Toward Content-Based Audio Indexing and Retrieval and a New Speaker Discrimination Technique

Lonce Wyse and Stephen W. Smoliar
National University of Singapore

Several techniques for identifying segment transitions in an audio stream are discussed. Gross features are first identified that control more detailed and computationally expensive analysis down stream. Pitch is tracked using some basic streaming principles, and then used as one cue to speaker transitions. A novel speaker discrimination technique is described that makes segmentation decisions when a continuously updated model of the current speaker suddenly ceases to sufficiently account for the input data.

23.1 INTRODUCTION

Despite the multimedia hype, video and audio information are not currently part of our everyday computing environment. We do not yet have the tools for manipulating this kind of information with the ease with which we manipulate text. The goal of the Video Classification Project at ISS is to automatically segment a stream of image and sound data into meaningful units which can then be used in a database system (Smoliar and Zhang, 1994). We consider the problems of parsing input streams, automatic indexing (labeling) of segments, and retrieval techniques. Such a system will support nonlinear browsing of material and the use of sound and image keys for retrieval, which are far more natural ways of interacting with multimedia data than simple linear scanning.

Currently, the audio and video stream parsing is done separately. However, the new systems will run together, because each separate media stream contains information that can help the other make parsing decisions. The work reported here focuses on the parsing and indexing of the audio stream.

The immediate goal of the audio processing is to identify transition points between segments and to do an initial content oriented labeling of the segments. We use a combination of signal processing techniques for feature extraction, and "intelligent" symbolic level processing for decision making. The two processes work together in the sense that some hypotheses are formed based on initial signal processing work which in turn controls further signal processing to test, verify or refine the initial hypotheses.

The symbolic processing includes knowledge about characteristics of some of the basic signal types that we expect to encounter. Currently our data testbed is news stories, and the signals can be grossly classified as "music," "speech," and "other," for the purpose of delineating meaningful segments. Speech is then further broken into segments at boundaries between different speakers.

23.2 INITIAL PROCESSING

The signal is passed first through a filter which measures the amplitude envelope. Labels are attached to the signal identifying regions where energy is at some threshold percentage below the average where some of the following stages do not need to do any work. A 256-point FFT is then performed.

23.3 MUSIC

The "music detector" is an extension of the work by Hawley (Hawley, 1993). No deep philosophical issues about what music is are being addressed here. The system computes peaks in the magnitude spectrum, then bases its decision on the average length of time that peaks exist in a narrow frequency region. We improved previous work by using an ERB (Equivalent Rectangular Bandwidth) scaling of the frequency region (Moore & Glasberg, 1983). Because this scaling is log-like above 500 Hz, it tends to be more robust than a linear representation because the sensitivity to peak movement is more uniform across frequency when the fundamental frequencies of speech or pitched musical instruments are nonstationary. Music detection is performed early because signals so labeled need no further analysis for our purposes. Sections that are not labeled as music are mined for more information.

23.4 PITCH

A spectrally based pitch detection algorithm (Cohen, Grossberg & Wyse, 1995) is employed which was designed to model aspects of human pitch perception. Also based on an ERB scaled energy representation of the signal, it employs an excitatory-center, inhibitory-surround mechanism that enhances peaks, and a weighted summation of regions around harmonics, to derive an activation strength function across pitch. It is robust under conditions of mistuned components and models human responses to rippled noise and noise-band edges in addition to simple harmonic complexes.

The pitch model is layered, and includes a spectral representation, a contrast-enhanced spectral representation and finally a pitch layer, where, in general, every pitch has some level of activation. The pitch detector is robust against the effects of certain kinds of noise. Broadband noise is ignored, for example, even when the signal to noise ratio (in dB) is negative. Due to the convolution with the "Mexican hat" on-center off-surround kernel, spectrally broad signals are suppressed before influencing the pitch layer. More compact signals, particularly those with energy across several harmonically related components, are represented in the pitch layer, but unless they are specially constructed to do so, tend not to shift the peaks due to other pitched signals. This robustness to noise does not make this a model of multiple source segregation, however. Even a single tone creates many peaks in the pitch layer (at all subharmonics, though only one is maximal), so there is no obvious way to associate source perception with any but the most salient peak.

In order to track the pitch of voiced speech over time, several auditory streaming constraints (Bregman, 1990) are embedded in a following processing stage. Because the pitch detector responds to peaked and rippled noise, noise from fricatives causes peaks to appear in the pitch activation function, and, especially if the fricative is unvoiced, a noise peak can be the most prominent one. The resulting trace of the maximally activated pitch makes jumps that are too far in frequency and too fast in time for humans to track as a single stream. By incorporating constraints concerning the relationship between the distance and the rate of frequency jumps that result in a sequence of tones either streaming together or breaking into several streams, we are able to keep the pitch tracker following the pitch of just the voiced portion of speech. Similar constraints concerning energy keep the tracker from being distracted by low level pitched sounds or brief nonspeech bursts.

23.5 SPEECH LABELING

At this point in the pipeline, we have several representations of the signal and a stream of time-stamped labels. To label a segment as "speech," the next stage examines the pitch track in segments not already carrying a label incompatible with speech. The speech label begins with a pitched (assumed now to be "voiced") segment. The label ends with the last pitched segment before a time interval greater than one second in which no pitched segment lasted more than 75 ms. These criteria were empirically determined.

23.6 SPEAKER DISCRIMINATION

Speaker discrimination is an important component of segmenting an audio stream into meaningful subunits. Understanding when speakers change is crucial for dialogue understanding. In the realm of newscasts, a change in speaker almost always corresponds to a change in the content of the news story. Speaker discrimination is related to speaker identification and verification, but the latter two processes are based on prior knowledge about a limited number of speaker identities and are usually text dependent. In speaker discrimination, only knowledge about speech in general is embedded in the system which is text independent. For the discrimination task, no matching of different segments to templates is done, only temporally local decisions about speaker changes are made. Despite the fact that "interspeaker variation" is the bane of speech recognition, actually extracting features that are invariant for one speaker, and that differ across speakers, is a challenging task.

Humans manage to recognize a change in speaker in a very short time, so averaging measures across tens of seconds should not be necessary. The methods used in our system combine pitch and spectral features and make use of timing cues as well. Before the discrimination processes run, a segment must first be labeled as speech. Potential speaker transitions are flagged by events such as lengthy segments of nonspeech, or sudden changes in pitch. Spectral features are extracted which are used for the final label assignment.

23.6.1 Pitch-Based Speaker Discrimination

Changes in pitch characteristics make an important contribution to speaker discrimination, but are neither necessary nor sufficient for identifying the transition. The cue is perhaps most reliable when the transition is between speakers of different gender, but the overlap of ranges is still considerable. Male vocal chords, tending to be longer and heavier than females', generally produce fundamental frequencies in the range between 80 Hz and 250 Hz,

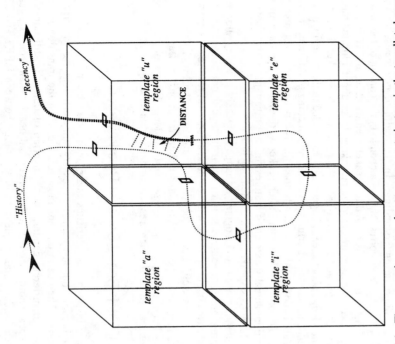

FIG. 23.1. The successive cepstral vectors trace a trajectory in the tessellated space, and vectors within the "recency" window (most recent .75 seconds) are compared to those in the "history" window (extending back 3 seconds) that were in the same template region. If the distance between a recency vector and the closest history vector exceeds a threshold, it adds to the novelty score.

Because one of the manifestations of speaker differences is that different vowels spoken by the respective speakers can overlap in formant space (Peterson & Barney, 1952), then a fairly complete speech recognition system would have to be a part of the discrimination mechanism and would thus carry a substantial computational burden. Another problem with this approach is that speaker discrimination would be language dependent, and people can normally detect speaker changes even when a language unknown to the observer is being spoken.

Our method, related to this same-phoneme comparison method, is to break up a spectral space into regions and compare new input only to stored data in the same spectral region that the input belongs to. This eliminates the need for phoneme identification (though at the expense of being able to use that

whereas those produced by females are generally in the range between 150 Hz and 500 Hz. The range for children is slightly higher than that for women.

Averaging of the speech signal over a window of time and looking for large changes in this measure is a possible technique, but we have found that pitch in a single utterance can vary widely even when averaged over a window of two or more seconds. Averaging also has the disadvantage of being too influenced by extremes; the more outlandish, the greater the influence. We have therefore adopted the use of a change in pitch range for flagging possible speaker transitions.

The range has two frequency bounds: one above which a certain percentage of input pitch values lie, the other below which a certain percentage lie over the duration of a time window. If a cutoff percentage parameter is set at 50%, for example, the mean is tracked. We are currently using a cutoff of 25% for both the upper and lower range, and a window of 2 seconds. The actual frequency of outliers thus have no effect on the range computation no matter how outlandish, making this method more robust than averaging with particularly "prosodic" speakers.

The temporal localization ability of the range change discrimination technique is better than the window size, since it depends upon the cutoff percentages as well. With cutoff percentages of less than 50%, the high bound is more sensitive (responds more quickly) to an increase in upper range than to a decrease, and the low bound is more sensitive to a decrease in the lower range than an increase. Changes to the range in the "sensitive direction" of the bound measures can happen as quickly as the cutoff percentage multiplied by the window length.

23.6.2 Spectrally Based Speaker Discrimination

Speaker variation is the bane of speech processors, and great pains are taken to normalize, compensate or otherwise make systems less sensitive to them. Sources of variation include regional accents, emotional stress, speaking rate, physical impediments, health, gender, and age, and chest, glottis, and vocal tract morphology. With so much interspeaker variability, it seems that automatic speaker discrimination should be easy. The difficulty, of course, lies in finding acoustic features that change less with one speaker than across many speakers.

We are currently exploring a spectrally based method. It is even more evident for spectra than for pitch that no average over a window short enough for reasonably fast detection of speaker change will be stationary over the course of a single speaker utterance.

One way to eliminate the effects of intraspeaker spectral variation would be to compare particular phonemes of one speaker to the same phonemes of another (recall that phonemes are linguistically, not acoustically, defined). This is one of the methods used in speaker identification and verification when comparing input to a known stored utterance (Furui, 1986). There are several problems with this approach. First, it involves the identification of the phonemes.

particular aspect of variation in the process), and turns the approach into a kind of spectral redundancy measure.

To break the representation space into regions, we recorded 15 different voiced sounds (vowels, liquids and fricatives) at as close to a steady state as they could be spoken. Sixteen LPC-derived cepstral coefficients were taken using 25 ms windows stepped every 10 ms, and the vectors were averaged to produce one representative vector for each sound.

During the processing of segments of the input stream that have already been labeled by our system as both "speech" and "pitched," the most recent 750 ms (the "recency" window) of input vectors are compared to the previous 3 seconds (the "history" window), and a novelty score is computed. If the novelty score exceeds a certain threshold, then a new speaker is flagged as starting at the time corresponding to the beginning of the recency window.

The way the novelty score is computed is by first identifying the region into which each input vector falls, and then finding the closest vector in the history window already stored in that region. Euclidean distance, a standard for comparing cepstral vectors, is used. If this distance exceeds a threshold parameter, then the input vector is flagged as novel (see Figure 23.1). If the number of vectors in the recency window that are flagged as novel is greater than a second threshold parameter (expressed as a percentage of the number of data points that the recency window holds), then the criteria for identifying a speaker transition is met.

A brief description of how the method works. The tessellation of cepstral space limits the range of history vectors that recent inputs are compared to. This is what prevents the intraspeaker spectral variation, due to different vowels, to influence the measure. Thus the number of regions must be large enough to prevent too many cross-vowel comparisons. Our tessellation corresponds roughly to the number of vowels and semivowels (glides and liquids) used in the English language. The number of regions must not be too large, lest there never be a "history" vector in the same region as the input for comparison. Similarly, the length of the history window, although needing to be as short as possible to achieve acceptable temporal resolution, needs to be long enough so that at any given time, there is a high probability that there are history window vectors in the same region as the input. The 3 seconds of "history" maintained provides reasonable assurance that much of the input will fall in regions with stored vectors. The recency window needs to be short for resolution, but long for robustness, and long enough so that history vectors in the same region are from a previous entry of the trajectory into the region. When the recency window is so short that this condition is not met, then the distance between a recency vector and a history vector is determined by their distance along the trajectory itself rather than a speaker-characteristic use of the region of cepstral space.

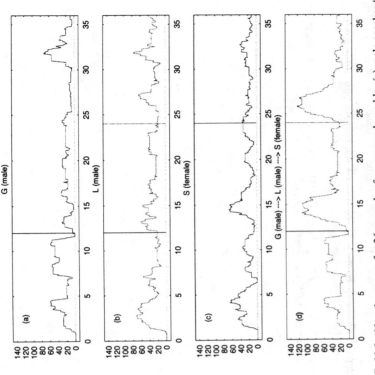

FIG. 23.2. Novelty scores for 36 seconds of a paragraph read by (a) male speaker "G," (b) male speaker "L," and (c) female speaker "S." (d) The novelty score for the same paragraph spliced together from the first 12 seconds from "L," the second 12 seconds from "G," and the last 12 seconds from "S." The traces of the individual speakers can be recognized in (d) except just after the speaker changes where the score suddenly jumps.

This spectral discrimination component of the system is still being developed, but preliminary results show some promise. Figure 23.2 (a,b,c) shows the running novelty score for 3 different speakers reading the same passage from a book. The maximum possible novelty score is 150 (if each of the 5 ms-spaced vectors in the .75 second recency windows was novel). The input for Figure 23.2 (d) was constructed from the first 12 seconds from the first reader, the second 12 seconds from the second reader and the final 12 seconds from the third reader. At each splice, the speaker changed in midsentence (though not midword), whereas the natural flow of the text was maintained. The novelty scores following each speaker changes can be seen to reach a peak higher than any of the individual speaker scores.

Preliminary investigations suggest that the method described is fairly robust, although the variations in a single speaker can still produce novelty scores in the vicinity of speaker-change peaks. The technique has the advantage

REFERENCES

Bloothooft, G. & Plomp, R. (1986). Spectral analysis of sung vowels, III. Characteristics of singers and modes of singing. *J. acoust. Soc. Am.*, 79(3), 852-864.

Bregman, A. (1990). *Auditory Scene Analysis*. Cambridge, MA: MIT Press.

Cohen, M., Grossberg, S., & Wyse, L. (1995). A spectral network model of pitch perception. *J. Acoust. Soc. Am.*, 98(2), 862-879.

Furui, S. (1986). Research on individuality features in speech waves and automatic speaker recognition techniques. *Speech Communication*, 5(2), 183-197.

Hawley, M. J. (1993). *Structure out of Sound*. Ph.D. Thesis, MIT

Hermansky, H. (1990). Perceptual linear predictive (PLP) analysis of speech. *J. Acoust. Soc. Am.*, 87(4), 1738-1752.

Moore, B., & Glasberg, B. (1983). Suggested formulae for calculating auditory filter bandwidths and excitation patterns. *J. Acoust. Soc. Am.* 74, 750-753.

Peterson, G. E. & Barney, H. (1952). Control methods used in a study of vowels. *J. Acoust. Soc. Am.*, 24(2), 175-184.

Smoliar, S. W., & Zhang, H. J. (1994). Content-based video indexing and retrieval. *IEEE Multimedia*, 1(2), 62-72.

of having a relatively light computationally load since it requires no speech or phoneme recognition, and because the input vector is only compared to a fraction of the recent speech utterance. The computation other than the distance measures is minimal. The method might also be useful for text-independent speaker identification and verification by concatenating stored speech of a known speaker with a new speech signal and deriving the novelty score.

There are a number of ways in which this spectral method might be improved. Using Perceptual Linear Predictive (PLP) analysis rather than Linear Predictive Coding (LPC) derived cepstral coefficients may prove beneficial since distances between PLP vectors have been shown to correlate more consistently with perceptual distance (Hermansky, 1990). The regions could be made adaptive with some continuously updated clustering method. Although most likely improving the performance over the a priori and arbitrary division of the representation space, this would add considerable computation time. It also appears that some of our representation regions are proving to be more useful for discrimination than others (which is suggested by the observation that parts of the spectrum are more useful than others in identifying voice types (Bloothooft & Plomp, 1986), and a systematic exploration of this will undoubtedly improve both the speed and the accuracy of this technique. Finally, other acoustic features that typically vary across speakers, but have a high intraspeaker variability with a high correlation to spectral variation (e.g., spectral tilt, relative levels of even and odd harmonics, breathiness) might be more usefully compared by region in the manner described herein.

23.7 DISCUSSION

In our video classification system, segment transition decisions in audio are based on less temporally localized information than are video transition decisions. However, all event labeling is done within 2 seconds of the event, and the processing runs in close to real time on a Sparc workstation, the actual run time being signal dependent.

The whole audio subsystem consists of some 20 or so different signal and symbol processing "filters" which can be run in a flexible ordering depending on the goals of the system. A uniform method of labeling and communication between processes has been developed which allows the information gleaned from one processes to control the processing parameters of another. Future work along these lines will make the flow of processing through the different filtering processes more flexible and integrated.

Open-Vocabulary Speech Indexing for Voice and Video Mail Retrieval

M. G. Brown[1]   *J. T. Foote*[2]   *G. J. F. Jones*[2,3]   *K. Spärck Jones*[3]   *S. J. Young*[2]

[1]Olivetti Research Limited, 24a Trumpington St., Cambridge, CB2 1QA, UK
[2]Cambridge University Engineering Department, Cambridge, CB2 1PZ, UK
[3]Cambridge University Computer Laboratory, Cambridge, CB2 3QG, UK

email: mgb@cam-orl.co.uk, {jtf,gjfj,sjy}@eng.cam.ac.uk, ksj@cl.cam.ac.uk

ABSTRACT

This paper presents recent work on a multimedia retrieval project at Cambridge University and Olivetti Research Limited (ORL). We present novel techniques that allow extremely rapid audio indexing, at rates approaching several thousand times real time. Unlike other methods, these techniques do not depend on a fixed vocabulary recognition system or on keywords that must be known well in advance. Using statistical methods developed for text, these indexing techniques allow rapid and efficient retrieval and browsing of audio and video documents. This paper presents the project background, the indexing and retrieval techniques, and a video mail retrieval application incorporating content-based audio indexing, retrieval, and browsing.

KEYWORDS:

audio indexing, speech recognition, word spotting, content-based retrieval, information retrieval, browsing

INTRODUCTION

Recent years have seen a rapid increase in the availability and use of multimedia applications. These systems can generate large amounts of audio and video data which can be expensive to store and unwieldy to access. The Video Mail Retrieval (VMR) project at Cambridge University and Olivetti Research Limited (ORL), Cambridge, UK, is addressing these problems by developing systems to retrieve stored video material using the spoken audio soundtrack [3, 25]. Specifically, the project focuses on the content-based location, retrieval, and playback of potentially relevant data. The primary goal of the VMR project is to develop a video mail retrieval application for the Medusa multimedia environment developed at ORL.

Finding the information content of arbitrary spoken documents is a difficult task. This paper presents methods of rapidly and automatically locating words spoken in voice and video mail messages. Unlike other approaches, these techniques do not depend on a limited-vocabulary recognition system or on "keywords" that must be known well in

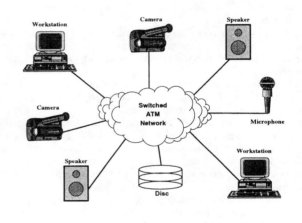

Figure 1. Connection of Medusa Network Endpoints to an ATM network

advance of search time [30] [21]. Given an estimate of word locations, we show that statistical retrieval methods can be used for efficient spoken document retrieval and browsing. These exploit a "phone lattice," which represents multiple acoustic hypotheses from which possible word occurrences can be inferred. This paper is organised as follows: after an overview of audio indexing methods, the multimedia environment and corpus of spoken documents is described. Further sections present the speech recognition and information retrieval methods used, and a final section describes how they are combined in a real-time open-vocabulary video mail retrieval system.

AUDIO INDEXING

The large computational cost of speech recognition is a fundamental obstacle to automatic audio indexing. Even using the most advanced decoders, recognition speed is seldom much faster than real-time, and often far slower. Though this may be acceptable for typical speech recognition applications such as dictation, it is clearly unacceptable to incur several hours of computation when searching an audio corpus of similar length.

The normal solution is to shift the computational burden ahead of need; thus for a voice-mail retrieval application, the expensive speech recognition is performed as messages are added to the archive. This allows rapid online searches as no recognition is done at search time: only the pre-computed index files need be interrogated. This approach has been used in cases where a "word spotting" and/or large-vocabulary recognition system generates text "pseudo-transcriptions" from the audio documents, which may then be rapidly searched. For example, previous work on the VMR project demonstrated practical retrieval of audio messages using fixed-vocabulary word spotting for content identification [12, 5], and more recent work has explored combining word spotting and large-vocabulary recognition for audio retrieval [14].

A similar approach is taken by most other groups working on audio indexing. In the Carnegie Mellon Informedia project, a combination of verbatim text transcriptions and large-vocabulary recogniser output are used for search indexes [23]. A large vocabulary system was used for topic spotting at BBN [16], while workers at Ensigma Ltd used keyword spotting for similar ends [31]. A novel approach is taken at ETH Zürich, where subword units are used as search indexes [28].

With the possible exception of work done at ETH Zürich, the drawback of these approaches is that index terms (the desired keywords or vocabulary) must be known well in advance of search time. A large-vocabulary system has the added drawback that a statistical "language model" (defining likely word tuples) must be available, otherwise the recognition search becomes computationally infeasible. To be useful, language models must be trained on example text (typically megawords) from a (hopefully) similar domain. While this may be possible for some domains (say broadcast news), it is much less practical for others, such as the video mail domain considered here, where there is unlikely to be sufficient training data.

This paper presents an alternative approach where a phone lattice is computed before search time. Though this takes substantial computation, it is less expensive than a large-vocabulary recognition system, and has the additional advantage that it requires no language model. Once computed, the phone lattice may be rapidly scanned using a dynamic-programming algorithm to find index terms [10]. This requires a phonetic decomposition of any desired words, but these are easily found from a dictionary or by a rule-based algorithm [4]. For comparison, the lexicon of our "large" vocabulary experiments was 20,000 words, while our phonetic dictionary has more than 200,000 entries.

This paper reports quantitative experiments demonstrating that Information Retrieval (IR) methods developed for searching text archives can accurately retrieve audio and video data using index terms generated on-the-fly from phone lattices. In addition, the same techniques can be used to rapidly locate interesting areas within an individual mail message. The paper concludes with the description of an on-line video mail retrieval application, including approaches to content-based audio browsing.

MEDUSA: MULTIMEDIA ON AN ATM NETWORK

The Medusa Project at ORL is a novel and extensive experiment in sending multiple simultaneous streams of digital audio and video over a prototype 100 Megabit-per-second switched ATM (Asynchronous Transfer Mode) network [7, 15]. A number of ATM Network Endpoints have been developed enabling the direct connection to the network of microphones, speakers, cameras, disk systems and LCD displays. This concept of exploding the workstation across the network has provided a very adaptable and easily

Figure 2. MDMail: Medusa video mail application

extensible environment for the work presented here. Some 200 of these Network Endpoints cover all laboratory rooms and optical fibre extends the ATM network to the University Engineering Department and the University Computer Laboratory. An ATM network's high bandwidth, low latency, and low transit time jitter make it an ideal transport medium for multimedia applications.

The Medusa software developed at ORL handles multimedia in a highly distributed environment. Medusa servers are run on each Network Endpoint and networked workstation in a peer-to-peer architecture. Software objects called Modules created within these servers provide media sources, sinks and pipeline processing components which can be connected together across the network in arbitrary ways. The software modules provide direct digital access to the audio and video data. This architecture enables expensive tasks like video processing and speech recognition to be sited on appropriate hardware, which can then offer its services to any source object connected to the network.

The Multimedia Repository

The Disc Endpoint, which is the size and shape of a small vertical format PC case, uses the ORL standard ATM network interface card plus a SCSI interface to make a RAID-3 array of discs available as a multimedia file server. The initial prototypes use five 2 Gbyte drives giving a storage capacity of 8 Gbytes per unit. Four Disc Bricks are currently deployed on ORL's ATM network. Disk capacities nearly double each year; it is now possible to construct 32 Gbyte devices and we anticipate 64 Gbyte ones within a year.

Medusa ATM camera Endpoints capture frames at a resolution of 176 x 128 pixels at a rate of 25 frames per second. With 5 bits per colour component packed into a 16 bit short word this equates to a raw data rate of 8.8 Megabits per second, though this may be lowered by reducing frame rate or size. Together with the 0.5 Megabits per second required for uncompressed 16-bit audio sampled at 32 KHz, a typical

30 second video mail message amounts to about 35 Mbytes of data. By pragmatically reducing the picture resolution it is possible to store over 1000 video mail messages on an 8 Gbyte device.

Recent developments have made available ATM-networked combined audio and video sources which deliver MPEG compressed data. This reduces these storage requirements dramatically, improving quality at the same time. It is now practical to build an archive containing hundreds of hours of audio/video material. As an example, a 64 Gbyte disc system could store over 90 hours of VHS quality material, equivalent to 11,000 typical video mail messages. If this were MPEG audio only some 88,000 audio mail messages could be stored. As archives with a capacity of this magnitude become more common, better ways of locating and retrieving information become essential.

THE VMR MESSAGE CORPUS

For research into the underlying speech recognition and information retrieval technologies, it was necessary to collect a corpus of mail messages and additional spoken data. (While other spoken data collections exist, they do not have the necessary information content for meaningful IR experimentation.)

The VMR message corpus is a structured collection of audio training data and information–bearing audio messages. Ten "categories" were chosen to reflect the anticipated messages of actual users, including, for example, "management" and "equipment." For the message data, speakers were asked to record a natural response to a prompt (with five prompts per category), for a total of 50 unique prompts. The messages are fully spontaneous, and contain a large number of disfluencies such as "um" and "ah," partially uttered words and false starts, laughter, sentence fragments, and informalities and slang ("'fraid" and "whizzo"). There were 6 messages (from 6 different users) for each of the 50 prompts. A more complete description of the VMR corpus may be found in [11].

There were fifteen speakers, of which 11 were male and 4 female. Data was recorded at 16 kHz from both a Sennheiser HMD 414 close-talking microphone and the cardioid far-field desk microphone used in the Medusa system, in an acoustically isolated room. Each speaker provided the following speech data:

- **Test:** 20 natural speech messages ("p" data): the response to 20 unique prompts from 4 categories.
- **Train:** Various additional training data for speech recognition models:
  - 77 read sentences ("r" data): sentences containing keywords, constructed such that each keyword occurred a minimum of five times.
  - 170 keywords ("i" data) spoken in isolation.
  - 150 read sentences ("z" data): phonetically-rich sentences from the TIMIT corpus.

All files were verified and transcribed at the word level; non-speech events and disfluencies such as partially spoken words, pauses, and hesitations were transcribed in accordance with the Wall Street Journal data collection procedures. Phonetic transcriptions were automatically generated from a machine-readable version of the Oxford Learners Dictionary. The standard reduced TIMIT phone set was augmented with additional vowels specific to British English pronunciation. The resulting 300 messages (5 hours of spoken data), along with their text transcriptions, serve as a test corpus for the speech recognition and IR experiments.

For a practical system, it cannot be assumed that speakers will be known, thus it is necessary to have speaker-independent acoustic models. To build such speaker-independent acoustic models, additional training data was obtained from the WSJCAM0 British English corpus, which consists of spoken sentences read from the Wall Street Journal. Data was collected for 100 British English speakers. The corpus contains a total of around 12 hours of spoken data. WSJCAM0 was collected at Cambridge University Engineering Department and further details may be found in [19].

ACOUSTIC INDEXING VIA PHONE LATTICES

Automatically detecting words or phrases in unconstrained speech is usually termed "word spotting;" this technology is the foundation of the work presented here. Conventional keyword spotters based on the same hidden Markov model (HMM) methods used in successful continuous-speech recognition [18]. A hidden Markov model is a statistical representation of a speech event like a word; model parameters are typically trained on a large corpus of labelled speech data. Given a trained set of HMMs, there exists an efficient algorithm for finding the most likely model sequence (the recognised words), given unknown speech data.

The work presented here takes a different approach, based on the work of James [9]. An off-line HMM system is used to generate a number of likely phone sequences, which may then be rapidly searched to find phone strings comprising a desired word. For HMM training and recognition, the acoustic data was parameterised into a spectral representation (mel-cepstral coefficients), and difference and acceleration coefficients were appended. The HTK tool set was used to construct both speaker-dependent (SD) and speaker-independent (SI) monophone models as well as speaker-independent biphone models [34]. All phone models have 3 emitting states, each with 8 Gaussian mixture diagonal-covariance output distributions.

Model Training

For every training utterance, a phone sequence was generated from the text transcription and a dictionary. These sequences were used to estimate HMM parameters as follows. Speaker-dependent "monophone" models were trained on the read messages ("r" data) and sentences from the TIMIT database ("z" data). Once single-mixture monophone models had been initialised, the number of mixture components was increased, and the parameters re-estimated. Re-estimation was halted at 8 mixture components, as additional components did not improve performance. Speaker-independent models were trained in a similar manner on the WSJCAM0 corpus of read speech, which contains more than one hundred speakers.

Though we rarely notice, phone pronunciation changes drastically depending on context (contrast the "T" sound in "attack" and "stain.") Automatic speech recognition improves substantially when phone models can be made context-dependent, thus the two "T" sounds above would have separate models because they occur in different contexts. Speaker-independent "biphone" models were constructed by "cloning" the 1-mixture speaker-dependent monophones such that each possible biphone was represented, then clustering similar states using a decision tree [32]. State parameters are tied across a cluster, then re-estimated in the usual way, once again up to 8 mixtures. An advantage of

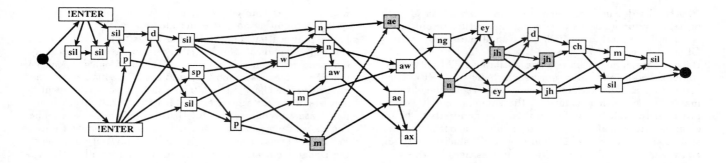

Figure 3. Phone lattice for word "manage" (m ae n ih jh)

this training method is that all possible biphones are modelled, yet because most states are tied, the full model set is relatively compact. There was insufficient training data to construct speaker-dependent biphones.

Lattice Generation

With a set of phone HMMs and a network of possible phone interconnections, it is possible to find the most likely sequence of phones given unknown acoustic data using an efficient search based on the Viterbi algorithm. An enhanced version of this algorithm can generate multiple hypotheses, representing the n most likely paths through the models. Such multiple hypotheses can be stored as a phone lattice: a directed acyclic graph where nodes represent phone start/end times and arcs represent hypothesised phone occurrences between them. Arcs are labelled with an acoustic score indicating the likelihood that the acoustic data over that interval corresponds with the particular phone model. To simplify searching, the lattices used here have the additional constraint that all paths must start at a particular start node and end at another special node.

The "depth" of a phone lattice is the number of phone hypotheses active at a given time. This parameter is critical to the performance of a lattice-based spotting system. If the lattice is too shallow, performance will be poor due to unavoidable phone recognition errors. Because the best phone recognition systems are little more than 70% accurate [20], the chance that a given phone string will be correctly identified in a 1-deep lattice is poor. On the other hand, if the lattice is too deep, too many phone sequences become possible, most of which will be incorrect. Another drawback is that the storage requirements and search time increase substantially with lattice depth. Failing to identify an uttered search word is termed a *miss* while hypothesising a word where none is present is a *false alarm*.

Lattice depth may be adjusted through several mechanisms. During generation, the number of active tokens at one time represents the n-best paths through the model lattice [33]. The more tokens used, the deeper the lattice. To speed lattice generation, a pruning threshold is used: this ensures that low-likelihood phone paths are not considered, saving substantial computation. The lower the pruning threshold, the more possible paths considered, and hence the deeper the resultant lattice. Figure 3 shows a lattice generated for the single utterance "manage." For clarity, acoustic scores and start/end times are not shown, though nodes are arranged in roughly chronological order. Four tokens were used in the decoding: the resultant lattice depth was 5 as 35 arcs were generated for the 7 phones actually uttered (m ae n ih jh plus beginning and ending silences).

Model type:	SI mono-phones	SD mono-phones	SI biphones
Phone Accuracy	41.1%	55.4%	51.7%
Figure of Merit	48.0%	73.6%	60.4%

Table 1. Speech recognition results for VMR corpus messages

Lattice Scanning

Once the lattices have been computed, it is relatively straightforward to scan them for a phone sequence constituting a given word. Once a string of the correct phones has been found, an acoustic score for the putative term is computed as the sum of the phone arc scores normalised by the best-path score. Deep lattices will result in many hypotheses for a given word (because of different paths starting or ending within a few milliseconds) so overlapping word hypotheses are eliminated by keeping only the best scoring one. For example, Figure 3 shows two possible paths for the phone sequence m ae n ih jh, because of the two instances of the phone jh following ih. This scanning procedure can be made extremely time-efficient, producing hypotheses in the order of a thousand times faster than the source audio.

Speech Recognition Results

Table presents the results of lattice scanning experiments using 6 tokens, on the VMR corpus messages. The phone accuracy is defined as the ratio of correctly recognised phones, minus deletions and insertions, to the actual number of phones, for the best path through the lattice. (Experiments on the WSJCAM0 read-speech corpus using the monophone models resulted in phone accuracies nearer 60%, indicating that the natural-speech VMR corpus is more difficult than read speech to recognise.)

Putative hits generated by a word spotting system generally have an associated acoustic score. Because low-scoring words are more likely to be false alarms, the operating point of the recognition system may be adjusted by ignoring terms with a score below a given threshold. Words with scores above the threshold are considered true hits, while those with scores below are considered false alarms and ignored. Choosing the appropriate threshold is a tradeoff between the number of Type I (miss) and Type II (false alarm) errors, with the usual problem that reducing one increases the other. The accuracy of a word spotter is thus dependent on the threshold and cannot be expressed as a single number if false alarms are taken into account. An accepted figure-of-merit (FOM) for word spotting is defined as the average percentage of correctly detected words as the threshold is varied from one to

Weight Scheme		Full Vocab.		
		uw	cfw	cw
Precision	5 docs	0.392	0.375	0.371
	10 docs	0.313	0.308	0.344
	15 docs	0.279	0.292	0.308
	20 docs	0.250	0.271	0.290
Average Precision		0.327	0.352	0.368

Table 2. Retrieval precision values using full text transcriptions (VMR Collection 1b)

ten false alarms per word per hour. These types of recognition error effect not only speech recognition but also information retrieval performance [12]. A drawback of the lattice scan approach is that it is not robust for short words – using lattices of the depth necessary to detect longer words results in a large number of false alarms for shorter ones. Though more sophisticated scoring mechanisms might improve this, the solution used here was to ignore very short words (3 or fewer phones), which are typically not information-rich anyway.

For comparison, the best FOMs obtainable using speaker-independent keyword models was 69.9%, but this additional accuracy was at the cost of having to explicitly search for the 35 particular keywords in the recognition phase, which is several orders of magnitude slower than the lattice-scan approach [5].

INFORMATION RETRIEVAL VIA ACOUSTIC INDEXES

Once words can be located in a speech corpus (using the techniques just described) they may be used for content-based message retrieval, by applying Information Retrieval (IR) techniques originally developed for text. IR techniques attempt to satisfy a user's information need by retrieving potentially relevant messages from a document archive.

In practice, the user composes a search "request" as a sentence or list of words from which a set of actual search "terms" is derived. A score can be computed for a document from the number or weights of matching "query" terms. Searching an archive of documents will deliver an output with documents ranked by matching score. The user can then browse high-ranking messages in this output to find desired information.

Prior to retrieval, conventional IR systems compute an "inverted file" structure where documents are indexed by term. This allows extremely rapid retrieval because documents containing a given term can be quickly located. In the VMR system described here, the actual word-level contents of message are unknown until search time and hence it is not possible to build the inverted file structure in advance. When a request is entered, the lattices are scanned for each search term, as described in the previous section; the putative hits are then used to construct an inverted file for retrieval. Ongoing retrieval efficiency is improved by preserving all lattice scan results in the inverted file, so that effort is not duplicated scanning for a term more than once.

Requests and Relevance Assessments

Evaluating retrieval performance is central to IR research. Evaluating an IR system requires a set of message requests, together with assessments of the relevance of each message to each of these requests. Though some previous experiments [3, 12] used a simulated request and assessment set, a more realistic set has since been collected from the user community that supplied the database messages, forming VMR Collection 1b.

A total of 50 text requests were collected from 10 users, each of whom generated 5 requests and corresponding relevance assessments. A request prompt for each category was formed from the 5 message prompts associated with the category. Users were asked to compose a natural language request after being shown the request prompt.

Ideally, the relevance of all archived messages should be assessed; however this is not practical even for our 300 message archive (which is considered a very small archive by the standards of text IR). A practical alternative is to assess only a subset chosen to contain (hopefully) all the relevant messages. A suitable assessment subset was formed by combining the 30 messages in the category to which the original message prompt belonged, plus 5 messages from outside the category having the highest query-message scores (using cfw weights, as in Section). Subjects were presented with the transcription of each message and asked to mark it as "relevant", "partially relevant", or "not relevant" to the request they had just composed. Messages were presented in random order to avoid possible sequencing effects during assessment. The following sections report results only for the set of messages assessed as highly relevant.

Text Preprocessing

In standard text retrieval systems, documents and requests are typically preprocessed to improve retrieval performance and storage efficiency. The first stage is usually to remove function words (such as "the," "which") which do not help retrieval. The remaining words are then stemmed to reduce word form variations that inhibit term matching between documents and requests.

Retrieval performance for spoken documents can be expected to suffer degradation due to recognition errors (either misses or false alarms on the search terms). In the VMR project, IR benchmarks are established using the full text transcriptions of the 300 messages. The relative degradation can then be computed by comparing retrieval performance with that for the text transcriptions.

The text transcriptions as well as the written requests were therefore preprocessed before search. Function words were removed using a standard "stop list" [27]. The remaining words were reduced to stems using a standard algorithm due to Porter [17]. For example, given the request

```
In what ways can the windows interface of a
workstation be personalised?
```

the following query is obtained:

```
wai window interfac workstat personalis
```

As the lattice is scanned only for the terms in the query, stop words are ignored, which is fortunate because they are generally short, and thus may not be reliably located by the lattice scanning method. The issue of suffix stripping is slightly more complex. There are several options: search only for the term as it appears in the request, search for the suffix stripped term, search for all terms which reduce to the same stem as the request term, or search for the shortest dictionary entry which reduces to this stem. The option taken here is to search for the term as it appears in the original request, although the other options are under investigation. Also the phonetic dictionary was expanded to include all search terms and hence rule-based phonetic prediction was not needed. Finally, search terms having 3 or

Weight Scheme		Average Precision (Relative %)		
		uw	*cfw*	*cw*
Text	Full Vocab	0.327 (100%)	0.352 (100%)	0.368 (100%)
Spoken Documents	SD monophones	0.262 (80.1%)	0.285 (81.0%)	0.315 (85.6%)
	SI monophones	0.174 (53.2%)	0.199 (56.5%)	0.222 (60.3%)
	SI biphones	0.224 (68.5%)	0.262 (74.4%)	0.277 (75.3%)

Table 3. Absolute and relative Average Precision for different lattice acoustic models (VMR Collection 1b)

fewer phones were excluded since they generate too many false alarms with the lattice depths used. For example, the word "date" was not searched for, as its typical phone decomposition (d ey t) was only three phones long. Though it is clearly not optimal to discard search terms, less than 10% of query terms not in the stop list were too short, and their absence did not harm retrieval performance unduly.

Message Scoring

Given a query, an estimate of each message's relevance depends on the number of terms in common. This estimate gives the query-document matching score, and allows all messages in the archive to be ranked in terms of potential relevance [27]. Considering search term presence/absence only, the simplest scoring method is just to count the number of terms in common, often called the *unweighted* (*uw*) score. Better retrieval can be achieved by weighting terms, for instance by the *collection frequency weight* (*cfw*),

$$cfw(i) = \log \frac{N}{n[i]}$$

where N is the total number of documents and $n[i]$ is the number of documents that contain search term i. This scheme favours rarer (and hence more selective) terms. The query-document matching score is then the sum of the matching query term weights. A more sophisticated weighting scheme takes into account the number of times each term occurs in each document, normalised by the document length. This latter factor is important since a document's relevance does not depend on its length, hence neither should its score. The well tested *combined weight (cw)*, described further in [26], is

$$cw(i,j) = \frac{cfw(i) \times tf(i,j) \times (K+1)}{K \times ndl(j) + tf(i,j)}$$

where $cw(i,j)$ represents the *cw* weight of term i in document j, the term frequency $tf(i,j)$ is the frequency of i in j, and $ndl(j)$ is the normalised document length. $ndl(j)$ is calculated as

$$ndl(j) = \frac{dl(j)}{\text{Average } dl \text{ for all documents}},$$

where $dl(j)$ is the length of j. The combined weight constant K must be determined empirically; after testing we set $K = 1$.

For full-text documents, the document length $dl(j)$ is simply the number of terms in document j. However, when deriving search terms from the phone lattice the situation is less clear. The simplest estimate of $dl(j)$ is the number of search terms actually located in the document. This is unsatisfactory for several reasons: for example, a short document with a large number of false alarms may appear comparatively long. This motivates other estimates of document length,

such as its length in time. Our experiments indicate that a better representation of $dl(j)$ is the number of phones in the the most likely phone sequence. This is easily computed during speech recognition and is intuitively a reasonable measure since the number of phones should be independent of speaking rate and hence is a better measure of the number of words actually spoken.

Measuring IR Performance

Given a query, a matching score may be computed for every document in the archive using the methods just described. Documents can then be ranked by score so that the highest-scoring documents (potentially the most relevant) occur at the top of the list. Retrieval performance is often measured by *precision*, the proportion of retrieved messages that are relevant to a particular query at a certain position in the ranked list. One accepted single-number performance figure is the *average precision*. For each query, the precision values are averaged for each relevant document in the ranked list. The results are then averaged across the query set, resulting in the average precision. Other less reductive retrieval evaluation metrics are available and generally preferable, but this single-number performance measure is a useful basic performance indicator.

Retrieval Results

This section presents experimental retrieval results for VMR Collection 1b, both for text transcriptions and for indexes derived from the monophone and biphone lattices discussed in Section . All results are for the *a posteriori* best acoustic threshold, and all *cw* scores estimate the document length as the number of phones. The basic comparisons are between monophone and biphone results, and between SI and SD model results. However, it is helpful to set this spoken document retrieval performance against reference performance for text.

Thus Table 2 shows retrieval performance using full open-vocabulary text transcriptions. These results confirm that more sophisticated weighting schemes improve retrieval performance. Note that the average precision score is the average of the precision values for the relevant documents in the ranked list. Figure 3 shows retrieval performance for the various models and weighting schemes for the spoken documents. Absolute average precision is shown, and also that relative to the average precision obtainable from text (which may be considered the best possible). Clearly the *cw* scheme produces the best retrieval performance. In addition, retrieval performance is well-correlated with speech recognition accuracy. Thus the SI biphones are better than the SI monophones, but the SD monophones are better still. It is not surprising that the SD monophones resulted in the best retrieval performance as they had the best phone recognition accuracy. But SD models limit the usefulness of the VMR system and hence the extension to SI modelling is important. Though the SI biphones do not perform as well as

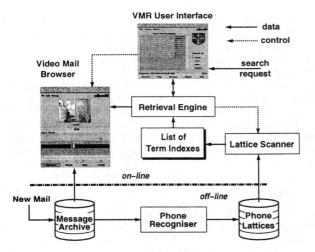

Figure 4. Block diagram of video mail retrieval system

the SD monophones, the speaker-independent models allow messages uttered by any speaker to be retrieved. It should be noted that one of the speakers is a native American and another speaker's accent is strongly influenced by his central European background. The British English models used here are not well matched to these speakers resulting in lower recognition performance. Nevertheless, reasonable retrieval performance can be obtained. Clearly spoken document retrieval is less good than the text case, but not disastrously so. More importantly, with the best weighting scheme (cw) the speaker independent biphone models perform respectably in themselves and not much worse than the speaker-dependent case.

A REAL-TIME VIDEO MAIL RETRIEVAL APPLICATION

At some point, results from both the keyword spotting and information retrieval must be presented to the user. The approach taken for the VMR user interface is the "message list filter." Upon startup, a scrollable list shows all available messages in the user's video mail archive. Using information in the mail message header, various controls let the user "narrow" the list, for example, by displaying only those messages from a particular user or received after a particular time. Unsetting a constraint restores the messages hidden by that constraint; multiple constraints can be active at one time, giving the messages selected by a boolean conjunction of the constraints.

A natural addition to this scheme is to add message attributes that reflect the information content of the audio portion, as determined using the retrieval methods described previously. In operation, the user types in a text search query. The resulting score for each message is computed by the retrieval engine, and the interface then displays a list of messages ranked by score. Scores are represented by bar graphs, as in Figure 5; messages with identical scores are ranked by time. In its simplest form, the keyword search resembles an "audio grep" that returns a list of messages containing a particular keyword. Because the search is phonetic rather than textual, certain "tricks" can be used to enhance search effectiveness:

- Concatenation: A "+" in the query instructs the dictionary lookup routine to concatenate two words into one long phone string. Example: to find the word "netscape" search for "nets+cape."

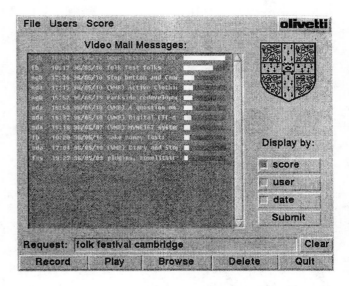

Figure 5. Video Mail User Interface application

- Word Stems: If a given search fails on a long word, shorter variants may work better. Example: To find "managerial" search for "manage."

- Homophones: If a given word is not in the dictionary, it may still be found using a homophone (exact rhyme). Example: to find "Basque" search for "bask."

- Phonetic representation: If not in the dictionary or amenable to the previous approaches, a word may still be found by entering its phonetic composition directly. Example: "Yeltsin" = "#y+#eh+#l+#t+#s+#ih+#n." The initial "#" is necessary to distinguish single-letter phones from single-letter words (eg "#b" ≠ "B" = "#b+#iy"). A help menu is available that displays a list of phones and their pronunciations.

All the above approaches may be used in conjunction; for example the following query would be useful to find the term "ATM" : "A+T+M eighty"

Figure 4 shows a block diagram of the video mail retrieval application. All archived messages have corresponding lattices, generated when the mail message was added to the archive. When the user types a search request into the interface, the information retrieval engine interrogates the inverted file to determine whether any previously unseen terms are present. If so, the lattice scan engine locates term occurrences in the available lattices. These new hypotheses are then added to the inverted file and preserved for future reference. The actual search time for unseen terms, though extremely rapid, is not instantaneous. In our demonstration system, searching more than an hour of audio data for these terms will take less than five seconds for a typical request. Once all available term hypotheses have been located, a ranked list of messages is computed, and returned to the GUI.

A Video Message Browser

After the ranked list of messages is displayed, the user must still investigate the listed messages to either find the relevant one(s) or determine that the retrieval was ineffective and that a new search is required. While there are convenient methods for the graphical browsing of text, e.g. scroll bars, "page-forward" commands, and word-search functions, existing video and audio playback interfaces almost universally adopt the "tape recorder" metaphor. To ensure that

Figure 6. Video mail browser showing detected keywords

nothing important is missed, an entire message must be auditioned from start to finish which takes significant time. In contrast, the transcription of a minute-long message is typically a paragraph of text, which may be scanned by eye in a matter of seconds. Even if there is a "fast forward" button it is generally a hit-or-miss operation to find a desired section in a lengthy message. We can, however use the term indexes to provide a reliably economical way to access and review audio/video data.

Our browser is an attempt to represent a dynamic time-varying process (the audio/video stream) by a static image that can be taken in at a glance. A message is represented as horizontal timeline, and events are displayed graphically along it. Time runs from left to right, and events are represented proportionally to when they occur in the message; for example, events at the beginning appear on the left side of the bar and short-duration events are short. When a particular file is selected for browsing, the list of term indexes (including exact times of search term occurrences) is available to the browser from the inverted file. For a selected message, the browser contents are computed dynamically for the current query by following a linked-list through the inverted file which links hypotheses pertaining to this particular message. Potentially interesting portions of the message are thus easily identified.

A simple representation is to display putative keyword hits on the timeline, as in Figure 6. The timeline is the black bar; the scale indicates time in seconds. When pointed at with the mouse, keyword names are highlighted in white (so it may be read in the presence of many other keyword hits). Clicking on the desired time in the time bar starts message playback at that time; this lets the user selectively play regions of interest, rather than the entire message. Figure 6 shows the keyword hits "folk" and "festival" (highlighted) displayed on the time bar, starting about eight seconds into the message; a time cursor (the triangle-bar) indicates the current playback time. This approach may be enhanced by displaying different search terms in different colours, and

weighting them according to term or document frequency (so less discriminating search terms appear less prominent in the display).

Due to false alarms, displaying all putative hits can sometimes give a misleading impression of the true relevance. Another approach to content-based browsing has been motivated by our work with broadcast news retrieval, where teletext transcriptions were used as indexing sources [2]. Individual keyword hits are not displayed in this approach; rather the message is considered as a series of overlapping "windows," consisting of a short, fixed interval. A query-window matching score can be computed for each interval, just as for an entire document. The window scores can then be displayed such that the higher-scoring windows appear brighter and more prominent. The resulting display is essentially a "low-pass filtered" version of the putative hits, and is thus less time-precise but less cluttered as well, and automatically incorporates the term weighting factors so that less-discriminating terms are not given undue importance. A similar approach is adopted in the "TileBars" data visualisation tool developed by Hearst [6], which displays document length and term relevance in the initial ranked list. This type of output could easily be incorporated into our ranked list display, allowing users to make a more informed choice of documents prior to browsing.

Video Cues

For the video mail application, we have focussed on the audio stream because that is where nearly all information of practical interest will be found. It is, in general, much more difficult to extract useful information from a video signal[1]. Image retrieval is a challenging task and many problems remain unsolved. Most work does not extend much beyond simple measures of colour or shape similarity [24, 1], although there is promising work based on wavelet analysis [8]. While efforts in face and gesture recognition are in progress at ORL and elsewhere [22], less sophisticated analyses can still yield information helpful for browsing. For example, a Medusa video analyser module can detect the activity in a video stream; one application uses this activity information to automatically select a preferred video stream from several available in each room. One simple strategy is to determine the "activity" of a video stream from an estimate of frame-to-frame difference. A large, impulsive value can indicate a new scene or camera, while moderate values over a period of time indicate subject or camera motion. Near-zero values mean a static (and therefore uninteresting) image. Though not yet implemented, current plans are to add this activity information to the browser, enabling automatic detection of a camera or scene change. In this case, a "thumbnail" image of the new view would be displayed on the timeline. Also, active areas could be highlighted to indicate that something of potential interest is occurring in the video stream.

FUTURE WORK AND CONCLUSIONS

The work presented here is only the latest step towards general audio and video retrieval. Previous work, by the VMR group and by others, has shown that spoken document retrieval using speech recognition is becoming practical [12, 9]. Future work in this project will be to integrate different audio index sources available from large vocabulary recognition and conventional as well as lattice-based word spotting

---

[1] This is particularly true in the video mail environment, where the vast majority of messages are just "talking head" images from a small pool of users, against static backgrounds.

[14, 13]. In addition, work will need to be done to make the system robust to environmental noise, microphone differences, accent variability, and telephone-bandwidth speech. Another promising area is to use other types of audio information, such as speaker or music identification, to help index multimedia streams [29]. In conclusion, this paper presents useful methods of indexing audio and video sources, and demonstrates a real-time audio retrieval application, although still on a small scale. Much more work needs to be done on scaling up, especially on handling large numbers of documents and their correspondingly large lattices. But as multimedia archives proliferate on the WWW and elsewhere, technology like that presented here will be become indispensable to locate, retrieve, and browse audio and video information.

ACKNOWLEDGEMENTS

The authors thank the following people for their invaluable assistance: David James for useful discussions, Steve Hedge for the network editor used to create Figure 3, Frank Stajano for Medusa application libraries, Julian Odell for decoder improvements, and Tony Robinson for compiling the BEEP British English pronunciation dictionary.
Olivetti Research Limited is an industrial partner of the VMR project. This project has been supported by the UK DTI Grant IED4/1/5804 and SERC (now EPSRC) Grant GR/H87629.

REFERENCES

1. R. Barber, C. Faloutsos, M. Flickner, J. Hafner, W. Niblack, and D. Petkovic. Efficient and effective querying by image content. *J. Intelligent Information Sys.*, (3):1–31, 1994.

2. M. G. Brown, J. T. Foote, G. J. F. Jones, K. Spärck Jones, and S. J. Young. Automatic content-based retrieval of broadcast news. In *Proc. ACM Multimedia 95*, pages 35–43, San Francisco, November 1995. ACM.

3. M. G. Brown, J. T. Foote, G. J. F. Jones, K. Spärck Jones, and S. J. Young. Video Mail Retrieval using Voice: An overview of the Cambridge/Olivetti retrieval system. In *Proc. ACM Multimedia 94 Workshop on Multimedia Database Management Systems*, pages 47–55, San Francisco, CA, October 1994.

4. C. Coker, K. Church, and M. Liberman. Morphology and rhyming: two powerful alternatives to Letter-to-Sound rules for speech synthesis. In *ESCA Workshop on Speech Synthesis*, pages 83–86, Autrans, France, Sept 1990. ECSA.

5. J. T. Foote, G. J. F. Jones, K. Spärck Jones, and S. J. Young. Talker-independent keyword spotting for information retrieval. In *Proc. Eurospeech 95*, volume 3, pages 2145–2148, Madrid, 1995. ESCA.

6. M. A. Hearst. TileBars: Visualisation of term distribution information in full text information access. In *Proceedings of the ACM SIGCHI Conference on Human Factors in Computing Systems (CHI)*, Denver, CO, May 1995. ACM.

7. A. Hopper. Digital video on computer workstations. In *Proceedings of Eurographics*, 1992.

8. C. E. Jacobs, A. Finkelstein, and D. H. Salesin. Fast multiresolution image querying. In *Proceedings of the SIGGRAPH 95 Conference*, pages 277–286, Los Angeles, CA, August 1995. ACM SIGGRAPH.

9. D. A. James. *The Application of Classical Information Retrieval Techniques to Spoken Documents*. PhD thesis, Cambridge University, February 1995.

10. D. A. James and S. J. Young. A fast lattice-based approach to vocabulary independent wordspotting. In *Proc. ICASSP 94*, volume I, pages 377–380, Adelaide, 1994. IEEE.

11. G. J. F. Jones, J. T. Foote, K. Spärck Jones, and S. J. Young. VMR report on keyword definition and data collection. Technical Report 335, Cambridge University Computer Laboratory, May 1994.

12. G. J. F. Jones, J. T. Foote, K. Spärck Jones, and S. J. Young. Video Mail Retrieval: the effect of word spotting accuracy on precision. In *Proc. ICASSP 95*, volume I, pages 309–312, Detroit, May 1995. IEEE.

13. G. J. F. Jones, J. T. Foote, K. Spärck Jones, and S. J. Young. Retrieving spoken documents by combining multiple index sources. In *Proc. SIGIR 96*, Zürich, August 1996. ACM.

14. G. J. F. Jones, J. T. Foote, K. Spärck Jones, and S. J. Young. Robust talker-independent audio document retrieval. In *Proc. ICASSP 96*, volume I, pages 311–314, Atlanta, GA, April 1996. IEEE.

15. I. Leslie, D. McAuley, and D. Tennenhouse. ATM Everywhere? *IEEE Network*, March 1993.

16. J. McDonough, K. Ng, P. Jeanrenaud, H. Gish, and J. R. Rohlicek. Approaches to topic identification on the switchboard corpus. In *Proc. ICASSP 94*, volume I, pages 385–388, Adelaide, 1994. IEEE.

17. M. F. Porter. An algorithm for suffix stripping. *Program*, 14(3):130–137, July 1980.

18. L. R. Rabiner. A tutorial on hidden Markov models and selected applications in speech recognition. *Proc. IEEE*, 77(2):257–286, February 1989.

19. T. Robinson, J. Fransen, D. Pye, J. Foote, and S. Renals. WSJCAM0: A British English speech corpus for large vocabulary continuous speech recognition. In *Proc. ICASSP 95*, pages 81–84, Detroit, May 1995. IEEE.

20. T. Robinson, M. Hochberg, and S. Renals. IPA: Improved phone modelling with recurrent neural networks. In *Proc. ICASSP 94*, volume 1, pages 37–40, Adelaide, SA, April 1994.

21. R. C. Rose. Techniques for information retrieval from speech messages. *Lincoln Laboratory Journal*, 4(1):45–60, 1991.

22. F. Samaria and S. J. Young. A HMM-based architecture for face identification. *Image and Vision Computing*, 12(8):537–543, October 1994.

23. M. A. Smith and M. G. Christel. Automating the creation of a digital video library. In *Proc. ACM Multimedia 95*, pages 357–358, San Francisco, November 1995. ACM.

24. S. W. Smoliar and H. J. Zhang. Content-based video indexing and retrieval. *IEEE Multimedia*, 1(2):62–72, Summer 1994.

25. K. Spärck Jones, J. T. Foote, G. J. F. Jones, and S. J. Young. Spoken document retrieval — a multimedia tool. In *Fourth Annual Symposium on Document Analysis and Information Retrieval*, pages 1–11, Las Vegas, April 1995.

26. K. Spärck Jones, G. J. F. Jones, J. T. Foote, and S. J. Young. Experiments in spoken document retrieval. *Information Processing and Management*, 32(4):399–417, 1996.

27. C. J. van Rijsbergen. *Information Retrieval*. Butterworths, London, 2nd edition, 1979.

28. M. Wechsler and P. Schäuble. Speech retrieval based on automatic indexing. In C. J. van Rijsbergen, editor, *Proceedings of the MIRO Workshop*, University of Glasgow, September 1995.

29. L. Wilcox, F. Chen, and V. Balasubramanian. Segmentation of speech using speaker identification. In *Proc. ICASSP 94*, volume S1, pages 161–164, Adelaide, SA, April 1994.

30. L. D. Wilcox and M. A. Bush. Training and search algorithms for an interactive wordspotting system. In *Proc. ICASSP 92*, volume II, pages 97–100, San Francisco, 1992. IEEE.

31. J. H. Wright, M. J. Carey, and E. S. Parris. Topic discrimination using higher–order statistical models of spotted keywords. *Computer Speech and Language*, 9(4):381–405, Oct 1995.

32. S. J. Young, J. J. Odell, and P. C. Woodland. Tree-based state tying for high accuracy acoustic modelling. In *Proc. ARPA Spoken Language Technology Workshop*, Plainsboro, NJ, 1994.

33. S. J. Young, N. H. Russell, and J. H. S. Thornton. Token passing: a simple conceptual model for connected speech recognition systems. Technical Report CUED/F-INFENG/TR.38, Cambridge University Engineering Department, July 1989. ftp://svr-ftp.eng.cam.ac.uk/pub/reports/young_tr38.ps.Z.

34. S. J. Young, P. C. Woodland, and W. J. Byrne. *HTK: Hidden Markov Model Toolkit V1.5*. Entropic Research Laboratories, Inc., 600 Pennsylvania Ave. SE, Suite 202, Washington, DC 20003 USA, 1993.

CHAPTER FOUR

Content–Based Image Indexing and Retrieval

HongJiang Zhang
Microsoft Research, China

LIKE AUDIO, visual data is a major media type in multimedia computing. In response to the need in multimedia applications, especially in digital libraries, where efficient image indexing and access tools are essential, substantial research efforts have been devoted to the problem of efficient and effective retrieval of vast amounts of image data. However, by and large, the earlier image database systems used in visual art archives, multimedia libraries, geographic information systems, CAD/CAM systems, and criminal identifications [1, 2, 3] have all taken a keyword or text-based approach for indexing and retrieval of image data. That is, as a database object, each image in the database is associated with a text description, in the form of either keywords or free text. These descriptors may be searched by standard Boolean queries, and retrieval may be based on either exact or probabilistic matching of the query text, often enhanced by thesaurus support [1, 3, 4]. Moreover, topical or semantic hierarchies may be used to classify or describe images using knowledge-based classification or parsing techniques; such hierarchies may then facilitate navigation and browsing within the data.

However, there are several limitations inherent in systems that are exclusively text-based [2, 5]. First, automatic generation of descriptive keywords or extraction of semantic information to build classification hierarchies for broad varieties of images is beyond the capability of current computer vision and intelligence technologies. Thus, these text descriptors have to be typed in by human operators.

Apart from the fact that this is a time-consuming process when indexing a large number of images, it is also often subjective, inaccurate, and incomplete. As a result, such an indexing scheme will not be able to support very broad varieties of user queries in searching images, unless users are forced to constrain their query to a given set of templates or a range of keywords. Moreover, certain visual properties, such as textures and color patterns, are often difficult, if not impossible, to describe with text in an objective way, at least for general-purpose usage.

The alternative to relying on text-based indexing of images is to work with descriptions based on properties that are inherent in the images themselves [5, 6, 7]. That is, the natural way to represent and index *visual* content is to base the representations on the *visual* features of an image: colors, textures, patterns, shapes, layouts, and locations of objects. For many applications, such indexing schemes may be either supplemental or preferable to text, and in some other cases they may be necessary. Furthermore, visual queries may simply be easier to formulate. For example, given a collection of fabric patterns, a fashion designer may want to retrieve specific images based on which color and texture patterns are present. Formulating a query for such a search would involve either selecting or creating one or more representative examples and then searching for images that resemble those examples. In other words, with visual feature-based indexing schemes, search is driven by first establishing one or more sample images, then identifying specific

247

features of those sample images, and finally using these features to match images in the database. Because the process focuses on those visual features themselves, we refer to such retrieval schemes as *content-based* image retrieval (CBIR).

CBIR requires a paradigm that differs significantly from both traditional databases and text-based image understanding systems. First, a search is based on *similarity* defined in terms of visual features. Formulating a query for such a search would involve either selecting or creating one or more representative examples and then searching for images which resemble those examples. This is the notion of *query by image example*. Consequently, in this paradigm, a query is more like an *information filter*, and a good filter should provide only a small number of relevant candidates for the user to examine after a query is submitted. This relationship implies that the functionality that supports interactivity between the user and the database through a *visual interface* is as significant as the ability to support image-based queries. Such interactivity enhances the user's ability to *define* queries, *evaluate* retrieval results, and *refine* queries on the basis of those evaluations.

Figure 1 illustrates a system diagram that supports this approach to CBIR. At the heart of this system is a metadata database where image features are stored. These content metadata are extracted for computing similarity during retrieval. The user interface then supports the "closing of the loop," which relates the formulation of queries to the browsing of retrieved data. This figure also illustrates the key issues in developing content-based image retrieval algorithms and systems as follows:

- selection and computation of image and object features that provide effective query representation
- retrieval methods based on similarity, as opposed to exact matching, and effective indexing schemes compatible with similarity-based search

- a user interface that supports the visual expression of queries and allows navigation of retrieval results and search refinement with relevance feedback

Because of CBIR's challenging nature and application potential, numerous research papers have been published in the area. For this chapter, I have selected six papers from the thousands of papers published in the last decade that address the key aspects of the research area. However, the field of CBIR is still progressing rapidly, and hundreds of new research papers and novel ideas are published each year in numerous conferences and workshops. Obviously, many more papers would be included if size of this collection allowed, and other papers might be more suitable in addressing a certain issue in the research. However, I believe these six papers do a fine job presenting a brief history of, the current state of, and the research challenges in the CBIR area. In the rest of this introduction I briefly preface each of the six papers from two key aspects of content-based image retrieval, *image feature and similarity; and browsing, learning, and feedback.*

IMAGE FEATURE AND SIMILARITY

Many image features have been studied for representing different aspects of image content. These images features can be classified into three major types: color, texture, and shape features. Each is associated with similarity metrics used to measure the similarity or distance between these features of two images or image objects. The first two types of features are used to represent both global and regional or object content of an image, whereas shape features are used only in describing image objects. There are also many derivative features of images, such as relations among objects in an image.

Color information is the most widely used feature for image retrieval because of its strong correlation with the underlying image objects or scenes. Compared to other low-level visual

Figure 1: Basic elements of content-based image retrieval systems.

information, color is more robust with respect to scaling, orientation, perspective, and occlusion of images. Several issues are commonly associated with the design of color features for image retrieval. First, we need to select a proper color space. Second, we need to choose a color quantization scheme to reduce the dimensions of a color feature. Last, but not least, we need to determine appropriate similarity/distance measures for comparing images based on their color features. I have selected two papers covering different color features for this chapter. The paper entitled "Color indexing," by M. J. Swain and D. H. Balllard, was the first paper to address the issue of indexing images in a large image database with the notion of retrieving images using color similarity. The paper introduced the color similarity measure, *color histogram intersection*, and presented a comprehensive study and evaluation of this color similarity in terms of accuracy and efficiency. After this study, this color similarity measure and its variations have become one of the most effective, efficient, and widely used color features in image databases that support color-based image retrieval. More detailed studies of other color histogram features and their applications in image retrieval have since been carried out [5, 6, 8–13].

There are also a number of other effective and widely used color features. These features include color moments [8], coherence vectors (CCV) [12], and correlograms [14]. The paper by by W. Y. Ma and H.J. Zhang [15] gives an overview of the effectiveness and efficiency of these color features. This paper presents a detailed performance comparison of these color features in image retrieval, including selection of color space, color quantization schemes, and appropriate similarity/distance measures for comparing images based on their color features.

Texture is an innate property of virtually all visual object surfaces, such as papers, clouds, woods, and fabrics. An image can be considered a mosaic of different texture regions, and the texture associated with each of these regions can be used as a representation of the region and used for image search and retrieval. Therefore, texture is another type of basic low-level image feature that has been used intensively for CBIR. Texture features that have been used frequently and proved to be effective in CBIR systems include Tamura features [16],

simultaneous auto-regressive (SAR) models, orientation features, Gabor texture features, and wavelet transform features. However, because of space limitations, please refer to the paper by Ma and Zhang [15] for a performance comparison of these texture features in image retrieval. The reference section at the end of this introduction offers some very good references that address in detail the definitions of these features and their associate similarity measures and applications in image databases [5, 7, 16–27].

Shapes of objects or regions of interest are another important feature for image content representation and thus for CBIR. In contrast with low-level color and texture features, shape features need good segmentation algorithms as a first step to detect object/region boundaries. Over the past few decades, many approaches to the characterization of shape have been proposed, which can be categorized: boundary-based or region-based. Boundary-based shape features include rectilinear shapes [28], polygonal approximation [29–31], finite element models [32], and Fourier-based shape descriptors [33–35]. Statistical moments [36, 37] provide an effective region-based shape feature. However, because robust and accurate image segmentation is difficult to achieve, the use of shape features for image retrieval has been limited to special applications where objects or regions are readily available. Furthermore, shape similarity is still a difficult problem and remains to be resolved, due to the requirement that a good shape representation feature for an object be invariant to translation, rotation, and scaling because human visual perception tends to be robust against such variations in object recognition. Although no paper is chosen for this chapter to describe shape features because of the size limitations of this collection, the references include papers that address different shape descriptors and their applications for image [28–37].

BROWSING, LEARNING, AND FEEDBACK

As discussed earlier, content-based image retrieval is like an information filtering process. A good filter should provide a high percentage of relevant candidates for the user to examine after a query is submitted. However, the similarity measures, such as color histograms, in general do not necessarily match the *perceptional semantics and subjectivity.* In addition, each type of image feature tends to capture only one of many aspects of image similarity, and it is difficult to require users to specify clearly which aspect exactly or what combination of these aspects they want to apply in defining a query. To address these problems, browsing and interactive relevance feedback techniques have been proposed. The idea is that we should incorporate human perception subjectivity into the retrieval process and provide users opportunities to *evaluate* retrieval results and automatically *refine* queries on the basis of those evaluations. Lately, this research topic has become the most challenging in content-based image retrieval research, and so we have chosen for this chapter three papers that address issues related to this topic.

One of the first attempts to solve the indexing problems associated with low-level feature-based image retrieval is to introduce a browsing notion using a hierarchical indexing scheme. This is the idea presented in the fourth paper in the chapter, "A scheme for visual feature based image indexing," by H.J. Zhang and D. Zhong. This paper presents a browsing scheme based on the Self-Organization Map (SOM). The advantage of this approach in addition to its indexing scheme is that it provides the user with a useful browsing tool to view the representative images of each class. This scheme was further applied in the work of Ma and Manjunath [38] to create a texture thesaurus for indexing a database of large aerial photographs.

Relevance feedback is the process of automatically refining an existing query using the information fed back by the user about the relevance of previously retrieved results. This technique has been widely used in information retrieval system. There are two basic ways of improving retrieval performance using feedback: modifying query vectors and modifying similarity measures. These feedback schemes have been adopted into feature-based image retrieval by replacing keywords and their weights in document retrieval with image feature vectors. An early example of this type of scheme is the MAR system [39]. Also, Huang and colleagues [40] used a similar relevance feedback scheme to improve the retrieval performance of the color correlogram, except that the negative examples were not used in the query refinement.

Another relevance feedback approach proposed by Huang, and colleagues, is to modify the weighted metric for computing the distance between feature vectors. The basic idea is to enhance the importance of dimensions of a feature that help retrieve the relevant images and to reduce the importance of dimensions that hinder this process. Instead of updating the individual components of a distance metric, we can begin with a set of predefined distance metrics and use the relevance feedback to automatically select the best one in the retrieval process. A simple algorithm based on this idea was described in the ImageRover system [41]. This algorithm automatically selects appropriate Minkowski distance metrics that minimize the mean distance between the relevant images specified by the user.

However, though the relevance feedback algorithms adapted from text document retrieval do improve the performance of feature-based image retrieval, they are still restricted by the limitations of low-level image features: even with feedback, it is difficult to capture the high-level semantics of images. Also, the potentially captured semantic knowledge in the relevance feedback processes in one query session is not memorized to continuously improve the retrieval performance of a system. To overcome this, another school of ideas is to use learning schemes in indexing and retrieving images based on low-level features. An early and representative work of this idea is presented in the paper chosen for this chapter entitled "Interactive learning with a 'society of models,'" by T. P. Minka and R. W. Picard. The key idea behind this approach is that each feature model has its own strength in representing a certain aspect of image content, and thus, the best way for effective content-based retrieval is to utilize "a society of models." This approach uses a learning scheme to dynamically determine which model or combination of models is best for subsequent retrieval, based on the user's inputs or feedback to the initial classification of objects or regions of images in the learning process. In other words, the system has the capability to learn user's subjectivity in terms of the best feature or feature set for representing a particular class of objects.

The *PicHunter* framework presented in the final paper in this chapter, "The Bayesian image retrieval system: *PicHunter* theory, implementation, and psychophysical experiments," by I. J. Cox and colleagues, further extend the relevance feedback and learning idea with a Bayesian approach. With an explicit model of what users would do, given what target image they want, *PicHunter* uses Bayes's rule to predict what is the target they want, given their actions. This prediction is made via a probability distribution over possible image targets, rather than by refining a query. To achieve this result, an entropy-minimizing display algorithm is developed that attempts to maximize the information obtained from a user at each iteration of the search. Also, this proposed framework makes use of hidden annotation rather than a possibly inaccurate and inconsistent annotation structure that the user must learn and make queries in. A good and related work is by Lee, Ma, and Zhang [42], in which a new scheme of integrating low-level feature retrieval and high-level learning in a feedback framework is proposed. This new framework maintains the strengths of feature-based image retrieval while incorporating learning and annotation in the relevance feedback processes. Experiments have shown that this new framework is effective not only in improving retrieval performance in a given query session, but in utilizing the knowledge learned from previous queries to reduce the number of iterations in following queries.

Finally, we have chosen "Query by image and video content: The QBIC system," by M. Flickner and colleagues, to be the first paper of this chapter. The QBIC work summarized in this paper is a pioneering effort in the field of CBIR, and marks a milestone in the history of CBIR research. This paper addresses all aspects of CBIR, including the user interface and indexing issues, and is one of the most widely referred to reference in the CBIR field. QBIC is also the first commercial CBIR product, though not a very successful one, following from which many experimental and prototype systems have been developed [7, 9, 41].

In summary, despite significant efforts from the researchers of CBIR, many challenging research topics remain unexplained in this area. In addition to the question of more effective visual features and similarity measures to represent image content and image similarity, how to utilize relevance feedback in image search is an intriguing research topic that is garnering interest. The issues of efficient indexing and database architecture for support of CBIR in large image databases will be addressed in more detail in Chapter 6.

REFERENCES

[1] S. K. Chang and A. Hsu, "Image information systems: Where do we go from here," *IEEE Transactions on Knowledge and Data Engineering* 4, no. 5 (Oct. 1992): 431–42.

[2] R. Jain, A. Pentland and D. Petkovic (eds.), *Workshop Report: NSF-ARPA Workshop on Visual Information Management Systems, Cambridge* (June 1995).

[3] A. E. Cawkill, "The British library's picture research projects: Image, word, and retrieval," *Advanced Imaging* 8, no. 10, (Oct. 1993): 38–40,

[4] S. Al-Hawamdeh et al, "Nearest neighbour searching in a picture archive system," *International Conference on Multimedia Information Systems* 91 (Singapore: World Scientific, Jan. 1991), 17–33.

[5] C. Faloutsos et al., "Efficient and effective querying by image content," *Journal of Intelligent Information Systems* (Nov. 1994): 231–62.

[6] B. Furht, S. W. Smoliar, and H.J. Zhang, *Image and Video Processing in Multimedia Systems,* (New York: Kluwer Academic Publishers, 1995).

[7] A. Pentland, R.W. Picard and S. Sclaroff, "Photobook: Content-based manipulation of image databases," in *Proceedings of SPIE Storage and Retrieval for Image and Video Databases II* 2185 (Feb. 1994): 34–47.

[8] M. Stricker and M. Orengo, "Similarity of color images," *Proceedings of SPIE Storage and Retrieval for Image and Video Databases III* 2185 (Feb. 1995): 381–92.

[9] J. R. Smith and S. F. Chang, "VisualSEEk: a fully automated content-based image query system," in *Proceedings of the 4th ACM International Multimedia Conference* (ACM, Nov. 1996): 87–98.

[10] H.J. Zhang et al., "Image retrieval based on color features: An evaluation study," in *Proceedings of the SPIE Conference on Digital Storage and Archival* (1995): 212–20.

[11] Y. Gong, H.J. Zhang, and T. C. Chua, "An image database system with content capturing and fast image indexing abilities," *Proceedings of the IEEE International Conference on Multimedia Computing and Systems* (IEEE, Oct. 1994), 121–30.

[12] J. Hafner et al., "Efficient color histogram indexing for quadratic form distance functions," *IEEE Transactions on Pattern Analysis and Machine Intelligence* 17, no. 7 (July 1995): 729–36.

[13] G. Pass and R. Zabih, "Histogram refinement for content-based image retrieval," in *Proceedings of the IEEE Workshop on Applications of Computer Vision* (1996): 96-102.

[14] J. Huang et al., "Image indexing using color correlogram," in *Proceedings of the IEEE International Conference on Computer Vision and Pattern Recognition* (San Juan: IEEE, June 1997), 762–68.

[15] W. Y. Ma and H.J. Zhang, "Benchmarking of image features for content-based image retrieval," in *Proceedings of the 32nd Asiloma Conference on Signal, Systems, and Computers* (Pacific Grove: IEEE, 1998), 253–57.

[16] H. Tamura, S. Mori, and T. Yamawaki, "Texture features corresponding to visual perception," *IEEE Transactions on Systems, Man, and Cybernetics* 8, no. 6 (June 1978).

[17] J. Mao and A. K. Jain, "Texture classification and segmentation using multiresolution simultaneous autoregressive models," *Pattern Recognition* 25, no. 2 (1992): 173–88.

[18] F. Liu and R. W. Picard, "Periodicity, directionality, and randomness: Wold features for image modeling and retrieval," *MIT Media Lab Technical Report*, no. 320 (Cambridge: MIT, 1994).

[19] R. W. Picard, T. Kabir, and F. Liu, "Real-time recognition with the entire Brodatz texture database," in *Proceedings of the IEEE International Conference on Computer Vision and Pattern Recognition* (New York: IEEE, June 1993), 638–39.

[20] B. S. Manjunath and W. Y. Ma, "Texture features for browsing and retrieval of image data," *IEEE Transactions on Pattern Analysis and Machine Intelligence* 18, no. 8 (Aug. 1996): 837–42.

[21] A. Kankanhalli, H.J. Zhang, and C. Y. Low, "Using texture for image retrieval," in *Proceedings of the 3rd International Conference on Automation, Robotics, and Computer Vision* (Singapore: IEEE, Nov. 1994), 935–39.

[22] M. M. Gorkani and R. W. Picard, "Texture orientation for sorting photos 'at a glance'," in *Proceedings of the International Conference on Pattern Recognition*, vol. 1 (IEEE, 1994), 459–64.

[23] R. Rao and B. G. Schunck, "Computing oriented texture fields," *CVGIP Graphical Models and Image Processing* 53, no. 2 (1991): 157–85.

[24] S. Chaudhuri et al., "A Fourier domain directional filtering method for analysis of collagen alignment in ligaments," *IEEE Transactions on Biomedical Engineering* 34, no. 7 (1987): 509–17.

[25] A. C. Bovic, M. Clark, and W. S. Geisler, "Multichannel texture analysis using localized spatial filters," *IEEE Transactions on Pattern Analysis and Machine Intelligence* 12 (Jan. 1990): 55–73.

[26] A. K. Jain and F. Farroknia, "Unsupervised texture segmentation using Gabor filters," *Pattern Recognition* 24, no. 12 (1991): 1167–86.

[27] W. Y. Ma and B. S. Manjunath, "A comparison of wavelet features for texture annotation," in *Proceedings of the IEEE International Conference on Image Processing* 2 (Washington D.C.: IEEE, Oct. 1995), 256–59.

[28] H. V. Jagadish, "A retrieval technique for similar shapes," in *Proceedings of ACM SIGMOD 91* (Denver: ACM, May 1991), 208–17.

[29] W. I. Grosky and R. Mehrotra, "Index based object recognition in pictorial data management," *CVGIP* 52, no. 3 (1990): 416–36.

[30] J. E. Gary and R. Mehrotra, "Shape similarity-based retrieval in image database systems," in *Proceedings of SPIE, Image Storage and Retrieval Systems* 1662 (1992): 2-8.

[31] E. M. Arkin et al., "An efficiently computable metric for comparing polygonal shapes," *IEEE Transactions on Pattern Analysis and Machine Intelligence* 13, no. 3 (1991): 209–26.

[32] S. Sclaroff and A. Pentland, "Modal matching for correspondence and recognition,"

IEEE *Transactions on Pattern Analysis and Machine Intelligence* 17, no. 6 (June 1995): 545–61.

[33] K. Arbter et al., "Application of affine-invariant Fourier descriptors to recognition of 3D objects," *IEEE Transactions on Pattern Analysis and Machine Intelligence* 12 (1990): 640–47.

[34] E. Persoon and K. Fu, "Shape discrimination using Fourier descriptors," *IEEE Transactions on Systems, Man, and Cybernetice* 7 (1977): 170–79.

[35] H. Kauppinen, T. Seppnäen, and M. Pietikäinen, "An experimental comparison of autoregressive and Fourier-based descriptors in 2D shape classification," *IEEE Transactions on Pattern Analysis and Machine Intelligence* 17, no. 2 (1995): 201–07.

[36] M. K. Hu, "Visual pattern recognition by moment invariants," in J. K. Aggarwal, R. O. Duda, and A. Rosenfeld, eds., *Computer Methods in Image analysis* (Los Angeles: IEEE Computer Society, 1977).

[37] D. Tegolo, "Shape analysis for image retrieval," in *Proceedings of SPIE, Storage and Retrieval for Image and Video Databases II* 2185 (Feb. 1994): 59–69.

[38] W. Y. Ma and B. S. Manjunath, "Image indexing using a texture dictionary," in *Proceedings of the SPIE Conference on Image Storage and Archiving Systems* 2606 (Philadelphia: SPIE, Feb. 1995), 288–98.

[39] Y. Rui et al., "A relevance feedback architecture in content-based multimedia information retrieval systems," in *Proceedings of the IEEE Workshop on Content-Based Access of Image and Video Libraries* (San Juan: IEEE, 1997), 82–9.

[40] J. Huang, S. R. Kumar, and M. Metra, "Combining supervised learning with color correlograms for content-based image retrieval," in *Proceedings of the 5th ACM International Multimedia Conference* (Seattle: ACM, Nov. 1997), 325–34.

[41] S. Sclaroff, L. Taycher, and M. L. Cascia, "ImageRover: A content-based image browser for the World Wide Web," in Proceedings of the IEEE Workshop on Content-Based Access of Image and Video Libraries (San Juan: ACM, 1997), 90–7.

[42] C. Lee, W.-Y. Ma, and H.J. Zhang, "A relevance feedback framework for content-based retrieval," Invited paper, in *Proceedings of the SPIE International Conference on Multimedia Storage and Archiving Systems IV* (Boston: SPIE, Sept. 1999), 294–304.

Query by Image and Video Content: The QBIC System

Myron Flickner, Harpreet Sawhney, Wayne Niblack, Jonathan Ashley, Qian Huang, Byron Dom, Monika Gorkani, Jim Hafner, Denis Lee, Dragutin Petkovic, David Steele, and Peter Yanker

IBM Almaden Research Center

QBIC* lets users

find pictorial information

in large image and video

databases based on color,

shape, texture, and sketches.

QBIC technology is part of

several IBM products.

*To run an interactive query, visit the QBIC Web server at http://wwwqbic. almaden. ibm. com/.

Picture yourself as a fashion designer needing images of fabrics with a particular mixture of colors, a museum cataloger looking for artifacts of a particular shape and textured pattern, or a movie producer needing a video clip of a red car-like object moving from right to left with the camera zooming. How do you find these images? Even though today's technology enables us to acquire, manipulate, transmit, and store vast on-line image and video collections, the search methodologies used to find pictorial information are still limited due to difficult research problems (see "Semantic versus nonsemantic" sidebar). Typically, these methodologies depend on file IDs, keywords, or text associated with the images. And, although powerful, they

- don't allow queries based directly on the visual properties of the images,
- are dependent on the particular vocabulary used, and
- don't provide queries for images similar to a given image.

Research on ways to extend and improve query methods for image databases is widespread, and results have been presented in workshops, conferences,[1,2] and surveys.

We have developed the QBIC (Query by Image Content) system to explore content-based retrieval methods. QBIC allows queries on large image and video databases based on

- example images,
- user-constructed sketches and drawings,
- selected color and texture patterns,

Semantic versus nonsemantic information

At first glance, content-based querying appears deceptively simple because we humans seem to be so good at it. If a program can be written to extract semantically relevant text phrases from images, the problem may be solved by using currently available text-search technology. Unfortunately, in an unconstrained environment, the task of writing this program is beyond the reach of current technology in image understanding. At an artificial intelligence conference several years ago, a challenge was issued to the audience to write a program that would identify all the dogs pictured in a children's book, a task most 3-year-olds can easily accomplish. Nobody in the audience accepted the challenge, and this remains an open problem.

Perceptual organization—the process of grouping image features into meaningful objects and attaching semantic

descriptions to scenes through model matching—is an unsolved problem in image understanding. Humans are much better than computers at extracting semantic descriptions from pictures. Computers, however, are better than humans at measuring properties and retaining these in long-term memory.

One of the guiding principles used by QBIC is to let computers do what they do best—quantifiable measurement—and let humans do what they do best—attaching semantic meaning. QBIC can find "fish-shaped objects," since shape is a measurable property that can be extracted. However, since fish occur in many shapes, the only fish that will be found will have a shape close to the drawn shape. This is not the same as the much harder semantical query of finding all the pictures of fish in a pictorial database.

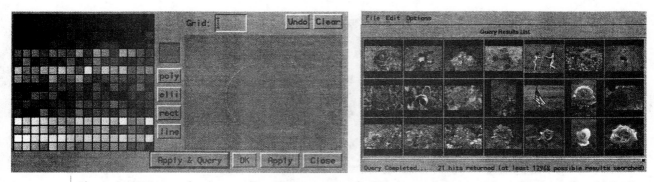

Figure 1. QBIC query by drawn color. Drawn query specification on left; best 21 results sorted by similarity to the query on right. The results were selected from a 12,968-picture database.

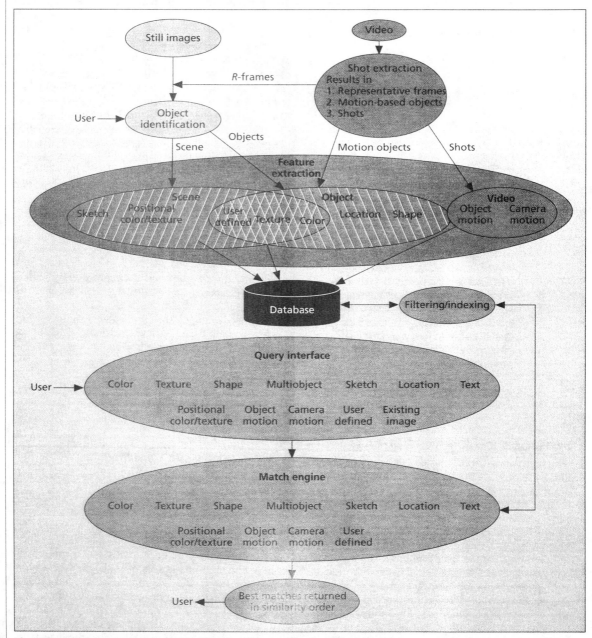

Figure 2. QBIC database population (top) and query (bottom) architecture.

- camera and object motion, and
- other graphical information.

Two key properties of QBIC are (1) its use of image and video content—computable properties of color, texture, shape, and motion of images, videos, and their objects—in the queries, and (2) its graphical query language in which queries are posed by drawing, selecting, and other graphical means. Related systems, such as MIT's Photobook[3] and the Trademark and Art Museum applications from ETL,[4] also address these common issues. This article describes the QBIC system and demonstrates its query capabilities.

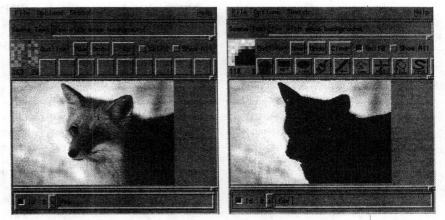

Figure 3. QBIC still image population interface. Entry for scene text at top. Tools in row are polygon outliner, rectangle outliner, ellipse outliner, paintbrush, eraser, line drawing, object translation, flood fill, and snake outliner.

QBIC SYSTEM OVERVIEW

Figure 1 illustrates a typical QBIC query.* The left side shows the query specification, where the user painted a large magenta circular area on a green background using standard drawing tools. Query results are shown on the right: an ordered list of "hits" similar to the query. The order of the results is top to bottom, then left to right, to support horizontal scrolling. In general, all queries follow this model in that the query is specified by using graphical means—drawing, selecting from a color wheel, selecting a sample image, and so on—and results are displayed as an ordered set of images.

To achieve this functionality, QBIC has two main components: database population (the process of creating an image database) and database query. During the population, images and videos are processed to extract features describing their content—colors, textures, shapes, and camera and object motion—and the features are stored in a database. During the query, the user composes a query graphically. Features are generated from the graphical query and then input to a matching engine that finds images or videos from the database with similar features. Figure 2 shows the system architecture.

Data model

For both population and query, the QBIC data model has

- still images or scenes (full images) that contain objects (subsets of an image), and
- video shots that consist of sets of contiguous frames and contain motion objects.

For still images, the QBIC data model distinguishes between "scenes" (or images) and "objects." A scene is an image or single representative frame of video. An object is a part of a scene—for example, the fox in Figure 3—or a moving entity in a video. For still image database population, features are extracted from images and objects and stored in a database as shown in the top left part of Figure 2.

Videos are broken into clips called shots. Representative

frames, or r-frames, are generated for each extracted shot. R-frames are treated as still images, and features are extracted and stored in the database. Further processing of shots generates motion objects—for example, a car moving across the screen.

Queries are allowed on objects ("Find images with a red, round object"), scenes ("Find images that have approximately 30-percent red and 15-percent blue colors"), shots ("Find all shots panning from left to right"), or any combination ("Find images that have 30 percent red and contain a blue textured object").

In QBIC, similarity queries are done against the database of pre-extracted features using distance functions between the features. These functions are intended to mimic human perception to approximate a perceptual ordering of the database. Figure 2 shows the match engine, the collection of all distance functions. The match engine interacts with a filtering/indexing module (see "Fast searching and indexing" sidebar, next page) to support fast searching methodologies such as indexing. Users interact with the query interface to generate a query specification, resulting in the features that define the query.

DATABASE POPULATION

In still image database population, the images are reduced to a standard-sized icon called a thumbnail and annotated with any available text information. Object identification is an optional but key part of this step. It lets users manually, semiautomatically, or fully automatically identify interesting regions—which we call objects—in the images. Internally, each object is represented as a binary mask. There may be an arbitrary number of objects per image. Objects can overlap and can consist of multiple disconnected components like the set of dots on a polka-dot dress. Text, like "baby on beach," can be associated with an outlined object or with the scene as a whole.

Object-outlining tools

Ideally, object identification would be automatic, but this is generally difficult. The alternative—manual identification—is tedious and can inhibit query-by-content

---

* The scene image database used in the figures consists of about 7,450 images from the Mediasource Series of images and audio from Applied Optical Media Corp., 4,100 images from the PhotoDisc sampler CD, 950 images from the Corel Professional Photo CD collection, and 450 images from an IBM collection.

Fast searching and indexing

Indexing tabular data for exact matching or range searches in traditional databases is a well-understood problem, and structures like *B*-trees provide efficient access mechanisms. In this scenario, indexing assures sublinear search while maintaining completeness; that is, all records satisfying the query are returned without the need for examining each record in the database. However, in the context of similarity matching for visual content, traditional indexing methods may not be appropriate. For queries in which similarity is defined as a distance metric in high-dimensional feature spaces (for example, color histogram queries), indexing involves clustering and indexable representations of the clusters. In the case of queries that combine similarity matching with spatial constraints on objects, the problem is more involved. Data structures for fast access of high-dimensional features for spatial relationships must be invented.

In a query, features from the database are compared to corresponding features from the query specification to determine which images are a good match. For a small database, sequential scanning of the features followed by straightforward similarity computations is adequate. But as the database grows, this combination can be too slow. To speed up the queries, we have investigated a variety of techniques. Two of the most promising follow.

Filtering

A computationally fast filter is applied to all data, and only items that pass through the filter are operated on by the second stage, which computes the true similarity metric. For example, in QBIC we have shown that color histogram matching, which is based on a 256-dimensional color histogram and requires a 256 matrix-vector multiply, can be made efficient by filtering. The filtering step employs a much faster computation in a 3D space with no loss in accuracy. Thus, for a query on a database of 10,000 elements, the fast filter is applied to produce the best 1,000 color histogram matches. These filtered histograms are subsequently passed to the slower complete matching operation to obtain, say, the best 200 matches to display to a user, with the guarantee that the global best 200 in the database have been found.

Indexing

For low-dimensional features such as average color and texture (each 3D), multidimensional indexing methods such as *R**-trees can be used. For high-dimensional features—for example, our 20-dimensional moment-based shape feature vector—the dimensionality is reduced using the K-L, or principal component, transform. This produces a low-dimensional space, as low as two or three dimensions, which could be indexed by using *R**-trees.

applications. As a result, we have devoted considerable effort to developing tools to aid in this step. In recent work, we have successfully used fully automatic unsupervised segmentation methods along with a foreground/background model to identify objects in a restricted class of images. The images, typical of museums and retail catalogs, have a small number of foreground objects on a generally separable background. Figure 4 shows example results. Even in this domain, robust algorithms are required because of the textured and variegated backgrounds.

We also provide semiautomatic tools for identifying objects. One is an enhanced flood-fill technique. Flood-fill methods, found in most photo-editing programs, start from a single object pixel and repeatedly add adjacent pixels whose values are within some given threshold of the original pixel. Selecting the threshold, which must change from image to image and object to object, is tedious. We automatically calculate a dynamic threshold by having the user click on background as well as object points. For reasonably uniform objects that are distinct from the background, this operation allows fast object identification

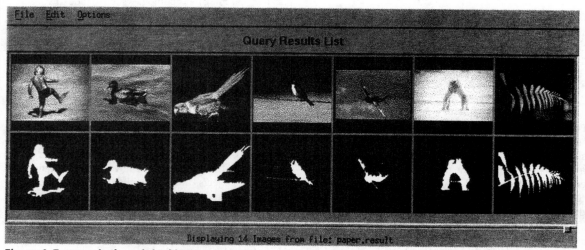

Figure 4. Top row is the original image. Bottom row contains the automatically extracted objects using a foreground/background model. Heuristics encode the knowledge that objects tend to be in the center of the picture.

without manually adjusting a threshold. The example in Figure 3 shows an object, a fox, identified by using only a few clicks.

We designed another outlining tool to help users track object edges. This tool takes a user-drawn curve and automatically aligns it with nearby image edges. Based on the "snakes" concept developed in recent computer vision research, the tool finds the curve that maximizes the image gradient magnitude along the curve.

The spline snake formulation we use allows for smooth solutions to the resulting nonlinear minimization problem. The computation is done at interactive speeds so that, as the user draws a curve, it is "rubber-banded" to lie along object boundaries.

Video data

For video data, database population has three major components:

- shot detection,
- representative frame creation for each shot, and
- derivation of a layered representation of coherently moving structures/objects.

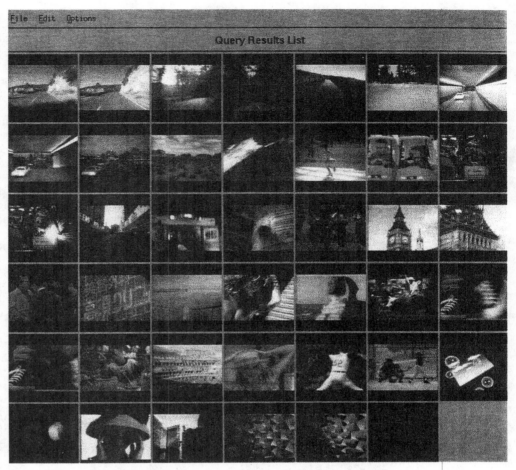

Figure 5. Scene cuts automatically extracted from a 1,148-frame sales demo from Energy Productions.

Shots are short sequences of contiguous frames that we use for annotation and querying. For instance, a video clip may consist of a shot smoothly panning over the skyline of San Francisco, switching to a panning shot of the Bay meeting the ocean, and then to one that zooms to the Golden Gate Bridge. In general, a set of contiguous frames may be grouped into a shot because they

- depict the same scene,
- signify a single camera operation,
- contain a distinct event or an action like a significant presence and persistence of an object, or
- are chosen as a single indexable entity by the user.

Our effort is to detect many shots automatically in a preprocessing step and provide an easy-to-use interface for the rest.

SHOT DETECTION. Gross scene changes or scene cuts are the first indicators of shot boundaries. Methods for detecting scene cuts proposed in the literature essentially fall into two classes: (1) those based on global representations like color/intensity histograms without any spatial information, and (2) those based on measuring differences between spatially registered features like intensity differences. The former are relatively insensitive to motion but can miss cuts when scenes look quite different but have similar distributions. The latter are sensitive to moving objects and camera. We have developed a method that combines the strengths of the two classes of detection. We use a robust normalized correlation measure that allows for small motions and combines this with a histogram distance measure.[5] Results on a few videos containing from 2,000 to 5,000 frames show no misses and only a few false cuts. Algorithms for signaling edit effects like fades and dissolves are under development. The results of cut detection on a video containing commercial advertisement clips are shown in Figure 5.

Shots may also be detected by finding changes in camera operation. Common camera transformations like zoom, pan, and illumination changes can be modeled as unknown affine 2×2 matrix transformations of the 2D image coordinate system and of the image intensities themselves. We have developed an algorithm[6] that computes the dominant global view transformation while it remains insensitive to nonglobal changes resulting from independently moving

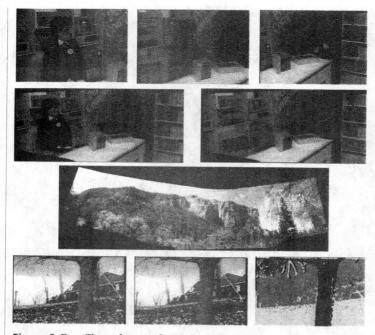

Figure 6. Top: Three frames from the *charlie* sequence and the resulting dynamic mosaics of the entire sequence. Below that is a mosaic from a video sequence of Yosemite National Park. Bottom: Original images and segmented motion layers for the flower garden sequence in which only the camera is moving. The flower bed, tree, and background have been separated into three layers shown in different shades of gray.

objects and local brightness changes. The affine transformations that result from this computation can be used for camera operation detection, shot boundary detection based on the camera operation, and creating a synthetic *r*-frame wherever appropriate.

Shot boundaries can also be defined on the basis of events: appearance/disappearance of an object, distinct change in the motion of an object, or similar events. For instance, segmenting an object of interest based on its appearance and/or motion, and tracking it throughout its significant presence may be used for defining shots.

REPRESENTATIVE FRAME GENERATION. Once the shot boundaries have been detected, each shot is represented using an *r*-frame. *R*-frames are used for several purposes. First, during database population, *r*-frames are treated as still images in which objects can be identified by using the previously described methods. Secondly, during query, they are the basic units initially returned in a video query. For example, in a query for shots that are dominantly red, a set of *r*-frames will be displayed. To see the actual video shot, the user clicks on the displayed *r*-frame icon.

The choice of an *r*-frame could be as simple as a particular frame in the shot: the

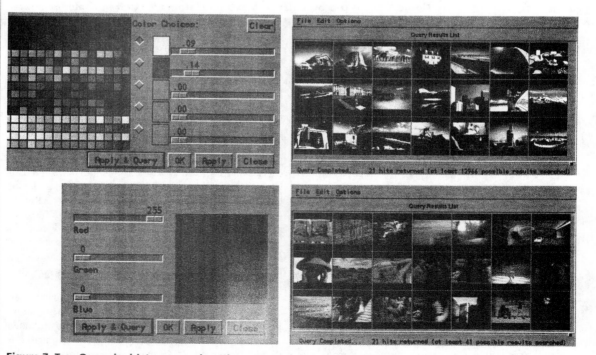

Figure 7. Top: Query by histogram color. Histogram color query specification on left; best 21 results from a 12,966-picture database on right. Bottom: A query for a red video *r*-frame. The color picker is on the left; the resulting *r*-frame thumbnails of the best matches are shown on the right. Each thumbnail is an active button that allows the user to play the shot.

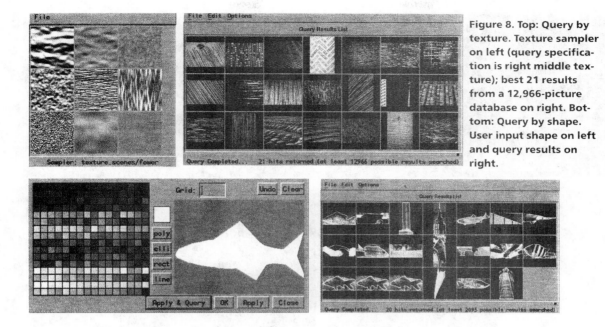

Figure 8. Top: Query by texture. Texture sampler on left (query specification is right middle texture); best 21 results from a 12,966-picture database on right. Bottom: Query by shape. User input shape on left and query results on right.

first, the last, or the middle. However, in situations such as a long panning shot, no single frame may be representative of the entire shot. We use a synthesized r-frame[7,8] created by seamlessly mosaicking all the frames in a given shot using the computed motion transformation of the dominant background. This frame is an authentic depiction of all background captured in the whole shot. Any foreground object can be superimposed on the background to create a single, static visual representation of the shot. The r-frame mosaicking is done by using warping transforms that result from automatic dominant motion computation. Given a video sequence with dominant motion and moving object(s), the 2D motion estimation algorithm is applied between consecutive pairs of frames. Then, a reference frame is chosen, and all the frames are warped into the coordinate system of the reference frame to create the mosaicked r-frame.

Figure 6 illustrates mosaic-based r-frame creation on a video sequence of an IBM commercial. Three frames of this sequence plus the final mosaic are shown. Two dominant-component-only mosaics of the *charlie* sequence are shown in Figure 6. In one case, the moving object has been removed from the mosaic by using temporal median filtering on the frames in the shot. In the other case, the moving object remains from the first frame in the sequence. We are also developing methods to visually represent the object motion in the r-frame.

LAYERED REPRESENTATION. To facilitate automatic segmentation of independently moving objects and significant structures, we take further advantage of the time-varying nature of video data to derive what is called a layered representation[9] of video. The different layers are used to identify significant objects in the scene for feature computations and querying. Our algorithm divides a shot into a number of layers, each with its own 2D affine motion parameters and region of support in each frame.[10]

The algorithm is first illustrated on a shot where the scene is static but the camera motion induces parallax

motion onto the image plane due to the different depths in the scene. Therefore, surfaces and objects that may correspond to semantically useful entities can be segmented based on the coherence of their motion. Figure 6 (bottom row) shows the results for the layers from the flower garden sequence.

SAMPLE QUERIES

For each full-scene image, identified image object, r-frame, and identified video object resulting from the above processing, a set of features is computed to allow content-based queries. The features are computed and stored during database population. We present a brief description of the features and the associated queries. Mathematical details on the features and matching methods can be found in Ashley et al.[11] and Niblack et al.[12]

Average color queries let users find images or objects that are similar to a selected color, say from a color wheel, or to the color of an object. The feature used in the query is a 3D vector of Munsell color coordinates. Histogram color queries return items with matching color distributions—say, a fabric pattern with approximately 40 percent red and 20 percent blue. For this case, the underlying feature is a 256-element histogram computed over a quantized version of the color space.

Figure 7 shows a histogram query on still images and a color query on video r-frames. Note that in the query specification for the histogram query of Figure 7, the user has selected percentages of two colors (blue and white) by adjusting sliders. Using such a query, an advertising agent could, for example, search for a picture of a beach scene, one predominantly blue (for sky and water) and white (for sand and clouds); or find images with similar color spreads for a uniform ad campaign. The average color query demonstrates a query against a video shot database where the user is searching for red r-frames. Again, the query specification is on the left and the best hits are on the right.

Figure 8 shows an example texture query. In this case, the query is specified by selecting from a sampler—a set of

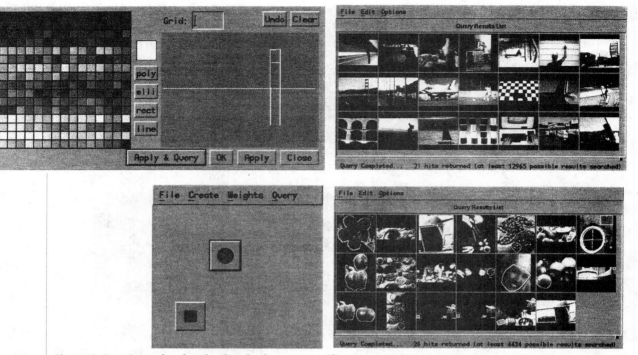

Figure 9. Top: Query by sketch. Sketched query specification on left; best 21 hits from a 12,965-image database on right. Bottom: A Multi-* object query. The query specification on the left describes a query for images with a red round object and a green textured object. Best 20 matches shown on right.

prestored example images. The underlying texture features are mathematical representations of coarseness, contrast, and directionality features. Coarseness measures the scale of a texture (pebbles versus boulders), contrast describes its vividness, and directionality describes whether it has a favored direction (like grass) or not (like a smooth object).

An object shape query is shown in Figure 8. In this case, the query specification is the drawn shape on the left. Area, circularity, eccentricity, major-axis direction, features derived from the object moments, and a set of tangent angles around the object perimeter are the features used to characterize and match shapes.

Figure 9 illustrates query by sketch. In this case, the query specification is a freehand drawing of the dominant lines and edges in the image. The sketch feature is an automatically extracted reduced-resolution "edge map." Matching is done by using a template-matching technique.

A multiobject query asking for images that contain both a red round object and a green textured object is shown in the bottom of Figure 9. The features are standard color and texture. The matching is done by combining the color and texture distances. Combining distances is applied to arbitrary sets of objects and features to implement logical And semantics.

WE HAVE DESCRIBED A PROTOTYPE SYSTEM that uses image and video content as the basis for retrievals. Technology from this prototype has already moved into a commercial stand-alone product, IBM's Ultimedia Manager, and is part of IBM's Digital Library and DB2 series of products. Other companies are beginning to offer products with similar capabilities. Key challenges remain in making this technology pervasive and useful.

ANNOTATION AND DATABASE POPULATION TOOLS. Automatic methods (such as our Positional Color query) that don't rely on object identification, methods that identify objects automatically as in the museum image example, fast and easy-to-use semiautomatic outlining tools, and motion-based segmentation algorithms will enable additional application areas.

FEATURE EXTRACTION AND MATCHING METHODS. New mathematical representations of video, image, and object attributes that capture "interesting" features for retrieval are needed. Features that describe new image properties such as alternate texture measures or that are based on fractals or wavelet representations, for example, may offer advantages of representation, indexability, and ease of similarity matching.

INTEGRATION WITH TEXT AND PARAMETRIC ANNOTATION. Query by visual content complements and extends existing query methods. Systems must be able to integrate queries combining date, subject matter, price, and availability with content properties such as color, texture, and shape.

EXTENSIBILITY AND FLEXIBILITY. System architectures must support the addition of new features and new matching/similarity measures. Real applications often require new features, say a face-matching module, to add to their existing content-based retrieval capabilities.

USER INTERFACE. The user interface must be designed to let users easily select content-based properties, allow these properties to be combined with each other and with text or parametric data, and let users reformulate queries and generally navigate the database.

INDEXING AND PERFORMANCE. As image and video collections grow, system performance must not slow down proportionately. Indexing, clustering, and filtering methods must be designed into the matching methods to maintain performance.

With these technologies, the QBIC paradigm of visual content querying, combined with traditional keyword and text querying, will lead to powerful search engines for multimedia archives. Applications will occur in areas such as decision support for retail marketing, on-line stock photo and video management, cataloging for library and museum collections, and multimedia-enabled applications in art, fashion, advertising, medicine, and science. ∎

References

1. IFIP, *Visual Database Systems I and II*, Elsevier Science Publishers, North-Holland, 1989 and 1992.
2. *Proc. Storage and Retrieval for Image and Video Databases I, II, and III*, Vols. 1,908; 2,185; and 2,420; W. Niblack and R. Jain, eds., SPIE, Bellingham, Wash., 1993, 1994, and 1995.
3. A. Pentland, R.W. Picard, and S. Sclaroff, "Photobook: Tools for Content-Based Manipulation of Image Databases," *Proc. Storage and Retrieval for Image and Video Databases II*, Vol. 2,185, SPIE, Bellingham, Wash., 1994, pp. 34-47.
4. T. Kato, T. Kurita, and H. Shimogaki, "Intelligent Visual Interaction with Image Database Systems—Toward the Multimedia Personal Interface," *J. Information Processing* (Japan), Vol. 14, No. 2, 1991, pp. 134-143.
5. A. Nagasaka and Y. Tanaka, "Automatic Video Indexing and Full-Video Search for Object Appearances," *Visual Database Systems, II, IFIP Trans. A-7*, Elsevier Science Publishers, North-Holland, 1992, pp. 113-127.
6. H.S. Sawhney, S. Ayer, and M. Gorkani, "Model-Based 2D & 3D Dominant Motion Estimation for Mosaicking and Video Representation," *Proc. Fifth Int'l Conf. Computer Vision*, Order No. PRO7042, IEEE CS Press, Los Alamitos, Calif., 1995, pp. 583-590; http://www.almaden.ibm.com/pub/cs/reports/vision/dominant_motion.ps.Z.
7. Y.T.A. Akutsu, K. Otsuji, and T. Sadakata, "VideoMAP and VideoSpaceIcon: Tools for Anatomizing Video Content," *ACM INTERCHI*, 1993, pp. 131-136.
8. L.A. Teodosio and W. Bender, "Salient Video Stills: Content and Context Preserved," *ACM Int'l Conf. Multimedia*, ACM, New York, 1993.
9. J.Y.A. Wang and E.H. Adelson, "Layered Representation for Motion Analysis," *Proc. Computer Vision and Pattern Recognition Conf.*, IEEE CS Press, Los Alamitos, Calif., 1993, pp. 361-366.
10. S. Ayer and H.S. Sawhney, "Layered Representation of Motion Video Using Robust Maximum-Likelihood Estimation of Mixture Models and MDL Encoding," *Proc. Fifth Int'l Conf. Computer Vision*, Order No. PRO7042, IEEE CS Press, Los Alamitos, Calif., 1995, pp. 777-784, http://www.almaden.ibm.com/pub/cs/reports/vision/layered_motion.ps.Z.
11. J. Ashley et al., "Automatic and Semiautomatic Methods for Image Annotation and Retrieval in QBIC," *Proc. Storage and Retrieval for Image and Video Databases III*, Vol. 2,420, SPIE, Bellingham, Wash., 1995, pp. 24-25.
12. W. Niblack et al., "The QBIC Project: Querying Images by Content Using Color, Texture, and Shape," *Proc. Storage and Retrieval for Image and Video Databases*, Vol. 1,908, SPIE, Bellingham, Wash., 1993, pp. 173-187.

Myron "Flick" Flickner *architected parts of QBIC and implemented several shape-matching methods and the database population GUI. His current research interests include image and shape representations, content-based image retrieval, and vision-based man-machine interaction.*

Harpreet "Video" Sawhney *has done much of the exploratory and implementation work to extend the QBIC system to video. The beautiful Yosemite mosaic is a direct result of his work. Sawhney's current research interests are in image and video analysis, representation, and indexing; 3D modeling from images; and multimedia information systems.*

Wayne "Dad" Niblack *is the manager of the Machine Vision group at IBM's Almaden Research Center and the project leader of Query by Image Content (QBIC). He implemented early versions of the color-matching code. Niblack's current interests are in image recognition and retrieval.*

Jonathan "Jaybird" Ashley *has been working on implementing positional color queries for QBIC. His current interests are in bird-watching, and in image processing and synthesis for holographic data storage.*

Qian "Cat" Huang *was a postdoctoral scholar at IBM during 1994-1995. She implemented the automatic object-identification program, whose results are shown in Figure 4. Her interests include computer vision, pattern recognition, medical imaging, artificial intelligence, multimedia, parallel computing, and cats.*

Byron "Bike" Dom *was manager of IBM's Machine Vision group before taking a sabbatical during 1995 to the K.U. Leuven in Belgium. Dom architected many parts of video QBIC as well as the automatic identification of objects by using image segmentation. His interests are segmentation, inspection, and information-theoretic approaches to vision.*

Monika "MPEG" Gorkani *was with IBM during 1994-1995 working on video QBIC. She enabled QBIC for MPEG video as well as implementing the warping code used for mosaicking. Her research interests include video understanding and texture analysis.*

Jim "Symbols-are-fun" Hafner *has solved many of the difficult mathematical problems related to QBIC. He has also implemented much of the positional and histogram color QBIC querying facility. His primary interests are in number theory, but he has worked in complexity theory, matrix theory, and image processing. Hafner loves to solve "impossible" integration problems.*

Denis "Software Wizard" Lee *designed and developed much of the QBIC system, including the graphical user interface, query engine, and World Wide Web server. His areas of interest include graphics, multimedia, computer-aided VLSI design, image processing, virtual reality, user interfaces, distributed systems, neural networks, and genetic algorithms.*

Dragutin "Human-in-the-loop" Petkovic *manages the Advanced Algorithms, Architectures, and Applications Department. Despite all the managerial responsibilities, he is still involved in marketing, applications, and testing much of the software the group creates. His research interests include image analysis applied to industrial, commercial, and biomedical problems, content-based search, large-image and multimedia databases, and advanced user interfaces.*

David "Chess" Steele*, a Canadian exiled to Silicon Valley since 1983, is involved in finding shots in video sequences as well as in the QBIC WWW server. The strongest chess player in the group, Steele is interested in machine vision, artificial intelligence, and decision analysis.*

Peter "Ski" Yanker *was involved in developing IBM Ultimedia Manager, a product that allows queries of images by color, texture, and shape. His current interests are video annotation, skiing, and hiking.*

Please direct e-mail correspondence to qbicwww@ almaden. ibm.com.

Color Indexing

MICHAEL J. SWAIN
Department of Computer Science, University of Chicago, Chicago, IL 60637

DANA H. BALLARD
Department of Computer Science, University of Rochester, Rochester, NY 14627

Received January 22, 1991. Revised June 6, 1991.

Abstract

Computer vision is embracing a new research focus in which the aim is to develop visual skills for robots that allow them to interact with a dynamic, realistic environment. To achieve this aim, new kinds of vision algorithms need to be developed which run in real time and subserve the robot's goals. Two fundamental goals are determining the location of a known object. Color can be successfully used for both tasks.

This article demonstrates that color histograms of multicolored objects provide a robust, efficient cue for indexing into a large database of models. It shows that color histograms are stable object representations in the presence of occlusion and over change in view, and that they can differentiate among a large number of objects. For solving the identification problem, it introduces a technique called *Histogram Intersection*, which matches model and image histograms and a fast incremental version of Histogram Intersection, which allows real-time indexing into a large database of stored models. For solving the location problem it introduces an algorithm called *Histogram Backprojection*, which performs this task efficiently in crowded scenes.

1 Introduction

In recent years a new set of ideas about the goals and the methods of computer vision has gained prominence, and may be on its way to becoming the dominant paradigm, because it promises the quickest route to constructing working vision systems. The term used to describe this set of ideas is *animate vision*, introduced by Ballard (1989, 1991). Similar ideas have recently been expressed using the terms *active perception* (Bajcsy 1985, 1988), *active vision* (Aloimonos et al. 1988; Aloimonos 1990), *qualitative vision* (Nelson 1989, 1991), *inexact vision* (Thompson 1986), and *dynamic vision* (Dickmanns 1988). As in many other areas of science and technology, one of the driving forces behind the change in research strategy has been the availability of new research tools. In this case it has been the advent of powerful real-time imaging-processing equipment, light-weight video cameras, and off-the-shelf computer-controlled motors which allowed movable camera setups to be constructed.

The real-time constraints of *animate vision* require fast algorithms that enable the robot to achieve its goals. Two such goals are determining the identity of an object with a known location, and determining the location of a known object. Color, because it is an identifying feature that is local, and largely independent of view and resolution, can be efficiently used for both tasks. The locality of color information leads to an efficient algorithm for recognizing three-dimensional objects from a variety of viewpoints. The color-identification algorithm can be used without first recognizing the object. The algorithm can be used to identify deformable objects and substances described by mass nouns, something that most other recognition algorithms cannot be used for because they are based on shape.

1.1 The Role of Color in Vision

The ease of recognition using color strands in contrast to the neglect given recently to color as a recognition cue, although it has been used in earlier work (Feldman & Yakimovsky 1974; Garvey 1976; Ohlander et al. 1978). Instead, much more attention has been given to geometric algorithms that extract shape from stereo, motion, and lighting cues. The fundamental reason that color has not been used may be that it is not intrinsically related to the object's class identity in the way that these other cues are. This view is well represented in Biederman (1985):[1]

> Surface characteristics such as color and texture will typically have only secondary roles in primal access... we may know that a chair has a particular color and texture simultaneously with its volumetric description, but it is only the volumetric description that provides efficient access to the representation of CHAIR.

The implicit claim made in the quotation above is that form follows function: Geometrical cues will be the most reliable of object identity. While this may be generally true, it may not be true for routine behavior (Chapman 1990). In such behavior, wherein familiar objects are interacted with repeatedly, color may be a far more efficient indexing feature.

Color may be used in other situations as well. There are many examples in nature where color correlates with the class identity of an object, because of pigments which form part of the function of the object, or because species use it to send messages of enticement or warning. Similarly, color is used as a trademark or identifying feature in objects that occur in artificial environments, such as packaged goods, advertising signs, road signs, etc. Shape cues, in contrast to color, are highly resolution dependent, include only a highly restricted set that is view invariant (e.g., corners, zeros of curvature), and may require elaborate processing to extract them from an image.

Robotic vision systems can also use representations that are heavily personalized to achieve efficient behaviors. For example, it may not be helpful to model coffee cups as being red and white, but *yours* may be, and that color combination is very useful in locating it and recognizing it. Recognition of a particular object is a task that is probably carried out as often as classification; and while classification may in some cases precede recognition of the individual this need not be true in general.

Another reason why color has not been used may have been the lack of good algorithms for *color constancy*, that is perceiving a stable perception of color over varying light conditions, as people do in most circumstances. However, recently there has been great progress in correcting both for the chromaticity of the illuminant (Maloney & Wandell 1986; Forsyth 1990; Rubner & Schulten 1989; Brainard et al. 1989; Novak & Shafer 1990) and for geometric effects such as specularity (Klinker et al. 1988). So there is good reason to believe that color can be used as an identifying invariant of object surfaces, even under varying light conditions.

1.2 What vs. Where

Eye traces of human observers suggest that we do not build categorical databases of the world around us independent of the task we are carrying out but that, instead, only highly selective regions of the scene are examined in detail, and these are highly dependent on the task being carried out. Furthermore, the sequential nature of the eye movement traces suggests that the visual architecture cannot analyze the entire picture at a glance but must break the analysis up into smaller sequential components. One gross distinction that we make is between *identification algorithms* that analyze the foveated area during fixation and *location algorithms* that direct the eyes to new targets.

Support for this *what/where* distinction comes from studies of human and primate brains. A significant feature of the gross organization of the primate visual brain is the specialization of the temporal and parietal lobes of visual cortex (Mishkin & Appenzeller 1987; Maunsell & Newsome 1987). The parietal cortex seems to be subserving the management of locations in space whereas the temporal cortex seems to be subserving the identification of objects in the case where location is not the issue. In a striking experiment by Miskin (Miskin & Appenzeller 1987), monkeys with parietal lesions fail at a task that requires using a relational cue, but have no trouble performing a very similar task that requires using a pattern cue. The reverse is true for temporal lesions. Why should the primate brain be specialized in this way? If we think generally about the problem of relating internal models to objects in the world, then one way to interpret this "What/Where" dichotomy is as a suggestion that image interpretation, the general problem of associating many models to many parts of the image simultaneously, is either too hard or unnecessary, or both (see table 1). In order to build vision systems that function in real time, perhaps the problem must be simplified. In sections 3 and 4, approaches to the identification and location problems are presented and tested.

Table 1. The biological organization of cortex into What/Where modules may have a basis in computational complexity. Trying to match a large number of image segments to a large number of models at once may be too difficult. (From Ballard (1991)).

		Object to Match Against	
		One	Many
Image Portions	One	Identification: trying to identify an object whose location can be fixated	Image interpretation: Too hard?
	Many	Location: trying to find a known object	

1.3 Outline

Section 2 introduces the multidimensional color histogram. Given a discrete color space, a color histogram counts how much of each color occurs in the image. Color histograms are invariant to translation, rotation about an axis perpendicular to the image, and change only slowly with rotation about other axes, occlusion, and change of distance to the object. On the other hand, histograms for different objects can differ markedly, and there are a huge number of possible histograms (exponential in the number of different colors in the color space). Therefore, the color histogram is an excellent representation to use for identifying objects.

Section 3 introduces a method of comparing image and model histograms called *Histogram Intersection*, which is especially suited to comparing histograms for recognition because it does not require the accurate separation of the object from its background or occluding objects in the foreground. Experiments show that Histogram Intersection can distinguish models from a large database, that it is robust to occlusion as well as image and histogram resolutuion, and that only a small number of histograms are needed to represent a three-dimensional object. They also show that an effective color-constancy algorithm will be needed for Histogram Intersection to work under variable light conditions. The section also describes a modification of Histogram Intersection called *Incremental Intersection* that allows efficient indexing into a very large database.

Section 4 shows how a model histogram can be used to find the location of a known object (the *target*). The algorithm to solve this problem is called *Histogram Backprojection*. It finds the region in the image where the colors in the model histogram show up together, relying more on those colors that show up as much as expected than those which show up much more, and therefore occur in other objects besides the target.

The experiments in section 4.1.2 show that Histogram Backprojection works well even when the objects containing the same colors occur in the image and when the object is partially occluded.

2 Color Histograms

Given a discrete color space defined by some color axes (e.g., red, green, blue), the color histogram is obtained by discretizing the image colors and counting the number of times each discrete color occurs in the image array. The image colors that are transformed to a common discrete color are usefully thought of as being in the same 3D histogram bin centered at that color. To illustrate, figure 1 (see color figures on page 29) shows the output from a color camera together with a color histogram obtained from the image.

Histograms are invariant to translation and rotation about the viewing axis, and change only slowly under change of angle of view, change in scale, and occlusion (see color figures 2 and 3 on page 30). Because histograms change slowly with view, a three-dimensional object can be adequately represented by a small number of histograms, corresponding to a set of canonical views (Koenderink & van Doorn 1976; Feldman 1985).

Histograms define an equivalence function on the set of all possible colors, namely that two colors are the same if they fall into the same bin. This equivalence function is not ideal for recognition, because the relative range of colors that are considered the same as a given color depend on where the given color is located within the bin. Ideally, the colors considered the same would be in a region centered on the color, or in some region whose shape depends on knowledge of the possible variations introduced by changes in lighting or noise in the sensors. It should be determined by the random effect of how the color happens to link up with respect to the tesselation of the discrete color space. Another

problem is that the equivalence is all or nothing. Presumably, as the difference in color of two object patches increases the probability of them being the same object patch decreases smoothly. The binary threshold used to define the tesselation serves as a crude approximation to the probability function.

Histograms whose bins define overlapping bell-shaped (e.g., Gaussian) functions of color space would address some of the concerns of the previous paragraph, as would interpolaion coding (Ballard 1987). Extensions such as these have not been considered because histograms in their simplest form have worked well. Why do histograms works, despite their inherent problems? Objects tend to have surfaces that are made up of regions of color. Because of shading and camera noise these regions are blurred in color space, and so span more than one bin in a histogram. When image and model histograms of the same object are matched, a high match value is obtained because the regions match well, even if point-by-point matches on the object's surface are not always reliable.

Strat (1990) has matched *cumulative histograms* with a match algorithm similar to Histogram Intersection to make a system that is robust to lighting changes. In a three-dimensional color space (x, y, z) the cumulative histogram is defined:

$$C(x, y, z) = \sum_{i=1}^{x} \sum_{j=1}^{y} \sum_{k=1}^{z} H(x, y, z)$$

where $H(x, y, z)$ is the non-cumulative histogram discussed above.

Both the object identification and object search implementations described in the following sections use color histograms to represent objects.

3 Identification

This section describes how to use the color histogram to identify an object whose approximate location is known, the "Identification" problem of table 1. To identify objects based on their color histogram, we must be able to judge the similarity of the color histogram of an image to the color histograms in the database. Section 3.1 introduces a method of comparing image and model histograms called *Histogram Intersection*, which tells how many of the pixels in the model histogram are found in the image. This method is especially suited to comparing histograms for recognition because

it does not require the accurate separation of the object from its background of occluding objects in the foreground, often a difficult task to perform before the object has been recognized. The results of the experimental section show that:

- Histogram Intersection can distinguish objects from a large database (66 objects).
- The Histogram Intersection match value is insensitive enough to rotation and moderate changes in distance so that only a small number of views is needed to represent a three-dimensional object (about 6).
- The range of colors that occur in the world need only be split into about 200 different discrete colors to distinguish a large number of objects, so color constancy to the degree demanded by the algorithm should be feasible. However, without transforming the input by a color-constancy algorithm, Histogram Intersection is sensitive to lighting changes.
- Identification can be done even when a significant amount of the object is *occluded* (not visible).
- Recognition accuracy is typically extremely insensitive to the histogram resolution used.

Section 3.2 describes an incremental version of Histogram Intersection, called *Incremental Intersection*. By matching the largest bins from the image and the models, Incremental Intersection allows extremely fast indexing into a large database. Experiments show that Incremental Intersection does not sacrifice accuracy because most of the information is carried by the largest bins of the histograms.

3.1 Histogram Intersection

Because the model database may be large, we can afford only a highly restricted amount of processing per model, but at the same time we must be able to overcome the problems that hinder recognition, most importantly

- distractions in the background of the object,
- viewing the object from a variety of viewpoints,
- occlusion,
- varying image resolution,
- varying lighting conditions.

The matching method proposed here, called *Histogram Intersection*, is robust to the first four problems; the last is left to a color-constancy module that operates on the input prior to the histogram stage.

3.1.1. *Description.* Given a pair of histograms, I and M, each containing n bins, the intersection of the histograms is defined to be

$$\sum_{j=1}^{n} \min(I_j, M_j).$$

The result of the intersection of a model histogram with an image histogram is the number of pixels from the model that have corresponding pixels of the same color in the image. To obtain a fractional match value between 0 and 1 intersection is normalized by the number of pixels in the model histogram. The match value is then

$$H(I, M) = \frac{\sum_{j=1}^{n} \min(I_j, M_j)}{\sum_{j=1}^{n} M_j}$$

The normalized histogram intersection match value is not reduced by distracting pixels in the background. This is the desired behavior since complete segmentation of the object from the background cannot be guaranteed. Segmentation is still a topic of active research, but the indications from the large amount of research done in the past are that complete, efficient, and reliable segmentation cannot be done prior to recognition. The histogram intersection match value is only increased by a pixel in the background if

— the pixel has the same color as one of the colors in the model, and
— the number of pixels of that color in the object is less than the number of pixels of that color in the model.

There are a number of ways of determining the approximate depth of an object, from laser or sonar range finders, disparity, focus, or touching the object with a sensor. The depth value combined with the known size of the object can be used to scale the model histogram. Alternatively, if it is possible to segment the object from the background and if it is not significantly occluded, the image histogram can be scaled to be the same size as the model histogram. Appendix A shows that when it is possible to segment the object from the background and thus scale the image histogram to be the same size as the model histogram, that Histogram Intersection is equivalent to the use of the sum of absolute differences or *city-block* metric. That is, if

$$\sum_{i=1}^{n} M_i = \sum_{i=1}^{n} I_i$$

then if we let T equal this value, we have

$$1 - H(I, M) = \frac{1}{2T} \sum_{i=1}^{n} |I_i - M_i|.$$

If images are scaled by depth then Histogram Intersection does not define a metric, since there is an asymmetry between the model and the image. That is, the model and image histograms are not constrained to contain the same number of pixels, so the normalization factor in the denominator will differ matching image to model as matching model to image. This asymmetry is a natural result of expecting background pixels in the image but not in the model.

Histogram Intersection is capable of differentiating among a large number of different objects. Appendix B shows that the fraction of the multidimensional space defined by the bins of the histogram occupied by a single model is at most

$$\frac{(2\delta)^{n-1}}{\sqrt{n}}$$

where $1 - \delta$ is the minimum Histogram Intersection match value allowed and n is the number of bins in a histogram.

For $\delta = 0.4$ (a reasonable number based on our experiments) and $n = 512$, the fraction is 1×10^{-51}. If histograms were distributed evenly throughout color space, the reciprocal of this number would approximate the carrying capacity of the histogram. But histograms are not distributed evenly throughout histogram space, as shown by figure 4 on page 30. For a back-of-the envelope calculation we can try to account for the unequal distribution by reducing the number of histogram bins to, say 100, as figure 2 would suggest. The fraction of histogram space is still very small, 3×10^{-11}. A more accurate analysis might consist of generating a Monte-Carlo distribution of histograms throughout color space and measuring their overlap.

3.1.2. *Experiments.* Experiments were performed to see if a large number of objects can be distinguished and to test the sensitivity of the recognition technique to changes in view, image resolution, and occlusion.

An experimental test of histogram intersection shows that the technique is capable of indexing into a large database, that is, eliminating most of the possible matches leaving only a small number for further consideration. The 32 images in figure 6 were matched to each of the 66 models in the database in figure 5 (see color figures on page 31). The color axes used for the histograms were the three *opponent color axes,* as defined as follows (Ballard & Brown 1982):

$$rg = r - g$$
$$by = 2 * b - r - g$$
$$wb = r + g + b$$

Here r, g, and b represent red, green, and blue signals, respectively. The rg, by, and wb axes are analogous to the opponent color axes used by the human visual system (Lennie & D'Zmura 1988). They were used here simply to allow the intensity (wb) axis to be more coarsely sampled than the other two, because the intensity axis is more sensitive to lighting variation from shadows and distance from the light source. The wb axis was divided into 8 sections, while the rg and by bins were each divided into 16 sections, for a total of 2048 bins. Because the total intensity limits the color differences possible, only a fraction of them can actually receive counts. For example, suppose the camera outputs a maximum M on each channel. Then if $wb = 0$ ($r = g = b = 0$) or $wb = 3M$ ($r = g = b = M$) then the variables by and wb must both take on the value 0 (see (Swain 1990a) for more details). Because most colors we experience are fairly unsaturated (i.e., close to the wb axis), even for objects such as ones in the database shown in figure 5, only about 200 (5×5×8) of the 512 receive an appreciable number of counts, as is discussed further below. So we are dividing up color space fairly coarsely.

For the 66-object database shown in Figures 5–8, the correct model is the best match 29 of 32 times and is always one of the top two matches. The three cases when the correct model was the second highest match are, listed in the format (*model: object receiving larger response*).

1. Crunchberries: Campbell's Special Request soup
2. Raisin Bran: Campbell's Chicken with Rice soup
3. Windsurfer shift: Ivory detergent bottle

Other, more expensive, matching techniques can be used to verify which of the top scoring models is the correct one, so it is not crucial that the correct model is always the best match. In the experiment the models were segmented from the background prior to generating the model histograms. No segmentation was performed on the images of the unknown objects.

In addition to using methods other than color to resolve ambiguous cases, there are steps that can be taken to improve the use of color information in the histogram intersection algorithm. All three of the models that received larger match values than the correct models had smaller numbers of pixels in their

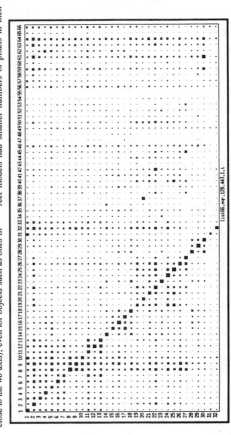

Fig. 7. The results of matching all combinations of image and database histograms displayed pictorially where the size of the squares are proportional to match values. The dominance of the diagonal values shows that the correct match is almost always selected. Twenty-nine of thirty-two matches are correct; in three cases the correct model received second-highest score. Models are along the horizontal axis; unknown objects are along the vertical axis.

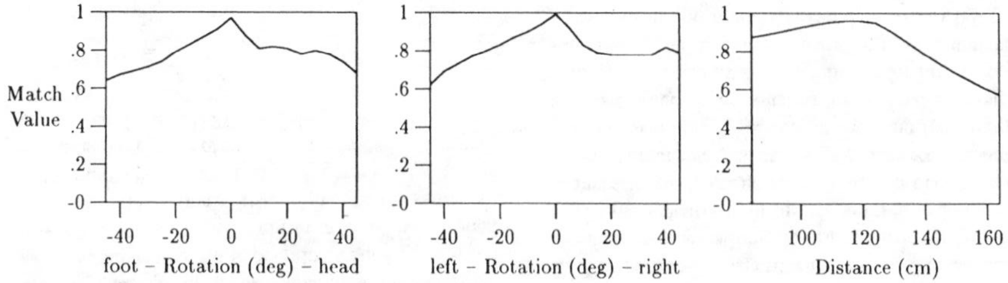

Table 2. Image resolution and match accuracy. The *Correct Match Placement* columns show the rank of the correct match for each of thirty-two images in figure 5 being matched to the sixty-six models in figure 4. The model histograms were obtained from images of 128×90, and scaled appropriately. See the text for the definition of *average match percentile.*

Image Size	Correct Match Placement				Average Match Percentile
	1st	2nd	3rd	> 3rd	
128 x 90	29	3	0	0	99.9
64 x 45	27	5	0	0	99.8
32 x 22	24	7	1	0	99.6
16 x 11	15	6	4	0	97.8
8 x 5	4	4	3	21	78.1

Table 3. Match accuracy with scaled image and model resolution. Both model and image histograms were generated from images of the same indicated size. Interpret the match data as in table 2.

Image Size	Correct Match Placement				Average Match Percentile
	1st	2nd	3rd	> 3rd	
128 x 90	29	3	0	0	99.9
64 x 45	29	3	0	0	99.9
32 x 22	28	4	0	0	99.8
16 x 11	23	5	3	1	99.3
8 x 5	17	7	2	6	97.7

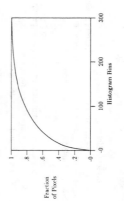

Fig. 12. Distribution of pixels across histogram bins for the database shown in figure 4 (black background removed). A point (x, y) on the curve indicates that fraction y of pixels fall into the x largest bins. There are a total of 512 bins in the entire histogram.

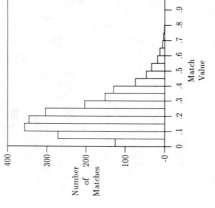

Fig. 8 Variation of the Histogram Intersection match value (see section 3 for definition) as the camera is moved with respect to a Snoopy doll. In the Distance graph the model image was taken at a distance of 124 cm. The match value changes slowly with changes in angle and distance.

histograms. It is easier to find evidence for a smaller object in any given image region than it is to find evidence for a larger object. A recognition system could choose to verify the large objects with high match values before the smaller ones. Alternatively, if the distance is known, objects could be categorized by their size before indexing using color.

One important claim is the insensitivity of the matching process to variations in view. To test this, the variation in match value with respect to view changes in a single model, the Snoopy Doll, was studied further. Figure 9 shows how the Histogram Intersection match value changes as the camera is rotated about the Snoopy Doll shown in figure 5, and moved closer and further from the doll. Compare these match values to the ones in figure 10. Even at 45 degrees rotation or 1⅓ times the original distance the match value (about 0.6) is higher than 99 percent of the false matches.

Another important claim is that recognition accuracy is fairly insensitive to image resolution. Table 2 shows how match success is affected by reducing the resolution of the images. The images were reduced in resolution by averaging the values of the pixels to be combined, and the histograms were taken from the reduced images. The model histograms were obtained from images of size 128×90 and scaled by the appropriate multiplicative factor prior to matching. For each image the match values to each model are sorted; the *rank* is the position of the correct match in this list. The match percentile for each image matched is then calculated as (*n*-models − rank) / (*n*-model − 1), where *n*-models is the number of models in the database (66). The match percentile is averaged over all 32 images in the experiment. A value of 100 indicates perfect matching; a value of 99 indicates that, on average, the correct match scored a higher match value that 99 of 100 of the

histograms of more highly textured objects could change more dramatically over scale. Images obtained from typical cameras contain 512×485 (about ¼ million) pixels, so these results suggest that color matching could be performed reliably on regions that cover as little as 1/1000 of the total image area, provided the camera was focused well enough that camera blur did not destroy detail in the image.

Table 3 shows that match success is improved for extremely low-resolution images by obtaining the model histograms from low-resolution images as well. Since it is unlikely that matching will be done to such small parts of the image, scaling the model histogram will do in most circumstances. What this does suggest is that a hypothetical extremely inexpensive system that operated on very low-resolution images would be able to recognize the dominant object in the image using color about as well as a full-resolution system. Examples of the reduced-resolution images are shown in color figure 6.

Recognition accuracy is also fairly insensitive to occlusion. To test this, subparts of the images were matched to the database. First, the bottom third of each image was removed (see color figure 11 on page 31) before matching to the database. Then, the right-hand third of the image was removed, leaving only 4/9th of the original image (color figure 12). This set was also matched to the database. The results are shown in

table 4. There is only slight degradation in the match accuracy with occlusion. The correct matches are still among the top three match values (out of sixty-six), even for the most severe occlusion.

These results demonstrate how match values will degrade under occlusion when the occluding object can be segmented from the object of interest. Matching in the presence of occlusion will be more difficult when segmentation cannot be achieved, because colors from the occluding object may also match to the models in the database. Nevertheless, other experiments have shown that matching can be achieved even with some occlusion of this sort (see Swain (1990b)).

Fig. 9. Distribution of match values for incorrect image-model matches for the models and images shown in figures 4 and 5. The values counted here are all the off-diagonal elements of the matrix shown in figure 7. The values for incorrect matches rarely exceed the values for different views of the same object (see figure 8), even when they are obtained from significantly different angles and distances.

other models, and so on. An average match percentile of 50 indicates the match selection is no better than random.

This experiment simulates matching to an object that covers only a small region of the image array. The match values are reasonable even for images of size 16×11, which is fewer than 200 pixels! The success of matching under low resolution can be explained by the fact that the images being matched to the database have fairly large regions of constant color. The color

Table 4. Occlusion and match accuracy.

Occluded Region	Correct Match Placement				Average Match Percentile
	1st	2nd	3rd	>3rd	
None (Figure 4)	29	3	0	0	99.9
Bottom (Figure 10)	27	4	1	0	99.7
Bottom, Side (Figure 11)	22	5	5	0	99.3

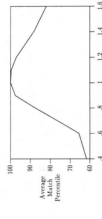

Fig. 13. Effects of changing histogram resolution on match success.

The number of bins in the opponent color histogram that receive a significant number of counts is much smaller than the total number of bins that could possibly receive counts. Figure 4 shows the distribution of counts for the histograms representing the models in figure 5. (Remember the background black is subtracted before creating the model histograms.) Sixty-five percent of the counts lie in the top fifty bins, eighty-three percent lie in the top one hundred bins, and ninety-six percent lie in the top two hundred. The bins that receive the most counts lie on the white-black (wb) axis. The numbers drop off with distance away from this axis.

The results of Histogram Intersection were extremely insensitive to the number of bins in the histogram used in the image and model histograms. Figure 13 shows the effects of varying the size of the histogram over two orders of magnitude, from 64 accessible bins (8×8×4 bins total) to 8125 accessible bins (40×40×20 bins total). There are only small changes in the match effectiveness over the entire range of histogram sizes. Note that matches in the high resolution histograms rely on the fact that there are smooth distributions of colors on the objects. These distributions arise from the large regions of constant color being blurred in color by shading and camera noise. In the highest resolution histograms the same pixels are not matching each other, but different pixels from the same color region.

In a set of real-time experiments employing a Datacube pipelined image processor, 8×8×8 (red, green, blue) histogram were used instead of the 16×8 opponent color histograms, with good results, so the choice of color axes is not crucial either. The color camera was mounted on our mobile robot platform and panned across a floor containing the database of colored shirts. The shirts were spread out on the floor, but no special effort was made to lay them perfectly flat or approximate the view in the database. Since this experiment tests the "what" or identification problem, the panning is done so that the image serves as a fovea, that is, each shirt, when centered, occupies the majority of the image. Nevertheless, the shirts are close enough that there is often another shirt in the background when a match is being done. The shirt occupying the major portion of the image is invariably the top notch.

As discussed at the beginning of this section, it is expected that a color-constancy algorithm be used before histogramming. Nonetheless, we tested Histogram Intersection in the presence of changing light intensity without color constancy. One aim is to see how necessary a color-constancy algorithm is. As we expected, changes in lighting conditions affect the match value considerably. More importantly, this experiment can be also used to test how well a color-constancy algorithm must work. Changing light intensity was simulated by multiplying the image pixel values by a constant factor ranging from 0.4 to 1.6. The resulting pixel values were constrained to be no greater than 255, as would occur in a camera. The transformed images were matched to the original models. The results are displayed in figure 14.

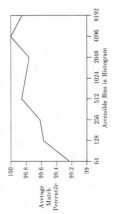

Fig. 14. Effects of changing intensity on match success.

It appears that with 16×16×8 opponent color histograms, where 8 is the number of bins along the white-black axis, good pruning of the possible matches can be achieved if the intensity is recovered to within about plus or minus 15 percent of the true values. Since one bin in the white-black direction only represents at most 12.5 percent of the maximum value in the histogram, the matching process can still work even if many of the counts fall in neighboring bins. This is because regions tend to cover a number of neighboring bins in color space, the same explanation for why fine-grain reso-

histograms can be used for accurate matching (see figure 13). When the multiplying factor is 0.4, a 60-percent decrease in light levels, the average match percentile is 61.7, not much better than random (50).

The simplest color constancy algorithm simply normalizes the red, green, and blue responses by their sum, that is:

$$r' = r/(r + g + b)$$
$$g' = g/(r + g + b)$$
$$b' = b/(r + g + b)$$

These new axes provide only two degrees of freedom, since the values of any two define the third. With 8×8 (r', g') histograms, an average match percentile of 98.0 was achieved (see table 5), with the worst ranking of an object matched to itself being a seventh place for the Raisin Bran box. The normalized intensity values are unaffected by changes in lighting intensity (assuming a linearized camera), making them much more effective than the 3D histograms in variable lighting conditions. By placing an object of known reflectance in the image and normalizing the responses with respect to it, a third axis of color information could be recovered under variable intensity lighting.

Table 5. Matching with normalized color signals.

Correct Match Placement				Average Match Percentile
1st	2nd	3rd	>3rd	
15	7	3	7	98.0

In summary, Histogram Intersection can successfully prune the number of candidates in a large database to a small number of possible matches. Because color histograms change only slowly over view, a small number of them can be used to represent a three-dimensional object. Histogram Intersection is robust to occlusion and changes in image and histogram resolution. With three sensors, three-dimensional histograms are sensitive to changing light conditions; and so, when the lighting is variable, it must be used after the pixel array has been transformed by an effective color-constancy algorithm. We demonstrated the effects of using the simplest color-constancy algorithm, scaling the color axes by the total intensity. The sensitivity to intensity variations was eliminated, as the cost of a moderate decrease in the ability to prune objects from the database under changing lighting conditions.

Histogram Intersection is an efficient way of matching histograms. Its complexity is linear in the number of elements in the histograms. Two 16×16×8 histograms can be matched in 2 milliseconds on a SUN Sparcstation 1 (a 12 MIP RISC machine). The histograms themselves are efficient to compute using parallel image processing hardware. For instance, generating a 16×16×8 histogram from a 512×485 image takes about 40 milliseconds using a Datacube FeatureMax board, including the time needed to transfer the histogram to the host.

Histogram intersection is efficient compared to most recognition schemes. Nevertheless, for large databases the linear dependence of the recognition scheme on database size will add up. Parallel processing is one way of attacking this problem, since the match over different models is easily parallelizable. Another way, which reduces the recognition complexity to constant time for a broad range of databases, is described in the next section.

3.2 Efficient Indexing into a Large Database

We introduce an algorithm, called *Incremental Intersection*, for indexing into a large database efficiently on a sequential computer. In this scheme, only the largest bins from the image and model histograms are compared, and a partial histogram intersection value is computed. The computation is incremental, so that the algorithm can be interrupted at any time after the sort with as good results as one could expect with the amount of time used. This last feature could prove to be important in a system that interacts with a dynamic world, in which the times that actions are taken are often dictated by outside events.

Incremental intersection is split into two phases, an off-line phase in which the data structure representing the database is generated and an on-line matching phase. In the off-line phase:

Table 6. Recognition times. Each histogram contains 2048 bins. Times (in milliseconds) were measured on a SUN SPARCstation 1.

	Database Size		
	19	37	70
Histogram Intersection	38	73	150
Incremental Intersection (B=10)	15	15	15

1. Assign to each bin in each model histogram a key which is the fraction of the total number of pixels in the histogram that fall in that bin.
2. Group the bins by index (color).
3. Sort each group by key.

In the on-line phase:

1. Sort the image histogram bins by size.
2. For the B largest image histogram bins, starting with the largest, match the image bin to all the model bins with the same index whose key is larger. If previously unmatched model bins are matched, match them to all larger image bins.

The efficiency of Histogram Intersection and Incremental Intersection is compared in table 6. A complexity analysis shows that the time for Histogram Intersection depends linearly on the product of the size of the histogram and the size of the database, i.e., the algorithm is $O(nm)$, where n is the total number of bins in the histogram and m is the number of models in the database. The asymptotic complexity of Incremental Intersection is $O(n \log n + cm)$, where c is the number of image bins used for indexing into the database. The complexity of Incremental Intersection is also linear in the size of the database. However, the constant factor is so low that for most databases the complexity is dominated by the sort of the image histogram bins.

Incremental Intersection only computes an approximation of the Histogram Intersection value, unless it is allowed to match every bin in the image histogram. One would think, therefore, that its performance would only be a fraction as good as complete Histogram Intersection. Figure 15 shows that the match effectiveness climbs very quickly and even surpasses that of Histogram Intersection using small numbers of image histogram bins. After examining 10 bins, Incremental Intersection matches the images to the models without error, whereas in three cases the Histogram Intersection match value for the correct match was the second highest. How can this happen? Most of the surface of each object in the test database consists of at most five or six different colors, so then histogram bins capture a good per-

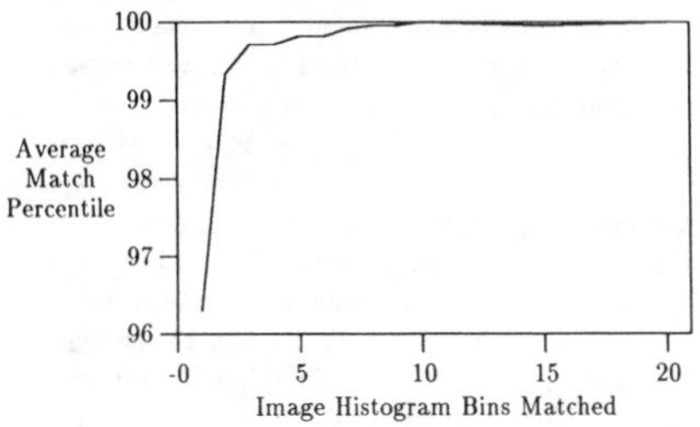

Fig. 15. Effectiveness of Incremental Intersection as function of the number of image histogram bins matched. For comparison, the average match percentile for Histogram Intersection is 99.86.

centage of the uncorrupted signal coming from the object, while the smaller bins are more likely to be noise.

4 Location

The previous section discussed recognizing an unknown object whose location is known, the ``Identification'' task in table 1. This section discusses the complementary ``Location'' box in table 1. Determining the location of an object is necessary when executing many tasks, not only looking for a ``lost'' object. Fixating a moving object, or a stationary object when the robot is moving, also requires keeping track of the location of the object (Coombs 1989). Verging a pair of cameras upon an object requires determining the location of an object in both images so that they can be registered (Olson & Coombs 1991). All these tasks can be accomplished using color histograms and an algorithm called *Histogram Backprojection.*

4.1 Histogram Backprojection

Histogram Backprojection answers the question ``Where in the image are the colors that belong to the object being looked for (the *target*)?'' The answer is

given in such a way so that the colors that appear in other objects besides the target are deemphasized so that they are less likely to distract the search mechanism. Experiments show that the technique works for objects in cluttered scenes under realistic conditions.

In Histogram Backprojection the model (target) and the image are represented by their multi-dimensional color histograms M and I as in Histogram Intersection. A *ratio histogram* R, defined as

$$R_i = \min\left(\frac{M_i}{I_i},\ 1\right)$$

is computed from the model and image histograms. It is this histogram R that is backprojected onto the image, that is, the image values are replaced by the values of R that they index. The backprojected image is then convolved by a mask, which for compact objects of unknown orientation could be a circle with the same area as the expected area subtended by the object. The peak in the convolved image is the expected location of the target, provided the target appears in the image.

4.1.1. Description. More precisely, let $h(c)$ be the histogram function that maps a color c (a three-dimensional value) to a histogram bin (another three-dimensional value). Let D^r be a disk of radius r:

$$D^r_{x,y} = \begin{cases} 1 & \text{if } \sqrt{x^2 + y^2} < r \\ 0 & \text{otherwise} \end{cases}$$

Define the ``loc'' function to return to pixel (x, y) with the value of its argument, and let the $*$ symbol denote convolution. Then Histogram Backprojection can be written

1. for each histogram bin j do

$$R_j := \min\left(\frac{M_j}{I_j},\ 1\right)$$

2. for each x, y do

$$b_{x,y} := R_{h(c_{x,y})}$$

3. $b := D^r * b$

4. $(x_t,\ y_t) := \text{loc}(\max_{x,y}\ b_{x,y})$

4.1.2. Experiments. As a demonstration of Histogram Backprojection, we consider figure 6 as a single crowded scene, and look for objects within it using the models from figure 5. The results are shown in figures 16 and

17 (see color figures on page 32). In all cases but four the largest peak in the convolved image corresponds to the correct object. The four cases in which it doesn't are listed below in the format (*target: objects receiving larger response*).

1. Wheaties: Manischewitz matzo farfel.
2. Campbell's clam chowder: red and white shirt, Campbell's chicken soup.
3. Charmin: orange White Cloud.
4. Mickey Mouse underwear: red and white shirt, USA Flyer.

The success rate is shown more graphically in table 7.

Because the convolution can be carried out on a reduced resolution image, Histogram Backprojection is very efficient. Its complexity on a sequential computer would be $O(I + c * I')$ where I is the number of pixels in the full-resolution image, I' is the number of pixels in the reduced resolution image, and c is the number of pixels in the convolution mask applied to the reduced resolution image.

Table 7. Performance of Histogram Backprojection. The number in each square is the rank of peak that falls into the corresponding square in figure 5 when looking for the model whose image is in that square. A ``1'' means the object has been correctly located, a ``2'' indicates the object created the second largest peak in the convolved backprojected image, etc.

1	1	1	1	1	1
2	1	3	1	1	1
1	1	2	1	1	1
1	3	1	1	1	1
1	3	1	1		
1	1				

Histogram Backprojection has been implemented in a Datacube image processor, with a Sun 4/260 workstation as its host. The Datacube can do histograms, subsample, and convolutions with 8×8 masks within a frame time. Using $8 \times 8 \times 8$ (512 total) size histograms and a reduced image of size 32×32 (1024 pixels) for the convolutions, the algorithm can be executed four times a second. The real-time experiments show that because Histogram Backprojection is extremely efficient it is useful not only for locating an object but also for tracking an object moving relative to the robot.

Histogram Backprojection, like Histogram Intersection, is robust to occlusion. If instead of using figure 6 as the crowded scene, we use figure 12 in which only four-ninths of the image of each object remains, the location of each object can be found almost as well as in the image with no occlusion. They only target for which the effectiveness of Histogram Backprojection suffers badly is that of Charmin paper towels, the object that already had a portion occluded in the original image. As for the previous experiment, we show the backprojected ratio histogram for the blue and white striped shirt (see figure 18 on color page 32) and the combined results of looking for each of the objects in the image (see figure 19 on color page 32). In all cases but six the largest peak in the convolved image corresponds to the correct object. The six cases in which it doesn't are listed below in the format (*target: objects receiving larger response*).

1. Campbell's clam chowder: red and white shirt.
2. Manischewitz chicken soup: Manischewitz bakit, Manischewitz matzo farfel.
3. Angelsoft: Charmin.
4. Charmin: orange White Cloud, Bakit, Northern, purple White Cloud, Campbell's Special chicken soup, Manischewitz chicken soup.
5. Balloons shirt: white with pink border shirt.
6. Mickey Mouse underwear: red and white shirt.

The success rate is shown diagrammatically in table 8.

Table 8 Performance of Histogram Backprojection under occlusion. The number in each square is the rank of peak that falls into the corresponding square in figure 11 when looking for the model whose image is in that square.

1	1	1	1	1	1	
1	2	1	1	3		
1	2	7	1	1	1	
2	1	1	1	1		
1	2	1	1	1		
1						

While the effects of occlusion are different for Histogram Intersection and Histogram Backprojection because the algorithms differ in how they process spatial information, the effects of changing image and histogram resolution are similar: Both algorithms will be successful if and only if the colors in the object stay in matching bins to the colors in the model. Since Histogram Intersection is very insensitive to changing the image or histogram resolution it is expected that Histogram Backprojection will be as well. Likewise, Histogram Backprojection is expected to be about as sensitive to failures of color constancy as Histogram Intersection.

5 Conclusion

The advent of real-time image-processing hardware is changing the research focus of computer vision in a fundamental way. Instead of attempting to build elaborate representations of the environment from static images, a new objective is to construct visual skills which allow a robot to interact with a dynamic, realistic environment. To achieve this objective, new kinds of vision algorithms need to be developed that are capable of running in real time and subserving the robot's goals. Two important skills for interacting with the environment are identifying an object in a known location and locating a known object. We have shown here how robust, extremely efficient algorithms for achieving these objectives can be designed using color histograms as their model and image representations. The robustness of the algorithms is directly related to their real-time performance. Since the algorithms function at or near video frame rates of 30 frames per second, they can fail on several frames per second and still achieve the overall goals of identification and location.

In the past research has concentrated on geometric cues. The shift toward real-time systems requires faster algorithms. For instance, in Rosenfeld's comprehensive 1989 bibliography, there are thirty-seven articles on recognition of three-dimensional objects, all of which use shape.[2] In contrast, there are no articles that use color for object identification. Color-based algorithms fulfill the requirement of such systems, because of their fast performance and capability of dealing with changes in view, object deformations, and inaccurate segmentation of objects from their backgrounds.

Because of color's important applications and ease of use, color cameras and digitizing facilities should be a feature of computer vision being considered in which color could play an important role. For instance, manufacturers of automated check-out devices in grocery stores are considering automating the identification of fruits and vegetables. Color would be an important identifying feature in this situation. As well, an aquarium is investigating installing equipment to automatically identify the fish swimming by a visitor to an aquarium. Again, the coloration of the fish could be an important identifying feature.

Color could also be used for vision systems in manufacturing environments provided the environment is color coded. Identification, location, and tracking

in such an environment using color would be straightforward. Color may be the easiest way to label objects and locations for a robot. Robots could pick up the tools they need based on color, follow lines on the floor of various colors to go to specific destinations, dangerous objects could be color coded in certain ways, the boundary of the workspace could be denoted by a colored band. The possibilities are numerous.

One especially convenient aspect of manufacturing environments is that the lighting can often be carefully controlled. Consistent lighting would avoid the necessity of solving the color constancy problem. Lighting which can be described by a small set of basis functions is easier to discount than lighting which may be from a variety of sources with different spectra. Only one basis function is needed when the light is from only one type of bulb. Similarly, color constancy is easier to achieve if the surface reflectances come from a known distribution which can be described by a small number of basis functions. This objective may be more easily achieved in a constrained manufacturing environment than in an unconstrained environment.

5.1 Future Work

One problem that requires much more careful analysis is the application of color recognition under varying light conditions. In addition to the simple normalization scheme described in the text, Novak and Shafer's the "guided" color-constancy algorithm of Novak and Shafer (1990) is a good one to try, because the large numbers of constraints introduced by the color chart they place in the scene should give it better color constancy than the algorithms that deduce the lighting from less reliable information. We conjecture that if the matching techniques introduced here don't work under variable lighting using Novak and Shafer's algorithm, they probably won't work with any of the other algorithms.

The light source does not have to be beyond the control of the robot or vision system. For instance, a robot could carry its own light source with it. If this light source were significantly stronger than the other lights in the room, only the intensity would change from image to image. If the distance to the object were known, even the intensity could be calculated. Some time of flight-range laser-range sensors also generate reflectance images. If a collection of lasers at different wavelengths were used, the reflectance images could be analyzed just as the color images are here.

A second challenging problem is identifying the region from which to extract the histogram for histogram intersection. Histogram intersection is fairly insensitive to pixels in the background, nonetheless, since they can cause mismatches and since cropping a portion of the object will diminish the match value, delimiting the object of interest is an interesting problem. The answer to this problem will probably not be a single solution, but a number of different ones each of which works better under a different situation. For isolating a moving object, motion cues should be used; for isolating an object separated from its background by depth, disparity cues or cues from an active depth sensor should be used. The visual motion and disparity cues or cues from an active depth sensor should be used. The visual motion and disparity cues may only be reliable at sparse points on the surfaces, and so they must be either extended by surface models or enclosed within a bounding region. A simple technique for eliminating background pixels based on verging on the object of interest and ignoring those pixels that do not register in the two eyes was demonstrated by Swain (1990a). Other techniques such as desensitization to a commonly occuring background could be used.

The algorithms have not been tested in cooperation with a method for estimating the depth of the object. Provided the object is within a fairly small distance, let's say 5 meters, the problem should be solvable using standard techniques. In this range, vergence (stereo), laser-range finders, and focus can recover approximate depth. A demonstration of this capability would be interesting. Estimating depth at long distances is more problematic, and may only be possible if other objects at a similar depth are first recognized and provide depth scale.

It may be possible to use other surface properties besides color for identification and location. The most obvious one to try is texture. Instead of histogramming colors, outputs of nonoriented and oriented spatial filters could be histogrammed. Malik and Perona (1990) have demonstrated a scheme for finding texture boundaries based on the output of such filters, but they have not investigated how to recognize texture. There is one problem to be overcome in texture recognition that does not occur in color recognition, viz., that the directionality of the filters does not make this scheme naturally orientation invariant. One approach to the solution of this problem would be to extract direction invariant measures from the output of the filters; another would be to attempt to align the image and model before comparison of the histograms. One drawback to the use of texture in machine vision systems is the large amount of computation needed. For instance, Malik and Perona employ the output of 192 different filters. Since Malik and Perona were proposing a biological model, cost of implementation in image processing hardware was not an issue. There may be ways of economizing on the use of filters using approaches such as suggested by Freeman and Adelson (1990).

Is it possible that a histogram-style approach can work for shape recognition? Pigeons can recognize Charlie Brown pictures in a variety of positions, orientations, and scales (Hernstein 1982). They do not distinguish, however, between a correct Charlie Brown figure, and a "jumbled up" version where the figure has been cut in half, and the two halves rearranged. It is possible, therefore, that they are using some sort of histogram-like data structure for recognition which counts the local features that show up but does not consider their relative orientation.

The *sum* and *minimum* and *division* operations needed for Histogram Intersection and Histogram Backprojection could easily be implemented in neural hardware. Could it be possible that algorithms similar to these are used in the brain? There are wavelength-sensitive cells in monkey Visual Area 4 that have large receptive fields and which could be loosely described as histogram cells. On the other hand, the work by Treisman (1985) and others on preattentive ("pop-out") phenomena suggests that people may have trouble searching for a conjunction of colors, as is done in the Histogram Backprojection algorithm. Until now, there has been no work on how color is used for identification or location in biological systems. This article provides computational models whose presence could be explored in biological systems.

Acknowledgments

Lambert Wixson, Chris Brown, Randal Nelson, and the Rochester vision group were a source of influential discussions and ideas. Thanks to Ketan Mulmuley for help with the theorem in Appendix B. Ray Rimey and the reviewers made careful comments on the manuscript. This work was supported by NSF research grant DCR-8602958 and ONR research grant N00014-91-J-1185.

Appendix A: Relation to Pattern Recognition

Each of the different bins of the histogram can be considered a different feature, as is done in pattern recognition (Young & Fu 1986). This approach to recognition has been studied extensively, and so it is important to discuss Histogram Intersection in relation to the approaches used in this discipline.

In pattern recognition, the set of features are designated to be axes in a *feature space*, in which the object is defined to be a point $(f_1, \ldots, f_n)$. A *metric* is defined on the space, and identification is done by finding the nearest object in feature space to the set of features extracted from the image. Recall that *metric space* is defined as follows:

Definition 1: A set X, whose elements we shall call *points*, is said to be a *metric space* if with any two points p and q of X there is associated a real number $d(p, q)$, called the *distance* from p to q, such that

1. $d(p, q) > 0$ if $p \neq q$; $d(p, p) = 0$;
2. $d(p, q) = d(q, p)$;
3. $d(p, q) \leq d(p, r) + d(r, q)$ for any $r \in X$.

Any function with these three properties is called a *distance function*, or a *metric*.

When the image and model histograms are scaled to be the same size, as can be done when the object in the image can be segmented from its background, then using Histogram Intersection is equivalent to using the sum of absolute differences or *city-block* metric, as is shown below.

Theorem 1. If

$$\sum_{i=1}^{n} M_i = \sum_{i=1}^{n} I_i$$

then

$$1 - H(I, M) = \frac{1}{2n} \sum_{i=1}^{n} |I_i - M_i|$$

Proof. The key to the proof is the identity shown in equation (1). To derive this identity, we note that

$$I_i = \min(I_i, M_i) + |I_i - M_i| \quad \text{if } I_i > M_i$$
$$I_i = \min(I_i, M_i) \text{ if } I_i \leq M_i$$

and

$$M_i = \min(I_i, M_i) \quad \text{if } I_i > M_i$$
$$M_i = \min(I_i, M_i) + |I_i - M_i| \quad \text{if } I_i \leq M_i \quad (1)$$

In either case

$$I_i + M_i = 2\min(I_i, M_i) + |I_i - M_i|$$

The proof follows easily. Let

$$\sum_{i=1}^{n} M_i = \sum_{i=1}^{n} I_i = k$$

Then, using equation (1),

$$k = \frac{1}{2} \sum_{i=1}^{n} (I_i + M_i)$$
$$= \sum_{i=1}^{n} \min(I_i, M_i) + \frac{1}{2} \sum_{i=1}^{n} |I_i - M_i| \quad (2)$$

By definition,

$$1 - H(I, M) = \frac{k - \Sigma_{i=1}^{n} \min(I_i, M_i)}{k}$$

and so

$$1 - H(I, M) = \frac{k - \Sigma_{i=1}^{n} \min(I_i, M_i)}{k}$$

Replacing the k in the numerator by the expression in equation (2) we have

$$1 - H(I, M) = \frac{1}{2k} \sum_{i=1}^{n} |I_i - M_i|$$

and the theorem is proven. Q.E.D.

If the model and image histograms do not contain the same number of pixels, that is, if

$$\sum_{i=1}^{n} M_i \neq \sum_{i=1}^{n} I_i$$

then the symmetry relation (axiom number 2) does not hold and Histogram Intersection is not a metric.

Appendix B: Representing a Large Database with Color Histograms

Consider the multidimensional space E defined by the bins of the histogram. That is, points in E are n-tuples $(c_1, c_2, \ldots, c_n)$ where n is the number of bins in the histogram, and c_i is the count in the ith bin. We ignore the discrete nature of histograms obtained from discrete images, and assume that the c_i are continuous values in the range $[0, n]$. We assume that image histograms are scaled to contain the same number of counts I as the model histograms, and so Histogram Intersection is equivalent to the use of the *city-block* metric (see Appendix A).

Define a city-block metric n-ball to be the following n-dimensional geometric figure:

$$\sum_{i=1}^{n} |x_i| \leq 1 \quad (3)$$

The theorem we wish to prove relies on the following lemma.

Lemma 2. *The volume of the intersection of a city-block metric n-ball of radius r and any $n - 1$ dimensional hyperplane through the origin is less than or equal to the area of the city-block $n - 1$ ball of radius r.*

Proof. From elementary multidimensional geometry we know that the intersection of the geometrical figure defined by equation (3) with an $n - 1$ dimensional hyperplane passing through the origin is of the form

$$\left(\sum_{i=1}^{n} |x_i'|^2\right) = \left(\sum_{i=1}^{n} |x_i|^2\right)^{1/2} \leq \sum_{i=1}^{n} |x_i| \leq 1$$

where the x_i' are defined with respect to a natural orthonormal coordinate system for the hyperplane in which the nth axis is perpendicular to it. Using the triangle inequality we have for all points in the n-ball

$$\sum_{i=1}^{n-1} |a_i x_i'| \leq 1$$

and so it follows that for all i, $|a_i| \geq 1$. Therefore, the intersection of the n-ball with the hyperplane could be contained within an $n - 1$ ball (in the coordinate system of the hyperplane), and so its is of smaller size. Q.E.D.

We can now show

Theorem 2. *The fraction of the volume of E occupied by a single model is at most*

$$\frac{(2\delta)^{n-1}}{\sqrt{n}}$$

where $1 - \delta$ is the minimum Histogram Intersection match value allowed and n is the number of bins in a histogram.

Proof. The points in E for which

$$\sum_{i=0}^{n} c_i = I$$

form an $n - 1$ dimensional subset of E, which we will call P. We can find the $n - 1$ dimensional volume of P by differentiating the n-dimensional volume of the set V, in which

$$\sum_{i=0}^{n} c_i \le I$$

By induction, it can be shown that the volume of V is

$$\nabla_V = \frac{I^n}{n!} \quad (4)$$

The volume of E is then

$$\nabla_P = \frac{(d/dI)\, \nabla_V(I)}{(d/dI)\, \mathcal{D}_P(I)} \quad (5)$$

where $\mathcal{D}_P$ is the distance from the origin to P.

To understand this formula think of the numerator multiplied by δI as the differential change in volume of V and the denominator multiplied by δI as the differential width of the volume.

Since the closest point to the origin in P is $(I/n, I/n, \ldots, I/n)$, we have

$$\mathcal{D}_P = \frac{I}{\sqrt{n}} \quad (6)$$

Differentiating equations (4) and (6) we have

$$\frac{d}{dI}\, \nabla_V(I) = \frac{I^{n-1}}{(n-1)!}$$

and

$$\frac{d}{dI}\, \mathcal{D}_P(I) = \frac{1}{\sqrt{n}}$$

Therefore, from (5),

$$\nabla_P = \frac{I^{n-1}\sqrt{n}}{(n-1)!} \quad (7)$$

We have found the volume of P. Now we need to find an upper bound on the volume occupied by a single model.

Under the city-block metric an n-ball has the shape of the region E in each quadrant. Since there are 2^n quadrants in n-dimensional Euclidean space, the volume of an n-ball of radius r is—using equation (4)

$$\frac{(2r)^n}{n!} \quad (8)$$

Using lemma 1 and equations (5) and (8), we have that the ratio ∇_m/∇_P of the volume occupied by a model and the total volume is bounded by

$$\frac{\nabla_m}{\nabla_P} \le \frac{\dfrac{(2I\delta)^{n-1}}{(n-1)!}}{\dfrac{I^{n-1}\sqrt{n}}{(n-1)!}}$$

$$= \frac{(2\delta)^{n-1}}{\sqrt{n}}$$

which is the required result.   Q.E.D.

Notes

1. A similar opinion is expressed by Ullman (1986): "For many objects color, texture, and motion play only a secondary role. In these cases, the objects are recognized by their shape properties. This is probably the most common and important aspect of visual recognition and therefore 'object recognition' is often taken to mean the visual recognition of objects based on their shape properties."

2. Resenfeld's bibliographies are available by anonymous FTP from ADSCOM (in the VISION-LIST-ARCHIEVE directory).

References

Aloimonos, J. 1990. "Purposive and qualitative active vision." Proc. Int. Conf. Pat. Rec., pp. 346-360.

Aloimonos, J., Weiss, I., and Bandyopadhay, A. 1988 "Active vision." Intern. J. Comput. Vision 1:436-440.

Bajcsy, R. 1985. "Active perception vs. passive perception." Workshop on Computer Vision: Representation and Control, pp. 55-59.

Bajcsy, R. 1988. "Active perception." Proc. IEEE 76:996-1005.

Ballard, D.H. 1987. "Interpolation coding: A representation for numbers in neural models." Biological Cybernetics, 57:389-402.

Ballard, D.H. 1989. "Reference frames for animate vision." Intern. Joint Conf. Artif. Intell., pp. 1635-1641.

Ballard, D.H. 1991. "Animate vision." Artificial Intelligence 48:57-86.

Ballard, D.H., and Brown, C.M. 1982. Computer Vision. Prentice Hall: New York.

Biederman, I. 1985. "Human image understanding: Recent research and a theory." Comput. Vision, Graph. Image Process. 32(1):29-73.

Brainard, D.H., Wandell, B.A., and Cowan, W.B. 1989. "Black light: How sensors filter spectral variation of the illuminant." IEEE Trans. Biomed. Engineer. 36:140-149.

Chapman, D. 1990. "Vision, instruction, and action." Technical Report 1204, Massachusetts Institute of Technology, Artificial Intelligence Laboratory, Cambridge, MA.

Coombs, D.J. 1989. "Tracking objects with eye movements." Proc. Topical Meet. Image Understand. Mach. Vision.

Dickmanns, E.D. 1988. "An integrated approach to feature based dynamic vision." Proc. IEEE Conf. Comput. Vision and Patt. Recog., pp. 820-825.

Feldman, J.A. 1985. "Four frames suffice: A provisional model of vision and space." Behav. Brain Sci. 8:265-289.

Feldman, J.A., and Yakimovsky, Y. 1984. "Decision theory and artificial intelligence: I. A semantics-based region analyzer." Artificial Intelligence 5:349-371.

Forsyth, D.A. 1990. "A novel algorithm for color constancy." Intern. J. Comput. Vision 5:5-35.

Freeman, W.T., and Adelson, E.H. 1990. "Steerable filters for early vision, image analysis, and wavelet decomposition." Proc. 3rd Intern. Conf. Comput. Vision, Osaka, pp. 406-415.

Garvey, T.D. 1986. "Perceptual strategies for purposive vision." SRI International, Technical Note 117.

Hernstein, R.J. 1982. "Objects, categories, and discriminative stimuli." Animal Cogn. Proc. Harry Frank Guggenheim Conf.

Klinker, G.J., Shafer, S.A., and Kanade, T. 1988. "The measurement of highlights in color images." Intern. J. Comput. Vision, 2:7-32.

Koenderink, J.J., and van Doorn, A.J. 1976. "The singularities of the visual mapping." Biological Cybernetics 24:51-59.

Lennie, P., and D'Zmura, M. 1988. "Mechanisms of color vision." CRC Crit. Rev. Neurobiol. 3:333-400.

Malik, J., and Perona, P. 1990. "Preattentive texture discrimination with early vision mechanisms." J. Opt. Soc. Amer. A7:923-932.

Maloney, L.T., and Wandell, B. 1986. "Color constancy: A method for recovering surface spectral reflectance." J. Opt. Soc. Amer. A 3(1):29-33.

Maunsell, J.H.R., and Newsome, W.T. 1987. "Visual Processing in monkey extrastriate cortex." Annu. Rev. Neurosci. 10:363-401.

Mishkin, M., and Appenzeller, T. 1987. "The anatomy of memory." Scientific American, June, pp. 80-89.

Nelson, R.C. 1989. "Obstacle avoidance using flow field divergence." IEEE Trans. Patt. Anal. Mach. Intell. 11:1102-1106.

Nelson, R.C. 1991. "Qualitative detection of motion by a moving observer." In this issue.

Novak, C.L., and Shafer, S.A. 1990. "Supervised color constancy using a color chart." School of Computer Science, Carnegie Mellon University, Technical Report CUM-CS-90-140.

Ohlander, R., Price, K., and Reddy, D.R. 1978. "Picture segmentation using a recursive region splitting method." Comput. Graph. Image Process. 8:313-333.

Olson, T.J., and Coombs, D.J. 1991. "Real-time vergence control for binocular robots." In this issue.

Rubner, J., and Schulten, K. 1989. "A regularized approach to color constancy." Biological Cybernetics 61:29-36.

Strat, T.M. 1990, personal communication.

Swain, M.J. 1990a. "Color indexing." Department of Computer Science, University of Rochester, Technical report 360.

Swain, M.J. 1990b. "Companion videotape to 'color indexing'."

Thompson, W.B. 1986. "Inexact vision." Workshop on Motion, Representation, and Analysis, pp. 15-22.

Treisman, A. 1985. "Preattentive processing in vision." Comput. Vision. Graph. Image Process. 31:156-177.

Ullman, S. 1986. "An approach to object recognition: Aligning pictorial descriptions." Artificial Intelligence Laboratory, Massachusetts Institute of Technology, Technical Report 931.

Yarbus, A.I. 1967. Eye Movements and Vision. Plenum Press: New York.

Young, T.Y., and Fu, K.S. eds. 1986. Handbook of Pattern Recognition and Image Processing. Academic Press: San Diego, CA.

COLOR FIGURES

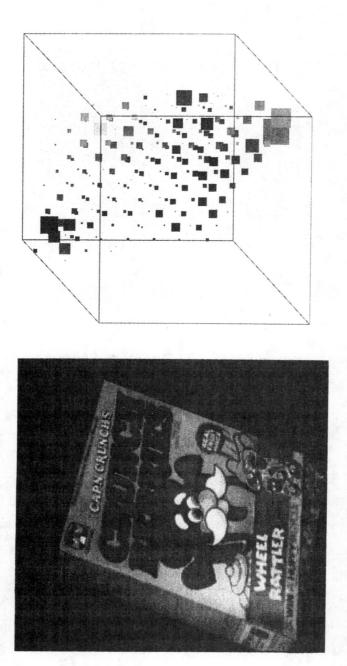

Fig. 1. Left: Image of a Crunchberries cereal box. **Right:** Three dimensional color histogram of the Crunchberries image with the black background substrated.

Fig. 4. Modeling indexing experiment based on color cues (continued in figures 6 and 8). Each of the sixty-six models shown here is represented by its color histogram.

Fig. 2. Four views of Snoopy.

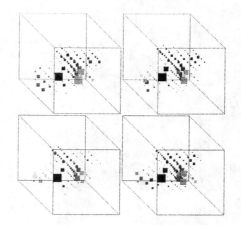

Fig. 3. Histograms of the four views of Snoopy.

Fig. 10. Images from figure 5, each with the bottom third removed. These images and the images below are used in the occlusion experiment (see table 4).

Fig. 11. Images from figure 10, each with the right-hand third removed. The upper left-hand corner (four ninths of the original image) is left.

Fig. 5. The unknown objects. Each is identified with the model color histogram that best matches its own color histogram. Compared to the models the unknown objects are translated (Ajax), rotated about various axes (Frankenberry, Ajax) scaled (USA Flyer), occluded (Charmin), partly outside of the field of view (red, white striped shirt), and deformed (Mickey Mouse underwear).

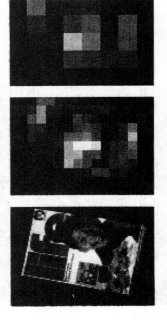

Fig. 6. Life cereal box image and reduced resolution copies. Left: 128×90 (1); Middle: 16×11 (2); Right 8×5 (30). The numbers in parenthesis indicate the rank of the match value for the Life cereal model. The middle image matches effectively, but the one on the right does not.

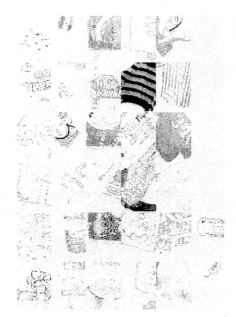

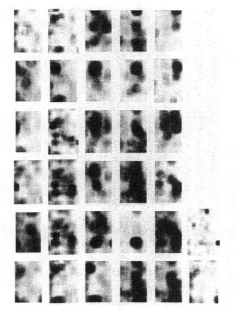

Fig. 18. Results of the ratio histogram backprojection step (2) of Histogram Backprojection when the objects are occluded. Figure 6 is the image and the striped blue and white shirt is the target.

Fig. 19. Results of the convolution step (3) of Histogram Backprojection, for the same image as above. The results of all the models are shown in the image, each in the rectangle corresponding to the location of that model in the composite photo. When the algorithm successfully finds the object, the darkest black dot in the small images is in the same location within that image as the image is in the composite. Compare with figure 17.

Fig. 16. Results of the ratio histogram backprojection step (2) of Histogram Backprojection, using figure 6 as the image and the striped blue and white shirt as the target. The blue hue is found in only a small area outside of the target, so it gives a strong response. White is found in many objects so it gives a weak response.

Fig. 17. Results of the convolution step (3) of Histogram Backprojection, for the same image as above. The results for all the models are shown in the image, each in the rectangle corresponding to the location of that model in the composite photo. When the algorithm successfully finds the object, the darkest black dot in the small image is in the same location within that image as the image in the component.

A Scheme for Visual Feature based Image Indexing

HongJiang Zhang and Di Zhong
Institute of Systems Science, National University of Singapore
Heng Mui Keng Terrace, Kent Ridge, Singapore 0511
Republic of Singapore

Tel: (65)772-6725, Fax: (65)778-2571, Email: {zhj,dzhong}@iss.nus.sg

ABSTRACT

As digital images are progressing into the mainstream of information systems, managing and manipulating them as images become an important issue to be resolved before we can take full advantage of their information content. To achieve content-based image indexing and retrieval, there are have been active research efforts in develop techniques to utilize visual features. On the other hand, without an effective indexing scheme, any visual content based image retrieval approach will lose its effectiveness as the number of features increases. This paper presents our initial work in developing an efficient indexing scheme using artificial neural network, which focuses on eliminating unlikely candidates rather than pin-pointing the targets directly. Experiment result in retrieving images using this scheme from a prototype visual database system is given.

Keywords: indexing; visual database; content-based retrieval; neural network, texture, color histogram.

1. INTRODUCTION

With rapid advances in electronic imaging, data storage, image compression, image processing and telecommunications, digital images have been progressing into the mainstream of information systems, taking their place alongside text and numeric data. As more and more image data are acquired, managing and manipulating them as *images* become an important issue to be resolved before we can take full advantage of their information content [1,2]. Therefore, many efforts to develop techniques for visual content based indexing have been carried out to utilize visual features, such as colors, textures, patterns and shapes of image objects, as well as related layout and location information. The idea behind this is that the natural way to retrieve *visual* data is by a query based on the *visual* content of an image. The most comprehensive examples of such work are IBM's QBIC[3], MIT Media Lab's Photobook[4] and ISS' SWIM(Show Me what I Mean) project[2].

However, when there are active research efforts in selecting and deriving visual features that effectively represent the image content, few have addressed the problems in developing an effective indexing scheme for image retrieval using these features. Without such a scheme, any visual content based image retrieval approach will lose its effectiveness especially in databases of large size, since the assumption is that a content based retrieval find its usefulness by reducing the search from a large and unmanageable number of images to a few that user can quickly brows. Another problem is that as the number of features increases, without an effective index scheme, retrieval will ultimately degenerate to sequential search. This paper presents our initial work in addressing this problem.

In the following sections, we first briefly discuss the general indexing problem for large image databases which employ visual content based retrieval, and introduce the index scheme, tree index by abstraction and classification. We then present our work in building such indexing trees automatically by abstraction using artificial neural network, the Self-Organization feature Map (SOM). Experiments to build the index tree using SOM based on textures and color features of images, evaluation result of using this scheme in retrieving images from a prototype visual database system are given in Section 3. Finally, conclusions and future works are presented in Section 4.

2. A HIERARCHICAL FEATURE INDEXING SCHEME

2.1. Multi-dimensional index: Problem definition

Generally speaking, an index in a database consists of a collection of entries, one for each data item, containing the value of a key attribute for that item and a reference pointer that allows immediate access to the item. Since in content based visual databases, all items (images or objects) are represented by pre-computed visual features, the key attribute for each image will be a feature vector which corresponds to a point in a multi-dimensional feature space; and search will be based on similarities between the feature vectors. Therefore, to achieve a fast and effective retrieval in content based image databases requires an efficient multi-dimensional indexing scheme.

We can formulate the image retrieval process as a nearest neighbor or range search process as follows: Given a feature vector Q, defined by or extracted from a query; then according to a similarity criterion S, a certain number (N) of feature vectors p_i ($i=1, ..., N$) in the complete vector set A_k of the visual database are found, whose similarities $S(p_i, q)$ are among the N largest ones. Based on this, the indexing process is to sort all the feature vectors in A_k to support effective search based on the similarity criterion. If more than one feature set (i.e. $A_1, A_2, ...$) are used, we have to sort feature vectors in all these feature spaces, and combine them into an integrated index structure.

There are three popular approaches to multi-dimensional indexing in traditional databases: R-trees (particularly the R*-tree); linear quadtrees; and grid files[5]. These indexing schemes use some partitioning methods to divide the multidimensional vector space into partitions so that finding the nearest neighbors of a given query point only needs to touch a small number of partitions. However, most of these multi-dimensional indexing methods explode geometrically as the number of dimensions increases; so for a sufficiently high dimensionality, the technique is no better than sequential scanning. For example, search time with linear quadtrees is proportional to the hypersurface of the query region; and the hypersurface grows geometrically with the dimensionally. With grid files it is the directory that grows geometrically with the dimensionality. Methods based on R-trees, on the other hand, can be efficient if the fan-out of the R-tree nodes remains greater than 2 and the dimensionality stays under 20[5].

The limitations of these indexing methods result from the two assumptions often made behind them: (a) a "distance" between two objects corresponding to the Euclidean distance of the points in the feature space; and (b) the dimensionality of the feature space is reasonably low. Both of these two assumptions may not be held in the image databases with content based retrieval, especially the second one, since a query to such database may use combination of different sets of features, which usually have very high dimensions. Also, these index schemes in general do not maintain the neighborhood information between points within a partition, especially the partition's boundary points, thus, are not suitable for nearest neighbor search.

To solve these problems, we need to employ a "signature" approach in which an efficient *filter* is used in a preprocessing step, allowing some false hits, but not false dismissals. There are two ways to build such an efficient index: to find a lower dimensional feature space for each set of visual features, or, to narrow the search space foe each query. However, both methods have to guarantee that a range query will not miss any actual hit, but may contain some false hits. In our study, our effort is concentrated in building an efficient index scheme using the second method. More specifically, to build an index tree by abstraction or classification using hierarchical *Self-Organization Maps* (SOM).

2.2. Tree Indexing by Abstraction and Classification

Let us consider a set of objects represented by $o_i\{(A_1, a_1), (A_2, a_2), ..., (A_n, a_n)\}$, where A_k is an attribute and a_j is an value of the attribute A_j. Then, a tree index can be constructed by the following steps[6, 7]:

1. **Labeling**: For a given attribute A_j, identify and label all objects (data items) which share the common attribute A_j by an identical value a_i, or with a certain range of a_i.

2. **Clustering**: The objects which have the same label are clustered together to form an abstraction of the objects, having a_i of the attribute A_j as its common label.

3. **Indexing**: The abstraction created at Step 2 can then be represented as a node in the index tree. After all possible abstracted objects have been created by the above two steps, a new class of abstracted objects is constructed and represented by the nodes of the same level of the index tree.

Applying above abstraction operations recursively, so that the index objects can again be labeled, clustered and indexed, until the root of the tree is reached. The root of the tree is then called an index tree of all objects with key attribute A_j. A similar, but reverse step will be able to constructed an index tree by classification[6]. The leaves of the tree could be images or objects which are very similar and does not need to be further divided into difference classes.

A major difference between such index trees in conventional database and the image database supporting content based retrieval is that the index tree in latter is usually not generated using only one key attribute, but one or more feature vectors. Thus, the clustering criterion and procedures used in Step 2 will again based on similarity or distance measures. Also, the different levels of index tree may employ different key attributes for the labeling and clustering.

For databases of a particular type of objects, the labeling process can also assign semantics to index nodes . More importantly, an iconic image of scenes or objects can be created to represent each node in the index, resulting an iconic index tree. A straight forward way to obtain such an icon image is to select an image from the images represented by the icon which is closest to the mean or centroid of them. Apart from indexing, such an iconic index provides user a useful browsing tool to quick view representative images of each type of images or objects. This will be further facilitated by allowing horizontal and vertical zooming of the iconic index trees.

2.3. Constructing Index Tree by Self-Organization Map

The abstraction or classification processes for building index tree presented above can be performed by Self-Organization feature Maps[8]. A typical two layer SOM network, shown as **Figure 1**, defines a mapping from the input data space R^n onto a regular two-dimension grid. The input layer receives input feature vectors and it has the same number of dimensions as the input feature vector, N. The output units are arranged as a two dimensional map and the number of nodes, M, in the map is more than the number of possible classes to be classified. Each node j in the input layer is connected to each node i in the map grid with an associated weight w_{ij}. All the weights associated to the node i in the map grid are defined as the reference vector of this node $m_i \in R^n$.

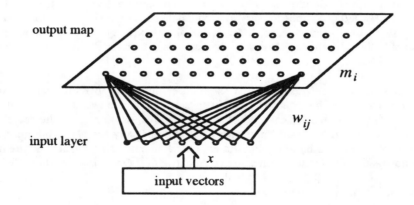

Figure 1: Architecture of SOM

In the competitive learning phase, all the reference vectors are compared with one input vector $x \in R^n$ according to certain metrics, such as Euclidean distance, to select one best-matching node c in the map, then the reference vectors of node c and its neighbors are updated. After large number of training steps the SOM map gradually adapts to the value and distribution of the input vectors at different nodes.

Several properties of such a feature map are desired for building an indexing structure.

- The map performs unsupervised learning to cluster feature data and adapts to changes over time;

- The map reflects the topological relationship (neighborhood) between input samples in the high dimensional space as faithfully as possible in the spatial arrangement of nodes on the map, thus, it is suitable for the nearest neighbor search;

- By using tow-dimension neural cell array, it is possible to make the neighborhood relationships visible and a representative image can be obtained for each map node to support visual query and browsing;

- The map allocating more nodes to more frequent input patterns and projecting the probability density function of high dimensional input data onto the map, such that each node will have approximately the same number of data points;

- It is suitable for clustering large amount of data that have a large number of classes and a small number of samples for each class, which is just the situation in a general image database.

On the basis of these considerations, we have developed a set of hierarchical self-organization maps (HSOMs) to construct an index tree which forms the *similarity space* of the feature data and provides a nearest neighbor searching method in this space.

The training(indexing) and searching processes based on this hierarchical structure of feature maps is illustrated in **Figure 2**.

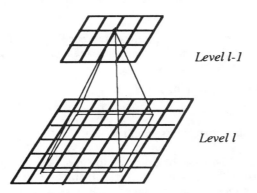

Level l-1

Level l

Figure 2: The hierarchical structure of feature maps.

First, the index map at the bottom level L is formed through competitive learning process. Each node in this map now represents a group of images which are close in term of similarity. The list of these image is called *searching list*, i.e., they will be searched when a query falls in the node. This training process corresponds to the labeling and clustering steps outlined in Section 2.2. A difference between the two methods is that, as we pointed out earlier, there will be more nodes in the map assigned to a class if it contains more images. In other words, the map automatically splits a class into sub-classes when the number of images in the class is large. In contrast, all images falling in a range from a class center will be classified into a single class.

The abstraction process presented before can then be adapted using SOM to construct high level maps of the hierarchy with the following clustering and projection processes.

Clustering:

1. Set the maximum number of nodes in one class, M and the maximum agglomeration distance, D; and set each node in map L as a class.

2. Calculate the distance between every two contiguous classes. (Two classes A, B are contiguous if there are at least one node $p \in A$ and one node $q \in B$ such that p and q are contiguous in the map, i.e. p is one of the 8 neighbors of q).

3. If the distance between every two contiguous classes is not smaller than D, end.

4. Find two closest classes; If the number of nodes in the two classes is larger than M, set distance between these two classes as D; else agglomerate the two classes. Replace the reference vector of the new class with the class center, i.e. the mean vector. Re-calculated the distances between the new class and its neighbors;

5. Go to Step 3.

As one can see, this clustering algorithm is a variation of conventional hierarchical clustering algorithm. Here, M can be defined according to the query requirement and database size. A large M will result in fewer classes, but each class will contain more images. On the other hand, a small M will result in more classes and/or a hierarchy of more levels.

After the set of classes, K, is formed by the clustering process, the smaller map of level l-1 is defined as follow:

Projection:

1. Set the size(number of nodes) of map of level l-1 as equal or slightly larger than the number of classes, K;

2. Find the largest class, A , from the class set K;

3. For each node in class A,

- Allocate a node, c, at level L-1 with coordinate at:

$$i_{l-1} = \left(\frac{S_{l-1}}{S_l} \right) i_l, \qquad j_{l-1} = \left(\frac{S_{l-1}}{S_l} \right) j_l$$

where S_{l-1} and S_l are the size of the map at level l and l-1, respectively; and (i_l, j_l) are the coordinate of a node at level l;

- If c has not been occupied by other classes, set the reference vector of c equal to the reference vector of class A.; otherwise, set the reference vector of c equal to the mean or centroid vector of the nodes in class A and the classes occupying the node;

- Attach the nodes in class A to the searching list of node c.

4. Delete class A from the class set K.

5. If no more classes left, end; otherwise, go to step 2.

Adapting such a projection process, the geometric distribution in the map of lower level will propagate to the map of higher level. Projecting large class first will allow smaller classes being kept in the new map, since in this way the small classes selected later may "eat" up the nodes that have been previously occupied by the larger classes. Also, the fact that large classes may occupy more nodes in the map of a given level may be used to determine if a higher level of the index is needed, while for small classes only few levels are needed. In addition, continuously attaching the nodes to the searching list will ensure that contiguous classes will be searched simultaneously while a query falls into the "boundary" of these classes.

A guided learning process can also be applied to the projection process, such that the nodes of the higher level map will be obtained by the using the nodes of a class in the lower level as training data and the centroid vector of the class as a reference vector. This process may be needed for large database. In addition, different features can be used for different levels in building the index tree using the algorithms presented above.

The clustering and projection processes can be applied iteratively until the number of nodes in top level of the hierarchy is equal or smaller than the required number of classes. Each node at a given level of the hierarchy has a reference vector and a searching list pointed to the son nodes in the lower map. Also, an icon image can be assigned to each node, which can be selected as, for instance, the one whose the feature vector is closest to the centroid of the class.

In the retrieval process, the nearest neighbor search can be started at any level of the hierarchy according to different requirements in terms of retrieval rate and time. If we start at the top level, the nearest neighbor search will be performed and all nodes of next level whose feature vectors are within the search range, and eventually all images at the bottom level represented by those nodes will be retrieved. In detail, given a query vector q, the search algorithm for level L of hierarchical index tree is as follows:

1. Set search start level $(=l)$, and search range (entire map); find the best matching node c_L for q.

2. If current level is the lowest level, go to *4*.

3. Go down to next level $(l+1)$, and set search range to the search list of node c_l; Then, find the best matching node, c_{l+1}, for q; Go to *2*.

4. Find the N-nearest neighbors of q in the node c_{L-1} (and its neighbors, if the number of feature vectors in nodes is smaller than N) in the map of the bottom level.

As such an index supports both tree structure and nearest neighbor search, as presented in the following section, high retrieval accuracy and speed can be achieved.

3. EXPERIMENTAL EVALUATIONS

While we are aiming at developing an indexing scheme for a general image database, textures and color distributions of the images have been used as the main descriptive features in our prototype system of image databases.

3.1 Texture Features based Index

Texture has been long and deeply studied with the development of image processing and pattern recognition, and is regarded as one of the most important features to identify different images. Some abstract concepts, such as uniformity, density, coarseness, roughness, regularity, direction, frequency and so on, can be reflected by texture features. However, there are still not a single model that can be used in general visual data recognition and classification. As the multi-resolution simultaneous auto-regressive(MRSAR) model of texture has been reported to has better performance[9-12], we use it as the basic texture feature set. In our attempt to improve the retrieval accuracy, we also experimented to combine MRSAR model with Tamura's Coarseness features[13] and gray histograms.

The experiments were accomplished on the entire Brodatz texture database, which contains 112 different texture classes, and each is a 512x512 8-bits image. Nine 128x128 subimages are extracted from the center of each Brodatz image, resulting in 112 classes of images with 9 images (subimages) in each class. In obtaining these results, each image in the database is used as a query image and the retrieval rate is calculated as the number (k) of retrieved subimages (the N-nearest neighbors of the query) that belong to the same class as the query image, dividing by N.

In our experiments, four spatial resolutions of each image were selected for the MRSAR features, i.e., 128x128, 64x64, 32x32 and 16x16, resulting in a 20 dimension feature vector for each image. It is found from our experiments that the retrieval rate of MRSAR model heavily depends on the coarseness of images, and low retrieval rates are expected for images whose coarseness values are larger. To improve this, we added coarseness measure[13] as an additional texture feature and extracted it at each of the four resolutions for each image, resulting a vector of 24 dimensions to represent image textures. Another feature set that may be combined with MRSAR features is gray histograms of images. This is due to the fact that by definition, SAR model only depends on the differences between pixels and absolute gray values have no influence on the value of SAR features. We added 6-level gray histogram into the MRSAR model, which together with coarseness and MRSAR features will form a 30 dimension feature vector for each image.

A three-level of hierarchical was constructed using the algorithm presented in the last section and based on the texture features. The map size at the bottom level is 30x24, the second level is 20x16 and the top level is 10x8. To construct the HSOM's, the maximum number of nodes in one class, M, was set to be 4 and the maximum agglomeration distance, D, was set to be ∞.

Within a class Mahalanobis distance was used as the similarity metric in SOM's due to its good performance in computing image similarity using MRSAR features. However, a problem in training SOM using Mahalanobis distance directly is that the input data need to be pre-clustered to obtain a scatter matrix of each class for calculating Mahalanobis distance. To avoid this, we start the training process with the Euclidean distance first, then, Mahalanobis distance when the initial classification of data is formed after a certain number of training steps (for example, 1000). The scatter matrix will then be calculated and updated continuously in the learning process of HSOM's with the developing of the clustering map. Another important issue in training the SOM's is that, because Euclidean distance depends on the scale of the components, the input feature data should be roughly normalized before they are presented to the map to avoid any possible effect on the clustering accuracy in the initial training process. This is especially important when MRSAR, coarseness and histogram features are combined in indexing images.

Figure 3 shows the retrieval performance from the experiments using the hierarchical tree index with three different sets of texture features. When MRSAR model was used alone, the retrieval rate for 9-nearest neighbors searching is about 74%, which is about the same as the result of conventional global searching method[9, 10, 11], while the retrieval speed is much faster. Our experiments indicate that the retrieval speed using the three level tree structure is at least 5 times faster than the global search method, even if there is no effort to optimize the programs.

When a feature vector of 24 dimensions, consisting of both MRSAR and coarseness features, was used, the retrieval rate for 9-nearest neighbors searching is about 78%, 4% higher than using MRSAR model alone. The performance of combined MRSAR, coarseness and histogram is also shown in Figure 3, and it is seen that another 2% improvement was achieved.

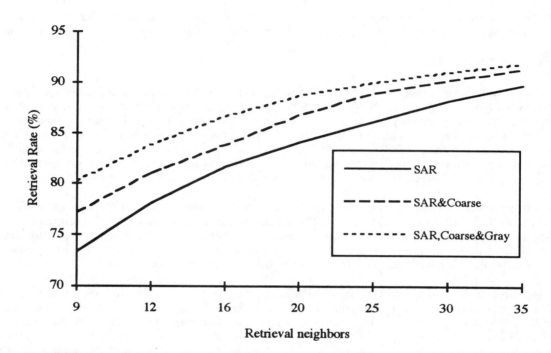

Figure 3: Retrieval performance using texture based hierarchical index tree. Three sets of texture feature were used: MRSAR (denoted as SAR), combination of MRSAR and coarseness (SAR & Coarse), and combination of MRSAR, coarseness and gray histogram (SAR & Coarse & gray).

As we mentioned earlier in this paper, an icon image can be assigned to each node at different level, thus resulting in an iconic index tree. Such an iconic index tree can present visually the content of images indexed by the tree, which will facilitate quick browsing of image database. An example of such iconic index is shown in **Figure 4**, where each image in the map represents a class of nodes or texture images at lower level map. Each node is represented by an icon image which is selected as the one whose the feature vector is closest to the node (centroid or mean of a class). It is observed that the concept areas in the map, such as bean, pellet, mesh, cane, crocodile skin, wood, etc., are very clear. A straight forward application of such a hierarchy of texture maps is for query compositions using templates in the user interface of image databases, where a user can brows through the texture maps to pick up templates. The navigation of images can be either horizontal in one map or vertical between different levels. Furthermore, these maps can be used to analyze performance of a type of feature model compared with human's visual perception.

The examples in Figure 4 and 5 show the abstraction process in terms of searching list from the bottom to the top levels. The searching list of node (5,5) at the top level has 4 nodes at the second level, and these 4 nodes in turn have 8 related nodes at the bottom level. It can be seen that the nodes need to be searched for a particular query in the bottom level have been reduced significantly compared with the conventional global search, thus fast retrieval speed can obtained .

Figure 4: The iconic map of Broads database: top level of three level index tree constructed by SOM's. Blank areas represent nodes that are not assigned any images from the database.

level 1

⇓ Searching list of the above node

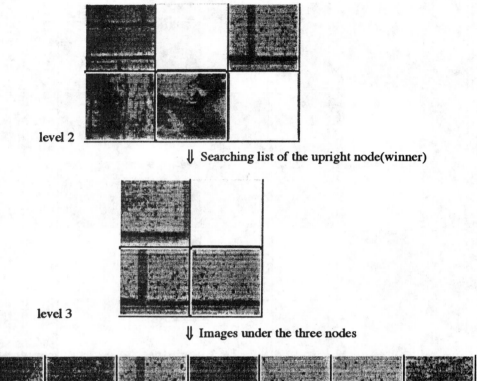

level 2

⇓ Searching list of the upright node(winner)

level 3

⇓ Images under the three nodes

Figure 5:   An example of index in the three-level HSOMs. Blank positions represent nodes that are not in the searching lists of the node at above level.

3.2. Color Histogram based Index

Another experiment on the tree index was to use color histogram of images in representing image content[14,15]. 317 color images from various sources were used in our tests. Among them, 106 images are classified into 7 classes of different visual objects: carton scenes, news anchorpersons, child faces, weather forecast shots, swimming suit models and green garden scenes, as listed and numbered in **Table 1**. The rest of images are not classified and are used as noise in the evaluation process.

	class1	class2	class3	class4	class5	class6	class7	other
Name	cartoon	bbcnews	children	weather	swim	green	red car	-
Number	25	12	10	16	11	13	19	211

Table 1: Color images for retrieval

We compared image indexing using color histograms in three different color spaces: RGB, $R_gB_yW_b$ [14] and LUV. In each case, SOM is used to generate a codebook [16] of the color distribution of all images, and then the color histogram of each image is calculated based on these color codes. For example, using a 8x4 map as a codebook, we can get a color histogram with 32 components. Two color histograms, 32 colors and 64 colors, were tested in each color space in our experiments.

Two-level HSOMs were constructed for the indexing of the color histograms. In the first level the map size is 10x5, and the second level is 30x15. The queries started from the top level and the comparing metric is Euclidean distance. The retrieval rates of the seven classes are shown in **Table 2**, where the number of the searching neighbors is 10.

RGB	class1	class2	class3	class4	class5	class6	class7	average
32 codes	77.6	55	50	78.8	34.5	48.5	29.5	55.9
64 codes	70.8	81.7	44	70.6	39.1	45.4	54.7	60.2

RBW	class1	class2	class3	class4	class5	class6	class7	average
32 codes	80.8	65.8	61	65	29.1	41.5	42.6	57.8
64 codes	86	67.5	69	78.1	36.4	56.2	38.9	63.9

LUV	class1	class2	class3	class4	class5	class6	class7	average
32 codes	83.6	68.3	100	69.4	34.5	56.2	68.42	70.1
64 codes	94.8	74.2	91	74.4	56.4	77.7	60	76.7

Table 2: Retrieval rates in percentage using color histograms.

Again, the retrieval accuracy is about the same as the global searching approach while the retrieval speed is much faster. Also, it is observed that LUV color space gives higher retrieval rates, because it approximates more closely to the color differences sensed by human.

4. CONCLUSION AND FURTHER WORKS

In this paper, we have presented our initial work in developing an effective indexing scheme for general image database. A hierarchical index scheme based on self-organization feature map, and the associated training, clustering and retrieval approaches have been developed. The experimental results demonstrate that such an indexing mechanism can achieve good performance when used in similarity based searching in high dimensional feature space.

We are currently working on several issues in applying the developed scheme in large image databases. An important issue is the dynamic maintenance of the indexing structure will be further studied to facilitate adding images to and/or purging images from the database. Another task is to find an optimal approach to integrating different features in constructing an index tree, since simple and direct addition of multiple feature sets may not necessarily improve the retrieval accuracy.

5. REFERENCES:

1. W. I. Grosky, Multimedia Information Systems, *IEEE Multimedia*, Spring, 1994, pp12-24.

2. H. J. Zhang and S. W. Smoliar, Developing Power Tools for Video Indexing and Retrieval, *Proc. IS&T/SPIE. on Storage and Retrieval for Image and Video Databases II*, San Jose, CA, 1994, pp.140-149.

3   W. Niblack, *et, al*, The QBIC Project: Querying Images by Content Using Color, Texture and Shape", *Proc. IS&T/SPIE. on Storage and Retrieval for Image and Video Databases I*, San Jose, CA, Februrary 1993.

4. A. P. Pentland, R. W. Picard and S. Scarloff, Photobook: tools for content-based manipulation of image database, *Proc. IS&T/SPIE. on Storage and Retrieval for Image and Video Databases II*, San Jose, CA, 1994, pp.34-47.

5.   C.Faloutsos, R Barber, M. Flickner, J. Hafner, W. Niblack, D. Peetkovic and W. Equitz, "Efficient and Effective Querying by Image Content", *Journal of Intelligent Information Systems* (1994), p231-262.

6.   S. K. Chang, *Principles of Pictorial Information Systems Design*, Prentice-Hall, Englewood Cliff, NJ, 1989.

7.   J. K. Wu and A. D. Narasimhalu, "Identifying Faces Using Multiple Retrievals", *IEEE Multimedia*, Summer, 1994, pp27-38.

8.   T.Kohonen, Self-Organization and Associative Memory, *.Proceedings of IEEE*, Vol.78, No.9, pp.1464-1480, 1989.

9   R.W.Picard and T.Kabir, Finding Similar Patterns in Large Image Databases, *Proc. IEEE conference on Acoustics, Speech and Signal Processing*, Minneapolis, MN, April 1993.

10.   R. W.Picard, T. Kabir and F. Liu "Real-time Recognition with the entire Broads Texture Database", CVPR, 1993.

11.   A. Kankanhalli, H. J. Zhang and C. Y. Low, Using Texture For Image Retrieval, *Proc. ICARCV'94*, November 1994, pp.935-939.

12.   A. Khotanzad and R. L.Kashyap, Feature Selection for Texture Recognition Based on Image Synthesis, IEEE Transactions on Systems, Man and Cybernetics, Vol SMC-17, No 6, Nov/Dec, 1987.

13.   H. Tamura, S. Mori, and T. Yamawaki, Texture Features Corresponding to Visual Perception, IEEE Transactions on System, Man and Cybernetics, Vol SMC-6, No.4, April 1976, pp.460-473.

14.   M. J. Swain, D. H. Ballard, Color Indexing, *International Journal of Computer Vision*, Vol 7, No 1, 1991, pp11-32.

15.   Y. Gong, H. J. Zhang and T. C. Chua, "An Image Database System with Content Capturing and Fast Image Indexing Abilities", *Proc. IEEE International Conference on Multimedia Computing and Systems*, Boston, 14-19 May, 1994, pp.121-130.

16.   S.-K. Kang, H.-Y. Kwon and I.-S. Han, Color Classification of Image Using Kohonen Neural Network Algorithm, *Proc. International Conference on Neural Information Processing'94*, Seoul, 1994.

Interactive Learning with a "Society of Models" *

Thomas P. Minka and Rosalind W. Picard

Vision and Modeling Group

MIT Media Laboratory

20 Ames Street; Cambridge, MA 02139

{tpminka, picard}@media.mit.edu

Abstract

Digital library access is driven by features, but the relevance of a feature for a query is not always obvious. This paper describes an approach for integrating a large number of context-dependent features into a semi-automated tool. Instead of requiring universal similarity measures or manual selection of relevant features, the approach provides a learning algorithm for selecting and combining groupings of the data, where groupings can be induced by highly specialized features. The selection process is guided by positive and negative examples from the user. The inherent combinatorics of using multiple features is reduced by a multistage grouping generation, weighting, and collection process. The stages closest to the user are trained fastest and slowly propagate their adaptations back to earlier stages. The weighting stage adapts the collection stage's search space across uses, so that, in later interactions, good groupings are found given few examples from the user.

1 Issues for digital libraries

One important issue for digital libraries is finding good models and similarity measures for comparing database entries (Figure 1). A part of this difficulty is that feature extraction and comparison methods are highly data-dependent. Similarity measures are also user and task dependent, as demonstrated by Figure 2. Unfortunately, these dependencies are not, at this point, understood well enough, especially by the typical digital library user, to permit careful selection of the optimal measure beforehand.

Next, the scope of queries that databases need to address is immense. Current computational solutions attempt to offer location of perceptual content ("find round, red objects") and objective content ("find pictures of people in Boston"). Desirable queries also extend to subjective content ("give me a scene of a romantic forest"), task-specific content ("I need something with open space, to place text"), and collaborative content ("show me pictures children like"). Answering such queries requires a variety of features, or metadata, to be attached to the data in a digital library, some of which may not be computable directly from the data. The implication for algorithms is that they cannot rely on one model or one small set of

*Supported in part by BT, Interval, HP Labs, and NEC.

carefully-picked features but will have to drink from a veritable "feature hydrant" from which only a few drops may be relevant for the query.

Some recent systems which perform retrieval on visual data are QBIC [9], SWIM [10], Photobook [11], and CORE [12]. A notable quality of these systems is that they present many different ways of organizing the data but offer little assistance in actually choosing one of these organizations or making a new one. Users are often forced to determine what features and feature combinations will be relevant to their intent, if any, instead of addressing their intent directly. Since intentions can vary greatly and features can be very opaque, another solution is needed. The example-based interaction in FourEyes, coupled with a learning element that selects and constructs organizations, provides such an alternative.

2 Multiple models

Dealing with these issues requires the use of multiple features, computed from the data or not, as well as ways to make informed, automatic selection of models and the features they describe. At this point in time, there seems to be no lack of specialized models, just a lack of knowing the best ways of utilizing them. Two well-known multiple model approaches are Bayesian combination [1] and the rule-based blackboard [2], but this paper advocates a different approach which is more desirable for the interactive digital library setting.

The approach described in this paper allows many different models to be easily incorporated without the computational complexity that usually plagues multi-model methods. The idea is to precompute many plausible groupings of the data, where groupings are induced by different models. Then the system selects and combines the groupings, based on positive and negative examples from the user. Relevance information, viz. which groupings were most useful, can then be fed back to modify these groupings or influence future grouping generation. In this way, the system is not only trained during individual example-based sessions with a user, but also trained across sessions to suit the tasks which it is asked to perform. This makes sure that the search space of groupings is always small but still contains desirable solutions.

An important optimization comes from the observation that when a reasonably large number of groupings

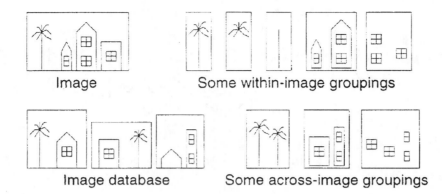

Figure 1: A basic task for image retrieval, segmentation, and annotation tools, which is addressed in this paper: recovering useful within-image or across-image groupings. A grouping is just a set of related regions. Note that useful groupings generally cannot be captured by a single model, or even a single partition or hierarchy, and the similarity measure required to induce these groupings may be quite complex.

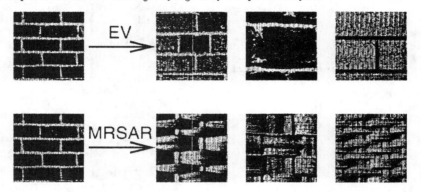

Figure 2: Task-dependent performance of texture models. The three patterns on the right are ordered by their similarity to the pattern on the left, given the particular model space EV or MRSAR. Both results capture the horizontal/vertical structure, but the EV returns a more semantically pleasing result since all images are bricks. However, these bricks are at different scales, and have different microtexture. Depending on the user's task, e.g. "find other images that look like bricks," the MRSAR result, or that of another model, may be preferable.

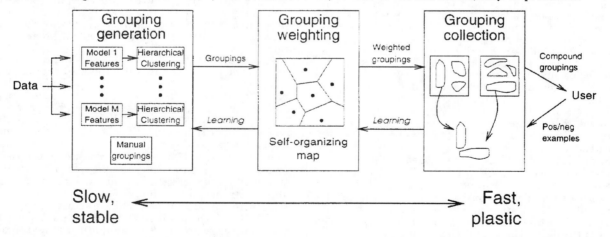

Figure 3: Interactive pattern recognition framework. The arrow at the bottom describes the rate at which the three stages learn.

is available, the correct groupings are usually present but are hard for the system to identify, given only a few training examples from the user. Therefore, the system can significantly improve itself just by changing the *relative weights* of groupings, not the groupings themselves. This optimization is realized by placing a separate weighting stage in between the generation and collection stages. Weighting does not change the size of the search space, but it does change the shape, by putting the "better" groupings first.

The resulting three-stage method, illustrated in Figure 3, differs from conventional feature extraction and classification in three crucial ways. First, the feedback arc between the classifier and the features is performed by the computer, not the designer. Second, each stage develops at different times and different rates, with the stages closest to the user changing fastest. This allows the computations to be distributed in time and space, facilitating interactive use and the incorporation of more complex models. This differs from Bayesian combination which essentially executes and adapts all stages at once, restricting the Bayesian approach to simple models for acceptable speed. Third, training is accumulated across sessions with the user, so that the system improves over time and can solve similar problems better, i.e. learn faster, the next time.

This paper describes an interactive-time learning system, called "FourEyes," which assists a user in finding groupings both within and across images based on features from a society of models. The current implementation obtains groupings for still images from color models, texture models, and the user. For images from a sequence, optical flow groupings are also used. The grouping representation used by FourEyes allows for a variety of arbitrary models, and could easily be extended to include audio, text, or other data. However, the focus in this paper is on visual data.

3 Generating groupings

A grouping is a set of image regions ("patches") which are associated in some way. The elements of a grouping may not necessarily come from the same image. This representation is useful since it admits different kinds of associations without adding complexity. For example, one set may represent "regions containing between 15% and 25% blue pixels" while another may represent "regions containing waterfalls" while yet another may represent "regions which were browsed very often this week." It also allows specific associations between patches to be weighted independently, since each set may have its own weight. This is important because, for example, lettering may be best grouped by shape whereas sky may be best grouped by brightness and location in the image. The notion of grouping, including the generation methods to be described, apply to all kinds of data, not just images.

FourEyes computes within-image groupings from a model feature, such as color or texture, in three steps as illustrated in Figure 4. This is the first stage of Figure 3. The result is a hierarchy of image regions for each image, for each model. Then it computes across-image groupings from a hierarchical clustering

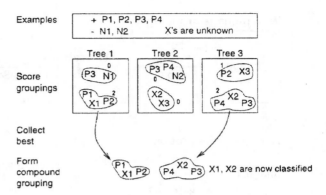

Figure 5: Collecting groupings

of a feature measured over the within-image groupings. The within-image groupings need not have been generated by the same feature used for across-image grouping; they may have come from optical flow or even manual outlining. For example, if a within-image grouping utilizes face detection to produce segments containing faces, the across-image grouping can use a face classifier. The clustering algorithm is described in [4], a longer version of this paper. All of these within-image and across-image groupings are computed off-line, before the user begins interaction with the system. On-line modification of groupings, included in the FourEyes model as the link from the second stage to the first, will be described in a future publication.

4 Collecting groupings

Once a set of groupings has been formed, the next task is to select or combine these to form compound groupings for the user. This is the third stage of Figure 3, referred to below as "the learner." At every point in the interaction, the learner must try to generalize from a set of examples provided by the user. The result is a set of image regions which contains all of the positive examples, and none of the negative. This set is formed from multiple groupings and so is called a compound grouping.

The learning algorithm used in FourEyes descends from AQ [5]. AQ is a greedy method that collects groupings one at a time, such that each one includes no negative examples but their union includes all positive examples. Starting from an empty union, the grouping which adds the most positive examples but no negative ones is iteratively added. Since the hierarchies generated in the first stage include the smallest-scale patches at the leaves, this algorithm can always satisfy any set of examples, no matter how arbitrary.

The algorithm used in FourEyes differs from AQ in its evaluation of the next grouping to add. Instead of choosing the grouping which simply maximizes the number of positive examples (as in our previous work [6]), it maximizes the product of this number and the *prior weight* of the grouping. This means that, e.g., a grouping with twice the prior weight can cover half as many positive examples before it is chosen. Thus the

Within-image grouping

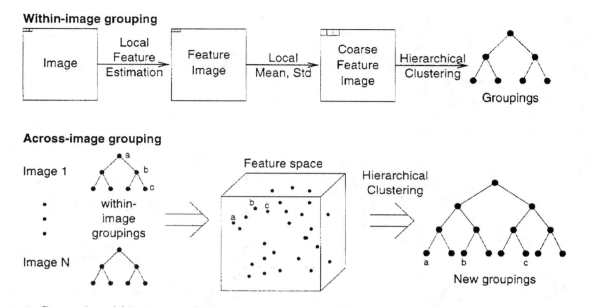

Across-image grouping

Figure 4: Computing within-image and across-image groupings. In image 1, grouping a contains b, which contains c; e.g. they might be house, door of the house, window on the door. When projected into feature space, they are considered individually, and look different. The resulting clustering says that a looks more like b than c.

prior weights directly influence the learner's inductive bias. The prior weights are determined from statistics collected over multiple learning sessions.

5   Weighting groupings

The learner in the third stage tries to find the best compound grouping according to consistency with the user's examples and an inductive bias. When the number of examples is large, consistency alone can serve to isolate good groupings. However, each example is expensive in terms of the user's time. When the number of examples is small, many groupings will be consistent; consequently, the bias is crucial in determining which groupings are chosen. Thus it is important that the learner have adaptive prior weights which change between interactions with the user, so that the groupings which were satisfactory this time will be selected earlier (i.e. with fewer examples) next time. This is the purpose of the second stage of Figure 3.

5.1   Modeling weight-space

FourEyes adapts to different learning problems by clustering weight-space. Currently this is done via a self-organizing map (SOM) [7]. During user interaction, each SOM unit (stored vector of weights) competes for consistency with the user's examples; the winning unit propagates its weights over the groupings. When the user is satisfied with the output of the learner, the winning unit is updated to more closely match the examples. In this way, the SOM defines a clustering of the weight-vectors for the problems it has seen, where each SOM unit is a cluster center. Note that a self-organizing map is typically used for the classification of feature vectors in a learning problem;

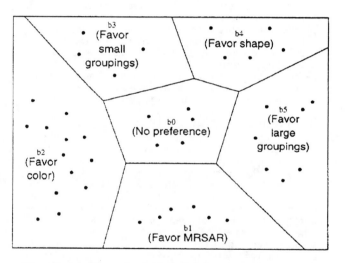

Figure 6: Hypothetical weight-space for learning. Each point is a vector of weights for all of the groupings. The optimal weights for different problem domains will fall into distinguished regions. These regions can be approximated by the Voronoi cells (in bold) of units in a self-organizing map, which clusters all of the points it sees. A unit which "favors color" weights most highly those groupings which come from a particular color model, from a combination of color models, or from non-color models that happen to be consistent with color.

here it is being used for classifying learning problems themselves, in terms of the grouping weights they favor. Each SOM unit then represents a prototypical learning problem.

Each SOM unit stores, for every grouping, the probability of including a positive or negative example. These probabilities are thus the "features" which are used to describe a learning problem. The distance function used to compute the winning unit is roughly the correlation between the probability distribution stored in a unit versus the actual distribution of the user's examples over the groupings (the precise function is described in [4]). When a unit is updated, the user's examples contribute to that unit's probability estimates.

5.2 Learning speedup

The learner described in Section 4 was modified in two ways:

1. After every e examples received, the SOM was consulted for each label to provide a prior weight to be used when selecting groupings for that label. The choice of e is a time/accuracy tradeoff, since SOM lookups are expensive; the experiments used $e = 10$.

2. When the learner was signaled that the learning task was completed, for each label it updated the SOM unit whose prior weight was selected for that label.

Experiments have shown that this self-organizing map approach is effective at learning good weights for several different learning problems simultaneously [4].

6   Performance on natural scenes

The performance of FourEyes was measured by its labeling performance on the natural scenes in the "BT images" (http://vismod.www.media.mit.edu/vismod/imagery/Bt_photos). In these images, the regions are of irregular shapes and sizes, and contain many different scales and inhomogeneous textures. Three human subjects were asked to freehand outline regions in 25 of the natural scenes and assign the seven labels "building," "car," "grass," "leaves," "person," "sky," and "water" to them. They were not asked to make precise boundaries or make decisions on a strictly perceptual basis (both of which would have aided FourEyes). Then a majority vote among the subjects was used to derive a single, approved ground-truth segmentation and labeling of those images. Since within-image groupings were computed using a 16×16 coarse feature image (Figure 4), the ground-truth segmentations were quantized to that resolution. Note that finer tessellation-sizes could be used, or overlapping tessellations, or even single pixels, if required by the application.

FourEyes was then used to simulate what the same labeling process would have been like with a computer assistant, where the user incrementally labels 32×32-pixel patches. This corresponds more closely to the database access scenario, where the user makes decisions while browsing the data, than the traditional

Groupings	Zero error	25% error
8×8	1.6	1.8
plus MRSAR	2.0	3.3
plus Ohta	2.4	5.7
second run	2.9	8.8
plus human	2.6	20
second run	2.9	28
plus ideal	38	47
second run	69	107

Table 1: Annotation savings for natural scenes. Numbers are the ratio between the total number of correctly labeled 32×32-pixel patches (4546 for zero error, 3410 for 25% error) and the number of examples. The higher the ratio, the more help the system is to the user.

train/test scenario. Five experiments were conducted with different sets of groupings in stage 1. Patch size varied in these groupings, but the results in Table 1 are given in terms of 32×32-pixel patches only. There were 4546 labeled 32×32-pixel patches and 7 classes so these are the theoretical maximum and minimum numbers of examples required to reach zero error, i.e. perfectly label all patches.

The baseline experiment (row 1 in Table 1) used a set of 1600 groupings corresponding to an 8×8 tessellation of each image, i.e. into groups of four 32×32-pixel patches. This corresponds to a simple bias toward giving nearby patches the same label. It required 2924 examples to reach zero error, for an annotation savings of 1.6:1.

Next, the feature set of FourEyes was enlarged to include within-image groupings computed from the MRSAR texture feature over 64×64-pixel patches (1740 groupings, or about 70 per image). This allowed FourEyes to achieve a savings of 2:1. Third, within-image groupings computed from the Euclidean distance between unnormalized histograms of 32×32-pixel patches in the Ohta color space [8] were added (1663 groupings), which raised the savings to 2.4:1.

Further improvement was found when the SOM was updated and run again on the same problem. Performance improved to 2.9:1, which is therefore the most that can be expected with these two models.

The learning curves exhibited diminishing returns after reaching 25% error; the last experiment spent 75% of its examples after this point. This indicates that the system is most effective at getting a quick first-cut labeling rather than a perfect labeling. Interestingly, adding across-image groupings computed from the MRSAR or Ohta histogram features did not improve performance. This indicates that the across-image perceptual variations in this data's semantic classes were high enough to confuse these image models. Another cause might be the scale-sensitivity of these particular across-image features.

The fourth test added human-provided within-image groupings to the first stage of FourEyes. This test would correspond to the system forming new groupings to better match that person's preferences.

The new groupings were provided by one of the sets from which the ground-truth was derived, but deliberately did not match exactly the ground-truth used in our tests. This raised the zero-error annotation savings slightly and allowed the learner to reach 25% error much faster. In the fifth test, the correct within-image groupings were added (an ideal situation) and FourEyes improved by an order of magnitude. This indicates that there is still room for improvement in the image groupings, either by using better models or by learning better groupings over multiple interactions.

7 Summary

The "FourEyes" learning system for assisting users in digital library segmentation, retrieval, and annotation, has been described. Digital library access requires the use of many context-dependent or noisy features, whose relevance is not always obvious. FourEyes addresses this problem on multiple fronts:

1. It first makes tentative organizations of the data, in the form of groupings. The grouping representation provides a common language for different measures of similarity. Groupings can be manually provided, induced by color/texture models, derived from optical flow information, etc. FourEyes uses both within-image groupings and across-image groupings composed of these.

2. The user no longer has to choose features or set feature control knobs. Instead, the user provides positive and negative examples which allow FourEyes to choose groupings (hence, similarity measures) automatically. The interaction is more like a conversation where both parties give each other prompt and relevant feedback in order to resolve ambiguities.

3. With many groupings to choose from, the number of examples required to isolate good groupings can get large. FourEyes circumvents this by having *prior weights* on the groupings and preferring groupings with more weight. These weights are learned across interactions with users, so that the system gets better, i.e. learns faster, from repeated use.

4. Since the optimal weights on groupings change with context, FourEyes employs a self-organizing map to remember useful weight settings. As the user interacts with it, FourEyes chooses the most appropriate weights in the map. This way, FourEyes can improve its joint performance on a wide range of tasks.

5. FourEyes offers interactive performance by explicitly separating these grouping generation, weighting, and collection stages. It does this without sacrificing adaptability or the use of multiple models, because feedback between the stages allows the whole system to learn, though each stage at a different rate.

References

[1] S. C. Zhu, T. S. Lee, and A. L. Yuille, "Region competition: Unifying snakes, region growing, energy/Bayes/MDL for multi-band image segmentation," in *Int. Conf. on Computer Vision*, (Boston, MA), pp. 416–423, 1995.

[2] T. M. Strat and M. A. Fischler, "Context-based vision: Recognizing objects using information from both 2-d and 3-d imagery," *IEEE T. Patt. Analy. and Mach. Intell.*, vol. 13, pp. 1050–1065, Oct. 1991.

[3] R. A. Jarvis and E. A. Patrick, "Clustering using a similarity measure based on shared near neighbors," *IEEE T. Comp.*, pp. 1025–1034, Nov. 1973.

[4] T. P. Minka and R. W. Picard, "Interactive learning using a 'society of models'," *Submitted for Publication*, 1995. Also appears as MIT Media Lab Perceptual Computing TR#349.

[5] R. S. Michalski, "A theory and methodology of inductive learning," *Artificial Intelligence*, vol. 20, no. 2, pp. 111–161, 1983.

[6] R. W. Picard and T. P. Minka, "Vision texture for annotation," *Journal of Multimedia Systems*, vol. 3, pp. 3–14, 1995.

[7] T. Kohonen, *Self-Organization and Associative Memory*. Berlin, Heidelberg: Springer, 1984. 3rd ed. 1989.

[8] Y.-I. Ohta, T. Kanade, and T. Sakai, "Color information for region segmentation," *Comp. Graph. and Img. Proc.*, vol. 13, pp. 222–241, 1980.

[9] W. Niblack, R. Barber, W. Equitz, M. Flickner, E. Glasman, D. Petkovic, P. Yanker, C. Faloutsos, and G. Taubin, "The QBIC project: Querying images by content using color, texture, and shape," in *Storage and Retrieval for Image and Video Databases* (W. Niblack, ed.), (San Jose, CA), pp. 173–181, SPIE, Feb. 1993.

[10] H.-J. Zhang and S. W. Smoliar, "Developing power tools for video indexing and retrieval," in *Proceedings SPIE Storage and Retrieval for Image and Video Databases II* (W. Niblack and R. C. Jain, eds.), (San Jose, CA), pp. 140–149, SPIE, Feb. 1994. Vol. 2185.

[11] A. Pentland, R. W. Picard, and S. Sclaroff, "Photobook: Tools for content-based manipulation of image databases," in *SPIE Storage and Retrieval of Image & Video Databases II*, (San Jose, CA), pp. 34–47, Feb. 1994.

[12] J. K. Wu, A. D. Narasimhalu, B. M. Mehtre, C. P. Lam, and Y. J. Gao, "CORE: a content-based retrieval engine for multimedia information systems," *Multimedia Systems*, vol. 2, pp. 25–41, Feb. 1995.

The Bayesian Image Retrieval System, *PicHunter*: Theory, Implementation, and Psychophysical Experiments

Ingemar J. Cox, *Senior Member, IEEE*, Matt L. Miller, Thomas P. Minka, Thomas V. Papathomas, and Peter N. Yianilos, *Senior Member, IEEE*

Abstract—This paper presents the theory, design principles, implementation, and performance results of *PicHunter*, a proto-type content-based image retrieval (CBIR) system that has been developed over the past three years. In addition, this document presents the rationale, design, and results of psychophysical experiments that were conducted to address some key issues that arose during *PicHunter*'s development. The *PicHunter* project makes four primary contributions to research on content-based image retrieval. First, *PicHunter* represents a simple instance of a general Bayesian framework we describe for using relevance feedback to direct a search. With an explicit model of what users would do, given what target image they want, *PicHunter* uses Bayes's rule to predict what is the target they want, given their actions. This is done via a probability distribution over possible image targets, rather than by refining a query. Second, an entropy-minimizing display algorithm is described that attempts to maximize the information obtained from a user at each iteration of the search. Third, *PicHunter* makes use of *hidden annotation* rather than a possibly inaccurate/inconsistent annotation structure that the user must learn and make queries in. Finally, *PicHunter* introduces two experimental paradigms to quantitatively evaluate the performance of the system, and psychophysical experiments are presented that support the theoretical claims.

Index Terms—Bayesian search, content-based retrieval, digital libraries, image search, relevance feedback.

I. INTRODUCTION

SEARCHING for digital information, especially images, music, and video, is quickly gaining in importance for business and entertainment. Content-based image retrieval (CBIR) is receiving widespread research interest [1]–[4], [6]–[20]. It is motivated by the fast growth of image databases which, in turn, require efficient search schemes. A search typically consists of a query followed by repeated relevance feedback, where the user comments on the items which were retrieved. The user's query provides a description of the desired image or class of images. This description can take many forms: it can be a set of keywords in the case of annotated image databases, or a sketch of the desired image [21], or an example image, or a set of values that represent quantitative pictorial features such as overall brightness, percentages of pixels of specific colors, etc. Unfortunately, users often have difficulty specifying such descriptions, in addition to the difficulties that computer programs have in understanding them. Moreover, even if a user provides a good initial query, the problem still remains of how to navigate through the database. After the query is made, the user may provide additional information, such as which retrieved images meet their goal, or which retrieved images come closest to meeting their goal. This "relevance feedback" stage differs from the query by being more interactive and having simpler interactions.

To date, there has been a distinct research emphasis on the query phase and therefore finding better representations of images. So much emphasis is placed on image modeling that relevance feedback is crude or nonexistent, essentially requiring the user to modify their query [7], [11], [17]. Under this paradigm, retrieval ability is entirely based on the quality of the features extracted from images and the ability of the user to provide a good query. Relevance feedback can be richer than this. In particular, the information the user provides need not be expressible in the query language, but may entail modifying feature weights [22] or constructing new features "on the fly "[23].

PicHunter takes this idea further with a Bayesian approach, representing its uncertainty about the user's goal by a probability distribution over possible goals. This Bayesian approach to the problem was pioneered by Cox *et al.* [3]. With an explicit model of a user's actions, assuming a desired goal, *PicHunter* uses Bayes's rule to predict the goal image, given their actions. So the retrieval problem is inverted into the problem of predicting users. Section IV describes how to obtain this predictive model.

An impediment to research on CBIR is the lack of a quantitative measure for comparing the performance of search algorithms. Typically, statistics are provided on the search length, e.g., the number of images that were visited before an image was found that was satisfactorily "similar" to a desired target image. The use of quotes around the word "similar" is deliberate; it is obvious that the search length depends on the content structure of the database and on how strict the criteria are for accepting an image as similar. In this context, searches can be classified into three broad categories.

Manuscript received November 30, 1998; revised July 27, 1999. The associate editor coordinating the review of this manuscript and approving it for publication was Dr. Hong Jiang Zhang. Portions of this paper were presented at various conferences, starting in 1996. The published record from these presentations is contained in [1]–[6].

I. J. Cox, P. N. Yianilos, and M. L. Miller are with NEC Research Institute, Princeton, NJ USA 08540 (e-mail: ingemar@research.nj.nec.com).

T. P. Minka is with the Massachusetts Institute of Technology Media Laboratory, Cambridge, MA 02139 USA.

T. V. Papathomas is with Laboratory of Vision Research and Department of Biomedical Engineering, Rutgers University, Piscataway, NJ 08854 USA.

Publisher Item Identifier S 1057-7149(00)00271-2.

1) Target-Specific Search or, Simply, Target Search: Users are required to find a specific target image in the database; search termination is not possible with any other image, no matter how similar it is to the singular image sought. This type of search is valuable for testing purposes (see Section V) and occurs, for example, when checking if a particular logo has been previously registered, or when searching for a specific historical photograph to accompany a document, or when looking for a specific painting whose artist and title escapes the searcher's memory.

2) Category Search: Users search for images that belong to a prototypical category, e.g., "dogs," "skyscrapers," "kitchens," or "scenes of basketball games;" in some sense, when a user is asked to find an image that is adequately similar to a target image, the user embarks on a category search.

3) Open-Ended Search—Browsing: Users search through a specialized database with a rather broad, nonspecific goal in mind. In a typical application, a user may start a search for a wallpaper geometric pattern with pastel colors, but the goal may change several times during the search, as the user navigates through the database and is exposed to various options.

The Bayesian approach described above can be adapted to accommodate all three search strategies. We focused on the target search paradigm for the reasons explained in Section V.

Another advantage of having a predictive model is that we can simulate it in order to estimate how effective a particular kind of interaction will be, and thereby design an optimal interaction scheme. In Section VII, we describe a novel display algorithm based on minimum entropy. This approach is evaluated by both simulation and psychophysical experiments.

Searching for images in large databases can be greatly facilitated by the use of semantic information. However, the current state of computer vision does not allow semantic information to be easily and automatically extracted.[1] Thus, in many applications, image databases also include textual annotation. Annotated text can describe some of the semantic content of each image. However, text-based search of annotated image databases has proved problematic for several reasons, including the user's unfamiliarity with specialized vocabulary and its restriction to a single language. Section VI examines this problem in more detail.

This paper presents an overview of *PicHunter*, a prototype image retrieval system that uses an adaptive Bayesian scheme, first introduced in 1996 [3], and continuously updated with improved features up to the present [1], [2], [4]–[6]. We present a conceptually coherent and highly expressive framework for the image retrieval problem, and report on validation of this framework using a simple system and careful experimental methods. Section II describes the theoretical basis for *PicHunter* and derives the necessary Bayesian update formulae. In order to implement the theoretical framework, it is necessary to decide upon a user interface and a model of the user. These are described in Sections III and IV. The user model is supported by psychophysical experiments that are also reported in Section IV. In order to evaluate the effectiveness of relevance feedback and a variety of other implementation issues, we introduce

two experimental paradigms that are described in Section V. We also provide experimental results that evaluate the performance of *PicHunter* with and without relevance feedback. Next, in Section VI, we describe how annotation can be hidden from the user yet still provide valuable semantic information to expedite the search process. Usually, the set of retrieved items that is displayed to a user is the closest set of current matches. However, such a scheme is not optimal from a search perspective. In Section VII, we describe a strategy for display which attempts to maximize the information obtained from the user at each iteration of the search. Theoretical and psychophysical studies demonstrate the utility of the information maximization approach. Finally, Section VIII describes possible extensions to the *PicHunter* model, Section IX details future avenues of research, and Section X concludes with a discussion of the contributions *PicHunter* makes to CBIR research together with a discussion of broader issues.

II. Bayesian Formulation

During each iteration $t = 1, 2, \cdots$ of a *PicHunter* session, the program displays a set D_t of N_D images from its database, and the user takes an action A_t in response, which the program observes. For convenience the *history* of the session through iteration t is denoted H_t and consists of $\{D_1, A_1, D_2, A_2, \cdots, D_t, A_t\}$.

The database images are denoted $T_1, \cdots, T_n$, and *PicHunter* takes a probabilistic approach regarding each of them as a putative target.[2] After iteration t *PicHunter*'s estimate of the probability that database image T_i is the user's target T, given the session history, is then written $P(T = T_i | H_t)$. The system's estimate prior to starting the session is denoted $P(T = T_i)$. After iteration t the program must select the next set D_{t+1} of images to display. The canonical strategy for doing so selects the most likely images, but other possibilities are explored later in this paper. So long as it is deterministic, the particular approach taken is not relevant to our immediate objective of giving a Bayesian prescription for the computation of $P(T = T_i | H_t)$. From Bayes' rule we have

$$P(T = T_i | H_t) = \frac{P(H_t | T = T_i) P(T = T_i)}{P(H_t)}$$
$$= \frac{P(H_t | T = T_i) P(T = T_i)}{\sum_{j=1}^{n} P(H_t | T = T_j) P(T = T_j)}.$$

That is, the *a posteriori* probability that image T_i is the target, given the observed history, may be computed by evaluating $P(H_t | T = T_i)$, which is the history's likelihood given that the target is, in fact, T_i. Here $P(T = T_i)$ represents the *a priori* probability. The canonical choice of $P(T = T_i)$ assigns probability $1/n$ to each image, but one might use other starting functions that digest the results of earlier sessions.[3]

---

[1]Color has proven to be an image feature with some capability of retrieving images from common semantic categories [19], [24]–[29].

[2]This amounts to the implicit assumption that the target is in the database, and this is indeed the case in all of our experiments. Formulations without this assumption are possible but are beyond the scope of this paper.

[3]The starting function must not assign probability zero to any image; otherwise the system's *a posteriori* estimate of its probability will always remain zero.

The *PicHunter* system performs the computation of $P(T = T_i|H_t)$ incrementally from $P(T = T_i|H_{t-1})$ according to

$$P(T = T_i|H_t) = P(T = T_i|D_t, A_t, H_{t-1})$$
$$= \frac{P(D_t, A_t|T = T_i, H_{t-1})P(D_t, T = T_i|H_{t-1})}{\sum_{j=1}^{n} P(D_t, A_t|T = T_j, H_{t-1})P(T = T_j|H_{t-1})}$$
$$= \frac{P(A_t|T = T_i, D_t, H_{t-1})P(T = T_i|H_{t-1})}{\sum_{j=1}^{n} P(A_t|T = T_j, D_t, H_{t-1})P(T = T_j|H_{t-1})}$$

where we may write $P(A_t|T = T_i, D_t, H_{t-1})$ instead of $P(D_t, A_t|T = T_i, H_{t-1})$ because D_t is a deterministic function of H_{t-1}.

The heart of our Bayesian approach is the term $P(A_t|T = T_i, D_t, H_{t-1})$, which we refer to as the *user model* because its goal is to predict what the user will do given the entire history D_t, H_{t-1} and the assumption that T_i is his/her target. The user model together with the prior give rise inductively to a probability distribution on the entire event space $\mathcal{T} \times \mathcal{H}^t$, where $\mathcal{T}$ denotes the database of images and $\mathcal{H}^t$ denotes the set of all possible history sequences $D_1, A_1, \cdots, D_t, A_t$. The particular user model used in our experimental instantiation of the *PicHunter* paradigm is described in section IV. Note that the user model's prediction is conditioned on image T_i and on all images that have been displayed thus far. This means that the model is free to examine the image in raw form (i.e., as pixels), or rely on any additional information that might be attached. In practice the model does not examine pixels directly but relies instead on an attached feature vector or other hidden attributes as described later in this paper.

Letting N_D denote the number of images in each iteration, our implementation assumes a space of $2^{N_D} + N_D + 1$ possible actions corresponding to the user's selection of a subset of the displayed images, or his/her indication that one of the N_D images is the target, or an "abort" signal respectively. But much more expressive action sets are possible within our framework (Section IX-C).

A contribution of our work is then the conceptual reduction of the image search problem to the three tasks: 1) designing a space of user actions, 2) constructing a user model, and 3) selecting an image display strategy.

Our implementation makes the additional simplifying assumption that the user model has the form $P(A_t|T = T_i, D_t)$, i.e., that the user's action is time-invariant. Note, however, that as a consequence of our Bayesian formulation, even this simple time-invariant model leads *PicHunter* to update its probability estimate in a way that embodies all the user's actions from the very beginning of the search.

Beyond the time-invariant user models of our experiments are models that fully exploit our Bayesian formulation and adapt their predictions based on the entire history. To preserve the possibility of incremental computation we introduce the notion of user models with *state* and write the *PicHunter* update equation as

$$P(T = T_i|H_t) = \frac{P(A_t|T = T_i, D_t, S_{t-1})P(T = T_i|H_{t-1})}{\sum_{j=1}^{n} P(A_t|T_j, D_t, S_{t-1})P(T_j|H_{t-1})}$$

(1)

where the model starts in some initial state S_0 and updates its state S_{t-1} to produce S_t after observing action A_t. Notice that we have said nothing of the structure of the state variable. But for efficiency's sake it makes sense to design it as a finite and succinct digest of the history H_t.

Equation (1) is, however, a fully general way to express *PicHunter* update since it spans the entire spectrum from time-invariant models where the state is trivial and constant, through models that carry forward a finite amount of state, to the original form $P(A_t|T = T_i, D_t, H_{t-1})$ where the state S_t is just H_t and grows without bound.

Finding effective models with state is an intriguing opportunity for future work within the *PicHunter* framework. We imagine that state might be used to carry forward estimates of feature relevancy, user type (e.g., expert versus beginner), general model type (e.g., color versus texture), and others.

III. USER INTERFACE

PicHunter uses a simple user interface designed to search for target images with minimum training. The rationale is that CBIR systems should ultimately be used as image-search tools by the general user on the World Wide Web, hence their usage should be effortless and self-explanatory. The user provides relevance feedback on each iteration of the search. The interface and user model (described in Section IV) are based on *relative similarity judgments* among images, i.e., "these images are more similar to the target than the others." If all images seem dissimilar to the target, the user can select none. Many systems instead use *categorical feedback*, where the user only selects the images that are in the same category as the target [16], [23]. However, this burdens the user to decide on a useful categorization of images in a possibly unfamiliar database, and is more suited to category search (Section I) than target search.

The user interface is shown in Fig. 1. It consists of a small number N_D of images; in this particular implementation $N_D = 9$. The initial display is determined by the display-update algorithm. The target is always present in the display to avoid possible interference from memory problems. Of course, the target could be in the form of a traditional printed photograph, but in such cases the CBIR system is unaware of what the target is. The user selects zero or more images that are similar to the desired target image by clicking on them with the mouse. If users wish to change their selection, they can unselect images by clicking on them again; the mouse clicks function as toggles in selecting/unselecting images. As mentioned above, users can select no images if they think that all images are dissimilar to the desired target image. After users are satisfied with their selection, they hit the "GO" button to trigger the next iteration. The program then interprets their selection based on the user model, and subsequently the display-update algorithm

Fig. 1.   *PicHunter*'s user interface.

(Section VII) decides which N_D images will be shown in the next iteration. The process is repeated until the desired image is found. When this is achieved, the user clicks the mouse button on the image identifier that is found directly above the image.

IV. USER MODEL: ASSESSING IMAGE SIMILARITY

As explained in the previous section, the key term in the Bayesian approach is the term $P(A_t|T = T_i, D_t, U)$, where U stands for the specific user conducting the search. Assume that $D_t = \{X_1, X_2, \cdots, X_{N_D}\}$. The task of the user model is to compute $P(A_t|T = T_i, D_t, U) = P(A_t|T = T_i, X_1, X_2, \cdots, X_{N_D}, U)$, in order to update the probability that each image T_i in the database might be the target image T. The first approximation we make is that all users respond in the same way, so that the dependence on U can be dropped. This approximation is not entirely supported by our human experiments, but we believe that more complex models should be motivated by the failure of a simple one. Kurita and Kato (1993) [30] reported work in taking account of individual differences.

The second approximation is that the user's judgment of image similarity can be captured by a small number of statistical pictorial features, in addition to some semantic labels, chosen in advance. That is, it is a function of some distance measure $d(\boldsymbol{f}(Y), \boldsymbol{f}(Z))$ between the feature values $\boldsymbol{f}(Y) = \{f_1(Y), f_2(Y), \cdots, f_F(Y)\}$ and $\boldsymbol{f}(Z) = \{f_1(Z), f_2(Z), \cdots, f_F(Z)\}$ of images Y and Z.

Psychophysical experiments helped us choose the distance measure as well as the form of the probability function. Different models are compared in terms of the probability they assign to the experimental outcomes; models which assign higher probability are preferred.

When $N_D = 2$ and the user must pick an image (A_t is either 1 or 2), the probability function that we found to perform best was sigmoidal in distance (in what follows, we drop the iteration subscript, t, for simplicity):

$$P_{sigmoid}(A = 1|X_1, X_2, T)$$
$$= \frac{1}{1 + \exp((d(X_1, T) - d(X_2, T))/\sigma)} \quad (2)$$

where σ is a parameter of the model chosen to maximize the probability of the data using a one-dimensional search.

When $N_D > 2$ and the user must pick $A = 1, \cdots, N_D$, a convenient generalization is the softmin

$$p_{\text{soft min}}(A = a|X_1, \cdots, X_{N_D}, T)$$
$$= \frac{\exp(-d(X_a, T)/\sigma)}{\sum_{i=1}^{N_D} \exp(-d(X_i, T)/\sigma)}. \quad (3)$$

Note that transitive ordering of the images is not required by this model.

When the user can pick any number of images, including zero, no complete model has been found. One approach is to assume that the user selects each image independently according to $p_{soft\ min}$. Another approach is to assume that the user first decides the number k of images to select and then chooses one of the $\binom{N_D}{k}$ possible selections of k images, according to a softmin. Both approaches achieved similar probabilities for the data once their weights were tuned. This paper reports on the latter approach. Unfortunately, both give a constant probability to selecting zero images, independent of the target and the choices, which is at odds with our experimental results and limits the accuracy of our simulations.

Two possible schemes for combining multiple distance measures were considered. The first scheme multiplied the softmin probabilities for each distance measure. The second scheme simply added the distance measures before computing the softmin. In both cases, each distance measure was multiplied by an adaptive scaling factor w_i, since distance measures are generally not on the same scale. These scaling factors were set to maximizing the probability of the training data, using gradient ascent. The second model achieved a higher maximum probability, so it was chosen for the *PicHunter* experiments. The resulting formula is

$$d(\boldsymbol{f}(Y), \boldsymbol{f}(Z)) = \sum_{i=1}^{F} w_i d_i(f_i(Y), f_i(Z)) \qquad (4)$$

The individual distance d_i was the simple L1 distance between feature $f_i(Y)$ and $f_i(Z)$.

A. Pictorial Features

This subsection deals with the pictorial features that the model uses for predicting human judgment of image similarity. It must be emphasized that we used rudimentary pictorial features, because our objective was not to test features as such, but only to use them as a tool to test the Bayesian approach and the entropy display-updating scheme. Hidden semantic features are covered in Section VI.

The original pictorial version of *PicHunter* [3] worked with 18 global image features that are derived for each picture in the database. These features are: the percentages of pixels that are of one of eleven colors (red, green, blue, black, grey, white, orange, yellow, purple, brown pink), mean color saturation of entire image, the median intensity of the image, image width, image height, a measure of global contrast, and two measures of the number of "edgels," computed at two different thresholds. Thus the dominant influence is that of chromatic content, in the form of the 11-bin color histogram. These features are admittedly not as sophisticated as those used in other CBIR systems, but they merely provided a starting point for experimenting with the initial system.

The current version of *PicHunter* incorporates some rudimentary information on the spatial distribution of colors, in addition to a conventional color histogram. The current version's pictorial features have the following three components.

1) HSV-HIST, a 64-element-long histogram of the HSV (Hue, Saturation, Value) values of the image's pixels.

These values are obtained after conversion to HSV color space and quantization into $4 \times 4 \times 4 = 64$ color bins.

2) HSV-CORR, a 256-element long HSV color autocorrelogram at distances 1, 3, 5, and 7 pixels [24]. The pixel values are subjected to the same preprocessing as HSV-HIST. The first 64 bins are the number of times each pixel of a given color had neighbors of the same color at distance 1. The next 64 bins are for distance 3, etc.

3) RGB-CCV, a 128-element long color-coherence vector of the RGB image after quantization into $4 \times 4 \times 4 = 64$ color bins. This vector is the concatenation of two 64-bin histograms: one for coherent pixels and one for incoherent pixels. A coherent pixel is defined as one belonging to a large connected region with pixels of the same color [25]

B. Relative—Versus Absolute-Distance Criteria

1) Relative-Distance Criterion: In this scheme, the set $Q = \{X_{q1}, X_{q2}, \cdots, X_{qC}\}$ of selected images in the display D_t, as well as the set $N = \{X_{n1}, X_{n2}, \cdots, X_{nL}\}$ of nonselected images, play a role in approximating the *user-model* term $P(A_t|T_i, D_t)$ by a function S [3], [4]. The distance difference $d(T_i, X_{qk}) - d(T_i, X_{nm})$ is computed for every pair $\{X_{qk}, X_{nm}\}$ of one selected and one nonselected image. This difference determines, of course, whether T_i is closer to X_{qk} or to X_{nm}; the difference is first transformed through a sigmoid function [(2) or (3)], and is then applied toward computing the function S. Thus, each pair $\{X_{qk}, X_{nm}\}$ increases the probabilities of images, T_c, that are closer to X_{qk}, and decreases the probabilities of images that are closer to X_{nm} in feature space.

2) Absolute-Distance Criterion: In this scheme, only one image X_q in the display D_t can be selected by the user in each iteration. The selection of X_q either increases or decreases the probability of an image T_i, depending on whether $d(T_i, X_q)$ is small or large, respectively. In our implementation of the absolute-distance criterion, this updating of the probability $P(T = T_i)$ takes the form

$$P(T = T_i) \leftarrow P(T = T_i)G(d(T_i, X_q))$$

where $G()$ is a monotonically decreasing function of its argument. One way to think about the updating of probabilities is to visualize the selected image X_q as defining an "enhancement region" in the F-dimensional feature space, centered at $\boldsymbol{f}(X_q)$. The probability of each image T_i in this region is enhanced, and the magnitude of the enhancement decreases as the distance from $\boldsymbol{f}(X_q)$ increases. After obtaining a new value $P(T = T_i)$ for each image by multiplying it by $G()$, each value is divided by the grand total $\sum_{i=1}^{n} P(T = T_i)$, such that the ultimate values at the end of each iteration sum up to 1. This post-normalization has the effect of enhancing or depressing the probabilities of images whose feature vectors are near or far, respectively, from the selected image $\boldsymbol{f}(X_q)$ in feature space, independently of the magnitude of $G()$; the only requirement is that $G()$ be monotonically decreasing. The series of iterations can be visualized as a series of enhancement regions that progress toward the target from one iteration to the next, getting progressively narrower as they converge to a small region that contains the

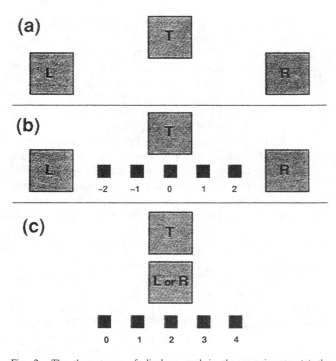

Fig. 2. The three types of displays used in the experiments: (a) the "2AFC" configuration, (b) the "relative-similarity" configuration, and (c) the "absolute-similarity" configuration.

target. In this scheme, the $(N_D - 1)$ nonselected images do not influence at all the distribution of probabilities in the database. Thus, this scheme can also be referred to as a "query-by-example" search, because only one image can be selected in each iteration, providing an example for converging to the target.

C. Experiments: Judgment of Image Similarity by Humans

This section deals with experiments that were designed to collect data on how humans judge image similarity, for use in developing a user model with some knowledge of human performance. In this experiment we used the three display configurations shown schematically in Fig. 2. The task of the user was always the same for a given configuration, but differed across configurations.

Fig. 2(a) shows the two-alternative forced-choice configuration, which we shall refer to simply as the "2AFC" configuration. Three images are presented on the screen: the target image on top, and two test images on the bottom. We will refer to the target, left test, and right test images in this and similar triplet configurations as T, L, and R, respectively; collectively, the set will be referred to as the LTR triplet. The user must select the test image that he/she thinks is more similar to the target image.

The second type of display, referred to as the "relative-similarity" configuration, is shown in Fig. 2(b). There are now five buttons between the bottom two images. The user clicks on one of the five buttons, depending on how he/she judges the relative similarities of the two test images are with respect to the target image, using the 5-point scale. If he/she thinks that one of them is clearly more similar to the target image, he/she clicks on the corresponding extreme button (left-most or right-most). If the

two test images seem to be equally similar or equally dissimilar to the target image, then the user clicks on the middle button. If one of the test images is somewhat more similar to the target image, then he/she clicks on the button immediately to the left or to the right of the center, as appropriate.

The third type of display, referred to as the "absolute-similarity" configuration, involves two images, one on top of the other, and five buttons at the bottom of the screen, as shown in Fig. 2(c). These buttons are used by the user to denote the degree of similarity of the two images, on a 5-point scale. The extreme left button indicates the least degree of similarity (0), and the extreme right one is used to show the maximum degree of similarity (4). If the two images have intermediate degrees of similarity, the user clicks on one of the intermediate three buttons, as appropriate.

The stimuli for this experiment consisted of a set of 150 LTR triplets, in all of which the L, T, and R images were randomly selected from a database of 4522 images. The user was presented with a sequence of trials, i.e., a sequence of randomly selected LTR triplets, and was asked to indicate his/her choices based on image similarity. Each triplet was shown in all three configurations of Fig. 2, and these three displays were randomly scattered among the 600 trials (150 of type 2a, 150 of type 2b, and 300 of type 2c, i.e., 150 for LT and 150 for RT pairings). Five users took part in this experiment. They were exposed to LTR triplets for about 20 min before the beginning of a session, so as to accustom themselves to the variety of images in the database and the range of similarities and dissimilarities. They were told that the images they were exposed to represented a good sample of all the images in the database. This exposure would allow them to calibrate their scales of similarity [31] to produce choices that are well distributed across the entire range, and this was indeed the case with most of the users. The results from these experiments indicated that 2AFC choices correlated very well with both the relative-similarity and the differences between the absolute-similarity judgments of the same LTR triplets. The data supported the idea of using some form of distance metric, and were used for adjusting the weights of the distance function for the pictorial features of the user model [see (4)].

V. EXPERIMENTAL PARADIGM—TARGET TESTING

The paradigm of *target testing* requires the user to find a specific target image in the database. When a user signifies that he/she has found the target, there are two possibilities: 1) if this is indeed the target, the search is terminated; 2) if the user mistakenly thinks that she/he found the target, then an appropriate message informs them of their mistake and instructs them to continue the search (the "ABORT" button is there for frustrated users who lose interest in finding the target after a lengthy search). This section presents more details on the implementation of the target testing paradigm that was used in the vast majority of our experiments. General remarks are made in Section V-A, and specific details on the databases are presented in Section V-B. Section V-C discusses two major memory schemes, and experimental results are given in the last two sections.

A. Rationale

The main problem with evaluating the performance of CBIR systems that terminate a search when the user finds an image which is "adequately similar" to a target image is that the similarity criteria can vary from user to user. This is reflected in the data we obtained in two different search-termination strategies: one in which users terminate the search when a "similar" image is encountered, and another employing target testing. The standard deviation across users is much higher in the former case (Section V-D), underlying the wide variability in judging image similarity. Thus it is very difficult to evaluate a CBIR system's performance under a category search, or a very-similar-to-target search termination scheme.

The main reason for deciding to employ target testing in *PicHunter* was precisely our belief that the use of more objective criteria of performance than category search results in more reliable statistical measures. The *performance measure* that has been used throughout our experiments is *the average number V of images required to converge to the desired specific target.* Typically, we obtained this average across 6–8 users, with each user's score averaged across searches of 10–17 randomly selected target images. This performance measure is extremely useful in two ways: 1) It provides a yardstick for comparing different *PicHunter* versions and evaluating new algorithmic ideas; 2) it is also a first step in the direction of establishing a benchmark for useful comparisons between CBIR systems, when coupled with a baseline search scheme, as explained in Section V-E.

B. Databases

The pictorial database was assembled using images from 44 Corel compact disks (CD's), each containing 100 images with a common theme such as horses, flower gardens, eagles, pictures of Eskimo everyday life, scenes from ancient Egyptian monuments, etc. [32]. To these 4400 images we added 122 images from a nonthematic Corel CD for a total of 4522 images. This database was used in all versions of *PicHunter* where the user model was based exclusively on pictorial features. In addition, we created a database of 1500 annotated images, which was a proper subset of the 4522-image set, from 15 thematic CD's. This semantic database is described in more detail in Section VI-A.

C. Schemes with and Without Memory

PicHunter differs from most CBIR systems along another dimension: how the user's relevance feedback is treated from the very beginning of a search. Whereas most systems tend to concentrate on the user's action only in the previous iteration, *PicHunter*'s Bayesian formulation empowers it with "long-term" memory: all the user's actions during a target search are taken into consideration. Nevertheless, the benefit of such memory has not been demonstrated experimentally. It is conceivable that performance gains from the inclusion of memory may depend on other conditions. Investigating such dependencies was the purpose of the experiments presented in Section V-D.

D. Experiments on Features, Distance, and Memory Schemes

All the experiments reported in this paper were conducted with the color images displayed on 1280 × 1024-pixel monitor screens, measuring 38 cm by 29 cm, viewed from a distance of about 70 cm. The programs ran on Silicon Graphics Indigo2 workstations. Individual images were either in "portrait" or in "landscape" format, and were referred to by their unique identification number. They were padded with dark pixels either horizontally or vertically to form square icons that measured 7.25 × 7.25 cm. All users tested perfect for color vision, scoring 15/15 on standard Ishihara test plates. All users were also tested for acuity, and found to have normal or corrected-to-normal visual acuity.

This set of experiments [5], [6] was designed to study the role of the following components: 1) memory during the search process; 2) relative-distance versus absolute-distance judgment of image similarity (Section IV-B); 3) semantic information (Section VI). Toward this goal, we tested six versions of *PicHunter*, which we code with trigraphs XYZ for mnemonic reasons. The letters in the trigraphs XYZ refer to components 1–3 above, in that order. Thus, the first letter X refers to memory: M or N denote that the algorithm did or did not use memory, respectively, in the search process. *M* refers to the standard Bayesian system of Section II. *N* refers to a system that bases its actions on the user's relevance feedback for only the last display. The second letter Y, referring to distance, can be either *R* or *A* to denote whether the model used relative or absolute distances, respectively. Finally, the last letter Z is devoted to semantic features, and it can have three possible values: *P*, or *S*, or *B* denote, respectively, that only pictorial features, or only semantic features, or both, are used in the user model for predicting judgments of image similarity. The pictorial features in these experiments were the 18 features described in Section IV-A. All the experiments of this section were run with algorithms that used the most-probable display-updating scheme of Section VII-A. Our previous experience indicates that some XYZ combinations are of little practical value, thus we concentrated on the following six versions.

1) MRB: Uses memory, relative distance, both semantic and pictorial features.
2) MAB: Same as MRB, but with absolute distance.
3) NRB: Same as MRB, but doesn't use memory.
4) NAB: Same as MAB, but doesn't use memory.
5) MRS: Same as MRB, but uses only semantic features.
6) MRP: Same as MRB, but uses only pictorial features.

Six first-time *PicHunter* users, naive as to the experimental purposes, participated in this study. They ran the experiment in a 6-users × 6-versions Latin-square design [33]. Each user went through 15 target searches, terminating the search under the target testing paradigm; all searches terminated successfully. The results of these experiments are shown in Table I. The first row has the average number V of 9-image displays visited before convergence to the target; smaller values of V denote better performances. The second row displays the standard error SE, and the third row shows the ratio SE/V, as a measure of the variability of V across users. Two experienced users also ran

TABLE I
RESULTS OF THE EXPERIMENT THAT WAS
DESIGNED TO TEST THE ROLES OF MEMORY, DISTANCE METRIC, AND
SEMANTIC FEATURES IN *PICHUNTER*. THE EXPECTED VALUE OF V UNDER
RANDOM SEARCH IS (1500/2)/9 = 83.3. IN THIS, AS WELL AS IN TABLES II,
IV, AND V, SMALLER VALUES OF V SIGNIFY BETTER PERFORMANCES

Version	MRB	MAB	NRB	NAB	MRS	MRP
No. displays, V	25.4	35.8	45.5	33.2	15.6	35.1
Standard Error, SE	2.35	2.37	2.48	2.44	1.76	2.11
Variability, SE/V	.093	.066	.055	.073	.113	.060
V, 2 exper. users	13.1	31.6	28.4	22.2	8.8	18.9

TABLE II
RESULTS OF THE EXPERIMENT WITH TARGET SEARCH AND CATEGORY
SEARCH. THE EXPECTED VALUE OF V UNDER RANDOM SEARCH IS 83.3. THE
ASTERISK ON RAND/C IS MEANT TO INDICATE THAT THIS IS NOT A
VERSION OF THE *PICHUNTER* CBIR SYSTEM

Version	MRB/T	MRS/T	MRB/C	RAND/C*
No. displays, V	25.4	15.6	12.2	19.7
Standard Error, SE	2.35	1.76	2.13	6.39
Variability, SE/V	0.093	0.113	0.175	0.324
V, 2 exper. users	13.1	8.8	8.9	20.1

the experiments under the same conditions. Their averages are shown below the data for the naive users.

The following main trends can be observed in the data. First, when one compares the results of the MRB and the MRS schemes, performance with the semantics-only features (MRS) is substantially better than with the semantics-plus-pictorial features (MRB). This is just the opposite of the expected behavior; namely, if the pictorial features were well chosen, their inclusion should improve, rather than worsen, performance (even if semantic features dominate in judgments of similarity, the addition of pictorial features should at worst keep performance the same). One obvious conclusion is that the 18 features of *PicHunter*'s original version need to be refined, and this is precisely what was done in the most recent version (see Section IV-A).

Second, the clear advantage of the MRS version over all others underscores the role played by semantic features in the search process. This fact is also corroborated by the experimental data of Sections VI-B and VII-E.

Third, pair-wise comparison of versions MRB to NRB and MAB to NAB show that the effect of memory depends on the distance criterion. The former comparison indicates that *memory improves the relative*-distance version, while the latter comparison shows that *memory slightly worsens the absolute*-distance version. This apparent paradox can be explained if one visualizes the search in the absolute-distance version as an enhancement region that moves toward the target across the iterations. Since probabilities are updated by multiplying factors cumulatively in long-memory versions, this memory adds a delay by introducing "inertia," due to the effect of all the previous iterations. By contrast, this accumulation is helpful in the the relative-distance versions, in which the target is approached as the feature space is successively partitioned in each iteration [5].

Fourth, other than the optimal scheme MRS, the next best one is the MRB scheme, which incorporates memory, a relative-distance measure, and both kinds of features; all other schemes perform somewhat worse than the two best schemes.

Fifth, as expected, the experienced users were substantially more efficient than the inexperienced ones.

E. Target and Baseline Testing as a Benchmark for Comparing CBIR Systems

As argued earlier, there is a great need for a benchmark for comparing CBIR systems. Such a benchmark can also be used for assessing the value of incorporating a new approach for a specific system, by comparing the new version's performance against that of the original version. Ideally, one hopes for an automated comparison, but this is not feasible at the present. Hence, our efforts must be focused on producing a benchmark, based on efficient experiments with as few human users as possible. The benchmark must yield a robust estimate of performance that is representative of performances of the population as a whole. In this section we describe such a scheme based on the target testing paradigm. Our experimental results tend to confirm our intuition, and in this sense are not surprising. But such confirmation is valuable in guiding the development of complex systems that interact with humans.

To be able to compare performances with systems that search for a similar-category image, rather than a unique image target, we need to establish a performance baseline against which to compare other versions. Such a baseline is provided by a similar-target search, with a random display update, since it is reasonable to determine what the performance would be in the complete absence of any relevance feedback from the user. This motivated the present set of experiments, that were conducted with six first-time *PicHunter* users, who were naive as to the purposes of the experiment [6]. These users were the same as those who participated in the experiments of Section V-D. We have just introduced a new option, namely whether searches are terminated under target testing (T), or under "category" search (C), in which an image similar to the target is found. Thus, MRB/T and MRS/T denote the same target-specific versions of *PicHunter* that were referred to as MRB and MRS, respectively, in Section V-D. Similarly, MRB/C is the MRB version that terminates searches when a similar image is found. In addition to MRB/T, MRS/T and MRB/C, the fourth scheme that we experimented with was RAND/C. RAND indicates that displays are updated at random, independently of the user's feedback, with the only restriction of not displaying images repeatedly, if they were already displayed in previous iterations.

The first three rows in Table II are the results with searches by these four schemes for the six naive users, each searching for the same 15 target images. In the XYZ/C searches, users were instructed to terminate the search when they encountered an image which looked similar to the target image. The entries of the Table follow the same convention as that of Table I. Namely, the first row shows the mean number V of 9-image displays required to converge to the target, averaged across the means of 6 users, where each user's performance was averaged across the 15 targets. The Table also includes the standard error SE, as well as the ratio SE/V, which is a measure of the relative variability of V across users. The last row has the averages V of the same two experienced users who also ran the experiments of Section V-D.

The entries for columns MRB/T and MRS/T are duplicated from Table I.

The following observations can be drawn from the data of Table II.

1) RAND/C converged rather fast to a picture that the average user judged to be similar to the target, establishing a high baseline standard. This makes it necessary to revisit results given in other reports where similar images are retrieved, but no baseline is established.

2) Despite this high standard, performance with the corresponding *PicHunter* scheme MRB/C is substantially better.

3) Variability in the baseline scheme RAND/C is markedly higher by a factor of 1.85 than that in MRB/C, which in turn is higher than that of the MRB/T scheme by a factor of 1.88. Since low variability allows efficient tests with few users, target search offers a valuable testing paradigm for getting representative performance data.

4) One must remark on the solid performance of the semantics-only target-search MRS/T version, which is comparable to the category-search MRB/C version, and better than the baseline.

5) Again, as expected, the performance of the experienced users was considerably better that of the naive ones, with the notable, but expected, exception of the random category search.

VI. HIDDEN ANNOTATION

Systems that retrieve images based on their *content* must in some way codify these images so that judgments and inferences may be made in a systematic fashion. The ultimate encoding would somehow capture an image's semantic content in a way that corresponds well to human interpretation. By contrast, the simplest encoding consists of the image's raw pixel values. Intermediate between these two extremes is a spectrum of possibilities, with most work in the area focusing on *low-level features*, i.e., straightforward functions of the raw pixel values (see [34], [21], [7], [35], [11], [12], [36], [17], [37]–[39], and [19]). Some such features, such as color, begin to capture an image's semantics, but at best they represent a dim reflection of the image's true meaning. The ultimate success of content-based image retrieval systems will likely depend on the discovery of effective and practical approaches at a much higher level. In this section we report conceptual and experimental progress toward this objective.

Any attempt to codify image semantics inevitably leads to design of a language with which to express them. If a human operator is required to formulate a query using this language, and interpret a database image's description in terms of the language, two serious problems arise. First, the language must not only be effective in theory, but must also serve as a natural tool with which a human can express a query. Second, inaccurate or inconsistent expression of each database image in terms of the language can lead to confusion on the part of the user, and ultimately undermine the effectiveness of, and confidence in, the system. The need for accurate and consistent expression can also limit the language's design.

For these reasons we are led to study *hidden languages* for semantic encoding, and in particular hidden Boolean attributes affixed to each database image.

A. Annotation Implementation

In an effort to characterize how CBIR performance is enhanced by the introduction of semantic cues, we created an annotated database of 1500 images from 15 thematic CD's of 100 images each. A set of approximately 138 keywords was identified by one of the authors who had extensive exposure to our experimental database of 1500 images taken from the Corel database [32]. The objective was to obtain a set of keywords that covered a broad spectrum of semantic attributes. Each image was then visually examined and all relevant keywords identified. An additional set of *category* keywords were then assigned automatically. For example, the "lion" attribute causes the category attribute "animal" to be present. Altogether there are 147 attributes. These supplement the pictorial features used by the basic *PicHunter* version, and described in [2]. The 147 semantic attributes are regarded as a boolean vector, and normalized Hamming distance combines their influence to form, in effect, an additional *PicHunter* feature. Table III shows representative semantic labels and suggests the level of semantic resolution. It must be emphasized that these semantic features are hidden: users are not required to learn a vocabulary of linguistic terms before using the system, or even use a particular language.

B. Experiments: Hidden Annotation and Learning

These experiments were designed to compare performances between the original pictorial-feature version of *PicHunter* [3] with a version that incorporated semantic features in addition to the image features. Furthermore, we examined whether user performances improved after they were explicitly taught which particular features were considered important by the algorithm's user model in both versions [1]. For notational purposes, we refer to the pictorial version as "P" and to the pictorial-*plus*-semantic version as "B" (B stands for *both*). The experiments involved eight first-time *PicHunter* users who were not aware of the purposes of the study. All sessions involved searches of a target image among the 1500 images in the database. There were a total of 17 target images that were selected randomly. Users were required to locate all 17 targets in one session for each *PicHunter* version. Both the P and the B versions were implemented with displays of nine images.

The experiments consisted of two major phases, each using the same 17 target images. In the first phase, the pre-explanation phase, users were told to use their own similarity criteria. The order of exposure was balanced: four users went through sequence (P,B), and the others through (B,P). The eight users were then divided in two groups of four, to balance within-group average performances and standard deviations for the two groups. This grouping was done on the basis of their performances in the first phase, and it was constrained by requiring that each group have two members that went through the (P,B) sequence, and the other two through the (B,P) sequence. In the second phase, users were first given explicit instructions for judging image similarity,

TABLE III
REPRESENTATIVE SEMANTIC LABELS IN THE ANNOTATED DATABASE

sky	cloud	ground
tree	one subject	aircraft
horse	two subjects	person
water	many subjects	lion
snow	sand	animal
rodent	arch	church
bicycle	field	shoe
Japan	Africa	woods
art	painting	umbrella
city	boat	night
interior	wall	autumn
mountain	close up	green grass
eagle	child	house
fish	pillar	texture

TABLE IV
EFFECT OF SEMANTICS AND EXPLANATIONS ON PERFORMANCE. THE
EXPECTED VALUE OF ENTRIES UNDER RANDOM SEARCH IS 83.3

	Before explanations	After explanations
Pictorial features only	17.1	13.2
Pictorial AND semantic	11.7	9.5

according to the user model. For the P model, we briefly explained to them the 18 features and their relative weights, and instructed them to ignore the images' semantic contents. For the B model, users were told to base similarity not only on image characteristics, but also on image semantics; they were shown the 42 words of Table III, to get an idea of how the B version was designed. This explanation was very brief, lasting at most 8 min for each of the two versions. Explanations were given separately for each version, and users started the 17-target search with that particular version of *PicHunter*. This was followed by explanations for the other version, and ended with a 17-target search with that other version. The order of versions, (P,B) or (B,P), was balanced in this second phase, as well.

The results are given in Table IV, the entries of which are the mean number V of nine-image displays that were required for users to locate the target, averaged across the eight users and the 17 targets. It is obvious from the entries of Table IV that both semantic features and training, in the form of explanations, improve users' performance. Specifically, the data indicate the following.

1) Without prior instruction, users took on average about 1/3 fewer displays to converge to the target with the B version than with the P version, underlying the importance of semantics.

2) After users were instructed on the similarity criteria, performance improved for both versions, as expected. Users took over 25% more displays prior to instruction,

when their performance is pooled over both versions of *PicHunter*.

3) In the P version the explanations reduced the search time to 77.8% of its original level; in the B version the search time was reduced to 81.2% of its original level. A 2×2 within-groups analysis of variance (ANOVA) was performed over both the version type and the instruction presence to look for an interaction between the two effects listed above. No such interaction was found ($F = 1.770; df = 1, 7; p = 0.225$). This shows that the instruction helped users equally with both versions.

Also, the issue of feature relevancy must be addressed. In observing the eight users' strategies, we observed that test images were sometimes selected because of similarity with the target in terms of, say, color ("it has as much blue as the target"), and other times because of similarity in, say, overall brightness. To the extent that a user relies on a small number of features during a session, it may be possible to learn which are being used, and in so doing improve performance. This is, in principle, possible using user models with state as described in Section II.

Because the attributes are hidden in our approach, we are free to consider attribute schemes in future work that might not work well in a traditional nonhidden approach. We might, for example, entertain a scheme that employs 10 000 attributes, far more than a human operator could reasonably be expected to deal with. Moreover, some of these attributes might correspond to complex semantic concepts that are not easily explained, or to overlapping concepts that do not fit well into the kind of hierarchies that humans frequently prefer. They might even include entirely artificial attributes that arise from a machine learning algorithm. Because the attributes are hidden, it may be that the system performs well despite considerable *error* in the assignment of attributes. For this reason we are free to consider attributes even if their proper identification seems very difficult.

We remark that there are errors and inconsistencies even in attributes assigned by humans. Here, the fact that the attribute values are hidden can result in more robust performance in the presence of error. We also observe that in some settings, such as the emerging area of Internet Web publication, authors are implicitly annotating their images by their choice of text to accompany them. Exploiting this textual proximity represents an immediate and interesting direction for future work and this general direction is explored in [27], [40]. Semantically annotated images are also appearing in structured environments such as medical image databases, news organization archives—and the trend seems to extend to generic electronic collections. In addition to using these annotations in a hidden fashion, mature image search systems may be hybrids that include an explicit query mechanism that corresponds to the space of available annotations. Even in query-based systems, learning may play a role as illustrated by related work in the field of textual information retrieval [41].

It is not clear how *high* in the semantic sense our approach of hidden attributes might reach. It is certainly conceivable that a large portion of an image's semantic content might be captured by a sufficiently large and rich collection of attributes—entirely obviating the need to produce a single succinct and coherent expression of an image's meaning.

VII. Display Updating Model

Once the user-model module of *PicHunter* updates the probability distribution across the entire database, the next task is to select the N_D images to be shown in the next display. We have experimented with several schemes in this area, but we report on the two that produced the best results: the most-probable scheme, and the most-informative scheme.

A. Most-Probable Display Updating Scheme

This is an obviously reasonable strategy: For the next display, choose the N_D images that possess the highest probabilities of being the target; possible ties are broken with random selections. This is the scheme that was used in all but the most recent version of *PicHunter*. It performed quite well, achieving search lengths that were about ten times better than random target-testing searches for purely picture-based features [2], [3]. Typically, this updating scheme produces displays whose images belong to a common theme, such as aircraft or horses, even with the purely pictorial feature user model, somehow exhibiting an ability to extract semantic content. However, this greedy strategy suffers from an over-learning disadvantage that is closely related to its desired ability to group similarly looking images. The problem is that, in a search of, say, an image of a jungle scene, *PicHunter* occasionally "gets stuck" by showing display after display of, say, lion pictures as a result of the user having selected a lion picture in an earlier display. This problem is addressed by the information-based scheme, described below.

B. Most-Informative Display Updating Scheme

Another approach is to attempt to minimize the total amount of iterations required in the search. The result is a scheme which tries to elicit as much information from the user as possible, while at the same time exploiting this information to end the search quickly.

At any time during the search, all of the knowledge *PicHunter* has about the target is concisely summarized by the distribution $P(T = T_i)$ over the database $\{T_1, T_2, \cdots, T_n\}$. The idea is to estimate the number of iterations left in the search, based on the distribution $P(T = T_i)$. Call this estimate $C[P(T)]$. Then the display scheme chooses the display which minimizes the expected number of future iterations, which is

$$C(X_1, \cdots, X_{N_D})$$
$$= P(\text{target not found}) \sum_a C[P(T|A = a)]$$
$$\cdot P(A = a|X_1, \cdots, X_{N_D})$$

where

$$P(A = a|X_1, \cdots, X_{N_D})$$
$$= \sum_{i=1}^n P(A = a|X_1, \cdots, X_{N_D}, T = T_i) P(T = T_i)$$

and

$$P(\text{target not found})$$
$$= 1 - P(T = X_1) - \cdots - P(T = X_{N_D})$$

and $p(T|A = a)$ is the distribution over targets after user response a.

Information theory suggests entropy as an estimate of the number of questions one needs to ask to resolve the ambiguity specified by $P(T = T_i)$

$$C[P(T)] \approx -\alpha \sum_{i=1}^n P(T = T_i) \log P(T = T_i) \qquad (5)$$

for some positive constant α which is irrelevant for the purpose of minimization. This offers an alternative interpretation of minimizing future cost: maximizing immediate information gain.

To illustrate this scheme, consider an ideal case when $N_D = 2$:

$$P_{\text{ideal}}(A = 1|X_1, X_2, T) = \begin{cases} 1, & \text{if } d(X_1, T) < d(X_2, T) \\ 0.5, & \text{if } d(X_1, T) = d(X_2, T) \\ 0, & \text{if } d(X_1, T) > d(X_2, T.) \end{cases}$$

If $A = 1$, all elements farther from T than X_1 will get zero probability. The remaining elements will have uniform probability (assuming no ties). The most-informative display updating scheme will therefore choose X_1 and X_2 so that the expected number of remaining elements is minimum. This minimum is achieved when the decision boundary $d(X_1, T) = d(X_2, T)$ exactly divides the set of targets in half. So in this idealized situation the most-informative display updating scheme behaves like the *vantage-point tree* algorithm of Yianilos [42], which is a kind of binary search on an arbitrary metric space.

Now consider the generalization

$$P_{sigmoid}(A = 1|X_1, X_2, T)$$
$$= \frac{1}{1 + \exp((d(X_1, T) - d(X_2, T))/\sigma)}.$$

When $\sigma \to 0$, this is the same as P_{ideal}. When $0 < \sigma < \infty$, there is a smooth transition from probability zero to probability one as T varies. When $\sigma \to \infty$, outcomes are completely random. This formula can be interpreted as P_{ideal} after corrupting the distance measurements with Gaussian noise. The parameter σ can therefore be interpreted as the degree of precision in the distance measurements.

Unfortunately, finding $X_1, \cdots, X_{N_D}$ to minimize $C(X_1, \cdots, X_{N_D})$ is a nontrivial task. An incremental approach in N_D does not seem possible, since an optimal display for $N_D - 1$ can be far from an optimal display for N_D. The problem is at least as hard as vector quantization, which we know can only be solved approximately by local search algorithms. Local search does not seem feasible here, since evaluating C is quite costly and there can be many local minima. One needs an optimization scheme which can give decent results with a small number of evaluations. Inspired by Yianilos's vantage-point tree algorithm, we chose a Monte Carlo approach: sample several random displays $X_1, \cdots, X_{N_D}$ from the distribution $P(T = T_i)$ and choose the one which minimizes C. Though crude, it still achieves considerable gains over the most-probable display update strategy.

C. Related Work

The general idea of maximizing the expected information from a query has also been pursued in the machine learning literature under the name "active learning" or "learning with

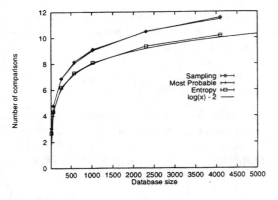

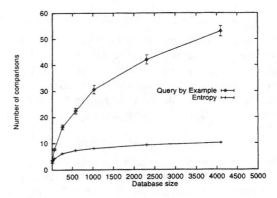

Fig. 3.   Number of iterations needed to find a target, for varying database sizes and search strategies. User actions were generated according to P_{ideal}.

Fig. 4.   Same as Fig. 3, but including the query-by-example method.

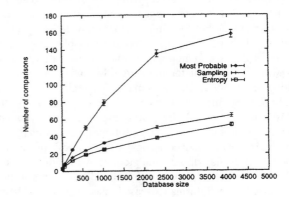

Fig. 5.   Here, user actions were generated according to $p_{sigmoid}$ with $\sigma = 0.1$.

queries" [43]. Active learning techniques have been shown to outperform simple probability ranking for document classification [44]. We know of no application of active learning techniques to database retrieval.

Comparison searching with errors has also been studied in the theoretical computer science literature. The algorithm of Rivest *et al.* [45] assumes that the number of errors has a known bound. Nevertheless, their algorithm is similar to the one presented here, in the sense that it minimizes at each step an information-theoretic bound on the number of future comparisons. The algorithm of Pelc [46] allows errors to occur at random but requires them to be independent of the comparison and the target and furthermore does not guarantee that the target is found. So while both of these algorithms run in provably logarithmic time, they also operate under more restrictive conditions than *PicHunter*.

D. Simulation Results

This section evaluates these two display update schemes (most-probable and most-informative) by comparing them to other plausible methods for choosing $X_1, \cdots, X_{N_D}$:

a) Sampling: Sample $X_1, \cdots, X_{N_D}$ from the distribution $P(T = T_i)$. This is a special case of the Most Informative scheme where only one Monte Carlo sample is drawn.

b) Query by example: Let $X_1, \cdots, X_{N_D}$ be the N_D closest items to the winner of the last comparison. This is a favorite approach in systems without relevance feedback [7]. It does not exploit memory or a stochastic user model. The idea is to simulate a user's responses by sampling from the stochastic user model. The database is synthetic, consisting of points uniformly-distributed inside the unit square. This allows databases of varying sizes to be easily drawn. The simulated users used the Euclidean distance measure.

1) Deterministic Case: Fig. 3 plots the empirical average search time for finding a randomly selected target as a function of database size, using the most probable, sampling, and most informative (entropy) schemes. The number of choices N_D was two. User actions were generated by the P_{ideal} model. In all experiments, the average is over 1000 searches, each with a different target, and the database was resampled ten times. Performance of these three schemes is comparable, scaling like $\log_2 n$. In particular, the Most Informative scheme is virtually

optimal, with deviations only due to a limited number of Monte Carlo samples. The query-by-example scheme is quite different, as shown in Fig. 4 note the change in vertical scale. The query-by-example method is not exploiting comparison information very well; its time scales as $n^{0.5}$. Increasing N_D or the dimensionality will reduce the difference between the four schemes.

2) Nondeterministic Case: Fig. 5 shows what happens when user actions are generated by the $p_{sigmoid}$ model, with $\sigma = 0.1$. Increasing the database size causes the unit square to be sampled more and more finely, while the distance uncertainty threshold σ remains the same. Thus it is much harder to isolate a particular target in a large database than in a small one, as would be true in a real situation. Again, the Sampling and Most Informative schemes are similar in search time, which scales like a square root. However, the fragility of the Most Probable scheme is evident here. Fig. 6 also reveals a large discrepancy in the query-by-example scheme. An explanation for this is that the most probable and query-by-example schemes tend to choose elements which are close together in feature space—exactly when comparisons are most unreliable. Entropy-minimization, by contrast, automatically chooses displays for which comparisons are reliable. The most probable scheme also does not properly exploit broad and nonuniform distributions, or distributions which are multimodal. Furthermore, a multimodal distribution causes this scheme to switch to different parts of the database between iterations, which is disconcerting to a real user.

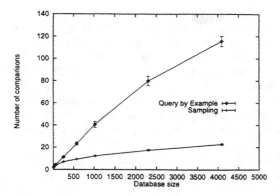

Fig. 6.   Same as Fig. 6. but including the query-by-example method. n square.

TABLE V

RESULTS OF THE EXPERIMENTS THAT TESTED ENTROPY-BASED DISPLAY UPDATING SCHEMES TO TRADITIONAL SCHEMES, AS WELL AS THE EFFECTIVENESS OF THE NEW PICTORIAL FEATURES. THE EXPECTED VALUE OF V UNDER RANDOM SEARCH IS 83.3

PicHunter Version	EB'	EP'	ES	RB' MRB'	AB' NAB'	RS MRS	RP MRP
No. displays, V	11.3	25.8	16.0	12.0	20.4	11.8	29.6
Standard Error, SE	1.16	3.40	1.74	1.17	2.52	.755	1.70
Variability, SE/V	.103	.132	.109	.098	.124	.064	.057
V, 2 exper. users	6.80	10.2	8.30	8.65	11.5		

E. Experiments on Updating Schemes

The most recent experiments on *PicHunter*, reported here for the first time, addressed two issues. 1) Compare performances with the two most promising display updating schemes. 2) Evaluate the new pictorial features introduced in Section IV-A. Toward this end, we tested seven versions of *PicHunter*, coded with a digraph notation XY that is analogous to that used in Section V-D. Some of these versions were the same as those tested previously (Section V-D); in these cases we label the scheme with the trigraph notation used in Section V-D next to the new digraph notation. The first letter X of the digraph XY represents the display-updating mode: E stands for the entropy-based "most-informative" updating. R stands for a relative-distance-based, most-probable scheme that uses memory. A is similar to R, but uses an absolute distance criterion without memory ("query-by-example"). The second letter Y of the digraph XY denotes the features used by the model for similarity judgments: P for pictorial only, S for semantic only, and B for both, with P' denoting the new pictorial features, and $B' = S + P'$ denoting the combination of the semantic features and the new pictorial features (the semantic features remained the same). The seven versions are the following: EB', EP', and ES, which are entropy-based schemes with S + P', P', and S, respectively; RB' and AB', which are the same as the versions denoted by MRB' and NAB' in the trigraph notation, but using the combination of the new pictorial features and the semantic features; finally, RS and RP, which are identical to versions MRS and MRP of Section V-D. All seven versions were run with the same set of 15 target images, which was different from the set of 15 images of the experiments of Section V-D. seven users, who were naive as to the purposes of the experiment and had never used *PicHunter* before, participated in the 7 × 7 Latin-square design [33]. The results are shown in Table V, which uses the same notation as that of Tables I and II. The same two experienced users who participated in all the previous experiments also ran a subset of the experiments.

The user model in the new version of *PicHunter* (the results of which are shown in the first five columns) differs from the old one (last two columns) in two major ways, besides the pictorial features. 1) The sigmoid slope *sigma* and the feature weights w_i are different, since they are based on more training data, and optimized in a better way than before. This affects the performance of individual metrics as well as combinations of metrics. 2) The user model in the old version was an approximate softmin while the new version uses an exact softmin.

One can make the following observations on the data of Table V. First, a comparison of the entropy-based schemes reveals that the combination of both semantic and pictorial features (EB') results in better performances than using either semantic (ES) or pictorial (EP') features alone, as expected. This expected behavior is unlike the surprising pattern of results of the experiments in Section V-D. One possibility for the difference is that the new set P' of pictorial features is better than the original ones P, hence they improve performance when they combine with the semantic features. Second, the best entropy-based scheme (EB') is at least as good as the best most-probable scheme (MRB'), and both are much better than the QBE search (NAB'). The superiority of the entropy-based scheme is even more evident in the results of the experienced users. It is interesting to note that such a display strategy produces a qualitatively different feel to the overall system. At the beginning of the search, the displayed set of images shows a large variety, which is in contrast to traditional display algorithms that attempt to display a set of very similar images. Third, the conditions RS and RP were used in order to compare the old version to the new one, where both were tested with the common new set of 15 target images. The data indicate that the combination of both S and P' features (RB') does not seem to yield an improvement over the semantics-only version (RS), which performs remarkably well. Parenthetically, one piece of useful data that would enable a complete comparison is performance of the most-probable scheme with the new pictorial features alone, i.e., the RP' scheme.

At this point, it is useful to reflect on the improvements of the present schemes as compared with earlier versions. In the original implementation, about half of the searches by first-time users were labeled "unsuccessful" in that users gave up after an excessive number of iterations. The average number of images visited *in the successful searches only* was 300 [3] which was 13.3% of the expected number under random search for the 4522-image database. This number must be at least doubled if we want to include the effect of the unsuccessful searches. By contrast, our users had only successful searches by definition, because they were required to continue searching until the target was found. This requirement necessitated some excessively long searches, which may be statistical outliers, yet their lengths inflate the mean value. Despite this, the improved schemes converged after visiting, on average, 100.8 images, which is still 13.4% of the expected number under random search for the

1500-image database. Experienced users do a lot better, averaging 8.2% of the expected length of random searches. Consistent users in *PicHunter* evaluations, in addition to the authors, report that present versions of *PicHunter* perform remarkably better than earlier versions in locating targets efficiently. It must be emphasized that these figures are for target testing, which is the most demanding of the search types.

VIII. EXTENSIONS

All *PicHunter* versions to date have been using the target search paradigm. However, when a user operates *PicHunter* to search for images that are similar to a prototype image, say, a North-Pole scene, the system quickly produces displays with similar images; in a lax sense, under these conditions, this type of search can be considered as a category search. More formally, however, *PicHunter* can become a *category-search* engine if the Bayesian scheme is modified to treat sets of images rather than individual images. The challenge for the system would be to discern the commonality of the features that specify a certain category that the user has in mind.

The main characteristic of *open-ended browsing* is that users change their goals during the search either gradually or quite abruptly, as a result of having encountered something interesting that they had not even considered at the beginning of the search. Accommodating these changes necessitates a modification of the probability distribution updating scheme. For the gradual changes one may assign weights to the probability updating factors that are strongest for the most recent iteration steps, and decay exponentially for distant past steps. For the abrupt changes, one option is to enable the user to indicate such switches, and then assign small weights to iterations prior to the abrupt change.

Although *PicHunter* was developed specifically for searching image databases, its underlying design and architecture make it suitable for other types of databases that contain digital data, such as audio passages or video-sequence databases.

IX. IDEAS FOR IMPROVEMENT

A. More Representative Databases

The main problem of the initial database, described in Section V-B, is that its images are clustered into thematic categories of 100 elements each. This results in a clustered distribution in feature space, which may not be representative of distributions in larger databases. *PicHunter*'s problem of occasionally "getting stuck," i.e., producing displays of a certain category in step after step (Section VII-A), may in fact turn out to be an advantage in databases that have a wider, nonclustered, distribution in feature space. A representative image database is needed by the CBIR community as a means toward establishing a benchmark for algorithm assessment.

B. More Relevant Image Features

PicHunter's performance improved when the new pictorial features were incorporated in the user model. The main advantage of the new features of the color autocorrelogram and the color-coherence vector is that they embody some measure of the spatial extent of each color, rather than a conventional color histogram's mere first-order statistics. Along the same lines, the user model can benefit by adding more information on the spatial properties of images, such as location, size, shape, and color of dominant objects in the image. The inclusion of spatial and figural features is especially important for the minority of color-blind people. Another feature can be the first few low-frequency Fourier components of the image's spectrum, or other measures of the distribution of spatial frequencies [17]. The need is evident for more psychophysical studies that investigate what criteria are used by humans in judging image similarity [47], [48]. Ultimately, some shape information [9] or object-based scene description [49] must be employed in CBIR systems.

C. More Complex User Feedback

PicHunter was deliberately designed with a very simple user interface, to concentrate on more fundamental issues in CBIR research. The items below remove this simplicity constraint by suggesting more complex ways of accepting users' feedback. Obviously, the user model needs to be adjusted accordingly to accommodate the additional feedback. Naturally, the introduction of new feedback modes has to be evaluated vis-a-vis the conflicting requirement for a simple user interface; appropriate experiments can decide whether there are any significant gains by the proposed idea to make it worth pursuing.

1) Specify Which Feature(s) are Relevant in a Selected Image: Post-experimental interviews with the users reveal that some of them followed a common strategy in selecting similar images in a display. They selected one image because it looked similar to the target in terms of, say, overall color, and another image for its similarity in, say, overall contrast. This suggests the possibility of allowing users to specify which feature(s) make a selected image desirable, and can be extended to cover semantic features as well.

2) Strength of Selected Image: Independently of specifying feature relevance, the user could also indicate the degree, or strength, of similarity between a selected image and the pursued target. This can be done by providing either a slide bar or a series of buttons below each image in the display.

3) Portions of Selected Image: Yet another independent form of more complex user feedback is to indicate the portion(s) of the image that is (are) similar to the target. The interface can still maintain simplicity by allowing the user to circumscribe relevant portions using the mouse.

D. More Complex Displays

The first three items below discuss how best to start the iteration process by using as informative an initial display as possible (the first item deals with expanding the current version by just providing more images in the initial display, the next two deal with initial queries). The last item provides the user with information on why images were selected to be included in the current display.

1) Initial Display: It would be helpful to give the user a head start by using a more complex initial display, keeping displays in the rest of the iterations as simple as described so far. For the particular database that we worked with, one idea that we experimented with was to take advantage of the fact that the database contained clusters in feature space. Thus we included in the first display a large number of images (50 or so), each being at the center of a cluster. This seemed to speed up search time but as yet we have no comprehensive data from such informal experiments.

2) Initial Query Template: PicHunter can be modified to add a feature that is common in many "query-by-example" CBIR systems that use a "sketch" to specify a template in order to start a search with a better-than-random initial display. The user can be given the option to select desirable values for the pictorial features by using, say, "slide bars." These bars can be used to specify mean brightness, luminance contrast, color content, etc. This will enable the user to start the search with a good guess in the first iteration.

3) Initial Query: Just as textual search engines do with words and phrases, CBIR systems may use Boolean expressions on semantics. The analogy is the following: with a database browser, one specifies logical expressions of words when searching for a paper in the literature; by analogy, one can use self-explanatory icons (such as for tree, house, animal, town, aircraft, person, crowd, lake, etc.), and build an interface for forming Boolean expressions that characterize the target image. This will enable users to start with an initial display that is very close to the desired target.

4) Which Features Caused an Image to be Displayed: The previous subsection dealt with allowing users to provide more complex feedback to the system. Reciprocally, users can benefit by knowing *PicHunter*'s current "beliefs," as this will give them an idea of how their choices affect the system. A simple way is to provide an indicator, next to each displayed image, on the system's relative strength of belief. A more complex display could indicate which feature(s) caused each image to be selected in the current display.

E. Improved User Model

One area in which the scheme can be improved is in handling the special case in which the user does not select any image in the current display before hitting the "GO" button to continue the search. This is an essential special case because users frequently find themselves forced to proceed to the next iteration without selecting any image. Currently, the program keeps the probability vector unchanged and then enters the display-update routine, in essence ignoring the user's action. However, some, perhaps most, users make this selection precisely to indicate that they want to avoid the types of displayed images. Experiments are needed to explore modifications to the algorithm for dealing with this special case.

X. Conclusions—Discussion

PicHunter's new approach is its formulation on a Bayesian framework, which tries to predict the user's actions for refining its answers to converge to a desired target image. The central data structure is a *vector of posterior probability distribution* across the entire database, i.e., each image has an entry in the vector that represents the probability of its being the target.

This distribution is updated based on the user action after each iterative display. This action is "interpreted" by the *user model*, which is the second major component of the system, together with the probability vector. This is an action-predictor model that uses rudimentary knowledge of humans' judgments of image similarity, based on empirically derived pictorial and semantic features. The user model was refined on the basis of data obtained from our similarity judgment experiments (Section IV-C). The third major component, the *display-updating scheme*, is concerned with how to select the images for the next iteration's display. We presented two major alternatives, a most-probable and a most-informative scheme, which exhibited considerably improved performances over alternative schemes. Overall, the system performs quite well for a wide spectrum of users tested on a wide variety of target images. The improvement over earlier versions, as verified by the reported experiments and attested by consistent users of the system, is very promising.

In comparing algorithms based on their performances under the target testing scheme, we make the implicit assumption that systems which are optimized under this target testing condition will also perform well in category searches and open-ended browsing. We reported on experiments that support this assumption when the target testing version is used for a form of category searching (Section V-E). Performance under open-ended browsing is much more difficult to quantify because of the vague nature of the task at hand. The main requirement in open-ended browsing is that the system display images that are similar to those selected by the user, and avoid displaying images that are similar to the nonselected images, resulting in appropriate changes to the display updating scheme. At the same time, because the goal changes during the search, the user must be allowed to reset the memory when he/she makes such a goal change, so that earlier choices no longer affect the display updating decisions.

It would be highly desirable to rank-order the various criteria used by humans for judging image similarity according to their importance. Weights can the be assigned to such criteria according to the role they play in predicting judgment of similarity by humans. Relevant research has been carried out on the application of multidimensional scaling (MDS) methods for finding principal attributes to characterize texture perception [47]. Much image processing research has also been conducted for utilizing texture as a pictorial feature in CBIR systems [14], [50], [51]. Rogowitz *et al.*[48] applied MDS analysis to humans' judgments of similarity using natural images; this task is quite complex, mainly due to the presence of semantics. An interesting experiment along these lines is to let humans play the role of *PicHunter*, to see what criteria they use, and to compare their performance with that of *PicHunter*.

The computation performed by *PicHunter* with each user interaction, and its main memory space requirements scale linearly with the number of images in the database assuming the user model requires constant time. Execution time is dominated by the user model,[4] and space by the storage of

---

[4]Any machine learning technique capable of producing a predictive model may be used to implement the required user model, so it is hard to say anything general about its computational burden.

feature vectors.[5] As such our approach might be expected to handle perhaps millions of images in today's technological environment, but not hundreds of millions. We remark that approximating its Bayesian update with a sublinear number of user model executions and the feature vectors in secondary storage, represents an interesting area for future theoretical and systems work.

While we have demonstrated search times that are much shorter than brute force, they are clearly not short enough to satisfy many users. It is possible that our pure relevance feedback approach might lead to a fully acceptable system, but it is also possible that a hybrid approach will prove best. That is, one that involves some explicit querying, but uses relevance feedback to further shorten the search.

Our experiments indicate that humans attend to the semantic content of images in judging similarity. Highly specialized databases, such as medical image databases in large medical centers, have started to get semantically annotated, and the trend appears to carry to images in generic electronic libraries. Thus, it seems that searching for an image will have much in common with searching for text documents in library databases.

In all our experiments, experienced users performed at a level that was considerably better than users with little experience, as expected. For example, they completed the average search by visiting only 65.4% and 53.2%, respectively, of the images visited by first-time users for the experiments reported in Sections V-D and VII-E. It must be noted, however, that even first-time users improve their scores substantially, after we explained to them the algorithm's user model (Section VI-B). This training was very brief, lasting less than 8 min, after which their (already good) pretraining performance improved by reducing the search length by about 20%. This substantial improvement after minimal training of nonexpert users is a desirable feature for a search engine, enabling the development of a short on-line training session for first-time users.

Most published papers provide data on the search length in terms of how many iterations are needed before users find an image that is similar to a desired target. This, however, may not be a reliable measure, because even a random search can produce relatively short search lengths, as shown in the experiments of Section V-E (column RAND/C in Table II). In fact, this latter search length could be used as a baseline against which to measure the performance of an algorithm under test. Even better, we believe that data under the target search paradigm offer an objective measure of performance. In addition, this measure exhibits small standard deviations across users' scores, when each user's score is averaged over an adequately large number of searches with different targets, whereas the corresponding random-search baseline measure exhibits much higher variability [5], [6]. Thus, target testing requires experiments with fewer users to establish the same degree of confidence in the statistics.

The experiments in this paper were designed with *PicHunter* in mind. Nevertheless, their results and findings are useful and potentially applicable to any CBIR system and, more generally, to any system that involves judgment of image similarity by humans.

ACKNOWLEDGMENT

The authors thank Y. Hara and K. Hirata, NEC Central Laboratories, for directing our attention to CBIR system research and for providing us with their system and image database; J. Ghosn, K. Lang, and S. Omohundro, who have contributed significantly in *PicHunter*'s development; B. Krovetz, T. Shamoon, and H. Stone for valuable discussions; the anonymous reviewers for their useful suggestion; E. Brooks, T. Conway, and S. Shah for administering experiments; and A. Feher for providing technical support.

REFERENCES

[1] I. J. Cox, J. Ghosn, M. L. Miller, T. V. Papathomas, and P. N. Yianilos, "Hidden annotation in content based image retrieval," in *Proc. IEEE Workshop on Content-Based Access of Image and Video Libraries*, 1997, pp. 76–81.

[2] I. J. Cox, M. L. Miller, S. M. Omohundro, and P. N. Yianilos, "Pichunter: Bayesian relevance feedback for image retrieval," in *Proc. Int. Conf. Pattern Recognition*, vol. 3, 1996, pp. 362–369.

[3] ——, "Target testing and the *PicHunter* Bayesian multimedia retrieval system," in *Proc. 3rd Forum on Research and Technology Advances in Digital Libraries, ADL'96*, 1996, pp. 66–75.

[4] I. J. Cox, M. L. Miller, T. P. Minka, and P. N. Yianilos, "An optimized interaction strategy for bayesian relevance feedback," in *Proc. IEEE Conf. Computer Vision and Pattern Recognition*, 1998, pp. 553–558.

[5] T. V. Papathomas *et al.*, "Psychophysical studies of the performance of an image database retrieval system," in *IS&T/SPIE Symp. Electronic Imaging: Science and Technology, Conf. on Human Vision and Electronic Imaging III*, 1998, pp. 591–602.

[6] T. V. Papathomas *et al.*, "Psychophysical evaluation for the performance of content-based image retrieval systems," *Investigative Ophthalmology and Visual Science*, vol. 39, no. 4, p. S1096, 1998.

[7] M. Flickner *et al.*, "Query by image and video content: The QBIC system," *Computer*, vol. 28, pp. 23–32, 1995.

[8] D. Forsyth, J. Malik, and R. Wilensky, "Searching for digital pictures," *Sci. Amer.*, vol. 276, pp. 88–93, 1997.

[9] B. Gunsel and A. M. Tekalp, "Shape similarity matching for query-by-example," *Pattern Recognit.*, vol. 31, pp. 931–944, 1998.

[10] B. Gunsel, A. M. Tekalp, and P. J. L. van Beek, "Content-based access to video objects: Temporal segmentation, visual summarization, and feature extraction," *Signal Process.*, vol. 66, pp. 261–280, 1998.

[11] K. Hirata and T. Kato, "Query by visual example: content based image retrieval," in *Advances in Database Technology—EDBT'92*, A. Pirotte, C. Delobel, and G. Gottlob, Eds. Berlin Germany: Springer-Verlag, 1992.

[12] T. Kato *et al.*, "Cognitive view mechanism for multimedia database system," in *IMS '91 Proc.: First Int. Workshop on Interoperability in Multidatabase Systems*, 1991, pp. 179–186.

[13] W. Y. Ma and B. S. Manjunath, "A texture thesaurus for browsing large aerial photographs," *J. Amer. Soc. Inform. Sci.*, vol. 49, pp. 633–644, 1998.

[14] B. S. Manjunath and W. Y. Ma, "Texture features for browsing and retrieval of image data," *IEEE Trans. Pattern Anal. Machine Intell.*, vol. 18, pp. 837–842, 1996.

[15] A. Pentland, R. W. Picard, and S. Sclaroff, "Photobook: Content-based manipulation of image databases," *Int. J. Comput. Vis.*, vol. 18, pp. 233–254, 1996.

[16] Y. Rui, T. S. Huang, and S. Mehrotra, "Content-based image retrieval with relevance feedback in MARS," in *Proc. IEEE Int. Conf. Image Processing*, Santa Barbara, CA, Oct. 1997.

[17] H. S. Stone and C.-S. Li, "Image matching by means of intensity and texture matching in the Fourier domain," in *Proc. SPIE Storage and Retrieval for Image and Video Databases*, 1996, pp. 337–349.

[18] Q. Tain and H. J. Zhang, "Digital video analysis and recognition for content-based access," *ACM Comput. Surv.*, vol. 27, no. 4, 1995.

[19] G. Yihong, Z. Hongjiang, and C. H. Chuan, "An image database system with fast image indexing capability based on color histograms," in *Proc. 1994 IEEE Region 10's Ninth Ann. Int. Conf. Theme: Frontiers of Computer Technology*, 1994, pp. 407–411.

---

[5]If an entropic display update is used, its computational burden is significant as well.

[20] H. J. Zhang, C. Y. Low, S. W. Smoliar, and J. H. Wu, "Video parsing, retrieval and browsing: An integrated and content-based solution," in *Proc. ACM Multimedia*, Nov. 1995.

[21] A. Del Bimbo, P. Pala, and S. Santini, "Visual image retrieval by elastic deformation of object sketches," in *Proc. IEEE Symp. Visual Languages*, 1994, pp. 216–223.

[22] Y. Rui, T. S. Huang, and S. Mehrotra, "Relevance feedback techniques in interactive content-based image retrieval," in *Proc. IS&T and SPIE Storage and Retrieval of Image and Video Databases VI*, San Jose, CA, Jan. 1998.

[23] T. P. Minka and R. W. Picard, "Interactive learning with a 'society of models'," *Pattern Recognit.*, vol. 30, pp. 565–581, 1997.

[24] J. Huang et al., "Image indexing using color correlograms," in *Proc. IEEE Computer Vision and Pattern Recognition Conf.*, San Juan, PR, June 1997, pp. 762–768.

[25] G. Pass, R. Zabih, and J. Miller, "Comparing images using color coherence vectors," in *Proc. 4th ACM Conf. Multimedia*, Boston, MA, Nov. 1996.

[26] E. Saber, A. M. Tekalp, R. Eschbach, and K. Knox, "Annotation of natural scenes using adaptive color segmentation," *Proc. SPIE*, vol. 2421, pp. 72–80, 1995.

[27] J. R. Smith and S.-F. Chang, "Visually searching the web for content," *IEEE Multimedia*, vol. 4, no. 3, pp. 12–20, 1997.

[28] M. Stricker and A. Dimai, "Color indexing with weak spatial constraints," in *Proc. SPIE Storage and Retrieval for Image and Video Databases*, 1996, pp. 29–40.

[29] H. J. Zhang, Y. Gong, C. Y. Low, and S. W. Smoliar, "Image retrieval based on color features: An evaluation study," in *Proc. SPIE Conf. Digital Storage and Archival*, Oct. 1995.

[30] T. Kurita and T. Kato, "Learning of personal visual impressions for image database systems," in *Proc. Second Int. Conf. Document Analysis and Recognition*, 1993, pp. 547–552.

[31] M. Eisenberg and C. Barry, "Order effects: A preliminary study of the possible influence of presentation order on user judgements of document relevance," *Proc. Amer. Soc. Information Science*, pp. 80–86, 1986.

[32] Corel Corp, , Corel stock photo library, Ont., Canada, 1990.

[33] G. E. P. Box, W. G. Hunter, and J. S. Hunter, *Statistics for Experimenters: An Introduction to Design, Analysis, and Model Building*, New York: Wiley , 1978.

[34] J. Barros, J. French, W. Martin, P. Kelly, and J. M. White, "Indexing multispectral images for content-based retrieval," in *Proc. 23rd AIPR Workshop on Image and Information Systems*, Washington, DC, Oct. 1994.

[35] M. Hirakawa and E. Jungert, "An image database system facilitating icon-driven spatial information definition and retrieval," in *Proc. 1991 IEEE Workshop on Visual Languages*, 1991, pp. 192–198.

[36] A. Pentland, R. W. Picard, and S. Sclaroff, "Photobook: Content-based manipulation of image databases," in *Proc. SPIE Storage and Retrieval for Image and Video Databases*, 1994, pp. 34–47.

[37] P. M. Kelly and T. M. Cannon, "Candid: Comparison algorithm for navigating digital image databases," in *Proc. 7th Int. Working Conf. Scientific and Statistical Database Management*, 1994, pp. 252–258.

[38] M. Stricker and M. Swain, "The capacity of color histogram indexing," in *Proc. 1994 IEEE Computer Soc. Conf. Computer Vision and Pattern Recognition*, 1994, pp. 704–708.

[39] M. J. Swain and D. H. Ballard, "Indexing via color histograms," in *Proc. 3rd Int. Conf. Computer Vision*, 1990, pp. 390–393.

[40] C. Frankel, M. J. Swain, and V. Athitsos, "Webseer: An image search engine for the world wide web," Dept. Comput. Sci., Univ. Chicago , Chicago, IL, Tech. Rep. TR-96-14, July 1996.

[41] D. Haines and W. B. Croft, "Relevance feedback and inference networks," in *Proc. 16th Annu. Int. ACM SIGIR Conf. Research and Development in Information Retrieval*, 1993, pp. 2–11.

[42] P. N. Yianilos, "Data structures and algorithms for nearest neighbor search in general metric spaces," in *Proc. 5th Annu. ACM-SIAM Symp. Discrete Algorithms (SODA)*, 1993.

[43] Y. Freund, H. S. Seung, E. Shamir, and N. Tishby, "Selective sampling using the query by committee algorithm," in *Advances in Neural Information Processing Systems*. Cambridge, MA: MIT Press, 1993.

[44] D. D. Lewis and W. A. Gale, "A sequential algorithm for training text classifiers," in *Proc. ACM-SIGIR Conf. R&D in Information Retrieval* Dublin, Ireland, July 1994.

[45] R. L. Rivest, A. R. Meyer, D. J. Kleitman, K. Winklmann, and J. Spencer, "Coping with errors in binary search procedures," *J. Comput. Syst. Sci.*, vol. 20, pp. 396–404, 1980.

[46] A. Pelc, "Searching with known error probability," *Theoret. Comput. Sci.*, vol. 63, pp. 185–202, 1989.

[47] R. A. Rao and G. L. Lohse, "Toward a texture naming system: Identifying relevant dimensions of texture," *Vis. Res.*, vol. 36, pp. 1649–1669, 1996.

[48] B. Rogowitz et al., "Perceptual image similarity experiments," in *IS&T/SPIE Symp. Electronic Imaging: Science and Technology, Conf. Human Vision and Electronic Imaging III*, 1998, pp. 576–590.

[49] J. Ponce, A. Zisserman, and M. Hebert, *Object Representation in Computer Vision—II*, ser. Number 1144 in LNCS. Berlin, Germany: Springer-Verlag, 1996.

[50] A. Kankanhalli and H. J. Zhang, "Using texture for image retrieval," in *Proc. ICARCV'94*, 1994.

[51] M. Beatty and B. S. Manjunath, "Dimensionality reduction using multi-dimensional scaling for content-based retrieval," in *IEEE Int. Conf. Image Processing*, 1997.

[52] W. Y. Ma and B. S. Manjunath, "Netra: A toolbox for navigating large image databases," in *IEEE Int. Conf. Image Processing*, 1997.

[53] W. Y. Ma and B. S. Manjunath, "Texture features and learning similarity," in *Proc. IEEE Conf. Computer Vision and Pattern Recognition*, 1996, pp. 425–430.

[54] V. Ogle and M. Stonebraker, "Chabot: Retrieval from a relational database of images," *Computer*, vol. 28, no. 9, pp. 40–48, 1995.

[55] R. Rickman and J. Stonham, "Content-based image retrieval using color tuple histograms," in *Proc. SPIE Storage and Retrieval for Image and Video Databases*, 1996.

[56] J. R. Smith and S.-F. Chang, "Visually searching the web for content," *IEEE Multimedia*, vol. 4, 1997.

[57] M. Davis, "Media Streams: An iconic visual language for video representation," in *Readings in Human-Computer Interaction: Toward the Year 2000*, 2nd ed, R. M. Baecker, J. Grudin, W. A. S. Buxton, and S. Greenberg, Eds. San Francisco, CA: Morgan Kaufmann , 1995, pp. 854–866.

[58] Y. Boykov, O. Veksler, and R. Zabih, "Disparity component matching for visual correspondence," in *Proc. IEEE Conf. Computer Vision and Pattern Recognition* , San Juan, PR, June 1997.

[59] G. Pass and R. Zabih, "Histogram refinement for content based image retrieval," in *Proc. IEEE Workshop on Applications of Computer Vision*, 1996, pp. 96–102.

[60] R. W. Picard and F. Liu, "A new Wold ordering for image similarity," in *Proc. IEEE Conf. Acoustics, Speech, and Signal Processing*, Adelaide, Australia, Apr. 1994, pp. V-129–V-132.

[61] D. E. Knuth, *The Art of Computer Programming*, 2nd ed. Reading, MA: Addison-Wesley, 1973, vol. 3.

[62] 94 704S. M. Omohundro, "Five balltree construction algorithms," Int. Comput. Sci. Inst., Berkeley, CA, Tech. Rep. TR-89-063, Dec. 1989.

[63] K. V. S. Murthy, "On growing better decision trees from data," Ph.D. dissertation, Johns Hopkins Univ., Baltimore, MD, 1995.

[64] W. H. Press, S. A. Teukolsky, W. T. Vetterling, and B. P. Flannery, *Numerical Recipes in C: The Art of Scientific Computing*, 2nd ed. Cambridge, U.K.: Cambridge Univ. Press, 1992.

[65] V. V. Federov, *Theory of Optimal Experiments*. New York, NY: Academic , 1972.

[66] F. Jelinek, J. D. Lafferty, and R. L. Mercer, "Basic methods of probabilistic context free grammars," in *Speech Recognition and Understanding*. ser. NATO Adv. Sci. Inst. Ser., P. Laface and R. De Mori, Eds. Berlin, Germany: Springer-Verlag, 1992, vol. F75, pp. 345–360.

[67] T. L. Booth and R. A. Thompson, "Applying probability measures to abstract languages," *IEEE Trans. Comput.*, vol. 22, pp. 442–450, 1973.

[68] N. Cressie, *Statistics for Spatial Data*, New York: Wiley, 1993.

[69] E. Saund, "A multiple cause mixture model for unsupervised learning," *Neural Comput.*, vol. 7, Jan. 1995.

[70] J. Smith and S.-F. Chang, "Tools and techniques for color image retrieval," in *Proc. SPIE Storage and Retrieval for Image and Video Databases*, 1996, pp. 426–437.

[71] R. W. Picard and T. P. Minka, "Vision texture for annotation," *J. Multimedia Syst.*, vol. 3, pp. 3–14, 1995.

[72] H. R. Turtle and W. B. Croft, "A comparison of text retrieval models," *Comput. J.*, vol. 35, pp. 279–290, 1992.

[73] A. R. Smith, "Color gamut transform pairs," *ACM Comput. Graph. (SIGGRAPH)*, vol. 12, pp. 12–19, 1978.

[74] D. Harman, "Relevance feedback revisited," in *Proc. 15th Ann Int. SIGIR*, Denmark, June 1992.

[75] I. J. Aalbersberg, "Incremental relevance feedback," in *Proc. 15th Ann Int. SIGIR* , Denmark, June 1992.

[76] M. Oda, "Context dependency effect in the formation of image concepts and its application," in *Proc. 1991 IEEE Int. Conf. Systems, Man, and Cybernetics. Decision Aiding for Complex Systems*, pp. 1673–1678.

[77] V. V. V. N. Gudivada and Raghavan, "Content-based image retrieval systems," *IEEE Computer*, vol. 28, pp. 18–22, Sept. 1995.

[78] T.-S. Chua, H.-K. Pung, G.-J. Lu, and H.-S. Jong, "A concept-based image retrieval system," in *Proc. 27th Annu. Hawaii Int. Conf. System Sciences*, 1994.

[79] C. C. Chang and S. Y. Lee, "Retrieval of similar pictures on pictorial databases," *Pattern Recognit.*, vol. 24, pp. 675–680, 1991.

[80] B. J. Oommen and C. Fothergill, "Fast learning automaton-based image examination and retrieval," *Comput. J.*, vol. 36, pp. 542–553, 1993.

[81] C. H. C. Leung, J. Hibler, and N. Mwara, "Content-based retrieval in multimedia databases," *Comput. Graph.*, vol. 28, 1994.

[82] G. Healey and D. Slater, "Global color constancy: Recognition of objects by use of illumination-invariant properties of color distributions," *J. Opt. Soc. Amer.*, vol. 11, 1994.

Thomas P. Minka received the M.Eng. degree in electrical engineering and computer science from the Massachusetts Institute of Technology (MIT) in 1996, and is currently pursuing the Ph.D. degree in electrical engineering and computer science at MIT.

He is a Research Assistant at MIT Media Laboratory. He strives for a formal Bayesian approach to statistical learning and pattern recognition problems. His interests in database retrieval include statistical models of content, relevance feedback, learning from multiple users, and adaptive visualization.

Ingemar J. Cox (M'83–SM'95) received the B.Sc. degree from the University College, London, U.K., and the Ph.D. degree from Oxford University, Oxford, U.K.

He was a Member of Technical Staff at AT&T Bell Laboratories, Murray Hill, NJ, from 1984 until 1989, where his research interests were focused on mobile robots. In 1989, he joined NEC Research Institute, Princeton, NJ, as a Senior Research Scientist in the computer science division. At NEC, his research shifted to problems in computer vision; he was responsible for creating the computer vision group at NEC. He has worked on problems related to stereo and motion correspondence and multimedia issues of image database retrieval and watermarking. He is the co-editor of two books, *Autonomous Robot Vehicles* (Berlin, Germany: Springer-Verlag, 1990), and *Partitioning Data Sets: With Applications to Psychology, Computer Vision and Target Tracking* (Providence, RI: Amer. Math. Soc.).

Dr. Cox is on the editorial board of the *International Journal of Autonomous Robots*.

Thomas V. Papathomas was born in Greece. He received the B.S., M.S., and Ph.D. degrees from Columbia University, New York.

He worked at Bell Laboratories, Murray Hill, NJ, from 1978 to 1989. Since 1989, he has been at Rutgers University, Piscataway, NJ, as Professor of biomedical engineering and Associate Director of the Laboratory of Vision Research. He is also associated with the NEC Research Center, Princeton, NJ, as a consultant. His research interests are in human and machine vision, and image processing. He is the Editor-in-Chief of *Early Vision and Beyond*, a volume of interdisciplinary research in vision (Cambridge, MA: MIT Press, 1995).

Dr. Papathomas is a member of the Editorial Board of the *International Journal of Imaging Systems and Technology*.

Matt L. Miller received the B.A. degree in cognitive science from the University of Rochester, Rochester, NY, in 1986.

He began working in computer graphics at AT&T Bell Laboratories, in 1979, after he became Lead Programmer at NPS, Sunnyvale, CA, a start-up developing color desktop publishing software. In 1987, he moved to Hollywood, CA, and divided his time between programming and working on film crews. Between 1990 and 1993, he delivered graduate-level lecture courses in color graphics at Aarhus University, Denmark, and Charles University and Czech Technical University, Prague. From 1993 to 1997, he divided his time between running Baltic Images, a company he founded in Lithuania, and consulting for NEC Institute, Princeton, NJ. In 1997, he sold Baltic Images and returned to Princeton to join Signafy Inc. He is currently with NEC Research Institute, Princeton, NJ.

Peter N. Yianilos (SM'86) received the B.S. and M.S. degrees from Emory University, Atlanta, GA, in 1978, and the Ph.D. degree in computer science from Princeton University, Princeton, NJ, in 1997.

In 1979, he founded Proximity Technology, Inc., Ft. Lauderdale, FL, which merged in 1988 to become Franklin Electronic Publishers, where he served as Chief Scientist and then President until 1991. At Franklin, his compression techniques, search algorithms, data structures, and product concepts formed the basis for the first hand-held electronic books, ranging from spellers and dictionaries to Bibles and encyclopedias. Since 1991, he has been a Senior Research Scientist at NEC Research Institute, Princeton. Within electronic publishing, his research interests include digital libraries, digital books, internet distributed storage systems, and information retrieval. Other research interests include machine learning and stochastic modeling, pattern recognition, nearest neighbor search, and data compression.

CHAPTER FIVE

Content-Based Video Browsing and Retrieval

HongJiang Zhang

Microsoft Research, China

CONSIDERING the great size of video data, developing means for management and relevance assessment of video documents is even more critical than the same process for other media types. The human production of text-based descriptive data of video content has the same shortcomings as text-based indexing of image data: It is subjective, inaccurate, and incomplete. Moreover, the manual production of video content description is even more time consuming—and thus more costly—to the point that it is almost impossible to generate descriptive text for the vast amount of video data available. Content-based image retrieval technologies can be extended to video retrieval. However, such extensions are not straightforward. Considering a video clip as a sequence of image frames, indexing each of them as a still image not only will introduce extremely high redundancy, but also will not be feasible given the number of frames in a video of even just one minute. Because video is a structured medium in which actions and events in time and space tell stories or convey particular visual information, a video program must be viewed as a document not a nonstructured sequence of frames. In other words, we need to identify structures of video, decompose video into basic components, and then build indices based on the structural information as well as the information from individual image frames.

In general, video indexing schemes involve three primary processes: *video parsing*, *content analysis* (feature extraction), and *abstraction*. These processes are significantly different and more complicated than those involved in image content indexing [1, 2]. Parsing is the process of temporal video structure segmentation. It involves the detection of temporal boundaries and identification of meaningful segments of video; thus it extracts structural information for video. Content feature extraction is similar to that of image feature extraction, but is extended to extraction of features that describe object motion, events, and actions in video sequences. Abstraction is the process of extraction or construction of a subset of video data from the original video such as key-frames or highlights as entries for shots, scenes, or stories. The result of the abstraction process forms the basis for content-based video representation and browsing. Based on the content features, often referred to as metadata, video indices can be built. As in image database systems, schemes and tools are needed to utilize the indices and content metadata to query, search, and browse large video databases to locate desired video clips. Figure 1 illustrates these processes.

Video content analysis, retrieval, and browsing as outlined above have attracted thousands of researchers from multiple research areas ranging from computer vision to signal processing to speech recognition, natural language processing, and databases. The breadth of background involved in this research is why video data requires analysis of different media and more importantly the integration of different media analyses. After a decade of many research efforts, video content analysis and retrieval has become

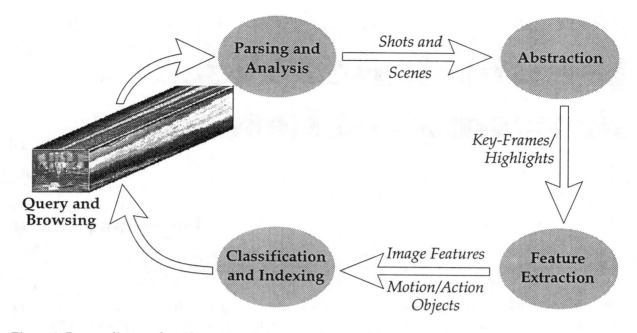

Figure 1: Process diagram for video content indexing and retrieval.

an active research field in which significant progress has been made. As a result, thousands of papers have been published and hundreds of papers are being published each year in conferences and journals.

For this chapter, we have chosen five works that represent significant milestones in the short history of this research field. Each of these five papers represents a classical approach to video structure analysis, abstraction, indexing, retrieval, and browsing. "Structured video computing," and "Video parsing, retrieval and browsing: An integrated and content-based solution," cover all aspects of video content analysis and indexing, including system designs. They, in particular, represent pioneering research efforts in this area.

VIDEO STRUCTURE PARSING

When text is indexed, a document may be first divided into smaller components such as sections, paragraphs, sentences, phrases, words, letters, and numerals, and indices can then be built on these components. In a similar way, a long video sequence has to be organized into smaller and more manageable components in order to identify index entries. These components should be organized in a hierarchy similar to storyboards used in film-making. Decomposing a long video sequence into its scenes and shots is the task of video structure parsing.

The basic structure unit for video indexing and retrieval is shots, consisting of a sequence of frames recorded contiguously and representing a continuous action in time or space. The basis for detecting shot boundaries is the fact that consecutive frames on either side of a boundary generally display a significant change in content. Hence, what is required is some suitable quantitative measure of the difference between a pair of frames. Difference metrics used in partitioning video can be divided into four major types: local pixel feature comparison [4, 6, 8], global features such as pixel histograms [4, 7, 13, 14], transform domain features such as DCT [11, 12], and motion features [5, 12]. These types of metrics have been implemented and integrated in a variety of ways to accommodate the idiosyncrasies of different video sources and have been successfully used in shot boundary detection. Several studies have compared various shot change detection algorithms [9, 10], concluding that histogram-based algorithms and MPEG compression domain feature-based algorithms outperform others in both accuracy and speed.

There are a number of different types of boundaries between shots. Cuts are the simplest boundaries and are relatively easy to detect using all the metrics. More sophisticated shot boundaries, such as dissolves, wipes, fade-ins, and fade-outs are much more difficult to detect because they involve much more gradual changes between consecutive frames. Also, changes resulting from camera operations, such as panning and zooming, may be of the same order as those from gradual transitions, which further complicates the detection. A robust partitioning algorithm should be able to detect all these different boundaries with accuracy. The first paper in this chapter, "Automatic partitioning of full-motion video," by H.J. Zhang, A. Konkanhalli, and S. W. Smoliar, is one of the classic works in the area of video parsing. This paper presents the first published algorithm—*twin-comparison*—for detecting gradual shot changes. This algorithm uses two comparisons: One looks at the difference between consecutive frames to detect sharp cuts; the other looks at accumulated difference over a sequence of frames to detect gradual transitions. This algorithm also applies a global motion analysis to filter out sequences of frames involving global or large moving objects, which may confuse the gradual transition detection. Experiments show that the twin comparison algorithm is very effective and achieves a very high level of accuracy.

The second paper in this chapter, "Structured video computing," by Y. Tonomura and colleagues, also presents a set of shot detection algorithms, as well as other video structuring and computing schemes and algorithms to be discussed later in this introduction.

The current algorithms for video structure partitioning are still limited to shot detection, and scene detection algorithms have only had limited success. Part of the problem is that scenes and stories in video are only logical layers of representation in a content of subjective semantics; there is no universal definition or rigid structure for scenes and stories. The process of detecting video scenes requires a very high level of content analysis.

Two different approaches have been taken for automatic video scene detection: one based on film production rules, the other based on *a priori* program models. Aigrain and colleagues have used filming rules to detect local (temporal) clues of macroscopic change [15]. These rules refer to transition effects, shot repetition, shot setting similarity, apparition of music in the soundtrack, editing rhythm, and camera work. The fourth paper in this chapter, "Extracting story units from long programs for video browsing and navigation," by M. Yeung and colleagues, presents a systematic

work on automated scene detection. They propose a so-called *time-constrained clustering* approach, in which they consider both visual similarity and temporal locality of shots in shot grouping and event detection. This approach is based on the idea that content presented in video programs tends to be localized in time. Two visually similar shots occurring next to each other may present a continuing event; whereas if they occurr far apart in time, they may belong to different scenes. Use of information of special temporal events, namely dialogue and fast action shots, is another essential part of this approach.

A priori model-based algorithms utilize specific structural models for video programs such as news and sports [16,17,18]. For those special video programs, the temporal structures are normally very rigid. Thus, if one can identify a few key types of shots, such as the anchors in a news video, then the rest of the shots can be classified according to the structural models, without sophisticated (and often impossible) semantic content analysis of the entire video.

In summary, general scene detection requires content analysis at a high level; the effectiveness of low-level feature-based analysis in automated scene detection is often limited. However, fusion of information from image, audio, and closed caption or transcript text analysis is a feasible solution. The work by Boreczky and Wilcox [21] is one of the many successful examples.

VIDEO ABSTRACTION AND SUMMARIZATION

When text documents are indexed, key words or summaries are used as index entries for sentences, paragraphs, chapters, or entire documents. Similarly, in video indexing, we can extract key-frames and highlight sequences as entries and visual abstractions for shots, scenes, or stories. In addition to browsing, key-frames can also be used in representing video in retrieval: A video index may be constructed based upon visual features of key-frames, and queries may be directed at key-frames using query-by-image-content techniques.

The first widely used visual abstract form of video is the key-frame, which is the still image extracted from the original video data that best represents the content of a shot in an abstract manner. The representational power of a set of key-frames depends on how they are chosen from all frames of a sequence. The challenge is that key-frame extraction must be automatic and content-based so that the key-frames retain the significant content of the video while removing all redundant information. In theory, semantic primitives of a video, such as interesting objects, actions, and events, should be used. However, such general semantic analysis is not currently feasible, especially when information from soundtracks and/or closed caption is not available. In practice, we have to rely on low-level image features and other readily available information instead. Many algorithms have been proposed for doing so.

The first effective approach to key-frame extraction using low-level image features was proposed by H.J. Zhang and colleagues, in "Video parsing, retrieval and browsing: An integrated and content-based solution," the third paper in this chapter. The fundamental idea of this approach is that the number of key-frames needed to represent a segment should be based on temporal variation of video content in the segment: If the temporal variation of content is large, the number of key-frames should also be large, and vice versa. That is, after shot segmentation, the key-frames in a shot will be selected based upon the amount of temporal variation in color histograms and motion in reference to the first frame or the last selected key-frame of the shot. According to the user studies, this approach achieves real-time processing speed, especially when MEPG compressed video is used, and reasonable accuracy. Since this paper was published, new algorithms have been proposed, many of which are capable of producing key-frames of high quality [23].

Another form of video abstraction is the "highlight" sequence, or a skimmed sequence extracted from the original video. A successful approach to such video summarization based on high-level video content analysis is to utilize information from multiple sources, including sound, speech, transcript, and image analysis of video. The last paper included in this chapter, "Video skimming and characterization through the combination of image and language understanding techniques," by M. A. Smith and T. Kanade presents the most influential work in video summarization by automated skimming, performed as part of the *Informedia* project. With this approach, low-level

and mid-level visual features, including shot boundaries, human faces, camera and object motions, and subtitles of video shots are integrated with keywords, spotted from text obtained from closed caption and speech recognition to identify video sequences that highlight the important contents. Experiments using this skimming approach have shown impressive results in generating video summaries on limited types of documentary video that have very clean speech or text (closed caption) contents, such as education video, news, or parliamentary debates.

Similar approaches to integrating audio, text, and image content analyses also have been performed by many other research groups, including with the AT&T Pictorial Transcript system [19, 20, 21]. Given the multimedia nature of video, the natural solution for content analysis and content-based indexing of video should be the utilization of content information available in all media forms. Hence, developing algorithms for such a solution is a new trend and focus in content-based video indexing research.

VIDEO CONTENT REPRESENTATION, INDEXING, AND RETRIEVAL

To support indexing and retrieval in large video databases, it is necessary to identify and compute representation primitives for video content, based on which the content of shots can be classified, indexed, and researched. These content primitives are often referred to as the content "metadata" for video, which is the focus of the new standard effort, MPEG-7.

If we consider shots as the basic indexing unit for video retrieval, then content representation of video should be based on shot features. There are two groups of such features: those associated with key-frames only and those associated with shots. The former are derived only from single key-frames, which capture representative information at only a few sampling points where key-frames are located. The latter are mostly derived from the sequence of frames of a shot. They include temporal variation of any given image feature, or feature set, and motions associated with the shot or some objects in the shot. Another effective way of representing shot content is object-based, in which visual features and motion of dominant objects in video shots are used [22, 24, 25]. This scheme is attractive because much of the object information is readily available in MPEG-4 video streams.

The third paper chosen for this chapter, presents in detail a system framework to represent and index video content using both structure data and low-level features of video. In this framework, a video document is represented at three structural levels: sequences, scenes, and shots. Shots are the basic indexing unit. The key-frames–based representation uses the same features as content-based still image retrieval (discussed in the previous chapter). In addition, high-level semantic features, such as objects (*e.g.*, a news anchor), in a key-frame [17] also are included. Shot-based features include statistical motion measures and the temporal mean and variance of color features over a shot, to provide information about activities and motion complexity and distribution that might be useful in queries. With this framework, content comparison can be performed based on key-frame–based features, shot-based temporal and motion features, object-based features, or a combination of the three. Experiments have shown that this set of features, obtained at a set of sampling points, is effective in representing motion information for shots and in retrieving shots of similar motion patterns.

Combining multiple features to define the content similarity between two video sequences of shots for retrieval is more challenging than in image retrieval, because more features, often with different importance, are involved. So far, there is very limited success in developing effective and efficient approaches to feature-based video retrieval, especially compared to retrieval of images.

VIDEO BROWSING SCHEMES

Content-based browsing is another significant issue for quick relevance assessment of video source material, given the huge data volume and the limitation of current specific goal or focus. For this reason, research on video browsing schemes is another very active and successful area in the field. The proposed browsing tools are mainly of two types: the traditional time-line and light-table display of video frames/icons [12, 26, 27, 28]; and the hierarchical or graph-based story board, based on structural and content features of video. Research in content-based video browsing has focused on the latter type of browsing schemes, and three of the five papers chosen in this chapter present a set of this type of browsing tools.

To achieve content-based browsing, we need a representation that presents the "information landscape" or structure of video in an abstracted or summarized manner. A video structure-based hierarchical browser is one of the most powerful content-based browsing tools. The first such browser was summarized in the third paper included in this chapter. In that paper's proposed framework, videos are segmented into trees, each of which represents stories, scenes, and shots, using key-frames. As we descend through the hierarchy, our attention focuses on scenes, groups of shots, single shots, and finally the key-frames of a specific shot and all frames of a shot. We also can view sequentially any particular segment of video selected from this browser at any level of the hierarchy by launching a video player.

Another hierarchical browsing scheme proposed in this paper was designed more for browsing a large collection of video clips, instead of a long video program. In this scheme, similar shots are grouped together by clustering shots or sequences based on similarity. That is, after clustering, each class of shots grouped by their similarity is represented by a key-frame determined by the centroid of the class, which is then displayed at a level of the hierarchical browser. With this type of browser, the viewer can get a rough sense of the content of the shots in a class without moving down to lower levels of the hierarchy.

An alternative approach to hierarchical browsers is the scene transition graph, proposed by M. Yeung and colleagues in "Extracting story units from long programs for video browsing and navigation," in the fourth paper in this chapter. By clustering visually similar shots into scenes, a directed graph with scenes for nodes is constructed. The resulting graph is displayed for browsing, with each node represented by a key-frame extracted from one of the shots in the node. Recent work has extended this framework to "video posters" [31].

In "Structured video computing," the second paper in this chapter, Y. Tonomura and colleagues also address the issues of content-based video browsing. In particular, they propose a video content visualization tool, VideoSpaceIcon, that utilizes camera motion information of shots to visualize the spatial and temporal content of video shots in an icon. Similar work has been explored for video browsing [3, 29, 30].

Browsing tools are particularly important for video applications on the Internet, since hierarchical browsing will allow for content selection without downloading or streaming of entire video clips, which is expensive and slow with today's Internet. To support the special needs of browsing video over the Internet, J. R. Smith proposed a system called VideoZoom to enable users to start with coarse, low-resolution views of the sequences and selectively zoom in in space and time [32]. VideoZoom decomposes the video sequences into a hierarchy of view elements, which are retrieved in a progressive fashion. The client browser incrementally builds the views by retrieving, caching, and assembling the view elements as needed. By integrating browsing and retrieval into a single progressive retrieval paradigm, VideoZoom provides a new and useful system for accessing video over the Internet.

SUMMARY

In summary, as with image retrieval, the current automated solutions for video browsing and retrieval still depend heavily, if not totally, upon the use of low-level visual features. On the other hand, the current video structure parsing, content representation, and browsing algorithms and tools can already increase productivity in video data browsing, management and other applications significantly more than in image databases. Also, when striving for visual content analysis and representation, the research community has recognized the importance of information fusion from different sources, such as speech, sound, text, and images in understanding and indexing video data. This is the trend and focus of video content analysis and content-based indexing research, and more and more of the published research will focus on this approach.

REFERENCES

[1] B. Furht, S. W. Smoliar, and H. J. Zhang, *Image and Video Processing in Multimedia Systems* (Kluwer Academic Publishers, 1995).

[2] P. Aigrain, H.J. Zhang, and D. Petkovic, "Content-based representation and retrieval of visual media: A state-of-the-art review," *International Journal of Multimedia Tools and Applications, Kluwer Academic Publishers* 3, no. 3 (1996).

[3] D. Zhong, H.J. Zhang, and S.-F. Chang, "Clustering methods for video browsing and annotation," in *Proceedings of the SPIE Conference on Storage and Retrieval for Image and Video Databases IV* (San Jose: SPIE, 1996), 239–46.

[4] A. Nagasaka and Y. Tanaka, "Automatic video indexing and full-search for video appearances," in E. Knuth and I. M. Wegener, eds., *Visual Database Systems 2*, (Amsterdam: Elsevier Science Publishers, 1992), 113–27.

[5] B. Shahraray, "Scene change detection and content-based sampling of video sequences," in *Proceedings of SPIE Conference on Digital Video Compression: Algorithm and Technologies* 2419 (Feb. 1995): 2–13.

[6] R. Zabih, K. Mai, and J. Miller, "A robust method for detecting cuts and dissolves in video sequences," in *Proceedings of the ACM 3rd International Multimedia Conference* (Nov. 1995), 189–200.

[7] P. Aigrain and P. Joly, "The automatic real-time analysis of film editing and transition effects and its applications," *Computers & Graphics* 18, no.1 (Jan.–Feb. 1994): 93–103.

[8] A. Hampapur, R. Jain, and T. E. Weymouth, "Production model based digital video segmentation," *Multimedia Tools and Applications* 1, no.1 (1995): 9–46.

[9] A. Dailianas, R. Allen, and P. England, "Comparison of automatic video segmentation algorithms," in *Proceedings of SPIE Photonics East* (Oct. 1995), 2–16.

[10] J. S. Boreczky and L. A. Rowe, "Comparison for video shot boundary detection techniques," in *Proceedings of the SPIE Conference on Storage and Retrieval for Image and Video Databases IV* (Feb. 1996): 170–79.

[11] F. Arman, A. Hsu, and M. Y. Chiu, "Feature management for large video databases," in *Proceedings of the SPIE Conference on Storage and Retrieval for Image and Video Databases I* (SPIE, 1993), 2–12.

[12] H.J. Zhang et al., "Video parsing using compressed data," in *Proceedings of the SPIE Conference on Image and Video Processing II* (Feb. 1994) 142–49.

[13] N. Vasconcelos and A. Lippman, "Statistical models of video structure for content analysis and characterization," *IEEE Transactions on Image Processing* 9, no. 1 (Jan., 2000): 3–19.

[14] I. S. Sethi and N. Patel, "A statistical approach to scene change," in *Proceedings of the SPIE Conference on Storage and Retrieval for Image and Video Databases III* (Feb. 1995): 329–38.

[15] P. Aigrain, P. Joly, and V. Longueville, "Medium-knowledge-based macro-segmentation of video into sequences," *Intelligent Multimedia Information Retrieval*, M. T. Maybury, ed., (Cambridge: AAAI/MIT Press, 1997), 159–73.

[16] D. Swanberg, C. F. Shu, and R. Jain, "Knowledge guided parsing in video databases," in *Proceedings of the SPIE Conference on Storage and Retrieval for Image and Video Databases I* (Feb. 1993): 13–24.

[17] H.J. Zhang et al., "Automatic parsing and indexing of news video," *Multimedia Systems* 2, no. 6 (1995): 256–65.

[18] Y. Gong et al., "Automatic parsing of TV soccer programs," in *Proceedings of the 2nd IEEE International Conference on Multimedia Computing and Systems* (May 1995): 167–74.

[19] B. Shahraray and D. Gibbon, "Automatic authoring of hypermedia documents of video programs," in *Proceedings of the 3rd ACM International Multimedia Conference* (Nov. 1995): 401–09.

[20] A. Merlino, D. Morey, and M. Maybury, "Broadcast navigation using story segmentation," in *Proceedings of the 5th ACM International Multimedia Conference* (1997): 381–88.

[21] J. S. Boreczky and L. D. Wilcox. "A hidden Markov model frame work for video segmentation using audio and image features," *Proceedings of ICASSP '98* (May 1998): 3741–44.

[22] A. Akutsu and Y. Tonomura, "Video tomography: An efficient method for camerawork extraction and motion analysis," in *Proceedings of the 1st ACM International Multimedia Conference* (Oct. 1993): 349–56.

[23] A. Hanjalic and R. L. Langendijk, "A new key-frame allocation method for representing stored video streams," in *Proceedings of the 1st International Workshop on Image Databases and Multimedia Search* (1996).

[24] N. Dimitrova and F. Golshani, "R for Semantic video database retrieval," in *Proceedings of the 2nd ACM International Multimedia Conference* (Oct. 1994): 219–26.

[25] S. F. Chang et al., "VideoQ: An automated content based video search system using visual cues," in *Proceedings of the 5th ACM International Multimedia Conference* (Nov. 1997): 313–24.

[26] S. Dagtas et al., "Models for motion-based video indexing and retrieval," *IEEE Transactions on Image Processing* 9, no.1 (Jan. 2000): 88–101

[27] T. G. Aguierre-Smith and G. Davenport, "The stratification system: A design environment for random access video," in *Proceedings of the 3rd International Workshop on Network and Operating System Support for Digital Audio and Video* (NDSSDAV, 1992): 250–61.

[28] H. Ueda, T. Miyatake, and S. Yoshisawa, "IMPACT: An interactive natural-motion-picture dedicated multimedia authoring system," in *Proceedings of the CHI '91* (New York: ACM, 1991), 343–50.

[29] L.Teodosio and W. Bender, "Salient video stills: Content and context preserved," in *Proceedings of the 1st ACM International Multimedia Conference* (Aug. 1993): 39–46.

[30] Y. Taniguchi, A. Akutsu, and Y. Tonomura, "PanoramaExcepts: Extracting and packing panoramas for video browsing," in *Proceedings of the 5th ACM International Multimedia Conference* (Dec. 1997): 427–36.

[31] M. M. Yeung and B.-L. Yeo, "Video visualization for compact presentation and fast browsing of pictorial content" *IEEE Transaxtions on Circuits and Systems for Video Technologies* 7, no. 5 (Oct. 1997): 971–85.

[32] J. R. Smith, "VideoZoom spatio-temporal video browser," *IEEE Transactions on Multimedia* 1, no. 2 (June 1999): 157–71.

Automatic partitioning of full-motion video

HongJiang Zhang, Atreyi Kankanhalli, Stephen W. Smoliar

Institute of Systems Science, National University of Singapore, Heng Mui Keng Terrace, Kent Ridge,
Singapore 0511, Republic of Singapore
e-mail: zhj@iss.nus.sg

Received January 10, 1993/Accepted April 10, 1993

Abstract. Partitioning a video source into meaningful segments is an important step for video indexing. We present a comprehensive study of a partitioning system that detects segment boundaries. The system is based on a set of difference metrics and it measures the content changes between video frames. A twin-comparison approach has been developed to solve the problem of detecting transitions implemented by special effects. To eliminate the false interpretation of camera movements as transitions, a motion analysis algorithm is applied to determine whether an actual transition has occurred. A technique for determining the threshold for a difference metric and a multi-pass approach to improve the computation speed and accuracy have also been developed.

Key words: Image difference analysis – Video partitioning – Video indexing – Multimedia

1 Introduction

Advances in multimedia technologies have now demonstrated that video in computers is a very important and common medium for applications as varied as education, broadcasting, publishing, and military intelligence (Mackay and Davenport 1989). The value of video is partially due to the fact that significant information about many major aspects of the world can only be successfully managed when presented in a time-varying manner. However, the effective use of video sources is seriously limited by a lack of viable systems that enable easy and effective organization and retrieval of information from those sources. Also, the time-dependent nature of video makes it a very difficult medium to represent and manage. Thus, much of the vast quantity of video that has been acquired sits on a shelf for future use without indexing (Nagasaka and Tanaka 1991). This is due to the fact that indexing requires an operator to view the entire video package and to assign index terms manually to each of its scenes. Between the abundance of unindexed video and the lack of sufficient manpower and time, such an approach is simply not feasible. Without an index, information retrieval

Correspondence to: H.J. Zhang

from video requires one to view the source during a sequential scan, but this process is slow and unreliable, particularly when compared with analogous retrieval techniques based on text. Unfortunately, when it comes to the problem of developing new techniques for indexing and searching of video sources, the intuitions we have acquired through the study of information retrieval do not translate very well into non-text media.

Clearly, research is required to improve this situation, but relatively little has been achieved towards the development of video editing and browsing tools (Mackay and Davenport 1989; Tonomura 1991). A growing interest in digital video has led to new approaches to image processing based on the creation and analysis of compressed data (Netravali and Haskell 1988; Le Gall 1991) but these activities are in their earliest stages. The Video Classification Project at the Institute of Systems Science (ISS) of the National University of Singapore (NUS) is an effort to change this situation. It aims to develop an intelligent system that can automatically classify the content of a given video package. The tangible result of this classification will consist of an index structure and a table of contents, both of which can be stored as part of the package. In this way a video package will become more like a book to anyone interested in accessing specific information.

When text is indexed, words and phrases are used as index entries for sentences, paragraphs, pages or documents. This process only selects certain key words or phrases as index terms. Similarly, a video index will require, apart from the entries used in text, key frames or frame sequences as entries for scenes or stories. Therefore, automated indexing will require the support of tools which can *detect* and *isolate* such meaningful segments in any video source. Content analysis can then be performed on individual segments in order to identify appropriate index terms.

In our study, a segment is defined as a single, uninterrupted camera shot. This reduces the partitioning task to detecting the boundaries between consecutive camera shots. The simplest transition is a *camera break*. Figure 1 illustrates a sequence of four consecutive video frames with a camera break occurring between the second and third frames. The

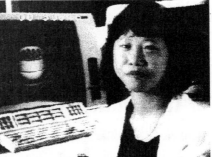

Fig. 1a–d. Four frames across a camera break from a documentary video. The first two frames are in the first camera shot, and the third and fourth frame belong to the second camera shot. There are significant content changes between the second and third frames

Fig. 2a–e. Frames in a dissolve. The first frame is the one just before the dissolve starts, and the last one is the frame immediately after the end of the dissolve. The rest are the frames within the dissolve

significant qualitative difference in content is readily apparent. If that difference can be expressed by a suitable metric, then a segment boundary can be declared whenever that metric exceeds a given threshold. Hence, establishing such metrics and techniques for applying them is the first step in our efforts to develop tools for the automatic partitioning of video packages.

The segmentation problem is also important for applications other than indexing. It is a key process in video editing, where it is generally called *scene change detection*. It also figures in the motion compensation of video for compression, where motion vectors must be computed *within* segments, rather than *across* segment boundaries (Liou 1991). However, accuracy is not as crucial for either of these applications; for example, in compression, false positives only increase the number of reference frames. By contrast, in video segmentation for indexing, such false positives would have to be corrected by manual intervention. Therefore, high accuracy is a more important requirement in automating the process.

A camera break is the simplest transition between two shots. More sophisticated techniques include dissolve, wipe, fade-in, and fade-out (Bordwell and Thompson 1993). Such special effects involve much more gradual changes between consecutive frames than does a camera break. Figure 2 shows five frames of a dissolve from a documentary video: the frame just before the dissolve begins, three frames within the dissolve, and the frame immediately after the dissolve. This sequence illustrates the gradual change that downgrades the power of a simple difference metric and a single threshold for camera break detection. Indeed, most changes are even more gradual, since dissolves usually last more than ten frames. Furthermore, the changes introduced by camera movement, such as pan and zoom, may be of the same order as that introduced by such gradual transitions. This further complicates the detection of the boundaries of camera shots, since the artefacts of camera movements must be distinguished from those of gradual shot transitions.

While there has been related work on camera break detection by other researchers (Tonomura 1991; Nagasaka and Tanaka 1991; Ruan et al. 1992), few experimental data have been reported. Also, the implementation of the difference metrics for practical video processing and an automatic determination of the cutoff threshold have not yet been addressed in the current literature. This paper presents a comprehensive experimental study of three difference metrics for video partitioning: pair-wise comparison of pixels, comparison of pixel histograms, and "likelihood ratio" comparison, where the likelihood ratio metric has not been previously discussed. It also discusses the automatic selection of the threshold for a chosen difference metric, which is a key issue in obtaining high segment accuracy, and a multi-pass technique that upgrades performance efficiency.

So far, there has been no report on algorithms that successfully detect gradual transitions. As a major contribution to the video segmentation problem, we suggest that this problem can be solved by a novel technique called twin-comparison. This technique first uses a difference metric with a reduced threshold to detect the potential frames where a gradual transition can occur; then the difference metric is used to compare the first potential transition frame with each following frame until the accumulated difference exceeds a second threshold. This interval is then interpreted to delineate the start and end frames of the transition. Motion detection and analysis techniques are then applied to distinguish camera movements from such gradual transitions. Experiments show that the approach is very effective and that it achieves a very high level of accuracy.

Before discussing the detection of gradual transitions, we first present a set of the difference metrics and their applications in detecting camera breaks in Sect. 2. In Sect. 3 we discuss how the use of a difference metric can be adapted to accommodate gradual transitions and present the twin-comparison approach. A motion analysis technique for eliminating false detection of transitions resulting from the artefacts of camera movements is presented in Sect. 3. This is followed by a discussion of automatic selection of threshold values and the multi-pass approach to improving computational efficiency in Sect. 4. Algorithmic implementation, evaluation of algorithm performance, and the application of these techniques to some "real-world" video examples are given in Sect. 5. Finally, Sect. 6 presents our conclusions and a discussion of anticipated future work.

2 Difference metrics for video partitioning

As observed in Sect. 1, the detection of transitions involves the quantification of the difference between two image frames in a video sequence. To achieve, this, we need first to define a suitable metric, so that a segment boundary can be declared whenever that metric exceeds a given threshold. Difference measures used to partition video can be divided into two major types: the pair-wise comparison of pixels or blocks, and the comparison of the histograms of pixel values. The blocks are compared with the *likelihood ràtio*, a statistic calculated over the area occupied by a given super-pixel (Kasturi and Jain 1991). These metrics can be implemented with a variety of different modifications to accommodate the idiosyncrasies of different video sources (Nagasaka and Tanaka 1991; Ruan et al. 1992) and have been used successfully in camera break detection. Details will now be discussed.

2.1 Pair-wise comparison

A simple way to detect a qualitative change between a pair of images is to compare the corresponding pixels in the two frames to determine how many pixels have changed. This approach is known as *pair-wise comparison*. In the simplest case of monochromatic images, a pixel is judged as changed if the difference between its intensity values in the two frames exceeds a given threshold t. This metric can be represented as a binary function $DP_i(k, l)$ over the domain of two-dimensional coordinates of pixels, (k, l), where the subscript i denotes the index of the frame being compared with its successor. If $P_i(k, l)$ denotes the intensity value of the pixel at coordinates (k, l) in frame i, then $DP_i(k, l)$ may be defined as follows:

$$DP_i(k, l) = \begin{cases} 1 & \text{if } |P_i(k, l) - P_{i+1}(k, l)| > t \\ 0 & \text{otherwise} \end{cases} \quad (1)$$

The pair-wise segmentation algorithm simply counts the number of pixels changed from one frame to the next according to this metric. A segment boundary is declared if more than a given percentage of the total number of pixels (given as a threshold T) have changed. Since the total number of pixels in a frame of dimensions M by N is $M * N$, this condition may be represented by the following inequality:

$$\frac{\sum_{k,l=1}^{M,N} DP_i(k,l)}{M * N} * 100 > T . \tag{2}$$

A potential problem with this metric is its sensitivity to camera movement. For instance, in the case of camera panning, a large number of objects will move in the same direction across successive frames; this means that a large number of pixels will be judged as changed even if the pan entails a shift of only a few pixels. This effect may be reduced by the use of a smoothing filter: before comparison each pixel in a frame is replaced with the mean value of its nearest neighbours. (We are currently using a 3×3 window centred on the pixel being "smoothed" for this purpose.) This also filters out some noise in the input images.

2.2 Likelihood ratio

To make the detection of camera breaks more robust, instead of comparing individual pixels we can compare corresponding *regions* (blocks) in two successive frames on the basis of second-order statistical characteristics of their intensity values. One such metric for comparing corresponding regions is called the *likelihood ratio* (Kasturi and Jain 1991). Let m_i and m_{i+1} denote the mean intensity values for a given region in two consecutive frames, and let S_i and S_{i+1} denote the corresponding variances. The following formula computes the likelihood ratio and determines whether or not it exceeds a given threshold t:

$$\frac{\left[\frac{S_i+S_{i+1}}{2} + \left(\frac{m_i-m_{i+1}}{2}\right)^2\right]^2}{S_i * S_{i+1}} > t . \tag{3}$$

Camera breaks can now be detected by first partitioning the frame into a set of sample areas. Then a camera break can be declared whenever the total number of sample areas whose likelihood ratio exceeds the threshold is sufficiently large (where "sufficiently large" will depend on how the frame is partitioned). An advantage that sample areas have over individual pixels is that the likelihood ratio raises the level of tolerance to slow and small object motion from frame to frame. This increased tolerance makes it less likely that effects such as slow motion will mistakenly be interpreted as camera breaks.

The likelihood ratio also has a broader dynamic range than does the percentage used in pair-wise comparison. This broader range makes it easier to choose a suitable threshold value t for distinguishing changed from unchanged sample areas. A potential problem with the likelihood ratio is that if two sample areas to be compared have the same mean and variance, but completely different probability density functions, no change will be detected. Fortunately, such a situation is very unlikely.

2.3 Histogram comparison

An alternative to comparing corresponding pixels or regions in successive frames is to compare some feature of the entire image. One such feature that can be used in segmentation algorithms is a histogram of intensity levels. The principle behind this algorithm is that two frames having an unchanging background and unchanging objects will show little difference in their respective histograms. The histogram comparison algorithm should be less sensitive to object motion than the pair-wise pixel comparison algorithm, since it ignores the spatial changes in a frame. One could argue that there may be cases in which two images have similar histograms but completely different content. However, the probability of such an event is sufficiently low that, in practice, we can tolerate such errors.

Let $H_i(j)$ denote the histogram value for the ith frame, where j is one of the G possible grey levels. (The number of histogram bins can be chosen on the basis of the available grey-level resolution and the desired computation time.) Then the difference between the ith frame and its successor will be given by the following formula:

$$SD_i = \sum_{j=1}^{G} |H_i(j) - H_{i+1}(j)| . \tag{4}$$

If the overall difference SD_i is larger than a given threshold T, a segment boundary is declared. To select a suitable threshold, SD_i can be normalized by dividing it by the product of G and $M * N$, the number of pixels in the frame.

Figure 3 shows grey-level histograms of the first three images shown in Fig. 1. Note the difference between the histograms across the camera break between the second and the third frames, while the histograms of the first and second frames are almost identical. Figure 4 illustrates the application of histogram comparison to a documentary video. The graph displays the sequence of SD_i values defined by Eq. 4 between every two consecutive frames over an excerpt from this source. Equation 4 was applied to grey-level intensities computed from the intensities of the three colour channels by the National Television System Committee (NTSC) conversion formula (Sect. 5.1). The graph exhibits two high pulses that correspond to two camera breaks. If an appropriate threshold is set, the breaks can be detected easily.

Equation 4 can also be applied to histograms of individual colour channels. A simple but effective approach is to use colour histogram comparison (Nagasaka and Tanaka 1991; Zhang et al. 1993): Instead of grey levels, j in Eq. 4 denotes a code value derived from the three colour intensities of a pixel. Of course, if 24 bits of colour data were translated into a 24-bit code word, that would create histograms with 2^{24} bins, which is clearly unwieldy. Consequently, only the two or three most significant bits of each colour component tend to be used to compose a colour code. A 6-bit code, providing 64 bins, has been shown to give sufficient accuracy. This approach is also more efficient for colour source material because it eliminates the need to first convert the colour intensities into grey levels.

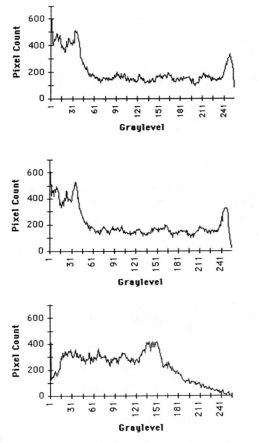

Fig. 3. Histograms of grey-level pixel values corresponding to the first three frames shown in Fig. 1

Nagasaka and Tanaka (1991) have also used the following χ^2-test equation,

$$SD_i = \sum_{j=1}^{G} \frac{|H_i(j) - H_{i+1}(j)|^2}{H_{i+1}(j)} \qquad (5)$$

to make the histogram comparison reflect the difference between two frames more strongly. However, our experiments show that while this equation enhances the difference between two frames across a camera break, it also increases the difference between frames representing small changes due to camera or object movements. Therefore, the overall performance is not necessarily better than that achieved by using Eq. 4, while Eq. 5 also requires more computation time.

2.4. Limitations

In addition to the weaknesses of each of the individual metrics that have already been cited, all three types of difference metric face a severe problem if there are moving objects (of either large size or of high speed) or a sharp illumination change between two frames in a common shot, resulting in a false detection of a camera break. Flashing lights and flick-ering objects (such as video monitors) are common sources of errors, as will be seen in Sect. 5.

When the illumination does not change over the entire frame, the problem can be overcome by a robust approach developed by Nagasaka and Tanaka (1991) to accommodate momentary noise. It is based on the assumption that such noise usually influences no more than half of an entire frame. Therefore, a frame can be divided into a 4 × 4 grid of 16 rectangular regions; and, instead of comparing entire frames, corresponding regions are compared. This yields 16 difference values, and the camera break detection is only based on the sum of the eight lowest difference values. Such a selection of data is meant to eliminate the errors introduced by momentary noise. We plan to test this technique, but we anticipate that its performance might be made more robust by taking the sum of the median eight difference values (eliminating the four extremes from both ends).

3 Gradual transition detection

We now present the twin-comparison approach that adapts a difference metric to accommodate gradual transitions, which is our main contribution to automatic video partitioning. This discussion will be based on the histogram-comparison difference metric. We also discuss how a technique based on motion detection and analysis can be used to identify intervals of camera movement that may be confused with gradual transitions between camera shots.

3.1 The twin-comparison approach for detecting special effects

As one can observe from Fig. 4, the graph of the frame-to-frame histogram differences for a sequence exhibits two high pulses that correspond to two camera breaks. It is easy to select a suitable cutoff threshold value (such as 50) for detecting these camera breaks. However, the inset of this graph displays another sequence of pulses the values of which are higher than those of their neighbour but are significantly lower than the cutoff threshold. This inset displays the difference values for the dissolve sequence shown in Fig. 2 and illustrates why a simple application of this difference metric is inadequate.

The simplest approach to this problem would be to lower the threshold. Unfortunately, lower thresholds cannot be effectively employed, because the difference values that occur during the gradual transition implemented by a special effect may be smaller than those that occur between the frames within a camera shot. For example, object motion, camera panning, and zooming also entail changes in the computed difference value. If the cutoff threshold is too low, such changes may easily be registered as "false positives". The problem is that a single threshold value is being made to account for all segment boundaries, regardless of context. This appears to be asking too much of a single number, so a new approach has to be developed.

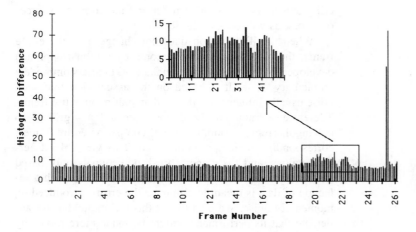

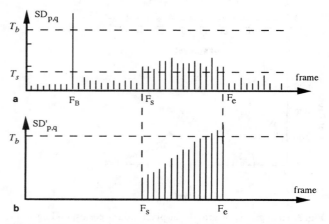

Fig. 4. A sequence of frame-to-frame histogram differences obtained from a documentary video, where differences corresponding to both camera breaks and transitions implemented by special effects can be observed

In Fig. 2 it is obvious that the first and the last frame are different, even if all consecutive frames are very similar in content. In other words the difference metric applied in Sect. 2.3 with the threshold derived from Fig. 4 would still be effective were it to be applied to the first and the last frame directly. Thus, the problem becomes one of detecting these first and last frames. If they can be determined, then each of them may be interpreted as a segment boundary, and the period of gradual transition can be isolated as a segment unto itself. The inset of Fig. 4 illustrates that the difference values between most of the frames during the dissolve are higher, although only slightly, than those in the preceding and following segments. What is required is a threshold value that will detect a dissolve *sequence* and distinguish it from an ordinary camera shot. A similar approach can be applied to transitions implemented by other types of special effects. We shall present this *twin-comparison* approach in the context of an example of dissolve detection using Eq. 4 as the difference metric.

Twin-comparison requires the use of two cutoff thresholds: T_b is used for camera break detection in the same manner as was described in Sect. 2. In addition, a second, lower, threshold T_s is used for special effect detection. The detection process begins by comparing consecutive frames using a difference metric such as Eq. 4. Whenever the difference value exceeds threshold T_b, a camera break is declared, e.g., F_B in Fig. 5a. However, the twin-comparison also detects differences that are smaller than T_b but larger than T_s. Any frame that exhibits such a difference value is marked as the potential start (F_s) of a gradual transition. Such a frame is labelled in Fig. 5a. This frame is then compared to subsequent frames, as shown in Fig. 5b. This is called an *accumulated comparison* since, during a gradual transition, this difference value will normally increase. The end frame (F_s) of the transition is detected when the difference between consecutive frames decreases to less than T_s, while the accumulated comparison has increased to a value larger than T_b.

Note that the accumulated comparison is only computed when the difference between consecutive frames exceeds T_s. If the consecutive difference value drops below T_s before the accumulated comparison value exceeds T_b, then the potential start point is dropped and the search continues for other

Fig. 5a,b. Illustration of twin-comparison. $SD_{p,q}$, the difference between consecutive frames defined by the difference metric; $SD'_{p,q}$, the accumulated difference between the current frame and the potential starting frame of a transition; T_s, the treshold used to detect the starting frame (F_s) of a transition; T_b, the threshold used to detect the ending frame (F_e) of a transition. T_b is also used to detect camera breaks and F_B is such a camera break. $SD'_{p,q}$ is only calculated when $SD_{p,q} > T_s$

gradual transitions. The key idea of twin-comparison is that two distinct threshold conditions be satisfied at the same time. Furthermore, the algorithm is designed in such a way that gradual transitions are detected *in addition* to ordinary camera breaks.

A problem with twin-comparison is that there are some gradual transitions during which the consecutive difference value *does* fall below T_s. This problem is solved by permitting the user to set a tolerance value that allows a number (such as two or three) of consecutive frames with low difference values before rejecting the transition candidate. This approach has proven to be effective when tested on real video examples.

3.2 Distinguishing special effects from camera movements

Given the ability to detect gradual transitions such as those that implement special effects, one must distinguish changes associated with those transitions from changes that are introduced by camera panning or zooming. Changes due to camera movements tend to induce successive difference values of the same order as those of gradual transitions, so that the problem cannot be resolved by introducing yet another cutoff threshold value. Instead, it is necessary to detect patterns of image motion that are induced by camera movement.

The specific feature that serves to detect camera movements is *optical flow*, a technique rooted in computer vision. The optical flow fields resulting from panning and zooming are illustrated in Fig. 6. In contrast, transitions implemented by special effects, such as dissolve, fade-in and fade-out, will not introduce such motion fields. Therefore, if such motion vector fields can be detected and analysed, changes introduced by camera movements can be distinguished from those due to special-effect transitions.

Optical flow computation involves representing the difference between two consecutive frames as a set of motion vectors. As is illustrated in Fig. 6a, during a camera pan these vectors will predominantly have the same direction. (Clearly, if there is also object movement in the scene, not all vectors need share this property.) Thus, the distribution of motion vectors in an entire frame resulting from a camera panning should exhibit a single strong modal value that corresponds to the movement of the camera. In other words, most of the motion vectors will be parallel to the modal vector. This leads to

$$\sum_{k}^{N} |\theta_k - \theta_m| \leq \Theta_p \tag{6}$$

where θ_k is the direction of motion vector k, θ_m is the direction of the modal vector, and N is the total number of motion vectors in a frame. $|\theta_k - \theta_m|$ is zero when the two vectors are exactly parallel. Equation 6 thus counts the total variation in direction of all motion vectors from the direction of the modal vector, and a camera pan is declared if this variation is smaller than Θ_p. Ideally, Θ_p should be zero, but we use a non-zero threshold to accommodate errors such as those that may be introduced by object motion.

In the case of zooming, the field of motion vectors has a minimum value at the focus centre, focus of expansion (FOE) in the case of zoom out, or focus of contraction (FOC) in the case of zoom in. Indeed, if the focus centre is located in the centre of the frame and there is no object movement, then the mean of all the motion vectors will be the zero vector. Unfortunately, determining an entire frame of motion vectors with high spatial resolution is a very time consuming process, so locating a focus centre is no easy matter.

Since we are only interested in determining that a zoom takes place over a sequence of frames, it is not necessary to locate the focus centre. If we assume that, in general, the focus centre of a camera zoom will lie within the boundary of a frame, we may apply a simpler vector comparison technique. In this approach we compare the vertical components of the motion vectors for the top and bottom rows of a frame, since during a zoom these vertical components will have opposite signs. Mathematically, this means that in every column the magnitude of the difference between these vertical components will always exceed the magnitude of both components. That is,

$$|v_k^{\text{top}} - v_k^{\text{bottom}}| \geq \max \left(|v_k^{\text{top}}| , |v_k^{\text{bottom}}| \right) . \tag{7.1}$$

One may again modify this "always" condition with a tolerance value, but this value can generally be low, since there tends to be little object motion at the periphery of a frame. The horizontal components of the motion vectors for the left-most and right-most columns can then be analysed the same way. That is, the vectors of two blocks located at the left-most and right-most columns but at the same row will satisfy the following condition:

$$|u_k^{\text{top}} - u_k^{\text{bottom}}| \geq \max \left(|u_k^{\text{top}}| , |u_k^{\text{bottom}}| \right) . \tag{7.2}$$

A zoom is said to occur when both conditions 7.1 and 7.2 are satisfied for the majority of the motion vectors.

The field of motion vectors that is required for this analysis can be computed by the *block-matching* algorithm commonly used for motion compensation in video compression (Netravali and Haskell 1988). This algorithm requires the partitioning of the frame into blocks, and motion vectors are computed for each block by finding the minimum value of a cost function over a set of trial vectors. Suppose each block is M lines high and N pixels wide; and, within a block, let $b(m, n)$ denote the intensity of the pixel with coordinates (m, n). Then one may define a cost function for block k between two consecutive frames, i and $i + 1$, in terms of an error-power function F as follows:

$$P_i(k) = \sum_{m}^{M} \sum_{n}^{N} F[b_i(m, n) - b_{i+1}(n, m)] . \tag{8}$$

Given a set of trial vectors, the vector that minimizes $P_i(k)$ can be assigned as the motion vector for block k. The calculation time to find a motion vector depends mainly on the number of trial vectors, which, in turn, is based on the possible maximum velocity of camera movement and the resolution of the field of motion vectors depends on the size of the blocks compared.

Apart from the approach just presented, one can also identify camera motion based on sophisticated optical flow analyses (Kasturi and Jain 1991). However, such a technique will require a much greater density of motion vectors (one vector per pixel, in principle). Computing such a resolution of motion vectors is very time consuming, requiring either iterative refinement of a gradient-based algorithm (Horn and Schunck 1981) or the construction of a hierarchical framework of cross-correlation (Anandan 1989). More importantly, although optical flow calculations have been under investigation by many researchers, besides the difficulties in obtaining high accuracy and robustness, the recovery of motion from optical flow and the application of smoothness constraints are still research issues (Kasturi and Jain 1991). Therefore, instead of waiting for more reliable algorithms for recovering camera motion from optical flow,

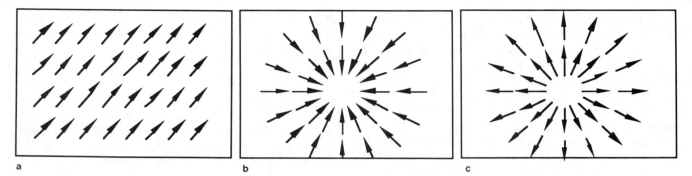

Fig. 6a–c. Motion vector patterns resulting from camera panning and zooming. **a** ╱ Camera panning direction. **b** Camera zoom-out. **c** Camera zoom-in

our current, more limited, motion vector analysis algorithm can provide reasonable accuracy, as one can see from the experimental results presented in Sect. 5.

In spite of the computational expense, there are still advantages to working with the block-matching algorithm. In the future we plan to make use of motion vectors retrieved from files of video that have been compressed by the motion-compensation technique. Such files can be computed already during a real-time scan of video input by video compression hardware, such as an MPEG (Moving Pictures Experts Group) chip (Ang et al. 1991).

4 Applying the comparison techniques

Before the difference metrics for transition detection can be applied to full-motion video, two practical issues have to be considered. First, how does one select the appropriate threshold values for a given video source and difference metric? Secondly, comparing each pair of consecutive frames of a video source (54 000 frames for half an hour's worth of material) is a very time consuming process; hence, a scheme to speed up the partitioning process needs to be considered. We discuss the solutions to these two issues.

4.1 Threshold selection

Selection of appropriate threshold values is a key issue in applying the segmentation algorithms described in Sect. 2 and 3. Thresholds must be assigned that tolerate variations in individual frames while still ensuring a desired level of performance. A "tight" threshold makes it difficult for "impostors" to be falsely accepted by the system, but at the risk of falsely rejecting true transitions. Conversely, a "loose" threshold enables transitions to be accepted consistently, at the risk of falsely accepting "impostors". In order to achieve high accuracy in video partitioning, an appropriate threshold must be found.

The threshold t, used in pair-wise comparison for judging whether a pixel or super-pixel has changed across successive frames, can be easily determined experimentally and it does not change significantly for different video sources. However, experiments have shown that the threshold T_b for

determining a segment boundary using any of the algorithms varies from one video source to another. For instance, "camera breaks" in a cartoon film tend to exhibit much larger frame-to-frame differences than those in a "live" film. Obviously, the threshold to be selected must be based on the distribution of the frame-to-frame differences of the video sequence.

Considerable research has been done on the selection of thresholds for the spatial segmentation of static images. A good summary can be found in *Digital Picture Processing* by Rosenfeld and Kak (1982). Typically, selecting thresholds for such spatial segmentation is based on the histogram of the pixel values of the image. The conventional approaches include the use of a single threshold, multiple thresholds and variable thresholds. The accuracy of single threshold selection depends upon whether the histogram is bimodal, while multiple threshold selection requires clear multiple peaks in the histogram. Variable threshold selection is based on local histograms of specific regions in an image. In spite of this variety of techniques, threshold selection is still a difficult problem in image processing and is most successful when the solution is application dependent. In order to set an appropriate threshold for temporal segmentation of video sequences, we draw upon the same feature, i.e., the histogram of the frame-to-frame differences. Thus, it is necessary to know the distribution of the frame-to-frame differences across camera breaks and gradual transitions.

The automatic selection of threshold T_b is based on the normalized frame-to-frame differences over an entire given video source. The dashed curve (M) in Fig. 7 shows a typical distribution of difference values. This particular example is based on the difference metric for comparison of colour code histograms obtained from a documentary video. The range of difference values is given on the horizontal axis, and the frequency of occurrence of each difference value is represented as a percentage of the total number of frame-to-frame differences on the vertical axis. This particular distribution exhibits a high and sharp peak on the left corresponding to a large number of consecutive frames that have a very small difference between them. The long tail to the right corresponds to the small number of consecutive frames between which a significant difference occurs. Because this histogram has only a single modal point, the approaches for threshold

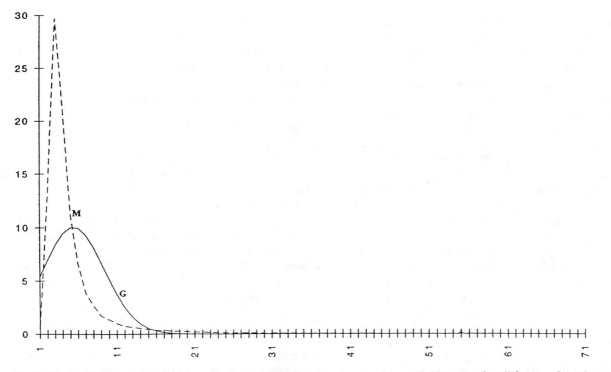

Fig. 7. M, distribution of computed frame-to-frame differences based on a colour code histogram for all frames of the documentary video; G, Gaussian distribution derived from the mean and variance of distribution M

selection already mentioned are not applicable. To solve this problem, we propose an alternative approach to selecting the threshold value T_b as follows.

If there is no camera shot change or camera movement in a video sequence, the frame-to-frame difference value can only be due to three sources of noise: noise from digitizing the original analog video signal, noise introduced by video production equipment, and noise resulting from the physical fact that few objects are perfectly still. All three sources of noise can be assumed to be Gaussian. Thus, the distribution of frame-to-frame differences can be decomposed into a sum of two parts: the Gaussian noises and the differences introduced by camera breaks, gradual transitions, and camera movements. Obviously, differences due to noise have nothing to do with transitions. Statistically, the second sum accounts for less than 15% of the total number of frames in a documentary video that we have used as a source of experimental data.

Let σ be the standard deviation and μ the mean of the frame-to-frame differences. If the only departure from μ is due to Gaussian noise, then the probability integral

$$P(x) = \int_0^x \frac{1}{\sqrt{2\pi}\sigma} e^{-\frac{(x-\mu)^2}{2\sigma^2}} \, dx \qquad (9)$$

(taken from 0 since all differences are given as absolute values) will account for most of the frames within a few standard deviations of the mean value. In other words, the frame-to-frame differences from the non-transition frames will fall in the range of 0 to $\mu + \alpha\sigma$ for a small constant value α. For instance, if we chose $\alpha = 3$, Eq. 9 will account

for 99.9% of all difference values. The black curve (G) in Fig. 7 shows the Gaussian distribution obtained from σ and μ for the frame-to-frame differences from which the M curve was calculated. Therefore, the threshold T_b can be selected as

$$T_b = \mu + \alpha\sigma \ . \qquad (10)$$

That is, difference values that fall out of the range from 0 to $\mu + \alpha\sigma$ can be considered indicators of segment boundaries. From our experiments, the value α should be chosen between five and six when the histogram comparison metric is used. Under a Gaussian distribution, the probability that a non-transition frame will fall out of this range is practically zero.

For detecting gradual transitions, another threshold, T_s, defined in Fig. 5, also needs to be selected. Experiments have shown that T_s should be selected along the right slope of the M distribution shown in Fig. 7. Furthermore, T_s should generally be larger than the mean value of the frame-to-frame differences of the entire video package. After examining three documentary videos, we observed that T_s does not vary significantly; and a typical value usually lies between eight and ten.

4.2 Multi-pass approach

Once threshold values have been established, the partitioning algorithms can be applied in "delayed real-time". Only one pass through the entire video package is required to determine all the camera breaks. However, the delay can be quite substantial given 30 fps of colour source material. In addition, such a single-pass approach has the disadvantage that it does not exploit any information other than the threshold values. Therefore, this approach depends heavily on the selection of those values.

A straightforward approach to the reduction of processing time is to lower the resolution of the comparison. This can be done in two ways – either spatially or temporally. In the spatial domain, one may sacrifice resolution by examining only a subset of the total number of pixels in each frame. However, this is clearly risky since if the subset is too small, the loss of spatial detail may result in a failure to detect certain segment boundaries. Also, resampling the original image may even increase the processing time, and that would run contrary to our goal of applying spatial resampling to reduce the processing time.

Alternatively, to sacrifice temporal resolution by examining fewer frames is a better choice, since in motion video temporal information redundancy is much higher than spatial information redundancy. For example, one could apply a "skip factor" of ten (examining only three frames/s of video time from a 30-frames/s source). This will reduce the number of comparisons (and, therefore, the associated processing time) by the same factor. An advantage of this approach is that it will also detect some of the transitions implemented by special effects as camera breaks, since the difference between two frames that are ten frames apart across such a transition could be larger than the threshold T_b. A drawback of this approach is that the accuracy of locating the camera break decreases with the same factor as the skip. Also, if the skip factor is too large, the change during a camera movement may be so great that it leads to a false detection of a camera break. (This was observed experimentally in a system that was limited to "grabbing" only one frame/s.)

To overcome the problems of low resolution in locating segment boundaries, we have developed a multi-pass approach that improves processing speed and achieves the same order of accuracy. In the first pass resolution is sacrificed temporally to detect *potential* segment boundaries. In this process twin-comparison for gradual transitions is not applied. Instead, a lower value of T_b is used; and all frames across which there is a difference larger than T_b are detected as potential segment boundaries. Due to the lower threshold and large skip factor, both camera breaks and gradual transitions, as well as some artefacts due to camera movement, will be detected; but any number of false detections will also be admitted, as long as no *real* boundaries are missed. In the second pass all computation is restricted to the vicinity of these potential boundaries. Increased resolution is used to locate all boundaries (both camera breaks and gradual transitions) more accurately. Also, motion analysis is applied to distinguish camera movements from gradual transitions.

With the multi-pass approach different detection algorithms can be applied in different passes to increase confidence in the results. For instance, for a given video package, we can apply either pair-wise or histogram comparison in the first, low resolution, pass with a large skip factor and a low value of T_b. Then, in the second pass, *both* comparison algorithms are applied independently to the potential boundaries detected by the first pass. The results from the two algorithms can then be used to verify each other, and positive results from both algorithms will have sufficiently high confidence to be declared as segment boundaries. As will be seen from the following experimental results, the multi-pass approach can achieve both high speed and accuracy.

Adaptive sampling in time can also be applied in the segmentation process to reduce processing time. That is, we only examine those frames with a high likelihood of crossing a segment boundary and skip the frames with a low likelihood. For instance, we can skip a number of frames after a camera shot boundary is detected since there are not likely to be two boundaries in very close succession. However, in general, it is difficult to obtain a priori knowledge about such likelihood. More importantly, we currently calculate the mean and variance for those frame-to-frame differences taken over an entire video sequence and sampled according to a constant skip factor; and those mean and variance values are used to determine the threshold for segment boundaries. That is, we need to calculate the threshold from the video sequence before the sequence is partitioned. An adaptive sampling technique that introduces variable skip factors, would destroy the statistical properties of those calculations, possibly resulting in an inadequate threshold. In addition, variable thresholds would be needed if adaptive sampling were to be applied, which would further complicate the processing. However, the detection process in the second pass (when the two-pass approach is used with the same metric in both passes) is, in fact, an adaptive sampling process in time, as only the frames close to the potential boundaries are examined in the second pass, while other frames between the potential boundaries are skipped. In this case, however, the threshold value is obtained from the first pass.

5 Implementation and evaluation

The partitioning algorithms described have been implemented and applied on a variety of video materials. The output of the segmentation process of a given video package is a sequence of segment boundaries. These boundaries are compared with those detected manually from the same video sources as a basis for evaluation. We shall now discuss the implementation of these algorithms, the experimental results, and the comparative value of each approach.

5.1 System and algorithm implementation

The implementation platform consists of a Macintosh IIfx connected to a Pioneer LD-V8000 video laser disc player, as shown in Fig. 8. The interface between the laser disc player and the computer is provided by a RasterOps Colorboard 364 video board, which combines the functions of a true colour frame buffer with hardware pan and zoom, "frame grabbing", and real-time video display at a rate of 30 frames/s. A software control panel for the video disc player has been developed and integrated with a user-friendly interface to control frame searching, input of algorithm parameters, monitoring of the segmentation process and display and storage of segmentation results.

During segmentation, the frames to be compared are directly grabbed from the laser disc rather than stored as a file of compressed digital video. The frames are of resolution 278 × 208 with each pixel represented by 32 bits of data: 8 bits for each of the three colour components and the first 8 bits unused. The colour intensities can then be transformed into a single 8-bit value of grey level or a 6-bit colour code, composed from the most significant 2 bits of each of the three colour components, as illustrated in Fig. 9. If grey-level intensities are used in the segmentation, they are computed from the three colour components according to the NTSC standard:

$$I = 0.299R + 0.587G + 0.114B . \qquad (11)$$

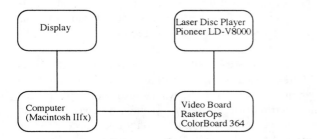

Fig. 8. Architecture of the automatic video segmentation system

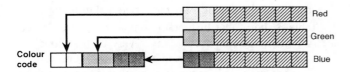

Fig. 9. Diagrammatic representation of colour code generation

In this formula R, G and B stand for the intensities of the red, green and blue components, respectively. This formula also gives the impact of individual colour changes on the overall grey level and indicates the significance of the green component. To increase the processing speed by avoiding the computation of this transformation, it is possible to compute differences using only the green component. However, this approach will miss any difference due to large changes in the red and blue components but a small change in the green component. Whether or not this information loss can be tolerated will depend on the nature of the video source.

Input to the segmentation system is provided by grabbing the frames for the sequence to be partitioned and digitizing each frame in the video board. The system first processes these input data by calculating the frame-to-frame differences between those frames determined by the skip factor; these difference values are then stored in an array. This array is then used to compute the mean and variance of those

difference values. Then the segmentation threshold is determined from these two quantities, as described in Sect. 4.2. Finally, segment boundaries are detected using the difference values in the array.

5.2 Experimental results

The algorithms described in this paper have been tested on a number of video sequences, including documentaries, educational material, and cartoons. However, we shall only present the results of the partitioning of a 7-min animated cartoon and two documentaries: The first is a 20-min local production about the Faculty of Engineering at NUS; the second is a 40-min commercial travelogue about Singapore. These video packages provide representative material for testing the algorithms. The cartoon employs few special effects, so while all "camera shots" are actually simulations in animation, they are all separated relatively conventionally. Therefore, this was excellent material for the initial testing and evaluation of our algorithms for camera break detection. The NUS documentary video provides a combination of live footage and a few animated sequences, along with the use of various special effects. The entire documentary consists of approximately 200 camera shots, and the transitions are implemented by both dissolves and camera breaks. There are also several sequences of camera panning and zooming, as well as object motion. This video thus provides suitable material for test and evaluation of algorithms for both camera break and gradual transition detection, as well as for the technique for camera movement detection. In the travel documentary there are many more camera breaks and camera movements, as well as more sequences where moving objects and lighting changes arising from flashing lights and the flickering of some objects occur. Thus, this video provides more data for testing the robustness and limitations of the partitioning algorithms.

Three experiments will now be discussed. The first is for proof-of-concept, testing the effectiveness of the difference metrics for segment boundary detection on the cartoon video. The second one presents both a much more in-depth analysis of the difference metrics and a test of twin-comparison for detecting gradual transitions. The comparison of histograms based on colour codes is further analysed by subjecting the complete travel documentary video to both twin-comparison and subsequent analysis for camera movement detection. Presentation of these results will include a detailed error analysis. The final experiment concentrates on the effectiveness of the camera movement detection techniques presented in Sect. 3.2.

5.2.1 Example 1: Camera break detection on a cartoon video

Table 1 lists the results of applying each of four difference metrics in a single pass to partition the cartoon video (12 990 frames). Since we were only concerned with testing the difference metrics, we were only interested in detecting camera

Table 1. Segmentation results of single pass algorithms

Algorithms	T_b	N_d	N_m	N_f	τ (seconds)
Pair-wise pixel, grey	77	51	2	6	71 320
Likelihood, grey	28	49	4	27	103 023
Histogram, grey	45	44	9	16	32 475
Histogram, colour	50	48	5	5	20 861

T_b, the threshold selected; N_d, the total number of camera breaks correctly detected by each algorithm; N_m, the number of boundaries missed; N_f, the number of boundaries misdetected; τ, the processing time

Table 2. Segmentation results of multi-pass algorithms

Algorithms	T_b	N_d	N_m	N_f	τ (seconds)
Pair-wise pixel, grey	77	49	4	6	17 386
Likelihood	28	49	4	25	19 546
Histogram	45	43	10	11	15 752
Hybrid	–	42	11	7	22 183

breaks. The performance was evaluated with respect to those segment boundaries detected by a manual analysis. The processing time (τ) for each algorithm is also shown in the table for the comparison of the processing load among the four difference metrics. Table 1 indicates that all algorithms detect camera breaks with satisfactory accuracy. The leading success of pair-wise comparison is partially due to the fact that its threshold was optimally tuned, which was not the case for the other algorithms. Nevertheless, it missed two transitions implemented as dissolves and falsely detected six artefacts of camera and object movements. Due to the high requirement of computation time for Eq. 3, the likelihood-ratio algorithm is slow. Of the four algorithms, the colour histogram gives the most promising overall result: both high speed and accuracy. The major sources of error in this case are due to camera panning, object motion, and improper threshold selection.

We have also tested the multi-pass concept on the cartoon video and the results are shown in Table 2. The first three results were obtained by using the same difference metric in both passes, while with the hybrid method, both the histogram comparison and likelihood criterion were applied; and the results from each of the algorithms were used to verify each other. As presented in Sect. 4.2, in the first pass a lower temporal resolution (skip factor of 3) was used. In using pairwise comparison, lower spatial resolution (averaging of 3×4 pixels) was also used in the first pass. The results in Table 2 indicate that this approach performs much faster than that of a single pass, with comparable or better accuracy. In the hybrid approach, a segment boundary is declared only if both algorithms detect it as a boundary. As indicated in the table, such a hybrid approach allows for high-confidence camera breaks to be detected and reduces the number of false detections.

5.2.2 Example 2: Transition detection on a documentary video

A more general test of segmentation, based on three different types of histogram comparison, was applied to the NUS documentary video. The twin-comparison approach was applied to detect both camera breaks and gradual transitions implemented by special effects. The reason that only histogram comparison algorithms were used in this experiment is that they are insensitive to object motion and they are faster than the two types of pair-wise comparison algorithms. The segmentation results are summarized in Table 3.

As in the case of Table 1 and Table 2, the camera breaks detected algorithmically, as well as those missed and misdetected, are listed. In addition, the same information is provided for gradual transitions. It should be noted that camera movements are also included here that may be subsequently detected by the technique discussed in example 3. Similar results, obtained from the differences of colour code histograms for the travel documentary are given in Table 4 as further evaluation of the performance and robustness of this particular algorithm, which will be seen later to be the optimal technique.

The first two rows of Table 3 show the results of applying difference metrics (4) and (5), respectively, to grey level histograms. The third row shows the results of applying difference metric (4) to histograms of the 6-bit colour code. In order to reduce computation time, only every second frame is compared (skip factor is 2), providing a temporal resolution of 15 frames/s. The last set of results were obtained by a two-pass algorithm: in the first pass the colour-code histogram was applied with a skip factor of 10 and a reduced threshold, and the second pass then used a skip factor of 2.

Table 3 shows that histogram comparison, based on either grey level or colour code, gives very high accuracy in detecting both camera breaks and gradual transitions. In fact, no effort has been made to tune the thresholds to obtain these data. Approximately 90% of the breaks and transitions are correctly detected. Among the three single-pass algorithms, colour gives the most promising result: besides the high accuracy, it is also the fastest of the three algorithms. (The 6-bit colour code requires only 64 histogram bins, instead of the 256 bins required for the 8-bit grey level.) The much smaller number of missing breaks suggests that the colour histogram is better than the grey level in detecting qualitative differences in content. In other words it would appear that 6 bits of a colour code provide more *effective* information than 8 bits of grey level. Similar accuracy in detecting both camera breaks and transitions is exhibited in Table 4, again using the colour histogram algorithm, though there are many more breaks and camera movements in this video.

Note that the χ^2-test histogram comparison algorithm does not yield a better result, even after tuning the threshold. In fact the number of missing and false detections in the second row of Table 3 is dramatically greater than those in the first row. This is contrary to the conclusions of Nagasaka and Tanaka (1991), where no experimental data were presented.

Table 3. Detection results for camera breaks and gradual transitions based on four types of twin-comparison algorithms applied to the NUS documentary video

Type of transitions	Camera breaks			Transitions + camera movements				
Algorithms used	N_d	N_m	N_f	N_d	N_m	N_f	N_P	N_Z
Grey level comparison	65	13	2	101	8	9	2	1
χ^2 grey level comparison	60	18	16	93	16	9	2	3
Colour code comparison	73	5	3	95	14	13	1	2
Colour code, 2 passes	71	7	3	88	21	18	3	2

N_d, the total number of camera breaks correctly detected by each algorithm; N_m, the number of boundaries missed; N_f, the number of boundaries misdetected; N_P, the number of "transitions" actually due to camera panning; N_Z, the number of "transitions" actually due to camera zooming

Also, χ^2-test comparison requires the longest computation time among the three algorithms. Therefore, we shall not discuss this algorithm any further, concentrating our attention on simple histogram comparison.

The multi-pass approach achieves similar accuracy, but it is almost three times faster than the single-pass colour code algorithm. The increased missing transitions were due to errors in the first pass and can be improved by either lowering the threshold or increasing the skip factor for the first pass. Accuracy may also be improved by increasing the search vicinity around the potential boundaries in the second pass.

Table 4. Results of applying the twin-comparison approach to camera break and transition detection and the camera movement detection approach on the travel documentary video. Differences were calculated from colour histograms

Camera breaks			Transitions + camera movements				
N_d	N_m	N_f	N_d	N_m	N_f	N_Z	N_P
280	2	10	104	6	19	20	22

N_d The total number of camera breaks correctly detected by each algorithm; N_m, the number of boundaries missed; N_f, the number of boundaries misdetected; N_Z, the number of "transitions" actually due to camera zooming; N_P, the number of "transitions actually due to camera panning

The missed camera breaks mainly result from the fact that the differences between some frames across a camera break are lower than the given threshold. Both the grey level and colour histogram comparison algorithms failed to detect the two frames across a camera break (Fig. 10), because the histograms of the two frames are similar. All missed camera breaks based on simple histogram comparison listed in Table 3 have resulted from this problem. The missing gradual transitions are mainly due to the same problem, as shown in Fig. 11. However, this problem cannot be solved simply by lowering the threshold because this will lead to an increase in the number of false detections. We have to accept the fact that, as in spatial segmentation in static image processing (Rosenfeld and Kak 1982), it is almost impossible to obtain a threshold that will achieve 100% accuracy. For this reason our segmentation system also provides a set of editing tools to enable the user to correct those few errors that result from the automatic partitioning process.

The second class of errors, false camera break detections, are mainly due to sharp changes in lighting arising from flashing lights and flickering objects, such as a computer screen, in the image. This type of error accounts for all the false breaks listed in all the rows of Table 3, except for some instances based on the χ^2-test histogram comparison, and four false breaks in Table 4. Such problems may be solved by using the robust algorithms presented in Sect. 4.2 if the large illumination changes only occur in a restricted portion of the entire frame. The rest of the false breaks listed in Table 4 result from dramatic content changes in short transitions of a length of 20 frames or less. That is, a short transition may be detected as one or more breaks due to the large content changes within the transition. This fact also accounts for four missing transitions that were falsely detected as breaks.

Flashing lights and flickering objects are also the major source of false detection of transitions: 9 out of 19 false transitions in listed in Table 4 resulted from such situations. In fact, gradual transitions are more sensitive than camera breaks to such changes, since even a gradual change of lighting can cause a false detection of a transition. Figure 12 shows an example of such a false transition where four frames from a shot of a colourful water fountain were detected as a transition due to the colour lighting changes.

Object movement is another main source of false detection of gradual transitions, and it accounts for most of the false transitions in both Table 3 and Table 4. Figure 13 shows an example of such a false detection. Movement of the large object results in large changes between consecutive frames that may far exceed the thresholds set for transitions. However, object motion in general tends not to induce the regular patterns in the motion field that arise from camera movements. Therefore, object motion cannot be detected by the technique developed for camera movement detection. An alternative is to identify a moving object as a cluster in the motion field and then use that cluster of vectors to track the object. One can then assume that a transition will not take place in the middle of an object's trajectory and thus eliminate false detection. Hence, detecting object motion is

a   b

Fig. 10a,b. Missed camera breaks: two frames across a camera break that both the grey-level and the colour-histogram comparison algorithms failed to detect because the histograms of the two frames are similar

a   b   c

d

Fig. 11a–d. A missed gradual transition: four frames from a dissolve transition that the twin-comparison approach, using the colour-histogram comparison as the difference metric, failed to detect, because the colour histograms of the two frames in the two shots are very close to each other

an important part of our efforts to improve the accuracy of video partitioning algorithms.

As a supplement to the data in Table 3, note that only nine of the errors of missing or false breaks or transitions are common to the analyses based on grey level and colour code histograms, respectively. Such overlap will be less likely if we compare the results from using pair-wise comparison and histogram comparison. In other words the results from the two different algorithms may compensate each other if we combine them in a proper way, rather than the exclusive verification used in the hybrid multi-pass approach presented in Table 2. However, if we use an opposite scheme where a segment boundary is declared whenever it is detected by *either* of the two algorithms, the number of false detections may increase. To avoid this, we are currently investigating the use of a *confidence measure* based on both the difference across two frames and the selected threshold. The concept of "fuzzy boundary" may be used in combining the segment boundaries obtained from different algorithms. While it should be relatively easy to improve the accuracy of camera

Table 5. Detection of camera movements by motion detection and analysis algorithms

Camera movements	N_d	N_m	N_f
Panning (skip = 1)	14	0	3
Zooming (skip = 1)	3	4	0
Zooming (skip = 5)	7	0	0

N_d, The number of camera movements detected by the algorithms; N_m, the number of camera movements missed by the algorithms; N_f, the number of false detections of camera movements

break detection, improving the accuracy in detecting gradual transitions will probably be much more difficult.

5.2.3 Example 3: Camera movement detection

Camera pan and zoom sequences are distinguished from gradual transitions by using the motion analysis techniques discussed in Sect. 3.2. Twenty blocks of 15×15 pixels, uniformly distributed in a frame as four rows of five columns,

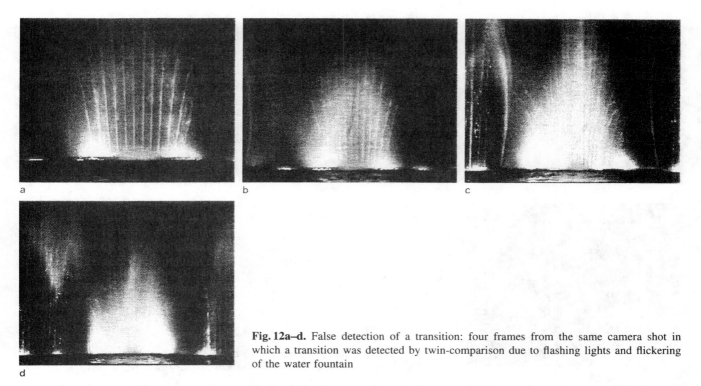

a

b

c

d

Fig. 12a–d. False detection of a transition: four frames from the same camera shot in which a transition was detected by twin-comparison due to flashing lights and flickering of the water fountain

are used to compute the motion vectors with the following cost function:

$$P_i(k) = \sum_m^M \sum_n^N |b_i(m, n) - b_{i+1}(m, n)| . \quad (12)$$

The search area for minimizing this cost function is crucial for obtaining accurate motion vectors and acceptable computation speed. In order to accommodate the video rate and the maximum velocity of camera movement, we have chosen 9 pixels per frame as the search area. It is not necessary to compare every pair of consecutive frames in a potential transition to determine if they resulted from a camera movement. Instead, only two pairs of consecutive frames are used to compute motion vectors, and the second pair is used to verify the first. If the motion vectors detected from the two pairs oppose each other, then they are probably not due to camera movements. If a potential transition lasts a large number of frames, it may be necessary to compute more than two pairs of frames in order to get higher confidence in the results.

Let (u_k, v_k) be a motion vector, where k ranges from 1 to N. Following the analysis in Sect. 3.2, let (u_m, v_m) be the modal value of these N motion vectors. Then a camera pan is detected if the fraction of motion vectors equal to the mode value exceeds a given threshold T_p. Camera zooms are detected using the comparison approach described in Sect. 3.2 that examines only the border rows and columns.

Our experiments show that those camera movements detected as potential transitions in Table 3 and Table 4 are correctly detected as camera pan or zoom instances. Figure 14 shows frames from a camera panning (moving from up to down) and zooming (moving from close to far), respectively, that were detected as transitions first and were

subsequently recognized as camera movement. This demonstrates that motion detection and analysis are effective in distinguishing camera movements from gradual transitions with a high degree of accuracy.

While identifying such distinctions was our primary purpose, we have also tried to classify camera movements over an entire video. This could provide useful information in video content analysis and in selecting representative frames for a detected segment. For instance, the end frame of a zoom can serve as the representative frame of a segment.

Our experiment consisted of applying the algorithm directly to the video package without first identifying potential transition frames. That is, the motion vector field between each pair of consecutive frames was computed and analysed to determine if there was a camera movement during a sequence of the frames. The results are summarized in Table 5. Two different skip factors were tested, and it was found that it is difficult to detect small zoom effects correctly with no skip (using every frame).

The motion of a large object in a camera shot is the major source of error for camera pan detection: two false detections of camera pans listed in Table 5 are due to this problem. Another one is due to erroneous motion vectors computed by the block-matching algorithm, which is inherently inaccurate when there are multiple motions inside a block. Therefore, to improve the accuracy of detecting camera movements, we need to apply a more accurate algorithm to determine motion vectors. Block-matching is particularly problematic during a zoom sequence because the area covered by the camera angle expands or contracts during a zoom. Also, *combinations* of pans and zooms make the detection of camera movement even more difficult. A more general-

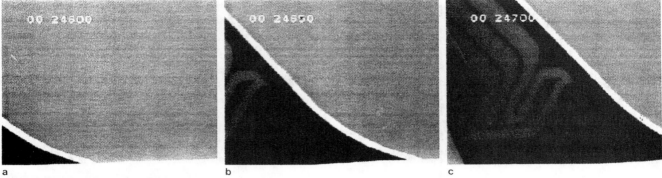

Fig. 13a–d. False detection of a transition: four frames from the same camera shot, detected as a transition by twin-comparison, due to the movement of an airplane rudder in the shot

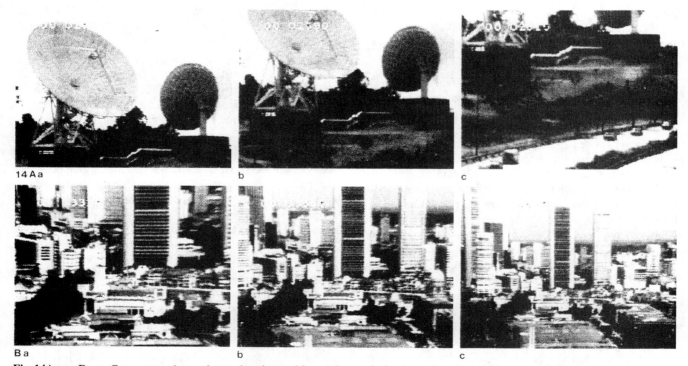

Fig. 14Aa–c, Ba–c. Camera panning and zooming detected by motion analysis: **Aa–c** three frames from a panning sequence; **Ba–c** three frames from a zooming sequence

ized motion classification approach is necessary, such as the global zoom/pan estimation algorithm proposed in Tse and Bakler (1991), which requires analysis of the motion field of a much higher density – a very time consuming process.

Another problematic situation occurs when the camera follows a moving object. The size of the object may be such that the background or foreground changes due to the camera panning exceed the threshold T_s; the sequence is then detected as a potential transition. If the moving object is not too large, the sequence can be detected as camera panning by motion vector analysis. However, if the object covers more than half the frame, there will not be a clear mode of motion vectors, and block matching will fail to detect camera panning. This accounts for a few of the false detections listed in Table 5. Such cases can no longer be treated as simple camera panning; rather the problem is one of *motion recovery*, which needs a more sophisticated analysis.

5.3 Summary and further discussion

These results demonstrate that segmentation can be performed with satisfactory accuracy. It has also been shown that, among a variety of difference metrics, comparison of colour code histograms is the optimal choice; it achieves both high accuracy and speed. The major sources of error in detecting breaks and transitions are object motion, lighting changes and a few inherent limitations of the segmentation processing, the effects of which need to be reduced to improve the performance of the algorithms further.

As was observed in the experiments, object motion is a major obstacle to segmentation and detection of camera movement. Fast motions of a single object or motion of several objects may induce a frame-to-frame difference that would be detected as a camera break, while any object motion will disrupt the visual flow required to identify pans and zooms. Distinguishing object motions from camera motion is much more difficult than distinguishing camera movement from gradual transitions, since object motions in a sequence of frames are usually not as regular as those introduced by camera movements. This problem is best solved by algorithms for object tracking. Indeed, continuous tracking of a set of objects can serve as an alternative criterion for setting segment boundaries, while the objects themselves are fundamental units for any indexing task. Therefore, the next phase of our project will involve an extensive study of object tracking algorithms. Again, optical flow analysis developed for robot navigation can be used for object tracking, though this particular analysis is still a very difficult task. Further study of optical flow analysis has been initiated as an important part of the project for both object tracking and camera movement detection.

Currently, computation of the field of motion vectors is implemented in software, but chips developed for video compression and transmission, using the H.261 (Ang et al. 1991) and MPEG (Le Gall 1991) standards, can be used for the same purpose. These chips compute a motion vector for every block of 8×8 pixels for motion-compensated interframe coding for video compression. When a video compression chip processes input from any video source, motion vectors are computed in real-time, thereby increasing the efficiency of computation with much higher spatial resolution than has been implemented in software. In addition, if the video material is stored as a compressed file, we can retrieve the motion vectors directly from that file. Once the dense motion field can be obtained accurately, algorithms to recover motion from optical flow (Kasturi and Jain 1991) may also

be used for camera movement detection. Such analysis may provide more accurate information about camera movement when both camera and object motion exist in the same frame sequence.

The study of object tracking and motion analysis is of importance not only for camera shot boundary detection but also for the classification of camera shots. Initially, the twin-comparison approach was introduced to detect gradual transitions but, as we have seen, it can also be used to detect potential sequences of camera and object motion. Such sequences can then be analysed further and classified as transitions, static camera shots, and shots with panning and zooming. Such a classification will provide useful information for content analysis of the video sequence.

If lighting changes only result in changes of pixel intensity, the problem of false detection can be avoided by using a colour histogram comparison algorithm suggested by Arman et al. (1993). This algorithm uses the two-dimensional hue and saturation (HS) histogram based on the hue, saturation and intensity (HSI) colour space. Only the hue and saturation information are used because past studies have shown that the hue of an object surface remains the same under different lighting intensities. However, since illumination changes may involve more than intensity change, the robustness of this algorithm may be limited.

6 Conclusions and future work

As an initial effort towards the automatic partitioning of a video package into meaningful segments, techniques for detecting camera breaks and gradual transitions implemented by special effects as well as the effects of camera movement, have been developed and implemented. The resulting algorithms have been tested on a variety of video sources. The segment boundaries detected by these algorithms have been compared with those detected by manual logging, and it has been demonstrated that the algorithms perform with satisfactory accuracy. Some future improvements were suggested in Sect. 5.3. We shall now consider several other important aspects of future work, including the development of more computer tools for video indexing.

6.1 Further enhancement of the video partitioning system

An important enhancement for video indexing is the capability to select a representative frame automatically so that it can be used as a visual cue for each segment determined by the partitioning process. Such cues are particularly valuable if one wishes to build an index based on a content analysis of each segment. Alternatively, an array of these representative frames can be used as an index itself through which a user can browse when searching for video source material. Our current effort toward automatic selection of representative frames focuses on developing algorithms that do not require any sophisticated (or computationally intensive) attempts at content analysis. For instance, in case there is a camera movement in a shot, then the end frame of the pan or zoom can be selected as the representative frame. Algorithms that find an average frame in a sequence may serve our purpose in case there are no other useful features.

As more and more video material becomes available in a compressed digital form, it would be advantageous to perform segmentation directly on that digital source in order to save on the computational cost of decompressing every frame. This is an important aspect of our current research. In general, compression of a video frame begins with dividing each colour component of the image into a set of 8×8 pixel blocks (Le Gall, 1991). The pixels in the blocks are then coded by the forward discrete cosine transform (DCT). The resulting 64 coefficients are then quantized and subjected to Huffman entropy encoding. This process is then reversed during decompression. Since these coefficients are mathematically related to the spatial domain, they can be used to detect the sorts of changes associated with segmentation. That is, the segment boundaries are detected by correlating the DCT coefficients of a set of blocks from each frame (Arman et al. 1993). Since only the differences between the *key frames* or *Intrapictures* in video compressed using MPEG, H.261 or Apple QuickTime standard contain scene change information (Le Gall, 1991; Liou, 1991; Apple Computer 1991), video partitioning can be based on only these frames. Thus, the processing time for correlating DCT coefficients can be reduced further. Our initial studies have shown promising results.

6.2 Video indexing: challenges

As we have already observed, the sort of automatic video partitioning reported here is only the first step in our effort towards computer-assisted video indexing. The next important step is to perform content analysis on individual segments to identify appropriate index terms. This is obviously a more challenging task. More sophisticated image processing techniques will be required to provide useful tools for automatic identification of index entries and content-based video retrieval.

Object tracking and motion analysis will not only improve the performance of video segmentation and camera shot classification, as pointed out in Sect. 5.3, but also they will supply the content information required for indexing. For instance, if we can extract a moving object from its background and track its motion, we should be able to construct a description of that motion that can be employed for subsequent retrieval of the camera shot. There is also the value of *identifying* the object, once it has been extracted; but even without sophisticated identification techniques, merely constructing an icon from the extracted image may serve as a valuable visual index term.

Besides images in video, another important source of information in most video packages is the audio track. As any film-maker knows, the audio signal provides a very rich source of information to supplement the understanding of any video source (Metz 1985); this information may also be engaged for tasks of segmentation and indexing. For instance, significant changes in spectral content may serve as segment boundary cues. Tracking audio objects will also provide useful information for segmentation and indexing. Therefore, an effective analysis of the audio track and its integration with information obtained from image analysis will be an important part of our future work on video segmentation and indexing.

Before a video index system can be developed, it will be necessary to develop an architectural specification. If one is working with a dynamic medium like video, any index that ultimately takes the form of a printed document is likely to be of limited value. It is preferable to view the index itself as a piece of computer software through which the user may interact with the video source material. This is a vision we share with the Visual Information System project (Swanberg et al. 1993), along with their specification of an architecture that integrates databases, knowledge bases, and vision systems. We can view the index construction process as one of data insertion in a video database. The index construction system (video parser) will first use the partitioning techniques to segment the video stream into representative clips. Once those clips are generated, the knowledge module should be able to feed components of the video sample into a parser that can compare the sample to the clips. When the parser identifies a matching clip or episode, it communicates its results with the knowledge base to determine an index term that can then be assigned. That is, the knowledge module should provide the connection between the vision system and a database of index categories. To support this activity, the parser should be able to both calculate similarities between video samples and extract a representative sample from a set of video clips. The building of such a parser system is the primary challenge we are facing, and it is the focus of our future work in developing a computer system for video indexing.

Acknowledgements. This research is carried out with support from the National Science and Technology Board of Singapore.

References

Anandan P (1989) A computational framework and an algorithm for the measurement of visual motion. Int J Comput Vision 2:283–310

Ang PH, Ruetz PA, Auld D (1991) Video compression makes big gains. IEEE Spectrum 28:16–19

Apple Computer (1991) Quick time developer's guide. Cupertino

Arman F, Hsu A, Chiu M-Y (1992) Feature management for large video databases. Proc SPIE Conf on Storage and Retrieval for Image and Video Databases, San Diego

Bordwell D, Thompson K (1993) Film art: An introduction, McGraw-Hill, New York

Horn BKP, Schunck BG (1981) Determining optical flow, Artif Intell 17:185–203

Kasturi R, Jain R (1991) Dynamic vision. In: Computer Vision: Principles, Kasturi R, Jain R (eds) IEEE Computer Society Press, Washington, pp. 469–480

Le Gall D (1991) MPEG: A video compression standard for multimedia applications. Commun ACM 34:47–58

Liou M (1991) Overview of the px64 kbit/s video coding standard. Commun ACM 34:59–63

Mackay W, Davenport G (1989) Virtual video editing in interactive multimedia applications. Commun ACM 32:802–810

Metz C (1985) Aural objects. In: Film sound: theory and practice. Weis E, Belton J (eds) Columbia University Press, New York, pp. 154–161

Nagasaka A, Tanaka Y (1991) Automatic video indexing and full-video search for object appearances. Proc 2nd Working Conf Visual Database Systems, pp. 119–133

Netravali AN, Haskell BG (1988) Digital pictures: representation and compression. Plenum, New York

Rosenfeld A, Kak AC (1982) Chapter 10: Segmentation. Digital Picture Processing, 2nd edn. Academic Press New York, pp. 57–190

Ruan LQ, Smoliar SW, Kankanhalli A (1992) An analysis of low-resolution segmentation techniques for animate video. Proc ICARCV '92. 1:CV-16.3.1–16.3.5

Swanberg D, Shu C-F, Jain R (1992) Knowledge guided parsing in video databases. Proc IS&T/SPIE's Symp Electronic Imaging: Sci Tech, San Jose

Tonomura Y (1991) Video handling based on structured information for hypermedia systems. Proc Int Conf Multimedia Information Syst, Singapore, pp. 333–344

Tse YT, Bakler RL (1991) Global zoom pan estimation and compensation for video compression. Proc ICASSP '91, pp. 2725–2728

Zhang HJ, Kankanhalli A, Smoliar SW (1993) Automatic video partitioning and indexing. Proc. IFAC '93, to appear. Detecting camera breaks in full-motion video, available from the authors upon request

HONGJIANG ZHANG obtained his Ph.D. from Technical University of Denmark in 1991 and his BSc from ZhengZhou University, China, in 1981, both in Electrical Engineering. He had also worked as an engineer at Shijiaz huang Communications Institute, China, before his Ph.D work. He joined the Institute of Systems Science at the National University of Singapore in December 1991 and is presently working on projects on video classification and moving object tracking and classification. His current research interests include image processing, computer vision, multimedia, digital video, and remote sensing.

ATREYI KANKANHALLI obtained the B.Tech. degree in electrical engineering from the Indian Institute of Technology, Delhi, in 1986 and the M.S. degree in electrical engineering from Rensselaer Polytechnic Institute, Troy, NY, in 1987. From 1988 to 1989, she was a graduate research assistant in the Biomedical Engineering Department at RPI. Since 1990, she is with the Institute of Systems Science, National University of Singapore, where she is working in the areas of image segmentation and object tracking.

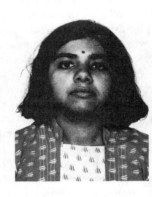

STEPHEN WILLIAM SMOLIAR obtained his PhD in Applied Mathematics and his BSc in Mathematics from MIT. He has taught Computer Science at both the Technion, Israel, and the University of Pennsylvania. He has worked on problems involving specification of distributed systems at General Research Corporation and has investigated expert systems development at both Schlumberger and the Information Sciences Institute (University of Southern California). He is currently interested in applying artificial intelligence to advanced media technologies. He joined the Institute of Systems Science at the National University of Singapore in May 1991 and is presently leading a project on video classification.

Structured Video Computing

**Yoshinobu Tonomura, Akihito Akutsu,
Yukinobu Taniguchi, and Gen Suzuki**
NTT Human Interface Laboratories

▬

Video is becoming increasingly important for multimedia applications, but computers should allow us to do more than just passively watch. They should broaden our viewing styles. We propose a way for computers to structure video and several new interfaces that make video easier to browse and search.

Video is becoming a very important medium, not only for professional and business use, but also for personal use. However, digital video technology implies much more than evidenced by current video applications, which just access and replay movies interactively. Computers offer the potential for different viewing styles and video use beyond the traditional mode of passive watching.

We propose a video processing method that first analyzes a video stream and automatically segments it into shots. Each shot is indexed using the extracted features, such as camera work information and representative colors. This is *video structuring,* and the resultant description is a structured video. As the basic interaction function, we introduce browsing methods based on these indexes. We also propose new video interfaces that allow users to intuitively grasp video content. The structuring process, interaction functions, and intuitive interfaces proposed here look promising for future video applications.

Video interaction

As video shows up increasingly often on computer screens, manipulation techniques once impossible are emerging, due to digital video compression, powerful CPUs, and high-capacity storage devices. However, these advances are not enough for future multimedia applications, because we still have problems manipulating video efficiently to perform such tasks as browsing, authoring, and retrieving video content. Most current video applications are based on three simple video functions: record, access, and replay.

Of the many issues in watching and actively using video, there are several that we want to tackle with computers: fast video browsing to grasp content in a very short time, quick search to find

a specific video segment, and inventing new ways to use video in future multimedia applications.

When you watch video, you watch it in actual replaying time: It takes two hours to watch a two-hour movie. We sometimes fast forward a video to get an overview or search for a specific part. It can be irritating to replay a sequential tape, because it takes time and often results in many unsuccessful attempts to locate a segment. Therefore, a method of fast video browsing that enables the viewer to grasp the idea of a lengthy video without watching it in its entirety is one of the most desired functions. To scan a specific video segment quickly, we need a more direct method than fast forwarding.

In addition to focusing on existing problems, we want to explore new ways to exploit video's possibilities, since this is a main goal of interactive video technology.

Interaction modes

Figure 1a shows our model of viewer-video interaction. The entire figure shows a simplified reference model on which our video-handling processes are based: video taking, video computing, and viewer interaction.

The interaction modes correspond to what we do with video: browse, watch, edit, search, analyze, and any other functions that may be added. Whenever we interact with video, we see visual cues that we associate with something in our memories. In browsing, the full video is not necessary, just enough representative information for a given purpose. Offering visual cues appropriate for the interaction mode is a central point underlying interactive issues. In one sense, this is the visualization of essential information. Therefore, the key technical issues are finding and managing that essential information and presenting it visually.

Video production

The first step for video computing is to consider the information related to video production. Figure 1c shows a flow model of the video-making process and related information. The first stage is obtaining source materials with a video camera. The camera's start and stop operations generate a segment of continuous video called a *take.* A *cut* is a point between adjacent takes on the sequential tape on which the video is recorded. Each take is considered a unit of source video that has a continuous video signal. The camera records object images under conditions controlled by the camera operator, such as panning, tilting, and zooming. These conditions are important information at this stage.

Next, at the editing stage source video materials are collected, examined, and selected. The selected takes are trimmed to *shots*, and are linearly edited into a single video stream. The splicing point between adjacent shots is also called a cut. Each shot is a minimum unit of continuous video, defined by the temporal positions of its beginning and ending points.

The resultant sequence implies the director's directions to the camera operator and the editor. Currently, the final result is just the video, and most of the other, nonvideo information related to video production is lost. However, rich information like the cut points and camera work conditions is embedded in the video. Moreover, the video stream has the implicit structure of the shot sequence.

Video computing

To tackle these issues, we have to process videos efficiently. Figure 1b shows our idea for a simplified video computing process. Since the final video has an implicit structure, the first step in video computing is to analyze the structure and make it explicit, which is the process of parsing the video. The links here, which reconnect the segmented shots, are established automatically. However, they can be established or edited by a human operator. Each shot is analyzed to get more features of the video content, called *video indexes*. The indexes are organized into two kinds of structures. The *link structure* describes the link relations between shots. The *content structure* has information about the scene and objects as obtained by shot analysis.

The next step is visualizing the information in the video using these structures and indexes. It is important to determine the essentiality of the visualized information. Computers do not have to "understand" video, but they need to have enough information to offer rich visual cues to the viewer.

Video structuring

One way to segment video into shots is by detecting cuts. Cut detection is not a new research topic. However, it was not until several years ago that cut detection was thought to be important for video computing. For video computing, cut detection should be as accurate as possible, because the resultant shots are processed further. Many of the developed algorithms detect the discontinuity of a certain video parameter using interframe differ-

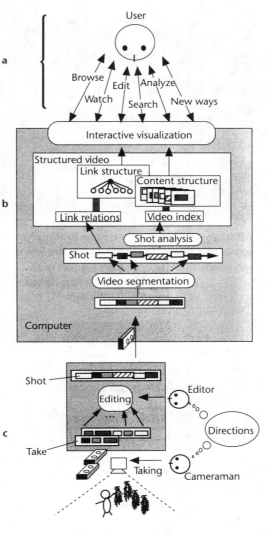

Figure 1. Reference model of the video handling process: (a) viewer interaction, (b) video computing, and (c) video production and editing.

ences.[1,2] These video parameters include intensity, RGB or hue color, and motion vectors.

The problem is that some video phenomena can cause misdetection, such as rapid object motion, telecine conversion (adapting a motion picture to a TV format), slow motion, animation, and strobe lighting. Such phenomena cause large interframe differences in many video parameters. Another problem is that tuning the algorithm parameters for all videos is not easy. The range in video content is extremely wide, from very dark to bright, from static to very lively, and from natural to artificial, such as computer graphics-based video. Also, cut points might not be perfect if they are spliced with a *wipe* or *dissolve*. Such effects weaken the interframe difference in video parameters. Conventional algorithms suffer from one or more weaknesses in these factors, and the result is a low detection rate.

Video computing: related works

The technical requirements for video computing center on

I   interfaces or tools rich in new functions,

I   the creation and management of structured video, and

I   processing structured videos.

A visual interface is essential to activate the

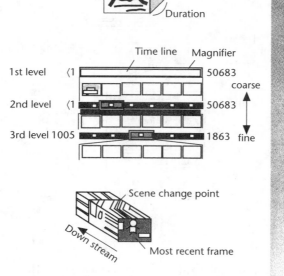

Figure A. Video icon, by Tonomura and Abe.[2]

Representative image

Duration

Figure B. Hierarchical video magnifier, by Mills, Cohen, and Wong.[3]

Time line   Magnifier

1st level ⟨1 50683   coarse

2nd level ⟨1 50683

3rd level 1005 .... 1863 fine

Figure C. Video Streamer.[4]

Scene change point

Down stream

Most recent frame

user's visual sense and stimulate the user's ability to manipulate video. Brondmo and Davenport introduced the micon (moving icon), an icon that displays moving images to represent video content. They used the micon to highlight the video sections of a hypermedia journal on a boat cruise on the Charles River.[1] Tonomura and Abe proposed a content-oriented visual interface using video icons and other visual interfaces for video handling.[2] The video icon is based on a structured icon model using information about video content. For example, its depth corresponds to the duration of the video segment—which appeals to the viewer's intuition (see Figure A). Mills, Cohen, and Wong proposed a hierarchical video magnifier that

offers a range of views from wide to close.[3] (See Figure B.) It allows a user to recursively magnify the temporal resolution of a video source while preserving magnification levels in a spatial hierarchy. The system does not use any video features, but it is effective for video manipulation.

Elliot's video interface, called the Video Streamer, shows spatiotemporal video streams in a box-style volume.[4] The viewer discerns object flows in a video from the patterns on the cube's side. Scene change points can be visually discerned from pattern discontinuities. The duration of shots, as well as the types of transition between them can also be identified visually (see Figure C). The research to date has aimed at developing effective visual interfaces, but they offer only limited cues to the user.

Video data management is important for establishing practical systems. The choice of management type revolves on two issues: determining which information is appropriate for representing video content and how to handle that information. Davenport, Aguierre, and Pincever proposed a framework that used layered information management.[5] They introduced the important idea of "granularity of meaning," which is the degree of information coarseness needed for efficient multimedia handling.

The development of a system supported by image processing is important because the index features of video content must be extracted automatically if we are to deal with a large video database. Ueda, Miyatake, and Yoshizawa reported an editing support system called Impact that used image analysis to achieve cut detection and image flow analysis. Software processed the images.[6] Teodosio and Bender proposed an image representation called Salient Video Stills, which created a combined still image, retaining spatial and temporal context from each video sequence.[7] The image created may have multiresolution patches or a larger field of view. The method includes optical flow analysis, affine transformation, and temporal processing such as weighted temporal median filtering. Tonomura proposed a video-handling architecture that used video indexes.[8] The primary level indexes are abstracted into higher level ones that describe the video's content structure. The primary indexes are created automatically by image analysis operations, such as interframe differences in the intensity histogram. Automatic cut detection is performed by thresholding the indexes.

Video computing: related works (continued)

References

1. H.P. Brondmo and G. Davenport, "Creating and Viewing the Elastic Charles—a Hypermedia Journal," in *Hypertext, State of the Art,* R. McAlesse and C. Greene, eds., Intellect, Ltd., Oxford, England, 1990.
2. Y. Tonomura and S. Abe, "Content-Oriented Visual Interface Using Video Icons For Visual Database Systems," *J. Visual Languages and Computing,* Vol. 1, No. 2, Academic Press, Orlando, Fla., 1990, pp. 183-198.
3. M. Mills, J. Cohen, and Y.Y. Wong, "A Magnifier Tool for Video Data," *Proc. CHI 92,* ACM Press, New York, 1992, pp. 93-98.
4. A. Davis, "Motion Image Processing: Striking Possibilities," *Advanced Imaging,* Vol. 7, No. 8, 1992, pp. 22-56.
5. G. Davenport, S. Aguierre, and N. Pincever, "Cinematic Primitives for Multimedia," *IEEE CG&A,* Vol. 11, No. 4, July 1991, pp. 67-74.
6. H. Ueda, T. Miyatake, and S. Yoshizawa, "Impact: An Interactive Natural-Motion-Picture Dedicated Multimedia Authoring System," *Proc. CHI 91,* ACM Press, New York, 1991, pp. 343-350.
7. L. Teodosio and W. Bender, "Salient Video Stills: Content and Context Preserved," *Proc. ACM Multimedia 93,* ACM Press, New York, 1993, pp. 39-46.
8. Y. Tonomura, "Video Handling Based on Structured Information For Hypermedia Systems," *Proc. ACM Int'l Conf. on Multimedia Information Systems,* ACM Press, New York, 1991, pp. 333-344.

Considering these weaknesses, we developed a filter that passes only short time projections, which can be found at instant cut points, of the interframe differences. We observe a few frames before and after the frame being checked for instant cut detection.[3] The accuracy of instant cut detection, calculated as the rate of correct detection minus that of wrong detection, ranged from 92 to 98 percent for various types of video including news programs, movies, and documentaries—all selected for having several types of potentially troubling phenomena. The tested video totaled more than 4.5 hours.

To handle gradual cuts, we enhanced our method by observing longer intervals than those used for instant cut detection. Differences in video parameters (such as intensity) between frame images are calculated for several intervals from minimum to long periods. The dynamic range of the parameter for each frame is automatically considered in evaluating the differences. The calculated results are evaluated for each interval, as shown in Figure 2. The principle behind this algorithm is that short interval observation is suitable for instant cuts, while longer ones are sensitive to gradual cuts. This algorithm worked very well, even for television advertisements, which have many kinds of special-effects cuts. The detection rate was over 90 percent in the evaluation of our algorithm using a video sequence in which one-third of all cuts are special-effect ones.

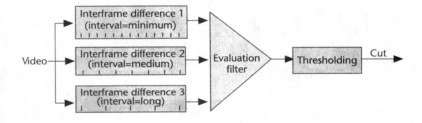

Figure 2. Cut detection processing. Differences between frames are calculated over varying intervals to detect a sequence cut.

Zhang, Kankanhalli, and Smoliar reported a cut detection algorithm that detects gradual cuts.[4] Their algorithm integrates the interframe difference of color value over a certain threshold and detects a cut if the integration result exceeds a threshold within a certain interval. Their method is based on the assumption that a gradual cut involves continuous changes. They reported a detection rate of 90 percent. With these levels of accuracy, we think either method can be applied with little human support.

Shot analysis

Roughly speaking, information contained in a shot is about the camera condition or the objects in the scene. It is not easy for computers to recognize each object unless the scene condition is limited to a specific application. However, we can extract video features that can be important as indexes for handling video.

Since a shot is a sequence of sampled frames that capture spatiotemporally projected images, it includes the scene's spatial and temporal context. We can extract this information using two methods: camera work information suggests the scene's

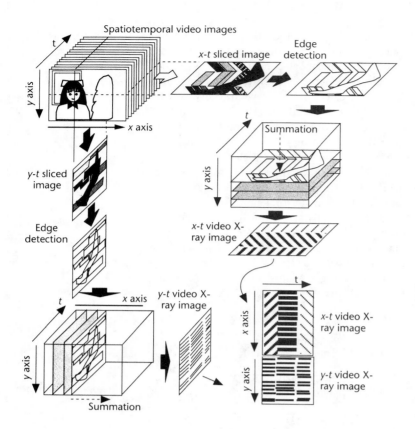

Figure 3. Creating a video X-ray image. Summing the edge-detected x-t sliced images on the vertical (y) axis produces an x-t video X-ray image. We can obtain a y-t video X-ray image in the same manner.

spatial situation and representative color information tells us something about the objects.

Camera work information extraction. When a camera moves, the captured objects show a global change. For example, if the camera is panned to the right, background and unmoving objects move to the left within the camera frame, and the traces of points generated by the objects can be extracted as motion vectors. By analyzing the flow of the motion vectors, camera work parameters can be detected to some extent. Our former research[5] and Ueda's prototype video editing system[6] are based on this method of optical flow analysis. Unfortunately, it takes some time to compute the results, and robustness suffers under various conditions.

In contrast, we propose a method based on video X-ray images. Easily calculated, it is robust enough to apply to general video. (An example of video X-ray images is shown at the bottom right of Figure 9 on page 40.) Video X-ray images are created from the spatiotemporal image sequence, as shown in Figure 3. We extract a sliced image from spatiotemporal images, based on video intensity data, at the y value. By this process we obtain an x-t image at y, then edge detect it to produce an x-t edge image. We repeat this process for all y values, then sum all the sliced x-t edge images on the y (vertical) axis to produce a gray-scale x-t video X-ray image. We obtain a y-t video X-ray image in the same manner. White pixels indicate the existence of many pixels at the image's edge on that axis. When the camera is fixed, the video X-ray images show lines parallel to the time line for the background and unmoving objects. When the camera pans, the lines become slanted. The degree of slanting indicates the panning speed. When the camera zooms in, the lines spread. If there is a moving object, we can detect patterns different from the global lines. Figure 4 explains basic camera operations, and Figure 5 shows corresponding video X-ray images. According to our experiments, as long as there is a background, global flow—which corresponds to camera work—is sufficient to calculate camera operation parameters.

Next, by analyzing the degree of slanting we extract the parameters for panning, tilting, and zooming. Extracting information about tracking and dollying awaits further study.

Representative color extraction. We get a strong impression from the major colors in a shot, such as background blue skies or green mountains. Each pixel's data in a video is translated into Munsel HVC (hue, value, and chroma) color data from RGB (red, green, and blue) data in our system because HVC data mirrors human color perception.[7] By extracting the two or three most frequent hue values for each frame, we can create a sequence of representative colors. The colors do not explicitly describe individual objects but reflect macro color features. By selecting the most frequent representative colors of frames in a shot, we can define the representative colors for the frame. (Figure 9 shows an example of a sequence of representative colors.) The representative colors reflect the background scene in a long shot and the object colors in a middle or close shot.

Figure 4. Basic camera operations.

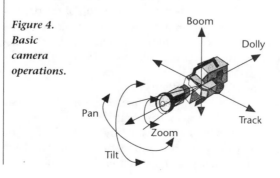

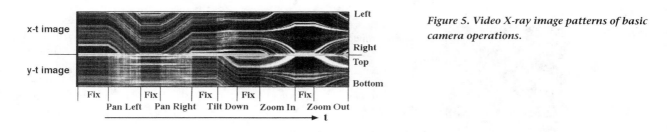

Figure 5. Video X-ray image patterns of basic camera operations.

Therefore, they are generally stable within a shot, and we can use them to locate a specific shot.

Interactive functions

Video can be viewed in different ways in different interaction modes. This is possible because video contains a lot of information, what it tells us is complex, and we watch and use video for various purposes. Here, we focus on visualization methods for video interaction: browsing and new styles of interaction.

Browsing

When we want to pay more attention to the sequential context or overview the video, it is sufficient to *browse*, to see only the essential visual cues without breaking the sequential context.

Figure 6 shows our model of grasping video content. Based on our experience, we divide it into three stages: no idea, rough idea, and full idea. This model may not fully reflect the process of a human understanding a video, but it approximates it for trial purposes. We are in the no idea stage when we have not seen the target video. By watching it in real time, we enter the full idea stage. However, as time passes, we revert to the rough idea, in which we remember only abstract images of the video. If we browse the video again, we easily return to the full idea stage, using the associations triggered by browsing key images. As browsing is quicker than full watching, it is a powerful method when we want to get only a rough idea of the video or recall video content previously seen.

To browse video quickly, it should be displayed either temporally compressed or spatially laid out. To do this, representative images, whether a sequence of still images or short moving images, should be properly extracted from the video. Since these images should efficiently support browsing, each representative image should correspond to a major event in the video. Assuming that each shot includes one major event, we extract one representative image for each shot for browsing.

We adopted the cut detection segmenting

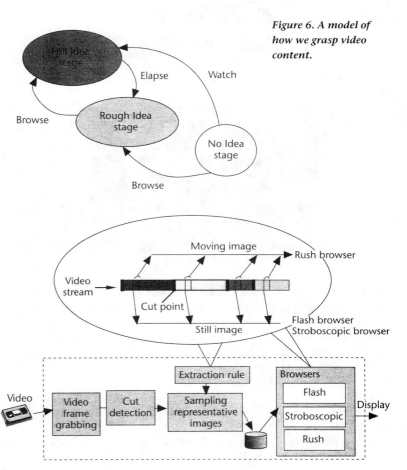

Figure 6. A model of how we grasp video content.

Figure 7. Computer processing for browsing.

technique to choose the images. Figure 7 shows how representative images are extracted using a rule. The rule is to sample at a constant time-offset from the cut point or at the first point after a cut where the frame image satisfies a quality condition, such as when a frame is not too dark or bright, or is not badly focused.

We named the temporal display of representative still images the *flash browser*, the sequence of representative moving images the *rush browser*, and the spatially developed representative still images the *stroboscopic browser*. The flash browser shows the sequence of still representative images like a picture-story show. The rush browser shows the

Figure 8. A browsing interface.

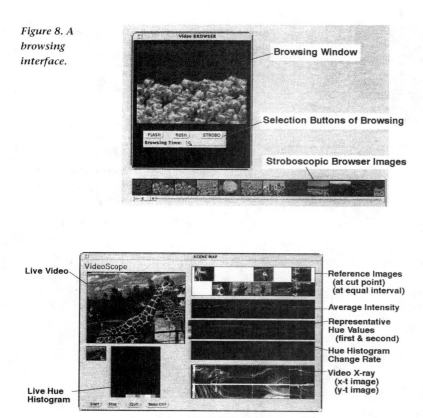

Figure 9. VideoScope interface. The upper left window shows the video. The images in the upper right windows represent reference images at cut points and at equal intervals. The graphs on the middle right represent average intensity, representative hue values, and the hue histogram change rate. Video X-ray images (x-t and y-t) are in the lower right corner. The updated hue histogram appears in the bottom left.

Figure 10. VideoSpaceIcon in its view window: (a) front view and (b) top left view. The front view gives us the panoramic view of the video space. The top-left view gives us a rough idea of both the vertical and horizontal camera work.

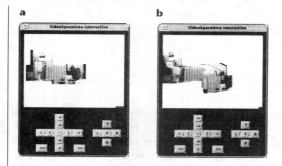

moving images instead. Each representative image is displayed for a period of time calculated by dividing the desired browsing time by the total number of shots. The stroboscopic browser displays the temporal context of the video content at a glance. Which rule to apply, and which browser to use, depends on the viewer's purpose and the video

content. Figure 8 shows a browsing interface.

In a preliminary evaluation experiment, we found the last part of each shot slightly better than the first part for browsing movies. This might have something to do with movie makers' editing methods. However, we need a more detailed evaluation to draw any conclusion.

New video interfaces

Conventional video displays are rectangles that display video in its original format. We propose several new interfaces for video viewing: Video-Scope, VideoSpaceIcon, Video Space Monitor, and PaperVideo. All offer spatial and temporal visual cues of video content.

VideoScope: visual analysis

We have developed a video content analyzer called VideoScope, which shows different types of video features in a way similar to an oscillograph analyzing an electronic device or a spectroanalyzer. This kind of analysis tool may not be used for normal video viewing, but we believe it is important for comprehensive digital video engineering.

Figure 9 shows the VideoScope interface. The top left image is the live video window, the top right one displays reference images sampled at cut points (upper images) and spaced at constant intervals (lower images). The top graph displays the average intensity of the current video frame, and the lines in the second graph correspond to the first and second representative hue values. The third graph displays the rate of change of the hue histogram, where a steep peak indicates a cut point, and the bottom patterns show x-t and y-t video X-ray images. In the video X-ray images, the left part of the y-t image indicates the camera tilting up, and the middle right part shows a zoom. The updated hue histogram is shown at the bottom left. These graphs show features extracted from the input video in real time. VideoScope allows us to see how each feature behaves at a glance.

VideoSpaceIcon: spatiotemporal context

VideoSpaceIcon is the visualization of spatial and temporal video features as an icon. It uses the camera work information extracted by the method explained above.

Conventional icons or video screens can only show actual frames, but a VideoSpaceIcon can show the entire physical space. We call this the video space. The conventional video display process employs only a time-oriented approach, but VideoSpaceIcon is space and time oriented; it allows us to grasp the physical space of the shot at a glance while maintaining temporal context. The three-dimensional figure of the icon allows us to grasp how the camera was operated at a glance.

Figure 10 shows an example of a Video-SpaceIcon with its viewer. It is an extended 3D rectangle, rather than the conventional square 2D image icon. The original video shot panned from left to right, following a woman who walked to the right and sat on a chair. The user can rotate the icon freely around its vertical and horizontal axes to grasp the icon's shape.

The VideoSpaceIcon is created by changing the image position and size for each frame according to the camera work parameters. To construct a VideoSpaceIcon, the icon image position shifts to indicate panning and tilting, while the image size changes to express zooming. Zooming has little effect on the video space itself, but the zoomed part has higher resolution than other parts.

One interesting aspect of the VideoSpaceIcon is that the viewer can reproduce object movement very simply. By overlapping sequential image frames in the video space, a moving object actually moves. In the example in Figure 11, the woman's image walks across the entire space of the shot. This new effect is not possible with traditional video. We can see the entire panoramic space captured by the video, which generates a more comprehensive view of the scene.

Video Space Monitor: no vibration

If we increase the size of the video space, it is no longer just an icon, but a display screen to view the space context of the entire video. We created two display modes: space oriented and anti-vibration. In the space-oriented mode, the front view of the video space is simply enlarged. In the anti-vibration mode, the vibrating frames are adjusted to compensate for vibration, and the video space is limited to frames in which rapid camera work is detected. In this mode, normal camera operations are observed.

Figure 12 shows these two modes. The camera was panned left and suffered strong vibration. In the space-oriented mode, we can see panoramic video. In the anti-vibration mode, the entire video space is not seen but vibration is removed.

The video space monitor differs from conventional monitor displays in that its screen shape dynamically changes, rather than remaining rectangular. However, we have not fully implemented this idea because of a problem with lens skew.

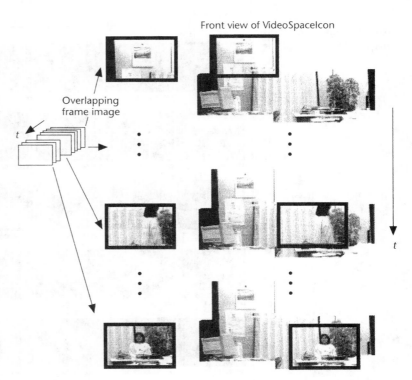

Front view of VideoSpaceIcon

Overlapping frame image

Figure 11. Creating a moving video space icon.

a   b

Given some reasonable constraints, we believe it is practical.

PaperVideo: video at a glance

We extended our idea of the stroboscopic browser to PaperVideo, which takes advantage of the browser's at-a-glance features to display on paper the video's sequence. The primary function of PaperVideo is for photo albums and video indexing. We noticed that, although more people are videotaping their daily lives, they watch the tapes only once or twice. Then the tapes are stockpiled, never to be seen again. This is partly because it is troublesome to find the right tape and locate the specific part through sequential video access. One idea to overcome this problem

Figure 12. Video Space Monitor: (a) the space-oriented mode shows the entire scene; (b) the anti-vibration mode adjusts images to compensate for vibration.

Figure 13. PaperVideo interface.

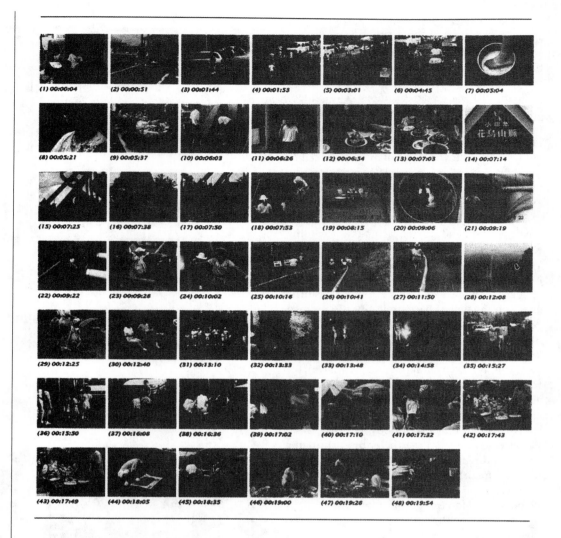

is to make a visual index that reproduces the video's temporal sequence on paper.

Paper can display only still information, but it is very handy and portable, and it needs no electricity or mechanism to see the information. We want to use paper as a bridge to video.

Figure 13 shows an example of PaperVideo in its most simple layout. This is the entire index for a 34-minute video comprised of 90 shots. Each small frame image is automatically sampled when the system detects cut points using the algorithm explained earlier. The time sequence runs from left to right and is carriage-returned left down, as with text. Time codes index each cut. The layout style and image size can be freely modified. In our prototype system, about a dozen template layout formats are available. PaperVideo allows us to clearly see what this video is about and what happened. It means more to the person who shot the

video. We have made PaperVideos for more than 100 hours of video for more than 60 people. Most are very satisfied with this new function.

Conclusion

Our approach to video computing includes making ordinary videos computer-processable and realizing new interactive interfaces. Video segmentation and camera work information extraction are central techniques for structuring video. We believe our ideas for various video browsing styles and new intuitive interfaces are very promising for future video usage and applications.

One thing to underline in handling video is that we should not stick to conventional styles of video processing and usage when we use computers for various applications. At the same time, one of the many things we should learn from movie making is the structure of film and video, because video structure is becoming more important for handling video on computers. We must also make an effort to retain video-related information during video production. **MM**

Acknowledgments

We are grateful to Tomio Kishimoto, Executive Manager of the Advanced Video Processing Laboratory, NTT Human Interface Laboratories, for his encouragement during this research. We would like to thank our colleagues for their helpful advice and discussions.

References

1. K. Otsuji, Y. Tonomura, and Y. Ohba, "Video Browsing Using Brightness Data," *Proc. SPIE Visual Comm. and Image Processing 91*, SPIE, Bellingham, Wash., Vol. 1606, 1991, pp. 980-989.

2. H. Ueda et al., "Automatic Structure Visualization for Video Editing," *Proc. InterCHI 93*, ACM Press, New York, 1993, pp. 137-141.

3. K. Otsuji and Y. Tonomura, "Projection Detecting Filter for Video Cut Detection," *Proc. ACM Multimedia 93*, ACM Press, New York, 1993, pp. 251-257.

4. H. Zhang, A. Kankanhalli, and S. Smoliar, "Automatic Partitioning of Full-Motion Video," *ACM Multimedia Systems*, ACM Press, New York, Vol. 1, 1993, pp. 10-28.

5. A. Akutsu et al., "Video Indexing Using Motion Vectors," *Proc. SPIE Visual Comm. and Image Processing 92*, SPIE, Bellingham, Wash., Vol. 1818, 1992, pp. 1522-1530.

6. H. Ueda, T. Miyatake, and S. Yoshizawa, "Impact: An Interactive Natural-Motion-Picture Dedicated Multimedia Authoring System," *Proc. CHI 91*, ACM Press, New York, 1991, pp. 343-350.

7. M. Miyahara and Y. Yoshida, "Mathematical Transform of (R,G,B) Color Data to Munsell (H, V, C) Color Data," *Proc. SPIE Visual Comm. and Image Processing 88*, SPIE, Bellingham, Wash., Vol. 1001, pp. 650-657.

Yoshinobu Tonomura is a senior research engineer and supervisor in the Advanced Video Processing Laboratory at NTT Human Interface Laboratories. He researches visual communication systems. He was a visiting researcher at the Media Laboratory at the Massachusetts Institute of Technology in 1987-88. He is working on video-handling techniques. Tonomura received BE and MS degrees in electronic engineering from Kyoto University in 1979 and 1981.

Akihito Akutsu is an engineer in the Advanced Video Processing Laboratory at NTT Human Interface Laboratories. He researches video-handling techniques based on image processing. He received BE and MS degrees in image science and engineering from Chiba University in 1988 and 1990.

Yukinobu Taniguchi is an engineer in the Advanced Video Processing Laboratory at NTT Human Interface Laboratories. His research interests include video-handling techniques and services. He received a BE in mathematical engineering and an MS in information physics from the University of Tokyo in 1990 and 1992.

Gen Suzuki is a group leader of the Visual Communication Environment Group in the NTT Human Interface Laboratories. Since he joined the NTT in 1973, he has worked on the research and development of intelligent terminals, electronic filing systems, video communication, ISDN terminals, and Cyberspace, the Networked Virtual Reality System. Suzuki received BE and ME degrees from Waseda University.

Contact Tonomura at 1-2356 Take, Yokosuka, Kanagawa, 235 Japan, e-mail tonomura@nttvdt.ntt.jp.

Video Parsing, Retrieval and Browsing:
An Integrated and Content-Based Solution

H. J. Zhang, C. Y. Low, S. W. Smoliar and J. H. Wu
Institute of Systems Science, National University of Singapore
Heng Mui Keng Terrace, Kent Ridge, Singapore 0511
Republic of Singapore
+65 772-6725
zhj@iss.nus.sg

ABSTRACT

This paper presents an integrated solution for computer assisted video parsing and content-based video retrieval and browsing. The uniqueness and effectiveness of this solution lies in its use of video content information provided by a parsing process driven by visual feature analysis. More specifically, parsing will temporally segment and abstract a video source, based on low-level image analyses; then retrieval and browsing of video will be based on key-frames selected during abstraction and spatial-temporal variations of visual features, as well as some shot-level semantics derived from camera operation and motion analysis. These processes, as well as video retrieval and browsing tools, are presented in detail as functions of an integrated system. Also, experimental results on automatic key-frame detection are given .

KEYWORDS

Video parsing, video indexing, video retrieval, video browsing, multimedia, database.

1. INTRODUCTION

Interfaces to multimedia information systems, such as video on demand (VOD), are in general very weak in interactive functionality (even if some are very visually appealing). Selection rarely involves anything better than key words; and any manipulation of the video itself is limited to the lowest level of VCR control. The problem is that, from the point of view of content, the resources managed by such systems are *unstructured*. The source material is not subject to any structural analysis (parsing) and therefore can be neither indexed nor accessed on the basis of structural properties. Fundamentally, such a system is a database which must support extended capabilities for retrieval (for the user) and insertion (for the system manager). Parsing is the primary extension which serves insertion, while retrieval must exploit parsing results. In addition, because of the subjective nature of the source material, retrieval must be supplemented by capabilities for browsing.

Our use of the term "parsing" differs slightly from linguistic conventions. We see it as encompassing two tasks: *temporal segmentation* of a video program into elemental units, and *content extraction* from those units, based on both video and audio semantic primitives [29]. Many effective algorithms are now available for temporal segmentation [17; 28]. However, fully automated content extraction is a much more difficult task, requiring both signal analysis and knowledge representation techniques; so human assistance is still needed. We thus feel the most fruitful research approach is to concentrate on *facilitating tools*, using low-level visual features . Such tools are clearly feasible and research in this direction should ultimately lead to an intelligent video parsing system [23, 30, 31].

Retrieval and browsing require that the source material first be effectively *indexed*. While most previous research in indexing has been text-based [6, 20], content based indexing of video with visual features is still an research problem. Visual features can be divided into two levels: low-level image features, and semantic features based on objects and events. To date automation of low-level feature indexing[8, 19, 10] has been far more successful than that of semantic indexing[6]. Perhaps the biggest problem with indexing video using the low-level image features of every frame is its enormous volume, but a viable solution seems to be to index representative key-frames [18] extracted from the video sources.

While we tend to think of indexing supporting retrieval, *browsing* is equally significant for video source material. By "browsing" we mean an informal perusal of content which may lack any specific goal or focus. The task of browsing is actually very intimately related to retrieval. On the one hand, if a query is too general, browsing is the best way to *examine the results*. This should provide some indication of *why* the query was poorly expressed; so browsing also serves as an aid to *formulating queries*, making it easier for the user to "just ask around" in the process of figuring out the most appropriate query to pose [32].

Unfortunately, the only major technological precedent for video browsing is the VCR (even available in "soft" form for computer viewing), with its support for sequential fast forward and reverse play. Browsing a video this way is a matter of skipping frames: the faster the play speed, the larger the skip factor. The "content-based" browser of [3] takes this approach, but a uniform skip factor really does not account for video content. Furthermore, there is always the danger that some skipped frames may contain the content of greatest interest. A *truly* content-based approach to video browsing should be based on some level of analysis of the actual image content, rather than simply providing a more sophisticated view of temporal context. However, only few research efforts published [31] that have discussed how parsing results may be applied to support more powerful browsing tools.

This paper presents our work on developing an integrated system to parsing, retrieval, and browsing based on three levels of automated content analysis. What makes our solution effective is its use of the content information represented by the visual feature extracted video parsing processes. There are three processes in our solution which capture different levels of content information: The first is temporal segmentation. At the second level each segment is abstracted into key-frames, based on a simple analysis of content variation which yields results far more useful than sub-sampling at a fixed rate. Finally, visual features, such as color and texture, are used to represent the content of key-frames. In addition, variations among key-frames from the same shot are calculated and integrated with information about camera operation and object motion to provide event-based cues. Indexing is then supported by a clustering process which classifies key-frames into different visual categories; this categorization may also support manual user annotation. These results facilitate retrieval and browsing in a variety of ways. Retrieval may be based on not only the annotated index but also low-level image features of key-frames and temporal variation, object motion and camera operation features of segments. The key-frames enable browsing with a fast forward/backward player, a hierarchical time-space viewer, and cluster-based clip windows.

This paper is organized as follows: Section 2 presents our approaches to video parsing, including a brief summary of temporal segmentation and a detailed discussion of key-frame extraction. Section 3 reviews the visual features of key-frames used in content representation. The resulting approach to retrieval and browsing is then presented in detail in Section 4. Finally, Section 5 offers concluding remarks and a brief view of our current and future work.

2. VIDEO PARSING: SEGMENTATION AND ABSTRACTION

2.1 Temporal Segmentation and Camera Operation Detection

The basic unit of video to be represented or indexed is usually assumed to be a single camera shot, consisting of one or more frames generated and recorded contiguously and representing a continuous action in time and space. Thus, temporal segmentation is the problem of detecting boundaries between consecutive camera shots. The general approach to the solution has been the definition of a suitable *quantitative* difference metric which represents significant *qualitative* differences between frames. Our

own system detects not only simple camera breaks but also gradual transitions implemented by special effects such as fades, wipes, and dissolves [28].

For compressed video data, it would be advantageous to segment it directly, saving on the computational cost of decompression and lowering the overall magnitude of the data to be processed. Also, elements of a compressed representation, such as DCT coefficients and motion vectors in JPEG and MPEG data streams, are useful features for effective content comparison [30, 27]. Our experiments have shown that proper use of both DCT coefficients and motion vectors can achieve both fast processing speed and very high segmentation accuracy [30].

To obtain motion features of video, our system also identifies frames involving camera operations, such as panning, tilting, and zooming, as false positives, and dominant object motions. The simple and effective approach in our system analyzes the characteristic patterns of motion vectors [28]. An alternative approach, implemented in our system, is to examine spatio-temporal slices of video sequences [1]. These images also provide characteristic patterns for camera operation, and they may be used for abstraction and representation of shot content [33].

2.2 Automated Video Abstraction: Key-Frame Extraction

Even when videos are compressed, it is rarely feasible or desirable to index and/or store all frames for retrieval purposes. Instead, an abstraction process is necessary, which may be effectively applied at the individual segment level. We view abstraction as a problem of mapping an entire segment to some small number of representative images, usually called *key-frames*. An index may be constructed from key-frames, and retrieval queries may be directed at key-frames, which can subsequently be displayed for browsing purposes. Also, if storage space is limited, only these key-frames need to be maintained on-line. Furthermore, aThese techniques will be discussed at greater length in the sequel.

Key-frames are still images which best represent the content of the video sequence in an abstracted manner, and may be either extracted or reconstructed from original video data. Key-frames are frequently used to supplement the text of a video log [18], but there has been little progress in identifying them automatically. The challenge is that the extraction of key-frames needs to be automatic and content based so that they maintain the important content of the video while remove all redundancy. In theory semantic primitives of video, such as interesting objects, actions and events should be used. However, because such general semantic analysis is not currently feasible, we have to rely on low-level image features and other readily available information instead. Based on these constraints, we have developed a robust key-frame extraction technique which utilizes information computed by the parsing processes:[1]

---

[1] US Patent pending.

- *Color features:* The basic representation of the color of a video frame is a histogram of the distribution of color components. Also, average brightness, color moments (including mean), dominant color are used. Our specific mathematical definitions will be presented in Section 3. If compressed data are used, these features may be calculated from DCT coefficients of video frames[27].

- *Motion:* Dominant motion components resulting from camera operations and large moving objects are the most important source of information, since motion is the major indicator or content change. For instance, a zoom shot is usually best abstracted by three frames—the first, the last, and one in the middle. When MPEG video is used, motion vectors from B and P frames can be directly extracted for motion analysis.

In our implementation, the key-frame extraction process is integrated with the processes of segmentation. Each time a new shot is identified, the key-frame extraction process is invoked, using parameters already computed during segmentation. Certain heuristics are also applied, such as the decision to use the first frame of every shot as a key-frame. In addition users can adjust several parameters to control the density of key-frames in each shot. The default is that at least two key-frames will be selected for each shot; and, in the simplest case, they could be the first and last frames of the shot. The process is faster with compressed video data, and real time extraction can be achieved.

2.3 Experimental Results

The performance of various temporal segmentation systems has been discussed elsewhere [17, 28, 3, 29, 27] and will not be repeated here. **Table 1** summarizes key-frame extraction results obtained from four test sets, which represent the effectiveness of the techniques described in Section 2.2 in abstracting different types of video material. The first test was based on two "stock footage" videos consisting of unedited raw shots of various lengths, covering a wide range of scenes and objects. "Singapore," the second test set, is travelogue material from an elaborately produced documentary which draws upon a variety of sophisticated editing effects. Finally, the "Dance" video is the entirety of *Changing Steps*, a "dance for television" containing shots with fast moving objects (dancers), complex and fast changing lighting and camera operations, and highly imaginative editing effects, many of which are far less conventional than those in "Singapore." We feel that these four source videos are representative of both the content material and style of presentation that one will generally find in professionally produced television and film.

Because key-frame extraction takes place at the segment level, segmentation results are also listed in **Table 1**. Furthermore, because it is hard to quantitatively measure the accuracy of key-frame extraction (even human selection can be subjective), only the number of key-frames extracted for each test is given. **Table 1** shows

that segmentation performs with an accuracy of over 95% (counting both missing and false detection as errors) in the first three tests. The dance video yields the lowest accuracy, due to the elaborate production technique, and can be considered the lowest achievable accuracy of the segmentation techniques. For all segments which were correctly detected, key-frames were correctly extracted, yielding an average of between two and three key-frames per shot, which tends to be a suitable abstraction ratio. In addition the test results demonstrate that camera operations (both panning and zooming) have been properly abstracted by the key-frames detected.

It is also worth observing that, particularly in the "Dance" example, key-frame extraction actually compensated for segmentation errors. That is, in many of the cases where a shot boundary was missed, one or more additional key-frames were detected to represent the material in the missed shot. In other words key-frame detection is more robust than shot boundary detection.

Video	Length (sec.)	N_d	N_m	N_f	N_k
Stock footage 1	451.8	35	1	1	116
Stock footage 2	1210.7	78	1	5	271
Singapore	173.8	31	1	0	71
Dance	2109.1	90	17	4	205

Table 1: Video segmentation and key-frame extraction results: N_d: number of shots correctly detected; N_m: number of shots missed by the detection algorithm; N_f: false detection of shot boundaries; N_k: number of key-frames extracted.

To systematically evaluate the effectiveness and accuracy of our key-frame extraction system, we conducted a user trial comparing automatic extraction with human identification of key-frames from the two stock footage videos listed in **Table 1**, which were provided by the Singapore Broadcasting Corporation (SBC).[2] Members of the SBC Film/Videotape Library staff were instructed to identify key-frames from these source tapes, on the basis of which they then evaluated the results of our system. Our system did not miss any of the key-frames selected by the librarians. The only difficulty was that our results were more "generous," extracting more key-frames than were selected manually; but this discrepancy has been remedied by providing user control of the density of frames selected. On the other hand the librarians agreed that our automatic extraction was more objective (our system always tried to identify at least one key-frame per shot), while they sometimes tended to ignore certain shots which they felt were not important.

3. SHOT CONTENT REPRESENTATION AND SIMILARITY MEASURES

After partitioning and abstraction the next step is to identify and compute *representation primitives*, based on which the content shot can be indexed, compared, and

---

[2] Now the Television Corporation of Singapore.

classified. Ideally these should be semantic primitives that a user can employ to define "interesting" or "significant" events. However, such an ideal solution is not feasible; so that our representation primitives are based on information accessible through the techniques described in Section 2. The resulting representation is divided into two parts: primitives based on key-frames and those based on temporal variation and motion information. These parts complement each other and can be used either separately or together.

3.1. Representation of Shot Content Based on Key-frame Features

Following the techniques used in image database systems[8, 19, 10], key-frames are represented by properties of color, texture, shape, and edge features, each of which will now be reviewed.

3.1.1 Color features

Color has excellent discrimination power in image retrieval systems. It is very rare that two images of totally different objects will have similar colors [22]. Our representation primitives for color features include mean brightness, color histogram, dominant colors, and statistical moments.

Color histogram: A histogram of the distribution of color intensities is a quantitative representation which is especially useful for textured images which are not well served by segmentation techniques. Also, color histograms are invariant under translation and rotation about the view axis and change only slowly under change of angle of view, change in scale, and occlusion [22]. We have chosen the Munsell space to define color histograms because it is close to human perception of colors [16]. As in QBIC, we have quantized the color space into 64 "super-cells" using a standard minimum sum of squares clustering algorithm [8]. A 64-bin color histogram is then calculated for each key-frame where each bin is assigned the normalized count of the number of pixels that fall in its corresponding supercell.

The distance between two color histograms, I and Q, each consisting of N bins, is quantified by the following metric :

$$D_{his}^2(I,Q) = \sum_i^N \sum_j^N a_{ij}(I_i - Q_i)(I_j - Q_j) \tag{1}$$

where the matrix a_{ij} represents the similarity between the colors corresponding to bins i and j, respectively. This matrix needs to be determined from human visual perception studies, and we have derived it using the method of [11]. Notice that if a_{ij} is the identity matrix, then this measure becomes Euclidean distance.

Dominant colors: Because, in most images, a small number of color ranges capture the majority of pixels, these dominant colors can be used to construct an approximate representation of color distribution. These dominant colors can be easily identified from color histograms of key-frames. Experiments have shown that using only a few dominant colors will not degrade the

performance of color image matching [22, 10]. In fact, performance may even be enhanced, since histogram bins which are too small are likely to be noise, thus distorting similarity computations. Our current implementation is based on twenty dominant colors, corresponding to the histogram bins contains the maximum numbers of pixels.

Color moments: Because a probability distribution is uniquely characterized by its moments, following [20] we represent a color distribution by its first three moments:

$$\mu_i = \frac{1}{N} \sum_{j=1}^N p_{ij} \tag{2}$$

$$\sigma_i = (\frac{1}{N} \sum_{j=1}^N (p_{ij} - \mu_i)^2)^{\frac{1}{2}} \tag{3}$$

$$s_i = (\frac{1}{N} \sum_{j=1}^N (p_{ij} - \mu_i)^3)^{\frac{1}{3}} \tag{4}$$

where p_{ij} is the value of the i-th color component of the j-th image pixel. The first order moment, μ_i, defines the average intensity of each color component; the second and third moments, σ_i and s_i, respectively, define the variance and skewness.

Using these three moments, distance may be computed as follows [21]:

$$D_{mom}(I,Q) = \sum_{i=1}^r (w_{i1}|\mu_i(I) - \mu_i(Q)| + w_{i2}|\sigma_i(I) - \sigma_i(Q)| + w_{i3}|s_i(I) - s_i(Q)|) \tag{5}$$

where r is the number of color components and the w_{ij} ($1 \le j \le 3$) weight the contributions of the different moments for each color component. As we use only a small set of moments, it is possible for two qualitatively different color images to have a D_{mom} value of 0. Nevertheless, experimental evidence has shown that this measure is more robust in matching color images than color histograms [21].

Mean brightness: This number reflects the overall lighting conditions, and is defined similar to and can be derived from (2).

3.1.2 Texture features

Texture has long been recognized as being as important a property of images as is color, if not more so, since textural information can be conveyed as readily with gray-level images as it can in color. Nevertheless, there is an extremely wide variety of opinion concerned with just what texture is and how it may be quantitatively represented [26]. Among all these alternatives we have chosen two models which are both popular and effective in image retrieval: Tamura features [25] and the Simultaneous Autoregressive (SAR) model [14].

Tamura Features: The Tamura features are *contrast*, *directionality*, and *coarseness*, which were introduced as quantification of psychological attributes. Coarseness is a measure of the granularity of the texture. It is derived from moving averages computed over windows of different sizes; one of these sizes gives an optimum fit in both the horizontal and vertical directions and is used to calculate the coarseness metric. Directionality is computed from distributions of magnitude and direction of gradient at all pixels. The quantification of contrast is based on the statistical distribution of pixel intensities [25].

SAR Model: Given an image of gray-level pixels, the SAR model provides a description of each pixel in terms of its neighboring pixels. For an $M \times M$ textured image, the intensity of a pixel at position $s = (s_1, s_2)$, $s_1, s_2 = 1$, ..., M, can be given by

$$g(s) = \mu + \sum_{r \in D} \theta(r) g(s+r) + \varepsilon(s) \tag{6}$$

The parameters for this model are as follows: μ is a bias value which depends on the mean gray-level of the entire image; θ is a set of model parameters which characterize the dependence of pixel s on its neighbors r; D is the set of neighbors; $\varepsilon(s)$ is an independent Gaussian random variable with zero mean whose variance σ^2 models the noise level. The effectiveness of the SAR model depends on the quality of estimates for θ and σ, which are usually determined by either least squares or maximum likelihood estimation.

Our implementation uses the multiresolution SAR (MRSAR) model [14] which describes textures at different resolutions in order to model different granularities. Images are represented by a multiresolution Gaussian pyramid obtained by low-pass filtering and subsampling operators applied at several successive levels. We have chosen four levels of resolution, and the collection of model parameters at each level is used as the texture features of each image.

Similarity: For either model texture is represented quantitatively as a feature vector X. For the SAR model the distance between two such vectors is given by the Mahalanobis function:

$$D_{Mahal} = \left(X^1 - X^2\right)^T C^{-1} \left(X^1 - X^2\right) \tag{7}$$

C is the covariance matrix which models pairwise relationships among the individual model features. Because the Tamura features are almost uncorrelated, the following simplified Mahalanobis function may be used instead:

$$D_{simp} = \sum_{i=1}^{J} \frac{\left(x_j^1 - x_j^2\right)^2}{c_j} \tag{8}$$

3.1.3 Shape Features
Dominant objects in key-frames represent important semantic content and are best represented by their shapes, if they can be identified by either automatic or semi-automatic spatial segmentation algorithms. In our implementation dominant objects in key-frames are obtained by a color-based segmentation algorithm [10] and an interactive outlining algorithm[5]. In comparing similarity between shapes, cumulative turning angles are used, because they provide a measure closer to human perception of shapes than algebraic moments or parameteric curves [2]. This metric also provides: 1) invariance under translation, rotation and scaling, 2) invariance with respect to convex and non-convex polygons, and 3) relatively easy computation.

3.1.4 Edge Features
Edges derived from an image using a technique such as a Sobel filter provide good cues for content: humans can easily identify some objects from their edge maps. We have derived such binary edge maps as a representation of key-frames. Two images can then be compared by calculating a correlation between their edge maps [13]. Key frames can also be retrieved based on such a similarity measure. However, these comparisons are limited by their dependency on image resolution, size, and orientation.

3.2. Temporal Features for Representation of Shot Content
Key frames utilize only spatial information and ignore the temporal nature of a video to a large extent. With such a representation only it will be difficult to support event-based classification and retrieval. An example is that frame-to-frame differences can be used to classify news video clips into anchorperson shots and news shots [31]. We shall now review some of the temporal features we are currently using to represent temporal characteristics at shot level.

Camera operations: We have already discussed the detection of camera operations, including panning, tilting, and zooming, by analyzing either motion fields or spatio-temporal images; this information provides a useful representation of temporal content for each shot.

Temporal variation of brightness and colors: They are represented by the mean and variance of average brightness and a few dominant colors calculated over all frames in a shot.

Salient stills: Salient stills are images that are constructed from the content of all the frames in a shot, which capture both the content and context of the entire shot [24]. However, constructing salient stills requires sophisticated motion analysis and segmentation and is computationally expensive. Though we are currently working on improving the accuracy and speed of constructing salient stills, we are not ready to integrate this representation into our current system.

Other features: Other temporal features for representing video content include global orientation parameters of spatio-temporal images and object motions. The spatio-temporal global orientation parameters calculated using steerable orientation filters provide additional information about motion in each shot and can be used to classify shots. Developing algorithms for moving object detection, tracking, and description is a longer-term research effort.

4. CONTENT-BASED RETRIEVAL AND BROWSING

Once a scheme for representation of video content has been established, tools for content-based retrieval and browsing can be built upon that representation; a set of such tools of our system will now be reviewed.

4.1 Content-Based Retrieval of Video Shots

With the representation and similarity measures described in Section 3, querying a video database to retrieve shots can be performed based on key-frame features, temporal shot features, or a combination of the two. The retrieval system we are building supports retrieval as a more interactive process than is provided by simply formulating and processing conventional queries, providing fewer constraints on the possibilities the user may with to explore. The query process is still iterative, with the system accepting feedback to narrow or reformulate searches or change its link-following behavior, and to refine any queries that are given.

4.1.1 Key-Frame-Based Retrieval

Once a video has been abstracted to key-frames, search becomes a matter of identifying those key-frames from the database which are similar to the query, according to the similarities defined in Section 3. To accommodate different user requests, three basic query approaches are supported: query by template manipulation, query by object feature specification, and query by visual examples. Also, the user can specify a particular feature set to be used for a retrieval.

Query by visual templates is based on the assumption

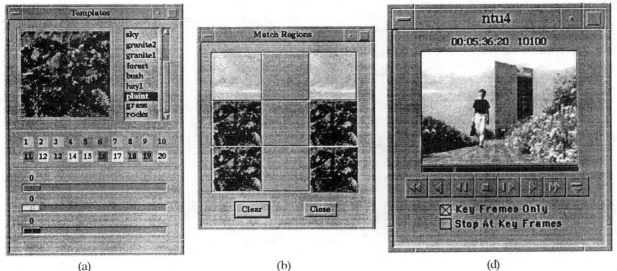

(a)   (b)   (d)

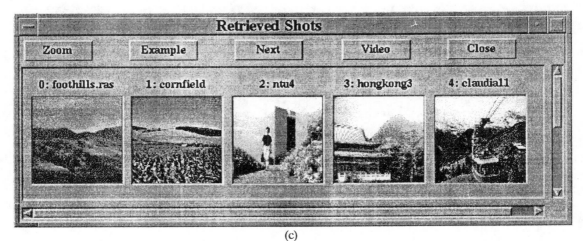

(c)

Figure 1:   Key-frame-based query of video database. (a) Template panel with color template selection and color manipulation tools; (b) Composed template image which forms a query; (c) Retrieved key-frames based on color similarity to the query; (d) A player to browse a shot represented by a key-frame retrieved.

that a user often wants to retrieve key-frame images which consist of some known color patterns, such as a sunny sky, sea, beach, lawn, or forest. These pre-defined templates are stored and displayed as color texture maps and can be selected by the user to form a query, as shown in *Figure 1(a)*. The color distribution of a selected template can also be manipulated: The color manipulator consists of three scalars, corresponding to red, green, and blue intensities, and a display of up to 20 significant colors in the selected template, in descending order of contribution to the template image. The user can modify the red, green, and blue content of any selection to approximate more closely what he/she has in mind. The manipulation is performed in real time, meaning that the user is able to see changes in the template color while making adjustments.

As shown in *Figure 1(b)*, it is not necessary that the entire area of the target image be filled by templates: images can be retrieved based on matching only those regions for which templates have been specified. For example, one can form a query by selecting a sky and a green area template and place them in the regions as shown in *Figure 1(b)*. This partially specified query resulted in the five best histogram-based matches displayed in *Figure 1(c)*.

Once a key-frame has been identified, the user may view its associated video clip by clicking the "Video" button in the "Retrieved Images" window. This initiates a video player, as shown in *Figure 1(d)*, which is cued by the location of the key-frame. That frame may also be used to derive a hierarchical display, as will be seen in *Figure 3*, in which the key-frames are elements of the lowest level. Retrieval may thus be followed by browsing as a means to examine the broader context of the retrieved key-frame. On the other hand a query can also be initiated from browsing. Thus, a user may select an image while browsing and offer it as a query: a request to find all key-frames which resemble that image.

4.1.2 Shot-Based Retrieval

Entire shots can also be retrieved based on their temporal features. Queries such as "find all shots with a camera panning at 10°/second" can be easily satisfied based on temporal representations. It is also possible to combine temporal and key-frame features in a single query, such as "query by example". *Figure 2* shows an example of such

(a)

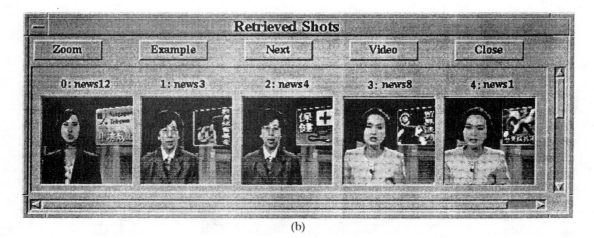

(b)

Figure 2: Shot based video retrieval. (a) Query formed by this example shot of anchorperson. (b) Retrieved shots represented by their key-frames from the video database based on their similarity to the query example in terms of shot features.

a query using an anchorperson shot, shown in *Figure 2(a)*, where retrieval is based on average colors, color histograms, and their temporal variations. This is, in fact, a general technique for distinguishing anchorperson shots from news shots.

4.2. CONTENT-BASED VIDEO BROWSING

As we pointed out earlier, the uniqueness of our browsing tools lies in their use of the content information obtained from video parsing including segment boundaries, camera operations, and key-frames. Our browsing tools support two different approaches to accessing video source data: *sequential* access and *random* access. In addition, these tools accommodate two levels of granularity—overview and detail—along with an effective bridge between the two levels.

Sequential access browsing takes place through the VCR-like interface illustrated in *Figure 1(d)*. Overview granularity is achieved by playing *only* the extracted key-frames at a selected rate. Detailed granularity is provided by normal viewing, with frame-by-frame single stepping; and this approach is further enhanced to "freeze" the

display each time a key-frame is reached. Finally, viewing at both levels of granularity is supported in the reverse, as well as forward, direction.

The hierarchical browser is designed to provide random access to any point in a given video: a video sequence is spread in space and represented by frame icons which functio n rather like a light table of slides [32]. In other words the display space is traded for time to provide a rapid overview of the content of a long video[15]. As shown in *Figure 3*, at the top of the hierarchy, a whole video is represented by five key-frames, each corresponding to a segment consisting of an equal number of consecutive camera shots. Any one of these segments may then be subdivided to create the next level of the hierarchy. As we descend through the hierarchy, our attention focuses on smaller groups of shots, single shots, the representative frames of a specific shot, and finally a sequence of frames represented by a key-frame. We can then move to more detailed granularity by opening the first type of video player to view sequentially any particular segment of video selected from this browser at any level of the hierarchy.

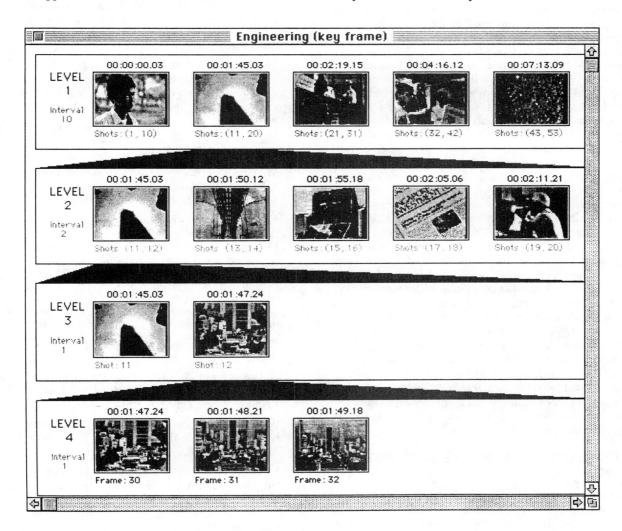

Figure 3: Key-frame-based hierarchical video browser.

As we pointed out earlier, another advantage to using key-frames in browsing is that we are able to browse the video content down to the key-frame level without necessarily storing the entire video. This is particularly advantageous if our storage space is limited. Such a feature is very useful not only in video databases and information systems but also to support previewing in VOD systems. What is particularly important is that the network load for transmitting small numbers of static images is far less than that required for transmitting video; and, because the images are static, quality of service is no longer such a critical constraint. Through the hierarchical browser, one may also identify a specific sequence of the video which is all that one may wish to "demand." Thus, the browser not only reduces network load during browsing but may also reduce the need for network services when the time comes to request the actual video.

The browsing tools presented above are basically *programs* or *clips* based. That is, video programs or clips are loaded into the browser either from a list of names specified by retrieval result, a database index or a user. As shown in Figure 3, the only criteria used to select the representative icons displayed at the top level of the hierarchy is time: they are the first key-frame of the first shot among all shots represented. In other words, the shots at the high levels are grouped only according to their sequential relations not their content. As a result, though random access is provided, a user has to browse down to the second or third level to get a sense of content of all shots in a group. This is less a problem if the browsing is launched from retrieval result such as shown in *Figure 1* and *Figure 2*, but it will not be very convenient when we use it to brows raw video data or parsing result.

To support *class-based* browsing, we have been working on clustering algorithms using the same content representation as used in retrieval. Two types of algorithms, ISODATA partitioning and hierarchical clustering[7], have been used for this task. With such clustering processes, when a list of video programs or clips are provided, the parsing system will use either key-frame and/or shot features to cluster shots into classes, each of which consists of shots of similar content. After such clustering, each class of shots can be represented by an icon, which can then be displayed at the high levels of hierarchical browser. As a result, user can know roughly the content of each calls of shots even without moving down to lower level of the hierarchy. Such clustering is also useful in index building and computer-assisted video content annotation. We are currently working on integrating this part into our system.

5 . CONCLUDING REMARKS AND FUTURE WORK

In this paper we have presented an overview of our work in developing an integrated and content-based solution for computer-assisted video parsing, abstraction, retrieval and browsing. The most important feature of our approach is its use of low-level visual features as a representation of video content and its automatic abstraction process. Such a representation and extracted key-frames, together with spatio-temporal features and some semantic primitives derived at shot level, can then be used to facilitate indexing, retrieval and browsing. Experimental results and usibility studies have shown that such a solution is effective and feasible and will be useful in many multimedia applications, though tranditional text-based indexing and retrieval tools will still be part of the integrated system.

We are now working on more robust algorithms to extract event-based features. Case studies on parsing and indexing news broadcasts have already allowed us to support queries such as "find me all interview shots in a news program" [31]. An inportant extension of our work is to incorporate audio analysis and text parsing into both video parsing and content representation[4].

6. REFERENCES

1. E. H. Adelson and J. R. Bergen, Spatiotemporal Energy Models for the Perception of Motion, *Journal of the Optical Society of America A* 2 (2), pp. 284-299, 1985.

2. E. M. Arkin *et al.*, An Efficiently Computable Metric for Comparing Polygonal Shapes, *IEEE Transactions on Patt. Analy. and Mach. Intell.*, 13 (3), pp. 209-216, 1991.

3. F. Arman *et al.*, Content-based Browsing of Video Sequences, *Proc. ACM Multimedia 94*, San Francisco, CA, 1994.

4. W. Bender and P. Chesnais, Network Plus, Proc. SPIE Electronic Imaging Device and Systems Symposium. Vol. 900, p81-86, 1988.

5. D. Daneels *et al.*, Interactive Outlining: An Improved Approach Using Active Geometry Features, *Proc. IS&T/SPIE. Conf. on Storage and Retrieval for Image and Video Databases II*, San Jose, CA, 1993.

6. M. Davis, Media Streams: An Iconic Visual Language for Video Annotation, *Proc. Symposium on Visual Languages*, Bergen, NORWAY, 1993.

7. R. Duda and P. Hart, *Pattern recognition and scene analysis*, Wiley, New York, 1973.

8. C. Faloutsos *et al.*, Efficient and Effective Querying by Image Content, *Journal of Intelligent Information Systems* 3, pp. 231-262, 1994.

9. W. T. Freeman and E. H. Adelson, The Design and Use of Steerable Filters, *IEEE Trans. on Patt. Analy. and Mach. Intell.*, 13 (9), pp. 891-906, 1991.

10. Y. Gong *et al.*, An Image Database System with Content Capturing and Fast Image Indexing Abilities, *Proc. International Conference on Multimedia Computing and Systems*, Boston, MA, 1994, pp. 121-130.

11. M. Gorkani and R. Picard, Texture Orientation for Sorting Photos at a Glance, *Proc. 112h International Conference on Pattern Recognition*, Jerusalem, ISRAEL, 1994.

12. M. Ioka, A Method Of Defining the Similarity of Images on the Basis Of Color Information, *Technical Report RT-0030*, IBM Tokyo Research Laboratory, 1989.

13. T. Kato *et al.*, A Sketch Retrieval Method for Full Color Image Database: Query by Visual Example, *Proc. 11th International Conference on Pattern Recognition*, Amsterdam, HOLLAND, 1992, pp. 530-533.

14. J. Mao and A. K. Jain, Texture Classification and Segmentation Using Multiresolution Simultaneous Autoregressive Models, *Pattern Recognition*, 25 (2), pp.173-188, 1992.

15. M. Mills, J. Cohen, and Y. Y. Wong, A Magnifier Tool for Video Data, *Proc. CHI '92*, Monterey, CA, pp. 93-98, 1992.

16. M. Miyahara, and Y. Yoshida, Mathematical Transform of (R,G,B) Color Data to Munsell (H,V,C) Color Data, *Proc. of SPIE Visual Communication and Image Processing*, 1001, pp. 650-657, 1988.

17. A. Nagasaka and Y. Tanaka, Automatic Video Indexing and Full-Video Search for Object Appearances, *Visual Database Systems, II*, E. Knuth and L. M. Wegner, editors, North-Holland, pp. 119-133, 1991.

18. B. C. O'Connor, Selecting Key Frames of Moving Image Documents: A Digital Environment for Analysis and Navigation, *Microcomputers for Information Management*, 8(2), pp. 119-133, 1991.

19. A. Pentland, R. W. Picard, and S. Scarloff, Photobook: Tools for Content-Based Manipulation of Image Databases, *Proc. IS&T/SPIE. Conf. on Storage and Retrieval for Image and Video Databases II*, San Jose, CA, 1994, pp. 34-47.

20. L. A. Rowe, J. S. Boreczky, and C. A. Eads, Indexes for User Access to Large Video Databases, *Proc. IS&T/SPIE Conf. on Storage and Retrieval for Image and Video Databases II*, San Jose, CA, 1994, pp. 150-161.

21. M. Stricker and M. Orengo, Similarity of Color Images, *Proc. IS&T/SPIE. Conf. on Storage and Retrieval for Image and Video Databases III*, San Jose, CA, 1995.

22. M. J. Swain and D. H. Balllard, Color Indexing, International Journal of Computer Vision, Vol.7, pp.11-32, 1991.

23. D. Swanberg, C.-F. Shu, and R. Jain, Knowledge Guided Parsing in Video Databases, *Proc. IS&T/SPIE Conf. on Storage and Retrieval for Image and Video Databases*, San Jose, CA, 1993.

24. L. Teodosio and W. Bender, Salient Video Stills: Content and Context Preserved, *Proc. ACM Multimedia 93*, Anaheim, CA, 1993, pp. 39-46.

25. H. Tamura, S. Mori, and T. Yamawaki, Texture Features Corresponding to Visual Perception, *IEEE Trans. on Syst., Man, and Cybern.*, 6 (4), pp.460-473, 1979.

26. M. Tuceryan and A. K. Jain, Texture Analysis, *Handbook of Pattern Recognition and Computer Vision*, C. H. Chen, L. F. Pau, and P. S. P. Wang, editors, World Scientific, pp. 235-276, 1993.

27. B.-L. Yeo and B. Liu, Rapid Scene Analysis on Compressed Video, *IEEE Transactions on Circuits and Systems for Video Technology*, to appear.

28. H. J. Zhang, A. Kankanhalli, and S. W. Smoliar, Automatic Partitioning of Full-motion Video, *Multimedia Systems* 1 (1), pp. 10-28, 1993.

29. H. J. Zhang and S. W. Smoliar, Developing Power Tools for Video Indexing and Retrieval, *Proc. IS&T/SPIE Conf. on Storage and Retrieval for Image and Video Databases II*, San Jose, CA, 1994, pp. 140-149.

30. H. J. Zhang *et al.*, Video Parsing Using Compressed Data, *Proc. IS&T/SPIE Conf. on Image and Video Processing II*, San Jose, CA, 1994, pp. 142-149.

31. H. J. Zhang *et al.*, Automatic Parsing and Indexing of News Video, *Multimedia Systems*, 2 (6), pp. 256-266, 1995.

32. H. J. Zhang, S. W. Smoliar, and J. H. Wu, Content-Based Video Browsing Tools, *Proc. IS&T/SPIE Conf. on Multimedia Computing and Networking 1995*, San Jose, CA, 1995.

33. H. J. Zhang and W. C. Ho, "Video sequence parsing," *Technical Report*, Institute of Systems Science, National University of Singapore, 1995.

Extracting Story Units from Long Programs for Video Browsing and Navigation

Minerva Yeung[†], Boon-Lock Yeo[‡] and Bede Liu[†]

[†] Department of Electrical Engineering
Princeton University
Princeton, NJ 08544
{mingy,liu}@ee.princeton.edu

[‡] IBM T.J. Watson Research Center
P.O. Box 704
Yorktown Heights, NY 10598
yeo@watson.ibm.com

Abstract

Content-based browsing and navigation in digital video collections have been centered on sequential and linear presentation of images. To facilitate such applications, nonlinear and non-sequential access into video documents is essential, especially with long programs. For many programs, this can be achieved by identifying underlying story structures which are reflected both by visual content and temporal organization of composing elements. In this paper a new framework of video analysis and associated techniques are proposed to automatically parse long programs, to extract story structures and identify story units. The proposed analysis and representation contribute to the extraction of scenes and story units, each representing a distinct locale or event, that cannot be achieved by shot boundary detection alone. Analysis is performed on MPEG-compressed video and without a prior models. The result is a compact representation that serves as a summary of the story and allows hierarchical organization of video documents.

Keywords: Hierarchical representation of video, scene identification, scene transition graph, time-constrained clustering, video browsing, video analysis.

"Cause and effect are mutually dependent, forwards and retrospectively. One begets the other by an inexorably ordained necessity, which would be fatal for us if we were able to discover all of the connections at once. The link of cause and effect, in other words the transition from one state to another, is also the form in which time exists, the means whereby it is materialized, in day to day practice. ..."

"Time itself, running through the shots, had met and linked together. ..."

"Time in the form of fact: ... The point is to pick out and join together the bits of sequential fact, knowing, seeing and hearing precisely what lies between them and what kind of chain holds them together. That is cinema." — Andrey Tarkovsky [7]

1. INTRODUCTION

Browsing and navigation are integral parts of interactive search to find clips of interest in large collections of video programs. To browse efficiently, the contents of video documents have to be succinctly presented to the users to enable understanding at a snapshot's notice. To navigate extensively, nonlinear access of video material must be provided, which means that structures have to be built to reflect the semantics of the video documents. Thus it is important to be able to automatically analyze video documents based on the contents, extract concisely the structures presented in the contents, and represent precisely the extracted structures to the users, in a way that implicitly or explicitly allows semantic understanding of the underlying contents as well as fast and meaningful nonlinear access to relevant materials.

Existing content-based analysis of video concentrates on detecting shot boundaries (commonly known as *scene change*[1] detection) based on objective visual primitives such as color, image correlations and sometimes motion parameters. By detecting the shot boundaries, individual shots are re-discovered and they represent the fundamental units of video. This is an important step towards content-based browsing: an image, usually the first frame, is chosen to represent the shot, and the collection of such images gives a "condensed" version of a given video sequence upon which the users can browse. This presentation format relieves the user from the need to watch the entire video during browsing. However, in many video programs, there are hundreds of shots: 500 is not uncommon in typical films [7]; in modern action movies, the number can be thousands (we counted 300 shots in a 15-minute segment of the "Terminator 2 — the Judgement Day", and the movie lasts 139 minutes.); an

---

[1] This is a misnomer of terms. These techniques detect the boundary when a camera shot transits to another. In film production, a scene may have many different shots. Throughout the paper, we call such operations "shot boundary detection" to distinct them from the actual segmentation of scenes.

half-hour episode of sitcom "Frasier" has about 300 shots. In addition, a frame taken from a shot often fails to represent the dynamic and time varying content within the shot. In such cases, presenting shots in a one dimensional image array does not offer the users an effective and efficient means to browse, navigate and search for any particular video segments. This presents a greater challenge for the user if the user has never watched the video in its entirety, and has no idea where in the time array the search should start.

Another approach of browsing is to differentiate the contents presented in the individual frames of video documents with predefined contexts and extract the more "important" frames for presentation. This can be achieved by extracting highlights[16] of sports events, detecting captions[13, 8], and spotting key words [8], etc. While such forms of video skimming cut significantly the time of browsing, the applications may be limited to certain types of video programming because of the underlying assumptions. Model-based parsing of video sequences has been proposed for news broadcasts[9, 17] to extract certain specialized semantic elements of the sequences based on *a priori* models.

In the above approaches, browsing is achieved on a sequential and linear presentation of the images, or from the results of parsing the video content using *a priori* models. To facilitate the process, we need nonlinear and nonsequential access into video documents to take full advantage of the digital media. In addition, *a priori* models may not be practical in many forms of video programs. In reality, video is a medium of presentation, a means of expression of ideas and in fact, a form of document. For many video documents, there are underlying storylines which are reflected by the visual contents and the temporal organization of the material presented. In view of such underlying structures, a video browser should allow the user to first identify the scenes taking place at that location using visual information, select the scene desired using temporal information, and similarly navigate through the various shots in the scene using both visual and temporal information. Thus there is a real need to identify both visual and temporal relationships to allow the user to recognize the underlying story structure and navigate to the desired point in the video. In the paper presented previously by Yeung *et. al* [15], the scene transition graph was proposed as a compact representation of story structures to allow efficient browsing and navigation. The structure was extracted automatically using visual and temporal information with no *a priori* knowledge of the content, by segmenting video clips into shots, condensing visually similar shots, and incorporating temporal relationships of the shots to build the graph. The representation is effective to present compactly the structures of shots and the temporal flow of the story for highly structured video programs.

However, in long programs, because of the change of scenes, locales and story content, visually similar shots,

when presented in different scenes or when separated far in time, may have different contexts. Visual contents alone cannot differentiate the difference in contexts. This can render the scene transition graph very complicated and not adequate for efficient analysis and browsing uses. A significant reserve of video programs, especially films and TV programs, simply last more than a few minutes. In this paper a general framework of video analysis and associated techniques are proposed to parse automatically long video programs to extract the story structures and identify individual story units. We first examine the role of "time" in the composition of video programs in Section 2, and provide a general framework of clustering of video shots on both visual similarities and temporal localities of the shots which we call *time-constrained clustering* in Section 3. We will look at the *Scene Transition Graph* and its analysis in details in Section 4. In Section 5, we will show that scene transition graph, when combined with time-constrained clustering, becomes a powerful tool to present not only the story structures, but also the flow of the story, and a means on which analysis can be performed to meaningfully segment individual units from the story. Each individual unit is a graph and the time line links the unit together to tell the underlying story. The block diagram, as well as some details, of an implementation of the concepts for the analysis of long programs are also presented. The experimental results are discussed in Section 7.

The framework presented and the subsequent analysis contributes to the extraction of scenes and story units which currently cannot be achieved by any means of shot boundary detection. In addition, the analysis and processing of video are carried out on greatly reduced data that are extracted directly from videos compressed using common compression standards like Motion JPEG and MPEG. Lastly, *a priori* knowledge of a video clip's story structure is not required as the structure is discovered through the analysis. Consequently, long programs can be automatically parsed to achieve a hierarchical decomposition of video, which in turn offers higher level of semantical understanding, and facilitates the browsing and navigation process in digital video libraries.

2. Dissecting Video

The fundamental unit of the production of video is the shot, which captures continuous action from a camera. A shot reflects a fragment of the story. A scene is "usually composed of a small number of interrelated shots that are unified by location or dramatic incident" [1]. At the higher level, several scenes can be composed into an act. The act-scene-shot decomposition forms an hierarchy of story units. The story line then chains the shots into scenes, the scenes into acts, and together they are linked to tell the story. The story structure and organization are commonly found in motion pictures, TV movies, sitcoms, etc, and are not confined to such: in many structured programs like news, documentaries, TV magazines, talk shows, etc., each program is a composition of distinctive segments, each of which represents a story unit with underlying messages. The segments are then linked together by some established shots like the shot of the anchor room or the host.

It is advantageous to be able to segment the story units from a program without very specific knowledge of the particular program selected, and instead segment based on the presentation along the time line and the visual contents. Consequently, long programs can be effectively broken down into meaningful segments, and the story can be further condensed and presented in a hierarchical fashion for efficient browsing applications. To do this, we first have to examine two characteristics of video presentation that are common in a variety of programs.

The most essential characteristic of motion picture presentation is the sequential montage. Montage "refers to the editing of the film, the cutting and piecing together of exposed film in a manner that best conveys the intent of the work" [3]. Montage was studied by Eisenstein [4] and other great Soviet directors. As described in [7], "One of the binding and immutable conditions of cinema is that actions on the screen have to develop sequentially, regardless of the fact of being conceived as simultaneous or retrospective... In order to present two or more processes as simultaneous or parallel you have necessarily to show them one after the other, they have to be in sequential montage." For example, in Hollywood the use of alternating close-up shots of two characters is common to convey conversations, innuendos and reactions[3]. Repeating shots of the same person or same settings, alternating or interleaving with other shots, are often seen in TV programs, news broadcasts, interviews, talk shows, etc. to convey parallel events in a scene.

In addition, contents in a motion picture and many video materials are localized in time. For example, given two shots of the same person, if the two shots are juxtaposed together, they are more likely to be of the same scene than if they are placed far apart in time from each other. Often time, a scene is made up of temporally adjacent shots indicating their interrelationships. And scenes, just like shots, can be alternating to convey an "image" of time.

The sequential montage has produced a distinctive consequence at the shot level: repetitive shots of similar contents interleaved by other shots with different contents. These shots may be the shots of the same person, taken from the same camera, at the same location, or about the same event. Most often, the similarities of contents are shown through similar visual characteristics of the compositing frames in the shots. This form of similarity measurement is independent of the featured video program, and does require any

specific knowledge of the underlying story. Hence we are able to classify the shots by grouping shots of similar visual contents into special classes of distinct labels. It provides a way to further condense the information presented and offers a better organization of the video.

However, because of the temporal locality of the contents, two visually similar shots, if occur far apart in the time line, may potentially represent different contents or locales in different scenes. For long programs, there is little justification for grouping shots into the same class based only on visual contents without regard to the timing of the context. On the contrary, such grouping may lead to shots from different story units (or *scenes* in script writers' terms) clustered together, which may not only complicate the understanding, but also make the segmentation of distinct scenes or story units very difficult, if not impossible.

In the following section, we will discuss how video shots can be clustered together based on visual similarities, and with constraints that reflect the temporal locality of contents. We call this time-constrained clustering of video shots. This clustering framework, when incorporated into the Scene Transition Graph (Section 4), is capable of capturing the flow of the story and allows broader segmentation of story units beyond the segmentation of video shots.

3. Time-Constrained Clustering of Video Shots

In this section, we formulate the problem of clustering in the context of video shots: clustering based on similarity distances of the shots such as visual primitives (like color and image correlations), and with additional temporal constraints to reflect the localities of video contents in time.

To proceed, assume there are N shots $S_1, S_2, \cdots S_N$. Each shot $S_i = \{f_{b_i}, \cdots f_{e_i}\}$ consists of images numbered $b_i, b_i + 1$, through e_i. Assume also that we have a distance $d(S_i, S_j)$ that compares the similarity between shots S_i and S_j. Section 5 discusses the nature of this $d(.,.)$ in more details.

We want to group shots that are both visually similar and temporally close together into a cluster. In addition, different clusters should have sufficiently different characteristics. We first define a modified distance between two shots to take also into account the temporal distances as follows:

$$\hat{d}(S_i, S_j) = \begin{cases} d(S_i, S_j), & d_t(S_i, S_j) \leq T; \\ \infty, & \text{otherwise,} \end{cases} \quad (1)$$

where $d_t(.,.)$ is the temporal distance between two shots:

$$d_t(S_i, S_j) = \begin{cases} \min(|b_j - e_i|, |b_i - e_j|), & i \neq j; \\ 0, & i = j. \end{cases} \quad (2)$$

The distance $d_t(.,.)$ is the distance in number of frames from the end of the earlier shot to the beginning of the latter one.

We propose to use a time-window parameter T (T is the elapsed number of frames) as a constraint on the clustering process: shots can be clustered together if they fall within the time window. This additional constraint means that, for any two shots S_i and S_j, $S_i \in C$ and $S_j \in C$ implies $d_t(S_i, S_j) \leq T$.

Denoting by C_i the ith cluster, and x, y and z elements of the cluster each of which is a video shot, we define the following criterion of time-constrained clustering:

[Time-constrained Clustering Criterion]

Given $x \in C_i$, define

$$\epsilon_i = \max_{y,z \in C_i} \hat{d}(y, z), \qquad (3)$$

then

$$\hat{d}(x, w) > \epsilon_i, \text{ for all } w \in C_j, j \neq i.$$

This criterion implies a strong condition on the similarity of shots in a cluster. It requires each shot to be similar to every other shot in a cluster. In this case, with each clustering C_i is an associated maximum dissimilarity ϵ_i defined by (3). It measures the maximum distance between any two shots in the cluster. Any other shot outside of the cluster must have a distance greater than ϵ_i relative to any shot in the cluster. In addition, each pair of shot in a cluster must be separated by no more than T frames apart.

Hierarchical clustering method based on *complete-link*, described in [6] and the references therein, generates clusters that satisfy the condition listed in the above criterion. Before describing the algorithms, we define the distance between two clusters C_i and C_j as

$$\hat{d}_{max}(C_i, C_j) = \max_{x \in C_i, y \in C_j} \hat{d}(x, y). \qquad (4)$$

The algorithm proceeds as follows:
    [**Algorithm** Complete-link Method]

1. Initially, there are N clusters $\{S_1\}, \{S_2\}, \cdots, \{S_N\}$. Each cluster contains a shot. Set $NumCluster \leftarrow N$.

2. Stop when

$$\hat{d}_{max}(A, B) > \delta, \text{ for all clusters } A \neq B.$$

    or $NumCluster = 1$.

3. Find the least dissimilar pair of clusters, R and S, according to (4), i.e., find R and S such that

$$\hat{d}_{max}(R, S) \leq \hat{d}_{max}(A, B), \text{ for all clusters } A, B.$$

4. Merge R and S into a new cluster. Set $NumCluster \leftarrow NumCluster - 1$.

5. Go to step (2).

The clustering parameter δ controls when the iteration stops. It is normalized to take on values from 0 and 1 and defines the minimum separation between any two resulting clusters. In practice, δ can be predefined. $NumCluster$ in the algorithm maintains the number of disjoint clusters formed. At each step, the algorithm merges two most similar clusters into a new cluster based on cluster distance (4). It is easy to see that at each step of the process, the time-constrained clustering criterion is always satisfied.

In implementation, the distances of the newly merged cluster to other clusters have to be updated accordingly at each iteration. One algorithm that implements such a clustering method is based on the proximity matrix $\mathcal{D}$ described in [6] and the references therein. An $N \times N$ proximity matrix $\mathcal{D} = [\hat{d}(S_i, S_j)]$ has entries the distance between two shots. At each step, the matrix is updated by deleting rows and columns corresponding to cluster R and S and adding a new row and column corresponding to the newly formed cluster $R \cup S$.

Specific realizations of the distance metric $d(., .)$ of video shots and the time window parameter T will be discussed in Section 5.

4. Scene Transition Graph and its Analysis

In this section we shall review the Scene Transition Graph, which is part of a more general model of Hierarchical Scene Transition Graph (HSTG) as presented in [15]. We will show how the STG and the time-constrained clustering together provide a representation that enable the partitioning of a video program into well-defined story units. The partitioning can be achieved by looking for *cut edges* in the STG.

Throughout this paper, we shall treat a *shot*, defined as a continuous sequence of actions, as a fundamental unit in a video sequence[2]. Physically a shot is a collection of image frames.

A Scene Transition Graph (STG) is a directed graphs with the following property:
$\mathcal{G}_0 = (\mathcal{V}_0, \mathcal{E}_0, \mathcal{F}_0)$, where $\mathcal{V}_0 = \{V_{0,i}\}$ is the node set and $\mathcal{E}_0$ is the edge set. $\mathcal{F}_0$ is a mapping that partitions the set of shots $\{S_i\}$ into $V_{0,1}, V_{0,2}, \cdots$, the members of $\mathcal{V}_0$. For given U, W in $\mathcal{V}_0$, (U, W) is a member of $\mathcal{E}_0$ if there exists some S_l in U and and S_m in W such that $m = l + 1$.

Thus, the collection of shots is partitioned into nodes of $\mathcal{G}_0$; each node represents a cluster of shots. $\mathcal{F}_0$ partitions $\{S_i\}$ into $V_{0,1}, V_{0,2}, \cdots$ such that nodes in each $V_{0,i}$ are *sufficiently similar*, according to some similarity metrics. A directed edge is drawn from node U to W if there is a shot

---
[2] Further subdivisions of shots into smaller units is possible and can be easily accommodated by the framework defined below.

represented by node U that immediately precedes any shots represented by node W.

In this case, shots that are *similar* to each other are clustered together. (In time-constrained clustering, the similarity metric has already incorporated an indication of the temporal distance.) Relations between clusters are governed by temporal ordering of shots within the two clusters. A simple example would be a scene of conversation between two persons; the camera alternates between shots of each person. The graph $\mathcal{G}_0$ consists of two nodes $V_{0,1}$ and $V_{0,2}$; $(V_{0,1}, V_{0,2})$ and $(V_{0,2}, V_{0,1})$ are both members of $\mathcal{E}_0$.

The STG representation allows some forms of analysis of video through the analysis of the graph. One important feature in a graph is a **cut edge** defined as follows: an edge is a *cut edge* in an undirected graph, if when it is removed, results in two *disconnected* graphs [2]. In the context of an STG, we treat a directed edge as a cut edge if the underlying undirected graph of $\mathcal{G}$ becomes disconnected after the removal of the edge. Note that the definition of the STG guarantees that when treated as an undirected graph, there always exists a path from any given node to any other node. Each connected subgraph after the removal of cut edges will then represent a *story unit*.

5. Analyzing Video and Extracting Story Units

In this section we will show a realization of the concepts of time-constrained clustering and scene transition graph presented in the previous sections to automatically parse a video program, extract story structures and identify story units. The resulting graph representation presents not only the story structures, but also the flow of the story, as well as a clear view of meaningful units of the story segmented.

Given a video program, it has many shots and a few scenes. To access this digital video document effectively and nonlinearly, there is the need to re-discover the composing shots and scenes, to find the structures of the document, to summarize the contents, and to present the structures and the contents to the users. More importantly, it is desirable to do most of the operations automatically.

The block diagram of the implementation is shown in Figure 1. Here are the key steps listed in the diagram for analyzing the video programs and extracting meaningful story units. For illustration purposes, we provide a sample video clip (R1) (which has several scenes, each scene is itself a story unit and contains several shots) and explain the results alongside the analysis steps. Individual components are discussed in the following sections. Note that in the diagram each shot is illustrated by an image, however, in the analysis process, the dynamics of content variations in the shot are represented by a collection of *key frames* instead.

1. *Shot Segmentation*: shot transitions (shot boundaries) are detected to segment individual video shots; The

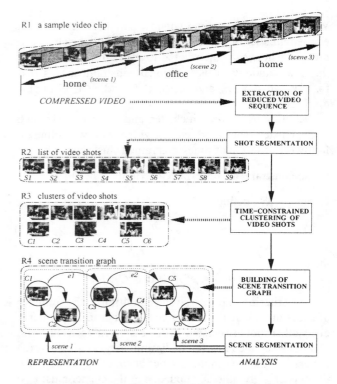

Figure 1. Block diagram of Proposed Framework

algorithm detects the boundaries of shots based on the changes of visual characteristics and gives a list of the video shots (R2) of the clip. For the sample clip, nine shots (S1 to S9) are segmented out.

2. *Time-constrained Clustering of Video Shots*: video shots are partitioned into distinct clusters based on visual similarities and temporal constraints. Given the list of video shots (R2), shots are matched and clustered based on their visual contents and temporal localities to further condense repetitive shots of similar contents. For example, the nine shots are matched and grouped to give 6 clusters in R3 (C1 to C6).

3. *Building of Scene Transition Graph*: A scene transition graph is built from the clustering results, and the temporal relationships of the shots in the clusters. A node represents a cluster and an edge shows the flow of story from one node to the next. The STG of the sample video is shown as R4.

4. *Scene Segmentation*: story units are extracted by finding the *cut edges* of the STG. Each unit is a connected subgraph by itself. In R4, two cut edges (e1 and e2) are found, thus segmenting the video clip into 3 scenes. Each scene indeed corresponds to the events

taking place at a specific locale.

The analysis steps do not require *a priori* models, and have been tested on a variety of programs with promising results. The steps are generic to both compressed and uncompressed videos, however, for compressed video, reduced image sequences are extracted directly from the compressed data stream upon which the subsequent analyses are based (*Extraction of Reduced Video Sequence*). The ability to carry out the analyses on compressed video is very important because many long programs are captured and stored directly in compressed formats like MPEG due to their inherent size of data. The details are presented in the following sections.

5.1. Extraction of Reduced Video Sequence from MPEG Video

We work with video compressed with MPEG-1 [5]. Since decompression of the video requires significant processing time and extra storage, we use the framework of processing directly on the compressed video proposed by Yeo [11] for the various image processing operations. In this framework, spatially reduced images are reconstructed from the compressed video without the full-frame decompression process. Two forms of reduced images are studied: the *DC* and *DC+2AC*. These images are reduced significantly in sizes but yet capture important global image features effective for low-level visual processing.-

We extract the DC images for video at a spatial resolution of 320×240 and the DC+2AC images for video at a spatial resolution of 160×240. In both situations, the reduced images are 40×30 and are sufficient for the processing requirements described in this paper. Significant speedup is obtained using the reduced images in applications like shot boundary detection. In expensive and non-sequential operations like video shot matching, the computational savings are especially noted.

5.2. Detection, Matching and Clustering of Video Shots

Since reduced images capture well the important global features of the images, they can be effectively used for detecting changes from one frame to the next. We use the algorithm proposed by Yeo and Liu [12] based on reduced images to detect both abrupt and gradual shot boundaries. The individual shots, once detected, are then used for shot matching and clusterings.

To compare one video shot to the next, we take into account the temporal variations in each shot. Based on difference metric $D()$ between two images, Yeung and Liu [14] define video shot similarity to be

$$d(S_i, S_j) = \min_{\substack{b_i \leq l \leq e_i \\ b_j \leq m \leq e_j}} D(f_l, f_m). \qquad (5)$$

The difference metric can be measured on color (histogram intersection measures), or pixel correlation (luminance projection), or a combination of both.

Such comparisons are inherently expensive since there are several comparisons of one shot to other shots. Because of the temporal redundancy inherent in video, [14] proposes the use of *keyframes*, selected in non-uniform manner in time, to approximate (5). More keyframes are selected in video shots with more variations and fewer in shots with little content changes. If we denote by $K_i \subset S_i$ the subset of keyframes of shot S_i, then we have

$$d(S_i, S_j) \approx \min_{f_l \in K_i, f_m \in K_j} D(f_l, f_m), \qquad (6)$$

for appropriately chosen set K_i and K_j. It is also reported in [14] that images of reduced spatial resolution (such as those extracted from MPEG using algorithms in [12]) are sufficient for low-level visual comparison of images. Through the use of keyframes, it is reported that only 2 % to 5 % of the number of frames are needed for accurate video shot matching. The use of reduced temporal resolution (through keyframes) and reduced spatial resolution (through reduced images from MPEG video) permit effective and efficient shot clustering to be performed.

Extracting story units involves the partitioning of the video program into distinct scenes. And the partitioning is first achieved through the time-constrained clustering. In time-constrained clustering, ideally, each cluster is a collection of shots with similar contents and in the same scene. Good clustering results in general depend both on the fidelity of distance metric selected to differentiate visual contents and the time-window parameter T chosen.

The time-window T optimally should be chosen to reflect the minimum temporal distance between two instances of the same scene, such that shots in these two instances are not grouped together (we shall call each such instance a scene by itself, or better, a story unit). Two alternating scenes are illustrated at the top of Figure 1. In the video clip, there are 2 scenes with the HOME setting, interleaved by a scene of the OFFICE. Each scene consists of several shots. T should be set to reflect the temporal length of the interleaved scene, such that the shots in scene 3, will not be in the same clusters that contains shots in scene 1, even if the visual characteristics may be quite similar.

However, such knowledge is not readily available. In practice, T can be chosen to be a sufficiently large fixed number. Here we assume that there are sufficient differences in the characteristics of one scene and those of the next scene, and the differences exhibited are good enough to segregate the shots from these adjacent but distinct scenes. (This is often the case because scene changes, unlike shot changes, often involve a change of locale and setting, different casts, etc. which are well reflected by changes in visual characteristics.) And a scene usually consists of several shots, thus lasts longer. In our experiments, we use $T = 3000$ for the programs tested, and the clustering results and the subsequent STG built are very satisfactory.

The clustering algorithm follows the algorithm presented in Section 3. The algorithm first groups the pair of shots that are most similar together, and then proceeds to group other shots by their proximity values. The proximity values between clusters are updated in the process. A dendrogram is built in the process and dissecting the dendrogram at a given index level (either by the number of clusters or proximity threshold desired) gives a corresponding partition of video shot clusters. The index level can be predefined or selected by the user for adjustments, or by automatic selection schemes.

5.3. Analysis of Scene Transition Graph

The clustering results, together with the temporal relations of the shots, are used to build the scene transition graph. Each node represents a collection of shots while an edge reflects the flow of story from one node to the next.

In a given scene, very often we find multiple elements co-exist (e.g., multiple casts), the shots of all these elements are juxtaposed and linked together, and very commonly we find multiple shots of the same element. Shots from different scenes cannot be juxtaposed, except at the transition from one scene to the next. We say that the two shots *interact* if they are juxtaposed side by side, that is, temporally adjacent to each other.

If the time-constrained clustering results are good — that is, shots of the same visual content falls in a category (e.g., a cluster of all the shots of the same person from the same camera in a given scene), and shots from different scenes (story units) are forced to fall under different categories, we can make the following observations: (1) shots in the same scene interact with other shots; and (2) shots from different scene do not interact, except at the transition of one scene to another.

In the STG, interactions are reflected by presence of cycles, edges connecting the nodes together and nodes with high degree of incoming or outgoing edges. Therefore, a scene in some way can be characterized by a connected subgraph. To be more precise, we use a story unit to approximate an actual scene. In a STG representation of video, the transition of one scene (or simply, a story unit) to the next will always occur on cut edge. This is because a cut edge represents a unique point of transition from a shot from a earlier story unit to the ensuing shot of the next story unit. The collections of cut edges in a STG then represent all the transitions from one unit to the next. By detecting the cut edges, individual story units can be segmented out.

These assumptions of video characteristics, and the subsequent segmentation procedures are not dependent on any *a priori* model of the specific nature of individual programs, and are applicable to a fairly wide variety of programming types. We will show later that story units can be successfully extracted from sitcoms, movies, cartoons, and documentaries.

6   Hierarchical Browsing and Navigation of Video

To better present the graph, an interface is built for the user to browse, navigate and understand the video programs. The scene transition graph makes use of the temporal relations to mark the edges of the directed graph. Individual units are clearly visible in the layout from its subgraph structure. The cut edges are shown with color. In the graph, the story units are linked from one to the next as the story unfolds. The content of each node can be presented in an expanded form to show the constituent shots upon a button click of the node.

The graph offers a condensed view of the contents, serves as the summary of the program and allows nonlinear access of the story elements. Browsing and navigation are achieved by identifying both content and structure of the program, and in a hierarchical manner. For example, given a STG of an episode of "Friends" (Figure 3), a user can get an overview by looking at the summary of story units presented by the visual contents in the nodes and associated edges, then navigate to a particular story unit (e.g., on Monica as shown by the highlighted nodes) by selecting the story. He can zoom into the story contents (Figure 2) to get more information; and then click on individual nodes to look at the video shots. He can then select any video shot to watch the key frames, or the entire sequence of frames in that particular shot, or listen to the associated audio track.

7. Results and Discussion

This section describes experimental results of the analyses applied to several test programs. The sequences are compressed with MPEG.

Figure 3 shows the STG constructed from an episode of the sitcom "Friends". There are 35575 frames. In this episode, there are 313 shots. From Figure 3, we can see clearly the individual story units. An example of a selected story unit is shown by highlighting the corresponding nodes. This STG is constructed with $T = 2000$ and $\delta = 0.3$.

We also see from this example that transition from a story unit to the next on the STG *always* occurs on a *cut edge* of the graph. The cut is shown by an highlighted edge. Each cut segments a subgraph into 2 disjoint subgraphs which are strongly connected. An example of such cut edge is the

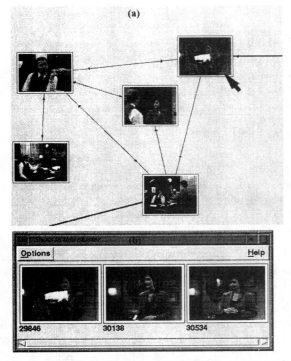

Figure 2. (a) Zoom in view of the story unit highlighted in Figure 3 (b) Shots presented in the selected node.

transition edges between the two subgraphs in the top left corner of the graph. Each cut edge in the STG represents a forward flow of story from one scene to the next. In general, there may be more cut edges than the actual transitions of scenes as described in the original script. Such instances are found when cut edges occur within a scene.

This example illustrates the power of time-constrained clustering of video shots to identify individual story units through the intense interactions between shots in an unit. Clustering procedures separate shots that are visually dissimilar into different clusters. The time constraints further segregate recurring scenes separated far apart in time. For example, in Figure 3, there are alternating scenes of events taking place at Monica's and Chandler's apartments. Other scenes with different casts and locales (cafe, office, etc.) are re-discovered as well. The highlighted edges (reflecting the cut edges) join the subgraphs together and present the flow of units in sequential order, linking one scene to the next as the story flows. The story structure is presented concisely and meaningfully this way. The segmentation of contents achieved is accurate and corresponds well to the program.

The STG permits rapid nonlinear browsing of long video program. The half-hour episode in this example is succinctly condensed to a graph which can be displayed in a screen. A user can quickly identify and zoom in to segments of interests without having to *linearly* view through the entire program.

A summary of the results are shown in Table 1. The tested sequences were digitized at 30 frames/sec except the "Democratic Convention 1992" which is digitized at 15 frames/sec. The sitcoms are half-hour episodes, with the commercials edited out; the movie segments are taken from "Aladdin" and "Dances with Wolves". For the results presented in Table 1, the time window is the same (100-second duration). This translates to $T = 3000$ for sequences digitized at 30 frames/sec, and $T = 1500$ for sequences digitized at 15 frames/sec. The clustering parameter $\delta = 0.3$. The results are used to illustrate the hierarchical decomposition of the video programs. Such an hierarchy, from frames, shots to story units, allows multilevel organization of video.

A breakdown of the timing performance of the entire algorithms applied to sequence "Frasier" is shown in Table 2. The table shows the time taken for different steps shown in Figure 1. The sequence was MPEG-1 compressed with GOP frame pattern IBBPBBPBBPBB. It has 37498 frames, each at a resolution of 320×240. Experiments were conducted on an 150 MHz SGI workstation. The time for each stage involves disk I/O time to read images from and write images to disk. We list only the timing for the first three stages, since a large amount of data has to be processed at these stages and that the processing time for the last two are insignificant by comparison. The codes have not been optimized for speed; in addition, further optimization can be achieved by combining the I/O flow from one stage to the next.

Stages	Timing (min:sec)
Extraction of Reduced Video Sequence	9:30
Shot Segmentation	0:25
Time-constrained Clustering	2:40
Total	12:35

Table 2. Breakdown of timing for different processing steps

In the results, the extraction of DC images averages 65 frames/second. The key frames selected in the "Frasier" test sequence constituted about 2% of the original number of frames. The good timing performance is achieved through processing on the reduced images extracted from compressed video, the selection of key frames for shot matching, and the time-constrained clustering framework. The process eliminates the need to perform decompression of the MPEG video streams and permits non-sequential operations to be done in an efficient way. The reduction both

Type	Sequence Name	# frames	# shots	# clusters	# story units
Sitcom	Friends	35575	313	105	18
Sitcom	Frasier	37427	318	99	19
Cartoon segment	Aladdin	23251	188	78	22
Movie segment	Dances with Wolves	21400	140	70	19
Documentary	Democratic Convention '92	14398	68	38	10

Table 1. Results of sample test sequences

in spatial and temporal domain renders the disk storage minimal for the processing of long video sequences.

We use graph layouts algorithms described in [10] for initial layout, and for simple graph layouts. For complex graphs, at the current stage the layout is user-assisted but we are working on efficient and automatic STG layout algorithms.

8. Conclusions

The video analysis framework and the associated techniques proposed in this paper have contributed to the extraction of scenes and story units that cannot be achieved by shot segmentation alone. In addition, the building of story structure gives non-sequential and non-linear access to a featured program and facilitates browsing and navigation. We have successfully segment story units which represent distinct events or locales from several types of video programs and the results are promising. We also are able to decompose the video into the hierarchy of story units (and scenes), clusters of similar shots, and shots at the lowest level. This helps further organization of video. We are currently testing the proposed scheme on more programs and on different programming types. We will further evaluate the performances, promises and limitations of such analysis.

Acknowledgments

This work was funded in part by the Intel Foundation Graduate Fellowship, the Wallace Memorial Fellowship in Engineering, and the Siemens Corporate Research. The computing facilities used in the research are supported by the National Science Foundation under Grant CDA-9216171.

References

[1] F. Beaver. *Dictionary of Film Terms*. Twayne Publishing, New York, 1994.

[2] J. A. Bondy and U. S. R. Murty. *Graph Theory with Applications*. The Macmilliam Press Ltd., 1976.

[3] Britannica online. http://www.eb.com:180/eb.html, Nov. 1995.

[4] S. Eisenstein. *The Film Sense*. Harcourt, Brace & World, New York, 1970.

[5] D. L. Gall. A video compression standard for multimedia applications. *Communications of the ACM*, 34(4):46–58, April 1991.

[6] A. K. Jain and R. C. Dubes. *Algorithms for Clustering Data*. Prentice Hall, 1988.

[7] Andrey Tarkovsky, translated by Kitty Hunter-Blaire. *Sculpting in Time — Reflections on the Cinema*. University of Texas Press, Austin, 1986.

[8] M. A. Smith and T. Kanade. Video skimming for quick browsing based on audio and image characterization. Technical Report CMU-CS-95-186, Carnegie Mellon University, July 1995.

[9] D. Swanberg, C. F. Shu, and R. Jain. Knowledge guided parsing in video databases. In *Storage and Retrieval for Image and Video Databases*, volume SPIE 1908, pages 13–25, 1993.

[10] L. Szirmay-Kalos. Dynamic layout algorithm to display general graphs. In P. Heckbert, editor, *Graphics Gems IV*, pages 505–517. Academic Press, Boston, 1994.

[11] B. L. Yeo. *Efficient Processing of Compressed Images and Video*. PhD thesis, Princeton University, Electrical Engineering Department, Jan. 1996.

[12] B. L. Yeo and B. Liu. Rapid scene analysis on compressed videos. *IEEE Transactions on Circuits and Systems For Video Technology*, 5(6):533–544, Dec. 1995.

[13] B. L. Yeo and B. Liu. Visual content highlighting via automatic extraction of embedded captions on MPEG compressed video. in *Digital Video Compression: Algorithms and Technologies 1996*, Feb. 1996.

[14] M. M. Yeung and B. Liu. Efficient matching and clustering of video shots. In *International Conference on Image Processing*, volume I, pages 338–341, 1995.

[15] M. M. Yeung, B. L. Yeo, W. Wolf, and B. Liu. Video browsing using clustering and scene transitions on compressed sequences. In *Multimedia Computing and Networking 1995*, volume SPIE 2417, pages 399–413, Feb. 1995.

[16] K. D. Yow, B. L. Yeo, M. M. Yeung, and B. Liu. Analysis and presentation of soccer highlights from digital video. In *Second Asian Conference on Computer Vision*, pages 499–503, Dec. 1995.

[17] H. J. Zhang, Y. H. Gong, S. W. Smoliar, and S. Y. Yan. Automatic parsing of news video. In *International Conference on Multimedia Computing and Systems*, pages 45–54, 1994.

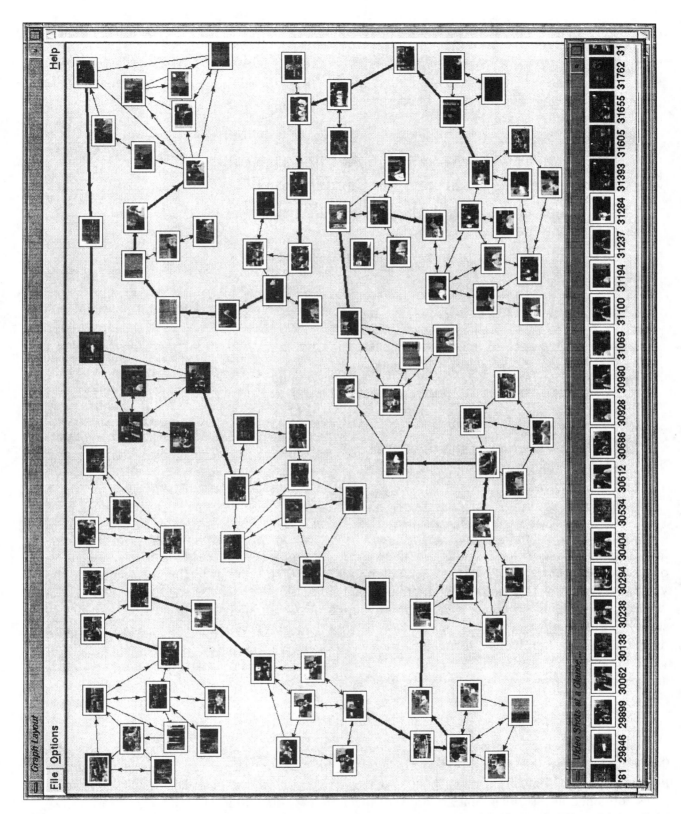

Figure 3. STG with time-constrained clustering for Friends (sitcom). A selected story unit and the cut edges are highlighted. The bottom window displays the shots of the highlighted story unit in temporal order.

Video Skimming and Characterization through the Combination of Image and Language Understanding Techniques

Michael A. Smith and Takeo Kanade
February 3, 1997
CMU-CS-97-111

School of Computer Science
Carnegie Mellon University
Pittsburgh, PA 15213

Abstract

Digital video is rapidly becoming important for education, entertainment, and a host of multimedia applications. With the size of the video collections growing to thousands of hours, technology is needed to effectively browse segments in a short time without losing the content of the video. We propose a method to extract the significant audio and video information and create a "skim" video which represents a very short synopsis of the original. The goal of this work is to show the utility of integrating language and image understanding techniques for video skimming by extraction of significant information, such as specific objects, audio keywords and relevant video structure. The resulting skim video is much shorter, where compaction is as high as 20:1, and yet retains the essential content of the original segment.

This research is sponsored by the National Science Foundation under grant no. IRI-9411299, the National Space and Aeronautics Administration, and the Advanced Research Projects Agency. Michael Smith is sponsored by AT&T Bell Laboratories. The views and conclusions contained in this document are those of the authors and should not be interpreted as necessarily representing official policies or endorsements, either expressed or implied, of the United States Government or AT&T Bell Laboratories.

1 Introduction

With increased computing power and electronic storage capacity, the potential for large digital video libraries is growing rapidly. These libraries, such as the Informedia[TM] Project at Carnegie Mellon [7], will make thousands of hours of video available to a user. For many users, the video of interest is not always a full-length film. Unlike video-on-demand, video libraries should provide informational access in the form of brief, content-specific segments as well as full-featured videos.

Even with intelligent content-based search algorithms being developed [5], [11], multiple video segments will be returned for a given query to insure retrieval of pertinent information. The users will often need to view all the segments to obtain their final selections. Instead, the user will want to "skim" the relevant portions of video for the segments related to their query.

Browsing Digital Video

Simplistic browsing techniques, such as fast-forward playback and skipping video frames at fixed intervals, reduce video viewing time. However, fast playback perturbs the audio and distorts much of the image information[2], and displaying video sections at fixed intervals merely gives a random sample of the overall content. Another idea is to present a set of "representative" video frames (e.g. keyframes in motion-based encoding) simultaneously on a display screen. While useful and effective, such static displays miss an important aspect of video: video contains audio information. It is critical to use and present audio information, as well as image information, for browsing. Recently, researchers have proposed browsing representations based on information within the video [8], [9], [10]. These systems rely on the motion in a scene, placement of scene breaks, or image statistics, such as color and shape, but they do not make integrated use of image and language understanding.

An ideal browser would display only the video pertaining to a segment's content, suppressing irrelevant data. It would show less video than the original and could be used to sample many segments without viewing each in its entirety. The amount of content displayed should be adjustable so the user can view as much or as little video as needed, from extremely compact to full-length video. The audio portion of this video should also consist of the significant audio or spoken words, instead of simply using the synchronized portion corresponding to the selected video frames.

Video Skims

Figure 1 illustrates the concept of extracting the most representative video frames and audio information to create the skim. The critical aspect of compacting a video is context understanding, which is the key to choosing the "significant images and words" that should be included in the skim video. We characterize the significance of video through the integration of image and lan-

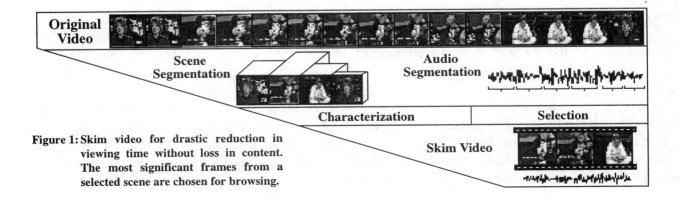

Figure 1: Skim video for drastic reduction in viewing time without loss in content. The most significant frames from a selected scene are chosen for browsing.

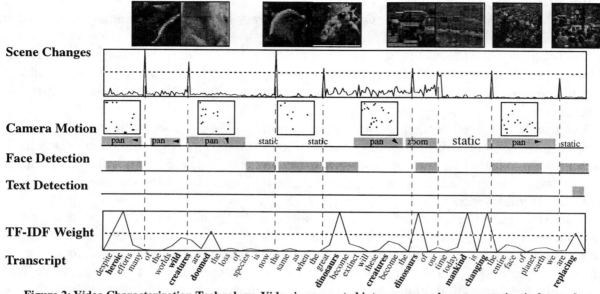

Figure 2: Video Characterization Technology. Video is segmented into scenes, and camera motion is detected along with significant objects (faces and text). Bars show frames with positive results.

guage understanding. Segment breaks produced by image processing can be examined along with boundaries of topics identified by the language processing of the transcript. The relative importance of each scene can be evaluated by 1) the objects that appear in it, 2) the associated words, and 3) the structure of the video scene. The integration of language and image understanding is needed to realize this level of characterization and is essential to skim creation.

In the sections that follow, we describe the technology involved in video characterization from audio and images embedded within the video, and the process of integrating this information for skim creation.

2 Video Characterization

Through techniques in image and language understanding, we can characterize scenes, segments, and individual frames in video. Figure 2 illustrates characterization of a segment taken from a video titled "Destruction of Species", from WQED Pittsburgh. At the moment, language understanding entails identifying the most significant words in a given scene, and for image understanding, it entails segmentation of video into scenes, detection of objects of importance (face and text) and identification of the structual motion of a scene.

2.1 Language Characterization

Language analysis works on the transcript to identify important audio regions known as "keywords". We use the well-known technique of TF-IDF (Term Frequency Inverse Document Fre-

$$TF\text{-}IDF = \frac{f_s}{f_c} \tag{1}$$

quency) to measure relative importance of words for the video document [5]. The TF-IDF of a word is its frequency in a given scene, f_s, divided by the frequency, f_c, of its appearance in a standard corpus. Words that appear often in a particular segment, but relatively infrequently in a standard corpus, receive the highest TF-IDF weights. A threshold is set to extract keywords from the TF-IDF weights, as shown in the bottom rows of Figure 2.

2.2 Scene Segmentation

Many research groups have developed working techniques for detecting scene changes [8], [3], [9]. We choose to segment video by the use of a comparative color histogram difference measure. By detecting significant changes in the weighted color histogram of each successive frame,

$$D(t) = \sum_{v=0}^{N} \left| H_t(v) - H_{t+1}(v) \right| \qquad (2)$$

$$H_t(v) : \text{Histogram of Color in Image}(t)$$

video sequences are separated into scenes. Peaks in the difference, $D(t)$, are detected and an empirically set threshold is used to select scene breaks. We have found that this technique is simple, and yet robust enough to maintain high levels of accuracy for our purpose. Using this technique, we have achieved 91% accuracy in scene segmentation on a test set of roughly 495,000 images (5 hours). Examples of segmentation results are shown in the top row of Figure 2.

2.3 Camera Motion Analysis

One important aspect of video characterization is interpretation of camera motion. The global distribution of motion vectors distinguishes between object motion and actual camera motion. Object motion typically exhibits flow fields in specific regions of an image. Camera motion is characterized by flow throughout the entire image.

Motion vectors for each 16x16 block are available with little computation in the MPEG-1 video standard [13]. An affine model is used to approximate the flow patterns consistent with all types

$$u\left(x_i, y_i\right) = ax_i + by_i + c \qquad (3)$$

$$v\left(x_i, y_i\right) = dx_i + ey_i + f \qquad (4)$$

of camera motion. Affine parameters $a,b,c,d,e,$ and f are calculated by minimizing the least squares error of the motion vectors. We also compute average flow $\bar{v}$ and $\bar{u}$.

Using the affine flow parameters and average flow, we classify the flow pattern. To determine if a pattern is a zoom, we first check if there is the convergence or divergence point (x_0, y_0), where $u\left(x_i, y_i\right) = 0$ and $v\left(x_i, y_i\right) = 0$. To solve for (x_0, y_0), the following relation must be true: $\begin{vmatrix} a & b \\ d & e \end{vmatrix} \neq 0$.

If the above relation is true, and (x_0, y_0) is located inside the image, then it must represent the focus of expansion. If $\bar{v}$ and $\bar{u}$, are large, then this is the focus of the flow and camera is zooming. If (x_0, y_0) is outside the image, and $\bar{v}$ or $\bar{u}$ are large, then the camera is panning in the direction of the dominant vector.

If the above determinant is approximately 0, then (x_0, y_0) does not exist and camera is panning or static. If $\bar{v}$ or $\bar{u}$ are large, the motion is panning in the direction of the dominant vector. Otherwise, there is no significant motion and the flow is static. We eliminate fragmented motion by averaging the results in a 20 frame window over time. Table 1 shows the statistics for detection

Table 1: Camera Motion Detection Results

Data(Images)	Regions Detected	Regions Missed	False Regions
Species I - II (20724)	23	5	1
PlanetEarthI-II (25680)	36	1	3
CNHAR News (30520)	14	1	2

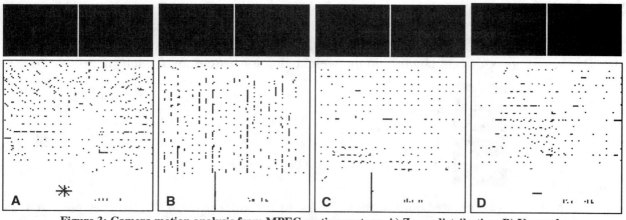

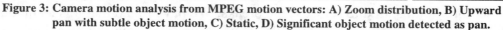

Figure 3: Camera motion analysis from MPEG motion vectors: A) Zoom distribution, B) Upward pan with subtle object motion, C) Static, D) Significant object motion detected as pan.

on various sets of images. Regions detected are either pans or zooms. Examples of the camera motion analysis results are shown in Figure 3.

2.4 Object Detection

Identifying significant objects that appear in the video frames is one of the key components for video characterization. For the time being, we have chosen to deal with two of the more interesting objects in video: human faces and text (caption characters). To reduce computation we detect text and faces every 15th frame.

Face Detection

The "talking head" image is common in interviews and news clips, and illustrates a clear example of video production focussing on an individual of interest. A human interacting within an environment is also a common theme in video. The human-face detection system used for our experiments was developed by Rowley, Baluja and Kanade [6]. It detects mostly frontal faces of any size and any background. Its current performance level is to detect over 86% of more than 507 faces contained in 130 images, while producing approximately 63 false detections. While improvement is needed, the system can detect faces of varying sizes and is especially reliable with frontal faces such as talking-head images. Figure 4 shows examples of its output, illustrating the range of face sizes that can be detected.

Figure 4: Detection of human-faces.

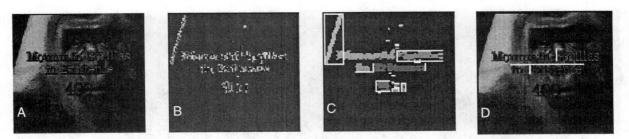

Figure 5: Stages of text detection: A) Input, B) Filtering, C) Clustering, and D) Region Extraction.

Text Detection

Text in the video provides significant information as to the content of a scene. For example, statistical numbers and titles are not usually spoken but are included in the captions for viewer inspection. A typical text region can be characterized as a horizontal rectangular structure of clustered sharp edges, because characters usually form regions of high contrast against the background. By detecting these properties we extract regions from video frames that contain textual information. Figure 5 illustrates the process of detecting text; primarily, regions of horizontal titles and captions.

We first apply a 3x3 horizontal differential filter to the entire image with appropriate binary thresholding for extraction of vertical edge features. Smoothing filters are then used to eliminate extraneous fragments, and to connect character sections that may have been detached. Individual regions are identified by cluster detection and their bounding rectangles are computed. Clusters with bounding regions that satisfy the following constraints are selected:

 $Cluster\ Size > 70 pixels$

$Cluster\ \ Fill Factor \geq 0.45$

$Horizontal - Vertical\ Aspect\ Ratio \geq 0.75$

A cluster's bounding region must have a large horizontal-to-vertical aspect ratio as well as satisfying various limits in height and width. The fill factor of the region should be high to insure dense clusters. The cluster size should also be relatively large to avoid small fragments. An intensity histogram of each region is used to test for high contrast. This is because certain textures and shapes appear similar to text but exhibit low contrast when examined in a bounded region. Finally, consistent detection of the same region over a certain period of time is also tested since text regions are placed at the exact position for many video frames. Figure 6 shows detection examples of words and subsets of a word. Table 2 presents statistics for detection on various sets of images.

Table 2: Text Region Detection Results

Data (Images)	Regions Detected	Regions Missed	False Detections
CNHAV News (1056)	26	1	3
CNHAR News (1526)	48	0	5
Species I (264)	12	2	0
Planet Earth I-II(1712)	0	0	2

3 Technology Integration and Skim Creation

We have characterized video by scene breaks, camera motion, object appearance and keywords. Skim creation involves selecting the appropriate keywords and choosing a corresponding set of images. Candidates for the image portion of a skim are chosen by two types of rules: 1)

Figure 6: Text detection results with various images.

Primitive Rules, independent rules that provide candidates for the selection of image regions for a given keyword, and 2) Meta-Rules, higher order rules that select a single candidate from the primitive rules according to global properties of the video. The subsections below describe the steps involved in the selection, prioritizing and ordering of the keywords and video frames.

3.1 Audio Skim

The first level of analysis for the skim is the creation of the reduced audio track, which is based on the keywords. Those words whose TF-IDF values are higher than a fixed threshold are selected as keywords. By varying this threshold, we control the number of keywords, and thus, the length of the skim. The length of the audio track is determined by a user specified compaction level.

Keywords that appear in close proximity or repeat throughout the transcript may create skims with redundant audio. Therefore, we discard keywords which repeat within a minimum number of frames (150 frames) and limit the repetition of each word.

Our experiments have shown that using individual keywords creates an audio skim which is fragmented and incomprehensible for some speakers. To increase comprehension, we use longer audio sequences, "keyphrases", in the audio skim. A keyphrase is obtained by starting with a keyword, and extending its boundaries to areas of silence or neighboring keywords. Each keyphrase is isolated from the original audio track to form the audio skim. The average keyphrase lasts 2 seconds.

3.2 Video Skim Candidates

In order to create the image skim, we might think of selecting those video frames that correspond in time to the audio skim segments. As we often observe in television programs, however, the contents of the audio and video are not necessarily synchronized. Therefore, for each keyword or keyphrase we must analyze the characterization results of the surrounding video frames and select a set of frames which may not align with the audio in time, but which are most appropriate for skimming.

To study the image selection process of skimming, we manually created skims for 5 hours of video with the help of producers and technicians in Carnegie Mellon's Drama Department. The study revealed that while perfect skimming requires semantic understanding of the entire video, certain parts of the image selection process can be automated with current image understanding. By studying these examples and video production standards [14], we can identify an initial set of heuristic rules.

The first heuristics are the primitive rules, which are tested with the video frames in the scene containing the keyword/keyphrase, and the scenes that follow within at least a 5 second window. A description of each primitive rule is given in order of priority below. The four rows above

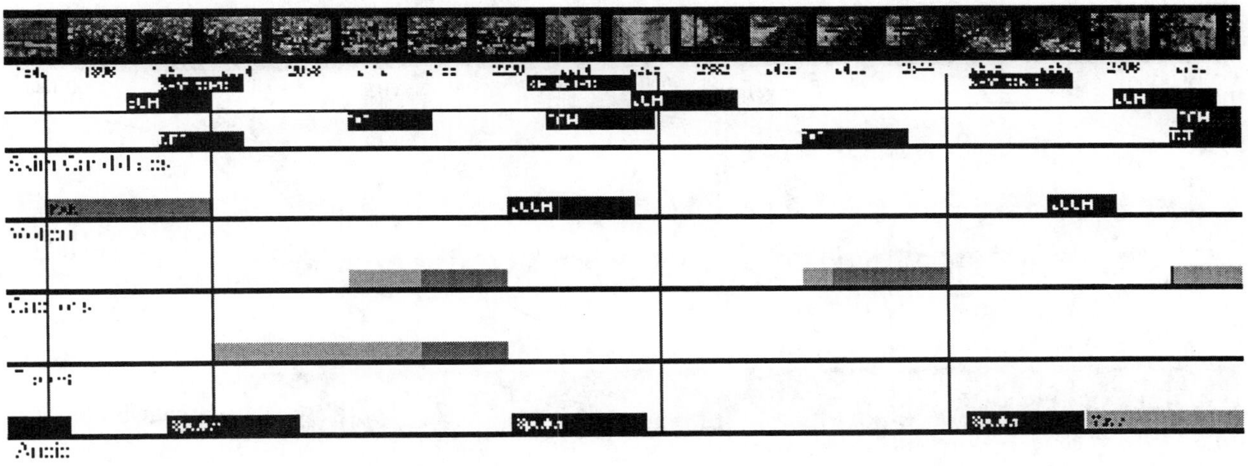

Figure 7:Characterization data with skim candidates and keyphrases for "Destruction of Species". The skim candidate symbols correspond to the following primitive rules: BCM, Bounded Camera Motion; ZCM, Zoom Camera Motion; TXT, Text Captions; and DEF Default. Vertical lines represent scene breaks.

"Skim Candidates", in Figure 7, indicate the candidate image sections selected by various primitive rules.

1.Introduction Scenes(INS)

The scenes prior to the introduction of a proper name usually describe a person's accomplishment and often precede scenes with large views of the person's face. If a keyphrase contains a proper name, and a large human face is detected within the surrounding scenes, then we set the face scene as the last frame of the skim candidate and use the previous frames for the beginning.

2. Similar Scenes(SIS)

The histogram technology in scene segmentation gives us a simple routine for detecting similarity between scenes. Scenes between successive shots of a human face usually imply illustration of the subject. For example, a video producer will often interleave shots of research between shots of a scientist. Images between similar scenes that are less than 5 seconds apart, are used for skimming.

3. Short Sequences(SHS)

Short successive shots often introduce a more important topic. By measuring the duration of each scene, we can detect these regions and identify "short shot" sequences. The video frames that follow these sequences and the exact sequence are used for skimming.

4. Object Motion(OBM)

Object motion is import simply because video producers usually include this type of footage to show something in action. We are currently exploring ways to detect object motion in video.

5. Bounded Camera Motion(BCM/ZCM)

The video frames that preceed or follow a pan or zoom motion are usually the focus of the segment. We can isolate the video regions that are static and bounded by segments with motion, and therefore likely to be the focal point in a scene containing motion.

6. Human Faces and Captions(TXT/FAC)

A scene will often contain recognizable humans, as well as captioned text to describe the scene. If a scene contains both faces and text, the portion containing text is used for skimming. A lower level of priority is given to the scenes with video frames containing only human-faces or text. For these scenes priority is given to text.

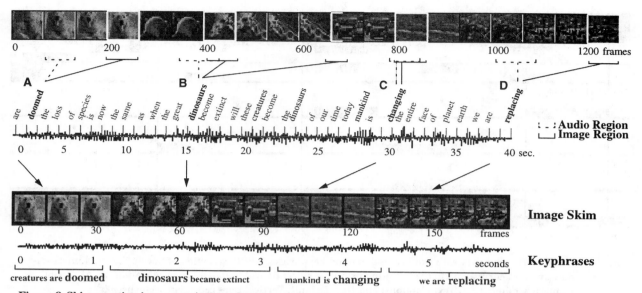

Figure 8: Skim creation incorporating word relevance, significant objects (humans and text), and camera motion: A) For the word "doomed", the images following the camera motion are selected, B) The keyphrase for "dinosaur" is long so portions of the next scene are used for more content, C) No significant structure for the word "changing", D) For the word "replacing" The latter portion of the scene contains both text and humans.

7. Significant Audio(AUD)

If the audio is music, then the scene may not be used for skimming. Soft music is often used as a transitional tool, but seldom accompanies images of high importance. High audio levels (e.g. loud music, explosions) may imply an important scene is about to occur. The skim region will start after high audio levels or music.

8. Default Rule(DEF)

Default video frames align to the audio keyphrases.

3.3 Image Adjustments

With prioritized video frames from each scene, we now have a suitable representation for combining the image and audio skims for the final skim. A set of higher order Meta-Rules are used to complete skim creation.

For visual clarity and comprehension, we allocate at least 30 video frames to a keyphrase. The 30 frame minimum for each scene is based on empirical studies of visual comprehension in short video sequences. When a keyphrase is longer than 60 video frames, we include frames from skim candidates of adjacent scenes within the 5 second search window. The final skim borders are adjusted to avoid image regions that overlap or continue into adjacent scenes by less than 30 frames.

To avoid visual redundancy, we reduce the presence of human faces and default image regions in the skim. If the highest ranking skim candidate for a keyphrase is the default, we extend the search range to a 10 second window and look for other candidates. The human face rule is limited if the segment contains several interviews. Interview scenes can be extremely long, so we look for other candidates in a 15 second search window.

Figure 8 illustrates the adjustment and final selection of video skims. It shows how and why the image segments, which do not necessarily correspond in time to the audio segments, are selected.

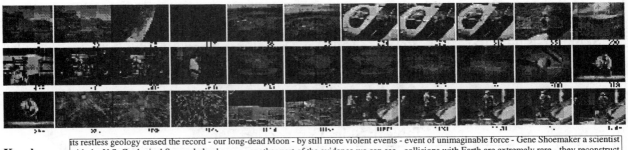

Keyphrases | its restless geology erased the record - our long-dead Moon - by still more violent events - event of unimaginable force - Gene Shoemaker a scientist with the U.S. Geological Survey helped prove - another part of the evidence we can see - collisions with Earth are extremely rare - they reconstruct these great collisions - O.K., Earl, let's shoot it - and we can see the ejecta curtain simply move out - these clumps eventually will impact the surface - now this is the edge of the target - if we step back we find - this is what makes up the crater rays - and the Moon's dark plains - as astronauts roam the Moon's surface - most Moon rocks were between three and four billion - the samples gathered so carefully were not part - the early chapters of the Moon's history began to emerge

Figure 9: Skim video frames and keyphrases for "Planet Earth - I" (10:1 compaction).

3.4 Example Results

Figure 9 shows the video frames and audio from the "Planet Earth" video. The image portion of the skim has captured information from 18 of the 64 total scenes in the video. With the exception of the scene at frame 585, which lasts over 1,300 frames in the original video, most scenes are small and provide maximum visual information. An error in scene segmentation, near frame 702, causes this scene to split and, therefore, it is used twice for separate keyphrases. The final scene in the original video is long and contains two keyphrases. In this case, the search window cannot extend to other scenes and these keyphrases must share image frames from the final scene. Introduction scenes, bounded camera motion and human faces dominate the image skims for this segment.

Figure 10 shows another example from the "Planet Earth" video with 16 of the 37 scenes represented. This segment contains many long outdoor scenes that provide little information. However, most primitive rules do not match these scenes so the search window is extended and they appear less frequently in the image skim. The scene at frame 828 is an interview scene which contains 3 keyphrases and lasts several frames. Even with an extended search window, the scenes that follow do not match any of the primitive rules so the image skim is rather long for this scene.

Figure 11 shows two types of skims for the "Mass Extinction" segment. Skim A was produced with our method of integrated image and language understanding. Skim B was created by selecting video and audio portions at fixed intervals. This segment contains 71 scenes, of which, skim A

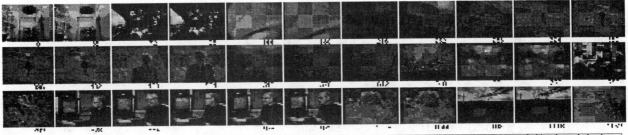

Keyphrases | to explore these neighboring planets - the first planet we would visit was Venus - it resisted exploration - our voyages revealed it - through the dense atmosphere winds up to two hundred miles an hour whip the clouds - no place can replicate the climate - but Death Valley, on a hot afternoon - how did it become the hot desolate planet - Jim Head, a planetary scientist at Brown University, is an authority - it's hot enough on the surface of Venus - the heat that comes into the surface can actually be - they radioed back images - and Jim Head and his colleagues had a global - we can also see some very distinctive highland - this one, Maxwell Montes - we have the same problem the resolution - Jim Head and his colleagues use a very special - the extensional forces are pulling

Figure 10: Skim video frames and keyphrases for "Planet Earth - II" (10:1 compaction).

has captured 23 scenes, and skim B has captured 17 scenes. Studies involving different skim creation methods are discussed in the next section.

Skim A has only 1632 frames, while the first scene of the original segment is an interview that lasts 1734 frames. The scenes that follow this interview contain camera motion, so we select them for the keyphrases towards the end of the scene. Charts and figures interleaved between successive human subjects are selected for the latter scenes.

Table 3: Skim Compaction Data

Title	Original(sec)	Skim (sec)	Comments
K'nex, CNN Headline News	61.0	7.13	MC-AS
Species Destruction I	68.65	6.40	MC-AS
Species Destruction II	123.23	12.43	MS
International Space University	166.20	28.13	MS
Rain Forest Destruction	107.13	5.36	MS
Mass Extinction	559.4	55.5	AC-AS
Human Archeology	391.2	40.8	AC-AS
Planet Earth I	464.5	44.1	AC-AS
Planet Earth II	393.0	40.0	AC-AS

Comments
MC- Manually Assisted CharacterizationAC- Automated Characterization
MS- Manual Skim CreationAS- Automated Skim Creation

3.5 User Evaluation

The results of several skims are summarized in Table 3. The manually created skims in the initial stages of the experiment help test the potential visual clarity and comprehension of skims. The compaction ratio for a typical segment is 10:1; and it was shown that skims with compaction as high as high as 20:1 still retain most of the content. Our results show the information representation potential of skims, but we must test our work with human subjects to study its effectiveness.

We are conducting a user-study to test the content summarization and effectiveness of the skim as a browsing tool in a video library. Subjects must navigate a video library to answer a series of questions. The effectiveness of each skim is based on the time to complete this task and the number of correct items retrieved. Although our evaluation results are tentative, the skim does appear to be an effective tool for browsing, as evident by the difference of time that subjects spend in skim mode versus regular playback mode.

We use various types of skims to test the utility of image and language understanding in skim creation. The following creation schemes are presently being tested:

        A - Image and Language Characterization
        B - Fixed Intervals (Default)
        C - Language Characterization Only
        D - Image Characterization Only

Figure 11 shows examples of skim type A and B. The visual information in skim A is less redundant and provides a greater variety of scenes. The audio for skim B is incoherent and considerably smaller. Although our skim does appear to provide more information, additional testing is needed.

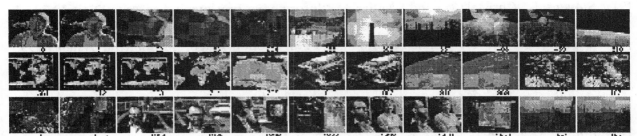

A: Our research shows us that mass extinctions are relatively common - this mass extinction is not triggered by some extraterrestrial phenomena - Man's destruction of the diversity of life - man has the technology to change the world - human waste are threatening the web of life - A tapestry of lights track the human presence - Fires in Africa fuel the struggle against famine - At NASA's Goddard Space Flight Center in Maryland Compton Tucker draws - past eight years Tucker has observed subtle shifts - Discovery returns to space on a mission to photograph the Earth - you see these incredibly large fires - Compton Tucker has been monitoring these fires - The destruction was triggered - homesteaders are transforming the wilderness - Norman Myers has voiced his concern - invited Myers to review his most recent findings - we could have 2 or 3 smaller fires burning - we're pushing species down the tubes on our own planet - What splendid creatures lived here

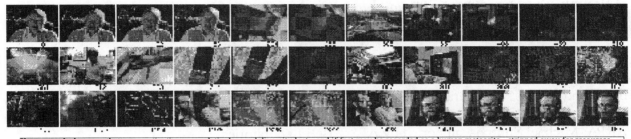

B: Our research shows us that mass extinctions are relatively - and diversity lost - and if fact may be regarded as a human meteorite - stripped away for resources - against famine in the Third World - At NASA's Goddard Space Flight - Houston Discovery - Amazon they are stunned by what they see - images confirm that in one - roads - visible from space - as - is particularly disturbing - fires there at about 2:45 in the afternoon - more probes sent off to have a look at this little - in the long run. It matters enormously - a few becomes many becomes too many

Figure 11: Image and text output for the "Mass Extinction" segment: A) Skim creation using image and language understanding, B) Skim creation using fixed intervals for image and audio.

4 Conclusions

The emergence of high volume video libraries has shown a clear need for content-specific video-browsing technology. We have described an algorithm to create skim videos that consist of content rich audio and video information. Compaction of video as high as 20:1 has been achieved without apparent loss in content.

While the generation of content-based skims presented in this paper is very limited due to the fact that the true understanding of video frames is extremely difficult, it illustrates the potential power of integrated language, and image information for characterization in video retrieval and browsing applications.

5 References

[1]   Akutsu, A. and Tonomura, Y. "Video Tomography: An efficient method for Camerawork Extraction and Motion Analysis," *Proc. of ACM Multimedia '94*, Oct.1994.

[2]   Degen, L., Mander, R., and Salomon, G. "Working with Audio: Integrating Personal Tape Recorders and Desktop Computers," *Proc. CHI '92*, May 1992, Monterey, CA.

[3]   Hampapur, A., Jain, R., and Weymouth, T. "Production Model Based Digital Video Segmentation," *Multimedia Tools and Applications* **1** March 1995.

[5]   Mauldin, M. "Information Retrieval by Text Skimming," PhD Thesis, Carnegie Mellon University. Aug. 1989.

[6]   Rowley, H., Baluja, S. and Kanade, K. "Neural Network-Based Face Detection," *Computer Vision and Pattern Recognition*, San Francisco, May 1996.

[7]   Stevens, S., Christel, M., and Wactlar, H. "Informedia: Improving Access to Digital Video" *Interactions* 1 Oct.94.

[8]   Zhang, H., *et a.l*, "Automatic Partitioning of Full-Motion Video," *Multimedia Systems* 1993 1, pp. 10-28.

[9]   Arman, F., Hsu, A., and Chiu, M-Y. "Image Processing on Encoded Video Sequences," *Multimedia Systems* 1994.

[10] Arman, F., *et al.*, "Content-Based Browsing of Video Sequences," *Proc. of ACM Multimedia '94*, Oct., 1994.

[11] "TREC 93," *Proceedings of the 2nd Text Retrieval Conference*, D. Harmon, Ed., sponsored by ARPA/SISTO, 1993.

[12] Hauptmann, A.G. and Smith, M, "Video Segmentation in the Informedia Project", IJCAI-95, *Workshop on Intelligent Multimedia Information Retrieval.* Aug. 1995.

[13] "MPEG-1 Video Standard", *Communications of the ACM*, April 1991.

[14] Smallman, K., "Creative Film-Making", 1st ed., Publisher Macmillan, New York 1970.

Acknowledgments

We thank Henry Rowley and Shumeet Baluja for the face detection routine; Michael Witbrock and Yuichi Nakamura for the keyword selection routines; and the Carnegie Mellon Drama Department for their insights on skim creation. This work is partially funded by NSF, NASA, and ARPA. Michael Smith is supported by AT&T Bell Laboratories.

PART II
SYSTEMS, NETWORKING, AND TOOLS

Introduction

Kevin Jeffay
University of North Carolina at Chapel Hill

PART I of this text presented the fundamentals of multimedia processing. We have seen how multimedia data can be efficiently coded, compressed, indexed, and searched. Solutions to these problems form the base technologies used to develop virtually all multimedia applications. However, to realize these applications, we must expand the discussion of multimedia processing to include a discussion of how multimedia data is stored in a computer system and how operating systems and network communication protocols must evolve to support the requirements of applications that process and communicate multimedia data types. For example, consider a simple movie player application. In Chapters 1 and 2, we saw how audio and video streams that make up a movie can be digitized and compressed. These streams can be stored in a file maintained by the operating system and later read by our movie player application, decompressed, and displayed on the screen. However, in this simple scenario, the question immediately arises of how the movie player application can ensure that frames of the movie are displayed continuously so that whatever motion is present in the video is maintained in the presentation of the movie on the screen. Similarly, how can the application ensure that the audio samples are decompressed and played continuously and are synchronized with the video? And if these problems can be solved for the case of playback on a single computer, how can this performance be approximated when the movie file to be played resides on a remote file or Web server?

The central issue is the fact that the multi-dimensional execution constraints of multimedia applications are not directly supported by traditional desktop operating systems or file servers. Multimedia data fundamentally differ from traditional data such as ASCII text in that multimedia data can have a temporal dimension to its acquisition and display. At first glance, whereas still images can be stored in and retrieved from a file system in a manner similar to text, moving images (video) cannot. For example, file systems are not designed to ensure that data from a video file can be read on a periodic basis or that a read operation on one file can be synchronized with a read operation on a second file. Moreover, even if a file system supported such read operations, these operations must be integrated with CPU scheduling. For example, in most operating systems, CPU scheduling is not performed in such a manner that an application can be guaranteed that once a video frame has been read from a disk in real-time, the application will be able to decompress and display the frame in real-time.

The simple movie player example illustrates some of the computer systems infrastructure necessary for the storage, communication, and processing of multimedia data types. In Part II of these readings we present the seminal papers from the literature in operating system and network support for multimedia. The goal is to discuss the primary systems problems that must be solved in order to effectively support the needs of multimedia system developers. In addition we discuss the primary systems software, or "middleware," that is essential for constructing effective multimedia

383

applications. Finally, we consider tools and toolkits supporting the creation and maintenance of multimedia documents and presentations. In all, we consider these issues:

- communicating audio and video streams across packet-switched networks such as the Internet
- storing and aiding the access of multimedia data in a file system
- allocating resources within an operating system and scheduling user processes so as to enable real-time processing and communication of media streams
- synchronizing the playout of media streams
- developing authoring tools to aid in the rapid development of multimedia documents and applications

The theme throughout is to identify how the unique structure and characteristics of multimedia data types can be leveraged to provide tools and services for meeting the logical and temporal requirements of multimedia applications. To illustrate many of the issues that supporting real-time, interactive multimedia in a distributed system face, we also consider a case study in the design of, and system support for, video conferencing systems.

Part II is composed of seven chapters:

- Multimedia Database Systems
- Multimedia Operating Systems
- Videoconferencing
- Networking and Media Streaming
- Multimedia Storage Servers
- Multimedia Synchronization
- Authoring Systems

For "Multimedia Databases," Aidong Zhang has organized a collection of readings in Chapter 6 that illustrate how database architectures and implementations have evolved to support the novel data modeling, querying, and indexing requirements for multimedia data types.

In Chapter 7, "Multimedia Operating Systems," Klara Nahrstedt has largely considered the problems of realizing real-time services for multimedia computing and networking. These include integrated, real-time resource allocation mechanisms and policies that allow multimedia data to "flow" from a source such as an acquisition or storage device, through the operating system to an application, and back through the operating system to a sink such as a network interface, display, or storage device.

Related to the research in operating systems is the work on multimedia servers. In Chapter 10, Prashant Shenoy and Harrick Vin have selected papers that consider both the low-level details of secondary storage management well as the higher-level issues of caching and batching of requests for common media files. The former problem domain includes a treatment of the components necessary for constructing a real-time file system. These include policies for disk-head scheduling, file placement, load balancing, and admission control. Regarding the latter domain, the chapter considers application-level server policies for maximizing the number of clients that can be served.

Multimedia servers typically exist to deliver multimedia content to remote clients over a network. In Chapter 9, Ketan Mayer-Patel summarizes the major developments in the area of networking and streaming of live and real-time multimedia. Included here are papers discussing the emerging standards for multimedia transport on the Internet RSVP, RTP, RTSP, and SIP. Motivating the need for better multimedia transport and quality of service on the Internet is a case study of the performance of a video conferencing system on the Internet.

A chapter on video conferencing (Chapter 8) is included both as a concrete example of the problem of managing real-time streams on the Internet today and as an example of complex distributed multimedia application design. I present papers on the topic ranging from user requirements for effective communication to application-level network transport protocols for ameliorating the effects of network congestion and contention for bandwidth. A case study is included here to highlight the impact of video conferencing technology on work processes.

Next we consider the fundamental problem of synchronizing the display of multiple media streams. This problem is critical for the use and acceptance of most multimedia applications and has received a great deal of attention in the literature. In Chapter 11, Larry Rowe surveys the field ranging from formal requirement specification methods to toolkits for achieving synchronization. Of particular interest here are case studies of measuring the effects of synchronized media playout.

Finally, Dick Bulterman considers the literature on methods and toolkits for the creation of multimedia and hypermedia documents and systems in Chapter 12. Included here is a discussion of high-level languages for specifying the temporal and spatial structure of multimedia presentations as well as tools and techniques for document creation. The work presented here can be viewed in essence as a form of user interface or API to much of the lower-level systems technology presented in the earlier chapters.

In total these chapters present a comprehensive picture of the state of the art in computer systems support for multimedia applications development. The papers included here should provide an excellent introduction to the technical problems and solutions in managing multimedia data and presentations in a distributed system. Moreover, the several case studies also included put this research in context by demonstrating both the real complexity of the problem and the limitations of current solutions.

CHAPTER SIX

Multimedia Database Systems

Aidong Zhang
State University of New York at Buffalo

THE NEED to handle multimedia data in database systems is growing rapidly in many fields, such as video-on-demand servers, education, and training; Web browsing; information retrieval; electronic commerce; and distributed publishing. To meet these demands, database systems must have the ability to efficiently model, store, access, and query multimedia data. Multimedia data refer to diverse media types representing text, audio, image, and video content. Such data usually contain large data objects, require real-time handling, and may be uninterpreted raw data, a characteristic that distinguishes these types from alphanumeric data. Conventional database systems were not designed with these characteristics of multimedia data in mind and, as a result, are not suitable to handle these types of new data. Research on multimedia database systems brings about a variety of interesting and challenging issues that are being studied by the multimedia database community.

Multimedia database systems are designed to efficiently store and manipulate multimedia data. Grosky gave a comprehensive introduction to the important research issues in multimedia database systems in 1994 [1]. Specific issues included in his discussion are multimedia data modeling, architecture, system design, query processing, and indexing. Since then, the importance of multimedia database systems has been realized in annual multimedia database workshops [2, 3], and several journal special issues on multimedia database systems have appeared. Two collections of research papers related to multimedia database systems have been published as well [4, 5].

Because of space considerations, this chapter includes only four papers, which address the issues of data modeling, architecture, query processing, and indexing. Other related topics such as synchronization, QoS, and content-based retrieval can be found in Chapters 4, 5, 9, and 11. In addition, many other research papers cover issues related to the design of multimedia database systems, such as disk scheduling and allocation strategies [6–9], buffer management for prefetching and maximizing buffer utilization [10–12], multimedia synchronization [13–15], collaboration between clients and servers [16–18], and QoS metrics for continuity and synchronization specifications [19, 20].

CONCEPTUAL MODELING

A number of studies have investigated the modeling of multimedia data from a conceptual perspective, including graphical models, Petri-Net based models, object-oriented models, collaborative models, and temporal abstraction models [21–24]. A general framework for multimedia data modeling has also been proposed [25]. Some of these models deal primarily with the synchronization aspects of multimedia data, whereas others are more concerned with facilitating the browsing of multimedia data. These models provide methods for specifying multimedia synchronization semantics at the application level. Accordingly, I have included as the first paper in the chapter, "A unified data model for representing multimedia, timeline, and simulation data," by J.D.N. Dionisio and A. F.

Cárdenas. This paper presents a data model that is a synthesis of entity-relationship and object-oriented data models. It defines a general framework for modeling and accessing various kinds of multimedia data, including images, sounds, long text, digital video, and integrated timelines. This data model organizes all multimedia types under a single hierarchy and layered structure, and its effectiveness is demonstrated in medical applications.

ARCHITECTURES

The research community has explored multimedia database architectures at different levels, including the system, schema, and functional levels, and various types of system architectures have been proposed. Gorsky defines a generic multimedia database architecture and identifies three logically independent repositories [1]. In a distributed environment, various types of system architecture are possible. Examples of such systems include GLOSS (from Stanford) [26], HARVEST (from University of Colorado) [27], WAIS (Wide Area Information Servers) [28], ImageRover [29], WebSeek [30], and MetaSEEk [31]. The third paper in this chapter, "NetView: Integrating large-scale distributed visual databases," address this issue. NetView supports global content-based query access to various visual databases over the Internet. An integrated metaserver consisting of a metadatabase, metasearch agent, and query manager facilitates such access. NetView significantly reduces the amount of time and effort that users spend finding information of interest. It also can further refine the metaserver's performance based on user feedback.

QUERYING

Querying a multimedia database consists of retrieving text, images, video, and audio simultaneously. Because the data in a multimedia database are usually not as structured as the data in a conventional database, querying multimedia data is not a trivial problem and has been a popular research area. Marcus and Subrahmanian define a structured multimedia database based on features and their relationships [32]. Media data can be queried based on such features and their relationships. Liu and colleagues have proposed a language called Hierarchical Temporal Logic (HTL) for expressing multimedia queries [33], in which temporal operators are used for similarity-based retrieval of video segments. I have selected

"Querying multimedia presentations based on content," by T. Lee and colleagues, to address this topic. This paper introduces an icon-based object-oriented graphical query language termed GVISUAL, in which multimedia presentations are modeled as directed acyclic graphs. For querying multimedia presentation graphs, GVISUAL incorporates temporal operators to specify query paths along a presentation graph. This paper also discussed query processing techniques that translate GVISUAL queries to an operator-based language.

MULTIDIMENSIONAL DATA INDEXING

Feature-based indexing and retrieval have been commonly used in multimedia database systems [34, 35]. However, images usually have high dimensional feature vectors, which are difficult to index. One popularly used index structure is the R-tree and its variants [36]. Such indexing approaches support nearest neighbor searches efficiently. One severe disadvantage of the R-tree and its variants is that the bounding rectangles associated with different nodes may overlap. Overlapping becomes more serious when dimensionality increases. When dimensions number more than 100, which is common in color and texture feature vectors, the advantage of the indexing will be diminished because of overlapping. The final paper in this chapter, "The X-tree: An indexing structure for high-dimensional data," by S. Berchtold, D. A. Keim, and H.-P. Kriegel, offers a case study on this topic. The X-tree is an R*-tree [37] based index structure that avoids a degeneration of the directory in high-dimensions using a special split algorithm and variably sized directory nodes. The experiments show that the X-tree outperforms the R-tree and other index structures.

The discussion above touches upon some key issues in multimedia database systems and provides an idea of the scope and future directions of the research in this important field. Today, multimedia database research has become an important field in both multimedia and database conferences. The main research topics such as multimedia analysis, multimedia data modeling, multimedia data synchronization, and content-based similarity retrieval of multimedia data will continue to be very active. Through these research activities, basic principles for the design of multimedia database systems will be formulated for long-term use. In addition, people also realize that multimedia technology can benefit database systems in assisting querying, browsing, and updating of the data in an intuitively interactive fashion. The integration of multimedia and database research will create the most powerful systems for supporting the application of digital libraries to areas such as education and training, Web browsing, information retrieval, distributed publishing, and electronic commerce. In summary, multimedia database systems will provide an innovative environment that can be used to support sophisticated applications requiring flexible and interactive construction and manipulation of data presentations from multimedia databases.

REFERENCES

[1] W. I. Grosky, "Multimedia information systems," *IEEE Multimedia* 1, no. 1 (1994): 12–24.

[2] 1996 International Workshop on Multi-media Database Management Systems. Blue Mountain Lake, New York, August 1996.

[3] 2nd International Workshop on Multimedia Information Systems, West Point, New York, September 1996.

[4] Special Issue on Multimedia Database Systems, *IEEE Multimedia* 4, no. 3 (1997).

[5] A. Ghafoor, ed., Special Issue on Multimedia Database Systems, *ACM Multimedia Systems* 3, no. 5/6 (1995).

[6] B. Ozden, R. Rastogi, and A. Silberschatz, "A low-cost storage server for movie on demand databases," in *Proceedings of the 20th VLDB Conference* (1994): 594–605.

[7] P. Venkat Rangan and H. M. Vin, "Efficient storage techniques for digital continuous multimedia," *IEEE Transactions on Knowledge and Data Engineering* 5, no. 4 (1993): 564–73.

[8] J. Gemmell and S. Christodoulakis, "Principles of delay-sensitive multimedia data storage and retrieval," *ACM Transactions on Information Systems* 10, no. 1 (Jan. 1992): 51–90.

[9] D. J. Gemmell, H. M. Vin, D. D. Kandlur, and P. V. Rangan, "Multimedia storage servers: A tutorial and survey," *Computer* 28, no. 5 (May 1995): 40–51.

[10] R. T. Ng and J. Yang, "Maximizing buffer and disk utilizations for news on-demand," in *Proceedings of the 20th VLDB Conference* (1994): 451–62.

[11] K.-L. Wu and P. S. Yu, "Consumption-based buffer management for maximizing system throughput of a multimedia system," in *Proceedings of the 3rd IEEE International Conference on Multimedia Computing and Systems (ICMCS 96)* (June 1996): 164–71.

[12] S. Gollapudi and A. Zhang, "Buffer model and management in distributed multimedia presentation systems," *ACM Multimedia Systems Journal* 6, no. 3 (May 1998): 206–18.

[13] R. Steinmetz, "Synchronization properties in multimedia systems," *IEEE Journal on Selected Areas in Communications* 8, no. 3 (April 1990): 401–12.

[14] D. P. Anderson and G. Homsy, "A communication media I/O server and its synchronization mechanisms," *IEEE Computer* 24, no. 10 (1991): 51–7.

[15] K. Nahrstedt, "End-to-end QoS guarantees in networked multimedia Systems," *ACM Computing Surveys* 27, no. 4 (Dec. 1995): 613–16.

[16] H. M. Vin, M. S. Chen, and T. Barzilai, "Collaboration management in DiCE," *The Computer Journal* 36, no. 1 (1993): 87–96.

[17] J. Hui, E. Karasan, J. Li, and J. Zhang, "Client-server synchronization and buffering for variable rate multimedia retrievals," *IEEE Journal on Selected Areas in Communications* 14, no. 1 (Jan. 1996): 226–37.

[18] Y. Song, M. Mielke, and A. Zhang, "NetMedia: Synchronized streaming of multimedia presentations in distributed environments," in *Proceedings of the IEEE Multimedia* (June 1999): 585–90.

[19] R. Staehli, J. Walpole, and D. Maier, "A quality-of-service specification for multimedia presentations," *ACM Multimedia Systems* 3, no. 5/6 (1995): 251–63.

[20] D. Wijesekera and J. Srivastava, "Quality of Server (QoS) metrics for continuous media," *The International Journal on Multimedia Tools and Applications* 3, no. 2 (Sep. 1996): 127–66.

[21] F. W. Tompa, "A data model for flexible hypertext database systems," *ACM Transactions on Information Systems* 7, no. 1 (1989): 85–100.

[22] Y. Deng and S. K. Chang, "A framework for the modeling and prototyping of distributed information systems," *International Journal of Software Engineering and Knowledge Engineering* 1, no. 3 (1991): 203–26.

[23] T. D.C. Little and A. Ghafoor, "Synchronization and storage models for multimedia objects," *IEEE Journal on Selected Areas in Communications* 8, no. 3 (April 1990): 413–27.

[24] Y. Masunaga, "Design issues of OMEGA: An object-oriented multimedia database management system," *Journal of Information Processing* 14, no.1 (1991): 60–74.

[25] S. Gibbs, C. Breiteneder, and D. Tsichritzis, "Data modeling of time-based media," in *Proceedings of SIGMOD 94* (May 1994): 91–102.

[26] L. Gavarno, H. Garcia-Molina, and A. Tomasic, "The effectiveness of GLOSS for the text database discovery problems," in *Proceedings of SIGMOD 94* (May 1994) 126–37.

[27] M. Bowman, P. Danzig, D. Hardy, U. Manber, and M. Schwartz, *HARVEST: A Scalable, Customizable Discovery and Access System*, Technical Report CU-CS732-94, Department of Computer Science, University of Colorado-Boulder, 1994.

[28] B. Kahle and A. Medlar, "An information system for corporate users: Wide area information servers," *ConneXions—The Interoperability Report* 5, no.11 (Nov. 1991): 2–9. WAIS is accessible at http://www.wais.com/newhomepages/techtalk.html.

[29] S. Sclaroff, L. Taycher, and M. La Cascia, "ImageRover: A content-based image browser for the World Wide Web," in *Proceedings of the IEEE International Workshop on Content-based Access of Image and Video Libraries* (1997): 2–9.

[30] J. R. Smith and S.-F. Chang, "Visually searching the Web for content," *IEEE Multimedia* 4, no. 3 (1997): 12–20.

[31] S. Chang, J. Smith, M. Beigi, and A. Benitez, "Visual information retrieval from large distributed online repositories," Communications of the ACM 40, no. 12 (Dec.1997): 63–71.

[32] S. Marcus and V. S. Subrahmanian, "Foundations of multimedia database systems," *Journal of the ACM* 43, no. 3 (1996): 474–523.

[33] K. L. Liu, P. Sistla, C. Yu, and N. Rishe, "Query processing in a video retrieval System, "in *Proceedings of the 14th International Conference on Data Engineering* (Feb. 1998): 276–83.

[34] B. S. Manjunath and W. Y. Ma, "Texture features for browsing and retrieval of image data," *IEEE Transactions on Pattern Analysis and Machine Intelligence* 18, no. 8 (Aug. 1996): 837–42.

[35] J. R. Smith and S. Chang, "Transform features for texture classification and discrimination in large image databases," in *Proceedings of the IEEE International Conference on Image Processing* (1994): 407–11.

[36] A. Guttman, "R-Trees: A dynamic index for geometric data," in *Proceedings of SIGMOD 84*, 47–57.

[37] N. Beckmann, H. P. Kriegel, R. Schneider, and B. Seeger, "The R*-tree: An efficient and robust access method for points and rectangles," in *Proceedings of SIGMOD 90* (May 1990): 322–31.

A Unified Data Model for Representing Multimedia, Timeline, and Simulation Data

John David N. Dionisio and Alfonso F. Cárdenas

Abstract—This paper describes a unified data model that represents multimedia, timeline, and simulation data utilizing a single set of related data modeling constructs. A uniform model for multimedia types structures image, sound, video, and long text data in a consistent way, giving multimedia schemas and queries a degree of data independence even for these complex data types. Information that possesses an intrinsic temporal element can all be represented using a construct called a stream. Streams can be aggregated into parallel multistreams, thus providing a structure for viewing multiple sets of time-based information. The unified stream construct permits real-time measurements, numerical simulation data, and visualizations of that data to be aggregated and manipulated using the same set of operators. Prototypes based on the model have been implemented for two medical application domains: thoracic oncology and thermal ablation therapy of brain tumors. Sample schemas, queries, and screenshots from these domains are provided. Finally, a set of examples is included for an accompanying visual query language discussed in detail in another document.

Index Terms—Multimedia database management, multimedia data model, timeline, simulation, visual data modeling, multimedia data streams, temporal databases, visual querying, multimedia querying, medical multimedia databases.

———————————————— ✦ ————————————————

1 INTRODUCTION

THIS paper describes a unified data model that we shall call M for representing multimedia, timeline, and simulation data. Our current research work in the Knowledge-Based Multimedia Medical Distributed Database (KMeD) project at UCLA has identified a number of data modeling needs that come from different application domains. Our investigation concluded that they can all be served using a single construct called a *stream*. Streams have been described in the literature, although within a narrower scope [25], [4], [39]. This paper describes how we have been able to generalize the *time-based stream* model so that it can fulfill the requirements of such diverse domains as simulation and validation, medical timelines, and multimedia visualization.

1.1 Background

Recent developments in scientific databases have identified new data modeling requirements for next-generation scientific databases. These developments involve areas which at first glance seem to be distinct and disjoint:

- *Multimedia.* In its fullest and most complete form, scientific data is multimedia in nature. It is fully visual, frequently three-dimensional, and spans the dimension of time [32]. Much work has focused in this area, and our work proceeds in a similar direction as in [31], [38], [12], [27].
- *Simulation and validation.* Harreld [27] and Anzai et al. [3] are evidence of an increasing need to integrate

simulation and database technologies. One potential benefit of this integration is the capability to validate simulation data by direct comparison to real-world, measured data.
- *Timelines.* Temporal, evolutionary, and process data models [15], [13], [35] have many potential applications in science and medicine. Much of medicine involves tracking the progress and history of a patient over time, while a large element of science is the study of processes and their effects over time. Scientific and medical *timelines* present the progress of a tumor, skeletal development, or other natural process as a series of still frames. If properly registered, timelines may be viewed as a short movie or animation clip.

The areas addressed by these application domains are linked by a number of common threads:

- *The element of time.* The above application domains all require data that changes over time: digital video, simulation data, timelines, etc. A data model supporting these application domains must be able to represent, query, and visualize this element of time. Better yet, this element of time must be captured in a uniform construct regardless of the time scale or data type.
- *Complex data structures.* Scientific data domains involve objects with complex structures and interrelationships with other objects. In the medical domain, for example, the Unified Medical Language System [23] defines a large and complex semantic network of objects, processes, subjects, synonyms, and relationships. Current relational data models do not easily capture and present such complex data without using artificial or arbitrary keys. A data model that

————————————————
- *The authors are with the Computer Science Department, School of Engineering and Applied Science, University of California at Los Angeles, 3732 Boelter Hall, Los Angeles, CA 90095-1596. E-mail: dondi@itmedicine.net, cardenas@cs.ucla.edu.*

takes this structural complexity to a higher level is thus required.

- *Multiple representations of objects.* The multimedia data generated by a scientific application domain results in the representation of any individual object in multiple data areas. For example, a tumor mass may be visible in multiple CAT scans and MRI scans. It may be mentioned in multiple lab or radiological reports, annotations, or voice transcriptions. Finally, it may be represented by numerical or tabular simulation data. A conventional database is capable of storing most of these data types, but a great deal of work is required to ensure that the word "tumor" or any concepts relating to it lead to any or all of these means of storage, and vice versa. Our data model attempts to resolve these multiple representations by making this concept a fundamental element of the model.

We address these needs by extending and integrating a number of data models already in the literature, as discussed in Section 2.

1.2 Contents of the Paper

After summarizing our model's primary contributions to the field in Section 1.3 and comparing related work in Section 2, we proceed with a review of the basic data modeling concepts upon which our model builds in Section 3.1.

Section 3.2, Section 3.3, Section 3.4, and Section 3.5 describe the focus of our new model: generalized constructs for representing various kinds of multimedia and time-based data. Section 4 outlines the application domains for which we intend to test its functionality. Section 5 and Section 7 provide a hint of things to come by giving an overview of the accompanying visual query language which we are designing.

1.3 Primary Contributions

The primary contributions of our data modeling work to the field can be described as follows:

- *Generalized multimedia types.* We define a general framework for modeling and accessing various kinds of multimedia data, including images, sounds, long text, digital video, and integrated timelines.
- *Generalized model for representing most kinds of time-based data.* In our data model, we have applied a time-based stream model that is common in multimedia work to other application domains. In particular, we use time-based streams to model evolutionary, simulation, and/or timeline data. Collaborative work with radiologists and clinicians, where prototype software using our generalized model was developed, has shown that this unified approach to representing time-based data results in greater ease of comprehension and specification of data models containing time-based entities [2].

Section 3.2, Section 3.3, Section 3.4, and Section 3.5 describe our data model, focusing on the constructs that specifically represent these contributions. We have asked users to both interpret and create different schema diagrams using our data model. These tests have shown that the new constructs make it easier for users to specify and express the multimedia and time-based components of a database.

2 PREVIOUS WORK

We compare our data model to three kinds of data models that exist today:

1) multimedia data models
2) general data models, and
3) multimedia file formats.

For each data model category, major models have been selected for comparison with our data model.

2.1 Multimedia Data Models

A number of data models that address the structure and semantics of multimedia data have been developed. These multimedia data models emphasize the modeling of images, sound, or video data. This approach simplifies the overall problem, because it assumes that a database consists only of this type of data. To our knowledge, only VIMSYS provides for a system that exists within the context of a broader database application, although emphasis remains within the realm of image data modeling [26].

Our work extends the modeling approach of the University of Geneva [25] with other general database modeling concepts, and also adds a query language. In addition, the major application of simulation and scientific computing extends the timed stream model to cover new areas such as interpolation and simulation validation. The Amsterdam Hypermedia Model [28] is extended in our model by adding a general query language and explicit support for simulation and scientific data. In addition, our work focuses on multimedia databases, and not on multimedia hypertext documents.

The M data model is also a superset of the capabilities of spatio-temporal logic [7] because it integrates spatial and temporal semantics with more general database constructs. Support for sound and simulation data is also added. Finally, we combine the multimedia modeling of time-based streams with the higher database functionality of VIMSYS [26], and add explicit support for simulation and scientific computing to both areas.

A number of more recent models have begun to tackle the modeling of digital video data. OVID [34], VideoMAP [40], and the concept of moving icons or "micons" [41] focus on digitized video and their semantics. The M data model applies the video-oriented ideas of OVID, VideoMAP, and micons within its definitions wherever they are appropriate.

2.2 General Data Models

Many current data models, though not explicitly directed toward multimedia applications, have a number of constructs that will nonetheless support current multimedia requirements. M uses the extended entity-relationship data model (EER) [33] as a basis for basic database concepts such as entities, relationships, and attributes. In addition, it adds new modeling constructs such as temporal and evolutionary relationships, a more explicit implementation of aggregation, and methods. Most importantly, multimedia modeling is incorporated into EER by this work.

The spatial temporal-evolutionary data model (SEDM) [15], [29] focuses primarily on semantic constructs over still images. Our model adds a stream construct that models time *within* an entity. Further, support for simulation data models is also added.

The object-oriented predicate calculus (OOPC) [6] provides a comprehensive model that is applicable to most of the object-oriented data models and database management systems that are present today. The M data model combines the visual effectiveness of EER with the rich constructs of OOPC to achieve a hybrid model with the advantages of both EER and OOPC. M's multimedia types, streams, and simulation modeling also serve as further enhancements to the basic framework established by OOPC.

The M data model provides the multimedia data integration in Jasmine [30] in addition to a rich multimedia model on a par with stand-alone models. Sound and video are modeled and integrated, and simulation and scientific data modeling constructs are added.

2.3 Multimedia File Formats

Multimedia file formats, though not formal data models, remain important to the field because they represent the most widespread and standardized means of distributing multimedia information. The steep requirements of multimedia data storage and management have given these file formats a degree of sophistication not previously found with simpler data types such as relational tables or text files.

The Moving Picture Experts Group (MPEG) [24] and QuickTime [4] formats are widely used for storing video data. They can be used as underlying storage formats for our higher-level models of digital video.

3 DATA MODEL

Because M is derived from a rich heritage of previous data modeling work, many of its fundamental notions correspond to current entity-relationship and object-oriented data models.

It should be noted that the M data model is an evolution of previous data modeling work by our research group. It functions as a superset of the constructs described before. This work includes the image stack data model, presented in [10].

Further, our stream data model interacts with the temporal evolutionary data model, or TEDM [15]. As will be discussed in Section 3.4 and Section 3.5, the combination of TEDM and our multimedia and stream models results in a set of constructs that can represent almost any type of temporal data, at varying logical levels.

3.1 Basic Concepts

The basic constructs of our model in graphical notation are shown in Fig. 1. They define the overall framework of the data model, synthesized from various data models such as those in [16], EER [33], OOPC [6], and Jasmine [30].

In general, our basic framework is a synthesis of entity-relationship (ER) and object-oriented (OO) data models. We have tried to combine the diagrammatic simplicity of ER with the richer semantics of OO. In later sections, we extend the model further with our own new constructs.

Databases and Knowledge Bases. A *database* is *a set of entities*. Each entity consists of *attributes, relationships,* and *methods*. Attributes and relationships describe the structure, content, and connectivity of an entity, while methods describe the behavior of that entity.

A *knowledge base* is *a structured repository of information, similar to a database in function but differing in content.* In general, knowledge bases contain stable or constant information that can be used as reference or resource material. It may be linked to the entities and other components of a database. Knowledge bases may be viewed as information resources that describe or characterize the information stored in a database. A knowledge base can take on many representations and formalisms. In the specific context of our research, we have focused on a *type abstraction hierarchy* representation of knowledge (see below).

Entities. An *entity* is *the database representation for a particular object in the real world, generally viewed as the "nouns" of a database.* It is notated as a labeled rectangle. If a data model diagram contains nonspecific entities (i.e., rectangles that may represent different kinds of entities), the label within the entity rectangle is italicized.

Inheritance is *the derivation of an entity from another entity.* The inheriting entity (called a *subclass*) possesses the attributes, relationships, and methods of its *superclass(es)*. Note that inheritance is really a special relationship called *is a* between the superclass and subclass entities. Our version of inheritance is semantically identical to the notion of inheritance found in today's object-oriented systems. It is notated as a double arrow, with arrowheads pointing toward the *subclass* entity.

Aggregation is *the composition of one or more entities as components of another entity.* It is generally used to express a *consists of* relationship. In Fig. 1, we may interpret A as being made up of an occurrence of B and C. A is the *aggregate* and B and C are its *components*. Aggregation is notated with a line that is connected to a circumscribed cross ($\oplus$) at the aggregate. No arrowhead is drawn at either the aggregate or the components.

Methods are *encapsulated modules of code that operate within the context of a particular entity.* Our model supports the specification of methods (or *functions*) for the different entities in the database. They are defined and used in this system in the same way that they are used in most object-oriented paradigms and can be applied in ways that will be familiar to those who use such systems:

- derivation of on-the-fly, calculated attributes,
- encapsulation of complex, highly domain-specific predicates (i.e., a *similarity* function that is tailored to a particular entity), and
- performing of nontrivial processing operations that require a general programming language.

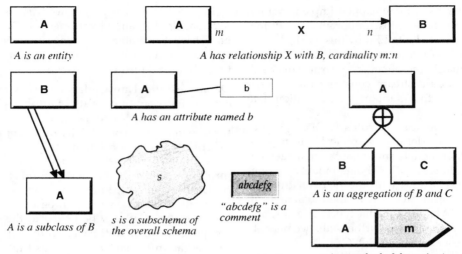

Fig. 1. Notational conventions for basic data model constructs.

In M, methods consist of a name, a set of named parameters and, if defined, a return value. Methods with or without an associated entity are supported. Methods that are associated with an entity can only be invoked from within the context of such an entity. This entity can be viewed as the *performer* of that method.

Relationships. *Relationships* are *constructs that define how different types of entities interact with each other.* They are named using verb expressions (i.e., *is a, contains objects,* etc.), and are notated as arrows between the participating entities. The diagram is read such that the arrowhead points to the receiver of the relationship: when "A contains objects B," the arrowhead points to the entity represented by B.

The degree or cardinality of the relationship among entities may be *one-to-one, one-to-many,* or *many-to-many,* and may involve any number of entities.

Attributes. An *attribute* is *a unit of information that qualifies or describes the entity to which it is attached.* It is notated as a dotted rectangle whose label states the attribute's name.

Attributes may be *atomic* or *complex.* Atomic attributes are thought of as the "basic data types" within the system: numbers, characters, strings, etc. In addition, images and audio data are also considered atomic in this work.

Complex attributes are attributes whose values are, in themselves, also entities within the database. They can also be thought of as nested entities. Thus, these attributes may have attributes, relationships, and methods of their own.

Attribute atomicity or complexity is not explicitly expressed by our notation. Further, our notation does not require that the data type of an attribute be set by the schema, nor does it indicate whether the attribute is stored or calculated by a method. Our intention in this design choice is to provide the user with as simple a view of the data as possible, without burdening him or her with details or restrictions such as data types, means of storage or calculation, etc.

Subschemas. A *subschema* is *a logical subset of a database's components that can be encapsulated as a single database node.* The size of a database schema may exceed the size of the medium on which it is presented (a piece of paper, a window on the screen, etc.). In this case, the schema may be broken up into logical pieces. Connections across schema portions may be indicated by a dotted curve, with the appropriate arrows or lines indicating how the current schema is connected to schemas on another page or screen.

Knowledge. *Knowledge* is *information that is stored not in the database, but in the knowledge base.* Thus, knowledge is precisely the information that was previously described as stable or constant, and usable as reference or resource material. For this work in particular, knowledge is used to describe or organize the data present in the system.

Within the specific context of our group's research, we focus on *type abstraction hierarchies* as our primary knowledge base construct. Full details on the use of type abstraction hierarchies and their role in cooperative query processing may be found in other publications [11], [17], [8]. More advanced forms of type abstraction hierarchies, called *multidimensional type abstraction hierarchies,* are used to perform query processing of spatial and similarity predicates. These are explored in [9].

Comments. A *comment* is *descriptive text that does not affect the structure or content of the database.* Comments are generally used to explain or clarify, for a human reader, certain portions of a database schema. They are notated as graphical boxes of italicized text. In an actual schema design environment, it may be useful to make the contents of these comments searchable by the user, to pinpoint sections of interest in the schema.

3.2 Multimedia Types

A *multimedia type* is defined as *an entity whose content is most meaningful when it is displayed or presented in a way that is directly perceivable by the human senses.* Images, for example, are seen; audio is heard; video is both seen and heard. These

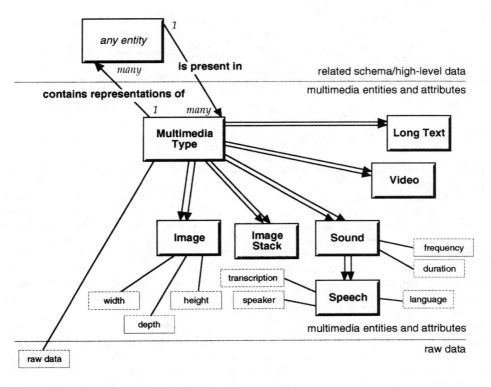

Fig. 2. Overall structure of a multimedia type, showing the layers which they occupy.

special entities form the foundation for the multimedia functionalities in this data model.

3.2.1 Structure of Multimedia Types

Multimedia types can be viewed as encapsulated "black boxes" by the user. They can be presented on a screen or a speaker, assigned to attributes, compared to other values, or manipulated through predefined operations and/or methods. Although the actual implementation of such black box functionality is, internally, much more complex than with numbers or characters, the user-level view of these operations remains the same.

If desired, multimedia types also provide a visible internal structure, illustrated in Fig. 2. This is analogous to our treatment of the string data type: we can assign, manipulate, and work with strings as if they were self-contained objects, but we can also access individual characters within a string. Thus, in our model, images and audio data may be displayed, compared, or manipulated as a whole, while supplementary information such as image dimensions or audio frequency are also available.

The structure that we define over a multimedia type consists of three layers. This structure is similar to the models that are found in [25], [28], [5], [4]. In our case, the multimedia types are integrated into the overall ER/OO framework described in Section 3.1 by placing all multimedia types under an entity **Multimedia Type**. The aforementioned structural layers are translated into attributes or relationships connected to this entity. Our discussion begins at the lowest, most physical level and focuses on increasingly logical or high-level constructs.

Raw Data. The *raw data* layer is the low-level, binary representation (i.e., file, byte stream, etc.) of a multimedia type: a raw sequence of bytes without any translation or interpretation. In Fig. 2, the raw data portion of **Multimedia Type** is notated as the attribute **raw data**.

Multimedia Entities and Attributes. The next layer, called the *multimedia entities* and *attributes* layer, describes the multimedia types such that they may be accessed as actual database entities. All entities representing a multimedia type are subclasses of **Multimedia Type**. Images are modeled either as **Image** or **Image Stack** entities,[1] audio samples are **Sound** entities, digitized video are **Video** entities, etc.

The attributes of a multimedia entity are frequently read-only, in the same way that a text string's length is read-only. For instance, you cannot directly assign a text string's length, but you can change it indirectly by modifying the contents of the string.

Fig. 2 presents some common multimedia entities and their attributes: width, height, and depth for images, or a transcription attribute for digitized speech.

Related Schema/High Level Data. Our *related schema/high level data* layer is similar to the semantic layers found in VIMSYS [26] and SEDM [29]. Most multimedia types need to be referenced by content or in terms of other entities (i.e., "Find images with the following tumor," "Find speeches that talk about the Gulf War," etc.). This higher level, semantic information is captured in logical entities

---

1. The difference between an image and an image stack is primarily cardinality, in that a single image can be thought of as a one-slice image stack.

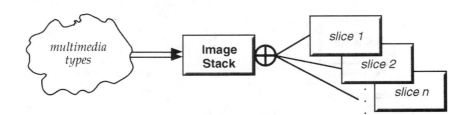

Fig. 3. The dynamic image stack model as represented in M.

that participate in specific relationships with the entity representing a multimedia type.

These entities are collectively labeled as "any entity" in Fig. 2. "Any entity" represents a set of any related database entities. These entities are identical to standard database entities, except that *they map to a particular portion of their underlying multimedia type*. For example, a tumor entity, with standard attributes such as a volume, type, and others, may also be connected to a region of an MRI image. Note that in order to be fully effective, this link is two-way—database entities point to their representative multimedia types, while multimedia types can list the database entities that are associated with them.

In Fig. 2, this bidirectional relationship is notated as the pair of one-to-many relationships *contains representations of* and *is present in*. Any entity in the database may participate in these relationships. A multimedia type itself may be viewed as a representation of another multimedia type. An example would be a thumbnail image which represents a preview version of a larger picture.

The high-level layer permits us to attach meaningful constructs to raw images and audio data, and thus permits us to query multimedia types on a level beyond just pixels or amplitudes. The use of this more logical level of access also permits integration with a knowledge base, thus providing even more contextual information for a user and serving as a guide when relaxing or modifying a query.

3.2.2 Basic Multimedia Types

Fig. 2 shows examples of the multimedia types that are common today. Fig. 2 can be expanded in one of two ways:

1) the addition of new, innovative multimedia types not currently envisioned by today's technology, and
2) the extension of a basic multimedia type (such as any of those shown in Fig. 2) to satisfy a highly specific application domain.

We now review the basic multimedia types that we see as forming the foundation of a multimedia database system.

Long Text. We have found that long text data, such as medical reports, book or article transcriptions, unstructured legacy data, etc., is very well-modeled if viewed as a multimedia type. This is due to a number of characteristics that long text shares with conventional multimedia types: high information content and/or volume, need for sophisticated search methods, and frequent interconnection with higher-level entities. Thus, long text fits very well within the three-layer structure that is described in the prior section.

Images. Images are the most ubiquitous and deeply researched multimedia types in the literature today. In our model, images are represented as entities in their own right. Structurally, they are two-dimensional arrays of picture elements or *pixels*, where each dimension is bounded by the attributes width and height. Each pixel takes up a particular number of bits, stored in the depth attribute. The Image entity defines methods for accessing the individual pixels of the 2D array. Other methods may also include filters or transformations, or operations for combination and convolution.

Subclasses of the Image entity may be defined for specific purposes or application domains. For example, a Radiologic Image may be defined, indicating specifically that a particular image was captured using a radiologic imaging device.

Image Stacks. An *image stack* is a logically related set of images. The model is based on previous work on pictorial database systems [10] and is ported into the data model as shown in Fig. 3. We represent an image stack as an aggregation of *slices*, each of which is given a unique name or numerical index within the stack. For example, slices of a geographical stack may represent elevation, amount of rainfall, etc., over the region covered by the stack. Alternatively, an image stack representing a magnetic resonance imaging (MRI) study may have slices numbered from 1 to 40.

Sound. Sounds are sequences of amplitude values played at a particular frequency. In addition to its actual data (a one-dimensional array of values), a Sound entity's primary attributes are its frequency and duration.[2]

Speech. Speech is a specific type of sound, restricted to digitized recordings of spoken language. Thus, speech inherits the structure and attributes of sound and adds a number of attributes specific to speech: language, speaker, and transcription. The transcription attribute to store a textual version of the speech object. The text may be derived either through manual interpretation (by a secretary, for example), or through automated speech recognition.

Video. Digital video is frequently called a *composite* multimedia type because it is made of other, simpler multimedia types. Digital video consists primarily of two *tracks*: a video track and a sound track. The video track is a sequence of images that is played back at a high rate to simulate

---

2. In this document, the term *frequency* refers not to the specific pitch or tone of a sound, but the rate at which a sound is digitally sampled.

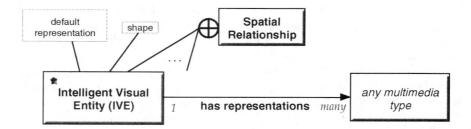

Fig. 4. Structure of an intelligent visual entity.

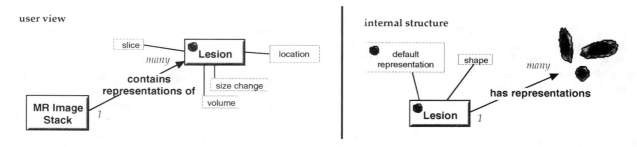

Fig. 5. Modeling a lesion entity in a database as an IVE.

motion. The sound track is sound data that is synchronized to produce audio that corresponds to the images on the video track.

3.3 Intelligent Visual Entities

In this section, we describe a construct that enables a user to ask questions about data in the most intuitive way possible—by "showing" the computer what he or she wants to retrieve.

3.3.1 IVE Definition and Semantics

An *intelligent visual entity* (IVE) is *an entity that stores visual information about itself in the database schema*. This information is then used to answer queries that are expressed as diagrams, sketches, or pictorial examples. Encapsulation is used to permit different IVEs to employ processing that is suited specifically to the application domain of each IVE.

Fig. 4 illustrates the special structure and appearance of an intelligent visual entity. An IVE has two appearances:

1) as a standard entity (with a special icon to show that it is an IVE), and
2) as a graphic "representative" of the instances of that entity.

In addition, an IVE has further properties that are typically not seen by a regular user. These properties are set by the database administrator or designer when defining the IVE.

As an example, consider a medical database that tracks various lesions within patients suffering from lung cancer. These lesions come in a wide variety of shapes and sizes, and may appear in many different locations. Thus, it is often insufficient for a radiologist to store these lesions based on artificial attributes such as an ID (i.e., "lesion 1") or oversimplified attributes such as a diameter or general location (i.e., "right lung," "left lung," etc.). Instead, a lesion can

be modeled as an IVE—it is characterized not by alpha numeric descriptors but by its visual appearance and spatial location. The radiologist is thus freed from remembering these sometimes unintuitive alphanumeric attributes and can, instead, refer to lesions as "lesions that look like the one in the current image." Fig. 5 illustrates how such a lesion entity may be modeled as an IVE. The left side of Fig. 5 shows how a database user perceives the IVE, while the right side shows the internal structure that the IVE encapsulates.

Internally, an IVE is linked via the relationship *has representations* to a set of instances of multimedia types, the most common of which would be images. These images are selected from the database as sufficient visual representations of the IVE. It is from these images that an IVE can choose its graphic appearance, as opposed to the generic entity-box look. A **default representation** indicates the type of display to which the IVE defaults when first presented to the user. This multiple representation approach is somewhat analogous to the views in [37], but applied to multimedia (primarily image) objects as opposed to alphanumeric data.

IVEs may also be aggregated into spatial relationship entities. Placing multiple IVEs under an entity specifically defined for a spatial relationship permits the database to store specific query processing methods into that relationship, so that interpreting or comparing relationships can be tailored to the actual application domain.

Note that the IVE structure complies with the multimedia type structure defined in Section 3.2.1. The IVE functions as the high-level, highly logical object, while its spatial relationships and multimedia types (as accessed by *has representations*) comprise the IVE's multimedia entities, attributes, and raw data.

3.3.2 Usage in Queries

The IVE model was designed specifically to support visual or by-example queries on objects that can be found in images, videos, and other multimedia data. Instead of translating spatial notions such as "looks like," "near to," or "touching" into textual operators (as some other multimedia databases do), the user is permitted to express a multimedia query *as is*—drawing a desired arrangement or appearance of objects retrieves the images or other data which look like that drawing.

Within the MQuery language, visual querying is triggered when one of the images for which the IVE *has representations* is selected as the current representation. The selected image now represents the IVE onscreen, and is used to make similarity comparisons with other images at query processing time. When multiple IVEs have been set to use images as their current representation, MQuery takes into account their positions relative to each other, and interprets this position as a desired set of spatial relationships come query time.

3.4 Streams

The term "stream" is generally used in the multimedia field to represent time-based data [25]. However, because our model generalizes this concept to include more that just multimedia information, the term "sequence" may be used instead. Typically, data are *temporally atomic*—viewing or perceiving them does not take up any time. However, present applications are increasingly producing data items that occupy an interval of time. Obvious examples include digitized sound and video. This section introduces our stream data model, followed by more detailed semantics in the next section.

3.4.1 Definitions

A *stream* is *an entity representing an ordered, finite sequence of entities, or values*. These entities or values are called *elements* of the stream. The sequencing is temporal: elements e_i and e_j of a stream entity S are distinguished by i and j being different instances in time. This temporal ordering is further described by a *frequency*, indicating the speed by which the elements of the stream travel through time.

Streams also have the notion of a *current time* from which the *current element* in the sequence can be determined. This is particularly useful when iterating over a stream's elements or when the passage of time is halted within a stream (i.e., viewing individual frames of a movie loop).

Substreams. A *substream* is a *stream that is itself an element of another stream*. They break up an overall sequence into semantically meaningful parts. For example, a stream that tracks changes in a tumor over time may group the first five tumor instances as a substream called "Phase A." The next seven instances may then be grouped into "Phase B," and so forth. Substreams permit our stream data model to interact with the temporal evolutionary data model previously defined by our research group [15]. In terms of digital video, a substream may be thought of as an individual *scene* out of an entire video sequence, and has been referred to as such in the literature [39].

The term "substream" was chosen over "scene" for its greater generality, as the term "scene" is too tightly connected to the area of multimedia and video.

Multistreams. A *multistream* is *an aggregation of streams combined and synchronized to form a new composite stream*. The canonical example for a multistream entity is digitized video with an associated soundtrack, which is an aggregation of synchronized video and audio streams. No limitation is placed on the type, frequency, or size of these component streams. However, the multistream that aggregates these streams must take care of managing and synchronizing their differing sizes, types, and frequencies.

3.4.2 Stream Notation

Fig. 6 illustrates the stream modeling concepts that have been defined so far. Due to the fact that sequencing or ordering is an intrinsic aspect of the data model, a new notation is introduced for representing a basic stream. Modeling the component entities as a 1-to-n relationship is not sufficient, because neither of these concepts have a sense of time or sequence.

To minimize any further notational complexity, the concepts of a substream and multistream build upon the new stream notation using known constructs. To express a substream, the elements of a stream are given unique names, and streams with these names are defined elsewhere in the diagram. Multistreams are expressed by aggregating separate streams into an entity. Multistreams may contain streams with varying frequencies or element durations, although this variation is not necessarily seen in the formal schema notation.

Streams, substreams, and multistreams are all special kinds of entities that, like standard entities, have attributes, have relationships with other entities, or participate in an inheritance ("is-a") hierarchy. In addition, the elements of a stream, when they are not substreams, are thought of as entities also. This permits the elements of a stream to have attributes, relationships, etc., that are separate from the attributes and relationships of the stream itself.

3.4.3 Practical Applications for Streams

In this section, we discuss the specific application of streams to a variety of domains. Previous work on this type of stream data structure has been, in general, applied only to multimedia data such as digitized video or music [25], [4], [39], [28]. It has not been framed within the greater context of a generalized database management system. The key idea that differentiates our stream work from the stream work of others in the field is our *application of the same general stream model to a diverse range of domains* that previously have been developed either in isolation of other subject areas or have not yet been sufficiently modeled in a database management system.

One of the most significant areas to which we are applying streams is to data resulting from *simulations*. The representation of simulation data into our stream structure has great potential for scientific database applications, which need to correlate *multiple* sets of simulated and real-world data in many domains.

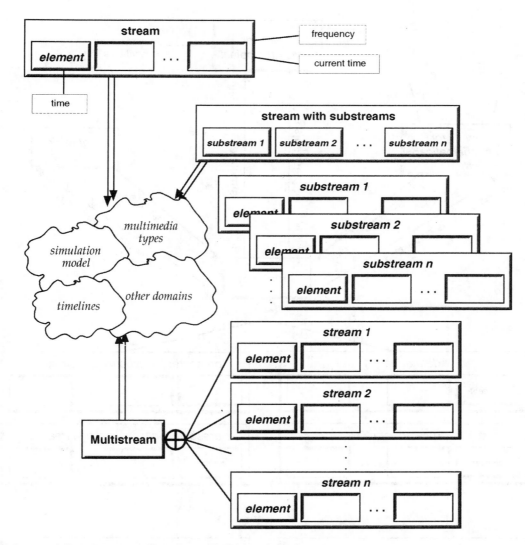

Fig. 6. Graphical diagram of abstract stream entity types and their internal structures.

Multimedia Types. Streams are highly applicable to multimedia data models. This is due primarily to the intrinsic temporal element behind such multimedia types as sound and video.

Sound, for example, has an intrinsic temporal quality. Sounds cannot be perceived instantaneously—listening to them *always* takes some finite amount of time. Thus, they are well-modeled as streams of samples at a given frequency. This approach permits sound data to be accessed and presented using the same notation and semantics as other higher-level streams (timeline histories, simulations, etc.), and is in fact an illustration of one of the significant contributions of this work.

Speech, since it is a subclass of sound, is also modeled as a stream. In addition, its transcription attribute may also be modeled as a stream, where individual words or even phonemes are sequenced over time. This makes possible queries such as "Retrieve dictations where the speaker mentions the word 'cancer' within five minutes of the recording." Although this particular avenue of research is not explored in depth by our work, it certainly holds interesting possibilities, and further illustrates the usefulness and versatility of our stream model.

Digital video, like sound and speech, is intrinsically time-based. An additional level of sophistication is necessary, however, due to the existence of multiple tracks (i.e., audio and video) that need to be synchronized during presentation. Thus, digital video is modeled as a multistream.

Simulations. Simulation data are easily represented using multistreams, managing the many parameters, mathematical models, geometries, and output sets of a simulated system. They also support relationships with real-world measurements and datasets that will aid the user in validating the accuracy of a simulation.

Simulations generally aggregate two kinds of streams:

1) a main data stream manages the actual, numeric output of a simulation, while
2) multiple presentation streams take care of any visualization or presentation of that data.

Thus, the elements of data stream are conventional entities with alphanumeric attributes, while the elements of the

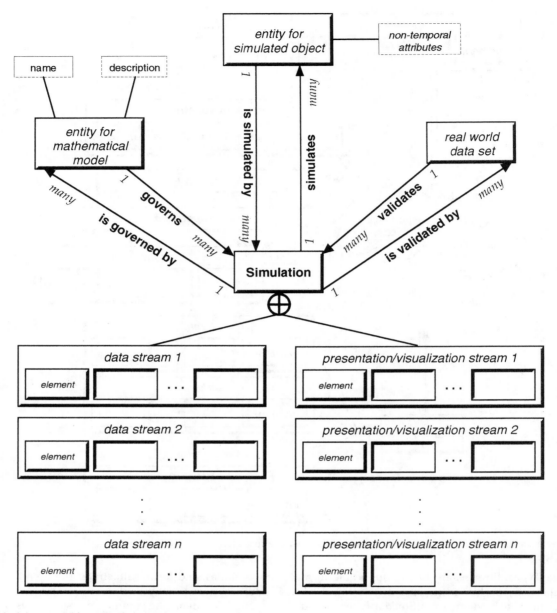

Fig. 7. Graphical data model for a simulation entity.

presentation streams may include images, three-dimensional meshes, graphs, or other presentation-oriented objects.

In our model, simulations participate in bidirectional relationships with two other kinds of entities: logical-level entities of the objects being simulated, and real-world measurements or datasets for those simulated objects. Fig. 7 illustrates the many relationships involved among these three entity types.

For example, a doctor may wish to simulate the behavior of a cerebral aneurysm. This system involves three types of database constructs: an entity representing the aneurysm and its attributes (such as patient ID, aneurysm type, etc.), a simulation entity that captures the mathematical model and other data relevant to the aneurysm's simulation, and a set of angiograms that represent actual, radiographic footage of the aneurysm in question. The aneurysm simulation

simulates the aneurysm entity, the aneurysm entity *is present in* the set of angiograms, while the angiograms themselves *validate* the accuracy of the aneurysm simulations. The database's knowledge of the semantics of these complex interrelationships will permit the doctor to manage all of this information in a unified and integrated fashion.

A new and significant aspect of using streams to model simulation data is the notion of *countability*. Although actual, stored simulation data are always *discrete* sets of values, the data modeler may choose to present them as if the data points existed along a *continuous* flow of time. The notion of being discrete or continuous does not directly affect the data model, or even the database, since digitally stored information is *always* discrete. However, if a continuous view of data is required, the necessary methods must be written to provide, perhaps dynamically, any data points

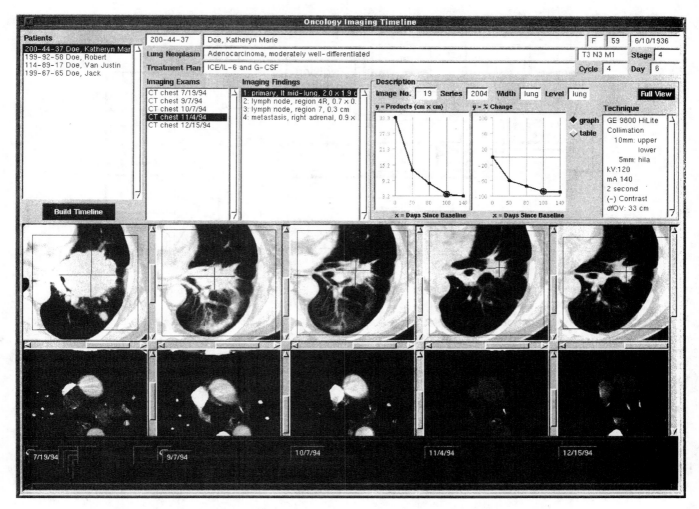

Fig. 8. A sample timeline that merges radiological images, reports, and graphs into a single overall view of a given patient.

that fall between the discrete time slices for which stored data points exist.

Timelines. Another effective application of streams and multistreams can be found in the representation and modeling of *timelines*. In radiology, our group has been exploring the use of timelines to concisely present the overall history of a patient, including images, reports, and graphs, in a single view. Fig. 8 illustrates an example of such a timeline.

Shown is an imaging timeline for thoracic oncology. On the upper-left corner of the window is a list of patients retrieved by a database query. A detailed view of the currently selected patient, including graphs for selected attributes, is shown to the right of this list. Below this alphanumeric data is the timeline multistream itself, divided into two panes. The upper pane is a timeline of images, showing one stream per lesion identified by the radiologist. The lower pane is a stream of other nonimage events in the patient's history. Different icons represent different kinds of events or data, such as a pathology test, radiological exam, etc.

Our stream-as-timeline model is applicable to diverse fields such as thoracic oncology and thermal ablation

therapy of brain tumors.[3] We have developed a prototype system for proof-of-concept, reported in [22]. Like an individual simulation data set, medical timelines are modeled as multistreams. Aggregated streams include various image streams, report streams, graph streams, and any number of other data types. Other potential aggregated streams include annotations, spoken recordings made by doctors, etc.

Doctors and radiologists have found timelines to be highly useful at presenting as much information about a patient as possible with a high degree of organization and clarity (as reported in [2]). Previous reporting methods either lacked the "big picture" view enabled by a timeline or lacked the amount of detail that most doctors require of their data.

Temporal Evolutionary Data Model. Temporal and evolutionary constructs, as defined in [15], may also be reformulated using a combination of intelligent visual entities and streams. Fig. 9 summarizes the new notation for the temporal evolutionary data model (TEDM).

---

3. Some readers may view such data, which are sampled at distant points in time, as versions of the medical image.

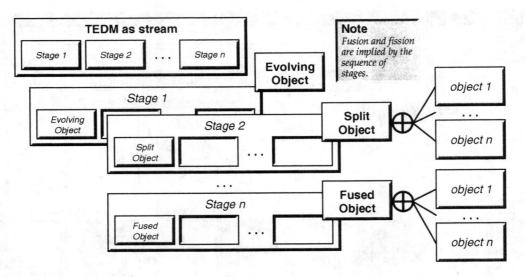

Fig. 9. Notational conventions for TEDM constructs.

The overall evolution of an object in TEDM is now captured in M as a stream or multistream. Stages within the evolution are translated into named substreams. The elements of these substreams represent individual instances of the evolving objects. When the elements of an evolutionary stage consist of multiple entities, the elements of that stage are modeled as aggregations of those entities (as can be seen from the *Split Object* and *Fused Object* entities in Fig. 9). The occurrence of fission and fusion are implied by the ordering of the stages—for example, if the elements of one stage are not aggregated entities and the next stage consists of aggregations, then the transition from one stage to another is fission.

3.5 Semantics of Streams

In this section, we formalize our stream data model and the concepts behind stream time. Our perspective of time views it from *within* an entity, and thus differs from other temporal models and algebras [15], [36] which study time's characteristics *outside of* the objects in the database. These temporal approaches focus on the history, evolution, or versioning of an object as time passes. With our stream model, time does not span over multiple separate objects. Instead, time passes *inside* an individual stream. Although a stream does consist of multiple elements, these objects are encapsulated within a single, larger construct, and can be manipulated collectively as a single entity instead of a linked set of entities. These two approaches to time are not mutually exclusive. They only look at time from different points of view.

Our model of time is based primarily on the models used in timed streams [25] and QuickTime [4]. It has been adapted so that it can be used for new domains such as simulation, medical imaging, and scientific computing.

3.5.1 Formal Definitions

A stream is either *discrete* or *continuous*, depending on the quantifiability of its elements.

DEFINITION 1. *A discrete stream S is a 6-tuple* $(f, d, t, \triangle t, n, E)$ *where:*

- f *is the* frequency *of the stream.*
- d *is the* duration *of the stream.*
- t *is the* current time *of the stream.*
- $\triangle t$ *is the stream's* time vector.
- n *is the* number of elements *in S.*
- E *is a sequence* e_0 *to* e_{n-1} *of elements* e_i.

In general, f is expressed in hertz (Hz) and its multiples. d, t, and $\triangle t$ *may be expressed in either ticks or seconds. n is a finite natural number, and* e_i *is as defined below.*

DEFINITION 2. *A continuous stream* S_∞ *is a 6-tuple* $(f, d, t, \triangle t, a, E)$ *where:*

- $f, d, t,$ *and* $\triangle t$ *are the same as in a discrete stream.*
- a *is a domain over which the elements of the stream may be "indexed."*
- E *is a continuum* $e(0)$ *to* $e(a)$ *of elements where* $e(x)$ *is a function in* $[0, a]$ *whose result is an element as defined below.*

DEFINITION 3. *An element* e_i *or* $e(x)$ *is a 4-tuple* (O, T, R, V) *where:*

- O *is the* index *of that element in the stream. In this definition,* $O = i$ *for discrete streams or* $O = x$ *for continuous streams.*
- T *is the* tick *of that element in the stream.*
- R *is the* time *of that element in the stream.*
- V *is the* value, *or data, stored by that element.*

V can be anything from an image or sound sample to a medical report from a timeline. V can also be another stream, in which case it is a substream of its owning stream S.

DEFINIITON 4. *A multistream M is a 7-tuple* $(f_M, d_M, t_M, \triangle t_M, n_M, \sigma, s)$ *where:*

- *The variables* f_M *to* $\triangle t_M$ *correspond to the variables for a stream S, except that they are now applied to the multistream.*

- n_M is the number of streams in M.
- σ is a set S_0 to S_{n_M-1} of streams S_k.
- s is an array of start times s_k for each stream S_k in σ.

For multistreams, the expressions f_k, d_k, etc., are used to denote the frequency, duration, or other attribute of the kth stream in the multistream.

The idea of continuous streams does not strictly contradict the earlier, more intuitive definition of streams as finite sequences of elements. Streams, after all, are ultimately stored as digital data, which is necessarily finite as stored. However, this finite data, through interpolation or dynamic calculations, can be used to provide the *appearance* of a continuous stream.

3.5.2 Time in Streams

The temporal basis of a stream entity is its *time scale*. A stream's time scale determines how the stream measures time when compared to our own sense of "real time." The succeeding sections define the concepts that are associated with a stream entity's time scale.

Real time is time as perceived and measured by human beings. In our model, real time is measured in *seconds*. All other temporal units are based on either fractions of or multiples of a real-time second. Real time is a *continuous* time scale, because every point in real time can be defined and isolated with infinite precision.

Streams measure time in terms of *ticks*. The passage of ticks, or *stream time*, represents a *discrete* time scale. Within an individual stream, time cannot be divided into units that are finer than the duration of an individual tick.

Frequency. Stream ticks are mapped into real-time seconds by their *frequency*. A stream's frequency is the *number of ticks per second*. The variable f is used to denote a stream's frequency, which is often measured in hertz (Hz) and its multiples. *Tick length* is the number of seconds between ticks, and is determined by calculating $1/f$. The amount of real time occupied by t ticks is thus t/f.

Duration. A stream occupies a finite span of time. Thus, it has a total *duration*. A stream's duration is the amount of time occupied by a stream, and it can be measured either continuously (in seconds) or discretely (in ticks). As a discrete measure, the duration d is the total number of ticks spanned by the stream. To convert this value into real time, d is divided by the stream's frequency f to arrive at the number of seconds spanned by a stream (d/f).

Current Time. There are instances when a user or system must access a stream during a specific point in time. These instances may occur during the "playback" of a stream, or when querying its data for a specific event or during a particular span of time. During these instances, the time value on which a stream is "focused" is defined as its *current time* or t. During playback, for example, a stream's current time is set to zero, then incremented at some predefined rate until it reaches the stream's duration.

The current time can be expressed either in a stream's ticks or in real-time seconds. Stream methods are available for converting between the two time scales.

Time Vectors. Another concept in time modeling is the notion of a *time vector* or $\triangle t$. Time vectors represent the state of time's movement within a stream: they express the *direction* (forward or backward) and *rate* (in ticks per second) of time's flow. Time vectors +1 and −1 represent playback and reverse playback at the stream's standard frequency. The special time vector 0 represents a state of "frozen time" within the stream entity.

Start Times. For multistreams, an additional time-related value called the *start time* is defined. One start time s_k is defined for each stream in the multistream. The start time denotes the time in a multistream M for which a given stream S_k starts to "play." Thus, if an element in a stream occurs τ seconds from the beginning of that stream, it is then invoked at $s_k + \tau$ seconds *in relation to the entire multistream*.

3.5.3 Precise Stream Element Access

Three options exist for directly accessing or locating an entity within a stream: *access by order*, *access by tick*, and *access by real time*. As we describe these forms of access, let S represent a given stream. For a discrete stream, n is the number of individual elements in S. Accessing methods to continuous streams are analogous to the discrete versions presented here.

Access By Order. The elements of a stream can be accessed in terms of their order within the stream. This order is defined purely by which entity comes before or after another. The length of time that passes *between* entities is not considered.

Access by *order* is notated as $S_O(i)$ for the ith element within the stream. Clearly, i is strictly an integer, and is defined as ranging from 0 to $n-1$. In a database schema, stream elements have an index attribute that indicates the element's position in the overall stream.

Access By Tick. Elements within S can be accessed in terms of the *tick* at which an element occurs within S. An element that occurs at tick j is written as $S_T(j)$, where j is an integer from 0 to $d-1$. Because not every tick in S is required to have a corresponding element, it is possible that $S_T(j)$ may be null. For database access, each stream element has a tick attribute that returns the value of j for that element.

Access By Real Time. An element of S can also be accessed in terms of the *seconds elapsed* between the real-time beginning of the stream and the occurrence of the element. An element that is accessed in this way is written as $S_R(\tau)$, where τ is a real number ranging from 0 to $(d-1)/f$.

The tick j represented by time τ is $j = \tau f$. As with access by tick, it is entirely possible that no element occurs precisely at $S_R(\tau)$. In that case, this expression has a value of null. A database or query language can access the time attribute to find out a particular element's timestamp.

3.5.4 Imprecise Stream Element Access

Not every tick (and certainly not every second or fraction thereof) will have a corresponding element. For example, a stream S may have an element occurring at the sixth tick, with the next element not occurring until the ninth tick. Thus, to be precise, no element exists at $S_T(7)$. However, it is often acceptable to think of an element as "applicable" or "active" until the next element in the stream comes along. One such instance is digital video, where a particular frame remains on display until the next frame comes along. Thus, an element *may* be defined to exist at $S_T(7)$.

In order to differentiate between precise (with nulls) and imprecise (without nulls) stream access, braces ({}) are used to designate imprecise access: for $\{S_T(j)\}$ or $\{S_R(\tau)\}$, if no element exists precisely at $S_T(j)$ or $S_R(\tau)$, then the element returned is the *last* element that occurred within the stream. Thus, in the digital video example, $\{S_T(7)\} = \{S_T(8)\} = S_T(6)$.

A domain for which imprecise stream access may not be acceptable is simulation. For example, if a particular simulation run only solved its equations every 10th of a second and the state of the system at 0.15 seconds is desired, returning the values at time = 0.10 seconds may not be acceptable. In this case, *interpolation* is the more desirable approach to returning the state of the stream at 0.15 seconds.

3.5.5 Stream Quantifiability and Interpolation

The multimedia application of streams can reasonably assume that streams are *discrete*—in other words, a stream's elements are countable, in the mathematical sense. However, when the notion of streams is expanded to cover other time-based data, this assumption becomes invalid. For example, in the case of simulation data, data points theoretically exist at every moment over the course of a simulation. Although it is true that these data points are never all calculated, from a modeling point of view it is incorrect to view the simulation stream as a discrete sequence of elements. We thus permit the notion of a *continuous* stream: streams which can be accessed only by real time or by tick, and not by order.

The entire data set of a continuous stream cannot be stored, so individual elements must be interpolated. The method of interpolation is very dependent on the application domain.

3.5.6 Composition of Multiple Streams

A time scale is only applicable to the specific stream entity for which it has been defined. Certain types of stream entities will share identical time scales: CD audio, for example, or standard NTSC video. However, most streams will have different time scales, particularly when dealing with simulation data, their visualization, and real measurements on the simulated object(s). It is thus necessary to look closely at what is needed in order to properly compose such streams into an integrated multistream entity.

Translating Times Among Streams. The time stream translation problem can be stated in this way:

> Given streams S and S' with differing time scales, where the current time in S is given as j_S ticks, find j_S' in terms of S' ticks such that in real time, $\tau_S = \tau_S'$. This translation is a fundamental step in performing more advanced operations such as synchronization and interpolation.

The translation algorithm is simple and universal. To determine the amount of real time (in seconds) represented

by a given number of ticks in a given frequency, we have the expression $\tau = j/f$. Therefore, the relationship between j_S and j_S' is:

$$\frac{j_S}{f_S} = \frac{j_{S'}}{f_{S'}} \tag{1}$$

Note that when f_S does not divide $j_S f_{S'}$ exactly, this equation will result in a noninteger value for j_S'. In this case, a ceiling or floor function (i.e., $\lceil j_{S'} \rceil$ and $\lfloor j_{S'} \rfloor$, respectively) may be necessary, depending on the purpose of the time stream translation. Alternatively, the system may *interpolate* the state of stream S' during that noninteger tick.

Synchronization of Time Among Streams. The need for synchronization arises when multiple streams with differing time scales are combined into a single multistream entity. The classic example of such synchronization is digitized video and sound. A video stream with a frequency of around 30 frames per second must be presented alongside an audio stream which, at CD-quality levels, can reach frequencies of up to 44,000 Hz.[4] The problem of synchronization lies in determining what corresponding components of each stream are simultaneously "active" at any given time. Inversely, if two events in two separate streams are required to occur simultaneously when the streams are aggregated into a multistream, the problem is to determine "when" in the overall multistream each local stream should start.

Conversion between the time scales of a stream and its aggregating multistream is straightforward: given S_k with frequency f_k and start time s_k, a tick j_{S_k} is easily translated into a tick j_M of the aggregating multistream M in this manner:

$$j_M = s_k + j_{S_k} \frac{LCM(f_0 \cdots f_{n_M-1})}{f_k} \tag{2}$$

Streams and multistreams defer to the approaches used in QuickTime [4] and the Amsterdam Hypermedia Model [28] when handling more complicated synchronization issues.

3.5.7 Interpolation Within Streams

In addition to synchronization, *interpolation* is another requirement that may arise from the aggregation of multiple streams with differing time scales into a single multistream. Interpolation is the *calculation of a new element based on the elements already present within a stream*. Specifically, if the state of a stream is required at a particular time or tick j and no element occurs (or is valid) precisely at that moment, interpolation can automatically generate a new element for j based on the element that precedes or succeeds this instant of time.

Our data model's approach to interpolation is simple: The ability to interpolate components of a stream may or not be present in that particular stream. If a stream entity is capable of interpolation, then it is an *interpolation-capable* stream, and this capability may either be enabled or disabled. Note that a continuous stream

---

4. Recall here that "frequency" in this document refers not to a sound's pitch but to the rate at which its waveform has been digitally sampled.

should always be interpolation-capable. Streams whose curves are not differentiable in the mathematical sense may define their own interpolation algorithms for dealing with any discontinuities.

4 SAMPLE APPLICATION AND PROTOTYPE

In this section, we describe a sample application that takes advantage of the new constructs presented in this paper, showing how their use greatly improves the usability and clarity of a database schema. The application is taken from the medical domain, and is first defined by its subject matter and requirements. The prototype that we developed using M is then presented.

4.1 Domain and Requirements

The example domain presented here is based on a multimedia database for thermal ablation therapy that has been developed by our group [22], [21]. However, we are also exploring other domains, such as thoracic oncology, though results are reported elsewhere [2].

Thermal ablation therapy is the use of focal heating for the treatment of tumors. Techniques for thermal ablation of brain tumors were pioneered in the 1960s, and have been further refined since then [18], [1], [3]. The procedure is particularly important in the treatment of brain tumors, where invasive surgery is either impossible or poses the risk of severe brain damage. Using specially designed interventional magnetic resonance instruments, a radiofrequency (RF) electrode is directed into the tumor with MR guidance. Instead of the usual surgical craniotomy exposure, a 2mm twist drill hole is used for access in the skull of the patient, who remains awake during the procedure.

The sample schema presented in this section maintains the patient records, models, and images that are relevant to the thermal ablation therapy application domain. Using the modeling constructs provided by M, an instantiation of the schema can store patient records and images, associate them with each other, and perform queries on this data based on features such as tumor volume or histology. In addition, the schema supports simulations of the heat transfer process that occurs during thermal ablation therapy, mapping these simulations to the appropriate patients where applicable.

4.2 Discussion of Schema

Fig. 10 shows the overall thermal ablation therapy schema that we have developed as a testbed for the M data model. The schema shown is actually a subset of a larger project between our Computer Science and Radiology Departments. A broader data model spanning many other areas of medical imaging is being developed as a part of that larger project.

4.2.1 Patients and Health Care Activities

The standard representation of a patient is shown in Fig. 10. This representation stores an individual **Patient** as an entity participating in the 1-to-n relationship *undergoes* with a **Health Care Activity** as its destination.

Patients have attributes such as a patient ID, name, and many others.

The sample database keeps track of two types of health care activities: **MR Examinations** and **Thermal Ablation** treatments. **MR Examinations** *generate* a set of MRI (magnetic resonance imaging) scans of the patient's brain and tumor. Thus, an **MR Image Stack** *contains representations of* the **Patient's Brain State** and any **Lesion States** at the time of the examination. This relationship shows an application of the multimedia type model illustrated in Fig. 2. In addition, **Brain States** and **Lesion States** are modeled as intelligent visual entities (IVEs), because they directly correspond to some visible region of interest in the **MR Image Stack**.

Thermal Ablations represent instances of actual thermal ablation procedures performed on the patient. They include information on the actual ablation procedure, such as the number of doses applied, whether or not a biopsy was taken, etc. Measurements tracking the brain's temperature are also taken during the procedure, and so a **Thermal Ablation** *contains* a stream of temperature values.

4.2.2 Brain, Lesion, and Temperature Streams

Our stream model is called upon frequently in Fig. 10. In one instance, as examinations accumulate over time, individual **Brain** and **Lesion States** (essentially snapshots at a particular moment in time) are collected into streams that fully represent the **Patient's Brain** and particular **Lesions** within the **Brain**.

The **Brain** entity belongs to an overall aggregation that represents the **Patient's** anatomical systems (other anatomical systems are not shown in Fig. 10, but may be explicitly modeled as necessitated by the application domain). The **Lesion** entity belongs under one of the pathologic functions for which a **Patient** *has processes*. In this case, it is a **Cerebral Neoplasm** disease process which *generates* one or more **Lesions**.

The third use of the stream construct lies in our representation of the **Temperature** entity as a stream of individual temperature values. **Temperature** is used in two places. In the first case, a **Thermal Ablation** *generates* a real-world stream of measurements, thus tracking the overall temperature of the tissue undergoing thermal ablation as it changes over time. Second, **Temperature** is one of the data streams of a **Lesion Simulation**. **Lesion Simulations** follow our simulation model (as seen in Fig. 7), capturing the heat transfer equations that theoretically characterize the thermal ablation process. Thus, instances of **Temperature** may be directly compared to determine the accuracy of simulated treatments against measurements taken during actual treatments.

5 QUERY LANGUAGE OVERVIEW

To accompany the data model presented in this paper, we propose a highly visual query language called MQuery that directly supports the new and unique concepts in our data model. MQuery is a next-generation evolution of the language PICQUERY+ [14]. We provide herein only an

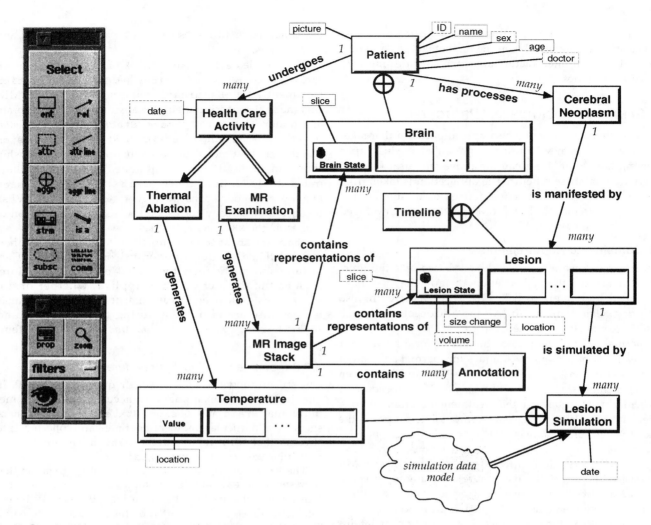

Fig. 10. Sample schema using the M data model for thermal ablation therapy data management.

overview of MQuery; a more detailed discussion of the language can be found in [19].

Queries with complex predicates (WHERE clause in an SQL statement) are more conveniently expressed in a tabular form. Thus, MQuery retains the capability to use PICQUERY+'s tabular format at the same time as its new visual constructs.

5.1 Multimedia Data Access: MQuery and Modules

With MQuery, we expand the idea of a query language beyond the conventional notion of a pure data retrieval system. Instead, the data retrieval functionality is only a module of the overall design. Other modules include:

- Schema designer, browser, and editor (called MSchema).
- Visual interface for inserting, modifying, retrieving, and deleting data.
- Information visualization and presentation.

Thus, MQuery serves as the front end for virtually all database operations. By interacting with the user during all phases of database design and manipulation, a high degree of integration and consistency across all of these stages is achieved. This level of integration permits features such as

"feedback" queries—where any query result or set of results may be used as input for new queries—and intensional queries, which permit the user to ask questions about the schema itself, as opposed to merely its data.

5.2 Query Formulation

The user forms a query in MQuery through a series of copy-paste actions. With a schema window on one side and a query window on another side of a display, the user "copies" desired schema elements and "pastes" them onto the query window. These actions result in the formation of what resembles a subschema in the query window.

When schema elements are pasted onto a query window, they can be filled out by the user to satisfy the conditions of the query. In addition, the desired query results are indicated. This is visually represented by an extra-thick border around the schema elements that have been designated as the desired query result. Fig. 11 and Fig. 12 show examples of visual queries formulated in this manner.

5.3 Sample Queries

The sample queries below have been separated into different categories in order to highlight selected features of MQuery.

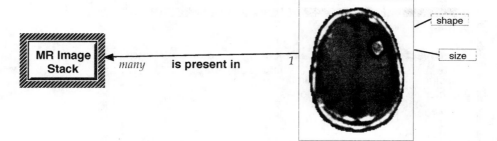

Fig. 11. MQuery expression for the query "Retrieve radiologic images which contain objects similar to the ones that I will place onscreen."

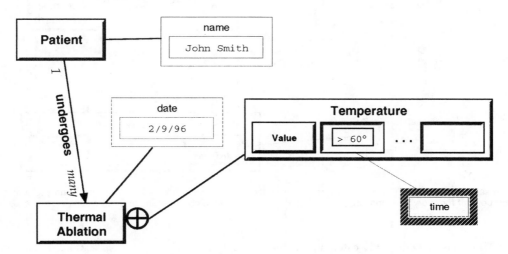

Fig. 12. MQuery expression for the query "When does the tissue in the lesion being treated for John Smith on February 9, 1996, become greater than 60°C?"

Note that these separate query categories can be arbitrarily mixed and matched to form queries that use more than one special MQuery feature at a time.

Alphanumeric Queries. Alphanumeric queries are well-handled by traditional alphanumeric commercial DBMS. MQuery contributes to this query category by providing a visual interface that simplifies operations including the equivalents of joins and subqueries.

Query 1. *Display a list of all the patients who are currently in the database.*

Query 2. *Display all reports generated concerning patient John Smith that are dated September 2, 1995, or later.*

Both of these queries can be expressed and answered by the current prototype.

Queries with Multimedia Results. These queries retrieve data that are not alphanumeric in nature. They highlight the multimedia types of the data model, and how they are closely coupled to the query language. Fig. 11 provides the MQuery diagram for Query 3.

Query 3. *Retrieve radiologic images which contain objects similar to the ones that I will place onscreen.*

Query 4. *Play back the voice recordings for images where Dr. Chan recommends chemotherapy.*

Query 5. *What are the radiologic/imaging appearances of a particular pathology?*

Query 3 can be expressed and answered by the current prototype. Query 4 and Query 5 can be expressed in the language given the right data model, but cannot yet be answered by the current prototype.

Queries with Multimedia Predicates. Multimedia data can be used in MQuery not only as query results but also as participants in the actual predicates. The queries below show predicates that cannot be answered solely from alphanumeric information.

Query 6. *Obtain the sex, age, and doctor of all patients with tumors similar in shape to the tumor currently being viewed.*

Query 7. *Locate other treated lesions in the database similar with respect to size, shape, intensity, and growth or shrink rate of the current case.*

Query 8. *Does the lesion overlap any of the activated areas from the functional MRI study?*

Query 6 and Query 7 can be expressed and answered by the current prototype, although better techniques for answering Query 7 are being investigated. Query 8 can be expressed but not answered by the current prototype.

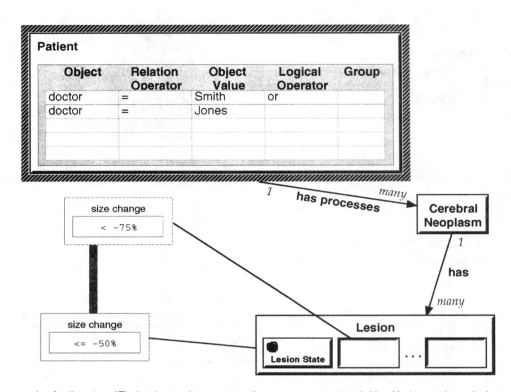

Fig. 13. MQuery expression for the query "Find patients who are currently on treatment protocols X or Y whose primary lesions exhibit a decrease in size by at least 50 percent for every examination since baseline, or have at least one examination that exhibits a decrease in size by greater than 75 percent."

Queries Over Time-Based Data. This category of queries highlights how our stream model makes querying over time-based data simpler and more intuitive. Fig. 12 provides the MQuery diagram for Query 10.

Query 9. *Retrieve and play back the thermal ablation simulation results for patient John Smith for any simulation runs performed after January 10, 1996.*

Query 10. *When does the tissue in the lesion being treated for John Smith on February 9, 1996, become greater than 60°C?*

Query 11. *How does the shape and volume of the left frontal lobe tumor of Jane Doe change with respect to time post therapy?*

Query 12. *Find all cases in which a tumor decreased in size for less than three months post treatment, then resumed a growth pattern after that period.*

All of these queries can be expressed in the current prototype, and all are theoretically answerable. However, lack of data, particularly in the area of simulations, has prevented the full implementation of this answering capability.

Feedback Queries. These queries show how MQuery's integrated modules make it simple to pass the results of one query into another.

Query 13. *What are the volumes of the tumors that were retrieved in the previous query?*

Query 14. *Where and when does maximum tissue heating take place for the simulation run that is currently on display?*

Query 15. *List other cases that have a meningioma of similar size to the case currently being viewed.*

Query 16. *What are the most up-to-date imaging and therapeutic methods for the pathologies currently displayed on the screen?*

These queries have been specified in the language but are not yet implemented in the current prototype. Specifically, linkages among queries and their results have not yet been implemented.

Queries With Multiple Predicates. A key challenge of a general query language is to permit the user to express complex Boolean predicates without detracting from the languages intuitiveness or usability. The following queries are intended to test the usability of MQuery's approach in expressing Boolean predicates. Fig. 13 provides the MQuery diagram for Query 17.

Query 17. *Find patients who are currently on treatment protocols X or Y whose primary lesions exhibit a decrease in size by at least 50 percent for every examination since baseline, or have at least one examination that exhibits a decrease in size by greater than 75 percent.*

Query 18. *Find cases which demonstrate a tumor in the posterior fossa adjacent to the dura or next to the fourth ventricle.*

Queries 17 and 18 can currently be expressed in the older PICQUERY+ language [14]. A PICQUERY+ compatibility module has been partially implemented in the current prototype. This module can express these queries within the newer MQuery environment, but cannot yet answer them.

5.4 Stream Query Processing

Stream predicates define logical conditions over streams. There are two types of stream predicates:

1) *Stream entity predicates* apply to an overall stream, such as "streams with more than 100 elements," or "streams over tumors of type X." These predicates are no different than standard predicates, in that they treat streams as straightforward, self-contained entities. For example, the predicate "performed after January 10, 1996," in Query 9 is a stream entity predicate.
2) *Stream element predicates* are stated in terms of a stream's elements. These predicates are repeatedly applied to the elements of a stream, returning either a **true** or **false** for each element. The predicate's result is a new stream consisting only of those elements that returned a **true** value for that predicate. For example, "greater than 60°C" in Query 10 is a stream element predicate.

As stream entity predicates are semantically no different from standard predicates applied to conventional entities, the discussion in this paper focuses on stream element predicates. In addition, the following definitions and results lead to indices over stored streams in a database, and thus focus on discrete streams or continuous streams with digitally stored representations (and are therefore discrete streams at that level).

5.4.1 Streams of Element Index Ranges

Queries 10, 11, 12, and 14 contain examples of stream element predicates. The formal definition of a stream element predicate is given below.

DEFINITION 5. *A stream element predicate P_S is a Boolean expression that can be applied to the elements $S_O(i)$ accessed by order from a stream S. $P_S(S_O(i))$ is the value of that predicate for a particular stream element $S_O(i)$, which is either* **true** *or* **false**.

DEFINITION 6. *Given a stream S = (f, d, t, $\triangle t$, n, E) and a stream element predicate P_S, the stream predicate result $P_S\{S\}$ is a stream $(f_P, d_P, t_P, \triangle t_P, n_P, E_P)$ where $E_P = \{e \mid (e \in E) \land P_S(e)\}$.*

The query "Retrieve lesions whose tissue temperature is greater than 60°C," which is a slight variation of Query 10, produces a stream predicate result consisting of lesions satisfying the stream element predicate "greater than 60°C." A stream of element indices can be derived from every stream predicate result (as in the above example). Further, consecutive indices can be concatenated into element index ranges, particularly when a stream element predicate holds true over an extensive subsequence of stream elements. This "stream of ranges" thus constitutes a storable index over a set of streams. Additional conventional indexing may then be performed over these sets of ranges, which are, at this point, composed of scalar values.

DEFINITION 7. *Given a stream predicate result $P_S\{S\}$ with element set E_P as defined previously, a stream of element indices S_I is a stream $(f_I, d_I, t_I, \triangle t_I, n_I, E_I)$ whose element set $E_I = \{e \mid e = O \forall (O, T, R, V) \in E_P\}$.*

DEFINITION 8. *The stream of element indices S_I constructed from a given stream S produces a stream of ranges $S_{[I]}$ such that the elements (O, T, R, V) of $S_{[I]}$ have $V = [O_j \ldots O_k]$ where $P_S(S_O(i))$ is* **true** $\forall i \in [O_j \ldots O_k]$.

Given $S_{[I]}$ for a particular predicate P_S, queries of the following forms may be answered without having to perform a complete scan of every instance of stream S in the database:

- Retrieve streams with elements that satisfy P_S (such as the modified Query 10).
- Retrieve the elements of some stream (perhaps specified by a stream entity predicate) that satisfy P_S (such as Query 12 and Query 14).
- Any other query that builds upon elements of a stream that satisfy the predicate P_S (such as Query 17).

The index $S_{[I]}$ can be constructed and maintained as stream instances are added to the database or deleted from it. If higher level indices have been constructed over $S_{[I]}$, these indices must also be maintained as well.

5.4.2 Streams of Satisfied Stream Element Predicates

The creation of streams of ranges $S_{[I]}$ facilitates the querying of streams based on the truth or falsehood of a single stream element predicate P_S. This approach results in one index for each predicate P_S of interest to the database's designers and target users. An alternative approach which constructs one index for a set of predicates is discussed in this section.

DEFINITION 9. *A stream element predicate partition φ for some stream S is a set of stream element predicates P_S such that $\forall$ elements e of S, $P_S(e)$ is* **true** *for no more than one $P_S \in \varphi$.*

Examples of these predicate partitions include $\{< x, > x, = x\}$ where x is some pivotal value (frequently zero, for streams that track rates of growth) and $\{= v_1, = v_2, \ldots, = v_n\}$ where $\{v_1, v_2, \ldots, v_n\}$ constitutes a finite range of values that can be taken on by some attribute of a stream's element. Query 11 and Query 12, which are interested in size changes, would benefit from such a partition. To index the growth or shrinkage of a tumor, the predicate partition $\{< 0, > 0, = 0\}$ may be used for that tumor's **volume** or **size** attributes.

The idea behind stream element partitions is to construct, for each stream instance, a sequence of element ranges for which some predicate in the partition is true. As with the previous approach, a higher-level index can then be constructed over these smaller streams of element ranges to streamline query processing even further.

DEFINITION 10. *Given a stream element predicate partition φ for some stream S, a stream of satisfied stream element predicates is a stream whose element set E_φ*

consists of element tuples $(O\varphi, T\varphi, R\varphi, V\varphi)$ where $V\varphi = (P_S, [O_j ... O_k])$, with $P_S \in \varphi$ and $[O_j ... O_k]$ is a range of indices for accesses by order in stream S such that $\forall S_O(o), o \in [O_j ... O_k], P_S(S_O(o))$ is `true`.

Query results from Query 12 would form a set of streams of satisfied stream element predicates. In this case, the partition φ is $\{\leq 0, > 0\}$ and the ranges $[O_j ... O_k]$ consist of elements that satisfy the ≤ 0 predicate prior to three months post treatment, then satisfy > 0 after that.

Note that our definitions permit the condition where *no* predicate in φ is true for a given element. This possibility is eliminated by choosing the predicates in φ such that $P_S(e)$ is `true` for one and only one $P_S \in \varphi$.

We observe, without presenting the complete (and lengthy) details, that satisfied stream element predicate streams are semantically related to the range streams defined in the previous section. Simply put, predicate streams can be constructed from a set of range streams and vice versa, as long as the stream element predicates involved satisfy the conditions in Definition 9. Though this may suggest, conceptually, that both stream indexing approaches require the same amount of storage and maintenance, differences in the actual data content of stream instances may make one approach better than the other.

6 PROTOTYPE IMPLEMENTATION

We have implemented the data model in this document with an interactive, visual schema design tool designed to support the entire M data model specification. The VisualWorks Smalltalk development environment from ParcPlace/Digitalk Inc. was used for this prototype.

6.1 Implementation Details

Schema diagrams are committed to a Gemstone database system, which is being extended in order to accommodate the more advanced data modeling constructs presented in this paper. Visualization and presentation can be done on VisualWorks, but can also use specialized packages such as IDL (Interactive Data Language) from Research Systems Inc.

An MQuery prototype has also been developed on the same platforms. At this point, MQuery can answer simple visual queries, including the brain and lesion objects for Query 3 and illustrated in Fig. 11. In PICQUERY+, which is a tabular and less visual subset of MQuery, we can answer thus far Query 1, Query 2, Query 12, Query 13, and Query 15.

The thermal ablation therapy application presented herein is discussed in depth in [21]. The initial data model and prototype use a subset of the M data model, and can perform queries on various brain tumors based on size and rate of growth. Query results are linked to an IDL 3D image visualization tool. Another major and concurrent effort is in thoracic oncology, including the necessary data model, timeline interface, and visualization facilities [2], [22].

6.2 Data Model Evaluation

The data model notation, and software implemented thus far, has been tested and evaluated by users with varied levels of formal database training (sometimes none at all). This section provides highlights of the testing process that was conducted. A full account, including more details and graphs of the testing results, is provided in a separate document [20].

Methodology. Users were tested in the areas of schema comprehension and definition or design. To separate the data model's usability from the software's usability, these tests were each conducted twice: once using pencil and paper, and again using the software prototype. Hands-on sessions were videotaped for later analysis.

After objective testing concluded, users were given a questionnaire where they provided subjective reactions to the data model and software. The questionnaire covered topics ranging from the usability of the data model to its potential application to real-world problem domains. Free-text comments were also solicited.

Results. In general, user feedback was very positive, particularly with regard to the ease of use of the model and notation and the ease by which multimedia types can be visualized and understood in schemas diagrammed with the model. On an objective level, users performed well in accomplishing the tasks given to them. Interpretations of schema diagrams were generally accurate and complete, as were the designs generated by the users with the data model notation. Subjectively, user responses in the questionnaire indicated a high degree of satisfaction with the data model.

7 CONCLUSIONS AND FUTURE WORK

We described the M data model which provides the following new constructs: an overall multimedia type model that organizes all multimedia types under a single hierarchy and layered structure, intelligent visual entities that are capable of answering queries on their appearance without depending on alphanumeric indexing, a stream construct that unifies data modeling requirements for time-based information, and a data model for simulation and visualization that takes advantage of our multimedia and stream models. Logical schemas defined in M are capable of capturing multimedia, simulation, temporal, and evolutionary data so that they may be represented, queried, and visualized.

M has an accompanying query language, MQuery, that takes advantage of the data model's special constructs. We showed examples of the query requirements in a number of application domains.

We indicate that prototype databases have been designed and implemented for thoracic oncology [2] and brain tumor thermal ablation therapy [21], illustrating a number of highlights. We are pursuing further implementation and use of the features presented in this article; modules that have been implemented thus far include schema design and basic querying and visualization. The schema design module already supports the complete data model, including multimedia types, intelligent visual entities, streams, and simulation.

All told, the data modeling concepts introduced herein are applicable to a wide variety of domains: multimedia digital libraries, medical imaging, medical records (via a visual timeline), engineering or scientific simulations, etc. Further, this broad set of domains is efficiently served by a small number of concepts and ideas, particularly multimedia types and streams.

Future work includes finalizing the detailed specification, implementation, and prototype testing of several parts of *MQuery*. MQuery will be visual in nature, and it will take full advantage of the special constructs defined by our model. Other research directions include advanced visualization, new interface paradigms (i.e., gestures, virtual reality, etc.), and the inclusion of hypertext or hypermedia data into the overall model.

ACKNOWLEDGMENTS

The authors thank the many colleagues, collaborators, and consultants who have motivated, inspired, and contributed to this work. Dr. Wesley W. Chu from the Computer Science Department and Dr. Ricky K. Taira from the Department of Radiological Sciences are the coprincipal investigators with Alfonso F. Cárdenas of the UCLA KMeD project. Drs. Denise R. Aberle, Gary R. Duckwiler, Jonathan Goldin, Robert B. Lufkin, Michael F. McNitt-Gray, and Fernando Viñuela of the UCLA School of Medicine have been invaluable in developing and evaluating the database requirements and proof-of-concept prototypes of real-world medical applications such as cerebral aneurysm embolization, thermal ablation therapy, and thoracic oncology imaging. Portions of this work were supported by grants from the National Science Foundation.

REFERENCES

[1] Y. Anzai, A. DeSalles, K. Black, K. Farahani, S. Sinha, D. Castro, and R.B. Lufkin, "Interventional MRI," *Radiographics*, 1993.

[2] D.R. Aberle, J.D.N. Dionisio, M.F. McNitt-Gray, R.K. Taira, A.F. Cárdenas, J.G. Goldin, K. Brown, R.A. Figlin, and W.W. Chu, "Integrated Multimedia Timeline of Medical Images and Data for Thoracic Oncology Patients," *Radiographics*, vol. 16, no. 3, pp. 669-681, May 1996.

[3] Y. Anzai, R.B. Lufkin, A. DeSalles, D.R. Hamilton, K. Farahani, and K.L. Black, "Preliminary Experience with MR-Guided Thermal Ablation of Brain Tumors," *Am. J. Neuroradiology*, vol. 16, no. 1, pp. 39-48 (discussion, pp. 49–52), Jan. 1995.

[4] Apple Computer, "QuickTime," *Inside Macintosh*, Addison-Wesley, 1993.

[5] E. Bertino, M. Damiani, and P. Randi, "An Approach to Integrate Multimedia Data in a Knowledge Representation System," T. Catarci, M.F. Costabile, and S. Levialdi, eds., *Proc. Int'l Workshop Advanced Visual Interfaces*, pp. 109-123, Rome, World Scientific, May 1992.

[6] E. Bertino, M. Negri, G. Pelagatti, and L. Sbattella, "Object-Oriented Query Languages: The Notion and the Issues," *IEEE Trans. Knowledge and Data Eng.*, vol. 4, no. 3, pp. 223-237, June 1992.

[7] A. Del Bimbo, E. Vicario, and D. Zingoni, "Symbolic Description and Visual Querying of Image Sequences Using Spatio-Temporal Logic," *IEEE Trans. Knowledge Data Eng.*, vol. 7, no. 4, pp. 609-622, 1995.

[8] W.W. Chu and Q. Chen, "A Structured Approach for Cooperative Query Answering," *IEEE Trans. Knowledge and Data Eng*, vol. 6, no. 5, pp. 738-749, Oct. 1994.

[9] W.W. Chu and K. Chiang, "Abstraction of High Level Concepts from Numerical Values in Databases," *Proc. AAAI Workshop Knowledge Discovery in Databases*, 1994.

[10] M. Chock, A.F. Cárdenas, and A. Klinger, "Manipulating Data Structures in Pictorial Information Systems," *Computer*, pp. 43-50, Nov. 1981.

[11] W.W. Chu, Q. Chen, R.-C. Lee, "Cooperative Query Answering via Type Abstraction Hierarchy," S.M. Deen, ed., *Cooperating Knowledge Based Systems*, Elsevier, 1990.

[12] *Workshop Advances in Data Management for the Scientist and Engineer*, W.W. Chu, A.F. Cárdenas and R.K. Taira, eds., National Science Foundation, Boston, Feb. 1993.

[13] W.W. Chu, A.F. Cárdenas, and R.K. Taira, "KMeD: A Knowledge-Based Multimedia Medical Distributed Database System," *Information Systems*, vol. 20, no. 2, pp. 75-96, 1995.

[14] A.F. Cárdenas, I.T. Ieong, R.K. Taira, R. Barker, and C.M. Breant, "The Knowledge-Based Object-Oriented PICQUERY+ Language," *IEEE Trans. Knowledge and Data Eng.*, vol. 5, no. 4, pp. 644-657, Aug. 1993.

[15] W.W. Chu, I.T. Ieong, R.K. Taira, and C.M. Breant, "A Temporal Evolutionary Object-Oriented Data Model and its Query Language for Medical Image Management," L.-Y. Yuan, ed., *Proc. 18th Int'l Conf. Very Large Databases*, pp. 53-64, Vancouver, Canada, Morgan Kaufmann, Aug. 1992.

[16] *Research Foundations in Object–Oriented and Semantic Database Systems*, A.F. Cárdenas and Dennis McLeod, eds., Prentice Hall, 1990.

[17] W.W. Chu, M.A. Merzbacher, and L. Berkovich, "The Design and Implementation of CoBase," *Proc. ACM SIGMOD*, pp. 517-522, Washington, D.C., 1993.

[18] D. Castro, R.E. Saxton, and R.B. Lufkin, "Interstitial Photoablative Laser Therapy Guided by Magnetic Resonance Imaging for the Treatment of Deep Tumors," *Seminars of Surgical Oncology*, vol. 8, pp. 233–241, 1992.

[19] J.D.N. Dionisio and A.F. Cárdenas, "MQuery: A Visual Query Language for Multimedia, Timeline, and Simulation Data," *J. Visual Languages and Computing*, vol. 7, pp. 377-401, 1996.

[20] J.D.N. Dionisio and A.F. Cárdenas, *A Methodology for User Evaluation of Visual Schema Designers and Query Languages*, under review, 1998.

[21] J.D.N. Dionisio, A.F. Cárdenas, R.B. Lufkin, K.L. Black, R.K. Taira, and W.W. Chu, "A Multimedia Database System for Thermal Ablation Therapy of Brain Tumors," *J. Digital Imaging*, vol. 10, no. 1, pp. 21-26, Feb. 1997.

[22] J.D.N. Dionisio, A.F. Cárdenas, R.K. Taira, D.R. Aberle, W.W. Chu, M.F. McNitt-Gray, J.G. Goldin, and R.B. Lufkin, "A Unified Timeline Model and User Interface for Multimedia Medical Databases," *Computerized Medical Imaging and Graphics*, vol. 20, no. 4, 1996.

[23] Dept. of Health and Human Services, National Institutes of Health, National Library of Medicine, *UMLS Knowledge Sources*, Aug. 1992.

[24] D. Le Gall, "MPEG: A Video Compression Standard for Multimedia Applications," *Comm. ACM*, vol. 34, no. 4, pp. 46-58, Apr. 1991.

[25] S. Gibbs, C. Breiteneder, and D. Tsichritzis, "Data Modeling of Time-Based Media," D. Tsichritzis, ed., *Visual Objects*, pp. 1-22, Centre Universitaire d'Informatique, Univ. of Geneva, 1993.

[26] A. Gupta, T. Weymouth, and R. Jain, "Semantic Queries with Pictures: The VIMSYS Model," G.M. Lohman, A. Sernadas, and R. Camps, eds., *Proc. 17th Int'l Conf. Very Large Databases*, pp. 69-79, Barcelona, Spain, Very Large Data Base Endowment, Morgan Kaufman, Sept. 1991.

[27] M.R. Harreld, "Brain Aneurysm Blood Flow: Modeling, Simulation, VR Visualization," PhD thesis, Univ. of California, Los Angeles, 1996.

[28] L. Hardman, D.C.A. Bulterman, and G. van Rossum, "The Amsterdam Hypermedia Model: Adding Time and Context to the Dexter Model," *Comm. ACM*, vol. 37, no. 2, pp. 50-63, Feb. 1994.

[29] I.T. Ieong, "Data Modeling and Query Processing for Image Management," PhD thesis, Univ. of California, Los Angeles, 1993.

[30] H. Ishikawa, F. Suzuki, F. Kozakura, A. Makinouchi, M. Miyagishima, Y. Izumida, M. Aoshima, and Y. Yamane, "The Model, Language, and Implementation of an Object-Oriented Multimedia Knowledge Base Management System," *ACM Trans. Database Systems*, vol. 18, no. 1, pp. 1-50, Mar. 1993.

[31] *Proc. NSF Workshop Visual Information Management Systems*, R. Jain, ed., Feb. 1992.

[32] P.R. Keller and M.M. Keller, *Visual Cues: Practical Data Visualization*, IEEE CS Press, Los Alamitos, Calif., 1993.

[33] V.M. Markowitz and A. Shoshani, "Representing Extended Entity-Relationship Structures in Relational Databases: A Modular Approach," *ACM Trans. Database Systems*, vol. 17, no. 3, pp. 423-464, Sept. 1992.

[34] E. Oomoto and K. Tanaka, "OVID: Design and Implementation of a Video-Object Database System," *IEEE Trans. Knowledge and Data Eng.*, vol. 5, no. 4, pp. 629-643, Aug. 1993.

[35] J.M. Pratt and M. Cohen, "A Process-Oriented Scientific Database Model," *SIGMOD Record*, vol. 21, no. 3, pp. 17-25, Sept. 1992.

[36] E. Rose and A. Segev, "A Temporal Object-Oriented Algebra and Data Model," technical report, Lawrence Berkeley Lab., June 1992.

[37] E. Sciore, "Object Specialization," *ACM Trans. Information Systems*, vol. 7, no. 2, pp. 103-122, Apr. 1989.

[38] M. Stonebraker, J. Chen, N. Nathan, C. Paxson, and J. Wu, "Tioga: Providing Data Management Support for Scientific Visualization Applications," *Proc. 19th Int'l Conf. Very Large Databases*, R. Agrawal, S. Baker, and D. Bell, eds., pp. 25–38, Dublin, Ireland, Very Large Data Base Endowment, Morgan Kaufmann, Sept. 1993.

[39] D. Swanberg, C.-F. Shu, and R. Jain, "Knowledge Guided Parsing in Video Databases, *Proc. Symp. Electronic Imaging: Science and Technology*, K.T. Knox and E. Granger, eds., San Jose, Calif., Soc. for Imaging Science and Technology and International Soc. for Optical Engineering, Jan.-Feb. 1993.

[40] Y. Tonomura, A. Akutsu, K. Otsuji, and T. Sadakata, "VideoMAP and VideoSpaceIcon: Tools for Anatomizing Video Content," *Proc. INTERCHI*, S. Ashlund, K. Mullet, A. Henderson, E. Hollnagel, and T. White, eds., pp. 131-136, Amsterdam, ACM, Apr. 1993.

[41] H. Ueda, T. Miyatake, S. Sumino, and A. Nagasaka, "Automatic Structure Visualization for Video Editing," *Proc. INTERCHI*, S. Ashlund, K. Mullet, A. Henderson, E. Hollnagel, and T. White, eds., pp. 137-141, Amsterdam, ACM, Apr. 1993.

John David N. Dionisio received his PhD degree in computer science at the University of California at Los Angeles in 1996. His dissertation, "An Integrated Data Model, Language, and User Interface for Knowledge, Multimedia, and Simulations," is based on multimedia database modeling and query languages, with particular interest in the medical domain. As a graduate student researcher, he was a member of the Knowledge-Based Multimedia Medical Distributed Database (KMeD) development team headed by Wesley W. Chu, Alfonso F. Cárdenas, and Ricky K. Taira. He is now the director of technology of the Telemedicine/ITMedicine Division of the Department of Radiological Sciences at UCLA. He is a member of the ACM, and has been inducted into the Pi Mu Epsilon mathematics honor society, the Alpha Sigma Nu Jesuit honor society, and the Tau Beta Pi engineering honor society.

Alfonso F. Cárdenas received the BS degree from San Diego State University, and the MS and PhD degrees in computer science from the University of California at Los Angeles in 1969. He is now a professor in the Computer Science Department of the School of Engineering and Applied Sciences at UCLA, and a consultant in computer science and management for the Computomata International Corporation. His major areas of research interest include database management, distributed multimedia (text, image/picture, voice) systems, information systems planning and development methodologies, and software engineering automation. He has been a consultant to users and vendors of hardware and software technology. He has served as chair and a member of organizational and program committees for many conferences, and has led many seminars and spoken before audiences in various countries. He is past-president of the Board of Trustees of the Very Large Data Base Endowment. He has been a member of review boards for the National Science Foundation, the National Institutes of Health, and various other institutions. He has authored numerous articles, and authored and/or edited three books.

Querying Multimedia Presentations Based on Content

Taekyong Lee, *Student Member, IEEE Computer Society*,
Lei Sheng, *Student Member, IEEE Computer Society*,
Tolga Bozkaya, *Student Member, IEEE Computer Society*,
Nevzat Hurkan Balkir, *Student Member, IEEE Computer Society*,
Z. Meral Özsoyoglu, *Member, IEEE Computer Society*,
and Gultekin Özsoyoglu, *Member, IEEE Computer Society*

Abstract—In this paper, we consider the problem of querying multimedia presentations based on content information. We believe that presentations should become an integral part of multimedia database systems and users should be able to store, query, and, possibly, manipulate multimedia presentations using a single database management system software. Multimedia presentations are modeled as presentation graphs, which are directed acyclic graphs that visually specify multimedia presentations. Each node of a presentation graph represents a media stream. Edges depict sequential or concurrent playout of streams during the presentation. Information captured in each individual stream and the presentation order of streams constitute the content information of the presentation. Querying multimedia presentation graphs based on content is important for the retrieval of information from a database. We present a graph data model for the specification of multimedia presentations and discuss query languages as effective tools to query and manipulate multimedia presentation graphs with respect to content information. To query the information flow throughout a multimedia presentation, as well as in each individual multimedia stream, we use revised versions of temporal operators *Next*, *Connected*, and *Until*, together with path formulas. These constructs allow us to specify and query paths along a presentation graph. We present an icon-based, graphical query language, GVISUAL, that provides iconic representations for these constructs and a user-friendly graphical interface for query specification. We also present an OQL-like language, GOQL (Graph OQL), with similar constructs, that allows textual and more traditional specifications of graph queries. Finally, we introduce GCalculus (Graph Calculus), a calculus-based language that establishes the formal grounds for the use of temporal operators in path formulas and for querying presentation graphs with respect to content information. We also discuss GCalculus/S (GCalculus with sets) which avoids highly complex query expressions by eliminating universal path quantifier, the negation operator, and the universal quantifier. GCalculus/S represents the formal basis for GVISUAL, i.e., GVISUAL uses the constructs of GCalculus/S directly.

Index Terms—Multimedia databases, graphical query languages, multimedia presentation.

——————————— ✦ ———————————

1 INTRODUCTION

MULTIMEDIA data is a combination of video, audio, text, graphics, still images, and animation data. A multimedia presentation is a synchronized and, possibly, interactive delivery of multimedia data to users. Multimedia presentations are used extensively in many applications such as computer-aided training, computer-aided learning, world wide web sites, product demonstrations, document presentations, online books, and electronic encyclopedias.

Presently, multimedia presentations are created by using commercial multimedia authoring tools and stored into persistent storage such as a CD medium. Recently, commercial multimedia authoring tools have added database access or a database front end to let users access media files and clip libraries. However, to the best of our knowledge, interaction between a multimedia authoring tool and a multimedia database is loose and the database is used for only very basic purposes. We believe that multimedia presentations should be managed by multimedia databases and queried by an integrated *presentation query* language to allow users to store or select multimedia presentations with respect to their content. The content of a multimedia presentation consists of the contents of the individual multimedia streams in the presentation, as well as the playout order of streams, which describes how the information is presented. Playout order is an important part of content, especially for querying purposes.

In this paper, we assume that multimedia presentations are created and stored in the form of multimedia presentation graphs, which can be viewed as high level abstractions for multimedia presentations. Simply, a multimedia presentation graph specifies the playout order of various types of streams making up the multimedia presentation, i.e., it is

————————————————
- *T. Lee is with Kyungsan University, College of Natural Sciences, Information and Science Department of Management Information Systems, Jomchon-Dong, San 75-Bonji, Kyongsan-City, Kyongsangbuk-Do, Korea. E-mail: tlee@ces.cwru.edu.*
- *L. Sheng, T. Bozkaya, N.H. Balkir, Z.M. Özsoyoglu, and G. Özsoyoglu are with the Department of Computer Engineering and Science, Case Western Reserve University, Cleveland, OH 44106. E-mail: {sheng, bozkaya, balkir, ozsoy, tekin}@ces.cwru.edu.*

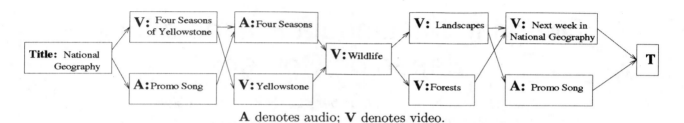

A denotes audio; V denotes video.

Fig. 1. A multimedia presentation graph.

a visual specification of a *presentation plan*. Using a graph model for presentations, this paper discusses languages for *querying* multimedia presentation graphs.

Each node of a presentation graph is a media stream and a directed edge between two nodes specifies the playout-time precedence relationship among the corresponding streams. Fig. 1 gives an example of a simple presentation graph entitled "National Geography" consisting of video streams "Four Seasons of Yellowstone", "Yellowstone", "Wildlife", "Landscapes", "Forests", and "Next week in National Geography", and audio streams "Promo Song" and "Four Seasons". In this paper, we illustrate our contributions using only the video multimedia data type.

A multimedia video stream consists of a sequence of video frames, each of which is associated with some *content* information, namely, a set of content objects and content relationships among its content objects. So, our object-oriented data model includes presentation graph, stream, frame and content-object classes whose objects represent, respectively, multimedia presentation graphs, multimedia streams, video frames, and content objects. Presentation node is also a class and inherits attributes of the stream class.

To query multimedia presentation graphs, this paper discusses GVISUAL, which is an icon-based object-oriented graphical query language. For comparison, we also introduce GOQL, an OQL-like language with constructs to create and manipulate presentation graphs. We also present GCalculus, which forms a formal basis for GVISUAL.

All three presentation graph languages are developed for querying presentation graphs using temporal operators *Next, Connected,* and *Until,* and path formulas. Paths of a multimedia presentation graph are specified by using *computational tree logic* [21] (extended with different semantics for path quantification [34]), and temporal operators of *propositional linear temporal logic* [21], [55] (extended with node and path variables). Path formulas not only can specify paths constructed by the nodes of a presentation graph, but also specify content changes among frames of streams and hierarchical relationships between a stream and its contents. We use temporal logic formulas for path formulas and introduce *node* and *path variables* to temporal logic formulas in order to identify distinct paths and to specifically refer to nodes in multimedia presentation graphs.

GVISUAL is a graphical icon-based query language for the graph data model and extends VISUAL [11]. For querying multimedia presentation graphs (or graphs in general), new constructs of GVISUAL that are graphical representations of temporal operators allow users to express relationships between nodes, edges, and paths along presentation graphs.

The rest of the paper is organized as follows: The data model for multimedia presentation graphs is given in Section 2. VISUAL is briefly reviewed in Section 3. GVISUAL and GOQL are discussed in Section 4. Section 5 presents GCalculus. In Section 6, we briefly discuss the expressive power and user friendliness of GVISUAL. Section 7 summarizes the GVISUAL implementation effort and the ongoing work on query processing in GVISUAL. Section 8 provides a discussion on related work. Section 9 concludes.

2   DATA MODEL FOR MULTIMEDIA PRESENTATION GRAPHS

In this section, we discuss the object-oriented data model used for representing multimedia presentation graphs. Each object o, defined below, has a *class (type)* c, $c \in C$. Objects may be of basic types (e.g., integers, strings), or structured types (e.g., complex objects) which may be constructed from the set of types and class names by using set, tuple or sequence constructors in any order. That is, structured objects may be (or may have components that are) tuples, sets or sequences [41].

EXAMPLE 2.1. A Pres_Node object in a multimedia presentation may be a tuple object with the following components (attributes) and also inherits from a stream object of type Stream.

> Pres_Node: inherits from Stream
> type [*graph-in*: Pres_Graph;
> *other attributes*]

where Pres_Graph is a class name. Stream is also a tuple type, as shown in Fig. 2. Thus, Pres_Node object is a tuple object which also has attributes of Stream class in addition to the attribute *graph-in*.

In order to give more formal definitions for the data model, we need the following pairwise disjoint sets [33], [41].

- D: set of atomic values in the union of four atomic type domains, *integer, float, string* and *Boolean*.
- A: set of symbols called *attributes,*
- I: set of *object identifiers,*
- C: set of *class names*.

We use the types defined as follows:

- Atomic types integer, float, Boolean, string are types, called the *basic types*.
- Class names in C are types.
- If $t_1, ..., t_n$ are types, then $[a_1 : t_1, ..., a_n : t_n]$ is a type, where $a_i \in A$, called the *tuple type*.

---

class Pres_Graph **type** [
    name: String;
    other attributes;
    Nodes: {Pres_Node};
    Edges: {<Pres_Node>}] ;
 	
class Stream **type** [
    name: String;
    type: String;
    pres_time: Real;
	frames: <Frame>;
	no_of_frames: Integer;
	topic: String;
	date: Date;
	other attributes];
	
	class Pres_Node : inherits from Stream
	type [
	    graph-in: Pres_Graph;
	    other attributes];
		class Frame **type** [
		    name: String,
		    objects: {C_Object};
		    other attributes];
		
		class C_Object **type** [
		    name: String;
		    type: String;
		    frame-in: Frame;
		    other attributes];

Notation: "{ }" denotes the set constructor, and "< >" denotes the sequence constructor.

Fig. 2. Data modeling of a presentation graph.

- If *t* is a type, then {*t*} is a type, called the *set type*.
- If *t* is a type, then <*t*> is a type, called the *sequence type*.

Using these types that are typically defined in object oriented data models, we also define, similar to [28], the following types to incorporate graphs into the data model:

- *Graph type* is a tuple type with two special attributes: *Nodes* and *Edges*, in addition to some other attributes, such as name. That is, [Nodes: {t_0}, Edges: {<*t*>}, $a_1 = t_1$, ..., $a_n = t_n$] is a graph type, where t_0 is a *node type*, <*t*> is an *edge type* as given below, and $t_1, ..., t_n$ are types, $a_i \in A$.
- *Node type* is an ordinary object type. In addition, we also have two special instances of node type called "Begin" and "Terminate" nodes.
- *Edge type* is a sequence type with two elements. <*t*>, | <*t*> | = 2, is an edge type, where t is a type, and the two elements of the sequence are also called *source* and *target* of the edge, respectively.
- *Path type* is a sequence type with one or more elements. That is, a sequence <*t*> is a path type, where | <*t*> | ≥ 1, and *t* is a type. If | <*t*> | = 2, then it is the same as an edge type; if | <*t*> | = 1, then it represents a type of a trivial path with a single node.

Let *T* denote the set of all types defined above. The set $\mathcal{V}$ of values are defined as usual [33], [41]:

- Every element of the set of atomic values *D* is a value, and special names such as Nil, Begin, End are values.
- Object identifiers are values.
- If $v_1, v_2, ..., v_n$ are values, then [$a_1 : v_1, ..., a_n : v_n$] is a (tuple) value. [] is the empty tuple value.
- If $v_1, ..., v_n$ are distinct values, then {$v_1, ..., v_n$} is a (set) value. {} is the empty set value.
- If $v_1, ..., v_n$ are values, then <$v_1, ..., v_n$> is a (sequence) value. <> is the empty sequence value.
- If $V = \{v_1, .., v_n\}$ is a set value, $E = \{<v_i, v_j> | v_i, v_j \in V\}$ is a set value, and $v_{n+1}, ..., v_{n+k}$ are values, then [Nodes: V, Edges: E, $a_1 : v_{n+1}, ..., a_k : v_{n+k}$] is a graph value. We will be dealing with acyclic graphs, so, for any <v_i, v_j> ∈ E, i < j.

Here, we need to elaborate on edges and paths in a graph. For both edges and paths to have valid values, the underlying graph needs to be specified. That is, an edge value <v_i, v_j> is a sequence value, but for a sequence value <v_i, v_j> to be an edge value, there needs to be a graph *g* such that v_i, v_j are elements of *g*.Nodes. Similarly, any path

is a sequence, but a sequence may not be a path. For a sequence value <$v_1, ..., v_n$> to be a path value in a graph *g*, we should have $v_i \in g$.Nodes for i = 1, ..., n and <v_i, v_{i+1}> ∈ *g*.Edges for i = 1, ..., n − 1.

An object *o* is a pair (*oid, v*), where *oid* is an identifier in *I* and *v* is a value in the set of values $\mathcal{V}$. A class is defined as the association of a class name in C with a type in T. The instances of a class are objects, and this association describes the structure of the values of the objects in the class [33]. The class hierarchy and subtyping are already defined for basic types, set, tuple, and sequence types [41]. Subtyping for graph types is also defined similarly since graph types are defined using tuple, sequence and set constructors.

The *database* is a structure M(C, I, $\mathcal{V}, \delta, \pi$) where C is the set of classes, I is the set of object identifiers, $\mathcal{V}$ is the set of all values, δ is a mapping from I to $\mathcal{V}$ such that every *oid* ∈ I is assigned to a value $v \in \mathcal{V}$, π is a function which assigns a finite set of oids in I to each class *c* in C.

Multimedia presentation graphs are directed acyclic graphs (DAG). Each presentation stream is a node in the presentation graph and edges describe sequential or concurrent playout of streams. Each presentation graph contains a *Title* node with attribute *type* value of *Begin* and a special node with attribute *type* value of *Terminate*.

In the following, we only give class definitions for the video data type as it is the richest multimedia data type. Each video stream consists of a sequence of (representative) Frames and each Frame has content objects and relationships among content objects. Please note that the same content object (with the same oid and the same value) *can* appear in multiple frames.

In this paper, we use class extents Pres_Graphs, Pres_Nodes, Streams, Frames, C_Objects for the classes Pres_Graph, Pres_Node, Stream, Frame, and C_Object, respectively.

In Fig. 3, we show the composition of the video stream "Wildlife" from the presentation graph of Fig. 1. There are five representative frames in the stream with names "deer", "deer-bird", "deer-river", "river-mountainlion", and "river-mountainlion-deer". The frames of the stream are about a deer hunted by a mountainlion, while drinking from the river. Note that, obviously, five frames cannot depict this scenario, however, it is common to model content information about *representative frames* in the database instead of all the frames, for querying purposes. A representative frame

Frames of the video stream "Wildlife"

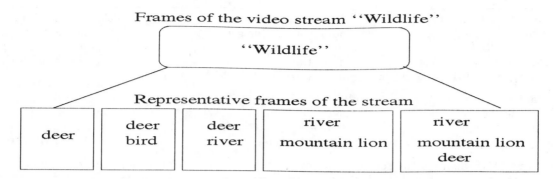

Fig. 3. Composition of the video stream "Wildlife",

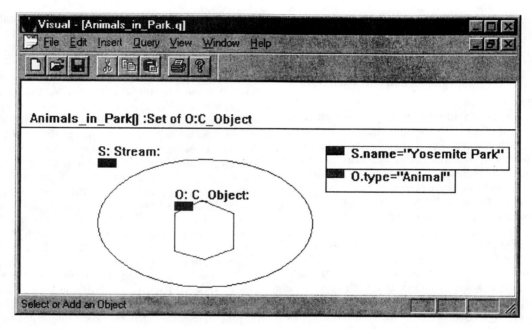

Fig. 4. Query Animals_in_Park.

simply represents the aggregate contents of a sequence of consecutive frames.

3 VISUAL

In this section, we summarize the basic features of VISUAL [11], [10], which is a graphical query language that provides user-friendly graphical tools to query and manipulate data objects. GVISUAL extends VISUAL to manipulate and query multimedia presentation graphs and GCalculus/S is the formal language behind it. In the rest of the paper, for each GVISUAL query, we also present the corresponding GOQL query. GVISUAL represents temporal operators *Next*, *Until*, and *Connected* graphically via different icons. Below, we review VISUAL with examples, and present the corresponding OQL queries.

3.1 Basic Features of VISUAL

A VISUAL query is represented by a window, or a set of windows that are arranged hierarchically. The query whose execution is to be requested is called the *main query*.

The top window always represents the main query. Each query can also contain *internal queries* and *external queries* and is composed of a *query head* and a *query body* (which are similar to rule head and rule body, respectively, in a Datalog rule). Query head contains the name of the query (a unique name that distinguishes the query), *query parameters* (a list of input and output objects), and the output type specification. Input list is defined by query parameters which function in different ways for different query types (internal, external, or main).

EXAMPLE 3.1. In Fig. 4, the main query is named "Animals_in_Park" and has no input parameters.

VISUAL is a strongly typed language and each output parameter is defined with a name and a type specification (after the query name), which can be a basic object type, a complex object type, or a class name. Query output is always a collection (set, bag, sequence) of object identifiers (oids) and, therefore, the output type specification defines the element type of the output collection. Query body may consist of iconized objects, a condition box, definitions of internal queries, and references to external or internal queries. The condition box may contain arithmetic expressions, set expressions, or aggregations.

VISUAL provides *the concept of a query and its subqueries*, the paradigm of "a program calling its procedures", A subquery can be "inside" or "outside" a query body, and it is called an internal or an external subquery, respectively.

EXAMPLE 3.2. In Fig. 4, the main query Animals_in_Park has one output parameter, namely, object *O* of type C_Object. The query output is a set of C_Object instances. The body of Animals_in_Park has the object *S* of type Stream, object *O* of type C_Object, and a condition box. The assertions specified in the condition box are (s_1.name = "Yosemite Park") and (*O*.type = "Animal"). The query in Fig. 4 has no external or internal queries.

Iconized objects represent data model objects, spatial and domain-specific methods involving data model objects and/or classes. There are three categories of iconized objects, and each category has unique properties (e.g., color or shape[1]) as defined in the query specification model:

1) *Domain objects* represent base objects or base classes that exist in the database,
2) *Method objects* represent domain-specific methods involving data model objects and/or classes (i.e., domain icons), and
3) *Spatial enforcement region object*.

EXAMPLE 3.3. The query Animals_in_Park has two domain objects as iconized objects, namely, oval-shaped icon for *S* object and colored-polygon-shaped icon for *O* object.

A domain object contains a variable name (or a constant), the corresponding type specification, and an iconic representation. A domain object within another domain object represents one of the three semantic relationships: composition, spatial, or collection membership.

EXAMPLE 3.4. Fig. 4 illustrates the composition relationship between two domain objects, i.e., stream *S* contains the content object *O*. The query returns all animals that appear in the stream Yosemite Park. This query can be specified in OQL as

> **select distinct** *o*
> **from** *s* **in** Streams, *f* **in** *s*.frames, *o* **in** *f*.objects
> **where** *s*.name = "Yosemite Park", *o*.type = "Animal"

We use the same two-dimensional window space to represent both composition hierarchies and spatial relationships among data model objects. A spatial attribute of a domain object specifies the object's geometric coordinates. For example, the content object *deer*'s x and y coordinates on a video frame is a spatial attribute. An object with spatial attributes is a spatial object (e.g., deer or Cuyahoga River); otherwise, it is a nonspatial object (e.g., frame or stream).

In VISUAL, spatial relationships among objects and classes are visually specified within a region in the query body, called the *spatial-enforcement region*, [2] which explicitly specifies a selected set of spatial relationships among spatial objects. Therefore, in a given query, if two spatial objects are in (or intersect with) the same spatial-enforcement region, then the query specifies the "user-chosen" set of spatial relationships (such as, is-left-of, is-below, is-above, etc.) between two spatial objects.

EXAMPLE 3.5. Assume that we specify a priori that the spatial enforcement region only enforces To-The-Left-Of spatial relationship. Consider the query "Find all streams with a frame that has two objects with names 'deer' and 'mountainlion', and that the deer is To-The-Left-Of the mountainlion". Fig. 5 illustrates the spatial relationship between content objects deer and mountainlion. The spatial relationship To-The-Left-Of is enforced only within the shaded area (the spatial enforcement region). The query outputs all streams with a frame in which the deer is to the left of the mountainlion. The corresponding OQL query is

> **select distinct** *s*
> **from** *s* **in** Streams, *f* **in** *s*.frames, o_1, o_2 **in** *f*.objects
> **where** *s*.type="video",
> o_1.name = "deer", o_2.name = "mountainlion",
>   *f.is_left_of*(o_1, o_2)

Here, is_left_of(o_1, o_2) is a method of Frame class which returns true if o_1 is to the left of o_2 in the frame, and false otherwise.

Users specify VISUAL queries using the *interpretation semantics*, which implies a subquery evaluation for every different instantiation of query variables (due to the hierarchically arranged window structure of VISUAL query objects). This means that, for every instantiation of query variable objects with the corresponding data model objects (or object components) in the database, methods and queries referred to within the query body are evaluated and conditions in the condition box are checked with the current instantiation. The outputs are then retrieved if all the conditions in the query are satisfied. Note that VISUAL *execution semantics* may be completely different than the interpretation semantics [11].

4 GVISUAL

GVISUAL adds temporal logic operators into VISUAL, namely, *Next*, *Until*, and *Connected*, graphically via different icons. However, the semantics of these operators are revised and are different than their counterparts in temporal logic. These three operators are overloaded in that they are used to specify assertions on both paths of graphs and on sequences. We also present an OQL-like (Object Query Language) [14] language, GOQL (Graph OQL), to query and manipulate presentation graphs. Below, we first illustrate the new icons of GVISUAL and basic building blocks

---

1. Each icon, once designed elsewhere in a "template," can be dropped and dragged to anywhere within the query using its "handle" (a rectangle underneath the object name). Also, users can scale an icon object up or down by clicking on its handle.

2. Our choice for the spatial-enforcement region object in this paper is shaded rectangle. Users of different applications can choose a different object with a different color or shape from the class of spatial-enforcement region objects of the query specification model.

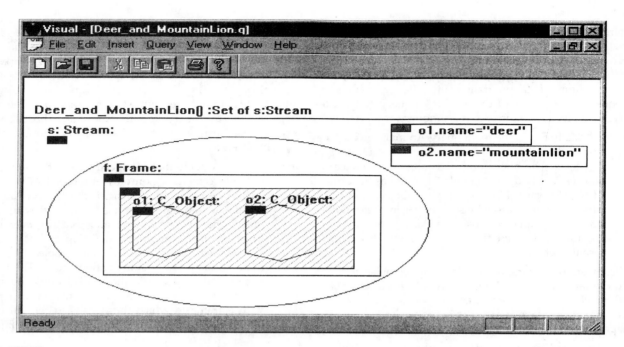

Fig. 5. VISUAL query.

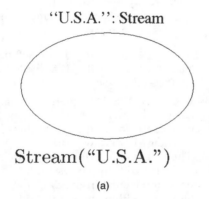

"U.S.A.": Stream

Stream("U.S.A.")

(a)

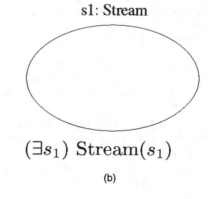

s1: Stream

$(\exists s_1)$ Stream(s_1)

(b)

Fig. 6. Object icons.

of GOQL. Then, we give examples of GVISUAL queries and illustrate them with the corresponding GOQL queries.

4.1 Icons and Expressions in GVISUAL

First, let us present the graphical constructs that are used to represent objects in a presentation graph in GVISUAL. The icon shapes, colors, and shading can be chosen arbitrarily by the user. For each nonshaded icon, *var-name* (or *object-name*): *class-name* (or *subquery-name*) is associated.

EXAMPLE 4.1. The oval icon in Fig. 6a represents the stream object instance "U.S.A.", i.e., the icon represents a constant. The oval icon in Fig. 6b states that a variable object s_1 of type Stream exists.

For visual specification of paths, we use different icons that represent an edge or a path between two objects. A straight arrow, illustrated in Fig. 7a, represents the relationship *Next* (denoted by X). A straight arrow with the optional label P from object A to object B states that, in the

graph containing A and B, there is an edge (also, a single-edge path) P from A to B.

EXAMPLE 4.2. Fig. 7d states that there is an edge from stream s_0 to stream s_1, and another edge from stream s_1 to stream s_2.

A dashed straight arrow, illustrated in Fig. 7b, represents the *Connected* relationship (denoted by C). A dashed straight arrow with optional label P from object A to object B states that, in the graph containing A and B, there is a path P from A to B.

EXAMPLE 4.3. Fig. 7e states that there is a path from stream s_0 to stream s_1, and an edge from stream s_1 to stream s_2.

A bold-faced oval with a solid arrow, illustrated in Fig. 7c, represents the *Until* relationship (denoted by $\mathcal{U}$). *Until* operator is used to express repetition: Starting at a node in a given presentation graph, a sequence **P** of nodes repetitively satisfying a given assertion p is encountered until a node satisfying assertion q is encountered.

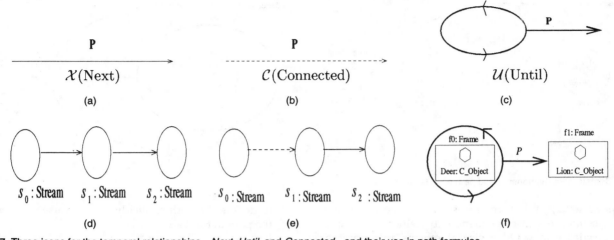

Fig. 7. Three icons for the temporal relationships—*Next, Until,* and *Connected*—and their use in path formulas.

Representation	Interpretation
a solid straight arrow	an edge between two nodes (next)
a dashed straight arrow	one or more edges between two nodes (connected)
a solid arrow with a bold-faced oval	"until" temporal operator

Fig. 8. Interpretations of icons in GVISUAL.

EXAMPLE 4.4. GVISUAL expression in Fig. 7f states that, starting at frame f_0 in a given stream (where f_0 is determined possibly through other conditions), f_0 and each consecutive frame contain the content object "deer" until a frame f_1 with the content object "lion" is encountered, and the resulting sequence (path) of frames constitutes P.

Fig. 8 summarizes the icons that represent the temporal relationships between two paths. We now discuss several semantic and syntactic differences between our temporal operators and those of temporal logic:

1) In temporal logic, formulas always apply starting from state 0 (at time 0) where "state" corresponds to "node" in a graph; in contrast, our temporal operators (including *Next*) can apply starting from any chosen node (i.e., state), called *the starting node*, in the graph. This allows for much simpler specifications of formulas about paths in a presentation graph.

2) We use the notion of *node variables* instantiated by nodes (e.g., streams s_0, s_1 and s_2 in Fig. 7d) which does not exist in temporal logic. The state (node) that is reached by temporal operators of temporal logic is identified *not* by the use of node variables, but, by the fact that temporal logic formulas always apply starting from a fixed state, i.e., state 0, and, thus, state reached for which state formulas apply is clear from the use of temporal logic operators. The use of node variables allows us to specify assertions in a straightforward manner.

3) In temporal logic, the sequence of states (i.e., paths in graphs) satisfying a "path formula" cannot be extracted and output. In GVISUAL, we use *path variables* to name and output such paths.

4) The *Next* operator that we use exploits the explicit specification of nodes by node variables and has two operands, e.g., for the *Next* icon from s_0 to s_1 in Fig. 7d, (state) formulas about the states s_0 and s_1 can be specified. In comparison, the *Next* operator of temporal logic [21] uses a single operand. Expressive power of our temporal operators is discussed in Section 6.1.

GVISUAL examples of Fig. 9 illustrate the use of containment relationships and path specifications simultaneously. Fig. 9a denotes that the presentation graph g_1 contains three consecutive streams s_0, s_1, and s_2, which, respectively, satisfy the assertions "s_0 contains a frame with the C_Object deer", "s_1 contains a frame with the C_Object river", and "s_2 contains a frame with the C_Object lion". The GVISUAL expression in Fig. 9b specifies that the presentation graph g_1 has a path of streams that start at s_0 and repetitively satisfy the assertion "the stream has a frame with the C_Object deer" until a stream that satisfies the assertion "the stream has a frame with the C_Object lion" is reached. Please note that whatever is specified inside the bold-faced oval of the *Until* icon is a path formula that is repetitively satisfied along a path (or a sequence).

4.2 GOQL and Its Building Blocks

GOQL is an extension of OQL (Object Query Language [14]) for querying and manipulating graphs [57] using the data model given in Section 2. GOQL uses the following methods for graphs and sequences:

paths(g, n_s, n_e): Returns the set of paths in graph g from node n_s to node n_e if n_s and n_e are connected in g. Otherwise, it returns an empty set.

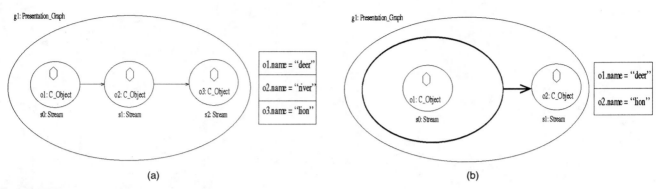

Fig. 9. Containment relationship and path specification.

subsequences(s, x, y): Returns the set of subsequences in a sequence s from element x to element y if x precedes y in s. Otherwise, it returns an empty set. Note that x, y can appear more than once in s.

Since paths are also sequences, usual sequence operators are also applicable to paths with minor modifications:

p.from: Returns the first node of the path p.

p.to: Returns the last node of the path p.

$p_1 \cdot p_2$: Path resulting from the concatenation of paths p_1 and p_2, where p_1 and p_2 are paths in the same graph g, and p_1.to is the same node as p_2.from. $p_1 \cdot p_2$ is also a path in g whose first node is p_1.from and the last node is p_2.to.

$p_1 + p_2$: The sequence resulting from the concatenation of the sequences corresponding to p_1 and p_2. Note that $p_1 + p_2$ is not necessarily a path in a graph g even if both p_1 and p_2 are paths in g.
    For $p_1 + p_2$ to be a path in g, in addition to p_1 and p_2 being paths in g, the edge $<p_1.\text{to}, p_2.\text{from}>$ must also be in g.

nodeset(p): Returns the set of nodes in path p.
    Note that nodeset(p) is very similar to listtoset(l) operator of ODMG object query language [14] which turns a list l into a set of its elements.

edgeset(p): Returns the set of edges in path p.

n in *p*: Returns *True* if n is a node in path p. Otherwise, it returns *False*.

e in *p*: Returns *True* if e is an edge in path p. Otherwise, it returns *False*.

x in *s*: Returns *True* if x is an element in sequence s. Otherwise, it returns *False*.

Temporal operators *Next*, *Connected*, and *Until* are utilized in GOQL to form Boolean expressions, i.e., path formulas, used as predicates for paths and sequences. A path formula is defined recursively as follows: Let p (also p_is) and n (also n_is) be variables denoting paths and nodes respectively in a graph g. Then,

1) Atomic path formula:
    $p : (n : q)$ is a path formula, where q is a Boolean condition on n. It returns *True* if p is a trivial path with a single node n which satisfies q consisting of built-in predicates involving arithmetic comparison, and set membership operators. $p : n$ is also used to denote $p : (n : True)$. The path p is omitted when there is no need

to denote the path explicitly, i.e., n is used to denote the path in this case.

2) Path formulas with one temporal operator:
    $p : e_1 \, \theta \, e_2$ is a path formula, where θ is one of temporal operators *Next*, *Connected*, and *Until*, and $e_i = p_i : (n_i : q_i)$, $i = 1, 2$, is an atomic path formula. It returns *True* if e_1 and e_2 are *True* and there is a path p in g which is defined for each temporal operator as follows:

   a) $\theta = Next$: p is a single edge from n_1 to n_2, i.e., $p = <n_1, n_2>$.

   b) $\theta = Connected$: p is a path from n_1 to n_2 with one or more edges.

   c) $\theta = Until$: p is a path from n_1 to n_2 such that all the nodes in the path up to n_2 (excluding n_2) satisfy the condition q_1 on n_1 and n_2 satisfies q_2.

The path formula returns *False* otherwise. Similar to atomic path formulas, condition q_is can be omitted if $q_i = True$, and the path variables are omitted if there is no ambiguity. For example, $p : (p_1 : (n_1 : True))$ *Connected* $(p_2 : (n_2 : True))$ is abbreviated as the path formula $p : n_1$ *Connected* n_2, which returns *True* if p is a path from n_1 to n_2.

3) Path formulas with more than one temporal operator:
    $p : e_1 \, \theta \, e_2$ is a path formula, where θ is a temporal operator (*Next, Connected, Until*), and $e_i = p_i : (w_i)$, $i = 1, 2$, is a path formula with one or more temporal operators. It returns *True* if e_1 and e_2 are *True*, and there is a path p in g from p_1.from to p_2.to which is defined for each temporal operator as follows:

   a) $\theta = Next$: $p = p_1 \cdot <p_1.\text{to}, p_2.\text{from}> \cdot p_2$ where "." denotes path concatenation. Note that the edge $<p_1.\text{to}, p_2.\text{from}>$ is the path p' which satisfies the path formula with one temporal operator $p' : (p_1.\text{to}$ *Next* $p_2.\text{from})$. The path p can also be expressed as $p = p_1 + p_2$ where "+" is sequence concatenation operator.

   b) $\theta = Connected$: $p = p_1 \cdot p' \cdot p_2$ where "." denotes path concatenation and p' is the path which satisfies the path formula with one temporal operator $p' : (p_1.\text{to}$ *Connected* $p_2.\text{from})$.

   c) $\theta = Until$: Let p' be another path instance for which $e' = p' : w_1$ returns *True*. Then, p satisfies either

   - $p : e_1$ *Next* e_2, or
   - $p : e_1$ *Next* e_1' *Until* e_2.

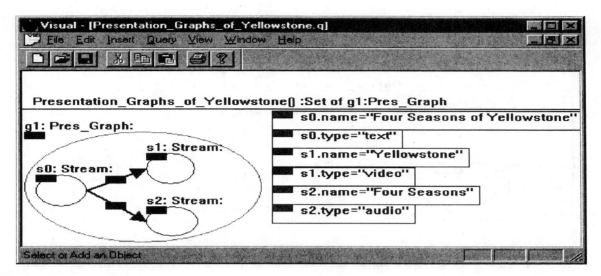

Fig. 10. GVISUAL query of Example 4.5.

That is, if p'_i, $1 \le i \le k$ are the paths such that the path formula $p'_i : w_1$ returns *True*, then the path p is:

$$p = p_1 + p_2, \text{ or}$$
$$p = p_1 + p'_1 + p'_2 + \ldots + p'_k + p_2,$$

where "+" is the sequence concatenation operator.

The path formula returns *False* otherwise. Similar to path formulas with one temporal operator, the intermediate path variables in a path formula can be omitted if there is no ambiguity.

Since paths are sequences, path formulas are defined on sequences similarly. For example, consider the sequence expression

$$ss : f_1 \text{ Next } ((f_2 : o_2 \text{ in } f_2.\text{objects}) \text{ Until } f_3)$$

in a GOQL query where f_1, f_2, f_3 denote frames and o_2 denotes a content object. This expression with intermediate path (sequence) variables is

$$ss : (p_1 : (f_1 : True)) \text{ Next } (p_4 : (p_2 : (f_2 : o_2 \text{ in } f_2.\text{objects})) \text{ Until } (p_3 : (f_3 : True))),$$

where p_i, i = 1, ..., 4, denote subsequences forming the sequence ss. This expression returns *True* if ss is a frame sequence from f_1 to f_3 such that f_1 is followed by one or more frame occurrences which have the content object o_2 and the last occurrence of such frames with the content object o_2 is followed by the frame f_3. That is, ss is a sequence of the form $f_1 f_2 f_3$ or $f_1 f_2 f'_1 f'_2 \ldots f'_k f_3$, where f_2 and f'_i, i = 1, 2, ..., k, each has a content object o_2.

4.3 GVISUAL Query Examples

In this section, we give examples for GVISUAL queries, and their specifications in GOQL.

EXAMPLE 4.5. Find a graph which has three streams: a text stream whose name is "Four Seasons of Yellowstone" followed concurrently by

1) a video stream and
2) an audio stream

whose names are "Yellowstone" and "Four Seasons", respectively.

This query (Fig. 10) illustrates the use of two *Next* operators in a graph and a condition box. Below, we specify the same query in GOQL.

> **select** g_1
> **from** g_1 **in** Pres_Graphs, s_0, s_1, s_2 **in** g_1.Nodes,
> p_1 **in** *paths*(g_1, s_0, s_1), p_2 **in** *paths*(g_1, s_0, s_2)
> **where** s_0.type = "text", s_0.name = "Four Seasons of Yellowstone",
> s_1.type = "video", s_1.name = "Yellowstone",
> s_2.type = "audio", s_2.name = "Four Seasons",
> $p_1 : s_0$ *Next* s_1, $p_2 : s_0$ *Next* s_2

Note that this query can also be expressed by simply checking whether the edges $<s_0, s_1>$ and $<s_0, s_2>$ are in the graph or not. That is,

> **select** g_1
> **from** g_1 **in** Pres_Graphs, s_0, s_1, s_2 **in** g.Nodes
> **where** s_0.type = "text", s_0.name = "Four Seasons of Yellowstone",
> s_1.type = "video", s_1.name = "Yellowstone",
> s_2.type = "audio", s_2.name = "Four Seasons",
> $<s_0, s_1>$ **in** g_1.Edges, $<s_0, s_2>$ **in** g_1.Edges

EXAMPLE 4.6. In all streams, find sequences of frames where the first frame has the content object "falcon", and the last frame has the content object "mountainlion".

This query (Fig. 11) illustrates the use of the *Connected* operator for sequence, and the output of sequences of frames. P denotes a sequence that satisfies the query.

Consider a stream instance with a sequence of frames f_3, f_4, f_5, f_6, where the content object with name "falcon" appears in f_3, f_4, f_5 and the content object with name "mountainlion" appears in f_6. The query of Fig. 11 returns the set of sequences $\{<f_3, f_4, f_5, f_6>, <f_4, f_5, f_6>, <f_5, f_6>\}$, that is, *all* sequences satisfying the path formula are returned. Also

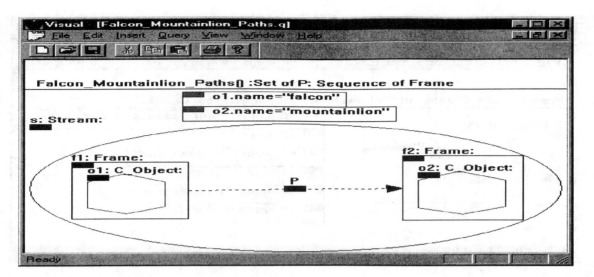

Fig. 11. GVISUAL query of Example 4.6.

note that the icons of temporal operators do not have the optional path variables as the query output does not need them.

> **select** p
> **from** s in Streams, f_1, f_2 **in** s.frames,
> o_1 **in** f_1.objects, o_2 **in** f_2.objects,
> p **in** *subsequences*(s.frames, f_1, f_2)
> **where** o_1.name = "falcon", o_2.name = "mountainlion"

In comparison with the GVISUAL query, the GOQL query does not use the temporal operator *Connected* explicitly.

EXAMPLE 4.7. Find video streams with a frame that contains the content object "river"; after that frame, there are repetitive frames with the content object "deer" until a frame with the content object "mountainlion" appears.

This query (Fig. 12) illustrates the use of a "path formula" with two temporal operators *Next* and *Until*. Below is the GOQL version of the same query.

> **select** s_1
> **from** s_1 **in** Streams,
> f_1, f_2, f_3 **in** s_1.frames,
> o_1 **in** f_1.objects, o_2 **in** C_Objects, o_3 **in** f_3.objects
> **where** o_1.name = "river", o_2.name = "deer",
> o_3.name = "mountainlion",
>   **exists** ss **in** *subsequences*(s_1.frames, f_1, f_3):
> $ss : f_1$ **Next** (($f_2: o_2$ **in** f_2.objects) **Until** f_3)

EXAMPLE 4.8. Find frames f_1, f_2, f_3 in a video stream where f_1 contains the content object "river", the next frame f_2 contains the content object "deer", followed by arbitrarily many frames each with the content object "deer" until a frame f_3 with the content object "mountainlion" is encountered.

This query has the same query body as in Fig. 12 and the query head is replaced by

> Frames_With_River_Deer_Mountainlion[ ]
> :Set of Sequence of f1:Frame, f2:Frame, f3:Frame

In other words, node (state) variables can also be used in the query output.

Similarly, in the GOQL version of the query, the *select* clause is replaced with

> **select** $<f_1, f_2, f_3>$.

The following example illustrates the use of *external queries* with presentation graphs. An external query is specified independently from the main query, and is provided with its input parameters. An external query can be independently saved into the database to make it persistent.

EXAMPLE 4.9. Find a presentation graph in which all streams have content objects "deer" and "mountainlion",

In this example (Fig. 13), the external queries All_ Streams and Streams_Having_D_and_M are called from the body of the main query with the input parameter g for both. Both external queries of the main query return a set of streams which are checked for set equality in the main query body. An external query has a name, input parameters, output parameters, and a query body with a condition box. In an external query call, the specifications inside "()" after the query name denote input parameters of the external query.

The GOQL version of this query is

> **select** g
> **from** g **in** Pres_Graphs, o_d, o_l **in** C_Object
> **where** o_1.name = "deer", o_2.name = "mountainlion",
>   **for all** s_1 **in** g.Nodes:(s_1.type = "Begin" **or** s_1.type
>   = "Terminate" **or**
>   (**exist** f **in** s_1.frames: o_1 **in** f_1.objects, **exist** f_2
>   **in** s_1.frames: o_2 **in** f_2.objects))

Note that, in this GOQL query, **"for all"** is used for universal quantification while, in the corresponding GVISUAL query, it is expressed using set comparison of subquery results. An equivalent query without utilizing **"for all"** which directly corresponds to the GVISUAL query is given below:

> **select distinct** g
> **from** g **in** Pres_Graphs

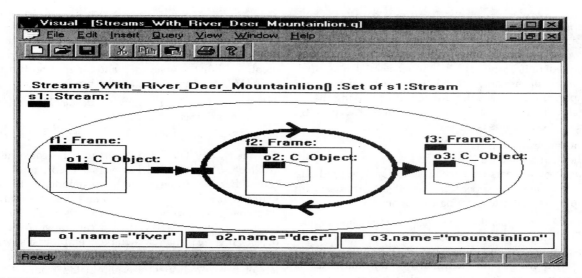

Fig. 12. GVISUAL query of Example 4.7.

where (**select** s_1
      from s_1 **in** g.Nodes
      where s_1.type != "Begin", s_1.type != "Terminate")
=
(**select** s_1
      from s_1 **in** g.Nodes
        where (**exists** f_1 **in** s_1.frames: (**exists** o_1 **in** f_1.objects: o_1.name = "deer"), **exists** f_2 **in** s_1.frames: (**exists** o_2 **in** f_2.objects: o_2.name = "mountainlion")))

EXAMPLE 4.10. Find presentation graphs which have a stream containing the content object "deer" and, along every path from this stream, a stream with the content object "river" is encountered.

This query (Fig. 14) illustrates the use of *internal queries* with presentation graphs. The two queries All_Paths_from_S1 and Paths_Having_Deer_and_River are internal queries of the query Graphs_Having_Deer_and_River. One advantage of internal queries is that objects defined in the query Graphs_Having_Deer_and_River can be directly referred to in internal queries, and do not need to be passed as arguments. Also, both internal query windows can be "closed" (i.e., reduced into their shaded-only forms in the body of Graphs_Having_Deer_and_River) if the user wants to reduce the visual complexity of the query.

Below is the GOQL version of the query:

select distinct g
from g **in** Pres_Graphs, s_1 **in** g.Nodes, f_1 **in** s_1.frames, o_1 **in** f_1.objects
where o_1.name = "deer",
    for all p **in** (**select** p
        from s_n **in** g.Nodes, p **in** $paths(g, s_1, s_n)$
        where s_n.type = "Terminate"):
    (**exist** s_2 **in** p: (**exist** f **in** s_2.frames:
        (**exist** o_2 **in** f.objects: o_2.name = "river")))

The equivalent GOQL query where universal quantification is expressed using set comparison operators is given below:

select g
from g **in** Pres_Graphs, s_1 **in** g.Nodes, f_1 **in** s_1.frames, o_1 **in** f_1.objects
where o_1.name = "deer",
    (**select** p
      from s_n **in** g.Nodes, p **in** $paths(g, s_1, s_n)$
      where s_n.type = "Terminate")
=
(**select** p
      from s_n **in** g.Nodes, p **in** $paths(g, s_1, s_n)$
      where s_n.type = "Terminate",
        exists s_2 **in** p: (**exists** f **in** s_2.frames:
          (**exists** o_2 **in** f.objects: o_2.name = "river")))

5 FORMAL BASIS OF GVISUAL: GCALCULUS/S

The formal basis of GVISUAL is provided by GCalculus/S, which is a revised version of GCalculus. Appendix 1 gives the full syntax, the semantics, and example queries of both GCalculus and GCalculus/S. Please note that Appendix 1 also provides formal definitions of all GVISUAL operators.

GCalculus is a calculus-based query language extended with temporal operators for the specification of paths in graphs. Revised versions of the existential and universal *path quantifiers* (**E** and **A**) of *Computational Tree Logic* (CTL*) [21] together with existential and universal quantifiers of relational calculus allow GCalculus to formulate queries over paths of multimedia presentation graphs.

The joint use of the universal quantifier and the negation operators result in complex GCalculus queries [50]. Similarly, the quantifier **A** and the negation operator together lead to highly complex query expressions. In Appendix 1.4, we describe GCalculus/S (GCalculus with Set Operators) which

1) replaces the universal path quantifier **A** and the negation operator with the existential quantifier ∃, the existential path quantifier **E** and set operators, and
2) uses negation only to the left of base predicates.

Removing the universal path quantifier **A** is needed for developing the user-friendly graphical language GVISUAL (based on GCalculus/S) because every object in GVISUAL is quantified uniformly only by the existential quantifier, the negation appears only to the left of base predicates, and set comparisons are naturally utilized, thus making the interface simple. To summarize, for defining GCalculus/S,[3] the syntax of GCalculus is revised as follows.

1) The quantifier **A** is not used.
2) The quantifier ∀ is not used.
3) Negation appears only to the left of a base predicate (i.e., it does not appear to the left of formulas with multiple predicates and logical connectives ∧ or ∨.)

Lemma A.1 in Appendix 1 specifies the translation of queries in GCalculus with **A**, ∀, and ∃ into ones in GCalculus/S with only **E** and ∃, and set operators. First, we translate formulas with the **A** path quantifier into formulas with ∀, ∃, and set operators. Then, we translate the resulting formulas (possibly still having ∀) into ones with ∃, **E**, and/or set operators, using the algorithms given in our earlier work [50]. The lemma below states that the translation of formulas with the **A** quantifier into ones with ∀, ∃, and set operators is always possible.

LEMMA 5.1. *Any formula in GCalculus with* **A**, ∀, *and* ∃ *quantifiers can be transformed into formulas with* **E**, ∃, *and set operators.*

PROOF. By Lemma A.1 in Appendix 1, formulas with quantifier **A** can be transformed into formulas with **E** and set operators. Formulas with the universal quantifier and negation can then be transformed into ones with the existential quantifier and set operators by lemmas and algorithms given in [50].   □

6 EXPRESSIVE POWER AND USER-FRIENDLINESS OF GVISUAL

VISUAL (and, thus, GVISUAL) uses a number of techniques designed to simplify the visual specifications of queries:

1) Visually incomplete specifications of containment relationships, class-subclass relationships, and paths are allowed. VISUAL relies on the database schema to convert a given query into an unambiguous one. For example, for the sake of visual simplicity, the user can skip the specification of object classes within multiply nested containment relationships, and the query processor derives this information from the database schema. GVISUAL extends this technique into visually incomplete path specifications [10], [35].
2) VISUAL allows the specification of spatial relationships to be observed in a query before the query session starts. For example, the user states that, in the queries to be specified, among all possible spatial relationships, only to_the_left_of relationship will be specified among object icons in a spatial enforcement region of queries.

Both (1) and (2) significantly simplify the visual complexity of queries. Ignoring (1) and (2) (as well as application-specific methods and functions of a given environment, arithmetic operators and aggregate functions) in GVISUAL, we have the following property.

THEOREM 6.1. *GVISUAL and GCalculus/S are equivalent in expressive power.*

PROOF. See Appendix 2.   □

That is, any GVISUAL query can be converted into a GCalculus/S query and vice versa. Theorem 6.1 holds because there is a one-to-one correspondence between the logical symbols of GCalculus/S and the (user-defined and user-changeable, icon-based) constructs of GVISUAL.

Since GCalculus/S variables can range over complex objects, it is clear that GCalculus/S employs a second-order logic. However, since **A** and ∀ and negation (except to the left of base predicates) are eliminated from GCalculus/S and, equivalently, from GVISUAL, query complexity is constrained. On the other hand, GCalculus/S (and GVISUAL) queries can contain arbitrarily nested sets (in GVISUAL, nested internal windows). In [35], [36], [1], we have described techniques that transform such queries into object-algebra [39], [40] expressions.

6.1 Temporal Operators vs. Regular Expressions

A *regular expression* over the alphabet Σ (a set of symbols) is a sequence of symbols formed by repeated applications of the following rules [13]:

1) ϕ (empty sequence) and each member of Σ is a regular expression,
2) If α and β are regular expressions, then so is $\alpha \odot \beta = \alpha\beta$, where $\alpha\beta$ denotes the concatenation of the expressions α and β,
3) If α and β are regular expressions, then so is $\alpha \oplus \beta = \{\alpha, \beta\}$, where $\oplus$ denotes the meta symbol for union.
4) If α is a regular expression, then so is α^+, where α^+ denotes $\alpha \oplus \alpha\alpha \oplus \alpha\alpha\alpha \oplus \ldots = \{\alpha, \alpha\alpha, \alpha\alpha\alpha, \ldots\}$.
5) If α is a regular expression, then so is α^* where α^* denotes $\phi \oplus \alpha \oplus \alpha\alpha \oplus \ldots = \{\phi, \alpha, \alpha\alpha, \alpha\alpha\alpha, \ldots\}$.

Regular expressions can also be used to specify path formulas. It is known that Propositional Linear Temporal Logic (PLTL) is strictly less expressive than regular expressions [64]. However, our operators, which are modified versions of PLTL operators, provide a higher expressive power than PLTL. We now compare our temporal operators and regular expressions.

A regular expression specifies a set of sequences created using symbols from Σ. To use regular expressions in a graph manipulation language and to compare their expressive power with our temporal operators, we need to map the sequences specified by regular expressions to path formulas, and give a semantics for each meta symbol of regular expressions. Let each symbol in the alphabet Σ denote an assertion about the state of a node. Let α and β denote regular expressions. Each of the truth value statements below is with respect to a path x in graph g and the starting node of x is s_t; however, we omit g and s_t for simplicity:

---

3. We actually use a safe subset of GCalculus/S, similar to [50].

1) $\alpha \odot \beta$ is *True* for x iff α is *True* for path x_1, β is *True* for path x_2, and $x = (x_1 + x_2)$ (i.e., x is a concatenation of two paths x_1 and x_2).

2) $\alpha \oplus \beta$ is *True* for x iff either α is *True* for x or β is *True* for x.

3) α^+ is *True* for x iff α is *True* for path x_i, $1 \le i \le n$, and $x = (x_1 + ... + x_n)$.

4) $\alpha\beta^*$ is *True* for x iff α is *True* for path x, or $\alpha\beta^+$ is *True* for x.

5) $\alpha^*\beta$ is *True* for x iff $\alpha^+\beta$ is *True* for x, or β is *True* for x.

We now show that GCalculus/S formulas can express regular expression path formulas that do not have any subexpression path formulas of the form exp^* or exp^+ with $\oplus$ appearing in exp.[4] All other regular expressions can be transformed as shown below. We first show the transformation rules for a regular expression with a single meta operator ($\odot$, $\oplus$, $^+$, or *). Assume that p and q below are single assertions on node variables. We omit the specifications of g, x, and s_t whenever there is no ambiguity:

1) $p \Rightarrow [[s_t]]p$

2) $pq \Rightarrow [[s_t]]p \ X \ [[s_j]]q$

3) $<<g, x, s_t>> p \oplus q \Rightarrow <<g, x, s_t>>[[s_t]]p \lor <<g, x, s_t>> [[s_t]]q$

4) $<<g, x, s_t>> p^+ \Rightarrow <<g, x, s_t>>[[s_t]]p \lor <<g, x, s_t>>[[s_t]]p \ \mathcal{U}[[s_j]]p$

5) p^* can only appear as a subexpression. This is because an atomic path formula $[[s_t]]p$ applies to a sequence of nonzero length.

6) $<<g, x, s_t>> p^*q \Rightarrow <<g, x, s_t>>[[s_t]]q \lor <<g, x, s_t>> [[s_t]]p \ \mathcal{U}[[s_j]]q$

Now, let us show the transformations for more complex regular expressions. Assume that α and β are regular expressions used to specify path formulas such that

$$<<g, x, n_i>> \alpha \Rightarrow <<g, x, n_i>> P,$$
$$<<g, x, n_j>> \beta \Rightarrow <<g, x, n_j>> Q,$$

and no node variable n_k appears in more than one of the path formulas P and Q. Then,

1) $<<g, x, n_i>> \alpha\beta \Rightarrow <<g, x, n_i>> P \ X \ Q$

2) $<<g, x, n_i>> \alpha \oplus \beta \Rightarrow <<g, x, n_i>> P \lor <<g, x, n_j>> Q$

3) $<<g, x, n_i>> \alpha^+ \Rightarrow <<g, x, n_i>> P \lor <<g, x, n_i>> P \ \mathcal{U} \ P$

4) $<<g, x, n_i>> \alpha^+\beta \Rightarrow <<g, x, n_i>> P \ \mathcal{U} \ Q$

5) Again, α^* can only appear as a subexpression.

6) $<<g, x, n_i>> \alpha^*\beta \Rightarrow <<g, x, n_j>> Q \lor <<g, x, n_i>> P \ \mathcal{U} \ Q$

6.2 User Friendliness

User friendliness of graphical languages, in general, and graphical database query languages, in particular, is an elusive issue [56], and can only be quantified by an extensive and controlled human factors study (e.g., please see [49], [53], [62]). Such a study is not yet done for GVISUAL (or GOQL).

High expressive power of GVISUAL comes at the expense of a number of highly advanced features, such as nested windows, set operators (to express the universal quantification), nested temporal operators, spatial

enforcement windows, parameter passing, etc. We have made an explicit attempt to simplify the specification and the look and feel of these features for user friendliness. Nevertheless, specifying complex queries in GVISUAL requires a degree of complexity and we expect that the advanced features of GVISUAL will be used by advanced users only. And, GVISUAL is designed to scale down into a much simpler language for simple queries of most users, i.e., a small simple subset of GVISUAL (e.g., single window queries, no parameter passing, single icon drag-and-drop query specification, etc.) will be used by most users. We have used GVISUAL in a graduate database course, and students did not report major problems in specifying complex queries. However, a human factors study of GVISUAL features remains to be done.

In designing graphical database query languages, there are two approaches:

1) Graphical objects and their placements imitate closely the reality. GVISUAL subscribes to this philosophy: Users employ icons that correspond to objects that they actually utilize in their applications to represent semantic relationships within data (e.g., composition hierarchies, containment, class-subclass hierarchies, spatial relationships). Application-specific methods and functions of the data model are also represented as graphical icons. And, icon (which is also a GVISUAL object) shapes and colors are designed by users (to recreate the environment that they are familiar with, and through a "template facility" in GVISUAL), and added to an icon class.

2) Graphical objects are based exclusively on domain-specific metaphors. This approach is mostly used for human-computer interfaces [3]. Gentner and Nielson criticize [24] the use of fixed metaphors for the limitations that they introduce for complex environments. GVISUAL does not use metaphors.

GVISUAL uses "closed (i.e., shaded)" icons to reduce the complexity of subquery specifications (internal or external subqueries) in a window. The use of closed icons allows users to control the visual complexity of a query. For example, in the GVISUAL query of Fig. 14, two internal queries, once understood by the user, can be removed to control the visual complexity.

The use of "incomplete expressions" in GVISUAL also reduces the visual complexity. As an example, in the external query "Stream_Having_D_and_M" of the GVISUAL query of Fig. 13, the content object icons o_1 and o_2 are inside the stream object s_1. To specify the containment relationship completely, there must also be frame objects between s_1 and (o_1 and o_2). The additional icon, which is unnecessary, would increase the visual complexity. We choose not to specify icons that are not necessary for the specification of containment relationships.

7 IMPLEMENTATION EFFORT AND GVISUAL QUERY PROCESSING

We have implemented a prototype client-server based database system ViSiOn [7] with a fully functional VISUAL

---

4. This is due to the fact that we do not allow disjunction in a path formula.

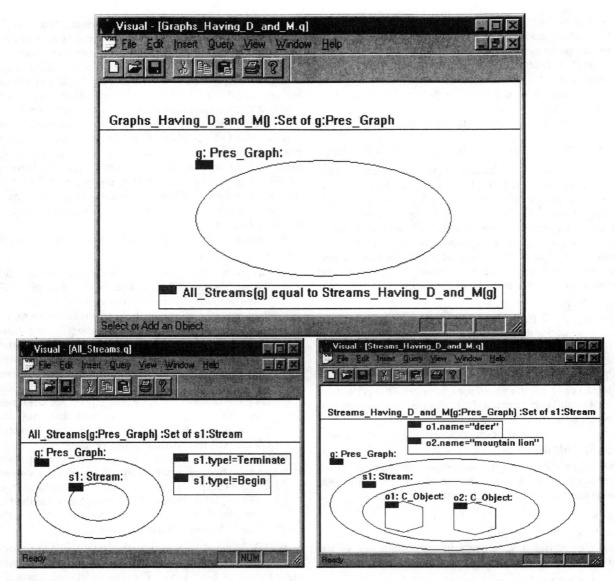

Fig. 13. GVISUAL query of Example 4.9.

user interface. ViSiOn runs on Windows NT or Windows 95, and is built using Visual C++, Microsoft MFC Class Library and OLE-based drag-and-drop programming [25], [52], [4]. GVISUAL query interface [1] is also functional. We are presently finishing the implementation of ViSiOn with

- GVISUAL query processing techniques [6], [35], [36], [1], [12],
- continuous multimedia storage servers that deliver presentations [5], and
- playout agents (as part of the browser) that play multimedia presentations.

GVISUAL clients (of ViSiOn) are

1) launched independently at different Windows NT/ Windows 95 sites,
2) registered and controlled by an administrative server [66], [63], similar to the registry of clients in distributed LAN systems,

3) fork out a GVISUAL interface to each user,
4) translate a GVISUAL query directly into the O-Algebra parse tree [39], [43]. Three new operators are added to O-Algebra to evaluate GVISUAL queries [35], [6], [36], namely, X^{next}, $X^{connect}$, and X^{until}, that correspond to the set-at-a-time evaluations of X(next), C(connected), and $\mathcal{U}$(until), respectively, of GVISUAL,
5) send the O-Algebra parse tree to a VStore client (through the administrative server) for the execution of the parse tree and receive the results back from VStore, and
6) call a browser (through the administrator server) to display (and play them out in the case of presentation objects) the objects of the query output.

To summarize, a ViSiOn client translates a GVISUAL query into O-Algebra, and submits the resulting O-Algebra expression to the Admission Server (over a socket interface) which, by using the system load, reroutes it to a storage

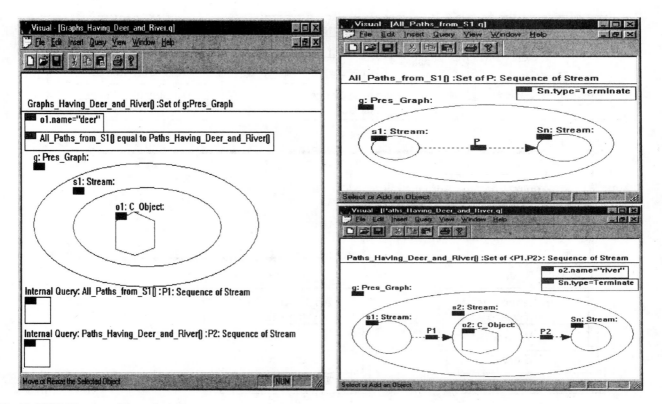

Fig. 14. GVISUAL query of Example 4.10.

manager, called the VStore [7] client. The VStore client contains an O-Algebra optimizer [22] and an O-Algebra engine [52], [60], together with an object repository called Disk Server. VStore is implemented and fully functional for multimedia objects and has a continuous multimedia storage server [5], [60]. Fig. 15 shows the architecture of the ViSiOn system.

In a GVISUAL query that involves path formulas for presentations, the operations to evaluate the query include traversals of presentation graphs. Confirming adjacency and connectiveness between nodes (required by operators X^{Next}, $X^{Connect}$, and X^{Until}) efficiently is important for efficient evaluations of presentation queries. One way to traverse presentation graphs is to use O-Algebra directly and employ a modified conventional depth-first search algorithm, i.e., given two paths, say p_1 and p_2, by using the tuples of O-Algebra "tables" (called *Collection of Objects*) directly, we visit every node along the paths starting from the last node of p_1 and check if we encounter the first node of p_2 along the paths. In this way, one can implement the operator $X^{Connect}$. However, this may lead to inefficient operator implementations.

Based on the observation that presentation graphs are not expected to be too large (e.g., around 50 nodes and sparse graphs), we have proposed the *nodecode* system [35], [36], [6] for efficient evaluations of queries on presentation graphs. In the nodecode system, nodes are assigned unique binary codes which are used to find out parent-child and ancestor-predecessor relationships between nodes. Each nodecode assigned to a node actually identifies a path from the source node to that node. If there is more than one different path connecting the source node to a node, that node

is assigned more than one (as many as the number of paths) nodecodes. Any path along a presentation graph can be identified by two nodecodes that belong to the beginning and the end node of the path. This makes it possible for set-at-a-time evaluations of queries with operators X, C, and U, avoiding extensive graph traversals. In [35], [36], we introduce the nodecode system and discuss how they are used in O-algebra for evaluations of presentation queries. In [6], we present efficient algorithms using nodecodes to find and extract paths along a presentation graph (or a DAG) with queries using X, C, and U. The nodecode system is currently being implemented [12] as part of VStore.

8 RELATED WORK

Querying multimedia information systems has been a popular research area [59]. Marcus and Subrahmanian [44] define the notion of a structured multimedia database system (SMDS), which is built on a set of media instances. Each media instance consists of "states" (video-clips, audiotracks), features (content objects) and their properties, and relationships between these features. Media instances can be queried based on these features and their relationships. They also define methodologies for relaxing queries and generation of media presentations from a sequence of queries. Although their query language can handle queries based on the content of the states of media instances, Marcus and Subrahmanian do not specify the tools to provide content based querying across the states of media instances. That is, queries like "Return all video-clips where a red

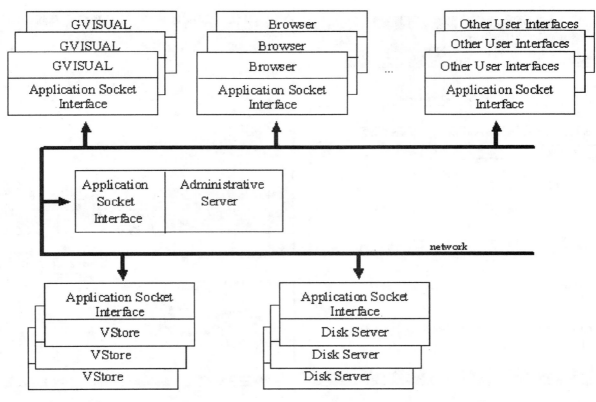

Fig. 15. Architecture of ViSiOn.

mustang" can only be expressed using complex expressions and long temporal constraints.

As part of a Video Retrieval System, called VIQS, Hwang and Subrahmanian [32] present an SQL-like video query language. They emphasize video queries that involve returning video segments (frame-request (FR)-queries) as opposed to queries that involve textual answers. While FR-queries are similar to our presentation query languages, in particular to GOQL, in the sense that both have an SQL-like syntax and can return frame sequences as answers, there are significant differences. Video database (Adali et al. [2]) of FR-queries is modeled in the form of a relational database in addition to some special data structures such as object array, event array, activity array. Frames have integer numbers associated with them. Queries return, in general, frame sequences containing certain activities and/or objects. In comparison, the data model we use is an object oriented model, which facilitates modeling sequences more naturally and also facilitates modeling and querying graphs. GVISUAL and GOQL query languages allow queries on not only content objects, but also on the relative ordering of nodes in paths and elements in sequences. Graph manipulation, including construction of graphs and paths, is also provided in GVISUAL and GOQL. The output of GVISUAL and GOQL queries is more general than frame sequences, and queries may return presentation paths, graphs, sets of video objects, etc.

Graphs in databases have been used by different researchers in different contexts. In the database query and

visualization system G^+ [17], [18] and Hy^+ [15], [16], the database is visualized as a graph and a query is formulated as a set of graphs which are viewed as patterns to be matched against the database. In the Graph-Oriented Object Database model [26], [27], [23], the emphasis is on representing the database scheme and the database instance as a graph. Database queries are expressed using five primitive graph operations (node and edge additions and deletions, and a duplicate eliminator). There is also a graphical user interface for formulating queries and visualization of results [23]. In this model, objects are represented as nodes in a graph, and relationships and properties of objects are represented as edges. Another alternative, which is used in many object-oriented data models, is to represent relationships of objects as object-valued attributes, and to use "path expressions" with an SQL-like language, such as OQL. However, for applications where graphs are needed to model data, supporting graphs explicitly in the data model and in the query language (in addition to supporting other bulk types such as lists and sets) is very beneficial. GraphDB is a good example which explicitly allows modeling and querying of graphs [28]. In GraphDB, there are three kinds of object classes, namely, simple classes, link classes, and path classes. A link class has references to source and target simple objects (in addition to having other components). Path objects are defined using regular expressions of link objects. For querying, GraphDB provides the *on...where...derive* statement. There are no nested subqueries in this language, but complex queries may be expressed in several steps, where each step may compute one or more classes of simple, edge, or path objects, or express a restriction of the database graph for the following steps. Since all of these steps are stated in the derive clause, the query structure may become very confusing when the query is complex.

GVISUAL is an extension of the object oriented graphical query language VISUAL [11] for querying and manipulating graphs. VISUAL is designed for applications where the data has spatial properties, also including sequences and complex objects, and queries are of exploratory in nature. VISUAL is nonprocedural, borrows the example-element concept of Query-by-Example [65] to formulate query objects, and uses such concepts as hierarchical subqueries, and internal and external queries. It has formal semantics, and derives its power from a small number of concepts and constructs. VISUAL graphical objects are not directly tied to the underlying formalism (e.g., DOODLE [19] and F-logic). VISUAL is fully implemented and functional.

In the context of multimedia databases, temporal operators such as *Next, Until, Eventually* have been used for expressing queries on multimedia streams. In a language called Hierarchical Temporal Logic (HTL) ([61] and [42]), these temporal operators are used for similarity based retrieval of video segments. Video streams are considered to consist of hierarchically structured video segments and temporal operators can be used to specify properties of sequences of video segments at any level. However, although video segment sequences can be queried at different levels, the segments in the same level appear to be in a single continuum, that is, without any branching. This is not the case when we consider paths in directed acyclic graphs that can only be modeled with branching time, as in *Computational Tree Logic* [21]. *Computational Tree Logic* uses universal and existential *path* quantifiers over infinitely long paths, and path formulas to specify and navigate paths representing branching timelines. Temporal operators of *Propositional Linear Temporal Logic* (PLTL) are used to construct path formulas as assertions that have to be satisfied by a single infinite path. The underlying nature of time in *PLTL* is linear, i.e., at each moment, there is a single timeline. In other words, there is only one possible *next* state. In terms of data structures, a list structure has a linear timeline and one possible *next* state. This nature of *PLTL* prevents it from being used directly for trees or graphs which have possibly several *next* states. Temporal operators of PLTL have also been used successfully to formulate and query lists (sequences) by Richardson [55].

To model the interactions between different types of multimedia data in a given multimedia presentation, many multimedia synchronization models are proposed in the literature [38], [58], [9], [29]. Most of these models are graph- and constraint-based, utilizing directed acyclic graphs or variants of petrinets.

Since multimedia authoring tools are used to publish (create and store into a persistent storage device such as a CD) multimedia presentations, we now briefly summarize the state of the art commercial multimedia authoring tools. Through a www search, we have observed more than 100 such tools that

1) provide a variety of features (such as dynamic updating, group authoring, object orientation, internet support),
2) contain a potpourri of separate software packages (such as enhanced text support, audio/video/frame/storybook/event editors, spell checkers, network managers), and
3) support quite complicated scripting languages (such as Lingo for Director[5] [51] and Script X of Kaleida Labs).

The visual interfaces provided by these commercial tools also vary widely, due to a lack of universal metaphor for building interactive multimedia presentations. Highly successful and most powerful authoring tools [45] (such as Macromedia's Authorware Professional, AimTech's IconAuthor, and Allen Communications' Quest [51]) use presentation graphs (or flowcharts) with icons and thumbnails (representing multimedia data) as nodes and edges for synchronization.

Along the lines of [8], [46], we classify the existing commercial multimedia authoring tools into four types:

1) *Presentation Graphics Tools* (e.g., Gold Disk's Astound [51] for Mac) allow a single timeline ordering of text, graphics, video clips, and animation, and buttons for branching to other parts of a presentation.
2) *Card-Based Authoring Tools* (e.g., Apple's Hypercard [51] for Mac) use stack-of-cards metaphor and powerful scripting languages (for, say, K-12 course authoring).
3) *Time-Based Tools* (e.g., Macromedia's Director [51]) display multitrack *scores* on the screen, with each track representing a multimedia item. In Director, each item's position and length in the score determines when it appears and disappears. Synchronization of items is usually through a scripting language (such as, say, the Lingo Language of Director).
4) *Presentation Graph-Based Tools* (e.g., Macromedia's Authorware Professional, AimTech's IconAuthor, Allen Communications' Quest [51]) use flowcharts (i.e., presentation graphs) with icons or thumbnails as nodes. These tools allow some form of interactivity using button clicks, menu selections, and navigational maps, and keep track of user responses (e.g., Authorware).

We have recently designed and implemented two prototype multimedia authoring tools for construction of presentation graphs [48], [54]. Both tools use drag-and-drop icons, dialog boxes, etc., to build multimedia presentations and store them into a multimedia database.

9 CONCLUSIONS

In this paper, by using graphs to model multimedia presentations, we have presented languages for querying multimedia presentations based on content information. Please

---

5. Information about these products is available on WWW, therefore, we only list a web address for the company marketing the related product as a reference.

note that this paper does not contribute to the multimedia data model research. Our goal is to design a query language for multimedia presentations. In principle, GVISUAL and GOQL work with "any" multimedia data model (as long as presentations are modeled as graphs) and are independent of the underlying data model. There are certainly very well designed multimedia data models in the literature, such as Day et al. model [20], and Little and Ghafoor's model [38]. For GVISUAL, by simply changing the data model schema (through the notion of "templates" [4], [1]), GVISUAL will work the same.

As for modeling presentations, there are again a large number of choices, ranging from variants of petrinets to graph-oriented models. And, extended versions of some types of graphs are invariably used by most of the advanced multimedia authoring tools. We have chosen the simplest model for presentations: directed acyclic graphs. Our motivation is not to give a rich and comprehensive model for multimedia presentations—in fact, presentation graphs are explicitly kept very simple (e.g., no labels on edges, no timing delays/constraints between presentation graph streams, etc.) for the sake of emphasizing the query language. By utilizing simple graphs as presentation models, GVISUAL and GOQL exploit

1) path specifications, and
2) graph traversals for querying presentations.

The content information of a multimedia presentation is not only the information stored in individual streams of the presentation. The flow of information during a multimedia presentation is an integral part of its information content. The flow of information constitutes the theme of the presentation. Tools for specification of patterns in information flow are required for querying the information content of multimedia presentations. In all the languages we discuss, namely, GVISUAL, GOQL, and GCalculus/S, we use the revised versions of the temporal operators *Next, Connected,* and *Until,* and path formulas for this purpose.

The semantics of these operators and their use in path formulas are presented by GCalculus. GCalculus uses path quantifiers (universal and existential), sequence variables, and temporal operators for querying paths in graphs and sequences. In GCalculus/S, the universal quantifier, the universal path quantifier, and the negation operator are eliminated to avoid highly complex expressions.

GVISUAL is an icon-based graphical query language that uses iconic representations of the constructs defined in GCalculus/S for querying presentation graphs. In other words, GCalculus/S provides the formal basis for GVISUAL. GVISUAL provides a user-friendly graphical interface for easy specification of queries on presentation graphs and media streams.

We also discuss an extension of OQL language, called GOQL (Graph OQL), with constructs for the specification of paths and sequences in presentation graphs. GOQL allows us to present more traditional and textual specifications of queries on presentations graphs. GOQL can also be used as a suplimental tool to provide a better understanding of GVISUAL queries.

GVISUAL is implemented on a prototype client-server based database system, called ViSiOn [7]. The query interface for GVISUAL is already functional. Query processing techniques have been investigated in [6], [35], [36], and they are being incorporated into ViSiOn.

APPENDIX 1
FORMAL BASIS OF GVISUAL: GCALCULUS/S

We first discuss GCalculus, which is a calculus-based query language extended with temporal operators for the specification of paths in graphs.

A1.1   Syntax
A1.1.1 Symbols of the Language

- Predicate symbols (1-ary): Examples are Pres_Graph(g), Pres_Node(p), Stream(s), Frame(f), and C_Object(o), where g, p, s, f, and o are either constant symbols or variable symbols.
- Constant symbols are typed and can be *atomic-valued, tuple-valued, sequence-valued, set-valued, node-valued,* or *graph-valued.*
- Variable symbols are typed and can be *atomic-valued, tuple-valued, sequence-valued, set-valued, node-valued,* or *graph-valued.*
- Arithmetic comparison symbols: $<, \leq, >, \geq, =, \neq$
- Set comparison and membership symbols: $\subset, \subseteq, \supset, \supseteq, \in, \notin$
- Set definition: $\{, \}$
- State formula for the starting node term and a path: $<<, >>$
- Node variable specification: $[[,]]$
- Sequence variable concatenation: $\cdot, +$
- Parentheses: $(,)$
- Quantification symbols: $\exists, \forall, \mathbf{E},$ and $\mathbf{A}$. The symbols $\exists$ and $\forall$ are existential and universal quantifiers for variables; and the symbols $\mathbf{E}$ and $\mathbf{A}$ are existential and universal quantifiers for paths.

Constants and variables are terms. Atomic-valued constants and variables are *simple-valued* (or *simple*) terms. Tuple-valued constants and variables are *tuple-valued* (or *tuple*) terms. Sequence-valued constants and variables are *sequence-valued* (or *sequence*) *terms.* Set-valued constants and variables are *set-valued* (or *set*) *terms.* Graph-valued constants and variables are *graph-valued* (or *graph*) *terms.* The terms which are used as nodes in a graph-valued term and elements in a sequence-valued term are called *node-valued* (or *node*) *terms.*

A1.1.2 Atomic State Formulas

(A1) $Cl(t)$ where Cl is a class name (object type) and t is a term of type Cl.

(A2) $t_1 \; \phi_1 \; t_2$ where $\phi_1 \in \{<, \leq, >, \geq\}$ and t_1, t_2 are simple terms.

(A3) $t_1 \; \phi_2 \; t_2$ where $\phi_2 \in \{=, \neq\}$ and t_1, t_2 are terms of the same type, i.e., t_1 and t_2 are of type either simple, tuple, sequence, set, node or graph.

(A4) $t_1 \phi_3 t_2$ where $\phi_3 \in \{\subset, \subseteq, \supset, \supseteq\}$, t_1 and t_2 are set-valued terms.

(A5) $t_1 \phi_4 t_2$ where $\phi_4 \in \{\in, \notin\}$, t_1 is a term, and t_2 is either a set or a sequence term whose elements are of type t_1.

(A6) $t_1 \phi_5 t_2$ where $\phi_5 \in \{<, \leqslant\}$, t_1 and t_2 are sequence terms. $<$ denotes *ProperSubsequenceOf* and $\leqslant$ denotes *SubsequenceOf*.

(A7) $t_1 \propto t_2$ where t_1 and t_2 are graph terms and $\propto$ denotes *SubgraphOf*.

A1.1.3 State Formulas

(C1) Each atomic state formula is a state formula.

(C2) $p \wedge q$, $p \vee q$, $\neg p$, (p) are state formulas where p, q are state formulas.

(C3) $(\exists y)p$, $(\forall y)p$ are state formulas where p is a state formula, y is a free variable in p (i.e., not bound to any quantifier in p). A variable in a formula is *free* if the variable is not bound to a quantifier appearing before the variable.

(C4) $<<g, x, s_t>>p$ is a state formula expressing that, starting at the node term s_t in graph g, the path formula p holds for path x. s_t is called the *starting node* term, and x is a sequence-valued variable or a concatenation of sequence-valued variables (where identical concatenated subsequence duplicates are eliminated).

(C5) $\mathbf{E}(x)<<g, x, s_t>>p$ and $\mathbf{A}(x)<<g, x, s_t>>p$ are state formulas where g is a graph or a sequence term, s_t is the starting node term, p is a *path formula*, and x is a sequence-valued variable or a concatenation of sequence-valued variables. $\mathbf{E}(x)<<g, x, s_t>>p$ states that, starting at the node term s_t, there exists a path x in the graph or sequence term g for which the path formula p holds. $\mathbf{A}(x)<<g, x, s_t>>p$ states that, for all paths x in g that begin at the node term s_t, the path formula p holds.

A1.1.4 Path Formulas

A *path formula* is

(P1) an *atomic path formula* $[[n]]p$ where n is a *node variable*, and p is a state formula that holds for n.

(P2) (p) where p is a path formula.

(P3) $p \; X : x \; q$ where p and q are path formulas, x is a sequence-valued variable, and X corresponds to the *Next* operator.

(P4) $p \; \mathcal{U} : x \; q$ where p and q are path formulas, x is a sequence-valued variable, and $\mathcal{U}$ corresponds to the *Until* operator.

(P5) $p \; C : x \; q$ where p and q are path formulas, x is a sequence-valued variable, and C corresponds to the *Connected* operator.

A1.1.5 Queries

A GCalculus query is of the form $\{x \mid \psi(x)\}$, where x (the "query output") is a variable and $\psi(x)$ is a state formula satisfying the property that the only free (nonquantified) variable in ψ is x.

A1.2 Semantics

We now define the meaning of all nonlogical symbols of GCalculus and, under a given interpretation, define the assignment of a truth value to a formula of GCalculus. The interpretation I is over a set of database values $\mathcal{V}$ and in terms of the database structure $M(C, I, \mathcal{V}, \delta, \pi)$ as defined in Section 2.

For convenience in representation, we do not use specific constant and variable names to denote the type of each variable. Instead, from the type of the object that instantiates a variable, we derive whether a variable is graph-valued, set-valued, sequence-valued, etc.

Let t be a tuple-valued term; then $t.AttrName$ is a term whose type is the type of the object referenced by $t.AttrName$. For example, $g.Nodes$ where g is graph-valued variable, refers to a set of streams, as defined in Section 2. Similarly, $n.frames.objects$ where n is a stream-valued term, refers to a set of content objects. In general, $t.a_1.a_2.a_3...a_n$ is a term whose type is the type of the object referenced by a_n (which is in turn referenced by a_{n-1} and so on). Let t be a sequence-valued or tuple-valued term; then, $t[i]$ is a term whose type is the type of the object referenced by the ith component of t. We allow the combinations of dot notation and component notation. For example, $n.frames[2].objects$ refers to content-objects in the second frame of the stream variable n.

We first give the interpretations of constants, variables and predicate symbols. That is, all instantiations of constants and variables come from the values $\mathcal{V}$ in the database.

1) for any constant c, $I(M, c) = c \in \mathcal{V}$,
2) for any variable y, $I(M, y) = y \in \mathcal{V}$.

A1.2.1 Atomic State Formulas

The interpretation I of a state formula p is written as $I(M, p)$. We write $M \models p$ to mean that $I(M, p)$ is true.

(A1) $M \models Cl(t)$ iff $I(M, Cl) = True$ where $I(M, t) = v$. That is, $Cl(x)$ denotes the assertion "x is in class Cl" which is either *True* or *False*.

(A2) $M \models t_1 \phi_1 t_2$ where $\phi_1 \in \{<, \leq, >, \geq\}$ iff $I(M, t_1) \phi_1 I(M, t_2) = True$.

(A3) $M \models t_1 \phi_2 t_2$ where $\phi_2 \in \{=, \neq\}$ iff $I(M, t_1) \phi_1 I(M, t_2) = True$.

(A4) $M \models t_1 \phi_3 t_2$ where $\phi_3 \in \{\subset, \subseteq, \supset, \supseteq\}$ and t_1, t_2 are set-valued terms iff $I(M, t_1) \phi_3 I(M, t_2) = True$.

(A5) $M \models t_1 \phi_4 t_2$ where $\phi_4 \in \{\in, \notin\}$ and t_1 is a simple term, and t_2 is either a set or sequence-valued term iff $I(M, t_1) \phi_4 I(M, t_2) = True$.

(A6)
- $M \models t_1 < t_2$ where t_1 and t_2 are sequence-valued terms iff $I(M, t_1)$ is a proper subsequence of $I(M, t_2)$.
- $M \models t_1 \leqslant t_2$ where t_1 and t_2 are sequence-valued terms iff $I(M, t_1)$ is a subsequence of $I(M, t_2)$.

(A7) $M \models t_1 \propto t_2$ where t_1 and t_2 are graph-valued terms iff $I(M, t_1)$ is a subgraph of $I(M, t_2)$.

A1.2.2 State Formulas

(C2)
- $M \models p \wedge q$ iff $M \models p$ and $M \models q$
- $M \models p \vee q$ iff $M \models p$ or $M \models q$
- $M \models \neg p$ iff $M \not\models p$
- $M \models (p)$ iff $M \models p$

(C3)

- $M \models (\exists y)p$ iff there exists an instantiation a for the free variable y in p such that $M \models p$ when every y in p is replaced by a.
- $M \models (\forall y)p$ iff whatever instantiation replaces all occurrences of the free variable y in p, we have $M \models p$

(C4) $M \models \langle\langle g, x, s_t\rangle\rangle p$ iff path x in graph g starts at node s_t, and the path formula p holds *True* for path x (i.e., as discussed next, $M, x \models p$).

(C5)

- $M \models \mathbf{E}(x) \langle\langle g, x, s_t\rangle\rangle p$ iff $\exists$ path x starting at node s_t in graph g, and the path formula p holds *True* for path x (i.e., $M, x \models p$).
- $M \models \mathbf{A}(x) \langle\langle g, x, s_t\rangle\rangle p$ iff $\forall$ paths x starting at node s_t in graph g, and the path formula p holds *True* for path x (i.e., $M, x \models p$).

A1.2.3 Path Formulas

Consider the state formulas $\langle\langle g, x, s_t\rangle\rangle p$, $\mathbf{E}(x)\langle\langle g, x, s_t\rangle\rangle p$, or $\mathbf{A}(x)\langle\langle g, x, s_t\rangle\rangle p$ where p is a path formula. The interpretation I of the path formula p over path x is written as $I(M, g, x, p)$ where x is a path in g, the starting node of x is s_t, and $I(M, g) = g$ is a graph object in M

1) with the node set $V = \{s_0, s_1, ..., s_v\}$ and the edge set $E = \{\langle s_i, s_j\rangle \mid i < j, 0 \le i, j \le v\}$,
2) g contains $I(M, s_t) = s_t$, $0 \le t \le v$, as a node in V,
3) g contains $I(M, x) = x$ as a path in g and the starting node of x is s_t.

We write $M, x \models p$ to mean that $I(M, g, x, p)$ is *True*. (We omit g for simplicity.) We now define the semantics of path formulas, recursively.

(P1) $M, x \models [[n]]p$ iff $x = \langle s_i\rangle$, p is a state formula with zero or more occurrences of term n, $I(M, n) = s_i$, $0 \le i \le v$, and $M \models p$.

(P2) $M, x \models (p)$ iff $M, x \models p$

To simplify the notation for the next three rules, we will assume that $s_t = s_1$ and $x = \langle s_1, ..., s_j\rangle$.

(P3) $M, x \models p \, \mathcal{X} : x \, q$ iff x is a concatenation of two paths $x_1 = \langle s_1, ..., s_i\rangle$ and $x_2 = \langle s_{i+1}, ..., s_j\rangle$ such that $M, x_1 \models p$, and $M, x_2 \models q$.

(P4) $M, x \models p \, C : x \, q$ iff x is a concatenation of three paths $x_1 = \langle s_1, ..., s_i\rangle$, $x_2 = \langle s_{i+1}, ..., s_k\rangle$, $x_3 = \langle s_{k+1}, ..., s_j\rangle$ such that $M, x_1 \models p$, $M, x_2 \models [[n_{i+1}]]True$, $I(M, n_{n+1}) = s_{i+1}$, $M, x_3 \models q$. Note that x_2 can be an empty path in which case $I(M, n_{i+1}) = s_{k+1}$.

(P5) We consider two cases for the interpretation of $p \, \mathcal{U} : x \, q$ path formula.

Case 1. p does not contain any C or $\mathcal{U}$ operators. Let the node variables in p be $n_1, ..., n_k$. Let p^i, $1 \le i \le m$, be a revised p where each n_r, $1 \le r \le k$, is replaced by a new node variable n_r^i. $M, x \models p \, \mathcal{U} : x \, q$ iff there exist subpaths x', x'', x_i, $1 \le i \le m$, where

$$x = x' \cdot x_1 \cdot x_2 \cdot ... \cdot x_m \cdot x'',$$

$$x' = \langle s_1, ..., s_k\rangle$$

$$x_1 = \langle s_{k+1}, ..., s_{2k}\rangle,$$

$$x_2 = \langle s_{2k+1}, ..., s_{3k}\rangle$$

$$\vdots$$

$$x_m = \langle s_{mk+1}, ..., s_{(m+1)k}\rangle,$$

$$x'' = \langle s_{(m+1)k+1}, ..., s_l\rangle, \text{ and}$$

$$M, x' \models p \ \left(\text{i.e., } I(M, n_j) = s_j, \ 1 \le j \le k\right)$$

$$M, x_i \models p^i \forall i \, 1 \le i \le m \ \left(\text{i.e., } I(M, N_j^i) = s_{ik+j}, \ 1 \le j \le k\right)$$

$$M, x'' \models q.$$

In other words, each node variable n_i in p is instantiated by the nodes in x', the first subpath in x where $M, x' \models p$. For all the following subpaths x_i in x where $M, x_i \models p$ holds, we use revised versions p^i of the path formula p with new node variables such that $M, x_i \models p^i$ holds for different node variable instantiations.

Case 2. p contains C or $\mathcal{U}$ operators. This case is similar to case 1 except that the lengths of the subpaths x' and x_i, $a \le i \le m$, are not necessarily the same due to C or $\mathcal{U}$ operators in p. That is,

$$x' = \langle s_1, ..., s_{k'}\rangle$$

$$x_1 = \langle s_{k'+1}, ..., s_{k_1}\rangle$$

$$\vdots$$

$$x_m = \langle s_{k_{m-1}+1}, ..., s_{k_m}\rangle$$

$$x'' = \langle s_{k_m+1}, ..., s_l\rangle.$$

A1.3 GCalculus Examples

We now give GCalculus formulas to illustrate the use of path formulas. For each path formula, we provide the specification of the starting node. In the examples below, state formulas are represented by p, q, r, etc., the nodes are represented by node variables n_0, n_1, n_2, etc., and a graph is represented by g.

EXAMPLE A.1.1. $\mathbf{E}(x_1 \cdot x_2)\langle\langle g, x_1 \cdot x_2, n_0\rangle\rangle[[n_0]]p \, \mathcal{X} : x_1 \, [[n_1]]q$
$\mathcal{X} : x_2 \, [[n_2]]r$

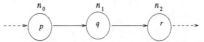

EXAMPLE A.1.2. $\mathbf{E}(x_1 \cdot x_2)\langle\langle g, x_1 \cdot x_2, n_0\rangle\rangle([[n_0]]p \, \mathcal{X} : x_1$
$[[n_1]]q) \, \mathcal{U} : x_2 \, [[n_2]]r$

Please note that the above path formula is not equivalent to $\mathbf{E}(x_1 \cdot x_2)\langle\langle g, x_1 \cdot x_2, n_0\rangle\rangle([[n_0]]p \, \mathcal{X} : x_1$
$([[n_1]]q \, \mathcal{U} : x_2 \, [[n_2]]r)$ which can be illustrated as applying to the following path.

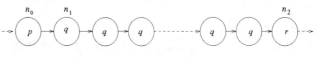

EXAMPLE A.1.3. $\mathbf{E}(x_1 \cdot x_2)<<g, x_1 \cdot x_2, n_0>>([[n_0]]p\ C : x_1$
$([[n_1]]q\ X : x_2\ [[n_2]]r)$

EXAMPLE A.1.4. $\mathbf{A}(x_1)<<g, x_1, n_0>>([[n_0]]p\ C : x_1\ [[n_1]]q) \wedge$
$\mathbf{E}(x_2 \cdot x_3)<<g, x_2 \cdot x_3, s_0>>\ ([[n_0]]p\ C : x_2\ [[n_1]]q\ X : x_3$
$[[n_2]]r)$

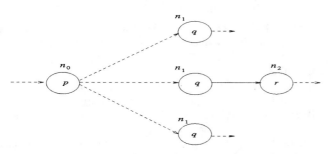

Note that C is a redundant operator defined for convenience. C is redundant in the sense that it can be represented
by the operators X and U. For example, the path formula
below can be represented by both $\mathbf{E}(x)<<g, x, n_0>>[[n_0]]p\ C :$
$x\ [[n_n]]q$ and $\mathbf{E}(x_1 \cdot x_2)<<g, x_1 \cdot x_2, n_0>>\ [[n_0]]p\ X : x_1$
$[[n_1]]True\ U : x_2\ [[n_n]]q \vee \mathbf{E}(x_3)<<g, x_3, n_0>>\ [[n_0]]p\ X : x_3$
$[[n_n]]q$ where $x = x_1 \cdot x_2$.

A1.4   GCalculus/S (GCalculus with Set Operators)

The use of the universal quantifier and the negation operators together result in complex relational calculus queries
[50]. Similarly, the quantifier $\mathbf{A}$ and the negation operator
together lead to highly complex query expressions. We now
describe GCalculus/S (GCalculus with Set Operators) which

1) replaces the universal path quantifier $\mathbf{A}$ and the negation operator with the existential quantifier $\exists$, the
   existential path quantifier $\mathbf{E}$ and set operators, and
2) uses negation only to the left of base predicates.

We give an example first.

EXAMPLE A.1.5. Consider the GCalculus query "Find presentation graphs that have a presentation node
(stream) containing the content object 'deer,' and
every adjacent node to that node contains the content
object 'lion'."

$\{g \mid$ Presentation-Graph$(g) \wedge$
$(\exists n_0, \exists n_1)($Stream$(n_0) \wedge$ Stream$(n_1) \wedge \{n_0, n_1\} \subseteq g.$Nodes $\wedge$
$\mathbf{A}(x)<<g, x, n_0>>\ [[n_0]](\exists o)(C_Object(o) \wedge o \in$
$n_0.$frames.objects $\wedge o.$name = "deer")
$X : x[[n_1]](\exists o_1)(C_Object(o_1) \wedge o_1 \in n_1.$frames.objects
$\wedge o_1.$name = "lion"))\}

Now, we remove the universal quantifier $\mathbf{A}$ from the
above GCalculus expression and replace it with set
operators as follows. S_p and S_q below are sets of paths.

$\{g \mid$ Presentation-Graph$(g) \wedge$
$(\exists n_0)$ (Stream$(n_0) \wedge n_0 \in g.$Nodes $\wedge S_p \subseteq S_q)\}$ where
$S_p = \{x \mid (\exists n_2)($Stream$(n_2) \wedge n_2 \in g.$Nodes $\wedge$
$<<g, x, n_0>>[[n_0]](\exists o)(C_Object(o) \wedge o \in$
$n_0.$frames.objects $\wedge o.$name = "deer")
$C : x\ [[n_2]]n_2.$type = "Terminate")$\}$ and
$S_q = \{x_1 \cdot x_2 \mid (\exists n_1, \exists n_2)($Stream$(n_1) \wedge$ Stream$(n_2) \wedge \{n_1, n_2\} \subseteq$
$g.$Nodes $\wedge$
$<<g, x_1 \cdot x_2, n_0>>\ [[n_0]](\exists o)(C_Object(o) \wedge o \in$
$n_0.$frames.objects $\wedge o.$name = "deer")
$X : x_1\ [[n_1]](\exists o_1)(C_Object(o_1) \wedge o_1 \in n_1.$frames.objects
$\wedge o_1.$name = "lion")
$C : x_2\ [[n_2]]n_2.$type = "Terminate")$\}$

The set S_p contains all the paths in g that start at n_0
and end at any terminate node. The set S_q contains all
the paths in g that start at n_0, continue with n_1 which
satisfies q, and end at a terminate node n_2.

Removing the universal path quantifier $\mathbf{A}$ is needed for
developing a user-friendly graphical language GVISUAL
based on GCalculus/S because every object in VISUAL is
quantified uniformly only by the existential quantifier, the
negation appears only to the left of base predicates, and set
comparisons are utilized, thus making the interface simple.

We now define GCalculus/S queries. The syntax defined
for GCalculus is revised as follows.

1) The quantifier $\mathbf{A}$ is not used.
2) The quantifier $\forall$ is not used.
3) Negation appears only to the left of a base predicate
   (i.e., it does not appear to the left of formulas with
   several predicates and logical connectives $\wedge$ or $\vee$.)

We now discuss how to translate queries in GCalculus
with $\mathbf{A}$, $\forall$, and $\exists$ into ones in GCalculus/S with only $\mathbf{E}$ and $\exists$,
and set operators. First, we translate formulas with $\mathbf{A}$ path
quantifier into formulas with $\forall$, $\exists$, and set operators. Second, we translate formulas that result from the first transformation (possibly still having $\forall$) into ones with $\exists$, $\mathbf{E}$,
and/or set operators using the algorithms given in our ear-
lier work [50].

LEMMA A.1. *Let* $\mathbf{A}(x)<<g, x, s_0>>P$ *be a state formula where P is
a path formula whose first and last node-valued terms are*
s_0 *and* s_j, *respectively, and p in P is an assertion associated
with* s_0. *The formula* $\mathbf{A}(x)<<g, x, s_0>>P$ *is equivalent (i.e.,
always has the same truth assignment) to* $S_p \subseteq S_q$, *where* S_p
$= \{x_1 \mid <<g, x_1, s_0>>[[s_0]]p\ C : x_1\ [[s_n]]s_n.$type = "Terminate"$\}$ *and* $S_q = \{x_1 \mid << g, x_1, s_0 >> \overline{P}\}$, *and if the state
formula for* s_j *contains the assertion* $s_j.$type = "Terminate",
then $\overline{P}$ *is defined as P, otherwise* $\overline{P}$ *is defined as* $P\ C :$
$x_2\ [[s_n]]s_n.$type = "Terminate".

PROOF. Let $S = \{x\}$ be the set of all paths from s_0 to any terminate node s_n. By definition, $S = S_p$.
Case 1. $s_j.$type = "Terminate" *holds.*

Assume $\mathbf{A}(x)<<g, x, s_0>>P$ holds. Since S_q can be
rewritten as $\{x_1 \mid <<g, x_1, s_0>>P\}$, we have $S = S_p = S_q$
and, thus, $S_p \subseteq S_q$ holds. Assume $\mathbf{A}(x)<<g, x, s_0>>P$

does not hold. Then, by the definitions of S_p and S_q, there is a path x' in S_p where s_n is a terminate node, and x' is *not* in S_q. Thus, $S_p \not\subseteq S_q$.

Case 2. s_j.type = "Terminate" does not hold.

Assume $\mathbf{A}(x)<<g, x, s_0>>P$ holds. Then, $S_q = \{x \cdot x_2 \mid <<g, x \cdot x_2, s_0>>(P\ C : x_2\ [[s_n]]s_n.\text{type} = \text{"Terminate"})\}$ and $S = S_p = S_q$ and, thus, $S_p \subseteq S_q$ holds. Assume $\mathbf{A}(x)<<g, x, s_0>>P$ does not hold. Then, a path x' in S_p is *not* in S_q, i.e., $S_p \not\subseteq S_q$. □

By Lemma A.1, formulas with quantifier $\mathbf{A}$ can be transformed into formulas with $\mathbf{E}$ and set operators. Formulas with the universal quantifier and negation can then be transformed into ones with the existential quantifier and set operators by lemmas and algorithms given in [50].

A1.5 GCalculus/S Query Examples

In this section, we give GCalculus/S queries for the example queries of Section 4.

EXAMPLE A.1.6 (EXAMPLE 4.5). Find a graph which has three streams: A text stream whose name is "Four Seasons of Yellowstone" followed concurrently by

1) a video stream and
2) an audio stream

whose names are "Yellowstone" and "Four Seasons", respectively.

GCalculus/S:
$\{g \mid \text{Presentation-Graph}(g_1) \wedge$
$(\exists n_0, \exists n_1, \exists n_2)(\text{Stream}(n_0) \wedge \text{Stream}(n_1) \wedge \text{Stream}(n_2) \wedge \{n_0, n_1, n_2\} \subseteq g.\text{Nodes} \wedge$
$\mathbf{E}(x_1)<<g, x_1, n_0>>([[n_0]](n_0.\text{name} = \text{"Four Seasons of Yellowstone"} \wedge n_0.\text{type} = \text{"text"})$
$\quad \mathcal{X} : x_1\ [[n_1]](n_1.\text{name} = \text{"Yellowstone"} \wedge n_1.\text{type} = \text{"video"})) \wedge$
$\mathbf{E}(x_2)<<g, x_2, n_0>>([[n_0]](n_0.\text{name} = \text{"Four Seasons of Yellowstone"} \wedge n_0.\text{type} = \text{"text"})$
$\quad \mathcal{X} : x_2\ [[n_2]](n_2.\text{name} = \text{"Four Seasons"} \wedge n_2.\text{type} = \text{"audio"})))\}$

EXAMPLE A.1.7 (EXAMPLE 4.6). In all streams, find sequences of frames where the first frame has the content object "falcon," and the last frame has the content object "mountainlion".

GCalculus/S:
$\{x \mid (\exists s, \exists n_0, \exists n_1)(\text{Stream}(s) \wedge \text{Frame}(n_0) \wedge \text{Frame}(n_1) \wedge \{n_0, n_1\} \subseteq s.\text{frames} \wedge$
$\quad <<s.\text{frames}, x, n_0>>[[n_0]](\exists o_1)(\text{C\_Object}(o_1) \wedge o_1.\text{name} = \text{"falcon"} \wedge o_1 \in n_0.\text{objects})$
$\quad C : x\ [[n_1]](\exists o_2)(\text{C\_Object}(o_2) \wedge o_2 \in n_1.\text{objects} \wedge o_2.\text{name} = \text{"mountainlion"}))\}$

EXAMPLE A.1.8 (EXAMPLE 4.7). Find video streams with a frame that contains the content object "river"; after the frame, there are repetitive frames with the content object "deer" until a frame with the content object "mountainlion" appears.

GCalculus/S:
$\{s \mid \text{Stream}(s) \wedge s.\text{type} = \text{"video"} \wedge$
$(\exists n_1, \exists n_2, \exists n_3)(\text{Frame}(n_1) \wedge \text{Frame}(n_2) \wedge \text{Frame}(n_3) \wedge \{n_1, n_2, n_3\} \subseteq s.\text{frames} \wedge$
$\mathbf{E}(x_1 \cdot x_2)<<s.\text{frames}, x_1 \cdot x_2, n_1>>[[n_1]](\exists o_1)\ (\text{C\_Object}(o_1) \wedge o_1 \in n_1.\text{objects} \wedge o_1.\text{name} = \text{"river"})$
$\quad \mathcal{X} : x_1\ ([[n_2]](\exists o_2)(\text{C\_Object}(o_2) \wedge o_2 \in n_2.\text{objects} \wedge o_2.\text{name} = \text{"deer"})$
$\quad \mathcal{U} : x_2\ [[n_3]](\exists o_3)(\text{C\_Object}(o_3) \wedge o_3 \in n_3.\text{objects} \wedge o_2.\text{name} = \text{"mountainlion"})))\}$

EXAMPLE A.1.9 (EXAMPLE 4.9). Find a presentation graph in which all streams have content objects "deer" and "mountainlion",

GCalculus/S:
$\{g \mid \text{Presentation-Graph}(g) \wedge \text{All\_Streams}(g) \equiv \text{Streams\_Having\_Deer\_and\_MountainLion}(g)\}$
$\text{All\_Streams} = \{s_1 \mid \text{Stream}(s_1) \wedge s_1 \in g.\text{Nodes} \wedge s_1.\text{type} \neq \text{"Terminate"} \wedge s_1.\text{type} \neq \text{"Begin"}\}$
$\text{Streams\_Having\_Deer\_and\_MountainLion} = s_1 \mid \text{Stream}(s_1)$
$\wedge s_1 \in g.\text{Nodes} \wedge (\exists o_1, \exists o_2)(\text{C\_Object}(o_1) \wedge \text{C\_Object}(o_2) \wedge \{o_1, o_2\} \subseteq s_1.\text{frames.objects} \wedge o_1.\text{name} = \text{"deer"} \wedge o_2.\text{name} = \text{"mountainlion"})\}$

EXAMPLE A.1.10 (EXAMPLE 4.10). Find graphs which have a stream containing the content object "deer" and, along every path from this stream, a stream with the content object "river" is encountered.

GCalculus/S:
$\{g \mid \text{Presentation-Graph}(g) \wedge$
$(\exists s_1)\ (\text{Stream}(s_1) \wedge s_1 \in g.\text{Nodes} \wedge (\exists o_1)(\text{C\_Object}(o_1) \wedge o_1.\text{name} = \text{"deer"} \wedge$
$\quad o_1 \in s_1.\text{frames.objects} \wedge \text{All\_Paths\_from\_S1} \equiv \text{Paths\_Having\_Deer\_and\_River})\}$
$\text{All\_Paths\_from\_S1} = \{x \mid (\exists s_2)(\text{Stream}(s_2) \wedge s_2 \in g.\text{Nodes} \wedge <<g, x, s_1>>[[s_1]]\textit{True}\ C : x\ [[s_2]]s_2.\text{type} = \text{"Terminate"})\}$
$\text{Paths\_Having\_Deer\_and\_River} = \{x_1 \cdot x_2 \mid (\exists s_2, \exists s_3)$
$(\text{Stream}(s_2) \wedge \text{Stream}(s_3) \wedge \{s_2, s_3\} \subseteq g.\text{Nodes} \wedge$
$\quad <<g, x_1 \cdot x_2, s_1>>[[s_1]]\textit{True}$
$C : x_1\ [[s_2]](\exists o_1)(\text{C\_Object}(o_1) \wedge o_1.\text{name} = \text{"river"} \wedge o_1 \in s_2.\text{frames.objects})$
$C : x_2\ [[s_3]]s_3.\text{type} = \text{"Terminate"})\}$

APPENDIX 2
PROOF OF THEOREM 6.1

We prove Theorem 6.1 by providing conversion from a GCalculus/S query into a GVISUAL query and vice versa.

Case 1. From GCalculus/S to GVISUAL:

1) Pick a suitable title for the GVISUAL query corresponding to the GCalculus/S query.
2) The output variables in the GCalculus/S query become the output variables in GVISUAL.
3) Transform the formula, say f, of the GCalculus/S query into the corresponding disjunctive normal form, say $e_1 \vee \dots \vee e_n, n \geq 1$. Every formula in $f_i, 1 \leq i \leq n$, has the form $g_1 \wedge \dots \wedge g_m, m \geq 1$.
4) For every e_i in Step 3, make a GVISUAL query definition with the same name obtained in Step 1 and the same output variables obtained in Step 2 using Steps 5 through 8.

5) For each variable defined in the GCalculus/S query, create an iconized object with the same name and the same domain. Each bounded variable of GCalculus/S is quantified by **E** or $\exists$. Similarly, iconized objects in GVISUAL are existentially quantified. This creates a one-to-one mapping between variables of GCalculus/S and GVISUAL.

6) For all formulas in the form of $x_1 \in s.atr_1.,,.atr_n$ or $\{x_1, .., x_m\} \subseteq s.atr_1.,,.atr_n$, where $atr_i, 1 \le i \le n$, is an attribute name, move the iconized objects corresponding to $x_j, 1 \le j \le m$, inside the icon corresponding to s.

7) For formulas in the form of $f_1 \; \theta : x \; f_2$, where θ is a temporal operator and x is a sequence-valued variable, draw the icon corresponding to θ between the two icons corresponding to f_1 and f_2 and put a variable x on the icon corresponding to the path captured in the temporal operator θ.

8) For formulas in the form of $f_1 \; \theta f_2$, where θ is a non-temporal operator:

8.1) When none of f_i, where $i = 1, 2$, is in the form of $\{t_i \mid l_i(t_1, v_1, ..., v_m)\}$, where $v_k, 1 \le k \le m$, are bounded variables and t_i is a free variable, specify the formulas in the condition box.

8.2) When either of f_i, where $i = 1, 2$, is in the form of $\{t_i \mid l_i(t_i, v_1, ..., v_m)\}$, where $v_k, 1 \le k \le m$, are bounded variables and t_i is a free variable, do the following:

8.2.1) If f_1 is in the form $\{t_1 \mid l_1(t_1, v_1, ..., v_m)\}$ use Steps 1 through 8 to obtain a subquery for f_1; let this subquery to have the name $name_1$; if not, $name_1$ is f_1.

8.2.2) If f_2 is in the form $\{t_2 \mid l_2(t_2, v_1, ..., v_m)\}$ use Steps 1 through 8 to obtain a subquery for f_2; let this subquery to have the name $name_2$; if not $name_2$ is f_2.

8.2.3) Write $name_1 \; \theta \; name_2$ in the condition box.

Case 2. From GVISUAL to GCalculus/S:

1) The output variables in the GVISUAL query become the output variables in the GCalculus/S query.

2) For each iconized object in the query body, write $\exists$ quantifier and, in its scope, the corresponding predicate which represents the type of the object.

3) For each containment relationship in the GVISUAL query, i.e., when the icon x_i is immediately inside the icon s, write the formulas in the form of $x_1 \in s.atr_1.,,.atr_n$ or $\{x_1, ..., x_m\} \subseteq s.atr_1, ..., atr_n$, where $x_i, 1 \le i \le m$, is in the composition hierarchy of $s.atr_1, ..., atr_n$.

4) For every path which is represented by n temporal operator icons and their n path variables $x_i, 1 \le i \le n$, do the following:

4.1) If any of the path variables x_i appears as an output variable for the query, then create a conjunct as $<<o.atr_1 ... atr_m, x_1 ,, x_n, s_t>>p$, where $m \ge 0$, o is the variable corresponding to the icon which immediately contains the node icons involved in the path expression, $o.atr_1 ... atr_m$ is the data model composition relation between the containing object and the contained objects, s_t is the variable corresponding to the starting node icon of the

path, and p is a path formula corresponding to the path.

4.2) If none of the path variables x_i appears as an output variable for the query, then create a conjunct as $E<<o.atr_1 ... atr_m, x_1 ,, x_n, s_t>>p$, where $m \ge 0$, o is the variable corresponding to the icon which immediately contains the node icons involved in the path expression, $o.atr_1 ... atr_m$ is the data model composition relation between the containing object and the contained objects, s_t is the variable corresponding to the starting node icon of the path, and p is a path formula corresponding to the path.

5) Each formula in the condition box of a GVISUAL query is converted to the corresponding formula of GCalculus/S by Steps 5.1 and 5.2. The formulas in a single GVISUAL query definition are connected by conjunctive connectives. Thus, formulas in the condition box of a query can be translated as conjuncts in the GCalculus/S query. For every formula in the condition box which is in the form of $f_1 \; \theta \; f_2$:

5.1) When none of f_i, $i = 1, 2$, is a subquery name:

5.1.1) If the formula is in the form of $o.atr_1.,,.atr_k \; \theta \; c$, where $k \ge 0$, c is a constant, and o is a node variable in a path, then write the formula in the scope of the node variable.

5.1.2) If the formula is in the form of $o_1.atr_1.,,.atr_k \; \theta \; o_2.atr_1.,,.atr_l$, where $k \ge 0$, $l \ge 0$, and o_1 and o_2 are node variables in a path, then write the formula in the scope which contains both node variables.

5.1.3) Otherwise, write the formula at the same scope in which f_1 and f_2 are defined.

5.2) When either of f_i, $i = 1, 2$, is a subquery name:

5.2.1) If f_1 is a subquery, use Steps 1 through 5 and obtain a formula in the form of $\{t_1 \mid \psi(t_1, v_1, ..., v_m)\}$, where t_1 is an output variable and $v_i, 1 \le i \le m$, are bounded variables outside of f_1, and $subquery_1 = \{t_i \mid \psi(t_1, v_1, ..., v_m)\}$; if not, $subquery_1$ is f_1.

5.2.2) If f_2 is a subquery, use Steps 1 through 5 and obtain a formula in the form of $\{t_2 \mid \psi(t_2, v_1, ..., v_n)\}$, where t_i is an output variable and $v_i, 1 \le i \le n$, are bounded variables outside of f_2, and $subquery_2 = \{t_2 \mid \psi(t_2, v_1, ..., v_n)\}$; if not, $subquery_2$ is f_2.

5.2.3) Write $subquery_1 \; \theta \; subquery_2$ in its scope.

By Cases 1 and 2, any GCalculus/S query can be transformed into the corresponding GVISUAL query, and vice versa. Thus, GVISUAL and GCalculus/S are equivalent in expressive power. $\square$

ACKNOWLEDGMENTS

We thank Abdullah Al-Hamdani for implementing the GVISUAL interface and providing GVISUAL figures in this paper. This research is supported by National Science Foundation Grants IRI 92-24660, IRI 96-31214, and CDA 95-29503.

REFERENCES

[1] A. Al-Hamdani, "Implementing GVISUAL for Multimedia Presentation Querying," MS thesis, Case Western Reserve Univ., June 1998.

[2] S. Adali, K.S. Candan, S.-S. Chen, K. Erol, and V.S. Subrahmanian, "The Advanced Video Information System: Data Structures and Query Processing," *ACM Multimedia Systems J.*, vol. 4, no. 4, pp. 172-186, 1996.

[3] Apple Computer, *Macintosh Human Interface Guidelines*. Reading, Mass.: Addison-Wesley, 1992.

[4] N.H. Balkir, "VISUAL," MS thesis, Computer Eng. and Science Dept., Case Western Reserve Univ., May 1995.

[5] N.H. Balkir and G. Özsoyoglu, "Multimedia Presentation Servers: Buffer Management and Admission Control," *Proc. 1998 IEEE Int'l Workshop Multimedia DBMSs*, Dayton, Ohio, Aug. 1998.

[6] T. Bozkaya, N.H. Balkir, and T. Lee, "Efficient Evaluation of Path Algebra Expressions," technical report, Case Western Reserve Univ., June 1997.

[7] N.H. Balkir, Y. Lin, N. Yazdani, G. Özsoyoglu, and Z.M. Özsoyoglu, "ViSiOn: VISUAL, VStore, and O-Algebra," unpublished manuscript, 1997.

[8] G. Beekman, "Multimedia Authoring Software," http://www.awl.com/he/is/bclink/bclink2/Authoring.html.

[9] G. Blakowski and R. Steinmetz, "A Media Synchronization Survey: Reference Model, Specification, and Case Studies," *IEEE J. Selected Areas in Comm.*, vol. 14, no. 1, Jan. 1996.

[10] N.H. Balkir, G. Özsoyoglu, and Z.M Özsoyoglu, "A Graphical Query Language: VISUAL," submitted for journal publication, 1997.

[11] N.H. Balkir, E. Sukan, G. Özsoyoglu, and Z.M Özsoyoglu, "VISUAL: A Graphical Icon-Based Query Language," *Proc. IEEE ICDE Conf.*, pp. 524-533, 1996.

[12] R. Cai, "Implementing Path Algebra Operators for the VStore System," MS project in progress, Case Western Reserve Univ., 1998.

[13] J. Carroll and D. Long, *Theory of Finite Automata with an Introduction to Formal Languages*. Prentice Hall, 1989.

[14] *The Object Database Standard: ODMG-93, Release 1.2*, R.G.G. Cattell, ed., 1996.

[15] M. Consens and A. Mendelzon, "GraphLog: A Visual Formalism for Real-Life Recursion," *Proc. ACM PODS Conf.*, 1990.

[16] M. Consens and A. Mendelzon, "Hy$^+$: A Hygraph-Based Query and Visualization System," *Proc. ACM SIGMOD Conf.*, 1993.

[17] I.F. Cruz, A. Mendelzon, and P.T. Wood, "A Graphical Query Language Supporting Recursion," *Proc. ACM SIGMOD Conf.*, 1987.

[18] I.F. Cruz, A. Mendelzon, and P.T. Wood, "G$^+$: Recursive Queries without Recursion," *Proc. Second Int'l Conf. Expert Database Systems*, 1988.

[19] I. Cruz, "Doodle: A Visual Language for Object-Oriented Databases," *Proc. ACM SIGMOD*, 1992.

[20] Y.F. Day, S. Dagtas, M. Iino, A. Khokhar, and A. Ghafoor, "An Object-Oriented Conceptual Modeling of Video Data," *Proc. IEEE ICDE Conf.*, pp. 401-408, 1995.

[21] E. Emerson, "Temporal and Modal Logic," *Handbook of Theoretical Computer Science*, J. Leeuwen, ed., chapter 16, pp. 995-1, 072. Elsevier, 1990.

[22] J. Gao, "OAOpt: An Optimizer's Design and Implementation for Object-Oriented Databases," MS project, Case Western Reserve Univ., Feb. 1997.

[23] M. Gyssens, J. Van Den Bussche, and J. Paradaens, "A Graph-Oriented Object Database Model," *IEEE Trans. Knowledge and Data Eng.*, Aug. 1994.

[24] D. Gentner and J. Nielson, "The Anti-Mac Interface," *Comm. ACM*, vol. 39, no. 8, pp. 70-82, Aug. 1996.

[25] M. Golebiewski, "Extending VISUAL with Drop-and-Drag Features," MS project, Case Western Reserve Univ., May 1996.

[26] M. Gyssens, J. Paradaens, and D. Van Gucht, "A Graph-Oriented Object Database Model," *Proc. ACM PODS Conf.*, 1990.

[27] M. Gyssens, J. Paradaens, and D. Van Gucht, "A Graph-Oriented Object Model for Database End-User Interfaces," *Proc. ACM SIGMOD Conf.*, 1990.

[28] R. Guting, "GraphDB: Modeling and Querying Graphs in Databases," *Proc. Int'l Conf. Very Large Data Bases*, pp. 297-308, 1994.

[29] M. Haindl, "A New Multimedia Synchronization Model," *IEEE J. Selected Areas in Comm.*, vol. 14, no. 1, Jan. 1996.

[30] V. Hakkoymaz, "A Constraint-Driven Methodology for Designing a Multimedia Presentation System from Multimedia Databases," PhD thesis, Computer Eng. and Science Dept., Case Western Reserve Univ., Dec. 1996.

[31] V. Hakkoymaz and G. Özsoyoglu, "Constrain-Based Automation of Multimedia Presentation Assembly," *ACM Multimedia Systems J.*, to appear 1998.

[32] E. Hwang and V.S. Subrahmanian, "Querying Video Libraries," technical report, Univ. of Maryland, College Park, June 1995.

[33] P. Kanellakis, C. Lecluse, and P. Richard, "Introduction to the Data Model," *Building an Object-Oriented Database System: The Story of O2*, pp. 61-76, Morgan-Kaufmann, 1992.

[34] T. Lee and G. Özsoyoglu, "On Presentation Languages for Multimedia Databases," Case Western Reserve Univ. technical report, 1996.

[35] T. Lee and G. Özsoyoglu, "Query Processing Techniques for Multimedia Presentations," *Proc. IEEE RIDE Conf.*, Feb. 1998.

[36] T. Lee, L. Sheng, N.H. Balkir, A. Al-Hamdani, G. Özsoyoglu, and Z.M. Özsoyoglu, "Query Processing Techniques for Multimedia Presentations," submitted for journal publication, Apr. 1998.

[37] O. Lichtenstein, A. Pneuli, and L. Zuck, "The Glory of the Past," Lecture Notes in Computer Science, vol. 193. Springer-Verlag, 1985.

[38] T.D.C. Little and A. Ghafoor, "Synchronization and Storage Models for Multimedia Objects," *IEEE J. Selected Areas in Comm.*, vol. 8, no. 3, Apr. 1990.

[39] J. Lin and Z.M. Özsoyoglu, "Processing OODB Queries by O-Algebra," *Proc. CIKM*, 1996.

[40] J. Lin, "Processing OODB Queries by O-Algebra," PhD thesis, Case Western Reserve Univ., May 1998.

[41] C. Lecluse and P. Richard, "Modeling Complex Structures in Object-Oriented Databases," *Proc. Symp. Principles of Database Systems*, pp. 360-368, 1989.

[42] K.L. Liu, A.P. Sistla, C. Yu, and N. Rishe, "Query Processing in a Video Retrieval System," *Proc. IEEE ICDE Conf.*, 1998.

[43] J. Lin, X. Zhang, and Z.M. Özsoyoglu, "A Complete Solution of Reducing OODB Nested Queries," submitted for publication, 1997.

[44] S. Marcus and V.S. Subrahmanian, "Foundation of Multimedia Information Systems," *J. ACM*, vol. 43, no. 3, May 1996.

[45] M. Magel, "Comparative Review of Authoring Tools," http://www.allencomm.com/p&s/software/quest/whtpgs/quwhite.html.

[46] A. Oeftering, "Picking a Multimedia Authoring Tool," http://www.datatech.com/hot/s96_3.htm.

[47] G. Özsoyoglu, V. Matos., and Z.M. Özsoyoglu, "Query Processing Techniques in the Summary-Table-by-Example Database Query Language," *ACM Trans. Database Systems*, vol. 14, no. 4, Dec. 1989.

[48] R. Ortega, "Design and Implementation of a Video Presentation Tool," MS project, Case Western Reserve Univ., May 1997.

[49] G. Özsoyoglu and W. Abdul-Qader, "Human Factors Study of Two Screen-Oriented Query Languages: STBE and QBE," *Information and Technology J.*, vol. 34, no. 1, pp. 3-15, Jan. 1997.

[50] G. Özsoyoglu and H. Wang, "A Relational Calculus with Set Operators, Its Safety, and Equivalent Graphical Languages," *IEEE Trans. Software Eng.*, vol. 15, no. 9, pp. 1, 038-1, 052, Sept. 1989.

[51] Products: Director, Authorware (*Company: Macromedia*) http://www.macromedia.com,
IconAuthor (*AIMTech*) http://www.aimtech.com,
Quest (*Allen Communications*) http://www.allencomm.com,
Astound (*Gold Disk*) http://www.golddisk.com,
Hypercard (*Apple*) http://www.hypercard.apple.com.

[52] B. Ramasamy, "Implementation of O-Algebra: An Algebra for OO Databases," MS project, Case Western Reserve Univ., Apr. 1996.

[53] P. Reisner, "Use of Psychological Experimentation as an Aid to Development of a Query Language," *IEEE Trans. Software Eng.*, pp. 218-229, Mar. 1977.

[54] K. Renganathan, "A Stand-Alone Multimedia Authoring Tool," MS project, Case Western Reserve Univ., Oct. 1997.

[55] J. Richardson, "Supporting Lists in a Data Model (A Timely Approach)," *Proc. VLDB Conf.*, 1992.

[56] B. Shneiderman, "Improving the Human Factors Aspect of Database Interactions," *ACM Trans. Database Systems*, vol. 3, no. 3, pp. 417-439, 1978.

[57] L. Sheng and Z.M. Özsoyoglu, "Querying Multimedia Presentation Graphs," Case Western Reserve Univ. technical report, 1997.

[58] R. Steinmetz, "Synchronization Properties on Multimedia Systems," *IEEE J. Selected Areas in Comm.*, vol. 8, no. 3, Apr. 1990.

[59] V.S. Subrahmanian, *Principles of Multimedia Database Systems.* Morgan Kaufmann, 1998.

[60] S. Subhani, "Implementing O-Algebra Operators in VStore," MS project in progress, Case Western Reserve Univ., 1998.

[61] A.P. Sistla, C. Yu, and R. Venkatasubrahmanian, "Similarity Based Retrieval of Videos," *Proc. IEEE Data Eng. Conf.*, 1997.

[62] J.C. Thomas and J.D. Gould, "A Psychological Study of Query by Example," *Proc. AFIPS Nat'l Conf.*, 1975.

[63] R. Touma, "ViSiOn Database Browser and Administration Server Upgrade," MS project, Case Western Reserve Univ., Nov. 1997.

[64] P. Wolper, "Temporal Logic Can Be More Expressive," *Proc. IEEE Symp. Foundations of Computer Science*, pp. 340-348, 1981.

[65] M.M. Zloof, "Query-by-Example: A Database Language," *IBM Systems J.*, vol. 21, no. 3, 1977.

[66] H. Yao, "Database Browser and Administration Server for VISUAL," MS project, Case Western Reserve Univ., June 1997.

Taekyong Lee received the bachelors degree in economics from Korea University; the masters degree in economics from Indiana University, Bloomington; and the PhD degree from Case Western Reserve University, Cleveland, Ohio, in computer science in 1998. He is currently a tenured lecturer at Kyungsan University, Korea. His research interests include multimedia data-bases, knowledge base systems, data mining, and artificial intelligence. He is a student member of the IEEE Computer Society.

Lei Sheng received a BS degree in computer science from Fudan University, China, in 1991; and an ME degree in computer engineering and science from Zhejiang University, China, in 1994. Currently, she is a PhD student in computer science at Case Western Reserve University, Cleveland, Ohio. Her research interests include database query languages, object-oriented databases, and multimedia databases. She is a student member of the IEEE Computer Society.

Tolga Bozkaya received a BSc degree in 1992 in computer science from Bilkent University, Ankara, Turkey; and his PhD from the Department of Computer Science and Engineering at Case Western Reserve University, Cleveland, Ohio, in 1998. He is now a member of the technical staff at Oracle Corporation. His primary work and research interests are indexing in temporal and spatial databases, similarity-based indexing for metric spaces, query languages, and query processing techniques for multimedia databases and multimedia presentations. He is a student member of the IEEE Computer Society.

Nevzat Hurkan Balkir received his MS degree from Case Western Reserve University and his BSc degree from Bilkent University, Ankara, Turkey, in 1995 and 1993, respectively. He is presently finishing his PhD degree studies in the Computer Engineering and Science Department, Case Western Reserve University, Cleveland, Ohio. His primary research interests are in the areas of object-oriented databases, multime-dia databases, and multimedia computing. He is a student member of the IEEE Computer Society.

Z. Meral Özsoyoglu has a BSc degree in electrical engineering and an MSc degree in computer science, both from Middle East Technical University, Turkey. She has a PhD degree in computer science from the University of Alberta, Canada. She is now a professor of computer engineering and science at Case Western Reserve University, Cleveland, Ohio, where she has been a faculty member since 1980. Her primary research work and interests are in the areas of principles of database systems, database query languages, database design, object-oriented databases, and complex objects with applications in scientific, temporal, and multimedia databases. She has published several papers on these topics in computer science journals and conference proceedings. She was ACM PODS program chair in 1997, and has served on organizing and program committees of several major conferences on databases. She has been a recipient of several National Science Foundation grants, as well as an IBM Faculty Development Award and an NSF FAW award. She is presently ACM SIGMOD vice chair and is a member of the IEEE Computer Society.

Gultekin Özsoyoglu received his PhD degree in computing science from the University of Alberta, Edmonton, Alberta, Canada, in 1980. He is now a professor in the Department of Computer Engineering and Science, Case Western Reserve University, Cleveland, Ohio. His current research interests include multimedia databases, multimedia computing, real-time databases, scientific and statistical databases, and graphical user interfaces. He has published in all of the major database conference proceedings and journals, such as *ACM Transactions on Database Systems, IEEE Transactions on Software Engineering, IEEE Transactions on Knowledge and Data Engineering*, and the *Journal of Computer and System Sciences*. He has served on program committees and panels of major database conferences, such as ACM SIGMOD, VLDB, and IEEE Data Engineering. He was an ACM national lecturer; program chair of the Third Statistical and Scientific Database Conference; workshop general chair of the CIKM '94 and CIKM '96 conferences; research prototypes chair of ACM SIGMOD '94 conference; and a guest editor for *IEEE Transactions on Knowledge and Data Engineering*. He is an associate editor of the *Journal of Database Administration*, and has served on National Science Foundation, National Research Council, and Ford Foundation panels. He is a member of the IEEE Computer Society.

NetView: Integrating Large-Scale Distributed Visual Databases

**Aidong Zhang, Wendy Chang, and
Gholamhosein Sheikholeslami**
State University of New York at Buffalo

Tanveer F. Syeda-Mahmood
Xerox Research Center

NetView supports global content-based query access to various visual databases over the Internet. An integrated metaserver consisting of a metadatabase, metasearch agent, and query manager facilitates such access. NetView significantly reduces the amount of time and effort that users spend in finding information of interest. It also can further refine the metaserver's performance based on user feedback.

The explosive growth and increasing popularity of the Internet and World Wide Web make it possible to access large image and video repositories distributed globally. Access to these repositories plays an increasingly important role in numerous applications such as geographic information systems, medical information systems, surveillance, and distributed publishing. The National Library of Medicine (NLM) is developing an electronic archive of digitized photographs, X rays, scanned articles, and digitized video with the goal of providing wide access to these collections via client-server systems. The National Aeronautics and Space Administration (NASA) also has terabytes of space data for exploring space and atmospheric sciences. In such applications, the search and retrieval of visual databases becomes an essential part of scientific research. In the commercial world, several products provide networked access to image databases. For example, ArtView lets art dealers display high-quality images of paintings and other artwork in various galleries to remote prospective buyers.

The enormous growth in the amount of image and video information has also created new issues for users. Internet users now face a problem of resource selection. That is, given a query, where should a user start a search? One example could be a graphic designer who looks for images with specific patterns as a background for a design. Experienced designers may already have a list of favorite image Web sites and will start the search from one of those sites. Less experienced designers will probably visit a well-known Web search engine—such as Yahoo—to get a list of stock photograph Web sites. In either case, the designers may need to search all the sites on the list to find the desired images. Furthermore, if the desired images can't be found, no specific approaches currently exist for the designer to obtain an alternate list of Web sites (except possibly by using a different search engine with an associated loss of context).

To deal with the increasing pool of visual data and the inherent complexity in visual data querying, it's crucial to carefully select database sites to support efficient queries. Designing a metaserver on top of various visual databases can help solve the problem. Given a query, the metaserver first ranks the database sites and then distributes the queries to the selected databases.

In recent research, database selection has focused on directing text queries to databases. For example, Web search engines such as Lycos and AltaVista currently create Web indices in their search engines by scanning potential Web sites periodically and using the text information in their resident Hypertext Markup Language (HTML) pages. But most implementations of text-based distributed systems don't perform site selection, often posing a query to all sites in parallel as done in the College Library Access and Storage System (Class) and the Networked Computer Science Technical Report Library (NCSTRL) systems at Cornell University.[1]

Also, information retrieval techniques handle intelligent resource site selection. Examples of such systems include the Glossary of Servers Server (Gloss)[2] from Stanford University, Palo Alto, California; WhoIs++[3] from Bunyip Corp., Montreal; and Harvest from the University of Colorado.[4] These systems use statistical approaches to record how often keywords appear in known sites to construct an index of relevant sites for directing a query. For example, Gloss keeps statistics on the available databases to estimate which databases prove useful for a given query using Boolean and vector-space models of document

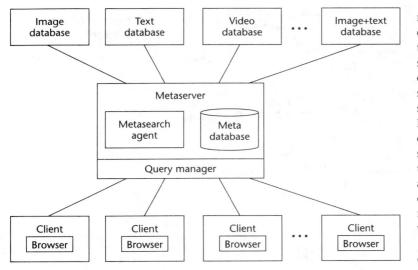

Figure 1. A distributed visual data retrieval system.

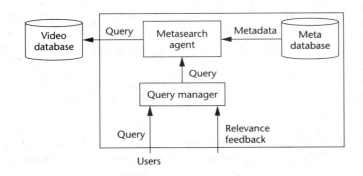

Figure 2. The metaserver architecture.

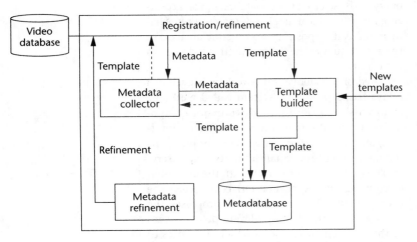

Figure 3. The metadatabase management system.

retrieval. Wide Area Information Servers (WAIS)[5] divides its indices among the databases into multiple levels with the top-level index containing a server directory. Given a query, the system searches the directory and then forwards the query to selected databases. Similar to the WAIS approach, several Web-based image search facilities such as ImageRover,[6] WebSeek,[7] and AltaVista maintain a centralized index on images in individual Web sites as specified through uniform resource locators (URLs), image file names, or manually generated text annotations. These search engines can combine text and image content queries and return a list of archival sites containing the images whose descriptions match the pattern.

MetaSeek[8]—a metaimage search engine for querying large distributed online visual information sources—comes closest to selecting relevant image databases (rather than images directly). MetaSeek's target search engines include VisualSeek,[9] Query by Image and Video Content (QBIC),[10] and Virage.[11] For each query, MetaSeek selects the target search engines that support the specified query method. It may select the desired results based on the performance metrics calculated from past queries. Users determine the query's performance metrics after viewing the responses from the search engines. While MetaSeek provides a novel approach for selecting search engines, the concept of selecting databases based on visual content has not, to our knowledge, been explored.

This article presents an approach to designing an integrated metaserver that supports intelligent resource selection based on the image queries' feature content. Given a visual query, the system returns a ranked list of potentially relevant database sites. Users can then follow the path recommended by the system, starting with the highest ranked sites. Such a framework lets users locate the resources quickly and dramatically reduces the overall time spent in retrieving the images of interest.

The metaserver contains three main components: the metadatabase, metasearch agent, and query manager. To support intelligent site selection, the metadata included in the metadatabase derives from the images' visual content, which is housed at each remote visual database. Image templates and statistical features characterizing the images' similarity distributions help summarize the images' visual content in each database. The metadatabase organizes into a hierarchical structure. The query manager extracts information in the query that matches the metadata. The query manager also refines the visual queries based on users' feedback. Various selection approaches for the metasearch agent—which use the metadata—can rank relevant database sites. We implemented a prototype system using Java in a Web-based environment and conducted experimental analysis.

System architecture

Figure 1 illustrates the system's overall architecture. This system contains three main parts: visual databases at remote sites, a metaserver, and a set of visual display applications at the client machines. We'll focus on the metaserver's design. The metaserver accepts user queries, extracts information in the query that matches the metadata, produces database site rankings, and distributes the queries to selected databases. Figure 2 shows the metaserver components, including the metadatabase, metasearch agent, and query manager.

The metadatabase houses both template and statistical metadata. The templates—feature vectors representing the component database images' feature vectors—and the statistical metadata record the relationships between the templates and database images (see the detailed discussion on metadata in the following section). Three additional modules—the metadata collector, template builder, and metadata refinement—support the metadata's interoperability and integrity. The metadatabase, together with the metadata collector, template builder, and metadata refinement module, constitute the metadatabase management system[12] shown in Figure 3. The collector gathers the metadata from the visual database either when the database registers with the metaserver or when the database resubmits its metadata. The template builder organizes and creates templates. The metadata refinement module initiates the metadata update process periodically by asking the database to resubmit its metadata.

The query manager consists of two modules: the query processing module and query refinement module. The query processing module accepts users' queries, extracts various feature vectors from them, and submits the feature vectors to the metasearch agent. During the feedback step, the query-processing module accepts images that users judge as relevant or irrelevant to the original query. It extracts various feature vectors from the images and forwards them to the query refinement module. The query refinement module constructs modified queries from the image-feature vectors sent by the query-processing module. Figure 4

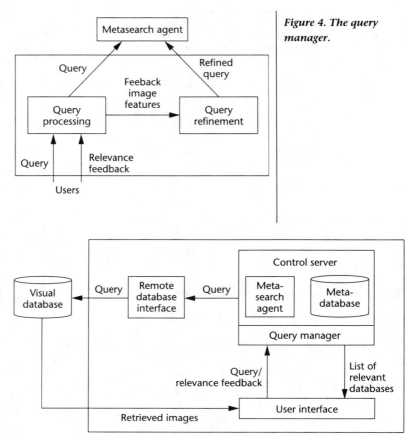

Figure 4. The query manager.

Figure 5. The NetView Web-based visual information system.

shows the query manager's functionalities.

The metasearch agent invokes the site selection algorithm, which matches the query features to templates of the databases' corresponding metadata, thus selecting the potentially relevant databases for the query. The system then forwards the query to the selected visual databases in an acceptable form. The local database's searching mechanism scans its repository for possible answers to the posed query. The answer then is fed back to the client.

Based on the above framework, we developed a Java-based prototype system called NetView. Figure 5 shows NetView's three major components: a central server, a remote database interface, and a user interface. NetView implements the metaserver functionalities in its central server. The central server interacts with the user interface through Java's socket interface to receive the user's query. The central server processes the query and returns a list of relevant database sites to the user. The user selects which databases to search. The central server then forwards the query to the remote database interface, which distributes

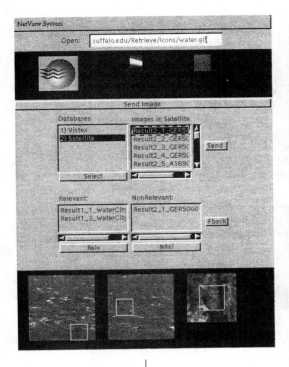

Figure 6. The NetView user interface.

queries to the chosen databases in an acceptable form. NetView currently supports image databases stored in file systems, Ardent Software's O2 databases, and Object Design's ObjectStore databases via the remote database interface.

NetView's user interface, an HTML form, can be invoked within a standard Web browser. The user interface handles interactions between users and the central server. Through a Java applet, the interface lets users submit queries, select the desired databases, initiate searches, mark the relevance of retrieved images, and initiate subsequent feedback searches. Figure 6 shows the NetView user interface.

Users can enter a query by typing a file name in the Open box. The query image then appears in the upper window. Any image accessible over the Internet can serve as a query. The query can either be the complete image or a portion of it (as marked by the user). Figure 6 shows queries of different sizes in the top window. The rightmost image represents the query for the retrieved images in the bottom window.

Next, the user sends the query to the server by clicking on the Send Image button. The user interface displays the relevant databases list upon receiving it from the metasearch agent. The user can then choose to search a database by highlighting the database name and clicking the Send button. The system forwards the query image to the chosen database. The local database searches its repository, and retrieved images are fed back to the user interface for viewing.

The remaining part of the user interface handles the relevance feedback mechanism. NetView asks the user to mark the retrieved images as relevant or irrelevant by highlighting the image name and clicking the corresponding buttons (Relv or NRel). Clicking the feedback (Fback) button sends these relevance indications to the system, thereby generating a refined list of relevant databases.

Metadata

We'll now outline the rationale of the metadata formulation we used to select relevant databases for a given visual query. It might seem that such a selection could be done using methods in text database discovery by maintaining a relevant site index (using text information associated with the database). Also, information such as monetary cost and latency of database sites can provide additional metadata to reduce costly sites. However, for visual querying, text information can only coarsely prune the database sites. For further refinement, the system must use the visual information in the query. But how can database relevance be determined for visual queries without examining all images in databases for possible matches? Clearly, it's not desirable to move the complete machinery of image content-based searches (used in the database engines) to the distribution site to determine database relevance. Also, it's impossible to create offline an indexed set of database sites containing relevant images to queries—that requires anticipating all possible visual queries. To address these problems, we propose an intermediate approach wherein the information in the database images is summarized in an abstract in the metadatabase.

Features such as texture, color, and shape can represent information in a visual object. Computationally, a set of numerical numbers—called a feature vector—typically represent an image's features. Visual queries can then be supported by matching the query's features with the feature vectors in the database using similarity metrics. Many approaches extract various features from visual data, including texture, color, and shape.[13,14] Figure 7 shows two examples of visual queries and their matched images retrieved using mechanisms presented elsewhere.[15-17] Figure 7 also shows texture and color queries and the matched segments within images. The similarity attached to each image demonstrates that the similarity between the query and the image increases as its content becomes more similar.

Templates

To support efficient retrieval, some approaches have categorized feature vectors as clusters based on features.[18,19] Each cluster can then be represented by a feature vector, denoted a *template*, which is generally the cluster's centroid. The cluster can further be classified into subclusters, represented by their centroids. A template at a higher level represents the coarse features that contain all the features its child templates represent. We

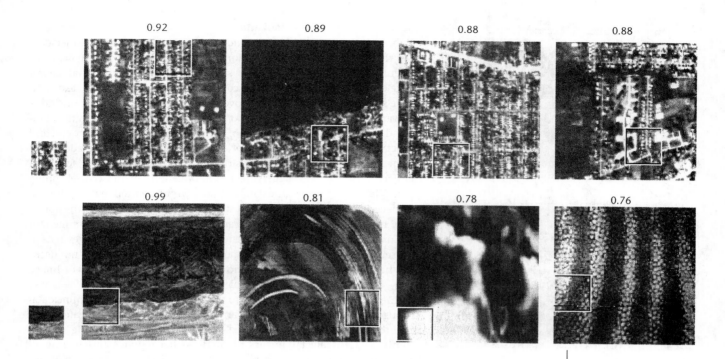

Figure 7. Visual queries and matched database images: (a) texture and (b) color.

observe that such templates can adequately represent the database's content. Thus, we collect templates from the component databases as part of the metadata in the metadatabase.

To find the templates, we first select sample images from all local databases. Then using a hierarchical clustering method, we build a tree-like structure called a dendrogram.[19,20] We can cut the dendrogram at different levels, resulting in different sets of clusters. We then use the resulting clusters' centroids as the templates. NetView applies this process for each feature class to find the corresponding templates. Thus, these templates can represent the images in all the local databases concisely. Moreover, the hierarchical template structure can search for matched templates for a given query efficiently. Other appropriate methods may also find a good set of templates that represent the databases' content well. The metaserver relates the databases' content to the templates by calculating each database's statistical metadata with respect to the templates. The site selection mechanism then uses this statistical metadata.

Statistical metadata

We can measure the visual data's similarity to the templates based on the templates collected from individual visual databases. Using these similarity measurements, the system computes statistical data, increasing the likelihood of selecting a database containing data relevant to a template.

Let *DB* denote the set of all databases and *sim* (i, t) denote the similarity between image i and template t, where $0.0 \le sim\ (i, t) \le 1.0$. The similarity between a database image and an image template can be measured using the methods Jain and Murthy[13] described. Figure 8 (next page) shows some similarity measure values between images and templates. As you can see, similar images tend to have a closer range of similarity measurement with the same template. We based our use of image templates for visual abstraction on this observation.

Assume that the feature extraction algorithms can generate feature vectors that lie close to each other in the feature space for similar images. Given a template t—the center of an image cluster—images similar to t usually have a high degree of similarity to t. Images not similar to t normally have a low degree of similarity to t. Consider an example of a texture template and its matched sample database images, shown in Figure 8 (next page). With respect to the template, cluster 4 (with similarity measures in the range of [0.02, 0.13]) proves the least similar set, while cluster 1 (with similarity measures in the range of [0.79, 0.85]) provides the most similar set.

Similarly, consider an example of a color template and its matched sample database images. Here cluster 4 proves the least similar set with similarity measures of 0.2, while cluster 1 offers the most similar set with similarity measures in the

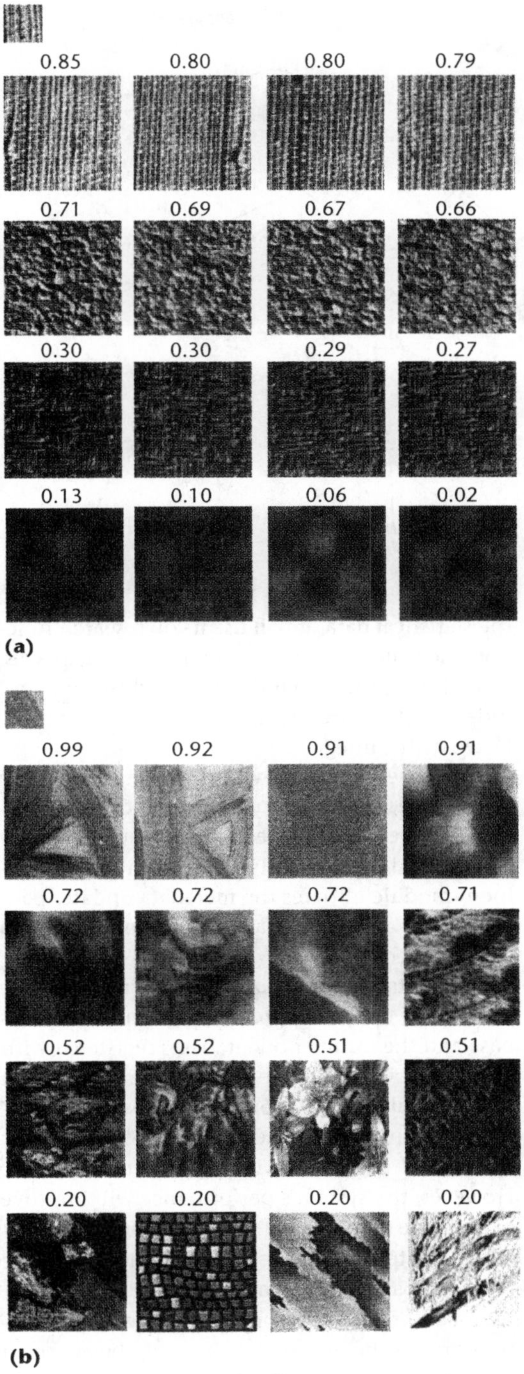

Figure 8. Templates and database images: (a) texture features and (b) color features.

(a)

(b)

range of [0.91, 0.99]. Thus, for image q, with a high similarity to template t, images similar to q will normally have a high similarity to q and a close degree of similarity to template t. Note that, in general, if two images have the same degree of similarity to a template, they're not necessarily similar to each other.

Various statistical data can be computed from the distributions of the similarities between database images and the templates and stored in the metadatabase. The statistical data represent the visual relationships between the databases and templates. The system can select the relevant databases for a given query by determining the query's similarity with metadatabase templates. It then ranks the database sites based on the visual relationships recorded between the databases and templates. Various database selection approaches can be developed corresponding to the statistical data.

The metadatabase hierarchy

The metadatabase follows a hierarchical structure. Figure 9 presents a conceptual view of the metadatabase. At the higher level, templates T_i ($1 \leq i \leq m$) are grouped according to features including texture, color, and shape patterns. The top-level nodes represent the most general categories of texture, color, and shape. To support efficient query retrieval, the system can index the templates in each feature class hierarchically. When the metadatabase is first initialized, we build the initial template hierarchy by clustering a set of sample images representing various application domains such as geography, medicine, industry, nature, and different types of video frames. At the lowest level, database sites group together under each template t_i ($1 \leq i \leq k$), and the groupings build on the database images' similarity to the template. We define an image as similar to a template if the similarity measurement between the two images exceeds a threshold. A database site db_i ($1 \leq i \leq n$) can be grouped under one or more templates.

The time it takes to initialize the metadatabase hierarchy depends on the number of sample images in the process. The larger the number of sample images required to configure the initial template hierarchy, the longer it takes to initialize the process. It took about six hours to build the initial metadatabase hierarchy with 3,000 sample images running on a dedicated Sun Ultra Enterprise 4000 with 1 Gbyte of memory and a 168-MHz UltraSparc CPU. The initial metadatabase hierarchy in our prototype consists of both texture and color features. Once initialized, the metadatabase expands to include new metadata.

Metadata gathering

The template builder adds new templates whenever a new visual database registers with the metaserver or when new images join the database. When a database registers with the metaserver, the system sends a set of representative image samples to the metaserver. If a visual database has already been clustered, the image samples will contain images chosen from each cluster. If a visual database has not yet been clustered, the system chooses the image samples randomly according to a uniform distribution. Based on our experiments, about 10 percent of the total number of images in a visual database suffice as image samples. The metaserver provides the sampling algorithm for the visual database. The metaserver then clusters the sample images to generate a set of image templates representing the visual database. (The clustering follows the strategy outlined previously.) Image templates representing the database then merge with the existing image templates housed at the metaserver.

Adding new images to a database doesn't always require new templates. New templates prove necessary only if the existing templates cannot adequately represent the new images' features. This can happen when the new images differ semantically from the existing images in the database. In such cases, the metadata collector collects the new sample images and configures the new templates. The template builder then merges the new templates into the metadatabase hierarchy. Once added to the metadatabase, a template will not be removed. Whenever a new template joins the metadatabase, all remote databases will be asked to provide the statistical metadata pertaining to the new template. There's no need to update the previously computed statistical metadata, since it's collected with respect to the existing templates.

Each visual database system may use different visual features, models, and similarity metrics. To maintain the visual databases' heterogeneity, the metadata collector provides the feature extraction and similarity measurement algorithms to gather the statistical metadata from the visual databases. When a database registers with the metaserver, the metadata collector sends a registration form, together with the image templates housed at the metaserver, to the database. The registration form contains the algorithms for calculating the metadata. It also requests information from the individual databases such as the type of data housed, the expected query form, the monetary cost, and the database site's latency. The database then computes the similarities of its images to all templates using the supplied algorithms and returns the statistics associated with each template, such as the number of samples, mean, variance, and histogram. The metadata collector then stores the metadata in the metadatabase. Note that although the visual database uses the algorithms supplied by the metaserver to compute

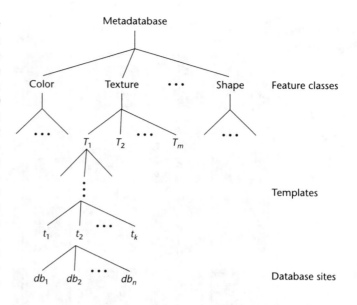

Figure 9. A conceptual view of the metadatabase.

the statistical data, it will use its own search function and similarity metrics when retrieving images. In addition, the visual database's clustering and indexing structures remain unchanged and unaffected by the integration.

Databases registered with the metaserver may be updated, rendering inaccurate statistical metadata recorded earlier. The metadata must therefore be updated dynamically. The metadata refinement module initiates the metadata updates periodically by asking databases to resubmit metadata to the collector.

The metadatabase's size depends largely on the number of templates presented at the metadatabase and the number of databases registered with the metaserver. Since the metadatabase stores a set of statistical metadata for each database and template pair, increasing the number of templates or number of databases will require more storage. However, the system's performance will improve because the templates can represent the visual databases' content more accurately. In addition, the metadatabase requires more storage to store the templates' feature vectors and database information such as the type of data housed, the expected query form, the specialized algorithms supported, the monetary cost, and the database sites' latency.

Much research has targeted to resource discovery over the Internet. Since our research doesn't focus on this aspect, we assume that the discovery of new database resources will be performed manually. Once discovered, the new database will be asked to register with the metaserver, following the steps outlined above.

Directing a visual query

For a given query, we use the following two-step process (using the metadatabase) to first find the relevant databases:

1. Select the templates that match the query (based on the query's similarity to the templates).

2. Determine the database sites' rankings based on the visual relationships recorded between the databases and selected templates. Users can then choose to send the query to the databases with the highest rankings.

In our system, a query is a still image. Upon receiving a query q, the query manager first extracts a set of subqueries $\{q_1,...,q_n\}$ from the query, with each subquery representing a feature class (that is, texture, color, and shape patterns). The system computes the similarities of each subquery q_i to the metadatabase templates. Let G denote the set of all templates existing in the metadatabase. A set of matched templates $T_{q_i}=\{t_1,...,t_{m_i}\}$ can be selected based on the following criterion:

$$T_{q_i} = \{t \,|\, \forall t \in G, sim\,(q_i,t) \geq \tau$$
$$\wedge (max_{t' \in T_{q_i}}\,(sim\,(q_i,t')) \qquad \textbf{(1)}$$
$$- sim\,(q_i,t)) \leq \varepsilon_{q_i}\}$$

where $sim\,(q_i, t)$ is the similarity between subquery q_i and template t, and τ and ε_{q_i} are given thresholds. The similarities between subquery q_i and the templates in T_{q_i} must exceed the given threshold τ. The templates in T_{q_i} have the highest similarities to q_i. If T_{q_i} is empty, the metaserver will ask the user either to submit a new query or distribute the query to all visual databases.

If a set of matched templates can be found for subquery q_i, the metasearch agent then invokes the selection approach, which uses the subquery similarity to matched templates and corresponding statistical metadata of databases db_i, $1 \leq i \leq n$, to return a list of relevant database sites for that specific subquery. The databases' rankings for all the subqueries then are merged to yield a final set of databases for the given query. Let q contain a set of subqueries $q_1,...,q_n$ and each q_i matches with multiple independent templates $t_1^{q_i},...,t_{m_i}^{q_i}$. Let D_1, $D_2,...,D_n$ be the sets of relevant databases for $q_1,...,q_n$, respectively. Since we look for databases containing images similar to all subqueries, the set of relevant databases for q, denoted DB_s, is calculated as the intersection of D_i, $i = 1,...,n$:

$$DB_s = D_1 \cap D_2 \cap ... \cap D_n \qquad \textbf{(2)}$$

Various selection approaches can be developed to determine D_i $(1 \leq i \leq n)$. For example, Chang et al.[21] developed a *histogram-based* selection approach, based on the similarity distribution's histogram.

Let $[a_{q_i,t},\ b_{q_i,t}]$, where $a_{q_i,t} = sim(q_i,t) - \delta_{q_i}$ and $b_{q_i,t} = sim(q_i,t) + \delta_{q_i}$, be the similarity interval for a subquery q_i with respect to a template t. δ_{q_i} is a predefined offset value for the given q_i. The interval $[a_{q_i,t},\ b_{q_i,t}]$ specifies a similarity range within which we wish to search for similar images to subquery q_i.

Given a database's similarity distribution with respect to a template t, let $h_{db,\,t}:[0.0,\ 1.0] \rightarrow I$ represent the histogram of the similarities of images in a database db to template t, where $h_{db,\,t}(x)$ is the number of images that have a similarity x. Let $num\,(db, t, s_1, s_2)$ be the number of images within database db with a similarity in the range of $[s_1, s_2]$, with respect to template t. For each subquery q_i that matches with a set of templates $\{t_1,...,t_{m_i}\}$, we calculate $num\,(db, t_i, a_{q_i,ti}, b_{q_i,ti})$ for each matched template t_i as

$$num\,(db, t_i, a_{q_i,t_i}, b_{q_i,t_i}) = \sum_{x \in [a_{q_i,t_i},\, b_{q_i,t_i}]} h_{db,t,t_i}(x) \qquad \textbf{(3)}$$

The value $num\,(db, t_i, a_{q_i,ti}, b_{q_i,ti})$ is the total number of database images falling within the similarity interval with respect to template t_i. We then sum $num\,(db, t_i, a_{q_i,ti}, b_{q_i,ti})$ over all matched templates $\{t_1,...,t_{m_i}\}$ and rank the databases in decreasing order of the summed value:

$$D_i = \{db \,|\, db \in DB \wedge \sum_{i=1}^{m_i} num\,(db, t_i, a_{q_i,t_i}, b_{q_i,t_i}) > 0$$
$$\wedge (max_{db' \in DB}\,(\sum_{i=1}^{m_i} num\,(db', t_i, a_{q_i,t_i}, b_{q_i,t_i})) \qquad \textbf{(4)}$$
$$- \sum_{i=1}^{m_i} num\,(db, t_i, a_{q_i,t_i}, b_{q_i,t_i})) \leq \xi\}$$

where DB is the set of databases registered with the metaserver and ξ is a given threshold. In determining the rank of each selected database db for subquery q_i, we use

$$\sum_{i=1}^{m_i} num\,(db, t_i, a_{q_i,t_i}, b_{q_i,t_i}) \,.$$

Figure 10 shows the relationships among a

query, templates, and databases. In this example, a subquery representing the query image's texture feature and a subquery representing its color feature are extracted from the query image. The texture subquery is matched with template t_1. The color subquery is matched with templates p_1 and p_2. The databases grouped under template t_1 are $db_1, ..., db_k$, the databases grouped under template p_1 are $db'_1, ..., db'_n$, and the databases grouped under template p_2 are $db''_1, ..., db''_m$. The metaserver then invokes the selection approach to determine which of the indexed databases relate to the specific subquery. For example, let $\{db_5, db_7, db_8\}$ be the top three ranked databases chosen for the texture subquery and $\{db_3, db_5, db_7\}$ be the top three ranked databases chosen for the color subquery. The selection approach returns the set of relevant databases for the query image as the intersection of the two sets, that is, $DB_s = \{db_5, db_7\}$.

Various models can merge the selections of multiple subqueries. For example, given a query $q = \{q_1, ..., q_n\}$, let $T_{qi} = \{t_1, ..., t_{mi}\}$ be the set of templates that match with subquery q_i using Equation 1 and $\tilde{a}$ be the average similarity between q_i and the templates in T_{qi}. Let $DB_s = \{db_1, ..., db_h\}$ be the final set of chosen databases for query q using Equation 2, and let $S^{q_i} = \{s^{q_i}_{db_1}, ..., s^{q_i}_{db_h}\}$ be the corresponding number of similar images used by the selection approach to rank databases for subquery q_i, where

$$s^{q_i}_{db} = \sum_{j=1}^{m_i} num\ (db, t_j, a_{q_i, t_j}, b_{q_i, t_j})$$

for the histogram-based approach. For each database db_j in DB_s, we compute the estimated score for the subquery q_i as

$$S_{c_{db_j, q_i}} = H_{q_i} \times \frac{\tilde{a}}{m_i} \times \frac{s^{q_i}_{db_j}}{\sum_{l=1}^{h} s^{q_i}_{db_l}} \qquad (5)$$

where H_{q_i} defaults to 1.0 and users can adjust it to satisfy their visual feature preferences.

The estimated score of database db_j for the query q can then be computed as $\sum_{i=1}^{n} (S_{c_{db_j, q_i}})$. The database sites in DB_s are then further ranked based on the decreasing order of $\sum_{i=1}^{n} (S_{c_{db_j, q_i}})$. As shown in Figure 10, the chosen databases in DB_s may be further ranked as $\{db_5, db_7\}$ using the merging algorithm.

We now estimate the time required for obtaining a ranked list of relevant databases for a given query. Let G denote the set of templates existing in the metadatabase and DB the set of databases registered with the metaserver. The computational complexity to choose the matching templates for a given query is $O(|G|)$. Since the maximum

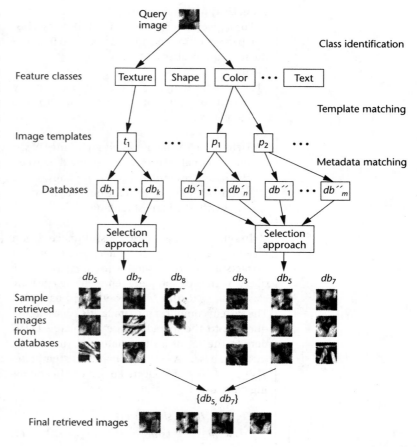

Figure 10. Relationships among a query, templates, and databases.

number of databases grouped under each template is $|DB|$, the computational complexity for applying the selection approach to the databases grouped under the matched templates in the worst case is $O(|DB|)$. Thus, the required time to obtain a ranked list of relevant databases for a given query in the worst case would be $O(|G|) + O(|DB|)$.

To improve efficiency in finding the templates matched to the query image, we can use the existing indexing methods such as R*-tree or its variants[22] to index the templates instead of a serial search. Thus, the computational complexity to choose the matching templates for a given query can be $O(\log |G|)$. In addition, the number of databases grouped under each template is generally much less than $|DB|$, which makes the average time complexity of finding the ranked list of databases less than $O(|G|) + O(|DB|)$. However, the average time needed to find similar images with respect to a given query depends largely on the effectiveness and efficiency of the selected local search engines. The network latency may also affect the response time.

Query refinement based on relevance feedback

Relevance feedback, first introduced in the mid-1960s, has been used extensively by the information retrieval community to improve a query's performance.[10,11] This process modifies the query formulations based on the user's judgment of the initial retrieved documents.[23] The main idea consists of adding or subtracting terms that the user has identified as relevant or irrelevant, and also altering term weights in a new query formulation. The system weights terms included in the previously retrieved relevant document higher and de-emphasizes terms included in the previously retrieved irrelevant document. This query alteration process obtains an optimal query in anticipation of retrieving more relevant documents and less irrelevant documents in a later search.

We implemented our query refinement with an interactive graphical display. After the initial search, a list of initial retrieved images appears on the screen. Users click a mouse pointer to designate images as relevant or irrelevant. The query process module extracts various features from each relevant or irrelevant image and forwards the features to the query refinement module.

Let $F = \{f_1, ..., f_n\}$ be a set of features, where $f_i \in$ {texture, color, shape, and so on}. Let $q = \{q_1, ..., q_n\}$ be the original query and $q_i \in F$. Let I_r be the set of relevant images the initial search retrieved and I_{ir} be the set of irrelevant images the initial search retrieved as determined by the user. Given an image $g = \{g_1, ..., g_n\}$, where $g \in I_r \cup I_{ir}$ and $g_i \in f_i$. Let $q_i^0 = q_i$. The query refinement module constructs a refined subquery $q_i^k (k \geq 1)$ by adding features in the relevant images and

Figure 11. Sample test images.

subtracting features in the irrelevant images:

$$q_i^k = \alpha q_i^{k-1} + \beta \frac{1}{N_r} \sum_{g \in I_r} g_i - \gamma \frac{1}{N_{ir}} \sum_{g \in I_{ir}} g_i \qquad (6)$$

where N_r is the number of the known relevant images in I_r, and N_{ir} is the number of known irrelevant images in I_{ir}. The weights α, β, and γ must be determined experimentally.

The metasearch agent then takes the modified subqueries $q_1^k, ..., q_n^k$ to produce a set of relevant database sites, D_i, for each subquery. The results then merge to generate a final list of relevant databases using Equation 2.

Performance evaluation

We now evaluate our design's effectiveness using the histogram-based selection approach and the merging algorithm introduced previously. We downloaded 8,722 flower, scenery, materials, and background images from the Internet and grouped them randomly into nine databases. The sizes of the databases ranged from 500 to 1,400 images. Figure 11 shows some sample test images. Using other techniques,[16,17] we extracted the texture and color features of the queries and database images.

In our experiments, we posed 35 queries. Each query decomposed into a texture subquery and a color subquery. The similarity values between all texture subqueries and texture templates ranged from 0.65 to 0.90. The similarity values between all color subqueries and color templates ranged from 0.50 to 0.95. Table 1 summarizes the number of queries with respect to the number of matched templates and different ranges of similarity. The δ offset that determines the similarity interval defaulted to 0.08. The ε threshold that selects templates is set at 0.05. By default, the perceptive weight H_{qi} was set to 1.0 for both color and texture subqueries.

We conducted all tests on a dedicated Sun Ultra Enterprise 4000 with 1 Gbyte of memory and a 168-MHz UltraSparc CPU. On average, the system took 0.48 second to return a list of relevant databases.

Selection effectiveness

Selection precision measures the accuracy of database selection against manually verified relevant databases. Given a query, let *selected_sites* be the set of top n database sites selected by the selection approach in response to the query and *relevant_sites* be the set of top m databases that have been manually judged to contain images relevant to the

Table 1. Distribution of number of queries based on the number of matched templates and similarity ranges.

| Number of Templates | | Similarity Ranges | | | Total |
Texture	Color	[0.80, 1.00]	[0.70, 0.79]	[0.60, 0.69]	Queries
1	1	9	3	4	16
1	2 or 3	2	1	1	
2 or 3	1	3	6	2	19
2 or 3	2 or 3	1	2	1	
Total Queries		15	12	8	35

query. The selection precision P is calculated as:

$$P = \begin{cases} \dfrac{|selected\_sites \cap relevant\_sites|}{|selected\_sites|} & \text{if } |selected\_sites| > 0, \\ 1 & \text{otherwise} \end{cases}$$

A higher P value indicates a better selection approach. The P values of all queries were calculated by comparing the top four manually ranked databases with the top four databases ranked by the selection approach (that is, $n = m = 4$). We assumed the manual ranking represents the achievable ideal ranking. Measuring the similarity between each given query to all database images helped us determine each database site's manual rank. For the subqueries, databases with at least 10 images that had a similarity ≥ 0.85 with respect to the given subquery were considered relevant to the subquery. For the query, databases with at least 10 images that had a similarity ≥ 0.80 with respect to both texture and color subqueries of the given query were relevant to the query. The system then ranked all relevant databases based on the number of highly similar images.

We used the top four ranked databases for the experiments as the top four relevant databases. All 35 queries in the experiments had at least one relevant database. Users weren't asked to determine the databases' rank because user judgments often prove subjective, and illustrative experimental results often cannot be generated based on such individual judgments. We measured the performance for each query at three levels of precision: 0.75, 0.50, and 0.25, representing high, medium, and low precision, respectively. Table 2 summarizes the experimental results, without query refinement, which shows the average P values as a function of the number of matched templates.

The relatively high selection precision (0.72) demonstrates the system's effectiveness in selecting relevant databases with respect to a query. Among the four selected databases, about three proved relevant to the given query. The system offers similar performance for queries matched with a single texture and color templates as well as queries matched with multiple texture and color templates. We observed that when the similarity between the query and the templates becomes low (generally below 0.6), the templates no longer provide a sound basis for the estimation. For a more detailed report on the experimental results, see Chang et al.[21]

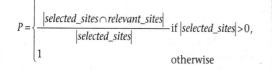

Table 2. Selection precision as a function of the number of matched templates.

| Number of Templates | | Similarity Ranges | | | Average |
Texture	Color	[0.80, 1.00]	[0.70, 0.79]	[0.60, 0.69]	Precision
1	1	0.75	0.83	0.58	0.73
1	2 or 3	0.75	0.75	0.50	
2 or 3	1	0.83	0.75	0.63	0.72
2 or 3	2 or 3	1.00	0.50	0.75	
Average Precision		0.78	0.73	0.60	0.72

Search efficiency

Search ratio S measures the query search efficiency that resulted from the database selection. Given a query, let $|DB_s|_{image}$ be the total number of images of the database sites selected by the selection approach in response to the query. Let $|DB|_{image}$ be the total number of images of all registered databases. We calculated the database search ratio as

$$S = \frac{|DB_s|_{image}}{|DB|_{image}}$$

We calculated the S values of all queries by comparing the total number of images included in the top four selected databases with the total number of images of all nine databases. A lower S value indicates that the system needs to search for fewer images with respect to the query, thus achieving more efficient image retrieval. In our experiments, the average S value of all 35 queries was 0.39. Thus, the image retrieval's overall efficiency significantly improved from searching against all 8,722 images to searching an average of 3,401 images for a given query. A low search ratio combined with a high selection precision shows how well our system performs.

Refinement

We chose the nine queries that had the lowest selection precision and applied the refinement process. The average selection precision of the queries before refinement was 0.47. We compared the selected databases returned by the refinement process to the results of the initial selection performed using the original query. Note that both the initial and refinement selections were conducted against all databases. The changes in precision helped us evaluate the refinement process' effect. For each query, the top five retrieved images returned by the top four selected databases (total of 20 images) were inspected and designated as relevant or irrelevant. In determining an image's relevancy, we used similarity measures instead of user judgments to achieve consistent results. Images that had a similarity greater than or equal to 0.80 with respect to both texture and color subqueries of the given query were considered relevant to the query—the rest of the images were considered irrelevant. The thresholds α, β, and γ were set to 0.5, 1.0, and 0.5, respectively. After the refinement, the average selection precision of the nine queries reached 0.58, a significant improvement with respect to the selection precision of 0.47 before the refinement. The result demonstrates that relevance feedback represents a powerful process for improving the retrieval system's output.

Discussion

We determined the retrieval system's robustness (whether or not all and only the relevant images for the query are retrieved) by the accuracy of the extracted features, similarity measures, and selected templates. Specifically, the site selection approach's effectiveness relies on the following factors:

■ The feature extraction algorithms can generate feature vectors that lie close to each other in the feature space for similar images.

■ The feature vectors' closeness can be represented by the high degree of similarity between the two vectors. In addition, a good similarity measurement should be consistent with human perception.

■ Templates can represent a database's content adequately. Thus, the sample images submitted by the visual databases for template configuration must adequately represent the underlying images included in the database.

Our proposed system generates reasonable texture and color feature vectors, and clusters the feature vectors using a hierarchical approach. We demonstrated the similarity measure's effectiveness in capturing visual similarity to templates by showing the existence of different similarity ranges for distinct clusters as shown in Figure 8. In our experiments, more than 85 percent of the 8,722 database images were matched to a single template with a high degree of similarity (≥ 0.80). This shows that the templates represent the majority of the database images adequately.

Future work

We developed the system framework NetView to support global visual query access to various visual databases over the Internet. This framework includes the creation of a metaserver and its major components: the metadatabase, the metasearch agent, and the query manager. We're currently using and testing our proposed framework at the Computer Science Department at the State University of New York at Buffalo. We're conducting further research to improve the system's performance and functionality by exploring new clustering approaches and supporting additional visual features such as shape. **MM**

Acknowledgments

We'd like to thank Deepak Murthy for his participation in designing the prototype for the NetView system.

References

1. C. Lagoze and J. Davis, "Dienst: An Architecture for Distributed Document Libraries," *Comm. ACM*, Vol. 38, No. 4, April 1995, p. 47.

2. L. Gavarno, H. Garcia-Molina, and A. Tomasic, "The Effectiveness of Gloss for the Text Database Discovery Problems," *Proc. ACM Sigmod 94*, ACM Press, New York, May 1994, pp. 126-137.

3. P. Deutsch et al., *Architecture of the WhoIs++ Service*, IETF RFC-1835, Aug. 1995, http://www.bunyip.com/research/papers/papers.html.

4. M. Bowman et al., *Harvest: A Scalable, Customizable Discovery and Access System*, Tech. Report CU-CS732-94, Dept. of Computer Science, University of Colorado, Boulder, Colo., 1994.

5. B. Kahle and A. Medlar, "An Information System for Corporate Users: Wide Area Information Servers," *ConneXions—The Interoperability Report*, Vol. 5, No. 11, Nov. 1991, pp. 2-9.

6. S. Sclaroff, L. Taycher, and M. La Cascia, "ImageRover: A Content-Based Image Browser for the World Wide Web," *Proc. IEEE Int'l Workshop on Content-Based Access of Image and Video Libraries*, IEEE CS Press, Los Alamitos, Calif., 1997, pp. 2-9.

7. J. Smith and S. Chang, "Visually Searching the Web for Content," *IEEE MultiMedia*, Vol. 4, No. 3, July-Sept. 1997, pp. 12-20.

8. S. Chang et al., "Visual Information Retrieval from Large Distributed Online Repositories," *Comm. ACM*, Vol. 40, No. 12, Dec. 1997, pp. 63-71.

9. J. Smith and S. Chang, "VisualSeek: A Fully Automated Content-Based Image Query System," *Proc. ACM Multimedia 96*, ACM Press, New York, 1996, pp. 87-98.

10. M. Flickner et al., "Query by Image and Video Content: The QBIC System," *Computer*, Vol. 28, No. 9, Sept. 1995, pp. 23-32.

11. J.R. Bach et al. "The Virage Image Search Engine: An Open Framework for Image Management," *Proc. SPIE on Storage and Retrieval for Still Image and Video Databases IV*, SPIE Press, Bellingham, Wash., Feb. 1996, pp. 76-87.

12. W. Chang and A. Zhang, "Metadata For Distributed Visual Database Access," *Proc. Second IEEE Metadata Conf.*, IEEE CS Press, Los Alamitos, Calif., Sept. 1997, http://computer.org/conferen/proceed/meta97/.

13. R. Jain and S.N.J. Murthy, "Similarity Measures for Image Databases," *Proc. SPIE Conf. Storage and Retrieval of Image and Video Databases III*, SPIE Press, Bellingham, Wash., 1995, pp. 58-67.

14. Special Issue on Content-Based Image Retrieval Systems, *Computer*, V.N. Gudivada and V. V. Raghavan, eds. Vol. 28, No. 9, 1995.

15. E. Remias et al., "Supporting Content-Based Retrieval in Large Image Database Systems," *The Int'l J. Multimedia Tools and Applications*, Vol. 4, No. 2, March 1997, pp. 153-170.

16. G. Sheikholeslami and A. Zhang, "An Approach to Clustering Large Visual Databases Using Wavelet Transform," *Proc. SPIE Conf. Visual Data Exploration and Analysis IV*, SPIE Press, Bellingham, Wash., Feb. 1997, pp. 322-333.

17. J. Wang, W. Yang, and R. Acharya, "Color Clustering Techniques for Color Content-Based Image Retrieval," *Proc. Fourth IEEE Int'l Conf. Multimedia Computing and Systems (ICMCS 97)*, IEEE CS Press, Los Alamitos, Calif., June 1997, pp. 442-449.

18. W. Wang, J. Yang, and R. Muntz, "Sting: A Statistical Information Grid Approach to Spatial Data Mining," *Proc. 23rd Very Large Data Base (VLDB) Conf.*, Morgan Kaufmann, San Francisco, 1997, pp. 186-195.

19. G. Sheikholeslami, A. Zhang, and L. Bian, "Geographical Data Classification and Retrieval," *Proc. 5th ACM Int'l Workshop on Geographic Information Systems*, ACM Press, New York, Nov. 1997, pp. 58-61.

20. A.D. Gordon, *Classification Methods for the Exploratory Analysis of Multivariate Data*, Chapman and Hall, London, 1981.

21. W. Chang et al., "Efficient Resource Selection in Distributed Visual Information Systems," *Proc. ACM Multimedia 97*, ACM Press, New York, Nov. 1997, pp. 203-213.

22. N. Beckmann et al., "The R*-Tree: An Efficient and Robust Access Method for Points and Rectangles," *Proc. ACM-Sigmod Int'l Conf. Management of Data*, ACM Press, New York, May 1990, pp. 322-331.

23. J. Rocchio, "Relevance Feedback in Information Retrieval," *The Smart System—Experiments in Automatic Document Processing*, Prentice Hall, Englewood Cliffs, N.J., 1971, pp. 313-323.

Aidong Zhang is an assistant professor in the Department of Computer Science at State University of New York at Buffalo. Her current research interests include transaction and workflow management, distributed database systems, multimedia database systems, educational digital libraries, and content-based image retrieval. She received a PhD in computer science from Purdue University, West Layfayette, Indiana, in 1994. She is an editor of the *International Journal of Multimedia Tools and Applications* and received the National Science Foundation Career award.

Wendy Chang is an assistant professor in the Department of Computer Engineering at the Rochester Institute of Technology, Rochester, New York. Her research interests include multimedia databases, information retrieval, distributed computing, and software engineering. She earned a PhD in electrical engineering from the State University of New York at Buffalo in 1998.

Gholamhosein Sheikholeslami is currently working toward a PhD in computer science at the State University of New York at Buffalo. He received a BS in computer science from Tehran University, Iran in 1989. He received an MS in computer science and an MS in electrical and computer engineering from the State University of New York at Buffalo in 1995 and 1996, respectively. His research interests include multimedia database systems, content-based image retrieval, data mining, and visual database clustering and indexing.

Tanveer Syeda-Mahmood is a member of the research staff at the Xerox Webster Research Center, Webster, New York, and is leading a program in image indexing of image databases. Her research interests are in computer vision and image databases. She earned her PhD in computer science from the Massachusetts Institute of Technology Artificial Intelligence Lab in 1993.

Contact Zhang at the Dept. of Computer Science, State University of New York at Buffalo, 226 Bell Hall, Buffalo, NY 14260-2000, e-mail azhang@cs.buffalo.edu.

The X-tree:
An Index Structure for High-Dimensional Data

Stefan Berchtold

Daniel A. Keim

Hans-Peter Kriegel

Institute for Computer Science, University of Munich, Oettingenstr. 67, D-80538 Munich, Germany
{berchtol, keim, kriegel}@informatik.uni-muenchen.de

Abstract

In this paper, we propose a new method for indexing large amounts of point and spatial data in high-dimensional space. An analysis shows that index structures such as the R*-tree are not adequate for indexing high-dimensional data sets. The major problem of R-tree-based index structures is the overlap of the bounding boxes in the directory, which increases with growing dimension. To avoid this problem, we introduce a new organization of the directory which uses a split algorithm minimizing overlap and additionally utilizes the concept of supernodes. The basic idea of overlap-minimizing split and supernodes is to keep the directory as hierarchical as possible, and at the same time to avoid splits in the directory that would result in high overlap. Our experiments show that for high-dimensional data, the X-tree outperforms the well-known R*-tree and the TV-tree by up to two orders of magnitude.

1. Introduction

In many applications, indexing of high-dimensional data has become increasingly important. In multimedia databases, for example, the multimedia objects are usually mapped to feature vectors in some high-dimensional space and queries are processed against a database of those feature vectors [Fal 94]. Similar approaches are taken in many other areas including CAD [MG 93], molecular biology (for the docking of molecules) [SBK 92], string matching and se

Proceedings ot the 22nd VLDB Conference
Mumbai (Bombay), India, 1996

quence alignment [AGMM 90], etc. Examples of feature vectors are color histograms [SH 94], shape descriptors [Jag 91, MG 95], Fourier vectors [WW 80], text descriptors [Kuk 92], etc. In some applications, the mapping process does not yield point objects, but extended spatial objects in high-dimensional space [MN 95]. In many of the mentioned applications, the databases are very large and consist of millions of data objects with several tens to a few hundreds of dimensions. For querying these databases, it is essential to use appropriate indexing techniques which provide an efficient access to high-dimensional data. The goal of this paper is to demonstrate the limits of currently available index structures, and present a new index structure which considerably improves the performance in indexing high-dimensional data.

Our approach is motivated by an examination of R-tree-based index structures. One major reason for using R-tree-based index structures is that we have to index not only point data but also extended spatial data, and R-tree-based index structures are well suited for both types of data. In contrast to most other index structures (such as kdB-trees [Rob 81], grid files [NHS 84], and their variants [see e.g. SK 90]), R-tree-based index structures do not need point transformations to store spatial data and therefore provide a better spatial clustering.

Some previous work on indexing high-dimensional data has been done, mainly focussing on two different approaches. The first approach is based on the observation that real data in high-dimensional space are highly correlated and clustered, and therefore the data occupy only some subspace of the high-dimensional space. Algorithms such as Fastmap [FL 95], multidimensional scaling [KW 78], principal component analysis [DE 82], and factor analysis [Har 67] take advantage of this fact and transform data objects into some lower dimensional space which can be efficiently indexed using traditional multidimensional index structures. A similar approach is proposed in the SS-tree [WJ 96] which is an R-tree-based index structure. The SS-tree uses ellipsoid bounding regions in a lower dimensional space applying a different transformation in each of the directory nodes. The second approach is based on the observation that in most high-dimensional data sets, a small number of the dimensions bears most of the information. The TV-tree [LJF 94], for example, organizes the directory in a way that only the information needed to distinguish between data objects is stored in the directory. This leads to a higher fanout and a smaller directory, resulting in a better query performance.

For high-dimensional data sets, reducing the dimensionality is an obvious and important possibility for diminishing the dimensionality problem and should be performed whenever possible. In many cases, the data sets resulting from reducing the dimensionality will still have a quite large dimensionality. The remaining dimensions are all relatively important which means that any efficient indexing method must guarantee a good selectivity on all those dimensions. Unfortunately, as we will see in section 2, currently available index structures for spatial data such as the R*-tree[1] do not adequately support an effective indexing of more than five dimensions. Our experiments show that the performance of the R*-tree is rapidly deteriorating when going to higher dimensions. To understand the reason for the performance problems, we carry out a detailed evaluation of the overlap of the bounding boxes in the directory of the R*-tree. Our experiments show that the overlap of the bounding boxes in the directory is rapidly increasing to about 90% when increasing the dimensionality to 5. In subsection 3.3, we provide a detailed explanation of the increasing overlap and show that the high overlap is not an R-tree specific problem, but a general problem in indexing high-dimensional data.

Based on our observations, we then develop an improved index structure for high-dimensional data, the X-tree (cf. section 3). The main idea of the X-tree is to avoid overlap of bounding boxes in the directory by using a new organization of the directory which is optimized for high-dimensional space. The X-tree avoids splits which would result in a high degree of overlap in the directory. Instead of allowing splits that introduce high overlaps, directory nodes are extended over the usual block size, resulting in so-called supernodes. The supernodes may become large and the linear scan of the large supernodes might seem to be a problem. The alternative, however, would be to introduce high overlap in the directory which leads to a fast degeneration of the filtering selectivity and also makes a sequential search of all subnodes necessary with the additional penalty of many random page accesses instead of a much faster sequential read. The concept of supernodes has some similarity to the idea of oversize shelves [GN 91]. In contrast to supernodes, oversize shelves are data nodes which are attached to internal nodes in order to avoid excessive clipping of large objects. Additionally, oversize shelves are organized as chains of disk pages which cannot be read sequentially.

We implemented the X-tree index structure and performed a detailed performance evaluation using very large

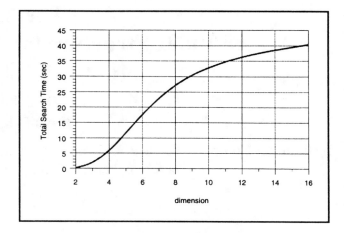

Figure 1: Performance of the R-tree Depending on the Dimension (Real Data)

amounts (up to 100 MBytes) of randomly generated as well as real data (point data and extended spatial data). Our experiments show that on high-dimensional data, the X-tree outperforms the TV-tree and the R*-tree by orders of magnitude (cf. section 4). For dimensionality larger than 2, the X-tree is up to 450 times faster than the R*-tree and between 4 and 12 times faster than the TV-tree. The X-tree also provides much faster insertion times (about 8 times faster than the R*-tree and about 30 times faster than the TV-tree).

2. Problems of (R-tree-based) Index Structures in High-Dimensional Space

In our performance evaluation of the R*-tree, we found that the performance deteriorates rapidly when going to higher dimensions (cf. Figure 1). Effects such as a lower fanout in higher dimensions do not explain this fact. In trying to understand the effects that lead to the performance problems, we performed a detailed evaluation of important characteristics of the R*-tree and found that the overlap in the directory is increasing very rapidly with growing dimensionality of the data. Overlap in the directory directly corresponds to the query performance since even for simple point queries multiple paths have to be followed. Overlap in the directory is a relatively imprecise term and there is no generally accepted definition especially for the high-dimensional case. In the following, we therefore provide definitions of overlap.

2.1 Definition of Overlap

Intuitively, overlap is the percentage of the volume that is covered by more than one directory hyperrectangle. This intuitive definition of overlap is directly correlated to the query performance since in processing queries, overlap of directory nodes results in the necessity to follow multiple paths, even for point queries.

---

1.   According to [BKSS 90], the R*-tree provides a consistently better performance than the R-tree [Gut 84] and R$^+$-tree [SRF 87] over a wide range of data sets and query types. In the rest of this paper, we therefore restrict ourselves to the R*-tree.

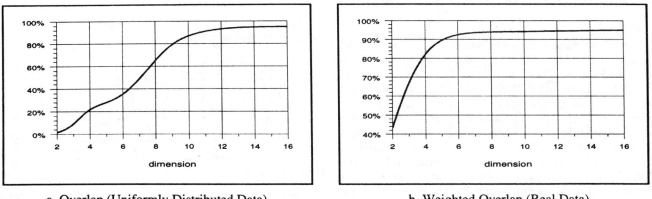

a. Overlap (Uniformly Distributed Data)   b. Weighted Overlap (Real Data)

Figure 2: Overlap of R*-tree Directory Nodes depending on the Dimensionality

Definition 1a (Overlap)

The overlap of an R-tree node is the percentage of space covered by more than one hyperrectangle. If the R-tree node contains n hyperrectangles $\{R_1, ... R_n\}$, the overlap may formally be defined as

$$Overlap = \frac{\left\| \bigcup_{i,j \in \{1...n\}, i \neq j} (R_i \cap R_j) \right\|}{\left\| \bigcup_{i \in \{1...n\}} R_i \right\|} . 1$$

The amount of overlap measured in definition 1a is related to the expected query performance only if the query objects (points, hyperrectangles) are distributed uniformly. A more accurate definition of overlap needs to take the actual distribution of queries into account. Since it is impossible to determine the distribution of queries in advance, in the following we will use the distribution of the data as an estimation for the query distribution. This seems to be reasonable for high-dimensional data since data and queries are often clustered in some areas, whereas other areas are virtually empty. Overlap in highly populated areas is much more critical than overlap in areas with a low population. In our second definition of overlap, the overlapping areas are therefore weighted with the number of data objects that are located in the area.

Definition 1b (Weighted Overlap)

The weighted overlap of an R-tree node is the percentage of data objects that fall in the overlapping portion of the space. More formally,

$$WeightedOverlap = \frac{\left| \left\{ p \mid p \in \bigcup_{i,j \in \{1...n\}, i \neq j} (R_i \cap R_j) \right\} \right|}{\left| \left\{ p \mid p \in \bigcup_{i \in \{1...n\}} R_i \right\} \right|} . 2$$

In definition 1a, overlap occurring at any point of space equally contributes to the overall overlap even if only few data objects fall within the overlapping area. If the query points are expected to be uniformly distributed over the data space, definition 1a is an appropriate measure which determines the expected query performance. If the distribution of queries corresponds to the distribution of the data and is non-uniform, definition 1b corresponds to the expected query performance and is therefore more appropriate. Depending on the query distribution, we have to choose the appropriate definition.

So far, we have only considered overlap to be any portion of space that is covered by more than *one* hyperrectangle. In practice however, it is very important how many hyperrectangles overlap at a certain portion of the space. The so-called multi-overlap of an R-tree node is defined as the sum of overlapping volumes multiplied by the number of overlapping hyperrectangles relative to the overall volume of the considered space.

In Figure 3, we show a two-dimensional example of the overlap according to definition 1a and the corresponding multi-overlap. The weighted overlap and weighted multi-overlap (not shown in the figure) would correspond to the areas weighted by the number of data objects that fall within the areas.

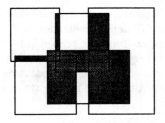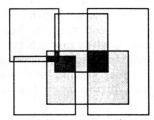

Figure 3: Overlap and Multi-Overlap of 2-dimensional data

---

1. $\|A\|$ denotes the volume covered by A.
2. $|A|$ denotes the number of data elements contained in A

2.2 Experimental Evaluation of Overlap in R*-tree Directories

In this subsection, we empirically evaluate the development of the overlap in the R*-tree depending on the dimensionality. For the experiments, we use the implementation of the R*-tree according to [BKSS 90]. The data used for the experiments are constant size databases of uniformly distributed and real data. The real data are Fourier vectors which are used in searching for similarly shaped polygons. The overlap curves presented in Figure 2 show the average overlap of directory nodes according to definition 1. In averaging the node overlaps, we used all directory levels except the root level since the root page may only contain a few hyperrectangles, which causes a high variance of the overlap in the root node.

In Figure 2a, we present the overlap curves of R*-trees generated from 6 MBytes of uniformly distributed point data. As expected, for a uniform distribution overlap and weighted overlap (definition 1a and 1b) provide the same results. For dimensionality larger than two, the overlap (cf. Figure 2a) increases rapidly to approach 100% for dimensionality larger than ten. This means that even for point queries on ten or higher dimensional data in almost every directory node at least two subnodes have to be accessed. For real data (cf. Figure 2b), the increase of the overlap is even more remarkable. The weighted overlap increases to about 80% for dimensionality 4 and approaches 100% for dimensionality larger than 6.

3. The *X-tree*

The X-tree (eXtended node tree) is a new index structure supporting efficient query processing of high-dimensional data. The goal is to support not only point data but also extended spatial data and therefore, the X-tree uses the concept of overlapping regions. From the insight obtained in the previous section, it is clear that we have to avoid overlap in the directory in order to improve the indexing of high-dimensional data. The X-tree therefore avoids overlap whenever it is possible without allowing the tree to degenerate; otherwise, the X-tree uses extended variable size directory nodes, so-called supernodes. In addition to providing a directory organization which is suitable for high-dimensional data, the X-tree uses the available main memory more efficiently (in comparison to using a cache).

The X-tree may be seen as a hybrid of a linear array-like and a hierarchical R-tree-like directory. It is well established that in low dimensions the most efficient organization of the directory is a hierarchical organization. The reason is that the selectivity in the directory is very high which means that, e.g. for point queries, the number of required page accesses directly corresponds to the height of the tree. This, however,

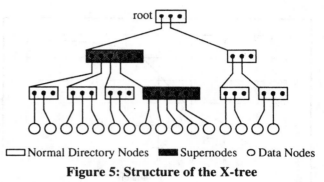

☐ Normal Directory Nodes ■ Supernodes ○ Data Nodes

Figure 5: Structure of the X-tree

is only true if there is no overlap between directory rectangles which is the case for a low dimensionality. It is also reasonable, that for very high dimensionality a linear organization of the directory is more efficient. The reason is that due to the high overlap, most of the directory if not the whole directory has to be searched anyway. If the whole directory has to be searched, a linearly organized directory needs less space[1] and may be read much faster from disk than a block-wise reading of the directory. For medium dimensionality, an efficient organization of the directory would probably be partially hierarchical and partially linear. The problem is to dynamically organize the tree such that portions of the data which would produce high overlap are organized linearly and those which can be organized hierarchically without too much overlap are dynamically organized in a hierarchical form. The algorithms used in the X-tree are designed to automatically organize the directory as hierarchical as possible, resulting in a very efficient hybrid organization of the directory.

3.1 Structure of the *X-tree*

The overall structure of the X-tree is presented in Figure 5. The data nodes of the X-tree contain rectilinear minimum bounding rectangles (MBRs) together with pointers to the actual data objects, and the directory nodes contain MBRs together with pointers to sub-MBRs (cf. Figure 5). The X-tree consists of three different types of nodes: data nodes, normal directory nodes, and supernodes. Supernodes are large directory nodes of variable size (a multiple of the usual block size). The basic goal of supernodes is to avoid splits in the directory that would result in an inefficient directory structure. The alternative to using larger node sizes are highly overlapping directory nodes which would require to access most of the son nodes during the search process. This, however, is more inefficient than linearly scanning the larger supernode. Note that the X-tree is completely different from an R-tree with a larger block size since the X-tree only consists of larger nodes where actually necessary. As a result, the structure of the X-tree may be rather heterogeneous as indicated in Figure 5. Due to the fact that the overlap is in-

| MBR$_0$ | SplitHistory$_0$ | Ptr$_0$ | | | | MBR$_{n-1}$ | SplitHistory$_{n-1}$ | Ptr$_{n-1}$ |

Figure 4: Structure of a Directory Node

---

1. In comparison to a hierarchically organized directory, a linearly organized directory only consists of the concatenation of the nodes on the lowest level of the corresponding hierarchical directory and is therefore much smaller.

creasing with the dimension, the internal structure of the X-tree is also changing with increasing dimension. In Figure 5, three examples of X-trees containing data of different dimensionality are shown. As expected, the number and size of supernodes increases with the dimension. For generating the examples, the block size has been artificially reduced to obtain a drawable fanout. Due to the increasing number and size of supernodes, the height of the X-tree which corresponds to the number of page accesses necessary for point queries is decreasing with increasing dimension.

Supernodes are created during insertion only if there is no other possibility to avoid overlap. In many cases, the creation or extension of supernodes may be avoided by choosing an overlap-minimal split axis (cf. subsection 3.3). For a fast determination of the overlap-minimal split, additional information is necessary which is stored in each of the directory nodes (cf. Figure 4). If enough main memory is available, supernodes are kept in main memory. Otherwise, the nodes which have to be replaced are determined by a priority function which depends on level, type (normal node or supernode), and size of the nodes. According to our experience, the priority function $c_t \cdot type + c_l \cdot level + c_s \cdot size$ with $c_t \gg c_l \gg c_s$ is a good choice for practical purposes. Note that the storage utilization of supernodes is higher than the storage utilization of normal directory nodes. For normal directory nodes, the expected storage utilization for uniformly distributed data is about 66%. For supernodes of size $m \cdot BlockSize$, the expected storage utilization can be determined as the average of the following two extreme cases: Assuming a certain amount of data occupies $X \cdot m$ blocks for a maximally filled node. Then the same amount of data requires $X \cdot \dfrac{m^2}{m-1}$ blocks when using a minimally filled node. On the average, a supernode storing the same amount of data requires $\left(X \cdot m + X \cdot \dfrac{m^2}{m-1}\right)/2 = X\left(\dfrac{m(2m-1)}{2m-2}\right)$ blocks. From that, we obtain a storage utilization of $m / \left(\dfrac{m(2m-1)}{2m-2}\right) = \dfrac{2 \cdot m - 2}{2 \cdot m - 1}$ which for large m is considerably higher than 66%. For $m=5$, for example, the storage utilization is about 88%.

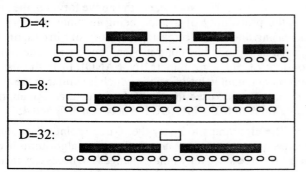

Figure 6: Various Shapes of the X-tree in different dimensions

There are two interesting special cases of the X-tree: (1) none of the directory nodes is a supernode and (2) the directory consists of only one large supernode (root). In the first case, the X-tree has a completely hierarchical organization of the directory and is therefore similar to an R-tree. This case may occur for low dimensional and non-overlapping data. In the second case, the directory of the X-tree is basically one root-supernode which contains the lowest directory level of the corresponding R-tree. The performance therefore corresponds to the performance of a linear directory scan. This case will only occur for high-dimensional or highly overlapping data where the directory would have to be completely searched anyway. The two cases also correspond to the two extremes for the height of the tree and the directory size. In case of a completely hierarchical organization, the height and size of the directory basically correspond to that of an R-tree. In the root-supernode case, the size of the directory linearly depends on the dimension

$$DirSize(D) = \frac{DatabaseSize}{BlockSize \cdot StorageUtil.} \cdot 2 \cdot BytesFloat \cdot D$$

For 1 GBytes of 16-dimensional data, a block size of 4 KBytes, a storage utilization of 66% for data nodes, and 4 bytes per float, the size of the directory is about 44 MBytes for the root-supernode in contrast to about 72 MBytes for the completely hierarchical directory.

3.2 Algorithms

The most important algorithm of the X-tree is the insertion algorithm. The insertion algorithm determines the structure of the X-tree which is a suitable combination of a hierarchical and a linear structure. The main objective of the algorithm is to avoid splits which would produce overlap. The algorithm (cf. Figure 7) first determines the MBR in which to insert the data object and recursively calls the insertion algorithm to actually insert the data object into the corresponding node. If no split occurs in the recursive insert, only the size of the corresponding MBRs has to be updated. In case of a split of the subnode, however, an additional MBR has to be added to the current node which might cause an overflow of the node. In this case, the current node calls the split algorithm (cf. Figure 8) which first tries to find a split of the node based on the topological and geometric properties of the MBRs. Topological and geometric properties of the MBRs are for example dead-space partitioning, extension of MBRs, etc. The heuristics of the R*-tree [BKSS 90] split algorithm are an example for a topological split to be used in this step. If the topological split however results in high overlap, the split algorithm tries next to find an overlap-minimal split which can be determined based on the split history (cf. subsection 3.3). In subsection 3.3, we show that for point data there always exists an overlap-free split. The partitioning of the MBRs resulting from the overlap-minimal split, however, may result in underfilled nodes which is unacceptable since it leads to a degeneration of the tree and also deteriorates the space utilization. If the number of MBRs in one of the partitions is below a given threshold, the split algorithm terminates without providing a split. In

```
int X_DirectoryNode::insert(DataObject obj, X_Node **new_node)
{
    SET_OF_MBR *s1, *s2;
    X_Node *follow, *new_son;
    int return_value;

    follow = choose_subtree(obj);       // choose a son node to insert obj into
    return_value = follow->insert(obj, &new_son); // insert obj into subtree
    update_mbr(follow->calc_mbr());     // update MBR of old son node

    if (return_value == SPLIT){
        add_mbr(new_son->calc_mbr());   // insert mbr of new son node into current node

        if (num_of_mbrs() > CAPACITY){  // overflow occurs
            if (split(mbrs, s1, s2) == TRUE){
                // topological or overlap-minimal split was successfull
                set_mbrs(s1);
                *new_node = new X_DirectoryNode(s2);

                return SPLIT;
            }
            else // there is no good split
            {
                *new_node = new X_SuperNode();
                (*new_node)->set_mbrs(mbrs);

                return SUPERNODE;
            }
        }
    } else if (return_value == SUPERNODE){ // node 'follow' becomes a supernode
        remove_son(follow);
        insert_son(new_son);
    }

    return NO_SPLIT;
}
```

Figure 7: X-tree Insertion Algorithm for Directory Nodes

this case, the current node is extended to become a supernode of twice the standard block size. If the same case occurs for an already existing supernode, the supernode is extended by one additional block. Obviously, supernodes are only created or extended if there is no possibility to find a suitable hierarchical structure of the directory. If a supernode is created or extended, there may be not enough contiguous space on disk to sequentially store the supernode. In this case, the disk manager has to perform a local reorganization. Since supernodes are created or extended in main memory, the local reorganization is only necessary when writing back the supernodes on secondary storage which does not occur frequently.

For point data, overlap in the X-tree directory may only occur if the overlap induced by the topological split is below a threshold overlap value (MAX_OVERLAP). In that case, the overlap-minimal split and the possible creation of a supernode do not make sense. The maximum overlap value which is acceptable is basically a system constant and depends on the page access time (T_{IO}), the time to transfer a block from disk into main memory (T_{Tr}), and the CPU time necessary to process a block (T_{CPU}). The maximum overlap value ($MaxO$[1]) may be determined approximately by the balance between reading a supernode of size 2*BlockSize

and reading 2 blocks with a probability of MaxO and one block with a probability of (1-MaxO). This estimation is only correct for the most simple case of initially creating a supernode. It does not take the effect of further splits into account. Nevertheless, for practical purposes the following equation provides a good estimation:

$$MaxO \cdot 2 \cdot (T_{IO} + T_{Tr} + T_{CPU}) + (1 - MaxO) \cdot (T_{IO} + T_{Tr} + T_{CPU})$$
$$= T_{IO} + 2 \cdot (T_{Tr} + T_{CPU})$$
$$\Rightarrow \quad MaxO = \frac{T_{Tr} + T_{CPU}}{T_{IO} + T_{Tr} + T_{CPU}}$$

For realistic system values measured in our experiments (T_{IO} = 20 ms, T_{Tr} = 4 ms, T_{CPU} = 1 ms), the resulting $MaxO$ value is 20%. Note that in the above formula, the fact that the probability of a node being in main memory is increasing due to the decreasing directory size in case of using the supernode has not yet been considered. The other constant of our algorithm (MIN_FANOUT) is the usual minimum fanout value of a node which is similar to the corresponding value used in other index structures. An appropriate value of MIN_FANOUT is between 35% and 45%.

The algorithms to query the X-tree (point, range, and nearest neighbor queries) are similar to the algorithms used in the R*-tree since only minor changes are necessary in accessing supernodes. The delete and update operations are also simple modifications of the corresponding R*-tree algorithms. The only difference occurs in case of an under-

---

1.   *MaxO* is the probability that we have to access both son nodes because of overlap during the search.

```
bool X_DirectoryNode::split(SET_OF_MBR *in, SET_OF_MBR *out1, SET_OF_MBR *out2)
{
    SET_OF_MBR t1, t2;
    MBR r1, r2;

    // first try topological split, resulting in two sets of MBRs t1 and t2
    topological_split(in, t1, t2);
    r1 = t1->calc_mbr(); r2 = t2->calc_mbr();

    // test for overlap
    if (overlap(r1, r2) > MAX_OVERLAP)
    {
        // topological split fails -> try overlap minimal split
        overlap_minimal_split(in, t1, t2);

        // test for unbalanced nodes
        if (t1->num_of_mbrs() < MIN_FANOUT || t2->num_of_mbrs() < MIN_FANOUT)
            // overlap-minimal split also fails (-> caller has to create supernode)
            return FALSE;
    }

    *out1 = t1; *out2 = t2;
    return TRUE;
}
```

Figure 8: X-tree Split Algorithm for Directory Nodes

flow of a supernode. If the supernode consists of two blocks, it is converted to a normal directory node. Otherwise, that is if the supernode consists of more than two blocks, we reduce the size of the supernode by one block. The update operation can be seen as a combination of a delete and an insert operation and is therefore straightforward.

3.3 Determining the Overlap-Minimal Split

For determining an overlap-minimal split of a directory node, we have to find a partitioning of the MBRs in the node into two subsets such that the overlap of the minimum bounding hyperrectangles of the two sets is minimal. In case of point data, it is always possible to find an overlap-free split, but in general it is not possible to guarantee that the two sets are balanced, i.e. have about the same cardinality.

Definition 2 (Split)

The split of a node $S = \{mbr_1, ..., mbr_n\}$ into two subnodes $S_1 = \left\{mbr_{i_1}, ..., mbr_{i_{s_1}}\right\}$ and $S_2 = \left\{mbr_{i_1}, ..., mbr_{i_{s_2}}\right\}$ $(S_1 \neq \varnothing$ and $S_2 \neq \varnothing)$ is defined as

$$Split(S) = \{(S_1, S_2) | S = S_1 \cup S_2 \wedge S_1 \cap S_2 = \varnothing \}.$$

The split is called
(1) overlap-minimal iff $\|MBR(S_1) \cap MBR(S_2)\|$ is minimal
(2) overlap-free   iff $\|MBR(S_1) \cap MBR(S_2)\| = 0$
(3) balanced   iff $-\varepsilon \leq |S_1| - |S_2| \leq \varepsilon$.

For obtaining a suitable directory structure, we are interested in overlap-minimal (overlap-free) splits which are balanced. For simplification, in the following we focus on overlap-free splits and assume to have high-dimensional uniformly distributed point data.[1] It is an interesting obser-

vation that an overlap-free split is only possible if there is a dimension according to which all MBRs have been split since otherwise at least one of the MBRs will span the full range of values in that dimension, resulting in some overlap.

Lemma 1

For uniformly distributed point data, an overlap-free split is only possible iff there is a dimension according to which all MBRs in the node have been previously split. More formally,

$$Split(S) \text{ is overlap-free} \Leftrightarrow$$
$$\exists\, d \in \{1, ..., D\} \;\; \forall mbr \in S:$$
$$mbr \text{ has been split according to } d$$

Proof (by contradiction):

" $\Rightarrow$ ": Assume that for all dimensions there is at least one MBR which has not been split in that dimension. This means for uniformly distributed data that the MBRs span the full range of values of the corresponding dimensions. Without loss of generality, we assume that the *mbr* which spans the full range of values of dimension d is assigned to S_1. As a consequence, $MBR(S_1)$ spans the full range for dimension d. Since the extension of $MBR(S_2)$ cannot be zero in dimension d, a split using dimension d as split axis cannot be overlap-free (i.e., $MBR(S_1) \cap MBR(S_2) \neq 0$). Since for all dimensions there is at least one MBR which has not been split in that dimension, we cannot find an overlap-free split.

" $\Leftarrow$ ": Assume that an overlap-free split of the node is not possible. This means that there is no dimension which can be used to partition the MBRs into two subsets S_1 and S_2. This however is in contradiction to the fact that there is a dimension d for which all MBRs have been split. For uniform-

---

1. According to our experiments, the results generalize to real data and even to spatial data (cf. section 4).

split tree

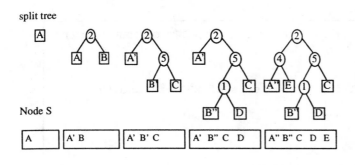

Node S

A	A' B	A' B' C	A' B" C D	A" B" C D E

Figure 9: Example for the Split History

ly distributed point data, the split may be assumed to be in the middle of the range of dimension d and therefore, an overlap-free split is possible using dimension d.[1] ∎

According to Lemma 1, for finding an overlap-free split we have to determine a dimension according to which all MBRs of S have been split previously. The split history provides the necessary information, in particular the dimensions according to which an MBR has been split and which new MBRs have been created by this split. Since a split creates two new MBRs from one, the split history may be represented as a binary tree, called the split tree. Each leaf node of the split tree corresponds to an MBR in S. The internal nodes of the split tree correspond to MBRs which do not exist any more since they have been split into new MBRs previously. Internal nodes of the split tree are labeled by the split axis that has been used; leaf nodes are labeled by the MBR they are related to. All MBRs related to leaves in the left subtree of an internal node have lower values in the split dimension of the node than the MBRs related to those in the right subtree.

Figure 9 shows an example for the split history of a node S and the respective split tree. The process starts with a single MBR A corresponding to a split tree which consists of only one leaf node labeled by A. For uniformly distributed data, A spans the full range of values in all dimensions. The split of A using dimension 2 as split axis produces new MBRs A' and B. Note that A' and B are disjoint because any point in MBR A' has a lower coordinate value in dimension 2 than all points in MBR B. The split tree now has one internal node (marked with dimension 2) and two leaf nodes (A' and B). Splitting MBR B using dimension 5 as split axis creates the nodes B' and C. After splitting B' and A' again, we finally reach the situation depicted in the right most tree of Figure 9 where S is completely filled with the MBRs A", B", C, D and E.

According to Lemma 1, we may find an overlap-free split if there is a dimension according to which all MBRs of S have been split. To obtain the information according to which dimensions an MBR X in S has been split, we only have to traverse the split tree from the root node to the leaf that corresponds to X. For example, MBR C has been split

according to dimension 2 and 5, since the path from the root node to the leaf C is labeled with 2 and 5. Obviously, all MBRs of the split tree in Figure 9 have been split according to dimension 2, the split axis used in the root of the split tree. In general, all MBRs in any split tree have one split dimension in common, namely the split axis used in the root node of the split tree.

***Lemma* 2** (Existence of an Overlap-free Split)
For point data, an overlap-free split always exists.

Proof *(using the split history):*

From the description of the split tree it is clear that all MBRs of a directory node S have one split dimension in common, namely the dimension used as split axis in the root node of the split tree. Let SD be this dimension. We are able to partition S such that all MBRs related to leaves in the left subtree of the root node are contained in S_1 and all other MBRs contained in S_2. Since any point belonging to S_1 has a lower value in dimension SD than all points belonging to S_2, the split is overlap-free[2]. ∎

One may argue that there may exist more than one overlap-free split dimension which is part of the split history of all data pages. This is true in most cases for low dimensionality, but the probability that a second split dimension exists which is part of the split history of all MBRs is decreasing rapidly with increasing dimensionality (cf. Figure 10). If there is no dimension which is in the split history of all MBRs, the resulting overlap of the newly created directory entries is on the average about 50%. This can be explained as follows: Since at least one MBR has not been split in the split dimension d, one of the partitions (without loss of generality: S_1) spans the full range of values in that dimension. The

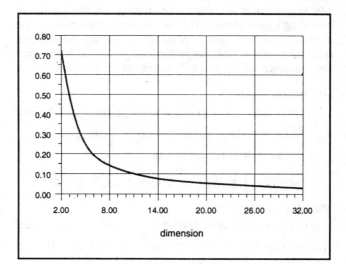

Figure 10: Probability of the Existence of a Second Overlap-free Split Dimension

---

1. If the splits have not been performed exactly in the middle of the data space, at least an overlap-minimal split is obtained.

2. Note that the resulting split is not necessarily balanced since sorted input data, for example, will result in an unbalanced split tree.

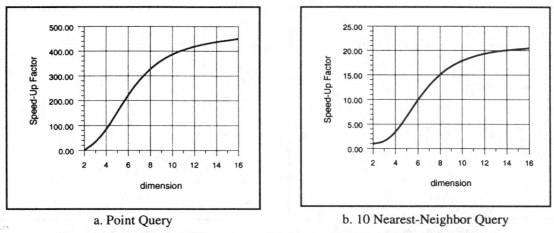

a. Point Query   b. 10 Nearest-Neighbor Query

Figure 11: Speed-Up of X-tree over R*-tree on Real Point Data (70 MBytes)

other partition S_2 spans at least half the range of values of the split dimension d. Since the MBRs are only partitioned with respect to dimension d, S_1 and S_2 span the full range of values of all other dimensions, resulting in a total overlap of about 50%.

The probability that a split algorithm which arbitrarily chooses the split axis coincidentally selects the right split axis for an overlap-free split is very low in high-dimensional space. As our analysis of the R*-tree shows, the behavior of the topological R*-tree split algorithm in high-dimensional space is similar to a random choice of the split axis since it optimizes different criteria. If the topological split fails, our split algorithm tries to perform an overlap-free split. This is done by determining the dimension for the overlap-free split as described above, determining the split value, and partitioning the MBRs with respect to the split value. If the resulting split is unbalanced, the insert algorithm of the X-tree initiates the creation/extension of a supernode (cf. subsection 3.2). Note that for the overlap-minimal split, information about the split history has to be stored in the directory nodes. The space needed for this purpose, however, is very small since the split history may be coded by a few bits.

4. Performance Evaluation

To show the practical relevance of our method, we performed an extensive experimental evaluation of the X-tree and compared it to the TV-tree as well to as the R*-tree. All experimental results presented in this sections are computed on an HP735 workstation with 64 MBytes of main memory and several GBytes of secondary storage. All programs have been implemented in C++ as templates to support different types of data objects. The X-tree and R*-tree support different types of queries such as point queries and nearest neighbor queries; the implementation of the TV-tree[1] only supports point queries. We use the original implementation

of the TV-tree by K. Lin, H. V. Jagadish, and C. Faloutsos [LJF 94].

The test data used for the experiments are real point data consisting of Fourier points in high-dimensional space (D = 2, 4, 8, 16), spatial data (D = 2, 4, 8, 16) consisting of manifolds in high-dimensional space describing regions of real CAD-objects, and synthetic data consisting of uniformly distributed points in high-dimensional space (D = 2, 3, 4, 6, 8, 10, 12, 14, 16). The block size used for our experiments is 4 KByte, and all index structures were allowed to use the same amount of cache. For a realistic evaluation, we used very large amounts of data in our experiments. The total amount of disk space occupied by the created index structures of TV-trees, R*-trees, and X-trees is about 10 GByte and the CPU time for inserting the data adds up to about four weeks of CPU time. As one expects, the insertion times increase with increasing dimension. For all experiments, the insertion into the X-tree was much faster than the insertion into the TV-tree and the R*-tree (up to a factor of 10.45 faster than the R*-tree). The X-tree reached a rate of about 170 insertions per second for a 150 MBytes index containing 16-dimensional point data.

First, we evaluated the X-tree on synthetic databases with varying dimensionality. Using the same number of data items over the different dimensions implies that the size of the database is linearly increasing with the dimension. This however has an important drawback, namely that in low dimensions, we would obtain only very small databases, whereas in high dimensions the databases would become very large. It is more realistic to assume that the amount of data which is stored in the database is constant. This means, however, that the number of data items needs to be varied accordingly. For the experiment presented in Figure 13, we used 100 MByte databases containing uniformly distributed point data. The number of data items varied between 8.3 million for D=2 and 1.5 million for D=16. Figure 13, shows the speed-up of the search time for point queries of the X-tree

---

1   We use the original implementation of the TV-tree by K. Lin, H. V. Jagadish, and C. Faloutsos [LJF 94].

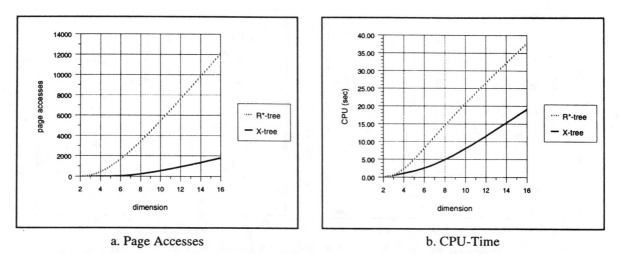

a. Page Accesses   b. CPU-Time

Figure 12: Number of Page Accesses versus CPU-Time on Real Point Data (70 MBytes)

over the R*-tree. As expected, the speed-up increases with growing dimension, reaching values of about 270 for D=16. For lower dimensions, the speed-up is still higher than one order of magnitude (e.g., for D=8 the speed-up is about 30). The high speed-up factors are caused by the fact that, due to the high overlap in high dimensions, the R*-tree needs to access most of the directory pages. The total query time turned out to be clearly dominated by the I/O-time, i.e. the number of page accesses (see also Figure 12).

Since one may argue that synthetic databases with uniformly distributed data are not realistic in high-dimensional space, we also used real data in our experiments. We had access to large Fourier databases of variable dimensionality containing about 70 Mbyte of Fourier data representing shapes of polygons. The results of our experiments (cf. Figure 11) show that the speed-up of the total search time for point queries is even higher (about 90 for D=4 and about

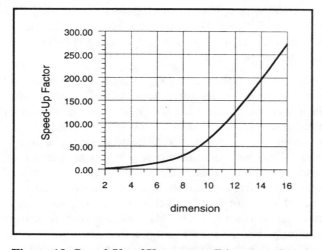

Figure 13: Speed-Up of X-tree over R*-tree on Point Queries (100 MBytes of Synthetic Point Data)

320 for D=8) than the speed-up of uniformly distributed data. This result was surprising but corresponds to the higher overlap of real data found in the overlap curves (cf. Figure 2). Additionally to point queries, in applications with high-dimensional data nearest neighbor queries are also important. We therefore also compared the performance of nearest neighbor queries searching for the 10 nearest neighbors. The nearest neighbor algorithm supported in the X-tree and R*-tree is the algorithm presented in [RKV 95]. The results of our comparisons show that the speed-up for nearest neighbor queries is still between about 10 for D=6 and about 20 for D=16. Since the nearest neighbor algorithm requires sorting the nodes according to the min-max distance, the CPU-time needed for nearest neighbor queries is much higher. In Figure 12, we therefore present the number of page accesses and the CPU-time of the X-tree and the R*-tree for nearest-neighbor queries. The figure shows that the X-tree provides a consistently better performance than the R*-tree. Note that, in counting page accesses, accesses to supernodes of size s are counted as s page accesses. In most practical cases, however, the supernodes will be cached due to the better main memory utilization of the X-tree. For practically relevant buffer sizes (1 MByte to 10 MBytes) there is no significant change of page accesses. For extreme buffer sizes of more than 10 MBytes or less than 1 MByte, the speed-up may decrease. The better CPU-times of the X-tree may be explained by the fact that due to the overlap the R*-tree has to search a large portion of the directory which in addition is larger than the X-tree directory.

Figure 14 shows the total search time of point queries depending on the size of the database (D=16). Note that in this figure we use a logarithmic scale of the y-axis, since otherwise the development of the times for the X-tree would not be visible (identical with the x-axis). Figure 14 shows that the search times of the X-tree are consistently about two orders of magnitude faster than those of the R*-tree

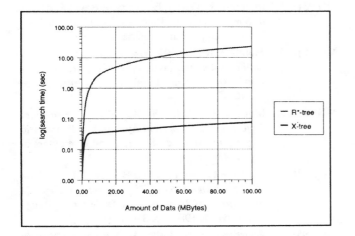

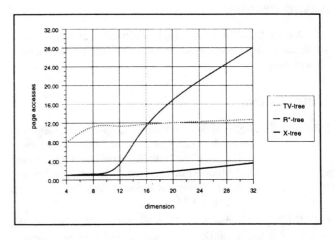

Figure 14: Total Search Time of Point Queries for Varying Database Size (Synthetic Point Data)

Figure 16: Comparison of X-tree, TV-tree, and R*-tree on Synthetic Data

(for D=16). The speed-up slightly increases with the database size from about 100 for 20 MBytes to about 270 for 100 MBytes. Also, as expected, the total search time of the X-tree grows logarithmically with the database size which means that the X-tree scales well to very large database sizes.

We also performed a comparison of the X-tree with the TV-tree and the R*-tree. With the implementation of the TV-tree made available to us by the authors of the TV-tree, we only managed to insert up to 25.000 data items which is slightly higher than the number of data items used in the original paper [LJF 94]. For the comparisons, we were therefore not able to use our large databases. The results of our comparisons are presented in Figure 16. The speed-up of the X-tree over the TV-tree ranges between 4 and 12, even for the rather small databases. It is interesting to note that the

performance of the R*-tree is better than the performance of the TV-tree for D smaller than 16.

In addition to using point data, we also examined the performance of the X-tree for extended data objects in high-dimensional space. The results of our experiments are shown in Figure 15. Since the extended spatial data objects induce some overlap in the X-tree as well, the speed-up of the X-tree over the R*-tree is lower than for point data. Still, we achieve a speed-up factor of about 8 for D=16.

5. Conclusions

In this paper, we propose a new indexing method for high-dimensional data. We investigate the effects that occur in high dimensions and show that R-tree-based index structures do not behave well for indexing high-dimensional spaces. We introduce formal definitions of overlap and show the correlation between overlap in the directory and poor query performance. We then propose a new index structure, the X-tree, which uses - in addition to the concept of supernodes - a new split algorithm minimizing overlap. Supernodes are directory nodes which are extended over the usual block size in order to avoid a degeneration of the index. We carry out an extensive performance evaluation of the X-tree and compare the X-tree with the TV-tree and the R*-tree using up to 100 MBytes of point and spatial data. The experiments show that the X-tree outperforms the TV-tree and R*-tree up to orders of magnitude for point queries and nearest neighbor queries on both synthetic and real data.

Since for very high dimensionality the supernodes may become rather large, we currently work on a parallel version of the X-tree which is expected to provide a good performance even for larger data sets and the more time consuming nearest neighbor queries. We also develop a novel nearest neighbor algorithm for high-dimensional data which is adapted to the X-tree.

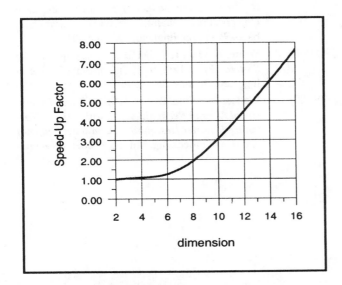

Figure 15: Speed-Up of X-tree over R*-tree on Real Extended Spatial Data

Acknowledgment

We are thankful to K. Lin, C. Faloutsos, and H. V. Jagadish for making the implementation of the TV-tree available to us.

References

[AFS 93] Agrawal R., Faloutsos C., Swami A.: *'Efficient Similarity Search in Sequence Databases'*, Proc. 4th Int. Conf. on Foundations of Data Organization and Algorithms, Evanston, ILL, 1993, in: Lecture Notes in Computer Science, Vol. 730, Springer, 1993, pp. 69-84.

[AGMM 90] Altschul S. F., Gish W., Miller W., Myers E. W., Lipman D. J.: *'A Basic Local Alignment Search Tool'*, Journal of Molecular Biology, Vol. 215, No. 3, 1990, pp. 403-410.

[BKSS 90] Beckmann N., Kriegel H.-P., Schneider R., Seeger B.: *'The R*-tree: An Efficient and Robust Access Method for Points and Rectangles'*, Proc. ACM SIGMOD Int. Conf. on Management of Data, Atlantic City, NJ, 1990, pp. 322-331.

[DE 82] Dunn G., Everitt B.: *'An Introduction to Mathematical Taxonomy'*, Cambridge University Press, Cambridge, MA, 1982.

[Fal 94] Faloutsos C., Barber R., Flickner M., Hafner J., et al.: *'Efficient and Effective Querying by Image Content'*, Journal of Intelligent Information Systems, 1994, Vol. 3, pp. 231-262.

[FL 95] Faloutsos C., Lin K.: *'Fastmap: A fast Algorithm for Indexing, Data-Mining and Visualization of Traditional and Multimedia Datasets'*, Proc. ACM SIGMOD Int. Conf. on Management of Data, San Jose, CA, 1995, pp. 163-174.

[Gut 84] Guttman A.: *'R-trees: A Dynamic Index Structure for Spatial Searching'*, Proc. ACM SIGMOD Int. Conf. on Management of Data, Boston, MA, 1984, pp. 47-57.

[GN 91] Günther O., Noltemeier H.: *'Spatial Database Indices For Large Extended Objects'*, Proc. 7th Int. Conf. on Data Engineering, 1991, pp. 520-527.

[Har 67] Harman H. H.: *'Modern Factor Analysis'*, University of Chicago Press, 1967.

[Jag 91] Jagadish H. V.: *'A Retrieval Technique for Similar Shapes'*, Proc. ACM SIGMOD Int. Conf. on Management of Data, 1991, pp. 208-217.

[Kuk 92] Kukich K.: *'Techniques for Automatically Correcting Words in Text'*, ACM Computing Surveys, Vol. 24, No. 4, 1992, pp. 377-440.

[KW 78] Kruskal J. B., Wish M.: *'Multidimensional Scaling'*, SAGE publications, Beverly Hills, 1978.

[LJF 94] Lin K., Jagadish H. V., Faloutsos C.: *'The TV-tree: An Index Structure for High-Dimensional Data'*, VLDB Journal, Vol. 3, 1995, pp. 517-542.

[MG 93] Mehrotra R., Gary J. E.: *'Feature-Based Retrieval of Similar Shapes'*, Proc. 9th Int. Conf. on Data Engineering, Vienna, Austria, 1993, pp. 108-115.

[MG 95] Mehrotra R., Gary J. E.: *'Feature-Index-Based Similar Shape retrieval'*, Proc. of the 3rd Working Conf. on Visual Database Systems, 1995, pp. 46-65.

[MN 95] Murase H., Nayar S. K: *'Three-Dimensional Object Recognition from Appearance-Parametric Eigenspace Method'*, Systems and Computers in Japan, Vol. 26, No. 8, 1995, pp. 45-54.

[NHS 84] Nievergelt J., Hinterberger H., Sevcik K. C.: *'The Grid File: An Adaptable, Symmetric Multikey File Structure'*, ACM Trans. on Database Systems, Vol. 9, No. 1, 1984, pp. 38-71.

[RKV 95] Roussopoulos N., Kelley S., Vincent F.: *'Nearest Neighbor Queries'*, Proc. ACM SIGMOD Int. Conf. on Management of Data, San Jose, CA, 1995, pp. 71-79.

[Rob 81] Robinson J. T.: *'The K-D-B-tree: A Search Structure for Large Multidimensional Dynamic Indexes'*, Proc. ACM SIGMOD Int. Conf. on Management of Data, 1981, pp. 10-18.

[SBK 92] Shoichet B. K., Bodian D. L., Kuntz I. D.: *'Molecular Docking Using Shape Descriptors'*, Journal of Computational Chemistry, Vol. 13, No. 3, 1992, pp. 380-397.

[SH 94] Shawney H., Hafner J.: *'Efficient Color Histogram Indexing'*, Proc. Int. Conf. on Image Processing, 1994, pp. 66-70.

[SK 90] Seeger B., Kriegel H.-P.: *'The Buddy Tree: An Efficient and Robust Access Method for Spatial Data Base Systems'*, Proc. 16th Int. Conf. on Very Large Data Bases, Brisbane, Australia, 1990, pp. 590-601.

[SRF 87] Sellis T., Roussopoulos N., Faloutsos C.: *'The R+-Tree: A Dynamic Index for Multi-Dimensional Objects'*, Proc. 13th Int. Conf. on Very Large Databases, Brighton, England, 1987, pp 507-518.

[WJ 96] White, D., Jain R.: *'Similarity Indexing with the SS-tree'*, Proc. 12th Int. Conf. on Data Engineering, New Orleans, LA, 1996.

[WW 80] Wallace T., Wintz P.: *'An Efficient Three-Dimensional Aircraft Recognition Algorithm Using Normalized Fourier Descriptors'*, Computer Graphics and Image Processing, Vol. 13, 1980, pp. 99-126.

CHAPTER SEVEN

Multimedia Operating Systems

Klara Nahrstedt

University of Illinois - Urbana-Champaign

MULTIMEDIA computing environments are composed of a variety of hard–real-time, soft–real-time and best effort (non–real-time) applications. In order to support the coexistence of these applications, multimedia computing requires a multimedia operating system framework. The reasons are as follows. In the past, two types of operating systems were used for multimedia applications: the general purpose operating system and the real-time operating system. The general purpose operating system serves non–real-time applications best and optimizes its resource management with respect to the throughput of schedulable units. It provides a fair coexistence among various applications. However, it does not deliver any timing guarantees to real-time applications. This means that multimedia applications running on this type of operating system experience undesirable gaps and large jitters in performance. The real-time operating system serves hard–real-time applications best and optimizes its resource management with respect to timing constraints of schedulable units. It does provide timing guarantees, which is very good for multimedia applications. However, it does not provide good throughput and fairness; hence non–real-time applications can experience starvation.

The analysis of the past existing operating systems shows that a multimedia operating system framework must solve the following problems:

- allow dynamic co-existence and cooperation of multiple independently authored real-time applications with varying timing and resource requirements in order to share the limited physical resources available to them
- allow for co-existence of real-time and non–real-time applications
- allow for scheduling of these different applications
- provide protections between various applications

Multimedia operating systems are currently moving in two basic directions to solve these problems: (1) reservation-based systems, which provide timing guarantees even in overload situations and (2) adaptation-based systems, which provide the best possible timing guarantees, but in case of scarce resources, achieve dynamic re-allocation of resources and deliver graceful degradation for multimedia applications. The reservation-based approach assumes timing constraints specification and admission control to provide and enforce a requested resource allocation, whereas the adaptation-based approach requires only importance information (weight), upon which metric the resource is allocated.

This chapter includes four papers that present innovative solutions for multimedia operating systems. The first two papers, authored by Jones and colleagues and by Rajkumar and others, represent the reservation-based direction. The second two, by Goyal and others and by Nieh and Lam, represent the adaptation direction.

"An overview of the Rialto real-time architecture," by M. B. Jones and colleagues, opens the chapter and discusses Microsoft's Rialto system. The primary focus of this paper is resource self-awareness of applications and scheduling framework utilizing this basic concept. This means that real-time programs, called activities, have mechanisms to allow them to become resource self-aware and negotiate their resource requirements with a per-machine resource planner. Each real-time program specifies timing constraints and requests a reservation from the planner. The resource planner arbitrates between programs requesting reservations and implements user-centric policies that choose which among the competing programs are granted reservations in case of conflicting requests. The CPU scheduling algorithm within Rialto is the *minimum-laxity-first* algorithm with preemption, and it is designed to honor the CPU reservations for activities, meet timing constraints deadlines if possible, provide fair-share scheduling of threads within activities, and prevent starvation of runnable threads. The results of the Rialto kernel, implemented on the x86 platform, show various models of consumer real-time and multimedia computing and the influence of their CPU reservations on the overall performance.

The second paper, "Resource kernels: A resource-centric approach to real-time and multimedia systems," by R. Rajkumar and colleagues, describes a resource management framework called Resource Kernels (RK) for supporting concurrent activities with different timing constraints. A resource kernel is a system entity that provides timely, guaranteed, and protected access to a system resource. The goals of a resource kernel are to allow an application to specify its timing constraints, to enforce maximum resource usage by applications, to support high utilization of system resources, and to allow an application simultaneous access to different system resources. The resource management consists of a set of resource kernels; it is based on resource reservation. The paper presents the processor resource kernel and the disk bandwidth resource kernel. The primary focus of this paper is not so much scheduling algorithms within the resource kernels as resolving the problem of simultaneous access to multiple resources by resource decoupling. The authors show results for the processor and the disk bandwidth reservation schemes separately and together, as well as evaluate their performance on a PC platform.

The third paper, "A hierarchical CPU scheduler for multimedia operating systems," by P. Goyal,

X. Guo and H. M. Vin, presents a hierarchical partitioning algorithm for CPU bandwidth to serve multimedia application classes with different timing requirements. This algorithm proposes support of multiple schedulers such as EDF (earliest deadline first), RM (rate-monotonic), and FIFO (first in first out) as the leaves of the hierarchy, and all these schedulers are coordinated by the start-time fair queuing (SFQ) scheduler, which represents an augmented weighted fair queuing (WFQ) algorithm. SFQ is a resource allocation algorithm that can be used for achieving fair CPU partitioning. SFQ's goals are fair allocation of the CPU regardless of variations in a server capacity, no *a priori* knowledge about the length of the quantum per thread, and bounded maximum delay and minimum throughput. The reader will find a detailed description of the SFQ algorithm, as well as extensive experimental evaluation of the hierarchical scheduler implementation, running on the SUN Sparc 10 platform.

The final paper, "The design, implementation and evaluation of SMART: A scheduler for multimedia applications," by J. Nieh and M. S. Lam, presents the SMART scheduler for support of multimedia applications. SMART's basic concept involves provision of soft–real-time guarantees with dynamic feedback to applications to allow them to adapt to the current load. The SMART scheduler integrates the real-time and non–real-time computations, allows the users to prioritize computations, and hence influences how the processor is to be shared among applications of the same priority. As the system load changes, SMART adjusts the allocation of resources dynamically, which means that it automatically sheds real-time tasks and regulates their execution rates in the overload state while fully utilizing the resources in the under-loaded conditions. The focus of the paper is the scheduling algorithm of SMART, which is based on priorities and weighted fair queuing (WFQ). This scheduling algorithm allows SMART to behave as a real-time scheduler when scheduling only real-time requests, as a conventional scheduler when scheduling only conventional requests, and as a hybrid scheduler in case of real-time and non–real-time requests, which ensures that more important tasks obtain their resource requirements. Results, measured under the Solaris 2.5.1 operating system, show in detail the adaptivity of applications under different load conditions.

In summary, the papers show clearly the trade-offs between the two approaches. Even within the same approach, different properties can be optimized, hence creating different solutions for the multimedia computing environments. Rialto and RK show that the advantage of reservation-based resource management is in timing guarantees of admitted schedulable units under any load conditions. However, disadvantages such as lower resource utilization, inflexible allocation in case of changes in the application behavior, fairness violation, and requirement of knowledge about execution times need to be carefully weighted when considering these solutions.

On the other hand, SMART and the hierarchical scheduler show that the advantage of the adaptation-based resource management is its high resource utilization and fairness. Both the hierarchical scheduler with the SFQ algorithm as well as the SMART scheduler show timing guarantees in underload and normal load situations. In case of overloads it comes to the adaptation choices, where, for example, SMART relies on dynamic feedback and application adaptation. Therefore, we must also consider seriously the disadvantages of this approach, such as the violation of deadlines in case of overloads and dependency on adaptive capabilities of running applications.

ADDITIONAL READINGS

K. Jeffay, D. L. Stone, and F. D. Smith, "Kernel support for live digital audio and video," in *Proceedings of the 2nd International Workshop on Network and Operating System Support for Digital Audio and Video (NOSSDAV 91)* (Nov. 1991): 10–21.

D. P. Anderson, "Meta-scheduling for continuous media" *ACM TOCS* 11, no. 3 (1993): 226–52

J. Nieh, J. G. Hanko, J. D.Northcutt, and G. A. Wall, "SVR4 UNIX scheduler unacceptable for multimedia applications," in *Proceedings of the 4th International Workshop on Network and Operating Systems Support for Digital Audio and Video (NOSSDAV 93)* (Nov. 1993): 35–48

C. W. Mercer, S. Savage, and H. Tokuda, "Processor capacity reserves: Operating system support for multimedia applications," in *Proceedings of the IEEE International Conference on Multimedia Computing and Systems (ICMCS 94)* (Boston: IEEE Computer Society, 1994), 1–10

Ian M. Leslie et al., "The design and implementation of an operating system to support of distributed multimedia applications," *IEEE Journal on Selected Areas in Communications* 14, no. 7 (1996): 1280–97

C. Lee, R. Rajkumar, and C. W. Mercer, "Experiences with processor reservation and dynamic QoS in real-time mach," in *Proceedings of the International Symposium on Multimedia Systems (IPSJ Multimedia Japan 96)* (Yokohama: Information Processing Society of Japan Press, 1996).

M. B. Jones, D. Rosu, and M.-C. Rosu, "CPU reservations and time constraints: Efficient, predictable scheduling of independent activities," in *Proceedings of the 16th ACM Symposium on Operating Systems Principles* (Saint Malo, France: ACM Press, 1997), 198–211.

K. Nahrstedt, H. Chu, and S. Narayan, "QoS-aware resource management for distributed multimedia applications," *Journal on High-Speed Networking* 7, no. 3, 4 (1998): 227–55.

H. H. Chu and K. Nahrstedt, "CPU service classes for multimedia applications," in *Proceedings of the IEEE International Conference on Multimedia Computing and Systems (ICMCS 99)* (Florence: IEEE Computer Society, 1999), 296–301.

An Overview of the Rialto Real-Time Architecture

Michael B. Jones, Joseph S. Barrera III, Alessandro Forin, Paul J. Leach, Daniela Roşu*, Marcel-Cătălin Roşu*

Microsoft Research, Microsoft Corporation
One Microsoft Way, Building 9s/1
Redmond, WA 98052

Abstract

The goal of the Rialto project at Microsoft Research is to build a system architecture supporting coexisting independent real-time (and non-real-time) programs. Unlike traditional embedded-systems real-time environments, where timing and resource analysis among competing tasks can be done off-line, it is our goal to allow multiple independently authored real-time applications with varying timing and resource requirements to dynamically coexist and cooperate to share the limited physical resources available to them, as well as also coexisting with non-real-time applications.

This paper gives an overview of the Rialto real-time architecture as it is implemented today and reports on some of the early results obtained. In particular, it describes the use of time constraints, activities, CPU and other resource reservation, and the system resource planner, and how they work together to achieve our goal of providing a flexible, dynamic real-time computing environment.

1. Introduction

The Rialto operating system has been designed and built from scratch to provide a basis for doing research in consumer real-time computing. Some of our goals are:

- Predictable concurrent execution of multiple real-time and non-real-time applications
- Timely service for application needs
- Small memory footprint
- Support for real-time distributed computing

This paper describes the system we have implemented to achieve those goals.

2. Time Constraints

One requirement of consumer real-time applications is to reliably execute pieces of code in a predictable and timely manner. Rialto supports this requirement via *time constraints*.

Time constraints allow a thread to specify the timeliness requirements for the execution of a block of code to the system, allowing the system to attempt to schedule execution of the code so as to be able to meet those requirements. Applications use time constraints primarily through the **BeginConstraint()** and **EndConstraint()** calls. This is a somewhat simpler mechanism than that which we originally proposed to implement in [Jones 93].

2.1 BeginConstraint() and EndConstraint()

The **BeginConstraint()** call takes the following parameters:

- **Start Time:** Earliest time to begin running the code.
- **Estimate:** Estimated time needed to execute code.
- **Deadline:** Latest time the code may finish running.
- **Criticality:** How important it is to meet the deadline.

It returns the boolean result:

- **Schedulable:** indicates whether the system believes that the deadline can be met.

The **EndConstraint()** call takes no parameters and returns the following result:

- **Time Taken:** amount of time spent running the code.

---

* Daniela Roşu and Marcel-Cătălin Roşu are Ph.D. students at the Georgia Institute of Technology.

The *start time* and *deadline* may both be either absolute or relative to the current time. *Estimate* specifies an elapsed time. Rialto measures time in 100 nanosecond units — the same as the Win32 **FILETIME** type.

Both the *estimate* parameter and the *time taken* result measure time as "standalone wall-clock time". For the *estimate*, this is the elapsed time that would be needed to execute the code in the absence of resource contention. In the case of *time taken*, this is the amount of elapsed time attributable to the code of the constraint. This includes time spent executing and doing I/O for the thread, but not any time that elapsed while other threads were scheduled.

The *criticality* parameter is a two-valued type informing the system how well the code handles occasional missed deadlines. The value **NONCRITICAL** specifies that the code can reasonably tolerate occasional missed deadlines; the value **CRITICAL** specifies that the code behaves badly if any deadlines are missed. For instance, video playback is an example of non-critical code; frames can typically be dropped without significant degradation of quality. Audio sample playback might be critical since dropping samples can lead to annoying pops, clicks, and silences. The default value is **NONCRITICAL**.

2.2 Time Constraint Usage

An application might request that a piece of code be executed by a particular deadline as follows:

```
Calculate constraint parameters
schedulable = BeginConstraint(
     start, estimate, deadline, criticality);
if (schedulable) {
     Do normal work under constraint
} else {
     Transient overload — shed load if possible
}
time_taken = EndConstraint();
```

The *start time*, *deadline*, and *criticality* parameters are straightforward to calculate since they are all directly related to what the code is intended to do and how it is implemented. The *estimate* parameter is the more interesting one, since predicting the run time of a piece of code is a hard problem (particularly in light of variations in processor speeds, memory speeds, cache & memory sizes, I/O bus bandwidths, etc., between machines).

Rather than trying to calculate the *estimate* in some manner from first principles (as might be done for some hard real-time embedded systems), the Rialto approach is to base the estimate on feedback from previous executions of the same code. In particular, the *time taken* result from the **EndConstraint()** provides the basis for this feedback. In simple cases, for instance, the *time taken* result might be directly used as the *estimate* for the next execution of the same code; that, or a simple function, such as an average or a maximum, of the last few results might be used. In more complex cases, where the expected runtime might be data-dependent, functions taking these data dependencies into account would be used.

Finally, note that the intended use of the *schedulable* result is to allow the code to be made aware of and react to transient overload conditions — specifically, when it is unlikely that *estimate* amount of work can be done by the *deadline*. In this case, the code can attempt to shed load, for instance, by skipping some of the work that would normally be done, doing only enough to maintain program invariants. By proactively shedding load when overload is detected the system as a whole can hopefully recover quickly, rather than oscillating out of control.

2.3 Time Constraint Properties

One important property of this approach is that all the knowledge needed to use time constraints is local. The *start time*, *estimate*, *deadline*, and *criticality* are all properties of the code being executed under the constraint. The *time taken* result is a local result.

The only globally-derived piece of information used in the method is the *schedulable* result. This result is calculated by the scheduler based on its global knowledge of the scheduling properties of all the other threads in the system. But viewed another way, this is also providing a piece of knowledge (the answer to the question: "Is it likely that *estimate* amount of work can be completed by *deadline*?") in such a manner that it can be effectively used locally — in this case to shed load if a transient overload occurs.

This use of strictly local knowledge in specifying timing properties of code is in marked contrast to priority-based approaches. For priority schemes to work, some person or algorithm must be used to assign global priority numbers across all threads in the system. While this is feasible for embedded systems where a static enumeration of the scheduled tasks is possible, assigning meaningful priorities in a dynamic environment where multiple independently authored real-time and non-real-time applications coexist is problematic (to say the least!). Thus, we have opted for the time constraints mechanism, in which timing specifications of code rely only on local information.

Time constraints affect CPU scheduling. However, they are also designed to be able to equally apply to all other forms of scheduling, such as scheduling I/O requests. Constraints provide the basis for a unified scheduling model.

Time constraints are transparently propagated across invocations to objects in other processes on the same machine. The calling thread's scheduling properties are applied to the server thread acting upon its behalf in the remote process. Likewise, we have a design for propagating constraints across cross-machine RPCs.

Time constraints are scheduled according to a modified minimum-laxity-first policy. If two constraints are in conflict with one another and have different criticalities, the critical constraint will be scheduled first. When not in overload, this policy can be optimal in the local machine case, and can also be meaningfully applied in cases involving remote procedure calls.

Of course, time constraints do not in any way guarantee a feasible schedule, and in fact, may behave very badly in overload conditions. Thus, higher level mechanisms are also needed to solve resource contention issues.

3. Real-Time Resource Management

In order to avoid persistent overload of resources needed by real-time applications and the resulting unpredictable execution, Rialto implements a real-time resource management mechanism. Since this mechanism has already been discussed in [Jones et al. 95], only an overview of its key concepts will be given here.

3.1 Resource Self-Awareness and Negotiation

The main idea is that in Rialto, real-time programs have mechanisms available to them allowing them to be *resource self-aware*. Programs can negotiate with a per-machine **resource planner** service for the resources that they need to obtain predictable real-time performance. Similarly to the feedback used with time constraints, this resource self-awareness is achieved by observing the resources actually used when doing specific tasks, and then reserving those resource amounts in order to be able to guarantee sufficient resources to do those tasks predictably on an ongoing basis.

The resource planner arbitrates between programs requesting resource reservations, and implements policies that choose which among the competing programs are granted resource reservations in cases of conflicting requests. The resource planner may request that a program relinquish all or a portion of a resource reservation already granted to it so as be able to grant those resources to another program. In such cases, programs may either choose to modify their behavior so as to be able to operate within the available resources, or if unable to do so, they may choose to terminate themselves.

It is our intent that the resource management policies be *user-centric*, meaning that their goal is to increase the user's perceived utility of the system as a whole. This, as opposed to, for instance, program-centric policies, in which each program tries to maximize its performance at the possible expense of any others, or first-come first-served policies, which may not make optimal use of the system's resources.

3.2 Resource Management Objects

The fundamental abstraction underlying resource management is that of a **resource**. By this, we mean any limited quantity, either hardware or software, that might be needed by a program for timely execution. Examples are CPU time, memory, network bandwidth, I/O bandwidth, and graphic processor time. Each resource is represented as a distinct object in Rialto.

A **resource set** object represents a collection of resources and associated amounts.

An **activity** object is the abstraction to which resources are allocated and against which resources usage is charged. Normally each distinct executing program or application is associated with a separate activity. Activities may span address spaces and machines and may have multiple threads of control associated with them. Each executing thread has an associated activity object. Examples of tasks that might be executed as distinct activities are playing a studio-quality video stream, recording and transmitting video for a video-conferencing application, and accepting voice input for a speech recognition system.

When threads execute, any resources used are charged against their activity. Both per-activity resource usage accounting, and resource reservation enforcement can be provided by resources, as appropriate.

4. Activity-Based CPU Reservation

One important resource object that is implemented in Rialto is the CPU resource. The primary operations on the CPU resource object are those to reserve a fraction of the total processor time (on an ongoing basis) for an activity, and to query the actual amount of processor time used by an activity. CPU reservations are similar to the processor capacity reserves described in [Mercer et al. 94].

The CPU scheduler allocates CPU time among activities with runnable threads based on the activity's CPU reservation. For instance, if activity A has a 40% CPU reservation, B has a 20% reservation, and C has a 10% reservation, then on average, the threads in A will accumulate twice as much runtime as the threads in B and four times as much runtime as the threads in C. Within an activity fair-share scheduling is done among runnable threads, although meeting time constraints takes precedence over fairness considerations.

Activities share unreserved CPU time equally among themselves. Activities without explicit reservations are scheduled as if they had reservations from the unreserved CPU pool.

Of course, due to time constraints and other factors, the scheduler uses a more involved algorithm than just a weighted round robin algorithm. What makes the scheduler interesting is that it has to balance both the requirement to meet as many time constraint deadlines as possible, while also respecting ongoing CPU reservations and preventing starvation. This algorithm is described in the next section.

5. Integrated Scheduling Algorithm

Rialto's CPU scheduling algorithm is designed to achieve a number of goals:
- Honor CPU reservations for activities
- Meet time constraint deadlines when possible
- Provide fair-share scheduling of threads within activities
- Prevent starvation of runnable threads

A description of our algorithm to achieve these goals follows.

The Rialto scheduler at its core uses a minimum-laxity-first based scheduling algorithm with preemption. Both threads with and without time constraints, and threads with and without reservations are scheduled in this manner.

For threads with time constraints the initial laxity is given by this formula:

$$laxity = deadline - current\ time - (estimate * scale\ factor)$$

Actually, the laxity amount is represented instead as a *run-by* time, where

$$run\text{-}by = current\ time + laxity = deadline - (estimate * scale\ factor)$$

The *run-by* time represents the latest time at which a constraint's code could be initially scheduled and still make the deadline (assuming that the estimate is accurate). The scale factor is the reciprocal of the fraction of the CPU that the thread's activity will receive during execution. (This will discussed in more detail shortly.)

While executing with a time constraint a thread's run-by time advances with real time times its activity's scale factor. For instance, if 3 ms of work is done for a constraint, the scale factor is 4 (corresponding to 25% of the CPU), and a context switch occurs, the remainder of the constraint's work can be started 12 ms later than its previous run-by time. Run-by times are constant while a thread is not running (which is why this representation was chosen).

Proportional and fair-share scheduling is achieved by also giving threads without constraints run-by times. While executing without a constraint a thread's run-by time is advanced inverse proportionately to its share of the CPU. For instance, if a thread should on average get 10% of the CPU and it is executed for 6 ms then at context-switch time its run-by time will be advanced by 60 ms. A thread's initial run-by time is simply the current time. Within an activity, with one exception, the thread with the earliest run-by time said to be the most *urgent* and is scheduled. The exception is that if any threads have constraints with **CRITICAL** criticality, then the thread among them with the earliest run-by time is the most urgent, and is scheduled, even if others may have earlier run-by times.

Proportional share scheduling between activities is achieved in exactly the manner described above, except that activities are given run-by times, and have no criticalities. After a thread has been run within an activity the activity's run-by time is advanced by the run time divided by the activity's CPU share. When a reschedule occurs, first the activity with the earliest run-by time with runnable threads is chosen; then the most urgent thread within that activity is chosen. This is the thread scheduled. First scheduling activities and then threads within those activities prevents threads within other activities from denying an activity its reserved CPU time.

Both any non-reserved CPU time and time reserved by activities with no runnable threads are divided up equally among activities. So, for instance, if there are three activities, with A having a 50% reservation, B having a 20% reservation, and C having no reservation, then each activity will get an equal share of the 30% remainder. In this example, A will actually get 60%, B will actually get 30%, and C will actually get 10%. The actual activity share for a thread's activity is currently computed when the thread is scheduled for execution, based on the number of activities with runnable threads and the amount of unreserved CPU time.

As noted above, the actual time estimates are scaled inversely with the activity's CPU share when computing run-by times for constraints. This is because, on average, threads in the activity can only proceed at a fraction of the CPU speed that is proportional to their activity's CPU share. Likewise, when executing in a constraint, the run-by time is advanced by the actual time run multiplied by the same scale factor. Run-by times for threads without constraints are advanced by the time run times the activity's scale factor times the number of runnable threads in the activity. This achieves fair-share scheduling among the threads without constraints in an activity.

Another detail of constraint execution is that when a constraint completes the thread's new run-by time will be updated to account for the time run under the constraint (as previously described) and then used as is. Nested constraints are implemented by keeping a stack of constraint objects associated with threads, with the top-most constraint being the active constraint. As above, when a constraint object is popped, the thread run-time will be adjusted to reflect work done under the previously active constraint.

Related to nested constraints is urgency inheritance. Whenever a thread owns an object (e.g., a mutex) it inherits the urgency of the most urgent thread waiting for that object. When the thread releases the object this inheritance is removed. This prevents situations analogous to priority inversion.

As previously mentioned, a server thread running on behalf of a client thread that makes a remote object invocation is scheduled as if it were, in fact, the client thread. In effect, the server thread assumes the client thread's scheduling identity and parameters while it is running on its behalf.

The schedulability test applied to constraints in the current implementation simply checks the sanity of the parameters and verifies that the resulting run-by time is after the present. This test is obviously overly optimistic and will be replaced shortly.

Currently when a thread sleeps or waits its run-by time is updated to reflect any run-time before the sleep or wait and then remains constant until it runs again. Changes are under consideration that would reset the thread's run-by time to the present time when it wakes up after sleeps or waits longer than some threshold so that when they wake up these threads don't effectively starve over threads in the same activity that continued to run. An activity's run-by time is never changed by a non-running thread.

A pure minimum laxity first scheduler with preemption would spend nearly all of its time context switching between threads with essentially equal run-by times. In order to prevent this hysteresis is introduced. In particular, threads are currently scheduled to be run for ten milliseconds unless a sleep wakeup or time constraint dictates a shorter run time.

Minimum-laxity first is used instead of earliest deadline first primarily because laxities can meaningfully be transmitted between and updated by components of a distributed system. This is important when a computation involves the sequential use of multiple machines (or equivalently, multiple resources). Each machine can make local laxity-based scheduling decisions, resulting in a globally correct schedule (if one is feasible). This would not be true for EDF since no meaningful deadlines are present for the different components of the computation.

Starvation is prevented in a simple fashion. A certain amount of CPU time is set aside and cannot be reserved, ensuring that there is always some unreserved CPU time to be shared. At present we only allow reservations up to 95% of the CPU (setting aside 5%).

6. Other Features

Rialto provides processes with protected address spaces and multiple threads per process. The kernel is itself a distinguished process and much of its code is mapped into other processes, resulting in significant code savings due to the ability to use kernel routines in user processes; in effect, the kernel serves as a shared library for all other processes. All functions available to user processes are also available in the kernel, allowing code to be developed in user processes and later run in the kernel completely unmodified, if so desired.

Synchronization between threads is provided via standard **Mutex** and **Condition Variable** objects. They are implemented in such as way as to provide *constraint inheritance*, a generalization of priority inheritance, preventing priority inversions from occurring.

Most services in Rialto are invoked via object invocation. Optimized cross-process object invocation is directly supported by the kernel, with a null RPC taking 47 microseconds on a 90 MHz Pentium workstation.

Besides the simple forms of the constraint calls discussed previously, there is also a form of **BeginConstraint()** that atomically ends one constraint and begins a new one. This is typically found in loops, where each loop iteration is required to execute by a deadline.

Likewise, there is a special **ConditionWaitAndBeginConstraint()** call that does a **ConditionWait()** and the atomically begins a new constraint as soon as the wait is satisfied. This allows code to be run with a deadline that is relative to an event signaled by another piece of code. For instance, device drivers or code handling user events such as mouse clicks can signal a condition, causing code handling the event to be executed subject to a constraint. If satisfiable, the constraint ensures that the event is handled within a bounded response time.

7. Related Work

The SMART scheduler work at Stanford [Nieh & Lam 96] is probably the closest to our own. They share the goals of allowing reasonable mixing of real-time and non-real-time applications on the same machines. Several significant differences are apparent. First, they introduce an explicit concept of virtual latency tolerance, which is used for determining how long "unfairness" can be tolerated by a task. They lack the concept of an activity; their weighted fair queueing based algorithm applies only to single tasks, not to activities with multiple threads. Finally, since their algorithm makes all timing decisions using periodic 10 ms clock interrupts instead of running the clock as an aperiodic device, they can only service deadlines at a 10 ms or larger granularity.

Mercer's processor capacity reserves [Mercer et al. 94] are similar in spirit to our activity-based CPU reservations. However, because the underlying system upon which it was built (RT-Mach and a Unix server) lacked the equivalent of Rialto's activity abstraction, server threads executing RPCs do not execute from the same reserve as the caller unless the server takes specific action to change its reserve to that of the caller.

Unlike the approaches above, the VuSystem work at MIT [Compton & Tennenhouse 93] takes the position that resource reservation is inappropriate and that applications should dynamically and cooperatively shed load when necessary, but they bemoan the crude measures available for deciding when to shed load. Rather than shedding load reactively, our work provides a means for programs to cooperatively reason about their resources in advance, proactively avoiding most dynamic load shedding situations.

8. Status and Results

The Rialto kernel is currently in use at Microsoft Research to provide a research testbed for investigating models of consumer real-time and multimedia computing. While most of the work is currently being done on the x86 platform, the system is portable. Versions are also in use on both the Mips and Arm processors. As typically configured, the kernel currently occupies approximately 175 kilobytes of memory on the x86.

Both native Rialto device drivers and some Windows/NT binary device drivers can be dynamically loaded. Devices currently used include the keyboard, serial lines, disks, several kinds display adapters including MPEG cards, some sound cards, several kinds of Ethernet cards and some ATM adapters, plus some custom devices.

Some of the applications currently running include real-time video players, interactive games, and ports of some Win32 applications, such as a web browser.

One of the key factors that differentiates this system from many being used for multimedia is that it was designed and implemented from the beginning with low latency as a goal. All services, including the kernel, are fully preemptible. Unlike traditional timesharing schedulers such as those used by UNIX or Windows/NT, we do not run the clock as a periodic device, with the only possible preemption points being at "tick" boundaries — typically 60 or 100 per second. For instance, on a 90 MHz Pentium workstation within one activity we can schedule two threads using constraints with periodic deadlines of 300 microseconds (during which essentially no work is done) against another thread that is spinning and reliably meet all of the deadlines.

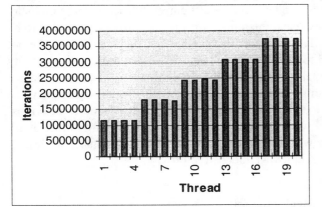

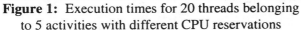

Figure 1: Execution times for 20 threads belonging to 5 activities with different CPU reservations

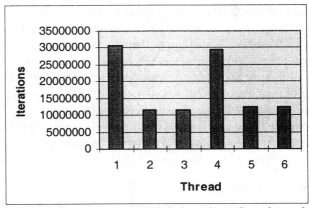

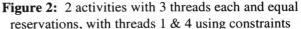

Figure 2: 2 activities with 3 threads each and equal reservations, with threads 1 & 4 using constraints

Figure 1 shows the results of a program that created five activities with four threads per activity, reserving 4%, 8%, 12%, 16%, and 20% of the CPU for the activities, for a total reservation of 60%. Each thread was running a simple loop and the number of loops executed are reported. The graph demonstrates several things.

First, it shows that CPU reservations do effectively control the amounts of CPU time granted to activities. It shows that fair share scheduling is done for threads within activities. Finally, notice that while the actual time granted to the activities increases linearly with their reservations that the ratios are not proportional to the actual reservations. This is because the unreserved CPU time is divided evenly among the activities, so each activity actually receives more time than it reserved.

Figure 2 shows the results of a program with two activities with equal 35% reservations and three threads each. Threads 1 and 4 (which are in different activities) use constraints to schedule execution of code that runs for 1.3 ms at every 5 ms. The other threads are running identical code without using constraints. This shows how constraints can be used to schedule more than a thread's "fair share" of time relative to other threads within an activity.

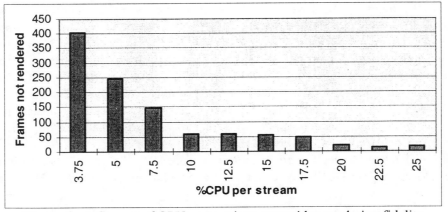

Figure 3: Influence of CPU reservations over video rendering fidelity

Figure 3 shows the result of varying the amount of CPU available to three simultaneously running AVI video player applications in terms of the average number of frames not successfully rendered per stream. Each player is rendering the same 3 minute, 45 second music video, which contains 3393 frames. In this experiment we vary the amount of CPU available to each AVI player by changing the reservation of a fourth application that merely spins.

The graph shows how the performance of the AVI players improves with increasing CPU availability. Note that the "obvious" experiment of varying the players' reservations does not give the same results without introducing and changing the reservation of the spinning application; unless CPU is denied to the players by the spinning application the players are able to use spare CPU to accomplish their (relatively constant work) rendering job.

While we are pleased with some of the preliminary results described in this paper, the scheduler work is by no means complete, and several deficiencies remain. The constraint schedulability test currently used is too simplistic. Certain code paths are known to be inefficient. While the *estimate* parameter and *time taken* result are intended to be standalone wall-clock time, they are actually just CPU time today; other resource providers, such as devices, are not yet contributing the time taken value when they cause a thread to block. Finally, we believe that the fact that activity run-by times completely dominate thread run-by times in scheduling decisions, even for threads with constraints, is a problem with the current algorithm. This can cause constraint deadlines to occasionally be missed even when sufficient CPU time is reserved for the constraint's activity to reliably meet the deadlines due to other activities' threads being scheduled at inopportune times. For this reason, we are re-thinking having activity run-by times at all, and are investigating replacing this portion of the algorithm with one using only thread run-by times, while still preserving the proportional scheduling properties for activities that it was intended to provide.

9. Conclusions

We have implemented the Rialto real-time kernel, which provides the following features:

- Low-latency real-time scheduling
- Dynamic time constraints
- Activity-based CPU reservations
- Extensible real-time resource management

While there is still additional work to do in refining the particular real-time scheduling algorithm used, we can report that it is both feasible and practical to provide unified support for this complimentary set of real-time features within a single system. Our initial experiments have shown that this approach can provide a promising platform for concurrently executing both traditional and highly responsive interactive and multimedia software.

References

[Compton & Tennenhouse 93] Charles L. Compton and David L. Tennenhouse. Collaborative Load Shedding. In *Proceedings of the Workshop on the Role of Real-Time in Multimedia/Interactive Computing Systems.* IEEE Computer Society, Raleigh-Durham, NC, November 1993.

[Jones 93] Michael B. Jones. Adaptive Real-Time Resource Management Supporting Composition of Independently Authored Time-Critical Services. In *Proceedings of the Fourth Workshop on Workstation Operating Systems*, pages 135-139. IEEE Computer Society, Napa, CA, October, 1993.

[Jones et al. 95] Michael B. Jones, Paul J. Leach, Richard P. Draves, Joseph S. Barrera, III. Modular Real-Time Resource Management in the Rialto Operating System. In *Proceedings of the Fifth Workshop on Hot Topics in Operating Systems*, pages 12-17. IEEE Computer Society, Orcas Island, WA, May, 1995.

[Mercer et al. 94] Clifford W. Mercer, Stefan Savage, Hideyuki Tokuda. Processor Capacity Reserves: Operating System Support for Multimedia Applications. In *Proceedings of the IEEE International Conference on Multimedia Computing and Systems (ICMCS),* May 1994.

[Nieh & Lam 96] Jason Nieh and Monica S. Lam. *The design of SMART: A Scheduler for Multimedia Applications.* Technical Report CSL-TR-96-697, Computer Systems Laboratory, Stanford University, June 1996.

Resource Kernels: A Resource-Centric Approach to Real-Time and Multimedia Systems

Raj Rajkumar, Kanaka Juvva, Anastasio Molano and Shuichi Oikawa
Real-Time and Multimedia Laboratory[1]
Department of Computer Science
Carnegie Mellon University
Pittsburgh, PA 15213
{raj+, kjuvva, amolano, shui}@cs.cmu.edu

Abstract

We consider the problem of OS resource management for real-time and multimedia systems where multiple activities with different timing constraints must be scheduled concurrently. Time on a particular resource is shared among its users and must be globally managed in real-time and multimedia systems. A resource kernel is meant for use in such systems and is defined to be one which provides timely, guaranteed and protected access to system resources. The resource kernel allows applications to specify only their resource demands leaving the kernel to satisfy those demands using hidden resource management schemes. This separation of resource specification from resource management allows OS-subsystem-specific customization by extending, optimizing or even replacing resource management schemes. As a result, this resource-centric approach can be implemented with any of several different resource management schemes.

We identify the specific goals of a resource kernel: applications must be able to explicitly state their timeliness requirements; the kernel must enforce maximum resource usage by applications; the kernel must support high utilization of system resources; and an application must be able to access different system resources simultaneously. Since the same application consumes a different amount of time on different platforms, the resource kernel must allow such resource consumption times to be portable across platforms, and to be automatically calibrated. Our resource management scheme is based on resource reservation [25] and satisfies these goals. The scheme is not only simple but captures a wide range of solutions developed by the real-time systems community over several years.

One potentially serious problem that any resource management scheme must address is that of allowing access to multiple resources simultaneously and in timely fashion, a problem which is known to be NP-complete [5]. We show that this problem of simultaneous access to multiple resources can be practically addressed by resource decoupling and resolving critical resource dependencies immediately.

Finally, we demonstrate our resource kernel's functionality and flexibility in the context of multimedia applications which need processor cycles and/or disk bandwidth.

1. Motivation for Resource Kernels

Example real-time systems include aircraft fighters such as F-22 and the Joint Strike fighter [19], beverage bottling plants, autonomous vehicles, live monitoring systems, etc. These systems are typically built using timeline based approaches, production/consumption rates [9] or priority-based schemes, where the resource demands are mapped to specific time slots or priority levels, often in ad hoc fashion. This mapping of resources to currently available scheduling mechanisms introduces many problems. Assumptions go undocumented, and violations go undetected with the end result that the system can become fragile and fail in unexpected ways. We argue for a resource-centric approach where the scheduling policies are completed subsumed by the kernel, and applications need only specify their resource and timing requirements. The kernel will then make internal scheduling decisions such that these requirements are guaranteed to be satisfied.

Various timing constraints also arise in desktop and networked multimedia systems. Multi-party video conferencing, mute but live news windows, recording of live video/audio feeds, playback of local audio/video streams to remote participants etc. can go on concurrently with normal computing activities such as compilation, editing and browsing. A range of implicit timeliness constraints need to be satisfied in this scenario. For example, audio has stringent jitter requirements, and video has high bandwidth requirements [8]. Disk accesses for compilation should take lower precedence over disk accesses for recording a live telecast.

Two points argue in favor of resource-centric kernels we call "resource kernels":

- Firstly, operating system kernels (including microkernels) are intended to manage resources such that application programs can assume in practice that system resources are made available to them as they need them. In real-time systems, system resources such as the disk, the network, communication buffers, the protocol stack and most obviously the processor are shared. If one applica-

[1]This research was supported by the Defense Advanced Research Projects Agency in part under agreement E30602-97-2-0287 and in part under agreement F30602-96-1-0160. Mr. Molano was funded by a research grant from the Community of Madrid and by the National R&D Program of Spain under contracts TIC96-0982 and TIC97-0438.

tion is using a large portion of the system resources, then it implies that other applications get a less portion of the system resources and consequently can take longer to execute. In other words, their timing behavior is adversely affected. Letting kernels take explicit control over resource usage is therefore a logical thing to do to prevent such unexpected side effects.

- Secondly, our resource model captures the essential requirements of many resource management policies in a simple, efficient yet general form. The implementation of the model can actually be done using any one of many popular resource management schemes (both classical and recent) without exposing the actual underlying resource management scheme chosen. User-level schemes can be used to dynamically downgrade (upgrade) application quality when new (current) resource demands arrive (leave). This feature of the resource model leads to minimal changes from existing infrastructure while retaining flexibility and offering many benefits.

Other alternatives to resource kernels include user-centric and application-centric kernels:

- A user-centric kernel can emphasize multi-user capabilities, and also track and facilitate the needs of specific users. Unix in general and Unix filesystems in particular can be viewed as providing such support. At the same time, Unix attempted to present and manipulate all system entities as files. In resource kernels, we adopt a similar approach and attempt to present all system resources using a uniform model for guaranteed access. Our implementation of the resource kernel is orthogonal to user-centricity, but tighter integration between the two may be possible. Currently, specific user-level requirements must be translated by intermediate layers into resource demands at the resource kernel interface.

- Application-centric kernels are typically custom executives with built-in support for the applications they are intended to serve. As an example, kernels used in telecommunication switches are application-centric and deal explicitly with the high-performance, upgrading, availability, billing and auditing requirements of telecommunication paths. Conceptually, the notions of resource kernels to guarantee timely access to resources can be applied to such kernels as well. For example, consider a postscript printer. It has an executive running a postscript interpreter and control of the physical printing operations. Precisely timed control and concurrency management of downloading new print tasks in such executives can also benefit from the support available in resource kernels.

1.1. Comparison with Related Work
A wealth of resource management schemes and scheduling algorithms exist from which one can draw. Our resource management work builds on and significantly extends established real-time scheduling theory and derived processor reservation work reported in [25]. The work in [25] did not deal with the management of multiple resource types, concurrent accesses to different resources, explicit timeliness control, feedback about resource usage, behavioral control on resource overruns, management of interactions between resource users, and considerations of portability, compatibility and automation. In brief, our resource management scheme supports the abstractions behind real-time priority-based scheduling for periodic activities, and service schemes for aperiodics in that framework.

Some of our goals (such as resource centricity and portability) are similar to those of Microsoft Research's Rialto kernel among others. The reservation model also has its counterparts in network reservation protocols as used in ATM and RSVP. However, the operating system problem seems more complex in one sense since inherently different resource types must be dealt with, while networks essentially deal with one type (namely network packets). In another sense, network reservations must be homogeneous, scalable and efficient, making its realization harder in a different sense.

Despite its origins in real-time scheduling theory, we expect our resource management model to be compatible with resource management schemes with their origins in networks such as proportional fair-sharing schemes such as PGPS, WF^2Q, virtual clocks and lottery scheduling. The notion of fairness has for long been deemed to be anti-thetic to real-time systems and the management of timeliness [38]. Weighted allocation schemes such as proportional fair-sharing, however, can still be applied to the real-time model. This can be done by dynamically recomputing the weights so as *not* to be proportional or fair, but instead to obtain a fixed share of a resource when new requests arrive or current requests complete. Our scheme employs a different period for each real-time activity, and guarantees a "share" of that period to the activity. As a result, the dynamic recomputing of weights in a proportional fair-share scheme can be viewed as a special case of our model as having a single (small) fixed period for all resource allocations. The primary difference that we see is that our work advances system capabilities to include non-traditional resources such as disk bandwidth that can be used in conjunction with processor scheduling.

Finally, Blazewicz et al. [5] have shown that the problem of scheduling activities which need multiple resources simultaneously and have timeliness constraints is NP-complete. In our work, we therefore strive for practical and acceptable alternatives which can guarantee access to different resource types.

1.2. Organization of the Paper
The rest of this paper is organized as follows. In Section 2, we present the goals to be satisfied in designing a resource kernel, and based on well-established principles of real-time resource management, defines a resource reservation model and its parameters. In Section 3, we describe the implementation of our resource reservation model in the context of processor scheduling, and evaluate it. In Section 4, we detail the implementation of the resource reservation model in the context of disk scheduling, and evaluate those schemes. In Section 5, we address other issues that arise in

the context of using the resource kernel in practice including calibrating an application's resource demands automatically and in portable ways. Finally, in Section 6, we conclude with some remarks outlining our research contributions and future work.

2. Designing a Resource Kernel

The challenges for a resource kernel are many. We characterize these challenges below as a set of goals that resource-centric kernels should aim to satisfy.

2.1. Design Goals of a Resource Kernel

G1. Timeliness of resource usage. An application using the resource kernel must be able to request specific resource demands from the kernel. If granted, the requested amount of resources must be guaranteed to be available in timely fashion to the application. An application with existing resource grants must also be able to dynamically upgrade or downgrade its resource usage (for adaptation and graceful degradation purposes). This implies that the kernel must support an admission control policy for resource demands. Conventional real-time operating systems do not provide any such admission control mechanisms, even though an equivalent feature (without enforcement capabilities) could be built at user level.

G2. Efficient resource utilization. The resource kernel must utilize system resources efficiently. For example, a trivial and unacceptable way to satisfy G1 would be to deny all requests for guaranteed resource access. In other words, if sufficient system resources are available, the kernel must allocate those resources to a requesting application. This goal implies that the admission control policy used by the resource kernel have provably good properties. Such proof may be analytical or empirical but our version of the resource kernel provides analytically proven properties. It must be noted that this goal is subordinated to G1, in that guaranteed resource access is the primary goal, and efforts to improve efficiency and throughput cannot happen at the expense of the guarantees.[2] Traditional real-time operating systems leaves the matter completely open to the developers, each of whom must use their own schemes to obtain better utilization for their applications.

G3. Enforcement and protection. The resource kernel must enforce the usage of resources such that abuse of resources (intended or not) by one application does *not* hurt the guaranteed usage of resources granted by the kernel to other applications. Traditional real-time operating systems such as those compliant with the POSIX Real-Time Extensions [30] do *not* satisfy this goal.

---

[2]This emphasis on guarantees and timeliness may understandably seem to bias the resource kernel away from multimedia systems. (In real-time systems, missed deadlines may potentially lead to system failure, and possible loss of life and/or property). However, we believe that as multimedia applications on desktops and internet appliances mature, users will come to expect smooth video frame changes, jitterless audio, and synchronized audio and video. It is to be noted that VCR/TV/satellite technologies have been delivering such guaranteed timing behavior for years. It seems rather illogical to expect anything less from computers at least when a user is willing to pay for it, particularly if virtual reality environments must seem real, or for applications such as tele-medicine and tele-surgery.

G4. Access to multiple resource types. The resource kernel must provide access to multiple resource types such as processor cycles, disk bandwidth, network bandwidth, communication buffers and virtual memory. The communication protocol stack on the system may potentially be viewed as a resource type as well, but in most systems, they use the processor and hence can be managed by appropriate scheduling and allocation of processor cycles. For example, see [23]. Traditional real-time operating systems provide mechanisms that can *only* be used to guarantee access to processor cycles.

G5. Portability and Automation. The absolute resource demands needed for a given amount of work can unfortunately vary from platform to platform due to differences in machine speed. For example, a signal processing algorithm can take 10ms on a 200MHz Pentium but take 20ms on a 100MHz Pentium. Ideally, applications must have the ability to specify their resource demands in a portable way such that the same resource specification can be used on different platforms. In addition, there must exist means for the resource demands of an application to be automatically calibrated.

G6. Upward compatibility with fielded operating systems. A large host of commercial and proprietary real-time operating systems and real-time systems exist. Many of these systems employ a fixed priority scheduling policy [12] to support provide real-time behavior, and the rate-monotonic [18] or deadline-monotonic [17] priority assignment algorithm is frequently used to assign fixed priorities to tasks. Basic priority inheritance [33] is used on synchronization primitives such as mutexes and semaphores to avoid the unbounded priority inversion problem when tasks share logical resources. For example, Solaris [11], OS/2, Windows, Windows NT, AIX, HP/UX all support the fixed priority scheduling policy. The Java virtual machine specification also does. Priority inheritance on semaphores is supported in all these OSs (except Windows NT). POSIX real-time extensions, Unix-derived real-time operating systems such as QNX and LynxOS, and other proprietary real-time operating systems such as pSOS, VxWorks, VRTX, OS/9000, and iRMX support priority inheritance and fixed priority scheduling. To be accepted, the resource kernel must be upward compatible with these schemes. The priority inheritance scheme is also used or being considered for use in multimedia-oriented systems [28, 40].

Goals G1-G4 are integral to resource kernels, while goals G5 and G6 are for practicality and convenience. Goals G1, G2, G5 and G6 can be satisfied by appropriate extensions to traditional real-time operating systems which support fixed priority CPU scheduling. For example, a user-level server can perform admission control using a resource specification model similar to ours, and assign fixed priorities based on the resource parameters used by our model. However, in order to satisfy goals G3 and G4, the internals of these operating systems need to be modified in ways similar to our resource kernel design and implementation.

2.2. An Historical Perspective of our Real-Time Resource Management Model

Many deployed real-time systems have been built and analyzed using the fixed priority periodic task model first proposed by Liu and Layland [18]. This model employs two parameters, a maximum computation time C needed every periodic interval T for each activity that needs to be guaranteed. The rate-monotonic scheduling algorithm [18] assigns fixed priorities[3] based only on T and is an optimal fixed priority scheduling algorithm. Instead of using priorities, if the $\{C, T\}$ model is directly used in a real-time system, the assumptions underlying the Liu and Layland model can be monitored and enforced at run-time. Following this strategy, the "aperiodic server" model [13, 37] uses artificially introduced C and T values for new "server tasks" which can then service aperiodic tasks within a periodic setting. This bounded periodic usage was adopted by the processor reservation work carried out in [25].

We build on this proven trend by identifying, designing, implementing and evaluating significant kernel extensions to the Liu and Layland work along multiple dimensions:

- using arbitrary deadlines [16, 17] to obtain fine-grained control timeliness of concurrent activities,

- applying the priority inheritance solutions explicitly to the unbounded priority inversion problem when activities share resources [2, 31, 34],

- dealing with new resource types such as disk scheduling, a problem which has not been studied in depth in the Liu and Layland model, and

- combining the scheduling of multiple resources into a single common framework observing that the problem of scheduling multiple resources with deadlines is known to be an NP-complete problem [5].

2.3. The Resource Reservation Model

The resource kernel gets its name from its resource-centricity and its ability of the kernel to

- apply a uniform resource model for dynamic sharing of different resource types,

- take resource usage specifications from applications,

- guarantee resource allocations at admission time,

- schedule contending activities on a resource based on a well-defined scheme, and

- ensure timeliness by dynamically monitoring and enforcing actual resource usage,

The resource kernel attains these capabilities by reserving resources for applications requesting them, and tracking outstanding reservation allocations. Based on the timeliness requirements of reservations, the resource kernel prioritizes them, and executes a higher priority reservation before a lower priority reservation if both are eligible to execute.

2.4. Explicit Resource Parameters

Our resource reservation model employs the following parameters: computation time C every T time-units for managing the net utilization of a resource, a deadline D for meeting timeliness requirements, a starting time S of the resource allocation, and L, the life-time of the resource allocation. We refer to these parameters, $\{C, T, D, S \text{ and } L\}$ as explicit parameters of our reservation model. The semantics are simple and are as follows. Each reservation will be allocated C units of usage time every T units of absolute time. These C units of usage time will be guaranteed to be available for consumption before D units of time after the begining of every periodic interval. The guarantees start at time S and terminate at time $S + L$.

2.5. Implicit Resource Parameter

If various reservations were strictly independent and have no interactions, then the explicit resource parameters would suffice. However, shared resources like buffers, critical sections, windowing systems, filesystems, protocol stacks, etc. are unavoidable in practical systems. When reservations interact, the possibility of "priority inversion" arises. A complete family of priority inheritance protocols [31] is known to address this problem. All these protocols share a common parameter B referred to as the blocking factor. It represents the maximum (desirably bounded) time that a reservation instance must wait for lower priority reservations while executing. If its B is unbounded, a reservation cannot meet its deadline. The resource kernel, therefore, implicitly derives, tracks and enforces the implicit B parameter for each reservation in the system. Priority (or reservation) inheritance is applied when a reservation blocks, waiting for a lower priority reservation to release (say) a lock. As we shall see in Section 4.5, this implicit parameter B can also be used to deliberately introduce priority inversion in a controlled fashion to achieve other optimizations.

2.6. Reservation Type

When a reservation uses up its allocation of C within an interval of T, it is said to be *depleted*. A reservation which is not depleted is said to be an *undepleted* reservation. At the end of the current interval T, the reservation will obtain a new quota of C and is said to be *replenished*. In our reservation model, the behavior of a reservation between depletion and replenishment can take one of three forms:

- *Hard reservations*: a hard reservation, on depletion, cannot be scheduled until it is replenished. While appearing constrained and very wasteful, we believe that this type of reservation can act as a powerful building block model for implementing "virtual" resources, automated calibration, etc.

- *Firm reservations*: a firm reservation, on depletion, can be scheduled for execution only if no other undepleted reservation or unreserved threads are ready to run.

- *Soft reservations*: a soft reservation, on depletion, can be scheduled for execution along with other unreserved threads and depleted reservations.

---

[3]A lower T yields a higher priority.

2.7. System Call Interface to Reservations

System Call	Description
Create	Create a reservation port
Request	Request resource on reservation port
Modify	Modify current reservation parameters
Notify	Set up notification ports for resource expiry messages.
Set Attribute	Set attributes of reservation (hard, firm or soft reservation)
Bind	Bind a thread to a reservation.
GetUsage	Get the usage on a reservation (accumulated or current).

Table 2-1: A subset of the reservation system call interface for each resource type.

Our resource reservations are *first-class* entities in the resource kernel. Hence, operations on the reservations must be invoked using system calls. A select subset of the system call interface for the resource reservation model is given in Table 2-1. A reservation modification call allows an existing reservation to be upgraded or downgraded. If the modification fails, the previous reservation parameters will be restored. In other words, if an application cannot obtain higher resources because of system load, it will at least retain its previous allocation. A notification registration interface allows the application to register a port to which a message will be sent by the resource kernel each time the reservation is depleted. A binding interface allows a thread to be bound to a reservation. More than one thread can be bound to a reservation. Query interfaces allow an application to obtain the current list of reservations in the system, the recent usage history of those reservations (updated at their respective T boundaries), and the usage of a reservation so far in its current T interval.

3. Processor Resource Management
In this section, we shall discuss and evaluate our implementation of the resource reservation model for the processor resource.

3.1. Admission Control

Description	Overhead (μs)
Processor admission control with 1 reservation	25
Processor admission control with 10 reservations	120
Processor admission control with 20 reservations	195
Processor reservation creation (excluding admission control)	150

Figure 3-1: Processor Admission Control Policy Overhead w/ Exact Schedulability Conditions

Our processor reservation scheme employs a fixed priority scheme due to its widespread popularity (as mentioned in the description of goal G6 in Section 2.1). In other words, each reservation is assigned a fixed priority, which is equal to its period T or deadline D, depending upon whether a rate-monotonic or a deadline-monotonic scheme is used respectively. Our admission control policy does *not* employ (oft-used) static utilization bounds (e.g as given in [18]) since they can be very pessimistic in nature [14]. Instead, we use an exact schedulability condition which provides the best admission control for a given set of real-time threads. This algorithm is described in detail in the Appendix (Section 2). The algorithm, being a complex non-linear function of the thread periods, their relationships and their computation times, does not have a standard degree of complexity. However, it is easily coded and can be computed efficiently. The computational cost of the scheme for a wide range of thread counts is shown in Figure 3-1. As can be seen, the overhead is acceptable. It is also incurred only when a thread requests a new reservation (or upgrades an existing reservation).

3.2. Tracking Implicit Parameter B
When a lower priority reservation blocks a higher priority reservation[4], the former inherits the reservation (and therefore its priority). When the higher priority reservation finally unblocks, the inheritance is revoked. However, the duration for which the inheritance was in place is priority inversion. The resource kernel tracks and accumulates the duration of priority inversion during a reservation's T. If it exceeds the maximum B that can be tolerated by that reservation, a message is sent to the reservation's notification port.

3.3. Performance Evaluation

Reservation Type	Initial Reservation				Upgraded to				Downgraded to			
	C_i (ms)	T_i (ms)	D_i (ms)	C_i/T_i	C_i (ms)	T_i (ms)	D_i ms)	C_i/T_i	C_i (ms)	T_i (ms)	D_i ms)	C_i/T_i
Hard	8	80	60	0.1	12	80	60	0.15	4	80	60	0.05
Firm	15	80	70	0.19	19	80	70	0.24	11	80	70	0.14
Soft	20	80	80	0.25	24	80	80	0.3	20	80	80	0.25

Table 3-1: The processor reservation parameters used for Figures 3-2, 3-3 and 3-4

We now evaluate the processor reservation scheme by running different workloads with and without the use of reservations. All our experiments use a PC using a 120MHz Pentium processor with a 256KB cache and 16MB of RAM. We illustrate two basic points in these experiments:

1. the nature of the three types of reservations, and

2. the flexibility to upgrade and downgrade different reservations. dynamically.

In the experiments of Figures 3-2 and 3-3, three threads running *simultaneously* in infinite loops are bound to the three reservations listed in Table 3-1. In the experiment of Figure 3-2, only these three threads are running. In contrast, in the experiment of Figure 3-3, many other unreserved threads in infinite loops are also running in the background and competing for the processor. The behavior of the three types of reservations is illustrated between these two figures.

---

[4]This terminology means that a thread bound to a lower priority reservation is blocking a thread bound to a higher priority reservation.

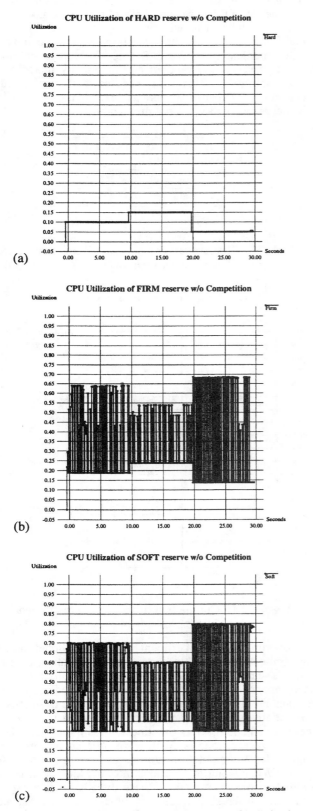

Figure 3-2: Behavior of *reserved* infinite loop threads *without* unreserved competition

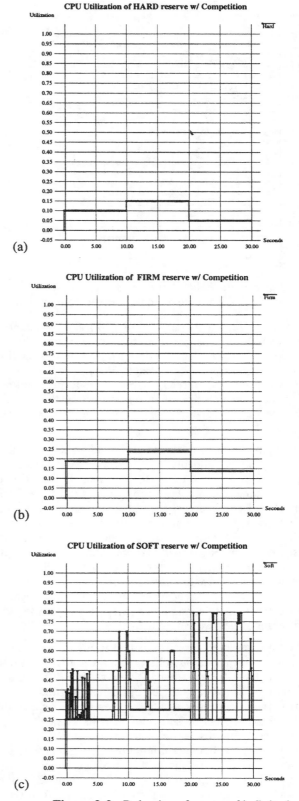

Figure 3-3: Behavior of *reserved* infinite loop threads *with* unreserved competition

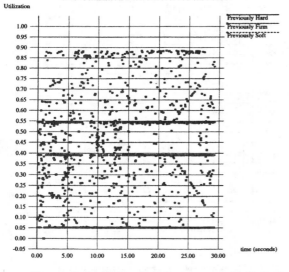

CPU Utilization with unreserved threads

Figure 3-4: Behavior of *unreserved* infinite loop threads with unreserved competition

- The first reserved thread is bound to a hard reservation and should not consume more than its granted utilization which is initially 10%, explicitly raised to 15% at time 10, and then explicitly dropped to 5% at time 20. As can be seen in (a), this thread, despite running in an infinite loop and the presence of many competing threads, obtains exactly this specified usage in *both* Figures 3-2 and 3-3.

- The second reserved thread is bound to a firm reservation, and is allocated 19% of the CPU initially, upgraded to 24% at time 10, and then downgraded to 14% at time 20. In Figure 3-2-(b), when there is no unreserved competition, this thread obtains a minimum of its granted utilization. In addition, it obtains "spare" idle cycles from the processor since there are no unreserved competing threads. However, in Figure 3-3-(b), when there is *always* unreserved competition, this thread obtains only its granted utilization. Thus, as intended, a firm reservation behaves like a hard reservation when the processor is *not* idle, and like a soft reservation when idle processor cycles are indeed available.

- The third reserved thread is bound to a soft reservation, which is allocated 25% initially, upgraded to 30% at time 10, and then downgraded to 25% at time 20. A soft reservation can compete for cycles left behind by any threads with currently undepleted reserves. As a result, this thread obtains more cycles than its granted utilization in both Figures 3-2-(c) and 3-3-(c). It must be noted that the thread obtains a minimum of its granted utilization during all its instances. It can also be seen that this thread obtains more processor cycles in Figure 3-2 since it competes only with one thread bound to a firm reservation.

It must be recalled that the three threads of Figures 3-2 and 3-3 are running simultaneously. The completion times of this same set of threads (with the background competition of Figure 3-3) when run without using any reservations are plotted in Figure 3-4. The same threads which behave extremely predictably in Figure 3-3 now exhibit an enormous amount of seemingly random and practically unacceptable unpredictability. This demonstrates that our resource management scheme works as expected; without the scheme, resource usage is not predictable.

C_i (ms)	T_i (ms)	D_i (ms)	$U_i=(C_i / T_i)$
5	20	10	25%
10	40	30	25%
10	60	45	16.66%

Table 3-2: The processor reservation parameters used for the experiment of Figures 3-5 and 3-6

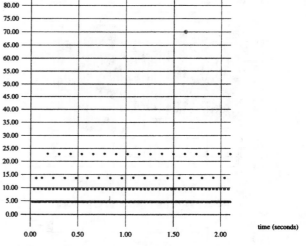
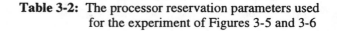
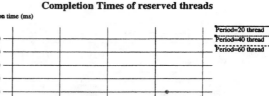

Completion Times of reserved threads

Figure 3-5: Completion times of reserved threads in the presence of competing threads

We now run another experiment where each thread imposes only finite demands, but the completion times of these demands can be predictable only with explicit resource management. The reservation parameters used for this experiment are listed in Figure 3-2. Note that the deadlines are substantially smaller than the reservation periods giving finer grained control over timeliness. One thread for each of the three reservations is created with the same period and (slightly less) computation time as its corresponding reservation. When using reservations in our resource kernel, the completion times for each of these threads as they execute with their different periods was time-stamped. The corresponding results are plotted in Figure 3-5. As can be seen, all the three threads complete their executions well ahead of their deadlines. Thread 2 also has a constant completion

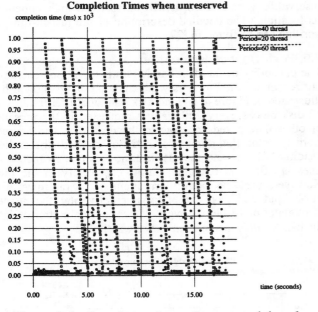

Figure 3-6: Completion times of unreserved threads with competing threads

time despite its lower priority because of its harmonicity with thread 1. The behavior of the completion times when no reservations are used is depicted in Figure 3-6. As can be seen, the same threads have widely varying completion times and also miss their deadlines rather frequently.

To summarize, the resource kernel provides a guaranteed slice of processor resources to applications independent of the behavior of other applications (including execution in infinite loops). Processor cycles that are idle can also be *selectively* allocated to running tasks.

4. Disk Bandwidth Resource Management

Traditional real-time systems have largely avoided the use of disks. This is in part because they may be relatively slow for some real-time applications. However, many real-time applications can benefit from the use of disks to store and access real-time data (such as real-time database applications). Unfortunately, the use of a disk can (a) introduce unpredictable latencies, and even worse (b) the disk access requests must now be managed in conjunction with the processor scheduling. On the processor side, fixed priority algorithms allow a mix of tasks with different periodicity, and hence the disk subsystem must do too. This problem has not been studied extensively partly because the multiple resource problem with deadlines is known to be NP-complete [5]. Some exceptions can be found in [1, 20, 21] but their resource specification models and metrics are very different from the ones we study. The closest scheduling model to ours is found in [6] but its approach is one of using fixed priority scheduling, minimizing blocking through the use of "chunking" and using a static task set. Also, only simulation studies were carried out. In contrast, we use dynamic priority scheduling, exploit blocking instead of minimizing it and evaluate an implementation within our resource framework. In addition, we deal with processor needs that must be dealt with concurrently

Desktop multimedia systems also need to read from (or write to) disk storage relatively large volumes of video and audio data. In addition, these streams represent continuous media streams, and must therefore be processed by the disk subsystem in real-time. In other words, it would be practically very useful in practice if disk bandwidth can also be guaranteed in addition to managing processor cycles.

In this section, we present a simplistic disk scheduling algorithm based on earliest deadline scheduling. We then improve the algorithm by exploiting "slack" in the reservations to obtain a hybrid of earliest deadline scheduling and a traditional scan algorithm. Our evaluations of these schemes that guaranteed disk bandwidth reservation can be obtained at only a small loss of system throughput.

4.1. Filesystem Bandwidth Specification

Our resource specification model for disk bandwidth is identical to that of processor cycles. In other words, a disk bandwidth reservation must specify a start time S, a processing time C to be obtained in every interval T before a deadline of D. The processing time C can be specified as # of disk blocks (as a portable specification) or in absolute disk bandwidth time in native-platform specification.

4.2. Admission Control

Our simplest disk head scheduling scheme employs the earliest deadline scheduling algorithm [18]. The earliest deadline scheduling algorithm is an optimal scheduling algorithm for our scheduling model and can guarantee 100% resource utilization under ideal conditions. In other words, a higher priority reservation must be able to preempt a lower priority preemption preemptively, and $D_i = T_i$. However, instantaneous preemptions are not possible in disk scheduling. An ongoing disk block access must complete before the next highest priority disk block access request can be issued. This introduces a blocking (priority inversion) factor of a single filesystem block access (as per [35]). Also, when $D_i < T_i$, the required earlier completion time (of $T_i - D_i$, must be added to the blocking factor. A detailed discussion of this admission control policy is beyond the scope of this paper and can be found in [27].

4.3. Scheduling Policy

Instances of a disk bandwidth reservation become eligible to execute *every* T_i units (at times S_i, $S_i + T_i$, $S_i + 2T_i$, $S_i + 2T_i$, $\cdots$). Consider an instance which arrives at time $S_i + nT_i$. This instance has a deadline of $S_i + nT_i + D_i$. Similarly, all instances of all outstanding disk bandwidth reservations have corresponding deadlines. After each disk block access is completed, the disk scheduler makes another scheduling decision. It picks the next ready reservation instance with the earliest deadline and issues a disk access command corresponding to that instance's next disk access request. If there are no pending requests, the disk remains idle.

4.4. The Architecture of the Reserved Filesystem

The architecture of the reserved filesystem follows a traditional scheme. A *Real-Time File Server* running on top of our resource kernel (based on the RT-Mach microkernel) manages the reserved real-time filesystem. RT-FS has multiple worker threads which receive and process filesystem access requests from real-time clients. Each worker thread stores the incoming request it is processing into a common io-request queue. The worker thread responsible for issuing the current disk block access waits for its completion. It then awakens, and determines the next request based on the scheduling policy above. If the next request corresponds to another worker thread, that thread is signaled. Else, the worker thread continues to service its remaining disk access requests, if any.

4.5. Exploiting 'B': Just-In-Time Disk Scheduling

The earliest deadline disk scheduling described above blindly picks the next block with the earliest deadline irrespective of the current position of the disk head. Since the physical movement of the disk head and the disk's rotational latencies constitute significant durations of time, such dynamic scheduling can result in significant disk subsystem throughput reductions particularly under heavy disk traffic. The reductions can be directly attributed to the time wasted by the disk head moving from one end to another and the disk's rotational time. In summary, the deadines are preferred over a block's physical location.

Traditional scan algorithms, in contrast, re-order the disk request queue such that the block closest to the current head position (in the direction of movement) is accessed next. As a result, a disk request which just arrived can be serviced before another disk request which has been waiting for a long time just because the latter is farther away from the head position. To summarize, the physical block location is favored over timeliness.

The earliest deadline scheduling algorithm and the scan algorithm are therefore at odds with one another. Fortunately, a hybrid scheme which can obtain all the benefits of the earliest deadline scheduling algorithm and at least part of the benefits of the scan algorithm is possible. In priority-driven scheduling, higher priority activities preempt lower priority activities. Since both lower and higher priority activities must be schedulable in an admission-controlled system, higher priority activities typically complete well ahead of their deadlines. In other words, such higher priority activities have a good amount of "slack" in their completion times. Based on this observation, we present a new algorithm we call "Just-in-time" disk scheduling. This algorithm exploits the slack available to higher priority tasks to schedule accesses of other disk blocks which are closer to the current head position.[5]

A brief description of the just-in-time disk scheduling algorithm is as follows. The maximum "slack" available to each disk reservation is computed whenever a new request is admitted (or an existing reservation is deleted). At run-time, if the current slack of higher priority reservations is non-zero, another unreserved (or lower priority reserved) request can be scheduled if closer to the disk head. If slack is stolen, the slack of higher priority reservations is reduced by one. This process is then repeated. If the slack of a high priority reservation goes to zero, it will be serviced independent of its location. The detailed description of the just-in-time algorithm can be found in [27].

4.6. Performance Evaluation

The capability of the disk bandwidth reservation scheme in our resource kernel to satisfy demands on disk bandwidth is illustrated in Figure 4-1. One disk bandwidth reservation of 12 disk blocks every 250 *ms* was requested in the presence of other unreserved accesses to the disk. As can be seen from the plot, this demand is satisfied by both the earliest deadline scheme and the just-in-time scheme; in fact, both lines are flat and coincide almost completely in the plot. However, the scan algorithm attempts to optimize disk throughput and pays for it by *not* delivering the needed throughput of 12 blocks every 250 *ms*. As a matter of fact, the bandwidth consumption varies widely.[6]

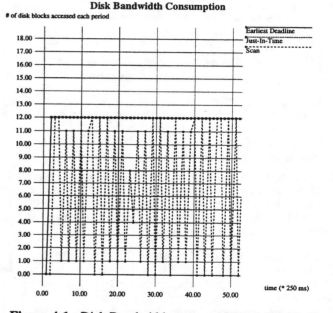

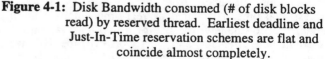

Figure 4-1: Disk Bandwidth consumed (# of disk blocks read) by reserved thread. Earliest deadline and Just-In-Time reservation schemes are flat and coincide almost completely.

We also imposed heavy disk traffic conditions and measured the throughput obtained under the scan and earliest deadline algorithms. This is shown in Table 4-1. As can be seen, the earliest deadline algorithm obtains only about 10% less throughput than the scan algorithm. This is the price to be paid for the predictable and guaranteed disk bandwidth obtained by the earliest deadline algorithm (as shown in Figure 4-1).

---

[5]Such "slack-stealing" has been done in the context of processor scheduling theory in order to provide better response to aperiodic activities [15]. The optimization, cost functions and implementation tradeoffs seem to be different for the processor and the disk, however.

[6]The pattern is more dramatic in a zoomed out view with the x-axis ranging upto 400 periods, but the lines/points are not clearly legible in a relatively small black-and-white graph.

Requested throughput (KB/s)	Throughput with Scan (KB/s)	Throughput for Earliest Deadline Scheduling (KB/s)	Throughput Degradation (%)
1158.6	856.36	764.88	10.68%

Table 4-1: Scan and EDF real-time filesystem throughput comparison

4.6.1. Synthetic Workload Behavior with both CPU and Disk Requirements

We next imposed a synthetic workload to determine the completion times of disk access requests, and to study the drop in disk throughput when the Scan policy is replaced with a policy which attempts to satisfy timing constraints in preference to enhancing disk throughput.

As illustrated in Figure 4-2, the real-time workload tested consists of two threads, *Thread 1* and *Thread 1b*. *Thread 1* reads periodically from disk and copies all the data into buffer A, while *Thread 1b* processes data previously stored in buffer B. At the end of the period, there is a buffer switch and the role of both buffers is interchanged. Buffers A and B have the same size. We bound disk bandwidth and CPU reserves to *Thread 1*, and a CPU reserve to *Thread 1b*, and traced the execution in terms of completion times, deadline misses and disk utilization. *Thread 1* makes use of relatively little cpu time and it sleeps till the beginning of the next period to invoke a new read operation. *Thread 1b* processes the data previously stored in the buffer. Both *Thread 1* and *Thread 1b* have a period of 250 *ms*. Also, *Thread 1* reads 44 KBytes during each of its instances, and has a deadline of 162 *ms* for completing its reads. Note that this deadline is shorter than its period of 250 *ms*, forcing a stringent test for the filesystem. *Thread 1b* is offset from *Thread 1* by 162 ms and has a deadline of 88 *ms*.

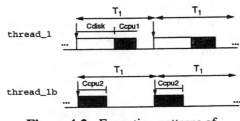

Figure 4-2: Execution patterns of *Thread 1* and *Thread1b*

Six periodic threads each with a different period (varying from 300 *ms* to 640 *ms*) and a different read-access load on the disk (varying from 8 KBytes to 200 KBytes per periodic instance of the thread) were introduced as competing threads without any reserved capacity on either the CPU or the disk bandwidth. We ran this workload for a duration of 100 seconds and measured the completion times of each periodic instance, and the total disk bandwidth consumed. The completion times are illustrated in Figure 4-3.

If we use EDF/EDF+JIT without reserving the CPU there

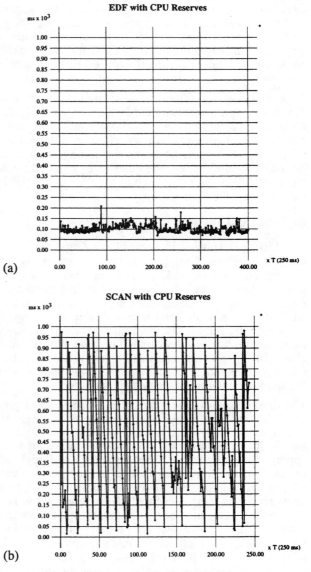

Figure 4-3: *Thread 1* Completion Times

are some deadlines misses (2 out of 400: periods 88 and 258). In these cases the task finished after 162 *ms* (but never after the period of 250 *ms*). These two deadline misses are due to the fact that our filesystem (extension of the Berkeley Fast FileSystem) does not allocate blocks contiguously on disk. So relatively high interblock seek times out of the cylinder group may happen from time to time even with requests for successive blocks within a file from the same thread. This can happen for each 1 MB of filesystem data according to the Berkeley FFS allocation algorithm and can lead to potential deadline misses. Accounting for the worst-case interblock seek times in the admission control test would avoid this problem, but can lead to extremely low guaranteed disk throughput. Thus, not withstanding our admission control test, some deadlines can be missed. However, as can be seen from our experiments, the deadline misses are rather infrequent. Conversely, in the Scan case there is no time to run the needed 400 disk accesses and only 248 accesses are completed within the experiment duration. The completion times are nearly always greater than the period itself (> 250 *ms*) and sometimes much greater. This shows that EDF w/ CPU reserves consistently meets the timeliness constraints of the real-time application accessing the disk.

Disk Throughput: The total disk bandwidth consumed in the above experiment was 16,464 KBytes with the EDF and CPU reserve policy, and 17,750 KBytes with the Scan policy. This represents only a performance throughput loss of 7.25%. In return, however, the timing constraints and periodic bandwidth requirements are satisfied with the EDF/CPU reserves policy, while they are dramatically unsatisfied with the Scan policy.

5. Practical Issues

5.1. Using Different Reservations Together
Consider a video display application which reads a video movie from the local disk and displays it on the screen. The movie is long enough that it does not fit into memory. As a result, subsequent video frames must be read from the disk while frames already read into a double buffer are being played on the screen. In this case, the video display algorithm must not only be scheduled on the CPU (where it can also do decompression or special signal processing) but also obtain guaranteed disk bandwidth to display the movie and its audio track without user-perceptible jitter.

The most straightforward way of approaching this problem is as follows: the application consists of a single thread which binds itself to a processor reservation and a disk bandwidth reservation with the same period, start time and appropriate computation times to satisfy the application's needs. There can be other threads in the system which use other combinations of resources (such as the processor and network bandwidth). Each of these reservations need to satisfy their associated deadlines given by the parameter D. However, it is known that the problem of scheduling concurrent tasks on multiple resources with timeliness constraints is NP-complete [5]. As a result, one faces the dilemma of finding a practical acceptable solution, since finding an optimal solution to the problem is very impractical. We address this problem next.

5.2. Resource Decoupling
Since simultaneous access to multiple resources is the problem we face, a natural solution to the practical dilemma one faces is to try to decouple the use of different resources, which can be used independent of one another. An end-to-end timing constraint problem is normally intractable as a single big problem, and is hence solved as a series of small problems where each problem only spans a single resource. For example, in an audio-conferencing application [23], the first pipeline stage occurs in the sound card which transfers data to the processor using *periodically self-initiated* DMA or multi-master bus transactions. A 2nd pipeline stage occurs on the processor to transmit the data and the next stage occurs in the network. The end-to-end delay for audio is the sum of the delays encountered in each of the audio pipeline stages. We refer to this strategy where each of the resources

involved are scheduled independent of one another as resource decoupling. When resources are decoupled, for example, the completion time test of Section 2 can be applied to each resource independently.

In the audio-conferencing application, the only coupling between the pipeline stages lies actually at the interface between stage 2 and the network (or the network and stage 4).[7] When the processor is ready to send out packets, the network must be able to transmit them. Memory buffers on the network interface card provide some decoupling by storing packets that the processor is ready to transmit, but the network is not ready to accept yet. We address this problem next.

5.3. Processor Co-Dependency
A phenomenon that we name *processor co-dependency* provides a hint to the solution. Complete resource decoupling seems possible between any two resources if neither of them is the processor. Since the processor is the brain of the system, communications between the network and the disk, for example, must go through the processor. The processor must obtain the network packets and then send them to the disk. In other words, a coupling problem which at first sight is between the disk and the network gets translated into two independent couplings between the disk and the processor, and between the processor and the network. The net result is that as soon as the disk (or the network) demand attention from the processor, the processor must be able to provide it.

5.4. "Immediate" or "System" Reservations
In our resource reservation model, we define the concept of a "system reservation" which is a highest priority reservation which does not get depleted. As a result, any thread or threads bound to a system reservation will be able to execute at the highest priority as soon as possible (subject only to other threads using a system reservation). We also sometimes refer to the system reservation as an "immediate reservation" because of the immediacy of its service. Clearly, the use of "system reserves" must be confined to trusted services only (to satisfy goal G3 of resource kernels), which must be trusted to use them only sparingly for relatively quick transfers of data. The worker threads in the reserved filesystem of Section 4.4 also fall into the category of system reservation users. It must be remembered that the usage of the system reservation will adversely affect new resource requests and must be accounted for in admission tests.

We measured the time consumed by components of a disk I/O to complete a filesystem block fetch of 4KB: time spent in core filesystem code = 532 μs, time spent in filesystem overhead (block map queries, etc.) = 171 μs, time spent in data copies = 131 μs, time spent in disk reserve overheads (scheduling, updating slack, etc.) = 230 υs, time spent in I/O = 2550 υs leading to a total elapsed time of 3082 υs. The CPU usage for the worker thread in the filesystem is there-

---

[7]If the network interface card hardware can be configured to be in auto-initiation mode as on the sound card, this coupling problem would disappear as well. This argues for better and more sophisticated support in interface cards and controllers. The trend towards MMX support and "software modems" is unfortunately in the opposite direction!

fore 532 vs out of 3082 μs = 17.26%. Since one worker thread can access the disk at any given time, this represents the worst-case processor requirement imposed by the real-time filesystem. However, due to the fact that disk seeks will not be issued continuously in a general system, this number will be lower in practice. Otherwise, for a disk-intensive context, this overhead is likely acceptable.

5.5. Calibrating an Application's Requirements

The computation time C needed for a reservation must be known in order to reserve processor time before it can be requested. It is, however, unknown practically before its actual execution since it heavily depends on a machine platform on which an application program runs. Even on machines with the same CPU and the same clock rate, the execution time may be affected by the presence of cache, the amount of memory, memory and system bus interface chip sets, and other I/O interface cards. Thus, we need to obtain C for the current platform by actually running an application on it. Obtaining C requires the kernel to support precise measurement of the processor time consumed by a certain thread. We now discuss how this can be obtained using only our resource kernel capabilities.

Our resource kernel supports hard reservations and also provides current and accumulated usage on a reservation by a program. The hard reservation ensures that any threads bound to it can only run upto its specified C. The execution time of the application program to be calibrated is then measured as follows. A new hard reservation, named (say) "calibration", is created, and the given application program is bound to it just for the purpose of measuring its execution time. The reservation will get depleted by the running of the application program, get replenished by the resource kernel, and the process will repeat until the application program completes execution. The accumulated usage on the hard reservation "calibration" now yields the execution time of the application program. An advantage of this method is that it is certain that a program can obtain its C even when the system is busy since it is guaranteed to receive a certain amount of processor time for its execution.

5.6. Portability Of Resource Specifications

As mentioned above, the absolute execution time of a program changes from platform to platform depending upon processor speed, etc. As a result, the specification of C in absolute time-units can become inherently not portable. Fortunately, portable time-units are available in the form of the number of clock ticks and the number of instructions executed for a given program segment on the processor. Of these two, the number of clock ticks is perhaps more portable since today's microprocessors contain on-chip clock counters which can not only provide high-accuracy resolution as well be inherently scalable across chips with lower or higher clock speeds. Similarly, C_i for disk bandwidth reservation can specify the number of disk blocks to be read, or better, the number of bytes to be read. The latter units will also be portable across platforms using different disk block sizes. Implementations of resource kernels must therefore provide convenience functions to translate "portable time-units" on a resource to native absolute time-units.

5.7. Adaptive QoS Management

User-level resource managers can be built on top of a resource kernel to react (or adapt to) to changes in application, system resources and the environment. In distributed real-time applications, such as video conferencing, the change in quality at one end-point typically implies that the other end-point must also adapt its quality correspondingly. Such distributed adaptations must clearly happen at a larger time-scale than single-node resource allocation changes. Similarly, we take the position that user-level application changes happen at a larger time-scale than the decisions made in the resource kernel to dynamically schedule activities on system resources. Such user-level resource managers can also potentially implement more complex resource management policies than the ones used by our resource model.

6. Concluding Remarks

We have presented a resource-centric approach to building real-time kernels, and we call the resulting kernel a resource kernel. The resource kernel provides timely, guaranteed and protected access to resources. We now compare our approach with two related approaches, and summarize our research contributions.

6.1. Resource Kernels and Related Approaches

We now compare the resource kernel notions with the approaches used by operating systems such as Nemesis [29] and Exokernel [7]. Nemesis and our resource kernel approach adopt a similar model of resource specification and allocation, based on the so-called $\{C, T\}$ model originally proposed by Liu and Layland [18]. Nemesis implicitly assumes a deadline of T before which the C units of time must be available. Our resource kernel also supports a deadline shorter than T[8]. The Nemesis approach to dealing with the problem of priority inversion, a potentially significant stumbling block of multi-tasking real-time systems, is rather unclear. In our resource kernel approach, bounding priority inversion is a key principle of managing interactions between concurrent real-time activities. Priority inversion, where a higher priority request is blocked by a lower priority activity, is unavoidable in the general case (such as critical sections, non-preemptible bus transactions and finite size ATM cells). However, it is imperative that unbounded priority inversion be eliminated, as in the use of semaphores in a priority-driven system [31, 35]. Such durations of priority inversion must be bounded and if possible minimized. Priority inheritance protocols have also been extended to dynamic priority algorithms [3, 9]. In resource kernels, we use priority inheritance in the form of reserve propagation [26] where a blocking thread inherits the scheduling priority of a higher priority reserved thread for the duration of the blocking.

Nemesis advocates the minimization of servers to enable correct "charging" of resource usage to applications. The Nemesis approch is to put 'server code' into client libraries, which would then use critical sections to enforce consistency requirements across multiple clients as necessary. Our

---

[8]A deadline longer than T is also possible.

resource kernel notions take a neutral stance on the topic of servers in that we (must) support configurations with and without servers. We do so for two fundamental reasons:

1. *Time and space are distinct*: Servers and critical sections executing in client space providing the given service are strictly analogous in a timing predictability sense, and differ only in a spatial organization sense. More precisely, the blocking (or priority version) factor is (almost) the same whether a service is implemented as a client library or within a server thread. Any difference arises only due to spatial overhead factors (primarily due to less context-switching in the case of client library implementations, for example see [24, 23]). This is hardly a fundamental question of functionality or capability. Consider a service S (such as a draw-in-window operation) executing in a real-time server like X. The server obtains requests from multiple clients. In a real-time system, the requests will be queued up in priority order *and* with support for priority inheritance to avoid unbounded priority inversion problems. If implemented as a client library, the critical section used within the library will use a mutex, which in turn will use a priority queue for waiting threads and support priority inheritance.[9]

2. *Sharing and interactions are in general unavoidable*: Concurrently running applications interact not only because they eventually share the same underlying physical resources, but also because of logical requirements above the physical layer. Shared display, shared files, concurrent access to bank accounts, shared data such as movies and databases are only some examples of these shared logical resources. As a result, critical sections which manage these shared *logical* resources are unavoidable in the context of multi-tasking and multithreaded systems. Whether these critical sections are organized in client space or in a dedicated server is only a question of convenience and flexibility with the time/space distintions coming into play. Anyhow, critical sections can be shortened or optimized but in general cannot be eliminated.[10]

Memory implications of using a client library (with a critical section) and a server also need to be considered. When a service is implemented as a server, it is relatively easy (for example) to wire down that server memory for predictable real-time performance. However, if clients used their own libraries (with critical sections), other relatively more complex issues must be addressed. In one case, each client can have its own copy of the library leading to higher memory usage. In contrast, if shared (dynamically linked) libraries are used, memory usage is the same as a server, but one must now be able to ensure that a shared library is wireable.

In other words, a finer granularity of memory control becomes necessary.

The Exo-kernel approach advocates that all policy decisions except for access protection reside in user-level programs. However, for real-time systems, the CPU scheduling policy must be centrally managed (at the "root") to ensure that an application group can satisfy its own timing constraints. This global scheduling policy *cannot* be delegated to individual applications. On the other hand, if the CPU resource management policy is deemed to be a temporal protection mechanism that resides in the exo-kernel, the resource kernel notion is actually compatible with the exo-kernel approach as well. Each application can then build its own local scheduler to use its allocated time in a way that it sees fit. However, in practice, we do not expect local schedulers in user space to provide significant added value. Instead, we propose a Quality of Service (QoS) manager running in user space (as a server) on top of the resource kernel [22, 32]. This QoS manager can arbitrate among competing requests when the maximal requests of all applications cannot be satisfied with the available resources.

6.2. Contributions

We have presented the notion of a resource kernel, which provides timely and protected access to machine resources. In this approach geared towards real-time and multimedia operating systems, guaranteed and protected access

- **Uniformity**: a single resource specification scheme can be applied to different time-shared resource types with timeliness control. The scheme can be locally optimized and applied for each resource type.

- **Resource management transparency**: the use of the exact resource management scheme is hidden from the application programs and changed transparently across different implementations. The implementation of the resource management scheme can use, among other things, fixed priority schemes such as rate-monotonic scheduling [18] and deadline-monotonic scheduling [17], dynamic priority schemes such as earliest-deadline-first [18], or processor sharing schemes such as PGPS, virtual clocks or WF^2Q [4]. We demonstrate two very different schemes for CPU and disk bandwidth management even though each uses the same resource specification model.

- **Resource composability**: We show that multiple resource types can be guaranteed at the same time with acceptable performance levels. In specific, reservations of different resource types can be independently created and then composed. We use the technique of *resource decoupling* [36] and management of *processor* co-dependency using higher priority *system reserves* to provide simultaneous access to CPU resource and another resource type simultaneously. We are unaware of other OS work where simultaneous access to two or more resources is addressed.

- *Hard* **resource reservation**: In this resource allocation scheme, the usage of a resource cannot exceed the allocated amount of the resource even if the resource is

---

[9]In the general case of this discussion, one should replace the notion of priority with the notion of 'scheduling attribute' which may be priorities or reserves with the basic concept remaining the same.

[10]Lock-free protocols exist but seem to be useful only under limited conditions.

idle. While this may sound draconian and wasteful, we expect that this will be a powerful building block for constructing virtual resources, which allow untrusted applications to be built and run in their own resource space with a pre-determined finite effect on other applications at all times.

- **Interactions and Disk bandwidth management:** The resource kernel is able to monitor and control priority inversion arising from the interactions between real-time tasks due to the use of common shared services. By deliberately introducing priority inversion in a controlled fashion, we demonstrate that there is no significant loss of disk subsystem throughput for acceptably substantial ranges of disk traffic while guaranteeing timely access to disk bandwidth for real-time and multimedia applications. This is achieved using a novel *just-in-time* disk scheduling scheme. Guaranteed access to disk bandwidth is obtained at the expense of a relatively small loss in throughput.

- **Flexibility of resource kernels:** Our resource kernel abstractions allow resource usage to be automatically calibrated, and to be portable across different hardware platforms.

6.3. Future Work
Our future work will include exploring network bandwidth reservation in conjunction with processor and disk reservation. Network bandwidth management has many implications in the context of a resource kernel: protocol stack overhead dominates on the CPU. As a result, network bandwidth management translates to both network reservation and CPU management. The times during which both network bandwidth and CPU cycles need to be available seem to be fairly limited, but remain to be verified.

The issue of CPU co-dependency needs to be addressed at greater length. Additional buffer space between different resource types with hardware buffers can also alleviate the problem; this is typical of today's hardware systems with self-triggered DMA on sound cards (such as the SoundBlaster 16), and bus-mastering on multi-master backplanes such as the PCI bus. Finally, distributed resource reservation in networked systems will open up another frontier of work.

Appendix: Admission Control Schemes

1. Resource Specification Notation
Let the set of n reservations requiring processor reservation be denoted as $\tau_1, \tau_2, \cdots, \tau_n$. Each reservation τ_i needs to obtain C_i units of time every T_i units of time. In addition, the C_i units of resource time must be available at or before D_i in each periodic interval separated by T_i.

2. Admission Control Using Fixed Priority Policies
The reservations are ordered in descending order of their fixed priorities such that for $i = 1$ to $n-1$, priority(τ_i) < τ_{i+1}.

In mathematical form, a necessary and sufficient condition for the schedulability of a set of periodic tasks using fixed priority scheduling is as follows [14]:

$$\forall i, 1 \leq i \leq n, \quad \min_{0 < t \leq D_i} \left(\sum_{j=1}^{i} \frac{C_j}{t} \left\lceil \frac{t}{T_j} \right\rceil \right) \leq 1$$

In algorithmic form, the completion time CT_i of a reservation τ_i with a resource allocation can be computed as follows using a recurrence relation [10, 39].

1. Let $w_i^0 := C_i$.

2. Compute $w_i^{k+1} := \sum_{j=1}^{i-1} C_j \left(\lceil \frac{w_i^k}{T_j} \rceil \right)$.

3. If $w_i^{k+1} > D_i$, $CT_i := \infty$. Skip to Step 6.

4. If $w_i^{k+1} = w_i^k$, $CT_i := w_i^k$. Skip to Step 6.

5. $k := k + 1$. Go to Step 2.

6. If $CT_i \leq D_i$, τ_i meets its deadline.

The completion time test is repeated for all reservations which need to be guaranteed. Even if one reservation will miss its deadline, the admission test will deny the newest incoming request.

3. Admission Control Based on Rate-Monotonic Priority Assignment
The rate-monotonic priority assignment algorithm is an optimal fixed priority algorithm when $D_i = T_i$ [18]. The reservations are ordered in descending order based on their rate-monotonic priorities (i.e., $T_i < T_{i+1}$). The admission control test use the scheme described in Section 2.

4. Admission Control Based on Deadline-Monotonic Priority Assignment
The deadline-monotonic priority assignment algorithm is an optimal fixed priority algorithm when $D_i \leq T_i$ [17]. The reservations are ordered in descending order based on their deadline-monotonic priorities (i.e. $D_i < D_{i+1}$). The admission control test uses the same scheme described in Section 2.

References

[1]   R. Abbott and H. Garcia-Molina. *Scheduling Real-Time Transactions with Disk Resident Data X Server.* Technical Report CS-TR-207-89, Department of Computer Science, Princeton University, February, 1989.

[2]   Baker, T. P. A Stack-Based Resource Allocation Policy for Real-Time Processes. *IEEE Real-Time Systems Symposium*, Dec., 1990.

[3]   Baker, T. Stack-Based Scheduling of Realtime Processes. *Journal of Real-Time Systems* 3(1):67--100, March 1991.

[4]   J. C. R. Bennett and H. Zhang. WF²Q: Worst-case Fair-Weighted Fair-Queueing. In *Proceedings of INFOCOM 96*. March, 1996.

[5]   J. Blazewicz, W. Cellary, R. Slowinski and J. Weglarz. Scheduling under Resource Constraints -- Deterministic Models. In *Annals of Operations Research, Volume 7*. Baltzer Science Publishers, 1986.

[6]   S. J. Daigle and J. K. Strosnider. Disk Scheduling for Multimedia Data Streams. *Proceedings of the SPIE Conference on High-Speed Networking and Multimedia Networking*, 1994.

[7]   D. R. Engler, M. F. Kaashoek and J. O. Toole, Jr. Exokernel: An Operating System Architecture for Application-Level Resource Management. *ACM Symposium on Operating System Principles*, December, 1995.

[8]   K. Jeffay, D. L. Stone and F. D. Smith. Kernel Support for Live Digital Audio and Video. In *Proceedings of the Second International Workshop on Network and Ope rating System Support for Digital Audio and Video*, pages 10-21. November, 1991.

[9]   K. Jeffay. Scheduling Sporadic Tasks with Shared Resources in Hard-Real-Time Systems. In *Proceedings of the 13th IEEE Real-Time Systems Symposium*, pages 89-99. IEEE, December, 1992.

[10]   Joseph, M. and Pandya. Finding Response Times in a Real-Time System. *The Computer Journal (British Computing Society)* 29(5):390-395, October, 1986.

[11]   Khanna, S., Sebree, M., and Zolnowsky, J. Real-Time Scheduling in SunOS 5.0. *The Proceedings of USENIX 92 Winter* :375-390, 1992.

[12]   Klein, M. H., Ralya, T., Pollak, B., Obenza, R. and Harbour, M. G. *A Practitioner's Handbook for Real-Time Analysis: Guide to Rate-Monotonic Analysis for Real-Time Systems.* Kluwer Academic Publishers, 1993. ISBN 0-7923-9361-9.

[13]   Lehoczky, J. P. and Sha, L. Performance of Real-Time Bus Scheduling Algorithms. *ACM Performance Evaluation Review, Special Issue Vol. 14, No. 1* , May, 1986.

[14]   Lehoczky, J. P., Sha, L. and Ding, Y. The Rate Monotonic Scheduling Algorithm --- Exact Characterization and Average-Case Behavior. *IEEE Real-Time Systems Symposium* , Dec, 1989.

[15]   Lehoczky, J. P., Sha, L., Strosnider, J. K. and Tokuda, H. Fixed Priority Scheduling Theory for Hard Real-Time Systems. *Technical Report, Department of Statistics, Carnegie Mellon University* , 1991.

[16]   Lehoczky, J. P. Fixed Priority Scheduling of Periodic Task Sets with Arbitrary Deadlines. *Proceedings of the IEEE Real-Time Systems Symposium* , Dec., 1990.

[17]   Leung, J. Y., and Whitehead, J. On the Complexity of Fixed-Priority Scheduling of Periodic, Real-Time Tasks. *Performance Evaluation* 2(4):237-250, Dec., 1982.

[18]   Liu, C. L. and Layland J. W. Scheduling Algorithms for Multiprogramming in a Hard Real Time Environment. *JACM* 20 (1):46 - 61, 1973.

[19]   Locke, C. D., Vogel, D. R., Lucas, L. Generic Avionics Software Specification. *Technical Report, Software Engineering Institute, Carnegie Mellon University* , 1990.

[20]   S. Chen, J. A. Stankovic, J. F. Kurose, D. Towsley. Performance Evaluation of Two New Disk Scheduling Algorithms for Real-Time Systems. *The Real-Time Systems Journal* 3:307-336, 1991.

[21]   P. Lougher and D. Shepherd. The Design and Implementation of a Continuous Media Storage Server . *Proceedings of the 3rd International Workshop on Network and Operating System Support for Audio and Video* , November, 1992.

[22]   C. Lee and R. Rajkumar and C. Mercer. Experiences with Processor Reservation and Dynamic QOS in Real-Time Mach. *In the proceedings of Multimedia Japan 96* , April, 1996.

[23]   C. Lee and K. Yoshida and C. Mercer and R. Rajkumar. Predictable Communication Protocol Processing in Real-Time Mach. *In the proceedings of IEEE Real-time Technology and Applications Symposium* , June, 1996.

[24]   C. Maeda and B. N. Bershad. Protocol Service Decomposition for High-Performance Networking. In *Proceedings of the Fourteenth ACM Symposium on Operating Systems Principles*, pages 244-255. December, 1993.

[25]   C. W. Mercer and S. Savage and H. Tokuda. Processor Capacity Reserves for Multimedia Operating Systems. In *Proceedings of the IEEE International Conference on Multimedia Computing and Systems.* May, 1994.

[26]   C. W. Mercer and R. Rajkumar. An Interactive Interface and RT-Mach Support for Monitoring and Controlling Resource Management. In *Proceedings of the IEEE Real-Time Technology and Applications Symposium.* May, 1995.

[27]   A. Molano, K. Juvva and R. Rajkumar. Real-Time Filesystems: Guaranteeing Timing Constraints for Disk Accesses in RT-Mach. In *IEEE Real-Time Systems Symposium.* December, 1997.

[28]   Needham, R. and Nakamura, A. An Approach to Real-Time Scheduling: Is it really a problem for multimedia? *The Third International Workshop on Network and Operating System Support for Multimedia* , 1992.

[29]   *Nemesis, the kernel: Overview* Dickson Reed and Robin Fairbairns, Editors, May 20, 1997.

[30]   *IEEE Standard P1003.4 (Real-time extensions to POSIX)* IEEE, 345 East 47th St., New York, NY 10017, 1991.

[31]   Rajkumar, R. *Synchronization in Real-Time Systems: A Priority Inheritance Approach.* Kluwer Academic Publishers, 1991. ISBN 0-7923-9211-6.

[32]   R. Rajkumar, C. Lee, J. P. Lehoczky and D. P. Siewiorek. A QoS-based Resource Allocation Model. *IEEE Real-Time Systems Symposium* , December, 1997.

[33]   Sha, L., Rajkumar, R. and Lehoczky, J. P. Task Scheduling in Distributed Real-Time Systems. *Proceedings of IEEE Industrial Electronics Conference* , 1987.

[34]   Sha, L., Rajkumar, R. and Lehoczky, J. P. Priority Inheritance Protocols: An Approach to Real-Time Synchronization. *Technical Report (CMU-CS-87-181), Department of Computer Science, CMU* , 1987.

[35]   Sha, L., Rajkumar, R. and Lehoczky, J. P. Priority Inheritance Protocols: An Approach to Real-Time Synchronization. *IEEE Transactions on Computers* :1175-1185, September, 1990.

[36]   Sha, L., Rajkumar, R. and Sathaye, S. Generalized Rate-Monotonic Scheduling Theory: A Framework for Developing Real-Time Systems. *Proceedings of the IEEE (journal)* , January, 1994.

[37]   Sprunt, H.M.B., Sha, L., and Lehoczky, J.P. Aperiodic Task Scheduling on Hard Real-Time Systems. *The Real-Time Systems Journal* , June, 1989.

[38]   John A. Stankovic. Misconceptions about Real-Time Computing. *Computer* 21(10):10-19, Oct., 1988.

[39]   Tindell, K. *An Extendible Approach for Analysing Fixed Priority Hard Real-Time Tasks.* Technical Report YCS189, Department of Computer Science, University of York, December, 1992.

[40]   C. A. Waldspurger and W. E. Weihl. Lottery Scheduling: Flexible Proportional-Share Resource Management. In *Proceedings of the First Operating Systems Design and Implementation*, pages 1-11. November, 1994.

A Hierarchical CPU Scheduler for Multimedia Operating Systems*

Pawan Goyal, Xingang Guo, and Harrick M. Vin

Distributed Multimedia Computing Laboratory
Department of Computer Sciences, University of Texas at Austin
Taylor Hall 2.124, Austin, Texas 78712-1188
E-mail: {pawang,xguo,vin} @cs.utexas.edu, Telephone: (512) 471-9732, Fax: (512) 471-8885
URL: http://www.cs.utexas.edu/users/dmcl

Abstract

The need for supporting variety of hard and soft real-time, as well as best effort applications in a multimedia computing environment requires an operating system framework that: (1) enables different schedulers to be employed for different application classes, and (2) provides protection between the various classes of applications. We argue that these objectives can be achieved by *hierarchical partitioning* of CPU bandwidth, in which an operating system partitions the CPU bandwidth among various application classes, and each application class, in turn, partitions its allocation (potentially using a different scheduling algorithm) among its sub-classes or applications. We present Start-time Fair Queuing (SFQ) algorithm, which enables such hierarchical partitioning. We have implemented a hierarchical scheduler in Solaris 2.4. We describe our implementation, and demonstrate its suitability for multimedia operating systems.

1 Introduction

Over the past few years, computing, communication, and video compression technologies have advanced significantly. Their synergistic advances have made the bandwidth and the storage space requirements of digital video manageable, and thereby have enabled a large class of multimedia applications (e.g., video conferencing, distance learning, news-on-demand services, virtual reality simulation of fire fighting, etc.). Since digital audio and video convey appropriate meaning only when presented continuously in time, such applications impose real-time requirements on the underlying storage, transmission, and processor sub-systems. Specifically, they require an

*This research was supported in part by IBM Graduate Fellowship, IBM Faculty Development Award, Intel, the National Science Foundation (Research Initiation Award CCR-9409666), NASA, Mitsubishi Electric Research Laboratories (MERL), and Sun Microsystems Inc.

operating system to allocate resources such as CPU, I/O bus, disk, and network bandwidth in a predictable manner as well as provide Quality of Service (QoS) guarantees (in terms of throughput, response time, etc.). Since no existing operating system meets these requirements, realizing such applications requires conventional operating systems to be extended along several dimensions. Design and implementation of a CPU allocation framework suitable for multimedia operating systems is the subject matter of this paper.

To determine suitable CPU scheduling algorithms, consider the requirements imposed by various application classes that may co-exist in a multimedia system:

- *Hard real-time applications*: These applications require an operating system to deterministically guarantee the delay that may be experienced by various tasks. Conventional schedulers such as the Earliest Deadline First (EDF) and the Rate Monotonic Algorithm (RMA) are suitable for such applications [12].

- *Soft real-time applications*: These applications require an operating system to statistically guarantee QoS parameters such as maximum delay and throughput. Since a large number of such applications are expected to involve video, consider the processing requirements for variable bit rate (VBR) video:

Due to inherent variations in scene complexity as well as the use of intra- and inter-frame compression techniques, processing bandwidth required for compression and decompression of frames of VBR video varies highly at multiple time-scales. For instance, Figure 1 illustrates that the processing bandwidth required for decompressing MPEG video varies from frame-to-frame (i.e., at the time scale of tens of milliseconds) as well as from scene-to-scene (i.e., at the time scale of seconds). Furthermore, these vari-

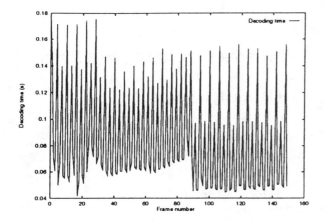

Figure 1 : Variation in decompression times of frames in an MPEG compressed video sequence

ations are unpredictable. These features lead to the following requirements for a scheduling algorithm for VBR video applications:

- Due to the multiple time-scale variations in the computation requirement of video applications, to efficiently utilize CPU, an operating system will be required to over-book CPU bandwidth. Since such over-booking may lead to CPU overload (i.e., cumulative requirement may exceed the processing capacity), a scheduling algorithm must provide some QoS guarantees even in the presence of overload.

- Due to the difficulty in predicting the computation requirements of VBR video applications, a scheduling algorithm must not assume precise knowledge of computation requirements of tasks.

EDF and RMA schedulers do not provide any QoS guarantee when CPU bandwidth is overbooked. Furthermore, their analysis requires the release time, the period, and the computation requirement of each task (thread) to be known a priori. Consequently, although appropriate for hard real-time applications, these algorithms are not suitable for soft real-time multimedia applications. Hence, a new scheduling algorithm that addresses these limitations is desirable.

- *Best-effort applications*: Many conventional applications do not need performance guarantees, but require the CPU to be allocated such that average response time is low while the throughput achieved is high. This is achieved in current systems by time-sharing scheduling algorithms.

From this, we conclude that different scheduling algorithms are suitable for different application classes in a multimedia system. Hence, an operating system framework that enables different schedulers to be employed for different applications is required. In addition to facilitating co-existence, such a framework should provide protection between the various classes of applications. For example, it should ensure that the overbooking of CPU for soft real-time applications does not violate the guarantees of hard real-time applications. Similarly, misbehavior of soft/hard real-time applications, either intentional or due to a programming error, should not lead to starvation of best-effort applications.

The requirements for supporting different scheduling algorithms for different applications as well as protecting application classes from one another leads naturally to the need for *hierarchical partitioning* of CPU bandwidth. Specifically, an operating system should be able to partition the CPU bandwidth among various application classes, and each application class, in turn, should be able to partition its allocation (potentially using a different scheduling algorithm) among its sub-classes or applications. In this paper, we present a flexible framework that achieves this objective.

In our framework, the hierarchical partitioning is specified by a tree. Each thread in the system belongs to exactly one leaf node, and each node in the tree represents either an application class or an aggregation of application classes. Whereas threads are scheduled by leaf node dependent schedulers (determined by the requirements of the application class), intermediate nodes are scheduled by an algorithm that achieves hierarchical partitioning. Specifically, intermediate nodes must be scheduled by an algorithm that: (1) achieves fair distribution[1] of processor bandwidth among competing nodes, (2) does not require a priori knowledge of computational requirements of threads, (3) provides throughput guarantees, and (4) is computationally efficient. We present Start-time Fair Queuing (SFQ) algorithm which meets all of these requirements. We further demonstrate that SFQ is suitable for video applications. We have implemented our hierarchical scheduling framework in Solaris 2.4. We describe our implementation and evaluate its performance. Our results demonstrate that the framework: (1) enables co-existence of heterogeneous schedulers, (2) protects application classes from each other, and (3) does not impose higher overhead than conventional time-sharing schedulers.

Observe that our hierarchical partitioning framework

---

[1]Intuitively, a CPU allocation is fair if, in every time interval, all runnable threads receive the same fraction of CPU bandwidth. This notion of uniform fairness generalizes to weighted fairness when threads have different weights and each thread receives CPU bandwidth in proportion to its weight. We will formalize this notion in Section 3.

also facilitates the development of a QoS manager that allocates resources as per the requirements of applications [10]. To illustrate, if an application requests hard (soft) real-time service, then the QoS manager can use a deterministic (statistical) admission control algorithm which utilizes the capacity allocated to hard (soft) real-time classes to determine if the request can be satisfied, and if so, assign it to the appropriate partition. On the other hand, if an application requests best-effort service, then the QoS manager would not deny the request but assign it to an appropriate partition depending on some other resource sharing policies. A QoS manager can also dynamically change the hierarchical partitioning to reflect the relative importance of various applications. For example, initially soft real-time applications may be allocated very small fraction of the CPU, but when many video decoders requesting soft real-time services are started (possibly as a part of a video conference), the allocation of soft real-time class may be increased significantly. The development of such policies, however, is the subject of future research and beyond the scope of this paper.

The rest of this paper is organized as follows. In Section 2, we introduce our hierarchical CPU scheduling framework. The Start-time Fair Queuing (SFQ) scheduling algorithm and its properties are described in Section 3. The details of our hierarchical SFQ scheduler implementation are described in Section 4. Section 5 describes the results of our experiments. We present related work in Section 6, and summarize our results in Section 7.

2 A Framework for Hierarchical CPU Scheduling

In our framework, the hierarchical partitioning requirements are specified through a *tree* structure. Each thread in the system belongs to exactly one leaf node. Each leaf node represents an aggregation of threads[2], and hence an application class, in the system. Each non-leaf node in the tree represents an aggregation of application classes. Each node in the tree has a weight that determines the percentage of its parent node's bandwidth that should be allocated to it. Specifically, if $r_1, r_2, ..., r_n$ denote the weights of the n children of a node, and if B denotes the processor bandwidth allocated to the parent node, then the bandwidth received by node i is given by:

$$B_i = \left(\frac{r_i}{\sum_{j=1}^{n} r_j} \right) * B$$

Furthermore, each node has a scheduler. Whereas the scheduler of a leaf node schedules all the threads that

---

[2] Threads are assumed to be the scheduling entities in the system.

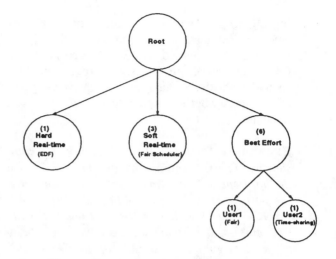

Figure 2 : An example scheduling structure

belong to the leaf node, the scheduler of an intermediate node schedules its child nodes. Given such a scheduling structure, the scheduling of threads occurs hierarchically: the root node schedules one of its child nodes; the child node, in turn, schedules one of its child nodes until a leaf node schedules a thread for execution. Figure 2 illustrates one such scheduling structure. In this example, the root class (node and class are used interchangeably) has three sub-classes: hard real-time, soft real-time and best-effort, with weights 1, 3, and 6, respectively. The bandwidth of the best-effort class has been further divided equally among leaf classes user1 and user2. Furthermore, whereas the soft real-time and user1 leaf classes employ a scheduler that fairly distributes its CPU allocation among its threads, the hard real-time and user2 classes have EDF and time-sharing schedulers, respectively.

Observe that the schedulers at leaf nodes in the hierarchy are determined based on the requirements of the applications. The requirements of a scheduling algorithm for intermediate nodes in the hierarchy, on the other hand, can be defined as follows:

1. To achieve hierarchical partitioning, the algorithm for scheduling intermediate nodes in the hierarchy should:

   - Partition the bandwidth allocated to a class among its sub-classes such that each sub-class gets its specified share.

   - Allocate the residual bandwidth fairly among its sub-classes. For example, in Figure 2, if there are no eligible threads in the hard real-time class, then its allocation should be partitioned between the soft real-time and best-effort nodes in the ratio 3:6.

Both these requirements would be met if the scheduling algorithm partitions the allocation of a class among its sub-classes in proportion to their weights, i.e., achieves weighted fairness. Moreover, as the following example illustrates, a key requirement for such an algorithm is that it should achieve weighted fairness even when the bandwidth available to a class fluctuates over time.

Example 1 *Consider the scheduling structure shown in Figure 2. Initially, let there be no threads in the hard and soft real-time classes. Consequently, the best-effort class receives the full CPU bandwidth. When threads join the hard and soft real-time classes, the bandwidth available to the best-effort class goes down to 60% of the CPU bandwidth. In such a scenario, to ensure that user1 and user2 continue to receive equal share of the available bandwidth, the scheduling algorithm for the best-effort class must remain fair even when the available bandwidth fluctuates over time.*

2. Since the computational requirements of tasks may not be known precisely, the scheduling algorithm should not assume a priori knowledge of the time duration for which a task executes before it is blocked.

3. To support hard and soft real-time application classes, the scheduling algorithm should provide bounds on minimum throughput and maximum delay observed by nodes. Furthermore, for the bounds to be useful, they should hold in realistic computing environments in which interrupts may be processed at the highest priority [9].

4. To be feasible in general purpose operating systems, the scheduling algorithm should be computationally efficient.

Recently, we have developed a packet scheduling algorithm, referred to as *Start-time Fair Queuing* (SFQ), which achieves fair allocation of network bandwidth [6]. In the next section, we present the algorithm and demonstrate that it meets the above requirements, and hence, is suitable for CPU scheduling in multimedia operating systems.

3 Start-time Fair Queuing

Start-time Fair Queuing (SFQ) is a resource allocation algorithm that can be used for achieving fair CPU allocation. Before we present SFQ, let us formalize the notion of fair allocation. Let r_f be the weight of thread f and $W_f(t_1, t_2)$ be the aggregate work done in interval $[t_1, t_2]$ by the CPU for thread f. For ease of exposition, let the work done by the CPU for a thread be measured by the

number of instructions executed for the thread. Then, a CPU allocation is considered to be fair if, for all intervals $[t_1, t_2]$ in which two threads f and m are runnable, the normalized work (by weight) received by them is identical (i.e., $\frac{W_f(t_1, t_2)}{r_f} - \frac{W_m(t_1, t_2)}{r_m} = 0$). Clearly, this is an idealized definition of fairness as it assumes that threads can be served in infinitesimally divisible units. Since the threads are scheduled for a quantum at a time, there will be some unfairness. Consequently, the objective of a fair scheduling algorithm is to minimize the resultant unfairness (i.e., ensure that $\left| \frac{W_f(t_1, t_2)}{r_f} - \frac{W_m(t_1, t_2)}{r_m} \right|$ is as close to 0 as possible)[3].

To achieve this objective, SFQ assigns a start tag to each thread and schedules threads in the increasing order of start tags. To define the start tag, let the threads be scheduled for variable length quantum at a time. Also, let q_f^j and l_f^j denote the jth quantum of thread f and its length[4] (measured in units of instructions), respectively. Let $A(q_f^j)$ denote the time at which the jth quantum is requested. If the thread is making a transition from a blocked mode to runnable mode, then $A(q_f^j)$ is the time at which the transition is made; otherwise it is the time at which its previous quantum finishes. Then SFQ algorithm is defined as follows:

1. When quantum q_f^j is requested by thread f, it is stamped with start tag S_f, computed as:

$$S_f = \max\{v(A(q_f^j)), F_f\} \qquad (1)$$

where $v(t)$ is the virtual time at time t and F_f is the finish tag of thread f. F_f is initially 0, and when j^{th} quantum finishes execution it is incremented as:

$$F_f = S_f + \frac{l_f^j}{r_f} \qquad (2)$$

where r_f is the weight of thread f.

2. Initially the virtual time is 0. When the CPU is busy, the virtual time at time t, $v(t)$, is defined to be equal to the start tag of the thread in service at time t. On the other hand, when the CPU is idle, $v(t)$ is set to the maximum of finish tag assigned to any thread.

3. Threads are serviced in the increasing order of the start tags; ties are broken arbitrarily.

---

[3] Several other definitions of fairness have been introduced in the networking and operating systems literature. A comparative evaluation of their relative merits, however, is beyond the scope of this paper.

[4] If l_f^j is the length of quantum q_f^j in terms of instructions, then its time duration is $t_f^j = \frac{l_f^j}{C}$ where C is the rate of execution of the CPU.

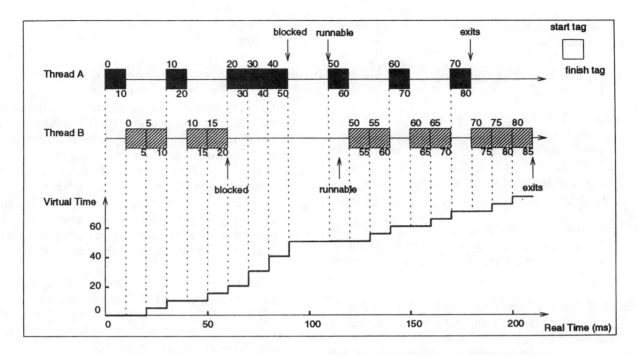

Figure 3 : Computation of virtual time, start tag, and finish tag in SFQ: an example

The following example illustrates the computation of the virtual time, as well as the start and the finish tags (and hence, the process of determining the execution sequence) in SFQ. Consider two threads A and B with weights 1 and 2, respectively, which become runnable at time $t = 0$. Let the scheduling quantum for each thread be 10ms and let $l_f = 10$. Let each thread consume the full length of the quantum each time it is scheduled. Initially, the virtual time $v(t) = 0$. Similarly, the start tags of threads A and B, denoted by S_A and S_B, respectively, are zero (i.e., $S_A = S_B = 0$). Since ties are broken arbitrarily, let us assume, without loss of generality, that thread A is scheduled first for one quantum. Since $v(t)$ is defined to be equal to the start tag of the packet in service, for $0 < t \leq 10 : v(t) = S_A = 0$. At the end of that quantum, the finish tag of A is computed as $F_A = 0 + \frac{10}{1} = 10$. Moreover, assuming that the thread remains runnable at the end of the quantum, it is stamped with $S_A = \max\{v(10), F_A\} = 10$. At this time, since $S_B < S_A$, the first quantum of thread B is scheduled. Note that since $S_B = 0$, the value of $v(t), 10 < t \leq 20$ continues to be equal to 0. At the end of this quantum, the finish tag for B is set to $F_B = 0 + \frac{10}{2} = 5$. Moreover, assuming that B remains runnable at the end of the quantum, we get $S_B = \max\{v(20), F_B\} = 5$. Carrying through this process illustrates that, before thread B blocks at time $t = 60$, threads A and B are scheduled for 20ms and 40ms, respectively, which is in proportion to their weights. When thread B is blocked, the entire CPU bandwidth is avail-

able to thread A, and the value of $v(t)$ changes at the beginning of each quantum of thread A. Now, when thread A blocks at time $t = 90$, the system contains no runnable threads. During this idle period, $v(t)$ is set to $\max\{F_A, F_B\} = \max\{50, 20\} = 50$. When thread A becomes runnable at time $t = 110$, $v(t) = 50$. Hence, thread A is stamped with $S_A = \max\{50, F_A\} = 50$, and is immediately scheduled for execution. On the other hand, when thread B becomes runnable at time $t = 115$, $v(t) = S_A = 50$. Hence, it is stamped with $S_B = \max\{50, F_B\} = \max\{50, 20\} = 50$. From this point, the ratio of CPU allocation goes back to 1:2. Finally, when thread A exits the system, the entire CPU bandwidth becomes available to thread B, until it completes execution. Figure 3 illustrates this complete execution sequence.

3.1 Properties of SFQ

In what follows, we describe the properties of the SFQ scheduling algorithm, and demonstrate that it meets the requirements of a hierarchical scheduler outlined in the previous section.

1. *SFQ achieves fair allocation of CPU regardless of variation in available processing bandwidth* and hence meets the key requirement of a scheduling algorithm for hierarchical partitioning. Specifically, in [6], we have shown that regardless of fluctuations in available processor bandwidth, SFQ guarantees that in any interval $[t_1, t_2]$ in which two threads f

and m are eligible for being scheduled, the following inequality holds:

$$\left| \frac{W_f(t_1, t_2)}{r_f} - \frac{W_m(t_1, t_2)}{r_m} \right| \leq \frac{l_f^{max}}{r_f} + \frac{l_m^{max}}{r_m} \quad (3)$$

where l_f^{max} and l_m^{max}, respectively, are the maximum length of quantum for which threads f and m are scheduled[5].   It has been shown in [4] that if a scheduling algorithm schedules threads in terms of quantums and guarantees that $\left| \frac{W_f(t_1,t_2)}{r_f} - \frac{W_m(t_1,t_2)}{r_m} \right| \leq H(f, m)$ for all intervals, then $H(f, m) \geq \frac{1}{2}(\frac{l_f^{max}}{r_f} + \frac{l_m^{max}}{r_m})$. Hence, SFQ is a near-optimal fair scheduling algorithm. In fact, no known algorithm achieves better fairness than SFQ.

2. *SFQ does not require the length of the quantum to be known a priori*: Since SFQ schedules threads in the increasing order of start tags, it does not need the length of the quantum of a thread to be known at the time of scheduling. The length of quantum q_f^j (namely, l_f^j) is required only when it finishes execution, at which time this information is always available. This feature is highly desirable in multimedia computing environments, where the computation requirements are not known precisely and threads may block for I/O even before they are preempted.

3. *SFQ provides bounds on maximum delay incurred and minimum throughput achieved by the threads in a realistic environment*: In most operating systems processing of hardware interrupts occurs at the highest priority. Consequently, the effective bandwidth of CPU fluctuates over time. SFQ provides bounds on delay and throughput even in such an environment. To derive these bounds, however, the variation in the CPU bandwidth has to be quantified. If the maximum rate of occurrence of interrupts and the CPU bandwidth used by the interrupts is known, the effective CPU bandwidth can be modeled as a Fluctuation Constrained (FC) server [11]. A FC server has two parameters; average rate C (instructions/s) and burstiness $\delta(C)$ (instructions). Intuitively, in any interval during a busy period, an FC server does at most $\delta(C)$ less work than an equivalent constant rate server. Formally,

Definition 1 *A server is a Fluctuation Constrained (FC) server with parameters $(C, \delta(C))$, if for all intervals $[t_1, t_2]$ in a busy period of the server,*

the work done by the server, denoted by $W(t_1, t_2)$, satisfies:

$$W(t_1, t_2) \geq C * (t_2 - t_1) - \delta(C) \quad (4)$$

If only bounds on the computation time required by the interrupts is known, then the FC server model is sufficient. However, if distributions of the computation time requirements for processing interrupts are known, then CPU is better modeled as an Exponentially Bounded Fluctuation (EBF) server [11]. An EBF server is a stochastic relaxation of FC server. Intuitively, the probability of work done by an EBF server deviating from the average rate by more than γ, decreases exponentially with γ. Formally,

Definition 2 *A server is an Exponentially Bounded Fluctuation (EBF) server with parameters $(C, B, \alpha, \delta(C))$, if for all intervals $[t_1, t_2]$ in a busy period of the server, the work done by the server, denoted by $W(t_1, t_2)$, satisfies:*

$$P\left(W(t_1, t_2) < C * (t_2 - t_1) - \delta(C) - \gamma\right) \leq Be^{-\alpha\gamma} \quad (5)$$

If CPU can be modeled as an FC or EBF server, then SFQ provides throughput and delay guarantees to each of the threads. To determine these guarantees, let the weights of the threads be interpreted as the rate assigned to the threads. For example, a thread that needs 30% of a 100MIPS CPU would have a rate of 30 MIPS. Let Q be the set of threads served by CPU and let $\sum_{n \in Q} r_n \leq C$ where C is the capacity of the CPU. Then, SFQ provides the following throughput and delay guarantees [6]:

Throughput Guarantee: If the CPU is an FC server with parameters $(C, \delta(C))$, then the throughput received by a thread f with weight r_f is also FC with parameters:

$$\left(r_f, r_f \frac{\sum_{n \in Q} l_n^{max}}{C} + r_f \frac{\delta(C)}{C} + l_f^{max} \right) \quad (6)$$

If, on the other hand, the CPU is an EBF server with parameters $(C, B, \alpha, \delta(C))$, then the throughput received by a thread f with weight r_f is also EBF with parameters:

$$\left(r_f, B, \frac{r_f}{C}\alpha, r_f \frac{\sum_{n \in Q} l_n^{max}}{C} + r_f \frac{\delta(C)}{C} + l_f^{max} \right) \quad (7)$$

Hence, if SFQ is used for hierarchical partitioning and if the CPU is an FC(EBF) server, then each of

---

[5] The maximum quantum length may be known a-priori or may be enforced by a scheduler by preempting threads.

the sub-classes of the root class are FC(EBF) servers. Using this argument recursively, we conclude that if the CPU is an FC(EBF) server, then each of the sub-classes are also FC(EBF) servers, the parameters of which can be derived using (6) and (7).

Delay Guarantee: If the CPU is a FC server, then SFQ guarantees that the time at which quantum q_f^j of thread f will complete execution, denoted by $L_{SFQ}(q_f^j)$, is given as:

$$L_{SFQ}(q_f^j) \leq EAT(q_f^j) + \sum_{n \in Q \wedge n \neq f} \frac{l_n^{max}}{C}$$
$$+ \frac{l_f^j}{C} + \frac{\delta(C)}{C} \qquad (8)$$

where $EAT(q_f^j)$ is the expected arrival time of quantum q_f^j. Intuitively, $EAT(q_f^j)$ is the time at which quantum q_f^j would start if only thread f was in the system and the CPU capacity was r_f. Formally,

$$EAT(q_f^j) = \max\{A(q_f^j), EAT(q_f^{j-1}) + \frac{l_f^{j-1}}{r_f}\}$$
$$(9)$$

where $EAT(q_f^0, r_f^0) = -\infty$.

If the CPU is an EBF server, then SFQ guarantees that $L_{SFQ}(q_f^j)$ is given as follows:

$$P \left(L_{SFQ}(q_f^j) \leq EAT(q_f^j, r_f^j) + \right.$$
$$\left. \sum_{n \in Q \wedge n \neq f} \frac{l_n^{max}}{C} + \frac{l_f^j}{C} + \frac{\delta(C)}{C} + \frac{\gamma}{C} \right)$$
$$\geq 1 - Be^{-\alpha\gamma} \quad 0 \leq \gamma \qquad (10)$$

The following example illustrates the delay guarantee of SFQ.

Example 2 *Consider a constant rate 100MIPS CPU that serves threads 1, 2, and 3. Let thread 1 reserve 30MIPS and execute 300K instructions every quantum. Also, let the other two threads execute at most 200K instructions every quantum. Then, since $\delta(C) = 0$ for a constant rate CPU, for thread 1, $\sum_{n \in Q \wedge n \neq f} \frac{l_n^{max}}{C} + \frac{l_f^j}{C} + \frac{\delta(C)}{C} = 7ms$. Since executing 300K instructions on a 30MIPS CPU takes 10ms, the expected arrival time of jth quantum of thread 1, assuming it remains runnable at the end of each of its allocated quantum, is $(j-1) * 10ms$. Hence, SFQ guarantees that j^{th} quantum of thread 1 will finish execution by $(j-1) * 10 + 7ms$.*

Thus, SFQ not only guarantees fair allocation of CPU to sub-classes, but also provides quantitative bounds on performance.

4. *SFQ is computationally efficient*: Whereas the computation of a start tag only requires one addition and one division, sorting can be efficiently done using a priority queue. The computational complexity of a priority queue is known to $O(logQ)$, where Q is the number of entities to be scheduled. Since the number of children of a node in a hierarchy are expected to be small (of the order of 2-10), this cost is insignificant when SFQ is used for hierarchical partitioning. Furthermore, no other known algorithm that simultaneously achieves predictable allocation and protection has a lower complexity. Although static priority algorithms have lower complexity, they provide no protection, and hence, have been found to be unsatisfactory for multimedia operating systems [15].

Recall from Section 1 that a scheduling algorithm suitable for video applications should: (1) provide QoS guarantees even in presence of overload, and (2) not require computation requirements to be known precisely. Since SFQ guarantees fair allocation of resources even in presence of overload and does not need computation requirements to be known precisely, it meets these requirements. Hence, it suitable for video applications as well.

4 Implementation

We have implemented our hierarchical CPU allocation framework in the Solaris 2.4 kernel, which is a derivative of SVR4 UNIX. Our framework utilizes SFQ to schedule all the intermediate nodes for achieving hierarchical partitioning. The requirements of hierarchical partitioning are specified through a tree referred to as a *scheduling structure*. Each node in the scheduling structure has a weight, a start-tag, and a finish-tag that are maintained as per the SFQ algorithm. A non-leaf node maintains a list of child nodes, a list of runnable child nodes sorted by their start-tags, and a virtual time of the node which, as per SFQ, is the minimum of the start-tags of the runnable child nodes. A leaf node has a pointer to a function that is invoked, when it is scheduled by its parent node, to select one of its threads for execution. Each node also has a unique identity and a name similar to a UNIX filename. For example, in the scheduling structure shown in Figure 2, the name of node user1 is "/best-effort/user1". The scheduling structure is created using the following system calls:

- int hsfq_mknod(char *name, int parent, int weight, int flag, scheduler_id sid): This system call creates a node with the given name as a child of node parent in the scheduling structure and returns the identifier of the new node. The flag parameter identifies the node to be created as a leaf or a non-leaf node. If the node is a leaf node, a pointer to the scheduling function of the class, identified by sid, is installed in the node.

- int hsfq_parse(char* name, int hint): This system call takes a name and resolves it to a node identifier in the scheduling structure. The name can be absolute or relative. If it is relative, it is considered to be relative to the node with identifier hint.

- int hsfq_rmnod(int id, int mode): This system call is used to remove a node from the scheduling structure. A node can be removed only if it does not have any child nodes.

- hsfq_move(int from, int to, ...): This system call is used to move a thread from one leaf node to another.

- hsfq_admin(int node, int cmd, void *args) : This system call is used for administration operations, other than those mentioned above, on the scheduling structure. Examples of administration operations include changing the weight of a node, determining the weight of a node, etc.

Given a scheduling structure, the actual scheduling of threads occurs recursively. To select a thread for execution, a function hsfq_schedule() is invoked. This function traverses the scheduling structure by always selecting the child node with the smallest start tag until a leaf node is selected. When a leaf node is selected, a function that is dependent on the leaf node scheduler, determined through the function pointer that is stored in the leaf node by hsfq_mknod(), is invoked to determine the thread to be scheduled. When a thread blocks or is preempted, the finish and the start tags of all the ancestors of the node to which the thread belongs have to be updated. This is done by invoking a function hsfq_update() with the duration for which the thread executed and the node identifier of the leaf node as parameters.

A node in the scheduling structure is scheduled if and only if at least one of the leaf nodes in the sub-tree rooted at that node has a runnable thread. The eligibility of a node is determined as follows. When the first thread in a leaf node becomes eligible for scheduling, function hsfq_setrun() is invoked with the leaf node's identifier. This function marks the leaf node as runnable and all the other ancestor nodes that may become eligible as a consequence. Note that this function has to traverse the path from the leaf up the tree only until a node that is already runnable is found. On the other hand, when the last thread in a leaf node makes a transition to sleep mode, function hsfq_sleep() is called with the leaf node's identifier. This function marks the leaf node as ineligible and all the other ancestor nodes that may become ineligible as a consequence. This function has to traverse the path from the leaf only until a node that has more than one runnable child nodes is found.

In our implementation, any scheduling algorithm can be used at the leaf node as long as it: (1) provides an interface function that can be invoked by hsfq_schedule() to select the next thread for execution, and (2) invokes hsfq_setrun(), hsfq_sleep(), and hsfq_update() as per the rules defined above. We have implemented SFQ as well as modified the existing SVR4 priority based scheduler to operate as a scheduler for a leaf node. The SVR4 leaf scheduler in our implementation, as in the standard release, uses a scheduling algorithm that is dependent on the scheduling class of a thread (e.g., time-sharing, interactive, system, etc.). Hence, in our implementation, a scheduler for a leaf node itself can use multiple scheduling policies.

Observe that the threads in a system may synchronize or communicate with each other, which can result in priority inversion (i.e., a scenario in which a lower priority thread may block the progress of a higher priority thread). The threads that synchronize/communicate may either belong to the same leaf class or different leaf classes. If the threads belong to different leaf classes, the notion of priority inversion is not defined. Furthermore, synchronization between threads belonging to different classes is not desirable, since that may lead to violation of QoS requirements of applications. For example, if a thread in the real-time leaf class synchronizes with a thread in the best-effort class, then, since the best-effort class does not perform any admission control, the QoS requirement of the thread may be violated. Techniques for avoiding priority inversion among threads belonging to the same leaf class, on the other hand, depend on the leaf class scheduler. For example, if the leaf scheduler uses static priority Rate Monotonic algorithm, then standard priority inheritance techniques can be employed [13, 14]. Similarly, when the leaf scheduler is SFQ, priority inversion can be avoided by transferring the weight of the blocked thread to the thread that is blocking it. Such a transfer will ensure that the blocking thread will have a weight (and hence, the CPU allocation) that is at least as large as the weight of the blocked thread.

We envision that our scheduling infrastructure would be used by a QoS manager [10] in a multimedia system (see Figure 4). Applications will specify their QoS requirements to the QoS manager which would: (1) determine the resources needed to meet the QoS requirements of the applications; (2) decide the scheduling class the application should belong to, and create the class if it does not exist; (3) employ class dependent admission control procedures to determine if the resource requirements can be satisfied (some classes may have no admission con-

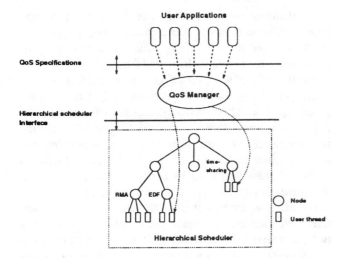

Figure 4 : Quality of Service Manager

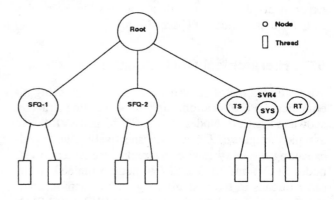

Figure 5 : Comparison of throughput of threads under SFQ and time-sharing schedulers

trol); and (4) allocate the resources to the application and move it to appropriate class. The QoS manager may also move applications between classes or change the resource allocation in response to change in QoS requirements. It would also dynamically change the relative allocations of different classes so as to effectively meet the requirements of the applications that may coexist at any time. The development of such policies is the subject of future research and beyond the scope of this paper.

5 Experimental Evaluation

We have evaluated the performance of our implementation using a Sun SPARCstation 10 with 32MB RAM. All our experiments were conducted in multiuser mode with all the normal system processes. Most of our experiments were carried out using the Dhrystone V2.1 benchmark, which is a CPU intensive application that executes a number of operations in a loop. The number of loops completed in a fixed duration was used as the performance metric. We evaluated several aspects of the hierarchical scheduler, the results of which are reported in the following sections.

5.1 Limitation of Conventional Schedulers

We had argued that conventional time-sharing schedulers are inadequate for achieving predictable resource allocation in multimedia operating systems. To experimentally validate this claim, we compared the throughput of 5 threads running Dhrystone benchmark under time-sharing and SFQ schedulers. Whereas in the case of SFQ all the threads had equal weight, in the case of time-sharing scheduler all the threads were assigned the same initial user priority. Figure 5 demonstrates that,

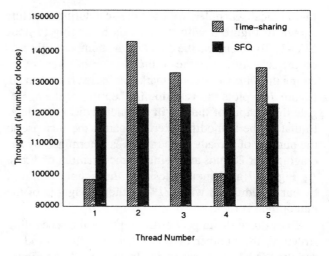

Figure 6 : Scheduling structure used for the experiments

in spite of having the same user priority, the throughput received by the threads in the time-sharing scheduler varies significantly, thereby demonstrating it's inadequacy in achieving predictable allocation. In contrast, all the threads in SFQ received the same throughput in conformance with the theoretical predictions. In [15], it has been demonstrated that when a multimedia application is run as a real-time thread in the SVR4 scheduler, the whole system may become unusable. This limitation of the SVR4 scheduler coupled with the unpredictability of time-sharing algorithm clearly demonstrates the need for a predictable scheduling algorithm for multimedia operating system.

5.2 Scheduling Overhead

A key concern in using dynamic priority-based algorithm such as SFQ is that the scheduling overhead may be high. To evaluate the overhead, we determined the ratio of the number of loops completed by a thread in our hierarchical scheduler and the unmodified kernel. In the hierarchical scheduler, we used the scheduling structure shown in Figure 6 with the threads belonging to node SFQ-1. To determine the effect of the number of threads on the scheduling overhead, the number of threads executing the Dhrystone benchmark was varied from 1 to 20. Figure 7(a) plots the variation in the ratio of the aggregate throughput of threads in our hierarchical scheduler to that in the unmodified kernel against the increase in the number of threads. The ratio was determined by averaging over 20 runs and using a time quantum of 20ms. As Figure 7(a) demonstrates, the throughput achieved by our scheduler is within 1% of the throughput of the unmodified kernel.

To evaluate the impact of the depth of the scheduling structure, the number of nodes between the root class and the SFQ-1 class was varied from 0 to 30. As Figure 7(b) demonstrates, in spite of the significant variation in the depth, the throughput remains within 0.2%. These experiments demonstrates that it is feasible to employ SFQ for hierarchical CPU scheduling.

5.3 Hierarchical CPU allocation

We evaluated the effectiveness of SFQ in achieving hierarchical CPU allocation using the scheduling structure shown in Figure 6. Nodes SFQ-1, SFQ-2 and SVR4 were assigned weights of 2, 6, and 1, respectively. Two threads executing the Dhrystone benchmark were added to leaf nodes SFQ-1 and SFQ-2 (SVR4 node contained all the other threads in the system). Figure 8(a) demonstrates that the aggregate throughput of nodes SFQ-1 and SFQ-2 (measured in terms of number of completed loops of the Dhrystone benchmark) are in the ratio 1:3 (i.e., in accordance to their weights). Observe that due to the variation in the CPU usage of the threads belonging to node SVR4, the aggregate throughput of nodes SFQ-1 and SFQ-2 fluctuates over time. In spite of this variation, nodes 1 and 2 receive throughput in the ratio 1:3, thereby demonstrating the SFQ achieves fair allocation even when the available CPU bandwidth fluctuates over time.

A key advantage of our hierarchical scheduler is that even though different leaf schedulers may be used, each node receives its fair allocation and is isolated from the other nodes. To demonstrate this, we used the scheduling structure shown in Figure 6 with 2 threads in SFQ-1 and 1 thread in SVR4. SFQ-1 as well SVR4 nodes were assigned the same weight. Figure 8(b) demonstrates that the threads in SFQ-1 node as well as SVR4 node make progress and are isolated from each other. Furthermore, both SFQ-1 and SVR4 nodes receive the same throughput. This is in contrast to the standard SVR4 scheduler where a higher priority class, such as the real-time class, can monopolize the CPU.

To demonstrate the feasibility of supporting hard real-time applications in our hierarchical scheduling framework, we used the scheduling structure shown in Figure 6, and executed two threads (namely, thread1 and thread2) in the RT class of the SVR4 node, and an MPEG decoder in SFQ-1 node. The SVR4 and the SFQ-1 nodes were given equal weights. Whereas thread1 executed for 10 ms every 60 ms, thread2 required 150 ms of computation time every 960 ms. Rate monotonic algorithm was used to schedule these two threads. For each thread, a clock interrupt was used to announce the deadline for the current round and the start of a new round of computation. The threads were scheduled for 25ms quantums. We measured the performance of the system using two parameters: (1) *scheduling latency*, which refers to the duration for which a thread has to wait prior to getting access to the CPU after its clock interrupt; and (2) *slack time*, which refers to the difference in time between the deadline and the time at which the current round of computation completes. Figure 9 depicts the variation in scheduling latency and slack time for each round for thread1. Whereas Figure 9(a) illustrates that thread1 gained access to the CPU within a bounded period of time (equal to the length of the scheduling quantum) after its clock interrupt, Figure 9(b) demonstrates that none of the deadlines for thread1 were violated (i.e., the slack time is always positive).

5.4 SFQ as a Leaf Scheduler

To evaluate the use of SFQ as a leaf scheduler, two threads with weights 5 and 10, each running the Berkeley MPEG video player, were assigned to node SFQ-1. Figure 10 plots the number of frames decoded by each thread as a function of time. It demonstrates that the thread with weight 10 decodes twice as many frames as compared to the other thread in any time interval.

5.5 Dynamic Bandwidth Allocation

A QoS manager may dynamically change the bandwidth allocation of classes to meet the application requirements. Hence, SFQ should be able to achieve fair allocation even when bandwidth allocation is dynamically varied. To evaluate this aspect of SFQ, two threads, each executing the Dhrystone benchmark, were run in the SFQ-1 node. The behavior of the threads was varied over time as follows:

- At time 0, both threads were assigned a weight of 4. Hence, the throughput ratio between threads was 4:4.

- At time 4, the weight of thread 2 was changed to 2. Hence, the throughput ratio became 4:2.

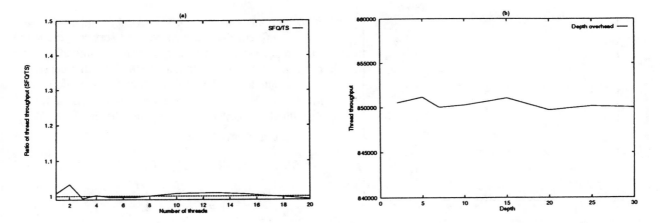

Figure 7 : (a) Ratio of number of loops executed in hierarchical and unmodified scheduler; (b) Variation in throughput with increase in depth of hierarchy

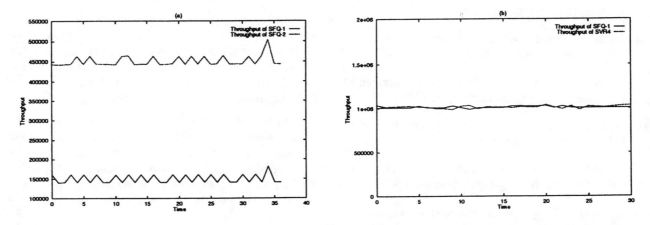

Figure 8 : (a) Aggregate throughput of nodes SFQ-1 and SFQ-2; (b) Throughput of nodes SFQ-1 and SVR4

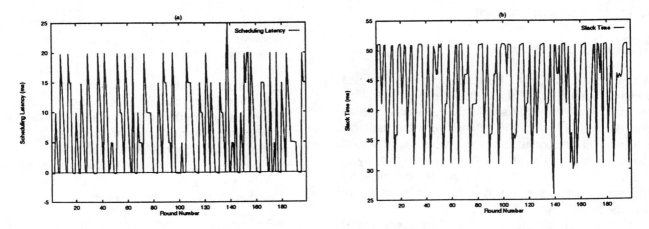

Figure 9 : Variation in: (a) scheduling latency and (b) slack time

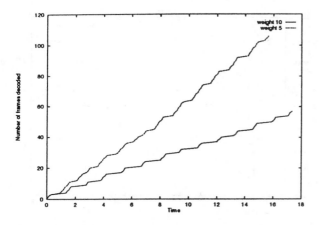

Figure 10 : Number of frames decoded as a function of time

- At time 6, thread 1 was put to sleep. Hence, the throughput ratio became 0:2.

- At time 9, thread 1 resumed execution. Hence, the throughput ratio became 4:2.

- At time 12, the weight of thread 1 was changed to 8. Hence, the throughput ratio became 8:2.

- At time 16, the weight of thread 2 was changed to 4. Hence, the throughput ratio became 8:4.

- At time 22, the weight of thread 1 was changed to 4. Hence, the throughput ratio became 4:4.

Figures 11(a) and 11(b), respectively, illustrate that the throughput of the threads (measured in terms of number of completed loops) and their ratio varies as per the changes in the weights of the threads. This demonstrates that SFQ can achieve fairness even in the presence of dynamic variation in weight assignments.

6   Related Work

We are not aware of any CPU scheduling algorithm that achieves hierarchical partitioning while allowing different schedulers to be used for different applications. However, since a fair scheduling algorithm is the basis for achieving hierarchical partitioning, we discuss other such algorithms proposed in the literature. Most of these algorithms have been proposed for fair allocation of network bandwidth; we have modified their presentation appropriately for CPU scheduling.

The earliest known fair scheduling algorithm is Weighted Fair Queuing (WFQ) [3]. WFQ was designed to emulate a hypothetical weighted round robin server in which the service received by each thread in a round is infinitesimal and proportional to the weight of the thread.

Since threads can only be serviced in quantums at a time, WFQ emulates a hypothetical server by scheduling threads in the increasing order of the finishing times of the quantums of the threads in the hypothetical server. To compute this order, WFQ associates two tags, a *start tag* and a *finish tag*, with every quantum of a thread. Specifically, the start tag $S(q_f^j)$ and the finish tag $F(q_f^j)$ of quantum q_f^j are defined as:

$$S(q_f^j) = \max\{v(A(q_f^j)), F(q_f^{j-1})\} \quad j \geq 1 \quad (11)$$

$$F(q_f^{j-1}) = S(q_f^{j-1}) + \frac{l_f^{j-1}}{r_f} \quad j \geq 1 \quad (12)$$

where $F(q_f^0) = 0$ and $v(t)$ is defined as the round number that would be in progress at time t in the hypothetical server. Formally, $v(t)$ is defined as:

$$\frac{dv(t)}{dt} = \frac{C}{\sum_{j \in B(t)} r_j} \quad (13)$$

where C is the capacity of the CPU measured in instructions/second and $B(t)$ is the set of runnable threads at time t in the hypothetical server. WFQ then schedules quantums in the increasing order of their finish tags. WFQ has several drawbacks for scheduling a CPU:

- As demonstrated in [6], WFQ does not provide fairness when the processor bandwidth fluctuates over time. Since fairness in the presence of variation in available CPU bandwidth is crucial for supporting hierarchical partitioning, WFQ is unsuitable for a CPU scheduler in a general purpose operating system.

- WFQ requires the length of the quantums to be known a priori. Though the maximum length of the quantum may always be known (as the scheduler can enforce it by preempting a thread), for environments in which the computation requirements are not known precisely, the exact quantum length may not be known. If WFQ assumes the maximum quantum length for scheduling and if the thread uses less than the maximum, the thread will not receive its fair share. On the other hand, if WFQ is modified to reflect the actual length of the execution (by changing the finish tag of a quantum after the end of its execution), then WFQ would have been modified in a non-trivial manner. Though WFQ is known to have bounded fairness, it is not known if the modified algorithm retains its fairness properties.

- WFQ requires the computation of $v(t)$, which, in turn, requires simulation of the hypothetical server. This simulation is known to be computationally expensive [4]. In contrast, SFQ computes the start and the finish tags efficiently.

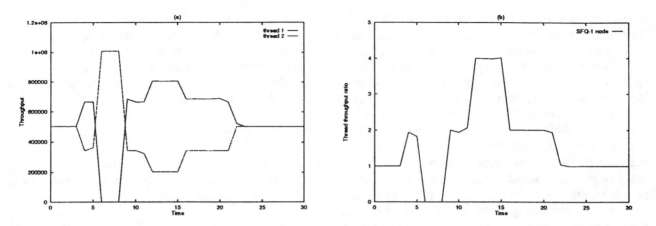

Figure 11 : (a) Throughput of threads 1 and 2; (b) Ratio of throughputs of threads 1 and 2

- The unfairness of WFQ, as derived in [16], is significantly higher than SFQ.

- WFQ provides high delay to low throughput applications. Specifically, it guarantees that quantum q_f^j will complete execution by:

$$EAT(q_f^j) + \frac{l_f^j}{r_f} + \frac{l^{max}}{C} \qquad (14)$$

where l^{max} is the maximum quantum length ever scheduled at the CPU. Hence, using (8), we conclude that the difference in maximum delay incurred in SFQ and WFQ, denoted by $\Delta(q_f^j)$, is given as:

$$\Delta(q_f^j) = \sum_{n \in Q \wedge n \neq f} \frac{l_n^{max}}{C} + \frac{l_f^j}{C} - \frac{l_f^j}{r_f} - \frac{l^{max}}{C} \qquad (15)$$

Now, if all quantums are of the same lengths, then $\Delta(q_f^j) < 0$ (i.e., SFQ provides a better delay guarantee) if $r_f \leq \frac{1}{|Q|-1}$. Since this condition is expected to hold for low throughput applications, we conclude that SFQ provides lower delay to low throughput applications. Since interactive applications are low throughput in nature, this feature of SFQ is highly desirable for CPU scheduling.

Fair Queuing based on Start-time (FQS) was proposed in [7] to make WFQ suitable for CPU scheduling when quantum length may not be known a priori. It computes the start tag and the finish tag of a quantum exactly as in WFQ. However, instead of scheduling quantums in the increasing order of finish tags, it schedules them in the increasing order of start tags. Since quantum length is not required for computing the start tag, it becomes suitable for CPU scheduling. However, its main drawbacks are that: (1) just as WFQ, it is computationally expensive, and (2) it does not provide fairness when the available

CPU bandwidth fluctuates over time, and consequently is unsuitable for hierarchical partitioning. Furthermore, it is not known to have any better properties than SFQ.

Self Clocked Fair Queuing (SCFQ), originally proposed in [2] and later analyzed in [4], was designed to reduce the computational complexity of fair scheduling algorithms like WFQ. It achieves efficiency over WFQ by approximating $v(t)$ with the finish tag of the quantum in service at time t. However, since SCFQ also schedules quantums in increasing order of finish tags, it is unsuitable for scheduling CPU in a multimedia operating system. Furthermore, although it has the same fairness and implementation complexity as SFQ, it provides significantly larger delay guarantee than SFQ. Specifically, it increases the maximum delay of quantum q_f^j by $\frac{l_f^j}{r_f}$ [6].

In the OS context, a randomized fair algorithm, termed lottery scheduling, was proposed in [19]. Due to its randomized nature, lottery scheduling achieved fairness only over large time-intervals. This limitation was later addressed by stride scheduling algorithm [18]. The stride scheduling algorithm is a variant of WFQ and, consequently, has all the drawbacks of WFQ. Furthermore, no theoretical properties of the stride scheduling algorithm are known. Recently, a proportionate share resource allocation algorithm, referred to as Earliest Eligible Virtual Deadline First (EEVDF), has been proposed [17].

Hierarchical partitioning of resource allocation was also proposed in [19] using the abstraction of tickets and currencies. In that framework, a thread is allocated tickets in some currency and the currency, in turn, is funded in terms of tickets of some other currency. The "funding" relationship is such that the value of a ticket in every currency can be translated to a value in the base currency. Every thread then is allocated resources in proportion to the value of its tickets in the base currency using lottery scheduling. This achieves hierarchical partitioning since if a thread becomes inactive, the value of the tickets of the threads that are funded by the same currency increases. This specification of hierarchical partitioning is similar to our scheduling structure. However, the key differences between our framework and the approach of [19] are as follows. First, our framework permits different scheduling algorithms to be employed for different classes of applications, whereas the framework of [19] does not. Second, hierarchical partitioning is achieved in [19] by re-computation of ticket values of every thread that are funded in the same currency or some ancestor of the currency every time a thread gets blocked or exits. This approach not only incurs additional overhead of computing ticket values, but also does not provide any guarantees. Hence, the requirements of hard and soft real-time applications can not be met in this framework. In contrast, our framework achieves hierarchical partitioning through a theoretically sound hierarchical scheduler.

Several other efforts have investigated scheduling techniques for multimedia systems [1, 5, 8, 13]. These scheduling algorithms are complementary to our hierarchical scheduler and can be employed as leaf class scheduler in our framework. Most of these algorithms require precise characterization of resource requirements of a task (such as computation time and period) as well as admission control to achieve predictable allocation of CPU. In contrast, SFQ requires neither of these; it just requires relative importance of tasks (expressed by weights) to be known. It requires admission control only if the applications desire a certain guaranteed minimum CPU bandwidth. Thus, SFQ allows a range of control over CPU allocation: whereas admission control can be used to guarantee a certain minimum CPU allocation to tasks and thus match the performance of the existing algorithms, admission control can be avoided when applications only require relative resource allocation. Such a flexibility is highly desirable in multimedia systems and the lack of it is one of the main disadvantage of existing algorithms. A detailed experimental investigation of the relative merits of these algorithms vis-a-vis SFQ as a leaf class scheduler is the subject of our current research.

7 Concluding Remarks

In this paper, we presented a flexible framework for hierarchical CPU allocation, using which an operating system can partition the CPU bandwidth among various application classes, and each application class, in turn, can partition its allocation (potentially using a different scheduling algorithm) among its sub-classes or applications. We presented the Start-time Fair Queuing (SFQ) algorithm, which enabled such hierarchical partitioning. We demonstrated that SFQ is not only suitable for hierarchical partitioning, but is also suitable for video applications. We have implemented the hierarchical scheduler in Solaris

2.4. We demonstrated that our framework: (1) enables co-existence of heterogeneous schedulers, (2) protects application classes from each other, and (3) does not impose higher overhead than conventional time-sharing schedulers. Thus, our hierarchical scheduling framework is suitable for multimedia operating systems.

References

[1] D. P. Anderson. Metascheduling for Continuous Media. *ACM Transactions on Computer Systems*, 11(3):266-252, August 1993.

[2] J. Davin and A. Heybey. A Simulation Study of Fair Queueing and Policy Enforcement. *Computer Communication Review*, 20(5):23-29, October 1990.

[3] A. Demers, S. Keshav, and S. Shenker. Analysis and Simulation of a Fair Queueing Algorithm. In *Proceedings of ACM SIGCOMM*, pages 1-12, September 1989.

[4] S.J. Golestani. A Self-Clocked Fair Queueing Scheme for High Speed Applications. In *Proceedings of INFOCOM'94*, 1994.

[5] R. Govindan and D. P. Anderson. Scheduling and IPC Mechanisms for Continuous Media. In *Proceedings of the 13th ACM Symposium on Operating System Principles*, pages 68-80, October 1991.

[6] P. Goyal, H. M. Vin, and H. Cheng. Start-time Fair Queuing: A Scheduling Algorithm for Integrated Services Packet Switching Networks. In *Proceedings of ACM SIGCOMM'96*, pages 157-168, August 1996.

[7] A. Greenberg and N. Madras. How Fair is Fair Queuing. *The Journal of ACM*, 39(3):568-598, July 1992.

[8] K. Jeffay, D. L. Stone, and F. D. Smith. Kernel Support for Live Digital Audio and Video. *Computer Communications*, 15:388-395, July/August 1992.

[9] K. Jeffay and D.L. Stone. Accounting for Interrupt Handling Costs in Dynamic Priority Task Systems. In *Proceedings of 14th IEEE Real-Time Systems Symposium Raleigh-Durham, NC*, pages 212-221, December 1993.

[10] M.B. Jones, P. Leach, R. Draves, and III J. Barrera. Support for User-Centric Modular Real-Time Resource Management in Rialto Oper-

ating System. In *Proceedings of NOSSDAV'95, Durham, New Hampshire*, April 1995.

[11] K. Lee. Performance Bounds in Communication Networks With Variable-Rate Links. In *Proceedings of ACM SIGCOMM'95*, pages 126–136, 1995.

[12] C.L. Liu and J.W. Layland. Scheduling Algorithms for Multiprocessing in a Hard-Real Time Environment. *JACM*, 20:46–61, January 1973.

[13] C. W. Mercer, S. Savage, and H. Tokuda. Processor Capacity Reserves: Operating System Support for Multimedia Applications. In *Proceedings of the IEEE ICMCS'94*, May 1994.

[14] T. Nakajima, T. Kitayama, H. Arakawa, and H. Tokuda. Integrated Management of Priority Inversion in Real-Time Mach. In *Proceedings of the 14th IEEE Real-Time Systems Symp.*, pages 120–130, December 1993.

[15] J. Nieh, J. Hanko, J. Northcutt, and G. Wall. SVR4UNIX Scheduler Unacceptable for Multimedia Applications. In *Proceedings of 4th International Workshop on Network and Operating System Support for Digital Audio and Video*, pages 41–53, November 1993.

[16] D. Stiliadis and A. Varma. Design and Analysis of Frame-based Fair Queueing: A New Traffic Scheduling Algorithm for Packet Switched Networks. In *Proceedings of SIGMETRICS'96*, May 1996.

[17] I. Stoica, H. Abdel-Wahab, and K. Jeffay. A Proportional Share Resource Allocation Algorithm for Real-Time, Time-Shared Systems. In *Proceedings of Real Time Systems Symposium (to appear)*, December 1996.

[18] C. Waldspurger and W. Weihl. Stride Scheduling: Deterministic Proportional-share Resource Management. Technical Report TM-528, MIT, Laboratory for Computer Science, June 1995.

[19] C. A. Waldspurger and W. E. Weihl. Lottery Scheduling: Flexible Proportional-share Resource Management. In *Proceedings of symposim on Operating System Design and Implementation*, November 1994.

The Design, Implementation and Evaluation of SMART: A Scheduler for Multimedia Applications

Jason Nieh[1,2] and Monica S. Lam[1]

[1]Computer Systems Laboratory, Stanford University

[2]Sun Microsystems Laboratories

Abstract

Real-time applications such as multimedia audio and video are increasingly populating the workstation desktop. To support the execution of these applications in conjunction with traditional non-real-time applications, we have created SMART, a Scheduler for Multimedia And Real-Time applications. SMART supports applications with time constraints, and provides dynamic feedback to applications to allow them to adapt to the current load. In addition, the support for real-time applications is integrated with the support for conventional computations. This allows the user to prioritize across real-time and conventional computations, and dictate how the processor is to be shared among applications of the same priority. As the system load changes, SMART adjusts the allocation of resources dynamically and seamlessly. SMART is unique in its ability to automatically shed real-time tasks and regulate their execution rates when the system is overloaded, while providing better value in underloaded conditions than previously proposed schemes. We have implemented SMART in the Solaris UNIX operating system and measured its performance against other schedulers in executing real-time, interactive, and batch applications. Our results demonstrate SMART's superior performance in supporting multimedia applications.

1 Introduction

The workload on computers is rapidly changing. In the past, computers were used in automating tasks around the work place, such as word and accounts processing in offices, and design automation in engineering environments. The human-computer interface has been primarily textual, with some limited amount of graphical input and display. With the phenomenal improvement in hardware technology in recent years, even highly affordable personal computers are capable of supporting much richer interfaces. Images, video, audio, and interactive graphics have become common place. A growing number of multimedia applications are available, ranging from video games and movie players, to sophisticated distributed simulation and virtual reality environments. In anticipation of a wider adoption of multimedia in applications in the future, there has been much research and development activity in computer architecture for multimedia applications. Not only is there a proliferation of processors that are built for accelerating the execution of multimedia applications, even general-purpose microprocessors have incorporated special instructions to speed their execution [20].

While hardware has advanced to meet the special demands of multimedia applications, software environments have not. In particular, multimedia applications have real-time constraints which are not handled well by today's general-purpose operating systems.

The problems experienced by users of multimedia on these machines include video jitter, poor "lip-synchronization" between audio and video, and slow interactive response while running video applications. Commercial operating systems such as UNIX SVR4 [39] attempt to address these problems by providing a real-time scheduler in addition to a standard time-sharing scheduler. However, such hybrid schemes lead to experimentally demonstrated unacceptable behavior, allowing runaway real-time activities to cause basic system services to lock up, and the user to lose control over the machine [29].

This paper argues for the need to design a new processor scheduling algorithm that can handle the mix of applications we see today. We present a scheduling algorithm which we have implemented in the Solaris UNIX operating system [11], and demonstrate its improved performance over existing schedulers on real applications.

1.1 Demands of multimedia applications on processor scheduling

To understand the requirements imposed by multimedia applications on processor scheduling, we first describe the salient features of these applications and their special demands that distinguish them from the conventional (non-real-time) applications current operating systems are designed for:

- *Soft real-time constraints.* Real-time applications have application-specific timing requirements that need to be met [31]. For example in the case of video, time constraints arise due to the need to display video in a smooth and synchronized way, often synchronized with audio. Time constraints may be periodic or aperiodic in nature. Unlike conventional applications, tardy results are often of little value; it is often preferable to skip a computation than to execute it late. Unlike hard real-time environments, missing a deadline only diminishes the quality of the results and does not lead to catastrophic failures.

- *Insatiable resource demands and frequent overload.* Multimedia applications present practically an insatiable demand for resources. Today, video playback windows are typically tiny at full display rate because of insufficient processor cycles to keep up at full resolution. As applications such as real-time video are highly resource intensive and can consume the resources of an entire machine, resources are commonly overloaded, with resource demand exceeding its availability.

- *Dynamically adaptive applications.* When resources are overloaded and not all time constraints can be met, multimedia applications are often able to adapt and degrade gracefully by offering a different quality of service [32]. For example, a video application may choose to skip some frames or display at a lower image quality when not all frames can be processed in time.

- *Co-existence with conventional computations.* Real-time applications must share the desktop with already existing conventional applications, such as word processors, compilers, etc. Real-time tasks should not always be allowed to run in preference to all other tasks because they may starve out important conventional activities, such as those required to keep the system running. Moreover, users would like to be able to combine real-time and conventional computations together in new applications, such as multimedia documents, which mix text and graphics as well as audio and video. In no way should the capabilities of a multiprogrammed workstation be reduced to a single function commodity television set in order to meet the demands of multimedia applications.

- *Dynamic environment.* Unlike static embedded real-time environments, workstation users run an often changing mix of applications, resulting in dynamically varying loads.
- *User preferences.* Different users may have different preferences, for example, in regard to trading off the speed of a compilation versus the display quality of a video, depending on whether the video is part of an important teleconferencing session or just a television show being watched while waiting for an important computational application to complete.

1.2 Overview of this paper

This paper proposes SMART (Scheduler for Multimedia And Real-Time applications), a processor scheduler that fully supports the application characteristics described above. SMART consists of a simple application interface and a scheduling algorithm that tries to deliver the best overall value to the user. SMART supports applications with time constraints, and provides dynamic feedback to applications to allow them to adapt to the current load. In addition, the support for real-time applications is integrated with the support for conventional computations. This allows the user to prioritize across real-time and conventional computations, and dictate how the processor is to be shared among applications of the same priority. As the system load changes, SMART adjusts the allocation of resources dynamically and seamlessly. SMART is unique in its ability to automatically shed real-time tasks and regulate their execution rates when the system is overloaded, while providing better value in underloaded conditions than previously proposed schemes.

SMART achieves this behavior by reducing this complex resource management problem into two decisions, one based on *importance* to determine the overall resource allocation for each task, and the other based on *urgency* to determine when each task is given its allocation. SMART provides a common importance attribute for both real-time and conventional tasks based on priorities and weighted fair queueing (WFQ) [7]. SMART then uses an urgency mechanism based on earliest-deadline scheduling [26] to optimize the order in which tasks are serviced to allow real-time tasks to make the most efficient use of their resource allocations to meet their time constraints. In addition, a bias on conventional batch tasks that accounts for their ability to tolerate more varied service latencies is used to give interactive and real-time tasks better performance during periods of transient overload.

This paper also presents some experimental data on the SMART algorithm, based on our implementation of the scheduler in the Solaris UNIX operating system. We present two sets of data, both of which are based on a workstation workload consisting of real multimedia applications running with representative batch and interactive applications. For the multimedia application, we use a synchronized media player developed by Sun Microsystems Laboratories that was originally tuned to run well with the UNIX SVR4 scheduler. It takes only the addition of a couple of system calls to allow the application to take advantage of SMART's features. We will describe how this is done to give readers a better understanding of the SMART application interface. The first experiment compares SMART with two other existing scheduling algorithms: UNIX SVR4 scheduling, which serves as the most common basis of work-station operating systems used in current practice [12], and WFQ, which has been the subject of much attention in current research [2, 7, 33, 38, 40]. The experiment shows that SMART is superior to the other algorithms in the case of a workstation overloaded with real-time activities. In the experiment, SMART delivers over 250% more real-time multimedia data on time than UNIX SVR4 time-sharing and over 60% more real-time multimedia data on time than WFQ, while also providing better interactive response. The second experiment demonstrates the ability of SMART to (1) provide the user with predictable control over resource allocation, (2) adapt to dynamic changes in the workload and (3) deliver expected behavior when the system is not overloaded.

The paper is organized as follows. Section 2 introduces the SMART application interface and usage model. Section 3 describes the SMART scheduling algorithm. We start with the overall rationale of the design and the major concepts, then present the algorithm itself, followed by an example to illustrate the algorithm. Despite the simplicity of the algorithm, the behavior it provides is rather rich. Section 4 analyzes the different aspects of the algorithm and shows how the algorithm delivers behavior consistent with its principles of operations. Section 5 provides a comparison with related work. Section 6 presents a set of experimental results, followed by some concluding remarks.

2 The SMART interface and usage model

The SMART interface provides to the application developer *time constraints* and *notifications* for supporting applications with real-time computations, and provides to the user of applications *priorities* and *shares* for predictable control over the allocation of resources. An overview of the interface is presented here. A more detailed description can be found in [30].

Multimedia application developers are faced with the problem of writing applications with time constraints. They typically know the deadlines that must be met in these applications and know how to allow these applications to degrade gracefully when not all time constraints can be met. The problem is that current operating system practice, as typified by UNIX, does not provide an adequate amount of functionality for supporting these applications. For example, in dealing with time under UNIX, an application can tell the scheduler to delay a computation by "sleeping" for a duration of time. An application can also obtain simple timing information such as elapsed wall clock time and accumulated execution time. However, it cannot ask the scheduler to complete a computation before a given deadline, nor can it ask the scheduler whether or not it is possible for the computation to complete before a given deadline. The lack of system support exacerbates the difficulty of writing applications with time constraints and results in poor application performance.

By providing explicit time constraints, SMART allows applications to communicate their timing requirements to the system. A time constraint consists of a deadline and an estimate of the processing time required to meet the deadline. An application can inform the scheduler that a given block of code has a certain deadline by which it should be completed, can request information on the availability of processing time for meeting a deadline, and can request a notification from the scheduler if it is not possible for the specified deadline to be met. Furthermore, applications can have blocks of code with time constraints and blocks of code that do not, thereby allowing application developers to freely mix real-time and conventional computations.

SMART also provides a simple upcall from the scheduler that informs the application that its deadline cannot be met. This upcall mechanism is called a notification. It frees applications from the burden of second guessing the system to determine if their time constraints can be met, and allows applications to choose their own

| | Real-Time Applications | Conventional Applications | |
		Interactive	Batch
Deadlines	Yes	No	No
Quantum of Execution	Service time: no value if the entire task is not executed	Arbitrary choice	Arbitrary choice
Resource Requirement	A slack is usually present	Relinquishes machine while waiting for human response	Can consume all processor cycles until it completes
Quality of Service Metric	Number of deadlines met	Response time	Program completion time

Table 1: Categories of applications

policies for deciding what to do when a deadline is missed. For example, upon notification, the application may choose to discard the current computation, perform only a portion of the computation, or change the time constraints of the computation. This feedback from the system enables adaptive real-time applications to degrade gracefully.

Time constraints and notifications are intended to be used by application writers to support their development of real-time applications; the end user of such applications need not know anything about time constraints. As an example, we describe an audio/video application that was programmed using time constraints in Section 6.1.

As users may have different preferences for how processing time should be allocated among a set of applications, SMART provides two parameters to predictably control processor allocation. These parameters can be used to bias the allocation of resources to provide the best performance for those applications which are currently more important to the user. The user can specify that applications have different priorities, meaning that the application with the higher priority is favored whenever there is contention for resources. Among applications at the same priority, the user can specify the share of each application, resulting in each application receiving an allocation of resources in proportion to its respective share whenever there is contention for resources. The notions of priority and share apply uniformly to both real-time and conventional applications. This level of predictable control is unlike current practice, as typified by UNIX time-sharing, in which all that a user is given is a "nice" knob [39] whose setting is poorly correlated to the scheduler's externally observable behavior [29].

Our expectation is that most users will run the applications in the default priority level with equal shares. This is the system default and requires no user parameters. The user may wish to adjust the proportion of shares between the applications occasionally. A simple graphical interface can be provided to make the adjustment as simple and intuitive as adjusting the volume of a television or the balance of a stereo output. The user may want to use the priority to handle specific circumstances. Suppose we wish to run the PointCast application [34] in the background only if the system is not busy; this can be achieved simply by running Point-Cast with a low priority.

3 The SMART scheduler

In the following, we first describe the principles of operations used in the design of the scheduler. We then give an overview of the rationale behind the design, followed by an overview of the algorithm and then the details.

3.1 Principles of operations

It is the scheduler's objective to deliver the behavior expected by the user in a manner that maximizes the overall value of the system to its users. We have reduced this objective to the following six principles of operations:

- *Priority.* The system should not degrade the performance of a high priority application in the presence of a low priority application.

- *Proportional sharing among real-time and conventional applications in the same priority class.* Proportional sharing applies only if the scheduler cannot satisfy all the requests in the system. The system will fully satisfy the requests of all applications requesting less than their proportional share. The resources left over after satisfying these requests are distributed proportionally among tasks that can use the excess. While it is relatively easy to control the execution rate of conventional applications, the execution rate of a real-time application is controlled by selectively shedding computations in as even a rate as possible.

- *Graceful transitions between fluctuations in load.* The system load varies dynamically, new applications come and go, and the resource demand of each application may also fluctuate. The system must be able to adapt to the changes gracefully.

- *Satisfying real-time constraints and fast interactive response time in underload.* If real-time and interactive tasks request less than their proportional share, their time constraints should be honored when possible, and the interactive response time should be short.

- *Trading off instantaneous fairness for better real-time and interactive response time.* While it is necessary that the allocation is fair on average, insisting on being fair instantaneously at all times would cause many more deadlines to be missed and deliver poor response time to short running tasks. We will tolerate some instantaneous unfairness so long as the extent of the unfairness is bounded. This is the same motivation behind the design of multi-level feedback schedulers [23] to improve the response time of interactive tasks.

- *Notification of resource availability.* SMART allows applications to specify if and when they wish to be notified if it is unlikely that their computations will be able to complete before their given deadlines.

3.2 Rationale and overview

As summarized in Table 1, real-time and conventional applications have very diverse characteristics. It is this diversity that makes devising an integrated scheduling algorithm difficult. A real-time scheduler uses real-time constraints to determine the execution order, but conventional tasks do not have real-time constraints. Adding periodic deadlines to conventional tasks is a tempting design choice, but it introduces artificial constraints that reduce the effectiveness of the system. On the other hand, a conventional task scheduler has no notion of real-time constraints; the notion of time-slicing the applications to optimize system throughput does not serve real-time applications well.

The crux of the solution is not to confuse *urgency* with *importance.* An urgent task is one which has an immediate real-time constraint. An important task is one with a high priority, or one that has been the least serviced proportionally among applications with the same priority. An urgent task may not be the one to execute if it requests more resources than its fair share. Conversely, an important task need not be run immediately. For example, a real-time task that has a higher priority but a later deadline may be able to tolerate the execution of a lower priority task with an earlier deadline. Our algorithm separates the processor scheduling decisions into two steps; the first identifies all the candidates that are considered important enough to execute, and the second chooses the task to execute based on urgency considerations.

While urgency is specific to real-time applications, importance is common to all the applications. We measure the importance of an application by a *value-tuple*, which is a tuple with two components: priority and the *biased virtual finishing time (BVFT)*. Priority is a static quantity either supplied by the user or assigned the default value; BVFT is a dynamic quantity the system uses to measure the degree to which each task has been allotted its proportional share of resources. The formal definition of the BVFT is given in Section 3.3. We say that task *A* has a higher value-tuple than task *B* if *A* has a higher static priority or if both *A* and *B* have the same priority and *A* has an earlier BVFT.

The SMART scheduling algorithm used to determine the next task to run is as follows:

1. If the task with the highest value-tuple is a conventional task (a task without a deadline), schedule that task.

2. Otherwise, create a candidate set consisting of all real-time tasks with higher value-tuple than that of the highest value-tuple conventional task. (If no conventional tasks are present, all the real-time tasks are placed in the candidate set.)

3. Apply the best-effort real-time scheduling algorithm [27] on the candidate set, using the value-tuple as the priority in the original algorithm. By using the given deadlines and service-time estimates, find the task with the earliest deadline whose execution does not cause any tasks with higher value-tuples to miss their deadlines. This is achieved by considering each candidate in turn, starting with the one with the highest value-tuple. The algorithm attempts to schedule the candidate into a working schedule which is initially empty. The candidate is inserted in deadline order in this schedule provided its execution does not cause any of the tasks in the schedule to miss its deadline. The scheduler simply picks the task with the earliest deadline in the working schedule.

4. If a task cannot complete its computation before its deadline, send a notification to inform the respective application that its deadline cannot be met.

The following sections provide a more detailed description of the BVFT, and the best-effort real-time scheduling technique.

3.3 Biased virtual finishing time

The notion of a *virtual finishing time (VFT)*, which measures the degree to which the task has been allotted its proportional share of resources, has been previously used in describing fair queueing algorithms [2, 7, 33, 38, 40]. We augment this basic notion in the following ways. First, our use of virtual finishing times incorporates tasks with different priorities. Second, we add to the virtual finishing time a bias, which is a bounded offset used to measure the ability of conventional tasks to tolerate longer and more varied service delays. The biased virtual finishing time allows us to provide better interactive and real-time response without compromising fairness. Finally and most importantly, weighted fair queueing executes the task with the earliest virtual finishing time to provide proportional sharing. SMART only uses the biased virtual finishing time in the selection of the candidates for scheduling, and real-time constraints

are also considered in the choice of the application to run. This modification enables SMART to handle applications with aperiodic constraints and overloaded conditions.

Our algorithm organizes all the tasks into queues, one for each priority. The tasks in each queue are ordered in increasing BVFT values. Each task has a *virtual time* which advances at a rate proportional to the amount of processing time it consumes divided by its share. Suppose the current task being executed has share *S* and was initiated at time τ. Let $v(\tau)$ denote the task's virtual time at time τ. Then the virtual time $v(t)$ of the task at current time t is

$$v(t) = v(\tau) + \frac{t - \tau}{S}. \qquad (1)$$

Correspondingly, each queue has a *queue virtual time* which advances only if any of its member tasks is executing. The rate of advance is proportional to the amount of processing time spent on the task divided by total number of shares of all tasks on the queue. To be more precise, suppose the current task being executed has priority *P* and was initiated at time τ. Let $V_P(\tau)$ denote the queue virtual time of the queue with priority *P* at time τ. Then the queue virtual time $V_P(t)$ of the queue with priority *P* at current time t is

$$V_P(t) = V_P(\tau) + \frac{t - \tau}{\sum\limits_{a \in A_P} S_a}, \qquad (2)$$

where S_a represents the share of application *a*, and A_P is the set of applications with priority *P*.

Previous work in the domain of packet switching provides a theoretical basis for using the difference between the virtual time of a task and the queue virtual time as a measure of whether the respective task has consumed its proportional allocation of resources [7, 33]. If a task's virtual time is equal to the queue virtual time, it is considered to have received its proportional allocation of resources. An earlier virtual time indicates that the task has less than its proportional share, and, similarly, a later virtual time indicates that it has more than its proportional share. Since the queue virtual time advances at the same rate for all tasks on the queue, the relative magnitudes of the virtual times provide a relative measure of the degree to which each task has received its proportional share of resources.

The virtual finishing time refers to the virtual time of the application, had the application been given the currently requested quantum. The quantum for a conventional task is the unit of time the scheduler gives to the task to run before being rescheduled. The quantum for a real-time task is the application-supplied estimate of its service time. A useful property of the virtual finishing time, which is not shared by the virtual time, is that it does not change as a task executes and uses up its time quantum, but only changes when the task is rescheduled with a new time quantum.

In the following, we step through all the events that lead to the adjustment of the biased virtual finishing time of a task. Let the task in question have priority *P* and share *S*. Let $\beta(t)$ denote the BVFT of the task at time t.

Task creation time. When a task is created at time τ_0, it acquires as its virtual time the queue virtual time of the its corresponding queue. Suppose the task has time quantum *Q*, then its BVFT is

$$\beta(\tau_0) = V_P(\tau_0) + \frac{Q}{S}. \qquad (3)$$

Completing a Quantum. Once a task is created, its BVFT is updated as follows. When a task finishes executing for its time quantum, it is assigned a new time quantum *Q*. As a conventional task accumulates execution time, a bias is added to its BVFT when it gets a new quantum. That is, let *b* represent the increased bias and τ be the time a task's BVFT was last changed. Then, the task's BVFT is

$$\beta(t) = \beta(\tau) + \frac{Q}{S} + \frac{b}{S}. \qquad (4)$$

The bias is used to defer long running batch computations during transient loads to allow real-time and interactive tasks to obtain better immediate response time. The bias is increased in a manner similar to the way priorities and time quanta are adjusted in UNIX SVR4 to implement time-sharing [39]. The total bias added to an application's BVFT is bounded. Thus, the bias does not change either the rate at which the BVFT is advanced or the overall proportional allocation of resources. It only affects the instantaneous proportional allocation. User interaction causes the bias to be reset to its initial value. Real-time tasks have zero bias.

The idea of a dynamically adjusted bias based on execution time is somewhat analogous to the idea of a decaying priority based on execution time which is used in multilevel-feedback schedulers. However, while multilevel-feedback affects the actual average amount of resources allocated to each task, bias only affects the response time of a task and does not affect its overall ability to obtain its proportional share of resources. By combining virtual finishing times with bias, the BVFT can be used to provide both proportional sharing and better system responsiveness in a systematic fashion.

Blocking for I/O or events. A blocked task should not be allowed to accumulate credit to a fair share indefinitely while it is sleeping; however, it is fair and desirable to give the task a limited amount of credit for not using the processor cycles and to improve the responsiveness of these tasks. Therefore, SMART allows the task to remain on its given priority queue for a limited duration which is equal to the lesser of the deadline of the task (if one exists), or a system default. At the end of this duration, a sleeping task must leave the queue, and SMART records the difference between the task's and the queue's virtual time. This difference is then restored when the task rejoins the queue once it becomes runnable. Let E be the execution time the task has already received toward completing its time quantum Q, B be its current bias, and $v(t)$ denote the task's virtual time. Then, the difference Δ is

$$\Delta = v(t) - V_P(t), \qquad (5)$$

where

$$v(t) = \beta(t) - \frac{Q-E}{S} - \frac{B}{S}. \qquad (6)$$

Upon rejoining the queue, its bias is reset to zero and the BVFT is

$$\beta(t) = V_P(t) + \Delta + \frac{Q}{S}. \qquad (7)$$

Reassigned user parameters. If a task is given a new priority, it is reassigned to the queue corresponding to its new priority, and its BVFT is simply calculated as in Equation (3). If the task is given a new share, the BVFT is calculated by having the task leave the queue with the old parameters used in Equation (6) to calculate Δ, and then join the queue again with the new parameters used in Equation (7) to calculate its BVFT.

3.4 Best-effort real-time scheduling

SMART iteratively selects tasks from the candidate set in decreasing value-tuple order and inserts them into an initially empty working schedule in increasing deadline order. The working schedule defines an execution order for servicing the real-time resource requests. It is said to be *feasible* if the set of task resource requirements in the working schedule, when serviced in the order defined by the working schedule, can be completed before their respective deadlines. It should be noted that the resource requirement of a periodic real-time task includes an estimate of the processing time required for its future resource requests.

To determine if a working schedule is feasible, let Q_j be the processing time required by task j to meet its deadline, and let E_j be the execution time task j has already spent running toward meeting its deadline. Let F_j be the fraction of the processor required by a periodic real-time task; F_j is simply the ratio of a task's service time to its period if it is a periodic real-time task, and zero otherwise. Let D_j be the deadline of the task. Then, the estimated resource requirement of task j at a time t such that $t \geq D_j$ is:

$$R_j(t) = Q_j - E_j + F_j \times (t - D_j), t \geq D_j. \qquad (8)$$

A working schedule W is then feasible if for each task i in the schedule with deadline D_i, the following inequality holds:

$$D_i \geq t + \sum_{j \in W | D_j \leq D_i} R_j(D_i), \forall i \in W. \qquad (9)$$

On each task insertion into the working schedule, the resulting working schedule that includes the newly inserted task is tested for feasibility. If the resulting working schedule is feasible and the newly inserted task is a periodic real-time task, its estimate of future processing time requirements is accounted for in subsequent feasibility tests. At the same time, lower value-tuple tasks are only inserted into the working schedule if they do not cause any of the current and estimated future resource requests of higher value-tuple tasks to miss their deadlines. The iterative selection process is repeated until SMART runs out of tasks or until it determines that no further tasks can be inserted into the schedule feasibly. Once the iterative selection process has been terminated, SMART then executes the earliest-deadline runnable task in the schedule.

If there are no runnable conventional tasks and there are no runnable real-time tasks that can complete before their deadlines, the scheduler runs the highest value-tuple runnable real-time task, even though it cannot complete before its deadline. The rationale for this is that it is better to use the processor cycles than allow the processor to be idle. The algorithm is therefore work conserving, meaning that the resources are never left idle if there is a runnable task, even if it cannot satisfy its deadline.

3.5 Complexity

The cost of scheduling with SMART consists of the cost of managing the value-tuple list and the cost of managing the working schedule. The cost of managing the value-tuple list in SMART is $O(N)$, where N is the number of active tasks. This assumes a linear insertion value-tuple list. The complexity can be reduced to $O(\log N)$ using a tree data structure. For small N, a simple linear list is likely to be most efficient in practice. The cost of managing the value-tuple list is the same as WFQ.

The worst case complexity of managing the working schedule is $O(N_R^2)$, where N_R is the number of active real-time tasks of higher value than the highest value conventional task. This worst case occurs if each real-time task needs to be selected and feasibility tested against all other tasks when rebuilding the working schedule. It is unlikely for the worst case to occur in practice for any reasonably large N_R. Real-time tasks typically have short deadlines so that if there are a large number of real-time tasks, the scheduler will determine that there is no more slack in the schedule before all of the tasks need to be individually tested for insertion feasibility. The presence of conventional tasks in the workstation environment also prevents N_R from growing large. For large N, the cost of scheduling with SMART in practice is expected to be similar to WFQ.

A more complicated algorithm can be used to reduce the complexity of managing the working schedule. In this case, a new working schedule can be incrementally built from the existing working schedule as new tasks arrive. By using information contained in the existing working schedule, the complexity of building the new working schedule can be reduced to $O(N_R)$. When only

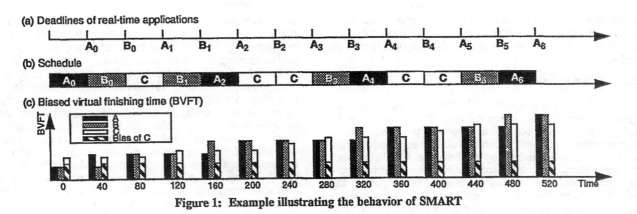

Figure 1: Example illustrating the behavior of SMART

deletions are made to the working schedule, the existing working schedule can simply be used, reducing the cost to $O(1)$.

3.6 Example

We now present a simple example to illustrate how the SMART algorithm works. Consider a workload involving two real-time applications, A and B, and a conventional application C. Suppose all the applications belong to the same priority class, and their proportional shares are in the ratio of 1:1:2, respectively. Both real-time applications request 40 ms of computation time every 80 ms, with their deadlines being completely out of phase, as shown in Figure 1(a). The applications request to be notified if the deadlines cannot be met; upon notification, the application drops the current computation and proceeds to the computation for the next deadline. The scheduling quantum of the conventional application C is also 40 ms and we assume that it has accumulated a bias of 100 ms at this point. Figure 1(b) and (c) show the final schedule created by SMART for this scenario, and the BVFT values of the different applications at different time instants.

The initial BVFTs of applications A and B are the same; since C has twice as many shares as A and B, the initial BVFT of C is half of the sum of the bias and the quantum length. Because of the bias, application C has a later BVFT and is therefore not run immediately. The candidate set considered for execution consists of both applications, A and B; A is selected to run because it has an earlier deadline. (In this case, the deadline is used as a tie-breaker between real-time tasks with the same BVFT; in general, a task with an early deadline may get to run over a task with an earlier BVFT but a later deadline.) When a task finishes its quantum, its BVFT is incremented. The increment for C is half of that for A and B because the increment is the result of dividing the time quantum by its share. Figure 1(c) shows how the tasks are scheduled such that their BVFT are kept close together.

This example illustrates several important characteristics of SMART. First, SMART implements proportional sharing properly. In the steady state, C is given twice as much resources as A or B, which reflects the ratio of shares given to the applications. Second, the bias allows better response in temporary overload, but it does not reduce the proportional share given to the biased task. Because of C's bias, A and B get to run immediately at the beginning; eventually their BVFTs catch up with the bias, and C is given its fair share. Third, the scheduler is able to meet many real-time constraints, while skipping tardy computations. For example, at time 0, SMART schedules application A before B so as to satisfy both deadlines. On the other hand, at time 120 ms into the execution, realizing that it cannot meet the A_2 deadline, it executes application B instead and notifies A of the missed deadline.

4 Analysis of the behavior of the algorithm

In the following, we describe how the scheduling algorithm follows the principles of operations as laid out in Section 3.1.

4.1 Priority

Our principle of operation regarding priority is that the performance of high priority tasks should not be affected by the presence of low priority tasks. As the performance of a conventional task is determined by its completion time, a high priority conventional task should be run before any lower priority task. Step 1 of the algorithm guarantees this behavior because a high priority task always has a higher value-tuple than any lower priority task.

On the other hand, the performance metric of a real-time application is the number of deadlines satisfied, not how early the execution takes place. The best-effort scheduling algorithm in Step 3 will run a lower priority task with an earlier deadline first, only if it can determine that doing so does not cause the high priority task to miss its deadline. In this way, the system delivers a better overall value to the user. Note that the scheduler uses the timing information supplied by the applications to determine if a higher priority deadline is to be satisfied. It is possible for a higher priority deadline to be missed if its corresponding time estimate is inaccurate.

4.2 Proportional sharing

Having described how time is apportioned across different priority classes, we now describe how time allocated to each priority class is apportioned between applications in the class. If the system is populated with only conventional tasks, we simply divide the cycles in proportion to the shares across the different applications. As noted in Table 1, interactive and real-time applications may not use up all the resources that they are entitled to. Any unused cycles are proportionally distributed among those applications that can consume the cycles.

4.2.1 Conventional tasks

Let us first consider conventional tasks whose virtual finishing time has not been biased. We observe that even though real-time tasks may not execute in the order dictated by WFQ, the scheduler will run a real-task only if it has an earlier VFT than any of the conventional tasks. Thus, by considering all the real-time tasks with an earlier VFT as one single application with a correspondingly higher share, we see the SMART treatment of the conventional tasks is identical to that of a WFQ algorithm. From the analysis of the WFQ algorithm, it is clear that conventional tasks are given their fair shares.

A bias is added to a task's VFT only after it has accumulated a significant computation time. As a fixed constant, the bias does not change the relative proportion between the allocation of resources. It only serves to allow a greater variance in instantaneous fairness, thus allowing a better interactive and real-time response in transient overloads.

4.2.2 Real-time applications

We say that a system is *underloaded* if there are sufficient cycles to give a fair share to the conventional tasks in the system while satisfying all the real-time constraints. When a system is underloaded, the conventional tasks will be serviced often enough with the left-over processor cycles so that they will have later BVFTs than real-time applications. The conventional applications will therefore only run when there are no real-time applications in the system. The real-time tasks are thus scheduled with a strict best-effort scheduling algorithm. It has been proven that in underload, the best-effort scheduling algorithm degenerates to an earliest-deadline scheduling algorithm [26], which has been shown to satisfy all scheduling constraints, periodic or aperiodic, optimally [8].

In an underloaded system, the scheduler satisfies all the real-time applications' requests. CPU time is given out according to the amounts requested, which may have a very different proportion from the shares assigned to the applications. The assigned proportional shares are used in the management of real-time applications only if the system is oversubscribed.

A real-time application whose request exceeds its fair share for the current loading condition will eventually accumulate a BVFT later than other applications' BVFTs. Even if it has the earliest deadline, it will not be run immediately if there is a conventional application with a higher value, or if running this application will cause a higher valued real-time application to miss its deadline. If the application accepts notification, the system will inform the application when it determines that the constraint will not be met. This interface allows applications to implement their own degradation policies. For instance, a video application can decide whether to skip the current frame, skip a future frame, or display a lower quality image when the frame cannot be fully processed in a timely fashion. The application adjusts the timing constraint accordingly and informs the system. If the application does not accept notification, however, eventually all the other applications will catch up with their BVFT, and the scheduler will allow the now late application to run.

Just as the use of BVFT regulates the fair allocation of resources for conventional tasks, it scales down the real-time tasks proportionally. In addition, the bias introduced in the algorithm, as well as the use of a best-effort scheduler among real-time tasks with sufficiently high values, allows more real-time constraints to be met.

5   Related work

Recognizing the need to provide better scheduling to support the needs of modern applications such as multimedia, a number of resource management mechanisms have been proposed. These approaches can be loosely classified as real-time scheduling, fair queueing, and hierarchical scheduling.

5.1   Real-time scheduling

Real-time schedulers such as rate-monotonic scheduling [24, 26] and earliest-deadline scheduling [8, 26] are designed to make better use of hardware resources in meeting real-time requirements. In particular, earliest-deadline scheduling is optimal in underload. However, they do not perform well when the system is overloaded, nor are they designed to support conventional applications.

Resource reservations are commonly combined with real-time scheduling in an attempt to run real-time tasks with conventional tasks [5, 22, 25, 28]. These approaches are used with admission control to allow real-time tasks to reserve a fixed percentage of the resource in accordance with their resource requirement. Any left-over processing time is allocated to conventional tasks using a standard timesharing or round-robin scheduler.

Several differences in these reservation approaches are apparent. While the approaches in [5, 25] take advantage of earliest-deadline scheduling to provide optimal real-time performance in underload, the rate monotonic utilization bound used in [28] and the time interval assignment used in Rialto [22] are not optimal, resulting in lower performance than earliest-deadline approaches. In contrast with SMART, these approaches are more restrictive, especially in the level of control provided for conventional tasks. They do not provide a common mechanism for sharing resources across real-time and conventional tasks. In particular, with conventional tasks being given leftover processing time, their potential starvation is a problem. This problem is exacerbated in Rialto [22] in which even in the absence of reservations, applications with time constraints buried in their source code are given priority over conventional applications [21].

Note that the use of reservations relies on inflexible admission control policies to avoid overload. This is usually done on a first-come-first-serve basis, resulting in later arriving applications being denied resources even if they are more important. To be able to execute later arriving applications, an as yet undetermined higher-level resource planning policy, or worse yet, the user, must renegotiate the resource reservations via what is at best a trial-and-error process.

Unlike reservation mechanisms, best-effort real-time scheduling [27] provides optimal performance in underload while ensuring that tasks of higher priority can meet their deadlines in overload. However, it provides no way of scheduling conventional tasks and does not support common resource sharing policies such as proportional sharing.

By introducing admission control, SMART can also provide resource reservations with optimal real-time performance. In addition, SMART subsumes best-effort real-time scheduling to provide optimal performance in meeting time constraints in underload even in the absence of reservations. This is especially important for common applications such as MPEG video whose dynamic requirements match poorly with static reservation abstractions [1, 16].

5.2   Fair queueing

Fair queueing provides a mechanism which allocates resources to tasks in proportion to their shares. It was first proposed for network packet scheduling in [7], with a more extensive analysis provided in [33], and later applied to processor scheduling in [40] as stride scheduling. Recent variants [2, 38] provide more accurate proportional sharing at the expense of additional scheduling overhead. The share used with fair queueing can be assigned in accordance with user desired allocations [40], or it can be assigned based on the task's resource requirement to provide resource reservations [33, 38]. When used to provide reservations, an admission control policy is also used.

When shares are assigned based on user desired allocations, fair queueing provides more accurate proportional sharing for conventional tasks than previous fair-share schedulers [9, 19]. However, it performs poorly for real-time tasks because it does not account for their time constraints. In underload, time constraints are unnecessarily missed. In overload, all tasks are proportionally late, potentially missing all time constraints.

When shares are assigned based on task resource requirements to provide reservations, fair queueing can be effective in underload at meeting real-time requirements that are strictly periodic in their computation and deadline. However, its performance is not optimal in underload and suffers especially in the case of aperiodic real-time requirements. To avoid making all tasks proportionally late in overload, admission control is used.

Unlike real-time reservation schedulers, fair queueing can integrate reservation support for real-time tasks with proportional sharing for conventional tasks [38]. However, shares for real-time applications must then be assigned based on their resource requirements; they cannot be assigned based on user desired allocations.

By providing time constraints and shares, SMART not only subsumes fair queueing, but it can also more effectively meet real-time requirements, with or without reservations. Unlike fair queueing, it can provide optimal real-time performance while allowing proportional sharing based on user desired allocations across both real-time and conventional applications. Furthermore, SMART also supports simultaneous prioritized and proportional resource allocation.

5.3 Hierarchical scheduling

Because creating a single scheduler to service both real-time and conventional resource requirements has proven difficult, a number of hybrid schemes [3, 6, 15, 16, 39] have been proposed. These approaches attempt to avoid the problem by having statically separate scheduling policies for real-time and conventional applications, respectively. The policies are combined using either priorities [6, 15, 39] or proportional sharing [3, 16, 18] as the base level scheduling mechanism.

With priorities, all tasks scheduled by the real-time scheduling policy are assigned higher priority than tasks scheduled by the conventional scheduling policy. This causes all real-time tasks, regardless of whether or not they are important, to be run ahead of any conventional task. The lack of control results in experimentally demonstrated pathological behaviors in which runaway real-time computations prevent the user from even being able to regain control of the system [29].

With proportional sharing, a real-time scheduling policy and a conventional scheduling policy are each given a proportional share of the machine to manage by the underlying proportional share mechanism, which then timeslices between them. Real-time applications will not take over the machine, but they also cannot meet their time constraints effectively as a result of the underlying proportional share mechanism taking the resource away from the real-time scheduler at an inopportune and unexpected time in the name of fairness [17].

The problem with previous mechanisms that have been used for combining these scheduling policies is that they do not explicitly account for real-time requirements. These schedulers rely on different policies for different classes of computations, but they encounter the same difficulty as other approaches in being unable to propagate these decisions to the lowest-level of resource management where the actual scheduling of processor cycles takes place.

SMART behaves like a real-time scheduler when scheduling only real-time requests and behaves like a conventional scheduler when scheduling only conventional requests. However, it combines these two dimensions in a dynamically integrated way that fully accounts for real-time requirements. SMART ensures that more important tasks obtain their resource requirements, whether they be real-time or conventional. In addition to allowing a wide range of behavior not possible with static schemes, SMART provides more efficient utilization of resources, is better able to adapt to varying workloads, and provides dynamic feedback to support adaptive real-time applications that is not found in previous approaches.

6 Experimental results

We have implemented SMART in Solaris 2.5.1, the current release of Sun Microsystems's UNIX operating system. To demonstrate its effectiveness, we describe two sets of experiments with a mix of real-time, interactive and batch applications executing in a workstation environment. The first experiment compares SMART with two existing schedulers: the UNIX SVR4 scheduler, both real-time (SVR4-RT) and time-sharing (SVR4-TS) policies, and a WFQ processor scheduler. The second experiment demonstrates the ability of SMART to provide the user with predictable resource allocation controls, adapt to dynamic changes in the workload, and deliver expected behavior when the system is not overloaded.

Three applications were used to represent batch, interactive and real-time computations:

- *Dhrystone* (batch) — This is the Dhrystone benchmark (Version 1.1), a synthetic benchmark that measures CPU integer performance.

- *Typing* (interactive) — This application emulates a user typing to a text editor by receiving a series of characters from a serial input line and using the X window server [35] to display them to the frame buffer. To enable a realistic and repeatable sequence of typed keystrokes for interactive applications, a hardware keyboard simulator was constructed and attached via a serial line to the testbed workstation. This device is capable of recording a sequence of keyboard inputs, and then replaying the sequence with the same timing characteristics.

- *Integrated Media Streams Player* (real-time) — The Integrated Media Streams (IMS) Player from Sun Microsystems Laboratories is a timestamp-based system capable of playing synchronized audio and video streams. It adapts to its system environment by adjusting the quality of playback based on the system load. The application was developed and tuned for the UNIX SVR4 time-sharing scheduler in the Solaris operating system. For the experiment with the SMART scheduler, we have inserted additional system calls to the application to take advantage of the features provided by SMART. The details of the modifications are presented in Section 6.1. We use this application in two different modes:

  - *News* (real-time) — This application displays synchronized audio and video streams from local storage. Each media stream flows under the direction of an independent thread of control. The audio and video threads communicate through a shared memory region and use timestamps to synchronize the display of the media streams. The video input stream contains frames at 320x240 pixel resolution in JPEG compressed format at roughly 15 frames/second. The audio input stream contains standard 8-bit μ-law monaural samples. The captured data is from a satellite news network.

  - *Entertain* (real-time) — This application processes video from local storage. The video input stream contains frames at 320x240 pixel resolution in JPEG compressed format at roughly 15 frames/second. The application scales and displays the video at 640x480 pixel resolution. The captured data contains a mix of television programming, including sitcom clips and commercials.

The experiments were performed on a standard, production SPARCstation™ 10 workstation with a single 150 MHz hyperSPARC™ processor, 64 MB of primary memory, and 3 GB of local disk space. The testbed system included a standard 8-bit pseudocolor frame buffer controller (i.e., GX). The display was managed using the X Window System. The Solaris 2.5.1 operating system was used as the basis for our experimental work.

The standard UNIX SVR4 scheduling framework upon which the Solaris operating system is based employs a periodic 10 ms clock tick. It is at this granularity that scheduling events can occur, which can be quite limiting in supporting real-time computations that have time constraints of the same order of magnitude. To allow a much finer resolution for scheduling events, we added a high res-

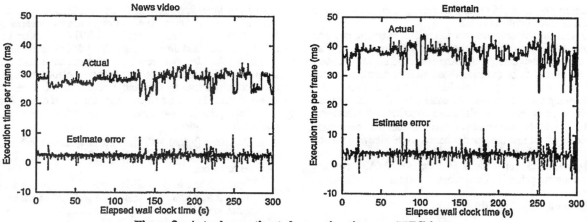

Figure 2: Actual vs. estimated execution time per JPEG image

olution timeout mechanism to the kernel and reduced the time scale at which timer based interrupts can occur. The exact resolution allowed is hardware dependent. On the testbed workstation used for these experiments, the resolution is 1 ms. The high resolution timing functionality was used for all of the schedulers to ensure a fair comparison.

All measurements were performed using a minimally obtrusive tracing facility that logs events at significant points in application, window system, and operating system code. This is done via a light-weight mechanism that writes timestamped event identifiers into a memory log. The timestamps are at 1 μs resolution. We measured the cost of the mechanism on the testbed workstation to be 2-4 μs per event. We created a suite of tools to post-process these event logs and obtain accurate representations of what happens in the actual system.

All measurements were performed on a fully functional system to represent a realistic workstation environment. By a fully functional system, we mean that all experiments were performed with all system functions running, the window system running, and the system connected to the network. At the same time, an effort was made to eliminate variations in the test environment to make the experiments repeatable. To this end, the testbed system was restarted prior to each experimental run.

6.1 Programming with time constraints

The SMART application interface makes it easier to develop a real-time application. The software developer can express the scheduling constraints directly to the system and have the system deliver the expected behavior. To illustrate this aspect of SMART, we first describe what it took to develop the IMS Player for UNIX SVR4, then discuss how we modified it for SMART.

6.1.1 Video player

The video player reads a timestamped JPEG video input stream from local storage, uncompresses it, dithers it to 8-bit pseudo-color, and renders it directly to the frame buffer. When the video player is not used in synchrony with an audio player, as in the case of *Entertain*, the player uses the timestamps on the video input stream to determine when to display each frame and whether a given frame is early or late. When used in conjunction with the audio player, as in the case of *News*, the video player attempts to synchronize its output with that of the audio device. In particular, since humans are more sensitive to intra-stream audio asynchronies (i.e. audio delays and drop-outs) than to asynchronies involving video, the thread controlling the audio stream free-runs as the master time reference and the video "slave" thread uses the information the audio player

posts into the shared memory region to determine when to display its frames.

If the video player is ready to display its frame early, then it delays until the appropriate time; but if it is late, it discards its current frame on the assumption that continued processing will cause further delays later in the stream. The application defines early and late as more than 20 ms early or late with respect to the audio. For UNIX SVR4, the video player must determine entirely on its own whether or not each video frame can be displayed on time. This is done by measuring the amount of wall clock time that elapses during the processing of each video frame. An exponential average [13] of the elapsed wall clock time of previously displayed frames is then used as an estimate for how long it will take to process the current frame. If the estimate indicates that the frame will complete too early (more than 20 ms early), the video player sleeps an amount of time necessary to delay processing to allow the frame to be completed at the right time. If the estimate indicates that the frame will be completed too late (more than 20 ms late), the frame is discarded.

The application adapted to run on SMART uses the same mechanism as the original to delay the frames that would otherwise be completed too early. We replace the application's discard mechanism with simply a time constraint system call to inform SMART of the time constraints for a given block of application code, along with a signal handler to process notifications of time constraints that cannot be met. The time constraint informs SMART of the deadline for the execution of the block of code that processes the video frame. The deadline is set to the time the frame is considered late, which is 20 ms after the ideal display time. It also provides an estimate of the amount of execution time for the code calculated in a similar manner as the original program. In particular, an exponential average of the execution times of previously displayed frames scaled by 10% is used as the estimate. Upon setting the given time constraint, the application requests that SMART provide a notification to the application right away if early estimates predict that the time constraint cannot be met. When a notification is sent to the application, the application signal handler simply records the fact that the notification has been received. If the notification is received by the time the application begins the computation to process and display the respective video frame, the frame is discarded; otherwise, the application simply allows the frame be displayed late.

Figure 2 indicates that simple exponential averaging based on previous frame execution times can be used to provide reasonable estimates of frame execution times even for JPEG compressed video in which frame times vary from one frame to another. Note that MPEG video would require averaging for each type of frame. Each graph shows the actual execution time for each frame, the

Name	Basis of Measurement	No. of Measurements	CPU Time Avg.	CPU Time Std. Dev.	% CPU Avg.
News audio	per segment	4700	1.54 ms	0.79 ms	2.42%
News video	per frame	4481	28.35 ms	2.19 ms	42.34%
Entertain	per frame	4487	39.16 ms	2.71 ms	58.55%
Typing	per character	1314	1.96 ms	0.17 ms	0.86%
Dhrystone	per execution	1	298.73 s	N/A	99.63%

Table 2: Standalone execution times of applications

Name	Quality Metric	On Time	Early	Late	Dropped	Avg.	Std. Dev.
News audio	Number of audio dropouts	100.00%	0.00%	0.00%	0.00%	0	0
News video	Actual display time minus desired display time	99.75%	0.09%	0.13%	0.02%	1.50 ms	2.54 ms
Entertain	Actual display time minus desired display time	99.58%	0.22%	0.13%	0.07%	1.95 ms	3.61 ms
Typing	Delay from character input to character display	100.00%	N/A	0%	N/A	26.40 ms	4.12 ms
Dhrystone	Accumulated CPU time	N/A	N/A	N/A	N/A	298.73 s	N/A

Table 3: Standalone application quality metric performance

average execution time across all frames, and the difference between the estimated and actual execution time for each frame. The slight positive bias in the difference is due to the 10% scaling in the estimate versus the actual execution time. As shown in the figure, there is a wide variance in the time it takes to handle a frame. The results also illustrate the difficulty of using a resource reservation scheme. Using the upper bound on the processing time as an estimate may yield a low utilization of resources; using the average processing time may cause too many deadlines to be missed.

6.1.2 Audio player

The audio player reads a timestamped audio input stream from local storage and outputs the audio samples to the audio device. The processing of the 8-bit μ-law monaural samples is done in 512 byte segments. To avoid audio dropouts, the audio player takes advantage of buffering available on the audio device to work ahead in the audio stream when processor cycles are available. Up to 1 second of workahead is allowed. For each block of code that processes an audio segment, the audio player aims to complete the segment before the audio device runs out of audio samples to display. The deadline communicated to SMART is therefore set to the display time of the last audio sample in the buffer. The estimate of the execution time is again computed by using an exponential average of the measured execution times for processing previous audio segments. Audio segments that cannot be processed before their deadlines are simply displayed late. Note that because of the workahead feature and the audio device buffering, the resulting deadlines can be highly aperiodic.

6.2 Application characteristics and quality metrics

Representing different classes of applications, *Typing*, *Dhrystone*, *News* and *Entertain* have very different characteristics and measures of quality. For example, we care about the response time for interactive tasks, the throughput of batch tasks and the number of deadlines met in real-time tasks. Before discussing how a combination of these applications executes on different schedulers, this section describes how we measure the quality of each of the different applications, and how each would perform if it were to run on its own.

Table 2 shows the execution time of each application on an otherwise quiescent system using the UNIX SVR4 scheduler, measured over a time period of 300 seconds. We note that there is no significant difference between the performance of different

schedulers when running only one application. The execution times include user time and system time spent on behalf of an application. The *Dhrystone* batch application can run whenever the processor is available and can thus fully utilize the processor. The execution of other system functions (fsflush, window system, etc.) takes less than 1% of the CPU time. The measurements on the real-time applications are taken every frame, and those for *Typing* are taken every character. None of the real-time and interactive applications can take up the whole machine on its own, with both *News* audio and *Typing* taking hardly any time at all. The video for *News* takes up 42% of the CPU, whereas *Entertain*, which displays scaled video, takes up almost 60% of the processor time.

For each application, the quality of metric is different. For *Typing*, it is desirable to minimize the time between user input and system response to a level that is faster than what a human can readily detect. This means that for simple tasks such as typing, cursor motion, or mouse selection, system response time should be less than 50-150 ms [37]. As such, we measured the *Typing* character latency and determine the percentage of characters processed with latency less than 50 ms, with latency between 50-150 ms, and with latency greater than 150 ms. For *News* audio, it is desirable not to have any artifacts in audio output. As such, we measured the number of *News* audio samples dropped. For *News* video and *Entertain*, it is desirable to minimize the difference between the desired display time and the actual display time, while maximizing the number of frames that are displayed within their time constraints. As such, we measured the percentage of *News* and *Entertain* video frames that were displayed on time (displayed within 20 ms of the desired time), displayed early, displayed late, and the percentage of frames dropped not displayed. Finally, for batch applications such as *Dhrystone*, it is desirable to maximize the processing time devoted to the application to ensure as rapid forward progress as possible. As such, we simply measured the CPU time *Dhrystone* accumulated. To establish a baseline performance, Table 3 shows the performance of each application when it was executed on its own.

While measurements of accumulated CPU time are straightforward, we note that several steps were taken to minimize and quantify any error in measuring audio and video performance as well as interactive performance. For *News* and *Entertain*, the measurements reported here are performed by the respective applications themselves during execution. We also quantified the error of these internal measurements by using a hardware device to externally measure the actual user perceived video display and audio display times [36]. External versus internal measurements differed by less than 10 ms. The difference is due to the refresh time of the frame buffer.

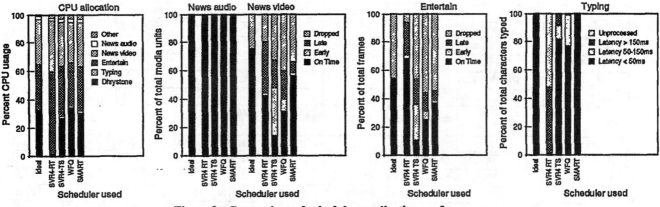

Figure 3: Comparison of scheduler application performance

For *Typing*, we measured the end-to-end character latency from the arrival of the character to the system in the input device driver, through the processing of the character by the application, until the actual display of the character by the X window system character display routine.

6.3   Scheduler characteristics

To provide a characterization of scheduling overhead, we measured the context switch times for the UNIX SVR4, WFQ, and SMART schedulers. Average context switch times for UNIX SVR4, WFQ, and SMART are 27 µs, 42 µs, and 47 µs, respectively. These measurements were obtained running the mixes of applications described in this paper. Similar results were obtained when we increased the number of real-time multimedia applications in the mix up to 15, at which point no further multimedia applications could be run due to there being no more memory to allocate to the applications.

The UNIX SVR4 context switch time essentially measures the context switch overhead for a scheduler that takes almost no time to decide what task it needs to execute. The scheduler simply selects the highest priority task to execute, with all tasks already sorted in priority order. Note that this measure does not account for the periodic processing done by the UNIX SVR4 timesharing policy to adjust the priority levels of all tasks. Such periodic processing is not required by WFQ or SMART, which makes the comparison of overhead based on context switch times more favorable for UNIX SVR4. Nevertheless, as tasks are typically scheduled for time quanta of several milliseconds, the measured context switch times for all of the schedulers were not found to have a significant impact on application performance.

For SMART, we also measured the cost to an application of assigning scheduling parameters such as time constraints or reading back scheduling information. The cost of assigning scheduling parameters to a task is 20 µs while the cost of reading the scheduling information for a task is only 10 µs. The small overhead easily allows application developers to program with time constraints at a fine granularity without much penalty to application performance.

6.4   Comparison of default scheduler behavior

Our first experiment is simply to run all four applications (*News*, *Entertain*, *Typing*, and *Dhrystone*) with the default user parameters for each of the schedulers:

- SVR4-RT: The real-time *News* and *Entertain* applications are put in the real-time class, leaving *Typing* and *Dhrystone* in the time-sharing class.

- SVR4-TS: All the applications are run in time-sharing mode. (We also experimented with putting *Typing* in the interactive application class and obtained slightly worse performance.)
- WFQ: All the applications are run with equal share.
- SMART: All the applications are run with equal share and equal priority.

Because of their computational requirements, the execution of these applications results in the system being overloaded. In fact, the *News* video and the *Entertain* applications alone will fully occupy the machine. Both the *Typing* and *News* audio applications hardly use any CPU time, taking up a total of only 3-4% of the CPU time. It is thus desirable for the scheduler to deliver short latency on the former application and meet all the deadlines on the latter application. With the default user parameters in SVR4-TS, WFQ, and SMART, we expect the remainder of the computation time to be distributed evenly between *News* video, *Entertain*, and *Dhrystone*. Even with an ideal scheduler, we expect the percentages of the frames dropped to be 25% and 45% for *News* video and *Entertain*, respectively.

Figure 3 presents the CPU allocation across different applications by different schedulers. It includes the percentage of the CPU used for executing other system functions such as the window system (labeled *Other*). The figure also includes the expected result of an ideal scheduler for comparison purposes. For the real-time applications, the figure also shows the percentages of media units that are displayed on-time, early, late, or dropped. For the interactive *Typing* application, the figure shows the number of characters that take less than 50 ms to display, take 50-150 ms to display, and take longer than 150 ms to display. Figure 4 presents more detail by showing the distributions of the data points. We have also included the measurements for each of the applications running by itself (labeled *Standalone*) in the figure. We observe that every scheduler handles the *News* audio application well with no audio dropouts. Thus we will only concentrate on discussing the quality of the rest of the applications.

Unlike the other schedulers, the SVR4-RT scheduler gives higher priority to applications in the real-time class. It devotes most of the CPU time to the video applications, and thus drops the least number of frames. (Nevertheless, SMART is able to deliver more on-time frames than SVR4-RT for the *News* video, while using less resources.) Unfortunately, SVR4-RT runs the real-time applications almost to the exclusion of conventional applications. *Dhrystone* gets only 1.6% of the CPU time. More disturbingly, the interactive *Typing* application does not get even the little processing time requested, receiving only 0.24% of the CPU time. Only 635 out of the 1314 characters typed are even processed within the 300 second duration, and nearly all the characters processed have an unacceptable latency of greater than 150 ms. Note that putting *Typing* in the

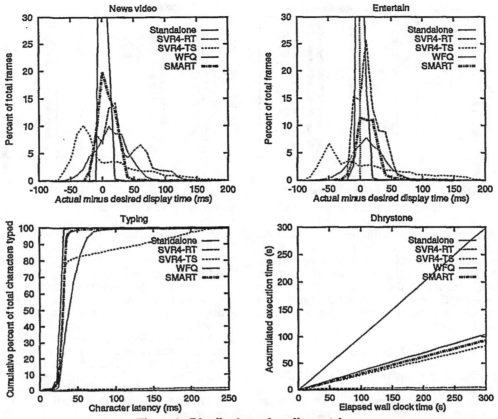

Figure 4: Distributions of quality metrics

real-time class does not alleviate this problem as the system-level I/O processing required by the application is still not able to run, because system functions are run at a lower priority than real-time tasks. Clearly, it is not acceptable to use the SVR4-RT scheduler.

All the other schedulers spread the resources relatively evenly across the three demanding applications. The SVR4-TS scheduler has less control over the resource distribution than WFQ and SMART, resulting in a slight bias towards *Entertain* over *Dhrystone*. The basic principles used to achieve fairness across applications are the same in WFQ and SMART. However, we observe that WFQ scheduler devotes slightly more (3.8%) CPU time to *Dhrystone* at the expense of *News* video. This effect can be attributed to the standard implementation of WFQ processor scheduling whereby the proportional share of the processor obtained by a task is based only on the time that the task is runnable and does not include any time that the task is sleeping.

Since the video applications either process a frame or discard a frame altogether from the beginning, the number of video frames dropped is directly correlated with the amount of time devoted by the scheduler to the applications, regardless of the scheduler used. The difference in allocation accounts for the difference in the number of frames dropped between the schedulers. We found that in each instance the scheduler drops about 6-7% more frames than the ideal computed using average computation times and the scheduler's specific allocation for the application.

The schedulers are distinguished by their ability to meet the time constraints of those frames processed. SMART meets a significantly larger number of time constraints than the other schedulers, delivering over 250% more video frames on time than SVR4-TS and over 60% more video frames on time than WFQ. SMART's effectiveness holds even for cases where it processes a larger total number of frames, as in the comparison with WFQ. Moreover, as

shown in Figure 4, the late frames are handled soon after the deadlines, unlike the case with the other schedulers. As SMART delivers a more predictable behavior, the applications are better at determining how long to sleep to avoid delay displaying the frames too early. As a result, there is a relatively small number of early frames. It delivers on time 57% and 37% of the total number of frames in *News* video and *Entertain*, respectively. They represent, respectively, 86% and 81% of the frames displayed.

To understand the significance of the bias introduced to improve the real-time and interactive application performance, we have also performed the same experiment with all biases set to zero. The use of the bias is found to yield a 10% relative improvement on the scheduler's ability in delivering the *Entertain* frames on time.

In contrast, the WFQ delivers 32% and 26% of the total frames on time, which represents only 53% and 58% of the frames processed. There are many more late frames in the WFQ case than in SMART. The tardiness causes the applications to initiate the processing earlier, thus resulting in a correspondingly larger number of early frames. The SVR4-TS performs even more poorly, delivering 15% and 11% of the total frames, representing only 22% and 21% of the frames processed. Some of the frames handled by SVR4-TS are extremely late, causing many frames to be processed extremely early, resulting in a very large variance in display time across frames.

Finally, as shown in Figure 4, SMART is superior to both SVRT-TS and WFQ in handling the *Typing* application. SMART has the least average and standard deviation in character latency and completes the most number of characters in less than 50 ms, the threshold of human detectable delay.

While both SMART and WFQ deliver acceptable interactive performance, *Typing* performs worse with WFQ because a task does not accumulate any credit at all when it sleeps. We performed

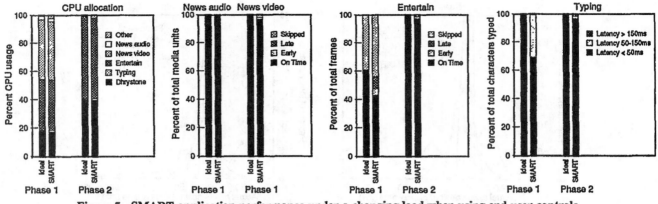

Figure 5: SMART application performance under a changing load when using end user controls

an experiment where the WFQ algorithm is modified to allow the blocked task to accumulate limited credit just as it would when run on the SMART scheduler. The result is that *Typing* improves significantly, and the video application gets a fairer share of the resources. However, even though the number of dropped video frames is reduced slightly, the modified WFQ algorithm has roughly the same poor performance as before when it comes to delivering the frames on time.

6.5   Adjusting the allocation of resources

Besides being effective for real-time applications, SMART has the ability to support arbitrary shares and priorities and to adapt to different system loads. We illustrate these features by running the same set of applications from before with different priority and share assignments under different system loads. In particular, *News* is given a higher priority than all the other applications, *Entertain* is given the default priority and twice as many shares as any other application, and all other applications are given the same default priority and share. This level of control afforded by SMART's priorities and shares is not possible with other schedulers. The experiment can be described in two phases:

- *Phase 1*: Run all the applications for the first 120 seconds of the experiment. *News* exits after the first 120 seconds of the experiment, resulting in a load change.
- *Phase 2*: Run the remaining applications for the remaining 180 seconds of the experiment.

Besides *News* and *Entertain*, the only other time-consuming application in the system is *Dhrystone*. Thus, in the first part of the experiment, *News* should be allowed to use as much of the processor as necessary to meet its resource requirements since it is higher priority than all other applications. Since *News* audio uses less than 3% of the machine and *News* video uses only 42% of the machine on average, over half of the processor's time should remain available for running other applications. As *Typing* consumes very little processing time, almost all of the remaining computation time should be distributed between *Entertain* and *Dhrystone* in the ratio 2:1. The time allotted to *Entertain* can service at most 62% of the deadlines on average. When *News* finishes, however, *Entertain* is allowed to take up to 2/3 of the processor, which would allow the application to run at full rate. The system is persistently overloaded in Phase 1 of the experiment, and on average underloaded in Phase 2, though transient overloads may occur due to fluctuations in processing requirements.

Figure 5 shows the CPU allocation and quality metrics of the different applications run under SMART as well as an ideal scheduler. (Distributions of the data points are not included here due to lack of space.) The figure shows that SMART's performance comes

quite close to the ideal. First, it implements proportional sharing well in both underloaded and overloaded conditions. Second, SMART performs well for higher priority real-time applications and real-time applications requesting less than their fair share of resources. In the first phase of the computation, it provides perfect *News* audio performance, and delivers 97% of the frames of *News* video on time and meets 99% of the deadlines. In the second phase, SMART displays 98% of the *Entertain* frames on time and meets 99% of the deadlines. Third, SMART is able to adjust the rate of the application requesting more than its fair share, and can meet a reasonable number of its deadlines. In the first phase for *Entertain*, SMART drops only 5% more total number of frames than the ideal, which is calculated using average execution times and an allocation of 33% of the processor time. Finally, SMART provides excellent interactive response for *Typing* in both overloaded and underloaded conditions. 99% of the characters are displayed with a delay unnoticeable to typical users of less than 100 ms [4].

7   Concluding remarks

Our experiments in the context of a full featured, commercial, general-purpose operating system show that SMART: (1) reduces the burden of writing adaptive real-time applications, (2) has the ability to cooperate with applications in managing resources to meet their dynamic time constraints, (3) provides resource sharing across both real-time and conventional applications, (4) delivers improved real-time and interactive performance over other schedulers without any need for users to reserve resources, adjust scheduling parameters, or know anything about application requirements, (5) provides flexible, predictable controls to allow users to bias the allocation of resources according to their preferences. SMART achieves this range of behavior by differentiating between the importance and urgency of real-time and conventional applications. This is done by integrating priorities and weighted fair queueing for importance, then using urgency to optimize the order in which tasks are serviced based on earliest-deadline scheduling. Our measured performance results demonstrate SMART's effectiveness over that of other schedulers in supporting multimedia applications in a realistic workstation environment.

Acknowledgments

We thank Jim Hanko, Duane Northcutt, and Brian Schmidt for their help with the applications and measurement tools used in our experiments. We also thank Jim, Duane, Amy Lim, Mendel Rosenblum, Alice Yu, Rich Draves, and the conference referees for helpful comments on earlier drafts of this paper. This work was supported in part by an NSF Young Investigator Award and Sun Microsystems Laboratories.

References

1. V. Baiceanu, C. Cowan, D. McNamee, C. Pu, J. Walpole, "Multimedia Applications Require Adaptive CPU Scheduling", *Proceedings of the IEEE RTSS Workshop on Resource Allocation Problems in Multimedia Systems*, Washington, DC, Dec. 1996.

2. J. C. R. Bennett, H. Zhang, "WF^{2}Q: Worst-case Fair Weighted Fair Queueing", *IEEE INFOCOM '96*, San Francisco, CA, pp. 120-128, Mar. 1996.

3. G. Bollella, K. Jeffay, "Support for Real-Time Computing Within General Purpose Operating Systems: Supporting Co-Resident Operating Systems", *Proceedings of the IEEE Real-Time Technology and Applications Symposium*, Chicago, IL, pp. 4-14, May 1995.

4. S. K. Card, T. P. Moran, A. Newell, *The Psychology of Human-Computer Interaction*, L. Erlbaum Associates, Hillsdale, NJ, 1983.

5. G. Coulson, A. Campbell, P. Robin, G. Blair, M. Papathomas, D. Hutchinson, "The Design of a QoS Controlled ATM Based Communications System in Chorus", *IEEE JSAC*, 13(4), pp. 686-699, May 1995.

6. H. Custer, *Inside Windows NT*, Microsoft Press, Redmond, WA, 1993.

7. A. Demers, S. Keshav, S. Shenker, "Analysis and Simulation of a Fair Queueing Algorithm", *Proceedings of SIGCOMM '89*, pp. 1-12, Sept. 1989.

8. M. Dertouzos, "Control Robotics: The Procedural Control of Physical Processors", *Proceedings of the IFIP Congress*, Stockholm, Sweden, pp. 807-813, Aug. 1974.

9. R. B. Essick, "An Event-based Fair Share Scheduler", *Proceedings of the 1990 Winter USENIX Conference*, Washington, DC, pp. 147-161, Jan. 1990.

10. S. Evans, K. Clarke, D. Singleton, B. Smaalders, "Optimizing Unix Resource Scheduling for User Interaction", *Proceedings of the 1993 Summer USENIX Conference*, Cincinnati, OH, pp. 205-218, June 1993.

11. J. R. Eykholt, S. R. Kleiman, S. Barton, R. Faulkner, A. Shivalingiah, M. Smith, D. Stein, J. Voll, M. Weeks, D. Williams, "Beyond Multiprocessing...Multithreading the SunOS Kernel", *Proceedings of the 1992 Summer USENIX Conference*, San Antonio, TX, pp. 11-18, June 1992.

12. P. Ffoulkes, D. Wikler, "Workstations Worldwide Market Segmentation", *Advanced Desktops and Workstations Worldwide*, Dataquest, June 1997.

13. N. G. Fosback, *Stock Market Logic*, Institute for Econometric Research, Ft. Lauderdale, FL, 1976.

14. L. Georgiadis, R. Guérin, V. Peris, K. N. Sivarajan, "Efficient Network QoS Provisioning Based on per Node Traffic Shaping", *IEEE/ACM Transactions on Networking*, 4(4), pp. 482-501, Aug. 1996.

15. D. B. Golub, "Operating System Support for Coexistence of Real-Time and Conventional Scheduling", Technical Report CMU-CS-94-212, School of Computer Science, Carnegie Mellon University, Nov. 1994.

16. P. Goyal, X. Guo, H. M. Vin, "A Hierarchical CPU Scheduler for Multimedia Operating Systems", *Proceedings of the Second Symposium on Operating Systems Design and Implementation*, Seattle, WA, pp. 107-122, Oct. 1996.

17. P. Goyal, Panel talk at the *IEEE RTSS Workshop on Resource Allocation Problems in Multimedia Systems*, Washington, DC, Dec. 1996.

18. J. G. Hanko, "A New Framework for Processor Scheduling in UNIX", Abstract talk at the *Fourth International Workshop on Network and Operating Systems Support for Digital Audio and Video*, Lancaster, U. K., Nov. 1993.

19. G. J. Henry, "The Fair Share Scheduler", *AT&T Bell Laboratories Technical Journal*, 63(8), pp. 1845-1858, Oct. 1984.

20. *IEEE Micro*, 15(4), Aug. 1996.

21. M. B. Jones, personal communication, July 1997.

22. M. B. Jones, D. Rosu, M-C. Rosu, "CPU Reservations and Time Constraints: Efficient, Predictable Scheduling of Independent Activities", *Proceedings of the Sixteenth ACM Symposium on Operating Systems Principles*, St. Malo, France, Oct. 1997.

23. S. J. Leffler, M. K. McKusick, M. J. Karels, J. S. Quarterman, *The Design and Implementation of the 4.3BSD UNIX Operating System*, Addison-Wesley, Reading, MA, 1989.

24. J. Lehoczky, L. Sha, Y. Ding, "The Rate Monotonic Scheduling Algorithm: Exact Characterization and Average Case Behavior", *Proceedings of the IEEE Real-Time Systems Symposium*, pp. 166-171, Dec. 1989.

25. I. M. Leslie, D. McAuley, R. Black, T. Roscoe, P. Barham, D. Evers, R. Fairbairns, E. Hyden, "The Design and Implementation of an Operating System to Support Distributed Multimedia Applications", *IEEE JSAC*, 14(7), pp. 1280-1297, Sept. 1996.

26. C. L. Liu, J. W. Layland, "Scheduling Algorithms for Multiprogramming in a Hard-Real-Time Environment", *JACM*, 20(1), pp. 46-61, Jan. 1973.

27. C. D. Locke, "Best-Effort Decision Making for Real-Time Scheduling", Ph.D. Thesis, Department of Computer Science, Carnegie Mellon University, May 1986.

28. C. W. Mercer, S. Savage, H. Tokuda, "Processor Capacity Reserves: Operating System Support for Multimedia Applications", *Proceedings of the IEEE International Conference on Multimedia Computing and Systems*, Boston, MA, pp. 90-99, May 1994.

29. J. Nieh, J. G. Hanko, J. D. Northcutt, G. A. Wall, "SVR4 UNIX Scheduler Unacceptable for Multimedia Applications", *Proceedings of the Fourth International Workshop on Network and Operating Systems Support for Digital Audio and Video*, Lancaster, U. K., pp. 35-48, Nov. 1993.

30. J. Nieh, M. S. Lam, "SMART UNIX SVR4 Support for Multimedia Applications", *Proceedings of the IEEE International Conference on Multimedia Computing and Systems*, Ottawa, Canada, pp. 404-414, June 1997.

31. J. D. Northcutt, *Mechanisms for Reliable Distributed Real-Time Operating Systems: The Alpha Kernel*, Academic Press, Boston, MA, 1987.

32. J. D. Northcutt, E. M. Kuerner, "System Support for Time-Critical Applications", *Proceedings of the Second International Workshop on Network and Operating Systems Support for Digital Audio and Video*, Lecture Notes in Computer Science, Vol. 614, Heidelberg, Germany, pp. 242-254, Nov. 1991.

33. A. K. Parekh, R. G. Gallager, "A Generalized Processor Sharing Approach to Flow Control in Integrated Services Networks: The Single-Node Case", *IEEE/ACM Transactions on Networking*, pp. 344-357, June 1993.

34. "PointCast Unveils First News Network that Reaches Viewers at Their Desktops", Press Release, PointCast Inc., San Francisco, CA, Feb. 13, 1996.

35. R. W. Scheifler, J. Gettys, "The X Window System, *ACM Transactions on Graphics*, 5(2), pp. 79-109, Apr. 1986.

36. B. K. Schmidt, "A Method and Apparatus for Measuring Media Synchronization", *Proceedings of the Fifth International Workshop on Network and Operating Systems Support for Digital Audio and Video*, Durham, NH, pp. 203-214, Apr. 1995.

37. B. Shneiderman, *Designing the User Interface: Strategies for Effective Human-Computer Interaction*, 2nd ed., Addison-Wesley, Reading, MA, 1992.

38. I. Stoica, H. Abdel-Wahab, K. Jeffay, "On the Duality between Resource Reservation and Proportional Share Resource Allocation", *Multimedia Computing and Networking Proceedings, SPIE Proceedings Series*, Vol. 3020, San Jose, CA, pp. 207-214, Feb. 1997.

39. *UNIX System V Release 4 Internals Student Guide*, Vol. I, Unit 2.4.2., AT&T, 1990.

40. C. A. Waldspurger, "Lottery and Stride Scheduling: Flexible Proportional-Share Resource Management", Ph.D. Thesis, Department of Electrical Engineering and Computer Science, Massachusetts Institute of Technology, Sept. 1995.

CHAPTER EIGHT

Videoconferencing

Kevin Jeffay

University of North Carolina - Chapel Hill

VIDEOCONFERENCING applications are an important area of study in multimedia computing and networking for two reasons. First and foremost, videoconferencing is a challenging real-time systems problem. By its nature, a videoconference is an interactive application with stringent latency and throughput requirements. In the ideal world, the video signal would be sent at full-motion video rates (*e.g.*, 30 frames per second for NTSC video), with sufficient resolution to create some semblance of the illusion of presence or co-location with remote conferees. Audio would be delivered reliably with an end-to-end delay approximating that of a telephone call (*e.g.*, delay less than 100 ms), and the end-system would synchronize the audio and video streams and present them to the user with minimal additional delay. Compounding the problem of realizing these real-time requirements is the fact that videoconferences often consume (or desire to consume) significant amounts of network bandwidth. This means videoconferences are both capable of congesting a network and are adversely effected when the network is congested.

The second reason for studying videoconferencing is the fact that it has frequently been touted as the "killer app" of multimedia computing. Videoconferencing has long been viewed as the application that would appeal to all computer users because it would provide a richer medium for person-to-person interaction than a telephone call. Moreover, it was felt that videoconferencing would enable or enhance collaborative work by fostering lightweight interactions and reducing the need for face-to-face meetings (thereby possibly reducing the need to travel to remote meetings). Videoconferencing, or more generally multipoint interactive video, was also envisioned as a key component of distance learning systems, remote consultation systems, and high-end gaming and tele-immersion systems. Thus solving the problems of network and operating system support for videoconferencing has implicitly been viewed as one of the linchpins for realizing next-generation communication services and applications on the Internet.

For this chapter I have selected three classes of papers on videoconferencing. The first class focuses on solutions to the primary technical problems encountered in trying to deliver and manage streams of audio and video in real-time over the Internet. The issues here are closely related to those discussed in Chapter 9, "Networking and Media Streaming," and indeed the papers I have included here complement those selected for Chapter 9 (and vice versa).

The second class of paper steps back from the technology to focus on the value of videoconferencing in fostering collaboration and group productivity in a distributed working environment. A preliminary conclusion from the first set of papers (and Chapter 9) is that although best-effort delivery of live audio and video data can be effective, it is frequently a poor approximation to real-time delivery. This raises the set of questions: What are the fundamental requirements for a videoconferencing system, what are the expected benefits from the use of videoconferencing technology, and are these benefits worth the cost?

Finally, I have included a case study in the design of a widely used Internet videoconferencing system called *vic*. This paper serves as an introduction to the major components of a videoconferencing system as well as a survey of the design issues faced in realizing such a system.

BEST-EFFORT DELIVERY OF LIVE DIGITAL AUDIO AND VIDEO

Given that today's Internet does not support real-time communications, the fundamental networking problem is that of coding the media streams and biasing how they are introduced into the network so as to maximize the probability that they can be received by conference participants and played out in a satisfactory manner. Chapter 9 introduces many of the classical problems and solutions to the best-effort multimedia networking problem. Here we focus on application-level techniques for dealing with the effects of network congestion that are particularly well suited to the transmission and playout of live media.

It is useful to differentiate between congestion in the small and congestion in the large. By congestion in the small, we refer to the state of the network wherein switches in the network are temporarily unable to forward all arriving packets in real-time and queues build up at the switches. As queues at switches grow and shrink, the end-to-end transmission delay experienced by packets corresponding to a videoconference will grow and shrink as well. This deviation in end-to-end delay is referred to as *delayjitter*. Delayjitter is problematic because applications such as videoconferencing typically require continual playout of media samples. Ideally, media samples such as video frames should be displayed continuously, with each successive frame displayed immediately after its predecessor. Because frames are typically generated and displayed at fixed intervals, it follows that continuous playout can occur only if each frame experiences the same end-to-end delay. The existence of delayjitter implies that continuous playout is, in general, impossible. Because of this limitation, a buffer is introduced at the receiver to smooth variation in end-to-end delay. However, the problem of setting the depth (size) of this buffer remains. A large buffer will ensure gross delayjitter can be accommodated but at the cost of

increasing the effective end-to-end delay (the transmission to playout delay) of the application. Given that latency is a key performance measure for videoconferencing, such a large buffer may be unacceptable, especially if such gross delayjitter is an infrequent occurrence. On the other hand, a small buffer will ensure minimal additional delay is incurred, but such a buffer will be ineffective in times of high delayjitter. In this case, the buffer may empty and the application be starved for new frames to display. This will result in a "gap" in the playout, an equally undesirable event.

Videoconferencing applications (as well as most streaming media applications) must explicitly manage the fundamental tradeoff between minimizing end-to-end display latency and minimizing the frequency with which gaps appear in the playout. This is done through what are known as *jitter-buffer* or *elastic queue management*, algorithms. These algorithms monitor changes in end-to-end delay and attempt to dynamically set a playout buffer depth at the receiver that is appropriate for the requirements of the application and the current perceived network conditions. The paper "An empirical study of delay jitter management policies," by D. L. Stone and K. Jeffay, presents two families of policies for adaptively setting the depth of the playout queue at the receiver and an empirical evaluation of the policies based on a set of network traces. These classic jitter-buffer algorithms represent the best practice for adaptive playout queue management.

Congestion in the large refers to the state of the network wherein queues at switches have filled to capacity and packets are dropped. When such a state is reached, applications must reduce their load on the network to ensure the network doesn't reach a state of congestive collapse. Whereas most applications reduce their load on the network in times of congestion by relying on the underlying transport protocol (most notably TCP) to reduce the transmission rate, videoconferencing and other streaming applications must develop their own means of reducing the load they generate. The process of modulating the bit-rate generated by a multimedia application to match a transmission rate that is sustainable in the network is called *media scaling*. The paper "Media scaling for audiovisual communication with the Heidelberg transport system," by L. Delgrossi and colleagues, presents a framework for addressing this problem for video streams. They present a taxonomy of methods for reducing the bit rate of a video stream and comment on the tradeoffs between the level of reduction achieved and the likely degradation in the perceptual quality of the stream that results.

Although media scaling attempts to reduce the load placed on the network by a videoconferencing application and thereby implicitly reduce the loss rate seen by the application, methods are still required to ameliorate the effects of packet loss. The final paper in this chapter, "Retransmission-based error control for interactive video applications over the Internet," by I. Rhee, considers a method for retransmitting lost video packets in videoconference. Retransmission requires the receiver to detect when a packet has been lost and to inform the sender of this fact, who will subsequently retransmit the packet. Because each stage in this process takes time, conventional wisdom held that retransmission would be ineffective for interactive applications such as videoconferencing because it would increase the end-to-end latency to unacceptable levels. Although this is indeed frequently the case, Rhee demonstrates that significant utility in retransmitting missing media samples remains. For example, although a retransmitted media sample may arrive too late to be played, in the case of inter-coded samples (such as MPEG video frames), the retransmitted sample may be used to improve the quality of the playout of future samples.

ON THE POWER AND PROMISE OF VIDEOCONFERENCING

To address the premise that videoconferencing is an important technology for distributed work groups, I have included the paper "What video can and can't do for collaboration: A case study," by E. A. Issacs and J. C. Tang. The paper reports on the effects of using workstation-based videoconferencing technology for communication between geographically distributed groups of software engineers. The authors conclude that although videoconferencing did not improve the product of the collaboration (*i.e.*, the software that was under construction), it did effect the process of collaboration in several observable (and positive) ways. Moreover, the authors document the effects that various video-conference performance parameters such as latency and throughput had on the collaboration process.

Although the conclusions are specific to a particular form and use of a videoconferencing system, they provide important insights into the likely effectiveness of best-effort videoconferencing technology for application domains such as distance learning and remote consultation.

A CASE STUDY ON THE DESIGN OF A VIDEOCONFERENCING SYSTEM

The final paper in this chapter is a case study in the design of the widely used Internet videoconferencing system called *vic*. The *vic* videoconferencing system has been used extensively by Internet researchers to broadcast meetings and hold videoconferences over the MBONE, an experimental multicast overlay network for the Internet.

The paper, entitled *"vic*: A flexible framework for packet video," by S. McCanne and V. Jacobson, provides an excellent introduction to some of the software engineering issues involved in the design of a network-centric video codec for real-time video transmission. In addition, the paper discusses the dominant (IETF-sanctioned) network transport protocol RTP (Real-Time Protocol) used for transmission of multimedia on the Internet as well as some of the related tools developed for conference management.

ADDITIONAL READINGS

E. Amir, S. McCanne, and H. Zhang, "An application-level video gateway," in *Proceedings of the 2nd ACM International Multimedia Conference* (Nov. 1995): 255–65.

H. Eriksson, "MBONE: The multicast backbone," *Communications of the ACM* 37, no. 8 (Aug. 1994): 54–60.

D. Ferrari, "Client requirements for real-time communication services," *IEEE Communications* (Nov. 1990): 65–72.

R. Fish, R. Kraut, R. Root, and R. Rice, "Video as a technology for informal communication," *Communications of the ACM* 36, no. 1 (Jan. 1993): 48–61.

A. M. Noll, "Anatomy of a failure: Picturephone revisited," *Telecommunications Policy* (May/June 1992).

R. Steinmetz and T. Meyer, "Multimedia synchronization techniques: Experiences based on different system structures," *IEEE*

Multimedia Workshop (1992).

C. Wolf, "Videoconferencing: Delay and transmission considerations," in *Teleconferencing and Electronic Communications: Applications, Technologies, and Human Factors,* L. Parker and C. Olgren, eds.

N. Yeadon, A. Mauthe, D. Hutchison, and F. Garcia, "QoS filters: Addressing the heterogeneity gap," *Lecture Notes in Computer Science* 1045, 227–44.

An empirical study of delay jitter management policies

Donald L. Stone*, Kevin Jeffay**

University of North Carolina at Chapel Hill, Department of Computer Science, Chapel Hill, NC 27599-3175, USA

Abstract. This paper presents an empirical study of several policies for managing the effect of delay jitter on the playout of audio and video in computer-based conferences. The problem addressed is that of managing the fundamental trade-off between display with low latency and display with few gaps. We describe a particular policy called *queue monitoring* which observes delay jitter over time and dynamically adjusts display latency in order to support low-latency conferences with an acceptable gap rate. Queue monitoring is evaluated by comparing it with two policies from the literature in a study based on measurements from a computer-based conferencing system. Our results show that queue monitoring performs as well or better than the other policies over the range of observed network loads. More importantly, we show that queue monitoring performs better on those network loads for which the other policies exhibit poor performance.

Key words: Delay jitter – Video conferencing

1 Introduction

This work concerns network and operating system support for computer-based video conferencing. Our goal is to support high-performance conferences using today's networks based on asynchronous communications (e.g., ethernet, token ring, FDDI, T3, etc.). In this environment, transmission times vary and hence audio and video data may occasionally arrive at their destination after the time at which they should have been displayed. When this occurs, a "gap" appears in the playout that can adversely affect users' perception of the conference. The problem we consider here is that of ameliorating the effect of variable network transmission delays in order to support good quality audio and video playout. In particular, we are interested in supporting small internetworks consisting of several physical networks connected via bridges and routers (e.g., a building or campus-area network). Support for such networks

This work was supported by the National Science Foundation (grant numbers CCR-9110938 and ICI-9015443), and by the IBM and Intel Corporations
*,** e-mail: {stone, jeffay}@cs.unc.edu
Correspondence to: K. Jeffay

will be necessary if, as we believe, conventional LANs continue to be widely used in the "last mile" to the desktop.

For the audio and video hardware considered in our work, data units called *frames* are acquired from an audio or video source at a precise rate (e.g., one frame every 33 ms for video), and must be delivered to a conference participant's display at the same precise rate. Prior to delivery, each frame must be digitized, compressed, transmitted over the network, and decompressed as shown in Fig. 1. Once decompressed, a frame is buffered in a *display queue* until it can be displayed.

For each conference receiver, the *display latency* of a frame is defined as the total time from acquisition at the sender to display at the receiver. For purposes of discussion, it is convenient to divide display latency into two components: the total time from acquisition to decompression, called the *end-to-end delay* of a frame, and the time a frame is buffered between decompression and display, called the *display queuing delay*. If we assume that the time required to digitize, compress, or decompress frames is not constant, or if we assume that the delays incurred in transmitting frames across the network can vary, then the end-to-end delays experienced by frames will vary. Variance in end-to-end delay is called *delay jitter*.

Ideally, frames should be displayed continuously with each successive frame displayed immediately after its predecessor. Since frames are generated and displayed at fixed intervals, continuous playout can occur only if each frame is played with the same display latency. Thus, if frames are to be played continuously, jitter in the end-to-end delay of each frame must be compensated for by varying the display queuing delay of the frame.

However, continuous playout is not always possible. For example, consider a case where a frame incurs a particularly long end-to-end delay. As a result, the frame may not be ready to be displayed at the time when the display of the preceding frame is complete. In such a case, there will necessarily be a *gap* in the playout (e.g., for a video stream, this would mean that no video frame is displayed for a 33 ms interval). More precisely, a gap will occur whenever a frame arrives with an end-to-end delay greater than the display latency of the previous frame.

In general, the lower the display latency, the higher the probability of encountering an end-to-end delay sufficient to cause a gap. Thus there is a fundamental tradeoff between dis-

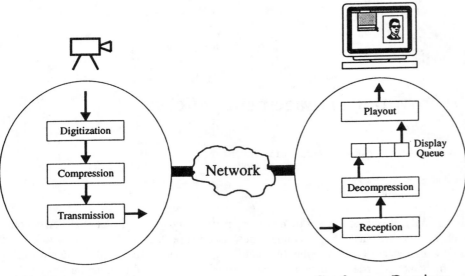

Fig. 1. System overview

play latency and gap frequency. A conferencing system must explicitly manage this tradeoff so as to provide good quality playout to the user.

One approach to managing this tradeoff is to prevent delay jitter completely by using a network that provides transmission with constant delay. This is the approach used in computer-based conferencing systems based on networks that provide isochronous services (such as ATM). Another approach is to minimize delay jitter by reserving resources in the network so as to provide guaranteed bounds on delay and delay jitter. For example, Ferrari [1] presents a scheme in which clients requiring real-time communication services specify their traffic characteristics and performance requirements. In response, the system reserves sufficient resources at each node on the network (e.g., processor capacity, buffer space) to guarantee the performance requirements of the client.

Unfortunately, isochronous delivery and resource reservation are not available in the network environments we wish to support. More importantly, even if the network supported transmission with constant delay, jitter in the end-to-end delay can occur as a result of variations in the time required to digitize, compress, and decompress frames, as well as variations in the time required to communicate data between the audio/video subsystem and the network transport system (all of which can be affected by operating system scheduling decisions). For each of these reasons, we assume that delay jitter is a fundamental phenomenon and therefore the tradeoff between display latency and gap frequency must be explicitly managed in any conferencing system.

In this paper, we evaluate three policies for managing the tradeoff between display latency and gap frequency. Two policies, the I-policy and the E-policy, are taken from the literature; the third, *queue monitoring*, is a new policy that we have developed. The performance of these policies is evaluated with an empirical study based on an experimental computer-based

video conferencing system (described in [3]). In the study, traces of the end-to-end delays experienced by frames are recorded during the execution of the conferencing system under a variety of (real) network loads. Each trace is used as input to a simulator which determines the display latency and gap rate that would result from applying each policy to a conference with the corresponding sequence of end-to-end delays. The simulation results demonstrate that queue monitoring always performs at least as well, and often performs better than either the I-policy or the E-policy over the range of observed network conditions.

The following section discusses the basic principles of managing the tradeoff between display latency and gap frequency, and describes the I- and E-policies. The queue monitoring policy is presented in Sect. 3. Section 4 discusses the metrics we propose for evaluating delay jitter management policies and the problems inherent in formulating such metrics. Section 5 describes the experiments and presents the results of the trace-driven simulations. We conclude in Sect. 6 with a summary of our findings.

2 Effect of delay jitter

In order to sustain continuous playout without gaps, every frame must be played with a fixed display latency that is greater than the worst-case end-to-end delay that will be encountered during a conference. It is not clear however that our primary goal should be playout with no gaps. Display latency is only one important factor in determining the perceived quality of the playout [2]. It is likely that in many conferencing applications, as long as gaps occur infrequently, playout with low latency and some gaps will be preferable to playout with high latency and no gaps. Therefore, if we always play frames with a display latency greater than the worst-case delay and if the worst-case delay is rarely observed in practice, then we will display most frames with latency higher than necessary to support good quality playout.

If we are willing to accept gaps in the playout, then we can choose to play frames with a display latency less than the worst-case end-to-end delay. However, we must now address the issue of what should be done with a frame that arrives after the time at which it should have been displayed. There are two choices: either the frame can be discarded or it can be displayed. These choices define two delay jitter management policies which Naylor and Kleinrock call the *I-Policy* and the *E-Policy* [6]. Under the I-policy, frames are displayed with a single fixed display latency which is a parameter of the policy, and each frame that arrives with an end-to-end delay greater than this latency is discarded. Under the E-policy, late frames are displayed at the next opportunity. This causes the display of all frames after the late frame to be delayed and thus the E-policy has the effect of increasing the display latency of all subsequent frames.

Figure 2 illustrates the behavior of the I- and E-policies in response to late frames. Figure 2a shows the acquisition and display times for eight frames. Tick marks on the upper timeline indicate *acquisition times*, the times at which new frames are acquired. Tick marks on the lower timeline indicate *display initiation times*, the times at which the new frames are displayed. Each diagonal arrow represents the end-to-end delay of an individual frame, extending from the time at which it was acquired to the time it is placed in the display queue. Throughout these examples, the acquisition time of a frame (i.e., points a, b, c, etc.) is used to refer to individual frames.

Figure 2b shows the effect of executing the I-policy on the pattern of acquisition times, display initiation times, and end-to-end delays shown in Fig. 2a. In this example, the display latency parameter of the I-policy is 2 frame times. (For simplicity in the examples, time is represented as multiples of the time taken to acquire or display a frame). The top graph in Fig. 2b shows the display queue length at each display initiation time. The bottom graph shows the display latency of the frame being displayed at each display initiation time. In addition, each latency bar is labeled with the acquisition time of the frame that is displayed at that display initiation time. In this example, frames b, d, and f arrive with end-to-end delays longer than 2 frame times and are discarded. Thus, use of the I-policy results in three gaps occurring in the playout at display initiation times 4, 6, and 8.

Figure 2c shows the effect of executing the E-policy. As with the I-policy, the late arrival of frame b causes a gap at display initiation time 4. However, after frame b arrives, it is placed in the display queue and eventually played at display initiation time 5, with a latency of 3 frame times. This delay results in each frame after b also being played with a display latency of 3 frame times. Because 3 frame times is longer than the end-to-end delay experienced by any frame after b, there are no gaps after display initiation time 4.

The example shown in Fig. 2 illustrates an advantage of the E-policy. The E-policy starts playing frames with the lowest possible initial display latency and then adjusts display latency

upward in response to delay jitter. The overall effect of the E-policy is to find a display latency which is sufficient to play frames without gaps by dynamically adjusting the latency to be higher than any end-to-end delay yet observed.

Figure 3 illustrates a situation in which the I-policy performs better than the E-policy. In this example, all frames except frames c and d arrive with an end-to-end delay of less than 1 frame time and experience negligible delay jitter. Frames c and d arrive late because of some temporary increase in network activity. Each policy results in gaps at display initiation times 4 and 5; however, the I-policy with a display latency of 1 frame time plays the frames after the gap with low latency while the E-policy plays the frames after the gap with high latency. Under the E-policy, a single "burst" of activity on the network that causes a few frames to arrive late results in a permanent increase in display latency.

In each policy, we are choosing a display latency at which to play frames, either explicitly in the case of the I-policy, or implicitly in the case of the E-policy. A good choice for display latency will depend on many factors. First, the acceptable rate of gaps and the acceptable display latency may vary depending on the application (e.g., speech and music may have different gap and latency requirements) and the current requirements of the user (e.g., a surgeon viewing an operation will have different requirements than participants in a televised lecture). Second, the display latency required to maintain an acceptable gap rate will depend on the expected level of delay jitter, which will vary as a result of congestion both at participants' machines and on the network. The dynamic nature of these factors motivates the design of a delay jitter management policy which dynamically chooses an appropriate display latency so as to adapt to new requirements and conditions.

3 Queue monitoring

The problem of choosing a display latency has been extensively studied in the context of packet audio systems (systems for the transmission of audio streams across packet-switched networks). In many applications, audio is modeled as a sequence of "talkspurts" (some period of time in which audio data must be acquired, transmitted, and played) separated by "silent periods" (some period of time in which there is no significant audio activity, so audio need not be acquired or played). Naylor and Kleinrock proposed that a display latency be chosen at the beginning of each talkspurt by observing the transmission delays of the last m audio fragments, discarding the k largest delays, and choosing the greatest remaining delay. For their particular model of audio quality, they stated a rule of thumb for choosing m and k ($m > 40$ and $k = 0.07 \times m$) which usually resulted in good quality audio. More recent work on practical solutions for the Internet (as exemplified by Nevot [7]) has also used a scheme by which a display latency is chosen at the beginning of each talkspurt on the basis of observed delay jitter.

More generally, consider an oracle that has perfect knowledge of the end-to-end delays of future frames and hence can choose the best display latency at which to play each

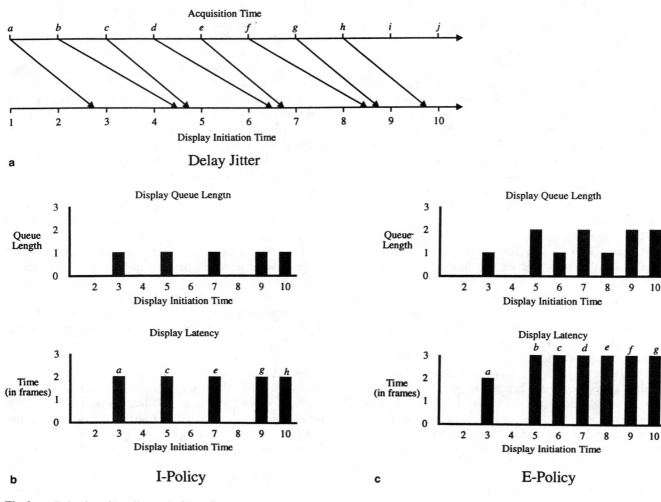

Fig. 2a–c. Behavior of I-policy and of E-policy

frame. Such an oracle can adjust display latency in response to changes in delay jitter (perhaps due to changes in network congestion) in order to achieve the best possible balance between display latency and gaps. Display latency can be adjusted upward by artificially introducing a gap (i.e., delaying the playout of the next frame) and can be adjusted downward by discarding frames.

If we assume that the delay jitter in the near future can be predicted by observing the delay jitter in the recent past, we can construct delay jitter management policies that are approximations to the oracle. (This is analogous to the working set concept of page replacement in virtual memory management.) The Naylor and Kleinrock policy for choosing a display latency is one example of such a policy. This policy, however, is difficult to implement as measuring end-to-end delays at runtime requires synchronized clocks.

Instead of measuring end-to-end delays, we can directly measure the impact of delay jitter at a receiver by observing the length of the display queue over time. Once every frame time, a frame is removed from the display queue to be played. For example, for video frames displayed at 30 frames per second, a frame is removed every 33 ms. Since frames are also acquired

and transmitted once per frame time, *on average* one frame will arrive and be placed in the display queue and one frame will be removed from the display queue during each frame time. If end-to-end delays are constant, the queue length measured at each display initiation time should be constant (as it was between display initiation times 7 and 10 in the example shown in Fig. 3c). If end-to-end delay increases sufficiently, it may happen that no frame arrives during the playout of a frame. In that case, the length of the display queue will decrease by one frame (e.g., display initiation time 6 in Fig. 2c). If end-to-end delays decrease sufficiently, more than one frame may arrive during the playout of a frame, and the length of the display queue will increase (e.g., display initiation time 6 in Fig. 3c).

Over time, the length of the display queue will vary depending on the range of end-to-end delays encountered by frames. If we assume the level of delay jitter in the near future will be the same as the level in the recent past, then while end-to-end delays may vary, they will not vary outside the range that we have observed recently. This implies that the length of the display queue will remain at least as long as the minimum length that has been observed in the recent past. Furthermore, as long as the display queue contains at least one frame at each

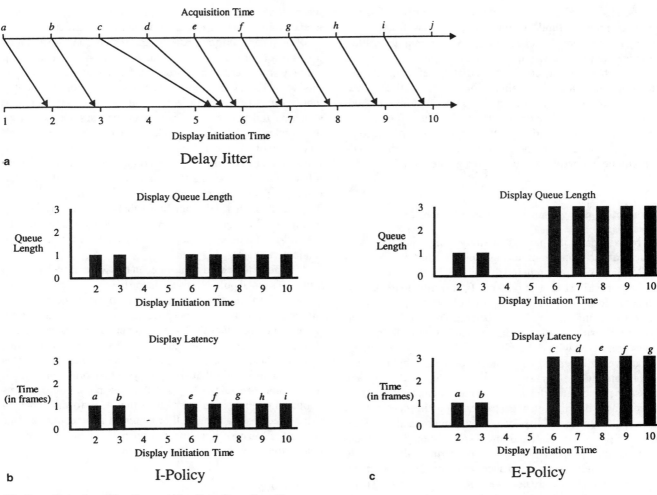

Fig. 3a–c. Behavior of I-policy and E-policy after a "burst"

display initiation time, there will be no gaps in the playout. Thus, if the minimum display queue length observed recently was at least two frames, we can discard a frame to reduce display latency without causing a gap.

A policy for decreasing display latency based on observing queue lengths has been used to govern the behavior of the audio display queue in the Pandora system [5]. Whenever frames are added to the display queue (called the *clawback buffer*), the length of the queue is checked against a target value. In the Pandora system, the target is two frames (which corresponds to 4 ms audio data). If the length of the display queue is greater than this target for a sufficiently long interval (8 s in the Pandora system), incoming audio frames are discarded. Because this has the effect of shortening the display queue, audio data that arrives after this time will be played with a lower display latency.

We propose a display queue management policy called *queue monitoring* that is a variation of the policy used in Pandora. For each possible display queue length we define a threshold value. The threshold value for queue length n specifies a duration (measured in frame times) after which, if the display queue has continuously contained more than n frames,

we will conclude that display latency can be reduced without increasing the frequency of gaps. Since we expect that large variations in end-to-end delay will occur infrequently, and small variations will occur much more frequently, threshold values for long queue lengths specify short durations while those for short queue lengths specify long durations. This policy has the effect of reducing display latency quickly after long delays due to large bursts of network traffic, but approaching minimal latency slowly.

To implement queue monitoring, we associate an array of counters and threshold values with the display queue. Each time we wish to display a new frame, we first perform a "thresholding operation." If the display queue has length m, then counters 2 through $m - 1$ are incremented and all other counters are reset. If any counter exceeds its associated threshold value, all the counters are reset and the oldest frame is discarded from the display queue. The oldest remaining frame is then displayed.

An important principle in this implementation is that the thresholding operation will never discard frames unless the display queue contains more than two frames. The last frame in the display queue should never be discarded because there must be a frame available for display after the thresholding operation completes. Similarly, if the second-to-last frame in the display queue were discarded, then even minimal delay jitter could potentially cause a gap. For example, this can occur in a situation where a frame arrives immediately before the thresholding operation and results in a display queue with length 2. If one of those frames is discarded and the other is displayed, then the queue would be empty. Then, if the next frame has a slightly larger end-to-end delay, it may not arrive in time to be displayed. Therefore, in the following discussion, thresholds will only be defined for queue lengths greater than 2.

4 Evaluating delay jitter management policies

The remainder of the paper is a study comparing the effectiveness of the queue monitoring policy to that of the I- and the E-policy. We are hampered in this task by the lack of metrics for comparing the performance of delay jitter management policies. Clearly, if policy A results in lower display latency and less gaps than policy B, it is performing better. However, if policy A results in a lower display latency and a higher gap rate as compared with policy B, which has performed better? The answer will depend on a number of factors including the display latency, the gap rate, the resolution of the display, and the user's particular audio and video requirements. It may also depend on the distribution of gaps throughout the measurement interval, the number of display latency changes, and the distribution of periods of high and low display latency throughout the interval. A proper standard for comparing policies would take each of these factors into account in making a judgment.

Unfortunately, we are not aware of such a standard. Therefore we have adopted a simple and arbitrary comparison rule for the analysis in this paper. The performance of a policy is evaluated along two dimensions: average display latency and average gap rate. We assume that only differences in display latency of more than 15 ms and differences in gap rate of more than 1 gap per minute are significant. Under these rules policy A is declared to have done better than policy B if it is better in one dimension and the same or better in the other dimension. Two policies are declared to have done equally well if they are the same in both dimensions and are declared to be incomparable if each has done better in one dimension.

Given this comparison rule, we can evaluate and compare the effectiveness of policies for a particular execution of the system. However, it is still difficult to compare results of multiple executions. One fundamental difficulty arises because the video hardware that acquires frames at the sender is not synchronized with the display at the receiver. To illustrate the effect this has on display latency, assume there is no end-to-end delay (i.e., acquisition and arrival of frames are simultaneous). Despite this fact, we must wait until the next display initiation time to display each new frame. Depending on the synchronization difference between the video hardware acquiring the frames and the display, each frame may have to wait up to 1 frame time before being displayed. This synchronization time is a random variable and varies between executions. Therefore,

when comparing results of multiple executions, differences in latency of as much as 1 frame time are not significant.

The second difficulty in comparing multiple executions arises from our working definition of the I-policy. Ideally, the I-policy should enforce a particular display latency. However, this would require that the clocks at the acquisition and display workstations be synchronized. In our work we only assume synchronized clocks for measurement purposes (i.e., we do not use synchronized clocks to guide the execution of the system), so we cannot completely implement such a policy. Instead, we use a variant of the I-policy which buffers the first frame for a fixed number of frame times before displaying it and then displays all subsequent frames with the same display latency. The effect of this definition is to make the display latency enforced by a particular I-policy in an execution, a function of the end-to-end delay of the first frame that is received (i.e., a random variable).

The goal of the study presented in this paper is to determine which of several policies results in the best quality playout. Because of the difficulties involved in comparing the results of multiple executions, and because our comparison rule determines relative, rather than absolute performance, we restrict direct comparisons to determining the relative performance of two policies on single conference executions. This allows us to conclude only that one policy outperforms another on a particular execution. To show that one policy outperforms another in general, we must show that it performs better on some executions and as well or better on all executions. This method of pairwise comparison is the basis of the performance evaluations presented in the next section.

5 The study

In this section, we present the results of a study that we have performed to gauge the effectiveness of the queue monitoring policy in a building-sized internetwork. In this study, we compared the performance of the queue monitoring policy with the performance of the I- and E-policies on video conferences transmitted over the main network supporting our department. The experiments presented were performed using the audio portion of an experimental video conferencing system that we have developed. In each experiment, we have recorded a trace of the end-to-end delay experienced by each frame. These traces are then used as input to a simulator which determines the average display latency and average gap rate that would result from applying each policy to a conference with the corresponding sequence of end-to-end delays. The results are compared using the comparison rule defined in Sect. 4.

The video conferencing system used for the experiments runs on IBM PS/2 workstations. These workstations run a real-time operating system and network transport software specially tailored for real-time communications. Network packets use the UDP/IP format. Acquisition and display of audio and video data is performed using IBM-Intel ActionMedia 750 hardware at a rate of 30 video frames per second (256×240 resolution and 8-bit color pixels; each compressed video frame occupies around 6000–8000 bytes) and 60 audio frames per second (a two-channel audio stream generated at a bit rate of 128 Kb per second and packaged into 16.5 ms "frames"). The full system has been extensively described elsewhere [3, 4].

The building network consists of several 10 Mb ethernets and 16 Mb token rings interconnect by bridges and routers. It supports approximately 400 UNIX workstations and Macintosh personal computers. The workstations share a common filesystem using a mix of NFS and AFS. The application mix running on these workstations should be typical of most academic computer science departments. We are linked to the Internet through the campus internetwork which also includes a number of other departmental networks (generally smaller than the one just described) connected via a central broadband network. In all, this environment should be typical of those generally found in the "last mile" to the desktop.

In each experiment, we acquired, transmitted, and displayed audio and video for a series of 10-min intervals. Audio frames were transmitted in individual packets and video frames were broken into 1350-byte fragments. Each packet was routed across a lightly loaded private token ring to a gateway, through a segment of the departmental ethernet to a bridge, through a second segment of the departmental ethernet to another gateway, and back across the private token ring to the display machine.

Twenty-four runs of the system were performed over the course of a typical day (between 6 a.m. and 5 p.m.) covering lightly and heavily loaded periods. Four additional runs were performed between midnight and 1 a.m. For each run, we recorded a trace of the acquisition time and the arrival time of each audio frame. In addition, we recorded each display initiation time (i.e., the times at which new frames were displayed). Before each run, we ran a protocol to measure the difference in clock times between the acquisition and display machines. After each run, the recorded times were adjusted to account for the difference in clock times and to account for clock drift (measured in a separate experiment). Finally, the traces were used as input for a trace-driven simulation of the display-side of a conference. For the given sequence of arrivals and display initiation times, the simulator determined the time at which each frame would be displayed under each of the three policies. The output of the simulator was the average display latency and average gap rate that would result from using each policy on the run.

Table 1 gives some basic data on the 28 runs. "Time of day" is the time the run was initiated. Average and maximum delays are calculated from the end-to-end delays experienced by audio frames. Lost and duplicate frames are counts of lost and duplicated packets which contained an audio frame. No out-of-order packets were observed.

Figure 4 provides a more detailed look at two runs, one with low delay jitter and one with high delay jitter. These figures are histograms of the end-to-end delays experienced by audio frames in runs 2 and 24. The y-axis shows a count of the number of frames with end-to-end delays within each 5-ms interval (e.g., a count of frames with an end-to-end delay of 30–35 ms). Note that the y-axis is plotted on a log scale.

Table 1. Study results: all runs, basic data

Run	Time of day	Avg. delay (ms)	Max. delay (ms)	Lost frames	Duplicate frames
1	06:03	38	76	1	0
2	06:25	38	88	3	0
3	06:36	37	171	5	0
4	06:47	37	105	1	0
5	08:03	38	115	1	0
6	08:14	37	73	2	0
7	08:25	38	184	7	0
8	08:36	39	157	1	0
9	10:02	41	186	23	0
10	10:16	40	124	4	0
11	10:31	41	213	7	0
12	10:49	40	140	6	0
13	11:57	39	110	5	0
14	12:08	41	138	5	0
15	12:19	41	133	3	0
16	12:34	40	187	11	0
17	14:02	41	189	11	0
18	14:13	42	141	3	0
19	14:42	39	107	4	0
20	14:54	40	131	12	0
21	16:01	39	171	9	0
22	16:21	39	128	2	0
23	16:33	39	86	2	1
24	16:55	42	242	14	1
25	00:05	38	80	4	0
26	00:16	38	128	0	0
27	00:27	38	134	8	0
28	00:38	38	83	2	0

Table 2 shows the simulation results for each of the 28 runs. For each, we simulated the queue monitoring policy with a threshold of 120 frame times at all queue lengths. The effect of these threshold settings is to reduce display latency by one audio frame time (i.e., 16.5 ms) whenever the display queue contains more than two audio frames for 120 continuous frame times (i.e., 2 s). We also simulated the E-policy and the (variant) I-policy with 2 and 3 frame times of display latency. In Table 2, these policies are labeled QM-120, E, I-2, and I-3 respectively. For each policy, the table shows the resulting average display latency (in milliseconds) and the average gap rate (in gaps per minute). For each run, the rightmost columns show the comparison between the queue monitoring policy and the other policies (using the comparison rule defined in Sect. 4). A "+" indicates that queue monitoring did better, a '0' means the two were equivalent, a "-" means that queue monitoring did worse, and a blank space means the two policies were incomparable.

Table 2 shows that the QM-120 policy performed as well or better than the I-2 policy for every run except run 11. For that run, QM-120 is incomparable with I-2 because it has a somewhat lower latency and a much higher gap rate. In particular, the gap rate produced by the I-2 policy is extremely high (approximately 1 gap every 2 s, compared with about 1 gap

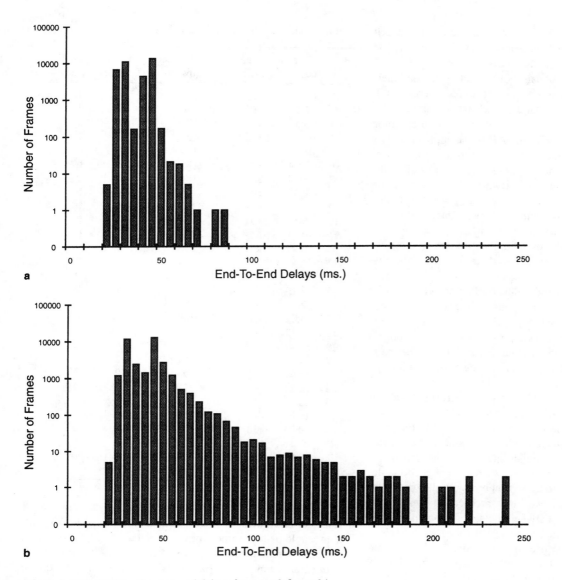

Fig. 4a,b. Distribution of end-to-end delays for **a** run 2, **b** run 24

every 12 s for the QM-120 policy). From these results, we can conclude that in general, the QM-120 policy is more effective than the I-2 policy.

The QM-120 policy also performed as well or better than the I-3 policy for every run except run 15. On that run, QM-120 policy is judged to perform worse than I-3 because the difference between the display latency produced by the QM-120 policy and that produced by the I-3 policy (13 ms) is not significant (according to the comparison rule), while the difference in gap rates (1.2 gaps per minute) is significant. Thus, we conclude that, in general, the QM-120 policy is more effective than the I-3 policy. Furthermore, QM-120 always results in a display latency lower than that produced by I-3. Therefore, all I-policies with display latencies larger than 3 frame times cannot perform better than the QM-120 policy (by our comparison rule). However, because gap rates for the I-policies with larger display latency will decrease, these policies may be incomparable with QM-120. Nevertheless, the QM-120 policy

resulted in relatively low gap rates for every run. Overall then, we conclude that if our goal in managing delay jitter is to minimize display latency with an acceptable gap frequency, then the QM-120 policy outperforms all I-policies. For other goals, we make no conclusions.

With respect to the E-policy, the QM-120 policy performs as well or better on 14 runs and is incomparable on 14 runs. The runs in which QM-120 performs as well or better tend to be the runs with low delay jitter (i.e., the early morning and late evening runs), while the incomparable runs are those with high delay jitter. In every run, QM-120 resulted in smaller display latency and a somewhat higher gap rate (5.2 gaps per minute is the largest difference). So again we conclude that if the goal in managing delay jitter is to minimize display latency with an acceptable gap frequency, then the QM-120 policy outperforms the E-policy. For other goals, we make no conclusions.

Table 2. Comparison of policies: results for all runs

Run	I-policy 2		I-policy 3		E-policy		QM-120		QM vs I-2	QM vs I-3	QM vs E
	Latency (ms)	Gaps /min	Latency (ms)	Gaps /min	Latency (ms)	Gaps /min	Latency (ms)	Gaps /min			
1	80	0.1	97	0.1	75	0.2	66	0.3	0	+	0
2	75	0.5	91	0.3	72	0.5	66	0.6	0	+	0
3	69	3.6	86	2.8	140	0.9	68	1.4	+	+	+
4	65	0.7	82	0.4	104	0.6	65	0.6	0	+	+
5	71	0.6	88	0.4	93	0.5	68	0.5	0	+	+
6	70	0.3	86	0.2	76	0.4	70	0.5	0	+	0
7	73	2.9	90	1.6	106	1.2	72	1.9	+	+	+
8	62	5.1	79	2.4	106	0.9	75	1.3	+	+	+
9	81	23.0	98	12.6	118	2.8	87	7.6	+	+	
10	70	14.6	87	3.6	113	0.8	78	3.9	+	0	
11	66	25.2	83	6.9	133	1.4	83	4.8		+	
12	71	9.6	87	3.4	114	0.9	76	2.7	+	0	
13	67	9.6	84	2.8	96	0.8	72	2.1	+	0	
14	72	15.1	88	3.9	101	1.1	80	3.9	+	0	
15	76	4.4	92	1.7	117	0.9	79	2.9	+	-	
16	68	18.6	85	8.0	114	1.8	80	6.6	+	+	
17	77	22.0	93	12.1	146	1.8	88	7.5	+	+	
18	76	13.0	93	4.1	131	0.7	85	4.8	+	0	
19	66	5.0	82	1.3	87	0.9	72	1.8	+	0	+
20	73	11.3	90	4.1	98	1.6	77	3.7	+	0	
21	70	12.8	87	6.1	159	1.5	76	3.6	+	+	
22	79	1.4	95	0.5	100	0.6	77	1.0	0	+	+
23	75	0.4	91	0.2	84	0.4	74	0.6	0	+	0
24	77	39.6	93	15.0	104	1.8	87	5.2	+	+	
25	65	0.8	81	0.4	66	0.7	65	0.7	0	+	0
26	64	5.4	81	0.9	122	0.6	69	1.5	+	0	+
27	70	7.8	87	3.8	107	1.3	73	3.5	+	0	
28	76	0.3	93	0.2	75	0.3	73	0.4	0	+	0
					QM better				18	18	8
					QM equivalent				9	9	6
					QM worse				0	1	0
					Incomparable				1	0	14

I-2, I-policy 2; I-3, I-policy 3; E, E-policy.

In the second part of the study, we investigated the effect of varying the threshold parameter on the effectiveness of the queue monitoring policy. For each of the 28 runs, we simulated the queue monitoring policy with a single threshold defined for all queue lengths. We considered thresholds of 30 frame times (0.5 s), 60 frame times (1 s), 120 frame times (2 s), 600 frame times (10 s), and 3600 frame times (1 min). Table 3 shows the simulation results. In the figure, these policies are labeled QM-30, QM-60, QM-120, QM-600, and QM-3600 respectively. The rightmost columns show the comparison between QM-120 and the other policies.

Table 3 shows that QM-600 performs best relative to QM-120. On 24 runs, QM-600 is judged to have provided better or equivalent performance. On the other four incomparable runs, QM-120 produced slightly better average display latency while QM-600 produced approximately one-third to one-quarter the number of gaps. QM-120 performed as well or better than QM-30 and QM-60 on every run. Finally, QM-120 performed as well or better than QM-3600 on half the runs and was incomparable on the remainder.

It is interesting to compare the performance of QM-30 and QM-60 with that of the I-2 policy. The QM-30 policy and QM-60 policy produced average display latencies that were similar to or better than those produced by I-2. Furthermore, both produced similar or better gap rates. For example, on run 9, the I-2 policy produced a display latency of 81 ms with a gap rate of 23.0 gaps/min. The QM-60 policy produced a display latency of 83 ms with a gap rate of 9.0 gaps/min. Thus, by choosing an appropriate threshold value, we can use queue monitoring to produce behavior similar to that produced by an I-policy, but with better performance on runs where an I-policy behaves badly.

The results for the QM-3600 policy are also interesting. In general, the QM-3600 policy produced results similar to those

Table 3. Queue monitoring policy: effect of varying thresholds

Run	QM-30		QM-60		QM-120		QM-600		QM-3600		120 vs 30	120 vs 60	120 vs 600	120 vs 3600
	Latency (ms)	Gaps /min	Latency (ms)	Gaps /min	Latency (ms)	Gaps /min	Latency (ms)	Gaps /min	Latency (ms)	Gaps /min				
1	64	0.3	65	0.3	66	0.3	73	0.3	75	0.2	0	0	0	0
2	65	0.7	65	0.7	66	0.6	66	0.6	67	0.6	0	0	0	0
3	67	1.7	67	1.4	68	1.4	74	1.4	103	1.1	0	0	0	+
4	65	0.6	65	0.6	65	0.6	69	0.6	83	0.6	0	0	0	+
5	67	0.5	68	0.5	68	0.5	69	0.5	81	0.5	0	0	0	0
6	70	0.5	70	0.5	70	0.5	70	0.5	76	0.4	0	0	0	0
7	70	2.3	71	1.9	72	1.9	77	1.7	95	1.4	0	0	0	+
8	68	2.0	70	1.5	75	1.3	83	1.0	97	1.0	0	0	0	+
9	77	13.1	83	9.0	87	7.6	102	4.9	117	3.0	+	+	-	
10	72	6.6	75	5.0	78	3.9	89	1.6	98	1.0	+	+	-	
11	72	8.3	76	6.3	83	4.8	98	3.4	124	1.7	+	+		
12	72	5.3	74	3.3	76	2.7	86	1.9	103	1.2	+	0	0	
13	69	3.5	70	2.7	72	2.1	82	1.4	91	1.0	+	0	0	
14	74	6.7	76	6.0	80	3.9	92	1.8	99	1.2	+	+	-	
15	76	3.1	77	3.1	79	2.9	89	1.7	106	1.2	0	0	-	
16	71	8.6	74	7.7	80	6.6	96	2.9	112	1.9	+	+		
17	79	10.0	83	8.9	88	7.5	106	3.9	131	2.2	+	+		
18	78	7.5	81	6.2	85	4.8	100	2.5	123	1.0	+	+		
19	68	3.0	69	2.3	72	1.8	80	1.1	86	0.9	+	0	0	0
20	74	5.0	74	4.3	77	3.7	85	2.3	94	1.7	+	0	-	
21	72	5.0	73	4.4	76	3.6	88	2.4	121	1.6	+	0	-	
22	70	1.6	72	1.3	77	1.0	79	0.9	90	0.7	0	0	0	0
23	73	0.6	74	0.6	74	0.6	74	0.6	81	0.5	0	0	0	0
24	81	8.5	83	6.4	87	5.2	97	2.7	104	1.9	+	+	-	
25	65	0.7	65	0.7	65	0.7	66	0.7	66	0.7	0	0	0	0
26	66	1.7	67	1.5	69	1.5	79	0.9	94	0.6	0	0	0	+
27	70	3.9	71	3.5	73	3.5	82	2.9	101	1.6	0	0	0	
28	73	0.4	73	0.4	73	0.4	73	0.4	74	0.4	0	0	0	0
QM-120 better											13	8	0	5
QM-120 equivalent											15	20	17	9
QM-120 worse											0	0	7	0
Incomparable											0	0	4	14

produced by the E-policy, with a slightly lower average display latency and a slightly higher gap rate. Thus, the QM-3600 policy is incomparable with the QM-120 policy on exactly the same runs that the E-policy was incomparable with the QM-120 policy. Again, by choosing an appropriate threshold value, we can use queue monitoring to produce behavior similar to that produced by the E-policy, but with better performance on runs where the E-policy behaves badly.

From these results, we conclude that thresholds are a useful tunable parameter for the general queue monitoring policy. A range of thresholds produces a range of results, from low latency with many gaps to high latency with few gaps. For our comparison rule and for the threshold values we examined, a threshold of 10 s for all queue lengths performs best. Given a particular network environment and a particular comparison rule, it should be possible to find an optimal threshold value.

The final part of the study examined the performance of the general queue monitoring policy. Recall that individual thresholds can be defined for each queue length, whereas in the previous simulations we used the same threshold value for all queue lengths. These thresholds can be arbitrary, but for purposes of this study, we defined a particular rule for setting the threshold values. This rule has two parameters: a threshold value for a queue of length 3, referred to as the *base threshold*, and a decay factor which specifies a rate at which the thresholds decrease with increasing queue length. For example, a queue monitoring policy with a base threshold of 3600 and a decay factor of 2 would have the threshold values: 3600 for queues of length 3, 1800 for queues of length 4, 900 for queues of length 5, etc. In Table 4, we show the results for three policies: base threshold 120 with decay factor 2, base threshold 600 with decay factor 2, and base threshold 3600 with decay factor 2. In the figure these are labeled QM-(120, 2), QM-(600, 2) and QM-(3600, 2). The figure also shows the QM-120 policy which is the base for comparison with the other policies.

Table 4. Queue measuring policy: effect of multiple thresholds

Run	QM-120 Latency (ms)	Gaps /min	QM-(120,2) Latency (ms)	Gaps /min	QM-(600,2) Latency (ms)	Gaps /min	QM-(3600,2) Latency (ms)	Gaps /min	120 vs (120,2)	120 vs (600,2)	120 vs (3600,2)
1	66	0.3	66	0.3	73	0.3	75	0.2	0	0	0
2	66	0.6	66	0.6	66	0.6	67	0.6	0	0	0
3	68	1.4	67	1.6	68	1.4	78	1.4	0	0	0
4	65	0.6	65	0.6	68	0.6	82	0.6	0	0	+
5	68	0.5	68	0.5	68	0.5	72	0.5	0	0	0
6	70	0.5	70	0.5	70	0.5	76	0.4	0	0	0
7	72	1.9	71	1.9	72	1.8	82	1.5	0	0	0
8	75	1.3	74	1.5	79	1.0	89	1.0	0	0	0
9	87	7.6	85	8.5	97	5.7	113	3.2	0	-	
10	78	3.9	78	4.2	88	1.7	97	1.0	0	-	
11	83	4.8	81	5.2	91	3.6	110	2.1	0	-	
12	76	2.7	75	2.8	82	2.0	94	1.3	0	0	
13	72	2.1	72	2.1	81	1.4	91	1.0	0	0	
14	80	3.9	79	4.0	90	2.0	99	1.2	0	-	
15	79	2.9	78	2.9	85	1.8	100	1.3	0	-	
16	80	6.6	77	7.1	90	3.6	106	2.1	0	-	
17	88	7.5	82	8.2	95	5.5	119	2.9	0	-	
18	85	4.8	84	4.9	98	2.7	120	1.1	0	-	
19	72	1.8	72	1.8	79	1.1	83	0.9	0	0	0
20	77	3.7	76	3.7	85	2.3	94	1.7	0	-	
21	76	3.6	74	3.9	82	2.6	98	1.8	0	-	
22	77	1.0	77	1.0	78	0.9	86	0.8	0	0	0
23	74	0.6	74	0.6	74	0.6	81	0.5	0	0	0
24	87	5.2	83	6.3	90	4.0	100	2.2	+	-	-
25	65	0.7	65	0.7	66	0.7	66	0.7	0	0	0
26	69	1.5	69	1.5	78	1.0	89	0.6	0	0	+
27	73	3.5	72	3.5	78	3.1	92	2.0	0	0	
28	73	0.4	73	0.4	73	0.4	74	0.4	0	0	0

							QM-120 better		1	0	2
							QM-120 equivalent		27	17	12
							QM-120 worse		0	11	1
							Incomparable		0	0	13

With a base threshold of 120 frame times, decreasing the thresholds for longer queue lengths did not improve the QM-120 policy. One run (run 24) was worse, and the runs that were equivalent according to the comparison rule generally had comparable latencies and slightly worse gap rates. On the other hand, for a base threshold of 600 frame times, decreasing the thresholds did improve the QM-600 policy. Relative to the QM-120 policy, QM-(600, 2) performed as well or better on every run. Furthermore, it performed better than QM-120 on 11 runs, where QM-600 only performed better than QM-120 on 7 runs. In general, QM-(600, 2) produced lower display latencies than QM-600 with only slightly higher gap rates. Decreasing the thresholds also helped to improve the performance of the QM-3600 policy. On a number of runs, the QM-(3600, 2) policy produced significantly lower display latencies than those produced by QM-3600 with only slightly higher gap rates. Relative to the QM-120 policy, QM-(3600, 2) performed somewhat better than QM-3600.

From these results, we conclude that the principle of decreasing thresholds has some utility. For low base thresholds, decreasing thresholds does not help, and may even hurt performance. But for higher base thresholds, decreasing the thresholds seems to help a great deal for some network conditions, without adversely affecting performance for other network conditions.

6 Summary and conclusions

If we wish to support computer-based video conferences transmitted over interconnected local-area networks based on ethernets and token rings, we must address the effect of variable network transmission delays (i.e., delay jitter) on the perceived quality of audio and video playout. The fundamental effect of delay jitter is to necessitate a tradeoff between display with low latency and display with few gaps. We have presented a new policy for managing this tradeoff called queue monitoring. This policy operates by observing delay jitter over time and dynamically adjusting display latency in order to support low-latency conferences with an acceptable gap rate. Overall, we conclude that queue monitoring can be an effective policy for ameliorating the effect of delay jitter in a building-sized internetwork.

In this paper, queue monitoring was evaluated by comparing it with two policies from the literature: the I-policy and the E-policy. The performance of these policies was evaluated by recording the end-to-end delays experienced by audio frames during video conferences run over our building network and simulating the effect of each policy on the resulting trace. In these conferences, the end-to-end delays experienced by most audio frames were in the range of 35–40 ms (including acquisition and processing time as well as network transmission time), but the variation in end-to-end delays was as much as 200 ms. Furthermore, even at times of day when there was little other activity on the network, end-to-end delays varied by as much as 80 ms. Over this range of network loads, queue monitoring consistently performed as well or better than either the I-policy or the E-policy. Our results have shown that queue monitoring with a base threshold of 600 frame times (10 s) and a decay factor of 2 resulted in the best performance.

Two runs best illustrate the advantages of the queue monitoring policy over the E-policy and the I-policy. Run 3 is an example of a run on which the E- policy performed poorly, producing an average display latency of 140 ms with a gap rate of 0.9 gaps/min. In contrast, the QM-(600, 2) policy produced an average display latency of 68 ms with a gap rate of 1.4 gaps/min. Run 24 is an example of a run on which the I-3 (and the other I-policies) performed poorly, producing an average display latency of 93 ms with a gap rate of 15.0 gaps/min. For this run, QM-(600, 2) produced an average display latency of 90 ms with a gap rate of 4.0 gaps/min. Together, these examples show that the queue monitoring policy can adapt to many network conditions to produce good quality playout.

Queue monitoring is also a flexible and tunable policy. Experiments with a range of thresholds produced a range of behaviors, from low display latency with frequent gaps to high display latency with few gaps. As a result, we believe that queue monitoring can be tuned to meet the requirements of particular applications and to adapt to the demands of particular network environments. In addition, queue monitoring has a simple and efficient implementation. A particularly important feature of this implementation is that it operates without feedback from the audio or video source and without synchronized clocks. Thus queue monitoring can be used effectively in computer-based conferences with many participants each of which may experience differing network delays.

There are a number of issues still to be addressed in evaluating the queue monitoring policy. First, in this paper we have compared queue monitoring to the I-policy in which the display latency remains fixed over an entire run. An alternative would be an I-policy for which we choose a new display latency at regular intervals, perhaps based on observations of delay jitter in the recent past.

Second, we have compared policies using average display latency and average gap rate. There are many other factors that can influence perceived quality including the distribution of gaps throughout a conference, the number of display latency changes, and the distribution of periods of high and low display latency throughout a conference. Ideally, policies should be compared using a more general measure of audio and video quality which accounts for all the factors which determine perceived quality.

Third, the study presented in this paper is based on audio and video data transmitted over a building-area network. We are also interested in determining the extent to which the queue monitoring technique scales. Future work will include repeating the study in this paper for a succession of larger networks. Such a study will help to identify the types of networks which can be supported without resorting to new specialized network services.

Fourth, the emphasis in this work has been on managing delay jitter. Another aspect of our work is a forward error correction (FEC) strategy for minimizing frame loss [4]. By decreasing loss, FEC will support the assumptions underlying queue monitoring, namely that display queue length only decreases as a result of late arrivals. However, frames that are recovered through FEC will incur longer end-to-end delays, thus increasing delay jitter. Because of these effects, we must investigate the impact of FEC and other mechanisms for reducing loss (e.g., timeouts and retransmission) on queue monitoring and the other policies.

Fifth, work must be done on choosing good threshold values, but this work will require a new quality measure. Simulation using a variety of threshold values indicates that large changes in threshold values may only produce small changes in average display latency and average gap rate. As such, work on choosing threshold values will involve making tradeoffs which result in small changes to display latency and gap rate. While simple measures of quality may be sufficient to evaluate the gross performance characteristics of a policy, proper evaluation of small tradeoffs will require a better quality measure than we currently have available.

Finally, the use of decreasing thresholds for longer queue lengths must be investigated further. While the study has shown that the principle of decreasing thresholds can improve performance, it is not yet clear what strategy should be used to set those thresholds. Among the possibilities are the geometric decrease in threshold values we used in this study, and a linear decrease in threshold values suggested by Jones and Hopper [5].

References

1. Ferrari D (1992) Delay jitter control scheme for packet-switching internetworks. Comput Commun 15:367–373
2. Issacs E, Tang JC (1993) What video can and can't do for collaboration: a case study. Proc. ACM Intl Conf on Multimedia, Anaheim Calif., August 1993 pp 199–205
3. Jeffay K, Stone DL, Smith FD (1992) Kernel support for live digital audio and video. Comput Commun 15:388–395

4. Jeffay K, Stone DL, Smith FD (1994) Transport and display mechanisms for multimedia conferencing across packet-switched networks. Comput Networks ISDN Syst 26:1281–1304

5. Jones A, Hopper A (1993) Handling audio and video streams in a distributed environment. ACM Operating Syst Review 27:231–243

6. Naylor WE, Kleinrock L (1982) Stream traffic communication in packet-switched networks: destination buffering considerations. IEEE Trans. Commun 12:2527–2534

7. Schulzrinne, Henning (1992) Voice communication across the iInternet: a network voice terminal. Technical Report, University of Massachusetts

KEVIN JEFFAY received a BS in Mathematics with Highest Distinction, University of Illinois at Urbana Champaign, in 1982, an MSc in Computer Science, University of Toronto, in 1984, and a PhD in Computer Science, University of Washington, in 1989. Since 1989 Dr Jeffay has been an Assistant Professor in the Computer Scinence Department of the University of North Carolina at Chapel Hill. His reseach interests are in operating systems, distributed and real-time systems, multimedia networking, computer-supported cooperative work, and scheduling theory. Dr Jeffay is a member of Phi Beta Kappa, ACM, and IEEE Computer Society.

DONALD L. STONE took his BS in Applied Mathematics/Computer Science, Carnegie-Mellon University, in 1985 and an MS in Computer Science, University of North Carolina at Chapel Hill, in 1992. He is currently a doctoral student in the Computer Science Department at the University of North Carolina at Chapel Hill. Research interests are software engineering and real-time systems. Mr Stone is a co-author of the book *IDL: The Language and its Implementation.*

Media Scaling for Audiovisual Communication
with the Heidelberg Transport System

Luca Delgrossi, Christian Halstrick, Dietmar Hehmann, Ralf Guido Herrtwich,
Oliver Krone, Jochen Sandvoss, Carsten Vogt

IBM European Networking Center
Vangerowstr. 18
D-6900 Heidelberg
Germany

Abstract: HeiTS, the Heidelberg Transport System, is a multimedia communication system for real-time delivery of digital audio and video. HeiTS operates on top of guaranteed-performance networks that apply resource reservation techniques. To make HeiTS also work with networks for which no reservation scheme can be realized (for example, Ethernet or existing internetworks), we implement an extension to HeiTS which performs media scaling at the transport level: The media encoding is modified according to the bandwidth available in the underlying networks. Both transparent and non-transparent scaling methods are examined. HeiTS lends itself to implement transparent temporal and spatial scaling of media streams. At the HeiTS interface, functions are provided which report information on the available resource bandwidth to the application so that non-transparent scaling methods may be used, too. Both a continuous and discrete scaling solution for HeiTS are presented. The continuous solution uses feedback messages to adjust the data flow. The discrete solution also exploits the multipoint network connection mechanism of HeiTS. Whereas the first method is more flexible, the second technique is better suited for multicast scenarios. The combination of resource reservation and media scaling seems to be particularly well-suited to meet the varying demands of distributed multimedia applications.

1 Introduction

The dispute of guaranteed vs. non-guaranteed communication is an unresolved argument in the multimedia community (as shown, for example, by recurring discussions at the first three International Workshops on Network and Operating System Support for Digital Audio and Video from 1990 till 1992). It is a repetition of the classical end-to-end argument: One group says that all mechanisms to cope with network bottlenecks should be included in the application; the other group says that only the underlying system is able to prevent network overload. In this paper, we propose a solution between the two extremes that offers both possibilities in an actual system. We favor this approach because different multimedia applications have different requirements on the network: There is virtually no way to recover from audio transmission errors so that the end user will not notice them. For everyday (consumer-quality) video on the other hand, it is fairly easy to live with network flaws and even with slight delay variations.

HeiTS, the Heidelberg Transport System [6, 7], facilitates the transmission of digital audio and video from a single origin to multiple targets. The transport and network layer protocols of HeiTS, HeiTP [3] and ST-II [15], allow the client to negotiate quality-of-service (QOS) parameters such as throughput and end-to-end delay for multimedia connections. In its original form, HeiTS depends on some type of bandwidth allocation mechanism in the underlying network to provide a transport connection with a guaranteed QOS. Some networks such as FDDI (with its synchronous mode) and ISDN implement this reservation. Other networks like Token Ring can be augmented with bandwidth allocation schemes [11]. However, not all kinds of networks support the reservation of bandwidth: as an example, Ethernet provides no guaranteed service at all due to the potential collisions of packets.[1] Hence, to use audio and motion video in such an "unfriendly" environment calls for additional techniques.

When reservation is not available, audio and motion video should be transported on a best-effort basis. From the start, HeiTS has supported some kind of best-effort QOS [18] which, however, is only a less strict version of guaranteed QOS. In this best-effort approach, resource capacities are reserved, but at the same time statistically multiplexed, that is, the sum of the portions of bandwidth allocated to the individual sessions is allowed to exceed the total resource capacity. Best-effort service with no reservation requires a different approach, which can work, for example, in a dynamic feedback fashion. Here, the system monitors how well it currently accomplishes the audiovisual data transport from one end to the other, then correspondingly determines the amount of audio visual data it forwards. We refer to this technique as *"media scaling"*.

Media scaling in different forms has been suggested and used in previous systems. Fluent, for example, bases its multimedia networking technology on a proprietary scaling scheme [16]. Tokuda et al. have developed a dynamic QOS management service which is intended to be used in conjunction with scaling techniques [14]. Clark et al. with their "predicted service" approach also assume in their networking architecture that some form of media scaling exists [2]. Our approach is special and different in that it shows how to combine resource reservation and media scaling methods.

This paper discusses several implementation alternatives for media scaling in HeiTS. Section 2 surveys scaling methods, concentrating on digital video. Section 3 introduces two different scaling methods for HeiTS. Section 4 specifies the changes to protocols and interfaces in HeiTS required to accommodate scaling.

---

1. For this reason, some "multimedia" solutions for the Ethernet use a 10BaseT hub and dedicate single Ethernet links to pairs of communication partners. This approach requires changes in the network infrastructure and still leaves unsolved the problem of conflicting uses of the dedicated links by multiple concurrent multimedia applications on the same machine.

2 Scaling Methods

Before describing the details of the HeiTS approach, we give a general overview of scaling techniques. We assume that the reader is familiar with typical encoding schemes for digital media.

'Scaling' means to subsample a data stream and only present some fraction of its original contents. In general, scaling can be done at either the source or the sink of a stream. Frame rate reduction, for example, is usually performed at the source whereas hierarchical decoding is a typical scaling method applied by the sink. Since in the context of this paper scaling is intended to reflect bandwidth constraints in the underlying resources, it is useful to scale a data stream before it enters a system bottleneck; otherwise it is likely to contribute to the overload of the bottleneck resource. Scaling at the source is usually the best solution here: there is no need for transmitting data in the first place if it will be thrown away somewhere in the system.

Scaling methods used in a multimedia transport system can be classified as follows:

- *Transparent scaling* methods can be applied independently from the upper protocol and application layers, that is, the transport system scales the media on its own. Transparent scaling is usually achieved by dropping some portions of the data stream. These portions – single frames or substreams – need to be identifiable by the transport system.
- *Non-transparent scaling* methods require an interaction of the transport system with the upper layers. In particular, this kind of scaling implies a modification of the media stream before it is presented to the transport layer. Non-transparent scaling typically require modification some parameters of the coding algorithm or even recoding of a stream that was previously encoded in a different format.

The following subsections investigate which kinds of compression schemes lend themselves to which scaling methods.

2.1 Scalable Elements in Media Streams

In a multimedia system, scaling can be applied to both audio and video data. For audio, transparent scaling is difficult because presenting only a fraction of the original data is easily noticed by the human listener. Dropping a channel of a stereo stream is an example. Hence, non-transparent scaling must be used for audio streams, for example, by changing the sampling rate at the stream source.

For video streams, the applicability of a specific scaling method depends strongly on the underlying compression technique, as will be explained in Section 2.2. There are several domains of a video signal to which scaling can be applied:

- *Temporal scaling* reduces the resolution of the video stream in the time domain by decreasing the number of video frames transmitted within a time interval. Temporal scaling is best suited for video streams in which individual frames are self-contained and can be accessed independently such as intra-pictures or DC-coded pictures for MPEG-coded video streams [9]. Interframe compression techniques are more difficult to handle because not all frames can be easily dropped.
- *Spatial scaling* reduces the number of pixels of each image in a video stream. For spatial scaling, hierarchical arrangement is ideal because it has the advantage that the compressed video is immediately available in various resolutions. Therefore, the video can be transferred over the network using different resolutions without applying a "decode → scale down→ encode" operation on each picture before finally transmitting it over the network.
- *Frequency scaling* reduces the number of DCT coefficients applied to the compression of an image. In a typical picture, the number of coefficients can be reduced significantly before a reduction of image quality becomes visible.
- *Amplitudinal scaling* reduces the color depths for each image pixel. This can be achieved by introducing a coarser quantization of the DCT coefficients, hence requiring a control of the scaling algorithm over the compression procedure.
- *Color space scaling* reduces the number of entries in the color space. One way to realize color space scaling is to switch from color to greyscale presentation.

Obviously, combinations of these scaling methods are possible.

Whether non-transparent scaling is possible depends strongly on the kind of data to be transmitted. For live video streams, it is easy to set all the coding parameters when an image is sampled at the source. For stored video, scaling may make a recoding of the stream necessary. As this may lead to more load on the system than actually transmitting the original stream, we concentrate on transparent scaling techniques that allow to scale without recoding. Temporal and spatial scaling fall into this category.

2.2 Scaling for Media Encoding Standards

The efficiency of a scaling algorithm strongly depends on the underlying compression technique. The format of the data stream produced by the coding algorithm determines which of the domains described in Section 2.1 are appropriate for scaling. The following enumeration gives a short overview of the applicability of scaling to some state-of-the-art compression techniques.

- *Motion JPEG.* The distinguished feature of Motion JPEG encoding (that is, the encoding of video as a sequence of JPEG frames [19]) is its robustness to transmission errors because of the independence of individual frames: a single error is not carried over from one frame to another. Obviously, temporal scaling is suited best for this compression technique as any frame can be left out without affecting its neighbors. Applying a hierarchical DCT-based compression method on every picture [16] enables spatial scaling methods. However, few existing JPEG implementations realize this hierarchical mode.
- *MPEG.* Since MPEG [9] is a context-sensitive compression method, temporal scaling is subject to certain constraints. Every compressed video stream consists of a sequence of intra-coded, predicted-coded, and bidirectionally-coded pictures. Temporal scaling of an MPEG coded video stream can be realized by dropping predicted and bidirectionally coded pictures. Assuming an intra-picture is inserted every 9th frame, this leads to a scaled frame rate of approximately 3 frames per second [13].

  The main improvement of *MPEG-2* over the original MPEG scheme is the support for scalable media streams [3, 4, 14]. It facilitates spatial and frequency scaling as well as temporal scaling methods. MPEG-2 uses a hierarchical compression technique which enables the compressed data stream to be demultiplexed into three substreams with different quality. Scaling can be achieved by transmitting only some but not all of the substreams. This method is particularly useful for the discrete scaling approach described in Section 3.2.
- *DVI.* Just like MPEG, DVI [10] uses a combination of intra- and intercoded frames. Thus, temporal scaling is restricted in the same way as described for MPEG-coded streams.
- *H.261 (px64).* The H.261 standard includes an amplitudinal scaling method on the sender side [20]. The coarseness of the quantization of the DCT coefficients determines the color depth of each image pixel. In addition to this, the intra-frame coding scheme which is similar to the intra-coded pictures of MPEG permits the easy use of temporal scaling.

Figure 1 demonstrates the effect of scaling when applied to a single image. We used JPEG to compress a picture with different granularities in the quantization tables for the DCT coefficients (frequency scaling). The picture on the left is compressed using a very coarse granularity, whereas an extremely fine granularity is used for the right one.

Figure 1: JPEG compressed pictures with different granularities.

3 Scaling in HeiTS

HeiTS is a rate-controlled transport system. For every data stream passing through a HeiTS connection, the system is informed about its message rate by means of an associated QOS parameter set. At the transport level interface, this rate is given in terms of logical data units (for example, video frames) per time period. HeiTS can use this information for monitoring the arrival of the packets. The late arrival of a packet is an indication of some bottleneck in the system, in which case the target can inform the origin about the overload and cause it to scale down the stream. Once the overload situation has passed, the stream may be scaled up again.

A scalable stream can be seen as composed of various substreams. For a spatially scaled stream this representation can, for example, consist of one substream with all odd/odd pixels, one substream with even/even pixels, etc. As an alternative, one could use one substream for intra-coded frames and one or even several other streams for the remaining frames, which implies that there are streams of different degrees of importance. A splitting of MPEG video streams based on DCT coefficients was described in [12].

In the scaling implementation of HeiTS, individual substreams are mapped onto different connections, each with its own set of QOS parameters. The transmission quality can then be adjusted either with fine granularity within a connection (substream) or with coarse granularity by adding and removing connections (substreams). We refer to these approaches as *continuous* and *discrete* scaling. They are discussed in the following subsections.

3.1 Continuous Scaling

In HeiTS, each packet has an expected arrival time, and a packet arriving later than expected is an indication of some bottleneck in the system. There are several possibilities to define this expected arrival time. One could, for example, define its value simply as the actual arrival time of the previous packet plus the period of the message stream (that is, the reciprocal value of its rate). Alternatively, the arrival time of the first packet of the stream (or any other earlier packet) rather than the arrival time of the previous packet could be used as an "anchor" for the calculation. This helps to avoid false indications of congestions in cases where the previous packet happend to arrive early and the current packet has a "normal" delay.

HeiTS calculates the expected arrival time as the "logical arrival time" of the previous packet plus the stream period. The logical arrival time is the arrival time observed when bursts are smoothed out, that is, when early packets are artificially delayed (for example, in a leaky bucket fashion) such that the specified stream rate is not exceeded (see [18] for details).

The lateness of a single packet should not immediately trigger the scaling down of a stream, because the congestion may only be short. However, if a sequence of packets are late (or some packets are missing because they were dropped due to buffer overflow), it can be assumed that there is congestion somewhere in the network. In this case, the receiver initiates a scale-down operation.

A major issue with the scaling procedure is the responsiveness, that is, how rapidly the traffic adapts to the available bandwidth. Wwe propose a scale-down scheme which consists of three stages.

- The first reaction on a congestion is to throw away excess or late packets. This usually happens within the network during a buffer overflow or at the receiver station that detects the lateness of a packet. An appropriate mechanism for lateness detection is included in HeiTP. Scaling by dropping packets is immediate and local, that is, it does not affect the sender, which continues to send at its full rate. Hence, scaling up can also be done very quickly by simply stopping to discard packets. As stated before, it makes sense not to immediately trigger the sender to scale down the stream, since the congestion may only be brief.

- When the number of late or lost packets exceeds a certain threshold, which can be defined heuristically, it is assumed that the congestion will last longer. In this case, the sender is triggered to throttle its traffic. As a first step, the sender reduces its sending rate – possibly down to zero. (Reducing the rate to zero makes no sense if all data are sent over only one connection. If continuous scaling is applied to one of several substreams, this substream may temporarily carry no data at all and the receiver will still receive information.) The connection, however, remains intact, along with its resource reservations.[2] This means that the resources can be temporarily used by other traffic, but the sender can scale the stream up immediately once the congestion is over.

- If the rate on a stream has been reduced to zero and the congestion is of a longer duration, that is, if several attempts of the sender to scale up the stream fail, the corresponding connection is terminated and all resources reserved for it are released. Since congestion typically occurs only at one bottleneck on the end-to-end connection (for example, on some subnetwork), the resources previously reserved on other subnetworks or nodes are made available for other connections. Scaling the stream up, however, requires the reestablishment of the connection, which takes some time.

This last step leads us directly to the discrete scaling approach which will be discussed in the next subsection.

The monitoring of a stream provides the receiving station with hints at congestion situations. This monitoring cannot, however, yield any information about the termination of a congestion. Assuming that the underlying network also does not give any explicit indication of congestions, the decision whether to scale up a stream must be based on heuristics. The only practical heuristic known is to scale up the stream when a certain time span after the previous scale down has elapsed.

A scale-up decision based on time spans can come either too early or too late. A scaling which is too late is not considered harmful if it happens within the range of a few seconds. If the transmission quality is temporarily reduced, a human user does not care much whether this lasts for three or five seconds. The effects of a scaling which is too early can be more severe. Scaling a stream up while the congestion situation is still present causes the receiver to trigger a new scale-down, and, in the extreme case, an oscillation of

---

2. Note that not only guaranteed connections but also best-effort connections in HeiTS may have resources reserved for them. However, the reservation for best-effort connections does not account for the worst possible case. Thus, in some situations the amount of reserved resources may not suffice which will lead to congestions. On the other hand, best-effort connections may temporarily use resources reserved for other connections as long as these connections do not need them.

the system. This implies an increased overhead for both end-systems and network and, additionally, can extend the phase of reduced quality longer than necessary.

To avoid oscillation, the scaling procedure of HeiTS scales up stepwise, as is done by other dynamic congestion control algorithms [1, 8]. After scaling down the stream, the sender transmits for a certain time span or a certain amount of data (for example, n packets for a fixed value of n) at the reduced rate. If after this period no scale-down message is obtained from the receiver, which means that, HeiTS could transfer the packets without any severe congestion, the sender increases its rate by some amount.[3] This procedure is continued until the maximum throughput for this stream is reached or until the receiver requests to scale down the stream again.

3.2 Discrete Scaling

The advantages of the continuous scaling technique are that scaling can be done at fine granularity and that in principle only one connection is required per stream. There are, however, some problems with this approach because it does not take into account two special features of HeiTS.

- HeiTS supports multicast. This implies that continuous scaling may lead to the following problem: If a receiver triggers the sender to scale down the rate, all receivers from that point on get data at the lower rate, that is, a multimedia stream of worse quality. This approach is "all-worst" (or socialistic, to use a historical term), since the worst path in the multicast tree determines the quality for every receiver.
- HeiTS supports different connection types. HeiTS has guaranteed connections for which all required resources are reserved in advance and hence the requested throughput can be guaranteed. Additionally, HeiTS supports best-effort connections, in which no resources or only part of the resources required are reserved in advance; thus congestion is possible.

The discrete scaling technique discussed in the following is based on splitting a multimedia stream into a set of substreams, as described in the beginning of Section 3. This technique can be used in a multicast environment and supports different rates for different receivers. It works in an "individual best" (capitalistic) fashion.

For each of the different substreams a separate network layer connection is established. ST-II, the network protocol of HeiTS, in principle treats each of these substreams independently. However, the "stream group identifier" of ST-II can be used to indicate that several network connections belong to a single transport connection. The system can then try to achieve roughly the same delay for each of these network connections which facilitates reassembly of the substreams as packets reach the target with approximately the same transit time.

For establishing a set of substreams, an application specifies the percentage of data which has to be transmitted to the receiver under any circumstance. If less data is transferred, a receiver cannot decode any useful information. This data is transferred over a guaranteed connection, if possible. If no guaranteed connections can be supported (for example, because there is an Ethernet in between), a best-effort connection is also used for this portion of the stream.

The rest of the stream is transferred over one or more best-effort connections. How many connections of this kind are required depends on the granularity of the data stream: Each part that provides a useful increase in quality is transferred over a separate best-effort connection.

Example: A video data stream is sent with 24 frames per second (fps). The sender decides that 6 fps have to be transferred under any circumstances to the receivers. These data are sent over the basic connection. The remaining 18 fps might be sent over two best-effort connections: 6 fps over the first and 12 fps over the second. In this example, the two best-effort connections have different throughput requirements. The video frames are then sent in the following order over the different connections:

1	2	3	4	5	6	7	8	9	...
bas	*be₂*	*be₁*	*be₂*	*bas*	*be₂*	*be₁*	*be₂*	*bas*	...

bas: sent over basic connection (guaranteed or best-effort)
be₁: first best-effort connection
be₂: second best-effort connection

If a receiver detects some congestion on any of these connections, it closes the least important connection (that is, *be₂* in the example). If we have a multicast connection, this disconnect does not necessarily imply a termination of the whole connection, but only of its last hop to the receiver. This means that the other receivers can still receive the stream in full quality.

Example: In Figure 2, Receiver 2 cannot keep up with the speed of the data stream. Thus, it has issued a disconnect request for the second best-effort connection. If after some time the receiver assumes that the congestion is over (see Section 3.1), it reconnects to the sender.

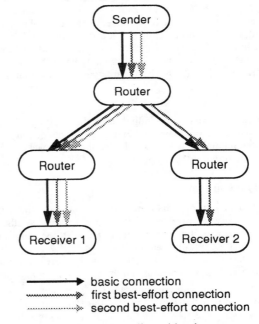

basic connection
first best-effort connection
second best-effort connection

Figure 2: Discrete scaling with substreams.

The discrete scaling approach has some advantages:

- It is applicable to multicast connections.
- The receivers are handled "individual best".
- Network routers require no knowledge of the traffic type.

However, the scheme implies that scaling can only be done only with a coarse granularity. Moreover, sending a stream over several connections leads to a non-negligible overhead for splitting and recombining the stream and the termination and re-establishment of connections (or parts of them).

In principle, it is possible to integrate the discrete and the continuous approachs by scaling continuously on a single substream

---

3. Note the difference between our scheme and the slow-start algorithm in TCP [8]. TCP's slow-start algorithm uses acknowledgements returned by the receiver to increase the traffic rate, whereas our scheme increases the rate in the absence of scale-down messages.

(preferably on the least important one) and deleting a connection (or parts of it) when the rate of the this substream has been reduced to zero. Section 3.1 already included some hints at this technique.

4 Extensions to HeiTP

HeiTP, the Heidelberg Transport Protocol [3], is a transport layer protocol for multimedia communication in an internet. HeiTP is designed to run on top of the ST-II network protocol. In the first design phase of HeiTP, multimedia data was assumed to travel along a privileged path in which services can be guaranteed by reserving the required resource capacities. As discussed in the introduction, this is not always possible. Hence, we have extended HeiTP by functions to transmit multimedia data also over best-effort connections which do not support resource reservation. These functions support media scaling and minimize the influence of packet losses caused by network congestions.

4.1 Extensions to HeiTP Functions

To support scaling, three major extensions were introduced to HeiTP. These additional features, which will be described in the next subsections, reflect the three stages of the scaling procedure described in Section 3.1.

The first step of congestion handling is to throw away packets-based on importance parameters that HeiTP associates with the packets. In the second step, the receiver, having detected the congestion, triggers the sender to lower the transmission rate. Reducing the rate is based on an extended HeiTP rate control mechanism. The third step in media scaling is the dynamic termination and reestablishment of network connections. This is provided by a call management mechanism which additionally helps the user to manage the transmission of a media stream over a group of substreams.

4.1.1 Importance

As a user should have some influence on the order by which individual packets are thrown away, HeiTP now includes *importance parameters* for packets. In case of a congestion, packets are discarded in the order of their importance.

4.1.2 Rate Control

In HeiTP, rate control mechanisms affect on one hand the transmission of data between peer transport entities, and on the other hand transmission across the user interfaces between the transport service users and the transport entities.

Rate control for transmission between transport entities is done in two different ways, depending on the type of the connection.

- For connections with guaranteed bandwidth, rate control mechanisms are realized locally within the transport entity on the sender side. The rate is static and determined at connection establishment time according to the application's requirements.
- In case of best-effort connections, a distributed mechanism with dynamic rate adjustment is required. Congestion detection is done at the transport entity on the target side as described in Section 3. When the number of late or lost packets exceeds a certain threshold, a scale-down message is sent to the transport entity on the sender side which lowers in response its transmission rate. Scaling up is done as discussed in Section 3.

Rate control for data transmission across the transport service interface is strongly coupled with transparent and non-transparent scaling. The application can decide which scaling method should be used by activating or deactivating this rate control.

- Transparent scaling is realized by switching off the rate control at the service interface. If the data rate of the application

exceeds the transmission rate supported by the connection, packets will be thrown away by the transport entity on the sender side without any indication to the application.
- Non-transparent scaling is realized by switching on the rate control. In this case, HeiTP informs the application when to reduce or increase the sending rate.

Supporting the selection of these services is in line with the underlying design principle of HeiTS not to impose services on an application if they are not used.

4.1.3 Call Management

A media stream can be transmitted as a collection of substreams of different degrees of importance (see Section 3.2). For the efficient handling of such structured streams, the function set of HeiTP was extended with a call management mechanism.

The call management provides functions required for the management of groups of substreams. Each substream is mapped on a separate transport connection with its own set of QOS parameters. Important substreams can be transmitted over connections with a guaranteed QOS. The reliability of these connections can be enhanced by using the error correction facilities provided by HeiTP. Less important substreams can be transmitted over best-effort connections.

For example, in the scenario described in Section 3.2, an MPEG video stream could be transmitted as two different substreams shown in Figure 3:

- One of the substreams contains the intra-coded I-frames which can be decoded independently from other frames and thus are important for restarting decoding after errors in previous frames have been found. I-frames should be transmitted over a guaranteed connection.
- The other substream contains the predicted coded or bidirectionally coded frames (P- and B-frames). Since P and B-frames are less important for error recovery than I-frames, they can be transmitted over a best-effort connection.

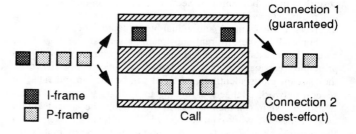

Figure 3: Splitting an MPEG stream into two substreams.

The call management provides functions to specify the relationship between the connections of a call. In the above MPEG scenario, the QOS parameters of each connection are handled separately, but the sequencing control has to be done together for both connections. The call management provides for this sequencing.

Discrete scaling is supported by defining some connections of a call as "optional". This means that these connections can be dynamically established and disconnected according to the available bandwidth (see Section 3.1). The termination and establishment is done by the call management transparently for the application. Optional connections are not necessarily required for the transmission of the data but, nevertheless, contribute to the quality of the stream. Connections not qualified as optional must be established with all targets participating. As described earlier, this mechanism is particularly important in the multicast case.

It is also possible to apply the discrete scaling approach statically at connection establishment time. This involves negotiation of connections between receivers and subsets of the stream. These subsets will not change during the whole lifetime of the stream.

4.2 Additions to the HeiTS Service Interface

As already stated, the application selects whether scaling has to be done transparently or whether it wants to be involved in the scaling process. In the latter case, it will get messages for up- and downscaling from HeiTP, as described in Section 4.1.2.

- HTP-DOWNSCALE triggers the user to reduce the transmission rate. In the current version of HeiTS, this does not contain any parameters. In further versions the user will get more information about the degree to which the rate should be changed.
- HTP-UPSCALE triggers an increase of the transmission rate.

For the call management we have added two more primitives:

- HTP-CALL allows the user to establish groups of connections. In addition to the parameters of the original HTP-CONNECT primitive, which establishes single connections, there are parameters for describing the relationship between the connections of a call. Examples are parallelism and sequence of TSDUs of different connections. Another parameter specifies whether a connection is mandatory or optional for a call.
- HTP-RELEASE can be used instead of the DISCONNECT primitive. Terminating a call means to disconnect all connections of a call.

The HTS-DATA primitive has been extended by an importance parameter.

5 Conclusion

Some existing networks, such as Ethernet, do not allow QOS management schemes that are based on bandwidth reservation. In such environments, it is not possible to supply multimedia connections with performance guarantees. In the networks, a temporary congestion is possible.

Within HeiTS, a media scaling strategy has been designed to allow multimedia communication over such networks even in case of congestion. Media scaling consists of reducing the amount of data that is forwarded. Since reducing audio information is easily detected by the human ear (at least in the case of transparent scaling methods), media scaling finds its best application in the case of video streams. Based on this consideration, we have shown how different scaling methods (temporal, spatial, frequency, amplitudinal, and color space) can be applied to some existing video encoding formats (Motion JPEG, MPEG, DVI, H.261).

We have shown how HeiTS enables transparent media scaling both in continuous and discrete mode and how the scaling methods apply to multi-destination environments. Extensions to the HeiTP protocol to accommodate the media scaling needs have also been presented. Experiments with implementing these mechanisms are currently done at the IBM European Networking Center in Heidelberg, based on IBM RS/6000s and PS/2s connected via Ethernet and running HeiTS 3.2.

Acknowledgement

The authors would like to thank Keith Hall for providing valuable comments on an earlier version of this paper. Thomas Käppner's experiments with video in a conferencing system were instrumental in identifying the need for media scaling functions in HeiTS.

References

[1] W. Bux, D. Grillo: *Flow Control in Local-area Networks of Interconnected Token Rings.* IBM Research Report No. 48243, 1984.

[2] D.D. Clark, S. Shenker, L. Zhang: *Supporting Real-Time Applications in an Integrated Services Packet Network: Architecture and Mechanism.* ACM SIGCOMM 92, Baltimore, 1992.

[3] L. Delgrossi, C. Halstrick, R.G. Herrtwich, H. Stüttgen: *HeiTP – A Transport Protocol for ST-II.* IEEE Globecom 92, Orlando, 1992.

[4] C.A. Gonzales, E. Viscito, T. McCarthy: *Scalable Motion-Compensated Transform Coding of Motion Video: A Proposal for the ISO/MPEG-2 Standard.* Research Report, IBM T.J. Watson Research Center, 1991.

[5] C. Gonzales, E. Viscito: *Flexibly Scalable Digital Video Coding.* Research Report, IBM T.J. Watson Research Center, 1992.

[6] D. Hehmann, R.G. Herrtwich, R. Steinmetz: *Creating HeiTS: Objectives of the Heidelberg High-Speed Transport System.* GI-Jahrestagung, Darmstadt, 1991.

[7] D. Hehmann, R.G. Herrtwich, W. Schulz, T. Schütt, R. Steinmetz: *Implementing HeiTS: Architecture and Implementation Strategy of the Heidelberg High-Speed Transport System.* Second International Workshop on Network and Operating System Support for Digital Audio and Video, Lecture Notes in Computer Science 614, Springer-Verlag, Heidelberg, 1992.

[8] V. Jacobson: *Congestion Avoidance and Control.* ACM SIGCOMM 88, 1988.

[9] D. LeGall: *MPEG: A Video Compression Standard for Multimedia Applications.* Communications of the ACM, Vol. 34, No. 4, 1991

[10] A.C. Luther: *Digital Video in the PC Environment.* McGraw-Hill, 1991.

[11] R. Nagarajan, C. Vogt: *Guaranteed-Performance Transport of Multimedia Traffic over the Token Ring.* IBM Technical Report No. 43.9201, 1992.

[12] P. Pancha, M. El Zarki: *Prioritized Transmission of Variable Bit Rate MPEG Video.* IEEE Globecom 92, Orlando, 1992.

[13] R. Steinmetz: *Kompressionsverfahren in der Übersicht.* To appear, 1993.

[14] H. Tokuda, Y. Tobe, S.T.-C. Chou, J.M.F. Moura: *Continous Media Communication with Dynamic QOS Control Using ARTS with an FDDI Network.* ACM SIGCOMM 92, Baltimore, 1992.

[15] C. Topolcic (Ed.): *Experimental Internet Stream Protocol, Version 2 (ST-II).* RFC 1190, October 1990.

[16] P. Uppaluru: *Networking Digital Video.* 37th IEEE COMPCON, 1992.

[17] E. Viscito, C. Gonzales: *The MPEG-1 Video Compression Standard*, Research Report, IBM T.J. Watson Research Center, 1991.

[18] C. Vogt, R.G. Herrtwich, R. Nagarajan: *HeiRAT: The Heidelberg Resource Administration Technique, Design Philosophy and Goals.* Kommunikation in verteilten Systemen, Munich, 1993 (also published as IBM Tech. Rep. No. 43.9213, 1992).

[19] G.K. Wallace: *The JPEG Still Picture Compression Standard.* Communications of the ACM, Vol. 34, No. 4, 1991.

[20] *Video Codec for Audiovisual Services at px64 kbit/s.* Recommendation H.261, CCITT Geneva, 1990.

Retransmission-Based Error Control for Interactive Video Applications over the Internet

Injong Rhee
Department of Computer Science
North Carolina State University
Raleigh, NC 27695-7534
E-mail: rhee@csc.ncsu.edu

Abstract

Retransmission has been known ineffective for interactive video transmission over the Internet. This paper challenges this view by presenting several retransmission-based error control schemes that can be used for interactive video applications. In particular, the schemes do not require any artificial extension of control time and play-out delays, and thus are suitable for interactive applications. They take advantage of the motion prediction loop employed in most motion compensation-based codecs. By correcting errors in a reference frame caused by earlier packet loss, the schemes prevent error propagation. Since a reference frame is arranged to be referenced for the construction of the current image much later than the display time of the reference frame, the delay in repairing lost packets can be effectively masked out. Internet video transmission experiments reveal the superior error resilience of the schemes.

1 Introduction

Video conferencing over the Internet has become increasingly popular because of the widespread use of the Internet and video compression technologies. However, high quality interactive video transmission over the Internet still remains challenging because of frequent occurrences of packet loss and limited bandwidth in the network. The problem mainly arises from the disparity of the operational models of traditional video coding standards and Internet-based video conferencing. Most of standard coding schemes, such as H261, H263, and MPEG, are not designed for transmission over a lossy packet switching network, but primarily for storage (CD or VHS tape). Although these schemes can achieve very high compression efficiency, even small packet loss could severely degrade video quality. This is due to motion compensation employed by these coding schemes to remove temporal redundancy in video stream. Motion compensation removes temporal redundancy in successive video frames (inter frame) by encoding only pixel value differences (prediction error) between a currently encoded image and a previously encoded image (reference frame). A single occurrence of packet loss can introduce an error in a reference frame, which can be propagated to its succeeding frames and gets amplified as more packets are lost.

Error propagation can be controlled by more frequently adding intra frames (which are coded temporally independently). However, the ratio of the compression efficiency of an intra-frame over an inter-frame is as large as 3 to 6 times. Increasing the frequency of intra-frames could increase the bandwidth requirement too much for video transmission over a bandwidth-constraint network. Nonetheless, the severe degradation of image quality due to error propagation has forced several popular video conferencing tools, such as `nv`[5], `vic`[7] and `CU-SeeMe`[4], to adopt an even more drastic approach. Using a technique called *conditional replenishment*, these tools filter out the blocks that have not changed much from the previous frame and intra-code the remaining blocks. Since all the coded blocks are temporally independent, packet loss affects only those frames contained in lost packets. However, this enhanced error resilience comes at the cost of low compression efficiency. Additional compression can always be obtained if temporal redundancy is removed from each coded block (i.e., by coding only their prediction error).

The goal is to find an error recovery scheme that solves the error propagation problem without much increase in the bandwidth requirement.

Retransmission-based error recovery (REC) can provide good error resilience without incurring much bandwidth overhead because packets are retransmitted only when some indications exist that they are lost. However, retransmission has been widely known ineffective for interactive video transmission because of the delay associated with detecting and recovering lost packets. Many researchers proposed to extend control or play-out times in order to allow enough time for retransmitted packets to arrive before their display times [11, 10, 6, 12]. This implies that the display time of a frame is delayed by at least three one-way trip times after its initial transmission (two for frame transmissions and one for a retransmission request). Under the current Internet environment, this delay can be as large as 400 ms to 600 ms. For instance, in a transatlantic transmission experiment, one round trip time delay is usually between 200 and 300 ms. When the network connection gets congested, the delay frequently rises beyond 400 ms. This latency significantly impairs the interact-ability of any real-time video applications.

In this paper, we present new REC schemes that do not require any additional control or play-out delay, and hence are suitable for real-time interactive applications. In addition, the proposed schemes do not require much change in existing standard codecs. We performed extensive transatlantic video transmission tests over the Internet to measure the effectiveness of the schemes. Our experiments indicate that REC can be a very effective error recovery technique for interactive video applications.

Section 2 describes the related work, Section 3 presents our REC schemes, Section 4 contains a discussion of the experimental results, and Section 5 contains the conclusion.

2   Related Work

Dempsey et al.[3] applied retransmission for the recovery of audio packets. They showed that by adding some delay before the play-out of each received audio packet, retransmission can be used to protect audio data from packet loss. Their work hinges on the earlier behavior study by Brady [2] showing that although less than 200 ms round trip delay is required for high quality voice applications, delays up to 600 ms can be tolerable by human ears.

Ramamurthy and Raychaudhuri [11] applied a similar technique to video transmission over ATM.

They analyzed the performance of video transmission over an ATM network when both retransmission and error concealment are used to repair errors occurring from cell loss. They analytically showed that for a coast-to-coast ATM connection, 33 ms to 66 ms play-out delay is sufficient to see a significant improvement in image quality.

Padopoulos and Parulkar [10] proposed an implementation of an ARQ scheme for continuous media transmission. Various techniques including selective repeat, retransmission expiration, and conditional retransmission are implemented inside a kernel. Their experiment over an ATM connection showed the effectiveness of their scheme.

Most recently, Li et al. [6] and Xu et al. [12] used retransmission in the recovery of lost packets for video multicasting. Li et al [6] proposed a novel scheme for distributing an MPEG-coded video over a best-effort network. By transmitting different frame types (I, P and B frames) of MPEG to different multicast groups, they implemented a simple layering mechanism in which a receiver can adjust frame play-out times during congestion by joining or leaving a multicast group. For instance, consider an MPEG picture pattern: IBBPBBPBBPBB. Their scheme delays the play-out times of frames for one frame interval. They call this delayed play-out time *adaptive playback point*. When a receiver leaves the B frame group, the adaptive playback point is additionally extended by three frame intervals because the next frame to be displayed after a P frame is at three frame intervals away. The scheme is shown effective for non-interactive real-time video applications.

In a video conference involving a large number of participants, different participants may have different service requirements. While some participants may require real-time interactions with other participants, others may simply want to watch or record the conference. Xu et al. [12] contend that retransmission can be effectively used for the transmission of high quality video to the receivers that do not need a real-time transfer of video data. They designed a new protocol called *structure-oriented resilient multicast* (STORM) in which senders and receivers collaborate to recover lost packets using a dynamic hierarchical tree structure.

3 Retransmission-Based Error Control (REC)

Our schemes are based on a careful observation on how video frames are encoded in most motion compensation-based codecs. We base our discussion mostly on H.261 from which many motion compensation-based video standards such as MPEG are designed. In H.261, a video sequence consists of two types of video frames: *intra-frame* (I-frame) and *inter-frame* (P-frame). I-frame removes only spatial redundancy present in the frame. P-frame is encoded through motion estimation using another P-frame or I-frame as a reference frame (R-frame). For each image block in a P-frame, motion estimation finds a closely matching block within its R-frame, and generates the distance between the two matching blocks as a motion vector. The pixel value differences between the original P-frame and a motion-predicted image of the P-frame obtained by simply cut-and-pasting the matching image blocks from its R-frame are encoded along with the motion vectors.

Most of the previously proposed retransmission schemes work as follows. When a packet containing the encoding of a frame is lost at a receiver, the receiver detects the loss after receiving a subsequent packet of the lost packet and sends a retransmission request to the sender. After receiving the request, the sender retransmits the packet. We define the *display time* of a packet to be the time that the frame whose encoding is contained in the packet is displayed at the receiver. If the retransmitted packet arrives before its display time, the frame can be fully restored. Otherwise, it is discarded and the displayed image contains some error. All the subsequently decoded frames will carry the same error unless a new I-frame is received.

Our scheme differs from others in that retransmitted packets arriving after their display times are not discarded but instead used to reduce error propagation. In motion compensation-based codecs, the correct image reconstruction of a currently displayed image depends on a successful reconstruction of its R-frames. The scheme allows that while a frames is being reconstructed, the "late" packets of an R-frame can be decoded and used for restoring the R-frame. This will stop possible error propagation because the next frame reconstructed would not carry over an error from the R-frame.

Figure 1 shows a H.261 decoder modified to handle the recovery of R-frames through retransmitted packets. The only difference from the original H.261 decoder is one additional frame buffer added to handle the recovery. When a packet is received and decoded into an image block, the decoder determines whether the block belongs to the current frame being decoded or its R-frame. If it is for the current frame, then the block is stored into frame buffer CP along with its motion vector. If it is for the R-frame, the block is added with its temporally dependent block in frame buffer R_0 and stored into R_1. Note that CP contains only the prediction error and motion vectors of the current frame while R_1 contains the fully motion compensated image of the R-frame of the current frame, and R_0 contains the R-frame of R_1. We call R_0 a *base reference frame buffer*. At the next display time, ' the current frame is constructed using the information in CP and R_1. After the display, R_1 is copied to R_0 and the displayed image are copied to R_1. In this scheme, as long as the packets belonging to R_1 arrive before the construction of the current frame, the packet can be used to help remove errors in the current frame. The *deadline of a packet* can be informally defined to be the arrival time of the packet at the receiver after which it is not useful for decoding any frame. Note that the decoder in Figure 1 extends the deadline of packets by one frame interval without delaying frame play-out times.

We can easily generalize the above scheme to extend packet deadlines beyond one frame interval. Below, we discuss three such schemes. Many different variations of the schemes are also possible.

In H.261, each R-frame temporally depends on the previous R-frames. Thus, by employing more R-frame buffers, the late packets can be decoded and used to restore their corresponding frames which are used as R-frames for the subsequent frames. Since a frame temporally depends on all the prior frames encoded after its immediately preceding I-frame, restoring a sequence of R-frames preceding to a frame contributes to reducing error propagation. Figure 2 illustrates this scheme, called *cascaded buffering*. The shaded squares represent image blocks and an arrow represents the temporal dependency between two blocks. Suppose that the current frame number is f. R_0 is the base reference frame buffer and contains the completely reconstructed image of frame $f-4$ while R_i ($1 \le i \le 4$) contains the prediction error and motion vectors of frame $f-4+i$. The image block that corresponds to b_3 can be constructed by adding b_0, b_1, b_2, and b_3. However this scheme has two drawbacks. First it requires many frame buffers if the

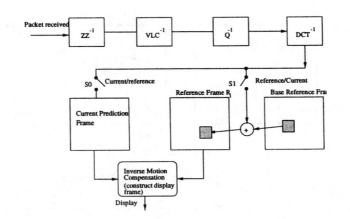

Figure 1: H.261 Decoder modified to handle the recovery of reference frames.

message delay is too long. Second, computational overhead might be large because all the R-frames in the decoder are needed to be added to construct the currently displayed frame.

Another way to extend the deadline is to increase the *temporal dependency distance* (TDD) of a frame which is defined to be the minimum number of frame intervals between that frame and its temporally dependent frame. Figure 3 shows an example where every frame has TDD 3. Each frame temporally depends on another frame sampled at three frame intervals away. The extended TDD essentially stretches the deadlines of packets because each displayed frame is referenced for the reconstruction of another frame only after one TDD period. We call this scheme *extended TDD* (ETDD). Because each frame within a TDD period depends on a frame in the previous TDD period, the receiver has to maintain all the reference frame buffers within a TDD period for the decoding of the frames in the next TDD period. In addition, to restore each R-frame through retransmission, each reference frame R should have one base reference frame. This scheme has another drawback. Since the prediction error of each frame is obtained from the frame that is at a few frame intervals away, it may reduce compression efficiency. However, the ETDD scheme does not require as much computational overhead as the cascade buffering scheme because the current decoded frame can be constructed from its R-frame and base reference frame.

Figure 4 shows another scheme, called *periodic TDD* (PTDD). In the scheme, only every ith frame has TDD i (we call this frame *a periodic frame*) while all the other inter-frames have TDD 1. This frame pattern is very similar to the picture group pattern of MPEG. All the periodic frames can be regarded as P-frames while the other frames as B-frame (except the first frame). Thus, this scheme can be easily incorporated into MPEG. PTDD is both computationally and spatially efficient since only periodic frames require two reference frame buffers. It would also give better compression efficiency than ETDD because every non-periodic frame has TDD 1. However, PTDD does not provide any protection for non-periodic frames from packet loss. An error in a non-periodic frame can propagate until the next periodic frame is received.

In all of the three schemes mentioned above, the packet deadline can be dynamically extended either by adding more frame buffers or extending the temporal dependency distance. For these schemes to be effective, an appropriate packet deadline needs to be selected that allows high compression efficiency as well as sufficient time for a large portion of retransmission packets to arrive before their deadlines. Finding the optimal packet deadline under a given network condition is left as future work.

4   Experimental Result

The main objective of the experiment is to show that a REC scheme is an effective error control scheme for a real-time interactive video transmission over the Internet. We show this through an Internet video transmission experiment between the University of Warwick, UK and Emory University, GA, USA. Among the three REC schemes mentioned in Section 3, we implement the periodic temporal dependency distance (PTDD) scheme by modifying a H.261 coder. The modified coder is called HP.261. The experiments with the other

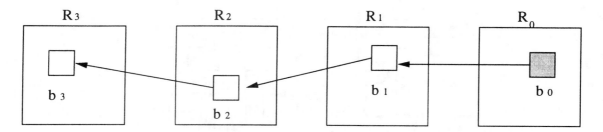

Figure 2: Cascaded Buffering

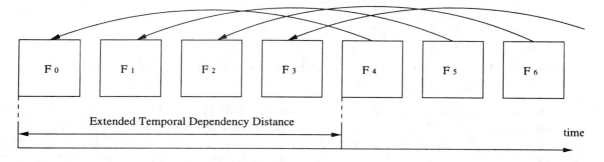

Figure 3: Extended Temporal Dependency Distance

REC schemes presented in this paper are left for future work.

The performance of HP.261 is compared to that of two other codecs. H.261 is used as a base case for the comparison. We implemented INTRA-H261 which is used in `vic`. INTRA-H261 is known for good error resilience under packet loss. INTRA-H.261 intra-codes every image block changed significantly much from the corresponding block in the previous frame. Section 4.1 describes the testing methodology and environment Section 4.2 presents the experimental result.

4.1 Testing Methodology

A test video sequence is obtained from a typical video conferencing session where one typical "talking head" engages in a conversation with the other party. The video is sampled at 5 frames/sec rate and each frame is captured in the color CIF YUV format (352×288). This video sampling rate allows us to achieve a bit rate suitable for a transatlantic transmission without imposing too much load on the network. Considering the long distance and limited bandwidth between the testing sites, this frame rate is not unusual. The target bit rate is around 250 Kbits/sec. In addition to the controlled sample rate, we use a conditional replenishment technique for all the tested schemes to obtain a desired bit rate. Adjusting quantization steps would

be a more common way to control the bit rate. However, since INTRA-H261 uses conditional replenishment, we use the same technique uniformly for all the schemes for fairness. Finding the optimal video quality for a given bit rate is outside the scope of this paper.

About 40 second length video sequence (total 190 frames) is obtained. The video sequence is replayed several times for five minute period for each experiment. The replay does not affect the integrity of the experiment because the first frame is always completely intra-coded (without any conditional replenishment). The 95th frame is intra-coded with conditional replenishment to remove any artifact due to the *decoder drift* effect. For all the schemes, we applied a default quantization step size 8, and for all the motion-compensated schemes, a full exhaustive search over search window size 15 by 15 is performed. We chose 5 frame intervals to be the TDD of all the periodic frames in HP.261. Given 5 frames/s frame rate, this TDD extends the deadlines of periodic frames up to 1 sec.

To see the compression efficiency of different schemes. we measure the average peak signal-to-noise ratio (PSNR) of decoded frames over various data rates. The data rate is measured by the average number of bytes required to compress a frame which is plotted in Figure 5. For a given data rate, INTRA-H.261 shows the worst video quality while H.261 shows the best. For instance, to obtain

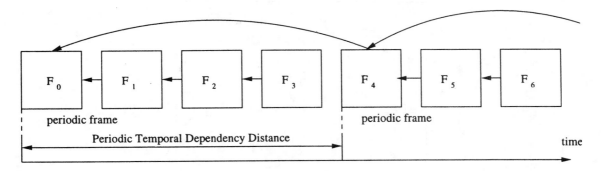

Figure 4: Periodic Temporal Dependency Distance

about 34 dB PSNR, INTRA-H.261 requires 80% (11KB/6KB) more bits per frame than the others.

For fairness, each scheme should use a similar bandwidth for transmission. Since H.261 gives the best compression efficiency, we chose the bandwidth requirement of H.261 under the given compression parameters (e.g., search window and quantization steps). H.261 gives the maximum PSNR around 240 Kbits/s.

We set the bit rates of other schemes to this bit rate. Figure 6 shows the chosen data rates. INTRA-H.261 is given a higher data rate because we could not get a finer precision on its data rate by varying only the conditional replenishment threshold. However this higher bit rate does not unfavorably affect the INTRA-H.261 because INTRA-H.261 is not actually transmitted. Instead, only the video sequence of HP.261 is transmitted and the other sequences are simply mapped to the obtained transmission traces of HP.261. More details about this mapping are given in the next section. HP.261 is given a bit lower data rates because the associated retransmission of lost packets would increase the actual data rate. We anticipate the actual data rate during a transmission test would be similar to the others. Figure 7 shows the PSNR of each frame compressed by three different schemes under the data rates given in Figure 6.

The test video sequence is first compressed using each of the three compression schemes and then packetized into approximately 512-byte packets. The packetized sequence of HP.261 is transmitted over the Internet. For each transmission test, we obtain a 5 minute trace that records the packet sequence numbers and arrival times of all the received packets. The transmission tests are conducted at every hour for 8 days between Oct. 20 to Oct. 27.

Each packet of a frame is transmitted at a reg-

ular interval determined by the given frame rate (5 frames/s) and the number of packets within the frame. For example, for the frame interval of 200 ms, if one frame consists of 10 packets, a packet in the frame is transmitted at 20 ms interval. Each transmitted packet is assigned a unique sequence number. Retransmitted packets are given the same sequence numbers as their original packets.

The ARQ scheme employed during the experiment works as follows. The receiver sends one acknowledgment to the sender for each received frame. An acknowledgment contains information about the missing packets of the last periodic frame that the receiver received. After retransmitting a packet, the sender does not retransmit the same packet for about three frame intervals. It may retransmit the packet if it receives another acknowledgment after the period indicating that the packet is lost. The receiver also does not request for the retransmission of packets whose deadlines are expired. These mechanisms reduce the number of unnecessary retransmissions.

Each trace is fed to an off-line decoder to measure the signal-to-noise of the received frames. To simplify the experiment, we did not add any jitter control time for frame play-out. Each frame is considered to be displayed at the arrival of the first packet of its next frame if that packet is received. If that packet is not received, the frame is considered to be displayed at 200 ms after its previous frame's play-out time. If no packet for the frame is received, any frame displayed last will be displayed for that frame. Retransmitted packets are not used for the display of their frames, but used only to restore their corresponding reference frames.

For a comparison purpose, we map each of the obtained traces T to the packetized sequence of H.261 and INTRA-H.261 as follows. We first obtain a 5 minute length of the packetized sequences

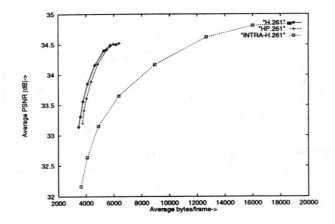

Figure 5: Compression Efficiency of Various Schemes

Compression scheme	Avg. bit rate Avg. Kbits/s	PSNR
H.261	240.6	34.50
HP.261	232.6	34.51
INTRA-H.261	247.77	33.65

Figure 6: Chosen data rates for network experiments, and their average PSNR's

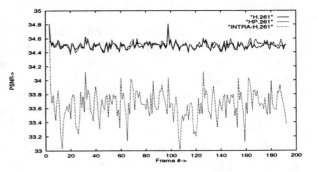

Figure 7: Video quality of encoded sequences

S of H.261 and INTRA-H.261 as if the sequences would have actually been transmitted. Each packet p in trace T is mapped to a packet q with the same sequence number as p. If packet p is received, we record q as received and assign the receiving time of p to q. Otherwise, we record that q is lost.

We obtained 168 traces of HP.261. Since many traces are obtained, it is difficult to present the result of each trace independently. So we classify the traces into several loss rate groups and present only the average behavior of the traces in each group. Table 1 shows the loss groups and their corresponding loss ranges. Since high loss cases are relatively infrequent, we set a larger range for high loss rates.

4.2   Performance of REC

In this section, we report the result of our experiment. Figure 8 shows the average PSNR's of H.261, INTRA-H.261 and HP.261 for various loss groups. H.261's PSNR drop considerably even under a small amount of packet loss showing the severe impact of error propagation. Both INTRA-H.261 and HP.261 exhibit generally good error re-

silience. Both show a similar PSNR for all loss groups. Under less than 10 % loss groups, HP.261 shows better PSNR than INTRA-H.261. Between 12% and 20% packet loss, the PSNR of HP.261 drops a little below INTRA-H.261. This is due to the drop in the REC recovery rates (see Figure 9).

Figure 10 shows a portion of one HP.261 trace with 10% packet loss. The figure on the top compares PSNR's of H.261 and HP.261 of all the frames received during the period. The figure on the bottom shows two kinds of data. The impulses indicate the ratio of the number of lost packets over the number of packets in a frame, and the line points indicate the ratio of the number of packets recovered by REC over the number of packets in a frame. When a point reaches the top of an impulse, it means all the lost packets in the frame are recovered. The line points are relatively sparse because only the packets belonging to periodic frames are retransmitted and no points are drawn for the frames that did not lose any packet.

Many packets are lost between sequence numbers 300 and 550. Accordingly the PSNR's of both HP.261 and H.261 drop significantly. How-

Loss group	0.025	0.05	0.075	0.1	0.125	0.15
Loss range	(0, 0.025)	[0.025,0.05)	[0.05,0.075)	[0.075,0.1)	[0.1, 0.125)	[0.125, 0.15)
Loss group	0.175	0.2	0.25	0.3	0.35	0.4
Loss range	[0.15, 0.175)	[0.175,0.2)	[0.2, 0.25)	[0.25,0.30)	[0.3, 0.35)	[0.35,0.40)

Table 1: Loss Rate Groups and their loss ranges

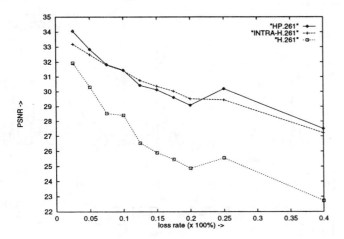

Figure 8: Mean PSNRs

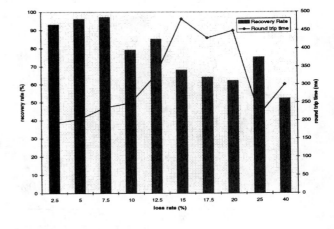

Figure 9: Mean round trip time, and recovery rate

ever, in HP.261, all the packets of periodic frames within that period are recovered by retransmission. Around packet 600, most frames are received without loss. In HP.261, those frames are displayed without an error since all the periodic frames that they temporally depend on are recovered fully before their reconstruction times. On the other hands, H.261 suffers severely from error propagation. The good receiving rate around packet 600 does not improve the PSNR of H.261 during that period.

If a periodic frame contains some error, all the frames before the next periodic frame will contain the same error. However, if the periodic frame is recovered later on before the next periodic frame is reconstructed, the error will disappear from the subsequent frames of the next periodic frame. The many peaks of PSNR shown in the top of Figure 10 illustrate this behavior.

There is a clear correlation between the round trip time and REC recovery rates. As the round trip times increase, the recovery rates of periodic frames also drop. When round trip times increase beyond 250ms, the recovery rates by REC are significantly reduced. This is because the increased network delay reduces the probability for retransmitted packets to meet their deadlines. However, the packet loss rates do not necessarily correlate

with the round trip times. The trace in 25% has the mean round trip times less than 250 ms, which contributes to the increases of the recovery rate up to 75% and PSNR to 30 dB. The trace contains a bulk loss in the middle of the experiment during which no packets are received.

A large amount of packet loss causes many retransmissions increasing the data rates. In Table 2, the data rates for HP.261 between 12.5% and 20% go beyond 260 Kbits/s, which means on an average about 5 to 6 packets/s are retransmitted. These data rates are slightly higher than those of INTRA-H.261 under some loss groups. We believe, however, that this is mainly due to the crudeness of the retransmission decision protocol (i.e., when to retransmit) we employed in the experiment. Use of a more sophisticated ARQ method such as the one used in [10] should reduce the data rates further.

5 Discussion

Retransmission has widely been known ineffective for recovering lost packets in real-time interactive video applications. This paper challenges the conventional wisdom and presents new retransmission-based error control techniques that do not incur any

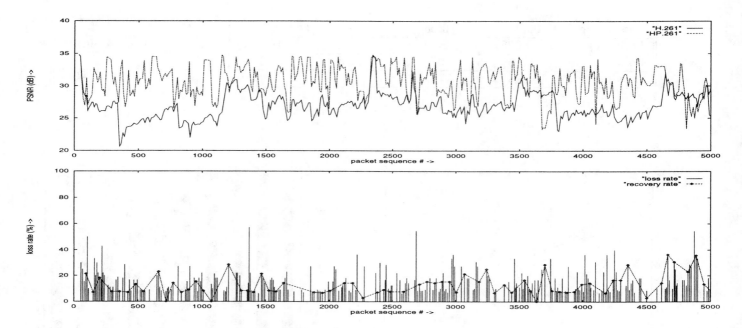

Figure 10: One trace of HP.261 with 10% packet loss – PSNR, and Loss and Recovery Rates

Loss Rate (%)	# of traces	H.261 Data Rate (Kbits/s)	HP.261			INTRA-H.261 Data Rate (Kbits/s)
			Data Rate (Kbits/s)	Recovery by REC(%)	RTT (ms)	
2.5	54	237.2	246.4	93.39	192.17	258.1
5.0	40	245.0	247.2	96.84	204.97	256.4
7.5	35	244.6	248.0	97.01	236.71	256.7
10.0	14	245.6	252.8	79.94	249.19	256.4
12.5	9	249.1	262.7	85.67	329.75	259.9
15.0	8	251.5	266.0	68.07	481.28	260.2
17.5	3	251.4	268.0	64.60	429.75	259.8
20.0	2	252.0	267.0	62.38	449.28	260.6
25.0	1	243.6	241.1	75.53	215.8	255.4
40.0	2	248.2	263.6	52.44	300.6	257.9

Table 2: Experimental Data based on HP.261 traces

additional latency in the frame play-out time, and hence are suitable for interactive applications.

One main implication of our work is that many motion compensation prediction-based codecs, such as MPEG, and H.261, are still useful for Internet interactive video transmission over a lossy network. Some of the disadvantages of the motion compensated codecs cited in the literature [8, 9, 7] include (1) computational complexity, (2) error resilience, (3) tight coupling between the prediction state at the encoder and that at the decoder, and (4) compute-scalable decoding. In this paper, we showed that the H.261 equipped with our REC schemes achieves comparable error resilience to that of INTRA-H.261. We also believe that some

of the other disadvantages can be overcome with a simple modification to the codecs. For instance, the compute-scalable decoding can also be achieved by decoding only periodic frames and shedding off the computational load for decoding non-periodic frames in PTDD.

Having said some of the disadvantages of motion-compensated codecs, we would like to emphasize one of their advantages over INTRA-H.261, which is high compression efficiency. Although INTRA-H.261 gives good error resilience, the low compression efficiency of INTRA-H.261 will make it very difficult to obtain very high quality video for a low bit rate transmission. As pointed out in [12], in a multicast group, while some receivers want real-time video, others may want to watch or record the transmitted video. These observers may want the highest quality that the video source could provide although they can tolerate a longer play-out delay. At the same time, they may have only a small amount of bandwidth allocated for the video.

Motion-compensated encoding allows much better video quality for a given data rate than intra-coding. Our scheme allows real-time receivers to view video in a comparable quality as intra-coding schemes. At the same time, it allows the same encoded video to be multicasted to other non-real-time receivers. These receivers can view the video in very high quality by adding an additional delay (i.e., control time) before the display of the first frame. On the other hand, for intra-coded video to be sent on a low bandwidth network, its quality needs to be reduced substantially. In this case, although real-time receivers may get the video in similar quality as the motion-compensation scheme with REC, non-real-time receivers will receive a poor quality video. Note that this feature is different from media scaling [8] where receivers with a higher network capacity always get a higher quality image. Here, this feature allows even the receivers with a low network capacity to get a high quality while trading interact-ability. The motion compensated codecs equipped with a REC scheme can provide this feature as they generally give better compression efficiency and lost packets can be recovered through retransmission.

References

[1] J. Bolot and A. Vega-Garcia, " The case for FEC-based error control for packet audio in the Internet," to appear in ACM Multimedia Systems.

[2] P. Brady, "Effects of Transmission Delay on Conversational Behavior on Echo-Free Telephone Circuits," *Bell System Technical Journal*, vol. 50, no. 1, pp. 115 – 134, Jan. 1993.

[3] B. Demsey, J. Liebeherr, and A. Weaver, "On retransmission-based error control for continuous media traffic in packet-switching networks," *Computer Networks and ISDN Systems*, 1996.

[4] T. Dorcey, "CU-SeeMe desktop videoconferencing software," *ConneXions*, vol. 9, no. 3, Mar. 1995.

[5] R. Fredrick, *Network Video(nv)*, Xerox Palo Alto Research Center.

[6] X. Li, S. Paul, P. Pancha, and M. Ammar, "Layered video multicast with retransmission (LVMR): evaluation of error recovery schemes," *Proceedings of the Sixth International Workshop on Network and Operating System Support for Digital Audio and Video*, St Louis, May 1997.

[7] S. McCanne and V. Jacobson, "*vic*: a flexible framework for packet video," in *Proceedings of ACM Multimedia'95*, San Francisco, CA, Nov. 1995, pp. 511–522

[8] S. McCanne, M. Verrerli, and V. Jacobson, "Low-complexity video coding for receiver-driven layered multicast," *IEEE Journal on Selected Areas in Communications*, vol. 16, no. 6, pp. 983-1001, August 1997

[9] S. McCanne, V. Jacobson, and M. Vetterli, "Receiver-driven Layered Multicast". *Proceedings of ACM SIGCOMM*, August 1996, Stanford, CA, pp. 117-130

[10] C. Papadopoulos and G. Parulkar, "Retransmission Based error control for continuous media applications," *Proceedings of the Sixth International Workshop on Network and Operating System Support for Digital Audio and Video*, pp. 5–12, 1996.

[11] G. Ramamurthy, and D. Raychaudhuri, "Performance of packet video with combined error recovery and concealment," *Proceedings of INFOCOM'95*, pp. 753–761, April 1995.

[12] R. Xu, C. Myers, H. Zhang, R. Yavatkar, "Resilient multicast support for continuous-media applications," *Proceedings of the Sixth International Workshop on Network and Operating System Support for Digital Audio and Video*, St Louis, May 1997.

What video can and cannot do for collaboration: a case study

Ellen A. Isaacs*, **John C. Tang****

SunSoft, Inc., 2550 Garcia Avenue, Mountain View, CA 94043, USA

Abstract. As multimedia become an integral part of collaborative systems, we must understand how to design such systems to support the user's rich set of existing interaction skills, rather than requiring people to adapt to arbitrary constraints of technology-driven designs. To understand how we can make effective use of video in remote collaboration, we compared a small team's interactions through a desktop video conferencing prototype with face-to-face interactions and phone conversations. We found that, compared with audio-only, the video channel of our desktop video conferencing prototype adds or improves the ability to show understanding, forecast responses, give nonverbal information, enhance verbal descriptions, manage pauses, and express attitudes. These findings suggest that video may be better than the phone for handling conflict and other interaction-intense activities. However, the advantages of video depend critically on the nearly-instantaneous transmission of audio, even if it means getting out of sync with the video image. Nonetheless, when compared with face-to-face interaction, it can be difficult in video interactions to notice peripheral cues, control the floor, have side conversations, point to things or manipulate real-world objects. To enable rich interactions fully, video should be integrated with other distributed tools that increase the extent and type of shared space in a way that enables natural collaborative behaviors within those environments.

Key words: Remote collaboration – Desktop video conferencing – Computer-supported cooperative work – User interfaces – Conversation

1 Introduction

Previous work on collaborative systems has revealed that building tools for groups of people involves specific challenges beyond those for single user systems. Collaborative systems must be designed so that they are both useful and usable enough to induce a critical mass of people to adopt the technology (Francik et al. 1991; Grudin 1988). When multimedia technology is included in collaborative systems, more

---

*   e-mail: isaacs@sun.com
**   e-mail: tang@sun.com
Correspondence to: E.A. Isaacs

design challenges are added, since so little is known about how to combine various media in ways that are effective and natural for people to use. At the very least, we know that incorporating multimedia into a computer system requires more than just attaching video or audio onto the front end without rethinking the entire user interface (Wulfman et al. 1988).

There has been particular interest in the use of video to enhance remote collaboration, which has traditionally been supported by voice-only (phone) or text-only (e-mail) interactions. Although video is often intuitively presumed to improve the quality of interactions among remote participants, many studies have found no evidence that groups are more effective or efficient at solving problems or making decisions when they are connected through a video and audio link than when they use only an audio link (Chapanis et al. 1972; Gale 1990; Ochsman and Chapanis 1974; Short et al. 1976; Williams 1977).

Did these previous studies somehow miss finding the effect of video, or are our intuitions about the value of video misleading? By re-examining some of the assumptions and conditions of the previous studies, we identified three reasons why they might not have detected any effect of video in support of interaction.

Firstly, the previous studies measured the *product* (e.g., decisions, quality of solutions, completion times) of short, problem-solving interactions. The effects of video are more likely to be visible when studying the *process* of interactions. For example, video is likely to be useful for managing the mechanics of conversations, e.g., turn taking, monitoring understanding, noting and adjusting to reactions (Clark and Schaefer 1987; Clark and Wilkes-Gibbs 1986; Isaacs and Clark 1987; Sacks et al. 1974; Williams 1977). If video is effective at enhancing the process of interaction, people may perceive their interactions to be more satisfying, and it may encourage coworkers to collaborate more frequently. If the process is important to collaboration, then the mechanics of interaction must be facilitated in the user interface so that users may take advantage of their rich set of existing skills in a natural and intuitive way.

Secondly, the effects of video in supporting interaction may be most visible over the long term, and may be too subtle or difficult to capture in short, laboratory experiments. As Gale (1990) notes:

The structure of groups is continually changing. The effects of technology on a group may take weeks, months, or even years before becoming apparent. These sort of effects cannot be fully explored in a one hour experiment.

We would expect that richer interactions would lead to more productive and/or higher quality results in the long term, although more research would be needed to test this hypothesis.

Thirdly, most of the previous studies were among strangers who were asked to accomplish an artificial task for the purposes of the study. That is, the participants did not have working relationships with each other, and were not dealing with an issue that highly motivated them. Yet the interactional cues that video transmits are likely to play a more important role among people who know each other and are accomplishing real work that requires complex social negotiation. Again, Gale (1990) notes:

> The results from this study suggest that by adding audio and video to the communications medium we allow groups to perform more 'social' activities. ... A possible reason for the lack of difference in the quality of the output of the groups is that the tasks used in this study were not sensitive to social factors.

Thus, previous studies may have missed the effects of video because they are too subtle to see among strangers carrying out impersonal tasks.

In this context, we believe there is still good reason to pursue video as an integral part of collaborative technology. To study the user-interface implications of using video for remote collaboration, we observed a team of engineers who were using a desktop video conferencing (DVC) prototype. The prototype enabled digital audio-video connections between workstation desktops. Rather than conducting a broad survey of users' reports of their perceptions in using this technology, we focused on studying the details of one group's behavior when using video and audio as compared with audio-only and face-to-face interactions. Our intention is to describe the evidence we found for the potential benefit of video in remote conversations compared with audio alone, and to point out how video interactions can fall short of, and in some ways offer advantages over, face-to-face interactions. We then discuss how our results may be applied to the design of effective video conferencing systems.

2 Method

We observed a team of five software engineers who were distributed across three sites. Two worked in a building in Billerica, Mass., two worked in a building in Mountain View, Calif., and one worked in another Mountain View building about 500 yds (ca. 450 m) away from the first. The team had previously worked together when they were all located in Billerica, but they had recently moved to their distributed locations for reasons unrelated to this study.

The DVC prototype provided a simple interface for requesting a desktop conference that followed a telephone model for making connections. The interface enabled a user to request a conference with one or two other people, and those people had to accept that conference request before audio-video connections were made. The interface allowed users to specify what kind of connections they wanted for a conference: audio, video, and/or a shared drawing tool called Show Me. Show Me allowed users to share an image of anything they could display on their screens. They could draw on top of shared images or construct a joint drawing from scratch. Within Show Me, users could type or draw at the same time, they could erase anyone else's work, and they could always see where everyone else was pointing with their cursors.

The default setting was to request audio, video, and Show Me connections with one other participant. Once a conference request was accepted, several windows popped up on each participant's workstation screen. Each person saw a video window showing the image of the other participant and a smaller preview window of the video image being sent to the other person. A full duplex audio connection was made with the other person. A Show Me window also popped up on each screen. (In a three-way connection, each person would see an additional video window of the second remote participant.)

The DVC prototype ran on Sun computer workstations with a prototype add-on board that enabled real-time video capture, compression, and display. For audio, the prototype used the 8 KHz μlaw encoding that is built into the workstation. At the time of this study, the prototype video board used the Intel RTV 1.5 video compression algorithm. The video windows had a video resolution of 120×128 pixels, although that resolution could be scaled to any arbitrary size window. The default video frame rate was 5 frames/s; due to some long-distance network bandwidth limitations, but the users could request a different video frame rate before starting a conference (although they did so only once). The quality of the video image was less than that of broadcast television and certain analogue desktop video conferencing systems such as Cruiser (Root 1988) (due to the lower refresh rate and lower effective resolution). But it was of higher quality than video conference systems than run over ISDN or conventional phone lines. More details on the technical description of the prototype can be found in Pearl (1992).

The data from this study was drawn from a larger study that observed the team's work activity under three conditions: (1) before installing the DVC prototype (to understand their baseline collaborative activity); (2) with the DVC prototype fully installed, including audio, video, and the shared drawing tool; and (3) with the video channel subtracted from the DVC prototype, leaving audio and the shared drawing capabilities still in place. [See Tang and Isaacs, (1993) for a further description of the results from the larger study.] Since the team that was observed was not involved in the development of the DVC prototype, they had never experienced using the prototype before it was installed during the second condition of the study. Each team member was given a short (less than 15 min) demonstration of the prototype to familiarize them with the prototype's capabilities and user interface.

Although we took many measures of their work activity, the data for this paper are based on videotapes of six inter-

Table 1. People involved in each observed interaction

DVC	Meeting	Phone
Kate, Jeff	Kate, Jeff	Jeff, Craig, Dave
Everyone	Everyone	Kate, Jeff, Jack, Dave

actions in three modalities: two desktop video conferences, two face- to-face interactions and two telephone conferences. Comparing interactions among the same people using various tools enabled us to isolate the effects of the tools on their interactions better. One of the DVC meetings included all five group members (call them Kate, Jeff, Jack, Dave, and Craig) and one was between just Kate and Jeff. Likewise, the two face-to-face meetings included the same sets of participants. We could not obtain phone-conference data among the same sets of people, so instead we studied a four-way call between Kate, Jeff, Jack and Dave, and a three-way call between Jeff, Craig and Dave. Table 1 shows the people in each interaction we observed.

The five-person DVC was a three-way connection where two people crowded around one camera and workstation at each of two sites. The four-person phone conference connected three sites; two people were in the same office sharing a speaker phone.

The videotapes of the six interactions were analyzed in the tradition of interaction analysis (Tang 1991a; Tatar 1989) to look for any changes in pattern among the three modalities. The qualitative analysis involved creating a detailed account of all the interactional behaviors among the group members, with a particular emphasis on behaviors that took advantage of audio and visual cues. The quantitative analysis involved comparing the mechanics of conversational turn taking (i.e., duration of turn, frequency of turn changes) between the face-to-face and DVC modalities.

3 Benefits of video over audio only

An analysis of the videotapes brought out the benefit of video conferencing compared to audio only. Specifically, participants used the visual channel to express understanding or agreement, forecast responses, enhance verbal descriptions, give purely nonverbal information, express attitudes through posture and facial expression, and manage extended pauses.

3.1 Expressing understanding

The most common use of the visual channel was to show understanding and, in some cases, agreement by nodding the head while someone was speaking. Research has shown that speakers are quite adept at adjusting the content of their utterances to their addressees' level of understanding (Clark and Schaefer 1987; Clark and Wilkes-Gibbs 1986; Isaacs and Clark 1987). Furthermore, they expect various degrees of feedback depending on the complexity of the topic (Isaacs and Clark 1987). Head nods are a subtle and nonintrusive way of conveying understanding (Duncan 1972), and they were used extensively throughout the DVCs. Participants nodded their heads to varying degrees and at varying rates, showing various levels of understanding. Sometimes they leaned forward to indicate they were still trying to understand, and other times they looked away and tilted their heads, indicating they were considering the idea.

For instance, during the two-way DVC, Kate explained a technical issue. At first, Jeff tilted his head and looked puzzled, but eventually he gave a slight head nod as he grasped the concept. Then he sighed and shook his head, acknowledging the issue as difficult. All these subtle reactions gave Kate a running commentary on the state of Jeff's understanding. Later, Kate asked him to confirm his understanding of an idea and he said "Uh huh," but then he looked down and pursed his lips as he considered the issue. Kate proceeded to elaborate, apparently responding to the visual, rather than the auditory feedback.

In contrast, during the phone conferences, speakers often explicitly asked for confirmation. In one instance, Dave said, "...we should probably take, like, the first part of the meeting and just go through and see what questions you guys have." After a 3-s pause, he said, "Okay? Then you can at least get your questions answered" (1 s pause). "And then we can hit you up for stuff that we want to know" (1 s). "Okay?" (1 s) "All right?" Finally, Jeff said "Yep" and continued. With no visual feedback, Dave had to explicitly request a response four times before getting one.

In DVCs, the video provided an effortless and ongoing feedback channel that gave the participants a fluid sense of each other's understanding throughout the conversation. Addressees could give visual feedback on the level of their understanding without interrupting the speaker. Without the video, the participants had to work harder to get much less information about each other's understanding.

3.3 Forecasting responses

In the DVC, the participants not only indicated their level of understanding, they also occasionally forecast their response to each others' remarks through their gestures. Often they indicated their responses by shaking their heads or making facial expressions. For example, in the two-way DVC, Kate made a point and Jeff tipped his head left and right in a gesture indicating "sort of." When she finished, he started his turn with "Yeah, but..."

Later, Kate started to nod in response to Jeff's comment but then stopped abruptly, indicating she thought she agreed but now was not sure. When she gave no indication of agreement at the end of his utterance, he prompted her with "Right?" He seemed to ask for explicit feedback because she stopped nodding in the middle of his utterance. Forecasting negative responses was just one way that participants seemed to use the visual channel to express and handle disagreement. Others will be discussed in the following examples.

Obviously it is impossible to use head gestures and expressions to forecast responses on the telephone. As a result, participants are unable to read each others' gestures and adjust their utterances in midcourse. Of course, addressees may recognize that their reactions are not being forecast and therefore explicitly express their reactions verbally. But doing so requires more effort, and thus people may be more inclined to let subtle problems pass. In particular, participants may prefer not to express disagreement verbally that might have been reflected on their faces. The speaker may therefore be unaware of a potential problem and cannot take steps to work out the disagreement.

3.4 Enhancing verbal descriptions with gestures

We also observed a variety of cases in which DVC participants made nonarbitrary gestures that emphasized their points. For example, Kate made a succession of gestures during her conference with Jeff. She said, "It really helps me when I draw little diagrams (makes a drawing gesture) just to make me think of how things (unintelligible) (interlocking her fingers, as shown in Fig. 1). There's so many functions now, the diagrams get all (flicked wrists back and forth showing a scattered feeling), get messy really quickly..." We cannot know whether Jeff understood the words we could not decipher, but her gesture indicates that she thinks the diagrams help her see how things *fit together*. Finally, she uses the "scattered" gesture to finish her thought and then follows it up with words. All these gestures convey shades of meaning that enhance Jeff's understanding.

In many cases, the gestures appeared to be made unconsciously, sometimes outside the view of the camera or when the other person was not looking. Many people gesture while talking on the phone, apparently because it helps them express themselves verbally. As a result, when people cannot see each other (as when on the phone), they may not express verbally the subtleties conveyed through their inadvertent gestures.

Fig. 1. Gesturing accompanying talking: a sequence of two images in time shows Kate (upper window) making a gesture to indicate *fit together*

3.5 Conveying purely nonverbal information

Not only did DVC participants use gestures to forecast their reactions and to emphasize their points, they occasionally responded solely with gestures, such as shaking or nodding their heads, shrugging, smiling, looking confused, or giving a meaningful gesture. For example, in the five-way DVC, Jack was frustrated about a decision, and asked "What does that benefit (this project)?" He then made a "zero" gesture with his hand and without saying any more. In the two-way DVC, Kate and Jeff finished discussing a problem that they were not in a position to resolve themselves. They looked at each other and made facial expressions that expressed "Oh well." Jeff shrugged and raised his hands, again as if to say, "such is life." They then moved on to the next topic. Of course they could have expressed their sentiments verbally, but this interaction highlights the ease and subtlety of interaction that video allows. It also illustrates that, in contrast to the predominantly serial nature of audio interaction, video supports concurrent interaction. Through their simultaneous gestures, they were able to realize that they both reached the same conclusion at the same time.

In another example of using visual information, Jeff noticed that another person, Ted, was walking behind Craig and Dave as they were discussing a technical matter. Ted happened to be knowledgeable about the matter, so Jeff suggested asking him to join the conversation, which he did. Clearly, it would be impossible for a phone conference participant to draw someone at a remote site into the conversation; only the person on that end could do so.

The participants could not convey information purely nonverbally over the phone. One interesting incident occurred in the four-way phone conference. During this call, two of the participants, Jack and Kate, were in the same office sharing a speaker phone, and so they could see each other. At one point, Jeff asked Jack, "I forget, how big of a pain is it to add new built-ins, Jack?" After a 3-s pause Kate observed, "He doesn't look too happy," and Dave burst out with a laugh. Had Kate not been able to see Jack, the pause would have indicated only that he was considering the answer; Jack's spontaneous unhappy expression would not have been communicated.

3.6 Expressing attitudes in posture and facial expression

The previous section described instances when informational content was conveyed visually. We also saw many instances in the DVCs when a person's *attitude* about verbal content was conveyed through posture and facial expression. The participants used facial expressions to indicate skepticism, surprise, amusement, confusion, conviction and so on. For example, at one point in the five-way DVC, Jack gave a treatise on an issue as he leaned forward, moved his torso around and gestured with his arms. There could be no question about the strength of his conviction.

Later in this conference, Jeff told the group that he had written a software utility they could use. They expressed interest, but then Craig teased Jeff, "As usual, no documentation." Jeff

Fig. 2. Visually demonstrating humor: Craig (upper left video window) throws head back when others smile, showing appreciation of humorous response

smiled and said, "It's not even done yet!" Craig threw his head back while smiling broadly, as shown in Fig. 2. Jeff's words could be construed as defensive, but the smiles and Craig's response made it clear to everyone that the conversation was in fun. In contrast, in the three-way phone conversation, Jeff teased Craig about how his wife would react when she learned he was planning to spend 3 straight weeks on business trips. He got a minimal response that did not acknowledge the tease, so he exaggerated it. Again, he got a noncommittal response, so he explicitly asked Craig to address the tease. Craig did, but without revealing whether he found the whole topic amusing. Had Jim been able to see Craig, he would have been better able to interpret the response and adjust if, in fact, he had hit a sore spot.

It was particularly interesting to see how participants used visual cues to convey disagreement. In many cases, participants looked away from a speaker when they disagreed with what that person was saying, sometimes returning their gaze as soon as they agreed with the speaker or when the topic changed. In other cases, they responded in understated terms, but looked down and sat back in their chairs while doing so. Previous research shows that people prefer to use unspoken cues to handle topics that raise politeness issues because it enables them to handle potentially threatening situations more gracefully and effectively (Brown and Levinson 1978; Isaacs and Clark; 1990). Over the phone, either the disagreement or misunderstanding is never communicated or the addressee must raise it explicitly, which can make it clumsy to resolve.

Of course, losing the shades of meaning conveyed in expressions and body position does not often cause dramatic effects, although there are cases when it would be critical to realize someone is not agreeing or that a comment is intended to be humorous. Our basic argument is that in the course of a conversation, or series of conversations, seeing each other's facial expressions, gestures, and posture generally increases the

participants' level of mutual understanding without requiring extra effort. Although any single instance of conveying these cues is expendable, their aggregation over time makes a substantial difference in the rapport and kind of interactions that occur between colleagues.

3.7 Managing pauses

Finally, the visual channel was particularly effective for interpreting the meaning of pauses, which can be helpful in determining someone's intention. The participants frequently interpreted pauses as indicating a lack of understanding and responded by elaborating further. However, we observed instances where the video indicated other meanings for a pause. For example, in the two-way conference, Kate responded to a question by looking to her left and consulting her notes for 13 s. Meanwhile, Jeff waited without trying to clarify his question. At another point, Jeff agreed to do something, and then scribbled a note to himself for the next 12 s. Kate looked up, saw what he was doing and waited until he had finished.

The video also made it easier to manage extended pauses, which generally must be explained in phone conversations. In one dramatic example during the five-way DVC, the two Billerica participants spent more than 2 min looking for an electronic mail message while the others waited. There were extremely long pauses, punctuated by the other three teasing the two in Billerica and having a casual conversation among themselves. The Mountain View participants were able to monitor the other two members' progress and adjust their expectations accordingly.

There were certainly instances of nonproblematic pauses during the phone conference as well. In fact, one lasted as long as 28 s. However, on the whole they were more likely to be explained explicitly. At one point in a phone conversation, Dave said "I'm trying to look down things that are open bugs," meaning that he was consulting a list. For the next 7 min, his participation in the conversation was minimal, until he said "I can't find anything else in here."

3.8 Design implications of adding video

Our results clearly show that even with its mediocre quality, the low-bandwidth video used in our prototype provided a great deal of information that participants used to enhance their interactions relative to phone conversations. People have extensive experience interpreting small changes in expressions, gestures, and body position and adapting their responses. The video channel enabled participants to take advantage of those cues. Our users appeared quite adept at transferring these skills from face-to-face interactions to a video-based link. Simply put, the video interactions were markedly richer, subtler, and easier than the telephone interactions.

One implication of this finding is that, relative to the phone, video should be most helpful in situations in which a rich set of interaction skills are most in demand. Our data suggest that one such case is the resolution of conflicts. Cultural norms tend to discourage people from handling disagreements directly, requiring them to rely more on subtle unspoken cues to interpret person's attitude. Through video, speakers may notice addressees' unconscious expressions or shifts in posture, and adjust their utterances in midstream to head off misinterpretations. This finding suggests that, relative to audio only, video would also be of use for handling other highly interactive situations when nonverbal cues are most helpful, such as negotiating or creating rapport. Finally, video should be more effective than the phone for people who are working together from different locations over a long period of time. If remote collaborators can communicate richer information more easily, they are likely to have fewer misunderstandings and more effective interactions. Of course, it would be better still to carry out such activities face-to-face, but these are at least a few areas where video and audio offer an advantage over audio alone.

It is important to note that although these subtle cues arrive through the visual channel, participants often use the audio channel to respond to the information. For example, after *seeing* someone show doubt, the participants in our study often *verbally* explained more fully, asked about the other person's concern, etc. Notice, also, that much of the speaker's adaptation depends on tightly integrated verbal exchanges. Previous studies show that small delays in the audio can seriously disrupt the participants' ability to reach mutual understanding and reduce their satisfaction with the conversation (Krauss and Bricker 1967; Tang and Isaacs 1993). This presents a design trade-off, because synchronizing video with audio is typically accomplished by delaying the audio until the more computationally-intensive video is processed. However, delaying the audio reduces the participants' ability to make use of the information in the video. In effect, delaying audio to provide synchronized video and audio generates a rich set of visual information, but people cannot effectively respond to it because of the delay. We have found that users of such a system feel far more frustration about this delay than they do about a lack of synchronization (Tang and Isaacs 1993).

In our DVC prototype, we transmitted the audio as fast as possible, without attempting to preserve synchrony with the video. One-way audio delays ranged from 0.32 to 0.44 s, while video arrived noticeably later. We found that, although the participants found it slightly disturbing when the video did not match the audio, they still had well-timed interactions that were far richer than those we have observed among people using a commercial video conferencing system, which delayed the audio by about 0.57 s (one-way) to synchronize with video (Tang and Isaacs 1993). In fact, one group who was using this audio-delayed commercial system decided to turn off the audio and use a half-duplex speaker phone connection instead, demonstrating their strong preference for instantaneous audio over synchronized audio and video.

It was somewhat surprising that the participants accomplished rich interactions using the DVC prototype with audio delays as long as 0.44 s. Still, our experience is consistent with a previous study that showed minimal detrimental effects of 0.3-s audio delays (one way) compared to 0.9-s delays (Krauss and Bricker 1967). We note that Wolf (1982) found that partici-

pants who interacted with a 0.420-s one-way audio delay rated the audio and interaction quality significantly lower than those who experienced 0.167-s delays. However, that study reported only the participants' *ratings* of audio quality and simultaneous speech rather than measuring *actual* audio problems and overlapping speech. Our experience concurs with Wolf's findings because our participants did notice and complain about the 0.32–0.44-s audio delays. Nonetheless, we found that they were able to compensate effectively for audio delays within that range.

4 Limitations of video

Despite the many advantages of having a video-and-audio channel rather than just audio, a comparison of the DVCs with face-to-face interactions revealed aspects of interactions that could not be accomplished through our DVC prototype, and in some cases, video in general. Interacting remotely through video makes it difficult or impossible for participants to manage turn-taking, control the floor through body position and eye gaze, notice motion through peripheral vision, have side conversations, point at things in each other's space, or manipulate real-world objects. Of course, some of these limitations may be overcome by providing additional capabilities, and we discuss these possibilities as design implications. However, some of these same drawbacks also create specific advantages. In particular, video interactions may not require as much social protocol and, in the case of DVC, people can spontaneously draw upon resources in their own environments as the conversation unfolds.

4.1 Managing turn taking

The participant's turn-taking patterns during face-to-face and DVC meetings were significantly different. In the five-way interactions, an analysis of variance showed that the participants exchanged more turns/min when talking face to face (4.2) than they did in DVC conversations (2.3) $[F(1,314) = 43.28, P < 0.0001]$, and their turns were shorter in duration (2.7 s/turn 4.5 s/turn) $[F(1,250) = 7.13, P < 0.008]$. In the two-way meetings, the participants again exchanged more turns/min face to face (7.8) than in a DVC (6.6) $[F(1,76) = 5.14, P < 0.026]$, but there was no difference in the duration of the turns (2.3 s/turn vs. 2.3 s/turn). Figure 3 graphs the mean number of turns/min and the mean duration for each condition. In this analysis, a turn length was defined as when a person started speaking to either when the speaker finished (e.g., denoted by a pause) or when someone else started speaking.

Exchanging shorter turns more frequently indicates that in the face-to-face encounters, the participants were able to coordinate their utterances more tightly, which, research has shown, enhances their ability to reach mutual understanding (Clark and Schaefer 1987; Clark and Wilkes-Gibbs 1986; Isaacs and Clark 1987). It is unclear why the participants in the two-way DVC and face-to-face meetings did not differ in their turn duration even though in the face-to-face meetings

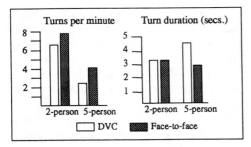

Fig. 3. Average number of turns/min and duration of turns/s during desktop video conferences (DVCs) versus face-to-face interactions in two- and five-person conversations

they exchanged turns more rapidly. Apparently, there was more silence between turns during the DVCs. Nonetheless, in both cases, the turn rate indicates that the participants coordinated their turn-taking more tightly. This finding indicates that while video improves the ability to handle conflict and confidential issues compared with the phone, face-to-face interactions are even better than video conferences for handling those types of sensitive issues.

It should be noted that this turn-taking finding is inconsistent with similar research. Sellen (1992) did not find a significant difference in number of turns when comparing two video conditions to face-to-face interactions. It seems plausible that the difference stems from the fact that her video setup used analog audio and video over short distances, which resulted in nearly no transmission delay. This would suggest that difficulties in managing turn taking are primarily a result of the audio delay and not an inherent limitation of video. However, Krauss and Bricker (1967) varied the audio transmission delay for an audio-only task, and they showed a difference in turn length only when the delay lasted 0.9 s, but not when there was no delay or a 0.3-s delay. They also found no difference in turn frequency in any condition. The difference in our findings may also be caused by our different measurement of "turns." Sellen (1992) did not count as turns short "backchannels" that lasted less than 1.5 s, whereas we used a cruder definition of turns that included any utterance that lasted at least 0.5 s. Perhaps the participants in our study used more backchannels when they were face-to-face than when they were talking over the DVC, which could account for the discrepancy in our findings.

4.2 Controlling the floor

In face-to-face interactions, we saw many instances of people using their eye gaze to indicate whom they were addressing and to suggest a next speaker (Sacks et al. 1974). In many instances when more than one person started speaking at the same time, the next speaker was determined by the eye gaze of the previous speaker. We even saw one interesting example of using a gesture to "reserve" a conversational turn. During a particularly active stretch of conversation, Jack and Jeff started speaking at the same time. As he spoke, Jeff reached over and touched Kate's document to make a point about it. He lost the turn, but he kept his finger on the document, essentially

reserving his right to the next turn, which in fact he took. Others have also noted the use of gestures to *prevent* others from taking a turn (Duncan 1972).

In contrast, in our desktop DVC prototype, it was impossible to direct attention toward a specific person in a multiway conference. Everyone sees a speaker through the same camera, so if the others are looking at the speakers video image, it appears to them that the speaker is looking at all of them. Not surprisingly, the participants of the DVCs did not seem to use body or eye position to control the floor. [However, see (Sellen 1992) for one way to overcome this obstacle.]

Instead, people tended to use names to address each other. For instance, at one point, Jack and Craig started talking at the same time and Jack got the turn. As Jack started speaking, Jeff overlapped with, "I didn't hear you, Craig" in an attempt to direct the next turn toward Craig. However, Jack held on to the turn, and after he finished speaking Jeff again explicitly asked Craig to take the next turn. Had they been face-to-face, Jeff might have used gestures to help Craig win the previous turn from Jack.

4.3 Using peripheral cues

We observed many instances during face-to-face meetings in which the participants used their peripheral vision to notice a change in each other's body, head, or eye position and then responded by coordinating their own activity. In our DVC, the video window on the screen was a small part of a participant's visual field. A participant who was not looking at or near that window was much less likely to notice motion in the window. Even large-scale motion on the other end, such as moving an arm to the face, translated into a small change in the remote participants' field of view and could easily be missed if that person was not looking near the video window. Changes in eye gaze were particularly unlikely to be noticed through peripheral vision.

For example, during a 30 s sequence of Jeff and Kate's face-to-face interaction, Jeff was talking and Kate was looking down as she took notes. Three times, Jeff looked up at Kate for confirmation, and each time, she nodded or replied "Yeah," without looking up or interrupting her writing. She was obviously able to sense his head position and eye gaze and recognize that he was seeking a response.

We did not see this kind of subtle coordination based on peripheral cues in DVCs. If anything, we saw many instances when the participants just missed each other's glances. [See (Heath and Luff 1991) for a discussion of similar problems.] In one typical example, Jeff glanced at Kate as he finished speaking, but looked away too soon to catch Kate's nod in response. At another point, Jeff missed Kate's smile, so he responded to her comment seriously.

4.4 Having side conversations

Side conversations were impossible with the DVC prototype because people could not address particular participants and because everyone shared a single audio channel. The closest we observed was two participants using the channel to discuss topics of interest to themselves while the others waited for the conversation to become more general.

In the five-way face-to-face meeting, the conversation occasionally broke into two parallel conversations and then seamlessly flowed back to a single conversation. For example, at one point Jack made a joke and everyone but Kate laughed. While the others continued with the conversation, Kate looked at Jack and asked him to repeat what he said, which he did. She commented on his joke and then they both refocused on the group's conversation. This side conversation was accomplished because the participants could "open" a second audio channel and because the visual cues enabled everyone to understand who was participating in which conversation when.

4.5 Pointing

If a participant in our DVC pointed to one of the video images on the screen, it was difficult for the others to use spatial position to figure out who was being addressed. They could use only the verbal context to make an educated guess. Pointing could be used, however, to focus attention on certain parts of their own environments.

We saw few instances of pointing in either the two-way or five-way DVC, even to indicate items in their own space. We saw one instance when Jeff pointed to his image of the two people in Billerica, but from the other participants' perspective, he simply appeared to be pointing to his screen. It was difficult for them to determine exactly which image he was indicating.

In contrast, we saw many instances of pointing during both face-to-face meetings. During the five-way meeting, the participants repeatedly pointed to places in their own documents and at times reached over to each other's documents to point out a particular line or diagram. In the two-way meeting, Kate pushed part of the document between her and Jeff, and they repeatedly pointed to various parts of it as they talked about it. We did see instances of this kind of pointing when the pariticipants used the Show Me shared drawing tool, but it was, of course, accomplished through a cursor on the shared window rather than over the video channel.

4.6 Manipulating real-world objects

The participants in our study never needed to observe, manipulate, or build an object jointly, but these activities present such an obvious limitation to remote video conferencing that we point it out. However, during both the two-way and five-way face-to-face interactions, the participants did review hard copy documents. By observing their joint behavior with the documents, we noticed at least two limitations of video in this regard: (1) it does not allow participants to build on each other's work, and (2) it does not allow them to "look over each other's shoulders" to gain another perspective.

We saw instances of both of these during face-to-face interactions, whereas no equivalent behavior was possible using our DVC, again unless they used the shared drawing tool. For example, when Kate pushed the document to the middle of the table, she and Jeff wrote and drew on it, at times building on each other's sketches or comments. They also continued to write on their own pads, moving easily between their own space and the shared space. In another simple example from the five-way meeting, Kate leaned over to look at Jack's copy of the document to see what he was looking at.

4.7 Advantages of video over face-to-face meetings

In addition to these limitations, we saw evidence of advantages of DVC over face-to-face meetings. First, we found, as have others, that video conferencing distanced our participants because they could not make eye contact or use peripheral cues to pick up on subtleties (Fish et al. 1990; Gale 1990; Mantei et al. 1991). As a result, there seems to be less pressure to carry out standard social practices that may make interactions "less efficient" (Fish et al. 1990). When someone physically drops by, we are often expected to ask how they are and have an introductory social conversation before getting down to business (Whittaker et. al. 1994). Kraut et. al. (1990) reported that 20% of the face-to-face office conversations they observed consisted of "social, non-task-oriented conversation," whereas only 5% of video conference conversations were social. This type of social interaction serves an important purpose, but it can be seen as reducing short-term efficiency. At least in those interactions when social chit-chat is less critical, people may choose to use DVC to help focus on the work at hand.

We see an interesting parallel with electronic mail, which people use, when, among other reasons, they want to handle certain factual or practical matters, perhaps without "bothering" with accompanying social interaction. Using e-mail does not mean people do not also use other communication techniques to handle more social or interactional matters. It merely provides another option when textual content is most important.

Participants in DVCs are normally in their own offices, with many resources at their disposal. All participants can spontaneously bring into the discussion both online and offline materials if they become relevant. In addition, if one person is looking for something or handles an interruption (a phone call, a person dropping by, or even an incoming e-mail message), the other members can draw on their own private space to use the time productively. As a result, meetings can and were used at times more like loose connections akin to sharing an office. In some cases, individual meetings smoothly shifted between focused conversations and loose, intermittent interactions. Users of other DVC systems have also been reported to open up video connections between offices to create virtual shared offices, while at other times they used the connection for focused interactions (Bly et al. 1992; Fish et al. 1992).

This kind of interaction may be inappropriate at times, and in fact members of the team we observed said they were sometimes annoyed when one member stopped participating as he read or answered an incoming e-mail message. But this type of "shared space" can be a useful environment for certain types of activities.

4.8 Design implications from the limitations of video

Comparing our DVC system with face-to-face meetings highlighted the possible shortcomings of video for remote collaboration. In particular, participants found it difficult to manage turn taking, control the floor, notice small movements through peripheral vision, have side conversations, point at things in each other's space, and manipulate real-world objects. One approach to compensating for these limitations is to use electronic means to directly substitute for some of the interactional mechanisms observed in face-to-face behavior. For example, one might provide an explicit visual mechanism for controlling the floor in group interactions or the ability to open a separate channel for side conversations.

One potential danger of such an approach is that it may force people to take explicit actions to carry out behaviors that are normally negotiated unconsciously. For example, requiring users to indicate explicitly when they want the next turn eliminates their ability to manage the politeness issues around floor control. Doing so may also eliminate cues about the degree of spontaneity and enthusiasm in a participants' desire to contribute. In addition, artificial behaviors may be interpreted differently by other participants. For instance, a person who would have been seen as enthusiastic might be perceived as dominating if that person uses an explicit mechanism rather than a socially negotiated one to manage floor control.

In general, we recommend thinking in terms of enabling a wider range of collaborative tasks by broadening the shared space among participants. This can be done by integrating other collaborative tools with a video-based system. Such a system may entail providing one or more mechanisms to enable particular collaborative activities (e.g., pointing, noticing motion), but it should also expand the participants' ability to handle collaboration issues through the standard social negotiation process.

The integration of the Show Me shared drawing program into the DVC prototype is an example of such an approach. Previous studies have shown that the ability to draw shared diagrams and pictures is an important aspect of many interactions (Olson and Bly 1991; Tang and Minneman 1991; Tang 1991b). We have mentioned some ways in which Show Me enabled a wider range of collaborative activities not available through video. It did so by increasing the nature of the shared space among the participants. Not only could participants bring any document or image from their workstations into discussion, but they could also use the cursor to point to parts of the image, and they could track each other's attention through their cursors. We did not build in protocols to prevent people from erasing each other's work, relying instead on the audio connection and social negotiation for people to manage its usage. Our intention was to enable a new type of activity (shared drawing), which involved building technology to support certain behaviors (showing certain objects, pointing, tracking attention) as well as relying on existing collaborative behaviors to handle many of the social interaction issues.

However, the tool was not as successful as we would have liked because it allowed the sharing of only one bitmap image at a time. If two people wanted to edit a document jointly, they could not work on the actual document. One person would have to make changes and then transmit a bitmap of the updates. To move on to another page, one person had to page the actual document and then transmit the image of the next page. The essential problem was that the shared space was not as broad as we would have liked, and that limitation did appear to reduce the usefulness of the tool.

Our observations lead us to conclude that tools designed to supplement a video conferencing system should:

− Broaden users' shared environment
− Enable behaviors associated with particular collaborative tasks
− Take advantage of users' existing collaboration skills
− Not require conscious actions for behaviors that are normally done unconsciously

We should not try to use a video conferencing system to carry out tasks that require manipulating objects, pointing, and other behaviors if they are not supported in the design of the system. For example, it would be unwise to attempt to use a simple video conference system to have a group video meeting about a controversial topic, expecting everyone to feel they had a chance to contribute. This situation depends too heavily on the ability to achieve smooth floor control among many people (and perhaps to have side conversations), which are weaknesses of a simple audio-video link. Similarly, it may be possible to use video to teach someone how to assemble a machine, but it will not be as effective as a face-to-face demonstration unless both the participants can point to and manipulate the objects together.

We hope that we have drawn attention to some limitations so that we may have more realistic expectations of video systems that do not specifically address them, and so that we may focus our development efforts on tools that help compensate for these drawbacks. In addition, our study identified some specific ways in which video affects the *processes* rather than the *products* of interaction compared to audio only and face-to-face. It remains to be shown if and how these *process* effects accumulate over time into *productivity* or *product quality* effects. More research is needed to explore these longitudinal effects of video support for remote collaboration.

Acknowledgements. We acknowledge the Digital Integrated Media Environment and the Conferencing and Collaboration Groups in Sun Microsystems Laboratories, Inc. for developing and studying the DVC prototype described in this paper. We also thank Jonathan Grudin for his helpful comments on an earlier draft. We especially thank the members of the team we observed for their cooperation.

References

Bly SA, Harrison SR, Irwin S (1993) Media spaces: bringing people together in a video, audio, and computing environment. Commun ACM 36:28–45

Brown P, Levinson S (1978) Universals in language usage: politeness phenomena. In: Goody E (ed) Questions and politeness, Cambridge University Press, Cambrdige, pp 56–311 University Press, 1978.

Chapanis A, Ochsman RB, Parrish RN, Weeks GD (1972) Studies in interactive communication: I. The effects of four communication modes on the behavior of teams during cooperative problem-solving. Human Factors 14:487–509

Clark HH, Wilkes-Gibbs D (1986) Referring as a collaborative process. Cognition 22:1–39

Clark HH, Schaefer EF (1987) Collaborating on contributions to conversations. Language and cognitive processes 2:19–41

Duncan S (1972) Some signals and rules for taking speaking turns in conversation. J Personality Soc Psychol 23:283–292

Fish RS, Kraut RE, Chalfonte BL (1990) The videowindows system in informal communications. Proceedings of the Conference on Computer-Supported Cooperative Work, Los Angeles, Calif., pp 1–11

Fish RS, Kraut RE, Root RW (1992) Evaluating video as a technology for informal communication. Proceedings of CHI '92 Human Factors in Computing Systems, Monterey, Calif., pp 37–48

Francik E, Ehrlich Rudman S, Cooper D, Levine S (1991) Putting innovation to work: adoption strategies for multimedia communication systems. Commun ACM 34:53–63

Gale S (1990) Human aspects of interactive multimedia communication. Interacting with Computers 2:175–189

Grudin J (1988) Why CSCW applications fail: problems pn the design and evaluation of organizational interfaces. Proceedings of the Conference on Computer-Supported Cooperative Work, Portland, Ore., pp 85–93

Heath C, Luff P (1991) Disembodied conduct: communication through video in a multimedia environment. Proceedings of the CHI '91 Conference on Human Factors in Computing Systems, New Orleans, La., pp 99–103

Isaacs EA, Clark HH (1987) References in conversation between experts and novices. Journal of Experimental Psychology: General 116:26–37

Isaacs EA, Clark HH (1990) Ostensible invitations. Language in society 19:493–509

Krauss RM, Bricker PD (1967) Effects of transmission delay and access delay on the efficiency of verbal communication. J Acoustic Soc Am 41:286–292

Kraut RE, Fish RS, Root RW, Chalfonte BL (1990), Informal communication in organizations: form, function and technology. In: Oshkamp S, Spacapan S (eds) People's Reactions to Technology. Sage Publications, Newbury Park, pp 145–199

Mantei MM, Baecker RM, Sellen, AJ, Buxton, WAS, Milligan T (1991) Experiences in the use of a media space. Proceedings of the CHI '91 Conference on Human Factors in Computing Systems, New Orleans, La., pp 203–208

Ochsman RB, Chapanis A (1974), The effects of 10 communication modes on the behavior of teams during co-operative problem-solving. Int J Man-Machine Studies, 6:579–619

Olson MH, Bly SA (1991) The Portland experience: a report on a distributed research group. Int J Man-Machine Systems 34:211–228. Reprinted in: Greenberg S (ed) Computer-supported Cooperative Work and Groupware, Academic Press, London, pp 81–98

Pearl A (1992) System support for integrated desktop video conferencing. Sun Microsystems Laboratories, Inc. Technical Report, TR-92-4

Root RW (1988) Design of a multimedia vehicle for social browsing. Proceedings of the Conference on Computer-Supported Cooperative Work, Portland, Ore., pp 25–38

Sacks H, Schegloff E, Jefferson G (1974) A simplest systematics for the organization of turn-taking for conversation. Language 50:696–735

Sellen AJ (1992) Speech patterns in video-mediated conversations. Proceedings of CHI '92 Human Factors in Computing Systems, Monterey, Calif., pp 49–59

Short J, Williams E, Christie B (1976) The social psychology of telecommunications. John Wiley, London

Tang JC (1991a) Involving social scientists in the design of new technology. In: Karat J (ed) Taking software design seriously: practical techniques for human-computer interaction. Academic Press, Boston, pp 115–126

Tang JC (1991b) Findings from observational studies of collaborative work. Int J Man-Machine Studies 34:143–160. Reprinted in: Greenberg S (ed) Computer-supported Cooperative Work and Groupware, Academic Press, London, pp 11–28

Tang JC, Isaacs EA (1993) Why do users like video? Studies of multimedia-supported collaboration. CSCW: Int J 1:163–196

Tang JC, Minneman SL (1991) VideoDraw: a video interface for collaborative drawing, ACM Trans Inform Syst 9:170–184

Tatar D (1989) Using video-based observation to shape the design of a new technology. SIGCHI Bulletin 21:108–111

Whittaker S, Frohlich D, Daly-Jones O, Informal workplace communication: What is it like and how might we support it?, Proceedings of the CHI '94 Conference on Human Factors in Computing Systems, Boston, Mass., pp 131–137

Williams E (1977) Experimental comparisons of face-to-face and mediated communication: a review. Psychol Bulletin 84:963–976

Wolf CG (1982) Video conferencing: delay and transmission considerations. In: Parker LA, Olgren CH (eds) Teleconferencing and electronic communications: applications, technologies and human factors, University of Wisconsin Extension Center for Interactive Programs, Madison, Wisconsin, pp 184–188

Wulfman CE, Isaacs EA, Webber BL, Fagan LM (1988) Integration discontinuity:rfacingusersandsystems.ProceedingsofArchitectures for Intelligent Interfaces: Elements and Prototypes, Monterey, Calif., pp 57–68

Dr. ELLEN ISAACS works at Sun-Soft in the Human Interface Engineering group. She spends part of her time working with the Collaborative Computing Group doing research on multimedia-supported collaborative work, and the rest of her time designing user interfaces for a variety of collaborative and single-user applications. Before coming to Sun, she worked at a Stanford University lab on a project to develop a speech interface to a medical expert system. She received her PhD in cognitive psychology from Stanford, where she studied language use and collaboration in conversation, and her bachelors from Brown Unversity, where she studied psychology and semiotics.

Dr. JOHN TANG works in the Collaborative Computing Group, an advanced development group within the Human Interface Engineering department at SunSoft, Inc. He studies collaborative work activity in order to guide the design and development of multimedia collaborative systems. Prior to joining Sun, John worked at Xerox PARC developing and studying several shared drawing prototype tools. His doctoral research at Stanford University was on studying group design activity. He received his degrees from Stanford University in the Mechanical Engineering Department, Design Division.

vic: A Flexible Framework for Packet Video

Steven McCanne
University of California, Berkeley
and Lawrence Berkeley Laboratory
mccanne@ee.lbl.gov

Van Jacobson
Network Research Group
Lawrence Berkeley Laboratory
van@ee.lbl.gov

ABSTRACT

The deployment of IP Multicast has fostered the development of a suite of applications, collectively known as the MBone tools, for real-time multimedia conferencing over the Internet. Two of these tools — *nv* from Xerox PARC and *ivs* from INRIA — provide video transmission using software-based codecs. We describe a new video tool, *vic*, that extends the groundbreaking work of nv and ivs with a more flexible system architecture. This flexibility is characterized by network layer independence, support for hardware-based codecs, a conference coordination model, an extensible user interface, and support for diverse compression algorithms. We also propose a novel compression scheme called "Intra-H.261". Created as a hybrid of the nv and ivs codecs, Intra-H.261 provides a factor of 2-3 improvement in compression gain over the nv encoder (6 dB of PSNR) as well as a substantial improvement in run-time performance over the ivs H.261 coder.

KEYWORDS

Conferencing protocols; digital video; image and video compression and processing; multicasting; networking and communication.

1 INTRODUCTION

Over the past few years, a collaborative effort in the network research community has produced a suite of tools for multimedia conferencing over the Internet [16, 25, 26, 39, 42]. The driving force behind these tools is Deering's IP Multicast [11], a technology which extends the traditional IP routing model for efficient multipoint packet delivery. The incremental deployment of IP Multicast has been realized by building a (temporary) virtual multicast network on top of the existing Internet, which Casner has dubbed the Multicast Backbone, or MBone [6].

Multimedia '95, San Francisco, CA USA
0-89791-751-0/95/11

The first applications to provide video over the MBone were the Xerox PARC Network Video tool, *nv*, and the INRIA Video Conferencing System, *ivs*. While these two systems share the goal of supporting low bit-rate multicast video over the Internet, their approaches are markedly different. Ivs is an integrated audio/video conferencing system that relies exclusively on H.261 [45] for video compression. By adopting a standardized algorithm, ivs can interoperate with a large installed base of H.320 video codecs as an H.320-compliant bit stream is easily generated from an H.261 packet stream by introducing H.221 framing in software [20].

In contrast, nv is a "video-only" application that utilizes a custom coding scheme tailored specifically for the Internet and targeted for efficient software implementation [17]. Because of its low computational complexity, the nv codec can run much faster than an H.261 codec. Even though H.261 has better compression performance than nv, nv is more often used by the MBone community because of its better run-time performance.

Inevitably, in pioneering work such as nv and ivs, restrictions must be imposed on the design process to facilitate experimentation. For example, the ivs design assumes video is represented as 4:1:1-decimated CCIR-601 YUV, while nv assumes 4:2:2 decimation. Extending nv to support H.261 or ivs to support nv-style compression would require non-trivial design changes. Also, since both systems are based on software compression, their video capture models were designed around uncompressed video. Extending either to support hardware-based compression engines would be relatively difficult.

In this paper, we describe a third model for a packet video application, realized in the UCB/LBL video conferencing tool, *vic*. Vic builds upon the lessons learned from ivs and nv by focusing on flexibility. It is an extensible, object-oriented, application framework that supports

- multiple network abstractions,

- hardware-based codecs,

- a conference coordination model,

- an extensible user interface, and

- diverse video compression algorithms.

Moreover, we have combined Frederick's insights from the nv codec with the compression advantages and standards compliance of H.261 in a novel scheme which we call *Intra-H.261*. Intra-H.261 gives significant gain in compression performance compared to nv and substantial improvement in both run-time performance and packet-loss tolerance compared to ivs.

Vic was originally conceived as an application to demonstrate the Tenet real-time networking protocols [14] and to simultaneously support the evolving "Lightweight Sessions" architecture [24] in the MBone. It has since driven the evolution of the Real-time Transport Protocol (RTP) [40]. As RTP evolved, we tracked and implemented protocol changes, and fed back implementation experience to the design process. Moreover, our experience implementing the RTP payload specification for H.261 led to an improved scheme based on macroblock-level fragmentation, which resulted in a revised protocol [44]. Finally, the RTP payload specification for JPEG [13] evolved from a vic implementation.

In the next section, we describe the design approach of the MBone tools. We then discuss the essentials of the vic network architecture. The network architecture shapes the software architecture, which is discussed in the following section. Finally, we discuss signal compression issues, deployment and implementation status.

2   COMPOSABLE TOOLS VS. TOOLKITS

A cornerstone of the Unix design philosophy was to avoid supplying a separate application for every possible user task. Instead, simple, one-function "filters" like *grep* and *sort* can be easily and dynamically combined via a "pipe" operator to perform arbitrarily complex tasks. Similarly, we use modular, configurable applications, each specialized to support a particular media, which can be easily composed via a *Conference Bus* to support the variety of conferencing styles needed to support effective human communication. This approach derives from the framework proposed by Ousterhout in [33], where he claims that large systems are easily composed from small tools that are glued together with a simple communication primitive (e.g., the Tk *send* command). We have simply replaced his *send* primitive with a well-defined (and more restrictive) Conference Bus protocol. Restricting the protocol prevents the evolution of sets of tools that rely on the specifics of each other's internal implementations. In addition to vic, our conferencing applications include the Visual Audio Tool (vat) for audio [26], a whiteboard (wb) for shared workspace and slide distribution [25, 15], and the Session Directory (sd) for session creation and advertisement [23].

This "composable tools" approach to networked multimedia contrasts with the more common "toolkit framework" adopted by other multimedia systems [10, 31, 37, 38]. Toolkits provide basic building blocks in the form of a code library with an application programming interface (API) to that library providing high-level abstractions for manipulating multimedia data flows. Each distinct conferencing style requires a different application but the applications are typically simple to write, consisting mostly of API calls with style-dependent glue and control logic.

The toolkit approach emphasizes the programming model and many elegant programming mechanisms have resulted

from toolkit-related research. To simplify the programming model, toolkits usually assume that communication is application independent and offer a generic, least-common-denominator network interface built using traditional transport protocols.

In 1990 Clark and Tennenhouse [8] pointed out that multimedia applications could be simplified and both application and network performance enhanced if the network protocol reflected the application semantics. Their model, Application Level Framing (ALF), is difficult to implement with toolkits (where application semantics are deliberately "factored out") but is the natural way to implement "composable tools". And ALF-based, media-specific tools offer a simple solution to multimedia's biggest problem — high rate, high volume, continuous media data streams. Since the tools are directly involved in processing the multimedia data flows, we can use ALF to tune all the performance-critical multimedia data paths within the application and across the network.

In addition to performance, flexibility is gained by composing simple tools rather than using a monolithic application built on top of some API. Since each tool deals directly with its media stream and sends only low-rate reports like "X has started/stopped sending" on the Conference Bus, the coordination agent necessary to implement a particular conferencing scenario can be written in a simple interpreted language like *Tcl* [34]. This allows the most volatile part of the conferencing problem, the piece that melds audio, video, etc., into a coordinated unit that meets particular human needs and expectations, to be simple and easy to evolve. It also ensures that the coordination agents are designed orthogonal to the media agents, enforcing a mechanism/policy separation: media tools implement the mechanism by which coordination tools impose the policy structure appropriate for some particular conferencing scenario, e.g., open meeting, moderated meeting, class, seminar, etc.

3   NETWORK ARCHITECTURE

While the freedom to explore the communications protocol design space fosters innovation, it precludes interoperability. Since the MBone was created to study multicast scaling issues, interoperability is especially important. Multicast use at an interesting scale requires that a large group of people spread over a large geographic region have some reason to send and receive data from the group. One good way to achieve this is to develop interoperable applications that encourage widespread use.

3.1   RTP

To promote such interoperability, the Audio/Video Transport Working group of the Internet Engineering Task Force (IETF) has developed RTP as an application level protocol for multimedia transport. The goal is to provide a very thin transport layer without overly restricting the application designer. The protocol specification itself states that "RTP is intended to be malleable to provide the information required by a particular application and will often be integrated into the application processing rather than being implemented as a separate layer." In the ALF spirit, the semantics of sev-

RTP		
UDP	RMTP	AAL5
IP	RTIP	ATM

Figure 1: RTP and the Protocol Stack

eral of the fields in the RTP header are deferred to an "RTP Profile" document, which defines the semantics according to the given application. For example, the RTP header contains a generic "marker" bit that in an audio packet indicates the start of a talk spurt but in a video packet indicates the end of a frame. The interpretation of fields can be further refined by the "Payload Format Specification". For example, an audio payload might define the RTP timestamp as a audio sample counter while the MPEG/RTP specification [22] defines it as the "Presentation Time Stamp" from the MPEG system specification.

Because of its ALF-like model, RTP is a natural match to the "composable tools" framework and serves as the foundation for vic's network architecture. Since RTP is independent of the underlying network technology, vic can simultaneously support multiple network protocols. Figure 1 illustrates how RTP fits into several protocol stacks. For IP and IP Multicast, RTP is layered over UDP, while in the Tenet protocols, it runs over RMTP/RTIP [2]. Similarly, vic can run directly over an ATM Adaptation Layer. In all these cases, RTP is realized in the application itself.

RTP is divided into two components: the data delivery protocol, and the control protocol, RTCP. The data delivery protocol handles the actual media transport, while RTCP manages control information like sender identification, receiver feedback, and cross-media synchronization. Different media of the same conference-level session are distributed on distinct RTP sessions.

Complete details of the RTP specification are provided in [40]. We briefly mention one feature of the protocol relevant to the rest of the paper. Because media are distributed on independent RTP sessions (and because vic is implemented independently of other multimedia applications), the protocol must provide a mechanism for identifying relationships among media streams (e.g., for audio/video synchronization). Media sources are identified by a 32-bit RTP "source identifier" (SRCID), which is guaranteed to be unique only within a single session. Thus, RTP defines a canonical-name (CNAME) identifier that is globally unique across all sessions. The CNAME is a variable-length, ASCII string that can be algorithmically derived, e.g., from user and host names. RTCP control packets advertise the mapping between a given source's SRCID and variable-length CNAME. Thus, a receiver can group distinct RTP sources via their CNAME into a single, logical entity that represents a given session participant.

In summary, RTP provides a solid, well-defined protocol framework that promotes application interoperability, while its ALF philosophy does not overly restrict the application

design and, in particular, lends itself to efficient implementation.

4 SOFTWARE ARCHITECTURE

The principles of ALF drove more than the vic network architecture; they also determined the overall software architecture. Our central goal was to achieve a flexible software framework which could be easily modified to explore new coding schemes, network models, compression hardware, and conference control abstractions. By basing the design on an objected-oriented ALF framework, we achieved this flexibility without compromising the efficiency of the implementation.

ALF leads to a design where data sources and sinks within the application are highly aware of how data must be represented for network transmission. For example, the software H.261 encoder does not produce a bit stream that is in turn packetized by an RTP agent. Instead, the encoder builds the packet stream fragmented at boundaries that are optimized for the semantics of H.261. In this way, the compressed bit stream can be made more robust to packet loss.

At the macroscopic level, the software architecture is built upon an event-driven model with highly optimized data paths glued together and controlled by a flexible Tcl/Tk [34] framework. A set of basic objects is implemented in C++ and are coordinated via Tcl/Tk. Portions of the C++ object hierarchy mirror a set of object-oriented Tcl commands. C++ base classes permit Tcl to manipulate objects and orchestrate data paths using a uniform interface, while derived subclasses support specific instances of capture devices, display types, decoder modules, etc. This division of low-overhead control functionality implemented in Tcl and performance critical data handling implemented in C++ allows for rapid prototyping without sacrifice of performance. A very similar approach was independently developed in the VuSystem [29].

4.1 Decode Path

Figure 2 roughly illustrates the receive/decode path. The elliptical nodes correspond to C++ base classes in the implementation, while the rectangular nodes represent output devices. A Tcl script is responsible for constructing the data paths and performing out-of-band control that might result from network events or local user interaction. Since Tcl/Tk also contains the user interface, it is easy to present control functionality to the user as a single interface element that might invoke several primitive control functions to implement its functionality.

The data flow through the receive path is indicated by the solid arrows. When a packet arrives from the network, the Network object dispatches it to the Demuxer which implements the bulk of the RTP processing. From there, the packet is demultiplexed to the appropriate Source object, which represents a specific, active transmitter in the multicast session. If no Source object exists for the incoming packet, an upcall into Tcl is made to instantiate a new data path for that source. Once the data path is established, packets flow from the source object to a decoder object. Hardware and soft-

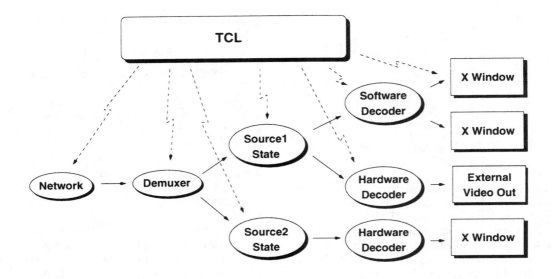

Figure 2: The receive/decode data path.

ware decoding, as well as multiple compression formats, are simultaneously supported via a C++ class hierarchy. When a decoder object decodes a complete frame, it invokes a rendering object to display the frame on the output device, either an X Window or external video output port.

Note that, in line with ALF, packets flow all the way to the decoder object more or less intact. The decoder modules are not isolated from the network issues. In fact, it is exactly these modules that know best what to do when faced with packet loss or reordering. C++ inheritance provides a convenient mechanism for implementing an ALF model without sacrificing software modularity.

While this architecture appears straightforward to implement, in practice the decode path has been one of the most challenging (and most revised) aspects of the design. The core difficulty is managing the combinatorics of all possible configurations. Many input compression formats are supported, and deciding the best way to decode any given stream depends on user input, the capabilities of the available hardware, and the parameters of the video stream. For example, DEC's J300 adaptor supports hardware decompression of 4:2:2-decimated JPEG, either to an X Window or an external output port. The board can be multiplexed between capture and decoding to a window but not between capture and decoding to the external port. Also, if the incoming JPEG stream is 4:1:1 rather than 4:2:2-decimated, the hardware cannot be used at all. Finally, only JPEG-compressed streams can be displayed on the video output port since the system software does not support a direct path for uncompressed video. Many other devices exhibit similar peculiarities.

Coping with all hardware peculiarities requires building a rule set describing legal data paths. Moreover, these rules depend intimately on how the application is being used, and therefore are complicated by user configuration. We have found that the Tcl/C++ combination provides a flexible solution for this problem. By implementing only the bare essentials in C++ and exporting a Tcl interface that allows easy creation, deletion, and configuration of C++ objects, the difficulty in managing the complexity of the data paths is greatly reduced.

4.2   Capture Path

We applied a similar architectural decomposition to the video capture/compression path. As with the decoder objects, encoder objects perform both compression and RTP packetization. For example, the H.261 encoder fragments its bit stream into packets on "macroblock" boundaries to minimize the impact of packet loss.

Different compression schemes require different video input formats. For instance, H.261 requires 4:1:1-decimated CIF format video while the nv encoder requires 4:2:2-decimated video of arbitrary geometry. One implementation approach would be for each capture device to export a common format that is subsequently converted to the format desired by the encoder. Unfortunately, manipulating video data in the uncompressed domain results in a substantial performance penalty, so we have optimized the capture path by supporting each format.

A further performance gain was realized by carrying out the "conditional replenishment" [32] step as early as possible. Most of the compression schemes utilize block-based conditional replenishment, where the input image is divided up into small (e.g., 8x8) blocks and only blocks that change are coded and sent. The send decision for a block depends on only a small (dynamically varying) selection of pixels of that block. Hence, if the send decision is folded in with the capture I/O process, most of the read memory traffic and all of the write memory traffic is avoided when a block is not coded.

4.3   Rendering

Another performance-critical operation is converting video from the YUV pixel representation used by most compression schemes to a format suitable for the output device. Since this rendering operation is performed after the decompression on uncompressed video, it can be a bottleneck and must be carefully implemented. Our profiles of vic match the experiences reported by Patel et al. [35], where image rendering sometimes accounts for 50% or more of the execution time.

Video output is rendered either through an output port on an external video device or to an X window. In the case of an X window, we might need to dither the output for a color-mapped display or simply convert YUV to RGB for a true-color display. Alternatively, HP's X server supports a "YUV visual" designed specifically for video and we can write YUV data directly to the X server. Again, we use a C++ class hierarchy to support all of these modes of operation and special-case the handling of 4:2:2 and 4:1:1-decimated video and scaling operations to maximize performance.

For color-mapped displays, vic supports several modes of dithering that trade off quality for computational efficiency. The default mode is a simple error-diffusion dither carried out in the YUV domain. Like the approach described in [35], we use table lookups for computing the error terms, but we use an improved algorithm for distributing color cells in the YUV color space. The color cells are chosen uniformly throughout the feasible set of colors in the YUV cube, rather than uniformly across the entire cube using saturation to find the closest feasible color. This approach effectively doubles the number of useful colors in the dither. Additionally, we add extra cells in the region of the color space that corresponds to flesh tones for better rendition of faces.

While the error-diffusion dither produces a relatively high quality image, it is computationally expensive. Hence, when performance is critical, a cheap, ordered dither is available. Vic's ordered dither is an optimized version of the ordered dither from nv.

An even cheaper approach is to use direct color quantization. Here, a color gamut is optimized to the statistics of the displayed video and each pixel is quantized to the nearest color in the gamut. While this approach can produce banding artifacts from quantization noise, the quality is reasonable when the color map is chosen appropriately. Vic computes this color map using a static optimization explicitly invoked by the user. When the user clicks a button, a histogram of colors computed across all active display windows is fed into Heckbert's median cut algorithm [21]. The resulting color map is then downloaded into the rendering module. Since median cut is a compute-intensive operation that can take several seconds, it runs asynchronously in a separate process. We have found that this approach is qualitatively well matched to LCD color displays found on laptop PCs. The Heckbert color map optimization can also be used in tandem with the error diffusion algorithm. By concentrating color cells according to the input distribution, the dither color variance is reduced and quality increased.

Finally, we optimized the true-color rendering case. Here, the problem is simply to convert pixels from the YUV color space to RGB. Typically, this involves a linear transforma-

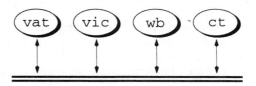

Figure 3: The Conference Bus.

tion requiring four scalar multiplications and six conditionals. Inspired by the approach in [35], vic uses an algorithm that gives full 24-bit resolution using a single table lookup on each U-V chrominance pair and performs all the saturation checks in parallel. The trick is to leverage off the fact that the three coefficients of the Y term are all 1 in the linear transform. Thus we can precompute all conversions for the tuple $(0, U, V)$ using a 64KB lookup table, T. Then, by linearity, the conversion is simply $(R, G, B) = (Y, Y, Y) + T(U, V)$.

A final rendering optimization is to dither only the regions of the image that change. Each decoder keeps track of the blocks that are updated in each frame and renders only those blocks. Pixels are rendered into a buffer shared between the X server and the application so that only a single data copy is needed to update the display with a new video frame. Moreover, this copy is optimized by limiting it to a bounding box computed across all the updated blocks of the new frame.

4.4   Privacy

To provide confidentiality to a session, vic implements end-to-end encryption per the RTP specification. Rather than rely on access controls (e.g., scope control in IP Multicast), the end-to-end model assumes that the network can be easily tapped and thus enlists encryption to prevent unwanted receivers from interpreting the transmission. In a private session, vic encrypts all packets as the last step in the transmission path, and decrypts everything as the first step in the reception path. The encryption key is specified to the session participants via some external, secure distribution mechanism.

Vic supports multiple encryption schemes with a C++ class hierarchy. By default, the Data Encryption Standard (DES) in cipher block chaining mode [1] is employed. While weaker forms of encryption could be used (e.g., those based on linear feedback shift registers), efficient implementations of the DES give good performance on current hardware (measurements are given in [27]). The computational requirements of compression/decompression far outweigh the cost of encryption/decryption.

4.5   The Conference Bus

Since the various media in a conference session are handled by separate applications, we need a mechanism to provide coordination among the separate processes. The "Conference Bus" abstraction, illustrated in Figure 3, provides this mechanism. The concept is simple. Each application can broadcast a typed message on the bus and all applications that are registered to receive that message type will get a copy. The figure depicts a single session composed of audio (vat), video (vic), and whiteboard (wb) media, orchestrated by a (yet to be developed) coordination tool (ct).

A complete description of the Conference Bus architecture is beyond the scope of this paper. Rather, we provide a brief overview of the mechanisms in vic that support this model.

Voice-switched Windows. A feature not present in the other MBone video tools is vic's voice-switched windows. A window in voice-switched mode uses cues from vat to focus on the current speaker. "Focus" messages are broadcast by vat over the Conference Bus, indicating the RTP CNAME of the current speaker. Vic monitors these messages and switches the viewing window to that person. If there are multiple voice-switched windows, the most recent speakers' video streams are shown. Because the focus messages are broadcast on the Conference Bus, other applications can use them for other purposes. For example, on a network that supports different qualities of service, a QoS tool might use the focus message to give more video bandwidth to the current speaker using dynamic RSVP filters [5].

Floor Control. All of the LBL MBone tools have the ability to "mute" or ignore a network media source, and the disposition of this mute control can be controlled via the Conference Bus. This very simple mechanism provides a means to implement floor control in an external application. One possible model is that each participant in the session follows the direction of a well-known (session-defined) moderator. The moderator can give the floor to a participant by multicasting a *takes-floor* directive with that participant's RTP CNAME. Locally, each receiver then mutes all participants except the one that holds the floor. Note that this model does not rely on cooperation among all the remote participants in a session. A misbehaving participant cannot cause problems because it will be muted by all participants that follow the protocol.

Synchronization. Cross-media synchronization can also be carried out over the Conference Bus. Each real-time application induces a buffering delay, called the *playback* point, to adapt to packet delay variations [24]. This playback point can be adjusted to synchronize across media. By broadcasting "synchronize" messages across the Conference Bus, the different media can compute the maximum of all advertised playout delays. This maximum is then used in the delay-adaptation algorithm. In order to assure accurate synchronization, the semantics of the advertised playback points must be the delay offset between the source timestamp and the time the media is actually transduced to the analog domain. The receiver buffering delay alone does not capture the local delay variability among codecs.

Device Access. Each active session has a separate conference bus to coordinate the media within that session. But some coordination operations like device access require interaction among different sessions. Thus we use a global conference bus shared among all media. Applications sharing a common device issue *claim-device* and *release-device* messages on the global bus to coordinate ownership of an exclusive-access device.

Conference Buses are implemented as multicast datagram sockets bound to the loopback interface. Local-machine IP multicast provides a simple, efficient way for one process to send information to an arbitrary set of processes without needing to have the destinations "wired in". Since one user may be participating in several conferences simultaneously, the transport address (UDP destination port) is used to create a separate bus for each active conference. This simplifies the communication model since a tool knows that everything it sends and receives over the bus refers to the conference it is participating in and also improves performance since tools are awakened only when there is activity in their conference. Each application in the conference is handed the address (port) of its bus via a startup command line argument. The global device access bus uses a reserved port known to all applications.

4.6 User Interface

A screen dump of vic's current user interface, illustrating the display of several active video streams, is shown in Figure 4. The main conference window is in the upper left hand corner. It shows a thumbnail view of each active source next to various identification and reception information. The three viewing windows were opened by clicking on their respective thumbnails. The control menu is shown at the lower right. Buttons in this window turn transmission on and off, select the encoding format and image size, and give access to capture device-specific features like the selection of several input ports. Bandwidth and frame rate sliders limit the rate of the transmission, while a generic quality slider trades off quality for bandwidth in a fashion dependent on the selected encoding format.

This user interface is implemented as a Tcl/Tk script embedded in vic. Therefore, it is easy to prototype changes and evolve the interface. Moreover, the interface is extensible since at run-time a user can include additional code to modify the core interface via a home directory "dot file".

A serious deficiency in our current approach is that vic's user interface is completely independent of the other media tools in the session. While this modularity is fundamental to our system architecture, it can be detrimental to the user interface and a more uniform presentation is needed. For example, vat, vic, and wb all employ their own user interface element to display the members of the session. A better model would be to have single instance of this list across all the tools. Each participant in the listing could be annotated to show which media are active (i.e., a participant may have audio but no video).

We intend to evolve our tools in this direction by merging the user interfaces of the different tools into an integrated interface. Each of the tools will be reduced to a bare application that performs only network and media processing. The integrated tool would orchestrate a given session structure by configuring the bare tools over the Conference Bus. Different application styles and arrangements could be easily implemented as separate programs, using the scripting language to realize the user interface and orchestration. Moreover, this decomposition makes the tools less dependent on the X environment. For example, the bare vic process would need only enough window system specific code to draw pixels into a display window. With the forthcoming port of Tcl/Tk to Windows95, our bare application framework should readily migrate to the PC environment.

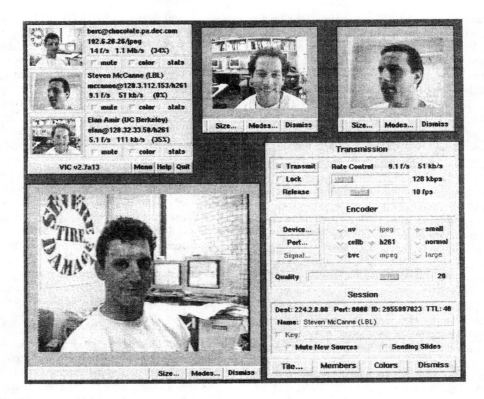

Figure 4: Vic's User Interface

5   SIGNAL COMPRESSION

The flexible software architecture presented in the previous section is well suited for experimentation with new signal compression schemes. This is especially important since video compression algorithms have been traditionally designed for constant bit-rate channels and new approaches are required for transmission over heterogeneous packet networks [18, 41] like the Internet. In its current form, the Internet is a relatively harsh environment for compressed video signals. Packet loss rates are often significant and loss patterns are bursty [4]. Compression schemes that rely on low bit error rate or on channel coding techniques to effectively reduce the bit error rate do not operate well under these conditions.

For compression algorithms like MPEG and H.261, packet loss causes sustained degraded quality. This is due to their method of removing temporal redundancy: Both use a motion-compensating predictor to predict blocks in the current frame from previous (or future) frames then code the residual prediction error. Because the prediction is based on the decoded signal, the model assumes the decoder shares an identical state. But when packet loss occurs, the decoder state becomes mismatched and quality degrades with each new frame. MPEG and H.261 both rely on intra-mode updates to eventually resynchronize, but at low bit rates, the resynchronization intervals can be tens or hundreds of frames so the probability of error in any given interval is high enough that the decoded bit stream is virtually never

error free. The solution is to reduce the resynchronization interval, in the extreme case, to a single frame. This is the model used in Motion-JPEG, where each frame is coded and transmitted independently of all others; but this approach results in low compression efficiency because much of the transmission is redundant.

Conditional replenishment. Another solution to this problem is to forego motion compensation, and instead employ a very rudimentary form of prediction. Frederick's insight in nv was to use an aggressive, block-based conditional replenishment scheme. In this model, each video frame is partitioned into small blocks and only the blocks that change (beyond some threshold) are transmitted. Furthermore, block updates are always intra-coded (i.e., dependent only on the current block) to avoid persistent errors in a predictor loop. At some low rate, a background process continuously refreshes all the blocks in the image to guarantee that lost blocks are eventually retransmitted.

Conditional replenishment works well in practice for several reasons. First, block updates are "self-correlated" in the sense that a block is usually transmitted because of motion in the scene. Therefore, that same block will likely be transmitted again in the next because of the spatial locality of the motion. Thus a lost block update is often retransmitted immediately as a side-effect of conditional replenishment. Second, the class of video currently sent over the Internet is primarily teleseminars and video conferences where large static backgrounds often dominate the scene and conditional replenishment is highly effective. Third, because the replenishment decision can be carried out in the pixel domain as the first step in processing, much of the encoder computation is shed by coding only small portions of the image. Finally, computational complexity is further reduced by the fact that a copy of the decoder need not be run at the encoder since there is no prediction carried out.

The Nv Codec. The high-level compression model utilized by nv is decomposed as follows [17]:

Here, 8x8 image blocks from the conditional replenishment stage are transformed using a Haar wavelet decomposition. A threshold is then applied to each coefficient such that coefficients with magnitude below the threshold are set to zero. This process creates runs of zeros, which are run-length coded in the last stage. Since the Haar transform requires only additions and subtractions and the threshold step requires only two conditionals, the algorithm has very low computational complexity. Unfortunately, compression performance suffers because the Haar transform provides relatively poor energy compaction of the signal [28] and the entropy coder is based exclusively on fixed size run-length codes.

The performance of the nv coder can be substantially improved with the following changes:

(i) Replace the Haar transform with the discrete cosine transform (DCT), which has good energy compaction for images [28].

(ii) Replace the coefficient threshold stage with a uniform quantizer to reduce the entropy of quantized coefficients.

(iii) Follow the run-length coder with a Huffman coder to further compress the symbol stream.

The modified encoder structure then becomes:

Intra-H.261. These changes amount to applying the compression advantages of the DCT-based approaches (JPEG, MPEG, and H.261) to nv's coder. Since the scheme so closely matches H.261, it makes sense to create an H.261 variant that leverages off the ideas from nv. In fact, it turns out that one can get the advantages of aggressive conditional replenishment and intra-coded blocks with a fully-compliant H.261 syntax.

In vic, we use this technique, which we call "Intra-H.261". Intra-H.261 uses only intra-mode H.261 macroblock types and uses macroblock addressing to skip over unreplenished blocks. Because the encoder uses only a small, simple subset of the H.261 specification, the implementation is straightforward (a few hundred lines of C++).

We achieve reasonable computational performance by folding quantization into the DCT computation and by using an efficient 80-multiply 8x8 DCT [36]. We experimented

with several vector-radix DCTs [7] but found that the separable row-column approach, though having asymptotically higher complexity, performed better in the 8x8 case because of reduced memory traffic. Furthermore, because Intra-H.261 never sends inter-coded blocks, the algorithm need not compute a prediction error signal. This prunes much of the computation because it eliminates the need to run a copy of the decoder within the encoder (i.e., it eliminates an inverse quantization and inverse DCT of every encoded block).

Performance. Because the Intra-H.261 and nv compression schemes use similar conditional replenishment algorithms, we can evaluate their relative compression performance simply by ignoring the temporal dimension and comparing only their 2D image compression performance. Figure 5 shows the performance of the two approaches for the canonical 8-bit, 512x512 grayscale "Lena" image. Both encoders were modified to omit block-addressing codes to allow the H.261 encoder to operate on a non-standard image size. This modification has little impact on the results since block-addressing accounts for a small fraction of the bit rate.

The peak signal-to-noise ratio (PSNR) is plotted against rate (in bits per pixel). Multiple points were obtained by varying the H.261 scalar quantizer and the nv dead-zone threshold. Note that the nv algorithm was intended to operate with a non-configurable, fixed threshold, but we explored other thresholds to complete a rate-distortion curve.

As seen in the graph, H.261 consistently outperforms the nv coder by 6-7dB. Since transmissions are typically rate-limited, we should consider a fixed distortion and compare the corresponding bit rates. From this perspective, the nv bit rate is two to three times that of H.261. For a rate-limited transmission, this translates into a factor of two to three decrease in frame rate.

Unfortunately, the compression advantages of H.261 come at the cost of increased computational complexity. Most modern workstations can handle the computational burden of H.261 for typical MBone rates (128kb/s). However, performance problems on lower end workstations have been reported. We believe these problems can be solved by gracefully shedding load to adapt to the available CPU resources. This work is currently underway.

We also compared the run-time performance of the H.261 encoders of vic and ivs. Vic version 2.6.2 and ivs version 3.4 were tested on an SGI Indy (133MHz MIPS R4600SC) with the built-in VINO video device. Both applications were compiled with gcc 2.6.2 using the -O2 flag. We ran the programs individually, giving each application a CIF-sized high-motion input and a low-motion input. In order to measure the maximum sustainable compression rate, we disabled the bandwidth controls in both tools and ran the test on an unloaded machine. We measured the resulting frame rates by decoding the streams on separate machines. The results are as follows:

	high-motion	low-motion	cpu. util.
ivs	3.5 f/s	20 f/s	100%
vic	8.5 f/s	30 f/s	40%

For the high motion case, almost all the blocks in each frame are coded, so this gives a worst-case performance bound. For the low-motion scene, vic ran at the full NTSC frame rate

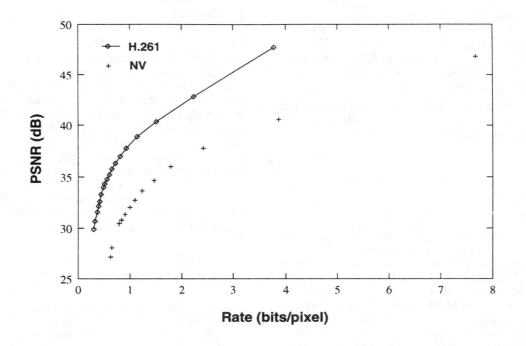

Figure 5: Relative compression performance of nv and Intra-H.261.

and thus was operating below 100% utilization of the CPU. We therefore measured the utilization and found it to be 40%, which adjusts the 30 f/s measure to 75 f/s.

Heterogeneous formats. While vic supports the Intra-H.261 scheme discussed above, it is also backward compatible with nv and supports several other formats. The philosophy is that any bit stream that can be produced by a sender must be decodable by any receiver. That is, even if a sender employs a hardware codec, all receivers must be able to decode the compressed stream in software. This means that we must implement a software decoder for each supported compression format. Vic currently supports H.261, the nv format, Sun's CellB format, and Motion-JPEG.

Motion-JPEG. The prevalence of Motion-JPEG hardware and widespread interest in using this medium over several high-speed testbeds motivated us to support hardware JPEG codecs in vic. Hence, vic must additionally be able to decode JPEG streams in software. However, the high data rates and temporal redundancy in Motion-JPEG lead to a computationally intensive decode process, which would perform poorly without tuning.

We applied several standard optimizations to our decoder (efficient DCT, inverse quantization folded with DCT, table driven Huffman decoding, minimization of memory traffic), but the most dramatic speedup was due to a novel computational pruning technique based on conditional replenishment. We maintain a reference cache of the six lowest frequency DCT coefficients of each block. As we decode a new block, we compare the reference coefficients against the newly decoded coefficients, and if the L^1 distance is below a configurable threshold, we skip the block entirely. Since JPEG does not carry out conditional replenishment in the compression algorithm itself, we apply conditional replen-

ishment at the receiver to prune unnecessary computation. A similar thresholding algorithm is described in [19], though it is used for a different purpose (i.e., motion detection at the encoder).

6 IMPLEMENTATION STATUS AND DEPLOYMENT

Source code for vic has been publicly available[1] since November 1994. Over 4000 retrievals of the software were made between the release date and March 1995. The common workstation platforms are all supported, and vic is rapidly being ported to unsupported systems by the user community.

Vic has been put to production use in several environments. An early version of vic was used by the Xunet research community to carry out distributed meetings in Fall 1993. Because bandwidth was plentiful, each site could (and did) transmit continuous video, placing the bottleneck in vic. This experience led to the voice-switched window feature and the model by which streams are only fully decoded when being displayed.

Vic has been used in several class projects at U.C. Berkeley as well as in several external research projects. It was the test application in a study of the Tenet real-time protocols over the Sequoia 2000 network [3].

In Fall 1994, vic was used on the U.C. Berkeley campus to distribute course lectures over the campus network. More recently, we have equipped a seminar room for MBone transmission and broadcast the Berkeley Multimedia and Graphics Seminar during Spring 1995.

---

[1] ftp://ftp.ee.lbl.gov/conferencing/vic/

In November 1994, a live surgery performed at the U.C. San Francisco Medical School was transmitted to a medical conference in Europe using vic's Intra-H.261. During the surgical demonstration, the surgeon lectured to medical students at Middlesex and Whittington Hospitals in London and in Gothenburg, Sweden.

Finally, vic has been used to broadcast several standard MBone events, including NASA's live space shuttle coverage, the IETF meetings, and USENIX keynote addresses.

7 FUTURE WORK

While the architecture is firmly in place and many features implemented, several unfinished pieces remain. The network delay-adaptation algorithm that is used in vat has not yet been implemented in vic. Instead, frames are rendered as soon as an end-of-frame packet arrives. Since small amounts of frame jitter are tolerated, this problem is not severe but lack of a playout schedule precludes cross-media synchronization. We plan to implement the playback point algorithm in vic and port vat to RTP in order to employ RTP cross-media synchronization between vic and vat.

One of the disadvantages of software-based compression schemes is the reliance on computational resources of the local host. If a hardware codec or a high end workstation sources a high rate video stream, a low end host might not be able to decode and render every frame in the stream. In this case, packets will be dropped by the operating system due to input buffer overflows, and quality will degrade dramatically. To address this problem, we are working on a scheme in which the application adapts gracefully to the available CPU resources by shedding load [12, 9]. While several mechanisms for shedding load are already in place, control algorithms to adapt to load fluctuations have not yet been implemented.

The Conference Bus is in place but still evolving. More work is needed on the coordination protocols and the user interfaces for the different media tools must move toward an integrated model.

Finally, while the Intra-H.261 coder is a step toward better compression schemes for Internet video, we have merely scratched the surface of this problem. In particular, since H.261 is a "single-layer" algorithm, a uniform quality of video is delivered to all receivers in a multicast transmission, even in the presence of heterogeneous link bandwidths and processing capabilities. We are currently using the vic framework to explore a new approach to the heterogeneous multicast video transmission problem, where we jointly design the video compression algorithm with the network transport protocol. We are developing a layered video codec [30] based on subband/wavelet decomposition and conditional replenishment, in tandem with an adaptive congestion control scheme. By striping the compression layers across different multicast groups [30, 43], receivers can locally adapt to fluctuations in network capacity by adding and dropping layers.

8 SUMMARY

In this paper, we described the network and software architectures of vic. By building the design around application-level framing, we achieved a highly flexible decomposition without sacrificing performance. A key benefit of this flexible framework is the ability to experiment with new video coding algorithms, which we exploited with the development of Intra-H.261. By applying elements of the nv codec design to the traditional H.261 compression algorithm, we produced a new coding scheme that balances the tradeoff between good compression gain and robustness to packet loss inherent in the Internet. Finally, we described our approach to building networked multimedia configurations out of composable tools, and the mechanisms we deployed in vic to support this composable architecture via the "Conference Bus".

9 ACKNOWLEDGMENTS

Domenico Ferrari originally proposed the development of a video application and provided support for much of the project. Hui Zhang and Elan Amir offered pointed advice on this paper's structure. We are grateful to Elan Amir, Domenico Ferrari, Sally Floyd, Ron Frederick, Amit Gupta, Deana Goldsmith, Fukiko Hidano, Vern Paxson, Hoofar Razavi, Michael Speer, Thierry Turletti, Martin Vetterli, and Hui Zhang for providing helpful comments on drafts of this paper. We thank the anonymous reviewers for their excellent and thorough feedback. Steven McCanne further thanks Martin Vetterli and Raj Yavatkar for encouraging him to write this paper. Finally, we would like to thank the users in the MBone community who have provided valuable feedback, contributed to the implementation, fixed and reported bugs, ported vic to numerous other platforms, and provided a tangible motivation for this work.

This work was co-sponsored by the Lawrence Berkeley National Laboratory and the Tenet Group of the University of California Berkeley and of the International Computer Science Institute. Support was provided by (1) an AT&T Graduate Fellowship; (2) for the Lawrence Berkeley National Laboratory: (i) the Director, Office of Energy Research, Scientific Computing Staff, of the U.S. Department of Energy, Contract No. DE-AC03-76SF00098, (ii) Sun Microsystems, and (iii) Digital Equipment Corporation; and (3) for the Tenet Research Group: (i) the National Science Foundation and the Advanced Research Projects Agency (ARPA) under Cooperative Agreement NCR-8919038 with the Corporation for National Research Initiatives, (ii) Digital Equipment Corporation, and (iii) Silicon Graphics, Inc.

References

[1] BALENSON, D. *Privacy Enhancement for Internet Electronic Mail: Part III: Algorithms, Modes, and Identifiers.* ARPANET Working Group Requests for Comment, DDN Network Information Center, Feb. 1993. RFC-1423.

[2] BANERJEA, A., FERRARI, D., MAH, B., MORAN, M., VERMA, D., AND ZHANG, H. The Tenet real-time protocol

suite: Design, implementation, and experiences. *To appear in IEEE/ACM Transactions on Networking* (1995).

[3] BANERJEA, A., KNIGHTLY, E., TEMPLIN, F., AND ZHANG, H. Experiments with the Tenet real-time protocol suite on the Sequoia 2000 wide area network. In *Proceedings of ACM Multimedia '94* (San Francisco. CA, Oct. 1994).

[4] BOLOT, J.-C. End-to-end packet delay and loss behavior in the Internet. In *Proceedings of SIGCOMM '93* (San Francisco, CA, Sept. 1993), ACM, pp. 289–298.

[5] BRADEN, R., ZHANG, L., ESTRIN, D., HERZOG, S., AND JAMIN, S. Resource reservation protocol (RSVP) – version 1 function specification, July 1995. Internet Draft expires 1/96.

[6] CASNER, S., AND DEERING, S. First IETF Internet audiocast. *ConneXions 6*, 6 (1992), 10–17.

[7] CHRISTOPOULOS, C. A., SKODRAS, A. N., AND CORNELIS, J. Comparative performance evaluation of algorithms for fast computation of the two-dimensional DCT. In *Proceedings of the IEFFF Benelux and ProRISC Workshop on Circuits, Systems and Signal Processing* (Papendal, Arnhen, Mar. 1994).

[8] CLARK, D. D., AND TENNENHOUSE, D. L. Architectural considerations for a new generation of protocols. In *Proceedings of SIGCOMM '90* (Philadelphia, PA, Sept. 1990), ACM.

[9] COMPTON, C., AND TENNENHOUSE, D. Collaborative load shedding for media-based applications. *International Conference on Multimedia Computing and Systems* (May 1994).

[10] CRAIGHILL, E., FONG, M., SKINNER, K., LANG, R., AND GRUENEFELDT, K. SCOOT: An object-oriented toolkit for multimedia collaboration. In *Proceedings of ACM Multimedia '94* (Oct. 1994), ACM, pp. 41–49.

[11] DEERING, S. E. *Multicast Routing in a Datagram Internetwork*. PhD thesis, Stanford University, Dec. 1991.

[12] FALL, K., PASQUALE, J., AND MCCANNE, S. Workstation video playback performance with competitive process load. In *Proceedings of the Fifth International Workshop on Network and OS Support for Digital Audio and Video* (Durham, NH, Apr. 1995).

[13] FENNER, W., BERC, L., FREDERICK, R., AND MCCANNE, S. *RTP Encapsulation of JPEG-compressed Video*. Internet Engineering Task Force, Audio-Video Transport Working Group, Mar. 1995. Internet Draft expires 12/1/95.

[14] FERRARI, D., AND VERMA, D. A scheme for real-time communication services in wide-area networks. *IEEE Journal on Selected Areas in Communications 8*, 3 (Apr. 1990), 368–379.

[15] FLOYD, S., JACOBSON, V., MCCANNE, S., LIU, C.-G., AND ZHANG, L. A reliable multicast framework for lightweight sessions and application level framing. In *Proceedings of SIGCOMM '95* (Boston, MA, Sept. 1995), ACM.

[16] FREDERICK, R. *Network Video (nv)*. Xerox Palo Alto Research Center. Software on-line.[2].

[17] FREDERICK, R. Experiences with real-time software video compression. In *Proceedings of the Sixth International Workshop on Packet Video* (Portland, OR, Sept. 1994).

[18] GARRETT, M. W., AND VETTERLI, M. Joint source/channel coding of statistically multiplexed real-time services on packet networks. *IEEE/ACM Transactions on Networking 1*, 1 (Feb. 1993), 71–80.

[19] GHANBARI, M. Two-layer coding of video signals for VBR networks. *IEEE Journal on Selected Areas in Communications 7*, 5 (June 1989), 771–781.

[20] HANDLEY, M. J. Using the UCL H.261 codec controller, Dec. 1993. On-line html document.[3].

[21] HECKBERT, P. Color image quantization for frame buffer display. In *Proceedings of SIGGRAPH '82* (1982), p. 297.

[22] HOFFMAN, D., FERNANDO, G., AND GOYAL, V. *RTP Payload Format for MPEG1/MPEG2 Video*. Internet Engineering Task Force, Audio-Video Transport Working Group, June 1995. Internet Draft expires 12/1/95.

[23] JACOBSON, V. *Session Directory*. Lawrence Berkeley Laboratory. Software on-line.[4].

[24] JACOBSON, V. SIGCOMM '94 Tutorial: Multimedia conferencing on the Internet, Aug. 1994.

[25] JACOBSON, V., AND MCCANNE, S. *LBL Whiteboard*. Lawrence Berkeley Laboratory. Software on-line.[5].

[26] JACOBSON, V., AND MCCANNE, S. *Visual Audio Tool*. Lawrence Berkeley Laboratory. Software on-line.[6].

[27] JACOBSON, V., MCCANNE, S., AND FLOYD, S. A privacy architecture for lightweight sessions, Sept. 1994. ARPA Network PI Meeting presentation [7]

[28] JAIN, A. K. *Fundamentals of Digital Image Processing*. Prentice-Hall International, Inc., 1989.

[29] LINDBLAD, C. J., WETHERALL, D. J., AND TENNENHOUSE, D. L. The VuSystem: A programming system for visual processing of digital video. In *Proceedings of ACM Multimedia '94* (Oct. 1994), ACM, pp. 307–314.

[30] MCCANNE, S., AND VETTERLI, M. Joint source/channel coding for multicast packet video. *IEEE International Conference on Image Processing* (Oct. 1995).

[31] MINES, R. F., FRIESEN, J. A., AND YANG, C. L. DAVE: A plug and play model for distributed multimedia application development. In *Proceedings of ACM Multimedia '94* (Oct. 1994), ACM, pp. 59–66.

[32] MOUNTS, F. W. A video encoding system with conditional picture-element replenishment. *Bell Systems Technical Journal 48*, 7 (Sept. 1969), 2545–2554.

[33] OUSTERHOUT, J. K. An X11 toolkit based on the Tcl language. In *Proceedings of the 1991 Winter USENIX Technical Conference* (Nashville, TN, Jan. 1991), USENIX.

[34] OUSTERHOUT, J. K. *Tcl and the Tk Toolkit*. Addison-Wesley, 1994.

[35] PATEL, K., SMITH, B. C., AND ROWE, L. A. Performance of a software MPEG video decoder. In *Proceedings of ACM Multimedia '93* (Aug. 1993), ACM, pp. 75–82.

---

[3] http://www.cs.ucl.ac.uk/mice/codec_manual/doc.html
[4] ftp://ftp.ee.lbl.gov/conferencing/sd
[5] ftp://ftp.ee.lbl.gov/conferencing/wb
[6] ftp://ftp.ee.lbl.gov/conferencing/vat
[7] ftp://ftp.ee.lbl.gov/talks/lws-privacy.ps.Z

---

[2] ftp://ftp.parc.xerox.com/net-research

[36] PENNEBAKER, W. B., AND MITCHELL, J. L. *JPEG Still Image Data Compression Standard.* Van Nostrand Reinhold, 1993.

[37] ROSEMAN, M., AND GREENBERG, S. GroupKit: A groupware toolkit for building real-time conferencing applications. In *Proceedings of the Conference on Computer-Supported Cooperative Work* (Oct. 1992).

[38] ROWE, L. A., PATEL, K. D., SMITH, B. C., AND LIU, K. MPEG video in software: Representation, transmission, and playback. In *High Speed Network and Multimedia Computing, Symp. on Elec. Imaging Sci. & Tech.* (San Jose, CA, Feb. 1994).

[39] SCHULZRINNE, H. Voice communication across the Internet: A network voice terminal. Technical Report TR 92-50, Dept. of Computer Science, University of Massachusetts, Amherst, Massachusetts, July 1992.

[40] SCHULZRINNE, H., CASNER, S., FREDERICK, R., AND JACOBSON, V. *RTP: A Transport Protocol for Real-Time Applications.* Internet Engineering Task Force, Audio-Video Transport Working Group, Mar. 1995. Internet Draft expires 9/1/95.

[41] TAUBMAN, D., AND ZAKHOR, A. Multi-rate 3-D subband coding of video. *IEEE Transactions on Image Processing 3,* 5 (Sept. 1994), 572–588.

[42] TURLETTI, T. The INRIA videoconferencing system (IVS). *ConneXions 8,* 10 (Oct. 1994), 20–24.

[43] TURLETTI, T., AND BOLOT, J.-C. Issues with multicast video distribution in heterogeneous packet networks. In *Proceedings of the Sixth International Workshop on Packet Video* (Portland, OR, Sept. 1994).

[44] TURLETTI, T., AND HUITEMA, C. *RTP payload for for H.261 video streams.* Internet Engineering Task Force, Audio-Video Transport Working Group, July 1995. Internet Draft expires 1/1/96.

[45] Video codec for audiovisual services at p*64kb/s, 1993. ITU-T Recommendation H.261.

CHAPTER NINE

Networking and Media Streaming

Ketan Mayer-Patel

University of North Carolina - Chapel Hill

THE ADVENT of broadband Internet access technologies like xDSL and cable modems are enabling streaming media applications. Driving applications include entertainment, IP telephony, and distance learning. The dynamics of streaming media through a network can be quite complex. This chapter identifies and characterizes some of the networking issues faced by media streaming. The papers included here discuss end-to-end strategies in the context of best-effort packet delivery, a description of the RSVP quality of service mechanism, and a discussion of the Internet Engineering Task Force (IETF) approach to protocol development and deployment in the context of IP telephony.

The characteristics of streaming media are often application-, media-, and transport protocol–specific. Interactive applications (e.g., videoconferencing, IP telephony, etc.) require low latency and delay jitter bounds. These requirements are particularly acute for audio applications because the ability to carry on a conversation becomes hampered by delays greater than 150 ms. Noninteractive applications do not require strict latency bounds and can alleviate delay jitter by using receiver-side buffers to smooth media playback. Different media types lend themselves to different network congestion adaptation strategies. For example, video bandwidth can be reduced by reducing the frame rate, resolution, color depth, or encoding quality. Audio data types have fewer dimensions of scalability. Unfortunately, a specific media encoding or representation may not lend itself to exploiting all (or in some cases any) of these techniques. The

use of multicast to efficiently distribute media to a group of receivers poses additional challenges not encountered in the unicast case. In particular, heterogeneous connectivity to receivers (i.e., some receivers with ample bandwidth available and some receivers with limited bandwidth) defeats source-controlled adaptation strategies because no one transmission rate is appropriate for all receivers. In addition, performance feedback information in multicast environments is probabilistic at best because explicit feedback from all receivers will not scale as group membership grows.

The perceived loss in quality that occurs with different packet loss and data rates is also media-specific and highly nonlinear. This complicates the design of any adaptation scheme. TCP-style congestion control and avoidance (i.e., slow-start, multiplicative decrease, etc.) is often not appropriate for continuous media applications because large and sudden changes in data rate result in extremely poor perceived media quality. The interaction between streaming media and network queue management policies such as RED, which were designed specifically for TCP-like congestion control, is complicated and not well understood. Cross-media relationships need to be considered as well. For example, given limited bandwidth in a videoconferencing application, perceived video quality should be sacrificed more readily than audio quality because audio is generally more important for the purposes of the conference participants. Prioritization between media streams, however, may be dynamic depending on how the application is used.

Dealing with all of these aspects of streaming media is a formidable challenge. The issues raised by high bandwidth streams (*e.g.*, video) center on effective network resource utilization and adapting to congestion. Among end-to-end strategies employed to cope with varying network conditions for high-bandwidth media streams are media scaling and media layering.

Media scaling schemes continually estimate network conditions and in response adjust media coding parameters. Typically, available bandwidth is estimated and frame rate or encoding quality is modulated to adjust bit rate to an appropriate level. The success of media scaling techniques depends on accurate estimates of network conditions and stable adaptation schemes. In the first paper of this chapter, "The performance of two-dimensional media scaling for Internet videoconferencing," by P. Nee, K. Jeffay, and G. Danneels, the technique is extended into a two-dimensional scheme for Internet videoconferencing. The authors differentiate between network capacity constraints and network access constraints and adapt independently along two different dimensions (bit rate and packet rate). The evaluation methodology in this work includes quantitative measures of latency and packet loss as well as qualitative measures of usability and quality.

The problem of heterogeneous receivers defeats media scaling techniques because no one transmission rate is appropriate for all receivers. In this setting, a receiver-driven adaptation scheme such as media layering is required. Media layering refers to encoded representations that can be separated into "layers" such that the quality of the reconstructed representation improves as additional layers are used. Receivers adapt to available bandwidth by subscribing to more or fewer layers in response to changing network conditions. Determining when to add or drop layers can be problematic. Although congestion is easily detected by observing packet loss rates, dropping layers too quickly makes the adaptation scheme acutely sensitive to transient congestion that may not warrant dropping a layer. The availability of additional bandwidth for an additional layer is not explicitly signaled to the application. Furthermore, the actions of receivers may interfere with each other. One receiver adding an additional layer may in turn create congestion, which other

receivers may react to by dropping layers. The problem of determining an appropriate subscription level is addressed in the paper included here by S. McCanne, V. Jacobson, and M. Vetterli, "Receiver-driven layered multicast." Their adaptation protocol includes mechanisms by which receivers coordinate their actions in a scalable manner.

Audio streaming is less concerned with effective network utilization because the bandwidth requirements for audio are significantly smaller than for video. The main issue for audio streaming is quality in the face of packet loss. The driving application for audio streaming is IP telephony, which requires low-latency audio streaming for two-way, interactive conversation. Packet loss in this context can not be remedied through request-based retransmission because of latency constraints. Instead, packet loss recovery techniques are employed. These techniques include interleaving audio samples and forward error correction. A survey of techniques by C. Perkins, O. Hodson, and V. Hardman, "A survey of packet loss recovery techniques for streaming audio," is also included here. The use of a specific technique, forward error correction, in an adaptive manner, is described by J.-C. Bolot, S. Fosse-Parisis, and D. Towsley in "Adaptive FEC-based error control for Internet telephony." In their system, the amount of bandwidth that should be used for forward error correction is cast as an optimization problem maximizing the utility of the recovered audio given an estimated packet loss rate and an adaptive rate control algorithm. An interesting result of this work is that the solution of the optimization problem is highly sensitive to the utility function (*i.e.*, qualitative worth) assigned to the recovered audio.

The end-to-end strategies described above assume only best-effort delivery from the underlying network architecture. Media streaming is simplified if the network can provide some quality-of-service (QoS) guarantees. If QoS can provide for bandwidth, delay, or jitter guarantees, dynamic adaptation is no longer required. QoS mechanisms, however, do not come without a cost. These costs may be incurred as under-utilized network resources, denial of service if sufficient resources are not available, and/or monetary premiums paid for receiving a higher level of service. Researchers have developed and experimented with a number of QoS schemes. Included here is the seminal work of L. Zhang, and colleagues, "RSVP: A new resource ReSerVation Protocol," which describes the resource ReSerVation Protocol (RSVP). This particular protocol is important because of its flexible design and its advancement within the Internet Engineering Task Force (IETF) as a proposed standard.

The IETF has been instrumental in the development of many media streaming protocols. The overall philosophy of these development efforts has been to create separate protocols for specific functions. For example, separate protocols exist for session initiation (SIP), media streaming (RTP), and media stream control (RTSP). Though RTP is a transport-level protocol for streaming media data, within its specification are mechanisms by which the protocol can be adapted to specific media types. The goal of this design philosophy is to maximize modularity, flexibility, and extensibility. The final paper in this section, "Internet telephony: Architecture and protocols—An IETF perspective," is a description by H. Schulzrinne and J. Rosenberg of how these IETF protocols can be used to support Internet telephony. The system described embodies the IETF design philosophy.

ADDITIONAL READINGS

E. Amir, S. McCanne, and R. Katz, "An active service framework and its application to real-time multimedia transcoding," in *Proceedings of ACM SIGCOMM 98* (Vancouver: ACM, 1998), 178–89.

J.-C. Bolot and A. V. Garcia, "The case for FEC-based error control for packet audio on the Internet," to appear in *ACM Multimedia Systems* (1997).

L. Delgrossi et al., "Media scaling for audiovisual communication for the Heidelberg transport system," in *Proceedings of the 1st ACM International Multimedia Conference* (Los Angeles: ACM, 1993), 99–104.

A. Fox, S. D. Gribble, E. A. Brewer, and E. Amir, "Adapting to network and client variation via on-demand dynamic transcoding," in *Proceedings of ASPLOS VII* (Oct. 1996): 160–70.

I. Kouvelas et al., "Redundancy control in real-time Internet audio conferencing," in *Proceedings of AVSPN 97* (1997): 195–201.

M. Podolsky, C. Romer, and S. McCanne, "Simulation of FEC-based error control for packet audio on the Internet," in *Proceedings of IEEE Infocom 98* (1998): 505–15.

M. Podolsky, S. McCanne, and M. Vetterli, "Soft ARQ for layered streaming media," *Journal of VLSI Signal Processing Systems for Signal, Image and Video Technology* (Special Issue on Multimedia Signal Processing) 27 (2001): 81–97.

R. Rejaie, M. Handley, and D. Estrin, "RAP: An end-to-end rate-based congestion control mechanism for realtime streams in the Internet," in *Proceedings of IEEE Infocom 99* (New York: IEEE, 1999), 1337–45.

R. Rejaie, M. Handley, and D. Estrin, "Quality adaptation for congestion controlled playback video over the Internet," in *Proceedings of ACM SIGCOMM 99* (Cambridge: ACM, 1999), 189–200.

J. Rosenberg and H. Schulzrinne, "An RTP payload format for generic forward error correction," IETF Proposal Standard RFC 2733, Dec. 1999.

L. Wu, R. Sharma, and B. Smith, "Thin streams: An architecture for multicasting layered video," in *Proceedings of the International Workshop on Network and Operating System Support for Digital, Audio, and Video (NOSSDAV 97)* (St. Louis: IEEE, 1997), 173–82.

The Performance of Two-Dimensional Media Scaling for Internet Videoconferencing*

Peter Nee   Kevin Jeffay

University of North Carolina at Chapel Hill
Department of Computer Science
Chapel Hill, NC 27599-3175
{nee,jeffay}@cs.unc.edu

Gunner Danneels

Intel Corporation
Intel Architecture Labs
Hillsboro, OR
Gunner_Danneels@ccm.jf.intel.com

http://www.cs.unc.edu/Research/dirt

Abstract: Until mechanisms for true real-time network communications are deployed and pervasive, one must rely on adaptive, best-effort congestion control methods to provide acceptable levels of service for interactive, real-time multimedia applications. Here we report on our experiences with a novel media-scaling congestion control scheme that was implemented in an experimental version of the Intel ProShare™ videoconferencing system and tested over the Internet. The media scaling scheme is unique in that it employs two-dimensional media scaling — the bit-rate and packet-rate of media streams are independently scaled. The goals of our study were (1) to empirically assess the performance improvement of two-dimensional media scaling over the simpler, and more commonly employed, one-dimensional scaling approaches and (2) to determine if it was possible to sustain ProShare conferences for a significant enough fraction of the time that two-dimensional scaling could be considered effective. We observed that systems using one-dimensional and two-dimensional scaling were both able to sustain conferences and that the two-dimensional scaling system always produced conferences with greater effective throughput. Our study provides empirical evidence that two-dimensional media scaling can be used effectively to ameliorate the effects of congestion in the Internet and can significantly extend the usability of an interactive multimedia application on the Internet.

1. Introduction

This paper presents the results of a set of experiments using an adaptive, best-effort videoconferencing system on the Internet. The system, a modified version of the Intel ProShare™ videoconferencing system, is novel in that it employs a two-dimensional media scaling algorithm to ameliorate the effects of congestion. Both the bit-rate of media streams and the partitioning of the streams into network packets (the packet-rate) are independently scaled

[9]. Our goal in this work was not to attempt to construct a videoconferencing system that would provide acceptable quality conferences under all network conditions, but rather to build a system that could sustain conferences over a sizable Internet path under daytime traffic conditions and to use the system as a testbed for the evaluation and comparison of adaptive scaling schemes. In particular, we were interested in the comparison between two-dimensional scaling schemes and conventional one-dimensional scaling in the Internet environment.

Our experience with this system and the experiments we performed highlight several of the issues surrounding real-time, low latency communications on current internetworks, and especially on the Internet itself. These issues include the practicality of videoconferencing on today's Internet, the applicability of adaptive scaling over a lengthy Internet path, the utility of two-dimensional scaling on the Internet, and the proper criteria for assessing the congestion control mechanisms of adaptive multimedia applications.

Our experiments show at least some promise for high-quality, low latency videoconferencing on the Internet. Although peak-period traffic makes conferences with our system infeasible, there are certain times during an average weekday at which we were able to routinely sustain quality conferences. Our experiments also indicate that adaptive techniques are able to function over Internet paths of some complexity. In addition we are able to measure a qualitative benefit of two-dimensional scaling over one-dimensional scaling.

The following section reviews the congestion control problem for interactive multimedia applications and describes some approaches reported in the literature for dealing with congestion. Section 3 presents the videoconferencing system used in this work and describes our two-dimensional media scaling scheme. Sections 4 and 5, respectively, describe our experimental method and the re-

* Supported by grants from the IBM and Intel Corporations, the National Science Foundation (grants IRIS-9508514 & CCR-9510156), and the Advanced Research Projects Agency (grant number 96-06580).

sults of using our system over the Internet over the course of three months. These experiments raise a number of issues such as the interplay between adaptive media scaling and TCP's congestion control. We discuss these and other issues in Section 6 and make the case for a definition of "network-friendly" application behavior that is consistent with the congestion control requirements of real-time multimedia applications. In addition, based on experiences with our system, we offer some insight into desirable attributes of scaleable audio and video codecs.

2. Background and Related Work

Current internetworks are built primarily from best-effort components. Paths between end systems are composed of elements such as shared media LANs, wide-area telecommunication links, and routers and switches that simply propagate packets as quickly as possible with no attempt to allocate resources or manage congestion. These best-effort components are cost effective and widely deployed. Therefore, even as more sophisticated components become available, best-effort networking will remain dominant for some time. The large investment in best-effort components and the availability of (presumably lower cost) best-effort service classes in proposed integrated network services for the Internet provide powerful economic incentives for the continued use of best effort services. Thus, the continued study of applications in a best-effort environment is important.

Videoconferencing is an application that is especially sensitive to network congestion. The goal of videoconferencing is to present elements of multimedia streams in a regular, periodic fashion with minimal latency to human participants. Network congestion can cause packet loss, which reduces the quality and regularity of the streams by introducing gaps in the playout of the streams. Congestion can also cause queuing at network elements such as routers, which introduces delays that impede interactivity. Finally, congestion can cause high variation in end-to-end delay (*delay-jitter*) which interferes with the smooth playout of a stream, even to the point where some portions of the stream, though successfully transmitted, arrive too late to be played and must be discarded.

Two primary methods of dealing with congestion for real-time multimedia applications have been proposed: *resource reservation*, and *adaptive media scaling*. Resource reservation schemes allocate network resources to a specific application or class of applications [2, 6, 11, 12]. Adaptive schemes monitor end-to-end performance and attempt to deal with congestion through adjustments to the attributes of media streams. The goal is to find a suitable set of at-

tributes that results in media streams that are deliverable in real-time in the current network conditions [1, 4, 5, 8, 9]. The primary advantage of reservation schemes is that with a suitable admission control policy, they can provide an *a priori* assessment of feasibility, and guarantee success if the conference is feasible. However, reservation schemes have two disadvantages. One is that the reservation of network resources must be done at every point in the path between the end systems. Otherwise, the feasibility of the transmission can be compromised at nodes supporting only best-effort service. This is a serious limitation as a broad deployment of reservation-capable network components remains some years away. Secondly, the static model of a reservation for a multimedia stream is overly restrictive. Multimedia applications are inherently scaleable, capable of conveying useful information over a wide range of quality/resource consumption tradeoffs. Making a reservation requires an arbitrary choice of a set of application operation parameters. Once this choice is committed by a reservation, it cannot easily be adjusted over time.

Adaptive methods are capable of operation over networks that are partially or completely made up of best-effort components. They exploit at least some of the scaleable attributes of multimedia streams, to make best use of the network under rapidly evolving conditions.

However, adaptive methods may exhibit decreasing effectiveness as the complexity of the network increases. Adaptive methods depend on feedback from the receiver to sample network conditions and attempt to operate at a stable point near the optimal for the current conditions. In a complex best-effort network, bottlenecks may appear and disappear at arbitrary locations, competing connections may come and go, and the availability of resources may fluctuate rapidly. If conditions evolve too rapidly for accurate sampling, the sender's adaptations will be ineffective. Indeed, there may exist significant periods of time during which there is no stable, sustainable mode of operation of the system. Experiments with our system indicate that such congestion is frequently experienced on a moderate length Internet path.

We characterize a videoconferencing system as a set of *operating points* in a bit-rate × packet-rate plane. Each point in this plane represents both a bit-rate that the system is capable of generating and a partitioning of the resulting media stream into network packets. The operating points for a videoconferencing system succinctly describe the cross-product of all the possible ways of operating the acquisition and compression hardware and all the possible ways of packaging data into packets and passing them to the network interface. The media scaling problem is that of choosing an operating point that is sustainable given the current network conditions.

To date, most adaptation schemes have been *one-dimensional*, that is, in times of congestion they primarily adjust the bit-rate of media streams. *Two-dimensional* scaling is a more sophisticated scheme that independently adjusts the bit-rates and the packet-rates of media streams [9]. Bit-rate scaling primarily ameliorates *capacity constraints* — a shortage of resources consumed by the transmission of bits. As an example, consider a router that is unable to transmit a packet from a stream in real-time. If the residence time for the packet at the router is dominated by the cost of physically transmitting the packet on an outbound link, or by the CPU time required to move data between buffers on router interfaces, then the stream is capacity constrained at that router. The benefit of two-dimensional scaling is that in addition to capacity constraints, it explicitly addresses constraints on the *access* to network resources. If the residence time for the packet at the router is dominated by the cost of per packet processing overhead (*e.g.*, route selection), or the media access time experienced when transmitting a packet on a shared media LAN, then the stream is access constrained at that router. Capacity constraints are alleviated only through a reduction in the bit-rate of a stream. Access constraints are alleviated only through a reduction in the packet-rate of a stream. In the latter case, this can be done by changing the packaging of a stream by simple techniques such as inter- or intra-stream aggregation of media units. In particular, one can often change the packaging of the stream with no reduction in throughput (bit-rate).

Previous work on two-dimensional scaling has shown that both types of constraints can arise on best-effort networks, and that independently adapting to both capacity and access constraints can greatly improve the quality of the delivered multimedia stream. Under certain network conditions two-dimensional scaling can even render a previously infeasible execution of a videoconferencing system feasible [9, 10].

Some adaptive schemes, such as temporal video scaling (*i.e.*, changing the video frame rate) adjust both packet-rate and bit-rate. However, these schemes are still one-dimensional in the sense that they do not independently adapt to both types of constraints, instead they adapt to the most severe and limiting of the two.

3. System Description

To experiment with the suitability of adaptive scaling schemes for an Internet application, we modified Intel's ProShare™ videoconferencing system (version 1.8) to support one- and two-dimensional media scaling. The ProShare™ system has many attributes well suited to our purposes. It generates low bit-rate, two-way audio and video streams. Although it was designed to operate at three preset, fixed data-rates (one data-rate for ISDN or LAN operation and two others for LAN operation only), we took advantage of an internal interface to the video codec to implement on-the-fly adjustments to the video bit-rate and frame-rate. The video frame rate was adjustable over the full range of frame-rates (from one to thirty frames per second). In addition, some flexibility in bits per frame was available. We exploited this bits per frame scalability to set three levels of compression, corresponding to 1,200 bytes per frame ("small size"), 2,100 bytes per frame ("medium size") and 2,800 bytes per frame ("large size"). In each case the compression scheme changes the number of bits per picture element in the image. These frame sizes correspond roughly to one Ethernet packet per video frame, one and one half Ethernet packets per video frame, and two Ethernet packets per video frame.

ProShare uses an interframe encoding scheme based on motion estimation. As a result of this, not all video frame rates are generated for each frame size. At frame rates below ten frames per second, the frames are generated so infrequently that the motion between frames is too great to sustain the small frame size. Conversely, at frame rates of twenty or above, frames are so frequent that the motion estimation typically works extremely well and the codec never generates more than 2,100 bytes per frame. Therefore the large frame size is not available above 19 frames per second.

ProShare generates audio at a single, aggressively compressed rate of ten 200 byte audio-frames per second. We are unable to adapt the bit-rate of the audio stream, and the low audio frame rate makes aggregation of two consecutive audio frames untenable; the introduced latency of 200 ms is just too great.

3.1 One-dimensional scaling implementation

There are numerous one-dimensional scaling schemes (see [5] for an excellent survey). Our one-dimensional scaling system was based on temporal video scaling (*i.e.*, scaling the video frame rate) using the medium level of compression. The frame rate was adjusted over a range from 6 frames per second to 30 frames per second. Because a medium video frame exceeds the size of an Ethernet MTU, each additional video frame has a cost of two packets. To minimize latency, no aggregation is performed. The fixed rate audio provides an additional ten packets and 16,000 bits per second. Since audio operates at a fixed point, we use the sum of the video operating point and the fixed audio overhead as the operating points of this system. A

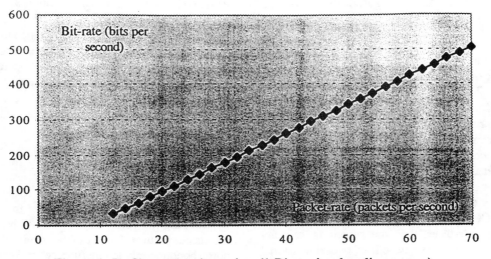

Figure 1: ProShare operating points (1-Dimensional scaling system).

plot of these combined operating points is provided in Figure 1. Note that while the operating points are plotted in the bit-rate × packet-rate plane, they all lie in a straight line in the plane. This is consistent with the thinking behind one-dimensional scaling schemes. The operating point set is geared toward scaling in the bit-rate dimension via frame rate adjustment, with the packet-rate at a fixed proportion to the bit-rate. No aggregation is attempted because that would only reduce the packet-rate, at the cost of increased latency. In a system that views bit-rate as the dominant constraint, there is no incentive to reduce the packet-rate at the cost of increasing latency.

We chose temporal video scaling for our one-dimensional system for several reasons. From a pragmatic standpoint, it is easy to implement and many of the other one-dimensional scaling schemes such as color-space scaling (reducing the color depth of images) require a more intimate knowledge of the internal workings of the codec than we possess. Second, we claim that all bit-rate scaling schemes yield sets of operating points that are similar to that shown in Figure 1. The slope of the line may change or the line may be translated vertically or horizontally in the plane, however, the result is essentially a line. As we will see shortly, our one-dimensional operating point set spans much of the same region in the plane as our two-dimensional point set. Therefore, the one-dimensional scaling scheme based on the point set in Figure 1 provides the best "competition" for the two-dimensional scheme.

All adaptive schemes use feedback from the receiver to detect congestion and adjust the stream appropriately. The adaptation process in one-dimensional schemes is straightforward as there is only one variable that is manipulated

(*i.e.*, bit-rate). When an adaptation is required, our one-dimensional system always attempts to adjust the bit-rate of the video stream by a constant fraction of the current frame rate. It does this by increasing or decreasing the frame rate by:

- one frame per second when the previous frame rate was in the range of one to nine frames per second,

- two frames per second when the previous frame rate was in the range of ten to 19 frames per second, and

- three frames per second when the previous frame rate was in the range of 20 to 29 frames per second.

If the conference is operating at 30 frames per second, a decrement of four frames per second is used when congestion is present. In addition to these rules, frame rates below six frames per second are not used due to excessive video latency and lack of motion in the playout.

Feedback is given by the receiver at one second intervals. Feedback messages include measurements of network packet loss and estimated round trip latency. Loss of more than two packets, or a latency increase of fifty percent over a moving average of the previous five measurements is taken to indicate congestion. Each time feedback indicates congestion the video frame rate is reduced. Thus, repeated reports of congestion lead to a rapid reduction in video frame rate. If four successive feedback messages indicate no sign of congestion, this is taken as an indication of congestion relief, and the video frame rate is increased as described above.

3.2 Two-dimensional scaling implementation

A two-dimensional scaling system values both packet-rate and bit-rate adjustments. For this type of system, an oper-

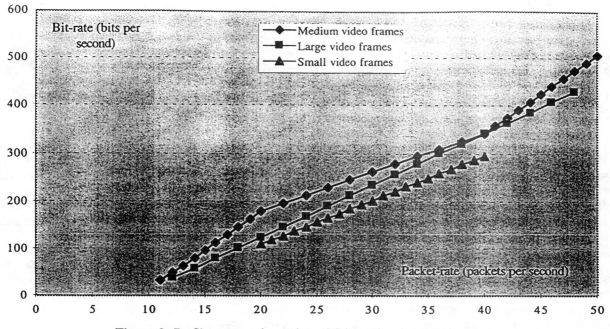

Figure 2: ProShare operating points (2-Dimensional scaling system).

ating point set that covers a large area in the bit-rate × packet-rate plane is desirable. However, with the video frame size as large or larger than the network MTU, and no possibility of audio adaptation, covering a sufficient area of the operating point plane is difficult.

Our two-dimensional system uses two strategies to increase coverage of the bit-rate × packet-rate plane. First, all three levels of video compression are used. Second, we use aggregation of audio frames with medium size video frames to "spread out" the operating points in the plane and thus provide more flexibility for two-dimensional adaptation of the video. To see this, it is useful to view each medium size frame as a one packet "body" and a half packet "tail." At frame rates of ten or below, each tail can be aggregated with an audio frame. Thus, each additional medium size video frame in this range raises the overall packet-rate by one, instead of by two as would be required without aggregation. (In theory this technique could also be applied to small size frames, however, in practice when application headers are factored in, the combination of a small video frame and an audio sample is often larger than a single Ethernet packet.)

In the range of 11 to 20 frames per second, there are too many video tails to aggregate with the audio frames, so each additional frame beyond 10 frames per second requires two additional packets. Above 20 frames per second, the video frames are generated close enough together in time that we can aggregate the tail of each additional frame with

the currently unaggregated tail of an adjacent frame with only a minimal impact on latency. Thus, in this range, each additional increase in video frame rate requires only one additional packet per second.

As always, there is some additional latency introduced by aggregation, but this rather complex arrangement ensures that the additional latency never exceeds 50 ms. In fact, the arrangement is implemented with a 50 ms timer for holding small packets that are candidates for aggregation.

The resulting operating points are plotted in Figure 2. The slope changes in the upper line (the medium frame rate) are the result of the changing number of packets per additional frame as we move from 10 and fewer frames per second (the region wherein we require one additional packet per additional frame) to the 10 to 20 frames per second range (two additional packets per additional frame) to the above 20 frames per second range (one additional packet per additional frame).

Note that the size of the range of bit-rates available varies at each packet rate. The bit-rate ranges are the largest in the twenty to forty packet range. This is the range in which this particular system is the most "two-dimensional," and, as we shall see, is the range of operation where two-dimensional scaling is the most beneficial for this system.

Our two dimensional system adapts the outgoing streams via two types of adjustments. We perform pure bit-rate scaling by moving between small, medium and large oper-

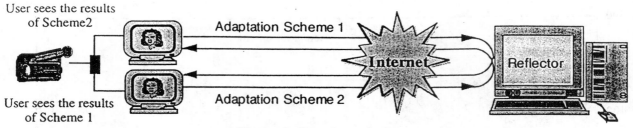

Figure 3: Experimental setup.

ating points while keeping the packet-rate constant. We also perform an adjustment in both bit- and packet-rate (but primarily in packet-rate) by temporal video scaling. We make the frame rate adjustments proportional to the current level of operation (*i.e.*, to change the bit-rate by a constant amount on each adaptation) as in the one-dimensional scaling scheme.

The mechanics of the adaptation process are more complicated in two-dimensional scaling than in one-dimensional scaling. With two-dimensional scaling there are two independent variables. However, both access and capacity constraints exhibit the same symptoms to end systems: increases in packet loss, packet latency, or packet delay-jitter. We use a "recent success" heuristic, which makes adjustments in one dimension in the bit-rate × packet-rate plane for as long as they seem effective. If adjustments in that dimension do not appear to alleviate congestion, recent success switches to adjustments in the other dimension. The contents of the feedback, as well as the criteria used to detect congestion and the relief of congestion, are identical to those used in the one-dimensional system described above.

4. Experimental Method

4.1 Setup

The goal of our experiments was to evaluate the performance of the modified ProShare system under real Internet traffic conditions. As each conference was competing with live Internet traffic, each experiment was non-repeatable and the results of different experiments were more or less incomparable. Therefore, to compare the relative performance of one- and two-dimensional scaling under comparable network congestion conditions, both scaling algorithms were run simultaneously using the configuration shown in Figure 3.

Each experiment consisted of a point-to-point, bi-directional conference between two machines located on a common Ethernet. One direction of the conference used a one-dimensional media scaling scheme to ameliorate the effects of congestion. A two-dimensional scheme was used in the other direction. Each conference end-point provided

the appropriate feedback to drive the adaptation process at the other end as described in Section 3. A single camera and audio source provided the same input to each system. Thus an observer could view the displays simultaneously and qualitatively compare the effects of each scaling scheme on the same inputs.

Although the two ProShare systems are attached to the same LAN, they exchange data streams via a remote reflector located at the University of Virginia (10 hops away). Therefore, each media stream traverses the path from UNC to UVA twice, traveling across 20 network hops.

Experiments consisted of 10 minute conferences run on weekdays during predetermined time slots over a three month period. Multiple experiments on a day were permitted, but experiments were always separated in time by at least two hours.

In addition to running experiments comparing the performance of one- and two-dimensional scaling, we also ran a small number of experiments comparing the two-dimensional adaptive system with the original version of the ProShare system that used fixed points of operation.

4.2 Evaluation Methodology

There were two aspects to the evaluation of each experiment. First, a human observer recorded a subjective impression of the utility of the conference based on direct observation of each system. The subjective evaluation was primarily based on an assessment of the quality of the audio playout and was used to judge the overall success of the conference. If the conference was judged too poor in quality for useful human-to-human communication it was judged a "failure." Second, detailed numerical measurements of conference quality were recorded by each system in an in-memory log to assess the relative performance of one-dimensional versus two-dimensional scaling. At the end of each experiment these logs were saved to disk for later analysis. The qualitative and quantitative analyses were combined as follows.

When an adaptive system operates over a wide range of conditions, we can evaluate it on three criteria:

- *Necessity of adaptation.* What network conditions constrain the system enough to require adaptation?

- *Feasibility of adaptation.* When adaptations are required, what network conditions permit the system to operate successfully with adaptation and what conditions preclude any adaptation from being successful?

- *Effectiveness of adaptation.* When adaptations are performed, what is the quality of the resulting conference?

For a given adaptive videoconferencing system, the first two criteria are determined by the extremal operating points. If there exist network conditions wherein the system's highest quality operating point (the operating point furthest from the origin — the operating point that generates the highest stream bit-rate and has the lowest latency due to packaging at the sender), can be routinely sustained, then adaptation is not necessary. Conversely, if there exist network conditions in which even the lowest quality operating point (the operating point closest to the origin — the operating point that generates the lowest stream bit-rate and has the greatest latency due to packaging at the sender), cannot be sustained, then operation of the system is not feasible.

Comparisons of adaptive videoconferencing systems based on these two criteria will hinge on the differences in the extremes of their operating point sets. For example, a system with operating points for highly compressed video will be feasible for a larger set of network conditions. A system with a maximum video frame rate of thirty frames per second will require adaptation of frame rate under more conditions than a system with a maximum video frame rate of fifteen.

For a given network, we can evaluate the utility of an adaptive videoconferencing system by the frequency with which conditions arise wherein adaptation is both necessary and feasible. Under these conditions, we can further compare videoconferencing systems by the effectiveness criterion. In this case (and only in this case), it is the richness of the interior space of the operating point set and the actual adaptation algorithm that are important. A rich operating point set gives a videoconferencing system the flexibility to closely

adapt to network conditions. A good algorithm finds the current appropriate operating point quickly, and without excessive adjustment. For a given network, we can evaluate the effectiveness of an adaptive videoconferencing system by performance measurements on the delivered media streams, such as latency, audio loss, and video frame rate. These comparisons are complicated by the fact that individual systems often make implicit tradeoffs between these measures such as increasing the quality of the displayed images by increasing the time required for processing samples (and hence the increasing the playout latency). However, if care is taken, meaningful comparisons can be made.

5. Experimental Results

We now turn to the evaluation of our two adaptive ProShare systems operating on a 20 hop Internet path under weekday conditions. First, with respect to necessity, not surprisingly, adaptation was required in all runs. Second, with respect to feasibility, we can use the observer's subjective assessment to differentiate between feasible and infeasible conferences. No significant difference in success-rate was noted for the one-dimensional and two-dimensional systems. Table 1 summarizes the utility of adaptive scaling by time of day. The results are consistent with naive expectations. The traffic starts out in mid-morning low enough to permit adaptive videoconferencing, builds to a peak during the late afternoon during which time our system was unable to sustain a quality videoconference, and then gradually recedes. Our results show a peak-period consistently centered in the afternoon. Since much of experimental path passed through academic environments, this peak may be skewed later in the day than for other parts of the Internet.

Finally, for conditions wherein scaling is necessary and feasible, our comparison of one-dimensional and two-dimensional scaling showed subtle but noticeable benefits for two-dimensional scaling by the effectiveness criterion. Primarily, two-dimensional scaling delivered better quality conferences by allowing the transmission of more video frames, especially in moderate traffic conditions. In heavy traffic conditions, two-dimensional scaling was not significantly more

Table 1: Summary of qualitative results

Time Slot	Number of Successes	Number of Failures	Success Percentage
10:00-12:00	6	3	67%
12:00-14:00	4	4	50%
14:00-16:00	1	11	8%
16:00-18:00	3	9	25%
18:00-20:00	4	5	44%
Percentage	36%	64%	

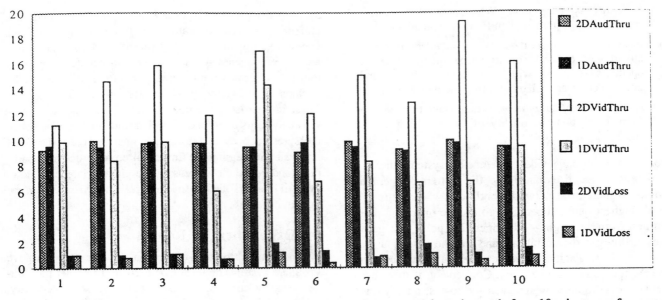

Figure 4: Video and audio throughput and video loss averaged over one minute intervals for a 10 minute conference.

effective than one-dimensional scaling. Since heavy traffic requires operation at the low end operating points (those closest to the origin), this is consistent with the lack of a significant difference in feasibility between the two systems.

Examination of the operating point plot provides insight here. First, any two-dimensional video scaling system provides less flexibility at the low end, since all the quality lines converge at the origin. Secondly, for our system, due to the constraints built-in, this was even more the case. For example, the small video frame size was only available at video frame rates above ten frames per second. Thus at low frame rates, less packet-rate scaling is possible. Also, at moderate frame rates, there were enough video tails available to take full advantage of packaging with audio. Thus, where our system is most able to take advantage of two-dimensional scaling, the middle range of operating points, is where we see a benefit typical of two-dimensional scaling: the ability to push more bits (higher quality) through by more attention to frame size and packaging. Therefore, our comparison to one-dimensional scaling shows that two-dimensional scaling is beneficial, and that the more the codec allows operating points spread out over the bit-rate × packet-rate plane, the greater the benefit.

Figure 4 shows a minute by minute plot of received audio frame rate, received video frame rate, and video frame loss (video generated and sent but not received) for both two-dimensional and one-dimensional scaling during a successful videoconference under moderate conditions. We see that the two adaptive schemes have no significant difference in

delivered audio or in video loss. However, the two-dimensional scheme delivers consistently more video frames. This pattern is typical for successful runs.

Figure 5 shows a more detailed second by second comparison of quality measurements for the two conferences in this same run. In the first row we again see the equivalent audio throughput and consistently higher video throughput for two-dimensional scaling. In the second row, we see equivalent patterns of audio latency for both schemes. (Since audio is synchronized with video, video latency is similar to audio and hence is omitted.) Finally, in that last row, we see that the two-dimensional scheme's higher video throughput does not come at the cost of higher packet loss. Both schemes exhibit an acceptable level of packet loss.

Finally, we briefly discuss runs of the original, unmodified ProShare system. As before, each direction of the conference used a different congestion control scheme. In this case one direction used two-dimensional scaling, and the other direction used a fixed operating point (*i.e.*, performed no adaptations). The audio and video throughput for one such conference is shown in Figure 6. We had hoped that in some cases the two-dimensional scheme would sustain a feasible conference while the fixed point operation did not, but this was not the typical case. Instead, we again saw the simultaneous success or failure of both sides of the conference. We hypothesize that the adaptations of the two-dimensional system were capable of sufficient adaptation to enable the success of the fixed operating point system. Figure 6 provides some support for this, since a second

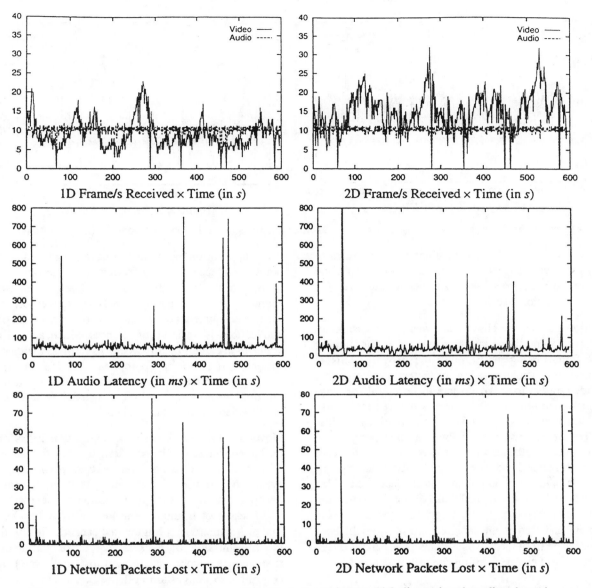

Figure 5: Sample conference performance with 1-dimensional and 2-dimensional media adaptations.

fixed operating point conferences would have exceeded the throughput that the adaptive method could sustain. Of course, there were also many runs where the level of network traffic exceeded the ability of the adaptive system to compensate for the fixed operating point system, and both sides of the conference were infeasible. The unfairness inherent in fixed point operation always severely degraded the performance of the adaptive side of the conference.

6. Discussion

Our results show that an adaptive approach to Internet videoconferencing is workable, and that receiver feedback is able to accurately characterize the level of congestion on a non-trivial Internet path. Further, at least in off-peak hours, adaptive videoconferencing is possible on today's Internet. The dynamic interplay of growth in the number of users and changes in usage and infrastructure makes the future availability of Internet resources purely a matter of speculation. However, our results provide support for a small measure of optimism for future videoconferencing and other best-effort real-time multimedia applications.

Our work further showed that it was possible to build a practical system incorporating two-dimensional scaling from an existing fixed-rate LAN videoconferencing system. This system benefited from two-dimensional scaling and benefited most in the area of operation with the greatest

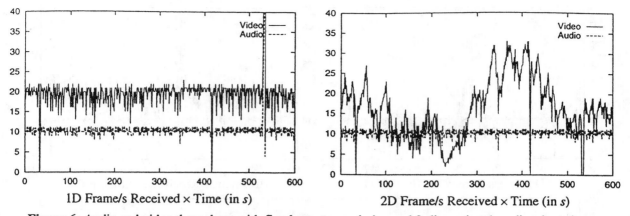

Figure 6: Audio and video throughput with fixed-rate transmission and 2-dimensional media adaptations.

range of bit-rate and packet-rate combinations. We surmise that systems with codecs expressly designed to provide even more combinations will reap even greater benefits from two-dimensional scaling.

An additional subjective observation was that occasionally the displayed video frame rate was lower than the number of video frames being sent through the network. This is attributable to synchronization or jitter problems that cause video frames to arrive too late to be useful for playout. Although infrequent, such video frames are essentially wasted transmissions, possibly as wasteful as a lost packet. (However, systems like ProShare that provide key frame data across all video frames may still benefit from the successful arrival and processing of unplayable frames.) In these cases, the detection of unplayable data in the video stream would be a useful additional factor in measuring congestion. Thus, we suggest that reports of frames usable for playout and frames unusable for playout would be a useful interface from media subsystems (*e.g.*, audio codec) to the transport layer performing congestion control.

We address our final remarks to a topic that must always be considered for high bandwidth applications that use best effort networks. This is the question of the impact of the application's congestion control mechanism on the network. An application's congestion control mechanism is most often evaluated by two criteria. First, its behavior must help protect the network from congestion collapse — a situation where the network is heavily utilized, but little or no useful throughput is achieved. Second, the high-bandwidth application's behavior must not negatively affect other applications.

We argue that the first criterion is appropriate, because an end-system application can readily assess network congestion through receiver feedback and can use this feedback to implement some form of congestion control. We note that

if an application does not aggravate congestion to the point of collapse, the only harm it can do to other applications is to use more than its "fair share" of network resources. Thus, if an application's congestion control scheme adequately protects the network, protection of other applications is an issue of fairness. Since an end-system application cannot readily assess its fairness to other applications, this is not an appropriate criterion for assessing its congestion control mechanism. Working from this position, we now examine the congestion control behavior of our videoconferencing application.

Floyd and Fall [7] give three application behaviors that lead to congestion collapse. First, there is the classic case of excessive and unnecessary retransmission, generally avoided by the use of conformant TCP implementations. Second, is the successful transmission of data that is unusable because of timing or the loss of related packets (*e.g.* loss of fragments of a fragmented packet). Finally, there is the transmission of packets that make partial progress through the network and are then lost. All three behaviors contribute to congestion collapse because they waste network resources when the network is most congested.

Our system avoids or attempts to avoid all these behaviors. First, our system does not use retransmission. Second, while our system does occasionally transmit data that is not useful to the receiver, these transmissions will be associated with a symptom of congestion and lead to adaptation. One example is a video frame spanning two packets, one of which is lost. In this case, our system detects a packet loss. A second example is an audio frame that arrives too late to be used for playout. In this case, our system detects an increase in network latency, another trigger for a congestion avoiding adaptation. As mentioned above, this second example could be even better dealt with if the audio codec had some way to indicate to the transport layer that the late frame was unusable. Finally, since our system measures and adapts to packet loss, it attempts to avoid losing packets in the network.

The TCP protocol provides applications a proven congestion control mechanism that helps the network avoid congestion collapse. Clearly, any application that shapes its traffic to closely resemble the behavior of a TCP application (*i.e.*, mimics slow start, uses a congestion window, employs multiplicative decrease, *etc.*) will also meet the congestion collapse avoidance criterion for effective congestion control. However, this approach is not the best choice for every application. The quality of service goals of the application may differ greatly from those, for example, of a bulk transfer stream. In videoconferencing, occasional loss is tolerable, retransmission is unhelpful, and drastic adjustments in data rate are undesirable. An adaptive scheme that takes into account the quality of service requirements of the application it supports will clearly do a better job of minimizing the impact of congestion on that application. For example, it may retreat more slowly to avoid a jarring adjustment in an audio stream.

In addition, an adaptive scheme may benefit from techniques incompatible with TCP behavior. For example, our adaptive scheme uses more detailed feedback than TCP, avoiding overreaction due to isolated packet loss, and anticipating congestion by monitoring average latency. Our adaptive scheme also uses two-dimensional scaling, which uses aggregation to balance a packet-rate versus latency tradeoff that is suitable to the current network conditions. A typical bulk transfer application will use fixed size packets near the network MTU, thus already effectively minimizing packet rate. This is an appropriate choice for bulk transfer, because the latency of data in the packet is irrelevant. Thus, for real-time multimedia, where each media frame has an inherent latency constraint, two-dimensional scaling is a useful way to adapt a tradeoff that is not a concern for many existing TCP applications.

An adaptive scheme that behaves differently from TCP may or may not adequately protect the network from congestion collapse. For each new adaptive scheme this is an open question until demonstrated through extensive experimentation. However, the steps taken by our adaptive scheme to avoid the underlying causes of congestion collapse, and our experience with it so far, provide compelling evidence that it meets the network protection criterion for effective congestion control.

We now consider the appropriateness of the effect on other applications as a criterion for assessing an application's congestion control scheme. A specific example is the concern is that an application that adapts to congestion differently than TCP may, under the right conditions, steal resources from TCP connections. In essence, this criterion places the burden for the protection of the existing body of applications on any, and every, new application that is introduced.

We believe this criterion is inappropriate because an application has no information about the effect of its traffic on the traffic of other applications. An application can only be fair to TCP applications by behaving exactly as TCP does. Again, TCP's behavior is at best suboptimal for many types of applications, and such applications may have compelling reasons to use congestion control that differs in behavior from TCP. Further, TCP is known to be unfair in some circumstances. For example, connections with a long round trip time get a smaller share of congested links than those with a shorter round trip time.

However, the concern over fairness to TCP is legitimate; our algorithm may scale back more slowly than TCP under certain conditions, and this may result in a shift of resources from TCP traffic to videoconferencing traffic. However, the end system congestion control scheme is not the place to address this. Fairness is properly dealt with in the intermediate nodes (routers and switches) of the network. Implementations for fairness by flow, by application type, and other criteria have already been proposed [3]. Intermediate network nodes have sufficient information to deal with fairness issues accurately and efficiently. End system congestion control mechanisms do not.

An additional objection to the application fairness criterion is a recognition that new applications will inevitably be deployed, and congestion control schemes specialized for these applications will inevitably be introduced. As additional congestion control techniques are deployed, the problem of assessing each congestion control protocol's interaction with each other protocol, or with a "reasonable" population of other protocols quickly becomes untenable.

We submit that fairness to other applications is not properly a criterion for assessing an application's congestion control mechanism. Policing resource competition between applications is a job for the network itself. A congestion control scheme for an application should be concerned with meeting the quality of service requirements of the application in a way that does not waste network resources and helps avoid congestion collapse. This is the most practical, reasonable criterion for assessing application-level congestion control and initial indications are that our two-dimensional ProShare system meets this criterion.

7. Summary and Conclusions

We have presented results from experiments with an adaptive videoconferencing system on the Internet. These experiments showed that an adaptive system using inexpensive components can, with a significant rate of success, provide usable videoconferences between widely separated points on the Internet. Further, our results demonstrated that two-dimensional scaling, with its attention to appropriate choice of both bit-rate and packet-rate, provides measurable quality improvements over one-dimensional scaling on an equivalent system. Our work also pointed to the desirability of media codecs that can cooperate with adaptive transport layers to more accurately assess the value of delivered packets, and can provide a flexible array of operating points enabling a rich set of bit-rate and packet-rate combinations. Finally, we argued that the behavior of our system is consistent with reasonable criteria for application-level congestion control. Our system avoids wasting network resources through congestion control scheme based on adaptive media scaling that is appropriate for the real-time multimedia application domain.

8. Acknowledgments

We are indebted to Jorg Liebeherr at the University of Virginia for the remote use of his facilities to perform the experiments reported herein.

9. References

[1] Bolot, J., Turletti, T., *A Rate Control Mechanism for Packet Video in the Internet*, Proc. IEEE INFOCOMM '94, Toronto, Canada, June 1994, pp. 1216-1223.

[2] Braden, R., D. Clark, and S. Shenker, *Integrated Services in the Internet Architecture: an Overview*, IETF RFC-1633, July 1994.

[3] Braden, R., *et al.*, *Recommendations on Queue Management and Congestion Avoidance in the Internet*, IETF End-to-End Research Group, Internet draft (work in progress), March 1997.

[4] Chakrabarti, S., Wang, R., *Adaptive Control for Packet Video*, Proc. IEEE International Conference on Multimedia Computing and Systems 1994, Boston, MA, May 1994, pp. 56-62.

[5] Delgrossi, L., Halstrick, C., Hehmann, D., Herrtwich, R., Krone, O., Sandvoss, J., Vogt, C., *Media Scaling for Audiovisual Communication with the Heidelberg Transport System*, Proc. ACM Multimedia '93, Anaheim, CA, Aug 1993, pp. 99-104.

[6] Ferrari, D., Banjea, A., and Zhang, H., *Network Support for Multimedia: A Discussion of the Tenet Approach*, Computer Networks and ISDN Systems, Vol. 26, No. 10 (July 1994), pp. 1267-1280.

[7] Floyd, S., Fall, K., *Router Mechanisms to support End-to-End Congestion Control*, Technical Report, 1997. URL *ftp://ftp.ee.lbl.gov/papers/collapse.ps*

[8] Hoffman, Don, Spear, M., Fernando, Gerard, *Network Support for Dynamically Scaled Multimedia Streams*, Network and Operating System Support for Digital Audio and Video, Proceedings, D. Shepard, *et al* (Ed.), Lecture Notes in Computer Science, Vol. 846, Springer-Verlag, Lancaster, UK, November 1993, pp. 240-251.

[9] Talley, T.M., Jeffay, K., *Two-Dimensional Scaling Techniques For Adaptive, Rate-Based Transmission Control of Live Audio and Video Streams*, Proc. Second ACM Intl. Conference on Multimedia, San Francisco, CA, October 1994, pp. 247-254.

[10] Talley, T.M., Jeffay, K., *A General Framework for Continuous Media Transmission Control*, Proc. 21st IEEE Conference on Local Computer Networks, Minneapolis, MN, October 1996, pages 374-383.

[11] Topolcic, C. (Ed.), *Experimental Internet Stream Protocol, Version 2 (ST-II)*. Network Working Group, RFC 1190, IEN-119, CIP Working Group, October 1990.

[12] Zhang, L., Deering, S., Estrin, D., Shenker, S., Zappala, D., *RSVP: A New Resource ReSerVation Protocol, IEEE Network*, Vol. 5, No. 5 (September 1993), pp. 8-18.

Receiver-driven Layered Multicast

Steven McCanne
University of California, Berkeley and
Lawrence Berkeley National Laboratory
mccanne@ee.lbl.gov

Van Jacobson
Network Research Group
Lawrence Berkeley National Laboratory
van@ee.lbl.gov

Martin Vetterli
University of California, Berkeley
martin@eecs.berkeley.edu

Abstract

State of the art, real-time, rate-adaptive, multimedia applications adjust their transmission rate to match the available network capacity. Unfortunately, this source-based rate-adaptation performs poorly in a heterogeneous multicast environment because there is no single target rate — the conflicting bandwidth requirements of all receivers cannot be simultaneously satisfied with one transmission rate. If the burden of rate-adaption is moved from the source to the receivers, heterogeneity is accommodated. One approach to receiver-driven adaptation is to combine a layered source coding algorithm with a layered transmission system. By selectively forwarding subsets of layers at constrained network links, each user receives the best quality signal that the network can deliver. We and others have proposed that selective-forwarding be carried out using multiple IP-Multicast groups where each receiver specifies its level of subscription by joining a subset of the groups. In this paper, we extend the multiple group framework with a rate-adaptation protocol called Receiver-driven Layered Multicast, or RLM. Under RLM, multicast receivers adapt to both the static heterogeneity of link bandwidths as well as dynamic variations in network capacity (i.e., congestion). We describe the RLM protocol and evaluate its performance with a preliminary simulation study that characterizes user-perceived quality by assessing loss rates over multiple time scales. For the configurations we simulated, RLM results in good throughput with transient short-term loss rates on the order of a few percent and long-term loss rates on the order of one percent. Finally, we discuss our implementation of a software-based Internet video codec and its integration with RLM.

SIGCOMM '96 8/96 CA, USA

1 Introduction

The Internet's heterogeneity and scale make multipoint communication design a difficult problem. For real-time multimedia, we would like to "broadcast" a live signal from any particular sender to an arbitrarily large set of receivers along paths with potentially high variability in bandwidth. The simplest solution to this problem is to distribute a uniform representation of the signal to all interested receivers using IP Multicast [8]. Unfortunately, this is suboptimal — low-capacity regions of the network suffer congestion while high-capacity regions are underutilized.

The problems posed by heterogeneity are not just theoretical, they impact our daily use of Internet remote-conferencing. For example, each week for the past year, U.C. Berkeley has broadcast a seminar over their campus network and onto the Internet. As depicted in Figure 1, a video application is run on a "seminar host" that sources a single-rate signal at 128 kb/s, the nominal rate for video over the Internet Multicast Backbone, or MBone [11]. However, a number of users on the local campus network have high bandwidth connectivity and would prefer to receive higher-rate, higher-quality video. At the other bandwidth extreme, many users have ISDN access and would like to participate from home, but a 128 kb/s video stream overwhelms an ISDN line.

In this open-loop approach, the sender broadcasts at some fixed rate without regard to changing network conditions. A better approach is to adjust the transmission rate to match the available capacity in the network, i.e., to react to congestion. Pioneering research in rate-adaptive video [1, 19, 23] has shown that this is feasible, but unfortunately, in the context of multicast, the notion of network capacity is ill defined. A control scheme that adjusts the rate of a single stream at the source simply cannot meet the conflicting requirements of a set of heterogeneous receivers.

An alternative approach is to combine a layered compression algorithm with a layered transmission scheme [29, 32]. In this approach, a signal is encoded into a number of layers that can be incrementally combined to provide progres-

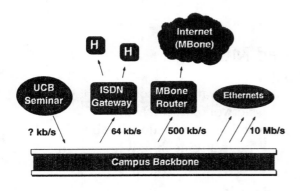

Figure 1: Network heterogeneity

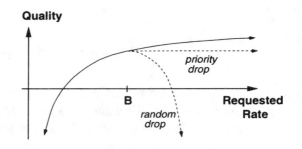

Figure 2: Priority-/Random-drop Tradeoff.

sive refinement. By dropping layers at choke points in the network — i.e., selectively forwarding only the number of layers that any given link can manage — heterogeneity is managed by locally degrading the quality of the transmitted signal.

This framework provides an elegant solution to heterogeneity but a crucial piece is missing. The system must have mechanisms for determining, communicating, and executing the selective forwarding of subflows along all the links in a distribution. While much of the previous work leaves this as an implementation detail, a novel mechanism based on IP Multicast was suggested by Deering [6] and elaborated on and/or independently reported in [4, 9, 20, 26, 33]. In this approach, the different layers of the hierarchical signal are striped across multiple multicast groups and receivers adapt to congestion by adding and dropping layers (i.e., joining and leaving multicast groups). Receivers implicitly define the multicast distribution trees simply by expressing their interest in receiving flows. Thus there is no explicit signaling between the receivers and routers or between the receivers and source.

While this general mechanism has been discussed in the research community, the problem has not been studied in detail, algorithms for adaptation have not been developed, and systems based on these ideas have not yet emerged. This paper addresses some of the open questions related to layered multicast transport through the design and simulation of an experimental network protocol called Receiver-driven Layered Multicast or RLM. In the following section we describe the network model assumed by RLM. Next we provide intuition for RLM and present the protocol in detail. We then explore its performance through simulation. Finally, we discuss the integration of RLM into a comprehensive systems framework, report on related work, and describe our future work.

2   The Network Model

RLM works within the existing IP model and requires no new machinery in the network. We assume:

- only best-effort, multipoint packet delivery, e.g., without guarantees for packet ordering, minimum bandwidth, etc.;

- the delivery efficiency of IP Multicast, i.e., that traffic flows only along links with downstream recipients; and,

- *group-oriented* communication: senders need not know that receivers exist and receivers can dynamically join and leave the communication group in an efficient and timely manner.

These three requirements are sufficient for single source distribution to arbitrary numbers of receivers under RLM. To handle multiple, simultaneous sources, RLM assumes that receivers can specify their group membership on a per-source basis (i.e., a receiver can ask for packets sent to some group but exclude packets from one or more sources)[1].

We refer to a set of end-systems communicating via a common set of layered multicast groups as a *session*. Because the IP Multicast service model does not export any of the routing mechanism, we cannot guarantee that all the groups of a single session follow the same distribution tree. That is, multicast routing can be carried out on a per-group basis and different groups can be routed along different spanning trees. Although RLM is most easily conceptualized in a network where all the groups follow the same route, this is not a requirement.

The relationship among the information contained across the set of groups in a session can either be cumulative or independent. In the cumulative case, each layer provides refinement information to the previous layers and the receiver must subscribe to all groups up to and including the highest group. In the independent case, each layer is independent and the receiver need only subscribe to one group. This latter scheme is often called *simulcast* because the source transmits

---

[1] Source-based pruning is not part of the current IP Multicast specification but is included in the next version, IGMP-3, which is under review by the IETF.

multiples copies of the same signal simultaneously at different rates (resulting in different qualities). In this paper, we focus on the cumulative model because it makes more effective use of bandwidth but RLM is also compatible with the simulcast model.

Instead of the best-effort, IP Multicast model described above, the universally cited approach to layered packet transmission adds a drop-preference packet discard policy to all the routers in the network. Under drop-preference, when congestion occurs, routers discard less important information (i.e., low-priority packets) before more important information (i.e., high-priority packets). Although this approach provides graceful degradation in the presence of packet loss, we believe it has scaling problems because it rewards poorly-behaved users.

This effect is illustrated in Figure 2, which plots the quality of a received signal vs. the requested bit rate for both priority-drop and random-drop policies. In both cases, the quality of the received signal increases with the requested rate up to the bottleneck capacity B but beyond this, the quality depends on the drop policy. With random-drop, quality degrades because packets are dropped uniformly across all layers, while with priority-drop the quality remains constant because only "enhancement" packets are dropped. The key distinguishing feature of these two curves is their convexity. Because the random-drop curve is strictly convex, it has a unique maximum. Thus we can design a control system that maximizes the quality metric and drives the system toward the stable, uncongested bottleneck rate B. The priority-drop curve has no unique maximum and hence does not admit a control system that optimizes delivered quality by converging to a single, stable operating point. In fact, a greedy or naive user would likely request a rate far above the bottleneck rate B, driving the network into a persistently congested state.

3 The RLM Protocol

Building on the best-effort IP-Multicast network model, we now describe RLM at a high-level to develop intuition for the protocol before discussing the low-level details. To first order, the source takes no active role in the protocol. It simply transmits each layer of its signal on a separate multicast group. The key protocol machinery is run at each receiver, where adaptation is carried out by joining and leaving groups. Conceptually, each receiver runs the following simple control loop:

- on congestion, drop a layer;

- on spare capacity, add a layer.

Under this scheme, a receiver searches for the optimal *level of subscription* much as a TCP source searches for the bottleneck transmission rate with the slow-start congestion avoidance algorithm [21]. The receiver adds layers until conges-

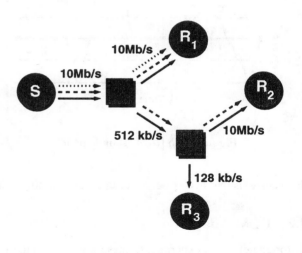

Figure 3: End-to-end adaptation.

tion occurs and backs off to an operating point below this bottleneck.

Figure 3 illustrates the RLM scheme. Suppose source S is transmitting three layers of video to receivers R_1, R_2, and R_3. Because the S/R_1 path has high capacity, R_1 can successfully subscribe to all three layers and receive the highest quality signal. However, if either R_2 or R_3 try to subscribe to the third layer, the 512 kb/s link becomes congested and packets will be dropped. Both receivers react to this congestion by dropping layer three, prompting the network to prune the unwanted layer from the 512 kb/s link. Finally, because of the limited capacity of the 128 kb/s link, R_3 might have to drop back all the way to a single layer. The effect is that the distribution trees for each layer have been implicitly defined as a side effect of the receiver adaptation.

3.1 Capacity Inference

To drive the adaptation, a receiver must determine if its current level of subscription is too high or low. By definition, the subscription is too high if it causes congestion. This is easy to detect because congestion is expressed explicitly in the data stream through lost packets and degraded quality. On the other hand, when the subscription is too low, there is no equivalent signal — the system continues to operate at its current level of performance. We must rely on some other mechanism to provide this feedback.

One source for this feedback might be to monitor link utilization and explicitly notify end-systems when capacity becomes available. However, this requires new mechanism in the network that renders deployment difficult. The approach we adopt in RLM is to carry out active experiments by spontaneously adding layers at "well chosen" times. We call this spontaneous subscription to the next layer in the hierarchy a *join-experiment*. If a join-experiment causes congestion, the receiver quickly drops the offending layer. If a join-experiment is successful (i.e., no congestion occurs), then

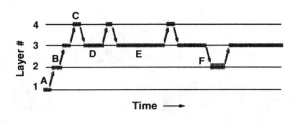

Figure 4: An RLM "sample path"

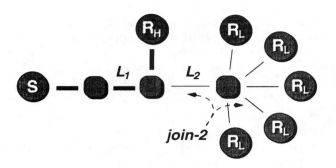

Figure 5: Shared Learning

the receiver is one step closer to the optimal operating point.

3.2 RLM Adaptation

Unfortunately, join-experiments cause transient congestion that can impact the quality of the delivered signal. Therefore, we need to minimize the frequency and duration of join-experiments without impacting the algorithm's convergence rate or its ability to track changing network conditions. This is done through a learning algorithm, where over time, each receiver determines the level of subscription that causes congestion. By doing join-experiments infrequently when they are likely to fail, but readily when they are likely to succeed, we reduce the impact of the experiments. We implement this learning strategy by managing a separate *join-timer* for each level of subscription and applying exponential backoff to problematic layers.

Figure 4 illustrates the exponential backoff strategy from the perspective of a single host receiving up to four layers. Initially, the receiver subscribes to layer 1 and sets a join-timer (A). At this point, the timer duration is short because the layer has not yet proven problematic. Once the join-timer expires, the receiver subscribes to layer 2 and sets another join-timer (B). Again, the timer is short and layer 3 is soon added. The process repeats to layer 4, but at this point, we will assume congestion occurs (C). A queue will then build up and cause packet loss. Once the receiver detects these lost packets, it drops back to layer 3. The layer 3 join-timer is then multiplicatively increased and another timeout is scheduled (D). Again, the process repeats, congestion is encountered, and the join-timer is further increased (E). Later, unrelated transient congestion provokes the receiver to drop down to layer 2 (F). At this point, because the layer 3 join-timer is still short, the layer is quickly reinstated.

In order to properly correlate a join-experiment with its outcome, we must know how long it takes for a local layer change to be fully established in the network and for the resulting impact to be detected back at the receiver. We call this time interval the *detection-time*. If a join-experiment lasts longer than the detection-time without congestion occurring, then we deem the experiment successful. On the other hand, if congestion occurs within the detection-time interval, we assume the experiment failed and increase the join-timer for that layer. Because the detection-time is un-

known and highly variable, we estimate it and its variance adaptively. We initialize our estimator (mean and deviation) with a conservative (i.e., large) value, and adapt it using failed join-experiments. That is, when an experiment fails, we update our estimator with the time interval between the start of the experiment and the onset of congestion.

3.3 Scaling RLM

If each receiver carries out the above adaptation algorithm independently, the system scales poorly. As the session membership grows, the aggregate frequency of join-experiments increases; hence, the fraction of time the network is congested due to join-experiments increases. Moreover, measurement noise increases because experiments tend to interfere with each other. For example, if one receiver is conducting an experiment on layer 2 and another begins an experiment on layer 4 that causes congestion, then the first receiver can misinterpret the congestion and mistakenly back off its layer 2 join-timer.

We can avoid these problems by scaling down the individual join-experiment rates in proportion to the overall group size. In other words, we can fix the aggregate join-experiment rate independent of session size much as RTCP scales back its control message rate in proportion to the group size [28]. However, reducing the experiment rate in this manner decreases the learning rate. For large groups, the algorithm will take too long to converge.

Our solution is "shared learning": Before a receiver conducts a join-experiment, it notifies the entire group by multicasting a message identifying the experimental layer. Thus all receivers can learn from other receivers' failed join-experiments. For example, Figure 5 shows a topology with a single source, one receiver R_H situated along a high-speed path (denoted by the thickened links) and a set receivers, each labeled R_L, situated at the far end of a low-rate link. Suppose a low-rate receiver decides to conduct a join-experiment on layer 2. It broadcasts a join-2 message to the group and joins the layer 2 multicast group. As a result, link L_2 becomes oversubscribed and congestion results, causing packets to be dropped indiscriminately across both layers.

At this point, all of the R_L receivers detect the congestion and since they know a layer 2 experiment is in progress, they all scale back their layer 2 join-timer. Thus all of the low-bandwidth receivers learn together that layer 2 is problematic. Each receiver need not run individual experiments to discover this on their own.

This learning process is conservative. Receivers make their decisions based on failed experiments not on successful experiments. Moreover, the success/failure decision is based on local observations, not on a global outcome. That is, each receiver decides whether the experiment succeeds based on the network conditions on the path from the source to that receiver, entirely independent of the receiver that instantiated the join-experiment. Hence, a given experiment may succeed for some receivers but fail for others.

Even though the shared learning process enhances the protocol's scalability by reducing convergence time, overlapped experiments can still adversely impact the learning rate. But because receivers explicitly announce the start of each experiment, the probability that an experiment overlaps with another can be substantially reduced by suppressing the start of a new experiment when one is outstanding. For example, if in Figure 5 receiver R_H decides to carry out a join-4 experiment that causes congestion on link L_1, then the low-rate receivers can misinterpret this as a failed join-2 experiment. But because R_H sees the explicit join-2 announcement, it will suppress the join-4 experiment and thereby limit the interference. Note that this exchange of information is merely an optimization. If the announcement packet is lost, the algorithm still works albeit with potentially reduced performance.

Because the shared learning process determines what does *not* work rather than what does work, each receiver can advance its level of subscription only through actual join-experiments. If the suppression algorithm were completely exclusionary, then the convergence time could still be very large because each receiver would have to wait its turn to run an experiment. Instead, we allow experimental overlap if the pending level is the same as or less than the level in progress. This gives newer receivers with lower levels of subscription an opportunity to conduct experiments in the presence of a large population of established receivers at higher levels of subscription. Although this mechanism allows experimental overlap, a receiver that causes an overlap can condition its response accordingly by reacting more conservatively than in the non-overlapped case. The intuition behind this scheme is that high-layer receivers allow low-layer receivers to quickly adapt to their stable level of subscription. As the low-layer receivers adapt, their join-experiment frequency falls off and the high-layer receivers will again find idle periods in which to conduct join-experiments.

This technique for sharing information relies on the fact that the network signals congestion by dropping packets across all layers of the distribution. Under a priority-drop policy, receivers not subscribed to the experimental layer would not see packet loss and would not know the experi-

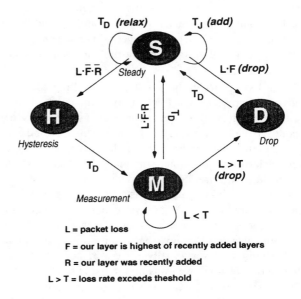

Figure 6: The receiver protocol state machine.

ment failed. In short, a priority-drop policy interferes with the scalability of RLM.

3.4 The RLM State Machine

Figure 6 elaborates the protocol sketched in the previous section. There are four states: steady-state (S), hysteresis state (H), measurement state (M), and drop state (D). Each state transition is labeled with the reason for the transition, either packet loss or a timeout. Actions associated with a transition are indicated in parentheses.

Join-timers (T_J) are randomized to avoid protocol synchronization effects [15], while detection-timers (T_D) are set to a scaled value of the detection-time estimator. The *add* action implies that we subscribe to the next layer in the multicast group hierarchy, while the *drop* action implies that we drop the current layer and multiplicatively increase the join-timer for that layer. The *relax* action implies that we multiplicatively decrease the join-timer for the current layer. There are two types of loss actions: a fast reaction to a single packet loss (indicated by L) and a slower reaction to a sustained loss rate. The loss rate is measured with a short-term estimator and action is taken if the estimator exceeds a configured threshold (indicated by $L > T$).

In the S state, there is always a pending join-timer (unless the receiver is subscribed to all available layers). When the join-timer expires, we broadcast an explicit notification message to the group and add a layer. Upon reception of the join-experiment message, a receiver notes the experiment start time for that layer. In this way, we track the join-experiment activity at each layer and deem an experiment "in progress" if the time since the experiment started is less than

$$k_1 \hat{T}_D + k_2 \hat{\sigma}_D$$

where $\hat{T}_D$ is the detection-time estimator, $\hat{\sigma}_D$ is the detection-time sample mean-deviation, and k_1 and k_2 are design constants. If a lower layer join-experiment is in progress, we ignore the current join-timer and simply schedule a new one.

When loss occurs in the S state, the resulting action depends on the presence of active join-experiments. If there is a join-experiment in progress and our level of subscription corresponds to the highest-level join-experiment in progress, we infer that our join-experiment has failed, drop the offending layer, back off the join-timer, and enter the D state. On the other hand, if we are locally conducting a join-experiment but a concurrent join-experiment is running at a higher layer, then it is likely that the higher layer experiment failed while ours did not but we cannot be certain. Hence, we enter the measurement state M to look for longer term congestion before dropping our layer. Finally, if we were not conducting a join-experiment at all, we transition to the H state.

The H state provides hysteresis to absorb transient congestion periods. This prevents a receiver in steady-state from reacting to join-experiments that are carried out by other receivers in the network or to transient network congestion. Once the detection-timer expires, we assume that any transient join-experiment is finished and transition to the measurement state and back to the S state after another detection time. If on other hand, the congestion is long-term (e.g., because of new offered load), then once we enter the M state, the loss rate estimator ramps up, exceeds the threshold, and forces the current layer to be dropped.

When a layer is dropped in response to congestion, the receiver enters the D state, sets the detection-timer, and ignores losses until the detection-timer expires. This prevents the receiver from (over-)reacting to losses that are unrelated to its current level of subscription. Once the receiver has waited long enough, the incoming packet stream will reflect the new level of subscription and the receiver can take action on the subsequent quality.

3.5   Protocol State Maintenance

In addition to the current state identifier, the receiver control algorithm must maintain the current subscription level, the detection-time estimator, and the join-timers. This state, along with several protocol design constants, is summarized in Table 1.

While the subscription level is trivial to maintain, the detection-time estimator and join-timers must be dynamically adapted to reflect changing network conditions. There are two operations performed on join-timers: backoff and relaxation. Call the mean of the join-timer for level-k, $\hat{T}_J^k$. Each timer interval is chosen randomly from a distribution parameterized by $\hat{T}_J^k$. When a join-experiment fails, the join-timer is multiplicatively increased:

$$\hat{T}_J^k \leftarrow \min(\alpha \hat{T}_J^k, T_J^{\max})$$

state	state identifier (S, H, M, D)
N	current level of subscription
$\hat{T}_J^k$	join-timer for level k
$\hat{T}_D$	detection-time sample mean
$\hat{\sigma}_D$	detection-time sample deviation
$T_J^{\min}$	minimum join-timer interval
$T_J^{\max}$	maximum join-timer interval
α	join-timer backoff constant
β	join-timer relaxation constant
k_1, k_2	detection-time estimator scaling term
g_1, g_2	detection-time estimator filter constants

Table 1: RLM State and Parameters

where $\alpha > 1$ is the backoff parameter and $T_J^{\max}$ is the maximum timeout. We clamp the backoff at a maximum to guarantee that a receiver will periodically probe for spare bandwidth. To scale to large session sizes, $T_J^{\max}$ is dynamically adjusted in proportion to the number of receivers. The number of receivers is in turn dynamically estimated through the exchange of session-wide control messages (e.g., as in RTCP [28]). Thus the aggregate join-experiment rate is fixed, independent of the session size, and packet loss induced by join-experiments does not increase with session size.

The join-timer undergoes relaxation in steady-state. The longer a receiver is in steady-state at some level, the more likely it is for that level to be stable. Thus the corresponding join-timer interval should be small. We adapt the join-timer by geometrically decreasing it at detection-timer intervals:

$$\hat{T}_J^k \leftarrow \max(\beta \hat{T}_J^k, T_J^{\min})$$

where $\beta < 1$ is the relaxation constant and $T_J^{\min}$ is the minimum join-timer interval.

While the join-timers are determined algorithmically, the detection-time estimate is derived directly from network measurements. The detection-time reflects the latency between time at which a local action is carried out and the time at which impact of that action is reflected back to the receiver. Note that this delay can be much larger than the time it takes for the network just to instantiate a new flow. If the new aggregate bandwidth exceeds the bottleneck link capacity by only a small amount, a long time may pass before a queue builds up and causes packet loss.

The detection-time estimate is computed by correlating failed join-experiment start times with the onset of congestion. Each time a join-experiment fails, the detection-time estimator is fed the new latency measurement. The measurement, D_i, is passed through first-order low-pass filters with gains g_1, g_2:

$$\hat{\sigma}_D \leftarrow (1 - g_2)\hat{\sigma}_D + g_2|D_i - \hat{T}_D|$$
$$\hat{T}_D \leftarrow (1 - g_1)\hat{T}_D + g_1 D_i$$

4 Simulations

In this section, we present simulation results of several simple network topologies to explore the scalability of RLM. This work is in an exploratory stage. Our simulations do not prove that RLM is definitively scalable. Rather, they demonstrate that the scaling behavior is consistent with our intuition and show that for simple scenarios, the protocol's performance is good. In a real network, performance will be affected by cross-traffic and competing groups, both of which add noise to the measurement process and introduce interactions that could result in oscillatory behavior. We will assess the impact of such interactions in future work.

We implemented the RLM protocol described above in the LBNL network simulator *ns* [24]. Not only did this implementation serve as a framework for evaluating the protocol's performance, but the simulator provided feedback that was critical to the design process. Ns is an event-driven packet-level simulator controlled and configured via Tcl [27]. Shortest-path routes are computed for the input topology and multicast packets are routed via reverse-path forwarding. A flooding algorithm similar to Dense-mode Protocol Independent Multicast (PIM) [7] handles forwarding and pruning of multicast flows.

Hierarchical sources are modeled as a set of constant-bit rate (CBR) streams with fixed packet sizes. Packets are generated at times defined by the following law:

$$
\begin{aligned}
T_0 &= 0 \\
T_k &= T_{k-1} + \Delta + N_k, \ \ k > 0
\end{aligned}
$$

where Δ is a fixed interval chosen to meet the target bit-rate and N_k is zero-mean noise process to model variable coding delays ($\{N_k\}$ is i.i.d. uniform on $[-\Delta/2, \Delta/2]$). Unfortunately, this simple model fails to capture the burstiness of real video streams [18]. Because convergence in RLM relies on matching the layered rates to available capacity, smooth sources are well-behaved and this traffic model is overly optimistic. On the other hand, a bursty source can be smoothed out by applying rate-control through adaptive quantization at the cost of variable quality. A topic for future research is whether RLM is amenable to bursty sources.

Before discussing the simulation results, we define the parameters we varied for the simulations and the metrics we used to evaluate the results. Variable parameters include network topology, link bandwidths and latencies, the number and rate of transmission layers, and the placement of senders and receivers. Fixed parameters include the routing discipline (drop-tail), the router queue size (20 packets), and the packet size (1 KB). In all of our simulations, the link bandwidths are 1.5 Mb/s, the traffic sources are modeled as a six-layer CBR stream at rates 32×2^m kb/s, $m = 0 \ldots 5$, and the start-time of each receiver is randomly chosen uniformly on the interval $[30, 120]$ seconds. The protocol constants from Table 1 have the following values: $\alpha = 2$, $\beta = 2/3$, $k_1 = 1$, $k_2 = 2$, $g_1 = 0.25$, $g_2 = 0.25$, $T_J^{\min} = 5$ sec, $T_J^{\max} = 600$

sec. Each join-timer interval is chosen from $\lambda/2 + X$, where X is a random variable with density

$$
f_X(x) = \left\{
\begin{array}{ll}
\lambda e^{-\lambda x}/(1 - e^{-4\lambda^2}) & 0 \leq x \leq 4\lambda \\
0 & \text{otherwise}
\end{array}
\right.
$$

and $\lambda = \hat{T}_j^k$. These protocol parameters were chosen heuristically based on experimentation with and intuition about the protocol. In future work, we plan to present a larger range of configurations and a study of the parametric sensitivity.

4.1 Evaluation Metrics

In our layered multicast transmission scheme, a traditional metric like aggregate throughput is not well defined because each user might receive a different bandwidth and experience different loss rates. Performance not only depends on aggregate metrics like overall loss rate, but also on the stability of the system and the time scales over which events occur. Moreover, we need to separate transient behavior from long-term behavior. For example, an aggregate loss rate can be made arbitrarily good by letting the simulation run arbitrarily long after reaching stability.

To address these issues, we rely on two metrics that (at least to first order) reflect the perceived quality of a real-time, loss-tolerant multimedia stream at the receiver. The first metric is the worst-case loss rate over varying time scales. By considering the short-term loss rates, we can assess the extent of congestion transients. Similarly, by considering long-term loss rates, we can determine how frequently congestion occurs in the steady-state (i.e., by the gap between the long-term and short-term rates).

Our second metric characterizes throughput. In all of the single-source simulations, each receiver eventually reaches the optimal level of subscription. Above this optimum, the network is congested, and below, the network is underutilized. Except for infrequent and brief excursions due to join-experiments, each receiver maintains this level. Accordingly, the throughput can be made arbitrarily close to optimal as described above. Thus we evaluate throughput based on the time it takes the system to converge to the optimal operating point. In an environment where capacity changes dynamically, this rate of convergence characterizes the proximity to optimal throughput. (We ignore the performance loss incurred by a mismatch between the discrete set of possible rates and the exact available bandwidth. In our simulations such mismatch is arbitrary but in practice is difficult to avoid.)

Neither loss rate nor throughput (as measured through convergence time) alone is a comprehensive metric. The system could have a low loss rate with poor throughput (e.g., send nothing), as well as good throughput with high loss rate (e.g., send too much). But taken together, acceptably low loss rates and fast convergence times imply a well-functioning system.

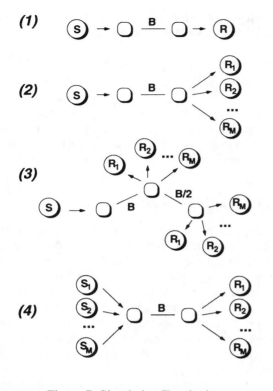

Figure 7: Simulation Topologies.

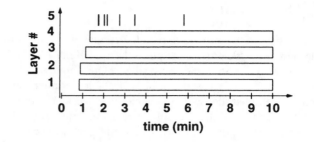

Figure 8: Simple sample path.

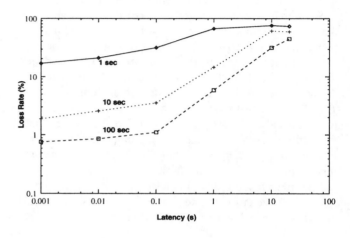

Figure 9: Latency Scalability.

4.2 Experiments

We have simulated RLM in a large number of topologies and configurations. Here we present a subset of the simulations that explores the scalability of RLM in simple environments. The four topologies are illustrated in Figure 7. Topology (1) consists of a single source and receiver separated by a bottleneck link. By analyzing the performance as we vary the latency on the bottleneck link , we explore the protocol's delay scalability.

Topology (2) extends topology (1) with multiple receivers. Here, we explore the scalability of the algorithm with respect to session size. As the size increases, we expect the join-experiment frequency during transients to increase and would like to assess the impact of this on the packet loss characteristic. Also, in large sessions join-experiments inevitably interfere with each other that lead to misinterpretation of the optimal capacity.

Topology (3) explores the performance in the presence of bandwidth heterogeneity by considering two sets of receivers. The first set is connected at the bottleneck rate B while the second set is connected at rate $B/2$. In this scenario, the receivers downstream of the lower speed link must be robust against the high-bandwidth join-experiments from the other set of receivers.

Finally, topology (4) considers the superposition of a large number of independent sessions.

4.3 Results

In this section, we present the results of simulations on the four topologies described above.

Latency Scalability. In the first experiment, we placed a hierarchical CBR source at S in topology (1), ran RLM at R, and fixed the link delay at 10 ms. The simulation was run for 10 (simulated) minutes. In this case, the behavior is predictable. The receiver ramps up to the number of layers supported by the link, then conducts join-experiments at progressively larger intervals until the maximum interval is reached. The duration of the join-experiment is roughly twice the link latency plus the queue build-up time; the impact of packet loss is proportional to the duration of the join-experiment, and thus proportional to the link latency.

This behavior is confirmed in Figure 8, which shows the level of subscription as it evolves over time for this simulation. Note that the receiver reaches the optimal layer subscription in about half a minute and at that point conducts join-experiments at progressively larger time intervals. Each join-experiment lasts less than a second.

To explore the delay sensitivity, we varied the link delay in topology (1) from 1 ms to 20 seconds and computed the worst-case loss rate over different time scales. For each re-

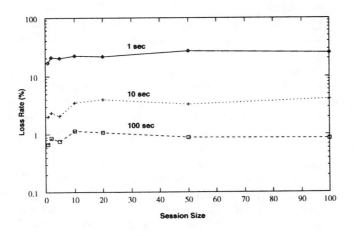

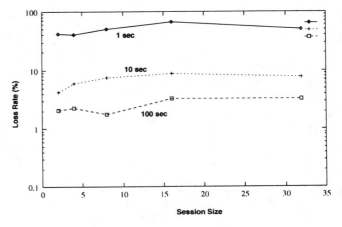

Figure 10: Session-size Scalability.

Figure 12: Bandwidth Heterogeneity.

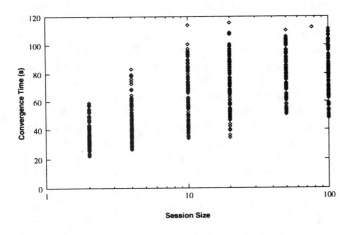

Figure 11: Rate of Convergence.

ceiver, we slide a measurement window (1, 10, or 100 seconds) over the arrival packet process. Within the window, we compute the fraction of lost to total packets and we take the maximum over all time offsets. As the latency increases, we expect the performance to decrease since it takes longer to learn that loss is occurring, prolonging congestion periods. Figure 9 plots the maximum loss rate for a given measurement window versus link latency. For the large measurement window (100 sec) and low delays (≤ 1 sec), the worst-case loss rates are under 1%. On the other hand, the short-term worst-case loss rate (window of 1 sec) ranges from 10 to 20% even for latencies below 100 ms. Finally, each curve has a knee that occurs roughly where measurement window size is twice the link latency. We expect this behavior because the join-experiment congestion period will last at least twice the latency, so the loss rate will be maximal for this size of measurement window.

Session Scalability. In the next experiment, we varied the session size as illustrated in topology (2). Again, we fixed the

link delays to 10 ms and ran each simulation for 10 minutes. Figure 10 shows the results. For each time scale, we plotted the maximum loss rate against the number of receivers. Because this configuration has multiple receivers, we compute the maximum loss rate by taking the maximum across the worst-case loss rates for each receiver (each computed as the supremum over the sliding window). The graph shows that the worst-case loss rates are essentially independent of the session size. And even for the largest sessions the long-term loss rate is only about 1%.

In this second experiment we also explored how the session size of topology (2) impacts the rate of convergence of each receiver to its optimal level of subscription. Figure 11 is a scatter plot collected over a number of simulation runs. Each point represents the time it took a receiver to reach and maintain its optimal level of subscription (aside from infrequent join-experiments). There is a linear trend in the log plot suggesting logarithmic dependence between convergence time and session size. As the number of receivers grows, we expect longer convergence times since a large number of receivers will suppress join experiments at higher layers. However, because information is shared on each failed join-experiment, receivers rapidly learn the state of the network.

Bandwidth Heterogeneity. Figure 12 illustrates that the algorithm works well even in the presence of large sets of receivers with different bandwidth constraints. The worst-case loss rates are comparable though somewhat higher than the homogeneous cases. The dependence on session size is more notable on short-term time scales because the larger session size increases the probability of colliding join-experiments. Thus, receivers that are genuinely responsible for congestion will transition through the M state before dropping the offending layer. Hence, short-term congestion periods can last longer at larger session sizes. However, the impact of this increase is limited by the detection time estimator, and hence does not increase without bound with the session size.

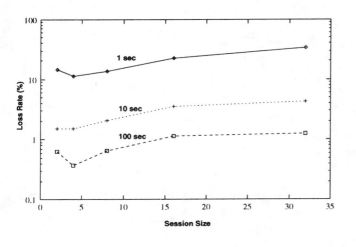

Figure 13: Superposition.

Superposition.   Topology (4) explores the performance of RLM when some number of independent single-source/single-receiver sessions share a common link. We ran several simulations and varied the number of source/receiver pairs. The bottleneck link bandwidth was scaled in proportion to the number of pairs and the router queue limit scaled to twice the bandwidth-delay product. Although each simulation converged to an aggregate link utilization close to one, the bandwidth allocation to each pair was often unfair (though no pair was ever starved of bandwidth, since a high-bandwidth session is more likely to experience loss during a join-experiment). Figure 13 illustrates the worst-case loss rate performance, which is consistent with our other simulations. Long-term loss rates are under 1% while medium-term rates are a few percent.

5   Network Implications

Although this paper focuses on the transmission mechanism for layered signals, RLM is only one component of an overall system for multimedia communication. In this section, we discuss some of the implications that RLM has on other components in a comprehensive system for layered multicast transmission.

Receiver-consensus An important requirement of RLM is that all users cooperate. The level of traffic on any given link requires consensus among all of the participants downstream from that link. If just one user in a large group defects and joins all the layers, then nothing can be done to counteract the resulting congestion. Of course, if everyone is running RLM, this will not happen. On the other hand, given the way multicast membership is managed and how RLM might be implemented, more subtle failure modes are possible. For example, a user might temporarily "suspend" an RLM-based application at an inopportune time, causing the end-host to be oversubscribed and unable to react to the resulting con-

gestion. This problem could be solved with the appropriate system fixes (e.g., by deactivating multicast group membership for suspended applications), but complicates deployment.

Group Maintenance. Our simulations show that the performance of RLM depends critically on the join/leave latencies. Once the receiver leaves a group, the network must suppress the flow in a timely manner because congestion persists as long as the network continues to deliver the offending layer. Similarly, to allow receivers to correlate join-experiments with resulting congestion periods, the network must instantiate a new flow expediently. In the case of IP Multicast, the Internet Group Management Protocol (IGMP) [12] carries out both of these operations on reasonable time scales. When a receiver joins a new group, the host immediately informs the next-hop router, which in turn, immediately propagates a *graft* message up the multicast distribution tree in order to instantiate the new group. If the flow already exists, the graft is suppressed. The leave-case is more complicated because the next-hop router must determine when all the hosts on a subnet have left the group. To do this, when a host drops a group, it broadcasts a "leave group" message on the subnet and the router responds by briefly accelerating its normal membership query algorithm. Upon quickly determining that no members remain, the router sends a *prune* message up the distribution tree to suppress the group.

Fairness. In a network with arbitrary numbers of senders each transmitting to an arbitrary number of receivers, each receiver should individually adjust its number of layers so that the aggregate system performance is "good". When there is only a single source sending some number of receivers, "good" is well-defined: each receiver should receive the maximum number of layers that the network can deliver. But when there are multiple sources, "good" is ill-defined because it depends on the relative importance of the users within and across sessions. In short, an aggregate performance metric depends on how group "fairness" is defined.

Rather than tackle the problem of defining fairness, we have placed our initial focus on the design of RLM in *isolation*, that is, when a single source sends to multiple receiver without interfering traffic. RLM alone *does not* provide fairness. In general it is not possible to achieve a "fair" allocation of bandwidth without some additional machinery in the network, even if all the end-nodes cooperate [22]. But, if machinery for fairness is added to the network, RLM should work effectively in concert with it.

Similar circumstance surrounds the design of TCP. TCP congestion control works well in isolation but in aggregation can be unfair [13]. As an optimization, network mechanism can be introduced to make TCP perform better: Random Early Detection (RED) [14] gateways or Fair Queuing (FQ) [10] routers minimize the interaction between connections to improve fairness. Similarly, we can design RLM to behave relatively well in a loosely controlled, drop-tail, best-effort network, and as an optimization add RED or FQ to the network (or to parts of the network) to improve aggregate performance.

All of our simulation results assume that routers drop packets on arrival when their queue is full. This widely deployed drop-tail discard policy is unfortunate because it delays the warning signal from the receivers until well after congestion has occurred. RED gateways, on the other hand, react to incipient congestion by discarding packets at the onset of congestion (i.e., when the rate of change of the queue size exceeds a threshold) [14]. RED's early reaction to congestion interacts nicely with RLM because it allows receivers to react to congestion before the bottleneck link becomes fully saturated. We have run simulations using RED gateways in place of drop-tail gateways and the loss rate performance indeed improves.

6   The Application

To complement the layered transmission system provided by RLM, we have developed a layered source coder adapted for this environment [26]. Our goal is to design, build, and evaluate all of the components that contribute to a scalable video transmission system, ensuring that the pieces of the design interact well with each other. To this end, our system is based on Clark and Tennenhouse's Application Level Framing (ALF) protocol architecture [5]. While ALF says that an application's semantics should be reflected in the design of its network protocol, we further believe that the "network's semantics" should also be reflected in the application design. For example, instead of designing an "optimal" framing protocol for a compressed-video bitstream emanating from a black box (i.e., reflecting application semantics in the protocol), we claim the compression format itself should be tailored to its environment (i.e., reflecting network constraints in the application design).

The ALF model is embodied in the co-design of RLM and our layered codec. The characteristic of the RLM communications environment substantially influences the design of our layered codec, while conversely, the layered compression model drives the design of RLM. Rather than design the sub-components in isolation, we design them jointly to complement each other and thereby produce an application with high performance not only over the network but also through the end-system and ultimately to the user.

Two key features of our layered coder are its resilience to packet loss and its low complexity. These characteristics make it especially well suited for scalable video transmission over the Internet. First, the scheme is robust to the RLM join-experiments (and the background transient congestion common in the Internet) since transient periods of congestion are gracefully accommodated through its loss resilience. Moreover, because join-experiments are announced to the group, the source can dynamically modify its coding algorithm to trade bandwidth for loss resilience. Second, the algorithm's low complexity admits an efficient software implementation that can be readily distributed to many users in the Internet.

Because RLM relies only on mechanisms that are already widely deployed in the Internet, we can field our system by building it into an application. We are currently implementing RLM and our layered codec in the UCB/LBNL video conferencing tool *vic* [25]. Vic's network transport is based on the Real-time Transport Protocol (RTP) [28], an application level protocol for multimedia transport standardized by the Internet Engineering Task Force. Although RTP has proven to be a solid foundation for interoperable real-time audio/video applications, it was designed without any explicit notion of a layered signal representation. In joint work, we have extended RTP for layered stream delivery [31] and are currently implementing our proposed changes in vic.

Since the RLM protocol processing is not in the "fast path", run-time performance is not critical. In fact, our prototype is implemented almost entirely in the interpreted language Tcl [27]. Vic's C++ packet processing code performs upcalls into Tcl when loss is detected. Tcl runs the adaptation algorithm and manipulates IP Multicast group membership via downcalls back to C++.

7   Related Work

The idea that the rate of an information source can be adjusted by degrading reconstruction quality was born in rate-distortion theory first developed by Shannon [30]. The rate-distortion framework forms the bedrock of traditional video codec design, where codec parameters (i.e., compression quality) are dynamically adjusted to match the transmission rate of a CBR communications channel. Gilge and Gusella [19] applied the CBR coding model to packet networks by viewing the network as the codec smoothing buffer. They proposed an end-to-end design that uses explicit feedback from the receiver to throttle the video transmission rate at the source.

Kanakia et al. [23] build on Gilge and Gusella's model with an architecture where the feedback signal is derived directly from the network. The bottleneck switch or router along the transmission path communicates its queuing delay back to the source. A controller uses this information to adjust the output rate of the source coder, allowing the source to react to queue buildup before packet loss occurs.

These source-based rate-adaptation schemes are poorly matched to multicast environments. QMTP [34] and the IVS congestion control scheme [1] adapt by soliciting feedback from the receivers in a scalable fashion, but these schemes do not cope well with bandwidth heterogeneity. Either low-capacity regions of the distribution are overwhelmed or high-capacity regions are underutilized.

Shacham proposed a scheme based on layered transmission and compression to solve the heterogeneity problem [29]. He focused on computing fixed, optimal routes for a given traffic mix and on error control procedures for coping with loss rather than reacting to it.

Taubman and Zakhor [32] have developed a layered video

compression algorithm that performs on par with the best non-layered schemes. Their focus is on the compression technology rather than the network, and their network model is based on signaling and packet discard policies that are not widely deployed.

The "Discrete Scaling" mechanism in the Heidelberg Transport System (HeiTS) [9] uses a receiver-oriented scheme for adapting to delivered bandwidth. Here, receivers open and close ST-II [3] multicast connections to adapt to bandwidth. The authors do not discuss adaptation algorithms or report any implementation results.

Deering first suggested that the IP Multicast be used as a layered transmission system where layers are individually mapped onto multicast groups [6]. Both Chaddha and Gupta [4] and Bolot and Turletti [33] describe this architecture but do not present an adaptation algorithm or implementation. Brown et al. have implemented a multi-resolution extension to the CU-SeeMe video conferencing system where IP Multicast receivers can subscribe to either a 160x120 or a 320x240 stream by joining either one or two multicast groups [2]. Receivers drop down to the 160x120 resolution when they detect high packet loss rates.

Concurrent with our work, Hoffman and Speer have built a similar system based on the layered multicast architecture [20]. They use multiple frame rates of JPEG video to generate a temporal hierarchy and employ two techniques for adaptation. Their first technique is a negotiation algorithm run by each receiver that obtains the highest available quality of service explicitly from the network (e.g., using RSVP [35]). Their second approach uses layered multicast with an aggressive adaptation scheme where a new receiver subscribes to all the layers in the distribution and drops layers until the quality of the delivered stream is adequate.

8   Future Work

RLM is the first comprehensive instance of a receiver-driven multicast adaptation algorithm and we have just scratched the surface of this problem. While we have evaluated RLM in terms of packet loss rates, the ultimate evaluation metric is the level of quality perceived by the user. We will soon carry out qualitative performance measurements both in a controlled environment as well as by fielding an implementation in the Internet. The litmus test will be whether or not the user community adopts the RLM and the layered codec as the preferred configuration.

We also plan to experiment with algorithms that dynamically adjust the bit-rate allocation of the different compression layers. Our compression scheme produces an *embedded code*, which has the property that any prefix of the compressed bitstream remains a valid representation at a lower quality. In other words, a given video frame can be successively refined at a very fine granularity. Using this property, we can partition the bit-rate arbitrarily among layers and vary this allocation dynamically, from frame to frame or slowly

over time. As an optimization, we can use scalable, low-rate feedback from the receivers (e.g., as provided by RTCP [28]) to tailor the rate allocation to the environment. For example, if the entire session is connected at high-rate, but one user is connected at ISDN rate, we could produce a two-layer stream rather than a higher-complexity multi-layer stream.

In an integrated services network, a receiver could explicitly negotiate with the network to determine the appropriate number of layers [20], with or without consideration of a pricing structure. In this case, RLM adaptation is not necessary. On the other hand, if the granularity of resource management were not as fine-grained, then RLM adaptation within an integrated services environment might still make sense. For example, Class Based Queuing (CBQ) [16] could be used to provide an "adaptive-rate video" traffic class with some specified bandwidth. Then within this CBQ class, video sessions could contend for the aggregate class bandwidth using RLM. This approach has the desirable side effect that RLM is shielded from interactions with other protocols.

The RLM framework could be combined with the Scalable Reliable Multicast (SRM) protocol [17] in the LBNL whiteboard, *wb*, to optimize the latency of rate-controlled transmissions. Because SRM uses a token-bucket rate-controller, it has the same limitations that single-layer video has in heterogeneous environments. On the other hand, several token-buckets with a range of rates could be used in tandem with multiple multicast groups and RLM. SRM would *simulcast* new data across all of the token-buckets to trade off bandwidth for latency. By spacing the rates exponentially, the overhead of the simulcast is minimized.

Our simulations explored interactions only among different instances of RLM. We plan to explore interactions with other bandwidth-adaptive protocols like TCP. Similarly, we are studying the interactions among multiple RLM sessions in the context of different scheduling disciplines. For example, fair-queuing (FQ) routers drop packets from sessions that use more than their proportion of bandwidth. Thus, if the FQ allocation granularity is the set of layered multicast groups, then RLM should converge to a fair operating point. Likewise, because RED gateways drop packets from connections with probability proportional to their bandwidth consumption, the system should converge to approximate fairness.

Finally, we intend to improve our modeling and analysis of the problem. We are developing a model for layered signal sources (based on our codec work) that expresses the dependencies between packets in different layers. This will allow us to develop better loss metrics since losses in the core layers tend to impact higher layers. We are also investigating a tractable analytic model of the protocol actions on simple topologies to characterize convergence and loss probabilities as a function of scale.

9 Summary

We have proposed a framework for the transmission of layered signals over heterogeneous networks using receiver-driven adaptation. We evaluated the performance of RLM through simulation and showed that it exhibits reasonable loss and convergence rates under several scaling scenarios. While many existing solutions are either network-oriented or compression-oriented, our focus is on the complete systems design. We described our work on a low-complexity, error-resilient layered source coder, which when combined with RLM, provides a comprehensive solution for scalable multicast video transmission in heterogeneous networks.

10 Acknowledgments

This work benefited from several thought-provoking discussions with Sally Floyd. Sally proposed the model where RLM is used within a CBQ class allocation. Elan Amir, Hari Balakrishnan, Sugih Jamin, Deana McCanne, Vern Paxson, Scott Shenker, and the anonymous reviewers provided thoughtful comments on drafts of this paper. Lixia Zhang inflicted an early version of this paper on her seminar at UCLA, which generated constructive feedback. Finally, Steve Deering participated in several early discussions of this work.

Support for this work was provided by the the Director, Office of Energy Research, Scientific Computing Staff, of the U.S. Department of Energy under Contract No. DE-AC03-76SF00098. Equipment grants and support were provided by Sun Microsystems, Digital Equipment Corporation, and Silicon Graphics Inc.

References

[1] BOLOT, J.-C., TURLETTI, T., AND WAKEMAN, I. Scalable feedback control for multicast video distribution in the Internet. In *Proceedings of SIGCOMM '94* (University College London, London, U.K., Sept. 1994), ACM.

[2] BROWN, T., SAZZAD, S., SCHROEDER, C., CANTRELL, P., AND GIBSON, J. Packet video for heterogeneous networks using CU-SeeMe. In *Proceedings of the IEEE International Conference on Image Processing* (Lausanne, Switzerland, Sept. 1996).

[3] CASNER, S., LYNN, J., PARK, P., SCHRODER, K., AND TOPOLCIC, C. *Experimental Internet Stream Protocol, version 2 (ST-II).* ARPANET Working Group Requests for Comment, DDN Network Information Center, SRI International, Menlo Park, CA, Oct. 1990. RFC-1190.

[4] CHADDHA, N., AND GUPTA, A. A frame-work for live multicast of video streams over the Internet. In *Proceedings of the IEEE International Conference on Image Processing* (Lausanne, Switzerland, Sept. 1996).

[5] CLARK, D. D., AND TENNENHOUSE, D. L. Architectural considerations for a new generation of protocols. In *Proceedings of SIGCOMM '90* (Philadelphia, PA, Sept. 1990), ACM.

[6] DEERING, S. Internet multicast routing: State of the art and open research issues, Oct. 1993. Multimedia Integrated Conferencing for Europe (MICE) Seminar at the Swedish Institute of Computer Science, Stockholm.

[7] DEERING, S., ESTRIN, D., FARINACCI, D., JACOBSON, V., GUNG LIU, C., AND WEI, L. An architecture for wide-area multicast routing. In *Proceedings of SIGCOMM '94* (University College London, London, U.K., Sept. 1994), ACM.

[8] DEERING, S. E. *Multicast Routing in a Datagram Internetwork.* PhD thesis, Stanford University, Dec. 1991.

[9] DELGROSSI, L., HALSTRICK, C., HEHMANN, D., HERRTWICH, R. G., KRONE, O., SANDVOSS, J., AND VOGT, C. Media scaling for audiovisual communication with the Heidelberg transport system. In *Proceedings of ACM Multimedia '93* (Aug. 1993), ACM, pp. 99–104.

[10] DEMERS, A., KESHAV, S., AND SHENKER, S. Analysis and simulation of a fair queueing algorithm. *Internetworking: Research and Experience 1* (1990), 3–26.

[11] ERIKSSON, H. Mbone: The multicast backbone. *Communications of the ACM 37*, 8 (1994), 54–60.

[12] FENNER, W. *Internet Group Management Protocol, Version 2.* Internet Engineering Task Force, Inter-Domain Multicast Routing Working Group, Feb. 1996. Internet Draft expires 8/31/96.

[13] FLOYD, S., AND JACOBSON, V. On traffic phase effects in packet-switched gateways. *Internetworking: Research and Experience 3*, 3 (Sept. 1992), 115–156.

[14] FLOYD, S., AND JACOBSON, V. Random early detection gateways for congestion avoidance. *IEEE/ACM Transactions on Networking 1*, 4 (Aug. 1993), 397–413.

[15] FLOYD, S., AND JACOBSON, V. The synchronization of periodic routing messages. In *Proceedings of SIGCOMM '93* (San Francisco, CA, Sept. 1993), ACM, pp. 33–44.

[16] FLOYD, S., AND JACOBSON, V. Link-sharing and resource management models for packet networks. *IEEE/ACM Transactions on Networking 3*, 4 (Aug. 1995), 365–386.

[17] FLOYD, S., JACOBSON, V., MCCANNE, S., LIU, C.-G., AND ZHANG, L. A reliable multicast framework for lightweight sessions and application level framing. In *Proceedings of SIGCOMM '95* (Boston, MA, Sept. 1995), ACM.

[18] GARRETT, M. W., AND WILLINGER, W. Analysis, modeling and generation of self-similar VBR video traffic. In *Proceedings of SIGCOMM '94* (University College London, London, U.K., Sept. 1994), ACM.

[19] GILGE, M., AND GUSELLA, R. Motion video coding for packet-switching networks—an integrated approach. In *Proceedings of the SPIE Conference on Visual Communications and Image Processing* (Boston, MA, Nov. 1991), ACM.

[20] HOFFMAN, D., AND SPEER, M. Hierarchical video distribution over Internet-style networks. In *Proceedings of the IEEE International Conference on Image Processing* (Lausanne, Switzerland, Sept. 1996).

[21] JACOBSON, V. Congestion avoidance and control. In *Proceedings of SIGCOMM '88* (Stanford, CA, Aug. 1988).

[22] JAFFE, J. M. Bottleneck flow control. *IEEE Transactions on Communications 29*, 7 (July 1981), 954–962.

[23] KANAKIA, H., MISHRA, P. P., AND REIBMAN, A. An adaptive congestion control scheme for real-time packet video transport. In *Proceedings of SIGCOMM '93* (San Francisco, CA, Sept. 1993), ACM, pp. 20–31.

[24] MCCANNE, S., AND FLOYD, S. *The LBNL Network Simulator*. Lawrence Berkeley Laboratory. Software on-line[2].

[25] MCCANNE, S., AND JACOBSON, V. *vic:* a flexible framework for packet video. In *Proceedings of ACM Multimedia '95* (Nov. 1995), ACM.

[26] MCCANNE, S., AND VETTERLI, M. Joint source/channel coding for multicast packet video. In *Proceedings of the IEEE International Conference on Image Processing* (Washington, DC, Oct. 1995).

[27] OUSTERHOUT, J. K. *Tcl and the Tk Toolkit*. Addison-Wesley, 1994.

[28] SCHULZRINNE, H., CASNER, S., FREDERICK, R., AND JACOBSON, V. *RTP: A Transport Protocol for Real-Time Applications*. Internet Engineering Task Force, Audio-Video Transport Working Group, Jan. 1996. RFC-1889.

[29] SHACHAM, N. Multipoint communication by hierarchically encoded data. In *Proceedings IEEE Infocom '92* (1992), pp. 2107–2114.

[30] SHANNON, C. E. A mathematical theory of communication. *Bell Systems Technical Journal 27* (1948), 379–423.

[31] SPEER, M. F., AND MCCANNE, S. *RTP usage with Layered Multimedia Streams*. Internet Engineering Task Force, Audio-Video Transport Working Group, Mar. 1996. Internet Draft expires 9/1/96.

[32] TAUBMAN, D., AND ZAKHOR, A. Multi-rate 3-D subband coding of video. *IEEE Transactions on Image Processing 3*, 5 (Sept. 1994), 572–588.

[33] TURLETTI, T., AND BOLOT, J.-C. Issues with multicast video distribution in heterogeneous packet networks. In *Proceedings of the Sixth International Workshop on Packet Video* (Portland, OR, Sept. 1994).

[34] YAVATKAR, R., AND MANOJ, L. Optimistic strategies for large-scale dissemination of multimedia information. In *Proceedings of ACM Multimedia '93* (Aug. 1993), ACM, pp. 1–8.

[35] ZHANG, L., DEERING, S., ESTRIN, D., SHENKER, S., AND ZAPPALA, D. RSVP: A new resource reservation protocol. *IEEE Network 7* (Sept. 1993), 8–18.

A Survey of Packet Loss
Recovery Techniques for Streaming Audio

Colin Perkins, Orion Hodson, and Vicky Hardman
University College London

Abstract

We survey a number of packet loss recovery techniques for streaming audio applications operating using IP multicast. We begin with a discussion of the loss and delay characteristics of an IP multicast channel, and from this show the need for packet loss recovery. Recovery techniques may be divided into two classes: sender- and receiver-based. We compare and contrast several sender-based recovery schemes: forward error correction (both media-specific and media-independent), interleaving, and retransmission. In addition, a number of error concealment schemes are discussed. We conclude with a series of recommendations for repair schemes to be used based on application requirements and network conditions.

The development of IP multicast and the Internet multicast backbone (Mbone) has led to the emergence of a new class of scalable audio/video conferencing applications. These are based on the lightweight sessions model [1, 2] and provide efficient multiway communication which scales from two to several thousand participants. The network model underlying these applications differs significantly from the tightly coupled approach in use for traditional conferencing systems. The advantage of this new, loosely coupled approach to conferencing is scalability; the disadvantage is unusual channel characteristics which require significant work to achieve robust communication.

In this article we discuss the loss characteristics of such an IP multicast channel and how these affect audio communication. Following this, we examine a number of techniques for recovery from packet loss on the channel. These represent a broad cross-section of the range of applicable techniques, both sender-driven and receiver-based, and have been implemented in a wide range of conferencing applications, giving operational experience as to their behavior. The article concludes with an overview of the scope of applicability of these techniques and a series of recommendations for designers of packet-based audio conferencing applications.

A number of surveys have previously been published in the area of reli-able multicast and IP-based audio-video transport. The work by Obraczka [3] and Levine and Garcia-Luna-Aceves [4] is limited to the study of fully reliable transport and does not consider real-time delivery. The survey by Carle and Biersack [5] discusses real-time IP-based audio-video applications and techniques for error recovery in this environment. However, that work neglects receiver-based error concealment techniques and focuses on sender-driven mechanisms for error correction.

Sender-driven and receiver-based repair are complementary techniques, and applications should use both methods to

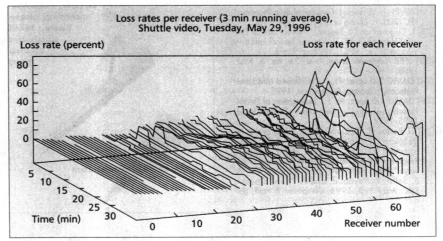

■ Figure 1. *Observed loss rates in a large multicast conference (from [7]).*

achieve the best possible performance. In contrast to previous work, we limit the focus of our article to streaming audio applications, and discuss both sender-driven repair and receiver-based error concealment techniques.

Multicast Channel Characteristics

The concept of IP multicast was proposed by Deering [6] to provide a scalable and efficient means by which datagrams may be distributed to a group of receivers. This is achieved by imposing a level of indirection between senders and receivers: packets are sent to a group address, receivers listen on that same address and the network conspires to deliver packets. Unless provided by an application-level protocol, the senders and receivers are decoupled by the group address: a sender does *not* know the set of hosts which will receive a packet. This indirection is important: routing decisions and recovery from network outages are purely local choices which do not have to be communicated back to the source of packets or to any of the receivers, enhancing scalability and robustness significantly.

Internet conferencing applications, based on IP multicast, typically employ an application-level protocol to provide *approximate* information as to the set of receivers and reception quality statistics. This protocol is the Real-time Transport Protocol (RTP) [8].

The portion of the Internet which supports IP multicast is known as the Mbone. Although some parts of the Mbone operate over dedicated links, the distinguishing feature is the presence of multicast routing support: multicast traffic typically shares links with other traffic. A number of attempts have been made to characterize the loss patterns seen on the Mbone [7, 9–11]. Although these results vary somewhat, the broad conclusion is clear: in a large conference it is inevitable that some receivers will experience packet loss. This is most clearly illustrated by the work of Handley [7], which tracks RTP reception report statistics for a large multicast session over several days. A typical portion of this trace is illustrated in Fig. 1. It can be seen that most receivers experience loss in the range of 2–5 percent, with some smaller number seeing significantly higher loss rates. The overwhelming cause of loss is due to congestion at routers. It is therefore not surprising that there is a correlation between the bandwidth used and the amount of loss experienced [7, 12], and the underlying loss rate varies during the day.

A multicast channel will typically have relatively high latency, and the variation in end-to-end delay may be large. This is clearly illustrated in Fig. 2, which shows the interarrival jitter for a series of packets sent from the University of Oregon to University College London on August 10, 1998. This delay variation is a reason for concern when developing loss-tolerant real-time applications, since packets delayed too long will have to be discarded in order to meet the application's timing

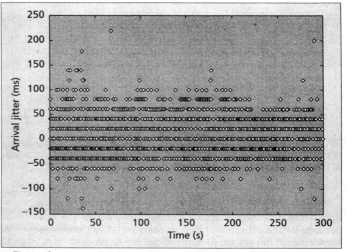

■ Figure 2. *Observed variation in end-to-end delay as seen by an Mbone audio tool (20 ms timing quantization).*

requirements, leading to the appearance of loss. This problem is more acute for interactive applications: if interactivity is unimportant, a large playout delay may be inserted to allow for these delayed packets. This problem and algorithms for playout buffer adaptation are studied further in [13–15].

Unlike other communications media, IP multicast allows for the trade-off between quality and interactivity to be made independently for each receiver in a session, since this is a local choice only and is not communicated to the source of the data. A session may exist with most participants acting as passive observers (high latency, low loss), but with some active participants (low latency, higher loss).

It should be noted that the characteristics of an IP multicast channel are significantly different from those of an asynchronous transfer mode (ATM) or integrated services digital network (ISDN) channel. The techniques discussed herein do not necessarily generalize to conferencing applications built on such network technologies.

The majority of these techniques are applicable to unicast IP, although the scaling and heterogeneity issues are clearly simpler in this case.

Sender-Based Repair

We discuss a number of techniques which require the participation of the sender of an audio stream to achieve recovery from packet loss. These techniques may be split into two major classes: active retransmission and passive channel coding. It is further possible to subdivide the set of channel coding techniques, with traditional forward error correction (FEC) and interleaving-based schemes being used. Forward error correction data may be either media-independent, typically based on exclusive-or operations, or media-specific based on the properties of an audio signal. This taxonomy is summarized in Fig. 3.

In order to simplify the following discussion we distinguish a *unit* of data from a *packet*. A unit is an interval of audio data, as stored internally in an audio tool. A packet comprises one or more units, encapsulated for transmission over the network.

Forward Error Correction

A number of forward error correction techniques have been developed to repair losses of data during transmission. These schemes rely on the addition of repair data to a stream, from which the contents of

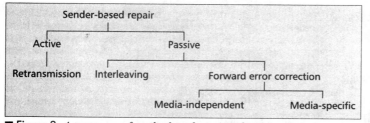

■ Figure 3. *A taxonomy of sender-based repair techniques.*

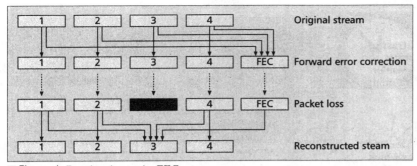

■ **Figure 4.** *Repair using parity FEC.*

lost packets may be recovered. There are two classes of repair data which may be added to a stream: those which are independent of the contents of that stream, and those which use knowledge of the stream to improve the repair process.

Media-Independent FEC — There has been much interest in the provision of media-independent FEC using block, or algebraic, codes to produce additional packets for transmission to aid the correction of losses. Each code takes a codeword of k data packets and generates $n - k$ additional check packets for the transmission of n packets over the network.

A large number of block coding schemes exist, and we discuss only two cases, parity coding and Reed-Solomon coding, since these are currently proposed as an RTP payload [16]. These block coding schemes were originally designed for the detection and correction of errors within a stream of transmitted bits, so the check bits were generated from a stream of data bits. In packet streams we are concerned with the loss of entire packets, so we apply block coding schemes across the corresponding bits in blocks of packets. Hence, the ith bit in a check packet is generated from the ith bit of each of the associated data packets.

In parity coding, the exclusive-or (XOR) operation is applied across groups of packets to generate corresponding parity packets. An example of this has been implemented by Rosenberg [17]. In this scheme, one parity packet is transmitted after every $n - 1$ data packets. Provided there is just one loss in every n packets, that loss is recoverable. This is illustrated in Fig. 4. Many different parity codes may be derived by XORing different combinations of packets; a number of these were proposed by Budge *et al.* and summarized by Rosenberg and Schulzrinne [16].

Reed-Solomon codes [18, 19] are renowned for their excellent error correcting properties, and in particular their resilience against burst losses. Encoding is based on the properties of polynomials over particular number bases. Essentially, RS encoders take a set of codewords and use these as coefficients of a polynomial, $f(x)$. The transmitted codeword is determined by evaluating the polynomial for all nonzero values of x over the number base. While this may sound complicated, the encoding procedure is relatively straightforward, and optimized decoding procedures such as the Berlekamp-Massey algorithm [20, 21] are available. In the absence of packet losses decoding carries the same computational cost as encoding, but when losses occur it is significantly more expensive.

There are several advantages to FEC schemes. The first is that they are media-independent: the operation of the FEC does not depend on the contents of the packets, and the repair is an exact replacement for a lost packet. In addition, the computation required to derive the error correction packets is relatively small and simple to implement. The disadvantages of these schemes are the additional delay imposed, increased bandwidth, and difficult decoder implementation.

Media-Specific FEC — A simple means to protect against packet loss is to transmit each unit of audio in multiple packets. If a packet is lost, another packet containing the same unit will be able to cover the loss. The principle is illustrated in Fig. 5. This approach has been advocated by Hardman *et al.* [22] and Bolot *et al.* [9] for use on the Mbone, and extensively simulated by Podolsky *et al.* [23].

The first transmitted copy of the audio data is referred to as the *primary encoding*, and subsequent transmissions as *secondary encodings*. It is the sender's decision whether the secondary audio encodings should be the same coding scheme as the primary, although usually the secondary is encoded using a lower-bandwidth, lower-quality encoding than the primary.

The choice of encodings is a difficult problem and depends on both the bandwidth requirements and the computational complexity of the encodings. Erdöl *et al.* [24] consider using short-term energy and zero crossing measurements as their secondary scheme. When loss occurs the receiver then interpolates an audio signal about the crossings using the short-term energy measurements. The advantage of this scheme is that it uses computationally cheap measures and can be coded compactly. However, it can only cover short periods of loss due to the crude nature of the measures. Hardman *et al.* [22] and Bolot *et al.* [9] advocate the use of low-bit-rate analysis-by-synthesis codecs, such as LPC (2.4–5.6 kb/s) and full rate GSM encoding (13.2 kb/s), which, although computationally more demanding, can tolerably cover the loss periods experienced on the Internet.

If the primary encoding consumes considerable processing power, but has sufficient quality and low bandwidth, then the secondary encodings may be the same as the primary. An example of this is the International Telecommunication Union (ITU) G.723.1 [25] codec which consumes a considerable fraction of today's desktop processing power, but has a low bandwidth (5.3/6.3 kb/s).

The use of media-specific FEC incurs an overhead in terms of packet size. For example, the use of 8 kHz PCM μ-law (64 kb/s) as the primary compression scheme and GSM [26] (13 kb/s) as the secondary results in a 20 percent increase in the size of the data portion of each packet. Like media-independent FEC schemes, the overhead of media-specific FEC is variable. How-

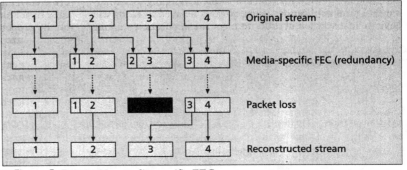

■ **Figure 5.** *Repair using media-specific FEC.*

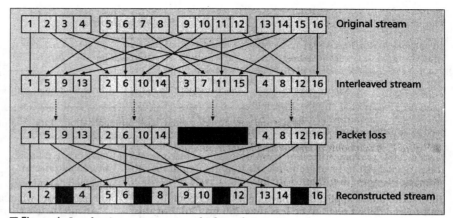

■ Figure 6. *Interleaving units across multiple packets.*

ever, unlike those schemes, the overhead of media-specific FEC may be reduced without affecting the number of losses which may be repaired; instead, the quality of the repair varies with the overhead. To reduce the overhead approximate repair is used, which is acceptable for audio applications.

It should be noted that it may often not be necessary to transmit media-specific FEC for every packet. Speech signals have transient stationary states that can cover 80 ms. Viswanathan *et al.* [27] describe LPC codecs where units of speech are only transmitted if the parameters of the codec are deemed to have changed sufficiently and achieve a 30 percent saving bandwidth for the same quality. A similar decision could be made about whether to transmit the FEC data, although this is likely to be codec-specific.

Unlike many of the other sender-based techniques discussed, the use of media-specific FEC has the advantage of low latency, with only a single-packet delay being added. This makes it suitable for interactive applications, where large end-to-end delays cannot be tolerated. If large end-to-end delay can be tolerated, it is possible to delay the redundant copy of a packet, achieving improved performance in the presence of burst losses [28].

At the time of writing, media-specific FEC is supported by a number of Mbone audio conferencing tools. The standard RTP payload format for media-specific FEC is described in [29].

Congestion Control — The addition of FEC repair data to a media stream is an effective means by which that stream may be protected against packet loss. However, application designers should be aware that the addition of large amounts of repair data when loss is detected will increase network congestion and hence packet loss, leading to a worsening of the problem which the use of FEC was intended to solve.

This is particularly important when sending to large multicast groups, since network heterogeneity causes different sets of receivers to observe widely varying loss rates: low-capacity regions of the network suffer congestion, while high-capacity regions are underutilized.

At the time of writing, there is no standard solution to this problem. There have been a number of contributions which show the likely form the solution will take [30–32]. These typically use some form of layered encoding of data sent at different rates over multiple multicast groups, with receivers joining and leaving groups in response to long-term congestion and with FEC employed to overcome short-term transient congestion.

Such a scheme pushes the burden of adaptation from the sender of a stream to the receivers, which choose the number of layers (groups) they join based on the packet loss rate they observe. Since the different layers contain data sent at different rates, receivers will receive different quality of service depending on the number of layers they are able to join. The precise details of these schemes are beyond the scope of this article; the reader is referred to the above references for further details.

Layered encoding schemes are expected to provide a congestion control solution suitable for streaming audio applications. However, this work is not yet complete, and it is important to give some advice to authors of streaming audio tools as to the behavior which is acceptable, until such congestion control mechanisms can be deployed.

It has been suggested that one heuristic suitable for determining reasonable behavior for unicast streaming media tools is to adapt the transmission rate to the approximate throughput a TCP/IP stream would achieve over the same path [33]. Since TCP/IP flows are the dominant form of traffic in the Internet, this would be roughly fair to existing traffic. Clearly such a scheme would not work for a multicast flow (although a worst case or average throughput to the set of receivers could be derived and used as the basis for adaptation), and clearly it does not capture the dynamic behavior of the connection, merely the average behavior; but it does provide one definition of reasonable behavior in the absence of real congestion control. In the long term, effective congestion control must be developed.

Note that the need for congestion control is *not* specific to FEC encoded audio streams. It should be considered for all streaming media.

Interleaving

When the unit size is smaller than the packet size and end-to-end delay is unimportant, interleaving is a useful technique for reducing the effects of loss [34]. Units are resequenced before transmission so that originally adjacent units are separated by a guaranteed distance in the transmitted stream and returned to their original order at the receiver. Interleaving disperses the effect of packet losses. If, for example, units are 5 ms in length and packets 20 ms (i.e., 4 units/packet), then the first packet would contain units 1, 5, 9, 13; the second units 2, 6, 10, 14; and so on, as illustrated in Fig. 6.

It can be seen that the loss of a single packet from an interleaved stream results in multiple small gaps in the reconstructed stream, as opposed to the single large gap which would occur in a noninterleaved stream. This spreading of the loss is important for two similar reasons: first, Mbone audio tools typically transmit packets which are similar in length to phonemes in human speech. Loss of a single packet will therefore have a large effect on the intelligibility of speech. If the loss is spread out so that small parts of several phonemes are lost, it becomes easier for listeners to mentally patch over this loss [35], resulting in improved perceived quality for a given loss rate. In a somewhat similar manner, error concealment techniques perform significantly better with small gaps, since the amount of change in the signal's characteristics is likely to be smaller.

The majority of speech and audio coding schemes can have their output interleaved and may be modified to improve the effectiveness of interleaving. The disadvantage of interleaving is that it increases latency. This limits the use of this technique for interactive applications, although it performs well for noninteractive use. The major advantage of interleaving is that it does not increase the bandwidth requirements of a stream.

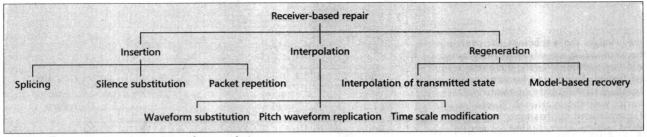

■ Figure 7. *A taxonomy of error concealment techniques.*

Retransmission

Interactive audio applications have tight latency bounds, and end-to-end delays need to be less than 250 ms [36]. For this reason such applications do not typically employ retransmission-based recovery for lost packets. If larger end-to-end delays can be tolerated, the use of retransmission to recover from loss becomes a possibility.

A widely deployed reliable multicast scheme based on the retransmission of lost packets is scalable reliable multicast (SRM) [1]. When a member of an SRM session detects loss, it will wait a random amount of time, determined by its distance from the original source of the lost data, and then multicast a repair request. The retransmission timer is calculated such that, although a number of hosts may miss the same packet, the host closest to the point of failure will most likely timeout first and issue the retransmission request. Other hosts which also see the loss, but receive the retransmission request message, suppress their own request to avoid message implosion.[1] On receiving a retransmission request, any host with the requested data may reply: once again, a timeout is used based on the distance of that host from the sender of the retransmit request, to prevent reply implosion. The timers are calculated such that typically only one request and one retransmission will occur for each lost packet.

While SRM and related protocols are well suited for reliable multicast of data objects, they are not generally suitable for streaming media such as audio. This is because they do not bound the transmission delay and, in the presence of packet loss, may take an arbitrary amount of time. A large number of reliable multicast protocols have been defined (see [4] for a survey) which are similarly unsuitable for streaming media and hence are not studied here. For similar reasons, TCP is not appropriate for unicast streaming audio.

That is not to say that retransmission-based schemes cannot be used for streaming media, in some circumstances. In particular, protocols which use retransmission but bound the number of retransmission requests allowed for a given unit of data may be appropriate. Such retransmission-based schemes work best when loss rates are relatively small. As loss rates increase, the overhead due to retransmission request packets increases. Eventually a cross-over point is reached, beyond which the use of FEC becomes more effective. It has been observed in large Mbone sessions that *most* packets are lost by at least one receiver [7]. Indeed, in their implementation of an SRM-like protocol for streaming audio [37], Xu *et al.* note that "In the worst case, for every multicast packet, at least one receiver does not receive the packet, which means that *every* packet needs to be transmitted to the whole group at least twice." In cases such as this, it is clear that the use of retrans-

mission is probably only appropriate as a secondary technique to repair losses which are not repaired by FEC.

An alternative combination of FEC and retransmission has been studied by Nonnenmacher *et al.* [38]. This work takes the approach of using parity FEC packets to repair multiple losses with a single retransmission, achieving substantial bandwidth savings relative to pure retransmission.

Furthermore, the retransmission of a unit of audio does not need to be identical to the original transmission: the unit can be recoded to a lower bandwidth if the overhead of retransmission is thought to be problematic. There is a natural synchrony with redundant transmission, and a protocol may be derived in which both redundant and retransmitted units may be accommodated. This allows receivers that cannot participate in the retransmission process to benefit from retransmitted units if they are operating with a sufficiently large playout delay.

The use of retransmission allows for an interesting trade-off between the desired playback quality and the desired degree of latency inherent in the stream. Within a large session, the amount of latency which can be tolerated varies greatly for different participants: some users desire to participate closely in a session, and hence require very low latency, whereas others are content to observe and can tolerate much higher latency. Those participants who require low latency must receive the media stream without the benefit of retransmission-based repair (but may use FEC). Others gain the benefit of the repair, but at the expense of increased delay.

Error Concealment

We consider a number of techniques for error concealment which may be initiated by the receiver of an audio stream and do not require assistance from the sender. These techniques are of use when sender-based recovery schemes fail to correct all loss, or when the sender of a stream is unable to participate in the recovery.

Error concealment schemes rely on producing a replacement for a lost packet which is similar to the original. This is possible since audio signals, in particular speech, exhibit large amounts of short-term self-similarity. As such, these techniques work for relatively small loss rates ($\leq$ 15 percent) and for small packets (4–40 ms). When the loss length approaches the length of a phoneme (5–100 ms) these techniques break down, since whole phonemes may be missed by the listener.

It is clear that error concealment schemes are not a substitute for sender-based repair, but rather work in tandem with it. A sender-based scheme is used to repair most losses, leaving a small number of isolated gaps to be repaired. Once the effective loss rate has been reduced in this way, error concealment forms a cheap and effective means of patching over the remaining loss.

A taxonomy of various receiver-based recovery techniques is given in Fig. 7. It can be seen that these techniques split into three categories:
- *Insertion*-based schemes repair losses by inserting a fill-in packet. This fill-in is usually very simple: silence or noise

---

[1] *The SRM protocol is designed to scale to very large groups. If request suppression were not used, a lost packet near the source would trigger simultaneous retransmission requests from many group members, which could overwhelm the sender (consider the effects in a group with many hundreds, or thousands, of members).*

are common, as is repetition of the previous packet. Such techniques are easy to implement but, with the exception of repetition, have poor performance.

- *Interpolation*-based schemes use some form of pattern matching and interpolation to derive a replacement packet which is expected to be similar to the lost packet. These techniques are more difficult to implement and require more processing when compared with insertion-based schemes. Typically performance is better.
- *Regeneration*-based schemes derive the decoder state from packets surrounding the loss and generate a replacement for the lost packet from that. This process is expensive to implement but can give good results.

The following sections discuss each of these categories in turn. This is followed by a summary of the range of applicability of these techniques.

Insertion-Based Repair

Insertion-based repair schemes derive a replacement for a lost packet by inserting a simple fill-in. The simplest case is splicing, where a zero-length fill-in is used; an alternative is silence substitution, where a fill-in with the duration of the lost packet is substituted to maintain the timing of the stream. Better results are obtained by using noise or a repeat of the previous packet as the replacement.

The distinguishing feature of insertion-based repair techniques is that the characteristics of the signal are not used to aid reconstruction. This makes these methods simple to implement, but results in generally poor performance.

Splicing — Lost units can be concealed by splicing together the audio on either side of the loss; no gap is left due to a missing packet, but the timing of the stream is disrupted. This technique has been evaluated by Gruber and Strawczynski [39] and shown to perform poorly. Low loss rates and short clipping lengths (4–16 ms) faired best, but the results were intolerable for losses above 3 percent.

The use of splicing can also interfere with the adaptive playout buffer required in a packet audio system, because it makes a step reduction in the amount of data available to buffer. The adaptive playout buffer is used to allow for the reordering of misordered packets and removal of network timing jitter, and poor performance of this buffer can adversely affect the quality of the entire system.

It is clear, therefore, that splicing together audio on either side of a lost unit is not an acceptable repair technique.

Silence Substitution — Silence substitution fills the gap left by a lost packet with silence in order to maintain the timing relationship between the surrounding packets. It is only effective with short packet lengths (< 4 ms) and low loss rates (< 2 percent) [40], making it suitable for interleaved audio over low-loss paths.

The performance of silence substitution degrades rapidly as packet sizes increase, and quality is unacceptably bad for the 40 ms packet size in common use in network audio conferencing tools [22]. Despite this, the use of silence substitution is widespread, primarily because it is simple to implement.

Noise Substitution — Since silence substitution has been shown to perform poorly, an obvious next choice is noise substitution, where, instead of filling in the gap left by a lost packet with silence, background noise is inserted instead.

A number of studies of the human perception of interrupted speech have been conducted, for example, that by Warren [41]. These have shown that *phonemic restoration*, the ability

of the human brain to subconsciously repair the missing segment of speech with the correct sound, occurs for speech repair using noise substitution but not for silence substitution.

In addition, when compared to silence, the use of white noise has been shown to give both subjectively better quality [35] and improved intelligibility [41]. It is therefore recommended as a replacement for silence substitution.

As an extension for this, a proposed future revision of the RTP profile for audio-video conferences [42] allows for the transmission of *comfort noise* indicator packets. This allows the communication of the loudness level of the background noise to be played, allowing for better fill-in information to be generated.

Repetition — Repetition replaces lost units with copies of the unit that arrived immediately before the loss. It has low computational complexity and performs reasonably well. The subjective quality of repetition can be improved by gradually fading repeated units. The GSM system, for example, advocates the repetition of the first 20 ms with the same amplitude followed by fading the repeated signal to zero amplitude over the next 320 ms [43].

The use of repetition with fading is a good compromise between the other poorly performing insertion-based concealment techniques and the more complex interpolation-based and regenerative concealment methods.

Interpolation-Based Repair

A number of error concealment techniques exist which attempt to interpolate from packets surrounding a loss to produce a replacement for that lost packet. The advantage of interpolation-based schemes over insertion-based techniques is that they account for the changing characteristics of a signal.

Waveform Substitution — Waveform substitution uses audio before, and optionally after, the loss to find a suitable signal to cover the loss. Goodman *et al.* [44] studied the use of waveform substitution in packet voice systems. They examined both one- and two-sided techniques that use templates to locate suitable pitch patterns either side of the loss. In the one-sided scheme the pattern is repeated across the gap, but with the two-sided schemes interpolation occurs. The two-sided schemes generally performed better than one-sided schemes, and both work better than silence substitution and packet repetition.

Pitch Waveform Replication — Wasem *et al.*, [45] present a refinement on waveform substitution by using a pitch detection algorithm either side of the loss. Losses during unvoiced speech segments are repaired using packet repetition and voiced losses repeat a waveform of appropriate pitch length. The technique, known as pitch waveform replication, was found to work marginally better than waveform substitution.

Time Scale Modification — Time scale modification allows the audio on either side of the loss to be stretched across the loss. Sanneck *et al.* [46] present a scheme that finds overlapping vectors of pitch cycles on either side of the loss, offsets them to cover the loss, and averages them where they overlap. Although computationally demanding, the technique appears to work better than both waveform substitution and pitch waveform replication.

Regeneration-Based Repair

Regenerative repair techniques use knowledge of the audio compression algorithm to derive codec parameters, such that audio in a lost packet can be synthesized. These tech-

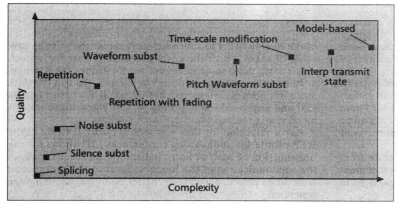

■ Figure 8. *Rough quality/complexity trade-off for error concealment.*

niques are necessarily codec-dependent but perform well because of the large amount of state information used in the repair. Typically, they are also somewhat computationally intensive.

Interpolation of Transmitted State — For codecs based on transform coding or linear prediction, it is possible that the decoder can interpolate between states. For example, the ITU G.723.1 speech coder [25] interpolates the state of the linear predictor coefficients either side of short losses and uses either a periodic excitation the same as the previous frame, or

gain matched random number generator, depending on whether the signal was voiced or unvoiced. For longer losses, the reproduced signal is gradually faded. The advantages of codecs that can interpolate state rather than recoding the audio on either side of the loss is that there is are no boundary effects due to changing codecs, and the computational load remains approximately constant. However, it should be noted that codecs where interpolation may be applied typically have high processing demands.

Model-Based Recovery — In model-based recovery the speech on one, or both, sides of the loss is fitted to a model that is used to generate speech to cover the period loss. In recent work by Chen and Chen [47], interleaved μ-law encoded speech is repaired by combining the results of autoregressive analysis on the last received set of samples with an estimate of the excitation made for the loss period. The technique works well for two reasons: the size of the interleaved blocks (8/16 ms) is short enough to ensure that the speech characteristics of the last received block have a high probability of being relevant. The majority of low-bit-rate speech codecs use an autoregressive model in conjunction with an excitation signal.

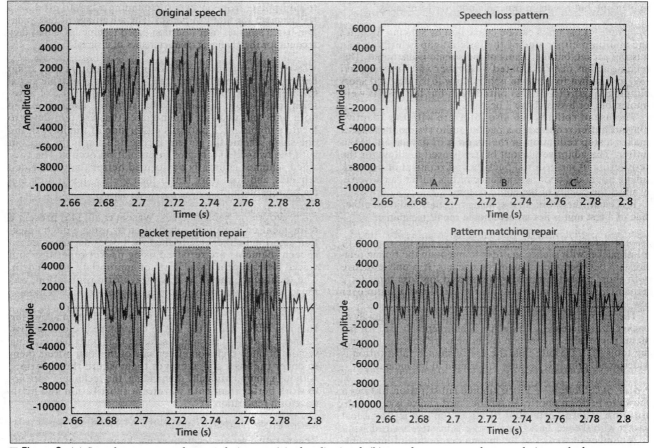

■ Figure 9. *(a) Sample error concealment techniques: original audio signal; (b) sample error concealment techniques: the loss pattern; (c) sample error concealment techniques; packet repetition; (d) sample error concealment techniques: one sided waveform substitution.*

Summary

It is difficult to obtain an accurate characterization of the performance and complexity of error concealment techniques since the measurements which may be performed are, due to the nature of the repair, subjective. However, based on our experience, we believe that Fig. 8 provides a reasonable illustration of the quality/complexity trade-off for the different repair techniques discussed.

The computation required to perform the more advanced repair techniques increases greatly relative to the simpler repair options. However, the improvement in quality achieved by these schemes is incremental at best. For this reason, the use of packet repetition with fading is recommended as offering a good compromise between achieved quality and excessive complexity. For comparison, an example using packet repetition and waveform substitution can be seen in Fig. 9.

Several of these techniques can be applied using data from one or both sides of the loss. Many audio and speech coders assume continuity of the decoder state. When a loss occurs, it may not be possible to decode audio data on both sides of the loss for use in the repair since the decoded audio after the loss may start from an inappropriate state. In addition, two-sided operations incur greater processing overhead and usually represent a marginal improvement. In the majority of cases one-sided repair is sufficient.

Recommendations

In this final section, we suggest which of these techniques should be considered for IP multicast applications in some common scenarios. We discuss the trade-off between achieving good performance with acceptable cost/complexity.

Noninteractive Applications

For one-to-many transmissions in the style of radio broadcasts, latency is of considerably less importance than quality. In addition, bandwidth efficiency is a concern since the receiver set is likely to be diverse and the group may include members behind low-speed links. The use of interleaving is compatible with both of these requirements and is strongly recommended.

Although interleaving drastically reduces the audible effects of lost packets, some form of error concealment will still be needed to compensate. In this case the use of a simple repair scheme, such as repetition with fading, is acceptable and will give good quality.

Retransmission-based repair is not appropriate for a multicast session, since the receiver set is likely to be heterogeneous. This leads to many retransmission requests for different packets and a large bandwidth overhead due to control traffic. For unicast sessions retransmission is more acceptable, particularly in low-loss scenarios.

A media-independent FEC scheme will perform better than a retransmission-based repair scheme, since a single FEC packet can correct many different losses and there is no control traffic overhead. The overhead due to the FEC data itself still persists, although this may be acceptable. In particular, FEC-protected streams allow for exact repair, while repair of interleaved streams is only approximate.

Interactive Applications

For interactive applications, such as IP telephony, the principal concern is minimizing end-to-end delay. It is acceptable to sacrifice some quality to meet delay requirements, provided that the result is intelligible.

The delay imposed by the use of interleaving, retransmission, and media-independent FEC is not acceptable for these applications. While media-independent FEC schemes do exist that satisfy the delay requirements, these typically have high bandwidth overhead and are likely to be inappropriate for this reason.

Our recommendation for interactive conferencing applications is that media-specific FEC is employed, since this has low latency and tunable bandwidth overhead. Repair is approximate due to the use of low-rate secondary encodings, but this is acceptable for this class of application when used in conjunction with receiver-based error concealment.

Error Concealment

Receivers must be prepared to accept some loss in an audio stream. The overhead involved in ensuring that all packets are received correctly, in both time and bandwidth, is such that some loss is unavoidable. Once this is accepted, the need for error concealment becomes apparent. Many current conferencing applications use silence substitution to fill the gaps left by packet loss, but it has been shown that this does not provide acceptable quality. A significant improvement is achieved by the use of packet repetition, which also has the advantages of being simple to implement and having low computational overhead. The other error concealment schemes discussed provide incremental improvements, with significantly greater complexity. Accordingly, we recommend the use of packet repetition since it is a simple and effective means of recovering from the low-level random packet loss inherent in the Mbone.

Acknowledgments

This work has benefited from the insightful comments of the reviewers and discussion with members of the networked multimedia research group at UCL. In particular, we wish to thank Jon Crowcroft and Roy Bennett for their helpful comments. We are grateful to Mark Handley for permission to use Fig. 1.

The authors are supported by the U.K. EPSRC project RAT (GR/K72780), the EU Telematics for research project MERCI (#1007), and British Telecommunications plc (ML72254).

References

[1] S. Floyd et al., "A reliable multicast framework for light-weight sessions and applications level framing," IEEE/ACM Trans. Networking, Dec. 1997.
[2] V. Jacobson, "Multimedia conferencing on the Internet," SIGCOMM Symp. Commun. Architectures and Protocols, tutorial slides, Aug. 1994.
[3] K. Obraczka, "Multicast transport mechanism: A survey and taxonomy," to appear, IEEE Commun. Mag., 1998.
[4] B. N. Levine and J. J. Garcia-Luna-Aceves, "A comparison of reliable multicast protocols," ACM Multimedia Sys., Aug. 1998.
[5] G. Carle and E. W. Biersack, "Survey of error recovery techniques for IP-based audio-visual multicast applications," IEEE Network, vol. 11, no. 6, Nov./Dec. 1997, pp. 24–36.
[6] S. Deering, "Multicast Routing in a Datagram Internetwork," Ph.D. thesis, Stanford University, Palo Alto, CA, Dec. 1991.
[7] M. Handley, "An examination of Mbone performance," USC/ISI res. rep. ISI/RR-97-450, Apr. 1997.
[8] H. Schulzrinne et al., "RTP: A transport protocol for real-time applications," IETF Audio/Video Transport WG, RFC1889, Jan. 1996.
[9] J.-C. Bolot and A. Vega-Garcia, "The case for FEC based error control for packet audio in the Internet," to appear, ACM Multimedia Sys.
[10] J.-C. Bolot and A. Vega-Garcia, "Control mechanisms for packet audio in the Internet," Proc. IEEE INFOCOM '96, 1996.
[11] M. Yajnik, J. Kurose, and D. Towsley, "Packet loss correlation in the Mbone multicast network," Proc. IEEE Global Internet Conf., Nov. 1996.
[12] O. Hermanns and M. Schuba, "Performance investigations of the IP multicast architecture," Comp. Networks and ISDN Syst., vol. 28, 1996, pp. 429–39.
[13] J.-C. Bolot, "End-to-end packet delay and loss behavior in the internet," Proc. ACM SIGCOMM '93, San Francisco, Sept. 1993, pp. 289–98.
[14] S. B. Moon, J. Kurose, and D. Towsley, "Packet audio playout delay adjustment algorithms: performance bounds and algorithms," Res. rep., Dept. of Comp. Sci., Univ. of MA at Amherst, Aug. 1995.
[15] R. Ramjee, J. Kurose, D. Towsley, and H. Schulzrinne, "Adaptive playout mechanisms for packetized audio applications in wide-area networks," Proc. IEEE INFOCOM, Toronto, Canada, June 1994.

[16] J. Rosenberg and H. Schulzrinne, "An RTP payload format for generic forward error correction," IETF Audio/Video Transport WG, work in progress (Internet-draft), July 1998.

[17] J. Rosenberg, "Reliability enhancements to NeVoT," Dec. 1996.

[18] H. F. Mattson and G. Solomon, "A new treatment of Bose-Chaudhuri codes," J. SIAM, vol. 9, no. 4, Dec. 1961, pp. 654–69.

[19] I. S. Reed and G. Solomon, "Polynomial codes over certain finite fields," J. SIAM, vol. 8, no. 2, June 1960, pp. 300–4.

[20] E. R. Berlekamp, Algebraic Coding Theory, McGraw-Hill, 1968.

[21] J. L. Massey, "Shift-register synthesis and BCH decoding," IEEE Trans. Info. Theory, vol. IT-15, 1969, pp. 122–27.

[22] V. Hardman et al., "Reliable audio for use over the Internet," Proc. INET '95, 1995.

[23] M. Podolsky, C. Romer and S. McCanne, "Simulation of FEC-based error control for packet audio on the Internet," Proc. IEEE INFOCOM '98, San Francisco, CA, Apr. 1998.

[24] N. Erdöl, C. Castelluccia, and A. Zilouchian, "Recovery of missing speech packets using the short-time energy and zero-crossing measurements," Trans. Speech and Audio Processing, vol. 1, no. 3, July 1993, pp. 295–303.

[25] ITU Rec. G.723.1, "Dual rate speech coder for multimedia communications transmitting at 5.3 and 6.3 kbit/s," Mar. 1996.

[26] M. Mouly and M.-B. Pautet, The GSM System for Mobile Communications, Europe Media Duplication, Lassay-les-Chateaux, France, 1993.

[27] V. R. Viswanathan et al., "Variable frame rate transmission: A review of methodology and application to narrow-band LPC speech coding," IEEE Trans. Commun., vol. COM-30, no. 4, Apr. 1982, pp. 674–87.

[28] I. Kouvelas et al., "Redundancy control in real-time Internet audio conferencing," Proc. AVSPN '97, Aberdeen, Scotland, Sept. 1997.

[29] C. S. Perkins et al., "RTP Payload for redundant audio data," IETF Audio/Video Transport WG, RFC2198, 1997.

[30] S. McCanne, V. Jacobson, and M. Vetterli, "Receiver-driven layered multicast," Proc. ACM SIGCOMM '96, Stanford, CA., Aug. 1996.

[31] L. Rizzo and V. Vicisano, "A reliable multicast data distribution protocol based on software fec techniques," Proc. 4th IEEE Wksp. Arch. and Implementation of High Perf. Commun. Sys. (HPCS '97), 1997.

[32] L. Vicisano, L. Rizzo, and J. Crowcroft, "TCP-like congestion control for layered multicast data transfer," Proc. IEEE INFOCOM '98, 1998.

[33] C. S. Perkins and O. Hodson, "Options for repair of streaming media," IETF Audio/Video Transport WG, RFC2354, June 1998.

[34] J. L. Ramsey, "Realization of optimum interleavers," IEEE Trans. Info. Theory, vol. IT-16, May 1970, pp. 338–45.

[35] G. A. Miller and J. C. R. Licklider, "The intelligibility of interrupted speech," J. Acoust. Soc. Amer., vol. 22, no. 2, 1950, pp. 167–73.

[36] P. T. Brady, "Effects of transmission delay on conversational behavior on echo-free telephone circuits," Bell Sys. Tech. J., vol. 50, Jan. 1971, pp. 115–34.

[37] R. X. Xu et al., "Resilient multicast support for continuous media applications," Proc. 7th Int'l. Wksp. Network and Op. Sys. Support for Digital Audio and Video (NOSSDAV '97), Washington Univ., St. Louis, MO, May 1997.

[38] J. Nonnenmacher, E. Biersack, and D. Towsley, "Parity-based loss recovery for reliable multicast transmission," Proc. ACM SIGCOMM '97, Cannes, France, Sept. 1997.

[39] J. G. Gruber and L. Strawczynski, "Subjective effects of variable delay and clipping in dynamically managed voice systems," IEEE Trans. Commun., vol. COM-33, no. 8, Aug. 1985, pp. 801–8.

[40] N. S. Jayant and S. W. Christenssen, "Effects of packet losses in waveform coded speech and improvements due to an odd-even sample-interpolation procedure," IEEE Trans. Commun., vol. COM-29, no. 2, Feb. 1981, pp. 101–9.

[41] R. M. Warren, Auditory Perception, Pergamon Press, 1982.

[42] H. Schulzrinne, "RTP profile for audio and video conferences with minimal control," IETF Audio/Video Transport WG, work in progress, Mar. 1997.

[43] ETSI Rec. GSM 6.11, "Substitution and muting of lost frames for full rate speech channels," 1992.

[44] D. J. Goodman et al., "Waveform substitution techniques for recovering missing speech segments in packet voice communications," IEEE Trans. Acoustics, Speech, and Sig. Processing, vol. ASSP-34, no. 6, Dec. 1986, pp. 1440–48.

[45] O. J. Wasem et al., "The effect of waveform substitution on the quality of PCM packet communications," IEEE Trans. Acoustics, Speech, and Sig. Processing, vol. 36, no. 3, Mar. 1988, pp. 342–48.

[46] H. Sanneck et al., "A new technique for audio packet loss concealment," IEEE Global Internet, IEEE, Dec. 1996, pp. 48–52.

[47] Y. L. Chen and B. S. Chen, "Model-based multirate representation of speech signals and its application to recovery of missing speech packets," IEEE Trans. Speech and Audio Processing, vol. 15, no. 3, May 1997, pp. 220–31.

Biographies

COLIN PERKINS (C.Perkins@cs.ucl.ac.uk) received the B. Eng. degree in electronic engineering from the University of York in 1992. In 1995 he received a D. Phil. from the University of York, Department of Electronics, where his work involved software reliability modeling and analysis. Since then he has been a research fellow at University College London, Department of Computer Science. His work at UCL has included development of the Robust-Audio Tool (RAT), audio transcoder/mixer design and implementation, and local conference coordination issues.

ORION HODSON (O.Hodson@cs.ucl.ac.uk) received a B.Sc. in physics and theory from the University of Birmingham, England, in 1993, and an M.Sc. in computation neuroscience from the University of Stirling, Scotland, in 1995. He is currently a Ph.D. candidate in the Computer Science Department of University College London. His research interests include voice over IP networks, multimedia conferencing, and real-time applications.

VICKY HARDMAN is a lecturer in computer science at University College London. She has a Ph.D. in speech over packet networks from Loughborough University of Technology, England, where she subsequently worked as a research assistant. Her research interests include multicast conferencing, speech over packet networks, audio in virtual reality environments, and real-time multimedia applications.

Adaptive FEC-Based Error Control
for Internet Telephony

Jean-Chrysostome Bolot   Sacha Fosse-Parisis
INRIA
2004 route des Lucioles
06902 Sophia Antipolis Cedex
France
www.inria.fr/rodeo/{bolot,sfosse}

Don Towsley
Department of Computer Science
University of Massachusetts at Amherst
Amherst, MA 01003-4610
USA
towsley@cs.umass.edu

Abstract—

Excessive packet loss rates can dramatically decrease the audio quality perceived by users of Internet telephony applications. Recent results suggest that error control schemes using forward error correction (FEC) are good candidates for decreasing the impact of packet loss on audio quality. With FEC schemes, redundant information is transmitted along with the original information so that the lost original data can be recovered at least in part from the redundant information. Clearly, sending additional redundancy increases the probability of recovering lost packets, but it also increases the bandwidth requirements and thus the loss rate of the audio stream. This means that the FEC scheme must be coupled to a rate control scheme. Furthermore, the amount of redundant information used at any given point in time should also depend on the characteristics of the loss process at that time (it would make no sense to send much redundant information when the channel is loss free), on the end to end delay constraints (destination typically have to wait longer to decode the FEC as more FEC information is used), on the quality of the redundant information, etc. However, it is not clear given all these constraints how to choose the "best" possible redundant information.

We address this issue in the paper, and illustrate our approach using a FEC scheme for packet audio recently standardized in the IETF. We show that the problem of finding the best redundant information can be expressed mathematically as a constrained optimization problem for which we give explicit solutions. We obtain from these solutions a simple algorithm with very interesting features, namely i) *the algorithm optimizes a subjective measure* (such as the audio quality perceived at a destination) as opposed to an objective measure of quality (such as the packet loss rate at a destination), ii) *it incorporates the constraints of rate control and playout delay adjustment schemes*, and iii) *it adapts to varying loss conditions in the network* (estimated online with RTCP feedback).

We have been using the algorithm, together with a TCP-friendly rate control scheme and we have found it to provide very good audio quality even over paths with high and varying loss rates. We present simulation and experimental results to illustrate its performance.

I. INTRODUCTION

The transmission of real time audio, and especially of real time voice, over the Internet has been much in the news recently. Traditional voice carriers, so-called next-

gen telcos, as well as manufacturers of gateways, phone-like appliances, and routers, have all become involved in some way or another with Internet telephony. Internet telephony is branded by the various parties as fitting anywhere between "the old-telco killer app" and "a toy for long distance lovers". In any case, it is clear that the field of packet voice over the Internet has matured and that the basic building blocks are available [25], ranging from high quality codecs to standardized packetization and signaling protocols such as RTP [24], H.323 [11], or SIP [26]. Still, Internet telephony has often been dismissed as a "real" application because of the mediocre quality experienced by many users of Internet voice software.

Audio quality problems are not so surprising because the current Internet provides users with a single class best effort service which does not promise anything in terms of performance guarantees. And indeed, measurements show persistent problems with audio quality caused by congestion in the network, and thus by the impact of traffic in the network on the streams of audio packets. In practice, this impact is felt via high loss rates, varying delay, etc.

In the absence of network support to provide guarantees of quality (such as a maximum loss rate or a maximum delay) to users of audio tools, a promising approach to tackle the problems caused by varying loss rates, delays, or available bandwidth, is to use application level control mechanisms. These mechanisms adapt the behavior of the audio application so as to eliminate or at least minimize the impact of loss, jitter, etc, on the quality of the audio delivered to the destinations.

Efficient playout adjustment mechanisms have been developed to minimize the impact of delay jitter [16]. Much recent effort has been devoted to developing mechanisms to minimize the impact of loss. Rate control mechanisms attempt to minimize the number of packets lost by ensuring that the rate at which audio packets are sent over a connection matches the capacity of the connection [5]. However, they typically do not prevent loss altogether. An error control, or loss recovery, mechanism is required if the number of lost audio packets is higher than that tolerated by the listener at the destination.

Typical mechanisms fall into one of two classes [19]. Automatic Repeat Request (ARQ) mechanisms are closed-loop mechanisms based on the retransmission of the packets that were not received at the destination. Forward Error Correction (FEC) mechanisms are open-loop mechanisms based on the transmission of redundant information along with the original information so that some of the lost original data can be recovered from the redundant information. ARQ mechanisms are typically not acceptable for live audio applications over the Internet because they dramatically increase end to end latency[1].

FEC is an attractive alternative to ARQ for providing reliability without increasing latency. FEC schemes send redundant information along with the original information so that the lost original data can be recovered, at least in part, from the redundant information. There are two main issues with FEC. First, the potential of FEC mechanisms to recover from losses depends in large part on the characteristics of the packet loss process in the network. Indeed, FEC mechanisms are more effective when the average number of consecutively lost packets is small. Second, sending additional redundancy increases the probability of recovering lost packets, but it also increases the bandwidth requirements and thus the loss rate of the audio stream. This means that the FEC scheme must be coupled to a rate control scheme. Furthermore, the amount of redundant information used at any given point in time should also depend on the characteristics of the loss process at that time (it makes no sense to send redundant information when the channel is loss free), on the end to end delay constraints (destination typically have to wait longer to decode the FEC as more FEC information is used), on the quality of the redundant information, etc. The problem, then, becomes a constrained optimization problem, namely: given constraints of the rate control mechanisms (i.e. given a total rate at which the source can send), find the combination of main and redundant information which provides the destination with the best perceived audio quality. It is precisely the goal of this paper to formalize this problem, solve it, derive a practical algorithm, apply it to the FEC scheme recently standardized in the IETF [18], and evaluate the performance of the algorithm in realistic Internet environments using a real Internet audio/telephony tool.

The paper is organized as follows. In Section II, we first briefly review recent results on the the loss process of audio packets in the Internet. We then describe a simple FEC scheme which uses these results to minimize an objective function (the loss rate after packet reconstruction) at

[1]However, they would be appropriate in low delay environments, or with relaxed end to end delay constraints [6].

the destination. However, that scheme turns out to have a number of drawbacks. We describe in Section III our main contribution, namely an adaptive algorithm for the IETF FEC scheme which incorporates the constraints of rate control and playout delay adjustment, which adapts to varying loss conditions, and which maximizes a subjective measure of quality (such as the perceived audio quality at a destination) as opposed to a measure such as the packet loss rate at a destination which does not reflect the quality perceived by the receiver. We present simulation and experimental results in Section IV to illustrate the performance of the algorithm.

II. A SIMPLE FEC-BASED ERROR CONTROL SCHEME

The loss process of audio packets

We mentioned in Section I that the characteristics of the loss process of audio packets are important in determining which type of error control scheme (ARQ or FEC) to use for error recovery. Recent work has shown that the correlation structure of the loss process of audio packets can be modeled by a low order Markov chain, such as a two state Gilbert model, and that the distribution of the number of packets lost in a loss period is approximately geometric, or, rather, that the head of the distribution is geometric, and that the tail includes a few events (which might contribute significantly to the overall loss rate, since a single event in the tail indicates that a loss period with a large number of lost packets) which appear not to have any specific structure [23], [4], [29], [31]. This is consistent with other, more general, results on end to end Internet loss characteristics (e.g. [3], [17]).

We will use in the rest of the paper a few basic results about the Gilbert model. Therefore, recall that a Gilbert model is a 2-state Markovian model in which one state (which we refer to as state 1) represents a packet loss, and the other state (which we refer to as state 0) represents a packet reaching the destination. Let p denote the probability of going from state 0 to state 1, and let q denote the probability of going from state 1 to state state 0. The probability that n consecutive packets are lost equals $(1-q)q^{n-1}$, and, thus, the residence time for state 1 is geometrically distributed. Refer to Figure 1. Note that when

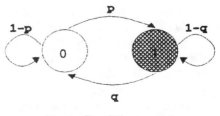

Fig. 1. The Gilbert model

$p + q = 1$, the model turns into a Bernoulli model.

The results on the loss process of audio packets in the Internet mentioned above show that the median number of consecutively lost packets is small, and thus, FEC is particularly well suited for live audio applications over the Internet. A large variety of FEC schemes have been proposed in the literature [19], based on parity and block erasure codes [21], convolutional codes [2], interleaving [14], or multiple description codes [28]. We consider in this paper another scheme, which was recently standardized in the IETF [18] and which, thus, we can expect many Internet audio applications to rely on for robustness with respect to packet loss. Furthermore, it appears to provide good subjective results even in the face of high loss rates [10].

This scheme evolved from an earlier scheme [7], in which a packet, say n, includes, in addition to its encoded samples, information about the previous packet, $n-1$. If packet $n-1$ is lost but packet n is not lost, then the destination can use that information to reconstruct (an approximation to) packet $n-1$. The information about packet $n-1$ considered in [7] includes a discretized energy envelope as well as the number and/or the location of zero crossings of the waveform encoded in packet $n-1$.

The IETF scheme relies on an idea similar to the above, i.e. packet n includes, in addition to its encoded samples, a redundant version of packet $n-1$. However, the redundant information about packet $n-1$ is now obtained with a low bit rate encoding of packet $n-1$. Consider for example the case when audio is sent using PCM encoding. Then LPC, GSM, or CELP coders could be used to obtain the redundant information. Clearly, the mechanism can be used to recover from isolated losses: if packet n is lost, the destination waits for packet $n+1$, decodes the redundant information, and sends the reconstructed samples to the audio driver. With redundant LPC audio, the output consists of a mixture of PCM- and LPC-coded speech. Somewhat surprisingly, the subjective quality of this reconstructed speech has been found to be quite good [10].

The scheme described above only recovers from isolated losses. However, it can be modified to recover from consecutive losses as well by including in packet n redundant versions of packets $n-1$ and $n-2$, or packets $n-1$, $n-2$ and $n-3$, or packets $n-1$ and $n-3$, etc. Note that the scheme then can be thought of as some kind of generalized interleaving: interleaving because the information relative to packet n is spread over multiple packets, and generalized because each interleaved chunk can be decoded by itself independent of the others. Also, it is clear that the more redundant information is added at the source, the more lost packets can be reconstructed at the destination. However, it would make little sense to add much redundant information when the loss rate is very low. Thus, we would like to choose the appropriate combination of redundant information given the loss process in the network at any given point in time. We consider this issue next.

A simple adaptive algorithm for the IETF FEC scheme

The choice of redundant information depends on the benefit we get from adding redundant information. To answer this question, we model the loss process in the presence of redundancy so as to find the perceived loss rate after reconstruction.

Recall that in the absence of redundant information, the loss rate is $\pi_1 = \frac{p}{p+q}$. Consider now the case when packet n includes redundant information about packet $n-1$ only: a packet is lost only if it cannot be reconstructed using the redundant information, i.e. the packet is lost and the next packet is lost as well. It is then straightforward to show that the loss rate after reconstruction is now

$$\pi_2 = \frac{p(1-q)}{p+q}$$

The ratio between π_2 and the loss rate without redundancy is equal to $(1-q)$. With q around 0.70 (a value we have typically found in traces collected between European universities), we see that adding one piece of redundancy decreases the perceived loss rate by 70%.

We can carry out a similar analysis and examine cases with two, three, four pieces of redundant information, etc. The results are summarized in Table I. In the column "Redundancy", the notation -1-3, for example, means that redundant information about packets $n-1$ and $n-3$ was sent in packet n.

Redun.	Loss rate after reconstruction
none	$p/(p+q)$
-1	$(p(1-q))/(p+q)$
-2	$(p^2 q + p(1-q)^2)/(p+q)$
-3	$p(3pq - p^2 q - 2q^2 p + 1 - 3q + 3q^2 - q^3)/(p+q)$
-1-2	$(p(1-q)^2)/(p+q)$
-1-3	$(p(1-q)(pq + 1 - 2q + q^2))/(p+q)$
-2-3	$(p(1-q)(pq + 1 - 2q + q^2))/(p+q)$
-1-2-3	$(p(1-q)^3)/(p+q)$

TABLE I

LOSS RATES AFTER RECONSTRUCTION

The simplest way to build a control mechanism is to have a target perceived loss rate (i.e. loss rate after reconstruction) at the destination, and to have the source choose the amount of redundant information that will yield the loss rate closest to the target loss rate. Of course, this requires that the source know p and q. Unfortunately, RTCP receiver reports (RRs) [24] only include information about the mean loss rate, i.e. $p/(p+q)$, but not about p and q separately. There are two ways around this. The first way is to use other fields in RTCP RRs to include p and q (we used the jitter field, which nobody seems to be using or intending to use). The other way is to assume that the loss process is Bernoulli, not Gilbert, i.e. to assume that

$p + q = 1$; then the loss rate p is the rate reported in the RTCP RRs.

Figure 2 shows the evolution with time of the loss rate measured over a connection between INRIA and London, and of the loss rate after reconstruction over the same connection when the algorithm described above is used, the target loss rate being 3%.

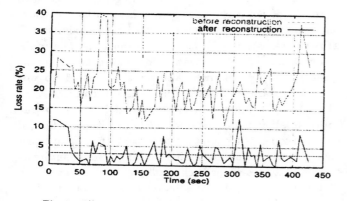

Fig. 2. Loss with and without FEC; target loss is 3%

The algorithm does provide the destination with a perceived loss rate which fluctuates around the desired loss rate, even though the loss rate in the network varies between 12 to 40%. The fluctuations are caused in part because the loss process in the network is not a Bernoulli process, and the value of p only is not enough to capture all of its characteristics, and in part because the RTCP feedback is sent back by the destination only every 5 seconds [24].

The figure above makes the algorithm appear attractive. However, it suffers from two drawbacks. First, it minimizes an objective performance measure (loss rate after reconstruction), instead of a measure tied to audio quality: in practice, it would make little sense to be able to reconstruct all lost packets if the quality of the information used for audio reconstruction (i.e. the quality of the redundant information) is too low to be understandable. Second, adding redundant information increases the bandwidth requirements of the source. Therefore, we need to tie the process of adding redundant information to a rate control scheme. In practice, we combine the rate control and the error control mechanisms into one joint rate/error control mechanism. The goal then is to adjust at the source both the send rate and the amount of redundant information to minimize the perceived loss rate at the destinations. We describe one such scheme next.

III. An optimal joint rate/FEC-based error control scheme

Main Results

Consider a voice source that has the flexibility to encode its samples at a rate $x \in [0, \infty)$ (or $[0, D]$ if one prefers).

The quality of the encoding of the sample is given by a function $f : \mathbb{R}^+ \to \mathbb{R}$ which is an increasing concave function with derivative g. Note that g is necessarily non-increasing.

The source transmits voice packets to a receiver over an unreliable network characterized by a two-state continuous time Markov chain $\{X_t\}$ where $X_t \in \{0, 1\}$ If a packet is transferred at time t, then the packet is not lost if $X_t = 0$; the packet is lost if $X_t = 1$. The infinitesimal generator of this Markov chain is

$$\mathbf{Q} = \begin{bmatrix} -\mu_0 & \mu_0 \\ \mu_1 & -\mu_1 \end{bmatrix}$$

The stationary distribution associated with this chain is $\pi = (\pi_0, \pi_1)$ where $\pi_0 = \mu_1/(\mu_0 + \mu_1)$ and $\pi_1 = \mu_0/(\mu_0 + \mu_1)$. Note that π_1 corresponds to the probability that a packet is lost.

We consider the case when we use the FEC-based error control scheme described earlier. Let $K - 1$ denote the maximum number of redundant pieces of information sent along with the main information. Thus, packet n carries information about at most (i.e. a subset of) packets $n - 1$, ..., $n - K + 1$. Therefore, the total number of copies (encoded at different rates, including 0) of a given audio packet sent by the source equals K. In practice, the larger K, the longer the destination has to wait to receive the redundant information to reconstruct missing packets, and thus the longer the end to end delay. We characterize the delay constraint of the interactive audio application of interest here by a delay T, which is the delay between sending the first and the last copy of a given packet.

The first question that we ask ourselves then is

Q1. Given that we will transmit K copies of each voice packet and we have a delay constraint of T by which the last packet can be transmitted, how should we space the packets so as to maximize the probability that at least one packet is received?

Before providing a more precise formulation of this problem, we introduce the following conditional probabilities. Let $p_{i,j}(t)$ denote the probability that the process is in state j at time $t + \tau$ given that it was in state i at time τ, $p_{i,j}(t) = P(X_{\tau+t} = j \mid X_\tau = i)$. These probabilities are easy to derive, for example

$$p_{11}(t) = (\mu_0 + \mu_1 \exp(-(\mu_0 + \mu_1)t)/(\mu_0 + \mu_1)$$
$$= \pi_1 + \pi_0 \exp(-(\mu_0 + \mu_1)t)$$

Let t_k denote the interval between the times at which the kth and $(k + 1)$-st copies of a voice packet are sent. The probability that the first $K - 1$ copies of a packet are lost is equal to $\pi_1 \prod_{k=1}^{K-1} p_{11}(t_k)$. Thus, question **Q1** above can be formulated as the optimization problem with linear constraints below:

Maximize $1 - \pi_1 \prod_{k=1}^{K-1} \left(\pi_1 + \pi_0 e^{-(\mu_0 + \mu_1) t_k} \right),$

such that $t_k \geq 0,$
                $\sum_{k=1}^{K} t_k \leq T$

It should be clear that the last constraint will always be satisfied with equality because the cost function is an increasing function of t_i. This problem falls in the general category of bit allocation problems with rate constraints [27], and use standard techniques based on Lagrange multipliers to solve it; refer to [1] for details. It is easy to show that $t_k = T/(K-1)$ is the optimal solution. This means that the K copies must be equally spaced in the interval $[0, T]$ including both endpoints. This is a welcome result and an *a posteriori* support for the FEC scheme under study here, since redundancy data in that scheme is sent precisely at regular intervals (piggybacked on audio packets).

We now address the following question:

Q2. Given that K copies are to be transmitted equally spaced in an interval of length T, what encoding rates should be used for each copy so as to maximize the quality of the transfer subject to a rate constraint?

Let R denote the rate available to the audio flow of interest. We assume that a value for R is available at any given point to the source, but we do not make any assumption as to how R is computed. In practice, R is obtained as a result of a rate control algorithm. In the current Internet, R might be computed using a linear-increase exponential decrease scheme or a TCP-friendly scheme [30], [15] (in practice, we use a scheme based on the result in [15]). However, R could also be computed using explicit feedback such as ECN bit(s) or the explicit rate messages in ABR.

Define the rv S to be $S = \{i \mid X_i = 0, i = 1, \ldots, K\}$, i.e. the set of copies of a packet that make it across the network. Question **Q2** can be stated mathematically as follows.

Maximize $\sum_{S \subseteq \{1, \ldots, K\}} P(S) \max_{i \in S} f(x_i)$

s.t. $x_i \geq r_0,$
                $\sum_{i=1}^{K} x_i \leq R$

where x_i is the encoding rate for the packet placed in the i-th position. Here r_0 is the minimum rate used to encode all samples.

It is important to observe that the formulation of the optimization problem above assumes that the different copies of an audio packet cannot be combined to produce a better quality copy of the original packet. Indeed, we measure quality at the destination using only the "best" (i.e. largest $f(x)$) copy of a packet. In other words, if the l-th best quality copy is not lost, it is used in the case that the best,

2-nd best, ... $(l-1)$-best quality copies are lost. The formulation would be different with layered or hierarchically encoded copies (we have examined those cases but do not report on them here because of lack of space). We focus on the formulation above in this paper because of space constraints, and because it ties in with the schemes proposed in [18].

The problem above appears to be, in general, difficult to solve. We do not derive the solution here for lack of space, but instead describe the results, which are as follows:
1) x_1 is greater than all other x_i's, meaning that **the main information should be encoded using the highest quality coding scheme (among those used to encode the main and the redundant information).**
2) $x_1 \geq x_K \geq$ other x_i's, meaning that **it pays to put more quality into the end packets.** In particular, if only two copies of a packet are to be sent, then these copies should be x_1 (main information) and x_K (redundant information that goes as far back as allowed).
3) for $K = 2, 3, 4, 5$, the solution tells us exactly which copies should be encoded with the better quality schemes.

The explicit results (result 3) have been obtained for $K = 2, 3, 4, 5$ only. However, it is important to observe that **results 1) and 2) are valid for any K.** Indeed, they essentially rely on the fact that $p_{10}(t)$ is an increasing function of t.

Discrete Rate Optimization

The analysis above assumes that the encoding rate at each copy of a packet could take on any real value. In practice, of course, there is a countable set of rates available to the encoder, say $\mathcal{R} = \{r_i\}_{i=0}^{n}$. Without loss of generality, we assume that $r_i < r_{i+1}$, $i = 0, 1, \ldots$. Let f remain non-decreasing concave. We now define the "derivative" of f as follows $g(i) = (f(r_i) - f(r_{i-1}))/(r_i - r_{i-1})$. The concavity of f implies that g is non-increasing. Our optimization problem can now be posed as follows

Maximize $\sum_{S \subseteq \{1, \ldots, K\}} P(S) \max_{i \in S} f(x_i)$

s.t. $x_i \in \mathcal{R},$
                $\sum_{i=1}^{K} x_i \leq R$

Again, this is not an easy problem to solve. However, the optimal solution exhibits some of the same properties as the solution to the continuous rate problem. The algorithm in Figure 3 provides a simple and computationally cheap [1] way to find an approximate solution to the above problem. The algorithm provides a non optimal solution, however with reasonable properties, in particular 1) the resulting solution is $x_i = r_{k_{i-1}}$, $i = 1, \ldots, n-1$, and the quality of the solution differs from that of the optimum by at most $(g(r_{k_j}) - g(r_{k_j - 1})) a_j$ where j resulted in the algorithm halting, 2) the solution can be improved by just checking to see if any of the other x_i's can be increased without violating the rate constraint, and 3) if $r_i = i \times r_0$, then the solution is optimal.

$S = \{1\}$; $n = 1$; $k_1 = 0$; $r = R$;
Repeat forever
    Choose $j \in S$ st $g(k_j)a_j$ is maximum;
    if $r_{k_j} - r_{k_j-1} \leq r$
    then
        $k_j = k_j + 1$;
        $r = r - r_{k_j} - r_{k_j-1}$
        if $j = n$ **then**
            $n = n + 1$; $k_n = 0$; $S = S \cup \{n\}$;
    else halt;

Fig. 3. Discrete rate optimization algorithm.

We have also examined the case of a non-concave utility function. We do not present it here for lack of space.

IV. Evaluating the scheme

We have implemented the joint rate/error control scheme described in the previous section in the FreePhone audio tool [8]. We next present some experimental results showing how the algorithm fares in practice. In particular, we consider how the optimal FEC allocation varies as a function of the utility function f, of the delay constraint T, and of the rate constraint R.

Utility functions

We have taken pain in the paper to consider mechanisms that would optimize a *subjective* measure of audio quality as perceived at a destination. Unfortunately, it is a well known fact that there is no agreed upon objective measure which captures the audio quality perceived by a user as a function of coding rate, loss rate in the network, etc. Subjective measures such as intelligibility, comfort of hearing, and mean opinion score (MOS), are hard to quantify. Objective measures such as loss rate or signal to noise ratio are related in complex and not always clear ways to subjective measures. For example, packet loss has a "generic" negative impact on quality because information is lost. However, it has a more subtle impact on quality depending on which type of coding scheme is used - for example, schemes that require that some state be kept about past packets to encode future packets (such as in G.729) are more sensitive to packet loss than other schemes [12], [22]. The signal to noise ratio, on the other hand, is sensitive to the characteristics of the signal, and hence to different sentences being spoken. Thus, in the absence of reliable objective functions, we have considered four sample functions, shown in Figure 4. The first function is defined by $f_0(x) = x$, the second function $f_1(x)$ was obtained by measurements of signal/noise ratios with the different codecs we consider here

(namely the LPC, GSM, ADM4, ADM6, and PCM coders mentioned earlier), the third curve $f_2(x)$ was obtained from values of MOS available in the literature for our codecs, and the last function $f_3(x)$ is defined by $f_3(x) = 1$ for $x \neq 0$ and $f_3(0) = 0$.

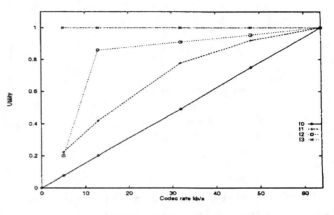

Fig. 4. Utility functions

We chose f_0 and f_3 because they yield two interesting ways of adding redundancy. Specifically, with f_0, the optimal allocation is always to send the main information encoded with the highest possible rate, and to send no redundant information at all[2]. Regarding f_3, note that f_3 is maximum as long as *some* information is received, no matter what the subjective quality of this information. Thus, using f_3 in our algorithm amounts to minimizing the loss rate after reconstruction at the destination, which is what we were doing back in Section II. It is easy to see that, in this case, the optimal policy is to send as many redundant packets as possible no matter how small the coding rate, as long as it fits within the constraints of the rate control mechanism.

How well does it work?

We have used adaptive FEC schemes in FreePhone for quite some time now and we have found them to provide very good average quality. This is illustrated in the figures below, which present measurements obtained over a connection between INRIA in southern France, and London in the UK. The loss rate over that connection is typically high, it was about 13% when the measures were taken. Suppose then that utility function f_3 has been chosen as the appropriate utility function, i.e. the goal is to minimize the number of lost packets at the destination. Figure 5 shows the evolutions as functions over time of the loss rate at the destination, computed over intervals of 128 packets, before and after reconstruction. For that experiment, we had $T = 4$.

---

[2]This can be derived by replacing $f(x_i)$ with x_i in section II and working out the optimization problem directly by hand.

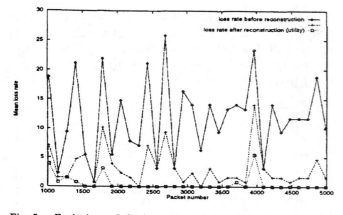

Fig. 5.   Evolutions of the loss rate and the utility (loss rate after reconstruction) over time, $f = f_3$

We observe that the loss rate after reconstruction is 0 much of the time, and it remains close to 0 even as the loss rate in the network varies between 1 and more than 25%. Clearly, the adaptive FEC scheme does a good job at improving utility even in the face of high and highly varying loss rate. Note also that the quality of the control scheme in Figure 5 is much better than that obtained with the simpler scheme in Figure 2 because i) the algorithm now takes into account bandwidth and delay constraints instead of just adding redundant information (and thus modifying bandwidth requirements) independent of the bandwidth available in the network for the connection, and ii) it finds the optimal combination of redundant information instead of just picking a combination in Table I which gives a loss rate after reconstruction close to a pre-specified target loss rate.

We have considered the case when the optimization is done for utility function f_3, because it makes it easier to compare with the earlier results in Figure 2. We have considered other functions as well. However, it is hard to illustrate the impact of subjective functions using objective measures, i.e. without listening to actual conversations or sound files sent over the Internet. We have found in practice that the best subjective quality by far is obtained with function f_2, i.e. the utility function which most closely matches MOS scores. We have also found that there is very little difference in terms of subjective quality between optimizing for f_0 ($f_0(x) = x$) and optimizing for f_1 (SNR). Recall that optimizing for f_0 amounts to not using any redundant information at all not matter what the loss rate; thus it is not surprising that the resulting quality is typically poor. This, however, also means that optimizing for the SNR (f_1) yields a poor quality as well, further proof that the SNR is not a reliable indicator of perceived audio quality.

Impact of the maximum delay T on quality

In the figures above, we had $T = 4$. Clearly, the higher T, the better the quality at the destination, but the larger the delay requirements. We now examine the impact of varying T on the quality achievable at the destination.

Figure 6 shows the average perceived quality at the destination for different values of T, and for the different utility functions described above. We make two observations.

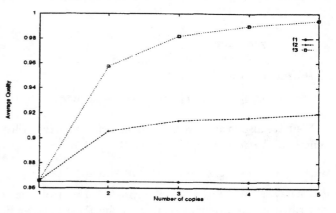

Fig. 6.   Perceived quality at the destination as a function of the delay T (or the number of redundant copies)

First, the quality increases dramatically as T goes from 1 to 2. This indicates that adding just one piece of redundant information about packet $n - 1$ in packet n makes a big difference in quality. This is consistent with the subjective results shown in [10]. We also observe that the quality perceived at the destination is essentially constant for f_1 now matter how much extra redundant information is added at the source. This is because f_1 is in fact very close to f_0, and f_0 yields an optimal FEC allocation that precisely does not include any redundant information at all (recall our discussion above).

The second observation is that the quality varies dramatically as a function of f. This indicates that i) algorithms that attempt to minimize an objective measure of quality such as the loss rate after reconstruction (i.e. they assume that $f = f_3$) yield very different performance from algorithms that maximize some kind of perceived audio quality, and thus that ii) it is important to get reliable data on subjective quality so as to be able to rely on reasonable curves for f.

V. CONCLUSION

Various FEC schemes for multimedia applications in the Internet have been proposed recently. However, they have to be handled carefully since adding FEC to a stream generated by a multimedia source increases the bandwidth requirements of that stream. The problem then is, given rate constraints imposed by a congestion control algorithm and given network conditions that can vary over time, to find the FEC information that will provide the destination with the best quality possible at any given point in time.

We have derived in this paper one such adaptive algorithm, which provides very good performance with the "signal processing" FEC scheme for audio recently standardized in the IETF. Of course, even our "optimal" scheme cannot provide guaranteed quality given the best effort service model of the current Internet. However, it puts us one step closer to quasi-constant quality audio even over connections with high or highly varying loss rates.

We are pursuing this work in several directions. One is to develop adaptive FEC schemes suitable for multicast groups (in the spirit of, for example, [13]). Another one is to consider more sophisticated FEC mechanisms, in particular mechanisms based on multiple description codes [28]. Yet another one is to use our technique to solve similar problems in other areas. Indeed, our approach is not restricted to the particular FEC scheme we focused on in this paper, nor to FEC schemes for audio applications only. One very interesting type of applications would be distributed gaming [9]. The idea there would be to use FEC to achieve an "almost reliable" *and* timely delivery of important information such as collisions/explosions or state changes. We can use the results in the paper to send multiple copies of the information encoded at different rates (and thus with different "granularities") so as to maximize the quality perceived by the destinations. Consider for example information about a bridge hit by a rocket. It is important for players to know whether the bridge can be crossed or not, less important to know the status of subparts of the bridge, etc. Thus, the information related to the bridge can be described with varying levels of detail, and thus sent with varying encoding rates (ranging from one bit "the bridge can be crossed or not" to as many bits as required for a full screen, accurate rendition of the bridge). The FEC scheme would then be supplemented by a reliable multicast delivery scheme such as SRM so as to make sure that information eventually gets delivered to all participants. We are currently evaluating such a scheme.

REFERENCES

[1]   D. Bertsimas, J. Tsitsiklis, *Introduction to Linear Optimization*, Athena Scientific, 1997.

[2]   R. Blahut, *Theory and Practice of Error Control Codes*, Addison-Wesley, 1983.

[3]   J-C. Bolot, "End-to-end packet delay and loss behavior in the Internet", *Proc. ACM Sigcomm '93*, San Fransisco, CA, pp. 189-199, Aug. 1993.

[4]   J-C. Bolot, A. V. Garcia, "The case for FEC-based error control for packet audio in the Internet", to appear in *ACM/Springer Multimedia Systems*, 1999.

[5]   J-C. Bolot, A. V. Garcia, "Control mechanisms for packet audio in the Internet", *Proc. IEEE Infocom '96*, San Fransisco, CA, pp. 232-239, Apr. 1996.

[6]   B. Dempsey, J. Liebeherr, A. Weaver, "On retransmission-based error control for continuous media traffic in packet-switching net-

works", *Computer Networks and ISDN Systems*, vol. 28, no. 5, pp. 719 - 736, March 1996.

[7]   N. Erdöl, C. Castelluccia, A. Zilouchian, "Recovery of missing speech packets using the short-time energy and zero-crossing measurements", *IEEE Trans. Speech and Audio Proc.*, vol. 1, no. 3, pp. 295-303, July 1993.

[8]   FreePhone http://www.inria.fr/rodeo/fphone

[9]   L. Gautier, C. Diot, "Design and evaluation of MiMaze, a multiplayer game on the Internet", *Proc. IEEE Multimedia Systems Conf.*, Austin, TX, June 1998.

[10] V. Hardman et al., "Reliable audio for use over the Internet", *Proc. INET '95*, Honolulu, HI, pp. 171-178, June 1995.

[11] ITU-T, *Recommendation H.323 - Visual Telephone Systems and Equipment for Local Area Networks which Provide Non-Guaranteed Quality of Service*, Feb. 1996.

[12] N. Jayant, S. W. Christensen, "Effects of packet losses in waveform-coded speech", *IEEE Trans. Comm.*, vol. COM-29, pp. 101-109, Feb. 1981.

[13] G. Karlsson, "Layered error-control coding for IP multicast", *Proc. HIPPARCH workshop*, Uppsala, Sweden, June 1997.

[14] A. Lapidoth, "The performance of convolutional codes on the block erasure channel using various finite interleaving techniques", *IEEE Tran. Information Theory*, vol. IT-40, pp. 1459-1473, Sept. 1994.

[15] M. Mathis, J. Semke, J. Mahdavi, T. Ott, "Macroscopic behavior of the TCP congestion avoidance algorithm", *Computer Comm Review*, vol. 27, no. 3, July 1997.

[16] S. B. Moon, J. Kurose, D. Towsley, "Packet audio playout delay adjustments: performance bounds and algorithms", *ACM/Springer Multimedia Systems*, vol. 5, pp. 17-28, Jan. 1998.

[17] V. Paxson, "End-to-end Internet packet dynamics", *Proc. ACM Sigcomm'97*, Cannes, France, Sept. 1997.

[18] C. Perkins et al., "RTP payload for redundant audio data", RFC 2198, Sept. 1997.

[19] C. Perkins, O. Hodson, "A survey of packet loss recovery techniques for streaming media", *IEEE Network*, Sept/Oct 1998.

[20] M. Podolsky, C. Romer, S. McCanne, "Simulation of FEC-based error control for packet audio on the Internet", *Proc. IEEE Infocom'98*, San Fransisco, CA, April 1998.

[21] L. Rizzo, "Effective erasure codes for reliable computer communication protocols", *Computer Communication Review*, April 1997.

[22] J. Rosenberg, "G.729 error recovery for Internet telephony", Columbia University report, spring 1997.

[23] H. Schulzrinne, J. Kurose, D. Towsley, "Loss correlation for queues with bursty input streams", *Proc. IEEE ICC '92*, Chicago, IL, pp. 219-224, 1992.

[24] H. Schulzrinne, S. Casner, R. Frederick, V. Jacobson, "RTP: A transport protocol for real-time applications", RFC 1889.

[25] H.Schulzrinne, J. Rosenberg, "Internet telephony, architecture and protocols: an IETF perspective", to appear in *Computer Networks and ISDN Systems*.

[26] H.Schulzrinne, J. Rosenberg, "Signaling for Internet telephony", *Proc. ICNP '98*, Austin, TX, Oct. 1998.

[27] Y. Shoham, A. Gersho, "Efficient bit allocation for an arbitrary set of quantizers", *IEEE Trans. Acoustics, Speech, Signal Proc.*, vol. 36, no. 9, pp. 1445-53, Sept. 1988.

[28] V. A. Vaishampayan, "Design of multiple description scalar quantizers", *IEEE Trans. Info. Theory*, vol. 39, no. 3, pp. 821-834, May 1993.

[29] D. Veitch, "Understanding end-to-end Internet traffic dynamics", *IEEE Globecom 98*, Sydney, Australia, Nov. 1998.

[30] L. Vicisano, L. Rizzo, J. Crowcroft, "TCP-like congestion control for layered multicast data transfer", *Proc. IEEE Infocom '98*, San Francisco, CA, March 1998.

[31] M. Yajnik, S. B. Moon, J. Kurose, D. Towsley, "Measurement and modeling of the temporal dependence in packet loss", *IEEE Infocom'99*, New York, NY, March 1999.

RSVP: A New Resource ReSerVation Protocol

Novel design features lead to an Internet protocol that is flexible and scalable.

■ ■ ■ ■ ■ ■ ■ ■ ■ ■

Lixia Zhang, Stephen Deering, Deborah Estrin, Scott Shenker, and Daniel Zappala

LIXIA ZHANG is a member of the research staff at Xerox PARC.

STEPHEN E. DEERING is a member of the research staff at Xerox PARC.

DEBORAH ESTRIN is an associate professor of computer science at the University of Southern California in Los Angeles.

SCOTT SHENKER is a member of the research staff at Xerox PARC.

DANIEL ZAPPALA is a doctoral student in computer science at the University of Southern California.

The current Internet architecture, embodied in the Internet Protocol (IP) network protocol, offers a very simple service model: point-to-point best-effort service. In recent years, several new classes of distributed applications have been developed, such as remote video, multimedia conferencing, data fusion, visualization, and virtual reality. It is becoming increasingly clear that the Internet's primitive service model is inadequate for these new applications; this inadequacy stems from the failure of the point-to-point best-effort service model to address two application requirements. First, many of these applications are very sensitive to the quality of service their packets receive. For a network to deliver the appropriate quality of service, it must go beyond the best-effort service model and allow flows (which is the generic term we will use to identify data traffic streams in the network) to reserve network resources. Second, these new applications are not solely point-to-point, with a single sender and a single receiver of data; instead, they are often multipoint-to-multipoint with several senders and receivers of data. Multipoint-to-multipoint communication occurs, for example, in multiparty conferencing where each participant is both a sender and a receiver of data, and also in remote learning applications, although in the latter case there are typically many more receivers than senders.

In recent years there has been a flurry of research activity devoted to the development of new network architectures and service models to accommodate these new application requirements. Even though fundamental differences exist between the proposed architectures, there is widespread agreement that any new architecture capable of accommodating multicast and a variety of qualities of service can be divided into five distinct components, which we identify and describe below.

Flow Specification — The network and the various data flows need a common language, so a source can tell the network about the traffic characteristics of its flow and, in turn, the network can specify the quality of service to be delivered to that flow. Thus, the first component of this new architecture is a flow specification, or "flowspec," which describes both the characteristics of the traffic stream sent by the source, and the service requirements of the application. In some sense, the flowspec is the central component of the architecture, since it embodies the service interface that applications interact with; the details of all of the other components of the architecture are hidden from applications. Two proposals for a flowspec are described in the literature [1,2].

Routing — The network must decide how to transport packets from the source to the receiver of the flow (or receivers of the flow, in the case of multicast). Thus, the second component of the architecture is a routing protocol that provides quality unicast and multicast paths. There are many approaches to unicast routing, and several different approaches to multicast routing exist as well [2-4]. None of the current proposals have yet dealt sufficiently with the interaction between routing and quality of service constraints; that is the subject of future research.

Resource Reservation — For the network to deliver a quantitatively specified quality of service (e.g., a bound on delay) to a particular flow, it is usually necessary to set aside certain resources, such as a share of bandwidth or a number of buffers, for that flow. This ability to create and maintain resource reservations on each link along the transport path is the third component of the architecture. Two approaches to resource reservation are described elsewhere [2,5]; in this article, we describe another.

Admission Control — Because a network's resources are finite, it cannot grant all resource reservation requests. In order to maintain the network load at a level where all quality of service commitments can be met, the network architecture must contain an admission control algorithm that determines which reservation requests to grant and which to deny, thereby maintaining the network load at an appropriate level. Two such admission control algorithms are described in the literature [6,7].

Packet Scheduling — After every packet transmission, a network switch must decide whether or not to transmit the next packet, and which is next. These decisions are controlled by the packet scheduling algorithm — which lies at the heart of any network architecture because it determines the qualities of service the network can provide. There are many proposed packet scheduling algorithms. A few examples are cited here [8-12].

In this article, we present our proposal for the third component of the architecture, a new resource ReSerVation Protocol (RSVP). Similar to previous work on resource reservation protocols, e.g., ST-II [2], RSVP is a simplex protocol, i.e., it reserves resources in one direction. However, several novel features in the RSVP design lead to the unique flexibility and scalability of the protocol. RSVP is receiver-oriented: The receiver of the data flow is responsible for the initiation of the resource reservation. This design decision enables RSVP to accommodate heterogeneous receivers in a multicast group; specifically, each receiver may reserve a different amount of resources, may receive different data streams sent to the same multicast group, and may "switch channels" from time to time (i.e., change which data streams it wishes to receive) without changing its reservation. RSVP also provides several reservation styles that allow applications to specify how reservations for the same multicast group should be aggregated at the intermediate switches; this feature results in more efficient utilization of network resources. Finally, by using "soft-state" in the switches, RSVP supports dynamic membership changes and automatically adapts to routing changes. These features enable RSVP to deal gracefully and efficiently with large multicast groups. While the motivation for RSVP arose within the Internet context, our design is intended to be fully general.

This article is organized as follows. We first list our design goals, and then discuss the basic design principles used to meet these goals. A more detailed description of the protocol operation is then given, followed by a simple example of how the protocol would work. Next, the current state of our RSVP implementation is described. We delay consideration of related work until later and follow that with a discussion of unresolved issues. Finally, we conclude with a brief summary.

RSVP Design Goals

In the traditional point-to-point case, one obvious reservation paradigm would have the sender transmit a reservation request towards the receiver, with the switches along the path either admitting or rejecting the flow. For the point-to-multipoint case, one may trivially extend this paradigm to have the sender transmit the reservation request along a multicast routing tree to each of the receivers. When we have multipoint-to-multipoint data transmissions, the straightforward extension of this paradigm would be to have each sender transmit a reservation request along its own multicast tree to each receiver. However, the special properties of having multiple, heterogeneous, receivers and/or multiple senders pose serious challenges that are not addressed by this simple extension of the basic reservation paradigm. We outline these various challenges below and detail how they are not met by the strawman proposal of straightforwardly extending the basic paradigm. In the process, we identify the seven goals which guided the design of RSVP.

In a wide area internetwork such as the Internet, receivers and paths to reach receivers can have very different properties from one another. In particular, one must not assume that all the receivers of a multicast group possess the same capacity for processing incoming data, nor even necessarily desire or require the same quality of service from the network. For instance, a source may be sending a layered encoding of a video signal; certain receivers decoding in software would only have sufficient processing power to decode the low-resolution signal, while those receivers with hardware decoding, or more processing power, could decode the entire signal. Furthermore, the paths to reach the receivers may not have the same capacity; in the layered encoding example above, certain receivers might only have low-bandwidth paths between them and the source and so could only receive the low-resolution signal. The strawman proposal above is incapable of dealing with the receivers individually, and so cannot address these heterogeneous needs. Therefore, our first design goal for RSVP is to provide the ability for heterogeneous receivers to make reservations specifically tailored to their own needs.

The presence of multiple receivers raises another issue; the membership in a multicast group can be dynamic. The strawman proposal would have to reinitiate the reservation protocol every time a new member joined or an existing member left the multicast group. Reinitiation of the reservation protocol is particularly burdensome for large groups because the larger the group size, the more frequent are changes in group membership. So our second design goal for RSVP is to deal gracefully with changes in the multicast group membership.

The strawman proposal deals with multiple senders by having each sender make an independent resource reservation along its own multicast routing tree. This approach results in resources being reserved along multiple, independent trees, even though the branches of different trees often share common links. Although appropriate for some applications, in other cases this duplication can lead to a significant wasting of resources. For example, in an audio conference with several people, usually only one person, or at most a few people, talk at any one time because of the normal dynamics of human conversation. Thus, instead of reserving enough bandwidth for every potential speaker to speak simultaneously, in many circumstances it is adequate to reserve only enough network resources to handle a few simultaneous audio channels. Our third design goal for RSVP is to allow end users to specify their application needs, so the aggregate resources reserved for a multicast group can more accurately reflect the resources actually needed by that group.

Furthermore, in a multiparty conference, a receiver may only wish to (or be able to) watch one or a few other participants at a time but would like the possibility of switching among various participants. The simple approach of delivering the data streams from all the sources and then

> ■ ■ ■ ■ ■
> Our first design goal for RSVP is to provide the ability for heterogeneous receivers to make reservations specifically tailored to their own needs.

The Seven Design Goals of RSVP

- Accommodate heterogeneous receivers.
- Adapt to changing multicast group membership.
- Exploit the resource needs of different applications in order to use network resources efficiently.
- Allow receivers to switch channels.
- Adapt to changes in the underlying unicast and multicast routes.
- Control protocol overhead so that it does not grow linearly (or worse) with the number of participants.
- Make the design modular to accommodate heterogeneous underlying technologies.

The Six Design Principles of RSVP

- Receiver-initiated reservation.
- Separating reservation from packet filtering.
- Providing different reservation styles.
- Maintaining "soft-state" in the network.
- Protocol overhead control.
- Modularity.

---

dropping the undesired ones at the receiver does not address network resource usage considerations (e.g., efficient use of limited bandwidth, or reducing the charges incurred for bandwidth usage). A receiver should be able to control which packets are carried on its reserved resources, not only what gets displayed on its local screen. Moreover, a receiver should be able to switch among sources without the risk of having the change request denied, as could occur if a new reservation request had to be submitted in order to "switch channels." Our fourth design goal for RSVP is to enable this channel changing feature.

RSVP is not a routing protocol and should avoid replicating any routing functions. RSVP's task is to establish and maintain resource reservations over a path or a distribution tree, independent of how the path or tree was created. In a large internetwork with a volatile topology and load, these routes may change from time to time. Adapting to such changes in topology and load is the explicit job of the routing protocol; it would be expensive and complicated to replicate such functions in RSVP. At the same time, however, RSVP should be able to cope with the resulting routing changes. Our fifth design goal is that RSVP should deal gracefully with such changes in routes, automatically reestablishing the resource reservations along the new paths as long as adequate resources are available.

The strawman proposal does not deal gracefully with changes in routes, because there is no mechanism to discover the change and trigger a new resource reservation request. One could introduce such a mechanism by having each source periodically refresh its reservation over the multicast routing tree. However, in large multicast groups such refreshing would lead to S messages arriving at every receiver during every refresh period, where S is the number of sources. Our sixth design goal is to control protocol overhead; by this we mean both avoiding the explosion in protocol overhead when group size gets large, and also incorporating tunable parameters so that the amount of protocol overhead can be adjusted.

Our last design goal is not specific to the problem at hand but rather is a general matter of modular design. We hope to make the general design of RSVP relatively independent of the architectural components listed in the first section of this paper. Clearly a particular implementation of RSVP will be tied quite closely to the flowspec and interfaces used by the routing and admission control algorithms. However, the general protocol design should be independent of these. In particular, our protocol should be capable of establishing reservations across networks that implement different routing algorithms, such as IP unicast routing, IP multicast routing [4], the recently proposed core-based tree (CBT) multicast routing [3], or some future routing protocols. This design goal makes RSVP deployable in many contexts. For optimally efficient routing decisions, however, routing selection and resource reservation should be integrated — so the choice of route can depend on the quality of service requested, and the stability of the route can be maintained over the duration of the reservation. Such an integration would lead to more coordination between the choice of which resources to reserve and the mechanics of establishing the reservation (which is RSVP's main focus). This integration is something that requires further research.

In summary, we have identified seven important design goals (see box this page). RSVP is primarily a vehicle used by applications to communicate their requirements to the network in a robust and efficient way, independent of the specific requirements. RSVP delivers resource reservation requests to the relevant switches but plays no other role in providing network services. Thus, RSVP communicates requirements for a wide range of network services but does not directly provide them. For instance, the synchronization requirements of flows or the need for reliable multicast delivery could be expressed in the flowspec that is distributed by RSVP and then realized by the switches. Similarly, the flowspec could also carry around information about advance reservations (reservations made for a future time) and preemptable reservations (reservations that a receiver is willing to have preempted). RSVP is capable of supporting the delivery of these and other services, whenever these network services rely only on the state being established at the individual switches along the paths determined by the routing algorithm. Thus, although we described RSVP as a resource reservation protocol, it can be seen more generally as a "switch state establishment" protocol.

Basic Design Principles

To achieve the seven design goals we used six basic design principles (see box this page). These principles are now described.

Receiver-Initiated Reservation

The strawman proposal discussed in the previous section — and all existing resource reservation protocols — are designed around the principle that the data source initiates the reservation request. In contrast, RSVP adopts a novel receiver-initiated design principle; receivers choose the level of resources reserved and are responsible for initiating and keeping the reservation active as long as they want to receive the data. We describe the motivation for this receiver-initiated approach below.

A source can always transmit data, whether or not adequate resources exist in the network to deliver the data. The receiver knows its own capacity limitations; furthermore, the receiver is the only one who experiences, and thus is directly concerned with, the quality of service of the incoming packets. Additionally, if network charging is deployed in the future, the receiver would likely be the party paying for the requested quality of service. Thus, it should be the receiver who decides what resources should be reserved.

One could imagine the receivers send this information to the source, which would use this information in sending out the reservation request. To handle heterogeneous requests, however, the sender would have to bundle all requests together and pass them to the network, and the network would determine how much resource to reserve on which links, according to the location of individual receivers. For large multicast groups, this will likely cause a multicast implosion at the sender. This implosion problem becomes more serious when the multicast group membership changes dynamically and the reservation has to be periodically renewed. Consider, as an extreme example, a cable TV firm broadcasting several channels of programs; while there are relatively few sources, there are perhaps hundreds of thousands of receivers, each watching only one or a few channels at a time. In the strawman proposal, whenever any individual receiver wants to switch between channels, it sends a message to the source. In this case, where there are many receivers and frequent switching between channels, each source has to accommodate a deluge of change requests. This overhead is superfluous, however, since the resulting broadcast pattern changes relatively slowly (because the resulting multicast trees are likely to be relatively stable except near the leaf nodes). Later in this paper, we show how our receiver-initiated design accommodates heterogeneity among group members yet avoids such multicast implosion.

The idea of the receiver-initiated approach was inspired by Deering's work on IP multicast routing [4]. The IP multicast routing protocol treats senders and receivers separately. A sender sends to a multicast group in exactly the same way as it sends to a single receiver; it merely puts in each packet a multicast group address in place of a host address. The multicast group membership is defined as the group of receivers. Deering's multicast routing design can be considered a receiver initiated approach: each receiver individually joins or leaves the group without affecting other receivers in the group, or affecting sources that send to the group. The routing protocol takes the responsibility of forwarding all multicast data packets to all the current members in the group. Analogous to our argument that a sender does not care whether adequate resources are available, a sender to a multicast group does not nece   know who is currently a member of the multicast group (i.e., receiving the data); in particular, it may not be a member of the multicast group itself.

Separating Reservation from Packet Filtering

A resource reservation at a switch assigns certain resources (buffers, bandwidth, etc.) to the entity making the reservation. A distinction that is rarely made which will be crucial to our ability to meet our design goals is that the resource reservation does not determine which packets can use the resources, but merely specifies what amount of resources are reserved for whom. Here, "whom" does not refer to "which packets" can use the reserved resources, it refers to "which entity" controls the resources.

A separate function, called a packet filter, selects those packets that can use the resources; it is set by the reserving entity. Moreover, it can be changed without changing the amount of reserved resources. One of the important design principles in RSVP is that we allow this filter to be dynamic; that is, the receiver can change it during the course of the reservation. This distinction between the reservation and the filter enables us to offer several different reservation styles, which we now describe.

Providing Different Reservation Styles

As we discussed briefly above, the service requirements of multicast applications dictate how the reservation requests from individual receivers should be aggregated inside the network. For example, the typical dynamics of human verbal interaction results in only one or a few people talking at any one time; thus, in many conferencing situations, it is feasible to have all senders of audio signals to a conference share the same set of reserved resources, where these resources were sufficient for a small number of simultaneous audio streams. In contrast, there are no analogous limitations on video signals. Therefore, if the conferencing application also includes video then enough resources must be reserved for the number of video streams one desires to watch simultaneously. As in the usual multicast paradigm, if two receivers downstream of a particular link are watching the same video stream for the lifetime of the application (e.g., when attending a remote lecture), only a single reservation need be made on this link to accommodate their needs. However, if these two receivers wish to occasionally switch among the senders during the application lifetime (e.g., when participating in a distributed group meeting), then separate reservations must be maintained. To support different needs of various applications, while making the most efficient use of network resources, RSVP defines different reservation styles which indicate how intermediate switches should aggregate reservation requests from receivers in the same multicast group. Currently there are three reservation styles: no-filter, fixed-filter, and dynamic-filter. We now describe these filter styles; for the sake of brevity we identify applications only by their multicast address, although in the current Internet context a multicast application may be identified by the IP multicast address plus destination port number.

When a receiver makes a resource reservation for a multicast application, it can specify whether or not a data source filter is to be used. If no filter is used, then any packets destined for that multicast group may use the reserved resources. (Although some enforcement mechanism is needed to ensure that the aggregate stream does not use more than the reserved amount, we will not discuss enforcement mechanisms here.) For example, the audio conference described above would use a no-filter reservation, so that a single reserved pipe can be used by whoever is speaking at the moment. If source filtering is needed, the filter is specified by a list of

■ ■ ■ ■ ■
Although we described RSVP as a resource reservation protocol, it can be seen more generally as a "switch state establishment" protocol.

Having several different reservation styles allows intermediate switches to decide how individual reservation requests for the same multicast group can be efficiently merged.

sources. (Again, in the Internet context, a data source can be specified by the source host address plus source port number; we only refer to the source host address here.) Only the packets from the specified sources can use the reserved resources. Filtered reservations are used to forward individual images in video conferencing, enabling participants to reserve resources for particular video streams.

A filtered reservation can be either fixed or dynamic. A "fixed-filter" reservation allows a receiver to receive data only from the sources listed in the original reservation request, for the duration of the reservation; a "dynamic-filter" reservation allows a receiver to change its filter to different sources over time.

To illustrate how intermediate nodes use these reservation styles to aggregate reservation requests, consider the case of several receivers in the same multicast group making fixed-filter reservations over a common link. These reservations may be shared if the source lists overlap, because the reservation will never be changed. Thus, only a single pipe (with the largest amount of resources from all the requests) is reserved for each source even when there are multiple requests. Such aggregation can occur when members of a multicast application all listen or watch the same audio or video signals, as in the case of a multicast lecture. Reservations using the no-filter style can also be aggregated in this manner; if a receiver does not discriminate between individual sources, it cannot switch among the sources either.

If a receiver expects to switch among different sources from time to time, it must make a dynamic filter reservation to avoid affecting the reception of other receivers in the same multicast application. The intermediate nodes cannot aggregate this style of reservation because the receiver can change the list of sources in the filter at any time during the course of the reservation. In fact, this separation between the resource reservation and the filter is one of the key facets of RSVP; the resource reservation controls how much bandwidth is reserved, while the filter controls which packets can use that bandwidth. In the dynamic-filter reservation case, each receiver requests enough bandwidth for the maximum number of incoming streams it can handle at once and the network reserves enough resources to handle the worst case when all the receivers that requested dynamic filter reservations take input from different sources, even though several receivers may actually tune to the same source(s) from time to time. However, note that the total amount of dynamic filter reservations made over any link should be limited to the amount of bandwidth needed to forward data from all the upstream sources.

In summary, having several different reservation styles allows intermediate switches to decide how individual reservation requests for the same multicast group can be efficiently merged. The dynamic filter reservation style allows receivers to change channels. Thus, we have met design goals 3 and 4. So far, RSVP has defined three reservation styles; other styles may be identified as new multicast applications with different needs are developed.

Maintaining "Soft-State" in the Network

The typical multipoint-to-multipoint applications we have considered are rather long-lived. Over the lifetime of such an application, new members may join, existing members may leave, and routes may change due to dynamic status changes at intermediate switches and links. To be able to adjust resource reservations accordingly, in a way transparent to end applications, RSVP keeps soft-state at intermediate switches and leaves the responsibility of maintaining the reservation to end users. The term "soft-state" was first used by Clark [13]. In our context, it refers to a state maintained at network switches which, when lost, will be automatically reinstated by RSVP soon thereafter. Thus, soft-state is appropriate in our context where frequent membership changes and occasional service outages would render a more brittle (i.e., less self-stabilizing) state to become, and perhaps remain, obsolete or incorrect.

More specifically, at each intermediate switch, RSVP distinguishes between state information of two kinds: path state and reservation state. Each data source periodically sends a Path message that establishes or updates the path state, and each receiver periodically sends a Reservation message that establishes or updates the reservation state (which is attached to the path state).

Path messages are forwarded using the switches' existing routing table; in other words, the routing decision is made by the network's routing protocol, not by RSVP. Each path message carries a flowspec given by the data source, as well as an F-flag indicating if the application wishes to allow filtered reservations. In processing each path message, the switch updates its path state containing information about 1) the incoming link upstream to the source, and 2) the outgoing links downstream from that source to the receivers in the group (as indicated by the multicast routing table). In addition, if the F-flag in the path message is on, the switch also keeps the information about the source and the previous hop upstream to reach the source; this information allows the switch to accommodate any style of reservation. If the F-flag is off, the switch does not maintain information about the specific source of the path message except for adding its incoming link to the path state; the state kept at the switch is thereby minimized. Consequently, only no-filter style reservations can be made for data streams from such sources. As we show later in an example, not maintaining per source information can, in some topologies, result in over-reserving resources over certain links.

Each reservation message carries a flowspec, a reservation style, and (if the reservation uses a fixed or dynamic filtered style) a packet filter. In processing each reservation message, the switch updates its reservation state (which contains information for the outgoing link the message came from) by recording 1) the amount of resources reserved, 2) the source filter for the reserved resource, 3) the reservation style, and 4) if the style is dynamic-filtered, the reserver (who is the sender of this reservation message, and one of the receivers of this multicast group). We see that the only time we need to keep per receiver information in the reservation table is when the reservations involve dynamic filters; when all reservations are either no-filter or fixed-filter we can assign the reservation to the multicast group as a whole and then only keep track of the total resources reserved on each downstream link.

Reservation messages are forwarded back towards the sources by reversing the paths of path messages. In fact, the path information is maintained solely for this reverse-path forwarding of reservation messages.

More specifically, reservation messages of the no-filter style are forwarded to all incoming links to the multicast group, and those of filtered styles are forwarded to the previous hops of the sources that are listed in the filters.

Both path messages and reservation messages carry a timeout value used by intermediate switches to set corresponding timers; the timers get reset whenever new messages are received. Whenever a timer expires, the corresponding state is deleted. This timeout-driven deletion prevents resources from being orphaned when a receiver fails to send an explicit tear-down message or the underlying route changes. It is also the only way to release the resources of no-filter or fixed-filter reservations; in these cases, the switch cannot determine if the reservation is being shared by multiple receivers, so the reservation can only be deleted when it times out. It is the responsibility of both senders and receivers to maintain the proper reservation state inside the network by periodically refreshing the path and reservation state.

When a route or membership changes, the routing protocol running underneath RSVP forwards future path messages along the new route(s) and reaches new members. As a result, the path state at switches is updated, causing future reservation messages to traverse the new routes or new route segments. Reservations along old routes, or along routes to inactive senders or receivers, time out automatically. Because path and reservation messages are sent periodically, the protocol tolerates occasional corruption or loss of a few messages. This soft-state approach adds both adaptivity and robustness to RSVP.

The advantages of the soft-state approach, however, do not come for free; the periodic refreshing messages add overhead to the protocol operation. We next discuss how RSVP controls protocol overhead.

Protocol Overhead Control

The RSVP overhead is determined by three factors: the number of RSVP messages sent, the size of these RSVP messages, and the refresh frequencies of both path and reservation messages. As we describe in more detail in the RSVP overview section, RSVP merges path and reservation messages as they traverse the network. The merging of path messages means that, in general, each link carries no more than a single path message in each direction during each path refresh period. Similarly, the merging of reservation messages means that each link carries no more than a single reservation message in each direction during each reservation refresh period. The maximum size of both the path and reservation messages on a particular link is proportional to the number of data sources upstream.

RSVP controls the third overhead factor, the refresh frequencies, by tuning the timeout values carried in path and reservation messages. The larger the timeout value, the less frequent the refresh messages have to be sent. There exists, however, a tradeoff between the overhead one is willing to tolerate and RSVP's responsiveness in adapting to dynamic changes. For instance, reservation messages are forwarded according to the path state maintained at intermediate switches, which in turn gets synchronized with the routing protocol state every time a path message is processed. When a route changes, reservations along the new route (or new route segments) are not established until a new path message is sent (causing the path state to be updated), and a new reservation message is sent along the new route.

Our current RSVP implementation uses static timer values chosen on the basis of engineering judgment; in the future, we will investigate adaptive timeout algorithms to optimally adjust the timer values according to observed dynamics in routes and membership changes, and the loss probability of RSVP messages.

Modularity

In the context of real-time, multicast applications, RSVP interfaces to three other components: 1) the flowspec, which is handed to RSVP by an application, or some session control protocol on behalf of the application, when invoking RSVP; 2) the network routing protocol, which forwards path messages towards all the receivers, causing the RSVP path state to be established at intermediate switch nodes; and 3) the network admission control, which makes an acceptance decision based on the flowspec carried in the reservation messages.

We list modularity as one of RSVP's design goals because we would like to make RSVP as independent from the other components as possible. We have attempted to make few assumptions about these other components, and those assumptions we have made are described explicitly.

We make no assumptions about the flowspec to be carried by RSVP. RSVP treats the flowspec as a number of uninterpreted bytes of data that need to be exchanged among only the applications and the network admission control algorithm. We assume that the admission control algorithm operates by having an RSVP reservation packet containing a flowspec pass through the switches along the delivery path for that flow (but obviously in the reverse direction), with each switch returning an admit or reject signal; the resource reservation is established only if all switches along the path admit the flow. We also assume that the packet scheduling algorithm can change packet filters without needing to establish a new reservation.

The only assumptions about the underlying routing protocol(s) are that it provides both unicast and multicast routing, and that a sender to a multicast group can reach all group members under normal network conditions; obviously, in the case of a network partition, no routing protocol can guarantee this reachability. We do not assume that a sender to a multicast group is necessarily a member of the group, nor do we assume that the route from a sender to a receiver is the same as the route from the receiver to the sender.

RSVP Operation Overview

RSVP, and indeed any reservation protocol, is a vehicle for establishing and maintaining state in switches along the paths that each flow's data packets travel. Because reservation messages are initiated by each receiver, RSVP must make sure that the reservation messages from a receiver follow exactly the reverse routes of the data streams from all the sources (that the receiver is interested in). In other words, RSVP must establish a sink tree from each receiver to all the sources to forward reservation messages.

■ ■ ■ ■ ■
This soft-state approach adds both adaptivity and robustness to RSVP.

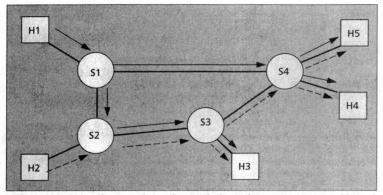

■ **Figure 1.** *A simple network topology with the multicast routing trees. H1 and H2 are data sources, and H3, H4, and H5 are receivers. The solid lines depict the routing tree of H1 and the dotted lines the routing tree of H2. In general, the set of sources and the set of receivers may overlap partially or completely. For the sake of clarity, here they are disjoint.*

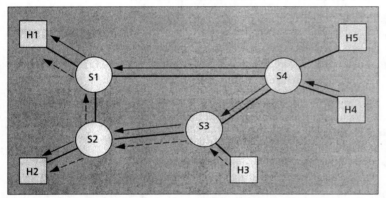

■ **Figure 2.** *A simple network topology with the sink trees. H1 and H2 are data sources, and H3, H4, and H5 are receivers (sinks). The dotted lines depict the sink tree of H3 and the solid lines the sink tree of H4. For clarity the sink tree of H5 is omitted.*

The sink tree for each receiver is formed by tracing the paths defined by the multicast routing protocol — in the reverse direction — from the receiver to each of the sources (Figs. 1 and 2). Periodic path messages are forwarded along the routing trees provided by the routing protocol, and reservation refresh messages are forwarded along the sink trees to maintain current reservation state. A reservation message propagates only as far as the closest point on the sink tree where a reservation level greater than or equal to the reservation level being requested has already been made.

Each switch uses the path states to maintain a table of incoming and outgoing interfaces for each multicast group. Each incoming interface keeps the information about the flowspecs it has forwarded upstream. (This information is needed in merging reservation requests from multiple downstream links.) For each outgoing link, there is a list of senders; associated with each sender is the previous hop address from which data from that sender arrives at the current switch. There is also a set of reservations. Generally speaking, each reservation consists of a reserver, a filter, and the amount of resources reserved. For no-filter reservations, the first two fields are not needed; and for fixed-filter reservations, the first field is not needed.

We now review the process of creating and maintaining reservations in more detail. Before or when each data source starts transmitting, it sends a path message containing the flowspec of the data source. When a switch receives a path message, it first checks to see if it already has the path state for the named target (which can be either a single host or a multicast group, plus the destination port number); if not it creates the path state for that target. The switch then obtains the outgoing interface(s) of the path message from the routing protocol in use, and updates its table of incoming and outgoing links accordingly; the source address (and port number in the Internet context) carried in the path message is also recorded if the path message indicates that the application may require a filtered reservation. This path message is forwarded immediately only if it is from a new source or indicates a change in routes. The switch can detect a change in routes by checking to see if the outgoing interfaces indicated by the routing protocol's routing table are different than the outgoing links maintained in the path state. Otherwise, the switch discards the incoming path message and instead periodically sends its own path messages which contain the path information carried in all the path messages that it has received so far.

When a receiver receives a path message from a source for whose data it would like to create a reservation, the receiver sends a reservation message using the (possibly modified) flowspec that came in the incoming path message. As described earlier, the reservation message is guided along the reverse route of the path messages to reach the data source(s). Along the way if any switch rejects the reservation, an RSVP reject message is sent back to the receiver and the reservation message discarded; otherwise if the reservation message requires a new reservation to be made, it propagates as far as the closest point along the way to the sender(s) where a reservation level equal or greater than that being requested has been made.

Once the reservation is established, the receiver periodically sends reservation refresh messages (which are identical in format to the original request). As the reservation requests are forwarded along the sink trees, the switches merge the requests for the same multicast group by pruning those that carry a request for reserving a smaller, or equal, amount of resources than some previous request. As an example, assume H1 is a video source, and H4 has reserved enough bandwidth to receive the full video data stream while H5 wants to receive only low resolution video data (Fig. 2). In this case, when the reservation request from H5 reaches S4, S4 makes the requested reservation over the link from S4 to H5 and then drops the request (i.e., does not forward it upstream) because sufficient resources have been reserved already by H4's request.

When a sender (receiver) wishes to terminate the connection, the sender (receiver) sends out a path (reservation) teardown message to release the path state or reserved resources. There is no retransmission timer for this teardown message. In cases where the teardown message is lost, the intermediate nodes will eventually time out the corresponding state. As we noted above, no-filter or fixed-filter reservations cannot be explicitly torn down because the switches do not maintain sufficient state.

Example

We consider a simple network configuration to illustrate in more detail how RSVP works. The network has five hosts connected by seven point-to-point links and three switches (Fig. 3). We assume that for links connecting hosts directly to a switch, the hosts act as switches in terms of reserving resources. To simplify the description, we assume adequate network resources exist for all reservation requests. Furthermore, the example involves only a single multicast group, so we do not discuss the addressing used to distinguish reservations made for one multicast group from reservations made for other multicast groups.

We describe the cases of no-filter and filtered reservations separately; we start with the simpler case, no-filter reservations, and then discuss the case of filtered reservations.

No-filter Reservations

Let us consider an audio conference among 5 participants, one at each of the 5 hosts (Fig. 3). In this case, each host behaves both as a source and a receiver at the same time. We make the following assumptions:
- The routing protocol has built a multicast routing tree so each sender can reach all the receivers.
- Each switch has received RSVP path messages (with the F-flag off from all the sources, so the switches do not record source information), and the complete path state for each switch has stored as described below, although in a real application sources may start at different times and the path state would be built up over time.
- No reservations have been made yet.

	S1	S2	S3
Incoming-links	L1, L2, L6	L5, L6, L7	L3, L4, L7

We now describe how reservations are created. H1 wants to receive data from all other senders to the multicast group but only wants enough bandwidth reserved to carry one audio stream; thus, it sends a reservation message R1 (B, no-filter) to S1, where B is the amount of bandwidth needed to forward one audio stream. When S1 receives R1 (B, no-filter), it first reserves resources over L1 (in the direction from S1 towards H1), then attaches the following reservation state to the path state to indicate the amount of the reservation made over L1.

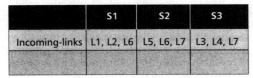

	S1		
Incoming-links	L1	L2	L6
Outgoing-links	L1(B)	L2	L6

Finally, S1 forwards R1 (B, no-filter) over all incoming-links, in this case L2 and L6. Note that the switch never forwards any RSVP message over the link the message came from.

The copy of R1 (B, no-filter) sent along L6 reaches S2, which reserves B over L6 and forwards the message to links 5 and 7. When the copy of R1

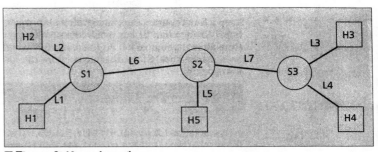

■ Figure 3. *Network topology.*

(B, no-filter) that was sent along L7 reaches S3, that switch reserves B over L7 and then forwards R1 (B, no-filter) over links 3 and 4.

When H2 wants to create a reservation, it sends a reservation message, R2 (B, no-filter), to S1. Upon receipt of R2 (B, no-filter), S1 first reserves B over L2, changing the path state to:

	S1		
Incoming-links	L1	L2	L6
Outgoing-links	L1(B)	L2(B)	L6

S1 then forwards R2 (B, no-filter) over L1 only, because it has forwarded an identical request over L6 previously.

After all the receiving hosts have sent RSVP reservation messages, an amount B of resources have been reserved over each of the seven links in each of the two directions.

Before leaving this example of no-filter reservation, consider the tradeoff between keeping extra state information and the possibility of over-reserving resources on certain links. In the above example, we assumed all the path messages had the F-flag off, so no per source information is kept at the switches. As a result, if each receiver requested 2B of bandwidth (i.e., an amount enough to carry two full audio streams), then 2B would be reserved on every link — even though on L1 (and similarly on L2, L3, L4, and L5) in the direction away from H1 we need only reserve B, since there is only a single source upstream on the link. In general, a no-filter reservation should indicate how much should be reserved as a function of the number of sources upstream; in this example it would be B units per upstream source. Unfortunately, one cannot know the number of sources upstream without keeping a list of the sources. If the F-flag was set in all the path messages, the switches would have kept track of individual sources and, by paying this extra cost in increased state, only the required resources would have been reserved along the links.

Not maintaining per source information can lead to an over-reserving of resources on some network links; but, in those applications involving many data sources with few resources required for each source (such as in a data-gathering application with many sensors), one may still choose to reduce the switch state at the possible expense of over-reserving resources over some links.

Filtered Reservations

Now consider the case where H2, H3, H4, and H5 are receivers (i.e., members of the multicast group), and H1, H4, and H5 are sources. All path message have the F-flag set, so each switch needs to keep a list of sources associated with their previous hops. Assume that S1 has received path messages from all of the sources but no reservations have yet been made. Thus, S1's path state contains the following entry:

S1				
Outgoing-links	L2(src:H1,H1	H4,S2	H5,S2)	L6(src:H1,H1)

The notation L2(src: H1, H1 | H4, S2 | H5, S2) indicates that data from sources H1, H4, and H5 are sent out along outgoing link L2; for each source, H1, S2, and S2 are the previous hop addresses from which data from that source arrives, respectively. H1 is not a receiver, so L1 is not among the outgoing links of S1.

Now assume that H2 sends a reservation message denoted R2(B, H4), that is, H2 wants to receive packets only from source H4 and is reserving an amount B, sufficient for one source. The reservation message R2(B, H4) reaches S1 via the L2 interface. S1 finds that H4 is indeed one of the sources it has heard, and that the packets from H4 come from S2. S1 reserves bandwidth B over L2, and forwards R2 (B, H4) over L6 to S2.

S2's path state contains the following entries.

S2				
Outgoing-links	L5(src:H1,S1 | H4,S3)	L6(src:H4,S3 | H5,H5)	L7(src:H1,S1 | H5,H5)

When S2 receives R2(B, H4), it reserves B over L6, and then forwards the message R2(B, H4) to S3, which is the previous hop towards H4.

S3's path state then has its entries changed to:

S3				
Outgoing-links	L3(src:H1,S2 | H4,H4)	H5,S2)	L4(src:H1,S2 | H5,S2)	L7(src:H4,H4

Upon receiving R2(B, H4), S3 reserves B over L7, and forwards the message to H4. When the message reaches H4, a pipe of B has been reserved from H4 to H2. This describes the reservation events surrounding the reservation request R2(B, H4).

Suppose that sometime afterwards, H5 sends the reservation message R5(2B, *), where * indicates a request for dynamic-filter reservation. When S2 receives this reservation message, it reserves 2B over L5 (at least 2 sources can go that direction) for H5, and forwards the reservation message R5(2B, *) over L6 and L7.

When S1 receives R5(2B, *), it finds out that there is only one source going out L6. It therefore reserves an amount B over L6 for R5 and then passes the reservation request on to H1. When S3 receives R5(2B,*), it finds out that there is only one source going out L7 and has a fixed-filter reservation already. S3 does not reserve any more, nor does it further forward the request to L4.

Suppose now that H4 terminates both receiving and sending without transmitting any teardown messages. As H4 no longer sends path or reservation refreshes, all H4 related state will time out, changing the outgoing-link entries in the various switches.

S1	L2(src:H1,H1 H5,S2)		L6(src:H1,H1)	
S2	L5(src:H1,S1)	L6(src:H5,H5)	L7(src:H1,S1	H5,H5)
S3	L3(src:H1,S2	H5,S2)		

S1 stops forwarding R2 (B, H4) from H2 and re- turns an RSVP error message to H2. S2 forwards future R5(2B, *) reservation refreshes to the L6 direction only since there are no more sources in L7 direction.

For the sake of simplicity, in the above example we assumed each data stream requires the same bandwidth to forward. RSVP is designed to handle cases where each source may demand different amounts of resources, and each receiver may receive only a subset of the data from each source. In fixed-filter reservations, this requires each source filter be associated with a specific amount of resources. In dynamic-filter reservations, the receiver must receive the same amount of data when "switching channels."

Implementation Status

This article illustrates how RSVP works at a general level. For the sake of brevity and clarity, many details have not presented; in particular, we have not described with any specificity the merging algorithm. We have, however, verified this design in a packet-level, interactive simulator, where all such details have been tested.

The simulator was written by one of the authors (LZ) and has been used in several previous simulation studies [8,6,14]. It provides modules that imitate the actual behavior of common network components, such as hosts, links, IP routers, and protocols such as IP, TCP, and UDP. We verified RSVP design by implementing the protocol in the simulator and then observing, step-by-step, how the protocol handles various dynamic events, such as new senders/receivers joining a multicast group, or existing members leaving. Indeed, the design of most protocol details emerged from an iterative process of simulation and redesign.

Using the simulator code as a starting point, the protocol was implemented by Sugih Jamin (USC) for experimentation on DARTnet, a cross-country T1 network testbed sponsored by ARPA, linking roughly a dozen academic and industrial research institutions. Preliminary tests have been performed on this implementation, but no systematic performance studies have been done as yet.

Related Work

In the course of exploring network algorithms that deliver quality of service guarantees, there have been several proposals and prototype implementations of network resource reservation algorithms over the last few years [9,15]. However, almost all of these prototypes deal exclusively with unicast reservations.

The Stream Protocol, ST [5], was a pioneering work in multicast reservation protocol design. ST was designed specifically to support voice conferencing and was capable of making both unicast and multicast resource reservations. At the time ST was proposed, there was no work on sophisticated multicast routing, so ST would make resource reservations over a single, duplex distribution tree which was created by blending the paths from unicast routing; this was done with the assumptions that the routes were reversible and the application data traffic would travel in both directions. However, ST requires a centralized

Access Controller to coordinate among all the participants and manage the tree establishment.

The successor to ST, ST-II [2], continues to create its own multicast trees by blending the paths from unicast routing; however, ST-II establishes multiple simplex reservations to eliminate the Access Controller. Each data source makes a resource reservation along a multicast tree that is rooted at the source and reaches out to all the receivers; the reservation made along the tree uses a single flowspec, so ST-II cannot accommodate heterogeneous receivers. Because each data source makes its reservation independently, a single pipe is reserved from every source to every receiver in the same multicast application group. An analysis of ST-II implementation and design issues is provided elsewhere [16].

Thus, neither ST nor ST-II provides a robust and efficient solution to the multipoint-to-multipoint resource reservation problem; they share several of the limitations of the strawman proposal described earlier. The RSVP design effort was initiated to fill this vacuum. Recently, however, there have been other proposals to fill this need. Pasquale et al. have proposed a dissemination-oriented approach in their work on multimedia multicast channels [17]. They share with us these viewpoints: to efficiently support heterogeneous receivers, each receiver must be able to specify a stream filter for the subset of the data it is interested in receiving; and, furthermore, not to waste network resources, the filters from all the receivers should be propagated towards the sender, so the subset of the data in which no one is interested would be stopped at the earliest point along the source propagation tree. However, they only considered single source applications (such as cable TV), as opposed to RSVP's functionality of supporting multipoint-to-multipoint applications, and they have mainly focused on the programming interface to applications, as opposed to our interest in designing a protocol that reserves resources inside the network and adjusts the reservation to dynamic environmental changes.

Unresolved Issues

While RSVP has been simulated and tested to some extent, we fully expect that further incremental design changes will be made as we gain experience with RSVP, both on DARTnet and also through further simulation. Besides these incremental changes, however, several larger design issues remain unresolved as follows.

RSVP was designed with minimal expectations of routing. Path states are used to essentially invert the routing tables, a function that routing could easily provide if it were so designed. If we were to design new routing algorithms, what routing support would we include to support resource reservation algorithms?

In this design, we have associated filters with resource reservations. In fact, filters could be applied to flows even without reserved resources. Furthermore, there are filter styles besides the ones described here that might be useful. For remote lectures with several speakers at separate sites, one might want a dynamic filtered reservation where the filter is the same for each receiver, as proposed by Jacobson [18]. This feature would allow the audience to switch (in unison) to different speakers with only one set of resources reserved. Thus, one unresolved issue is defining the general service model and interfaces for such filters, where these definitions are not specifically tied to the presence of resource reservations.

Our current simulations and tests deal only with reasonably small networks and small multicast groups. We do not yet understand how RSVP performs when the size of the multicast groups gets very large. Can one use caching strategies to avoid the router state explosion when S (the number of senders) and/or R (the number of receivers) gets very large? This issue is particularly relevant to the case of cable TV, where every home would want a dynamic reservation but the switches obviously would not want to keep an individual reservation state for each home.

Summary

RSVP's architecture is unique in that: 1) it provides receiver-initiated reservations to accommodate heterogeneity among receivers as well as dynamic membership changes; 2) it separates the filter from the reservation, thus allowing channel changing behavior; 3) it supports a dynamic and robust multipoint-to-multipoint communication model by taking a soft-state approach in maintaining resource reservations; and 4) it decouples the reservation and routing functions and thus can run on top of, and take advantage of, any multicast routing protocols.

We have verified the first RSVP design by detailed simulation and a preliminary implementation. Much testing remains to be done in the context of larger scale simulations, as well as in real prototype networks such as DARTnet.

Acknowledgments

We would like to gratefully acknowledge useful conversations with Bob Braden, David Clark, Ron Frederick, Shai Herzog, Sugih Jamin, and Danny Mitzel.

References

[1] C. Partridge, "A Proposed Flow Specification," Internet RFC-1363, July, 1992.

[2] C. Topolcic, "Experimental Internet Stream Protocol: Version 2 (ST-II)," Internet RFC 1190, October, 1990.

[3] A. Ballardie, P. Tsuchiya, and J. Crowcroft, "Core Based Trees (CBT)," Internet Draft, November, 1992.

[4] S. Deering, "Multicast Routing in a Datagram Internetwork," Tech. Report No. STAN-CS-92-1415, Stanford University, December, 1991.

[5] J. Forgie, "ST — A Proposed Internet Stream Protocol," Internet Experimental Notes IEN-119, September 1979.

[6] S. Jamin, S. Shenker, L. Zhang, and D. Clark, "Admission Control Algorithm for Predictive Real-Time Service," Proc. 3rd International Workshop on Network and Operating System Support for Digital Audio and Video, November, 1992.

[7] J.M. Hyman, A.A. Lazar, and G. Pacifici, "Joint Scheduling and Admission Control for ATS-based Switching Nodes, Proc. ACM SIGCOMM '92, August, 1992.

[8] D.D. Clark, S. Shenker, and L. Zhang, "Supporting Real-Time Applications in an Integrated Services Packet Network: Architecture and Mechanism," Proc. ACM SIGCOMM '92, August, 1992.

[9] D. Ferrari, A. Banerjea, and H. Zhang, "Network Support for Multimedia: A Discussion of the Tenet Approach," Technical Report TR-92-072, Computer Science Division, University of California at Berkeley, November 1992.

[10] S.J. Golestani, "Duration-Limited Statistical Multiplexing of Delay Sensitive Traffic in Packet Networks," Proc. INFOCOM '91, 1991.

[11] C. Kalmanek, H. Kanakia, and S. Keshav, "Rate Controlled Servers for Very High-Speed Networks," Proc. GlobeCom '90, pp. 300.3.1-300.3.9, 1990.

[12] J. Hyman, A. Lazar, and G. Pacifici, "Real-Time Scheduling with Quality of Service Constraints," IEEE JSAC, vol. 9, no. 9, pp. 1052-63, September 1991.

■ ■ ■ ■ ■

We expect that further incremental design changes will be made as we gain experience with RSVP, both on DARTnet and also through further simulation.

■ ■ ■ ■ ■

Much
testing
remains to
be done in
the context
of larger
scale
simulations.

[13] D.D. Clark, "The Design Philosophy of the DARPA Internet Protocols," *Proc. ACM SIGCOMM '88*, August, 1988.

[14] L. Zhang, "A New Architecture for Packet Switching Network Protocols," Technical Report TR-455, Laboratory for Computer Science, Massachusetts Institute of Technology, 1989.

[15] I. Cidon, A. Segall, "Fast Connection Establishment in High Speed Networks," *Proc. ACM SIGCOMM '90*, September, 1990.

[16] C. Partridge and S. Pink, "An Implementation of the Revised Internet Stream Protocol (ST-2)," *Internetworking: Research and Experience*, vol. 3, no. 1, pp. 27-54, March 1992.

[17] J. Pasquale, G. Polyzos, E. Anderson, and V. Kompella, "The Multimedia Multicast Channel," *Proc. 3rd International Workshop on Network and Operating System Support for Digital Audio and Video*, November, 1992.

[18] V. Jacobson, private communication.

Biographies

LIXIA ZHANG received her B.S. degree in physics from Heilongjiang University, China, in 1976, M.S. degree in electrical engineering from California State University, Los Angeles, in 1981, and Ph.D. degree in computer science from Massachusetts Institute of Technology in 1989. Since 1989, she has been a member of the research staff at Xerox PARC. Her research interest includes network architecture and protocols, network performance analysis, and distributed systems.

STEPHEN E. DEERING received his B.Sc. in 1973 and M.Sc. in 1982, from the University of British Columbia, and his Ph.D. in 1991, from Stanford University. He has been studying, designing, and implementing computer communication protocols since 1978. He is currently a member of the research staff at Xerox PARC, where he is continuing his work on multicast routing and applications and investigating new communication architectures and services. He is an active member of the Internet End-to-End Research Group and the Internet Engineering Task Force (IETF).

DEBORAH ESTRIN [M] is an associate professor of computer science at the University of Southern California in Los Angeles, where she joined the faculty in 1986. She received her M.S. in technology policy and Ph.D. in computer science in 1982 and 1985, respectively, both from the Massachusetts Institute of Technology. She received her B.S. (1980) from U.C. Berkeley. She is currently involved in standardization efforts within the IETF in the areas of inter-domain and multicast routing and acts as a reviewer and program committee member for several IEEE and ACM journals and conferences. She is a member of IEEE, ACM, AAAS, and CPSR.

SCOTT SHENKER received his Sc.B. degree from Brown University in 1978, and his Ph.D. degree in theoretical physics from the University of Chicago in 1983. Since 1984, he has been a member of the research staff at Xerox PARC. In addition to network architecture and performance, his research interests include game theory, economics, dynamical systems, and performance analysis.

DANIEL ZAPPALA is currently a doctoral student in computer science at the University of Southern California. He received his B.S. in electrical engineering from Stanford University in 1990. At USC he has collaborated on several projects, including the design and implementation of the source demand routing protocol (SDRP) and simulation studies of adaptive routing. He spent the summer of 1992 as a summer intern at Xerox PARC working on RSVP.

Internet Telephony: architecture and protocols – an IETF perspective

Henning Schulzrinne [a,*], Jonathan Rosenberg [b,1]

[a] *Department of Computer Science, Columbia University, New York, NY 10027, USA*
[b] *Bell Laboratories, Lucent Technologies, Holmdel, NJ 07974-0616 USA*

Abstract

Internet telephony offers the opportunity to design a global multimedia communications system that may eventually replace the existing telephony infrastructure. We describe the upper-layer protocol components that are specific to Internet telephony services: the Real-Time Transport Protocol (RTP) to carry voice and video data, and the Session Initiation Protocol (SIP) for signaling. We also mention some complementary protocols, including the Real Time Streaming Protocol (RTSP) for control of streaming media, and the Wide Area Service Discovery Protocol (WASRV) for location of telephony gateways. © 1999 Published by Elsevier Science B.V. All rights reserved.

Keywords: Internet telephony; Internet multimedia; SIP; RTSP; RTP

1. Introduction

Internet telephony, also known as voice-over-IP or IP telephony (IPtel), is the real-time delivery of voice (and possibly other multimedia data types) between two or more parties, across networks using the Internet protocols, and the exchange of information required to control this delivery. Internet telephony offers the opportunity to design a global multimedia communications systems that may eventually replace the existing telephony infrastructure, without being encumbered by the legacy of a century-old technology.

While we will use the common term of "Internet telephony", it should be understood that the addition of other media, such as video or shared applications, does not fundamentally change the problem. Also, unlike in traditional telecommunications networks where distribution applications (radio, TV) and communications applications (telephone, fax) are quite distinct in terms of technology, user interface, communications devices and even regulatory environments, this is not the case for the Internet. The delivery of stored ("streaming") media and telephone-style applications can share almost all of the underlying protocol infrastructure. Indeed, in the model presented here, the same end user application may well serve both. This affords new opportunities to integrate these two modes. Consider, for example, the simple act of rolling a VCR into a conference room to either playback or record a session. The equivalent function requires specialized equipment in the phone system, but is easy to implement in the system to be described here. As another example, it may be desirable to jointly view stored or live

* Corresponding author. Tel.: +1-212-939-7042; fax: +1-212-666-0140; e-mail: hgs@cs.columbia.edu.
1 E-mail: jdrosen@bell-labs.com.

broadcast events, in a kind of "virtual couch", where friends, distributed across the Internet, could share the same movie, as well as side comments and conversations.

Internet telephony differs from Internet multimedia streaming primarily in the control and establishment of sessions, the "signaling". While we generally assume that a stored media resource is available at a given location, identified at different levels of abstraction by a URI (Uniform Resource Identifer) or URL (Uniform Resource Locator), participants in phone calls are not so easily located. Personal mobility, call delegation, availability, and desire to communicate make the process of signaling more complex. On the other hand, streaming media can make use of time-axis manipulations, such as fast-forward or absolute positioning. In the Internet, the Real Time Streaming Protocol (RTSP) [1] is the standard protocol for controlling multimedia streams. Section 5 describes the Session Initiation Protocol (SIP) [2] co-developed by the authors for signaling Internet telephony services.

Both RTSP and SIP are part of a protocol stack that has recently emerged from the Internet Engineering Task Force (IETF) – the *Internet Multimedia Conferencing Architecture* [3]. The protocols encompass both IPtel services and stored media services in an integrated fashion. Fig. 1 depicts the stack, along with other protocols likely to be used for both Internet streaming media and Internet telephony. Unlike circuit-switched telephony, Internet telephony services are built on a range of packet switched protocols. For example, the functionality of the SS7 ISUP and TCAP [4] telephony signaling protocols encompass routing, resource reservation, call admission, address translation, call establishment, call management and billing. In an Internet environment, routing is handled by protocols such as the Border Gateway Protocol (BGP) [5], resource reservation by the Resource Reservation Protocol (RSVP) [6] or other resource reservation protocols [7]. SIP, described here, translates application-layer addresses, establishes and manages calls. There is currently no Internet telephony billing protocol in the Internet, although RADIUS [8] or DIAMETER [9], in combination with SIP authentication, may initially serve that purpose for calls through Internet telephony gateways. Having a number of different protocols, each serving a particular function, allows for modularity, flexibility, simplicity, and extensibility. End systems or network servers that only provide a specific service need only implement that particular protocol, without interoperability problems. Furthermore, protocol components can be reused in other

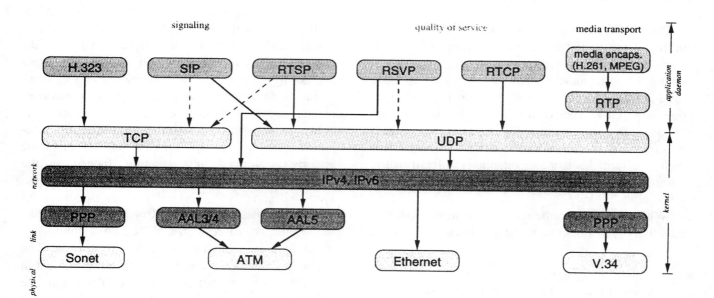

Fig. 1. Internet telephony protocol stack.

applications, avoiding re-invention of specific functions in each application.

Even though the term Internet telephony is often associated with point-to-point voice service [10], none of the protocols described here are restricted to a single media type or unicast delivery. Indeed, one of the largest advantages of Internet telephony compared to the Plain Old Telephone System (POTS) is the transparency of the network to the media carried, so that adding a new media type requires no changes to the network infrastructure. Also, at least for signaling, the support of multiparty calls differs only marginally from two-party calls.

The protocols mentioned, and the rich services they provide, are just one part of the picture for IPtel. As it was designed for data transport, the Internet currently offers only best effort service. The result is that voice packets suffer heavy losses and significant delays when there is network congestion, making the speech quality poor. A number of efforts in the area of Quality of Service (QoS) management are underway in order to address this issue.

The remainder of the paper is organized as follows. Section 2 discusses the differences between the general switched telephone network (GSTN, i.e., the current phone system) and the Internet telephony architecture. Section 3 then discusses how these differences translate into some of the advantages of Internet telephony. We then discuss the key protocol components of Internet telephony. Section 4 discusses the Real Time Transport Protocol (RTP), and addresses some of the efforts underway to resolve the QoS problems with voice transport. Section 5.1 discusses SIP and Section 6 discusses some additional protocols, including a call processing language and service location, which form pieces of the overall puzzle. We then put them all together in Section 7. We conclude in Section 8 and present ideas for future work.

2. Differences between Internet telephony and the GSTN

Internet telephony differs in a number of respects from the GSTN, both in terms of architecture and protocols. These differences affect the design of telephony services.

Fundamentally, IPtel relies on the "end-to-end" paradigm for delivery of services. Signaling protocols are between the end systems involved in the call; network routers treat these signaling packets like any other data, ignoring any semantics implied by them. Note, however, that IPtel can make use of "signaling routers" (which are effectively proxies) to assist in functions such as user location. In this case, these proxies can be used for routing only of initial signaling messages. Subsequent messages can be exchanged end-to-end. As a consequence of the end-to-end signaling paradigm, call state is as well end to end, as are instantiation of many telephony features.

The Internet itself is both multi-service and service-independent. It provides packet-level transport, end-to-end, for whatever services are deployed at the end systems through higher layer protocols and software. This leads to tremendous flexibility and extensibility. New application level services, such as the web, email, and now IPtel, can be created and deployed by anyone with access to the Internet.

IPtel separates call setup from reserving resources. In the Internet, protocols such as RSVP [6] are used to reserve resources. These protocols are application independent, and reservations may take place before or after actual flow of data begins. When used after the flow of data begins, the data will be treated as best effort. As a result, IPtel can be used without per-call resource reservation in networks with sufficient capacity. On the other hand, removing the "atomicity" of call setup found in the current telephone system also breaks the assumption of "all or nothing" call completion: since call setup and resource reservation are distinct, one may succeed, while the other may fail. If resources are reserved first, the caller may incur a cost for holding those resources while "the phone rings", even though the call is not answered. (If the network does not charge for reservations that are not actually used, the network becomes vulnerable to denial-of-service attacks, where the attacker can block others from making reservations.) Also, in the phone system, the resource needs for a single leg of a call are known ahead of time; this is clearly not the case for Internet telephony calls, where the callee may choose to communicate with only a subset of the media offered by the caller.

Due to the limited signaling abilities of GSTN end systems, GSTN addresses (phone numbers) are overloaded with at least four functions: end point identification, service indication, indication of who pays for the call and carrier selection. The GSTN also ties call origination with payment, except as modified by the address (800 numbers) or specific manual features (such as collect calls). IPtel addresses, which are formulated as URL's, are used solely for endpoint identification and basic service indication. The other functions, such as payment and carrier selection, are more readily handled by the protocols, such as RSVP and RTSP, which carry the addresses.

Internet telephony offers a larger degree of freedom to allocate functions between network servers and user-supplied and operated end systems. For example, because of the end-to-end signaling, phone services such as distinctive ringing based on call urgency, media-based endpoint selection, and cryptographically authenticated caller id (in addition to features available from POTS phones, such as speed dialing and caller ID) may be accomplished trivially by even standalone IP telephones, resulting in better scaling.

The phone system employs different signaling protocols between a user and the "network" (User–Network Interface – UNI) as compared to between (implicitly trusted) network elements (Network–Network Interface – NNI). This makes certain features (such as mumber translation) unavailable to end users, or leads to classifying end users as "networks", with the attendant security implications in the access to databases and network resources. The UNI/NNI distinction does not exist on the Internet, both at the level of data transport and signaling. SIP can set up calls between two end systems just as easily as creating a "channel" on an aggregated RTP session (see Section 4.3).

The open, multi-service, end-to-end nature of the Internet also means that various components of telephony services can be provided by completely different service vendors (of course, agreement on protocols is necessary for interoperability). For example, one vendor can provide a name to IP address mapping service, another can provide voice-mail, another can provide mobility services, while yet another can provide conferencing services. Furthermore, the end-

to-end nature of the Internet means that anyone with an Internet connection can run and operate such a service. This leads to an easy-entry, highly competitive marketplace for all Internet services, such as IPtel.

This separation of functionality also simplifies the number portability problem. As an organization may provide just a name mapping service, a user can change other service providers (such as their voice-mail provider or ISP) without a change in name [2]. Changing name mapping providers may require a change in name. However, automated white-pages services, such as those run by Four11, allow another layer of indirection which further alleviates the number portability problem.

3. Features of Internet telephony

The architectural differences described in the previous section lead to a number of advantages from both a user perspective and a carrier perspective [12], beyond just "cheaper phone calls":

Adjustable quality: While IPtel currently has the reputation for tin-can quality (due to low bitrate codecs, in part) there is no reason (except lack of bandwidth) why the same technology cannot supply audiophile-quality music. Because the Internet is not a service-specific network, the media exchanged is chosen entirely by end systems. As such, end systems can control the amount of compression based on network bandwidth [13] or the content to be transmitted. For example, music-on-hold (as it is not speech) is not suitable for very low bit-rate speech codecs.

Security: The Internet has the reputation as being insecure, even though it is probably easier to tap a telephone demarc box than a router. SIP can encrypt and authenticate signaling messages; RTP supports encryption of media. Together, these provide cryptographically secure communications.

User identification: Standard POTS and ISDN telephone service offers caller id indicating the number (or, occasionally, name) of the caller, but during

---

[2] There is a more difficult issue of maintaining the same IP network address when changing providers [11].

a bridged multi-party conference, there is no indication of who is talking. The real-time transport protocol (RTP) [14] used for Internet telephony easily supports talker indication in both multicast and bridged configurations and can convey more detailed information if the caller desires.

User interface: Most POTS and ISDN telephones have a rather limited user interface, with at best a two-line liquid crystal display or, in the public network, cryptic commands like "*69" for call-back. Advanced GSTN features such as call-forwarding are rarely used or customized, since the sequence of steps is typically not intuitive. This is due in part to the limited signaling capabilities of end systems, and the general notion of "network intelligence" as compared to "end system intelligence". As IPtel end systems have much richer signaling capabilities, the graphical user interface offered by Internet telephony can be more readily customized and offer richer indications of features, process and progress.

Computer-telephony integration: Because of the complete separation of data and control paths and the separation of phone equipment from the PC's controlling them, computer-telephony integration (CTI) [15] is very complex, with specs [16] running to 3300 pages. Much of the call handling functionality can be easily accomplished once the data and control path pass through intelligent, network-connected end systems.

Feature ubiquity: The current phone system offers very different features depending on whether the parties are connected by the same Private Branch Exchange (PBX), reside within the same local calling area or are connected by a long-distance carrier. Even trivial features such as caller ID only work for a small fraction of international calls, for example. A PBX may not allow a call to be forwarded outside that PBX, or cause the forwarded call to still go through the PBX. Internet telephony does not suffer from this problem. This is because the Internet protocols are internationally used, and because services are defined largely by the end systems.

Multimedia: As pointed out, adding additional media such as video, shared whiteboards or shared applications is much easier in the Internet environment compared to the POTS and ISDN, as multiplexing is natural for packet networks. This makes signaling protocols simpler as well, as issues such as B-channel allocation and synchronization are non-existent in the Internet.

Carriers benefit as well:

Silence suppression and compression: Sending audio as packets makes it easy to suppress silence periods, further reducing bandwidth consumption, particularly in a multi-party conference or for voice announcement systems. Unlike the GSTN, which generally does such silence suppression across trans-continental links, IPtel performs silence suppression at the endpoints. Furthermore, as packet networks are much more suitable to multiplexing, no network support is required to take advantage of end system silence suppression. This leads to a reduction in cost to perform the silence suppression (as it's distributed to end systems where it can be done cheaply), and an improvement in the scope of its benefits. Furthermore, compression can be used at end systems to reduce bandwidth consumption across the entire network. Unfortunately, compression is at odds with enhanced voice quality services described above. However, there exist codecs which can compress wideband speech to 16 kb/s, which can give both excellent voice quality and reduced bandwidth compared to the GSTN. Note that silence suppression and compression compensate for the decreased efficiency of packet switching.

Shared facilities: The largest operational savings can probably come from provisioning and managing a single, integrated network, rather than separate voice, data and signaling networks.

Advanced services: From first experiences and protocols, it appears to be far simpler to develop and deploy advanced telephony services in a packet-switched environment than in the GSTN [17,18]. Internet protocols, such as SIP [2] that support standard CLASS (Custom Local Area Signaling Services) [19] features (such as Call Forward No Answer) take only a few tens of pages to specify. They can perform the functions of both the user-to-network signaling protocols such as Q.931 as well as the network signaling (ISUP, Signaling System 7).

Separation of voice and control flow: In telephony, the signaling flow, even though carried on a separate network, has to "touch" all the intermediate switches to set up the circuit. Since packet forwarding in the Internet requires no setup, Internet call control can concentrate on the call (rather than connection) functionality. For example, it is easy to avoid triangle-routing when forwarding or transferring calls; the transferring party can simply inform the transferred party of the address of the transferred-to party, and the two can contact each other directly. As there is no network connection state, none needs to be torn down.

4. RTP for data transport

Real-time flows such as IPtel voice and video streams have a number of common requirements that distinguish them from "traditional" Internet data services:

Sequencing: The packets must be re-ordered in real time at the receiver, should they arrive out of order. If a packet is lost, it must be detected and compensated for without retransmissions.

Intra-media synchronization: The amount of time between when successive packets are to be "played-out" must be conveyed. For example, no data is usually sent during silence periods in speech. The duration of this silence must be reconstructed properly.

Inter-media synchronization: If a number of different media are being used in a session, there must be a means to synchronize them, so that the audio that is played out matches the video. This is also known as lip-sync.

Payload identification: In the Internet, it is often necessary to change the encoding for the media ("pay-load") on the fly to adjust to changing bandwidth availability or the capabilities of new users joining a group. Some kind of mechanism is therefore needed to identify the encoding for each packet.

Frame indication: Video and audio are sent in logical units called frames. It is necessary to indicate to a receiver where the beginning or end of a frame is, in order to aid in synchronized delivery to higher layers.

These services are provided by a *transport protocol*. In the Internet, the RTP [14] is used for this purpose. RTP has two components. The first is RTP itself, and the second is RTCP, the Real Time Control Protocol. Transport protocols for real time media are not new, dating back to the 1970's [20]. How-

ever, RTP provides some functionality beyond resequencing and loss detection:

Multicast-friendly: RTP and RTCP have been engineered for multicast. In fact, they are designed to operate in both small multicast groups, like those used in a three-person phone call, to huge ones, like those used for broadcast events.

Media independent: RTP provides services needed for generic real time media, such as voice and video. Any codec-specific additional header fields and semantics are defined for each media codec in separate specifications.

Mixers and translators: Mixers are devices which take media from several users, mix or "bridge" them into one media stream, and send the resulting stream out. Translators take a single media stream, convert it to another format, and send it out. Translators are useful for reducing the bandwidth requirements of a stream before sending it over a low-bandwidth link, without requiring the RTP source to reduce its bitrate. This allows receivers that are connected via fast links to still receive high quality media. Mixers limit the bandwidth if several sources send data simultaneously, fulfilling the function of conference bridge. RTP includes explicit support for mixers and translators.

QoS feedback: RTCP allows receivers to provide feedback to all members of a group on the quality of the reception. RTP sources may use this information to adjust their data rate, while other receivers can determine whether QoS problems are local or network-wide. External observers can use it for scalable quality-of-service management.

Loose session control: With RTCP, participants can exchange identification information such as name, email, phone number, and brief messages.

Encryption: RTP media streams can be encrypted using keys that are exchanged by some non-RTP method, e.g., SIP or the Session Description Protocol (SDP) [21].

4.1. RTP

RTP is generally used in conjunction with the User Datagram Protocol (UDP), but can make use of any packet-based lower-layer protocol. When a host wishes to send a media packet, it takes the media, formats it for packetization, adds any media-specific packet headers, prepends the RTP header, and places it in a lower-layer payload. It is then sent into the network, either to a multicast group or unicast to another participant.

The RTP header (Fig. 2) is 12 bytes long. The **V** field indicates the protocol version. The **X** flag signals the presence of a header extension between the fixed header and the payload. If the **P** bit is set, the payload is padded to ensure proper alignment for encryption.

Users within a multicast group are distinguished by a random 32-bit synchronization source **SSRC** identifier. Having an application-layer identifier allows to easily distinguish streams coming from the same translator or mixer and associate receiver reports with sources. In the rare event that two users happen to choose the same identifier, they redraw their SSRCs.

As described above, a mixer combines media streams from several sources, e.g., a conference bridge might mix the audio of all active participants. In current telephony, the participants may have a hard time distinguishing who happens to be speaking at any given time. The Contributing SSRC (CSRC) list, whose length is indicated by the CSRC length field, lists all the SSRC that ''contributed'' content to the packet. For the audio conference, it would list all active speakers.

RTP supports the notion of media-dependent framing to assist in the reconstruction and playout process. The marker (**M**) bit provides information for this purpose. For audio, the first packet in a voice talkspurt can be scheduled for playout independently of those in the previous talkspurt. The bit is used in this case to indicate the first packet in a talkspurt. For video, a video frame can only be rendered when its last packet has arrived. Here, the marker bit is used to indicate the last packet in a video frame.

The **payload type** identifies the media encoding used in the packet. The **sequence number** increments sequentially from one packet to the next, and is used to detect losses and restore packet order. The **timestamp**, incremented with the media sampling frequency, indicates when the media frame was generated.

The payload itself may contain headers specific for the media; this is described in more detail below.

4.2. RTCP: control and management

The Real Time Control Protocol, RTCP is the companion control protocol for RTP. Media senders (sources) and receivers (sinks) periodically send RTCP packets to the same multicast group (but different ports) as is used to distribute RTP packets. Each RTCP packet contains a number of elements, usually a sender report (SR) or receiver report followed by source descriptions (SDES). Each serves a different function:

Sender Reports (SR) are generated by users who are also sending media (RTP sources). They describe the amount of data sent so far, as well as correlating the RTP sampling timestamp and absolute (''wall clock'') time to allow synchronization between different media.

Receiver Reports (IR) are sent by RTP session participants which are receiving media (RTP sinks). Each such report contains one block for each RTP source in the group. Each block describes the instantaneous and cumulative loss rate and jitter from that source. The block also indicates the last timestamp and delay since receiving a sender report, allowing sources to estimate their distance to sinks.

Source Descriptor (SDES) packets are used for session control. They contain the CNAME (Canonical Name), a globally unique identifier similar in format to an email address. The CNAME is used for resolving conflicts in the SSRC value and associate different media streams generated by the same user. SDES packets also identify the participant through its name, email, and phone number. This provides a

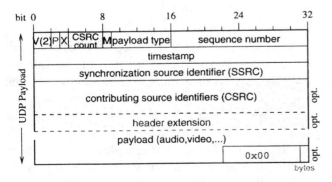

Fig. 2. RTP fixed header format.

simple form of session control. Client applications can display the name and email information in the user interface. This allows session participants to learn about the other participants in the session. It also allows them to obtain contact information (such as email and phone) to allow for other forms of communication (such as initiation of a separate conference using SIP). This also makes it easier to contact a user should he, for example, have left his camera running.

If a user is leaving, he includes a *BYE* message. Finally, *Application (APP)* elements can be used to add application-specific information to RTCP packets.

Since the sender reports, receiver reports, and SDES packets contain information which can continually change, it is necessary to send these packets periodically. If the RTP session participants simply sent RTCP packets with a fixed period, the resulting bandwidth used in the multicast group would grow linearly with the group size. This is clearly undesirable. Instead, each session member counts the number of other session members it hears from (via RTCP packets). The period between RTCP packets from each user is then set to scale linearly with the number of group members. This ensures that the bandwidth used for RTCP reports remains fixed, independent of the group size. Since the group size estimate is obtained by counting the number of other participants, it takes time for each new participant to converge to the correct group size count. If many users simultaneously join a group, as is common in broadcast applications, each user will have an incorrect, and very low estimate of the group size. The result is a flood of RTCP reports. A back-off algorithm called reconsideration [22] is used to prevent such floods.

4.3. Payload formats

The above mechanisms in RTP provide for services needed for the generic transport of audio and video. However, particular codecs will have additional requirements for information that needs to be conveyed. To support this, RTP allows for payload formats to be defined for each particular codec. These payload formats describe the syntax and se-

mantics of the RTP payload. The particular semantic of the payload is communicated in the RTP payload type indicator bits. These bits are mapped to actual codecs and formats via a binding to names, registered with the Internet Assigned Numbers Authority (IANA), and conveyed out of band (through SDP, for example). Any number of bindings can be conveyed out of band; this allows an RTP source to change encoding formats mid-stream without explicit signaling. Furthermore, anyone can register a name (so long as it has not been used), and procedures are defined for doing so. This allows for RTP to be used with any kind of codec developed by anyone.

RTP media payload formats have been defined for the H.263 [23], H.261 [24], JPEG [25] and MPEG [26] video codecs, and a host of other audio and video encoders are supported with simpler payload formats [27].

Furthermore, RTP payload formats are being defined to provide some generic services. One format, for redundant audio codings [28], allows a user to transmit audio content using multiple audio codecs, each delayed from the previous, and of a lower bitrate. This allows for lost packets to be recovered from subsequent packets, albeit with a lower quality codec. Another payload format is being defined for parity and Reed Solomon like forward error correction (FEC) mechanisms, to allow for recovery of lost packets in a codec-independent manner [29]. Yet another format is being introduced to multiplex media from multiple users into a single packet [30]. This is particularly useful for trunk replacement between Internet telephony gateways, where it can provide a significant reduction in packet header overheads.

4.4. Resource reservation

Given the importance of telephony services, we anticipate that a significant fraction of the Internet bandwidth will be consumed by voice and video, that is, RTP-based protocols. Due to its tight delay constraints, IPtel streams are also likely candidates for guaranteed QOS. Unfortunately, existing proposals such as RSVP [6] are rather complex, largely due to features such as receiver orientation and support for receiver diversity that is likely to be of limited use for Internet telephony. We have proposed [7] to dispense with a separate resource reservation protocol altogether and simply use RTCP messages to tell routers along the path to reserve sufficient resources. To determine the amount of bandwidth for the reservation, RTCP sender reports (SR) can be used as is (by observing the difference between two subsequent SR byte counts), or an additional field can be inserted that specifies the desired grade of service in more detail. RTCP messages carrying reservation requests are marked for special handling by a router alert option [31]. The receiver reports back whether the reservation was completely or only partially successful.

Similar proposals of simplified, sender-based resource reservation protocols can be found (albeit not using RTCP) in the Scalable Reservation Protocol (SRP) [32].

The issue of reservations for IPtel services has another facet: if a reservation fails, the call can still take place, but using best effort transport of the audio. This is certainly preferable to a fast-busy signal, where no communications at all are established. This introduces the possibility of completely removing the admission decision all together. On each link in the network, sufficient bandwidth for voice traffic can be allocated. Time-honored approaches to telephone network engineering can be used to determine the amount of allocation needed. The remaining bandwidth on links will be used for other services, and for best effort. Incoming packets can be classified as voice or non-voice. Should there be too many voice connections active at any point in time (possible since there is no admission control), the extra calls can simply become best effort. Good network engineering can place reasonably low probabilities on such an event, and the use of "spillover" best effort bandwidth can eliminate admission control to handle these unlikely occurrences.

The above mechanism is generally referred to as part of the class of IP service referred to as *differentiated services*. These rely on user subscription (to facilitate network engineering) and packet classification and marking at network peripheries. From the above discussion, IPtel is a prime candidate for such a service. In fact, the *premium service* [33] provides almost no delay and jitter for its packets, making it ideal for real-time voice and video.

5. Signaling: Session Initiation Protocol

A defining property of IPtel is the ability of one party to signal to one or more other parties to initiate a new call. For purposes of discussing the SIP, we define a call is an association between a number of participants. The signaling association between a pair of participants in a call is referred to as a connection. Note that there is no physical channel or network resources associated with a connection; the connection exists only as signaling state at the two endpoints. A session refers to a single RTP session carrying a single media type. The relationship between the signaling connections and media sessions can be varied. In a multiparty call, for example, each participant may have a connection to every other participant, while the media is being distributed via multicast, in which case there is a single media session. In other cases, there may be a single unicast media session associated with each connection. Other, more complex, scenarios are possible as well.

An IPtel signaling protocol must accomplish a number of functions:

Name translation and user location involve the mapping between names of different levels of abstraction, e.g., a common name at a domain and a user name at a particular Internet host. This translation is necessary in order to determine the IP address of the host to exchange media with. Usually, a user has only the name or email address of the person they would like to communicate with (j.doe@company.com, for example). This must be translated into an IP address. This translation is more than just a simple table lookup. The translation can vary based on time of day (so that a caller reaches you at work during the day, and at home in the evening), caller (so that your boss always gets your work number), or the status of the callee (so that calls to you are sent to your voice mail when you are already talking to someone), among other criteria.

Feature negotiation allows a group of end systems to agree on what media to exchange and their respective parameters, such as encodings. The set and type of media need not be uniform within a call, as different point-to-point connections may involve different media and media parameters. Many software codecs are able to receive different encodings within a single call and in parallel, for example, while being restricted to sending one type of media for each stream.

Any call participant can invite others into an existing call and terminate connections with some (*call participant management*). During the call, participants should be able to transfer and hold other users. The most general model of a multi-party association is that of a full or partial mesh of connections among participants (where one of the participants may be a media bridge), with the possible addition of multicast media distribution.

Feature changes make it possible to adjust the composition of media sessions during the course of a call, either because the participants require additional or reduced functionality or because of constraints imposed or removed by the addition or removal of call participants.

There are two protocols that have been developed for such signaling operations, SIP [2], developed in the IETF, and H.323 [34], developed by the ITU. In the next section, we will discuss SIP, while H.323 is covered by Toga et al. within this issue.

5.1. SIP overview

SIP is a client-server protocol. This means that requests are generated by one entity (the client), and sent to a receiving entity (the server) which processes them. As a call participant may either generate or receive requests, SIP-enabled end systems include a protocol client and server (generally called a user agent server). The user agent server generally responds to the requests based on human interaction or some other kind of input. Furthermore, SIP requests can traverse many *proxy servers*, each of which receives a request and forwards it towards a next hop server, which may be another proxy server or the final user agent server. A server may also act as a *redirect server*, informing the client of the address of the next hop server, so that the client can contact it directly. There is no protocol distinction between a proxy server, redirect server, and user agent server; a client or proxy server has no way of knowing which it is communicating with. The distinction lies only in function: a proxy or redirect server cannot accept or reject a request, whereas a user agent server can. This is similar to the Hypertext Transfer Protocol (HTTP) model of clients, ori-

gin and proxy servers. A single host may well act as client and server for the same request. A connection is constructed by issuing an INVITE request, and destroyed by issuing a BYE request.

As in HTTP, the client requests invoke *methods* on the server. Requests and responses are textual, and contain header fields which convey call properties and service information. SIP reuses many of the header fields used in HTTP, such as the entity headers (e.g., Content-type) and authentication headers. This allows for code reuse, and simplifies integration of SIP servers with web servers.

Calls in SIP are uniquely identified by a call identifier, carried in the Call-ID header field in SIP messages. The call identifier is created by the creator of the call and used by all call participants. Connections have the following properties: The *logical connection source* indicates the entity that is requesting the connection (the originator). This may not be the entity that is actually sending the request, as proxies may send requests on behalf of other users. In SIP messages, this property is conveyed in the From header field. The *logical connection destination* contained in the To field names the party who the originator wishes to contact (the recipient). The *media destination* conveys the location (IP address and port) where the media (audio, video, data) are to be sent for a particular recipient. This address may not be the same address as the logical connection destination. *Media capabilities* convey the media that a participant is capable of receiving and their attributes. Media capabilities and media destinations are conveyed jointly as part of the payload of a SIP message. Currently, the Session Description Protocol (SDP) [21] serves this purpose, although others are likely to find use in the future [3]. SDP expresses lists of capabilities for audio and video and indicates where the media is to be sent to. It also allows to schedule media sessions into the future and schedule repeated sessions.

SIP defines several methods, where the first three manage or prepare calls and connections: INVITE invites a user to a call and establishes a new connection, BYE terminates a connection between two users

---

[3] In fact, H.245 capability sets can be carried in SDP for this purpose.

in a call (note that a call, as a logical entity, is created when the first connection in the call is created, and destroyed when the last connection in the call is destroyed), and OPTIONS solicits information about capabilities, but does not set up a connection. STATUS informs another server about the progress of signaling actions that it has requested via the Also header [4] (see below). ACK is used for reliable message exchanges for invitations. CANCEL terminates a search for a user. Finally, REGISTER conveys information about a user's location to a SIP server.

SIP makes minimal assumptions about the underlying transport protocol. It can directly use any datagram or stream protocol, with the only restriction that a whole SIP request or response has to be either delivered in full or not at all. SIP can thus be used with UDP or TCP in the Internet, and with X.25, AAL5/ATM, CLNP, TP4, IPX or PPP elsewhere. Network addresses within SIP are also not restricted to being Internet addresses, but could be E.164 (GSTN) addresses, OSI addresses or private numbering plans. In many cases, addresses can be any URL; for example, a call can be "forwarded" to a mailto URL for email delivery.

5.2. Message encoding

Unlike other signaling protocols such as Q.931 and H.323, SIP is a text-based protocol. This design was chosen to minimize the cost of entry. The data structures needed in SIP headers all fall into the parameter-value category, possible with a single level of subparameters, so that generic data coding mechanisms like Abstract Syntax Notation 1 (ASN.1) offer no functional advantage.

Unlike the ASN.1 Packed Encoding Rules (PER) and Basic Encoding Rules (BER), a SIP header is largely self-describing. Even if an extension has not been formally documented, as was the case for many common email headers, it is usually easy to reverse-engineer them. Since most values are textual, the space penalty is limited to the parameter names, usually at most a few tens of bytes per request.

(Indeed, the ASN.1 PER-encoded H.323 signaling messages are larger than equivalent SIP messages.) Besides, extreme space efficiency is not a concern for signaling protocols.

If not designed carefully, text-based protocols can be difficult to parse due to their irregular structure. SIP tries to avoid this by maintaining a common structure of all header fields, allowing a generic parser to be written.

Unlike, say, HTTP and Internet email, SIP was designed for character-set independence, so that any field can contain any ISO 10646 character. Since SIP operates on an 8-bit clean channel, binary data such as certificates does not have to be encoded. Together with the ability to indicate languages of enclosed content and language preferences of the requestor, SIP is well suited for cross-national use.

5.3. Addressing and naming

To be invited and identified, the called party has to be named. Since it is the most common form of user addressing in the Internet, SIP chose an email-like identifier of the form "*user@domain*", "*user@host*", "*user@IP_address*" or "*phone-number@gateway*". The identifier can refer to the name of the host that a user is logged in at the time, an email address or the name of a domain-specific name translation service. Addresses of the form "*phone-number@gateway*" designate GSTN phone numbers reachable via the named gateway.

SIP uses these addresses as part of SIP URLs, such as sip:j.doe@example.com. This URL may well be placed in a web page, so that clicking on the link initiates a call to that address, similar to a mailto [35] URL today.

We anticipate that most users will be able to use their email address as their published SIP address. Email addresses already offer a basic location-independent form of addressing, in that the host part does not have to designate a particular Internet host, but can be a domain, which is then resolved into one or more possible domain mail server hosts via Domain Name System (DNS) MX (mail exchange) records. This not only saves space on business cards, but also allows re-use of existing directory services such as the Lightweight Directory Access Protocol (LDAP) [36], DNS MX records (as explained below) and

---

[4] The Also and Replaces headers and the STATUS method are part of the SIP call control extensions.

email as a last-ditch means of delivering SIP invitations.

For email, finding the mail exchange host is often sufficient to deliver mail, as the user either logs in to the mail exchange host or uses protocols such as the Internet Mail Access Protocol (IMAP) or the Post Office Protocol (POP) to retrieve their mail. For interactive audio and video communications, however, participants are typically sending and receiving data on the workstation, PC or Internet appliance in their immediate physical proximity. Thus, SIP has to be able to resolve "*name@domain*" to "*user@host*". A user at a specific host will be derived through zero or more translations. A single externally visible address may well lead to a different host depending on time of day, media to be used, and any number of other factors. Also, hosts that connect via dial-up modems may acquire a different IP address each time.

5.4. Basic operation

The most important SIP operation is that of inviting new participants to a call. A SIP client first obtains an address where the new participant is to be contacted, of the form *name@domain*. The client then tries to translate this domain to an IP address where a server may be found. This translation is done by trying, in sequence, DNS Service (SRV) records, Canonical Name (CNAME) and finally Address (A) records. Once the server's IP address has been found, the client sends it an INVITE message using either UDP or TCP.

The server which receives the message is not likely to be the user agent server where the user is actually located; it may be a proxy or redirect server. For example, a server at example.com contacted when trying to call joe@example.com may forward the INVITE request to doe@sales.example.com. A Via header traces the progress of the invitation from server to server, allows responses to find their way back and helps servers to detect loops. A redirect server, on the other hand, would respond to the INVITE request, telling the caller to contact doe@sales.example.com directly. In either case, the proxy or redirect server must somehow determine the next hop server. This is the function of a *location server*. A location server is a non-SIP entity which has information about next hop servers for various users. The location server can be anything – an LDAP server, a proprietary corporate database, a local file, the result of a finger command, etc. The choice is a matter of local configuration. Figs. 3 and 4 show the behavior of SIP proxy and redirect servers, respectively.

Proxy servers can forward the invitation to multiple servers at once, in the hopes of contacting the user at one of the locations. They can also forward the invitation to multicast groups, effectively contacting multiple next hops in the most efficient manner.

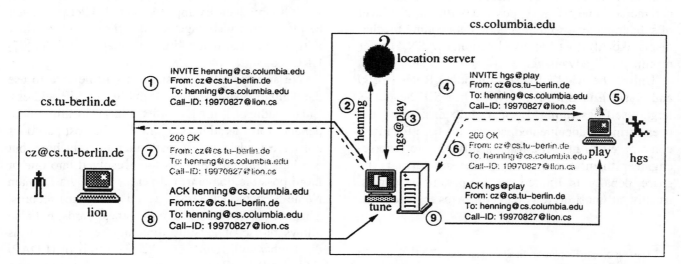

Fig. 3. SIP proxy server operation.

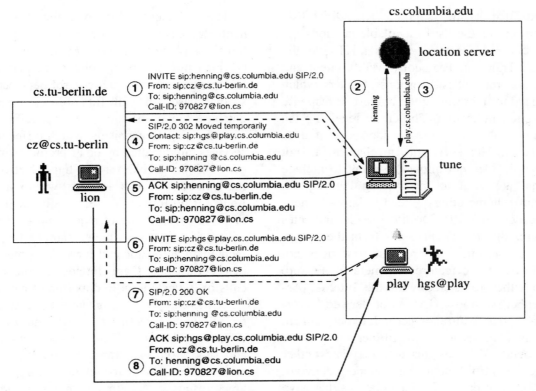

Fig. 4. SIP redirect server operation.

Once the user agent server has been contacted, it sends a response back to the client. The response has a response code and response message. The codes fall into classes 100 through 600, similar to HTTP.

Unlike other requests, invitations cannot be answered immediately, as locating the callee and waiting for a human to answer may take several seconds. Call requests may also be queued, e.g., if the callee is busy. Responses of the 100 class (denoted as 1xx) indicate call progress; they are always followed by other responses indicating the final outcome of the request.

While the 1xx responses are provisional, the other classes indicate the final status of the request: 2xx for success, 3xx for redirection, 4xx, 5xx and 6xx for client, server and global failures, respectively. 3xx responses list, in a Contact header, alternate places where the user might be contacted. To ensure reliability even with unreliable transport protocols, the server retransmits final responses until the client confirms receipt by sending an ACK request to the server.

All responses can include more detailed information. For example, a call to the central "switchboard" address may return a web page that includes links to the various departments in the company, providing navigation more appropriate to the Internet than an interactive voice response system (IVR).

5.5. Protocol extensions

Since IPtel is still immature, it is likely that additional signaling capabilities will be needed in the future. Also, individual implementations and vendors may want to add additional features. SIP is designed so that the client can either inquire about server abilities first or proceed under the assumption that the server supports the extension and then "back off" if the assumption was wrong.

Methods: As in HTTP, additional methods can be introduced. The server signals an error if a method requested by a client is not supported and informs it with the Public and Allow response headers about the methods that it does support. The OPTIONS request also returns the list of available methods.

Request and response headers: As in HTTP or the Simple Mail Transport Protocol (SMTP), client and server can add request and response headers which are not crucial to interpreting the request or response without explicit indication. The entity receiving the header simply silently ignores headers that it does not understand. However, this mechanism is not sufficient, as it does not allow the client to include headers that are vital to interpreting the request. Rather than enumerating "need-to-know" nonstandard headers, the SIP Required header indicates those features that the client needs from the server. The server must refuse the request if it does not understand one of the features enumerated. Feature names are either registered with the Internet Assigned Number Authority (IANA) or derived hierarchically from the feature owner's Internet domain name, giving hints as to where further information might be found. SIP uses this to ascertain whether telephony call-control functions are supported, avoiding the problem of partial implementations that have unpredictable sets of optional features.

Status codes: Status codes returned in responses are classified by their most-significant digit, so that the client knows whether the request was successful, failed temporarily or permanently. A textual status message offers a fall-back mechanism that allows the server to provide further human-readable information.

5.6. Telephony services

SIP takes a different approach than standard telephony in defining services. Rather than explicitly describing the implementation of a particular service, it provides a number of elements, namely headers and methods, to construct services. The two principle headers used are Also and Replaces. When present in a request or response, the Also header instructs the recipient to place a call to the parties listed. Similarly, Replaces instructs the recipient to terminate any connections with the parties listed. An additional method, called STATUS, is provided to allow a client to obtain results about progress of calls requested via the Also header.

These elements, along with the basic SIP components, are easily used to construct a variety of traditional telephony services. *700, 800 and 900* services (permanent numbers, freephone and paid information services) are, from a call control perspective, simply special cases of call forwarding, governed by a database lookup or some server-specified algorithm. The charging mechanisms, which differ for the three services, are handled by other protocols in an orthogonal fashion. Unlike for Intelligent Networking (IN), the number of such lookups within a call is not limited. Call forwarding services based on user status or preferences similarly require no additional protocol machinery. As a simple example, we have implemented an automatic call forwarding mechanism that inspects a callee's appointment calendar to forward calls or indicate a more opportune time to call back.

While *call forwarding* precedes a call, *call transfer* allows to direct a call participant to connect to a different subscriber. Transfer services include blind and supervised call transfer, attendant and operator services, auto-dialer for telemarketing, or interactive voice response. All are supported through use of the Also header combined with programmed behavior specific to the particular service. For example, blind transfer is implemented by having the transferring party send a BYE to the transferred party containing an Also header listing the transferred-to party.

In SIP, call setup and session parameter modification are accomplished by the same (INVITE) request, as all SIP requests are idempotent.

In an Internet environment, no "lines" are tied up by active calls when media is not being sent. This means an IP telephone can support an unlimited number of active calls at one time. This makes it easy, for example, to implement call waiting and camp-on.

5.7. Multi-party calls

SIP supports the three basic modes of creating multiparty conferences (and their combinations): via network-level multicast, via one or more bridges (also known as multipoint control units) or as a mesh of unicast connections. Multicast conferences require no further protocol support beyond listing a group address in the session description; indeed, the caller does not even have to be a member of the multicast group to issue an invitation. Bridges are introduced like regular session members; they may take over branches of a mesh through the **Replaces** header, without the participants needing to be aware that there is a bridge serving the conference. SIP also supports conferences through full-mesh, also known as *multi-unicast*. In this case, the client maintains a point to point connection with each participant. While this mode is very inefficient, it is very useful for small conferences where bridges or multicast service are not available. Full meshes are built up easily using the **Also** header. For example, to add a participant C to a call between users A and B, user A would send an **INVITE** to C with an **Also** header containing the address of B. Mixes of multi-unicast, multicast, and bridges are also possible.

SIP can also be used to set up calls to several callees. For example, if the callee's address is a mailing list, the SIP server can return a list of individuals to be called in an **Also** header. Alternatively, a single address, e.g., sysadmin@acme.com, may reach the first available administrator. Servers can fan-out invitation requests, including sending them out via multicast. Multicast invitations are particularly useful for inviting members of a department (product_team@example.com) to a conference in an extremely efficient manner without requiring centralized list administration.

Multicast invitations also allow a small conference to gradually and smoothly migrate to a large-scale Mbone-type conference (such as the ones described by Handley in this issue) without requiring separate protocols and architectures.

6. Additional protocols

We have so far touched on the two major protocol components required for Internet telephony, namely RTP and SIP. However, a number of other protocol components are very useful for more rich services; we briefly mention them here.

When an IP host wishes to communicate with a GSTN endpoint, it must do so by means of an Internet Telephony Gateway (ITG). This will generally require the host, or a proxy for the host, to eventually find the IP address of a telephony gate-

way appropriate for terminating the call. The selection of such a gateway is not an easy problem. There are many factors which contribute to the process: cost of completing the call, billing methods supported (credit card, debit card, e-cash), signaling protocols supported (SIP, H.323), media codecs supported, service provider, etc. Generally, the client will need to provide input, indicating many of these preferences, for the selection to take place. In essence, a telephony gateway is a service, and the client desires to select a server for this service based on some criteria. Extensions to the Service Location Protocol [37] for discovery of wide area services [38] have been proposed which seem applicable to telephony gateways [39].

As discussed in Section 5.1, SIP can be used to translate addresses as the request moves from SIP server to SIP server. This translation can be based on any criteria, such as caller and time of day. However, there is no currently defined mechanism for allowing a user to express its preference for how an address is to be translated. For example, if alice@acme.com calls bob@widgets.com, Alice will send a SIP request to the SIP server at widgets.com. Bob would like the calls forwarded to his PC if he is connected and if Carol calls, but the calls should be forwarded to his voice mail (through an ITG) otherwise. This requires Bob to express preferences for such translations to the server. We are currently developing a call processing syntax which can be uploaded to a server in a SIP **REGISTER** message. Such a language is to be standardized in the IETF iptel (IP Telephony) working group.

With widespread use of IP telephony, IP telephony voicemail is likely to follow. In order to support retrieval and recording of voicemail (which could easily include video), a protocol is necessary to give a user VCR-like controls over the voicemail server. The RTSP [40] is used for this purpose. RTSP allows a client to instruct a media server to record and playback multimedia sessions, including functions such as seek, fast forward, rewind, and pause. RTSP, like SIP, is a textual protocol similar in format to HTTP. RTSP integrates easily with SIP, in fact. A user can use SIP to invite a media server or voicemail server to a multimedia session, and then use RTSP to control operation of the during the session.

7. Protocol integration

The previous sections have described the basics of the protocol mechanisms for Internet telephony: SIP, RTP, wide area service location, and RTSP. In this section, we put the elements together and show how they can be used for a complex service.

Fig. 5 shows an IP network consisting of three Internet Service Providers (ISP's), A, B, and transit ISP C. ISP A provides a SIP proxy server A, and a wide area service location (WASRV) server. ISP B provides a SIP proxy server as well, in addition to an RTSP server for voicemail. ISP C provides a telephony gateway (ITG). User A in ISP A wishes to call user B in ISP B. User A's SIP user agent client is configured to use SIP server A as a proxy for all call requests. To call B, A sends a SIP INVITE message to the SIP Server A (1), indicating the name of user B in the To field (john_b@ispb.com). SIP server A looks up the domain ispb.com in DNS, and obtains the IP address of server B. Acting as a proxy, it forwards the SIP INVITE to SIP server B (2). Server B checks its records, and finds a set of call processing instructions for the user. The instructions indicate that the user is first to be contacted, via proxy, at their PC. If no one answers, the server should return two alternate locations for user B to

the requester: a telephone number and a voicemail server. The SIP server then follows these instructions, and forwards the INVITE message to user B's PC (3).

User B has instructed his SIP user agent server software not to accept any calls. User B's SIP user server thus responds with an error message to SIP server B (4). The SIP server then sends a redirect response to SIP server A (5). The response is in the 300 class set, and includes in the Contact fields two alternate addresses. The first is a telephone URL (tel: // + 1-732-555-1212), and the second an RTSP URL for a media server. The location headers can indicate preferences, and the response indicates that the caller should try the phone URL first.

The SIP server A then tries to call the user at the GSTN number. To do this, it first queries a WASRV server (6). It provides the server with the telephone number to contact, and user preferences about billing methods (such as credit card payment). These preferences can be supplied to the SIP server by the user in any number of ways, including manual entry by a administrator. The WASRV server queries its database, and returns the address of an appropriate gateway (7).

The SIP server then sends the original SIP INVITE to the gateway (8). The gateway makes a call

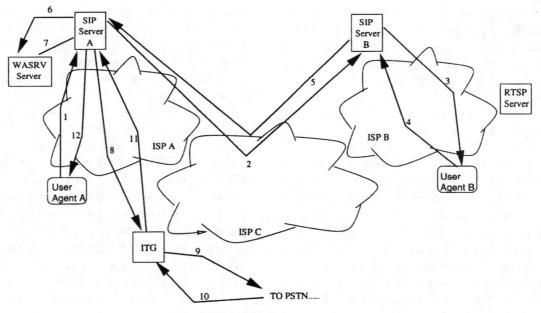

Fig. 5. Internet telephony components.

to the PSTN (9), but the line is busy (10). The gateway indicates this to the server via a SIP error message (11). The server A still has the RTSP URL as a potential contact point for the client. Since it does not understand how to process RTSP URL's, it returns this URL to A's user agent client via a SIP redirection response (12). User A can then contact the RTSP server, and leave a message for user B.

This example illustrates a number of different facets of the architecture. The first is the "hopping" of SIP INVITE requests between elements, with each element accessing directories (such as a WASRV server) or databases as needed. The behavior of each SIP server is dependent on its local programming and implementation. In the example here, SIP server B had been programmed with user preferences about call handling. Server A was programmed with user preferences about billing, and had access to WASRV services to complete calls to PSTN destinations. This heterogeneity allows for the definition of new services, and for differentiation among servers.

Another facet of the architecture is the smooth integration with other services (such as tel: and rtsp:). SIP allows for any type of URL to be carried in the From, To, Contact, and Also fields. This allows calls to be handed off to other protocols and services when needed.

8. Conclusion and future work

We have presented a portion of a protocol suite for supported advanced IP telephony services on the Internet. This suite includes the RTP for transport, the SIP for signaling, and the RTSP for stored media retrieval. These protocols are independent and modular, and when combined with billing, service discovery, and resource reservation protocols, form a complete architecture for future services.

However, much work remains. While IPtel promises to add greater flexibility to telephony services and speed their implementation, IPtel first has to overcome a number of well-known problems, including unpredictable quality of service in the wide area, the lack of reliable and cheap end systems, Internet unreliability, and the lack of a billing infrastructure.

The Internet also currently lacks a generally accepted reliable multicast protocol. Application sharing, voting (i.e., distributed counting) and floor control (i.e., a distributed queue) require such reliability.

As mentioned earlier, gateways to existing telecommunications systems will have to play a large role in the transition to an Internet-based telecommunications infrastructure. We are currently investigating the interconnection of SIP servers with the SS7 (ISUP) protocol [4], so that a gateway can become a first-class citizen in the telephone network (in other words, interface to the telephone network using an NNI as opposed to UNI). Gateways of SIP to H.323 are also under study.

References

[1] H. Schulzrinne, A comprehensive multimedia control architecture for the Internet, Proc. Int. Workshop on Network and Operating System Support for Digital Audio and Video (NOSSDAV), St. Louis, MO, May 1997.

[2] M. Handley, H. Schulzrinne, E. Schooler, J. Rosenberg, SIP: Session initiation protocol, Internet Draft, Internet Engineering Task Force, October 1998. Work in progress.

[3] M. Handley, J. Crowcroft, C. Bormann, J. Ott, The Internet Multimedia Conferencing Architecture, Internet Draft, Internet Engineering Task Force, July 1997, Work in progress.

[4] T. Russell, Signaling System #7, McGraw-Hill, New York, 1995.

[5] Y. Rekhter, T. Li, A Border Gateway Protocol 4 (BGP-4), Request for Comments (Draft Standard) 1771, Internet Engineering Task Force, March 1995.

[6] B. Braden, L. Zhang, S. Berson, S. Herzog, S. Jamin, Resource ReSerVation Protocol (RSVP) – Version 1 Functional Specification, Request for Comments (Proposed Standard) 2205, Internet Engineering Task Force, October 1997.

[7] P. Pan, H. Schulzrinne, Yessir: A simple reservation mechanism for the Internet, Technical Report RC 20697, IBM Research, Hawthorne, New York, September 1997.

[8] C. Rigney, RADIUS Accounting, Request for Comments (Informational) 2139, Internet Engineering Task Force, April 1997.

[9] A. Rubens, P. Calhoun, DIAMETER Base Protocol, Internet Draft, Internet Engineering Task Force, March 1998, Work in progress.

[10] International Telecommunication Union, Terms and Definitions, Recommendation B.13, Telecommunication Standardization Sector of ITU, Geneva, Switzerland, 1988.

[11] L. Zhang, A. Mankin, J. Stewart, T. Narten, M. Crawford, Separating Identifiers and Locators in Addresses: An Analysis of the GSE Proposal for IPv6, Internet Draft, Internet Engineering Task Force, March 1998, Work in progress.

[12] H. Schulzrinne, Re-engineering the telephone system, Proc.

IEEE Singapore Int. Conf. on Networks (SICON), Singapore, April 1997.

[13] I. Busse, B. Deffner, H. Schulzrinne, Dynamic QoS control of multimedia applications based on RTP, Computer Communications 19 (1996) 49–58.

[14] H. Schulzrinne, S. Casner, R. Frederick, V. Jacobson, RTP: A Transport Protocol for Real-time Applications, Request for Comments (Proposed Standard) 1889, Internet Engineering Task Force, January 1996.

[15] C. Strathmeyer, Feature topic: Computer telephony, IEEE Communications Magazine 34 (1996) .

[16] Versit Consortium, Computer Telephony Integration (CTI) Encyclopedia, Tech. Rep. Release 1.0, Versit Consortium, October 1996.

[17] C. Low, The internet telephony red herring, Proc. Global Internet, London, England, November 1996, pp. 72–80.

[18] C. Low, Integrating communications services, IEEE Communications Magazine 35 (1997) .

[19] P. Moulton, J. Moulton, Telecommunications technical fundamentals, technical handout, The Moulton Company, Columbia, MD, 1996, see http://www.moultonco.com/semnotes/telecomm/teladd.htm.

[20] D. Cohen, A protocol for packet-switching voice communication, Proc. Computer Network Protocols Symp., Liege, Belgium, February 1978.

[21] M. Handley, V. Jacobson, SDP: Session Description Protocol, Request for Comments (Proposed Standard) 2327, Internet Engineering Task Force, April 1998.

[22] J. Rosenberg, H. Schulzrinne, Timer reconsideration for enhanced RTP scalability, Proc. Conf. on Computer Communications (IEEE Infocom), San Francisco, CA, March/April 1998.

[23] C. Zhu, RTP Payload Format for H.263 Video Streams, Request for Comments (Proposed Standard) 2190, Internet Engineering Task Force, September 1997.

[24] T. Turletti, C. Huitema, RTP Payload Format for H.261 Video Streams, Request for Comments (Proposed Standard) 2032, Internet Engineering Task Force, October 1996.

[25] L. Berc, B. Fenner, R. Frederick, S. McCanne, RTP Payload Format for JPEG-compressed Video, Request for Comments (Proposed Standard) 2035, Internet Engineering Task Force, October 1996.

[26] R. Civanlar, G. Fernando, V. Goyal, D. Hoffman, RTP Payload Format for MPEG1/MPEG2 Video, Request for Comments (Proposed Standard) 2250, Internet Engineering Task Force, January 1998.

[27] H. Schulzrinne, RTP Profile for Audio and Video Conferences with Minimal Control, Request for Comments (Proposed Standard) 1890, Internet Engineering Task Force, January 1996.

[28] O. Hodson, I. Kouvelas, O. Hodson, M. Handley, J. Bolot, RTP Payload for Redundant Audio Data, Request for Comments (Proposed Standard) 2198, Internet Engineering Task Force, September 1997.

[29] J. Rosenberg, H. Schulzrinne, An RTP Payload Format for Generic Forward Error Correction, Internet Draft, Internet Engineering Task Force, March 1998, Work in progress.

[30] J. Rosenberg, H. Schulzrinne, An RTP Payload Format for User Multiplexing, Internet Draft, Internet Engineering Task Force, January 1998, Work in progress.

[31] D. Katz, IP Router Alert Option, Request for Comments (Proposed Standard) 2113, Internet Engineering Task Force, February 1997.

[32] W. Almesberger, J.-Y.L. Boudec, T. Ferrari, Scalable resource reservation for the Internet, Proc. IEEE Conf. on Protocols for Multimedia Systems – Multimedia Networking (PROMS-MmNet), Santiago, Chile, November 1997, Technical Report 97/234, DI-EPFL, Lausanne, Switzerland.

[33] K. Nichols, V. Jacobson, L. Zhang, A Two-bit Differentiated Services Architecture for the Internet, Internet Draft, Internet Engineering Task Force, November 1997, Work in progress.

[34] International Telecommunication Union, Visual Telephone Systems and Equipment for Local Area Networks Which Provide a Non-guaranteed Quality of Service, Recommendation H.323, Telecommunication Standardization Sector of ITU, Geneva, Switzerland, May 1996.

[35] P. Hoffman, L. Masinter, J. Zawinski, The mailto URL scheme, Request for Comments (Proposed Standard) 2368, Internet Engineering Task Force, July 1998.

[36] T. Howes, S. Kille, M. Wahl, Lightweight Directory Access Protocol (v3), Request for Comments (Proposed Standard) 2251, Internet Engineering Task Force, December 1997.

[37] J. Veizades, E. Guttman, C. Perkins, S. Kaplan, Service Location Protocol, Request for Comments (Proposed Standard) 2165, Internet Engineering Task Force, June 1997.

[38] J. Rosenberg, H. Schulzrinne, B. Suter, Wide Area Network Service Location, Internet Draft, Internet Engineering Task Force, December 1997, Work in progress.

[39] J. Rosenberg, H. Schulzrinne, Internet telephony gateway location, Proc. Conf. on Computer Communications (IEEE Infocom), San Francisco, CA, March/April 1998.

[40] H. Schulzrinne, R. Lanphier, A. Rao, Real Time Streaming Protocol (RTSP), Request for Comments (Proposed Standard) 2326, Internet Engineering Task Force, April 1998.

 **Henning Schulzrinne** received his undergraduate degree in economics and electrical engineering from the Technische Hochschule in Darmstadt, Germany, in 1984, his MSEE degree as a Fulbright scholar from the University of Cincinnati, OH and his Ph.D. degree from the University of Massachusetts in Amherst, Massachusetts in 1987 and 1992, respectively. From 1992 to 1994, he was a member of technical staff at AT&T Bell Laboratories, Murray Hill. From 1994–1996, he was associate department head at GMD-Fokus (Berlin), before joining the Computer Science and Electrical Engineering departments at Columbia University, New York. His research interests encompass real-time network services, the Internet and modeling and performance evaluation.

Jonathan Rosenberg is currently a Member of Technical Staff in the High Speed Networks Research Department, Bell Labs, Lucent Technologies, in Holmdel, NJ. After completing his Masters from MIT, he came to work at Bell Labs, where he worked on development and implementation of low bitrate video codecs. His current research interests include IP voice transport, signaling protocols and architectures for IP telephony, and service discovery. Mr. Rosenberg is currently pursuing a part-time Ph.D. at Columbia University, working with Prof. Henning Schulzrinne on IP telephony. He has published numerous papers, and filed over a dozen patents, in the general areas of multimedia and networking. He is active in the IETF, where he chairs the newly formed iptel working group.

CHAPTER TEN

Multimedia Storage Servers

Prashant J. Shenoy
University of Massachusetts - Amherst

Harrick M. Vin
Universtiy of Texas - Austin

RAPID advances in computing, communication, and compression technologies coupled with the dramatic growth of the Internet has led to the emergence of a wide variety of multimedia applications—such as distance learning, interactive multiplayer games, online virtual worlds, and scientific visualization of multiresolution imagery. These applications differ from conventional applications in at least two ways. First, they involve storage, transmission, and processing of heterogeneous data types—such as text, image, audio, and video—that differ significantly in their characteristics (*e.g.*, size, data rate, real-time requirements, etc.). Second, unlike conventional best-effort applications, these applications impose diverse performance requirements—for instance, with respect to timeliness—on the networks and operating systems. Because of these differences, techniques employed by conventional file systems for managing textual files do not suffice for managing multimedia objects. In this chapter, we discuss storage and retrieval techniques employed by multimedia storage servers.

STORAGE TECHNIQUES

Digitization of audio yields a sequence of samples and that of video yields a sequence of frames. A media stream refers to a continuously recorded sequence of audio samples or video frames. Because of the large sizes and data transfer rates of

media streams, multimedia servers are founded on disk arrays. To effectively utilize a disk array, multimedia servers stripe each media stream across disks in the array. The striping unit, also referred to as a media block, denotes the maximum amount of logically contiguous data stored on a single disk. Each media block may contain either a fixed number of media units (*e.g.*, video frames or audio samples) or a fixed number of storage units (*e.g.*, bytes). If a media stream is compressed using a variable bit rate (VBR) compression algorithm, then the storage space requirement may vary from one media unit to another. Hence, a server that constructs a media block using a fixed number of media units will be required to store variable-size media blocks on the array. On the other hand, if media blocks are of fixed-size, then they will contain a variable number of media units. Thus, depending on the placement policy, accessing a fixed number of media units for a stream will require the server to retrieve either a fixed number of variable-size blocks, or a variable number of fixed-size blocks. Because of the sequentiality of media stream playback, the variable-size block placement policy yields predictable access patterns for the disk array, and thereby simplifies disk bandwidth management. This, however, comes at the expense of increased complexity of storage space management. The fixed-size block placement policy simplifies storage space management at the expense of more complex disk bandwidth management

655

algorithms. Hence, the variable-size blocks are suitable for predominantly read-only environments (*e.g.*, video-on-demand [VOD] servers), whereas fixed-size blocks are better suited for environments that involve frequent creation, deletion, and modification of media streams (*e.g.*, multimedia file systems).

To maximize the throughput of a disk array, load on disks should be balanced. Multimedia servers attempt to balance the load across the disks by using a combination of static and dynamic load-balancing techniques.

Static Load Balancing

With static load balancing, a multimedia server attempts to balance load across disks by selecting for each media stream an appropriate (1) stripe unit size, (2) degree of striping, and (3) amount of replication.

Conventional file systems select stripe unit sizes that minimize the average response time while maximizing throughput. In contrast, to decrease the frequency of playback discontinuities, a multimedia server should select a stripe unit size that minimizes the variance in response time while maximizing throughput. Whereas small stripe units result in a uniform load distribution among disks in the array (and thereby decrease the variance in response times), they also increase the overhead of disk seeks and rotational latencies (and thereby decrease throughput). Large stripe units, on the other hand, increase the array throughput at the expense of increased load imbalance and variance in response times. To maximize the number of clients that can be serviced simultaneously, the server should select a stripe unit size that balances these tradeoffs.

The degree of striping for media streams is dependent on the number of disks in the array. In relatively small disk arrays, striping media streams across all disks in the array (wide-striping) yields a balanced load and maximizes throughput. For large disk arrays, however, to maximize the throughput, the server may need to stripe media streams across subsets of disks in the array and replicate their storage to achieve load balancing.

The amount of replication for each media stream depends on the popularity of the stream and the total storage space constraints.

Dynamic Load Balancing

Load across disks within a multimedia server may become unbalanced, at least transiently, because of the arrival pattern of requests. To smooth out this load imbalance, multimedia servers employ dynamic load-balancing techniques. If multiple replicas of the requested media stream are stored on the array, then the server can attempt to balance load across disks by servicing the request from the least loaded disk containing a replica. Further, the server can exploit the sequentiality of audio and video retrieval to pre-fetch data for media streams to smooth out variation in the load imposed by an individual media stream.

Fault-tolerance is another issue that arises with increase in number of disks in a multimedia server. Multimedia servers should provide mechanisms to recover from a disk failure without losing data or taking the system offline. Conventional disk arrays either replicate data on separate disks or use error-correcting codes (*e.g.*, parity encoding) to recover from a disk failure. These approaches, however, can significantly increase the load on the surviving disks in the event of a disk failure, resulting in deadline violations in the playback of media streams. To prevent such a scenario, with conventional fault-tolerance techniques, servers must operate at low levels of disk utilization during the fault-free state. Multimedia servers can reduce this overhead by exploiting the characteristics of media streams. In particular, there are two general techniques that a multimedia server may use. First, a multimedia server can exploit the sequentiality of audio and video access to reduce the overhead of online recovery in a disk array. Specifically, by computing parity information over a sequence of blocks belonging to the same media stream, the server can ensure that media blocks retrieved for recovering a block stored on the failed disk are requested by the client in the near future. By buffering such blocks and then servicing the requests for their access from the buffer, this method minimizes the overhead of the online failure recovery process. Second, because human perception is tolerant to minor distortions in media playback, a multimedia server can reduce the overhead of failure recovery by approximating data stored on the failed disk using spatial and temporal redundancies inherent in media streams. This method integrates the media decoding process with failure recovery and hence distributes the task of failure recovery among client sites.

RETRIEVAL TECHNIQUES

A multimedia server needs to choose from two

fundamentally different paradigms to schedule retrieval of media streams: server-push or client-pull. Because of the periodic nature of media playback, a multimedia server using server-push architecture can service multiple streams by proceeding in *rounds*. During each round, the server retrieves a fixed number of media units for each stream. To ensure continuous playback, the number of media units accessed for each stream must be sufficient to sustain its playback rate, and the service time (*i.e.,* the total time spent retrieving media units during a round) should not exceed the duration of a round. In client-pull architecture, on the other hand, the server retrieves media units for a client only in response to an explicit read request. Whereas the server needs to maintain client states in the server-push mode, the client-pull mode is inherently stateless. The primary advantage of server-push architecture is that it optimizes array utilization by batching read/write operations. Furthermore, it is easier for such servers to enforce quality of service guarantees provided to clients.

In both of these architectures, a multimedia server employs admission control algorithms to ensure that the resources required by a new request do not affect the real-time requirements of streams already being serviced. An admission control algorithm determines the resource requirements of a request by estimating its bit rate and the disk access times. Depending on the nature of this estimate, admission control algorithms can be classified into three categories:

- *Deterministic* admission control algorithms make worst-case estimates of the bit rate and disk access times of user requests and are used when clients cannot tolerate any deadline violations.
- *Statistical* admission control algorithms use probability distributions to estimate the bit rate and disk access time variations of user requests to guarantee that deadlines will be met with a certain probability. Such algorithms achieve much higher utilization than deterministic algorithms and are used when clients can tolerate some, but only a bounded number of, deadline violations.
- *Measurement-based* admission control algorithms use past variations in bit rate and disk access times of media streams as an indicator of future variations. They achieve

the highest disk utilization but provide the weakest guarantees.

In addition to admission control algorithms, a multimedia server needs to employ a disk scheduling algorithm that can meet the performance requirements of multimedia applications. Typically, disk requests issued by multimedia servers have deadlines. Conventional disk scheduling algorithms—such as SCAN and shortest access time first (SATF)—schedule requests based on their physical location on disk (so as to reduce disk seek and rotational latency overheads) and ignore other requirements such as deadlines. To service requests with deadlines, several disk scheduling algorithms have been proposed. The simplest of these scheduling algorithms is earliest deadline first (EDF). EDF schedules requests in the order of their deadlines but ignores the relative positions of requested data on disk. Hence, it can incur significant seek time and rotational latency overhead. This limitation has been addressed by several disk scheduling algorithms, including priority SCAN (PSCAN), earliest deadline SCAN (ED-SCAN), feasible deadline SCAN (FD-SCAN), SCAN-EDF, and shortest seek earliest deadline by order/value (SSEDO, SSEDV). These algorithms start from an EDF schedule and reorder requests without violating their deadlines such that the seek time and rotational latency overhead is reduced.

To maximize the number of clients that can be serviced simultaneously, multimedia servers also rely on *caching* and *batching* techniques.

Caching

Caching involves using the buffer space at the server to store recently accessed data and subsequently using the cached data to service new requests. Traditional caching techniques based on the least recently used (LRU) policy yield poor hit ratios for sequential data accesses. In fact, because of the periodic and sequential nature of media streams, the buffer allocated to a block can be reassigned immediately after use. However, if another user is accessing the same data, within a short time interval, the block can be retained in the buffer for the later user. Algorithms such as interval caching and distance caching exploit this observation; they cache intervals formed by consecutive accesses to the same media stream. The two requests that form such a consecutive pair are called the writer and the reader; the writer causes media data to be written into the cache, and the reader reads the cached data.

Batching

Batching delays a new user request, for a duration referred to as the batching interval, with the expectation that more requests for the same media stream may arrive within that duration. If multiple requests are indeed received for the same media stream within the batching interval, then the server can service all the requests by retrieving a single stream from the disks. The longer the batching interval, the larger is the probability of receiving multiple requests for the same media stream within the interval, and hence the larger is the gain because of batching. However, the larger the batching interval, the larger is the startup latency for requests. Batching policies attempt to find a balance between these concerns. One approach for reducing the startup latency is called piggybacking (or catching). In this technique, requests are serviced immediately upon their arrival. However, if the server began servicing a request for the same media stream sometime in the recent past, then the server attempts to service the two requests in a manner such that the servicing of the new request catches up with that of the previous request. If this is successful, the server then services both of these requests as a single stream from the disks.

Finally, a user may access a media stream in fast-forward or rewind modes. Hence, a multimedia server is required to support these VCR control operations. The main challenge in supporting VCR control operations is that fast-forward or rewind operations generally impose higher disk bandwidth requirements than normal retrieval. Hence, if a multimedia server performs admission control based on the bandwidth requirement for normal playback, then on receiving requests for fast-forward or rewind, the server may not be able to meet the real-time performance requirements of clients. To address this issue, a server may employ techniques that range from degrading the quality of media streams (possibly by using multiresolution encoding of media streams) while maintaining roughly the same bandwidth requirement during VCR control operations to optimistically reserving some fraction of the total disk bandwidth for servicing such VCR control requests.

CASE STUDIES

Over the past several years, several academic and commercial institutions have developed multimedia servers. Commercial multimedia servers range from low-end PC-based multimedia servers designed to serve small work groups to high-end large-scale servers that can serve thousands of video-on-demand users.

The low-end servers are targeted for a local area network environment, and their clients are personal computers, equipped with video-processing hardware, connected on a LAN. They are designed for applications such as on-site training and information kiosks, and the multimedia files consist of short audio and video clips. They are also used as small-scale video servers for environments such as hotels and conference centers.

High-end servers are targeted for applications such as video-on-demand, in which the number of simultaneous streams is expected to be in the thousands, and the distribution system is expected to be cable-based or telephone-wire–based. In order to provide a large collection of videos in a cost-effective solution, these servers generally are based on a hierarchy of storage devices, ranging from high-cost, high-bandwidth semiconductor memory through disk storage to low-cost, high-capacity tape/CD/DVD libraries.

CONCLUDING REMARKS

Multimedia storage servers differ significantly from conventional storage servers in their design. These differences are wide in scope, influencing everything from the selection of storage hardware to the choice of disk scheduling algorithms. This chapter provides an introduction to the problems involved in multimedia storage server design and to the various approaches to solving these problems. The chapter consists of six recent articles. The first article, "Multimedia storage servers: A tutorial," by D. J. Gemmell and colleagues, provides an overview of the architectures and algorithms required for designing multimedia servers. The second article, "Random RAIDs with selective exploitation of redundancy for high performance video servers," by Y. Birk, deals with placement, fault-tolerance, and performance issues. The article shows how redundant information stored by a multimedia server for fault-tolerance can also be employed for improving response times in the absence of faults. Specifically, the proposed technique treats an overloaded disk on the server like a failed disk and uses redundant information stored on the remaining disks to reconstruct data requested from the overloaded disk (which reduces the load on this disk and improves response times).

The next two articles deal with retrieval issues. The first of these, "Disk scheduling in a multimedia I/O system" by A. L. Narasimha Reddy and J. Wyllie, discusses a scheduling algorithm that takes deadlines of real-time disk requests into account while optimizing disk seek overheads. This process is achieved by combining the earliest deadline first (EDF) algorithm with the SCAN disk scheduling algorithm; the resulting algorithm is referred to as SCAN-EDF. The second article, "A statistical admission control algorithm for multimedia servers," by H. M. Vin and colleagues, deals with admission control issues. It shows how probability distributions of the client load and disk service times can be employed to provide statistical performance guarantees to clients in a multimedia server.

The final two articles deal with techniques for maximizing the number of clients that can be supported by a multimedia server. The first of these, "A generalized interval caching policy for mixed interactive and long video workloads," by A. Dan and D. Sitaram, discusses techniques for efficiently utilizing the buffer cache at the server. The final article, "On optimal piggyback merging policies for video-on-demand systems," by C. Aggarwal, J. Wolf, and P. S. Yu, discusses batching policies for improving the number of clients supported by the server.

✦✦✦

ADDITIONAL READINGS

Case Studies

D. Anderson, Y. Osawa, and R. Govindan, "A file system for continuous media," *ACM Transactions on Computer Systems* 10, no. 4 (April 1994), 311–37.

W. Bolosky et al., "The tiger video file server," in *Proceedings of the 6th International Workshop on Network and Operating System Support for Digital Audio and Video (NOSSDAV 96)* (April 1996): 97–104.

M. Buddhikot, G. Parulkar, and J. Cox, "Design of a large scale multimedia storage server," *Journal of Computer Networks and ISDN Systems* (Dec. 1994): 504–24.

R. Haskin, "Tiger Shark—A scalable file system for multimedia," *IBM Journal of Research and Development* 42, no. 2 (March 1998): 185–97.

C. Martin, P. Narayan, B. Ozden, R. Rastogi, and A. Silberschatz, "The Fellini multimedia storage server," in *Multimedia Information Storage and Management*, S. M. Chung, ed. (Aug. 1996).

D. Pegler, D. Hutchison, P. Lougher, and D. Shepherd, "A scalable architecture for multimedia storage," in *High-Speed Networking for Multimedia Applications*, W. Effelsberg, O. Spaniol, A. Danthine, and D. Ferrari (eds.), (1996): 127–63.

P. J. Shenoy, P. Goyal, S. S. Rao, and H. M. Vin, "Symphony: An integrated multimedia file system," in *Proceedings of the ACM SPIE Conference on Multimedia Computing and Networking* (MMCN 98) (1998): 124–38.

Retrieval Issues

P. Barham, "A fresh approach to file system quality of service," in *Proceedings of the 7th International Workshop on Network and Operating System Support for Digital Audio and Video (NOSSDAV 97)* (May 1997): 119–28.

E. Chang and A. Zakhor, "Cost analyses for VBR video servers," in *Proceedings of the SPIE ACM Conference on Multimedia Computing and Networking (MMCN 96)* (Jan. 1996): 381–97.

A. Dan, D. Sitaram, and P. Shahabuddin, "Scheduling policies for an on-demand video server with batching," in *Proceedings of the 2nd ACM International Multimedia Conference* (Oct. 1994): 15–23.

S. Sahu, Z. Zhang, J. Kurose, and D. Towsley, "On the efficient retrieval of variable bit rate video in a multimedia server," in *Proceedings of the IEEE International Conference on Multimedia Computing Systems (ICMCS 97)* (June 1997): 46–53.

P. Shenoy and H. M. Vin, "Cello: A disk scheduling framework for next generation operating systems," in *Proceedings of ACM SIGMETRICS 98* (June 1998): 44–55.

Placement Issues

S. Berson, S. Ghandeharizadeh, R. Muntz, and X. Ju, "Staggered striping in multimedia information systems," in Proceedings of ACM SIGMOD (1994): 79–90.

T. Chiueh and R. Katz, "Multi-resolution video representation for parallel disk arrays," in *Proceedings of the 1st ACM International Multimedia Conference* (Aug. 1993): 401–09.

J. R. Santos, R. Muntz, and B. Rabeiro-Nato, "Comparing random data allocation and data striping in multimedia servers," in *Proceedings of ACM SIGMETRICS 2000* (June 2000): 44–55.

R. Tewari, D. Dias, R. Mukherjee, and H. Vin, "Design and performance tradeoffs in clustered multimedia servers," in *Proceedings of the IEEE International Conference on Multimedia Computing Systems (ICMCS 96)* (June 1996): 144–150.

R. Tewari, R. King, D. Kandlur, and D. Dias, "Placement of multimedia blocks on zoned disks," in *Proceedings of the ACM/SPIE Conference on Multimedia Computing and Networking (MMCN)* (June 1996): 360–7.

P. J. Shenoy and H. M. Vin, "Efficient striping techniques for multimedia file servers," in *Proceedings of the 7th International Workshop on Network and Operating System Support for Digital Audio and Video (NOSSDAV 97)* (May 1997): 25–36.

Fault Tolerance

S. Berson, L. Golubchik, and R. Muntz, "Fault tolerant design of multimedia servers," in *Proceedings of ACM SIGMOD 95* (1995): 364–75.

P. Shenoy and H. M. Vin, "Failure recovery algorithms for multimedia servers," *ACM/Springer Multimedia Systems Journal 8*, no. 1 (Jan. 2000): 1–19.

Miscellaneous Issues

A. L. Drapeau and R. H. Katz, "Striping in large tape libraries," in *Proceedings of Supercomputing 93* (Nov. 1993): 378–387.

W. Feng, B. Krishnaswami, and A. Prabhudev, "Proactive buffer management for the delivery of stored video across best-effort networks," in *Proceedings of the 6th ACM International Multimedia Conference* (Sept. 1998): 285–90.

L. Golubchik, J.C.S. Lui, and R. R. Muntz, "Reducing I/O demand in video-on-demand storage servers," in *Proceedings of ACM SIGMETRICS 95* (May 1995): 25–36.

B. Ozden, R. Rastogi, and A. Silberschatz, "Buffer replacement algorithms for multimedia storage systems," in *Proceedings of the IEEE International Conference on Multimedia Computing Systems (ICMCS 96)* (June 1996): 172–80.

J. Rexford, S. Sen, J. Dey, W. Feng, J. Kurose, J. Stankovic, and D. Towsley, "Online smoothing of live, variable-bit-rate video," in *Proceedings of the 7th International Workshop on Network and Operating Systems Support for Digital Audio and Video (NOSSDAV 97)* (May 1997): 249–58.

J. Salehi, Z. Zhang, J. Kurose, and D. Towsley, "Supporting stored video: Reducing rate variability and end-to-end resource requirements through optimal smoothing," in *Proceedings of ACM SIGMETRICS 96* (May 1996): 222–31.

P. Shenoy, P. Goyal, and H. M. Vin, "Architectural considerations for next generation file systems," in *Proceedings of the 7th ACM International Multimedia Conference* (Nov. 1999): 457–468.

D. Venkatesh and T.D.C. Little, "The use of media characteristics and user behavior for the design of multimedia servers," in *Multimedia Information Storage and Management*, S. M. Chung, ed. (1996): 95–116.

R. Tewari, H. Vin, A. Dan, and D. Sitaram, "Resource Based Caching for web servers," in *Proceedings of the ACM SPIE Conference on Multimedia Computing and Networking (MMCN 98)* (Jan. 1998).

Multimedia Storage Servers: A Tutorial

D. James Gemmell
Simon Fraser University

Harrick M. Vin
University of Texas at Austin

Dilip D. Kandlur
International Business Machines

P. Venkat Rangan
University of California at San Diego

Lawrence A. Rowe
University of California at Berkeley

Real-time processing of multimedia data is required of those who offer audio and video on-demand. This tutorial highlights the unique issues and data storage characteristics that concern designers.

Recent advances in computing and communication make on-line access to multimedia information—like books, periodicals, images, video clips, and scientific data—both possible and cost-effective. The architecture for these services consists of multimedia storage servers connected to client sites via high-speed networks (see Figure 1). Clients can retrieve multimedia objects from the server for real-time playback. Furthermore, access is interactive because clients can stop, pause, and resume playback and, in some cases, perform fast-forward and rewind operations.

Some media (such as audio and video) are classified as *continuous* because they consist of a sequence of media *quanta* (such as audio samples or video frames), which convey meaning only when presented in time. The design of services to support continuous media (CM) differs significantly from that of services to support only traditional textual and numeric data because of two fundamental CM characteristics:

- *Real-time storage and retrieval*: CM recording devices (such as video cameras) generate a continuous stream of media quanta that must be stored in real time. CM playback is essentially recording in reverse: The media quanta must be presented using the same timing sequence with which they were captured. Any deviation from this timing sequence can lead to artifacts such as jerkiness in video motion, pops in audio, or possibly complete unintelligibility. Furthermore, media components can be combined in a fashion requiring synchronization. For example, a slide presentation must synchronize audio (music and commentary) with images.
- *High data transfer rate and large storage space*: Digital video and audio playback demands a high data transfer rate (see Table 1), so storage space is rapidly filled. Thus, a multimedia service must efficiently store, retrieve, and manipulate data in large quantities at high speeds.

Consequently, the critical components in the design of multimedia services are

1. *multimedia storage servers* that support continuous media (CM) storage and retrieval, and
2. *network subsystems* that synchronously deliver media information, on time, to the client sites.

Our focus is to survey the design issues of digital multimedia storage servers. We describe the design issues of multimedia, and we assume a network subsystem (or transmission channel) that delivers CM information according to its real-time specifications. The network can be simply telephone lines of sufficient bandwidth, which clients can call for server access.

CONTINUOUS MEDIA RECORDING AND RETRIEVAL

Video digitization yields a sequence of continuously recorded video frames; audio digitization yields a sequence of continuously recorded audio samples. Because media quanta, as we mentioned earlier, convey meaning only when presented continuously in time, a multimedia server must ensure that the recording and playback of each media stream proceeds at its real-time data rate. During recording, for example, a server must continuously store the data produced by an input device (such as a microphone or camera) to prevent buffer overruns at the device. During playback, on the other hand, the server must retrieve data from the disk at a rate that prevents an output device (such as a speaker or video display) from starving. Although semantically different, both operations are mathematically equivalent with respect to their real-time performance requirements.[1] For simplicity, we discuss techniques only for retrieving media information for real-time playback, although real-time recording can be similarly analyzed.

Single-stream playback

A media stream's continuous playback is a sequence of periodic tasks with deadlines. Tasks correspond to retrievals of media blocks from disk, and deadlines correspond to the scheduled playback times. Although it's conceivable that multimedia systems could fetch media quanta from disk just in time to be played, in practice the retrieval is likely to be bursty. Media blocks will need to be buffered when retrieval gets ahead of playback.

The server's challenge, consequently, is to supply the stream buffers with enough data to ensure that the playback processes do not starve[2] (see Figure 2). Continuous playback can be assured simply by buffering the entire stream before initiating the playback; however, this requires a large buffer and will cause a lengthy latency for initiating playback of large files. Efficiently servicing a single stream is thus a threefold problem: preventing starvation while minimizing the buffer space requirement and the initiation latency. These two minimization problems are, in fact, the same—minimizing one will

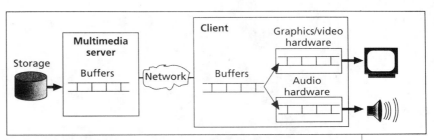

Figure 1. Data flow for a multimedia network server.

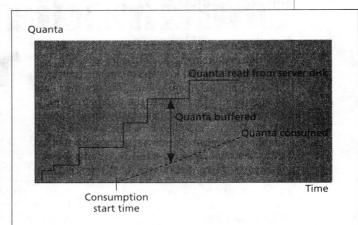

Figure 2. Ensuring continuous retrieval of a media stream from disk.

minimize the other.[2] Furthermore, because disk data transfer rates are significantly higher than a single stream's real-time data rate, even a small buffer will let conventional file and operating systems support continuous storage and retrieval of a few media streams. (Consider that the maxi-

Table 1. Storage space requirements for uncompressed digital multimedia data.

Media type	Specifications	Data rate (per second)
Voice-quality audio	1 channel, 8-bit samples at 8 kHz	64 Kbits
MPEG-encoded audio	Equivalent to CD quality	384 Kbits
CD-quality audio	2 channels, 16-bit samples at 44.1 kHz	1.4 Mbits
MPEG-2-encoded video	640 × 480 pixels/frame, 24 bits/pixel	0.42 Mbytes
NTSC-quality video	640 × 480 pixels/frame, 24 bits/pixel	27 Mbytes
HDTV-quality video	1,280 × 720 pixels/frame, 24 bits/pixel	81 Mbytes

mum throughput of modern disks is around 3 to 4 Mbytes per second while that of an MPEG-2-encoded video stream is 0.42 Mbytes and uncompressed CD-quality stereo audio is about 0.2 Mbytes.)

Multistream retrieval

In practice, a multimedia server must process retrieval requests for several streams simultaneously. Even when multiple streams access the same file (such as a popular movie), different streams might access different parts of the file at the same time.

A simple way to guarantee meeting the real-time requirements of all streams is to dedicate a disk head to each stream and treat each disk head as a single-stream system. This however limits the total number of streams to the number of disk heads. Because disk data rates significantly exceed those of single streams, the number of streams that can be serviced simultaneously can generally be increased by multiplexing a disk head among several streams. In doing so, the server must meet the continuous playback requirements of all streams through carefully scheduling disk requests so that no individual stream starves. Furthermore, the server must ensure that it can in fact schedule disks by limiting the number of streams serviced at any given time.

Disk scheduling

Servers traditionally employ disk-scheduling algorithms—such as first come, first served; shortest seek time first; and Scan—to reduce seek time and rotational latency, to achieve high throughput, or to provide fair access to each stream. Real-time constraints, however, reduce the direct application of traditional disk-scheduling algorithms to multimedia servers.

The best-known algorithm for real-time scheduling of tasks with deadlines is the *earliest deadline first* algorithm. This algorithm schedules the media block with the earliest deadline for retrieval. Scheduling of the disk head based solely on EDF policy, however, is likely to yield excessive seek time and rotational latency, and poor server-resource utilization can be expected.

One variant of this basic algorithm combines Scan with EDF and is called the Scan-EDF scheduling algorithm.[3] The Scan algorithm scans the disk head back and forth across the disk's surface and retrieves a requested block as the head passes over the surface. By limiting the amount of backtracking that the disk head does, Scan can significantly reduce seek latencies. Scan-EDF services the requests with earliest deadlines first, just like EDF; however, when several requests have the same deadline, their respective blocks are accessed with the Scan algorithm. Clearly, the Scan-EDF technique's effectiveness depends on the number of requests having the same deadline. When deadlines for media block retrieval are batched (for example, by initiating media strand playbacks only at certain intervals), Scan-EDF is reduced to Scan only.

Scan-EDF is a unique disk-scheduling algorithm for CM because it does not intrinsically batch requests. All other algorithms typically process requests in *rounds*. During

> **S**ervers **traditionally employ disk-scheduling algorithms to reduce seek time and rotational latency, to achieve high throughput, or to provide fair access to each stream.**

each round, the multimedia server retrieves a media block sequence of arbitrary length (even zero) for each stream. Processing requests in rounds is more than a convenience; it also exploits the periodic nature of CM playback.

Each round still requires a disk-scheduling algorithm, the simplest of which is the *round-robin* algorithm. This services streams in a fixed order that does not vary from one round to the next. Round-robin scheduling's major drawback is that it, like EDF, does not exploit the relative positions of the media blocks being retrieved during a round. For this reason, data-placement algorithms that inherently reduce latencies are sometimes used in conjunction with round-robin scheduling.

Round length and latency trade-offs

Applying the Scan algorithm to reduce round latencies is simple. For CM servers, minor alterations to Scan can minimize both the seek latencies and the round length.[4] In addition to round-length minimization, latencies between successive stream retrievals are also an issue for the CM server. In the round-robin algorithm, the order in which streams are serviced is fixed across rounds. Therefore, the maximum latency between retrieval times of streams' successive requests is bounded by a round's duration. With Scan, the relative order for servicing streams depends solely on the placement of blocks being retrieved; thus a stream can receive service at the beginning of one round and at the end of another round.

The latency between successive stream retrievals has several implications for playback initiation delay and buffer requirements. For round-robin, playback can be initiated immediately after all blocks from the stream's first request have been retrieved. With Scan, however, playback must wait until the end of the round. To prevent output device starvation, round-robin needs enough buffer space to satisfy data consumption for one round, while Scan needs enough to satisfy consumption for nearly two rounds. However, because Scan's rounds are shorter, there is a trade-off between round length and latency between successive stream retrievals.

To exploit this trade-off, a disk-scheduling algorithm known as the *grouped sweeping scheme* (GSS) partitions each round into groups. Each stream is assigned to a group, and the groups are serviced in a fixed order in each round. The Scan disk-scheduling algorithm is used in each group. If all streams are assigned to the same group, GSS reduces to Scan. On the other hand, if each stream is assigned to its own unique group, GSS degenerates to round-robin. By optimally deriving the number of groups, the server can balance the reduction of round length against the latency of successive stream retrievals (see Figure 3).

Reading and buffering requirements

As mentioned, nearly all multistream CM retrieval approaches involve processing stream requests in rounds. Another almost universal practice found in the literature is to ensure that production matches consumption in each round. During a round, the amount of data retrieved for a stream is at least equal to the amount consumed by the stream's playback. This means that, on a round-by-round basis, data production never lags consumption, and there is never a net decrease in the amount of buffered data. Algorithms having this property are referred to as *work-ahead-augmenting*[1] or *buffer-conserving*.[4]

An algorithm could conceivably be developed that proceeds in rounds but is not buffer-conserving. Such an algorithm would allow production to fall behind consumption in one round and compensate for it in a later round, although this would be more complex. Furthermore, while buffer conservation is not a necessary condition for preventing starvation, it can be used as a sufficient condition. For instance, before initiating playback, if enough data is prefetched to meet the consumption requirements of the longest possible round and if each round thereafter is buffer-conserving, it is clear that starvation is impossible.

To ensure continuous playback of media streams, a sufficient number of blocks must be retrieved for each client during a round to prevent the output device's starvation for the round's entire duration. To determine this number, the server must know the maximum duration of a round. As round length depends on the number of blocks retrieved for each stream, some care should be taken that unnecessary reads are not performed. In particular, a simple scheme that retrieves the same number of media blocks for each stream will be inefficient because the stream with the maximum consumption rate will dictate the number of blocks to read. This will cause streams with smaller consumption rates to read more than they need. To minimize round length, the number of blocks retrieved for each stream during each round should be proportional to the stream's consumption rate.[1-2, 5-6]

Managing buffers for maximum consumption

Naturally, a server must manage its buffers to leave sufficient free space for the next reads to be performed. On a per-stream basis, the most suitable buffer model is a first-in, first-out queue. Using a FIFO, contiguous files, and round-robin scheduling, the buffer size can approximate the size of the maximum required read. In this case, each stream's FIFO can simply be "topped up" in each round (that is, enough data is read to fill the FIFO). In contrast, a Scan strategy would require at least a double-buffered scheme, where each buffer is the size of a maximum read. This is because Scan can schedule the reads for a stream so that the stream is serviced last in one round and first in the next (back to back). If a buffer is not completely empty when it is time for reading, the topping-up strategy can still be used.

With a topping-up strategy, the amount read for a stream in each reading period will vary with the amount of free buffer space. When files are not stored contiguously but are split into blocks, variable read amounts might mean that the data to be retrieved is split across two blocks, causing an extra intrafile seek. One solution to this problem uses three block-sized buffers. With three buffers, the only time a whole block cannot be read is when at least two buffers are full; buffering is otherwise sufficient so that reading is not necessary until the next round. Other solutions with fewer than three buffers are also possible.[4]

Admission control

Given streams' real-time performance requirements, a multimedia server must employ admission control algorithms to determine whether a new stream can be serviced without affecting streams already being serviced. So far we have assumed that stream performance requirements

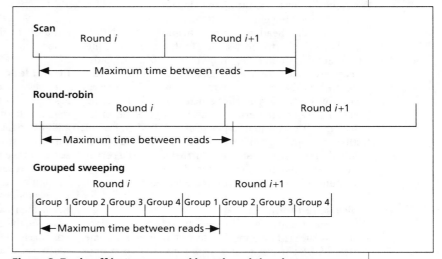

Figure 3. Trade-off between round length and time between service for Scan, round-robin, and grouped sweeping scheme.

include meeting all real-time deadlines; however, some applications can tolerate missed deadlines. For example, a few lost video frames or a pop in the audio can occasionally be tolerated, especially if such tolerance is rewarded with a reduced cost of service. To guarantee that a server meets all real-time deadlines, worst-case assumptions must be made by the server regarding seek and rotational latencies, although the seek time and rotational latency incurred are generally shorter than those in a worst case. A multimedia server might therefore accommodate additional streams through an admission control algorithm that exploits the statistical variation in media block-access times from disk (or statistical variations in compression ratios, where applicable).

In admitting streams, CM servers can offer three broad quality-of-service categories:

- *Deterministic*. All deadlines are guaranteed to be met. For this level of service, the admission control algorithm considers worst-case scenarios in admitting new streams.
- *Statistical*. Deadlines are guaranteed to be met with a certain probability. For example, a client subscribes to a service that guarantees meeting 90 percent of deadlines over an interval. To provide such guarantees,

admission control algorithms must consider the system's statistical behavior while admitting new streams.

- *Background.* No guarantees are given for meeting deadlines. The server schedules such accesses only when there is time left over after servicing all guaranteed and statistical streams.

To implement deterministic service, resources are reserved in worst-case fashion for each stream. Before admitting another stream and lengthening the round's duration, the server must ensure that buffering for existing streams is adequate to prevent starvation.[1,6] Some schemes dynamically change the stream buffer spaces based on the current round's length. Alternately, all stream buffer spaces can be allocated assuming a maximum round length and, for admission, the new round length need only be compared to the maximum.[4]

Techniques for managing disk storage include optimally placing data blocks on disk, using multiple disks, adding tertiary storage to gain additional capacity, and building storage hierarchies.

Statistical service implementation resembles that of deterministic service, but instead of the server's computing the change to round length based on worst-case values, the computation is based on statistical values. For instance, the computation can use an average rotational-delay value that would be expected to occur with a certain probability based on a random distribution of rotational delays.

In servicing streams during a round, deterministic streams must be guaranteed service before any statistical streams, and all statistical streams must similarly be serviced before any background streams. Missed deadlines should be distributed fairly so that the same streams are not dropped each time.

Dealing with service guarantees and deadlines

When variable-rate compression is used, a media block will decompress into a variable amount of media quanta. Therefore, the number of blocks that must be retrieved will vary according to the compression ratio achieved for each block. In a like manner when dealing with variable disk latencies, deterministic service for such data could use worst-case compression figures, and statistical service could use probabilistic figures. With compressed data, a further option is to record the compression ratios achieved. Deterministic service could then be based on actual rather than worst-case figures, and statistical service could be based on the files' actual statistics rather than on the statistics for the compression algorithm in general.

For background and statistical traffic, different strategies are available to resolve missed deadlines. For example, although it might be desirable not to skip any data blocks to ensure that the information received is intelligible, this technique would lengthen the playback duration of media streams. On the other hand, if the playback of multiple media streams is being temporally coordinated, dropping media blocks might be preferable.

Techniques that dynamically vary media resolution levels to accommodate an overloaded server significantly depart from these simplistic schemes. For example, audio quality can be degraded simply by transmitting only the higher order bits. Similarly, some compression schemes can be made scalable—that is, data is encoded so that subsets of the media stream can be extracted and decoded to achieve lower resolution output. To deal with missed deadlines, techniques for varying resolution are generally similar to those used for implementing fast forward.

MANAGING DIGITAL MULTIMEDIA STORAGE

A multimedia server must divide video and audio files into blocks while storing them on disk. Each data block can occupy several physical disk blocks. Techniques for managing disk storage include optimally placing data blocks on disk, using multiple disks, adding tertiary storage to gain additional capacity, and building storage hierarchies.

Placing data blocks for optimal service

A file's blocks can be stored contiguously or scattered about the storage device. Contiguous files are simple to implement but subject to fragmentation. They also can necessitate enormous copying overheads during insertions and deletions to maintain contiguity. In contrast, scattered placements avoid fragmentation and copying overheads. Contiguous layouts are useful in read-only systems, such as video-on-demand, but not for read-write servers.

CONTIGUOUS PLACEMENT. For continuous media, the choice between contiguous and scattered files relates primarily to intrafile seeks. When reading from a contiguous file, only one seek is required to position the disk head at the start of the data. However, when reading several blocks in a scattered file, a seek could be incurred for each block read. Furthermore, even when reading a small amount of data, it is possible that half of the data might be stored in one block and the other half in the next block, thereby incurring intrafile seeks.

Intrafile seeks can be avoided in scattered layouts if the amount read for a stream always evenly divides a block. One approach to achieve this result is to select a sufficiently large block size and read one block in each round. This technique has several advantages, especially for large video servers. It improves disk throughput substantially, thereby increasing the number of streams that can be served by the disk. Furthermore, since a file system has to maintain indexes for each media block, choosing a large block size also reduces the overhead for maintaining indexes.

CONSTRAINED PLACEMENT. If more than one block is required to prevent starvation prior to the next read, intrafile seeks are necessary. Instead of avoiding intrafile seeks, another approach is to reduce them to a reasonable bound. This is referred to as the *constrained placement* approach.[1,7] Constrained placement techniques ensure that the separation between successive file blocks is bounded. The bound on separation is generally not enforced for each pair of successive blocks but only on average over a finite sequence of blocks (see Figure 4).

Constrained placement is particularly attractive when the block size must be small (for example, when using a conventional file system with block sizes tailored for text). Implementing constrained placement can require elaborate algorithms to assure that separation between blocks conforms to the required constraints. Furthermore, for constrained latency to yield its full benefits, the scheduling algorithm must immediately retrieve all blocks for a given stream before switching to any other stream. An algorithm like Scan, which orders blocks regardless of the stream they belong to, highly reduces the impact of constrained placement.[4]

LOG-STRUCTURE PLACEMENT. One way to reduce disk seeks is to adapt "log-structured" file systems.[5] When modifying blocks of data, log-structured systems do not store modified blocks in their original positions. Instead, all writes for all streams are performed sequentially in a large contiguous free space (see Figure 4). Therefore, instead of requiring a seek (and possibly intrafile seeks) for each stream writing, only one seek is required prior to a batch of writes. This leads to a dramatic performance improvement during recording.

A log-structured approach, however, does not guarantee any improvement in playback performance and is more complex to implement because modified blocks may change position. Consequently, log-structured file systems are best suited for multimedia servers that support extensive editing and are inappropriate for systems that are primarily read-only (for example, video-on-demand servers, which could likely implement writes in non-real time).

Special placement considerations apply when the media is encoded with variable bit-rate compression. Conventional fixed-sized clusters correspond to varying amounts of time, depending on the compression achieved. Alternately, the system can store data in clusters that correspond to a fixed amount of time, with a variable cluster size. Furthermore, compressed media quanta might not correspond to an even number of disk sectors, which raises questions about "packing" data.[2] With scalable compression, data must be carefully placed and managed to ensure efficient extraction of low-resolution subsets.

Data striping and data interleaving

If an entire multimedia file is stored on one disk, the number of concurrent accesses to that file are limited by disk throughput. One approach to overcome this limitation is to maintain multiple copies of the file on different disks, but this is expensive because it requires additional storage space. A more effective approach is to scatter the multimedia file across multiple disks. This scattering can be achieved by using two techniques: data striping and data interleaving.

RAID (redundant array of inexpensive disks) technology has popularized the use of parallel access to an array of disks. Under the RAID scheme, data is "striped" across each disk (see Figure 5). Physical sector 1 of each disk is accessed in parallel as a large logical sector 1. Physical sector 2 of each disk is accessed as logical sector 2, and so on. In this configuration, the disks in the set are *spindle synchronized* and operate in lock-step parallel mode. Because accesses are performed in parallel, logical and physical blocks have identical access times. Therefore, the transfer rate is effectively increased by the number of drives involved.

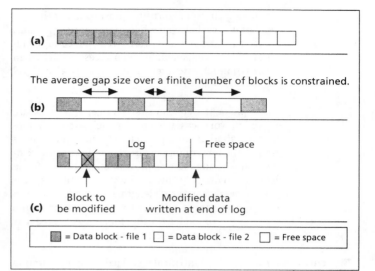

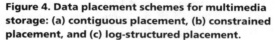

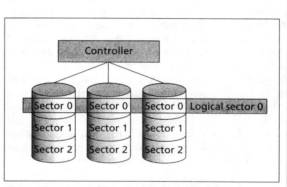

The average gap size over a finite number of blocks is constrained.

Figure 4. Data placement schemes for multimedia storage: (a) contiguous placement, (b) constrained placement, and (c) log-structured placement.

Figure 5. Striped data accessed in parallel.

With their increased transfer rates, disk arrays are a good solution to the problem of the CM's high bandwidth requirements. However, striping cannot improve the seek time and rotational latency incurred during retrieval. The throughput of each disk in the array is still determined by the ratio of the useful read time to the total (read plus seek) time. As with the single disk configuration, disk throughput can be improved by increasing the size of the physical block. However, this would also increase the logical block size and consequently lengthen startup delays and enlarge buffer space requirements per stream.

In *data interleaving*, the blocks of the media file are interleaved across the disk array for storage, with successive file blocks stored on different disks. A simple interleave pattern stores the blocks cyclically across an array of *N* disks. The disks in the array are not spindle synchronized, and they operate independently.

Two data retrieval methods can be used with this organization. The first one follows the data striping model, whereby one block is retrieved from each disk in the array for each stream in every round. This method ensures a balanced load for the disks but requires more buffer space per stream. In the second method, data is extracted from one of the disks for a given stream in each round (see Table 2). Data retrieval for the stream thus cycles through all disks in N successive rounds. In each round, the retrieval load must be balanced across the disks to maximize throughput of N disks. Because each stream cycles through the array, this load can be balanced by staggering the streams. With staggering, all streams still have the same round length, but each stream considers the round to begin at a different time, so that their requests are staggered rather than simultaneous.

A combination of data striping and data interleaving can scatter the media file across a large number of disks attached to a networked cluster of servers. This technique lets a scalable video server be constructed that can serve many streams from a single copy of the media file. Moreover, redundancy techniques can be applied to the media file to increase availability and throughput.

Tertiary storage and hierarchies

Although the performance of fixed magnetic disks makes them desirable for CM applications, their high cost per gigabyte makes them impractical as the sole storage medium for a large-scale server (such as a video-on-demand server with hundreds of feature-length titles, each being several Gbytes in size even with MPEG-2 compression). For large-scale servers, economics will dictate the use of large tertiary storage devices such as tape and optical jukeboxes.

Tertiary storage devices are highly cost-effective and offer enormous storage capacities by means of robotic arms that serve removable tapes or disks to a few reading devices (see Table 3). However, their slow random access—due to long seeking and loading times—and relatively low data transfer rates make them inappropriate for CM playback. Consequently, large-scale servers will need to combine the cost-effectiveness of tertiary storage with the high performance of fixed magnetic disks. The storage subsystem will need to be organized as a hierarchy and the magnetic disks used as a cache for the tertiary storage devices.

Several approaches are possible for managing such a storage hierarchy. One approach is to use the magnetic disks only as storage for the beginning segments of the multimedia files. These segments can reduce the start-up latency and ensure smooth transitions

in the playback.[8] When media files are to be played back, another alternative is to move the entire file from tertiary storage to the disks. A drawback with this approach is that the startup delays associated with loading the entire file will be very high for large files like videos. Fortunately, for applications like video-on-demand, relatively few titles will generally be popular at any given time, while older and more obscure titles will be seldom accessed. Thus a policy of replacing the least recently used titles to make room in the cache for requested items is likely to be effective.

Additionally, for a large class of applications, the user access pattern is often predictable well in advance. For example, an instructor may predict that recent class lectures as well as material related to an upcoming test are more likely to be accessed than other class material. Distributed hierarchical storage extends these ideas by distributing multiple magnetic disk-based caches across a network. Although distributed caches in general must deal with cache consistency, this problem will not apply to most CM applications, which will generally be read-only or will have single-user access (it's hard to imagine widespread demand for simultaneous editing of the same audio or video file among multiple users).

The architecture of a proposed distributed hierarchical storage management system will consist of several video storage servers that act as on-line cache for information stored permanently on archive servers (see Figure 6).[9,10] In addition to maintaining one or more tertiary storage devices that contain the video files as well as the corresponding metadata, each archive server will also provide an interface to let users query the database to locate pertinent video files and schedule their retrieval.

IMPLEMENTING A MULTIMEDIA FILE SYSTEM

Designers of a multimedia file system must concern themselves with client/server interaction, tracking data through file structures, and creating, editing, and retrieving multimedia objects.

Table 2. Reading interleaved data (method 2).

Round	Disk 1	Disk 2	Disk 3
1	File A, block 1	File B, block 1	File C, block 1
2	File C, block 2	File A, block 2	File B, block 2
3	File B, block 3	File C, block 3	File A, block 3
4	File A, block 4	File B, block 4	File C, block 4

Table 3. Tertiary storage devices in a multimedia system.

Feature	Magnetic disk	Optical disk	Low-end tape	High-end tape
Capacity	9 Gbytes	200 Gbytes	500 Gbytes	10 Tbytes
Mount time	None	20 seconds	60 seconds	90 seconds
Transfer rate (per second)	2 Mbytes	300 Kbytes	100 Kbytes	1 Mbyte
Cost	$5,000	$50,000	$50,000	$500,000–$1,000,000
Cost per Gbyte	$555	$125	$100	$50

Interfacing with the client

Multimedia storage servers can be classified as *file-system oriented* or *stream oriented*. A client of a file-system-oriented server sees the multimedia object as a large file and uses typical file system operations such as open, close, and read to access the file. The client issues read requests to the server periodically to read data from the file. The server can use the open operation to enforce admission control and initiate prefetching of the multimedia file. The server can also periodically prefetch from the disk system into memory buffers to service read requests with minimal delay. In this model, the client can implement operations, such as pause and resume, by simply ceasing to issue read requests.

The client of a stream-oriented multimedia server issues commands such as *play, pause,* and *resume* to the server. The server uses the stream concept to deliver data continuously to the client. After the client initiates stream playback, the server periodically sends data to the user at the selected rate without further read requests from the user.

Moving data is another key issue in the client/server interface. Typically, data being transferred from one process (such as the server kernel) to another process (such as the client) is copied. For CM streams, copying is unnecessary, takes extra time, and produces extra traffic on the system bus. Because of CM's high throughput requirements, it is desirable to share memory or remap the memory into another address space to avoid data copying.

File-retrieval structures

A fundamental issue in implementing a file system is to keep track of which disk blocks belong to each file, keeping a map, essentially, of how to travel from block to block in a file. Of course this is not a concern for contiguous files. File mapping for scattered files can be accomplished in several ways, each with its own merit.

A simple solution for mapping blocks is a *linked list*, where each block contains a pointer to the next block in the file. The file descriptor only needs to contain a pointer to the first block of the file. A serious limitation of this approach, however, is that random access is highly inefficient as accessing a random block requires accessing all previous blocks.

To improve random-access performance, some conventional file systems (like DOS) have used a file allocation table, with a table entry for each block on the disk. Each table entry maintains a pointer to the next block of a file. Assuming that the entire FAT is kept in main memory, random access can be very fast. However, it might not be possible to keep a FAT in main memory for the large file systems expected in multimedia servers.

INDEXES. A FAT contains information about the entire file system, but only a portion of this information relating to currently open files is needed. Storing an index for each

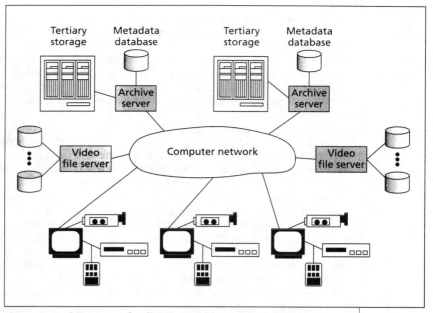

Figure 6. Architecture of a distributed hierarchical video-on-demand server.

file separately (for instance, I-nodes in Unix) can exploit this situation. These indexes can be simple lists or hierarchical structures such as binary trees (to make the process of searching more efficient). Rapid random access is still possible, but the need to keep the entire FAT in main memory is lessened.

A potential drawback to storing file indexes separately occurs when all open file indexes cannot be kept in main memory in their entirety, as is possible with large CM files. (For example, a server with a small selection of long videos may have all the videos open for playback at once. The open indexes would therefore map all the allocated file space.) Retrieving a CM file involves retrieving blocks of the index in real time, in addition to the blocks of the file itself. It is true that the index retrieval demands less in terms of bandwidth, but it nonetheless consumes resources. In fact, managing such small bandwidth streams might require special algorithms to keep them from using a disproportionate amount of system resources.

A HYBRID SOLUTION. An obvious solution to excessively using resources is to implement a linked list so that real-time playback can follow pointers contained in the data blocks. Random seeks can be achieved quickly through the index without reserving real-time resources. This would add system overhead in keeping both the index and the link pointers up to date, but for applications that perform little editing, such as video-on-demand, the overhead might be worthwhile. (To support fast forward and rewind, it may be necessary to store extra pointers, as the blocks will not be visited in normal sequential order.)

Finally, a multimedia server must accommodate the fact that each multimedia object can contain media information in various formats (such as video, audio, and textual).

Besides maintaining file maps for each media file, the server must maintain characteristics of each multimedia object, such as its creator, length, access rights and, most important, intermedia synchronization relationships.

Editing multimedia objects

Multimedia objects comprise media components (such as audio or video files, images, and text) that are presented to the user in a coordinated fashion. When a large media component is copied into more than one object, the copying operation consumes significant time and space. To minimize copying, the multimedia file system can consider media component files immutable and enable editing by manipulating pointers to the media component files (or portions of files). Once a media component file has no multimedia object referring to it, it can be deleted by the server to reclaim memory. A "garbage collection" algorithm that uses a reference count mechanism called *interests*, such as the one presented by Terry and Swinehart[11] in the Etherphone system, can be used for this purpose.

When performing small insertions, using a pointer may not be worthwhile (or feasible) in terms of maintaining continuous playback. Also, CM files might need small deletions. As small as such operations might be, the naive approach—simply rewriting the file from the edited point on—can be extremely time-consuming for large CM files. If the section being inserted or deleted is an integral number of blocks, then the file map could simply be modified, but usually the section will not be such a convenient size. It is possible to perform insertion and deletions in time, proportional to the size of the insertion/deletion rather than to the whole file, by implementing a scheme where blocks must be filled to a certain minimum level to support continuous retrieval. The insertion/deletion will consist of some number of full blocks plus a remaining partially filled block. All the blocks are then inserted/deleted by modifying the file map, and then data is distributed among adjacent blocks of the file to meet the required fill level.

INTERACTIVE CONTROL FUNCTIONS. A multimedia server must also support interactive control functions such as pause/resume, fast forward, and fast backward. The pause/resume operations pose a significant challenge for buffer management because they interfere with the sharing of a multimedia stream among different viewers.[12] The fast-forward and fast-backward operations can be implemented either by playing back media at a higher rate than normal or by continuing playback at the normal rate while skipping some data. Since the former approach can significantly increase the data rate, its direct implementation is impractical. The latter approach, on the other hand, can also be complicated by the presence of interdata dependencies (for example, compression schemes that store only differences from previous data).

ACHIEVING FAST FORWARD. Several approaches can achieve fast forward through data skipping. One method is to create a separate, highly compressed (and lossy) file. For example, the MPEG-2 draft standard proposes the creation of special, highly compressed D video frames that do not have any interframe dependency to support video browsing. During retrieval, when fast-forward operation is required, the playback would switch from the normal file (which could itself be compressed but still maintain acceptable quality levels) to the highly compressed file. This option is attractive because it does not require any special storage methods or file postprocessing. It does however require additional storage space and, moreover, the resulting output has poor resolution because of the high compression.

Another way to achieve fast forward is to categorize each block as either relevant or irrelevant to fast forward. During normal operation, both types of blocks are retrieved, and the media stream is reconstructed by recombining the blocks either in the server or in the client station. Alternatively, during fast-forward operation only the fast-forward blocks are retrieved and transmitted.

Scalable compression schemes are readily adapted to this sort of use, although the drawback here is that it poses additional overheads for splitting and recombining blocks. Furthermore, with compression schemes that store differences from previous data, most data will be relevant to fast forward. For example, the I and P frames of MPEG are much larger than the average frame size. This means that the data rate required during fast-forward operations would be higher than normal.

Chen, Kandlur, and Yu[13] offer a different solution for fast-forward operations on MPEG video files. Their method performs block skipping through an intelligent arrangement of blocks (called segments) that takes into account the interframe dependencies of the compressed video. Entire video segments are skipped during fast-forward operations, and the viewer sees normal resolution video with gaps. Their solution also addresses the placement and retrieval of blocks on a disk array using block interleaving.

MULTIMEDIA STORAGE SERVERS DIFFER FROM conventional storage servers to an extent that requires significant changes in design. Graphical user interfaces have already tremendously influenced computing, calling for faster and more efficient hardware, and for specialized algorithms. Multimedia interfaces, and CM in particular, are even more revolutionary because they introduce real-time demands and consume system resources in unprecedented quantities.

Commercially available multimedia server products underscore progress made thus far. For example, in the LAN environment, products like IBM's LANServer Ultimedia serve video and audio to suitably equipped PCs. In the video-on-demand arena, there are products like Oracle's Media Server, which is slated to deliver approximately 25,000 video streams.

The study of multimedia systems continues to flourish and to confirm that merely tacking multimedia onto conventional systems is inadequate. If multimedia is to succeed, fundamental changes must be made with respect to real-time issues: The services supported by an operating system or network must be expanded, data must be stored and retrieved for real-time retrieval rates and to meet client expectations, and user interfaces must be rethought once again to fulfill multimedia's promise of interactivity.   ∎

Acknowledgments

The authors acknowledge the coordination and detailed suggestions of Arturo Rodriguez. This work was partially supported by MPR Teltech Ltd. and the British Columbia Science Council.

References

1. D. Anderson, Y. Osawa, and R. Govindan, "A File System for Continuous Media," *ACM Trans. Computer Systems*, Vol. 10, No. 4, Nov. 1992, pp. 311-337.

2. D.J. Gemmell and S. Christodoulakis, "Principles of Delay Sensitive Multimedia Data Storage and Retrieval," *ACM Trans. Information Systems*, Vol. 10, No. 1, Jan. 1992, pp. 51-90.

3. A.L. Narasimha Reddy and J.C. Wyllie, "I/O Issues in a Multimedia System," *Computer*, Vol. 27, No. 3, Mar. 1994, pp. 69-74.

4. D.J. Gemmell and J. Han, "Multimedia Network File Servers: Multichannel Delay Sensitive Data Retrieval," *Multimedia Systems*, Vol. 1, No. 6, Apr. 1994, pp. 240-252.

5. P. Lougher and D. Shepherd, "The Design of a Storage Server for Continuous Media," *The Computer J.*, Vol. 36, No. 1, Feb. 1993, pp. 32-42.

6. H.M. Vin and P. Venkat Rangan, "Designing a Multi-User HDTV Storage Server," *IEEE J. Selected Areas in Comm.*, Vol. 11, No. 1, Jan. 1993, pp. 153-164.

7. P. Venkat Rangan and H.M. Vin, "Efficient Storage Techniques for Digital Continuous Multimedia," *IEEE Trans. Knowledge and Data Engineering*, Vol. 5, No. 4, Aug. 1993, pp. 564-573.

8. T. Mori et al., "Video-on-Demand System using Optical Mass Storage System," (Japanese) *J. Applied Physics*, Vol. 1, No. 11B, Nov. 1993, pp. 5,433-5,438.

9. C. Federighi and L.A. Rowe, "The Design and Implementation of the UCB Distributed Video-On-Demand System," *Proc. IS&T/SPIE 1994 Int'l Symp. Electronic Imaging: Science and Technology*, Int'l Soc. for Optical Eng., P.O. Box 10, Bellingham, Wash., 98227-0010, 1994, pp. 185-197.

10. L.A. Rowe, J. Boreczky, and C. Eads, "Indexes for User Access to Large Video Databases," *Proc. IS&T/SPIE 1994 Int'l. Symp. Electronic Imaging: Science and Technology*, Int'l Soc. for Optical Eng., P.O. Box 10, Bellingham, Wash., 98227-0010, 1994, pp. 150-161.

11. D.B. Terry and D.C. Swinehart, "Managing Stored Voice in the Etherphone System," *ACM Trans. Computer Systems*, Vol. 6, No. 1, Feb. 1988, pp. 3-27.

12. A. Dan, D. Sitaram, and P. Shahabuddin, "Dynamic Batching Policies for an On-Demand Video Server," *Proc. ACM Multimedia 94*, ACM Press, New York, Oct. 1994, pp. 15-24.

13. M. Chen, D.D. Kandlur, and P.S. Yu, "Support for Fully Interactive Playout in a Disk-Array-Based Video Server," *Proc. ACM Multimedia 94*, ACM Press, New York, Oct. 1994.

D. James Gemmell *is a PhD candidate at Simon Fraser University. His research interests include delay-sensitive multimedia systems, focusing on server storage and retrieval.*

Gemmell received a BSc degree from Simon Fraser University in 1988 and an MSc degree from the University of Waterloo in 1990, both in computer science.

Harrick M. Vin *is an assistant professor of computer science and the director of the Distributed Multimedia Computing Laboratory at the University of Texas at Austin. His research interests are multimedia systems, high-speed networking, mobile computing, and large-scale distributed systems. He has co-authored more than 35 papers in leading journals and conferences on multimedia systems.*

Vin received a BTech degree in computer science and engineering in 1987 from the Indian Institute of Technology in Bombay. He received an MS in 1988 from Colorado State University and a PhD in 1993 from University of California at San Diego, both in computer science.

Dilip D. Kandlur *is on the research staff at the IBM T. J. Watson Research Center in Yorktown Heights, N.Y., where he has worked on designing and implementing the Multimedia Multiparty Teleconferencing system. His research interests include video/audio support for desktop collaboration, multimedia networking, and multimedia storage management.*

Kandlur received a BTech degree in computer science and engineering from the Indian Institute of Technology in Bombay in 1985. He received MSE and PhD degrees, also in computer science and engineering, from the University of Michigan, Ann Arbor, in 1987 and 1991 respectively. Kandlur is a member of the IEEE Computer Society.

P. Venkat Rangan *founded and directs the Multimedia Laboratory at the University of California at San Diego, where he is also associate professor of computer science. His research interests include multimedia on-demand servers, media synchronization, and multimedia communication and collaboration.*

Rangan received a PhD degree in computer science from the University of California at Berkeley in 1988, and a BTech degree in electrical engineering from the Indian Institute of Technology in Madras in 1984, where he received the President of India gold medal. Rangan recently received the National Science Foundation Young Investigator Award. He is editor-in-chief of the ACM/Springer-Verlag Multimedia Systems journal. Rangan is a member of IEEE.

Lawrence A. Rowe *is a coguest editor of this theme issue. His biography appears following the guest editors' introduction on p. 22.*

Readers can contact James Gemmell at the School of Computer Sci., Simon Fraser Univ., Burnaby, B.C. Canada, V5A 1S6, e-mail dgemmell@sfu.ca; Harrick Vin at Dept. of Computer Sci., Univ. of Texas at Austin, 78712-1188, e-mail vin@cs.utexas.edu; Dilip Kandlur at IBM, T.J. Watson Research Ctr., 30 Saw Mill River Rd., Hawthorne, N.Y. 10532 e-mail kandlur@watson.ibm.com; and Venkat Rangan at Computer Sci. Dept., Univ. of California at San Diego, 92093-0114, e-mail venkat@chinmaya.ucsd.edu.

Random RAIDs with Selective Exploitation of Redundancy for High Performance Video Servers*

Yitzhak Birk

birk@ee.technion.ac.il

+972 4 829 4637

Electrical Engineering Department

Technion – Israel Institute of Technology

Haifa 32000, ISRAEL

Abstract

This paper jointly addresses the issues of load balancing, fault tolerance, responsiveness, agility, streaming capacity and cost-effectiveness of high-performance storage servers for data-streaming applications such as video-on-demand. Striping the data of each movie across disks in a "random" order balances the load while breaking any correlation between user requests and the access pattern to disks. Parity groups are of fixed-size, comprising consecutive blocks of a movie and a derived parity block, and resulting in "random" disk-members of any given group. Consequently, the load of masking a faulty disk is shared by all disk drives, minimizing the degradation in streaming capacity. By using the redundant information to avoid accessing an overloaded disk drive, the occasional transient imbalance in disk load due to the randomization is partly prevented and, when occurring, can be circumvented. Finally and most important, making a distinction between data blocks and redundant blocks and using redundant blocks only when necessary is shown to substantially reduce required buffer sizes without giving up the benefits. The result is a simple, flexible and robust video-server architecture.

1 Introduction

A "video server" is a storage and communication system for data-streaming applications. These include the viewing of movies and video clips, and listening to audio. The primary measure of a video server's performance is the number of concurrent video streams that it can supply without glitches, subject to a sufficiently

prompt response to user requests.

As depicted in Fig. 1, a video server usually stores movies on magnetic disk drives, from which they are read into RAM buffers and are subsequently "streamed" onto a distribution network. The RAM serves as an adapter between the disk drives and the network: it receives data from disk in bulk, thereby permitting efficient operation of the drives; the interleaving of data for different streams onto the distribution network is carried out with a much finer granularity, thereby avoiding undesirable burstiness over the network. The use of tertiary storage for video servers has been shown to be mostly ineffective [1].

The need for a video server to be fault-tolerant and highly available used to be questioned: the viewing of movies is not a critical application, and loss of data is not an issue since additional copies of movies are always available. Moreover, disk drives and electronic components are extremely reliable, so a mean time between failures of weeks if not months can be assumed even for fairly large servers. However, for reasons such as load-balancing that will be explained shortly, the *failure mode* of such servers is problematic: the failure of a single disk drive is likely to result in an interruption of all active streams. A "blackout" every three months is clearly much more visible than independent interruptions to individual streams at the same rate. For this reason, high availability is a must.

The design of a video server is not a matter of feasibility. Rather, the issue is cost-effectiveness. Also, despite the fact that it is often viewed primarily as a storage server, its bandwidth often affects cost at least as much as storage capacity.

In this paper, we will exploit the unique characteristics of video servers in jointly addressing cost, performance and fault-tolerance, and providing various

---

*This work was begun while at Hewlett Packard Company Labs in Palo Alto, and parts of it may be covered by U.S. Patents. The author is grateful to Scientific and Engineering Software, Inc., for providing the Workbench simulation package.

DISK DRIVES

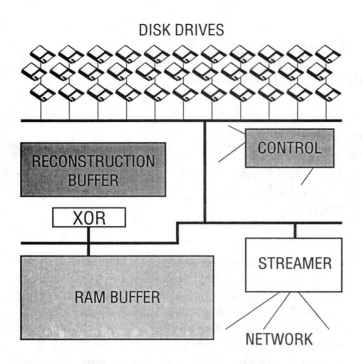

Figure 1: A typical video server. Data is stored on disk, read into RAM buffers, and then streamed onto a distribution network. Components also include intra-server communication, control and possible processing of the data for purposes such as fault-tolerance.

additional benefits. Our focus is on inter-disk data layout and scheduling. (Intra-disk issues, especially the accommodation of multi-zone recording, are addressed in [2][3][4].) We begin with a careful review of the characteristics of a video server and the applications for which it is used. The implications of those on the design are then examined, and current approaches to the design of servers are discussed in this context. We then present a new video-server architecture that jointly addresses all the problems that arise in the storage subsystem (including storage bandwidth and capacity, RAM buffers, intra-server communication overhead and fault-tolerance), and present simulation results that indicate the promise of our approach. The key idea in our approach is the use of randomization in data layout in order to solve certain problems, along with the selective exploitation of redundancy for the purpose of taming the randomization and sharply mitigating its undesirable side-effects. The result is a simple, cost-effective, agile and easily-testable server architecture.

The remainder of the paper is organized as follows. In section 2, we characterize a video server and the

requirements imposed on it, and raise a number of important issues pertaining to the cost-effectiveness of a design. In section 3, we progress through a sequence of video-server designs, solving certain problems and identifying new ones as we go along. In section 4 we present our approach, and simulation results are presented in section 5 along with additional insights. Section 6 discusses our approach, and section 7 offers concluding remarks.

2   Characteristics of a video server

In most applications of storage systems, the semantics of requests are "provide all the requested data as soon as possible", and a server is measured on the time until the last byte is received. In contrast, the intent of a request from a video server is "begin providing data as soon as possible, then continue providing it at the prescribed *rate*". The primary measure of a video server's performance is the number of concurrent video streams that it can supply without glitches, subject to a sufficiently prompt response to user requests.

A video server is a "real-time" system in the sense that it must provide a given amount of data per unit time (with some tolerance in one direction, namely excess data, and none in the other) and in the sense that it must respond to user requests within a short period of time. At the "micro" level, however, it differs dramatically from a true "real-time" system since, once the viewing of a video stream has started, the sequence of requests for data is known and requests occur at times that can be determined in advance. Moreover, since all the data (movie) is available at the outset, the server may mask disk latency by prefetching data into its buffers. With the exception of response to new user requests, a video server is thus best viewed a "data pump" rather than as an interactive system.

The two primary resources of a video server are its storage capacity and its storage (communication) bandwidth. Unfortunately, the two are embodied in disk drives and are thus coupled. So, in order to claim that a server can supply a given set of video streams based on the server's aggregate storage bandwidth, one must balance the communication load among all disk drives at all times, independently of viewing choices.

In many cases, the system cost for supporting a disk drive is independent of the drive's storage capacity, and even the cost of a disk drive is the sum of a fixed component and a linear one across a large range of capacities. It is therefore desirable to use high-capacity disk drives. However, using fewer storage devices means that each one must have higher bandwidth in order to meet the aggregate bandwidth requirement. Consequently, disk drives must be operated efficiently. This can be done by efficient seek algorithms in conjunction with early submission of requests (so as to effectively extend deadlines and permit more flexible disk-scheduling) [5] as well as by reading large chunks of data in each access.

"Video" is often associated with very high data rates. However, compressed digital video, which is being considered in this paper, requires very modest data rates, ranging from 150KB/s to some 600KB/s. The transfer rate of a modern disk drive is on the order of 5MB/s, i.e., much higher than the video rate. Throughout the paper, we will consider the ratio between a disk drive's effective transfer rate and the rate of a video stream, denoted dvr, and will show that it is a very important parameter.

RAM buffers in a video server are required for two purposes:

- *Starvation prevention.* Whenever there is a delay in the response of a disk drive to a read request, data is streamed from the buffer in order to mask the delay and prevent a glitch (starvation).

- *Overflow prevention.* Any data that is prefetched, e.g., to permit efficient operation of the disk drive, must be buffered. The large dvr, in conjunction with the desire to operate the disk drives efficiently, implies that data read from disk is held in RAM buffer for a long time (proportional to dvr), which increases the required amount of overflow buffer space.

Despite the fact that the two types of buffers are embodied in the same memory, it is important to observe an important difference between them: buffers for starvation prevention must be allocated in advance to every stream and filled with data, since when trouble strikes it is too late. In contrast, overflow buffers can be allocated dynamically on a need basis. We will return to this issue when simulation results are presented. For the above reasons and other ones, the required amount of RAM must not be overlooked when designing a video server.

3 Successive refinements of a basic architecture

The controllable components of server cost are RAM buffers and various overheads (storage capacity and bandwidth, for example). In this section, we discuss data layout and access scheduling in order to better understand the issues. We begin with data layout, and then move on to scheduling. We will use a

sequence of design approaches in order to unveil fundamental problems. These will later be addressed in our architecture.

3.1 Data striping for load-balancing

The only way of avoiding communication hot spots is to distribute the communication load among all disk drives uniformly under all circumstances. This can only be done by splitting the data of each movie among the drives in sufficiently small pieces, as this "striping" guarantees that all drives are equally utilized at all times. Moreover, since a disk drive's transfer rate is much higher than the data rate of a single video stream, frequent seeks are unavoidable and are not caused by the striping. So, striping each movie across many or all disks is a widely accepted approach.

The amount of data read from disk in a single access should be sufficiently large so as to keep the seek overhead in check, and the striping granularity should be equal to this amount. Throughout most of the paper, we will ignore seek overhead.

3.2 Fault tolerance

A disk drive can be modeled as either providing correct data or declaring itself faulty. Consequently, parity (XOR) information can be used to correct a single disk failure. This is exploited in various ways in redundant arrays of inexpensive disks (RAID)[6] in order to provide fault tolerance. An alternative approach is duplication of data, also referred to as "mirroring". Throughout the remainder of the paper, we will use M to denote the total number of disk drives in the server, and the size of a parity group will be denoted by $k + 1$. (In the case of mirroring, $k = 1$.)

3.3 RAID 3: a buffer-explosion problem

In a RAID 3 organization [6], data is striped very thinly across all disk drives ($k = M - 1$), and all are accessed simultaneously to service a single request. (One of the drives contains parity information which can be used to overcome a single disk failure.) The disk array thus has the appearance of a single high-capacity, high-bandwidth, highly-available disk drive.

Since, in a video server, the duration of a read is dictated by disk-efficiency considerations, accessing all disks concurrently on behalf of the same stream would result in a per-stream buffer size that is proportional to the number of disk drives. Since the server's streaming capacity is also proportional to the number of drives, total buffer size would increase quadratically with the number of drives. This approach, which has been employed in small video servers [7], is therefore indeed limited to very small servers.

3.4 Other regular layout and scheduling schemes

When viewed simplistically, the data-retrieval requirements imposed on a video server lend themselves to a round-robin layout of the data for any given movie across the disk drives, and an associated round-robin access schedule on behalf of the different video streams.

Approaches along this line include, for example, striping data across all drives but partitioning the drives into several parity groups. The access schedules to the different groups can be staggered relative to one another in order to prevent the buffer-explosion problem.

Unfortunately, and regardless of details, the placement of consecutive data chunks of any given movie in consecutive disks gives rise to several salient properties:

- There is a high correlation between the timing of user requests for streams from the same or different movies and the (temporal) load patterns on the disks. Moreover, patterns that arise tend to persist. This, combined with the limited scheduling flexibility, can create hot spots which must be masked by large buffers or restrict operation to low loads. Finally, even if one offers an algorithmic solution, it is extremely difficult to prove its potency in all cases, since it depends on user-generated scenarios.

- The round-robin data layout along with fixed-size parity groups results in a significant performance degradation upon disk failure. The group of $k+1$ drives that includes the failing drive loses $\frac{1}{k+1}$ of its bandwidth and is the weak link of a chain. Rebuilding the missing data onto a fresh replacement drive may even take up all the bandwidth.

- The apparent simplicity and efficiency of the "law and order" approach of highly regular layout and scheduling are not viable in practice: variability in disk performance, variable compression ratio, variable transfer rate (multi-zone recording) and other factors all break the regularity and mandate operation at light loads in order to provide sufficient slack. (The problem is akin to that of designing a synchronous pipeline from stages with variable execution times: the design must be based on the worst case.)

3.5 Randomized layout

Here, consecutive chunks of data for any given movie are stored on randomly-ordered disk drives. (In practice, we use some rules to govern the randomness so as to guarantee "short term" equal distribution of data across disks.) Moreover, fixed-size parity groups ($k << M$) are used to avoid the buffer-explosion problem. This randomization achieves two important goals:

1. It breaks the aforementioned correlations.

2. Any given disk drive equally participates in parity groups with all other disk drives. Consequently, when a drive fails, the load of covering for it is shared equally among all the remaining drives. Accordingly, performance degradation is minimal and remains small even during rebuild. A similar approach was proposed in a different context in [8] under the name "parity declustering". A much more restricted form of declustering was discussed in [9] in the context of fault-tolerant video servers, but ignored any variability in disk performance or video rate.

Unfortunately, randomization leaves problems such as the determination of performance by the slowest disk unsolved, and even creates a new problem, namely short-term hot spots. The former is due to the fact that, regardless of the details of the data layout, the load is distributed uniformly across all drives. The latter is due to the fact that, regardless of the exact arrival process of read-requests to the system, the process as seen by any given disk drive is similar to a Poisson process, and a disk can thus be viewed approximately as an M/D/1 queue. The "meaningfully thick" tail of the queue-length distribution of such a queue at heavy loads is long, and so is the delay that must be maskable with starvation buffers.

An alternative (or complementary) approach entails "scheduling into the future": if, when looking at the schedule, one observes that a presently-idle disk drive is soon to become overloaded, one reads from that drive in advance of the schedule in order to "smooth" the load [10]. This approach, however, cannot help when the load on the disks is unequal or their performance is not identical, since it is akin to taking a loan which must be repaid. One must also watch the impact on overflow buffer requirements very carefully.

3.6 Exploitation of redundancy for load balancing

Although redundancy was originally intended for fault-tolerance, its usefulness for performance enhancement has also been noted: in 1975, Maxemchuk proposed to partition a message into m packets, compute r redundant ones such that the original message can be reconstructed from any sufficiently large subset of the $m + r$ packets, send those packets over different paths and use the earliest arrivers to reconstruct the message [11]. He showed that this substantially reduced delay and provided fault-tolerance. Similar observations were later made by Rabin [12] and dubbed "information dispersal algorithm". This approach, cast in terms of disk arrays, would entail submitting requests to all the disk drives holding a given parity group, and using the first ones that arrive to reconstruct the data. With parity groups of size $k + 1$, this would entail a storage-bandwidth overhead of $1/k$, which is undesirable. This is alluded to by Bestavros [13] in a paper that focuses on the fault-tolerance advantages of IDA over multi-parity schemes.

Unlike in communication networks, in storage systems it is often possible to know the expected response time of different disk drives at any given time, based on the pending requests. Accordingly, one may select a subset of size k from among the $k + 1$ disks holding the chunks comprising a parity group based on this information and submit requests only to those, thereby avoiding the bandwidth overhead. This approach, used here and developed independently by Berson, Muntz and Wong [14], eliminates the storage-bandwidth overhead. As shown in [14] and in a later section of this paper, this use of redundancy effectively "clips" the tail of the queue-length distribution, resulting in the ability to guarantee low response times with very high probability. This, in turn, sharply reduces the requirement for "starvation" buffers whose purpose is to mask the delays. Additional important observations are included in the next section, in which we present our new architecture.

4   Selective exploitation of redundancy
4.1   Motivation and the basic scheme

In the cited work on exploitation of redundancy for load balancing, no distinction was made between "data" chunks and "redundant" chunks. Thus, a simple policy for exploitation of redundancy for the purpose of delay (and buffering) reduction in a video server might entail, for every parity group, reading from the k (out of $k + 1$) disk drives with the shortest queues.

In applications such as on-line transaction processing, wherein one typically accesses a single block that resides on a single disk drive, avoiding the reading of a particular data block would require the reading of the remainder of its parity group, namely k blocks. The resulting storage-bandwidth overhead is obviously unacceptable, so one would always access the data block unless the disk holding it is faulty.

At the other extreme, in applications that entail reading large amounts of contiguous data as fast as possible, the entire parity group is required as soon as possible, so (from a storage-bandwidth perspective) it doesn't mater which k of the $k + 1$ drives are accessed.

A video server presents yet another situation: the chunks comprising a parity group are all required, since they are consecutive chunks of the same movie. However, they are not all required immediately: if only data chunks are read, they can be read one at a time; in contrast, if parity is read instead of one of them, k chunks must be read before the one that wasn't read can be reconstructed. Those that are read prematurely can be thrown away and read again when needed, but this would double the required storage bandwidth, which is unacceptable. The alternative is to buffer them in "overflow" RAM until needed for streaming.

The above observations have led us to realize the importance of a distinction between the mere inclusion of redundancy and its actual exploitation: storing a parity chunk for every k data chunks is the inclusion, whereas reading it instead of a data chunk constitutes exploitation. Inclusion is a largely "static" decision, whereas exploitation can be decided dynamically. With a parity group of size $k + 1$, the required buffer size per stream is smaller by approximately a factor of $k/2$ if data chunks are read one at a time.

When no distinction is made between data chunks and redundant ones, the redundant chunk is exploited with probability $k/(k + 1)$, so buffer requirements would be almost as if k chunks must be read concurrently.

Based on the above, one might jump to the conclusion that the redundant chunks should not be used unless absolutely necessary to prevent buffer starvation for the stream. However, the issue is more subtle: in addition to solving an immediate problem for the stream in question, refraining from accessing an overloaded disk drive also helps balance queue lengths, and thus has both a remedial and a preventive effect. Exploiting the redundancy only when absolutely necessary would thus increase the frequency of "emergencies". It would, in fact, increase the frequency of emergencies that cannot be treated in full (more than one overloaded disk among those holding a parity group).

Our approach is therefore to strike a balance between the desire for greedy, short-term minimization of required buffer space and the need for a preventive load-balancing action. For example, we exploit the redundant chunk if and only if the queue length to one of the disks holding a data chunk is longer than a certain value and the queue to the disk holding the parity chunk is sufficiently shorter. We refer to our approach as *selective exploitation of redundancy*, and apply it in conjunction with randomized layout.

4.2   Fine tuning

Fine tuning is possible in numerous ways, some of which we explain below along with the rationale.

Choice of k. The straightforward trade-off is due to the fact that smaller k increases the flexibility of avoiding congested disk drives, but increases storage overhead. However, as pointed out in [14], as k approaches the number of disk drives, and especially when $k + 1$ equals the number of drives, load-balancing is guaranteed at all times. In the context of video servers, there are additional considerations that favor small k:

- The amount of data that must be buffered when reconstruction is employed is proportional to k. Taken to the extreme ($k = M - 1$), this becomes the buffer-explosion problem.

- In deciding whether to exploit the redundancy, we must consider the next k chunks of the movie. This, in turn, corresponds to a time window (into the future) whose size is proportional to k (the size of a data chunk is dictated by disk-efficiency considerations). As the window size increases, the snapshot of queue lengths becomes less and less relevant since many things can change by the time the data chunk of interest will have to be read. (Note that priorities are based on deadlines rather than FCFS.)

- The performance reduction during rebuilding increases as k increases, since more blocks must be read per single-block reconstruction.

In view of the above and due to the fact that the incremental storage-overhead savings with an increase in k diminish rather quickly, values of k between 3 and 5 appear the most sensible.

Criteria for redundancy-exploitation. Frequent exploitation of redundancy increases the required amount of "overflow" buffer space, since more chunks are read prematurely and must be buffered until streaming time. It also increases the memory-bandwidth overhead and the computation overhead. However, frequent (more aggressive) exploitation of redundancy improves load balancing, thereby helping clip the tails of the queue-length distributions. This, in turn, reduces the delay that must be maskable by buffers, thereby reducing the required amount of per-stream "starvation" buffers. The actual choice of parameters is best left to an implementation. Nonethe-

less, following is a brief description of the policies used in our simulations.

- The choice whether to exploit redundancy for a given sequence of k data chunks is based on the number of requests in the queue of the drive holding the first (earliest) data chunk and on that in the queue of the drive holding the parity chunk. This reflects the fact that the "normal" reading time of that data chunk is the soonest, and its queue length is the most meaningful. For redundancy to be exploited, we require that the "data" queue exceed a certain length, and that the "parity" queue be shorter by at least a certain amount. The choice of numbers is a simulation parameter; we used 8 and 4, respectively.

- Having decided to exploit parity, the $k - 1$ data chunks that are read and the parity chunk are all read with the same urgency. Consequently, the original reason for giving preference to the earliest chunk is largely gone. So, despite the fact that the decision whether or not to reconstruct one of the data chunks was made based on the earliest chunk, the data chunk that is reconstructed is the one whose drive is the most congested. It should be noted that, unless there is an immediate problem for the earliest chunk, the choice of a chunk for reconstruction should be biased against this chunk, since reconstruction can only be completed when all other chunks have arrived (maximum of several i.i.d. random variables), and the earliest chunk is the most vulnerable to a missed deadline.

- Basing our decision whether or not to exploit redundancy solely on queue lengths appears strange. For example, if the queue to the disk holding the first (earliest streaming) chunk is long, this doesn't necessarily imply a long delay for that chunk, since its priority may be high. However, whenever a queue is of a certain length, at least one of the enqueued requests will have to wait for a time corresponding to the length of that queue. Recalling that the role of load-balancing as a preventive measure is as important to our scheme as its role as a quick fix, and that with proper tuning our exploitation of redundancy is normally done as a preventive measure, explains our decision.

Submission of requests. Having made the decision which of $k + 1$ chunks (k data and one parity) to read, requests must be submitted to the individual disk queues. This entails two decisions: time of submission and priority. We next discuss those.

- A chunk's priority is determined by its streaming time. If needed for reconstruction, it is determined based on the earlier of its streaming time and that of the chunk for whose reconstruction it is required. (In our simulation, we always used the streaming time of the earliest chunk whenever redundancy was exploited. This was done in part for simplicity and in part in order to counteract the fact that reconstruction can only be completed when all chunks have been read.)

- Our decision whether or not to exploit redundancy is based only on queue lengths, regardless of priority. Accordingly, the mere enqueuing of a request in a drive's queue may discourage other arrivals to that queue, even if their priority is higher than those of already-enqueued requests. Whenever reconstruction is not used, we therefore intentionally delay the submission of requests for "late" chunks until a fixed time prior to their streaming time.

Possible extensions and refinements. One possible extension is to simulate a future time window (excluding new user requests) and use that in refining the policies. This would be an extension of the approach suggested in [10] to our case. Numerous others are possible as well, but we prefer to refrain from those if a simple approach works sufficiently well and leaves little room for improvement.

5 Simulation results

In this section, we present simulation results. The intention is not an exhaustive search through the design space. Rather, it is a demonstration of the merits of our approach even with limited optimizations. Also, in order to focus on first-order effects and since randomization tends to mask details, we kept things simple whenever possible.

We simulated a 30-disk system. A sequence of random permutations was used as the disk-order in laying out the chunks of any given movie. (Whenever $k+1$ divides M, this guarantees that the same disk is not used twice by the same parity group. In other cases, alternate permutations are picked randomly, and a constrained random permutation is placed between successive independent ones. This guarantees that a disk is never used twice by any given parity group while preventing sequences of dependencies from forming.)

Other approaches may be equally viable. Disk service time was assumed fixed and served as our unit of time. Seek and rotational latency were ignored (incorporated into the effective disk transfer rate). k-chunk requests for the different streams arrive in round-robin order, and the inter-arrival time is distributed uniformly between 0.5 and 1.5 times the mean value. Most of the studies were carried out with $k = 5$ and $dvr = 10$, but $k = 1, 4$ and $dvr = 5$ were used for comparison.

The system was simulated with no disk failures under a load of 0.95, and with a single disk failure under a load of 0.9 (this is actually a load of 0.93 because there are only 29 operational disk drives). Also, in both cases we introduced a small percentage ($\frac{2}{k}\%$) of "urgent" requests, corresponding to the need to respond promptly to viewer requests.

Requests for the first chunk in a group of k were submitted to the disk queues 20 time units prior to the streaming time; subsequent chunks were delayed by the inter-streaming times (dvr time units between consecutive chunks).

The figures below focus on the probability that the disk response time exceeds various values. This is a good indication of the ability to "clip" the tails of the queue-length distribution. However, the buffer sizes and response time to urgent chunks (representing viewer requests) are the true measures for comparison. We will discuss those as well.

In the figures, NER, FER and SER correspond to no-, full- and selective-exploitation of redundancy, respectively.

Fig. 2 depicts the probability that disk response time exceeds various values for the case of no faulty drives and no urgent requests. The load is 0.95, which is very high. The dramatic effect of exploitation of redundancy is clearly visible. (Note the logarithmic scale.) For example, the response time that is exceeded with probability of at most 0.0001 (corresponding to once per 100-minute movie) is reduced by a factor of two when redundancy is exploited with $k = 5$ and by another factor of two when mirroring is employed.

The difference between full exploitation of redundancy (picking the parity chunk whenever the queue to its disk is shorter than one of the queues to the data chunks) and selective exploitation is small. However, there is a big difference in the overhead due to exploitation of redundancy, as will be seen later.

Fig. 3 depicts similar plots for the case of a faulty drive and/or a small percentage of urgent chunks. The top curve depicts the case of a faulty drive (R=0.90)

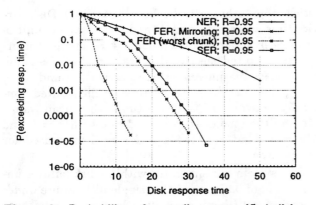

Figure 2: Probability of exceeding a specified disk response time vs. that response time: no exploitation of redundancy, selective exploitation, full exploitation and mirroring. No disk failures. $k = 5$; $dvr = 10$.

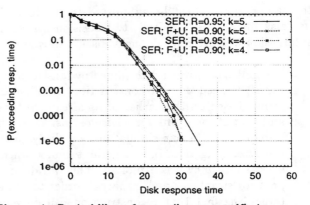

Figure 4: Probability of exceeding a specified response time vs. that response time: selective exploitation of redundancy. $k = 4, 5$; with and without faulty disk and urgent requests.

and exploitation of redundancy only when the faulty drive contains a requested data chunk. The cluster of curves includes the cases of selective exploitation for all the combinations of urgent chunks and/or a faulty drive, as well as the cases of no faulty drives (R=0.95). The leftmost plot depicts the response time to urgent requests. Again, the benefits of exploitation of redundancy are very clear, and the scheme works well even with a faulty drive at a very high load of 0.93 (on the remaining disks).

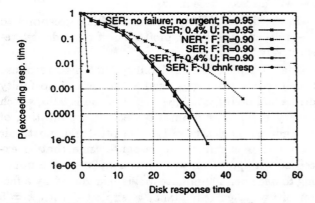

Figure 3: Probability of exceeding a specified response time vs. that response time: exploitation of redundancy only for fault tolerance; selective exploitation. With and without a faulty disk and urgent requests. Prompt response to urgent chunks is shown on the left. $k = 5$; $dvr = 10$.

Fig. 4 depicts similar plots for $k = 5$ and $k = 4$, focusing on selective exploitation. A small advantage for $k = 4$ is visible.

The simulation also tracked the total buffer occupancy and, for each chunk, recorded the difference

between its streaming time and the time at which it emerged from the disks into the buffer. Dividing the buffer occupancy by the number of streams yields the required per-stream (amortized) overflow buffer size. (The number of streams equals the number of drives times dvr.) If chunks arrive post-deadline by t time units, a glitch could have been avoided if a starvation buffer of size $\frac{t}{dvr}$ were allocated to each stream. Consequently, by picking an acceptable glitch probability, one can compute the total amount of required buffer space as well as the amount of data that should be buffered for a stream before its streaming commences.

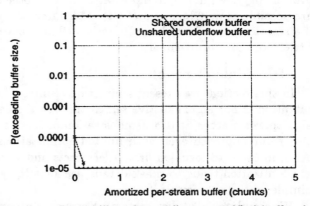

Figure 5: Probability of exceeding a specified buffer size (per stream). The overflow buffer is shown on the right and the underflow (starvation) — on the left. Selective exploitation of redundancy; faulty drive and urgent requests; $R = 0.90$; $k = 5$; $dvr = 10$.

Fig. 5 depicts the results for the case of selective exploitation of redundancy with a faulty disk and urgent chunks. One can see that a buffer of size 2.6 per chunk suffices. These results are the most meaningful ones,

Red. Exp.	Load	k	dvr	F	U	S.T.	Tot. Buff	Buff/ strm	pExp
NER	0.95	5	10	n	n	−35	675	5.75	0
FER	0.95	1	10	n	n	4.5	539	1.2	0.35
FERw	0.95	5	10	n	n	−05	991	3.8	0.75
FER1	0.95	5	10	n	n	−02	876	3.1	0.44
SER	0.95	5	10	n	n	−02	724	2.6	0.15
SER	0.95	5	10	n	y	−05	722	2.6	0.15
SER	0.90	5	10	y	n	−02	750	2.7	0.26
SER	0.90	5	10	y	y	−03	749	3.8	0.26
NER*	0.90	5	10	n	y	−20	718	4.4	0.16
SER	0.95	5	5	n	n	−07.3	450	4.5	0.13
SER	0.90	5	5	y	y	−13.6	460	5.7	0.26
SER	0.95	4	10	n	n	−01.3	685	2.4	0.13
SER	0.90	4	10	y	y	−01.0	686	2.4	0.22

Table 1: Summary of results for a permissible glitch probability of 10^{-4}. The first columns refers to redundancy exploitation (FERw and FER1 correspond, respectively, to full exploitation based on a comparison between the parity queue and the longest data queue or that of the first data chunk; NER* refers to exploitation of redundancy only when a requested data chunk resides in the faulty drive). F and U refer to faulty drive and urgent chunks, respectively. S.T. is the spare time remaining between the arrival of a chunk into the buffer and its streaming time (negative corresponds to a missed deadline). Tot. Buff. is the total overflow buffer used, and Buff/strm is the derived amortized per-stream total buffer requirement. Finally, pExp is the probability of exploiting redundancy.

since a change of policy can shift buffer requirement from one type to the other.

The most interesting results are depicted in Table 1. In the first batch of rows, we see that the required amount of RAM with selective exploitation is actually smaller than with full exploitation and has a much lower computation and memory-bandwidth overhead (lower probability of exploitation and the resulting need to reconstruct a data chunk).

The second batch shows that SER maintains a substantial advantage over NER even in the presence of a faulty drive. A lower value of dvr increases buffer size, since each chunk suffices for less streaming time.

Finally, $k = 4$ requires substantially smaller buffers in the presence of a faulty drive.

Simulations with different arrival patterns and variable disk service time yielded similar results. This also suggests that the variable transfer rate due to multi-zone recording can be accommodated automatically so long as placement is also randomized at the intra-disk level.

6 Discussion

We have seen that randomized (or other irregular) data layout in conjunction with selective exploitation of redundancy for load-balancing and avoiding occasional trouble permits operation at extremely heavy loads with very reasonable buffering and excellent response to urgent requests. We now shift our attention to other issues, such as communication overhead.

Storage-bandwidth overhead with our scheme is zero, since we read the same number of chunks regardless of whether redundancy is exploited. Similarly, communication overhead on the distribution network is zero, since reconstruction of missing chunks is carried out in the server.

Storage overhead is minimal ($1/k$) and is required for fault-tolerance. The same goes for computation of XOR and related memory traffic, since we exploit redundancy for load balancing with a relatively low probability.

Burstiness of traffic within the server is minimal, since we are operating at heavy load and the disks send data most of the time, regardless of what streams or parity groups the data belongs to. Also, the queueing delays were included in the simulation and starvation buffers were added as required. Finally, with the emergence of very-high-bandwidth disk interconnects, we expect burstiness of traffic within the server not to be very important.

We are presently in early stages of implementation of our architecture. We are constructing a Pentium-Pro based server with between 16 and 24 disk drives. The distribution network will include four 100base T Fast Ethernet lines and possibly a 155Mbps ATM line. The project is being carried out under Windows NT.

If one assumes the availability of some storage at the user end, a distributed implementation is also possible. One option would be a central server which delegates the XOR operations to the clients; another would distribute the server.

Design and operation become simpler when one employs replication instead of lower-overhead schemes such as parity. The main reason is that no operations need to be carried out among blocks. An interesting server that employs duplication is Microsoft's Tiger [15]. However, Tiger exploits the redundancy only when the primary copy is on a faulty disk or computer. Also, the operation of Tiger assumes streams with fixed data rates and identical disk drives. It may be interesting to apply our approach to Tiger, thereby increasing its robustness and agility, and permitting it to operate at very heavy loads without simplifying assumptions. One must, of course, carefully consider control traffic and latencies in this case.

Finally, it is important to summarize some of the key observations that underly our approach:

- Exploitation of redundancy in video servers is costly, since data that is read prematurely must be buffered.

- The high ratio of disk rate to video rate sharply reduces the amount of buffer space that is required to mask queuing delays.

- Related to the above, it is permissible to encounter queues that are not empty or nearly so.

- Once the operating point does not assume nearly-empty queues, there is a possibility for carrying out some seek-related optimizations in the disk drives. These could improve the results.

- For the same reason, the sensitivity to variability in disk service time is sharply reduced.

7　Conclusions

The use of randomized layout in conjunction with selective exploitation of redundancy for load-balancing solves a large number of problems that arise in the design of a video server, paving the way to the construction of a simple, robust, flexible, high-performance video server. Any number of non-identical disk drives can be employed; streams needn't have fixed data rates; urgent user requests can be handled immediately without causing glitches in ongoing streams. Also, performance evaluation is simple since the randomized layout makes system performance depend only on the aggregate load. Finally, all this is attained with very small buffer requirements due to the selective exploitation of redundancy. Interestingly, this stochastic design enables us to give firmer (and higher) performance guarantees than would be possible with a more regular design. The reason, of course, is the underlying uncertainty regarding viewer requests and resulting load patterns.

The difference between architectures that do not exploit redundancy for load-balancing (e.g., use only smart scheduling, looking into the future, etc.) and the architecture described in·this paper is fundamental: with the former schemes, the amount of work that must be done by any given disk cannot be changed, whereas the exploitation of redundancy permits it to

be changed to some extent. While scheduling-only approaches can provide a some of the features claimed for our architecture, they are inherently incapable of providing others.

Finally, selective exploitation of redundancy appears to be useful in a variety of application domains, as demonstrated in [16] for distributed systems. We are continuing to explore its applicability and merits in various contexts.

Acknowledgment. The simulations were carried out using the Workbench simulation package by Scientific and Engineering Software, Inc.

References

[1] M.G. Kienzle, A. Dan, D. Sitaram and W. Tetzlaff, "Using tertiary storage in video-on-demand servers", *Proc. IEEE CompCon*, 1995, pp. 225–233.

[2] S.R. Heltzer, J.M. Menon and M.F. Mitoma, "Logical data tracks extending among a plurality of of zones of physical tracks of one or more disk devices", *U.S. Patent No. 5,202,799*, April 1993.

[3] Y. Birk, "Track-Pairing: a novel data layout for VOD servers with multi-zone-recording disks", *IEEE 1995 Int'l conf. on Multimedia Comp. and Sys.* (ICMCS95), Washington, D.C., May 15-18, 1995. Also, Hewlett Packard Technical Report HPL-95-24, March 1995.

[4] S. Chen and M. Thapar, "Zone-Bit-Recording Enhanced Video Data Layout Strategies", *Proc. of 4th Int'l Workshop on Modeling, Analysis, and Simulation of Computer and Telecommunication Systems (MASCOTS'96)*, San Jose, CA, Feb. 1996, pp.29-35. Also, Hewlett Packard Technical Report HPL-TR-95-124.

[5] A.L. Narasimha Reddy and J. Wyllie, "Disk scheduling in a multimedia I/O system," *Proc. ACM Multimedia* 1993, pp. 225–233.

[6] D.A. Patterson, G. Gibson and R.H. Katz, "A case for redundant arrays of inexpensive disks (RAID)", *Proc. ACM SIGMOD*, pp. 109–116, June 1988.

[7] F.A. Tobagi, J. Pang, R. Baird and M. Gang, "Streaming RAID — A disk array management system for video files", *Proc. 1st ACM Int'l Conf. on Multimedia*, Aug. 1–6, 1993, Anaheim CA.

[8] M. Holland and G.A. Gibson, "Parity declustering for continuous operation in redundant disk

arrays," *Fifth Int'l Conf. on Architectural Support for Programming Lang. and Operating Sys. (ASPLOS-V)* SIGPLAN Not. (USA), SIGPLAN Notices, vol.27, no.9, p. 23-35 1992.

[9] S. Berson, L. Golubchik and R.R. Muntz, "Fault tolerant design of multimedia servers," *Proc. SIGMOD '95*, San Jose, CA, May 1995. (Also, Technical Report No. CSD-940040, UCLA, October 1994.)

[10] H.M. Vin, S.S. Rao and P. Goyal, "Optimizing the placement of multimedia objects on disk arrays", *Proc. Int'l Conf. on Multimedia Comp. and Sys.*, pp. 158-165, May 1995.

[11] N.F. Maxemchuk, "Dispersity Routing", *Proc. Int'l Commun. Conf.*, pp. 41.10-41.13, 1975.

[12] M.O. Rabin, "Efficient Dispersal of Information for Security, Load Balancing, and Fault tolerance", *J. ACM*, vol. 36, pp. 335-348, Apr. 1989.

[13] A. Bestavros, "IDA Disk Arrays", *Proc. PDIS'91, the First Int'l Conf. on Parallel and Distributed Information Systems, Miami Beach, Florida*, IEEE Computer Society Press, December, 1991.

[14] S. Berson, R.R. Muntz and W.R Wong, "Randomized Data Allocation for Real-time Disk I/O", *Proc. IEEE Compcon'96* vol. 11, no. 4, pp. 631-640, May. 1996.

[15] W. Bolosky, J.S. Barrera, III, R.P. Draves, R.P. Fitzgerald, G.A. Gibson, M.B. Jones, S.P. Levi, N.P. Myhrvold, R.F. Rashid, "The tiger video fileserver", *Proc. NOSSDAV96*, April 1996. Also Microsoft report MSR-TR-96-09.

[16] Y. Birk and N. Bloch, "Prioritized dispersal: a scheme for selective exploitation of redundancy in distributed systems", *Proc. 8th Israeli Conf. on Computer Sys. And Software Engr. (ISySE'97)*, June 1997 (to appear).

Disk scheduling in a multimedia I/O system

A. L. Narasimha Reddy
Jim Wyllie

IBM Almaden Research Center
650 Harry Road
San Jose, CA 95120.

Abstract

In this paper, we look at the problem of disk scheduling in a multimedia I/O system. In a multimedia server, the disk requests may have constant data rate requirements and need guaranteed service. We propose a new scheduling algorithm, SCAN-EDF, that combines the features of SCAN type of seek optimizing algorithms with Earliest Deadline First (EDF) type of real-time scheduling algorithms. We compare SCAN-EDF with other scheduling strategies and show that SCAN-EDF combines the best features of both SCAN and EDF. We also investigate the impact of buffer space on the maximum number of video streams that can be supported. We show that by making the deadlines larger than the request periods, a larger number of streams can be supported.

1   Introduction

Future I/O systems will be required to support continuous-media such as video and audio. Continuous media put different demands on the system than data streams such as text. The real-time demands of the requests need to be taken into account in designing a system. In this paper, we will use the terms, real-time, video and multimedia interchangeably to describe requests that have constant data rate requirements. We also use the terms, server and I/O system interchangeably.

A real-time request is denoted by two parameters (c,p), where p is the period at which the real-time requests are generated and c is the service time required in each period. When c is a fixed value, it is easy to specify a real-time request with these two variables. But, the disk service time for a request depends on the random components of seek time and latency time. Hence, we will specify the real-time requests by specifying the required data rate in kbytes/sec.

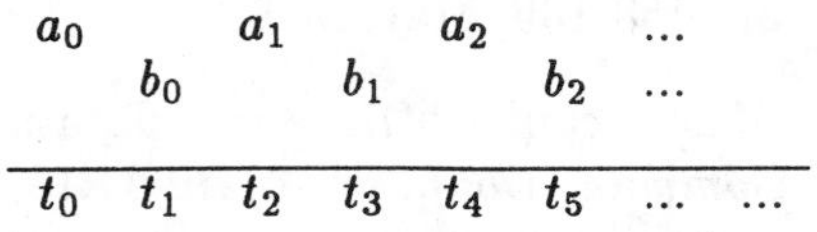

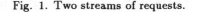

Fig. 1. Two streams of requests.

The time at which a periodic stream is started is called the *release time* of that request. The time at which the request is to be completed is called the *deadline* for that request. Requests that do not have real-time requirements are termed *aperiodic* requests. Fig. 1 shows the terminology used in this paper. Fig. 1 shows two streams of requests a and b that are released at times t_0 and t_1 respectively. Stream a is represented by a string of requests a_0, a_1, a_2 ... and similarly b is represented by b_0, b_1, b_2 ....

In real-time systems, when requests may have to be satisfied within deadlines, algorithms such as earliest deadline first, and least slack time first are used. Earliest deadline first (EDF) algorithm is shown to be optimal [1] if the service times of the requests are known in advance. However, the disk service time for a request depends on the relative position of the request from the current position of the read-write head. The original EDF algorithm assumed that the tasks are preemptable with zero preemption cost and showed that tasks can be scheduled by EDF if and only if the task utilization $\sum_{i=1}^{n} c_i/p_i < 1$. Current disks are however not preemptable. Recently it is shown that even when the tasks are non-preemptable, EDF is an optimal policy [2]. However, due to the overheads of seek time, strict real-time scheduling of disk arm may result in excessive seek time cost and poor utilization of the disk.

Traditionally, disks have used seek optimization techniques such as SCAN or shortest seek time first (SSTF) for minimizing the arm movement in serving the requests. These techniques reduce the disk arm utilization by serving requests close to the disk arm. The request queue is ordered by the relative position of the requests on the disk surface to reduce the seek overheads. Even though these techniques utilize the disk arm efficiently, they may not be suitable for real-time environments since they do not have a notion of time or deadlines in making a scheduling decision.

Continuous-media I/O systems may have to serve aperiodic requests also. In such environments, it is necessary to ensure that periodic requests do not miss their deadlines while giving reasonable response times for aperiodic requests. A similar problem is studied in [3]. I/O requests are known to be bursty. A burst of aperiodic requests should not result in missing the guarantees for the periodic requests. At the same time, aperiodic requests should not be starved of service.

The scheduling algorithm should be fair. For example, shortest seek time first, is not a fair scheduling algorithm since requests at the edges of the disk surface may get starved. If the scheduling algorithm is not fair, an occasional request in the stream may get starved of service and hence will result in missing the deadlines. Hence, we will not use SSTF kind of algorithms in our discussion. For the same reasons, the policy proposed in [4] is not suitable for this application.

Available buffer space has a significant impact on the performance of the system. The constant data rate of real-time requests can be provided in various ways. When the available buffer space is small, the request stream can ask for small pieces of data in each period. When the available buffer space is large, the request stream can ask for larger pieces of data with correspondingly larger periods between requests. This tradeoff is significant since the efficiency of the disk service is a varying function of the request size. We will study the impact of buffer space on the performance of the various scheduling policies. We also show that by deferring deadlines, which also increases the buffer requirements, the performance of the system can be improved significantly. We will describe in the next section, how buffers can be used to improve the throughput of the I/O system.

Anderson *et al* [5] present a comprehensive treatment of this problem. A work-ahead scheduling algorithm based on least slack time first is presented. Worst-case service time is assumed to estimate the number of supportable streams. Effect of buffers on performance is also studied. The proposed policies do not optimize the disk schedule to reduce the seek time costs.

A periodic fill policy is proposed in [6] for scheduling multi-media requests at the disk. Worst-case (seek and latency) overheads are assumed as part of the service time in calculating the schedule. The proposed solution does not address serving aperiodic requests. A file system for handling audio/video data is presented in [7, 8].

To prove the correctness of the schedule, worst-case assumptions about seek and latency overheads have to be made. When worst-case overheads are assumed, random disk service times can be bounded to some constant service time. Another approach to making service times predictable is to make the request size so large that the overheads form a smaller fraction of the request service time. This approach may result in large demands on buffer space. Our approach to this problem is to reduce the overheads in service time by making more efficient use of the disk arm either by optimizing the service schedule and/or by using large requests. By reducing the random overheads, we make the service time more predictable. We utilize deadline extensions to reduce the uncertainties of meeting the deadlines. Guaranteeing the correctness of the schedule and admission policy controls are discussed in a later section.

In this paper, we propose a new scheduling algorithm, SCAN-EDF. SCAN-EDF is a hybrid algorithm that incorporates the real-time aspects of EDF and seek optimization aspects of SCAN, CSCAN and other such seek optimization policies. We will show that SCAN-EDF has good characteristics for supporting multimedia requests. We also study the impact of buffer availability on the number of streams that can be supported.

The rest of the paper is organized as follows. Section 2 describes SCAN-EDF scheduling algorithm in detail. Section 3 describes the possible tradeoff with available buffer space. Section 4 presents an evaluation of the different scheduling algorithms. Section 5 presents a simple analysis of SCAN-EDF for multimedia scheduling and also presents an admission control policy that can be used with SCAN-EDF. Section 7 presents some conclusions and the future work.

2   SCAN-EDF scheduling algorithm

SCAN-EDF disk scheduling algorithm combines seek optimization techniques and EDF in the following way. Requests with earliest deadline are served first. But, if several requests have the same deadline, these requests are served by their track locations on the disk or by using a seek optimization scheduling algorithm for these requests. In this paper, deadlines are always in multiples of request periods. This strategy combines the benefits of both real-time and seek-optimizing scheduling algorithms. Requests with earlier deadlines are served first, but requests with the same deadline make use of seek optimization techniques to reduce the disk utilization.

SCAN-EDF applies seek optimization to only those requests having the same deadline. Its efficiency depends on how often these seek optimizations can be applied, or on the fraction of requests that have the same deadlines. The following techniques make it possible for various requests to have the same deadlines. SCAN-EDF prescribes that the requests have release times that are multiples of the period p. This results in all the requests to have deadlines that are multiples of the period p. This enables the requests to be grouped in batches and served accordingly. When the requests have different data rate requirements, SCAN-EDF can be combined with a periodic fill policy [6] to let all the requests have the same deadline. Requests are served in a cycle with each request getting an amount of service time proportional to its required data rate, the length of the cycle being the sum of the service times of all the requests. All the requests in the current cycle can then be given a deadline at the end of the current cycle. These two techniques enhance the possibility of applying seek optimization in SCAN-EDF.

A more precise description of the algorithm is given below.

SCAN-EDF algorithm
Step 1: let T = set of tasks with the earliest deadline
Step 2: if $|T| = 1$, (there is only a single request in T),

service that request.

else let t_1 be the first task in T in scan direction, service t_1.

go to **Step 1**.

The scan direction can be chosen in several ways. In Step 2, if the tasks are ordered with the track numbers of tasks such that $N_1 <= N_2 <= ... <= N_l$, then we obtain a CSCAN type of scheduling where the scan takes place only from smallest track number to the largest track number. If the tasks are ordered such that $N_1 >= N_2 >= ... >= N_l$, then we obtain a CSCAN type of scheduling where the scan takes place only from largest track number to the smallest track number. If the tasks can be ordered in either of the above forms depending on the relative position of the disk arm, we get (elevator) SCAN type of algorithm.

SCAN-EDF can be implemented with a slight modification to EDF. Let D_i be the deadlines of the tasks and N_i be their track positions. Then the deadlines can be modified to be $D_i + f(N_i)$, where $f()$ is a function that converts the track numbers of the tasks into small perturbations to the deadlines. The perturbations have to be small enough such that $D_i + f(N_i) > D_j + f(N_j)$, if $D_i > D_j$ and requests i and j are ordered in the SCAN order when $D_i = D_j$. We can choose $f()$ in various ways. Some of the choices are $f(N_i) = N_i/N_{max}$ or $f(N_i) = N_i/N_{max} - 1$, where N_{max} is the maximum track number on the disk or some other suitably large constant. For example, let tasks A, B, and C and D have deadlines 500, 500, 500 and 600 respectively and ask for data from tracks 347, 113, 851, and 256 respectively. If $N_{max} = 1000$, the modified deadlines of A, B, C and D become 499.347, 499.113, 499.851 and 599.256 respectively when we use $f(N_i) = N_i/N_{max} - 1$. When these requests are served by their modified deadlines, requests A, B and C are served in the SCAN order of B, A and C and request D is served later.

3   Buffer space tradeoff

Real-time requests typically need some kind of response before the next request is issued. Hence, the deadlines for the requests are made equal to the periods of the requests. The multimedia I/O system needs to provide a constant data rate for each request stream. This constant data rate can be provided in various ways. When the available buffer space is small, the request stream can ask for small pieces of data in each period. When the available buffer space is large, the request stream can ask for larger pieces of data with correspondingly larger periods between requests. This tradeoff is significant since the efficiency of the disk service is a varying function of the request size. The disk arm is more efficiently used when the request sizes are large and hence it may be possible to support larger number of multimedia streams at a single disk. A stream of requests described by (c,p) supports the same data rate as a stream of requests of (2c,2p) if larger buffers are provided.

Each request stream requires a buffer for the consuming process and one buffer for the producing process (disk). If we decide to issue requests at the size of S, then the buffer space requirement for each stream is $2S$. If the I/O system

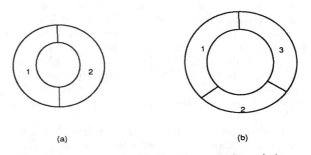

(a)   (b)

Fig. 2. Arrangement of buffers for a single real-time stream.

supports n streams, the total buffer space requirement is $2nS$. Figure 2(a) shows the usage of the buffers for this process. In Fig. 2(a), while buffer 1 is being consumed, an outstanding request tries to fill buffer 2 and when buffer 2 is being consumed, an outstanding request tries to fill buffer 1.

There is another tradeoff that is possible. The deadlines of the requests need not be chosen equal to the periods of the requests. For example, we can defer the deadlines of the requests by a period and make the deadlines of the requests equal to $2p$. This gives more time for the disk arm to serve a given request and may allow more seek optimizations than that is possible when the deadlines are equal to the period p. This results in a scenario where the consuming process is consuming buffer 1, the producing process (disk) is reading data into buffer 3 and buffer 2 is filled earlier by the producer and waiting consumption. Hence, this raises the buffer requirements to $3S$ for each request stream. This is shown in Fig. 2(b) where three buffers 1, 2 and 3 are used circularly for satisfying the requests of a single stream. In general, when the requests are allowed to have deadlines that are mp, the buffer requirements for each stream are $(m + 1)S$, where S is the size of the request in each period. We will show in next section that this strategy has significant benefits. The extra time available for serving a given request allows seek optimization techniques to be applied more number of times to the request queue at the disk. This results in more efficient use of disk arm and as a result, larger number of request streams can be supported at a single disk. A similar technique called work-ahead is utilized by Anderson *et al* [5].

In [9], it is shown that when all the deadlines are extended by a multiple of the periods, monotonic scheduling achieves higher useful utilization of the resource. In [10], it is shown that if the periods of all the requests are extended by the largest period, a modified rate monotone scheduling algorithm is optimal. Both these studies assume that the tasks are preemptable.

Both these techniques, larger requests with larger periods and delayed deadlines, increase the latency of service for a real-time stream. When the deadlines are delayed, the multimedia data stream cannot be consumed till two buffers are filled as opposed to waiting for one filled buffer when deadlines are equal to periods. When larger requests are

Table 1. Disk parameters.

Time for one rotation	11.1 ms
Avg. seek	9.4 ms
sectors/track	84
sector size	512 bytes
tracks/cylinder	15
cylinders/disk	2577
seek cost function	nonlinear
Min. seek time s_0	1.0 ms

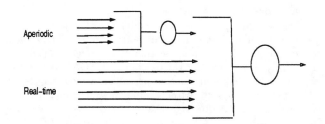

Fig. 3. Service model for serving real-time and aperiodic requests.

employed, similarly longer time is taken before a buffer is filled and hence a longer time before the multimedia stream can be started. Larger requests increase the response time for aperiodic requests as well since the aperiodic requests will have to wait for a longer time behind the current real-time request that is being served. The improved efficiency of these techniques needs to be weighed against the higher buffer requirements and the higher latency for a request service.

We discussed two techniques, deferring deadlines and employing larger requests, in which the buffer space can be traded off to improve the efficiency of disk scheduling. Quantitative evaluation and comparison of these techniques will be provided in a later section.

4   Performance Evaluation

In this section, we present the simulation model and the results obtained through simulations.

4.1   Simulation model

A disk with the parameters shown in Table 1 is modeled. It is assumed that the disk uses split-access operations or zero latency reads. In split-access operation, the request is satisfied by two smaller requests if the read-write head happens to be in the middle of the requested data at the end of the seek operation. The disk starts servicing the request as soon as any of the requested blocks comes under the read-write head. For example, if a request asks for reading blocks numbered 1,2,3,4 from a track of eight blocks 1,2,...8, and the read-write head happens to get to block number 3 first, then blocks 3 and 4 are read, blocks 5,6,7,8 are skipped over and then blocks 1 and 2 are read. In such operation, a disk read/write of a single track will not take more than one single revolution. Split access operation of the disk is shown to improve the response time of the disk considerably in [11]. Split-access operation, besides reducing the service time of a request, also helps in reducing the variability in service time.

Each real-time request stream is assumed to require a constant data rate of 150 kB/sec. This roughly corresponds to the data rate requirements for a CDROM data stream. Each request stream is modeled by an independent request generator. The release times of the requests are dependent on the scheduling policy employed and is as described below. The number of streams is a parameter to the simulator.

Aperiodic requests are modeled by a single aperiodic request generator. Aperiodic requests are assumed to arrive with an exponential distribution. The mean time between arrivals is varied from 25 ms to 200 ms. If we allow unlimited service for the aperiodic requests, a burst of aperiodic requests can disturb the service of real-time requests considerably. It is necessary to limit the number of aperiodic requests that may be served in a given period of time. A separate queue could be maintained for these requests and these requests can be released at a rate that is bounded by a known rate. A multimedia server will have to be built in this fashion to guarantee meeting the real-time schedules. Hence, we decided to model the arrival of aperiodic requests by a single request generator. In our model, if the aperiodic requests are generated faster than they are being served, they are queued in a separate queue. This model of service is shown in Fig. 3.

The service policy for aperiodic requests depended on the scheduling policy employed. In EDF, SCAN-EDF and STAGEDF, they are served using the immediate server approach [3] where the aperiodic requests are given higher priority over the periodic real-time requests. The service schedule for these three policies allows a certain number of aperiodic requests each period and when sufficient number of aperiodic requests are not present, the real-time requests make use of the reamining service period. This policy of serving aperiodic requests is employed so as to provide reasonable response times for both aperiodic and periodic requests. This is in contrast to earlier approaches where the emphasis has been only on providing real-time performance guarantees. In CSCAN, aperiodic requests are served in SCAN order and in PCSCAN, aperiodic requests are served as explained earlier.

Each aperiodic request is assumed to ask for a track of data. With split-access operations, the service time for a request asking for less than or equal to a track of data is bounded by the service time for a track. Hence, this assumption is equivalent to assuming that no aperiodic request asks for more than a track of data at a time. The request size for the real-time requests is varied among 1, 2, 5, or 15 tracks. The effect of request size on number of supportable streams is investigated. The period between two requests of a real-time request stream is varied depending on the request size to support a constant data rate of 150 kB/sec. The requests are assumed to be uniformly distributed over the disk surface.

Five scheduling policies are modeled. EDF is the strict earliest deadline first scheduling policy. SCAN-EDF is the policy proposed earlier in Section 2. We used $f(N_i) = N_i/N_{max} - 1$ to modify the deadlines. CSCAN is the policy where the disk arm moves from the outermost request to the innermost request. After serving the innermost request, the disk arm jumps back to the outermost request waiting to be served. PCSCAN is a slight modification of CSCAN where aperiodic requests that are less than half the number of tracks behind the disk arm are served immediately i.e., out of the CSCAN arm movement order. STAGEDF is EDF policy with staggered release times. For this policy, the release times of request streams are equally placed between 0 and the period p. For all the other policies, the release times are at time zero. Relative merits of the various scheduling policies are studied.

Two systems, one with deadlines equal to the request periods and the second with deadlines equal to twice the request periods are modeled. A comparison of these two systems gives insight into how performance can be improved by deferring the deadlines.

Two measures of performance are studied. The number of real-time streams that can be supported by each scheduling policy is taken as the primary measure of performance. We also look at the response time for aperiodic requests. The response time for aperiodic requests cannot be unduly large. A good policy will offer good response times for aperiodic requests while supporting large number of real-time streams.

Each experiment involved running 50,000 requests of each stream. The maximum number of supportable streams n is obtained by increasing the number of streams incrementally till $n + 1$ where the deadlines cannot be met. Twenty experiments were conducted, with different seeds for random number generation, for each point in the figures. The minimum among these values is chosen as the maximum number of streams that can be supported. Each point in the figures is obtained in this way. The minimum is chosen (instead of the average) in order to guarantee the real-time performance. We confirm the simulations later through analysis.

4.2   Results

4.2.1   Maximum number of streams

Fig. 4 shows the results from simulations. The solid lines correspond to a system with extended deadlines (=2p) and the dashed lines are for the system where deadlines are equal to periods.

It is observed that deferring deadlines improves the number of supportable streams significantly for all the scheduling policies. The performance improvement ranges from 4 streams for CSCAN to 9 streams for SCAN-EDF at a request size of 1 track.

When deadlines are deferred, CSCAN has the best performance. SCAN-EDF has performance very close to CSCAN. EDF has the worst performance. EDF scheduling results in random disk arm movement and this is the reason for poor performance of this policy. Fig. 4 clearly shows the advan-

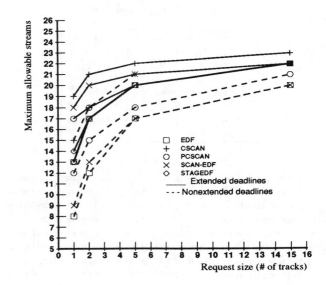

Fig. 4. Performance of different scheduling policies.

tage of utilizing seek optimization techniques.

Fig. 4 also presents the improvements that are possible by increasing the request size. As the request size is increased from 1 track to 15 tracks, the number of supportable streams keeps increasing. The knee of the curve seems to be around 5 tracks or 200 kbytes. At larger request sizes, the different scheduling policies make relatively less difference in performance. At larger request sizes, the transfer time dominates the service time. When seek time overhead is a smaller fraction of service time, the different scheduling policies have less scope for optimizing the schedule. Hence, the performance of all the scheduling policies does not differ significantly at larger request sizes. At a request size of 5 tracks, i.e., 200 kbytes/buffer, minimum of 2 buffers/stream corresponds to 400 kbytes of buffer space per stream. This results in a demand of 400 kbytes * 20 = 8Mbytes of buffer space at the I/O system for supporting 20 streams. If deadlines are deferred, this corresponds to a requirement of 12 Mbytes. When such amount of buffer space is not available, smaller request sizes need to be considered.

At smaller request sizes, deferring the deadlines has a better impact on performance than increasing the buffer size. For example, at a request size of 1 track and deferred deadlines (with buffer requirements of 3 tracks) EDF supports 13 streams. When deadlines are not deferred, at a larger request size of 2 tracks and buffer requirements of 4 tracks, EDF supports only 12 streams. A similar trend is observed with other policies as well. A similar observation also seems to hold when request sizes of 2 and 5 tracks are compared.

Fig. 4 also shows that staggering the deadlines of the requests had an impact on the number of supportable streams when the deadlines are not extended. When deadlines are not extended, STAGEDF has considerably better perfor-

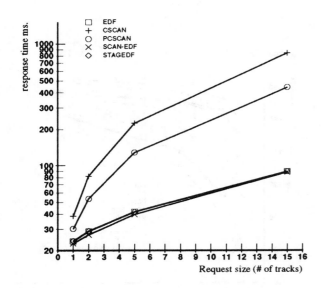

Fig. 5. Aperiodic response time with different scheduling policies.

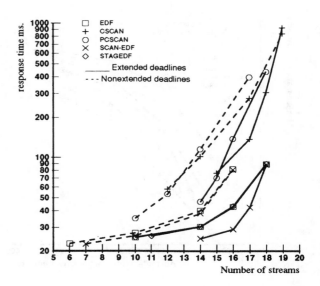

Fig. 6. Aperiodic response time as a function of number of streams.

mance than EDF. But, when deadlines are extended, the two policies have almost no difference in performance. In general, staggering deadlines is not exactly feasible. When all the requests arrive at once, it is possible to make the release times uniformly distributed between 0 and p. In our simulations, we assumed this scenario. But when requests are incrementally allowed to arrive, this uniform distribution will not be possible.

4.2.2 Aperiodic response time

Fig. 5 shows the response time for aperiodic requests. The figure shows the aperiodic response time when 8, 12, 15, 18 real-time streams are being supported in the system at request sizes of 1, 2, 5, and 15 tracks respectively. It is observed that CSCAN has the worst performance and SCAN-EDF has the best performance. With CSCAN, on an average, an aperiodic request has to wait for half a sweep for service. This may result in waiting behind half the number of real-time requests. In SCAN-EDF, EDF, STAGEDF, aperiodic requests are given higher priorities by giving them shorter deadlines (100 ms from the issuing time). In these strategies, requests with shorter deadlines get higher priority. As a result, aperiodic requests typically wait behind only the current request that is being served. As a result, aperiodic requests have to wait, on an average, for about half the service time of a single real-time request. Among these three policies, the slightly better performance of SCAN-EDF is due to the lower arm utilizations.

From Figures 4 and 5, it is seen that SCAN-EDF performs well under both measures of performance. CSCAN performs well in supporting real-time requests but does not have very good performance in serving the aperiodic requests. EDF, does not perform very well in supporting real-

time requests but offers good response times for aperiodic requests. SCAN-EDF supports almost as many real-time streams as CSCAN and at the same time offers the best response times for aperiodic requests. When both the performance measures are considered, SCAN-EDF has better characteristics.

When deadlines are deferred, smaller request sizes can be used to support the same number of real-time streams at the disk. This improves the aperiodic request response time besides reducing the demand on the buffer space needed at the I/O system. When deadlines are not deferred, the aperiodic requests have to wait behind larger requests (for supporting the same number of real-time streams). Hence, the aperiodic response time suffers. Effect of this is shown in Fig. 6. Fig. 6 shows the aperiodic response time with various scheduling policies at 80% of the maximum number of supportable streams. Fig. 6 shows that, it is better to defer the deadlines than to use a larger request size since better aperiodic response times are obtained.

4.2.3 Effect of aperiodic request arrival

Fig. 7 shows the effect of aperiodic request arrival rate on the number of real-time streams that can be supported. It is observed that aperiodic request arrival rate has a significant impact on all the policies. Except for CSCAN, all other policies support less than 5 streams at an inter-arrival time of 25 ms. Figure 7 shows that the inter-arrival time of aperiodic requests should not be below 50 ms if more than 10 real-time streams need to be supported at the disk. CSCAN treats all requests equally and hence higher aperiodic request arrival time only reduces the time available for the real-time request streams and does not alter the schedule of service. In other policies, since aperiodic requests are

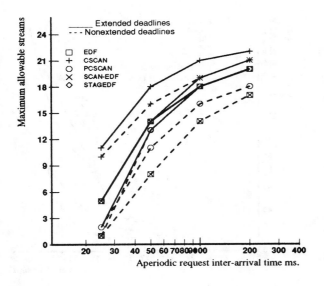

Fig. 7. Effect of aperiodic request arrival rate on the number of streams.

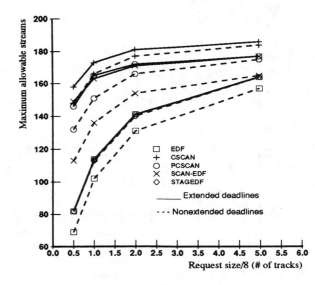

Fig. 8. Performance of various policies with a disk array.

given higher priorities, higher aperiodic request arrival rate results in less efficient arm utilization due to more random arm movement. Hence, other policies see more impact on performance due to higher aperiodic request arrival rate.

4.2.4   Performance with an array

Fig. 8 shows the performance of various policies, at an aperiodic request inter-arrival time of 200 ms, when an 8-disk array is employed in a RAID3 configuration without parity protection (i.e., all the 8 disk arms tied together with a transfer rate of 8 times that of a normal disk). This configuration is shown to offer good performance for sequential transfers [12, 13, 14, 15]. Performance of all the policies is improved by nearly 8-fold. It is observed that the performance differences between SCAN-EDF and EDF are higher with an array than with a single disk. This is primarily due to the fact that seek time is a bigger fraction of the service time in the array.

4.2.5   Multiple data rates

Fig. 9 shows the performance of various scheduling policies when requests with different data rates are served. The simulations modeled equal number of three different data rates of 150 kB/sec, 8 kB/sec and 176 kB/sec with aperiodic requests arriving at a rate of 200ms. Even with multiple data rate requirements, SCAN-EDF supports almost as many streams as CSCAN and more than EDF.

5   Analysis of SCAN-EDF

In this section, we will present an analysis of SCAN-EDF policy and show how request service can be guaranteed. We

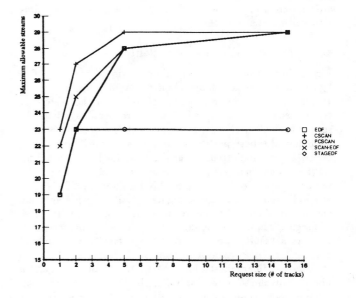

Fig. 9. Performance of various policies with multiple data rates.

assume that the disk seek time can be modeled by the following equation $s(m) = s_0 + m * s_1$, where $s(m)$ is the seek time for m tracks, s_0 is the minimum seek time. This equation assumes that the seek time is a linear function of the number of tracks. This is a simplifying assumption to make the analysis easy (in simulations earlier, we used the actual measured seek function of one of the IBM disks). The value of s_1 can be chosen such that the seek time function $s(m)$ gives an upper bound on the actual seek time. Let M denote the number of tracks on the disk and T the track capacity. We will denote the required data rate for each stream by C. We also assume that the disk requests are issued at a varying rate, but always in multiples of track capacity. Let kT be the request size. Since C is the required data rate for each stream, the period for a request stream $p = kT/C$. If r denotes the data rate of the disk in bytes/sec, $r = T/(rotation\ time)$. Disk is assumed to employ split-access operation and hence no latency penalty. This analysis assumes that there are no aperiodic requests. These assumptions are made so that we can establish an upper bound on performance.

SCAN-EDF serves requests in batches. Each batch is served in a scan order for meeting a particular deadline. We assume that the batch of n requests are uniformly placed over the disk surface. Hence the seek time cost for a complete sweep of n requests can be given by $s_1 * M + n * s_0$. This assumes that the disk arm sweeps across all the M tracks in serving the n requests. The read time cost for n requests is given by $n * kr$. The total time for one sweep is the time taken for serving the n requests plus the time taken to move the disk arm back from the innermost track to the outermost track. This innermost track to outermost track seek takes $s_0 + M * s_1$ time. Hence, the total time for serving one batch of requests is given by $Q = (n * s_0 + M * s_1 + n * kr) + s_0 + M * s_1 = n * (s_0 + kr) + 2M * s_1 + s_0$. The worst-case for a single stream results when its request is the first request to be served in a batch and is the last request to be served in the next batch of requests. This results in roughly $2Q$ time between serving two requests of a stream. This implies the number of streams n is obtained when p = 2Q or $n = (kT/C - 4M * s_1 - 2 * s_0)/2 * (s_0 + kr)$. However, this bound can be improved if we allow deadline extension. If we allow the deadlines to be extended by one period, the maximum number of streams n is obtained when $n = (kT/C - 2M * s_1 - s_0)/(s_0 + kr)$.

The time taken to serve a batch of requests through a sweep, using SCAN-EDF, has little variance. The possible variances of individual seek times could add up to a possible large variance if served by a strict EDF policy. SCAN-EDF reduces this variance by serving all the requests in a single sweep across the disk surface. SCAN-EDF, by reducing the variance, reduces the time taken for serving a batch of requests and hence supports larger number of streams. This reduction in the variance of service time for a batch of requests has a significant impact on improving the service time guarantees. Larger request sizes, split-access operation of disk arm also reduce the variance in service time by limiting the variable portions of the service time to a smaller fraction.

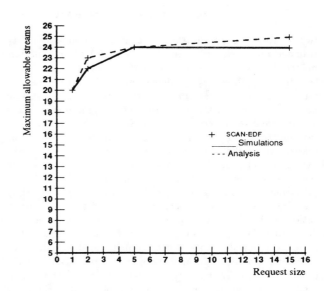

Fig. 10. Comparison of analysis with simulation results.

Fig. 10 compares the predictions of analysis with results obtained from simulations for extended deadlines. For this experiment, aperiodic requests were not considered and hence the small difference in the number of streams supportable by SCAN-EDF from Fig. 4. It is observed that the analysis is very close to the simulation results. The error is within one stream.

5.1   Admission Control

A slight modification of the above analysis also gives us an admission control policy. When the nth request is issued, it is checked to see if the service time for a batch of n requests plus the worst-case estimate of service time for any aperiodic requests, is less than the smallest period p of the requests. The time for n periodic requests can be calculated from the above equations. We use the immediate server approach of [3] for serving the aperiodic requests. If l aperiodic requests are allowed to be served in each sweep of n periodic requests, the total time taken for the sweep can be bounded by $Q <= n*(s_0 + kr) + 2M * s_1 + s_0 + l * T_{worst}$, where T_{worst} is the worst-case interruption of service time to the periodic requests due to an aperiodic request. If the period $p > Q$, then the new request can be admitted.

When multiple data rates are handled, the above analysis needs to be modified. SCAN-EDF would then be combined with a periodic fill policy where requests are served in cycles. The period p is made equal to the total time allocated for a cycle of service. The total time Q required for serving the real-time requests and the aperiodic requests is computed as above and the request is allowed if $p > Q$.

6   General Discussion

In a multimedia system, the real-time requirements of data transfer put a different emphasis on I/O system performance. In this paper, we looked at the aspect of disk scheduling. However, in delivering the multimedia I/O streams to the workstation, several aspects of the system need to be investigated. In an I/O system, several disks are attached to the controller through a single communication link/channel such as SCSI or IPI interface. Real-time scheduling of disk-controller channel needs to be investigated. We also need to look at the problems of delivering real-time I/O over the local area network. Several of these problems remain to be solved. The bottleneck in supporting real-time I/O may be determined by one of these communication problems. A complete study remains to be done to determine the performance of the complete system. In this paper, we looked at one of the problems, disk scheduling.

Several practical problems remain to be solved for the potential of SCAN-EDF to be realized. Some of the current disks utilize zone-bit recording which makes the track capacity a variable depending on the location of the track on the disk. This results in variable data rate depending on the track location. Some of the compression algorithms such as MPEG yield streams that have variable data rate requirements over the length of the stream. These issues complicate the scheduling problem. These issues are currently being investigated.

7   Conclusions

In this paper, we presented a new disk scheduling algorithm, SCAN-EDF. SCAN-EDF is a hybrid scheduling policy that combines the features of real-time scheduling policies and the traditional seek optimization policies. SCAN-EDF with deferred deadlines is shown to perform well in multimedia environments. SCAN-EDF employs immediate server approach to provide reasonable performance to aperiodic requests at the same time supporting a large number of real-time streams. Larger requests and deferred deadlines are shown to improve the performance significantly. We have done comparative evaluation of these techniques to show that, for a given amount of buffer space, deferring deadlines is a better tradeoff than using larger requests in a multimedia I/O system. We also observed that other factors such as network delay and the disk-controller channel delay need to be accounted for in guaranteeing the end-to-end delay bounds for a multimedia stream.

8   Acknowledgements

Discussions with Barbara Simons and Robert Morris, and Roger Haskin, IBM Almaden Research Center, have helped in clarifying the presentation.

References

[1] C. L. Liu and J. W. Layland. Scheduling algorithms for multiprogramming in a hard real-time environment. *Journal of ACM*, pages 46–61, 1973.

[2] K. Jeffay, D. F. Stanat, and C. U. Martel. On non-preemptive scheduling of periodic and sporadic tasks. *Proc. of Real-time Systems Symp.*, pages 129–139, Dec. 1991.

[3] T. H. Lin and W. Tarng. Scheduling periodic and aperiodic tasks in hard real-time computing systems. *Proc. of SIGMETRICS*, pages 31–38, May 1991.

[4] R. K. Abbott and H. Garcia-Molina. Scheduling I/O requests with deadlines: a performance evaluation. *Proc. of Real-time Systems Symp.*, pages 113–124, Dec. 1990.

[5] D. P. Anderson, Y. Osawa, and R. Govindan. Real-time disk storage and retrieval of digital audio/video data. *Tech. report UCB/CSD 91/646, Univ. of Cal., Berkeley*, Aug. 1991.

[6] J. Yee and P. Varaiya. Disk scheduling policies for real-time multimedia applications. *Tech. report, Univ. of California, Bekeley*, Aug. 1992.

[7] H. M. Vin and P. V. Rangan. Designing file systems for digital video and audio. *Proc. of 13th ACM Symp. on Oper. Sys. Principles*, 1991.

[8] P. V. Rangan, H. M. Vin, and S. Ramanathan. Designing an on-demand multimedia service. *IEEE Comm. magazine*, pages 56–64, July 1992.

[9] J.P. Lehoczky. Fixed priority scheduling of periodic task sets with arbitrary deadlines. *Proc. of Real-time Systems Symp.*, pages 201–212, Dec. 1990.

[10] W. K. Shih, J. W. Liu, and C. L. Liu. Modified rate monotone algorithm for scheduling periodic jobs with deferred deadlines. *Tech. Report, Univ. of Illinois, Urbana-Champaign*, Sept. 1992.

[11] A. L. Narasimha Reddy. A study of I/O system organizations. *Proc. of Int. Symp. on Comp. Arch.*, May 1992.

[12] D. A. Patterson, G. Gibson, and R. H. Katz. A case for redundant arrays of inexpensive disks (RAID). *ACM SIGMOD Conference*, June 1988.

[13] M. Y. Kim. Synchronized disk interleaving. *IEEE Trans. Comput.*, C-35, no. 11:978–988, Nov. 1986.

[14] K. Salem and H. Garcia-Molina. Disk striping. *Int. Conf. on Data Engineering*, pages 336–342, 1986.

[15] A. L. Narasimha Reddy and P. Banerjee. An evaluation of multiple-disk I/O systems. *IEEE Trans. Comput.*, C-38, no. 12:1680–1690, Dec. 1989.

A Statistical Admission Control Algorithm for Multimedia Servers

Harrick M. Vin, Pawan Goyal, Alok Goyal, and **Anshuman Goyal**

Department of Computer Sciences, University of Texas at Austin
Taylor Hall 2.124, Austin, Texas 78712-1188
E-mail: {vin,pawang,alok,anshu}@cs.utexas.edu, Telephone: (512) 471-9732, Fax: (512) 471-8885

Abstract

A large-scale multimedia server, in practice, has to service a large number of clients simultaneously. Given the real-time requirements of each client and the fixed data transfer bandwidth of disks, a multimedia server must employ admission control algorithms to decide whether a new client can be admitted for service without violating the requirements of the clients already being serviced. In this paper, we present an admission control algorithm for multimedia servers which: (1) exploits the variation in access times of media blocks from disk as well as the variation in client load induced by variable rate compression schemes, and (2) provides statistical service guarantees to each client. The effectiveness of the algorithm is demonstrated through trace-driven simulations.

1 Introduction

1.1 Motivation

Recent advances in computing and communication technologies have made it feasible as well as economically viable to provide on-line access to a variety of information sources (such as reference books, journals, newspapers, images, video clips, scientific data, etc.) over high speed networks. The realization of such information management systems of the future, however, will require the development of high performance, scalable multimedia servers which can provide a wide range of services to a large number of clients [4]. The fundamental problem in developing such multimedia servers is that images, audio, video, and other similar forms of data differ from numeric data and text in their characteristics, and hence require totally different techniques for their organization and management.

The most critical of these characteristics is that digital audio and video streams consist of a sequence of media quanta, such as video frames or audio samples, which convey meaning only when presented continuously in time (unlike text in which spatial continuity is sufficient). Hence, a multimedia server must ensure that recording and retrieval of media streams to and from disks proceed at their real-time rates. The development of techniques that enable a multimedia server to provide real-time performance guarantees to a large number of clients simultaneously is the subject matter of this paper.

1.2 Relation to Previous Work

Digitization of audio yields a sequence of samples, and that of video yields a sequence of frames. We refer to a continuously recorded sequence of audio samples or video frames as a *strand*. A multimedia server can organize the storage of such media strands on disk in terms of fixed size *media blocks*. Due to the periodic nature of media playback, a multimedia server can service multiple clients simultaneously by proceeding in *rounds*, retrieving a fixed number of media blocks for each client during each round. The number of blocks of a media strand retrieved during a round is dependent on its playback rate requirement, as well as the buffer space availability at the client [10]. Ensuring continuous retrieval of each strand requires that the *service time* (i.e., the total time spent in retrieving media blocks during a round) does not exceed the minimum of the playback durations of the blocks retrieved for each strand during a round. Hence, before admitting a new client, a multimedia server must employ admission control algorithms to decide whether a new client can be admitted without violating the continuous playback requirements of the clients already being serviced.

The precise formulation of the admission control algorithm is dependent on the quality of service requirements of the clients. If the entire clientele of a multimedia server desires deterministic service guarantees (i.e., their continuous playback requirements should never be violated for the entire service duration), the corresponding admission control algorithm will be characterized by worst-case assumptions regarding the service time [1, 2, 6, 8, 10, 11]. Notice, however, that due to the human perceptual tolerances as well as the inherent redundancy in continuous media streams, most clients of a multimedia server are tolerant to brief distortions in playback continuity as well as occasional loss of media information. Therefore, providing deterministic service guarantees to all the clients is superfluous. Furthermore, the worst-case assumptions that characterize deterministic admission control algorithms needlessly constrain the number of clients that can be serviced simultaneously, and hence, lead to severe under-utilization of server resources.

As a first step towards exploiting the human perceptual tolerances as well as the differences between the average and the worst-case performance characteristics of a multimedia server, we have recently proposed an *observation-based admission control algorithm*, in which a new client is admitted for service only if the prediction from the status quo measurements of the server performance characteristics indicate that the service requirements of all the clients can be met satisfactorily [9]. It is based on the assumption that the average amount of time spent in retrieving a media block from disk does not change significantly even after a new client is admitted by the server. In fact, it uses the average access time of a media block from the server and its standard deviation observed over a finite period to predict the access times of media blocks in future rounds. A multimedia server that employs such an observation-based approach is referred to as providing *predictive* service guarantees to clients.

1.3   Research Contributions of This Paper

The deterministic algorithms (which provide strict performance guarantees) and the observation-based algorithms (which offer a fairly reliable service, but no absolute guarantees) define two ends of the spectrum. In this paper, we analyze the continuum between these two extremes and develop admission control algorithms which use *distributions* (rather than worst-case and average-case values) of: (1) access times of media blocks from disk, and (2) playback rate requirements of media strands encoded using variable bit rate compression techniques; and provide *statistical* service guarantees to each client (i.e., the continuity requirements of at least a fixed percentage of media units is ensured to be met). The proposed algorithm improves the utilization of server resources by employing an aggressive admission control criteria: new clients are admitted for service as long as the *statistical estimation* of the aggregate data rate requirement (rather than the corresponding peak data rate requirement) can be met by the server. The statistical multiplexing of the server resources resulting from the admission of such clients, however, may occasionally lead to violation of the continuous playback requirements of some of the clients. To ensure that the statistical service guarantees being provided to the clients are not violated, we propose a technique for judiciously distributing such violations among multiple clients. Finally, to demonstrate the effectiveness of our statistical admission control algorithm, we have carried out extensive simulations. We present and analyze our simulation results.

The rest of the paper is organized as follows: In Section 2,

we present the statistical admission control algorithm. Techniques for meeting the service requirements of clients are outlined in Sections 3. Our simulation results are described in Section 4, and finally, Section 5 summarizes our results.

2   Statistical Admission Control Algorithm

Consider a multimedia server that is servicing n clients, each retrieving a video strand (say $S_1, S_2, ..., S_n$, respectively). Let the service requirements of client i be specified as a percentage p_i of the total number of frames that must be retrieved on time. A multimedia server can service these clients by proceeding in periodic *rounds*, retrieving a fixed number of frames for each client during each round. Let $f_1, f_2, ..., f_n$ denote the number of frames of strands $S_1, S_2, ..., S_n$ retrieved during each round. Then, assuming that $\mathcal{R}_{pl}^i$ denotes the playback rate (expressed in terms of frames/sec) of strand S_i, the duration of a round, defined as the minimum of the playback durations of the frames accessed during a round, is given by:

$$\mathcal{R} = \min_{i \in [1,n]} \left(\frac{f_i}{\mathcal{R}_{pl}^i} \right)$$

In such a scenario, ensuring continuous playback of each media strand requires that the total time spent in retrieving media blocks from disk during each round (referred to as *service time* τ) should not exceed $\mathcal{R}$. The service time, however, is dependent on the number of media blocks being accessed as well as their relative placement on disk. Since each media strand may be encoded using a variable bit rate compression technique (e.g., JPEG, MPEG, etc.), the number of media blocks that contain f_i frames of strand S_i may vary from one round to another. This difference, when coupled with the variation in the relative separation between blocks, yields different service times across rounds. In fact, while servicing a large number of clients, the service time may occasionally exceed the round duration (i.e., $\tau > \mathcal{R}$). We refer to such rounds as *overflow* rounds. Given that each client may have requested a different quality of service (i.e., different values of p_i), meeting all of their service requirements will require the server to delay the retrieval of or discard (i.e., not retrieve) media blocks of some of the more tolerant clients during overflow rounds[1]. Consequently, to ensure that the statistical quality of service requirements of clients are not violated, a multimedia server must employ admission control algorithms that restrict the occurrence of such overflow rounds by limiting the number of clients admitted for service.

To precisely derive an admission control criterion that meets the above requirement, observe that for rounds in which $\tau \leq \mathcal{R}$, none of the media blocks need to be discarded. Therefore, the total number of frames retrieved during such rounds

---

[1] The choice between delaying or discarding media blocks during overflow rounds is application dependent. Since both of these policies are mathematically equivalent, in this paper, we will analyze only the discarding policy.

is given by $\sum_{i=1}^{n} f_i$. During overflow rounds, however, since a few media blocks may have to be discarded or delayed to yield $\tau \leq \mathcal{R}$, the total number of frames retrieved will be smaller than $\sum_{i=1}^{n} f_i$. Given that p_i denotes the percentage of frames of strand S_i that must be retrieved on time to satisfy the service requirements of client i, the *average* number of frames that must be retrieved during each round is given by $p_i * f_i$. Hence, assuming that q denotes the overflow probability (i.e., $P(\tau > \mathcal{R}) = q$), the service requirements of the clients will be satisfied if:

$$q * \mathcal{F}_o + (1 - q) \sum_{i=1}^{n} f_i \geq \sum_{i=1}^{n} p_i * f_i \qquad (1)$$

where $\mathcal{F}_o$ denotes the number of frames that are guaranteed to be retrieved during overflow rounds. The left hand side of Equation (1) represents the lower bound on the expected number of frames retrieved during a round and the right hand side denotes the average number of frames that must be accessed during each round so as to meet the service requirements of all clients. Clearly, the effectiveness of this admission control criteria, measured in terms of the number of clients that can be admitted, is dependent on the values of q and $\mathcal{F}_o$. In what follows, we present techniques for accurately determining their values.

2.1 Computing the Overflow Probability

While servicing multiple clients simultaneously, an overflow is said to occur when the service time exceeds the playback duration of a round. Whereas the playback duration $\mathcal{R}$ of a round is fixed (since the server is accessing a fixed number of frames for each client), the service time varies from round to round. Let the random variable τ_k denote the service time for accessing k media blocks from disk. Then overflow probability q can be computed as:

$$q = P(\tau > \mathcal{R}) = \sum_{k=k_{min}}^{k_{max}} P(\tau > \mathcal{R}|\mathcal{B} = k)P(\mathcal{B} = k)$$

$$= \sum_{k=k_{min}}^{k_{max}} P(\tau_k > \mathcal{R})P(\mathcal{B} = k) \qquad (2)$$

where $\mathcal{B}$ is the random variable representing the number of blocks to be retrieved in a round, and k_{min} and k_{max}, respectively, denote its minimum and maximum values. Hence, computing the overflow probability q requires the determination of probability distribution functions for τ_k and $\mathcal{B}$, as well as the values of k_{min} and k_{max}, techniques for which are described below.

- **Service time characterization**:

  Given the number of blocks to be accessed during a round, since the service time is dependent only on the relative placement of media blocks on disk and the disk scheduling algorithm, and is completely independent of

the client characteristics, service time distributions are required to be computed only *once* during the lifetime of a multimedia server, possibly at the time of its installation.

The server can derive a distribution function for τ_k by empirically measuring the variation in service times yielded by different placements of k blocks on disk. The larger the number of such measurements, the greater is the accuracy of the distribution function. Starting with the minimum number of blocks that are guaranteed to be accessed during a round (i.e., the value of k_d derived in Section 2.2), the procedure for determining the distribution function for τ_k should be repeated for $k = k_d, k_d + 1, ..., k_{end}$, where k_{end} is the minimum value of k for which $P(\tau_{k_{end}} > \mathcal{R}) \simeq 1$. Using these empirically derived distribution functions, the probability $P(\tau_k > \mathcal{R})$, for various values of k, can be easily computed.

- **Client load characterization**:

  Since f_i frames of strand S_i are retrieved during each round, the total number of blocks $\mathcal{B}$ required to be accessed is dependent on the frame size distributions for each strand. Specifically, if the random variable $\mathcal{B}_i$ denotes the number of media blocks that contain f_i frames of strand S_i, then the total number of blocks to be accessed during each round is given by:

$$\mathcal{B} = \sum_{i=1}^{n} \mathcal{B}_i$$

Since $\mathcal{B}_i$ is only dependent on the frame size variations within strand S_i, $\mathcal{B}_i$'s denote a set of n *independent* random variables. Therefore, using the *central limit theorem*, we conclude that the distribution function $\mathcal{G}_{\mathcal{B}}(b)$ of $\mathcal{B}$ approaches a normal distribution [5]. Furthermore, if $\eta_{\mathcal{B}_i}$ and $\sigma_{\mathcal{B}_i}$ denote the mean and standard deviation of random variable $\mathcal{B}_i$, respectively, then the mean and standard deviation for $\mathcal{B}$ are given by:

$$\eta_{\mathcal{B}} = \sum_{i=1}^{n} \eta_{\mathcal{B}_i}, \quad \sigma_{\mathcal{B}}^2 = \sum_{i=1}^{n} \sigma_{\mathcal{B}_i}^2 \qquad (3)$$

Consequently,

$$\mathcal{G}_{\mathcal{B}}(b) \simeq \mathcal{N}\left(\frac{b - \eta_{\mathcal{B}}}{\sigma_{\mathcal{B}}}\right) \qquad (4)$$

where $\mathcal{N}$ is the standard normal distribution function. Additionally, since $\mathcal{B}_i$'s denote discrete random variables that take only integral values, they can be categorized as *lattice-type* random variables [5]. Hence, using the central limit theorem, the point probabilities $P(\mathcal{B} = k)$ can be derived as:

$$P(\mathcal{B} = k) \simeq \frac{1}{\sigma_{\mathcal{B}}\sqrt{2\pi}} e^{-\frac{(k-\eta_{\mathcal{B}})^2}{2\sigma_{\mathcal{B}}^2}} \qquad (5)$$

Finally, computing the overflow probability q using Equation (2) requires the values of k_{min} and k_{max}. If b_i^{min} and b_i^{max}, respectively, denote the minimum and the maximum number of media blocks that may contain f_i frames of strand S_i, then the values of k_{min} and k_{max} can be derived as:

$$k_{min} = \sum_{i=1}^{n} b_i^{min}; \quad k_{max} = \sum_{i=1}^{n} b_i^{max} \qquad (6)$$

Thus, by substituting the values of k_{min}, k_{max}, $P(\tau_k > \mathcal{R})$, and $P(\mathcal{B} = k)$ in Equation (2), the overflow probability q can be computed.

2.2 Determination of $\mathcal{F}_o$

The maximum number of frames $\mathcal{F}_o$ that are guaranteed to be retrieved during an overflow round is dependent on: (1) the number of media blocks that are guaranteed to be accessed from disk within the round duration $\mathcal{R}$, and (2) the relationship between the media block size and the maximum frame sizes.

To compute the number of media blocks that are guaranteed to be accessed during each round, worst-case assumptions (similar to those employed by deterministic admission control algorithms) regarding the access times of media blocks from disk may need to be employed. To illustrate the procedure, consider a multimedia server that employs the SCAN disk scheduling algorithm [7]. Let k denote the number of media blocks that are to be retrieved during a round. Since, in the worst-case, each media block may be placed on a different cylinder, the disk head may have to be repositioned onto a new cylinder at most k times. Furthermore, while accessing these blocks, the disk head may have to move from the inner-most cylinder to the outer-most cylinder, or vice versa. Hence, assuming that the disk contains C cylinders and the seek time incurred while moving the disk head from cylinder c_1 to c_2 is given by $l_{seek}(c_1, c_2) = a + b * |c_1 - c_2|$ where a and b are constants, the upper bound on the total seek time incurred during each round can be computed as: $(a * k + b * C)$. Similarly, assuming that the retrieval of each media block may, in the worst case, incur maximum rotational latency (denoted by l_{rot}^{max}), the total service time for each round can be computed as:

$$\tau = b * C + (a + l_{rot}^{max}) * k \qquad (7)$$

Since $\tau \leq \mathcal{R}$, the number of media blocks, k_d, that are guaranteed to be retrieved during each round is bounded by:

$$k_d \leq \frac{\mathcal{R} - b * C}{(a + l_{rot}^{max})} \qquad (8)$$

Now, assuming that $f(S_i)$ denotes the minimum number of frames that may be contained in a block of strand S_i, the lower bound on the number of frames accessed during an overflow round is given by:

$$\mathcal{F}_o = k_d * \min_{i \in [1,n]} f(S_i) \qquad (9)$$

2.3 Admitting a New Client

Consider the scenario that a multimedia server receives a new client request for the retrieval of strand S_{n+1}. In order to validate that the admission of the new client will not violate the service requirements of the clients already being serviced, the server must first compute the overflow probability assuming that the new client has been admitted. In order to do so, the server must determine:

1. The mean and the standard deviation of the number of media blocks that may contain f_{n+1} frames of strand S_{n+1} (denoted by $\eta_{\mathcal{B}_{n+1}}$ and $\sigma_{\mathcal{B}_{n+1}}$, respectively), to be used in Equations (3) and (4);

2. The minimum and the maximum number of media blocks that may contain f_{n+1} frames of strand S_{n+1} (denoted by b_{n+1}^{min} and b_{n+1}^{max}, respectively), to be used in Equation (6); and

3. The minimum number of frames contained in a media block of strand S_{n+1} (denoted by $f(S_{n+1})$), to be used in Equation (9).

Since all of these parameters are dependent on the distribution of frame sizes in strand S_{n+1}, the server can simplify the processing requirements at the time of admission by precomputing these parameters while storing the media strand on disk.

These values, when coupled with the corresponding values for all the clients already being serviced as well as the predetermined service time distributions will yield new values for q and $\mathcal{F}_o$. The new client is then admitted for service if the newly derived values for q and $\mathcal{F}_o$ satisfy the admission control criteria:

$$q * \mathcal{F}_o + (1 - q) \sum_{i=1}^{n+1} f_i \geq \sum_{i=1}^{n+1} p_i * f_i$$

3 Enforcing Statistical Service Guarantees

Meeting the admission control criteria (i.e., Equation 1) ensures that the lower bound on the expected number of frames retrieved during a round is at least as large as the average number of frames that must be accessed during each round to meet the service requirements of all clients. Stated differently, the total number of frames discarded by the multimedia server during overflow rounds will not exceed the cumulative loss tolerance of all the clients. However, to ensure that the individual service requirements of the clients are not violated, the server must judiciously distribute the discarded frames among all the clients. The sequential nature of video playback facilitates the prediction of the set of blocks to be accessed in a round prior to its initiation, and thereby enables a server to employ various policies for discarding media blocks during overflow rounds.

To precisely formulate the selection criteria, let us assume that $\mathcal{T}_i$ denotes the entire playback duration of strand S_i. Since $\mathcal{R}_{pl}^i$ and p_i denote the playback rate of strand S_i (expressed in frames/sec) and the service requirement of the client i, respectively, the number of frames of strand S_i which can be discarded over the entire playback duration, without violating the requirements of client i, is bounded by:

$$\mathcal{F}_i = \lfloor (1 - p_i) * \mathcal{R}_{pl}^i * \mathcal{T}_i \rfloor \qquad (10)$$

Since $\mathcal{R}$ denotes the duration of a round, the retrieval of strand S_i from disk will be spread across $r = \lceil \frac{\mathcal{T}_i}{\mathcal{R}} \rceil$ rounds. In order to achieve an equitable distribution of the discarded frames throughout the playback duration of a strand, and hence to minimize the perceptual loss of media information, we define *loss affordability* of client i during round j (denoted by $\chi_{i,j}$) as $\chi_{i,j} = L_{i,j} - l_{i,j}$, where:

$$L_{i,j} = \lfloor j * (1 - p_i) * f_i \rfloor ; \quad l_{i,j} = \sum_{m=1}^{j-1} \widehat{l_i^m}$$

where $\widehat{l_i^m}$ denotes the number of frames of strand S_i discarded during the mth round. The server can then select a set of media blocks to be discarded during an overflow round based on the relative values of $\chi_{i,j}$. Since $L_{i,j}$ gradually increases from one round to the next, employing such a policy will enable the server to disperse the frame losses throughout the playback duration of the strand.

To minimize the number of media blocks discarded during an overflow round, we now present a two-step algorithm for selecting a set of media blocks to be discarded during a round based both on the loss affordability of the clients and their relative placement on disk. In the first step, the server can compare the loss affordability of client i with the number of frames contained in each block of strand S_i to be retrieved during the round, and label them as either *can-be-discarded* or *can-not-be-discarded*. Clearly, this labeling procedure is dependent on the video compression scheme. For instance, if all the frames in a video strand are considered equally important (e.g., intra-coded frames in a JPEG video clip), then if the loss affordability $\chi_{i,j}$ is smaller than the number of frames contained in a media block of strand S_i, the block must be labeled as *can-not-be-discarded*. Otherwise, the block is labeled as *can-be-discarded*. On the other hand, for an MPEG-encoded video strand, since discarding an I-frame effectively eliminates all the succeeding P- and B-frames until the next I-frame can be accessed, the loss affordability must be compared with the *effective* frame loss, rather than just the number of frames contained in the block.

Once all the blocks have been labeled, the server must judiciously select and discard a subset of the *can-be-discarded* blocks. To minimize the number of frames discarded during this process, the selection criteria must be governed by the reduction in service time obtained by discarding a block as well as the number of frames contained in it. Specifically, if $\psi(z)$ and $f(z)$ denote the reduction in service time yielded

by discarding media block z and the number of frames contained in block z, respectively, then a gain function $g(z)$ can be defined as:

$$g(z) = \frac{\psi(z)}{f(z)}$$

The server can then minimize the cumulative frame loss by discarding *can-be-discarded* media blocks in the decreasing order of $g(z)$.

Regardless of the labeling algorithm as well as the selection policy, once a media block to be discarded is determined, the multimedia server can recompute the service time τ_{new}. If $\tau_{new} > \mathcal{R}$, then the number of media blocks discarded need to be progressively increased until the new retrieval sequence yields $\tau_{new} \leq \mathcal{R}$. If, even after discarding all the *can-be-discarded* media blocks, the service time continues to be greater than the duration of the round, then $L_{i,j}$ can be set to $\mathcal{F}_i$, and the above process can be repeated. Since the clients are admitted by the server only when the admission control criteria (Equation (1)) is satisfied, it is guaranteed that the total number of frames discarded will never exceed $\sum_{i=1}^n \mathcal{F}_i$. Hence, the server is guaranteed to find a subset of media blocks which when discarded yield sufficient reduction in service time, while ensuring that the service requirements of the clients are not violated.

4 Experimental Evaluation

In this section, we demonstrate the viability of the statistical admission control algorithm through trace-driven simulations. The simulations were carried out in an environment consisting of a synchronous disk array with 16 disks. The characteristics of each disk are shown in Table 1. For the purposes of the simulations, each video strand is assumed to be encoded using a Variable Bit Rate (VBR) compression technique, and striped across the entire disk array. Successive blocks of a strand are assumed to be stored on the disk using the random placement model [3]. A *greedy* disk scheduling algorithm, which derives a retrieval sequence of media blocks from disk so as to simultaneously minimize both seek time and rotational latency, was employed for the simulations [9]. Furthermore, the playback rate of each video strand is assumed to be 30 frames/sec. The trace data for frame size variation yielded by VBR encoding techniques was obtained from Bellcore, University of California at Berkeley, and Columbia University.

4.1 Computing the Overflow Probability

For a multimedia server servicing n clients, an overflow is said to occur when the service time τ exceeds the playback duration $\mathcal{R}$ of a round. For various values of $\mathcal{R}$, we have computed the overflow probability q by determining distribution functions for: (1) service time τ_k for various values of k, and (2) the number of blocks $\mathcal{B}$ accessed during a round.

To illustrate, consider the scenario in which a multimedia server is retrieving 30 frames for each client during each

Disk capacity	4 GBytes
Number of disks in the array	16
Number tracks per disk	1024
Disk block size	32 KBytes
Rate of disk rotation	3600 RPM
$l_{seek}(t_1, t_2)$	$4 + 0.02 * |t_1 - t_2|$ ms
Maximum seek time	24.48 ms
Maximum rotational latency	16.66 ms

Table 1 : Disk parameters assumed in the simulation

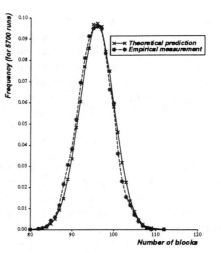

Figure 1 : Comparison of the empirically derived variation in the number of blocks accessed during each round for sixty clients and the theoretically derived normal distribution function

round. Since the playback rate for all the clients is assumed to be 30 frames/sec, we get $\mathcal{R} = 1$ sec. Using Equation (8), the minimum number of blocks that are guaranteed to be retrieved within time $\mathcal{R}$ can be derived as $k_d = 48$. Starting with $k = k_d$, the process of computing service time distributions was repeated, by incrementing the value of k by 1 for each iteration, until for a particular value of $k = k_{end}$, $P(\tau_{k_{end}} > \mathcal{R}) \simeq 1$. For our environment, this termination condition was satisfied for $k_{end} = 170$. Notice that since the service time distributions are required to be computed only once during the lifetime of a multimedia server, the complexity of the above procedure is not very critical. Furthermore, since the variation in service times for different values of k follow the same pattern, instead of generating service time distribution functions for all values of $k \in [k_d, k_{end}]$, standard statistical modeling techniques can be employed to characterize the observed values of τ_k as a well-known distribution function. For instance, assuming that media blocks of each strand have been placed on disk using the random placement model, it can be shown that the service time yielded by SCAN disk scheduling algorithm is characterized by a normal distribution function. Once such a distribution function is determined, it can be parameterized appropriately to obtain the service time distribution functions for various values of k.

In order to validate our hypothesis that the total number of media blocks accessed during a round is normally distributed, we experimentally measured the variation in the number of blocks accessed during a round for different numbers of clients. Figure 1 shows one such distribution function obtained for 60 clients. As is evident from the figure, the empirically derived distribution function is closely approximated by the normal distribution.

Finally, using the distribution functions for service time and the number of blocks accessed during a round, we derived the overflow probability q (using Equation (2)), and studied its variation with increase in the number of clients n and the playback duration $\mathcal{R}$ (see Figure 2). As depicted in Figure 2, the value of q rises very slowly for small values of n, grows very rapidly over a small range of values of n, and finally

saturates at large values of n. This is because, for small n, the value of k_{max} derived using Equation (6) is sufficiently small such that the distribution function for $\tau_{k_{max}}$ is completely to the left of $\mathcal{R}$, and hence, $q \approx 0$. Similarly, for large values of n, the value of k_{min} derived using Equation (6) is sufficiently large such that the distribution function for $\tau_{k_{min}}$ is completely to the right of $\mathcal{R}$, yielding $q \approx 1$. For all the values of n between these extremes, the sudden rise in the value of q can be attributed to the bell-shaped curve for the distribution functions. Figure 2 also demonstrates that as the number of frames accessed for each client during a round increases (i.e. $\mathcal{R}$ increases), the server can accommodate a larger number of clients for the same value of q, albeit at the cost of increased latency. The rate of increase in the number of clients, however, decreases with increase in $\mathcal{R}$.

4.2 Evaluating the Statistical Admission Control Algorithm

We have compared the performance of our statistical admission control algorithm with conventional deterministic admission control algorithms [1, 2, 10, 11] (see Figure 3). As is depicted in Figure 3, the statistical admission control algorithm achieves a 200% increase in the number of clients that can be serviced simultaneously by the server.

Furthermore, to evaluate the effectiveness of the statistical admission control algorithm, we have compared its performance with theoretically derived as well as empirically observed bounds on the maximum number of clients that can be serviced simultaneously by a multimedia server. The theoretical upper bound, denoted by n_{max}, is defined as the ratio of the average data transfer bandwidth from the disk to the average data rate requirement of the clients. The empirically observed bound, denoted by n_{obs}, is derived by continuously

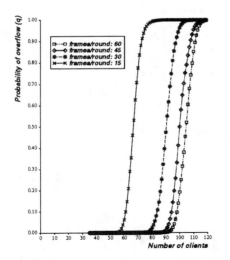

Figure 2 : Variation of the overflow probability with number of clients

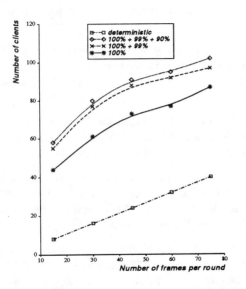

Figure 3 : Comparison of the statistical admission control algorithm with its deterministic counterpart

increasing the number of clients being serviced by the server until the service requirements of at least one of the clients are violated. Finally, n_{stat} denotes the maximum number of clients that can be admitted for service by the statistical admission control algorithm proposed in this paper. For various values of the desired quality of service (i.e., p_i), Figure 4 depicts the variation in n_{max}, n_{obs}, and n_{stat} with increase in round duration $\mathcal{R}$.

Figure 4 demonstrates that the number of clients admitted by the statistical admission control algorithm increases with decrease in p_i. However, the rate of increase in n_{stat} decreases with decrease in p_i. To explain this behavior, consider the statistical admission control criteria (i.e., Equation (1)). Since the value of $q * \mathcal{F}_o$ is likely to be very small as compared to the term $(1 - q) * \sum_{i=1}^{n} f_i$, the maximum

permissible value of the overflow probability can be approximated as: $q \approx (1 - p_i)$. Thus, for the region of interest depicted in Figure 4 (namely, $0.9 \leq p_i \leq 1$), the overflow probability q must be bounded within $[0.0, 0.1]$. Within this region, relaxing the requirements of the clients from $p_i = 1.0$ to $p_i = 0.99$, and thereby increasing the maximum tolerable overflow probability from $q = 0.0$ to $q = 0.01$, enables the server to exploit the statistical variation in service times, and admit a much larger number of clients. However, as depicted in Figure 2, once the overflow probability is about 0.01, the server operates in a state where each increase in the number of clients results in a sharp increase in the value of q. Hence, relaxing the service requirements of the clients further, and thereby increasing the maximum tolerable value of overflow probability, does not yield the same rate of increase in n_{stat}. Figure 4 also demonstrates that, in the region of interest, the value of n_{max} increases linearly with the reduction in p_i. In comparison, the rate of increase in n_{stat} is higher when $(1 - p_i) \leq 0.3$, and lower for all higher values of $(1 - p_i)$. Hence, the difference between the values of n_{max} and n_{stat} decreases when p_i reduces from 1.0 to 0.97, (see Figures 4(a) and 4(b)), but starts to increase once $p_i < 0.97$ (see Figures 4(b) and 4(c)).

Figure 4 also demonstrates the values of n_{stat} supported by the statistical admission control algorithm are inherently more conservative than n_{obs}. This is because, for all n, $n_{stat} \leq n \leq n_{max}$, although the statistical analysis predicts that there exists a sequence of access patterns which may result in the violation of service requirements of some of the clients, it may not be encountered during the finite playback times of each media strand. Furthermore, in order to ensure that satisfying the admission control criteria (i.e., Equation (1)) is sufficient for meeting the statistical service requirements of all the clients, the value of $\mathcal{F}_o$ was derived by making worst-case assumptions (Section 2.2). In practice, however, employing the techniques for judiciously selecting a set of blocks to be discarded during overflow rounds (outlined in Section 3) may successfully retrieve a much larger number of frames as compared to $\mathcal{F}_o$. Hence, in practice, n_{obs} is ensured to be at least as large as n_{stat}. The difference between n_{obs} and n_{stat}, however, can be bridged by utilizing the available service time distributions and deriving $\mathcal{F}_o$ as:

$$\mathcal{F}_o = k_{stat} * \min_{i \in [1,n]} f(S_i)$$

where k_{stat} is the maximum value of k for which $P(\tau_k \leq \mathcal{R}) \simeq 1$.

5   Concluding Remarks

In this paper, we have presented a statistical admission control algorithm which improves the utilization of server resources by exploiting the variation in the access times of media blocks from disk, as well as the variation in playback rate requirement induced by variable rate compression techniques. The

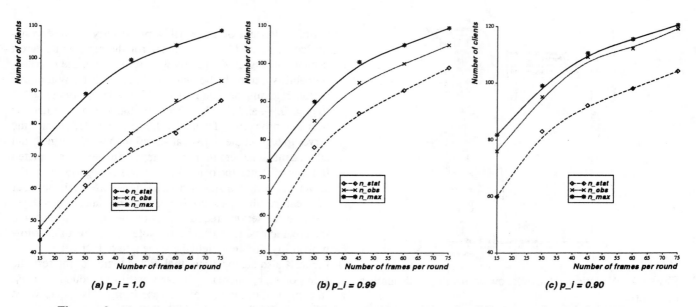

Figure 4 : Variation in n_{max}, n_{obs}, and n_{stat} with increase in round time for different service requirements

main goals of our admission control algorithm are to: (1) accept enough traffic to efficiently utilize the server resources, while not accepting clients whose admission may lead to the violations of the service requirements of clients, and (2) provide statistical service guarantees to each client. We have demonstrated the effectiveness of the statistical admission control algorithm through extensive simulations. Our simulation results reveal that, as compared to its deterministic counterpart, the statistical admission algorithm achieves a 200% increase in the number of clients serviced simultaneously. A prototype multimedia server, based on the algorithms presented in this paper, is being implemented at the UT Austin Distributed Multimedia Computing Laboratory.

REFERENCES

[1] D. Anderson, Y. Osawa, and R. Govindan. A File System for Continuous Media. *ACM Transactions on Computer Systems*, 10(4):311–337, November 1992.

[2] J. Gemmell and S. Christodoulakis. Principles of Delay Sensitive Multimedia Data Storage and Retrieval. *ACM Transactions on Information Systems*, 10(1):51–90, 1992.

[3] M. K. McKusick, W. N. Joy, S. J. Leffler, and R. S. Fabry. A Fast File System for UNIX. *ACM Transactions on Computer Systems*, 2(3):181–197, August 1984.

[4] G. Miller, G. Baber, and M. Gilliland. News On-Demand for Multimedia Networks. In *Proceedings of ACM Multimedia'93, Anaheim, CA*, pages 383–392, August 1993.

[5] A. Papoulis. *Probability, Random Variables, and Stochastic Processes*. McGraw Hill, 1991.

[6] A.L. Narasimha Reddy and J. Wyllie. Disk Scheduling in Multimedia I/O System. In *Proceedings of ACM Multimedia'93, Anaheim, CA*, pages 225–234, August 1993.

[7] T. Teorey and T. B. Pinkerton. A Comparative Analysis of Disk Scheduling Policies. *Communications of the ACM*, 15(3):177–184, March 1972.

[8] F.A. Tobagi, J. Pang, R. Baird, and M. Gang. Streaming RAID: A Disk Storage System for Video and Audio Files. In *Proceedings of ACM Multimedia'93, Anaheim, CA*, pages 393–400, August 1993.

[9] Harrick M. Vin, Alok Goyal, Anshuman Goyal, and Pawan Goyal. An Observation-Based Approach For Designing Multimedia Servers. In *Proceedings of the IEEE International Conference on Multimedia Computing and Systems, Boston, MA*, pages 234–243, May 1994.

[10] Harrick M. Vin and P. Venkat Rangan. Designing a Multi-User HDTV Storage Server. *IEEE Journal on Selected Areas in Communications*, 11(1):153–164, January 1993.

[11] P. Yu, M.S. Chen, and D.D. Kandlur. Design and Analysis of a Grouped Sweeping Scheme for Multimedia Storage Management. *Proceedings of Third International Workshop on Network and Operating System Support for Digital Audio and Video, San Diego*, pages 38–49, November 1992.

A GENERALIZED INTERVAL CACHING POLICY FOR MIXED INTERACTIVE AND LONG VIDEO WORKLOADS

Asit Dan, Dinkar Sitaram
IBM T.J.Watson Research Center
Hawthorne, NY

e-mail:{asit,sitaram} @ watson.ibm.com

In a video server environment, some video objects (e.g., movies) are very large and are read sequentially. Hence it is not economical to cache the entire object. However, caching random fractions of a multimedia object is not beneficial. Therefore, traditional cache management policies such as LRU are not effective. The sequential access of pages can be exploited by caching only the intervals between two successive streams on the same object, i.e., by retaining the pages brought in by a stream for reuse by a closely following stream and subsequently discarding them. In contrast to the movie-on-demand workload, an interactive workload is composed of many short video clips (e.g., shopping). Hence, concurrent access to the same video clip will be infrequent and interval caching policy will not be effective. In this paper, we propose a *Generalized Interval Caching policy* that caches both short video objects as well as intervals or fractions of large video objects. To study the efficacy of the GIC policy, we also propose a model for mixed short interactive and long video workloads. The proposed policy is shown to effectively reduce disk overload and hence to increase the capacity of the video server.

1 Introduction

In a video server environment, to guarantee continuous delivery of video streams to the clients sufficient resources need to be reserved on the server [15, 6]. For an environment with a large number of users, the required disk bandwidth can be very high. With falling memory prices, caching of video data can be cost-effective in reducing the disk bandwidth requirement. Two types of applications may co-exist in such environments: interactive and movie-on-demand. An interactive application consists of many small video clips that are displayed in response to client commands. In contrast, under a movie-on-demand application a single long video may be watched for a long duration (say two hours). Hence it is necessary to develop caching techniques that handle both large as well as short video objects. In addition, such a policy should adapt quickly to a change in workload. Hence, fixed allocation of cache to different objects will not be effective.

Traditional cache management policies employed by various software systems are based upon the concept of a *hot set* of data which is much smaller in size than the total set of data [3, 14]. Generalizing the idea of a hot set to the video-on-demand environment (i.e. storing the most frequently accessed videos in the cache) may not be very useful, since multimedia objects (e.g. movie) may be very large. Hence, caching even a small number of popular movies will require a very large memory space. Caching policies which operate at the block level (e.g. single page) and caches unrelated set of blocks (e.g., LRU) can not guarantee continuous delivery of streams.

For movie-on-demand and other applications with large video objects, we proposed an *Interval Caching Policy* that caches only the small intervals between successive streams [5]. The pages brought in by a preceding stream are retained in the cache for reuse by a following stream being served from cache. By caching only the smallest intervals from a large sample of intervals, the policy exploits the statistical variation in interval size. Such a policy is shown to be superior, in terms of the cache hit ratio, to the policy of caching the hottest movies. In addition, the policy dynamically adapts to the changing frequency of access to different movies unlike the static caching policy. Interval caching policy, however, is not directly applicable for an *interactive workload* consisting of small videos. This is because concurrent accesses to small video objects are infrequent and hence, there are very few intervals that can be cached.

We extended the interval caching policy to handle any mix of interactive and long video workloads. The new policy is referred to as the *Generalized Interval Caching (GIC)* policy since it is based on the generalization of the concept of interval. For the short video objects where the concurrent accesses are unlikely, the interval is defined as the time between successive accesses to the same object, and is referred to as the *predictive interval*. The policy still caches the shortest intervals whether the interval encompasses the entire video object or just a segment as in the interval caching policy. This uniform approach to caching allows the GIC policy to handle both interactive and movie-on-demand applications while retaining the benefits of interval caching such as superior performance and adaption to changing access frequency.

Earlier works in multimedia buffer management have studied the buffer requirements for various disk scheduling algorithms [15, 1]. In these works, the video data block is discarded once it has been transmitted to the clients and is not retained for subsequent re-use by other clients. The idea of using alternatives to LRU and CLOCK for sequential access patterns has been used in several contexts in database environments [18, 11, 2, 17, 16]. In a general database environment, various queries and transactions follow different access patterns [2, 17, 4]. The concept of query hot set is exploited in [2, 17, 12] for allocation of cache to various queries. Various prefetching strategies based on the dynamic identification of sequential access have been used in [16, 4]. The objective in all of the above work has been to minimize the overall response time and cache miss probability. Hence these algorithms may not provide continuous delivery of a stream from the cache. The algorithm that is closest to the current work is [16] which tries to retain the page that will be accessed earliest for concurrently executing queries in a batch environment. The objective of the algorithm is to minimize the total completion time of all jobs and hence to be fair in terms of cache miss to all jobs. Note that this does not translate into a continuous delivery guarantee.

Research Contributions: The contribution of this paper is twofold. First, we propose a a model for *interactive workloads* that can be used to study system performance under interactive applications, e.g., medical, shopping, etc.

We next propose a stream dependent caching policy (as opposed to traditional block level caching policy) for both short video clips as well as long videos. In a mixed workload environment, where both long videos and short clips are present [8], we use the notion of predictive intervals to extend the basic interval caching policy that we had proposed in [5]. The basic policy was shown to be adaptable to load change in [5] and cost-effective in [10] for long video workload.

This extended policy is referred to as the *Generalized Interval Caching Policy*. Here, we also provide an overview of the GIC policy.

The remainder of this paper is organized as follows. In section 2, we discuss client behaviour, the types of applications studied and the server environment. We discuss the details of the GIC policy in Section 3. In section 4, we study the performance of this policy using a detailed simulation. Finally, we summarize our results in section 5.

A more detailed version of this paper [7] describes the implementation of the GIC policy and demonstrates its cost-effectiveness.

2   Video Applications

Two different types of applications may be possible in video-on-demand servers. In an interactive application, short video clips are displayed in response to frequent client commands. An example is a shopping application where a video catalog consisting of short product advertisements may be browsed by clients. Alternatively, in a movie-on-demand applications clients view long running movies (typically 1-2 hours long) and client commands are infrequent once the selected movie starts playing (e.g. occasional pause/resume). Since the performance of the GIC policy will depend on the type of application, both types of applications are considered in the paper.

2.1   Interactive Application

Under an interactive application, the server contains a video catalog consisting of short clips of varying length. The interactive application workload is characterized by the following three parameters:

Access skew across the clips. We will use the notation $x - y$ to represent that x fraction of the viewing requests go to the y fraction of the clips in the database.

Clip length distribution. The length of any clip is assumed to be distributed between L_{min} and L_{max}.

Viewing time per individual clip. Many interactive applications may use *video banners* consisting of a short clip that is displayed repeatedly (e.g. a logo that is shown until the client makes a selection). To model this kind of behaviour, each clip is assumed to be viewed for a random viewing time. Viewing time is assumed to be independent of the length of a clip, and can be smaller than the playback duration of an entire clip. Therefore, general viewing time, T_v, is modeled as a random variable.

Client session duration. Each client session is modeled as a set of clips selected using the above parameters and the session duration is assumed to be of length $T_{session}$. The client selects playing of a new clip until the session duration exceeds $T_{session}$.

2.2   Movie-on-demand application

In a pure movie-on-demand application, clients may choose movies according to an access distribution. The access distribution is based on the empirical data on video rentals in various video stores during a particular week [19]. The empirical data can be fitted using a Zipf distribution over 92 movies with the parameter 0.271 [5]. In our paper, the Zipf distribution is used to generate accesses to video files. Each client session is assumed to be the playback of a single movie.

A mixed workload environment is modeled by randomly classifying a client during the session open time as interactive or movie-on-demand clients. A control parameter called the *interactive probability* determines the ratio of interactive and movie-on-demand sessions. The client arrival process is modeled as a Poisson proces with a mean inter-arrival duration of T seconds.

2.3   Server Environment

A video server may contain various software processes such as a disk manager that reads data from disk, a communication manager that transmits data to clients, and a cache manager that determines which blocks are to be retained in the cache [5]. The cache space is subdivided into a number of blocks, and the

blocks containing valid data are in the cache pool while the rest of the blocks are in the free pool. During normal operation, for each data stream the disk manager acquires a free block, inserts it into the cache pool and starts the disk I/O to read data into that block. The communication manager on the other hand sends previous data blocks of a stream stored in the cache to the corresponding client process.[1] In the absence of any long term caching, at the completion of the communication I/O for each data block, the data in that block is discarded by returning the block to the free pool. Hence, only two cache blocks per stream are required.

The data brought in by a stream however can be reused by other closely following streams, if sufficient cache space is available to retain the data blocks in the cache. Upon completion of the communication I/O for each data block the cache manager is invoked to decide whether the block should be returned to the free pool or retained in the cache pool for reuse by other streams. Note that the processes share blocks by the exchange of pointers and not by copying data. We next describe the GIC policy and detail the implementation issues.

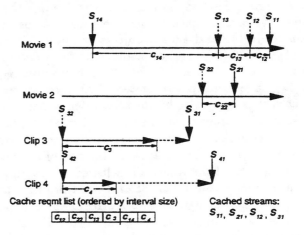

Figure 1: Generalized Interval Caching policy

3   Overview of the Proposed Policy

The main idea behind the proposed policy is illustrated using Figure 1. The small arrows marked by

---

[1] The same data may be sent to multiple client processes if playback of the video by multiple clients are synchronized [6].

S_{11} through S_{42} represent the pointers corresponding to the various playback streams on the large movies 1 and 2, and video clips 3 and 4. In the interval caching policy [5], two streams, S_{ij} and S_{ik} accessing the same video object are defined as *consecutive* if S_{ik} is the stream that next reads the data blocks that have just been read by S_{ij}; and a pair of consecutive streams is referred to as an *interval*. The two streams of an interval are referred to as the *preceding* and the *following* streams. By caching the blocks brought in by the preceding stream, it is possible to serve the following stream from the cache. The *cache requirement* of an interval is defined to be the number of blocks needed to store the interval and is a function of the time-interval between the two streams and the compression method used. The interval caching policy selects the intervals to be cached so as to maximize the number of streams served from cache. It orders the intervals in terms of their cache requirements and caches the shortest intervals.

Figure 1 illustrates how the definition of an interval is extended to small video objects that are not being accessed concurrently. Arrows S_{32} and S_{42} represent two streams presently reading small video objects 3 and 4. Arrows S_{31} and S_{41} represent the position that would have been reached by the previous streams accessing objects 3 and 4 if the objects had been larger. (S_{31}, S_{32}), and (S_{41}, S_{42}) are defined to form two intervals for objects 3 and 4 even though streams S_{31} and S_{41} have already terminated. The *interval size* in this case is defined to be the time-interval between two successive accesses on the same object. However, the cache requirement is smaller than the interval size times the data rate and is equal to the size of the object. Therefore, if the interval is selected for caching, the entire video object will be cached. Note that at the time of allocating cache to a stream there is no concurrent following stream on that object. The sizes of the previous intervals provide an indication of the anticipated interval size for that object. In this paper, we will assume the size of the last interval as the anticipated interval size.

The GIC policy thus caches intervals which may be either video segments or entire video objects. The policy orders all intervals (current or anticipated) in terms of increasing interval size (see, Figure 1). As before, it then allocates cache to as many of the intervals as possible. Hence, with a larger number of video segments and video objects, the GIC policy still maximizes the number of streams served from the cache.

The ability to choose a small set of intervals from a large set of samples allows the policy to exploit the variation in cache requirements across all intervals due to size, the variation in inter-arrival times and/or different compression rates for different videos.

Changes to the interval list may occur due to the arrival of a new stream or termination of a current stream. Therefore, the algorithm for reordering of the interval list and the allocation and deallocation of cache to intervals is executed only at the time of arrival or ending of a playback stream (the finer details of selecting the intervals to be cached and switching of a stream from cache to disk and vice versa are discussed in later subsections). Since only simple modifications are required when opening or closing a video file, the policy is simple to implement.

OPEN:

```
Form new interval with previous stream;
Compute cache requirement
    and interval size;
Reorder cache requirement list;
If not already cached
    If space available,
        Cache this new interval;
    else if this interval is smaller
        than existing cached intervals
      and sufficient cache space
            can be released
        Release cache space from
            larger intervals;
        Cache this new interval;
```

Figure 2: Details of OPEN in generalized interval caching policy

3.1 Details of implementation

Figure 2 shows the actions taken when an open request is received from an user. As described earlier, a new interval is formed by the new request and the preceding stream. The cache requirement and interval size of this new interval are computed. Successive requests to a small video object may result in all the blocks of the object being retained in the cache. Hence, if the open request is for a small video object, the interval may already be in the cache.

If the interval is not already cached, the cache manager determines if it is desirable to cache the interval as follows. Since the cache manager attempts to retain the blocks with the lowest interval size, it determines the total cache space available in intervals with a larger interval size and the free pool. If this space is larger than the cache requirement of the new interval, the new interval is allocated cache space from the free pool as well as the intervals with the largest interval sizes. In the case where the free space by itself is sufficient, the cache manager need not release cache from intervals with larger sizes. The decision to cache an interval has different results depending on whether the interval is formed by two concurrent streams or not. In the former case, blocks brought in by the preceding stream are retained in the cache and used to serve the new request. Caching an anticipated interval results in retaining the blocks brought in by the new request for use by a later stream.

CLOSE:

```
If following stream of an interval
    Delete the interval;
    Free allocated cache;
    If next largest interval can
            be cached
        Cache next largest interval;
```

Figure 3: Details of CLOSE in generalized interval caching policy

Figure 3 summarizes the steps needed during when the client finishes viewing a video. When a close request is received, the interval in which the client was the following stream is deleted. If the interval is a segment of a video object, it is unlikely that there will be any benefit to retaining it in the cache. Hence the cache management process releases the space being held by the interval. The cache management process then considers the interval with the smallest interval size to determine if it should be allocated cache using the same algorithm used during the arrival of a new stream.

3.2 VCR control

Video-on-demand systems may allow clients to pause and restart viewing at arbitrary times. At such times, the stream dependencies will change. The problem of providing VCR control capabilities exists even in the absence of a caching policy, since the resources released during a pause may not be available in general at the time of a resume request. In [6] it is proposed that pause and resume requests be handled by setting aside a small pool of channels called *contingency channels*. The method provides a *statistical guarantee* that with high probability (e.g. 99%) a resume request can be serviced within a small pre-specified delay. It is shown in [9] that this method is more efficient than reserving resources for all paused streams. Details of an integrated GIC policy under VCR control can be found in [7].

4 Simulation and Results

In [5], it is shown that the analysis of the interval caching policy can be related to the general problem of obtaining order statistics and that obtaining explicit expressions may be quite a difficult task. Hence, simulation is used to study the effectiveness of the GIC policy. In the simulation, clients made random requests to a server. The server disks were assumed to be striped together into a single striping group with a pre-specified bandwidth. The simulation modelled the change in disk load due to arrival and ending of client requests, or switching between cache and disk. Requests for videos that would result in overloading of disk bandwidth are rejected. However, individual block I/Os are not modelled. The cache is modelled as a collection of 1MB blocks. While computing the amount of cache space required for a cachable segment, the computation is rounded up to the nearest megabyte. In order to estimate the length of the simulation, trial runs are made using the method of batch means. It is found that with a simulation duration of 8 hours, after ignoring the initial transient (1.5 hours), 99% confidence intervals of less than 10% are obtained for important quantities such as the average number of streams reading from the cache. Thus the simulations are run, in general, for 8 hours.

4.1 Workload Parameters

The client inter-arrival time, T, is assumed to be 6.25 seconds corresponding to a server simultaneously serving on an average 400 streams. This value is typical of the range of active clients expected for video-on-demand servers [13]. The mixed workload is modeled by varying the control parameter *interactive probability*. Unless mentioned otherwise, this parameter is taken to be 0.8. The duration of an interactive session, T_s, is assumed to be 30 minutes. Therefore, 50% of all I/O requests are made by the interactive sessions. All videos are assumed to be MPEG-1 with a delivery rate of 192 KB/s. The length of the movies is assumed to be approximately ninety minutes long so that the total amount of storage required per movie is one GB. The movie library consists of 92 movies with an access skew parameter of 0.271.

For interactive applications, in the base case, a video catalog of 500 MPEG-1 video clips with viewing time uniformly distributed up to 30 seconds was stored on the server. Thus in the base case, the total size of the video catalog was 125 minutes. The number of video clips was varied in the simulation to study its impact on the server capacity. A clip access distribution of 80-20 was studied. The length of a clip is uniformly distributed between 1 second and 30 seconds. For modelling video banners, each clip was viewed for an exponentially distributed viewing time with an average of 30 seconds. However, the minimum viewing time of a clip is set to 5 seconds. Experiments varying other parameters are reported in [7].

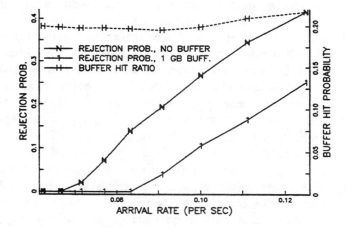

Figure 4: Rejection probability; 400 stream disk capacity

4.2 Admission Control

In the presence of caching, the number of streams that can be served by a video server depends on the number of streams that can be served from the cache. The capacity of a system can be measured as the request rate that can be supported with no or a small

rejection probability. Figure 4 shows the rejection probability as a function of the arrival rate for a system with a disk capacity of 400 streams. The two curves are for a system without any cache and a system with 1 GB cache. In both cases, the rejection probability is 0 initially and then rises approximately linearly. Considering the arrival rates where the rejection probabilities become non-zero (.067/sec and .085/sec) it can be seen that the effect of caching is to increase the system capacity by 25%. Figure 4 also shows the corresponding overall cache hit ratios, defined as the number of reads served from the cache as a fraction of the total number of reads. From the graph it can be seen that the hit ratio is 0.22 which translates to a 25% increase in system capacity. Hence, in the following results, only the cache hit ratio is studied since the increase in system capacity due to caching is proportional to the cache hit ratio.

4.3 Cache hit ratios

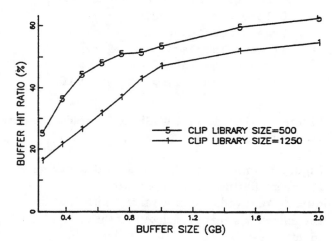

Figure 5: Overall cache hit ratio for mixed workload

In the following, we show that high hit ratios are possible with the generalized interval caching policy under a wide range of variation in the workload parameters. Figure 5 shows the variation of the overall cache hit ratio as a function of the cache size for the base mixed workload. The two curves are for an interactive library size of 500 clips and 1250 clips. For a given cache size, the overall hit ratio with 500 clips is higher than that with 1250 clips since with a smaller number of clips, a larger fraction of the accesses falls on the clips retained in the cache. Figure 6 shows the hit ratios of the individual components of the workload. The clip hit ratio is defined as the fraction of clip reads satisfied from the cache. Similarly, the movie hit ratio is the fraction of movie reads serviced from the cache. The access to the short videos are more likely to be found in the cache, and only the shortest intervals of long videos are satisfied from cache. However, both clip and movie hit ratios are smaller for the workload with 1250 clips.

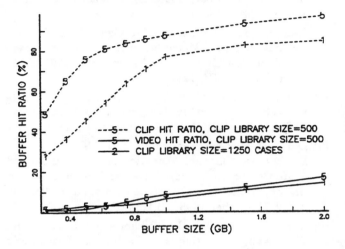

Figure 6: Interactive and movie cache hit ratios for mixed workload

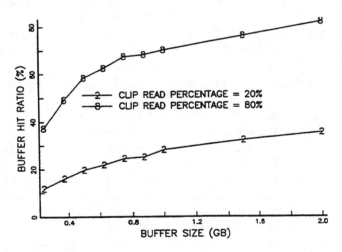

Figure 7: Effect of varying interactive fraction on overall cache hit ratio

The variation of the overall cache hit ratio with the cache size for different fractions of short video clips is shown in Figure 7. The interactive library size contains 500 clips as in the base workload. The two curves shown are for workloads where the fraction of accesses to the short clips are 20% and 80%, respectively. The cache hit ratio is much larger for the workload with the read percentage to interactive

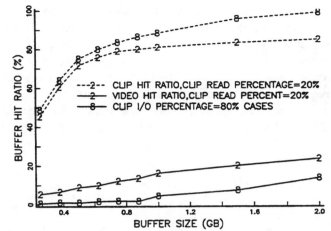

Figure 8: Effect of varying interactive fraction on interactive and movie cache hit ratios

clips as 80%, since by caching the hot clips in a small amount of cache, a larger fraction of the accesses can be served from the cache. Figure 8 shows the hit ratios for the interactive clips and the movies seperately for the two different values of read percentage to interactive clips. The dotted lines are for the interactive clips while the solid lines are for the movies. In both cases, the cache hit ratio for the clips is higher than that for the movies. However, the clip hit ratio for the 80% read case is higher than that for the 20% read case while the relationship is reversed for the movie hit ratios. This is because with decreasing clip access frequency, a smaller number of hot clips are retained in the cache, leading to a lower clip cache hit ratio and a higher movie cache hit ratio.

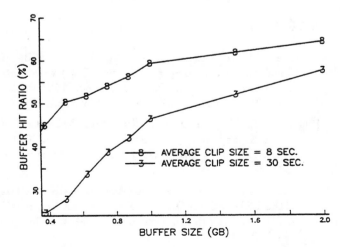

Figure 9: Effect of varying average clip size on overall cache hit ratio

Figure 9 plots the cache hit ratio against the cache size for two different values of average clip size (8 seconds and 30 seconds). The cache hit ratio with an average clip size of 8 seconds is higher than that for an average clip size of 30 seconds, since less cache is required when the clip size is smaller. At large cache sizes, however, the difference in hit ratio is reduced, since in both cases most of the hot clips can be stored.

5 Conclusions

In this paper, we proposed a model for interactive workload consisting of short video clips. We then used the notion of predictive intervals to extend the basic stream dependent caching policy (*Interval Caching* policy [5]) for handling mixed workloads consisting of long movies and short interactive clips. The extended policy is referred to as the *Generalized Interval Caching (GIC)* policy. The implementation of GIC policy requires only a small modification to the video server access path during start, resume, pause or stop of videos. Hence, it is easy to implement in any existing multimedia server. Since analytical modelling of the policy is intractable, the performance of the generalized interval caching (GIC) policy is studied by simulation. A mixed workload consisting of an interactive application and a movie-on-demand application was used in the simulation. It is shown that the GIC policy has high cache hit ratios with small size of cache with varying mixes of the two application types and with varying parameters of the workloads.

References

[1] Chen, M., D. Kandlur, and P. Yu, "Optimization of the Grouped Sweeping Scheduling (GSS) with Heterogenous Multimedia Streams", *Proc. ACM Multimedia 93*, Anaheim, CA, Aug. 1993, pp. 235–242.

[2] Chou, H. T., and D. J. Dewitt, "An Evaluation of Buffer Management Strategies for Relational Database Systems," *VLDB Conf.*, Stockholm, Sweden, 1985.

[3] Dan, A., and D. Towsley, "An Approximate Analysis of the LRU and FIFO Buffer Replacement Schemes," *ACM SIGMETRICS*, Denver, CO, May 1990, pp. 143–152.

[4] Dan, A., P. Yu, and J. Y. Chung, "Characterization of Database Access Patterns for Analytic Pre-

diction of Buffer Hit Probability", *The VLDB Journal*, Vol. 4, No. 1, January 1995, pp. 127–154.

[5] Dan, A., and D. Sitaram, "Buffer Management Policy for an On-Demand Video Server", *IBM Research Report, RC 19347*, Yorktown Heights, NY, 1993.

[6] Dan, A., D. Sitaram, and P. Shahabuddin, "Scheduling Policies for an On-Demand Video Server with Batching", *Proc. ACM Multimedia 94*, San Fransisco, CA, October, 1994. An extended version to appear in *ACM Multimedia Systems*.

[7] Dan, A., and D. Sitaram, "A Generalized Interval Caching Policy for Mixed Interactive and Long Video Workloads", *IBM Research Report, RC 20206*, Yorktown Heights, NY, 1995.

[8] Dan, A., and D. Sitaram, "An Online Video Placement Policy based on Bandwidth to Space Ratio (BSR)", *Proc. SIGMOD'95*, San Jose, May 1995.

[9] Dan, A., P. Shahabuddin, D. Sitaram, and D. Towsley, "Channel Allocation under Batching and VCR Control in Video-On-Demand Servers", *Journal of Parallel and Distributed Computing*, Vol. 30, No. 2, November 1995, pp. 168–179.

[10] Dan, A., D. M. Dias, R. Mukherjee, D. Sitaram and R. Tewari, "Buffering and Caching in Large-Scale Video Servers", *IEEE CompCon'95*.

[11] Effelsberg, W. and T. Haerder, "Principles of Database Buffer Management", *ACM Trans. Database Systems*, Vol. 9, No. 4, Dec. 1984, pp.560–595.

[12] Faloutsos, C., R. Ng, and T. Sellis, "Predictive Load Control for Flexible Buffer Allocation," *VLDB Conf* Barcelona, Spain, 1991, pp. 265–274.

[13] *Electronic Engineering Times*, March 15, 1993, pp 72.

[14] Nicola, V. F., A. Dan, and D. M. Dias, "Analysis of the Generalized Clock Buffer Replacement Scheme for Database Transaction Processing", *ACM SIGMETRICS*, 1992, pp. 35–46.

[15] Rangan, P. V., H. M. Vin, and S. Ramanathan, "Designing an On-Demand Multimedia Service," *IEEE Communication Magazine*, Vol. 30, July 1992, pp. 56–65.

[16] Rahm, E., and D. Ferguson, "Cache Management Algorithms for Sequential Data Access" *IBM Research Report, RC15486*, Yorktown Heights, NY, 1993.

[17] Sacco, G. M., and M. Schkolnick, "Buffer Management in Relational Database Systems", *ACM Trans. Database Systems*, Vol. 11, No. 4, Dec. 1986, pp. 473–498.

[18] Teng, J. Z., and R. A. Gumaer, "Managing IBM Database 2 Buffers to Maximize Performance", *IBM Systems Journal*, Vol.23, No.2, 1984, pp.211–218.

[19] *Video Store Magazine*, Dec. 13, 1992.

On Optimal Piggyback Merging Policies for Video-On-Demand Systems

Charu Aggarwal*, Joel Wolf† and Philip S. Yu†
* Massachusetts Institute of Technology, Cambridge, Massachusetts
† IBM T.J. Watson Research Center, Yorktown Heights, New York
charu at mit.edu, jlw at watson.ibm.com, psyu at watson.ibm.com

Abstract A critical issue in the performance of a video-on-demand system is the I/O bandwidth required in order to satisfy client requests. A number of techniques have been proposed in order to reduce these bandwidth requirements. In this paper we concentrate on one such technique, known as adaptive piggybacking. We develop and analyze piggyback merging policies which are optimal over large classes of reasonable methods.

1 Introduction

In a video-on-demand (VOD) system, subscribers can choose both the movie they wish to view and the time at which they wish to view it. Such systems are becoming feasible because of recent technological advances, and will presumably become popular in the consumer market. The quality of service can be characterized in terms of the *latency time* of a customer request, defined as the length of time between the arrival of the request and the initiation of service. The latency of a request is influenced by a number of factors, which we shall outline in this section.

A VOD system may be modeled as a client-server architecture. The clients essentially consist of the cus-tomers, who access the videos stored on disks in the server. (For the purposes of this paper we shall consider only videos stored on disk. Less frequently accessed videos may reside on tertiary storage. The most frequently accessed videos may possibly be stored in memory.) Whenever there is a request for a particular video, it is accessed from the disks in the storage server, transmitted to the central processor, and then routed to the client. Thus an I/O stream needs to be scheduled. Since I/O bandwidth is costly, such streams are key resources in a VOD system, and need to be managed carefully.

One simple way of reducing the bandwidth requirements is known as *batching*. In batching, we intentionally delay the initiation of requests by some amount of time, called a *batching interval*, so that subsequent requests for the same video arriving during the current batching interval may be serviced using a single I/O stream. This trades off reduced I/O stream requirements for increased latency, of course, so large batching intervals would seem to be incompatible with the notion of a VOD system. More work on batching may be found in [1, 2, 4].

A second technique to reduce the I/O bandwidth requirements is called *bridging*. In this technique, we use memory in the central processor as a buffer. If some fixed number of frames behind a particular video stream is buffered, then any subsequent request for that video within the corresponding time interval can be read from buffer rather than from disk. This technique has the disadvantage that a considerable amount of buffer space may be required in order to build bridges large enough to yield substantial savings in bandwidth. More details on the bridging technique may be found in [6, 8].

Recently an elegant technique called *adaptive piggy-*

SIGMETRICS '96 5/96 PA, USA
© 1996 ACM 0-89791-793-6/96/0005...$3.50

backing was proposed by Golubchik, Lui, and Muntz [5]. This approach assumes the capability of altering the display rates of videos while they are in progress. (It has been established that small differences in the display rates, for example those which deviate at most 5% from the normal display rate, are not perceived by the viewer. So from the customer's perspective this notion appears feasible. We comment a bit about technical feasibility later in the paper.) Suppose two streams are displaying the same video a small number of frames apart. The idea is to display the leading stream at a slower rate, and the trailing stream at a faster rate. Then, assuming this interval is sufficiently small, the faster stream will eventually catch up with the slower stream. At that point the streams can be piggybacked, or *merged*. That is, they can be played thereafter at a single speed, and one stream can be dropped. In a sense adaptive piggybacking is similar in spirit to batching, but it avoids the extra latency which is inherent in the batching interval.

In this paper we will concentrate on adaptive piggybacking. The issue, of course, is to find piggybacking policies for which there are maximum savings in bandwidth. Three basic types of piggybacking policies were discussed in the seminal paper [5]. In approximate order of worst to best performance, these include the *simple merging* policy, the *odd-even* policy, and the *greedy* policy. The first two of these can be characterized as *elementary* in the sense that they involve at most a single change of speed for each video stream. (The greedy algorithm is not elementary.) We should note that by its nature the odd-even policy can have at most 50% improvement in the number of streams saved, because it pairs off subsequent streams.

The contribution of the current paper is twofold. First, we develop a generalization and optimal variant of the simple merging policy which appears to perform better (both empirically as well as analytically) than the version presented in [5]. Second, we propose an entirely new policy, called the *snapshot algorithm*, which will be seen to be optimal over a large class of reasonable piggybacking policies.

Ultimately, our revised simple merging algorithm, which is still elementary, will be seen to have performance nearly equal to that of greedy, the best overall algorithm of [5]. Our snapshot algorithm, which is not elementary, appears to have better performance than any known adaptive piggybacking algorithm.

This paper is organized as follows. In Section 2 we shall develop the generalized simple merging policy. We then focus on the optimal variant, and show its properties. Section 3 describes the snapshot algorithm, which is based on dynamic programming. We show that this policy is optimal over a large class of piggybacking policies. Experimental results are presented in Section 4, and a conclusion is presented in Section 5.

2   Generalized Simple Merging Policy

We shall begin by describing a slightly generalized version of the *simple merging policy* developed in [5]. Consider a single video whose length, in frames, is given by L. Initially we will not consider special features such as pause-resume, fast-forward or rewind. Assume there are two possible display speeds (in frames/second) at which the display may take place – a *slow* speed denoted by S_{min}, and a *fast* speed denoted by S_{max}. (A third, *normal* speed is also considered in [5]. We prefer to assume that the normal and slow speeds are identical, giving customers the most for their money. Less charitable authors might adopt the maxim originally attributed to P.T. Barnum: "This way to the egress." In other words, they would employ the fast speed in normal situations, simultaneously shortening the videos and encouraging customers to watch more of them. However, this and other minor changes in assumptions to the original algorithms presented in [5] are not critical. The reader can easily modify the algorithms and analysis as appropriate.) Define the *maximum catchup window size W_m*, measured in frames, as the latest position in the video at which a slow stream can be overtaken by a fast stream starting at the beginning of the video by the time the video completes at frame L. Given the difference in speed, this can be computed as

$$W_m = \frac{S_{max} - S_{min}}{S_{max}} \cdot L. \qquad (1)$$

We define the generalized simple merging policy in terms of a parameter W also measured in frames, called the *window size*. (We require that $0 \leq W \leq W_m$.)

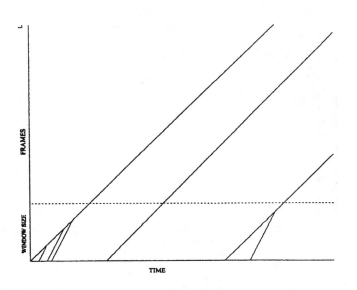

Figure 1: Generalized Simple Merging Policy

Specifically, a new arrival is designated to be a fast stream if a slow stream exists within W frames of it. Otherwise, the stream is designated to be a slow stream. If a fast stream merges with a slow stream, the fast stream is dropped, and the slow stream proceeds. Figure 1 illustrates the algorithm, the x-axis representing (increasing) time and the y-axis representing the position of the video in frames. (The window size and length L of the video are also shown.) Note that there is always a single slow stream associated with each distinct window. On the other hand there can be any number of fast streams, including 0.

Pseudocode for the generalized simple merging policy is as follows:

Algorithm Generalized Simple Merging Policy (W)
Case: Arrival of stream i
If no stream within W is moving at S_{min}
  Set Speed $= S_{min}$
Else
  Set Speed $= S_{max}$
Case: Merge of streams i and j
Drop stream i
Set Speed $= S_{min}$

Now in [5] the window size W used is exactly equal to the maximum catchup window size. That is, they set $W = W_m$. We plan, instead, to optimize W as a function of the forecasted arrival rate. Assume, for simplicity, that requests for the video arrive according to a simple Poisson process with rate λ. (This assumption will not, of course, be perfectly accurate.)

The tradeoffs for different size values of W are as follows:

(1) When the window size is big, a larger number of fast streams can be merged into one slow stream. But they tend to be merged at later stages, with less benefit.

(2) When the window size is small, merges tend to occur at earlier stages. But there are fewer of them.

In order to quantify the savings due to piggybacking, recall that whenever a slow stream is merged with a fast stream, both streams combine into one slow stream. In effect, we assume that the fast stream exists only until that time. Thus we will charge a fast stream only the number frames needed to reach the merge point.

We first proceed to build a model which expresses the expected number of frames for a randomly chosen display stream as a function of the window size W. Consider a new video stream arrival, which may be either fast with probability P_{fast} or slow with probability $P_{slow} = 1 - P_{fast}$. The expected number $E[F]$ of frames read by a randomly chosen display stream is the weighted average of the expected number $E[F_{fast}]$ of frames if the stream is fast and the expected number $E[F_{slow}]$ of frames if the stream is slow. In other words,

$$E[F] = P_{fast} \cdot E[F_{fast}] + P_{slow} \cdot E[F_{slow}]. \quad (2)$$

By our frame charging assumption we have that F_{slow} is deterministically equal to L, and hence $E[F_{slow}] = L$ as well. It is only slightly more complicated to calculate the number of frames charged when the stream is fast. Suppose the nearest slow stream beyond it is p frames ahead. The number of frames required by this fast stream to catch up with the slow stream is given by

$$F_{fast} = \frac{p \cdot S_{max}}{S_{max} - S_{min}}. \quad (3)$$

Note that the algorithm is designed in such a way to ensure that $p \leq W$. Since the arrival rate is uniform it follows by symmetry that p is uniformly distributed between zero and W. Thus

$$E[F_{fast}] = \frac{W/2 \cdot S_{max}}{S_{max} - S_{min}}. \qquad (4)$$

It now remains to calculate the probability that a randomly chosen stream will be fast. Note that all streams which are within W frames of a slow stream (or, equivalently, arrive within W/S_{min} time units of a slow stream) are fast. Hence for each slow stream, the expected number of fast streams following it consecutively equal to $\lambda \cdot W/S_{min}$. Consequently, the fraction of fast streams in the system is approximately equal to

$$P_{fast} = \frac{\lambda W/S_{min}}{\lambda W/S_{min} + 1}. \qquad (5)$$

Substituting the above values in Equation 2, we obtain the following relationship:

$$E[F] = \frac{\lambda W}{\lambda W + S_{min}} \cdot \frac{W S_{max}}{2(S_{max} - S_{min})} + \frac{S_{min}}{\lambda W + S_{min}} \cdot L. \qquad (6)$$

We now minimize this equation subject to the constraint that a new fast stream must always be able to catch up with a slow stream if the slow stream is at most W frames ahead the fast one. This constraint amounts to:

$$W \cdot \frac{S_{max}}{S_{max} - S_{min}} \leq L. \qquad (7)$$

Ignoring the constraint for the time being, we set

$$\frac{dE[F]}{dW} = 0. \qquad (8)$$

On expanding the resulting equation for W and simplifying, we obtain:

$$W^2 + \frac{2 S_{min}}{\lambda} \cdot W - \frac{L S_{min}(S_{max} - S_{min})}{\lambda \cdot S_{max}} = 0. \qquad (9)$$

Solving the above quadratic for W (and ignoring the negative root), we obtain:

$$W^* = -\frac{S_{min}}{\lambda} + \sqrt{\left(\frac{S_{min}}{\lambda}\right)^2 + 2 \cdot \frac{L S_{min}(S_{max} - S_{min})}{\lambda S_{max}}}. \qquad (10)$$

The second derivative is positive, and an easy check shows that this value of W^* automatically satisfies constraint 7. Consequently, W^* is the optimal window size.

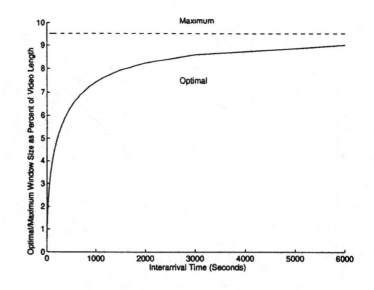

Figure 2: Optimal and Maximum Catchup Window Sizes

Figure 2 shows the relative values of W_m and W^* as a function of interarrival time (the reciprocal of λ). (These are normalized as a percentage of the total number of frames in the video.) These numbers were evaluated for a two hour video with $S_{min} = 28.5$ and $S_{max} = 31.5$. Notice that the optimal window size is always smaller than the maximum catchup window size, sometimes considerably so. However, W^* asymptotically approaches W_m as the interarrival time increases.

We briefly discuss the modifications required to the generalized simple merging policy to handle special customer features such as pause, resume, fast-forward and rewind. One must be able to accomodate the addition of new streams at arbitrary positions within the video, and similarly the elimination of existing streams from arbitrary positions. To handle the addition of a new stream, notice that currently playing streams can be partitioned at any point in time into groups of two different types. The first group will consist of a slow stream followed by one or more consecutive fast streams which will ultimately merge with the slow one. The second group consists of solitary slow streams. If a new video arrives at a position between the first and last members of a group of the first kind, it should be assigned a fast speed and eventually merged with the slow stream. A new video arriving outside the range of a group of the first kind should be assigned a fast speed if it is behind a slow stream at position less than W, and a slow speed otherwise. To handle the elimination of an existing slow stream, do nothing if the stream trailing it is also slow (or nonexistent). If the stream trailing it is fast, change its speed to slow. Nothing need be done to handle the elimination of an existing fast stream. Remember, of course, that many customers may be piggybacked onto a single stream, so the removal of one such customer does not necessarily imply that the stream itself will be dropped. The policy just described remains elementary in the sense that streams will change speeds at most once. We have developed an approximation algorithm to compute the optimal window size for such a scenario, but details are complicated and we omit them in the current paper.

3   The Snapshot Algorithm

Consider again a single video consisting of L frames. Suppose that at a fixed point T in time there are a total of n streams of this video playing. Denote the positions of these streams, measured in terms of frames, by $f_1, ..., f_n$, respectively. Without loss of generality we can assume that $f_1 \geq ... \geq f_n$. Ignore for the time being any other requests for this video which may appear later, and the manner in which the streams reached their current positions. Also assume that there are no pauses, resumes, fast-forwards or rewinds. This scenario is entirely deterministic, and it is therefore meaningful to attempt to find the precise piggybacking strategy which minimizes the total number of frames required from time T onward. We begin the section by solving this optimization problem via a dynamic programming algorithm.

As before, the two speeds are denoted by S_{max} and S_{min}. We can assume in an optimal solution that the stream farthest along (in this case the one initially corresponding to f_1) proceeds at speed S_{min}, while the stream least farthest along (corresponding initially to f_n) proceeds at speed S_{max}: It is never *more* profitable not to do so. For the same reason, of course, we always merge two streams which coalesce. While we will certainly have to account for the costs correctly, pretend for the moment that merges can occur at any point, including possibly past the length L of the video. We can then envision each potentially optimal piggybacking

policy as a binary tree. The leaf nodes correspond to the original streams, while interior nodes correspond to merges. The root node corresponds to the final merge of all the n original streams. Left arcs correspond to the fast speed, and right arcs correspond to the slow speed. *Past* the root node there exists only one stream, which can proceed at either speed. We don't explicitly consider this as part of the binary tree, but assume the speed is S_{min} as before. Some of the merges close to the root node may never actually take place. This depends on whether or not they would occur past position L.

Looked at in this light there is a one-to-one correspondence between the set of binary trees with n leaf nodes and all potentially optimal piggybacking policies for n streams.

Figure 3 shows the 5 possible binary trees for a scenario in which there are $n = 4$ original streams. Here we have reversed the roles of the x- and y-axes from that of Figure 1, in order to draw the binary trees in something like standard orientation. Thus the x-axis corresponds to position and the y-axis to time. (We actually show a little more structure, namely the relative positions of the initial streams, the two speeds, and so on. The area of the histogram underneath each binary tree illustrates the cost, in frames, of implementing that particular piggybacking strategy, assuming the final merge at the root occurs *before* L. Note that the root always occurs at the same position, and the cost remaining is the difference between that position and L. This is a constant, and like the remaining single stream is not illustrated. Being a constant, this term is also irrelevant to the optimization problem. If L occurs before the final merge, the actual cost would correspond to integrating the curve *up to L*.)

We note in passing that the *odd-even* policy described in [5] pairs up successive streams which start no more than a fixed window size apart, by playing one at S_{min} and the other at S_{max} until they merge. The *greedy* policy developed in [5] iterates this process recursively with successive merged pairs. Thus, roughly speaking, the greedy policy results in binary trees of the form shown in (d) of the figure.

We recall that the number of binary trees with n leaf nodes (streams) is given by the $(n-1)$st *Catalan*

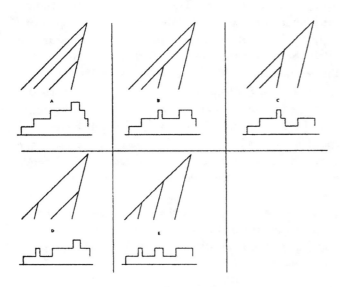

Figure 3: Typical Binary Tree Alternatives and Costs

number

$$b(n-1) = \frac{1}{n}\binom{2n-2}{n-1}. \tag{11}$$

See [3] for details. The Catalan number $b(n)$ can be approximated via Stirling's approximation as

$$b(n) \approx \frac{4^n}{\sqrt{\pi}n^{3/2}}. \tag{12}$$

So the Catalan numbers grow very rapidly, and searching all binary trees for any reasonable value of n will be impractical. Fortunately, there is a better way:

Let i and j denote two streams between 1 and n, with $i \leq j$. Let $P(i,j)$ denote the hypothetical position in frames at which streams i and j would merge in an optimal policy for the case in which only the arrivals $i, ..., j$ occur. This value may possibly be greater than L, and is also the position at which streams i and j would merge if they were the *only* streams. The point is that $P(i,j)$ is well-defined because this optimal policy would involve stream i moving at the maximum speed and stream j moving at the minimum speed. So we obtain

$$P(i,j) = f_j + \frac{S_{min} \cdot (f_j - f_i)}{S_{max} - S_{min}} \tag{13}$$

via our standard analysis if $i < j$, and

$$P(i,i) = f_i. \tag{14}$$

This value can thus be computed for each relevant pair i and j, and is independent of all other streams. Now let $C(i,j)$ denote the cost of an optimal policy in which only the arrivals $i, ..., j$ occur. Denote the corresponding binary tree by $\mathcal{T}(i,j)$. It is easy to see that

$$C(i,i) = L - f_i \tag{15}$$

for each i. In order to compute $C(i,j)$ for $i < j$ we observe that the principal of optimality holds here: For the optimal policy there will exist a stream k with $i \leq k < j$ such that the left subtree will contain the leaf nodes corresponding to streams $i, ..., k$ and the right subtree will contain the leaf nodes corresponding to streams $k+1, ..., j$. Furthermore, both the left and right subtrees themselves will be optimal. That is, they will be $\mathcal{T}(i,k)$ and $\mathcal{T}(k+1,j)$, respectively. Such a binary tree has cost $C(i,k) + C(k+1,j) - max(L - P(i,j), 0)$, the last term indicating the (potential) savings of the final merge at position $P(i,j)$. Thus the optimal policy in which only arrivals $i, ..., j$ occur has a left subtree with leaf nodes corresponding to $i, ..., k^*$ and a right subtree with leaf nodes corresponding to $k^* + 1, ..., j$, where

$$k^* = \text{argmin}_{i \leq k < j}\{C(i,k) + C(k+1,j) - (L - P(i,j))^+\}. \tag{16}$$

The overall optimal cost $C(1,n)$ and its corresponding piggybacking policy can therefore be calculated in a bottom up fashion by dynamic programming: Starting with the initial trees $\mathcal{T}(i,i)$ and costs $C(i,i)$, compute all trees $\mathcal{T}(i,i+1)$ and costs $C(i,i+1)$, then all trees $\mathcal{T}(i,i+2)$ and costs $C(i,i+2)$, and so on. Ultimately, we compute the optimal tree $\mathcal{T}(1,n)$ and its optimal cost $C(1,n)$.

Pseudocode for the dynamic programming algorithm is as follows:

Algorithm Dynamic Programming
For $i = 1$ to n do
   Initialize $P(i,i), C(i,i)$ and $\mathcal{T}(i,i)$ via Equations 14 and 15
End
For $m = 1$ to $n - 1$ do
   For $i = 1$ to $n - m$ do
      Compute $P(i, i+m), C(i, i+m)$ and $\mathcal{T}(i, i+m)$ via Equations 13 and 16
   End
End

It remains to compute the computational complexity:

Theorem 3.1 *The dynamic programming algorithm finds the optimal merging policy and requires $O(n^3)$ iterations, where n is the number of streams to be merged.*

Proof After initialization there are $O(n)$ iterations of the outer loop and $O(n)$ iterations of the inner loop. The calculation of the positions, costs and trees requires $O(n)$ comparisons.

We comment that the dynamic program algorithm presented has analogues in the problem of optimal polygon triangulation via the natural correspondence between binary trees and convex polygons [3, 7]. This, in turn, has led to algorithms for parse trees and the like.

We now incorporate the deterministic dynamic programming technique discussed above into a practical window-based piggybacking policy known as the *snapshot* algorithm. Assume at first that there are no pauses, resumes, fast-forwards or rewinds. The algorithm is based on the idea of taking snapshots of the positions of the streams at fixed time intervals, say of I units each. We will call these the *snapshot* intervals. The first stream arriving within a snapshot interval is assigned a speed of S_{min}. All other arriving streams within this same snapshot interval are assigned a speed of S_{max}. Suppose there are n such streams, with stream 1 being slow and streams $2, ..., n$ being fast. This mimics the original and generalized simple merging policy described in [5] and the previous section. Notice that all n streams will lie within a window, measured in frames, of length $W = I \cdot S_{max}$. We shall refer to W as the *snapshot window size*. We will choose I in a way that ensures that the snapshot window size is less than or equal to the maximum catchup window size W_m. By the end of the snapshot interval some of our initial n streams may have merged. We shall use our dynamic programming algorithm in order to modify the speeds of all the remaining streams that were initiated in the interval. We do not affect the speeds of streams from previous snapshot intervals.

Actually, many variants of this snapshot algorithm are possible. One could, for example, solve the overall dynamic programming problem for all currently playing streams, not just the ones within the most recent snapshot interval. This approach would appear to be too costly, given the complexity of the dynamic programming algorithm. Of course, the effectiveness of the algorithm itself will cause the number of surviving streams to be significantly reduced relative to the number of original customer requests. Conversely, the ratio of surviving streams relative to original requests should decrease throughout the lifetime of the video. Thus it is more important to perform the dynamic programming algorithm for earlier rather than later streams anyway. A second apparently reasonable algorithmic variant might group streams together according to their arrival snapshot interval, and resolve the dynamic programming problem for each such group at the end of every snapshot interval during its lifetime. These groupings would appear plausible in the sense that the last stream from one snapshot interval and the first stream from the next snapshot interval are naturally moving away from each other anyway. But a little thought will show that all subsequent solutions to the dynamic programming problem will be identical to the original one. Thus the snapshot algorithm we have presented appears to represent the best tradeoff among various reasonable alternatives.

Pseudocode for the snapshot algorithm is as follows:

Algorithm Snapshot Policy (W)
Compute snapshot interval I
Start interval counter
Case: Arrival of stream i
If first stream is within interval
    Set Speed $= S_{min}$
Else
    Set Speed $= S_{max}$
Case: End of interval counter
Solve dynamic programming problem on remaining new streams
Reset interval counter
Case: Merge of streams i and j
If within initial interval follow generalized simple merging rules
Else follow dynamic programming rules

The dynamic programming policy is optimal for streams which survive past the snapshot interval. Because it employs a generalized simple merging policy to deal with non-deterministic arrivals until the end of that interval it may not be quite optimal during that region of time. But if the snapshot interval is small relative to the total time of the video (or, equivalently, if W is small relative to L), then we may ignore this effect. In other words, no window-based policy will outperform the snapshot algorithm under these conditions. As we shall see, the snapshot algorithm gives the best experimental results of any of the tested piggyback policies as well.

We should point out that we do not have an analytic method for deriving the optimal snapshot window size. So we have adopted the optimal window size of the generalized simple merging policy instead. Fortunately, we will show experimentally that the performance of the snapshot algorithm is fairly insensitive to the choice of window size.

Special customer features such as pause, resume, fast-forward and rewind can be accomodated in the context of a snapshot algorithm. However, they involve complicated heuristics, and we omit details.

4   Experimental Results

In this section we discuss the empirical results of simulations in which we compare the various piggybacking policies. No batching or bridging was considered in any of these experiments, in order to isolate the benefits of piggybacking policies from any other effects. In all our experiments we assumed a fast speed of $S_{max} = 31.5$ frames per second and a slow speed of $S_{min} = 28.5$ frames per second. All simulations were performed assuming Poisson arrivals with a parameter of λ. Each graph discussed in this section shows the percentage of frames saved as a result of piggybacking.

Figure 4 shows the performance of the original simple merging and greedy policies of [5] and our new optimal simple merging policy. Here we fix the length of the video to be 2 hours, and vary the interarrival time $\gamma = 1/\lambda$ between 15 and 500 seconds. As we see, employing the optimal rather than maximum catchup window size can have a large effect on the performance of the generalized simple merging policies, at least when the interarrival time is small (or equivalently, when the arrival rate is large). Furthermore, the optimal simple

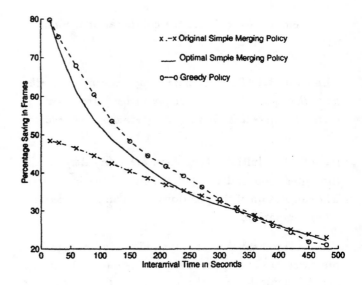

Figure 4: Comparisons for Varying Interarrival Rates

merging policy now appears to be nearly competitive with the more elaborate greedy policy. Recall that the former algorithm is *elementary*, while the latter is not. For high interarrival times all three algorithms have essentially equal performance. As one would expect, the performance of each algorithm decreases as a function of increasing interarrival time.

Figure 5 shows the performance of the generalized simple merging policy as a function of window size W. Here we fix the length of the video to be 2 hours, and the interarrival time to be 30 seconds. The optimal window size W^* is also shown, and matches the best performance of the generalized simple merging policy. Differing from the optimal window size by too much in either direction causes the performance to degrade. Note that our optimal window size is computed in terms of the arrival rate λ, which is by necessity a forecast. Fortunately the figure shows relatively stable performance for values of W close to optimal, so errors in forecasts will probably not have major negative effects on the optimal policy.

Figure 6 shows the performance of the original and optimal simple merging policies and the snapshot algorithm as a function of video length. Here we fix the interarrival time to be 30 seconds. Notice that optimal simple merging policy always outperforms the original policy, and the improvement grows as a function of the video length. In fact, the performance of the original

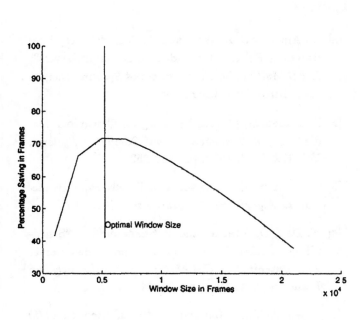

Figure 5: **Generalized Simple Merging Performance for Varying Window Sizes**

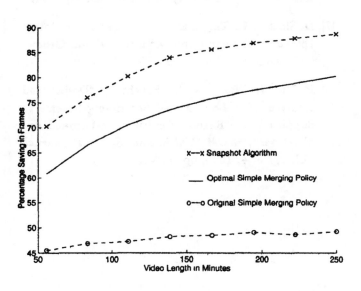

Figure 6: **Comparisons at Varying Video Lengths**

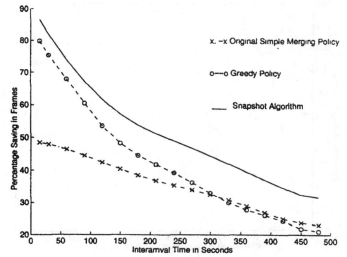

Figure 7: **Comparisons for Varying Interarrival Times**

simple merging policy is relatively flat. The snapshot algorithm outperforms both of the other policies, and the improvement relative to the optimal simple merging policy remains more or less constant.

Figure 7 shows the performance of the original simple merging and greedy policies of [5] and the snapshot algorithm. Again we fix the length of the video to be 2 hours, and vary the interarrival time γ between 15 and 500 seconds. Notice that snapshot does clearly better than the greedy algorithm, and this difference is even more pronounced for higher interarrival times.

Figure 8 shows the performance of the snapshot algorithm as a function of window size W, which we normalize as a fraction of the maximum catchup window size. Again we fix the length of the video to be 2 hours, and the interarrival time to be 30 seconds. Recall that this is important because we do not have a method to determine the optimal value of W for snapshot. Fortunately, the curve is quite flat in the range we are concerned about.

5   Conclusions

Based on the original idea of Golubchik, Lui and Muntz, we have in this paper devised and analyzed two piggybacking algorithms for VOD systems. The first is a generalized version of their simple merging policy, for which

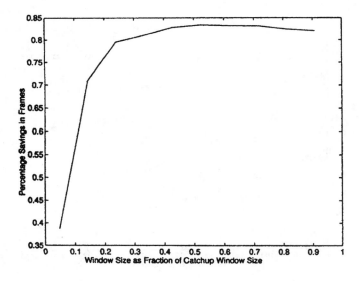

Figure 8: Snapshot Performance for Various Window Sizes

we find the optimal window size. The second is a snapshot algorithm based on dynamic programming. The snapshot algorithm apparently outperforms all existing policies, while the performance of the optimal simple merging policy is nearly equal to that of the best previously known policy.

Some concern has been raised regarding the ease of implementation of on-the-fly piggybacking schemes, given current MPEG standards. That is, it may be difficult to create a fast version of a video in real time from a slow version. (There certainly exists equipment today which can vary speeds of videos off-line.) We believe that the notion of piggybacking is very appealing, however, especially as an alternative and/or companion to batching. Piggybacking results in improvements similar to those of batching, and yet does not require additional latency for customers. Thus piggybacking would seem to be more in the spirit of VOD. In any case, there is an alternative to on-the-fly piggybacking. As noted in [5], one could pre-store on disk fast speed initial segments of the most popular videos. Since most of the good effects of piggybacking will occur early in video showing, it should be possible to derive most of the benefits, at the cost of a small amount of additional disk space.

References

[1] C. Aggarwal, J. Wolf and P. Yu, "On Optimal Batching Policies for Video-on-Demand Servers", *IEEE Multimedia Computing and Systems Conference*, Hiroshima, Japan, 1996.

[2] D. Anderson, "Metascheduling for Continious Media", *ACM Transactions on Computer Systems*, Vol. 11, No. 3, 1993, pp. 226-252.

[3] T. Cormen, C. Leiserson and R. Rivest, *Introduction to Algorithms*, McGraw Hill, 1986.

[4] A. Dan, D. Sitaram and P. Shahabuddin, "Scheduling Policies for an On-Demand Video Server with Batching", *ACM Multimedia Conference*, San Francisco, CA, 1994, pp. 15-24.

[5] L. Golubchik, J. Lui and R. Muntz, "Reducing I/O Demand in Video-on-Demand Storage Servers", *ACM Sigmetrics Conference*, Ottawa, Canada, 1995, pp. 25-36.

[6] M. Kamath, D. Towsley D., and Ramamritham, "Buffer Management for Continuous Media Sharing in Multi-Media Database Systems *Technical Report 94-11*, University of Massachusetts, 1994.

[7] D. Sleator, R. Tarjan and W. Thurston, "Rotation Distance, Triangulations and Hyperbolic Geometry", *JACM*, 1986, pp. 122-135.

[8] P. Yu, J. Wolf and H. Shachnai, "Design and Analysis of A Look-Ahead Scheduling Scheme to Support Pause-Resume for Video-on-Demand Applications", *ACM Multimedia Systems Journal*, Vol. 3, No. 4, 1995, pp. 137-150.

CHAPTER ELEVEN

Multimedia Synchronization

Lawrence A. Rowe

University of California - Berkeley

MULTIMEDIA synchronization deals with the problem of playing media from different sources or locations to create a desired effect that can be perceived by the user. The media can be text, images, audio, video, or animations or combinations of media as in a lecture with synchronized audio, video, and slides. The content being played may be synchronous, as in a live n-way videoconference, or asynchronous, as in a recording of a music recital. And, the application may include user interaction that changes the behavior of what is played. For example, while playing back a recorded lecture with slides, the user might want to step through the slides to look at the material the speaker talked about in the past or will be talking about in the future without stopping the audio and video. In other words, the user wants to turn off slide synchronization with the video. Then, after examining the slides, the user might want to turn on synchronization and set the play out clock to the current video position or to the current slide.

Multimedia synchronization researchers have solved problems ranging from modeling and specifying timing requirements between multimedia objects to developing systems and algorithms to play out content captured at different times and locations and stored on distributed systems. In other words, the application must assure the correct temporal alignment of media events relative to the play out clock. The papers in this section present important experimental results on human perception and system behavior, reference models for temporal specifications, and examples of specification

language implementations that simplify multimedia content authoring.

The first paper, "A temporal reference framework for multimedia synchronization," by M. J. Pérez-Luque and T.D.C. Little, presents a reference framework for comparing different synchronization models and specification languages. In the simplest terms, a synchronization model must specify when events must occur. These events might include playing a segment of continuous media (*e.g.*, audio, video, or animation) or presenting an image or dialog box. Pérez-Luque and Little describe different models of time and show how they can be incorporated into a temporal specification scheme that can be implemented by a synchronization mechanism. This framework is then used to compare the expressive power of different temporal specification schemes and their implementation in a distributed multimedia system.

The most important variable to be optimized when playing multimedia content for a user, whether live or on-demand, is how the human perceives the experience. "Human perception of media synchronization," by R. Steinmetz and C. Engler presents the results of an extensive study of human perception of synchronization. For example, we are all familiar with the problem of "lip-sync" in which video images of a person talking must be synchronized with the audio so that the motion of the speaker's lips corresponds to what we hear. Steinmetz and Engler carefully measure human perception of lip-sync by playing the sound earlier or later than when it should be played. Their experiments show that sound will be perceived as "in synchronization" if it is played within one video frame time of when it should be played (*i.e.*, +/− 30 ms for NTSC video and +/− 40 ms for PAL/SECAM video). Lip-sync is an example of fine-grained synchronization because the time constraints are short (*e.g.*, several milliseconds). Pointer-audio synchronization, that is, motion of a remote pointer on an image with audio describing the image, is an example of course-grained synchronization because the time constraints are longer (*e.g.*, hundreds of milliseconds or seconds). The Steinmetz and Engler paper presents facts that anyone designing and implementing a synchronization model or system must accommodate. It is also an important result for application developers because it establishes bounds on performance.

Similar research was done in the middle of the twentieth century on the communication delay in a telephone system that would interfere with natural interaction when speaking [1]. Those studies showed that if the round-trip communication time was greater than 300 ms, people talked to each other unnaturally. This constraint is important for multimedia synchronization because content play out from a distributed collaboration application in which the participants are at different geographic locations must satisfy it. Because early international telephone calls used satellite links that introduced a round-trip delay greater than 500 ms, people had to adopt a strict turn-taking protocol commonly used on simplex radio communication systems. For example, one person talks and then says "over" to signal the other user that he or she can talk. Modern international telephone calls use optical fibers laid on the ocean floor, which reduce the round-trip delay to well below 300 ms. As a result, calling someone half-way around the world sounds the same as calling someone next door.

The third paper, "Improved algorithms for synchronizing computer network clocks," by D. L. Mills, describes the algorithms used to implement the Internet Network Time Protocol (NTP), which synchronizes computer clocks to international standard clocks. Most multimedia applications operate on a distributed system. In other words, the content storage, users, or both are located on different computers. These computers might be on the same local area network as, for example, in a distributed media server in which data is stored

on different systems and delivered to the user's computer where it is synchronized for play out. Or, the computers might be at different geographical locations as in an *n*-way videoconference. These distributed multimedia applications must synchronize events happening on these different computers. NTP was originally developed in the early 1970s to solve the problem of maintaining consistency in transport protocols and applications such as e-mail. As it turns out, distributed multimedia applications need the same services, namely synchronization of time on different computers. This paper presents the protocols and algorithms used in NTP version 3, which was deployed on more than 100,000 computers on the Internet when the paper was written in 1994–95. A subsequent paper describes NTP version 4, which improved on these algorithms [2], but the paper included in this collection presents a better description of the fundamental ideas and algorithms.

This paper is also included in this collection in part because too many multimedia application developers re-invent the ideas and solutions of NTP, often not as well. Some researchers, myself included, argue that all computer system clocks should be synchronized with NTP so that problems associated with time on geographically distributed systems will be solved. Several years ago, other researchers argued against this position, but today nearly all computers run time synchronization clients to manage general system events such as modification times on files in network file systems and scheduling backups. The concepts and algorithms in the work by Mills are fundamental to the problems of synchronization in multimedia applications.

The fourth paper, "Nsync—A toolkit for building Intractive Multimedia Presentations," by B. Baily and colleagues, describes the design and implementation of a specific multimedia synchronization toolkit, called Nsync, developed by J. Konstan and his students at the University of Minnesota. The key features of this toolkit are that it supports synchronous and asynchronous interaction and fine- and coarse-grained relationships as well as combinations of these interactions and relationships. It also supports multiple timelines. Synchronization specifications are concise because Nsync is a declarative language implemented efficiently with a predictive logic. A scheduler and change monitor execute the application until an event happens that requires the computation to change. Nsync is a modern, expressive synchronization system that illustrates the features that the emerging SMIL multimedia synchronization standard, being developed by the World Wide Web Consortium (W3C) [3], should provide. The Nsync toolkit also shows how a powerful synchronization system can be implemented in relatively few lines of code (*e.g.*, 3,500) if the underlying primitives required to implement it are available. The implementation reported in the paper can enforce coarse-grained synchronization constraints because the overhead for detecting a change and responding to it is less than 200 ms, as measured using 1998 computers. Making the system efficient enough to enforce fine-grained synchronization constraints remains a challenge for future research.

The last paper in this section, "A method and apparatus for measuting media synchronization," by B. K. Schmidt, J. D. Northcutt, and M. S. Lam, addresses the problem of measuring media synchronization. Synchronization specification languages that can describe complex relationships are only as good as their implementations. You compare specification languages by the expressiveness of the languages, the length of specifications written in different languages, the ease of learning the language, and the ease of reading and comprehending a specification. The question is: How do you measure quantitatively the performance of a synchronization implementation? Schmidt, Northcutt, and Lam answer this question by describing a hardware and software system that can measure synchronization quality. They define the fundamental variables to be measured, namely, skew, drift, and jitter, and they show how these variables can be calculated for a specific application and synchronization implementation. Finally, they use their methodology to compare various streaming audio/video players to assess the causes of asynchrony in modern systems. The major finding of the paper is that internal assessments of synchronization cannot accurately measure event times, so an external event timestamping and recording device is needed. The design and use of the device they developed is described in the paper.

Synchronization is a relatively mature field in that fundamental solutions to many problems have been developed. The major problem today, from an application developer's perspective, is that a well-defined standard with independent implementations on all the major platforms is unavailable. Many organizations have attempted to create such a standard, including, among others, the International Telecommunication Union (ITU), the International Multimedia Systems Consortium, and the W3C. The best candidate for a widely adopted and supported standard today is SMIL, but unfortunately, the current standard is severely limited in functionality and there are few implementations. Hopefully, both these problems will be remedied in the next few years.

On the research front, problems that still can be explored include the design and implementation of distributed synchronization systems and the previously mentioned problem of enforcing fine-grained synchronization.

REFERENCES

[1] G. A. Miller and J.C.R. Licklider, "The intelligibility of interrupted speech," *Journal of the Acoustics Society of America* 22, no. 2 (1950): 167–73.

[2] D. L. Mills, "Adaptive hybrid clock discipline algorithm for the Network Time Protocol," *IEEE/ACM Transactions on Networking* 6, no. 5 (Oct. 1998): 505–14.

[3] W3C Recommendation, "Synchronized Multimedia Integration Language (SMIL) 1.0 Specification," June 15, 1998.

ADDITIONAL READINGS

G. Blakowski, J. Huebel, and U. Langrehr, "Tools for specifying and executing synchronized multimedia presentations," in *Proceedings of the 2nd International Workshop on Network and Operating system support for Digital Audio and Video (NOSSDAV 91)* (1991).

T.D.C. Little, "A framework for synchrounous delivery of time-dependent multimedia data," *Multimedia Systems* 1, no. 2 (1983): 87–94.

D. L. Mills, "Network Time Protocol (version 3) specification, implementation and analysis," RFC 1305, March 1992.

D. L. Mills, "Simple Network Time Protocol (SNTP) version 4 for IPv4, IPv6, and OSI," RFC 2030, October 1996.

K. Rothemel and T. Helbig, "An adaptive protocol for synchronizing media streams," in *Proceedings of the IEEE* 5, no. 5 (1997): 324–36.

A Temporal Reference Framework
for Multimedia Synchronization

María José Pérez-Luque and Thomas D. C. Little, *Member, IEEE*

Abstract—The synchronization problem for audio/visual reproduction has consumed engineers since the advent of recorded audio and images and the first multimedia productions. As computers have evolved to support programmed reproduction of multimedia information, the complexity but not the character or interest have changed. In the digital domain, synchronization problems exist due to data distribution and communications, random events caused by human–computer interaction, and general computer and communications performance limitations. This rich research domain has led to numerous approaches to the modeling and execution of multimedia synchronization scenarios. Unfortunately, these approaches are difficult to compare and evaluate due to their varied theoretical bases and modeling techniques.

In this paper we develop a uniform, theoretical foundation for discussing multimedia synchronization and temporal specification. We propose a temporal reference framework and use it to compare existing temporal specification schemes and their relationships to multimedia synchronization. The ensuing comparison of existing specification and synchronization techniques demonstrates the utility of the framework.

Index Terms—Models of time, temporal specification, temporal reference framework, multimedia synchronization.

I. INTRODUCTION

MULTIMEDIA synchronization is about providing coherent playout of orchestrated audio and visual information. It is a controversial topic in the multimedia computing community. On the one hand, providing "lip-sync" or "slide-show" capability requires no more than fast buses, buffering, and hardware decompression devices. On the other hand, complex multi-party human–computer interaction coupled with live and preorchestrated presentations are difficult to deal with in any formal or ad hoc manner. For these scenarios (e.g., the construction of virtual environments), the behavior of each participant must be understood and represented in the temporal domain. Once such a characterization is achieved, the nuances of the operating environment (communications, operating system, and playout devices) must be dealt with to achieve the desired multimedia presentation outcome.

For this reason, we divide the general multimedia synchronization problem into two parts. The first is one of

Manuscript received August 5, 1994; revised April 10, 1995. This work was supported, in part, by the National Science Foundation under Grant IRI-9211165.

M. J. Pérez-Luque is with Facultad de Ciencias de la Información, Universidad de Navarra, 31080 Pamplona, Spain (e-mail: mjpl@mmlab.unav.es).

T. D. C. Little is with the Multimedia Communications Laboratory, Department of Electrical, Computer, and Systems Engineering, Boston University, Boston, MA 02215 USA (e-mail: tdcl@bu.edu).

Publisher Item Identifier S 0733-8716(96)00234-X.

modeling, representing, and specifying timing requirements of multimedia scenarios. The second problem is to achieve the temporal specification via synchronization. In this decomposition, synchronization reduces to the rendering of a temporal specification using some technique. In this paper we focus on the former problem: that of the specification of timing requirements. However, we also show the relationship between temporal specification and the rendering of a temporal specification (synchronization).

To appreciate the temporal specification problem (modeling and representing included) requires a basic understanding of formal specification techniques. These techniques isolate a *semantic domain* (i.e., the meaning of a specification and language) and a *syntactic domain* (i.e., the alphabet, and grammar of the specification language). Theory focuses on the semantics; however, the theory must be supported by models which require tools for visualization. These visualization tools exist as a syntax. Therefore, when we think we deal only with semantics, we are often crippled by a syntax as well. We have found this problem to arise quite frequently when considering models of time and their use in specifying *temporal scenarios*, i.e., sequences of events in time.

Consider the analogous problem of specifying or representing physical objects by computer. Computers can provide artificial representations of our real world (e.g., three-dimensional rendering of objects on a computer screen). For obtaining these representations we need to find models to capture the nature of the real objects, mechanize the models, and find algorithms to transform (render) the mechanized models (representations) into the display space of the computer. Usually, more than one model can be found to represent a single object from the real world. For example, Fig. 1 shows simple models characterizing a table from the real world. The left-hand side describes the table. The middle illustrates three models and their corresponding representations. The right-hand side shows the object rendered on a computer display. The example illustrates different geometric modeling and representation approaches that can yield equivalent renderings of the synthesized object.

Time is another aspect of the real world that can be modeled. As in the case of the spatial example of Fig. 1, several models of time can be used to represent the same sequence of events. Consider Fig. 2 as an example of a short movie that has been recorded from the real world. We present four possible ways to describe the sequence of events in the time domain.

1) **An English description**: The car was initially stopped. Subsequently, the traffic light turned green and the car

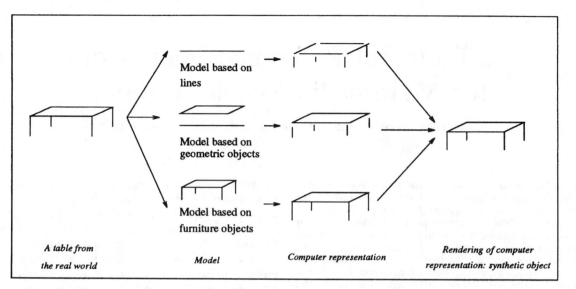

Fig. 1.   Geometric representations of a table.

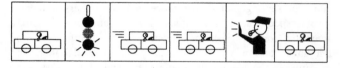

Fig. 2.   Frames representing a movie recorded from the real world.

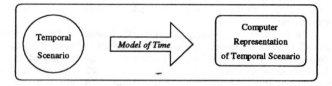

Fig. 3.   Modeling temporal information.

began moving. The car remained in motion until a gendarme signaled it to stop.

2) **A time of occurrence description**: At $t = 0$, the stopped car appears (beginning of the movie). At $t = 5$, the traffic light turns green. At $t = 5$, the car starts moving. At $t = 25$, a gendarme signals the car to stop and the car stops immediately. At $t = 29$, the movie ends.

3) **An instant-based/temporal relationship description**: The car started moving at the same time the traffic light turned green. The car stopped moving at the same time the gendarme signaled the car to stop.

4) **An interval-based/temporal relationship description**: The car was initially stopped for 5 seconds; the traffic light was red for the same 5 seconds. After the first period, the car traveled for 20 seconds. Subsequently, the car stopped for 4 seconds (until the end of the movie) while the gendarme signaled the car to remain stopped.

Like the rendering of the table (Fig. 1), any of the descriptions above will lead to an appropriate temporal sequence for the movie, provided that we have suitable rendering mechanisms. This example illustrates how a single scenario can be modeled by a range of different approaches (models of time). The ensuing representations can be very different yet yield the same results. In the example, four different models capture the same scenario.

The process of modeling temporal information is represented in Fig. 3. The left-hand side captures the *temporal scenario* that we seek to model. The right-hand side captures the representation of the scenario. The transformation from the scenario to the representation is achieved by various temporal

modeling techniques. Once a representation is achieved, mechanisms are required for final rendering in the time domain. For multimedia data presentation, this is equivalent to multimedia synchronization.

Our contribution is the development of a *temporal reference framework*: a uniform, theoretical basis for discussing multimedia synchronization and temporal specification. The proposed framework is most useful in the comparison and synthesis of temporal specification schemes. The remainder of the paper deals with the modeling and rendering process for temporal information in multimedia systems. In Section II, we characterize temporal scenarios and present our terminology for models of time. Section III describes the proposed temporal reference framework. In Section IV, we show how the framework can be used to compare various existing specification approaches for multimedia object timing. Section V concludes the paper.

II. MODELING TEMPORAL INFORMATION

To develop a unified theory for multimedia synchronization and representation, we require common terminology. Here we develop and define the basic terms that we use in the framework development, introduce and characterize the models of time used for multimedia specification, and present representations suitable for mechanization.

First we consider a definition of the temporal activities we wish to model within the realm of computer-based multimedia applications.

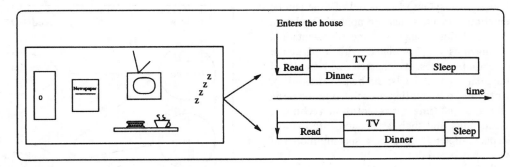

Fig. 4. Example of an indeterminate temporal scenario.

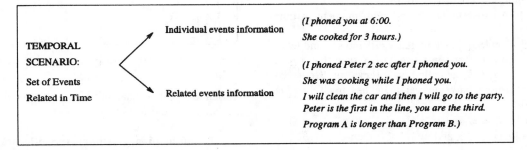

Fig. 5. Possible descriptions of a temporal scenario.

A. Temporal Scenarios

A **Temporal Scenario** represents an instance of a set of activities that are in some way related in time. For example, consider the temporal scenario describing an instructor lecturing with slides. The time that each slide stays in the projector depends on the time expended in explanation. In this way, the activity called "slide in projector" is dependent on the activity called "instructor explains slide." These two activities are *related* in time as well as *dependent* on time. This relation/dependency must be captured by a model of time.

There are two types of temporal scenarios: **determinate**, and **indeterminate**. Determinate temporal scenarios represent a set of real-world activities. As they are real-world activities, the temporal constraints are completely defined and determined by the physical world. There is no indeterminacy in the temporal scenario. Fig. 2 is an example of such a scenario.

For indeterminate temporal scenarios there is uncertainty or nondeterminism. Fig. 4 shows an example of such a case. The left-hand side of the figure describes a symbolic description of an indeterminate temporal scenario. It consists of a common sequence of activities that an individual might do in the evening: opening the door, reading the newspaper, watching TV while eating dinner, and sleeping. This temporal scenario is the same every evening, but each day it has different realizations (e.g., arrival time, time spent reading the newspaper). Two of these realizations are illustrated on the right hand side of the figure. In these cases we need models of time that can deal with indeterminate cases.[1] When

generating a model, we have sufficient information to describe the indeterminate temporal scenario, but the final realization is not specified or determined. Therefore, the description of the temporal scenario represents a superset of all possible final realizations. Ultimately, the final rendering or realization of the temporal scenario depends on external factors (e.g., human interaction). These cases of indeterminacy contrast scenarios that are determinate and therefore possess a unique temporal realization (e.g., the movie of Fig. 2).

Note that a temporal scenario does not imply a specific temporal model.[2] Temporal models should be able to capture the relationships and dependencies among activities for both determinate and indeterminate temporal scenarios. We now consider models of time for translation of temporal semantics to formal specification languages.

B. Models of Time

Activities in the temporal scenario are called **events**. To clarify this term, it is defined as follows

Definition 1: An **event** is an occurrence in time that can be instantaneous or can occur over some time period.

Using an English language description, Fig. 5 presents examples of descriptions of a temporal scenario. Note that we can describe the temporal scenario either as a set of independent events (top of Fig. 5) or as a description that captures some temporal relationships among the events (bottom of Fig. 5).

In order to capture and describe the temporal scenario, we require the services of a model of time. The use of such a model forces us to stray from a discussion of only semantics

---

[1] Indeterminate temporal scenarios are studied because in multimedia systems there are two clear sources of indeterminacy: user interaction, in which the final realization is not known until the user interacts, and system failures, where the final realization is not known until run-time.

[2] *Model of time* and *temporal model* are used interchangeably throughout the paper.

(i.e., we must choose some syntax).[3] A model of time can be viewed as the temporal semantics that are applied to yield a formal specification technique, language, and representation. Typically, these semantics are associated with a particular syntax for visualization purposes. We characterize a **model of time** through three related components: the **basic time unit** of the model, the **contextual information** associated to the basic time units and, the **type of time representation technique** expressing the basic units and their associated information. These three concepts completely describe a specific model of time and its power of expressivity.

The *basic time unit* is the temporal unit used in characterizing a temporal scenario. There are two types of basic units: instants and intervals, defined as follows:

Definition 2: An **instant** is a zero-length moment in time [15].

Definition 3: Let $[S, \leq]$ be a partially ordered set, and let a, b be any two elements (time instances) of S such that $a \leq b$. The set $\{x \mid a \leq x \leq b\}$ is called an **interval** of S denoted by $[a, b]$. Furthermore, any interval $[a, b]$ has the following properties [26]:

1) $[a, b] = [c, d] \Longleftrightarrow a = c \wedge b = d$,
2) if $c, d \in [a, b], e \in S$ and $c \leq e \leq d$ then $e \in [a, b]$,
3) $\#([a, b]) \geq 1$.

The events of the temporal scenario are modeled through the basic time unit. Fig. 6 shows the relationships among the events in the temporal scenario and the basic time units of a model of time. The mapping from the temporal scenarios to the models of time is described by the following:

- Models of time with intervals as basic time units can only model interval events.
- Models of time with instants as basic time units can model interval, instants, and interval & instants together.[4]

Contextual Information: The *contextual information* comprising the model of time specifies the type of temporal information that can be associated with the basic time units of the model. The contextual information is a key principle in the selection of a model of time that is capable of expressing the semantics of a temporal scenario (relations/dependencies among events and indeterminacy included). The contextual information can be described as either quantitative or qualitative:

Quantitative information: Quantitative information is temporal information that can be expressed in time units (e.g., $t_1 = 6$ pm; $\#[a, b] = 3$ hours). Quantitative information can refer to any temporal axis (*absolute* or *relative*) and can be expressed using a real or virtual measure of time (e.g., seconds, minutes, or bits in a constant-bit-rate stream).

Qualitative information: Qualitative information is the temporal information that is not quantifiable. For example, total and partial orderings of basic time units represent qualitative

---

[3] Recall from Section I, formal language of specification technique is comprised of syntactical and semantic components.

[4] We could also think of modeling instants through intervals and consider the possibility of modeling interval & instants together through intervals. However, modeling instants through intervals is not very useful. Moreover, modeling instants and intervals through intervals is not always achievable. To the knowledge of the authors, there are no temporal techniques developed for this approach and we do not pursue the topic further.

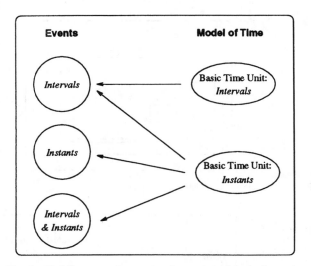

Fig. 6.   Modeling events in a temporal scenario with basic time units.

information. Other qualitative information relating basic time units are the following:

- The **basic binary temporal relationships between instants** define the three ways in which two instants can be related [34]: before, after, and at_the_same_time. Only one basic temporal relation can hold between two instants.

- The **basic binary temporal relationships between intervals** define the thirteen ways in which two intervals can be related [15]. Only one basic temporal relation can hold between two intervals. These relationships are illustrated elsewhere [26]. Similarly, n-**ary temporal relationships among intervals** define the ways in which n intervals can be related in time [28]. Like the binary temporal relations, there are thirteen possible n-ary temporal relations, which reduce to the seven cases after eliminating their inverses; and a set of constraints can be identified for the timing parameter relationships among intervals of the n-ary cases.

- **Indefinite temporal relationships** are those temporal relations between basic time units that are not explicitly or unambiguously given. Usually, these indefinite relations are expressed as disjunctions of the basic temporal relationships. The number of indefinite relationships is calculated as the set of all possible disjunctions of the basic ones. For instance, there are three basic binary relations between instants, therefore, the number of indefinite relations is $2^3 = 8$. Two examples are the following {before or at the same time}, {at the same time or after}. For intervals, there are thirteen basic binary relations between intervals. Therefore, the number indefinite relations is $2^{13} = 8192$. Three examples are the following {starts or equals}, {finishes or overlaps}, {meets or after or overlaps}. An enumeration of these indefinite temporal relationships has been performed by Ladkin [23] and van Beek [33].

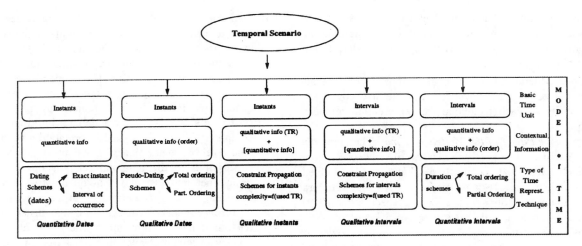

Fig. 7.   General models of time.

- **Duration relationships** describe how the durations of two temporal intervals can be related [1]. Considering two intervals, $[a, b]$ and $[c, d]$, some examples are the following:

  1) $[a, b]$ is shorter than $[c, d]$ iff $\#[a, b] < \#[c, d]$,

  2) $[a, b]$ is longer than $[c, d]$ iff $\#[a, b] > \#[c, d]$.

  Duration relationships are usually specified in conjunction with temporal relationships among intervals.

Time Representation Techniques: A time representation technique describes how time can be captured and mechanized in a computer environment. A particular representation occurs as a result of the application of a model of time. This is a concept that is intrinsically associated with the basic time units and contextual information of a model of time, i.e., a particular model of time will produce a specific time representation and will indicate the theory that will be required to interpret a resultant temporal specification.

To identify the type of time representation technique we follow Allen's terminology and classification [2]. There are three types of time representation techniques: dating schemes, constraint propagation schemes, and duration schemes. A more detailed analysis of representation techniques is described by Pérez-Luque [31].

- A **dating scheme** is a representation technique that expresses time in the form of dates or times of occurrence. These techniques consider either the exact times of occurrence (e.g., 6 pm), or intervals of possible times of occurrence (e.g., between 6:00 pm and 6:02 pm). Related to dating is pseudo-dating. Pseudo-dating does not use absolute time units (e.g., 6 pm), but units of ordering that indirectly express time of occurrence. This order means partial ordering and total ordering [3].

- A **constraint propagation scheme** is a representation technique that expresses time in the form of temporal constraints. Examples of temporal constraints include temporal relationships and duration relationships. Propagation of the constraints is provided by application of temporal logic.

- A **duration scheme** is a representation technique that expresses time in the form of temporal durations (e.g., 3 s). Additional total or partial ordering information can be added to this representation to yield a complete temporal specification.

1) Classification of Models of Time: The three previous concepts, the basic time unit, contextual information, and type of time representation, completely describe a *specific* model of time. There are five general types of models of time to which we have assigned names (Fig. 7). These are:

1) **Quantitative dates.** The basic time unit is an instant. The associated information is quantitative. The type of time representation technique used is a dating scheme. The specific value of the contextual information (exact date, or interval of occurrence) determines the specific model of time within this general category.

2) **Qualitative dates.** The basic time unit is an instant. The associated information is qualitative in the form of ordering information. The type of time representation technique used is a pseudo-dating scheme. The specific contextual information (total order or partial order) determines the specific model of time within the category.

3) **Qualitative instants.** The basic time unit is an instant. The associated information is qualitative (temporal relationships) with optional quantitative information. The type of time representation technique used is a constraint representation for instants. The specific contextual information (type of temporal relationships used) determines the specific model of time within the category.

4) **Qualitative intervals.** The basic time unit is an interval. The associated information is qualitative (temporal relationships) with optional quantitative information. The type of time representation technique used is a constraint representation technique for intervals. The specific contextual information (type of temporal relationships used) determines the specific model of time in the category.

5) **Quantitative intervals.** The basic time unit is an interval. The associated information is quantitative (durations) and qualitative (ordering). The type of time

representation technique used is a duration-based. The specific contextual information (type of ordering information used) determines the specific model of time within the category.

With this general classification of temporal modeling approaches we now seek to identify the expressive power and general utility of each technique for representing temporal scenarios.

2) Expressive Power of the Models of Time: The previous section described five general classes of models of time from which a temporal specification scheme can be derived. However, when one seeks to model a particular temporal scenario, many questions arise: Can a specific model be used for a given temporal scenario or for a set of temporal scenarios? Do certain models have the same power of expressivity (i.e., are they equivalent)? How can we study the equivalences? To answer these questions, we first evaluate the expressive power of each model and then provide a comparison (Section II-B.3).

The expressive power describes the ability of a model of time to represent temporal scenarios. It can tell us about the expression of semantics for the temporal scenario and the type of events that can be modeled; the way relations/dependencies among events and the indeterminacy in the temporal scenario are captured by the model. Note that the expressive power characterizes the model of time rather than the temporal scenario. It is not possible to define the set of temporal scenarios that can be modeled with a model of time. The expressive power for each general class of models of time is as follows:

1) **Quantitative dates.** This class models dates (times of ocurrence). The relations among events in the temporal scenario are captured through the specification of the appropriate dates; however, this model does not directly express any type of temporal relation. The associated information is quantitative. If the contextual information corresponds to the exact date of occurrence, then no indeterminacy can be described with this model. If the contextual information corresponds to the modeling of the exact interval of occurrence then a limited indeterminacy can be described by specifying the two extremes of possible occurrence. This can be useful for instants, intervals, and instant & intervals.

2) **Qualitative dates.** This class models dates in the form of qualitative ordering information. The temporal scenario can only be described with ordering relationships. As the contextual information is qualitative, indeterminacy in temporal scenarios can also be modeled. The level of indeterminacy depends on the contextual information. If it corresponds to fully ordered information, then the indeterminacy refers to the exact date of occurrence, but the order of occurrence is completely determined. On the other hand, if it corresponds to partially ordered information, then the indeterminacy is captured in the order of occurrence, and therefore, on the exact dates of occurrence. This scheme is useful for instants, intervals, and instant & intervals.

3) **Qualitative instants.** The model characterizes temporally related events through temporal relationships between the basic units of the model (instants). Apart from the qualitative information, the model can also use quantitative information. The temporal scenarios that can be modeled range from completely defined (using quantitative information) to completely indeterminate (using only qualitative and indefinite information). The complexity of the contextual information gives the specific level of indeterminacy. The contextual information corresponds to the temporal relationships among the basic time units (instants). If no quantitative information is added, there is indeterminacy in the exact instant of occurrence (e.g., one can specify that an instant is `after` the other, but not how much after); but also indeterminacy in temporal relationships can be specified (i.e., by the use of indefinite temporal relations). Therefore, the specific expressive power must be determined as a function of the contextual information. This is useful for instants, intervals, and instant & intervals.

4) **Qualitative intervals.** This model considers that the events in the temporal scenario are related and model the relation through different types of temporal relationships among intervals. It uses qualitative information and quantitative information optionally. This approach can model completely defined temporal scenarios as well as temporal scenarios with indeterminacy, depending on the contextual information used. If quantitative information is not specified, indeterminacy in the duration of the intervals can be described. Also, indeterminacy in the temporal relationships between basic time units (intervals) can be specified by the use of indefinite relationships. The specific contextual information within this general class dictates the level of indeterminacy that can be described. This scheme is useful only for intervals.

5) **Quantitative intervals.** This model considers that the events in the temporal scenario occur over a period of time and models this time (duration) directly. The fact that the events are related is understood as an ordering relationship. The scheme uses quantitative information and additional qualitative information. The duration of the intervals is always defined, and therefore no indeterminacy in durations can be specified. The model uses qualitative information, in the form of ordering relationships (fully or partially ordered). Therefore, indeterminacies in the specific dates of occurrence (beginning of the interval) can be modeled. This is useful only for intervals.

The statements above delineate the expressive power of the general models of time. However, as mentioned, each model must be supplemented by the use of contextual information. For example, consider two models of time belonging to the general category *qualitative intervals*. Model 1 uses basic binary relations between two intervals. Model 2 uses indefinite binary relations, i.e., it can model more than one basic relation between two intervals. They belong to the same general category and they can model interval events, but the use of

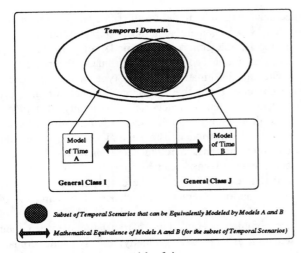

Fig. 8.   Equivalences among models of time.

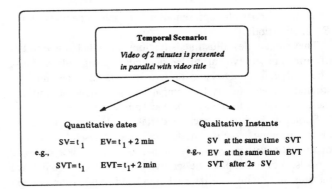

Fig. 9.   Example 1: Equivalent models of time for a determinate temporal scenario.

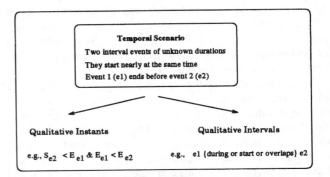

Fig. 10.   Example 2: Equivalent models of time for an indeterminate temporal scenario.

different contextual information leads to different powers of expression. Model 2 can define indeterminacy in the temporal relationships between two intervals while Model 1 can only model one fixed temporal relation.

3) Equivalent Models of Time: The previous section presented the concept of the expressive power for a model of time. As we saw in the example illustrated in Fig. 2, two or more models of time can be used to capture the same multimedia scenario. In this case the models are equivalent for the scenario; however, they are not necessarily completely equivalent. In this section we analyze the equivalences between the models of time.

Fig. 8 presents a graphical description of the possible equivalences between two models of time. Model of time A, belonging to the general class I, is able to describe a subset of temporal scenarios within the temporal domain[5] (ellipse on the left).[6] Model of time B, belonging to the general class J, is able to describe another subset of temporal scenarios within the temporal domain (ellipse on the right). If they were completely equivalent the two ellipses would coincide. In the figure, the two models of time are equivalent for a subset of temporal scenarios (the greyed circle), i.e., they can model equivalently the marked subset of temporal scenarios (intersection of subsets of model A and model B). This intersection cannot easily be identified because the concept of an temporal scenario is too abstract; however, the equivalence of the corresponding descriptions following the different models of time can be identified mathematically, and transformations among them can be found. If the temporal semantics are equivalent (horizontal grayed arrow between the models), transformation between the syntactic domains is possible. If two models of time are partially equivalent, the translation from the less powerful to the more powerful is always achievable.

[5] The set of all temporal scenarios (TS) comprise the **Temporal Domain** (*TD*), i.e., TS$_i$ ⊂ TD, the universe of temporal scenarios.

[6] The symbols A, B, I, and J, have no particular meaning except to distinguish themselves.

The following are two examples of equivalent models of time for *particular* temporal scenarios. The first one considers the case of modeling a determinate temporal scenario that it is completely defined a priori. It is a temporal scenario composed of interval events. The second example considers an indeterminate temporal scenario comprised of interval events.

Example 1: A video of 2 minute duration is presented in parallel with its video title. There is no indeterminacy in the temporal scenario. In this example, we can think of at least two equivalent models of time for that particular scenario: *quantitative dates* (i.e., a definition of the exact dates for the starting and endings points of both events), and *qualitative instants* with three basic binary relationships plus quantitative information (i.e., a definition of the equivalent temporal relationship between the starting and ending points of the events). Fig. 9 presents these two cases and a possible representation for each of them (S means Starts, E Ends, V Video, and VT Video Title).

Example 2: There are two events of unknown duration; they start at nearly the same time; event 1 finishes before event 2. For this example, we require a model of time that is capable of describing an indeterminate temporal scenario (i.e., a unique description that can yield a range of different realizations). Two equivalent models are apparent: *qualitative instants* with the three basic binary relationships, and *qualitative intervals* with indefinite binary temporal relationships. Here we cannot use a quantitative date model because its expressivity does not include the required indeterminacy. Fig. 10 presents these two cases with a possible representation for each (*S* denotes Starts, *E* denotes Ends).

These examples illustrate situations in which the models of time are equivalent for a *particular* temporal scenario. The *complete* equivalence of two models of time must be studied mathematically by comparing the basic time unit and the contextual information for each model of time.

Some studies have been undertaken to determine equivalences among existing models of time. These demonstrate mathematically the complete or partial equivalence of some models. For example, the equivalence between qualitative instants and qualitative intervals models in which the contextual information consists of temporal relations is extensively studied by Ladkin [23] and van Beek [33] (e.g., the indefinite temporal relations between instants is equivalent to 181 indefinite temporal relations between intervals). Wahl and Rothermel [35] have also studied these equivalences. For example, they demonstrate that a qualitative dates model (for the exact time of occurrence) is equivalent to the rest of the models if the temporal scenario is determinate.

We can also examine the equivalences among other models of time (e.g., qualitative dates model with partial ordering as contextual information versus qualitative intervals model with the thirteen basic relationships). These comparisons are yet to be undertaken. We know that the general models can be used for representing the same particular temporal scenarios, but the complete (or partial) equivalence among them is still unknown.

C. Computer Representations

The goal of modeling temporal information is to find techniques for representing temporal scenarios for subsequent computer rendering and reproduction (Fig. 3). Following our terminology, we say that a mechanized representation corresponds to a *temporal specification*. More formally, a temporal specification is defined below.

Definition 4: A **temporal specification** is a well-formed sentence satisfying a particular temporal specification language.

A specification language is the result of the definition of semantic and syntactic domains. Section II-B deals with the temporal semantics of the modeling process. Here we introduce the concept of syntactic domain and its influence in the resulting specification language.

The syntactic domain is defined in terms of a set of symbols (constants, variables, operators, etc.) and a set of grammatical rules. These symbols can either be textual or graphical in nature. The external appearance of a specification language corresponds to the combination of the syntactic symbols following the syntactic grammar. Many different specification languages can and have been defined for temporal representations because (1) different temporal semantics can be used for the same temporal scenario and (2) the same semantics can be represented in very different syntactic domains.

As long as the semantics of a specification language are correct, we can use any of the representations to describe a particular temporal scenario. Therefore, many different tempo-

ral specifications can be found for the same temporal scenario. In Section IV we compare some of these representations.

In synopsis, the concept of a model of time has been introduced as influenced by three attributes: the basic time unit, contextual information, and the type of time representation technique. From these attributes, models of time are classified in five general categories. The ability of a model of time to describe a temporal scenario is determined by the expressivity of the model. The general class to which the model belongs provides a rough characterization. However, its specific expressiveness can be identified. More than one model of time can be found for the description of a concrete temporal scenario. Complete equivalence of two models of time must be demonstrated mathematically. If two models of time are completely equivalent, a translation between their representation is achievable. Finally, the syntactic domain must be selected to achieve a specification language for a model of time, and this can be achieved with diverse syntax.

III. TEMPORAL REFERENCE FRAMEWORK

Based on the terminology and concepts presented in Section II, we now introduce our framework for the modeling and comparison of multimedia specification and synchronization techniques.

Multimedia synchronization techniques have been developed for the satisfaction of multimedia scenarios specified in some temporal language. In the design of these techniques, there are three processes that are clearly different (1) the definition of the specification language for a set of temporal scenarios, (2) the description of the multimedia scenario with the specification language, and (3) the creation of the synchronization mechanisms to render descriptions within the specification language. To clarify the relationship between a multimedia scenario and a temporal scenario we present the following definition:

Definition 5: A **multimedia scenario** is the spatial and temporal semantics of a multimedia presentation session, i.e., the orchestration of media in time and space that should be delivered to a user.

A temporal specification language is used to provide a temporal specification for a multimedia scenario.[7] The synchronization mechanisms try to achieve the multimedia scenario that is described in the temporal specification. These terms and their relationships are illustrated in Fig. 11 and are defined as follows.

Definition 6: A **temporal specification scheme** is a specification language that is used to describe multimedia scenarios.

This specification language is defined by a semantic and a syntactic domain. The temporal specification scheme is equivalent to the time representation scheme. In multimedia scenarios, the former usually is not restricted to temporal information, and we distinguish the two definitions. We also reiterate our distinction between specification and satisfaction of a specification in the definition of a synchronization mechanism.

---

[7] In the remainder of the paper we only consider the temporal aspect of multimedia scenarios.

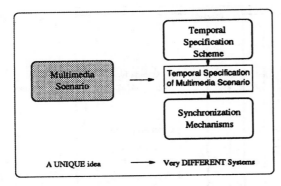

Fig. 11.   General view of multimedia synchronization techniques.

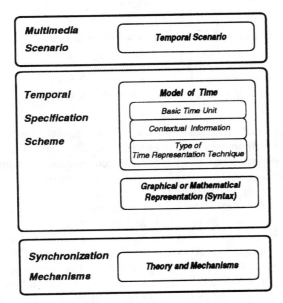

Fig. 12.   The temporal reference framework.

Definition 7: A **synchronization mechanism** is a service or process that realizes a multimedia scenario.

The synchronization mechanisms can be one that interprets general temporal specifications (e.g., from authoring tools) or one that is restricted to particular applications (e.g., lip-sync in audio and video). These mechanisms are varied and depend on the infrastructure, the architecture of the system, and the specific media types. Therefore, although they each share the common objective of satisfaction of a temporal specification (the multimedia scenario), they must combine temporal information with other types of atemporal information in different ways.

Fig. 12 shows the integrated view of the temporal reference framework: the **multimedia scenario**, the **temporal specification scheme**, and the **synchronization mechanisms**. On the left-hand side of the figure are the multimedia definitions; on the right-hand side are the corresponding temporal definitions.

Our temporal reference framework aims to facilitate the system analysis process by providing the necessary concepts for a unified temporal study. By comparison of components, we can use the framework to compare many synchronization techniques that attempt to realize the same multimedia sce-

narios. This is represented in Fig. 11: the unique idea of the left hand side does not lead to a unique solution on the right hand side. Several temporal specification schemes can be used for the temporal specification of the same multimedia scenario and several mechanisms can be designed for the enforcement of the same temporal specification scheme. As a result, very different system realizations can accomplish the same goal.

In a distributed multimedia system (DMS), the synchronization is achieved by the combined effort of the different parts of the system (databases, network, operating systems, etc.). We call this integration the system realization, defined below.

Definition 8: The **system realization** is the specification of system components, temporal specifications, and mechanisms to carry out the multimedia scenario in a distributed multimedia system.

Our temporal reference framework is also useful in the analysis of the components of distributed multimedia systems. It can help to identify the temporal specification schemes of each component and the exchange of temporal information among the different parts of the system.

IV.   USE OF THE FRAMEWORK FOR ANALYSIS AND COMPARISON OF APPROACHES

In this section, we analyze a number of temporal specification and synchronization techniques that have appeared in recent literature. Our analysis, based on the temporal reference framework, focuses on models of time and begins with an investigation of temporal specification schemes and concludes with a study of the temporal aspects of several distributed multimedia systems.

A. Temporal Specification Schemes

Recent temporal specification schemes include Firefly [6], OCPN [26], and many others. To compare these schemes we apply the proposed temporal reference framework as a guide. Each temporal specification scheme is compared in terms of structure of specification language (semantic and syntactic domain) and equivalence of the models of time used (at the semantic level). The main differences between techniques are illustrated with figures.

Fig. 13 shows a comparison of temporal specification schemes for (1) the timeline, (2) Firefly, and (3) the OCPN. As summarized in the figure, these three temporal specification schemes are distinct because of their different use of models of time. Therefore, they belong to different categories of our classification scheme. The timeline representation belongs to *quantitative dates,* Firefly belongs to *qualitative instants,* and OCPN belongs to *qualitative intervals.* As they use different models of time, they also use different syntax in their specification. Each is described in the following.

The Timeline Approach The timeline representation is the most basic method used for temporal specification. It consists of a dated timeline. A synchronization mechanism for this representation scheme can interpret the timeline and execute the appropriate actions at the indicated moments in time. Several synchronization systems use a timeline for the representation

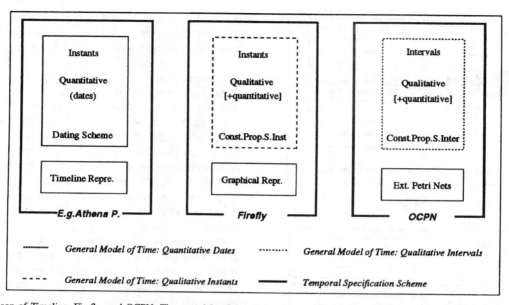

Fig. 13. Comparison of Timeline, Firefly, and OCPN: Three models of time belonging to different classes of the general classification.

of the timing constraints (e.g., the Athena Muse Project [16] and Gibbs *et al.* [13], [14]).

The model of time used for the timeline belongs to the general category of *quantitative dates*. The contextual quantitative information corresponds to the exact date ("at") of the basic time unit. The scheme can only temporal scenarios with no indeterminacy.

Firefly Buchanan and Zellweger [6], [7] propose a temporal specification scheme for the definition of general multimedia scenarios. They also develop algorithms for deriving the appropriate schedules for achieving the specified scenario.

The model of time used by Firefly belongs to the general category of *qualitative instants*. The contextual information corresponds to the basic binary temporal relationships between instants (i.e., only a single relationship between two instants). Associated quantitative information can also be used optionally. For modeling instants in the temporal scenario, no indeterminacy can be expressed in the temporal relations. For modeling intervals in the temporal scenario, indeterminacy in the temporal relationships can be expressed by a combination of the basic binary relationships between basic time units (instants). In any case, indeterminacy in the exact instant of occurrence can be described. A graphical representation (syntax) is used to capture the relations between the specified instants.

OCPN Little and Ghafoor [26] proposed the OCPN, a temporal specification scheme for the description of general multimedia scenarios. The authors also present algorithms for deriving a playout schedule from a specification of a temporal scenario [27], [12].

The model of time used for the OCPN belongs to the general category of *qualitative intervals*. The contextual information is both qualitative and quantitative. The temporal relationships

considered are the thirteen basic binary temporal relationships. No indeterminacy can be expressed in the temporal scenario because the temporal relations are fixed (no indefinite temporal relations), and modified by quantitative information, which completely determines the scenario. The graphical representation (syntax) is based on an extended type of Petri net and retains most conventional Petri net semantics.

Fig. 14 shows a comparison of three related temporal specification schemes: Hoepner's path operators, the OCPN, and Wahl and Rothermel's operators [35]. In this comparison, the models of time of the temporal specification schemes belong to the same general category: *qualitative intervals*. The particular models of time used by each differ because of the contextual information that they consider. Furthermore, each technique uses a different representation. They are described in the following.

Hoepner's Path Operators Hoepner [17], [18] defines a temporal specification scheme for the description of general multimedia scenarios. Her scheme consists of a set of path operators with an associated graphical representation. These operators are valid for any synchronization mechanism that can interpret them. One such mechanism is described in reference [18].

The model of time used belongs to the general category *qualitative intervals*. The specific contextual information for the qualitative information corresponds to a subset of the basic binary relationships (three) and to a subset of the indefinite temporal relationships (four) between intervals. In this temporal specification scheme, the syntax limits the extent of the possible temporal semantics, i.e., the path operators limit the number of binary temporal relationships that can be modeled. The expressive power is reduced to model only a subset of the possible temporal relations of the intervals in the temporal scenario. Indeterminacy in the temporal relationships (four indefinite relations) can be expressed.

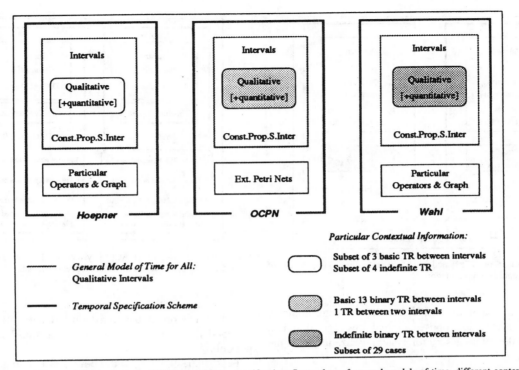

Fig. 14.   Comparison of Hoepner's Path operators, OCPN, and Wahl's specification: Same class of general models of time, different contextual information.

Wahl and Rothermel's Temporal Specification Scheme Wahl and Rothermel [35] have proposed a temporal specification scheme for multimedia scenarios. A common set of operators describe the temporal relationships between intervals and the possible variations due to user interaction. A synchronization mechanism for realizing the specification has not been reported.

For this scheme, the model of time belongs to the general category of *qualitative intervals*. The contextual information is qualitative and can use quantitative information optionally. The temporal relationships considered are a set of 29 indefinite binary temporal relationships. Ten operators are used in conjunction with parameters to cover all possible cases and can be illustrated graphically. Indeterminacy of interval durations in the temporal scenario can be expressed in addition to indefinite temporal relationships between pairs of intervals.

Figs. 15 and 16 present comparisons of temporal specification schemes with identical temporal semantics but different syntactic domains. In the case illustrated by Fig. 15, the model of time used is *qualitative instants* with the three basic binary relationships between instants and quantitative information. In the case illustrated by Fig. 16, both approaches use a *qualitative interval* model with the thirteen basic binary relationships and quantitative information. Emery's and Filali's approaches are explained as follows. (The expressivity of these models is equivalent to Firefly and the OCPN, respectively.)

Emery's Temporal Specification Scheme Emery [8] *et al.* propose a temporal specification scheme for the description of general multimedia scenarios. The temporal semantics are the same as Buchanan's approach. (In this comparison we do

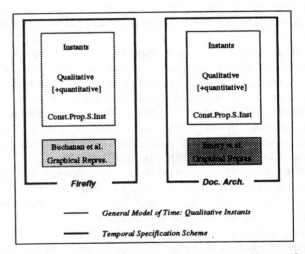

Fig. 15.   Comparison of Firefly and Emery's document architecture: Same model of time, different graphical representations.

not consider the concept of flexibility that is introduced by Buchanan; we are comparing this from the temporal specification perspective.) The graphical representation is different as are the synchronization rendering mechanisms of the system. Buchanan's approach has been developed in conjunction with a scheduling system, while Emery's has been developed for a run-time system.

Filali's Temporal Specification Scheme Filali [11] has proposed a formal language for the definition of multimedia scenarios. The syntactic domain corresponds to the elements and the grammar of the specification language. The temporal

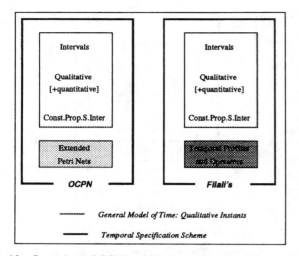

Fig. 16.   Comparison of OCPN and Filali's specification: Same model of time, different graphical representations.

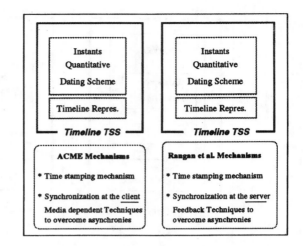

Fig. 17.   Comparison of the ACME system and the system of Rangan *et al.*: Same temporal specification scheme, different mechanisms.

semantics are the same as OCPN, but the syntactic domains are different. He has also proposed a scheduling algorithm, i.e., the associated theory necessary for system realization from the formal language.

Fig. 17 illustrates two synchronization mechanisms that have been designed for the same temporal scenario: the synchronized delivery of audio and video. In both cases, the temporal specification is created in run-time with a time-stamping mechanism.

In this case, the re-synchronization mechanisms are different: the ACME [4] system tries to overcome asynchronies at the client side, while the system proposed by Rangan *et al.* [32] tries to solve the asynchronous at the server side. The different architectures of the systems also has an influence on the mechanisms. We illustrate these approaches to highlight that a temporal specification can be achieved by very different system architectures and mechanisms.

Discussion: The aforementioned specification schemes can be examined for equivalence of temporal specification schemes. Fig. 18 shows a multimedia scenario and three possible temporal specification schemes for its representation. Using a natural language, the scenario can be described as a video of a person anchoring the news, a title of the broadcast company presented for the duration of the news broadcast, and two graphics that appear during the exposition. The Timeline, Firefly and OCPN schemes can be used for its specification. The resultant temporal specifications are shown at the bottom of Fig. 18. The temporal specifications are different but equivalent for this particular multimedia scenario.

Although several temporal specification schemes might be equivalent for a particular multimedia scenario (e.g., Fig. 18), this does not imply that their temporal semantics are equivalent in all cases. In the analysis of equivalence (and translation) of temporal specification schemes, three steps are required: (1) separation of the syntactic domain from the temporal semantic domain for each specification scheme under evaluation, (2) evaluation of the equivalences at the semantic level (Section II-B.3); two temporal specification schemes are equivalent

if and only if their models of time are equivalent, and (3) identification of the translation at the syntactic level. If the models of time are equivalent, the translation is always possible.

Few studies dealing with equivalent temporal specification schemes have been reported. Wahl and Rothermel [35] present a mathematical comparison of the equivalences among some temporal specification schemes: Timeline (e.g., [16]), OCPN [26], Firefly [6], MHEG [21], and Wahl and Rothermel's operators [35]. The results of this study indicate that the listed approaches are equivalent for scenarios with no indeterminacy; however, only two of them (Firefly and Wahl and Rothermel's technique) can be used for modeling indeterminate scenarios. Fig. 19 illustrates four of these schemes and the scenarios that they can model. Although this study effectively compares the equivalences at the semantic level, it does not examine translations among the schemes at the syntactic level.

In contrast, Erfle [9] studies possible translations among three temporal specification schemes. He proposes translations at the syntactic level, but does not use an adequate theoretical foundation for sufficient comparison at the semantic level. Compared schemes are OCPN [26], MODE [5], and Firefly [6], studied for the purpose of translation into HyTime [20, 29]. Because HyTime uses a timeline model [22, 30], the study results in a comparison of four temporal specification schemes. He demonstrates that HyTime is able to specify the same temporal constraints as the other three schemes, and details the equivalent syntactic translations for particular temporal scenarios. He admits that for user interaction (indeterminate temporal scenarios), there are some indeterminate semantics that cannot be translated directly to HyTime. A mathematical justification for these results (with the exception of MODE) can be found in reference [35].

Iino *et al.* [19] propose an object-oriented scheme for spatio-temporal synchronization of multimedia information. They also study the translation between the OCPN [26] and their proposed model. Their temporal specification scheme differs from the OCPN in two respects: (1) the contextual information associated with the OCPN consists of the basic binary temporal

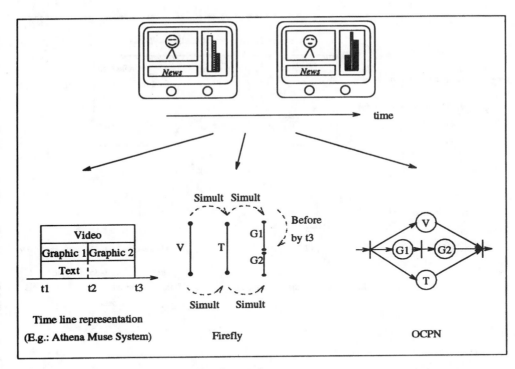

Fig. 18. Several temporal specifications of a particular multimedia scenario.

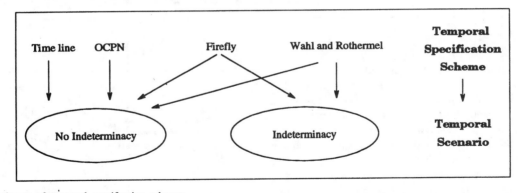

Fig. 19. Equivalences of temporal specification schemes.

relationships, while the their model considers the *n-ary* basic temporal relationships [28]; and (2) the syntax of their model includes additional spatial and "processing" capabilities. We note that any scenario modeled with the OCPN can also be modeled with Iino's scheme. The translation between the two temporal specification schemes is achievable.

B. Distributed Multimedia Systems

It is particularly interesting to observe how the various system components follow different models of time in a complete distributed multimedia system. In this section we briefly show the utility of the temporal reference framework in the analysis of distributed multimedia systems. Again, our focus is on the identification of the different models of time used in each component.

Fig. 20 illustrates a system realization of the Firefly system (temporal specification plus scheduler). The figure shows the temporal specification scheme for a multimedia scenario that considers user interaction, i.e., indeterminacy in the final realization. With a language description it can be described as follows: "Object 2 is presented before object 3, and during the presentation of objects 2 and 3, object 1 is presented. Also, two related unpredictable events are also considered, event 4 triggers event 5 after 2 seconds, and they end together (the end is unpredictable)." For this system we see two models of time appearing: the Firefly temporal specification scheme, and the derived schedules. The former originates from the Firefly authoring tool in the specification of the multimedia scenario (*qualitative instants*), and the latter from the presentation playout schedules of the presentation system (*quantitative dates*). Because user interaction is considered, the derived presentation schedules are provisional, and they are merged properly in real-time following the user's interaction.

Fig. 21 illustrates the operation of the distributed system proposed by Little and Ghafoor [27] for the same multimedia

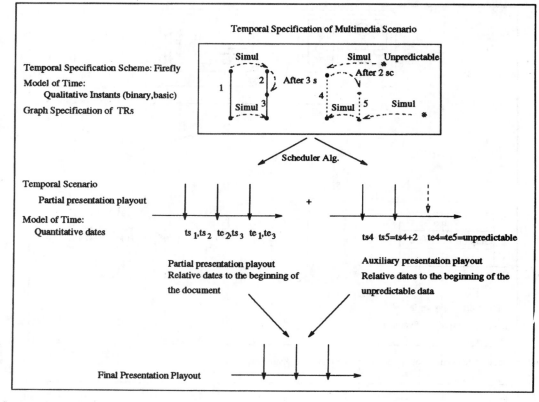

Fig. 20. Firefly.

scenario of the previous example (unpredictable events are not considered here). The system uses a derivation of a playout schedule for presentation. As it assumes a distributed architecture, delay and jitter variations are anticipated during the presentation process. To overcome these problems, a secondary schedule is derived [12]. The system shown uses a scenario specification through the OCPN (*qualitative intervals*), and a playout specification (*quantitative dates*). The communication system also works according to the same model of time as the playout schedule. The quantitative information in the case of the playout schedule is different than the information used in the retrieval schedule (here, the dates are derived from the presentation playout schedule).

The identification of temporal structures in the overal multimedia system is very useful for comparison. Systems that are intended for different applications, and that appear to have little resemblance can have identical temporal structures. Fig. 22 compares temporal structures of two distributed multimedia systems: the OCPN system presented above, and a possible implementation following the temporal specification scheme proposed by Li *et al.* [24]. In this case, the systems have the same temporal structure: (1) a temporal specification scheme for the multimedia scenario, on the left-hand side, OCPN, on the right-hand side, Temporal Graph Model (TGM); (2) the presentation system, both of them follow a presentation schedule that has been derived from the specification of the multimedia scenario (a *quantitative dates* model of time); (3) a communication system that follows a retrieval schedule that

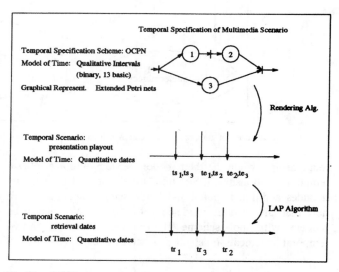

Fig. 21. OCPN system.

has been derived from the presentation schedule. Although the temporal specification schemes and the theory and mechanisms to derive the schedules and carry them out are different, the temporal structures are the same.

Discussion: The identification of the temporal models used in each component of the system clarifies the way in which different approaches can be combined. For example, Amer *et al.* [3] have designed a communications protocol which

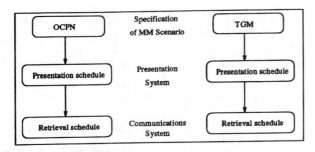

Fig. 22.   Comparison of systems derived from Li *et al.* and the OCPN.

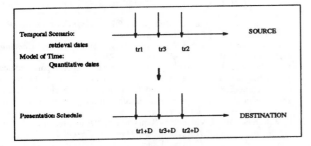

Fig. 23.   The flow synchronization protocol.

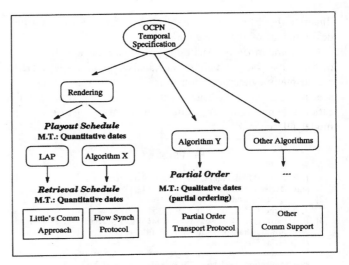

Fig. 24.   Using the OCPN with different communications protocols.

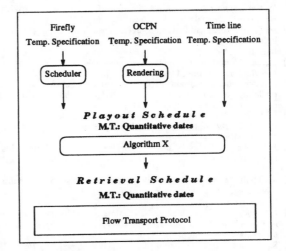

Fig. 25.   Using the flow synchronization protocol for several temporal specification schemes.

takes advantage of partial orderings to improve transmission bandwidth utilization. One can envision the use of a specification scheme such as the OCPN for the description of a multimedia scenario, the use of a presentation schedule for the playout mechanism, and the use of the aforementioned communications protocol for the transmission of the media units. To achieve this combination we need an algorithm that generates a partial ordering from the OCPN temporal specification.

Escobar has proposed another protocol for the communication system: Flow Synchronization Transport Protocol [10]. It has been designed for media units generated in real-time, and provides a constant virtual delay between sources and destinations. This protocol can also be used for the transmission of stored data by using a prespecified retrieval schedule (Fig. 23).

Fig. 24 illustrates several alternatives for the construction of distributed multimedia systems by combining a temporal specification scheme with different mechanisms for satisfying the communications component. The models of time for each part of the system are highlighted. In this figure, an OCPN specification is shown with a rendering algorithm that generates quantitative dates. This is linked to the LAP algorithm and might also be linked to Escobar's flow synchronization protocol through some (undefined) algorithm X. The OCPN can also be applied to techniques such as the partial order protocol of Amer *et al.* through some (undefined) translation Y or to other communications approaches not considered here. In all cases the unifying basis is a model of time.

Fig. 25 shows another example of the combination of techniques to yield multimedia synchronization. Here we use the same communication system for different temporal specification schemes when uncertainties do not exist. From any of the temporal specification schemes we can derive a presentation

schedule. With some (undefined) algorithm (X) we can transform presentation schedules into retrieval schedules, and then use the flow transport protocol for communications.

V. CONCLUSION

In this paper we have divided the general multimedia synchronization problem into two parts: one of modeling, representing, and specifying timing requirements of multimedia scenarios; and the other of achieving a temporal specification via synchronization methods. The former problem was the focus in our development of a temporal reference framework that can be used to evaluate and synthesize temporal specification schemes for the support of multimedia synchronization.

The temporal reference framework is based on existing temporal theory and modeling techniques and attempts to unify the terminology applied toward temporal specification for multimedia. The framework was applied to the comparison of existing approaches for multimedia synchronization to illustrate the differences of modeling power and to justify the development of the framework.

Our comparison of existing approaches indicates the utility of the framework. In addition, the analysis explains why there are so many synchronization frameworks, how a multimedia scenario can be represented with different temporal specification schemes, and why some specification schemes cannot model all scenarios.

REFERENCES

[1] J. F. Allen, "Maintaining knowledge about temporal intervals," *Commun. ACM*, vol. 26, no. 11, pp. 832–843, Nov. 1983.

[2] ———, "Time and time again: The many ways to represent time," *Int. J. Intelligent Syst.*, no. 6, pp. 341–355, 1991.

[3] P. D. Amer, C. Chassot, T. J. Connolly, M. Díaz, and P. Conrad, "Partial order transport service for multimedia and other applications," *IEEE/ACM Trans. Networking*, vol. 2, no. 5, pp. 440–456, Oct. 1994.

[4] D. Anderson and G. Homsy, "A continuous media I/O server and its synchronization mechanism," *Computer*, pp. 51–57, Oct. 1991.

[5] G. Blakowski, J. Hübel, and U. Langrehr, "Tools for specifying and executing synchronized multimedia," in *Proc. Network and Operating System Support for Digital Audio and Video*, R. G. Herrtwich, Ed. Berlin, Germany: Springer–Verlag, 1991, pp. 271–282.

[6] M. C. Buchanan and P. T. Zellweger, "Specifying temporal behavior in hypermedia documents," in *Proc. ACM Eur. Conf. on Hypertext*, Milan, Italy, Dec. 1992, pp. 262–271.

[7] ———, "Automatic temporal layout mechanisms," in *Proc. ACM Multimedia '93*, Anaheim, CA, Aug. 1993, pp. 341–350.

[8] J. Emery and A. Karmouch, "A multimedia document architecture and rendering synchronization scheme," in *2nd Int. Conf., Broadband Islands (Bridging the Services Gap)*, 1993, pp. 59–69.

[9] R. Erfle, "Hytime as the multimedia document model of choice," in *Proc. IEEE Int. Conf. Multimedia Computing and Systems*, Boston, MA, May 1994, pp. 445–454.

[10] J. Escobar, D. Deutsch, and C. Partridge, "Flow synchronization protocol," *IEEE/ACM Trans. Networking*, vol. 2, no. 2, pp. 111–121, Apr. 1994.

[11] M. Filali, "The specification of the temporal behavior for multimedia scheduling," *Ann. Telecommunications*, vol. 49, nos. 5-6, pp. 315–323, May–June 1994.

[12] J. Gibbon and T. D. C. Little, "Real-time data delivery for multimedia networks," in *Proc. 18th Annual Conf., Local Computer Networks*, Minneapolis, MN, Sept. 1993, pp. 7–16.

[13] S. Gibbs, "Composite multimedia and active objects," in *Proc. Object-Oriented Programming Systems, Languages and Applications (OOPSLA '91)*, 1991, pp. 97–112.

[14] S. Gibbs, L. Dami, and D. Tsichritzis, "An object oriented framework for multimedia composition and synchronization," in *Proc. Eurographics Multimedia Workshop*, Stockholm, Sweden, 1991.

[15] C. L. Hamblin, "Instants and intervals," in *Proc. 1st Conf. Int. Society for the Study of Time*, New York, 1972.

[16] M. Hodges and R. Sasnett, "Synchronization," *Multimedia Computing: Case Studies from MIT Project Athena*. Reading, MA: Addison-Wesley, 1993.

[17] P. Hoepner, "Presentation scheduling of multimedia objects and its impact on network and operating system support," in *Proc. Network and Operating System Support for Digital Audio and Video*, R. G. Herrtwich, Ed. Berlin, Germany: Springer-Verlag, 1991, pp. 132–143.

[18] P. Hoepner, "Synchronizing the presentation of multimedia objects," *Computer Commun.*, vol. 15, no. 9, pp. 557–564, Nov. 1992.

[19] M. Iino, Y. F. Day, and A. Ghafoor, "An oject-oriented model for spatio-temporal synchronization of multimedia information," in *Proc. IEEE Intl. Conf. Multimedia Computing and Systems*, Boston, MA, May 1994, pp. 110–119.

[20] ISO, "Hypermedia/timed based document structuring language (hytime)," *ISO/IEC IS 10744*, Apr. 1992.

[21] ISO, "Information technology coded representation of multimedia and hypermedia information objects (MHEG)," *ISO/IEC JTC1/SC29/WG12*, Feb. 1993.

[22] J. F. Koegel, L. W. Rutledge, J. L. Rutledge, and C. Keskin, "Hyoctane: A hytime engine for and MMIS," in *Proc. ACM Multimedia '93*, Anaheim, CA, Aug. 1993, pp. 129–136.

[23] P. Ladkin and R. Maddux, "On binary constraint networks," Krestel Institute, Palo Alto, CA, Technical Report, 1988.

[24] L. Li, A. Karmouch, and N. D. Georganas, "Multimedia teleorchestra with independent sources: Part 1—Temporal modeling of collaborative multimedia scenarios," *ACM/Springer Multimedia Syst.*, vol. 1, no. 4, pp. 143–153, 1994.

[25] ———, "Multimedia teleorchestra with independent sources: Part 2—Synchronization algorithms," *ACM/Springer Multimedia Syst.*, vol. 1, no. 4, pp. 154–165, 1994.

[26] T. D. C. Little and A. Ghafoor, "Synchronization and storage models for multimedia objects," *IEEE J. Select. Areas Commun.*, vol. 8, no. 3, pp. 413–427, Apr. 1990.

[27] ———, "Scheduling of bandwidth-constrained multimedia traffic," *Computer Commun.*, vol. 15, no. 6, pp. 381–387, July/Aug. 1992.

[28] ———, "Interval-based conceptual models for time-dependent multimedia data," *IEEE Trans. Knowledge Data Eng.*, vol. 5, no. 4, pp. 551–563, Aug. 1993.

[29] B. D. Markey, "Hytime and MHEG," in *Proc. COMPCON Spring 1992*, San Francisco, CA, Feb. 1992, pp. 25–40.

[30] S. R. Newcomb, N. A. Kipp, and V. T. Newcomb, "Hytime," *Commun. ACM*, vol. 34, no. 11, pp. 67–83, Nov. 1991.

[31] M. J. Pérez-Luque, "Un marco de referencia temporal para técnicas de sincronización multimedia," Ph.D. dissertation, E. T. S. Ingenieros de Telecomunicación, Universidad Politécnica de Madrid, 1995; also available in English: "A temporal reference framework for multimedia synchronization techniques."

[32] P. V. Rangan, H. M. Vin, and S. Ramanathan, "Designing an on-demand multimedia service," *IEEE Commun. Mag.*, pp. 56–64, July 1992.

[33] P. van Beek and R. Cohen, "Exact and approximate reasoning about temporal relations," *Computational Intelligence*, no. 6, pp. 132–144, 1990.

[34] M. Vilain and H. Kautz, "Constraint propagation algorithms for temporal reasoning," in *Proc. AAAI-86, Artificial Intelligence*, Philadelphia, PA, Aug. 1986, pp. 377–382.

[35] T. Wahl and K. Rothermel, "Representing time in multimedia systems," in *Proc. IEEE Intl. Conf. Multimedia Computing and Systems*, Boston, MA, May 1994, pp. 538–543.

María José Pérez-Luque received her major and Ph.D. degrees in signal and communication theory (Dr. Ingeniero de Telecomunicación) from the Universidad Politécnica de Madrid, in 1991 and 1995, respectively.

She is a professor in the Facultad de Ciencias de la Información at the Universidad de Navarra, and Director del Laboratorio de Comunicación Multimedia. She is currently involved in research and development projects for the application of multimedia technologies to the communication field: journalism, film, television, public relations, and advertising.

Dr. Pérez-Luque is a member of the IEEE Computer Society and the Association for Computer Machinery.

Thomas D. C. Little (S'90–M'91) received the B.S. degree in biomedical engineering from Rensselaer Polytechnic Institute in 1983, and the M.S. degree in electrical engineering and the Ph.D. degree in computer engineering from Syracuse University, in 1989 and 1991, respectively.

He is an assistant professor in the Department of Electrical, Computer, and Systems Engineering at Boston University. He is the director of the Multimedia Communications Lab at Boston University, where he is involved in the development of enabling technologies and applications for interactive multimedia systems. He serves on the editorial board of IEEE MULTIMEDIA and ACM/Springer *Multimedia Systems* and on various program committees for ACM and IEEE.

Human Perception of
Media Synchronization

Ralf Steinmetz
Clemens Engler

Technical Report 43.9310

IBM European Networking Center
Vangerowstraße 18 • 69115 Heidelberg • Germany

Phone: +49-6221-59-3000 • Fax: +49-6221-59-3400

steinmet, engler @ dhdibml .bitnet
steinmet @ heidelbg.vnet

Abstract: Multimedia synchronization comprises the definition and the establishment of temporal relationships among audio, video, and other data. The presentation of 'in sync' data streams by computers is essential to achieve a natural impression. If data is 'out of sync', the human perception tends to identify the presentation as artificial, strange, or annoying. Therefore, the goal of any multimedia system is to present all data without synchronization errors. The achievement of this goal requires a detailed knowledge of the synchronization requirements at the user interface. This paper presents the results of a series of experiments about human media perception. It leads to a first guideline for the definition of a synchronization quality of service. The results show that a skew between related data streams may still let data appear 'in sync'. It also turned out that the notion of a synchronization error highly depends on the types of media. We use our findings to develop a scheme for the processing of non-trivial synchronization skew between more than two data streams.

in Section 3. Section 4 describes the test strategy, how the results were achieved including influencing factors. Section 5 presents the results on pointer synchronization, remaining types of media synchronization are discussed in Section 6. The aggregation of various individual media synchronization results is analyzed in Section 7 and Section 8 defines and summarizes the results in terms of the required quality of service parameters. The appendix of this paper includes an example of the questionnaire used by test participants.

2 The Lip Synchronization Experiment

'Lip synchronization' denotes the temporal relationship between an audio and a video stream where speakers are shown while they say something. The time difference between related audio and video LDUs is known as the 'skew'. Streams which are perfectly 'in sync' have no skew, i.e., 0 ms. We conducted experiments and measured which skews were perceived as 'out of sync' for audio and video data. In our experiments, users often mentioned that something is wrong with the synchronization, but this did not disturb their feeling for the quality of the presentation. Therefore, we additionally evaluated the tolerance of the users by asking if the data out of sink affects the quality of the presentation (see also the questionnaire in Appendix B).

In several discussions with experts working with audio and video, we noticed that most of the personal experiences were derived from very specific situations. As an immediate consequence we have been confronted with a wide range and tolerance levels up to 240 ms. A comparison and a general usage of these values is doubtful because the environments from which they resulted were were comperable. In some cases we encountered the 'head view' displayed in front of some single color background on a high resolution professional monitor. In another set-up a 'body view' was displayed in a video window at a resolution of 240*256 pixels in the middle of some dancing people. In order to get the most accurate and stringent affordable skew tolerance levels, we selected a speaker in a TV news environment as a 'talking head' (see Figure 1). In this scenario, the viewer is not disturbed by background information. The user is attracted by the gestures, eyes, and lip movement of the speaker. We selected a speaker who makes use of gestures and articulates very accurately.

We recorded the presentation and then played it back in our experiments with artificially introduced skew that was adjusted according to the frame rate, i.e., n times 40 ms, that was introduced by professional video editing equipment. We conducted some experiments with a higher resolution time scale by cutting the material with the help of a computer where it was possible to introduce a smaller delay in the audio stream. It turned out that there was no need for any test with higher granularity than 40 ms.

Figure 1: Left: Head View, Middle: Shoulder View, Right: Body View[1]

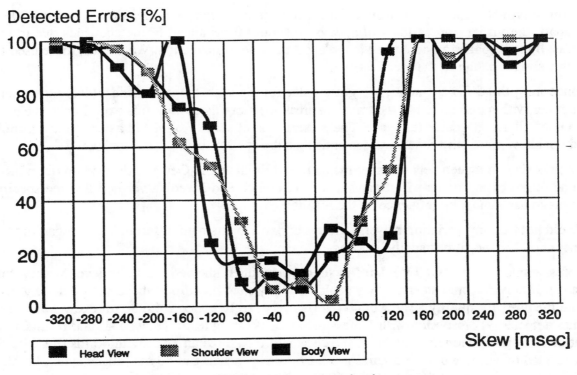

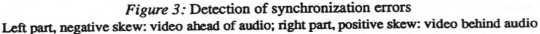

Figure 3: Detection of synchronization errors
Left part, negative skew: video ahead of audio; right part, positive skew: video behind audio

The left side of the figure relates to negative skew values, where video is ahead of audio. In our daily life, we experience this situation whenever we talk to some distant located person. All three curves are, in general, flat in this region. Since we are not accustomed to hearing speech ahead of the related visual impression, the right side of the curves turns out to be steeper.

The 'body view' curve is broader than the 'head view' curve, at the 'head view' a small skew was easier to notice. This was more difficult in the 'body view'. The 'head view' is also more asymmetric than the 'body view'. Basically, the further away we are situated, the less noticeable the error is.

At a fairly high skew, the curves show some periodic ripples. This is more obvious in the case of audio being ahead of video. It means that some people had difficulties in identifying the synchronization error even with fairly high skew values. A careful analysis of this phenomenon lead to the following explanation; At the relative minima, the speech signal was closely related to the movement of the lips which tends to be quasi periodic. Errors were easy to notice at the start, at the end, at the borders of pauses, and whenever changing drastically the mood (e.g., from an explanation style to a sudden aggressive comment). Errors were more difficult to notice in the middle of sentences. A subsequent test containing video clips with skews according to these minima (without pauses and not showing the start, the end, and changes of mood) caused problems in identifying if there was indeed a synchronization error.

This asymmetry is very plausible: In a conversation where two people are located 20 m apart, the visual impression will always be about 60 ms ahead of the acoustics due to the fast light propagation compared to the acoustic wave propagation. We are just more used to this situation than to the previous one.

Concerning the different areas, we got similar results with the noise and video experiment (hammer with nails) although the transient areas are more narrow. In this experiment, the type of view had a negligeable influence. The presentation of some violinist in a concert and a choir did not show more stringent skew demands than the speaker being synchronized.

A comparison between sets of experiments ran in English and German showed no difference. Some minor experiments with Spanish, Italian, French and Swedish verified that the specific language has almost no influence on the results.

We did not find any variation between groups of participants with different habits regarding the amount of TV and films usually watched.

Professionals (cutters and TV related technical personnel) showed a smaller level of skew tolerance. If they detected an error, they could correctly state if audio is ahead of or behind video. With the used TV quality a skew of 40 ms was very rarely noticed, the 80 ms skew was sometimes detected. A discussion with professional video cutting teams showed similar results. One out of three professionals stated that she/he would recognize an error with 40 ms of skew, all mentioned that they would recognize a 'lip sync error' starting at 80 ms 'out of sync', but that this might not influence the quality of the perceived information [Rau93].

3 Quality of Lip Synchronization

Figure 3 and Figure 4 outline the perception of synchronization errors. More important than just to notice the error is the effect of such an 'out of sync' video clip on the human perception. If in an extreme case all people tend to like audio data to be, e.g., 40 ms ahead of video, we should take it into account. Therefore the test candidates were asked to qualify a detected synchronization error in terms of being acceptable, indifferent, or annoying (see Question 3 at Appendix B). Out of these answers we derived the 'level of annoyance' which quantifies the quality of synchronization.

Figure 5 shows by which degree a skew was believed to be acceptable or intolerable. We used the 'talking head' experiment and depict here the 'shoulder view' as it is a compromise between the 'head' and the 'body view'. The diagrams of the other views are included in the appendix.

The envelope curve defines the amount of candidates who detected a synchronization problem, i.e., if candidates did not notice an error, they can hardly determine if the error is acceptable or not. This is the same curve for the 'shoulder view' as shown in Figure 3 and Figure 4 without a spline interpolation.

4 Test Strategy

For each person, the lip synchronization test took approximately 45 minutes. The experiment was intentionally carried out with the same audio and video over and over again. This led to some concentration problems during the whole test, which was alleviated by introducing breaks.

We always ran all tests related to one view in one session. Then, the second and the third view were shown in their sessions. The order of the sessions had no effect. Individual probes, each having a different skew, were shown randomly. This led to sequences of probes as summed up in Table 3 in the Appendix.

Initial experiments showed that a total length of about 30s with a small subsequent break is sufficient for getting the users impression. All experiments with longer video clips did not provide any additional new or different results. With some test candidates, were more experienced with video technology and synchronization issues, 5s turned out to be sufficient. Nevertheless we sticked to have 30s for each probe.

The background of all scenes was static (i.e., not moving) and out of focus in order to keep the distraction to a minimum. In short clips with a moving background the viewer is sometimes more attracted by the actions occurring behind the speaker than by the speaker himself. This would lead to more larger skew values for the perception of synchronization errors. We focussed on the detection of such errors in the most challenging set-ups, this allowed the determination of skew values independently from the actual content of the video and audio data. In these experiments the viewer should never have been distracted by the background.

The same consideration, i.e. background vs. foreground, can be applied to the audio data. The voice of the speaker can be mixed with some background noise or music. In order to differentiate between foreground and background, the volume of the speaker should be at least twice the volume of the background audio. In contrast to the video analogy discussed in the previous paragraph, any background audio did not influence our results. Background noise in the audio channel had no effect on the experiments.

The group of people was selected according to an equal distribution of sex and ages. To have a representative distribution we did not take into account habits (like the time spent for watching TV) and the social status or any other characteristics of the test candidates.

It would have been very interesting if, before presenting each probe to the candidates, they were not aware of the fact that we were looking for synchronization issues. As soon as the test candidates noticed the first time a synchronization fault, they would not have been allowed to continue the experiment with further skews. This would have led to results for casual unexperienced users. As a matter of fact, we started to run the experiment in this way with a very few people. It turned out, that lip synchronization is not detected so easily leading to a broader range of the 'in sync' zone. In order to provide results for building multimedia systems for all types of users, we have to make the assumption that a user can also make frequent use of such a system and interact for a longer time with the application. Therefore, the results of users being aware of possible synchronization faults provide the correct basis.

Figure 7: Pointer synchronization experiment based on a map and on a technical sketch

We generated two experiments:

- In the first experiment some technical items of a sailing boat are explained while a pointer locates the aread of interest (see Figure 7, right side). The shorter the explanation, the more crucial the synchronization turns out to be.

- Therefore we additionally made a second experiment with the explanation of a travelling route on a map as seen on the left side of Figure 7.

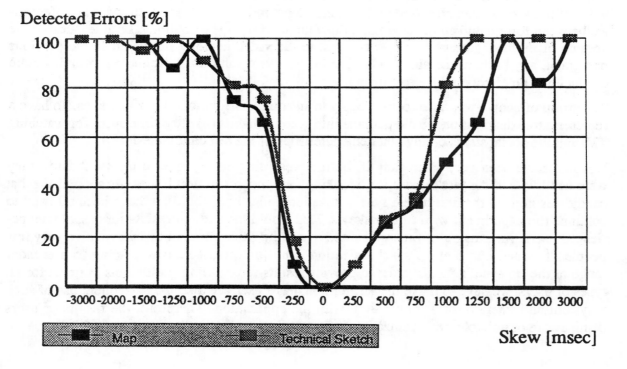

Figure 8: Detection of the pointer synchronization errors
Left part, negative skew; pointer ahead of audio; right part, positive skew; pointer behind audio

detected the fault, but did not object at all to work with such a skew. Therefore, we encounter a broad "in sync' and 'transient' area.

6 Elementary Media Synchronization

Lip synchronization and pointer synchronisation were investigated by us because of the contradictory results available to us from other sources. In the following, we will summrize other synchronization results which we found to provide less diverse statements. We do this to arrive at a more complete picture of synchronization requirements.

Since the beginnings of digital *audio* the ('affordable') *jitter* and the jitter to be tolerated by dedicated hardware has been studied. In discussions with Dannenberg, he provided us some references and the following explanations of these studies: In [Bles78] the maximum allowable jitter in a sample period for at 16 bit quality audio is mentioned to be 200ps, this is explained as the error equivalence to the magnitude of the LSB (least significant bit) of a full-level maximum-frequency 20KHz signal. In [Stoc72] some perception experiments recommend an allowable jitter in an audio sample period between 5 and 10 ns. Further perception experiments were carried out by [Lick51] and [Wood51], the maximum spacing of short clicks to obtain fusion into a single percept was mentioned to be 2ms (as cited by [RuAv80]).

The combination of *audio and animation* is usually not as stringent as lip synchronization. A multimedia course on dancing, e.g., comprises the dancing steps as animation with the respective music. By making use of the interactive capabilities, individual sequences can be viewed and listened to over and over again. In this example the synchronization between music and animation is particulary important. Experience showed that a skew of +/- 80 ms fulfills all user demands even though some jitters may occur. Nevertheless, the most challenging issue is the correlation between a noisy event and its visual representation, e.g. a simulated crash of cars. Here we encounter the same constraints as for lip synchronization, +/- 80 ms.

Two audio tracks can be tightly or loosely coupled, the effect of related audio streams depends heavily on the content:

- A stereo signal usually contains information about the location of the sources of audio and is *tightly coupled*. The correct processing of this information by the human brain can only be accomplished if the phases of the acoustic signals are delivered correctly. This demands for a skew less than the distance between consecutive samples leading to the order of magnitude of 20 µs. [DaSt93] reports that the perceptible phase shift between two audio channels is 17µs. This is based on a headphone listening experiment. Since a varying delay in one channel causes the apparent a sound's source location to move, Dannenberg proposed to allow an audio sample skew between stereo channels within the boundaries of +/- 11µs. This is derived from the observation that a one-sample offset at a sample rate of 44kHz can be heard.

- *Loosely coupled* audio channels are a speaker and, e.g., some background music. In such scenarios we experience an affordable skew of 500 ms. The most stringent loosely coupled configuration has been the playback of a dialogue where the audio data of the participants originate from different sources. The experienced acceptable skew was 120 ms.

The combination of *audio with images* has its initial application in slide shows. By intuition a skew of about 1s arises which can be explained as follows [Dann93]: Consider that it takes a second or so to advance a slide projector. People sometimes comment on the time it takes to

Sometimes *video* is combined *with animation* as there may be a film where some actors become animated pictures. But, for the following short reasoning of synchronization between video and animation let us go back to the example of a video showing the stroke of a billiard ball and the image of the actual 'route' of this ball. Instead of the static image, the track of the ball can be followed by an animation which displays this route at the time the ball is moving on the table. In this example any 'out of sync' effect is immediately visible. In order for humans to be able to watch the ball with the perception of a moving picture, this ball must be visible in several consecutive adjacent video frames at a slidely different position: a good result can be achieved, if in every 3 subsequent video frames, the ball moves by the distance of it's diameter. Less frames will result in the problem of visibility of what occurs, e.g., in tennis, and it may lead to difficulties with the notion of continuity. Derived from this number of 3 subsequent frames, we allow the equivalent skew of 120 ms to occur. This is very tight synchronization, and we have not found any practical requirement which cannot be handled with this value of the affordable skew.

Multimedia systems also incorporate the real-time processing of *control data* and the presentation of this data using various media. A tight timing requirement occurs if the person has to react to this displayed data. No overall timing demand can be stated as these issues highly depend on the application itself.

7 Aggregation of Media Synchronization

So far, media synchronization has been evaluated as the relationship between two kinds of media or two data streams. This is the canonical foundation of all types of media synchronization. In practice, we often encounter more than two related media streams: A sophisticated multimedia application scenario incorporates the simultaneous handling of various sessions. Take as an example an ongoing conference where a video window displays the actual speaker, the audio data is his/her voice as he/she explains some technical details of a new space command station.

Figure 10: Aggregation of media at the user interface

6. max skew (audio_spanish ahead_of audio_english) = 160 ms

In the following step any set of linear independent synchronization requirements can be chosen to be used as it may be the following set.

max skew (video ahead_of audio_english) = 80 ms
max skew (audio_english ahead_of video) = 80 ms
max skew (audio_english ahead_of audio_spanish) = 160 ms
max skew (audio_spanish ahead_of audio_english) = 160 ms

In summary, the above sketched procedures allow to solve two related problems:

- If the applications impose a set of related synchronization requirements on a multimedia system , we are now able to find out the most stringent demands.

- If a set of individual synchronization requirements between various data streams is provided, we are now able to compute the required relationships between each individual pair of streams.

Both issues arise at non-trivial systems when estimating, computing or negotiating the quality of service as it is outlined in the next section.

8 Synchronization Quality of Service

The control of synchronization in distributed multimedia systems requires a knowledge of the temporal relationship between media streams. The result of this study is of service to this management component. Synchronization requirements can be expressed by a quality of service (QoS) definition. This QoS parameter defines the acceptable skew within the involved data streams, it defines the affordable synchronization boundaries. The notion of QoS is well established in communication systems, in the context of multimedia, it also applies to local systems. If the video data is to be presented simultaneously to some audio and, both are stored as different files or as different entries in a database, lip synchronization according to the above mentioned results has to be taken into account.

In this context we want to introduce the notion of *presentation* and *production level synchronization*:

- *Production level synchronization* refers to the QoS to be guaranteed prior to the presentation of the data at the user interface. It typically involves the recording of synchronized data for a subsequent playback. The stored data should be captured and recorded with no skew at all, i.e. it is achieved totally "in sync". This is of particular interest if the file is stored in an interleaved format applying multiplexing techniques. Imagine a participant of an audio-video conference who additionally records this audiovisual data to be playbacked later for a remote spectator. At the conference participant's site, the actual incoming audiovisual data is 'in sync' according to the defined lip synchronization boundaries. Let the data arrive with a skew of +80 ms and let audio and video LDUs be transmitted as a single multiplexed stream over the same transport connection. It is displayed to the user and directly stored on the harddisk (still having this skew). Later on, this data is presented simultaneously at a local workstation and to the remote spectator. For a correct data to be deliverable, the QoS should be specified as being between -160 ms and 0 ms. At the remote viewer's station - without this additional knowledge of the actual skew - it might turn out that by applying these boundaries twice, data is not 'in sync'. In general, any synchronized data which will be further processed should be synchronized according to a production level quality, i.e. with no skew at all.

9 Outlook

Synchronization QoS parameters allow the builders of distributed multimedia and communication systems to make use of the affordable tolerances. In our Heidelberg multimedia system [Herr92], the HeiRAT component [VHNa92] is in charge of the resource management. HeiRAT accepts QoS requests from the applications and serves for this QoS demands as interface to the whole distributed system. It makes use of the flow specification of the ST-II multimedia internetwork protocol to negotiate them among the whole set of involved system components [DHHo93]. It provides a QoS calculation by optimizing one QoS parameter dependent on the resource characteristics. Subsequently resources are reserved according to the QoS guarantees. At the actual data transfer phase, resources are scheduled according to the provided guarantees.

Synchronization is a crucial issue of multimedia systems. In local systems it is often easy to provide because there are sufficient resources or it is a single user configuration. In networked systems we encounter a plethora of concurrent processes making use of the same scarce resources. A skew between media easily arises.

This paper provides a set of quality of service values for synchronization. It is a feather in our cap to reach results for wide range of media synchronization with extensive user interface experiments. The enforcement of which remains to be a different item which already has been addressed by several systems. The presentation of audio and video, according to some logical time system is one of the possible solutions.

10 Acknowledgments

We would like to acknowledge the help of Wieland Holfelder in producing the basic video material as well as the patience and accuracy of all our test candidates. Roger Dannenberg, CMU Pittsburgh, provided many valuable hints concerning jitter of audio samples and synchronization related to music. Ralf Guido Herrtwich substantially commented the final version of this paper. Thank you.

References

[AnHo91]   David P. Anderson, George Homsy: *Synchronization Policies and Mechanisms in a Continuous Media I/O Server*, International Computer Science Institute, Technical Report no. 91-003, Berkeley, 1991.

[Blak92]   Gerold Blakowski, Jens Huebel, Ulrike Langrehr, Max Muhlhaeuser: *Tools Support for the Synchronization and Presentation of Distributed Multimedia*, computer communications, vol. 15, no. 10, December 1992.

[Bles78]   Barry Blesser: *Digitization of Audio: A Comprehensive Examination of Theory, Implementation, and Current Practice*, Journal of the Audio Engineering Society, JAES 26(10), October 1978, pp. 739-771.

[Clyn85]   M. Clynes: *Secrets of Life in Music: Musicality Realized by Computer* in Proceedings of the 1984 International Computer Music Conference, San Francisco, International Computer Music Association, 1985.

[Dann93]   Roger Dannenberg: *Personal communication on sound effects and video synchronization and on music play back and visualization of the corresponding strokes*, 1993.

[Stei90]   Ralf Steinmetz: *Synchronization Properties in Multimedia Systems*, IEEE Journal on Selected Areas in Communication, vol. 8, no. 3, April 1990, pp. 401-412.

[Stei92]   Ralf Steinmetz: *Multimedia Synchronization Techniques: Experiences Based on Different System Structures*, IEEE Multimedia Workshop '92, Monterey, April 1992.

[Stei93]   Ralf Steinmetz, *Multimedia-Technology: Fundamentals (in German)*, Springer-Verlag, September 1993.

[Stew87]   M. Stewart: *The Feel Factor: Music with Soul*, Electronic Musician, vol. 3, no. 10, pp. 55-66, 1987.

[StHe91]   Ralf Steinmetz, Ralf Guido Herrtwich: *Integrated Distributed Multimedia-Systems*, Informatik Spektrum, Springer Verlag, vol.14, no.5, October 1991, pp.280-282.

[Stoc72]   T. Stockham: *A/D and D/A Converters: Their Effect on Digital Audio Fidelity*, in Digital Signal Processing, L. Rabiner and C. Rader, (Eds.), IEEE Press, NY 1972.

[VHNa92]   Carsten Vogt, Ralf Guido Herrtwich, Ramesh Nagarajan: HeiRat: *The Heidelberg Resource Administration Technique Design Philosophie and Goals*, IBM Technical Report 43.9307, IBM European Networking Center, Heidelberg 1992.

[Wood51]   H. Woodrow: *Time Perception*, in S. S. Stevens, (Ed.) Handbook of Experimental Psychology, Wiley, 1951.

Correctly Detected Errors [%]

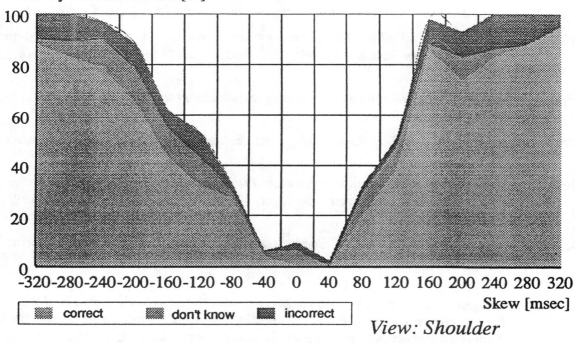

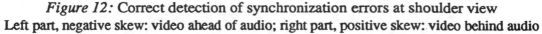

View: Shoulder

Figure 12: Correct detection of synchronization errors at shoulder view
Left part, negative skew: video ahead of audio; right part, positive skew: video behind audio

Correctly Detected Errors [%]

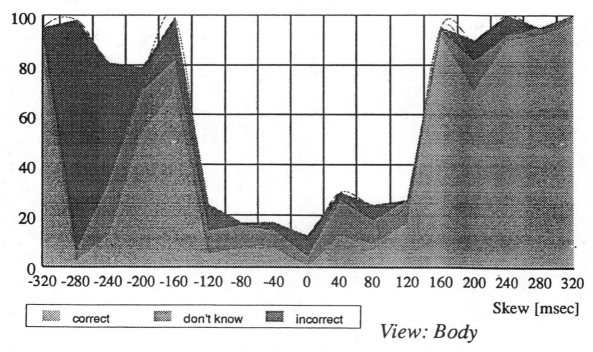

View: Body

Figure 13: Correct detection of synchronization errors at body view
Left part, negative skew: video ahead of audio; right part, positive skew: video behind audio

Level Of Annoyance [%]

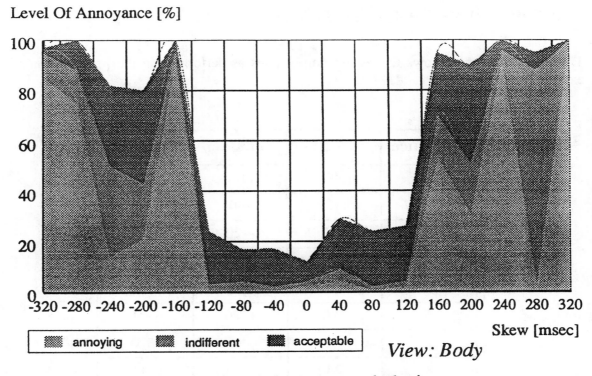

View: Body

Figure 16: Level of Annoyance at body view
Left part, negative skew: video ahead of audio; right part, positive skew: video behind audio

Appendix C: Sequencing of Clips

The following Table shows the sequencing of clips as performed in the lip synchronisation experiments.

Sequence	Head	Shoulder	Body
1	-80	+160	+120
2	+120	-40	-160
3	+40	-120	-40
4	-200	+240	+160
5	0	-160	-240
6	+80	+280	+80
7	-40	-80	-320
8	+240	-240	0
9	-120	+200	+240
10	+160	+320	-200
11	-240	+40	-120
12	-160	-120	+320
13	+200	-320	-40
14	-320	0	-280
15	-120	-40	+40
16	0	+80	+280
17	-280	-280	-80
18	-40	-200	+200
19	+320	+120	-120

Table 2: Ordering of the Probes

Improved Algorithms for Synchronizing Computer Network Clocks

David L. Mills, *Member, IEEE*

Abstract— The Network Time Protocol (NTP) is widely deployed in the Internet to synchronize computer clocks to each other and to international standards via telephone modem, radio and satellite. The protocols and algorithms have evolved over more than a decade to produce the present NTP Version 3 specification and implementations. Most of the estimated deployment of 100 000 NTP servers and clients enjoy synchronization to within a few tens of milliseconds in the Internet of today.

This paper describes specific improvements developed for NTP Version 3 which have resulted in increased accuracy, stability and reliability in both local-area and wide-area networks. These include engineered refinements of several algorithms used to measure time differences between a local clock and a number of peer clocks in the network, as well as to select the best subset from among an ensemble of peer clocks and combine their differences to produce a local clock accuracy better than any in the ensemble. This paper also describes engineered refinements of the algorithms used to adjust the time and frequency of the local clock, which functions as a disciplined oscillator. The refinements provide automatic adjustment of algorithm parameters in response to prevailing network conditions, in order to minimize network traffic between clients and busy servers while maintaining the best accuracy. Finally, this paper describes certain enhancements to the Unix operating system kernel software in order to realize submillisecond accuracies with fast workstations and networks.

I. INTRODUCTION

A COMPUTER CLOCK (or simply *clock*) is an ensemble of hardware and software components used to provide an accurate, stable and reliable time-of-day function for the computer operating system and its clients. In order that multiple distributed computers sharing a network can synchronize their operations with each other, a *synchronization protocol* is used to exchange time information and synchronize the clocks. In this paper the term *local clock* identifies the clock in a particular computer as distinguished from a *peer clock* in another computer with which it exchanges time information. If the clocks are to agree with Coordinated Universal Time (UTC) (sic), a radio clock (usually a special-purpose radio or satellite receiver) must be provided to synchronize one or more of them to UTC as disseminated by various means [14].

Computer clocks can be synchronized typically within a few tens of milliseconds in the global Internet of today

Manuscript received December 6, 1994; approved by IEEE/ACM TRANSACTIONS ON NETWORKING Editor R. Guerin. This work was supported by the Advanced Research Projects Agency under NASA Ames Research Center Contract NAG 2-638, the National Science Foundation under Grant NCR-93-01002, and the U.S. Navy Surface Weapons Center under Northeastern Center for Engineering Education Contract A30327-93.

The author is with the Department of Electrical Engineering, University of Delaware, Newark, DE 19716 USA (e-mail: mills@udel.edu).

IEEE Log Number 9412272.

[12]. However, as computers and networks become faster, there is every expectation that future applications will require accuracies better than a millisecond. This requires in essence a complete reexamination of all elements of the timekeeping apparatus described originally in [9], including the protocols which exchange timekeeping messages and the algorithms which process the data and discipline the local clock. This paper examines in detail the various design issues necessary to achieve this goal and, in particular, describes a suite of algorithms designed to exchange data with possibly many redundant peer clocks and to select an accurate, stable and reliable set of clocks from among them. Besides some new results, it contains some previous work published only in technical reports.

In this paper the Network Time Protocol (NTP) developed for the Internet is used as an example application of the new algorithms, but others, such as the Digital Time Synchronization Service (DTS) [2] could be used as well. After a review of terms and notation in Section II, Section III gives an overview of NTP. Section IV summarizes the clock filter, clustering and combining algorithms, which select the best measurement samples from among possibly several peers and combine them to produce the best available time.

The main results of this paper are in Sections V through VII. Section V describes the intersection algorithm, which is used to separate the *truechimers*, which represent correct clocks, from *falsetickers*, which may not. Section VI contains an analysis of the local clock model, including the effects of oscillator jitter and wander. Section VII details the local clock discipline, which is implemented as a hybrid phase/frequency-lock loop. These algorithms are primarily responsible for the increased accuracy and reliability of the current protocol compared to previous versions.

Section VIII contains a summary of related improvements and extensions of previous algorithms, including those utilizing special PPS and IRIG signals generated by some radio clocks. It also contains a description of certain modifications to four different Unix operating system kernels which provide extremely precise control of the clock time and frequency. Section IX discusses the present status of NTP in the Internet, Section X outlines future plans, and Section XI is a summary of this paper.

II. TERMS AND NOTATION

In this paper the terms *epoch, timescale, oscillator, tolerance, clock,* and *time* are used in a technical sense. Strictly speaking, the epoch of an event is an abstraction which determines the ordering of events in some given frame of reference or timescale. An oscillator is a generator capable of precise frequency (relative to the given timescale) within a specified tolerance, usually expressed in parts-per-million (ppm). A clock is an oscillator together with a counter which records the number of cycles since being initialized with a given value at a given epoch. The value of the counter at epoch t defines the time of that epoch $T(t)$. In general, time is not continuous and depends on the precision of the counter.

Let $T(t)$ be the time displayed by a clock at epoch t relative to the standard timescale:

$$T(t) = T(t_0) + R(t_0)[t - t_0] + 1/2D(t_0)[t - t_0]^2 + \epsilon(t) \quad (1)$$

where $T(t_0)$ is the time at some previous epoch T_0, $R(t_0)$ is the frequency (rate) and $D(t_0)$ is the drift (first derivative of frequency) per unit time. In the conventional (stationary) model used in the literature, T and R are estimated by some disciplining process and the second-order term D is ignored. The random nature of the clock is characterized by ϵ, usually in terms of phase or frequency spectra or measurements of variance [15].

In this paper the *stability* of a clock is how well it can maintain a constant frequency, the *accuracy* is how well its time compares with UTC and the *precision* is to what degree time can be resolved in a particular timekeeping system. These terms will be given precise definitions when necessary. The *time offset* of clock i relative to clock j is the time difference between them $x_{ij}(t) \equiv T_i(t) - T_j(t)$ at a particular epoch t, while the *frequency offset* is the frequency difference between them $y_{ij}(t) \equiv R_i(t) - R_j(t)$. It follows that $x_{ij} = -x_{ji}, y_{ij} = -y_{ji}$ and $x_{ii} = y_{ii} = 0$ for all t. When clear from context, the subscripts i and j will be omitted. In this paper, reference to simply "offset" means time offset, unless indicated otherwise. The term *jitter* refers to differences between the elements of a series $\{y_k\}$; similarly, *wander* refers to differences in $\{y_k\}$ where the peers involved are understood. Finally, the *reliability* of a timekeeping system is the fraction of the time it can be kept connected to the network and operating correctly relative to stated accuracy and stability tolerances.

In order to synchronize clocks, there must be some way to directly or indirectly compare them in time and frequency. In network architectures such as DECnet and Internet, local clocks -synchronize to designated *time servers*, which are timekeeping systems belonging to a *synchronization subnet*. At the root of the subnet are the *primary servers*, which synchronize to external sources (e.g., radio clocks) and are assigned a *stratum number* of 1. *Secondary servers*, which synchronize to primary servers and each other, are assigned stratum numbers equal to the minimum subnet hop count from the root. In general, synchronization proceeds in a hierarchical fashion from the root in increasing stratum numbers along the edges of a minimum spanning tree. In this paper to *synchronize frequency* means to adjust the subnet clocks to run at the same frequency, to *synchronize time* means to set them to agree at a particular epoch with respect to UTC and to *synchronize clocks* means to synchronize them in both frequency and time.

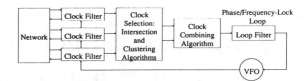

Fig. 1.   Network time protocol.

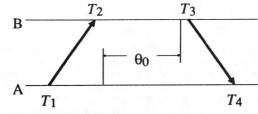

Fig. 2.   Measuring delay and offset.

III. NETWORK TIME PROTOCOL

The Network Time Protocol (NTP) is used by Internet time servers and their clients to synchronize clocks, as well as automatically organize and maintain the time synchronization subnet itself. NTP and its implementations have evolved and proliferated in the Internet over the last decade, with NTP Version 3 adopted as a Internet Standard (Draft). A detailed description of the architecture and service model is contained in [9], while the current formal protocol specification is defined in RFC-1305 [10].

Fig. 1 shows the overall organization of the NTP time server model. *Timestamps* are exchanged between the client and each of possibly several other subnet peers at intervals ranging from a few seconds to several hours. These are used to determine individual roundtrip delays and clock offsets, as well as provide error estimates. As shown in the figure, the computed delays and offsets for each peer are processed by the clock filter algorithm to reduce incidental jitter.

The clock selection algorithm determines from among all peers a suitable subset capable of providing the most accurate and trustworthy time. This is done using a cascade of two subalgorithms, one based on interval intersections to cast out falsetickers and the other based on clustering and maximum likelihood principles to improve accuracy. The resulting offsets of this subset are first combined on a weighted-average basis and then used to drive the clock-discipline algorithm, which is implemented as a feedback loop. In this loop the combined offset is processed by the loop filter to control the variable frequency oscillator (VFO) frequency. The VFO is implemented as a programmable counter using a combination of hardware and software components. It furnishes the time reference to produce the timestamps used in all timing calculations.

Fig. 2 shows how NTP timestamps are numbered and exchanged between peers A and B. Let T_1, T_2, T_3, T_4 be the values of the four most recent timestamps as shown and, without loss of generality, assume $T_3 > T_2$. Also, for the moment assume the clocks of A and B are stable and run at the same frequency. Let

$$a = T_2 - T_1 \quad and \quad b = T_3 - T_4.$$

If the network delay difference from A to B and from B to A, called *differential delay*, is small, the clock offset θ and roundtrip delay δ of B relative to A at time T_4 are close to

$$\theta = \frac{a+b}{2} \cdot \quad \text{and} \quad \delta = a - b. \tag{2}$$

Each NTP message includes the latest three timestamps T_1, T_2 and T_3, while the fourth T_4 is determined upon arrival. Thus, both peers A and B can independently calculate delay and offset using a single bidirectional message stream. This is a symmetric, continuously sampled, time-transfer scheme similar to those used in some digital telephone networks [6]. Among its advantages are that errors due to missing or duplicated messages can be avoided.

In [11] an exhaustive analysis is presented of the time and frequency errors that can accrue as the data are processed and refined at various levels in the subnet hierarchy. While the analysis is too long to repeat here, the results define the maximum error that can accrue under any operational condition, called the *synchronization distance* λ, and the error expected under nominal operating conditions, called the *dispersion* ϵ. There are several components of ϵ, including:

1) The maximum error in reading the local clock and each peer clock, which depends on the clock resolution and method of adjustment.
2) The maximum error due to the frequency tolerance of the local clock and each peer clock since the time either was last set.
3) The estimated error contributed by each peer clock due to delay variations in the network and statistical latencies in the operating systems on the path to the primary reference source, which depends on differences between successive measurements for each peer clock. This is called the *peer dispersion*.
4) The estimated error contributed by the combined set of peers used to discipline the local clock, which depends upon the differences between individual members of the set. This is called the *select dispersion*.

In practice, errors due to network delays usually dominate ϵ. However, it is not possible to characterize these delays as a stationary random process, since network queues can grow and shrink in chaotic fashion and packet arrivals are frequently bursty. However, the method of calculating ϵ defined in [10] represents a conservative estimate of the errors due to each of the above causes.

In [11] it is shown that, given ϵ calculated as above, $\lambda = \frac{\delta}{2} + \epsilon$ is a good estimate of the maximum error contribution due to all causes. In other words, if θ is the measured offset of the local clock relative to the primary reference source, then the true offset θ_0 relative to that source must with high probability be somewhere in the interval

$$\theta - \lambda \leq \theta_0 \leq \theta + \lambda \tag{3}$$

which is called the *confidence interval*.

The ϵ and λ are used as metrics in the various algorithms presented in following sections. They determine the peers selected by the intersection and clustering algorithms, the weight factors used by the clock combining algorithm, and the calculation of various error statistics. While the basic design of these algorithms is developed using sound engineering and statistical principles, there are a number of intricate details, such as various weights used in the filter and selection algorithms, which can only be determined using simulation and experiment. In general, however, the metrics used are based on the pragmatic observation that the highest reliability is usually associated with the lowest stratum and synchronization distance, while the highest accuracy is usually associated with the lowest stratum and dispersion.

IV. Clock Filter, Combining and Clustering Algorithms

The clock filter, clustering and combining algorithms shown in Fig. 1 operate essentially as described previously in [9], however all three have been refined and defined formally in [10]. In order to understand the other algorithms described in this paper, it will be useful to briefly summarize the operation of these three algorithms.

The clock filter algorithm operates on a moving window of samples to produce three statistical estimates: *peer delay*, *peer offset* and *peer dispersion*. We will use θ, δ and ϵ for these quantities when their distinction from the previous use is clear. A discussion of the design approach, implementation and performance assessment is given in [9] and will not be repeated here. However, the design described there, which can be described as a *minimum filter*, has been enhanced to include the peer dispersion contributions due to the frequency tolerance of the local clock and the interval between T_1 and the present time, which must be recorded with every data sample.

There are usually some offset variations among the peers surviving the intersection algorithm (described later), due to differential delays, radio clock calibration errors, etc. The clustering algorithm is designed to select the best subset of this population on a maximum likelihood basis. It first ranks the peers by stratum, then by λ. For each peer it computes the select dispersion, defined as the total weighted time offsets of that peer relative to all the others. It then ejects the outlyer peer with greatest select dispersion and repeats the process until either a pre-specified minimum number of peers has been met or the maximum select dispersion is less than or equal to the minimum peer dispersion for all peers in the surviving population.

The termination condition is designed to maximize the number of peers for the combining algorithm, yet to produce the most accurate time. Since discarding more outlyers can neither increase the select dispersion nor decrease the peer dispersion, further discards will not improve the accuracy. As incorporated in NTP Version 3, the increase in dispersion as samples grow old helps to reduce errors resulting from local clock instability.

For each selected peer i the clock combining algorithm constructs a weight

$$w_i = \frac{1}{\epsilon_i \sum_j \frac{1}{\epsilon_j}}$$

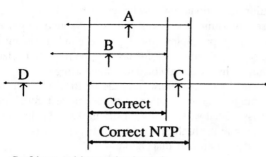

Fig. 3.   Confidence and intersection intervals.

where j ranges over all contributors. The algorithm then computes ensemble averages

$$\overline{\theta} = \sum_j w_j \theta_j \quad and \quad \epsilon = \sum_j w_j \epsilon_j.$$

V. INTERSECTION ALGORITHM

When a number of peer clocks are involved as in Fig. 1, it is not clear beforehand which are truechimers and which are falsetickers. In order to provide reliable synchronization, NTP relies on multiple peers and disjoint peer paths whenever possible. Crucial to the success of this approach is a robust algorithm which finds and discards the falsetickers from among these peers. Criteria for evaluation include a suite of sanity checks, consistency checks and the intersection algorithm described in this section.

Recall that the true offset θ_0 of a correctly operating clock relative to UTC must be contained in the confidence interval (3). Marzullo and Owicki [7] devised an algorithm designed to find an appropriate interval containing the correct time given the confidence intervals of m clocks, of which no more than f are considered incorrect. The algorithm finds the smallest *intersection interval* containing points in at least $m - f$ of the given confidence intervals.

Fig. 3 illustrates the operation of this algorithm with a scenario involving four clocks A, B, C and D, with the peer offset θ (shown by the ↑ symbol) along with the confidence interval for each. For instance, any point in the A interval may represent the actual time associated with that clock. If all clocks are correct, there must exist a nonempty intersection including points in all four confidence intervals; but, clearly this is not the case in the figure. However, if it is assumed that one of the clocks is incorrect (e.g., D), it might be possible to find a nonempty intersection including all but one of the intervals. If not, it might be possible to find a nonempty intersection including all but two of the intervals and so on.

The algorithm used by DEC in DTS is based on these principles. The algorithm finds the smallest intersection containing at least one point in each of $m - f$ confidence intervals, where m is the total number of clocks and f is the number of falsetickers, as long as the $f < \frac{m}{2}$. For the scenario illustrated in Figure 3, it computes the intersection for $m = 4$ clocks, three of which turn out to be correct and one not. The interval marked DTS is the smallest intersection containing points in three confidence intervals, with one interval outside the intersection considered incorrect.

There are some cases where this algorithm can produce anomalistic results. For instance, consider the case where the left endpoints of A and B are moved to coincide with the left endpoint of D, so that $f = 0$. In this case the intersection interval extends to the left endpoint of D, in spite of the fact that there is a subinterval that does not contain at least one point in all confidence intervals. Nevertheless, the assertion that the correct time lies in the intersection interval remains valid.

One problem is that, while the smallest interval containing the correct time may have been found, it is not clear which point in that interval is the best estimate of the correct time. Simply taking the estimate as the midpoint of the interval throws away a good deal of useful statistical data and results in large jitter, as confirmed by experiment. Especially in cases where the network jitter is large, some or all of the calculated offsets (such as for C in Fig. 3 may lie outside the intersection. For these reasons, in the NTP algorithm the DEC algorithm is modified so as to include at least $m - f$ of the peer offsets. The revised algorithm finds the smallest intersection of $m - f$ intervals containing at least $m - f$ peer offsets. As shown in Figure 3, the modified algorithm produces the intersection interval marked NTP and including the calculated time for C.

The algorithm starts with a set of peers which have passed several sanity checks designed to detect configuration errors and defective implementations. In the NTP Version 3 implementation, only the ten peers with the lowest λ are considered to avoid needless computing cycles for candidates very unlikely to be useful. For each peer the algorithm constructs a set of three tuples of the form [*offset, type*]: $[\theta - \lambda, -1]$ for the lower endpoint, $[\theta, 0]$ for the midpoint, and $[\theta + \lambda, +1]$ for the upper endpoint. These entries are placed on a list sorted by increasing *offset*.

The job of the intersection algorithm is to determine the lower and upper endpoints of an interval containing at least $m - f$ peer offsets. As before, let m be the number of entries in the sorted list and f be the number of presumed falsetickers, initially zero. Also, let *lower* designate the lower limit of the final confidence interval and *upper* the upper limit. The algorithm uses *endcount* as a counter of endpoints and *midcount* as the number of offsets found outside the intersection interval.

1) Set both *endcount* and *midcount* equal to zero.
2) Starting from the beginning of the sorted list and working toward the end, consider each entry [*offset, type*] in turn. As each entry is considered, subtract *type* from *endcount*. If $endcount \geq m - f$, the lower endpoint has been found. In this case set *lower* equal to *offset* and go to step 3. Otherwise, if *type* is zero, increment *midcount*. Then continue with the next entry.
3) At this point a tentative lower endpoint has been found; however, the number of midpoints has yet to be determined. Set the *endcount* again to zero, leaving *midcount* as is.
4) In a similar way as step 2, starting from the end of the sorted list and working toward the beginning, add the value of *type* for each entry in turn to *endcount*. If $endcount \geq m - f$, go to step 5. Otherwise, if *type* is

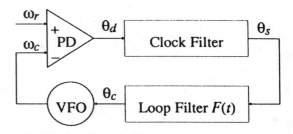

Fig. 4.   Disciplined oscillator model.

TABLE I
PEER CONFIGURATION FOR SERVER *pogo*

Code	Server (Location)	Stratum	Source	θ	δ	ε	λ	Lower	Upper
*	GPS	0	GPS	0.117	0.0	1.01	1.01	-0.89	1.13
	churchy	2	*pogo*	-1.080	0.42	1.36	4.07		
+	*rackety*	1	GPS	0.563	3.83	0.73	2.65	-2.08	3.21
+	*barnstable*	1	GPS	0.618	4.04	0.60	2.62	-2.00	3.24
+	*tick* (USNO)	1	ATOM	0.357	49.84	3.42	28.34	-27.98	28.70
+	*time* (NIST)	1	ACTS	0.635	101.72	4.14	55.00	-54.37	55.64
x	*err* (Switzerland)	1	DCF77	5.420	140.69	18.43	88.78	-83.36	94.20
x	*lucifer* (Germany)	1	GPS	9.863	183.36	36.62	128.30	-118.44	138.16
+	*time1* (Sweden)	1	ATOM	0.544	155.70	124.02	201.87	-201.33	202.41
−	*terss* (Australia)	1	OMEGA	1.088	767.40	69.05	452.75	-451.66	453.84

zero, increment *midcount*. Then continue with the next entry.

5) If *lower* ≤ *upper* and *midcount* ≤ *f* , then terminate the procedure and declare success with *lower* equal to the lower endpoint and *upper* equal the upper endpoint of the resulting confidence interval. Otherwise, increment *f*. If $f \geq \frac{m}{2}$, terminate the procedure and declare failure. If neither case holds, continue in step 1.

The original (Marzullo and Owicki) algorithm produces an intersection interval that is guaranteed to contain the correct time as long as less than half the clocks are falsetickers. The modified algorithm produces an interval containing the original interval, so the correctness assertion continues to hold. However, so long as the clock filter produces statistically unbiased estimates for each peer, the new algorithm allows the clustering and combining algorithms to produce unbiased estimates as well.

Table I shows a typical configuration for NTP primary server *pogo*. The data used to construct tables such as this are collected by each server on a regular basis and automatically retrieved by monitoring hosts using scripts and programs designed for the purpose. Using these data, operators can quickly spot trouble in either the servers or the network.

The peers located in Europe, Australia, National Institute of Standards and Technology (NIST) in Boulder, CO, and U.S. Naval Observatory (USNO) in Washington, DC, are identified in the table; the others are located at the University of Delaware. The entry identified as GPS and assigned pseudo-stratum zero is a precision timing receiver synchronized by the Global Positioning System (GPS) and connected to *pogo*. Note that this receiver is treated like any other peer, so that possible malfunctions can be detected and avoided. The synchronization source for each peer is shown by dissemination service if stratum 0 or 1, or by another peer if higher. GPS, DCF77 and OMEGA use radio and satellite, ATOM is a national standard cesium clock ensemble, and ACTS is the Automated Computer Time Service operated by NIST [4].

The offset θ, delay δ, dispersion ε and synchronization distance λ for each peer are shown in the table, as well as the lower and upper endpoints used in the clock selection algorithm, all in milliseconds. Peer *churchy* is ineligible for selection because it is operating at a stratum higher than *pogo*, so would not normally provide better time, and in addition, it is synchronized to *pogo*, so would cause a synchronization loop. This peer would be considered for synchronization only if the GPS receiver and all other stratum-1 sources were to fail.

The remaining peers are eligible for processing by the intersection and clustering algorithms. The synchronization status is shown by the Code column. Those marked "x" have been discarded by the intersection algorithm as falsetickers, while those marked "-" have been discarded by the clustering algorithm as outlyers. Note that the truechimer offsets all fall within the smallest intersection interval, while the falseticker offsets do not. Obviously, the ensemble average is improved by discarding falsetickers and outlyers.

The peers marked "*" and "+" have survived both algorithms and the one marked "*" has been identified as the pick of the litter. All of these peers will be considered by the combining algorithm; however, the NTP Version 3 implementation includes an option: If a designated peer has survived both algorithms, it is the sole source for synchronization and the combining algorithm is not used. This is useful in special cases where known differential delays are relatively severe or when the lowest possible jitter is required.

VI. LOCAL CLOCK MODELS

The local clock is commonly implemented using a hardware counter and room-temperature quartz oscillator. Such oscillators exhibit some degree of temperature-induced frequency instability in the order of 1-2 ppm due to room-temperature variations. The NTP clock discipline continuously corrects the time and frequency of the local clock to agree with the time as determined from the synchronization source(s).

A significant improvement in accuracy and stability is possible by modeling the local clock and its adjustment mechanism as a *disciplined oscillator*. In this type of clock the time and frequency are controlled by a feedback loop with a relatively long time constant, so the frequency is "learned" over some minutes or hours of integration. Besides improving accuracy, a disciplined oscillator can correct for the intrinsic frequency error of the oscillator itself, so that much longer intervals between timestamp messages can be used without significant accuracy degradation.

A disciplined oscillator can be implemented as the feedback loop shown in Fig. 4. The variable ω_r represents the reference signal and ω_c the variable frequency oscillator (VFO) signal, which controls the local clock. The phase detector (PD) produces a signal θ_d representing the instantaneous phase difference between ω_r and ω_c. The clock filter functions as a tapped delay line, with the output θ_s taken at the sample selected by the clock filter algorithm. The loop filter, with impulse response $F(t)$, produces a VFO correction θ_c, which controls the oscillator frequency ω_c and thus its phase. The

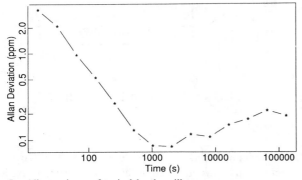

Fig. 5. Allan variance of typical local oscillator.

characteristic behavior of this model, which is determined by the $F(t)$, is studied in many textbooks and summarized in [11].

As reported in [12], the major source of error in most configurations is the stability of the local clock oscillator. The stability of a free-running frequency source is commonly characterized by a statistic called *Allan variance* [1], which is defined as follows. Consider a series of time offsets measured between a local clock and some external standard. Let x_k be the kth measurement and τ_k be the interval since the previous measurement. Define the *fractional frequency*

$$y_k = \frac{x_k - x_{k-1}}{\tau_k} \qquad (4)$$

which is a dimensionless quantity. Now, consider a sequence of N independent fractional frequency samples $y_k (k = 0, 1, \cdots, N - 1)$. If the averaging interval $\tau = \tau_k$ is the same as the interval between measurements, the 2-sample Allan variance is defined

$$\sigma_y^2(\tau) \equiv \frac{1}{2}\langle (y_k - y_{k-1})^2 \rangle$$
$$= \frac{1}{2(N-2)\tau^2} \sum_{k=2}^{N-1} (x_k - 2x_{k-1} + x_{k-2})^2.$$

The Allan variance $\sigma_y^2(\tau)$ (or Allan deviation $\sigma_y(\tau)$) is particularly useful when designing the clock discipline, since it determines the optimum impulse response $F(t)$, time constants and update intervals. Fig. 5 shows the results of an experiment designed to determine the Allan deviation of a typical workstation under normal room-temperature conditions. For the experiment, the local clock was first synchronized to a primary server on the same LAN using NTP to allow the frequency to stabilize, then uncoupled from NTP and allowed to free-run for about seven days. The local clock offsets during this interval were measured at the primary server using NTP. This model is designed to closely duplicate actual operating conditions, including the jitter of the LAN and operating systems involved.

It is important to note that both the x and y scales of Fig. 5 are logarithmic, but the axes are labeled in actual values. Starting from the left at $\tau = 16$, the plot tends to a straight line with slope near -1, which is characteristic of white phase noise [15]. In this region, increasing τ increases the frequency stability in direct proportion. At about $\tau = 1000$ the plot has an upward inflection, indicating that the white phase noise

becomes dominated first by white frequency noise (slope -0.5), then by flicker frequency noise (flat slope), and finally by random-walk frequency noise (slope +0.5). In other words, as τ is increased, there is less and less correlation between one averaging interval and the next.

The Allan deviation can be used to determine the best clock discipline method to use over the range of τ likely to be useful in practice. At the lowest τ the errors due to phase noise dominate those due to frequency stability. A phase-lock loop (PLL) clock discipline provides the best performance in such cases. As the PLL time constant increases and with it τ, the PLL low-pass filter characteristic tends to reduce the phase noise, as well as compensate for any systematic (constant) local clock frequency error. However, while the phase averaging interval in a PLL increases directly as the time constant, the frequency averaging interval increases as the square. The price paid for this at the longer τ is an extremely sluggish adaptation to oscillator frequency wander.

On the other hand, at the highest τ, the errors due to frequency stability dominate those due to phase noise. A frequency-lock loop (FLL) clock discipline provides the best performance in such cases. In order to provide the most rapid adaptation to frequency wander, while avoiding spurious disruptions due to phase noise, the best τ would seem from Fig. 1 to be about 1000 s. However, it is apparent from (4) that the FLL can become seriously vulnerable to phase spikes at τ much below this. These conclusions were verified In a series of experiments and simulations using the algorithms developed in the next section.

VII. The NTP Clock Discipline

The Unix 4.3bsd timekeeping functions are implemented using a hardware timer interrupt produced by an oscillator in the 100-1000 Hz range. Each interrupt causes an increment *tick* to be added to the kernel *time* variable. The value of *tick* is chosen so that *time*, once properly initialized, is equal to the present time of day in seconds and microseconds relative to a given epoch. When *tick* does not evenly divide 1 s (1 000 000 μs), an additional increment *fixtick* is added to *time* once each second to make up the difference.

The oscillator can actually run at three different frequencies, one at the intrinsic oscillator frequency, a second slightly higher and a third slightly lower . The adjtime() system call is used to select one of the three frequencies and how long δt to run, in order to amortize the specified offset. The NTP clock discipline uses the adjtime() mechanism to control the VFO and implements the impulse response $F(t)$ using the algorithm described below.

The new clock discipline differs from the one described in the NTP specification and previous reports. It is based on an adaptive-parameter, hybrid PLL/FLL design which gives good performance with update intervals from a few seconds to tens of kiloseconds, depending on accuracy requirements and acceptable costs. As before, let x_k be the time and y_k be the frequency at the kth update. Let $\overline{y}_k$ be the mean oscillator frequency determined from past offsets $\{x_i\}$ and intervals $\{\tau_i\}$. In the most general formulation, an algorithm that corrects for clock time and frequency errors computes a prediction

$$\hat{x}_k = x_{k-1} + \overline{y}_{k-1}\tau. \tag{5}$$

The clock discipline operates as a negative-feedback loop to minimize $\hat{x}_k$ for all k. As each update x_k is measured, the clock time is adjusted by $-x_k$, so that it displays the correct time. In addition, the mean frequency $\overline{y}_k$ is adjusted to minimize the time adjustments in future. Subsequently, the oscillator runs at this frequency until the next update.

Between updates, which can range from seconds to hours, the clock discipline amortizes x_k in small increments at adjustment intervals $t_A = 1s$, in order to prevent timescale discontinuities and to conform to monotonic requirements. At each interval the value

$$ax + \overline{y}_k t_A \tag{6}$$

is added to the clock time, where a is a constant between zero and one ($a = 2^{-6}$ in the current implementation) and x is a variable defined below. In the NTP daemon for Unix, these adjustments are implemented by the adjtime() system call; while, in the modified kernel described in [13], correspondingly scaled adjustments are performed at each timer interrupt. The constant a is used as a gain factor in the following way. Let the value x be the residual in the adjustment whose initial value is x_k. At each interval the time is adjusted by ax and the residual by $-ax$. This provides a rapid adjustment when x is relatively large, together with a fine adjustment (low jitter) when x is relatively small.

In the original type-II PLL design of [9], the frequency is determined as past accumulations of time. In this case,

$$\overline{y}_k = b \sum_{i=1}^{k} x_i \tau_i \tag{7}$$

where b is a constant between zero and one ($b = 2^{-16}$ in the current implementation). In order to understand the dynamics, it is useful to consider the limit as τ approaches zero. In a type-II PLL, the oscillator frequency $y(t)$ is determined by the measured offset $x(t)$:

$$y(t) = ax(t) + b \int_0^t x(t)dt.$$

Since phase is the integral of frequency, the integral of the right hand side represents the overall open-loop impulse response of the feedback loop. Taking the Laplace transform, we get

$$\theta(s) = \frac{x(s)}{s}\left(a + \frac{b}{s}\right)$$

where the extra pole $\frac{1}{s}$ at the origin is due to the integration which converts the frequency $y(s)$ to phase $\theta(s)$. After some rearrangement, the magnitude of the right hand side can be written

$$\frac{\omega_c^2}{s^2}\left(1 + \frac{s}{\omega_z}\right)$$

where $\omega_z = \frac{b}{a}$ and $\omega_c^2 = b$. From elementary theory, this is the transfer function of a type-II PLL which can control both time

and frequency. In practice, the damping factor $\eta = \frac{\omega_c}{2\omega_z} = 4$ for good transient response. In order to simplify the presentation, this model does not include the time constant, which is used to control the loop response. The detailed design and behavior of the PLL is treated in great detail in [11] and will not be repeated here.

The new clock discipline is a hybrid PLL/FLL design in which the original PLL is used for $\tau \leq 1024$ and the FLL used otherwise. The FLL design, adapted from [5], operates in a manner identical to the PLL, except that the mean frequency $\overline{y}(t)$ is determined as an average, rather than an integral. In the FLL, $\overline{y}(t)$ is directly adjusted in order to minimize the time error $x(t)$. While a number of methods could be used to compute $\overline{y}_k$, a convenient one is the weighted average

$$\overline{y}_k = \overline{y}_{k-1} + w(y_k - \overline{y}_{k-1}) \tag{8}$$

where $w = 0.25$ is a weight factor determined by experiment. The goal of the clock discipline is to adjust the clock time and frequency so that $\hat{x}_k = 0$ for all k. To the extent this has been successful in the past, we can assume corrections prior to x_k are all zero and, in particular, $x_{k-1} = 0$. Therefore, from (4) and (8) we have

$$\overline{y}_k = \overline{y}_{k-1} + w\frac{x_k}{\tau}. \tag{9}$$

It may seem strange that the coefficient a in (6) is used in both the FLL and PLL modes. The primary reason is to avoid discontinuities when the offset x_k is very large, e.g., over 100 ms. A secondary reason is to reduce the effects of phase noise, since in the NTP model the local clock of one stratum can be used to discipline clocks at the next higher stratum. While in the PLL $a < 1$ is necessary for stability, its affect on dynamics when the FLL is in use is minor.

A key feature of the NTP design is the selection of τ in response to measured local clock stability. When the PLL is in use, the time constant is directly proportional to τ. At $\tau = 64s$, this results in a 90% time response of about 900 s and a 63% frequency response of about 3600 s, which is a useful compromise under most operating conditions. The time constant is not used when the FLL is in use.

The sum of the peer dispersion and select dispersion is used as a measure of oscillator instability in both the PLL and FLL modes. If $|\theta|$ exceeds this sum, the oscillator frequency is deviating too fast for the clock discipline to follow, so τ is reduced. In the opposite case holds for some number of updates, τ is increased. Under typical network conditions, τ hovers close to the maximum; but, on occasions when the oscillator frequency wanders more than about 1 ppm, τ quickly drops to lower values until the wander subsides.

VIII. Additional Improvements

In a perfect world, the NTP clock discipline would be implemented as an intrinsic feature of the kernel with standardized interfaces for the user and daemon processes and with a precision oscillator available as a standard option. However, during the development and deployment of NTP technology, there was considerable reluctance to intrude on kernel hardware or nonstandard software features, since this would impede portability, maintainability and perhaps reliability. In addition, manufacturers were understandably reluctant to provide a precision oscillator option, since there were not many customers to justify the development expense.

We have explored both the kernel discipline and external oscillator options. A Unix kernel implementation of the discipline has been developed for four popular workstations, the Ultrix kernel for the DEC 5000 series, the OSF/1 kernel for the DEC 3000 series, the SunOS kernel for the Sun SPARCstation series, and the HP-UX kernel for the Hewlett Packard 9000 series. As described in [12], the kernel discipline provides a time resolution of 1 μs and a frequency resolution of parts in 10^{11} (with an appropriately stable external oscillator). In addition, the modified kernels provide new system calls so that applications can learn the local clock status and error estimates determined by the daemon.

A special pulse-per-second (PPS) signal is available from sources such as cesium clocks and precision timing receivers. It generally provides much better accuracy than the serial ASCII timecode produced by an ordinary radio clock. The new kernel software uses a modem control lead of a serial port to produce an interrupt at each PPS pulse. The interrupt captures a timestamp from the local clock and computes the offset modulo 1 s. Assuming the seconds numbering of the clock counter has been determined by a reliable source, such as the ASCII timecode or even other NTP peers, the PPS offset is used to discipline the local clock. Using this feature on a typical workstation with a PPS signal from a GPS receiver, jitter is reduced to few tens of microseconds [12].

Some radio clocks can produce a special IRIG signal, which encodes the day and time as a modulated audio signal compatible with the audio codec native to some workstations. A particularly interesting feature of the NTP design described in [12] is an algorithm that processes codec samples to demodulate the signal, extract the time information and discipline the local clock. The scheme requires very few external components, but achieves a jitter comparable to the PPS signal.

However, neither the PPS or IRIG signals improve the stability of the local clock oscillator itself, since wander-induced time errors usually dominate the error budget. We have experimented with external oscillators, both using commercial bus peripherals and bus peripherals of our own design. An external clock for the Sun SBus has been constructed using FPGA technology. It includes a pair of counters that can be read directly in Unix *timeval* format and an oven-compensated precision oscillator with stability of a few parts in 10^9. In experiments where a host equipped with this device was synchronized to a primary server using NTP, the wander was measured at a few parts in 10^8, about two orders of magnitude better than the original undisciplined oscillator.

Perhaps the most useful and inexpensive approach is an auxiliary feedback loop designed to discipline the oscillator frequency directly to an external PPS signal. In this design, the PPS timestamps are used at intervals τ from 4 to 256 s to calculate a vernier frequency adjustment as in (9). This adjustment is added to the mean frequency $\bar{y}_k$ in (6). The result is that the oscillator frequency is disciplined to the PPS signal

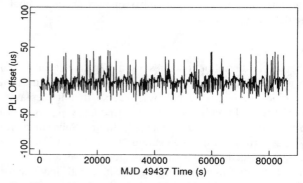

Fig. 6.   Offsett with   kernel PLL and PPS signal.

and the wander considerably reduced. However, the external corrections provided by NTP continue to function as usual. Measurements show that, using this scheme with a typical workstation and PPS signal from a GPS receiver results in performance comparable to the precision external oscillator.

Fig. 6 shows the performance using the native oscillator, kernel discipline and PPS signal over the Modified Julian Day (MJD) 49437.[1] In this experiment, measurements were made about every 64 s of the local clock offset relative to the PPS signal of a cesium clock and the results graphed. The server involved, a SPARCstation IPC, had about 400 NTP clients on the day of the experiment. The maximum jitter over the day is about 45 μs, primarily due to collisions between the timer interrupt and PPS signal interrupt. This represents probably the best performance possible with this generation of machines.

IX. PRESENT STATUS AND DEPLOYMENT

Software support for NTP is available for a wide variety of workstations and mainframe computers manufactured by DEC, IBM, Hewlett Packard, Sun Microsystems, Silicon Graphics, Cray Research and many others. One manufacturer (Bancomm) markets a dedicated NTP server integrated with a GPS receiver and another (Cisco) markets a router with integrated NTP support. The software is available for public access or as a standard option in some software products. A client running this software can synchronize to one or more NTP servers or radio timecode receivers and at the same time provide synchronization to a number of dependent clients, in some cases in excess of 500, while requiring only a small fraction of available processor and memory resources.

In the most cherished of Internet traditions, the worldwide NTP synchronization subnet is not engineered in any specific way other than informal, voluntary compliance to a set of configuration rules. To protect the primary servers, potential stratum-2 peers are invited only if they serve a sizable population of stratum-3 and higher peers. Operators are cautioned that reliable service is possible only through the use of redundant servers and diverse network paths. A typical configuration for a campus serving several hundred clients includes three stratum-2 servers, each operating with two different primary

---

[1] MJD is derived from a scheme invented in the 16th century to number the days since an historically eclectic epoch at noon on the first day of the year 4713 BC.

servers, each of the other campus servers and at least one stratum-2 server at another institution. Department servers then operate with all three campus servers and each other, which simplifies configuration table management. Department servers offer service to client hosts, either individually or using the NTP broadcast mode.

In a previous paper [8] the number of NTP-synchronized peers was estimated at 1000 on the basis of an systematic survey of all known Internet hosts. Today, such a survey would be very difficult and probably be considered rude at best. However, it is known that there are at the time of writing about 100 NTP primary servers located in North America, Europe and the Pacific, almost half of which are advertised for public access. These peers are synchronized to national time standards using all known computer-readable time-dissemination services in the world, including the U.S. (ACTS, WWVB, WWV and WWVH), Canada (CHU), U.K. (MSF), Germany (DCF77) and France (TDF), as well as the GPS, OMEGA and LORAN navigation systems, and the GOES environmental satellite. In addition, NTP primary servers at NIST and USNO, as well as the national time standards laboratories of Norway and Australia, are directly synchronized to national standard clock ensembles.

It is difficult to estimate the number of NTP secondary (stratum-2 and higher) peers in the global Internet. A recent informal estimate puts the total number of Internet hosts over 1.7 million. An intricate check of the monitoring information maintained by some public NTP servers reveals about 8,000 stratum-2 and stratum-3 dependents; however, this survey grossly undercounts the population, since only a fraction of the servers retain this information and many thousands of known dependents are hidden deep inside corporate networks, either independently synchronized or carefully peeking out through access-controlled gateways. Informal estimates based on anecdotal information provided by various network operators suggest the total number of hosts running NTP is probably in excess of 100 000.

The earlier survey presented error measurements for various paths between NTP primary servers in the U.S. and concluded reliable time synchronization could be obtained "...in the order of a few tens of milliseconds over most paths in the Internet of today." As reported in [12], while there are exceptions, this claim remains generally valid in the much larger worldwide Internet of today. With the software and hardware improvements described herein for the NTP Version 3 specification and implementations, and with suitable allowance for differential delays, most places in the worldwide Internet are able to maintain an accuracy better than 10 ms and those on LAN's and high speed WAN's better than 1 ms.

X. Current Work and Future Plans

As time moves on, so do NTP versions. A summary of current work and future plans for Version 4 of the protocol are given in [13]. They include refinement of the broadcast/multicast protocol modes, automated peer discovery and implementation of a new feature called *distributed mode.*

In cases where a moderate loss in accuracy can be tolerated, such as most workstations on a LAN subnet, the NTP broadcast mode greatly simplifies client configuration and network management. In this mode, client workstations automatically survey their environment and configure themselves without requiring pre-engineered configuration files. After joining the subnet, a client listens for broadcasts from one or more servers on the LAN. Upon hearing one, the client exchanges messages with the server in order to determine the best time and calibrate the broadcast propagation delay. When calibration is complete, generally after a few message exchanges, the client again resumes listening for broadcasts. In broadcast mode the NTP filter, selection and combining algorithms operate as in the client/server modes, with resulting accuracy usually in the order of a few milliseconds on an Ethernet.

We have recently extended the NTP broadcast mode to use IP multicast facilities [3] for wide-area time distribution. The NTP multicast mode operates in the same way as the broadcast mode, so that clients can discover servers wherever IP multicast facilities and connectivity to the Internet MBONE are available. At the present time, experimental servers have been established in the U.S., U.K., and Germany, with clients in these and other countries. The accuracies that have been achieved vary widely, depending on the particular server and path. For instance, with typical U.K. servers and clients in the U.S., the accuracies vary from 10 to 100 ms, depending on particular server configuration and ambient network traffic levels.

While we have proof of concept that time distribution using IP multicast is practical, there are many remaining problems to be resolved, such as how to avoid sending messages all over the world from possibly many multicast servers, how to authenticate and select which ones a particular client or client population chooses to believe, and how to allocate and manage possibly many multicast group addresses.

In other future plans, we expect to make use of IP multicast to maintain timekeeping data not only between peers, but between other members of the synchronization subnet as well. This scheme, called distributed mode, will allow additional opportunities to discover potential peers, as well as reduce errors due to differential delays. In addition, we expect to participate in a comprehensive design exercise involving the Domain Name System to discover domain-based time servers and to distribute authentication information.

XI. Summary

This paper has presented an in-depth analysis of certain issues important to achieve accurate, stable and reliable time synchronization in a computer network. These issues include the design of the synchronization protocol, the local clock, and the algorithms used to filter, select and combine the reading of possibly many peer clocks. The intersection algorithm presented in this paper is designed to distinguish truechimers from among a population possibly including falsetickers. The local clock is modeled as a disciplined oscillator and implemented as a hybrid PLL/FLL feedback loop. The behavior of the model is controlled automatically for oscillators of varying stability and network paths of widely varying characteristics.

The NTP Version 3 implementations have been widely deployed to probably over 100 000 installations in the Internet of today. Surveys using previous versions of NTP have found synchronization to UTC can be generally maintained to within a few tens of milliseconds. With NTP Version 3 and the hardware and software improvements described in this paper, synchronization can be generally maintained with some exceptions to within 10 ms on typical Internet paths and within 1 ms on LAN's and WAN's with high speed (over 1 Mb/s) transmission paths. The exceptions are in all known cases due to either severe network congestion or differential path delays, which in principle can be calibrated out.

REFERENCES

[1] D. W. Allan, Time and frequency (time-domain) estimation and prediction of precision clocks and oscillators. *IEEE Trans. on Ultrasound, Ferroelectrics, and Frequency Contr.* vol. UFFC-34, pp. 647-654, Nov. 1987. Also in "Characterization of clocks and oscillators," D. B. Sullivan, D. W. Allan, D. A. Howe, and F.L. Walls, Eds., U.S. Dep. Commerce, 1990, NIST Tech. Note 1337, pp. 121–128.

[2] *Digital Time Service Functional Specification Version T.1.0.5*, Digital Equipment Corp., 1989.

[3] S. E. Deering and D. R. Cheriton, "Multicast routing in datagram internetworks and extended LAN's," *ACM Trans. Comput. Syst.* , vol. 8, no. 2, pp. 85-100, May 1990.

[4] J. Levine, M. Weiss, D. D. Davis, D. W. Allan, and D. B. Sullivan, "The NIST automated computer time service," *J. Res. Nat. Inst. Standards and Technol. 94*, Sept.–Oct. 1989, vol. 5, pp. 311–321.

[5] J. Levine, "An algorithm to synchronize the time of a computer to universal time," *IEEE Trans. Networks*, vol. 3, pp. 42-50, Feb. 1995.

[6] W. C. Lindsay and A. V. Kantak, "Network synchronization of random signals," *IEEE Trans. Commun.*, vol. COM-28, pp. 1260-1266, Aug. 1980.

[7] K. Marzullo, and S. Owicki. "Maintaining the time in a distributed system," *ACM Oper. Syst. Rev.*, vol. 19, no. 3, pp. 44-54, July 1985.

[8] D. L. Mills, "Measured performance of the network time protocol in the Internet system," *ACM Comput. Commun. Rev.*, vol. 20, no. 1, pp. 65-75, Jan. 1990.

[9] ———, "Internet time synchronization: The network time protocol," *IEEE Trans. Commun.*, vol. 39, pp. 1482-1493, Oct. 1991. Also in *Global States and Time in Distributed Systems*, Z. Yang, and T. A. Marsland, Eds. Los Alamitos, CA: IEEE Press, pp. 91-102.

[10] ———, "Network time protocol (Version 3) specification, implementation and analysis," Univ. Delaware, DARPA Network Working Group Rep. RFC-1305, Mar. 1992, 113 pp.

[11] ———, "Modeling and analysis of computer network clocks," Elec. Eng. Dep. Rep. 92-5-2, Univ. Delaware, May 1992, 29 pp.

[12] ———, "Precision synchronization of computer network clocks," *ACM Comput. Commun. Rev.*, vol. 24, no. 2, 16 pp., Apr. 1994.

[13] ———, "Network time protocol version 4 proposed changes," Elec. Eng. Dep. Rep. 94-10-2, Univ. Delaware, Oct. 1994, 46 pp.

[14] *NIST Time and Frequency Dissemination Services* . NBS Special Publication 432 (Revised 1990), Nat. Inst. of Sci. and Technol., U.S. Dep. of Commerce, 1990.

[15] S. R. Stein, "Frequency and time - their measurement and characterization (Chapter 12)," in *Precision Frequency Control, Vol. 2*, E.A. Gerber and A. Ballato Eds. New York: Academic, 1985, pp. 191-232, pp. 399-416. Also in: *Characterization of Clocks and Oscillators*, D. B. Sullivan, D. W. Allan, D. A. Howe, and F. L. Walls, Eds. Nat. Inst. Standards and Technol. Tech. Note 1337, U.S. Government Printing Office, Jan., 1990, TN61-TN119.

David L. Mills (M'86) received the M.S. degree in electrical engineering and the Ph.D. degree in computer science from the University of Michigan in 1963 and 1971, respectively.

He is a Professor of Electrical Engineering at the University of Delaware. His research activities are in the areas of computer network architecture and modeling, protocol engineering and experimental studies using the Internet system. He was formerly a Directorat M/A-COM Linkabit and a Senior Scientist at COMSAT Laboratories, where he worked in the areas of computer network and satellite systems.

Dr. Mills has been a member of the ACM since 1964.

Nsync - A Toolkit for Building Interactive Multimedia Presentations

Brian Bailey, Joseph A. Konstan, Robert Cooley, and Moses Dejong

{bailey, konstan, cooley, dejong}@cs.umn.edu

University of Minnesota
Department of Computer Science and Engineering
Minneapolis, MN 55455

1. Abstract

Creating innovative interactive multimedia presentations requires a great deal of time, skill, and effort. We have developed a multimedia synchronization toolkit, called Nsync (pronounced 'in-sync'), to address the complicated issues inherent in designing flexible, interactive multimedia presentations. The toolkit consists of two primary components, a declarative synchronization definition language and a run-time presentation management system. The synchronization definition language supports the specification of synchronous interaction, asynchronous interaction, fine-grained relationships, and combinations of each through the use of conjunctive and disjunctive operators. Pre-computed playout schedules are too inflexible to deal with asynchronous interaction, and a more adaptive presentation management system is required. Nsync's run-time system uses a novel predictive logic to predict the future behavior of a presentation. As the viewer makes decisions, the presentation is updated and new predictions are made in order to maintain consistency with the viewer's wishes and the integrity of the presentation's message.

2. Introduction

Interactive multimedia presentations represent an asynchronous collaboration between the presentation author and the presentation viewer. The role of the presentation author is to design an interactive presentation at the *present* time that will result in an individual experience for a variety of potentially unknown viewers at a *future* time. To aid in designing this individual experience, the author must be able to request viewer participation at key points within the presentation, and also must be able to specify the action to take based on the result of the viewer's response. Here viewer *participation* is defined as the ability to respond to requests; such as a multi-choice question, or as the ability to navigate within the presentation, choosing one of

several different possible playout paths. The role of the presentation viewer is to cognitively absorb the message inherent within the presentation and to provide responses when viewer participation is requested. The viewer should also be allowed to exercise control over the playback of the presentation. Here *control* is defined as the ability to skip ahead, skip behind, or adjust the playback rate at any point within the presentation.

In order to build a complex, interactive multimedia presentation, a presentation author must rely on a flexible synchronization model in order to specify:

- The temporal layout, or *synchronization*, of the different media objects involved in the presentation. This includes both fine-grained relationships, which are *within* and *between* media objects, and coarse grained relationships, which are primarily *between* media objects; i.e., between their start and end events.

- The participation required and/or requested from the viewer.

- The behavior of the presentation when the viewer provides input or exercises control over the presentation in an unpredictable way.

The author must be able to specify each of the above in order to ensure that the integrity of the presentation's message is not blurred as the result of unpredictable viewer input or control actions. As an example of a blurred message, consider a virtual tour of a home consisting of a sequence of slides along with accompanying narrations. If the viewer were to delay the slide transitions for a closer look, yet the narration was inadvertently advanced to the next location, the viewer might be misled or possibly confused.

Synchronization models typically determine the types of relationships that can be expressed among different media objects, and to some extent, the set of allowable media objects themselves. For example, some synchronization models do not support media objects of unknown durations [2, 8, 10, 12]. Exactly how a presentation author uses a synchronization model to define a presentation depends on the temporal layout and interactive

ACM Multimedia'98, Bristol, UK
© 1998 ACM 1-58113-036-8/98/0008 $5.00

requirements of the presentation being defined, the synchronization model being used, and the author's ability to understand and express the desired relationships using that model. Designing interactive presentations is a difficult task primarily because most synchronization models either do not directly support viewer participation [1, 8, 10, 14, 18, 20, 21], or only support viewer participation or control actions at predefined locations in the presentation [4, 9, 19]. Desirable properties of flexible synchronization models have been outlined in [9], but here we more clearly identify the interactive requirements of a synchronization model useful in building interactive presentations:

- The ability to specify *synchronous* interaction. Synchronous interaction is defined as a specific time point where viewer participation is requested and the presentation halts until a response is given.

- The ability to specify *asynchronous* interaction. Asynchronous interaction is defined as an interaction that may occur at any point within a specified temporal interval, where that interval may span from only a few seconds to the entire presentation.

- The ability to specify a wide variety of fine and coarse-grained relationships among different media objects. We use the term *temporal constraint* to refer to these relationships in general.

- The ability to specify combinations of synchronous interactions, asynchronous interactions, and temporal constraints.

3. Related Work

One method for building a synchronization model with these properties would be to extend an already existing synchronization model. Prabhakaran *et.al.* used this approach when augmenting object composition petri nets to support viewer input and control [19]. Although useful for modeling synchronous interaction, dynamic timed petri nets do not model asynchronous interactions well. To model an asynchronous interaction, an interrupt arc would have to be added to each place in the net where the interaction could potentially occur. Similarly, because all petri net based models are bipartite *directed* graphs, modeling reverse play would essentially require duplicating the graph and reversing each one of the arcs. For designing highly interactive presentations, this approach would soon become tedious and potentially confusing.

The MODE [4] system supports both fine and coarse-grained synchronization, and also supports interaction through the use of explicit interaction objects. Although these objects allow the viewer to control aspects such as the starting, stopping, or playback rate of a media object, it is unclear as to how the viewer's input can affect the synchronization decisions over the lifetime of the

presentation. Nsync allows the viewer's input to be explicitly included as part of the synchronization definitions. The Firefly multimedia document system [7] is perhaps the most similar to the Nsync toolkit in that it distinctly supports both synchronous and asynchronous interaction. However, asynchronous interaction can only be tied to synchronous events [7], whereas in Nsync, asynchronous interaction may have a *deferred* implication. This means that the interaction does not have an immediate visible affect on the presentation; rather, it affects a *future* synchronization decision. Another distinction is that Firefly uses a single document clock whereas Nsync supports multiple coordinated timelines. Nsync also supports the specification of continuous synchronization such as skew control.

Macromedia's Lingo [16] is the scripting language designed to allow multimedia authors to include interactivity to their Director-based presentations. Because Director only supports a single timeline, interactive presentation authors typically divide it into different logical segments, and then map each presentation segment into one of these logical segments; effectively giving multiple timelines, but where only one can be active at any given point. Lingo is then used to control when and how viewers may switch between these different segments (timelines). However, Lingo does not offer any special control structures to assist the author in this process, whereas this is one of the primary goals of the Nsync synchronization language. Nsync also allows multiple timelines to be active at any point within the presentation; e.g., to allow a continuous animation and an audio segment to be played and controlled separately.

SMIL [25] is a W3C recommended markup language for publishing synchronized multimedia presentations via the Internet. The core synchronization mechanisms of SMIL are based on the sequential and parallel grouping tags. SMIL also supports link-style navigation (asynchronous interaction) within a presentation. This is accomplished using mechanisms similar to those used within HTML, but with the added ability to specify temporal subparts of media objects. However, as with MODE, it is unclear as to how the viewer's input can affect the synchronization decisions over the lifetime of the presentation.

MHEG-5 [10] is an effort to standardize an encoding format describing multimedia applications. This interoperable format would allow presentation authors to use their favorite authoring tool, yet be able to produce a common encoding format. MHEG-5 does not specify an authoring environment nor does it specify an architecture for a playback engine. We believe several of the techniques and mechanisms presented in this paper; e.g., the ability to combine interactive events along with temporal events, and also the predictive logic, would be of interest to both the SMIL and MHEG-5 working groups and also to the implementers of these standards.

In the next section, we lay the foundation of the Nsync synchronization toolkit and also compare the model to current and past-related work. In section 5, we describe the synchronization definition language and illustrate its use in expressing viewer participation, viewer control, and temporal constraints. In section 6 we describe the implementation and workings of the run-time system including a novel predictive logic used in maintaining the integrity of the synchronization relationships. In section 7, we give some concluding thoughts and ideas for future work.

4. Model

In this section we describe the foundation of the Nsync toolkit and briefly describe how the model relates to other work. Our approach was to start with an existing media based toolkit [21] and build a synchronization layer on top of it [3]. This synchronization layer, called Nsync, provides the ability to express:

- Synchronous interactions. An example would be to present a multi-choice question to the viewer and freeze the presentation until a response is received.

- Asynchronous interactions. As an example, consider a presentation which narrates an intriguing question to the viewer in order to peak the viewer's interest. As soon as the question begins, a set of possible answers are presented to the viewer. The viewer should then be allowed to make a selection as soon as an answer is known (asynchronous interaction), rather than being forced to wait until the question has been completed before a selection could be made (synchronous interaction). Viewer control is an example of asynchronous interaction which spans the entire presentation.

- Fine-grained temporal relationships. Examples would be to express tight, or loosely coupled skew relationships, or to synchronize events at specific time points within a media object.

- Conjunctions and disjunctions involving each of the above items. An example would be the ability to specify within a single synchronization specification that a loosely coupled skew relationship should be enforced *only* (conjunction) if requested by the viewer.

The goal of the Nsync toolkit is to support fine-grained relationships in conjunction with viewer participation and control.

4.1 Fine-grained Synchronization

In general, coarse-grained models cannot be used to express fine-grained relationships; however, fine-grained relationships *can* be used to express coarse-grained semantics as long as the fine-grained model supports multiple timelines [3]. To support rich synchronization semantics, temporal constraints in Nsync are expressed as fine-grained relationships involving multiple clock objects (clocks will be discussed in Section 4.3). This allows temporal constraints both within and between media objects to be expressed. For example, the following specifications are possible in Nsync:

- A second narration should start after the first one has ended. See Figure 1a.

- A loosely coupled skew relationship between a narration and background music. See Figure 1b.

- Mute, or turn down the audio volume whenever the presentation is not being viewed at normal speed; i.e., the viewer is rewinding or fast-forwarding the presentation. See Figure 1c.

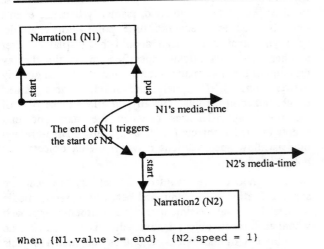

```
When {N1.value >= end}  {N2.speed = 1}
```

Figure 1a: A second narration (N2) should start after the first narration (N1) has reached its endpoint. The value of the first narration's endpoint is assumed to be stored in the variable end.

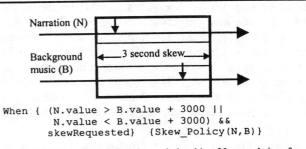

```
When { (N.value > B.value + 3000 ||
        N.value < B.value + 3000) &&
       skewRequested}  {Skew_Policy(N,B)}
```

Figure 1b: A loosely coupled skew relationship of 3 seconds is enforced between the narration (N) and the background music (B) only if requested by the viewer, perhaps through a toggle button. The viewer's response is held in the variable skewRequested.

```
When {Audio.speed == 1} {Volume = 1}
When {Audio.speed != 1} {Volume = 0}
```

Figure 1c: The above specifications state that whenever the audio is played at anything other than normal speed (1), the volume should be turned off; signified by setting it to zero.

4.2 Media objects

Within Nsync, media objects may be either static (time-independent) or continuous (time-dependent) media. Examples of static media would be text, images, or graphics, whereas examples of continuous media would be audio, video, or animations. Because our work primarily focuses on providing support for the synchronization and interaction aspects of multimedia presentations, we have looked to other sources to provide the necessary content. For continuous media support, we have chosen the Continuous Media Toolkit (CMT) [21] from the University of California-Berkeley. In CMT, *clock* objects provide the necessary time source for intra-stream synchronization (synchronizing the individual media frames). Thus, a continuous media object can be controlled simply by manipulating its corresponding clock object. By attaching multiple continuous media objects to the same clock, a lip-sync quality coupling can be achieved. However, loosely coupled skew relationships, interaction, or any another type of synchronization are not supported by CMT. For time-independent media, we use the functionality of Tcl/Tk [17].

4.3 Clock Objects

Every media object in the Nsync system is assumed to be associated with a distinct clock object. A clock provides a linear mapping from system time to *media-time*. *Media-time* has no start or end and can be thought of as an infinite timeline in both directions. For continuous media, *media-time* provides the time source for synchronized playback. For time-independent media, *media-time* can be used as a "stopwatch" to time the overall length of display.

Clocks maintain three attributes: *value*, *speed*, and *offset*. *Value* represents the current *media-time* of the clock which can be set to a new value in order to support skip ahead or skip behind operations. *Speed* represents the ratio of *media-time* progression to that of real-time[1]. For example, a speed of 2.0 for continuous media indicates that the media is being played at twice its normal playout rate and a speed of -1.0 indicates that is being played in reverse at normal speed. Rate control is achieved simply by adjusting the speed of the clock. *Offset* is a scalar that is used to complete the mapping between *media-time* and real-time:

```
Media-Time = Speed * Real-Time + Offset
```

A clock can be set by setting any two of {*value*, *speed*, *offset*} and the third will be computed.

Clocks exhibit several useful properties [3], but for this discussion, the relevant properties are:

- Different clocks can be perfectly synchronized by setting their speeds and offsets to identical values. Since *media-time* is computed from real-time, two clocks with the same *speed* and *offset* will always have the same *media-time*.

- *Speed* and *offset* do not change during normal play-out without intervention by either the viewer or other system events.

- Clocks always progress in a piecewise linear fashion. See Figure 2 below. As a result, the time it will take a clock, given its current *value*, *speed*, and *offset*, to reach a future time instant can be predicted.

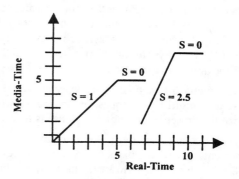

Figure 2: A graph demonstrating the media-time mapping as well as the piecewise linearity of the clock object. At real-time 7, a skip behind has been performed by setting the clock's value attribute back to media-time 2, and the speed (S) is also set to 2.5.

4.4 Multiple timelines

Using a single timeline as the basis of a synchronization model [2, 10, 12, 16, 21] provides a natural and intuitive method for synchronizing events *within* a media object.

For example, specifying that a narration start at time 2 is trivial. However, for more complex applications a single timeline proves to be too rigid, primarily because events must be tied to a specific time point. For example, specifying that one image should be displayed after another cannot be directly specified unless the display duration of the first image is known exactly (rules out any viewer control). On the other hand, coarse-grained synchronization models generally do allow these type of incomplete specifications between the start and end events of media objects [1, 14, 23]. Thus, coarse-grained models allow specifications *between* media objects, but not *within* them.

In our model, we wanted the ability to capture synchronization both within and between different media objects. To do this, Nsync uses a multi-timeline approach where each media object is attached to its own clock. The coordination of the clocks, and thus the media objects themselves, is specified using the synchronization definition language (discussed in section 5). The language

---

[1] For this paper, real-time and system-time are synonymous.

allows a wide variety of relationships involving zero or more timelines to be defined; thus relationships both within and between media objects can easily be specified. Consider the example shown in Figure 1a. Each narration is attached to its own clock (timeline) and thus maintains its own media-time mapping. The two clocks are then coordinated using the synchronization definition language.

4.5 Interaction

In general, *interaction* refers to an asynchronous collaboration between the presentation author and the presentation viewer. Interactive presentation authors create a kind of "presentation roadmap," where the particular path that is navigated and exactly how that path is traversed, is ultimately up to the viewer. However, providing even the simplest form of interaction within a synchronization model is a difficult task. Several issues need to be addressed in order to provide interaction:

- A bi-directional communication path must be established between the viewer and the run-time system responsible for presentation playout. Requests and responses from both the viewer and the run-time system follow along this path. For example, the presentation may present the user with a multi-choice question and request a response. Upon making a selection, the viewer's response must then be communicated back to the playout mechanism which then determines the appropriate action to take. This implies that presentation schedules should not be statically pre-computed; rather, they should be managed at run-time so that viewer responses can influence future presentation playout.

- A mechanism for detecting and then handling asynchronous events, such as when the viewer decides to skip ahead or behind within the presentation.

- Communication with a user interface toolkit in order for things like choice boxes to be displayed.

In Nsync, these issues are addressed by allowing both variables and clock attributes {*value*, *speed*, and *offset*} to be included in the synchronization specifications along with a mechanism for detecting changes to any of them [22]. This addresses the first two issues, but also creates additional problems. Supporting the combination of these non-temporal elements (variables plus the *speed* and *offset* attributes of clocks) along with temporal elements (the *value* attribute of a clock) in the same specification is non-trivial. The solution was to use conjunctive and disjunctive operators and evaluate the specifications according to a *predictive* logic. See Section 6.

Finally, the last issue was addressed by using the Tcl/Tk scripting language and toolkit [17] for the implementation

of our system. Because Tcl is an interpreted language, communicating with the Tk widget set is trivial.

5. Synchronization Definition Language

At the core of Nsync is a declarative synchronization definition language used to express the synchronization relationships. The language is formally described by an LL(1) BNF grammar[2]. The language allows the following synchronization specifications to be defined:

- *Non-temporal constraint.* An expression consisting of constants, scalar variables, arithmetic operators, equality or inequality relationships, boolean connectives, negations, and references to a clock's *speed* or *offset* attribute. An example is Figure 1c.

- *Temporal constraint.* An expression consisting of constants, scalar variables, arithmetic operators, equality or inequality relationships, boolean connectives, negations, and at least one reference to a clock's *value* attribute. Examples are shown in Figures 1a and 1b.

- *Combinations* of temporal and non-temporal constraints. Both disjunctive (| |) and conjunctive (&&) operators can be applied to any combination of temporal or non-temporal constraints. An example is shown in Figure 1b.

Each constraint specification is made using the following syntax[3]:

```
When {expression} {action}
```

Where When is the main procedure name, expression is the synchronization relationship that needs to be monitored, and action is the command associated with expression. Upon definition, each synchronization expression is compiled into an equivalent stack-based representation for efficient evaluation [3]. Semantically, the syntax states:

"Whenever expression ***becomes*** true (transitions from false to true) invoke the corresponding action."

For example, the first specification in Figure 1a states, *whenever the value of N1* ***becomes*** *greater than end, start the second narration.* The key here is that this transition may occur as the result of normal playout or due to a skip operation.

The When command differs from the traditional if control structure found in most programming languages in that it is *persistent*, meaning that the synchronization expression is continuously monitored by the Nsync run-time system. An if command would only check the logic

---

[2] The BNF grammar is available upon request.

[3] The syntax used for the When expression and all examples demonstrating its use are based on the Tcl language.

status of the synchronization expression at a particular moment in time. One may also think of the synchronization expression as a description of a particular system state, such that *whenever* the system state is entered, the associated action is invoked. It is also important to realize that since asynchronous skips and speed manipulation are allowed, synchronization expressions may make multiple logic transitions and must be monitored throughout presentation playback.

Because the implementation of Nsync was done using the Tcl/Tk scripting language, the *action* associated with a synchronization definition may be *any* Tcl command, which has proven to be extremely flexible.

5.1 Usage examples

Here we present two examples of how to use the synchronization definition language to specify interaction within a presentation. The first example demonstrates how to specify asynchronous interaction and have the implication of that interaction affect a later synchronization decision, or *deferred* synchronization. The second example demonstrates how to specify an asynchronous interaction; i.e., a multi-choice question, and enforce that the viewer has responded to the question at a future point within the presentation.

5.1.1 A Virtual Home Tour

The overall goal of this example is to lead the viewer on a narrated tour of a home. The tour begins with the display of an image of the kitchen along with an accompanying narration. The kitchen display also contains a *hold* toggle button which allows the viewer to express an interest in the current location, thus inhibiting the next scheduled transition. This is not a pause operation because selecting the toggle does not freeze the presentation; rather, its implication is deferred until a later point in the presentation. Note that this is similar to, but not the same as restricted blocking [24]. Based on the specifications and the initial state of the system; i.e., the hold toggle is not currently selected, the run-time system predicts (schedules) the transition into the dining room. However, if the viewer selects the hold toggle during the kitchen presentation, the run-time system catches the change, re-evaluates the specifications, and as a result, schedules the additional information regarding the kitchen. For simplicity, we assume that these details are provided by simply continuing on with the current narration, although an alternative narration track could also be started. This example and the necessary Nsync synchronization specifications are shown in Figure 3.

5.1.2 A Virtual Murder Mystery

The overall goal of this example is allow the viewer to choose a particular character role within a virtual murder mystery. After a few preliminary instructions are given,

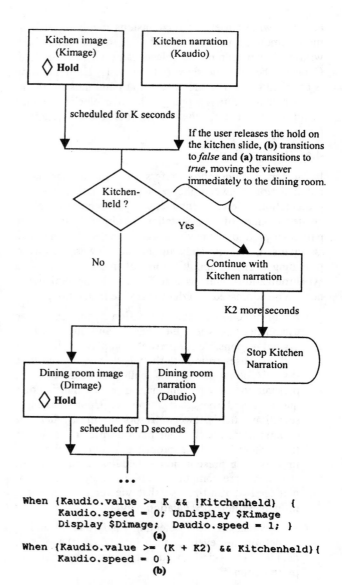

```
When {Kaudio.value >= K && !Kitchenheld}  {
      Kaudio.speed = 0;  UnDisplay $Kimage
      Display $Dimage;  Daudio.speed = 1; }
                         (a)
When {Kaudio.value >= (K + K2) && Kitchenheld}{
      Kaudio.speed = 0 }
                         (b)
```

Figure 3: The virtual home tour begins in the kitchen which is scheduled to last for K seconds. Unless the viewer selects the hold toggle, the run-time system schedules the transition to the dining room; however, if the viewer does select the hold toggle, then the run-time system catches the change, re-evaluates the specifications, and as a result, schedules the additional kitchen information. At any point during the detailed kitchen description, the viewer may unselect the hold toggle, which will immediately transition them to the dining room as expected. The specifications to capture these semantics are shown in (a) and (b) above. The variable Kitchenheld represents the current state of the kitchen hold toggle.

the viewer is presented with a multi-choice dialog box allowing them to begin thinking about which role they want to fulfill within the mystery (asynchronous interaction). Instructions continue until a point is reached where the viewer must have responded to the multi-choice question before further instructions can be given. If not, the presentation will freeze until such a choice is made

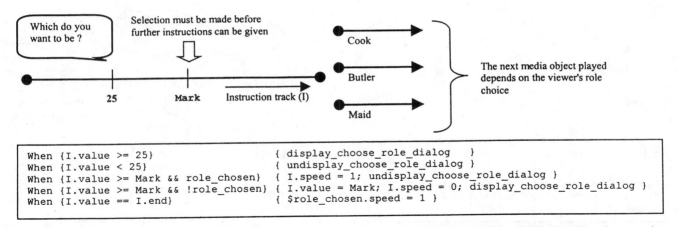

```
When {I.value >= 25}                    { display_choose_role_dialog    }
When {I.value < 25}                     { undisplay_choose_role_dialog }
When {I.value >= Mark && role_chosen}   { I.speed = 1; undisplay_choose_role_dialog }
When {I.value >= Mark && !role_chosen}  { I.value = Mark; I.speed = 0; display_choose_role_dialog }
When {I.value == I.end}                 { $role_chosen.speed = 1 }
```

Figure 4: A virtual murder mystery begins with some preliminary instructions. Once the preliminary instructions are finished (I = 25), a character role dialog box is displayed so that the viewer may begin thinking about which role they want to fulfill within the story. Additional instructions continue for a period of time (Mark seconds) until a point is reached where the viewer must have responded to the multi-choice question before any further details can be given. If not, the presentation will freeze until such a choice is made. Once the role is chosen, the instructions are completed and the story-line continues based upon the chosen character role. At any point within the instruction segment, the viewer is also permitted to skip ahead or behind, perhaps to change the role they have initially chosen or to skip instructions they have heard before. The synchronization specifications to capture these semantics are shown above.

(synchronous interaction). Once the role has been chosen and instructions completed, the virtual mystery continues based upon which character role was chosen. The viewer is also permitted to skip ahead or behind within the instruction segment in order to change the chosen character role, or to skip instructions they have heard before. However, the viewer must not be allowed to skip past the selection of a character role; otherwise, the integrity of the presentation would be violated. This example and the necessary synchronization specifications are shown in Figure 4.

6. Presentation Management System Implementation

Because Nsync supports synchronous and asynchronous interaction, pre-computing presentation playout schedules before run-time does not provide the necessary flexibility. Thus we have designed a more flexible run-time presentation management system which can evaluate combinations, expressed through conjunctive and disjunctive operators, of non-temporal constraints, temporal constraints, and interactive behaviors. The run-time presentation management system is composed of three inner components:

- *Evaluator*. Determines the current logic value of a synchronization expression according to the predictive logic presented in Section 6.1. If the expression evaluates to *WBT(x)* or *WBF(x)*, then the predicted time *x*, along with the associated action, is given to the Scheduler.

- *Change Monitor*. Watches the *relevant* clock attributes and variables to determine if new predictions need to be made by the Evaluator.

Relevant means that the variable or clock attribute has been used in at least one synchronization expression. If a change is detected, both the Scheduler and Evaluator are notified.

- *Scheduler*. Maintains and schedules all of the predictions made by the Evaluator. As these predicted times arrive, the associated actions are invoked.

The interaction among these components is shown in Figure 6.

6.1 Evaluator

The Evaluator is responsible for determining the current truth-value of a synchronization expression. Recall that synchronization expressions are persistent; i.e., the expressions are continuously monitored for logic transitions throughout presentation playback. Because these expressions may contain clock objects, whose values are continuously changing when their rates are non-zero, the logic state of the expression could change at any time. The goal is to capture these logic transitions so that the appropriate actions can be invoked. One approach would be to poll the expressions at regular intervals; however, this wastes precious cpu cycles and also competes for the cpu with the rest of the presentation playback. As a result, the Evaluator uses a newly designed *predictive* logic that has four possible truth-values:

- *FALSE*. The synchronization expression is currently FALSE, and will remain FALSE at least until a clock's attribute or scalar variable used within the synchronization expression changes.

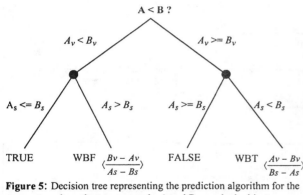

Figure 5: Decision tree representing the prediction algorithm for the < operator where the two operands, A and B, are clock objects. Decision trees for <=, >, >=, are similar.

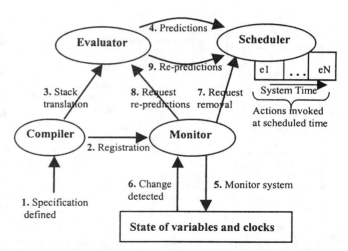

Figure 6: Graphical view of how synchronization expressions are created, monitored, and maintained at run-time.

- *TRUE.* The synchronization expression is currently TRUE, and will remain TRUE at least until a clock's attribute or scalar variable used within the synchronization expression changes.

- *WBT(x).* The synchronization expression is currently FALSE, but *will become true* in a predictable amount of time, x, given the current system state.

- *WBF(x).* The synchronization expression is currently TRUE, but *will become false* in a predictable amount of time, x, given the current system state[4].

The prediction x represents an offset from the current system time, *not* media-time. Recall that the action associated with a synchronization expression is only invoked when the expression makes a logic transition from FALSE to TRUE and not from TRUE to FALSE. We made this decision for two reasons:

- To keep the semantic meaning of the When command unambiguous. Invoking different actions depending on the logic transition may lead to confusion as to the correct specification technique.

- Any synchronization expression which needs its action invoked when the synchronization expression becomes FALSE rather than TRUE, can simply negate its expression clause and use the current When semantics.

In order to evaluate the expression stack, the top element is popped from the stack and each of its operands is recursively evaluated. Each operand is evaluated according to the following rules:

- Constants are promoted to a temporary clock object with a speed of zero, and with a value set equal to the constant.

- Scalar variables have their values dynamically retrieved and are then promoted to a temporary clock object in the same manner as constants.

- Arithmetic operators (+, -, *, /) are evaluated by applying the operator to each respective attribute of the clock objects. Because of constant and scalar variable promotions, each operand of the arithmetic operator is guaranteed to be a clock object.

- The inequality and equality operators (>, >=, <, <=, ==) are evaluated by first determining if either clock's *speed* is non-zero (operands are guaranteed to be clock objects due to previous promotions). If the *speed* of each clock is zero, then the *value* attribute of each clock is compared using the corresponding operator and TRUE or FALSE is returned. However, when one of the clock's *speed* attribute is non-zero, then a prediction algorithm is invoked which may return TRUE or FALSE, or, WBF or WBT along with a predicted time. A decision tree for the < operator is shown in Figure 5 above. The remaining operators work similarly.

- The conjunctive (&&) and disjunctive (| |) operators are evaluated according to Tables 1 and 2 listed below.

Every time a synchronization expression is evaluated, the Evaluator applies the above rules to determine the current logic value of the synchronization expression. If the expression evaluates to

- *FALSE.* No action is taken.

- *TRUE.* The Scheduler is called upon to invoke the enforcement action immediately (prediction value of 0) as long as a logic transition actually did occur. In other words, the action is invoked only if the previous logic value was FALSE; otherwise, the

---

[4] The reader may realize that TRUE = WBF(∞) and FALSE = WBT(∞); however, for the purposes of explanation, we choose to use the four distinct values.

expression has *remained* TRUE and a logic transition did not actually occur.

- *WBT(x)*. The Scheduler is called upon to invoke the enforcement action at the predicted time.

- *WBF(x)*. The Scheduler is called upon to invoke an internal system function which simply marks the fact that this expression is now FALSE, so that the next transition to TRUE will trigger the associated action.

Table 1 Truth Table for Predictive AND

AND	TRUE	FALSE	WBT_{x2}	WBF_{y2}
TRUE	TRUE	FALSE	WBT_{x2}	WBF_{y2}
FALSE	FALSE	FALSE	FALSE	FALSE
WBT_{x1}	WBT_{x1}	FALSE	WBT $max(x1,x2)$	*
WBF_{y1}	WBF_{y1}	FALSE	†	WBF $min(y1,y2)$

* if $(x1 < y2)$ then $\{WBT_{x1}, WBF_{y2}\}$ else FALSE
† if $(x2 < y1)$ then $\{WBT_{x2}, WBF_{y1}\}$ else FALSE

Table 2 Truth Table for Predictive OR

OR	TRUE	FALSE	WBT_{x2}	WBF_{y2}
TRUE	TRUE	TRUE	TRUE	TRUE
FALSE	TRUE	FALSE	WBT_{x2}	WBF_{y2}
WBT_{x1}	TRUE	WBT_{x1}	WBT $min(x1,x2)$	*
WBF_{y1}	TRUE	WBF_{y1}	†	WBF $min(y1,y2)$

* if $(x1 > y2)$ then $\{WBF_{y2}, WBT_{x1}\}$ else TRUE
† if $(x2 > y1)$ then $\{WBF_{y1}, WBT_{x2}\}$ else TRUE

6.2 Change Monitor

As shown in Figure 2, clocks progress at a predictable rate until one of the attributes, *value*, *speed*, or *offset* is explicitly changed. If any clock attribute or variable used in synchronization expression changes, then all of the expressions referencing it need to be re-evaluated. The Change Monitor performs this monitoring function, and if any changes do occur, it notifies both the Scheduler and Evaluator.

6.3 Scheduler

The Scheduler is responsible for invoking a specification's *action* at the future time predicted by the Evaluator. To perform this function, the Scheduler maintains a timed event queue where the events are ordered by their predicted times. Recall that predictions are given as an offset to the current system time, thus ordering them is

straightforward. Here the term "event" represents a transition in the logic state of a synchronization expression. Once the predicted amount of time has elapsed, the corresponding synchronization expression will have just changed logic states, and the corresponding specification's action should, and will be invoked. Recall that transitions from FALSE to TRUE result in the invocation of a specification action; whereas a transition from TRUE to FALSE results in the invocation of a system action which simply notes the change. If the Change Monitor notifies the Scheduler that a dependent clock attribute or variable has changed, the Scheduler removes all associated events from the queue. The Change Monitor also notifies the Evaluator of the change. The Evaluator then re-evaluates any synchronization expression referencing the changed clock attribute or variable and the new predictions, if any, are given back to the Scheduler. This entire process is depicted in Figure 6.

7. Discussion and Future Work

The Nsync toolkit has been completely implemented in the Tcl/Tk scripting language. The total implementation effort was about 3,500 lines of Tcl code extending over a 6 month period. The number of lines of code per component is listed in Table 3 below.

Table 3: Number of lines of Tcl code within Nsync

Component	Lines of Tcl code
Compiler	1,000
Evaluator	1,500
Change Monitor	750
Scheduler	200
Total	**3,450**

Because presentation playback is monitored at run-time, performance is an obvious issue. For an expression representing skew control, we have measured the overhead of the system to be around 200 milliseconds[5]. This measurement represents the time from the initial detection of a relevant change for an expression that was currently FALSE, to the time at which the Evaluator determined that the expression transitioned to TRUE. For coarse-grained relationships, this is very reasonable as studies have shown that the viewer can tolerate up to a 500 millisecond transition period. However, for fine-grained relationships; e.g., skew control, this is unacceptable as it typically needs to be under 80 milliseconds. Thus, although Nsync can model any granularity of skew relationship, it cannot currently enforce them. To address this issue, some parts of the

---

[5] Measured on an SGI IP22 with an R5000 processor, 32 MB RAM, and running Irix 6.2 operating system.

system would need to be re-implemented in a lower-level programming language such as C or C++.

We believe that Nsync represents a significant improvement over many of the current synchronization models in its ability to model combinations of synchronous interactions, asynchronous interactions, and fine-grained relationships. However, we are also looking into several extensions to the Nsync toolkit:

- *Verification.* Nsync analyzes the synchronization expression, but not the action portion of the When command. Thus, it is currently not possible to prove consistency among all the different specifications made.

- *Synchronization library.* As experience is gained from using the system, action behaviors found to be useful across different presentations in similar circumstances could be provided in a library for future authors to reuse.

- *Priorities.* Each synchronization expression has an equal priority in the system. Experience has shown that when multiple specifications share some of the same dependencies, the order of evaluation becomes important. One method to help alleviate this problem would be to extend the specification language to include priorities.

In summary, we have identified many of the necessary requirements for authoring highly innovative, interactive multimedia presentations, and have demonstrated through explanations and examples how the Nsync toolkit meets these requirements.

8. Acknowledgements

This work was supported by a grant from the National Science Foundation (IRI 94-10470) and the Distributed Multimedia Research Center. The authors would also like to thank Duminda Wijesekara for his valuable knowledge of temporal logics and insight when designing our predictive logic.

9. References

[1] Allen, J.F. Maintaining Knowledge about Temporal Intervals. *CACM.* November 1983.

[2] Apple Computer. Inside Macintosh: QuickTime. *Addison-Wesley Publishing Company*, 1997.

[3] Bailey, B., and Konstan, J. Nsync - A Constraint Based Toolkit for Multimedia. *Proceedings of the 1997 Tcl/Tk Workshop.*

[4] Blakowski, G., Huebel, J., and Langrehr, U. Tools for Specifying and Executing Synchronized Multimedia Presentations. *Proc. NOSSDAV* 1991. Heidelberg, Germany.

[5] Blakowski, G., and Steinmetz, R. A Media Synchronization Survey: Reference Model, Specification, and Case Studies. *IEEE JSAC.* January 1996.

[6] Buchanan, C., and Zellweger P. Scheduling multimedia documents using temporal constraints. *Proc. NOSSDAV.* November 1992.

[7] Buchanan, C. and Zellweger, P. Specifying Temporal Behavior in Hypermedia Documents. *Proc. ACM ECHT Conference*, 1992.

[8] Candan, K., et.al. CHIMP: A Framework for Supporting Multimedia Document Authoring and Presentation. *Proc. ACM Multimedia*, 1996.

[9] Courtiat, J.P., and De Oliveira, R.C. Proving Temporal Consistency in a new Multimedia Synchronization Model. *Proc. ACM Multimedia*, 1996.

[10] Drapeau, G.D. Synchronization in the MAEstro Multimedia Authoring Environment. *Proc. ACM Multimedia*, 1993.

[11] Echiffre, M., et.al. MHEG-5-Aims, Concepts, and Implementation Issues. *IEEE Multimedia.* 5(1), 1998.

[12] Herlocker, J., and Konstan, J. Commands as Media: Design and Implementation of a Command Stream. *Proc. ACM Multimedia*, 1995.

[13] Iyengar, S., and Konstan, J. TclProp: A Data-Propagation Formula Manager for Tcl and Tk. *Proceedings of the 1995 Tcl/Tk Workshop.*

[14] Little, T.D.C, and Ghafoor, A. Interval-Based Conceptual Models for Time-Dependent Multimedia Data. *IEEE TKDE*, 5(4):551-563, 1993.

[15] Little, T.D.C, and Ghafoor, A. Synchronization and Storage Models for Multimedia Objects. *IEEE JSAC*, 8(3):413-427, April, 1990.

[16] Learning Lingo. *Macromedia Press*, March, 1997.

[17] Ousterhout, J.K. Tcl and the Tk Toolkit. *Addison-Wesley Publishing Company*, 1994.

[18] Pazandack, P. Multimedia Language Constructs and Execution Environments for Next-Generation Interactive Applications. *Ph.D. Thesis.* University of Minnesota, 1996.

[19] Prabhakaran, B., and Subrahmanian, S.V. Synchronization Models For Multimedia Presentation With User Input. *Multimedia Systems*, 2(2):53-62, August 1994.

[20] Rothermel, K., and Helbig, T. Clock Hierarchies: An Abstraction for Grouping and Controlling Media Streams. *IEEE JSAC.* January 1996.

[21] Rowe, L., and Smith, B. A Continuous Media Player. *Proc. NOSSDAV*, 1992.

[22] Safonov, A. Extending Traces with OAT: an Object Attribute Trace package for Tcl/Tk. *Proceedings of the 1997 Tcl/Tk Workshop.*

[23] Schnepf, J., Konstan, J., and Du, D. Doing FLIPS: FLexible Interactive Presentation Synchronization. *IEEE JSAC.* January 1996.

[24] Steinmetz, R. Synchronization Properties in multimedia systems. *IEEE JSAC.* April 1990.

[25] The CWI SMIL page. http://www.cwi.nl/SMIL.

A Method and Apparatus for Measuring Media Synchronization

Brian K. Schmidt†, J. Duane Northcutt‡, and Monica S. Lam†

†Computer Systems Laboratory, Stanford University, Stanford, CA 94305
‡Sun Microsystems Laboratories, 2550 Garcia Avenue, Mountain View, CA 94043

Media synchronization is widely regarded as a fundamental problem in the field of multimedia. While much work has been conducted in this area, and many different solutions have been proposed, no method for obtaining a repeatable, objective measure of synchronization performance exists. Thus, there has been no means for determining the effectiveness of potential media synchronization solutions. In this paper we present an experimental methodology for quantitatively measuring the performance of different media synchronization schemes. We describe a complete (hardware and software) test environment for measuring audio/video synchronization quality of various media players, and we also present empirical performance measurements of an example media player. The results show that external observation is necessary for accurate assessments of synchronization performance. This test and evaluation methodology is applicable to other media delivery systems and can serve as the first step in isolating and quantifying the effects of individual components of a media delivery system.

1 Introduction

Multimedia refers to the use of one or more types of *media data* — data designed to be consumed by humans, such as text, graphics, audio, and video. These data typically possess timeliness requirements with respect to their presentation. For example, digital audio samples may be required to be displayed at a uniform rate of 48KHz. The media synchronization problem is to assure the correct temporal alignment of such time-critical activities relative to a physical clock.

Although there is a relatively large body of research describing various solutions to the synchronization problem, no metrics have been defined to measure the performance and efficacy of this work. Effectiveness assessments have been largely subjective in nature, thus making comparisons between different approaches quite difficult. To determine the degree to which media synchronization is achieved, a means for obtaining a repeatable, objective measure of (externally visible) system performance must exist. We present such a scheme below.

1.1 Background

To help characterize the media synchronization problem we present the following terminology. A *media element* is a single unit of a multimedia data type, such as a video frame, or audio sample. A *media stream* (or *stream*) is a series of media elements. Common examples of streams include video clips and audio sound bites. A time-ordered collection of media streams is termed a *media sequence* (or *sequence*). A good example of a sequence is a music album, i.e. a set of audio streams (songs). Given these definitions we decompose the media synchronization problem space into three classes: event-based, stream-based, and element-based.

Event-based synchronization refers to synchronization activities performed in response to external events such as user input, whereas *stream-based* and *element-based synchronization* refer to activities which attempt to control the timely interactions between related media data. The units of synchronization for stream-based and element-based synchronization are media streams and media elements respectively. The interactions between synchronization units may be within the same sequence (intra-sequence), across different sequences (inter-sequence), within the same stream (intra-stream), or across different streams (inter-stream).

Several methods have been proposed to address all or part of the media synchronization problem. One common approach for dealing with the case of inter-stream element-based synchronization (e.g. managing lip sync in movie clips) is to interleave the associated media streams. However, this scheme suffers from a number of different shortcomings — including the coupling of failure modes resulting from packet loss during transmission, and the inability to prioritize the data streams or handle them in a manner appropriate to their data type ([7], [8], [10]). An approach which attempts to address all types of element-based synchronization is to assign each media element a timestamp that represents the time at which it must be displayed ([1], [4]). While this scheme has the benefit of simplicity, it does not take into account the variations between the different physical clocks involved in actual systems (i.e. system, frame buffer, and audio codec clocks). Some approaches designed to provide general support for media synchronization in distributed settings are based on the use of synchronized system clocks ([5], [14]), while others employ centralized synchronization servers ([13], [15]). Work has also been done in other areas, such as operating systems ([3], [11], [12]) and network protocols ([6], [9], [18]), to provide support for media synchronization. These approaches have vastly different properties and address different aspects of the problem. Without a means for quantitatively measuring their performance, it is difficult to accurately and objectively determine what impact these schemes have on the achieved quality of media synchronization.

1.2 System Overview

This paper presents a methodology for quantitatively measuring the performance of media delivery systems. Below, we present an overview of a complete framework for measuring synchronization quality. In Section 2 we outline our experimental methodology, and Section 3 describes the implementation of our framework. Section 4 presents some experimental results, and we conclude in Section 5.

A generalized media delivery system is capable of capturing, manipulating, and presenting synchronized media data. Evaluating the performance of such a system requires a repeatable procedure for presenting the system with a stimulus and quantitatively measuring its output relative to an ideal response. To meet this goal we have developed a complete synchronization test environment as depicted in Figure 1. The environment is comprised of three components: the media delivery system being tested, a stimulus production system, and a measurement system. The components execute on separate machines in order to avoid interference effects.

The stimulus production system must generate a controlled stimulus and present it as input to the system under test. This stimulus must be a well-defined media sequence that requires synchronization, and it must be produced in a reliable, accurate, and repeatable manner. In practice, a media delivery system typically receives its input either from a storage system (as in a movie player) or from a live analog source (as in a teleconferencing application). To simulate typical use, the stimulus production system must be able to generate a sequence for both situations.

system provides an indication of the end-to-end synchronization performance of the system under test, and it can be used to isolate and quantify the effects of individual system components.

2 Experimental Methodology

Since displaying synchronized audio and video is such a common activity in practice, we have chosen to measure element-based intra-stream audio, intra-stream video, and inter-stream audio/video synchronization as the initial test cases. We use a timestamp-based audio/video test generator and a timestamp-based movie player as two sample media delivery systems. However, since we make no *a priori* assumption on the manner in which the problem is attacked, any system capable of displaying audio and video can be measured. We will conduct experiments with other media delivery systems in the future, and we also plan to measure other forms of synchronization performance. This section presents the design issues of the input sequence as well as the types of synchronization measurements that can be made.

2.1 Designing a Media Sequence for Controlled Input

To provide reliable measurements, the media sequence which is used as a controlled input must be well-defined so that all timing information is known *a priori*. Thus, given that the ideal display time of each media event is known, and since the actual display time is measurable, it is possible to detect any deviations. The sequence must also be defined in such a manner that the measurement system can reliably quantify these timing differences. For example, typical quartz oscillators have a frequency offset from ideal which is on the order of 100 parts per million (ppm). Without some method of compensation, this error accumulates over time and will result in media elements being displayed increasingly farther from their ideal presentation times. This effect is usually termed *drift*. Since this type of error becomes noticeable (to a human) only very slowly, the test sequence must be sufficiently long-running to allow the potential error to accumulate to an appreciable level. Also, the event inter-arrival times must be varied in order to avoid resonance effects with any other clocks in the system. For instance, if the scheduler executes every 10ms, a media delivery system displaying a stream with a period of 30ms between element presentation times may appear to have better (or worse) performance than the same system displaying a stream with a 33ms period.

For our initial experiments with simple audio/video synchronization, we defined the following sequence to satisfy the above requirements. To simplify matters, monaural audio is used, and the video is comprised of only two different frames: a solid black frame, and a black frame with a white square in the center. Two types of media events are recognized by the measuring device: video events, and audio events. A *video event* occurs whenever the type of video frame being displayed is changed, and an *audio event* occurs when a click sound is played. The sequence is defined so that audio and video events should occur simultaneously. This limits the granularity of synchronization to a video frame time. Clearly, this is the smallest meaningful unit for intra-stream video and inter-stream audio/video synchronization, but intra-stream audio synchronization could be measured at a finer granularity. While this is possible, it adds unneeded complexity since measuring the rate at which audio samples are output from the system can be much more easily achieved by monitoring the output voltage levels of the audio codec (a technique supported by the system we have implemented).

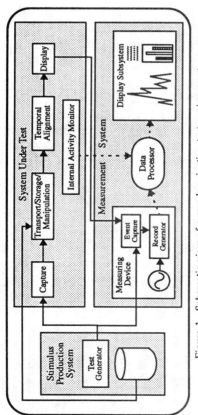

Figure 1. Schematic view of a synchronization test environment.

A stored sequence can be generated once and recorded in a file (in a format suitable for input by the system under test). All timing information of the media elements within the sequence can then be recovered by simply examining the properties of the stored data. If, however, live data are to be used, it is necessary to produce the sequence using a test sequence generator — a specialized media delivery system. The test generator must be able to display the defined sequence in a repeatable fashion and with a small error bound. In addition, the accuracy of the generated sequence must exceed the acquisition and synchronization accuracy of the system under test. Although the sequence generated by this method may be highly accurate, it is still not perfect. So, the output from the test generator is not only sent to the media capture device(s) of the system under test, but it is also sent to the measurement system (described below), which then characterizes the actual sequence timing for later comparison with the output from the system being tested.

Once the sequence is input to the test system, it may be stored, manipulated, transmitted across a network, etc. When the system is ready to display the sequence, it will analyze the synchronization requirements, attempt to temporally align the media elements to their ideal presentation times, and then finally display them. The system under test might also make record information regarding its activity and pass it to the measurement system (described below). This information can then be correlated with the measured output of the system to establish causal relationships between externally- and internally-observed system behavior.

The measurement system contains three components: a measuring device, a data processor, and a display subsystem. The measuring device is responsible for collecting the output of both the test generator and the system under test. It then analyzes these data, looking for particular *media events*. A media event corresponds to the display of one or more semantically meaningful media elements, e.g. an audible click, a certain type of video frame, etc. For each media event that it receives, the measuring device generates an *event record* (or record). Records consist of a timestamp and an identifying tag. All generated records are output to the data processor, which is responsible for analyzing the data from the measuring device and compiling statistics on the timing of events. These statistics are then passed to the display subsystem, which presents graphical and tabular summaries of media synchronization quality for the system being tested. The measurement

The test sequence runs for at least two hours — a sufficient length to allow drift to accumulate to a noticeable level. The sequence displays video at rates of 30Hz, 29.97Hz, 29Hz, and then cycles down to 1Hz with a step size of 1Hz. For each rate, the ratio of the duty cycles of white-square frames to black frames is varied as follows: 1:1 (one white-square frame, then one black frame), 1:2, 1:3, 1:5, 1:7. A pseudo-random sequence of frame types is also displayed for each rate. The sequence is defined in this way to avoid any possible resonance effects with clocks in the system. This pattern is repeated until the time limit for the test is reached.

2.2 Performance Measurements

The above measurement environment is defined in such a way that for each media event ε, the following values are available: the generation time $\tau_G(\varepsilon)$, the ideal display time $\tau_I(\varepsilon)$, and the actual display time $\tau_A(\varepsilon)$. Based on these values, we define six quantitative performance measurements. The *end-to-end latency* of a media event is defined as $\lambda_\varepsilon = \tau_A(\varepsilon) - \tau_G(\varepsilon)$. *Absolute asynchrony* represents the deviation of a particular media event from its ideal display time and is given by $\delta_\varepsilon = \tau_A(\varepsilon) - \tau_I(\varepsilon)$. *Relative asynchrony* is given by $\pi_{\varepsilon_i \varepsilon_j} = \tau_A(\varepsilon_i) - \tau_A(\varepsilon_j)$, where ε_i and ε_j denote events from streams i and j respectively. It corresponds to the relative display time of nominally simultaneous events from different streams.

With these measures we can derive additional quantities for *skew*, *drift*, and *jitter*. Intuitively, given two sets of values over time (e.g. actual and ideal presentation times of media elements from a given stream), skew refers to a constant offset between pairs of values, drift denotes the amount by which the difference between value pairs changes over time, and jitter is characterized by the instantaneous variations in these values when skew and drift effects have been removed. These quantities can be computed for both absolute and relative asynchrony through simple statistical analysis techniques. For example, given a series of media events $\varepsilon_1, \varepsilon_2, ..., \varepsilon_N$ and the corresponding series of absolute asynchronies $\delta_{\varepsilon_1}, \delta_{\varepsilon_2}, ..., \delta_{\varepsilon_N}$, for each event ε_i we can plot absolute asynchrony (δ_{ε_i}) vs. ideal display time $(\tau_I(\varepsilon_i))$ on a graph and use a curve interpolation technique (e.g. linear least squares) to fit a straight line through these points. Then, the skew is given by the intercept of this line on the absolute asynchrony axis, the drift corresponds to the slope, and the dispersion about the line gives an indication of the amount of jitter. We can also plot a series of relative asynchrony values $(\pi_{\varepsilon_i \varepsilon_j})$ against a series of actual display time values $(\tau_A(\varepsilon_i))$ and perform a similar analysis to yield skew, drift and jitter figures for stream i.

For our audio/video experiment, analyzing the statistical distributions of the absolute asynchronies for either type of stream provides an indication of intra-stream synchronization quality, while the distribution of relative asynchronies describes the effectiveness of inter-stream synchronization. The relative importance of each of the above measures is application- and media-dependent. For example, low latency is extremely important for interactive applications, and drift is only a concern for long-running sequences. Also, the level at which jitter becomes noticeable depends on the media type (e.g., tolerable video jitter is large compared to tolerable audio jitter). Further, the extent to which asynchronies can be tolerated by a viewer is dependent upon human perceptual limits as well as personal taste. Steinmetz and Engler conducted user studies in [17], and they report several figures of merit for quantifying tolerable asynchrony limits. This type of information must be taken into account when judging the merits of any media delivery system.

3   System Design

Utilizing the above experimental methodology, we implemented a complete test environment for measuring the synchronization performance of arbitrary media delivery systems. As an initial exercise of the capabilities of this system, our test generator and a locally developed media player were used as test cases for measurement. In this section we describe the implementations of our example media player, test sequence generator, and measurement system.

3.1   Media Player Implementation

The chosen test case media player was developed at Sun Microsystems Laboratories. It is a timestamp-based system capable of playing synchronized audio, video, and text streams. Media data are displayed at a single site, but may originate from arbitrary sources, including network connections and local capture devices. Each media stream flows under the direction of an independent thread of control. At the receiver, these threads communicate through a shared memory region, and use time stamps to synchronize the display of their media elements.

Since humans are more sensitive to intra-stream audio asynchronies (i.e. audio delays and drop-outs) than to asynchronies involving the video or text, the clock from the audio codec is used as a master reference to which all threads attempt to synchronize the display of their media elements. The thread controlling the audio stream free-runs, and the other "slave" threads use the information it posts into the shared memory region to determine when to display their elements. If a slave thread is ready to display its element early, then it delays until the appropriate time; but if it is late (>20ms behind audio), it discards its current element on the assumption that continued processing will cause further delays later in the stream.

The player uses the following data format. Video frames are captured at 320x240 pixel resolution and stored using JPEG compression. The audio data are standard 8-bit μ-law monaural samples. The average decompression and display time for the black and white-square frames was measured to be about 33.5ms on a Sun SparcStation 20, and the maximum data rate required is 7.8KB/s for audio and 60.4KB/s for video. Given these values, the media player should be able to sustain the necessary display rates without encountering frequent overload conditions.

In addition, the environment we used to conduct our experiments provides a lightweight event tracing facility. Applications can make calls to tracing routines in order to log the time (relative to the system clock) that some internal event occurred. These tracing routines are very low-cost (a few microseconds). Thus, when used judiciously, they do not significantly perturb an application's normal behavior. By inserting tracepoints into the system under test, it is possible to correlate tracing information to the measured output data so that causal relationships between system activity and noted asynchronies can be determined.

3.2   Test Generator Implementation

We implemented a test generator capable of producing the audio/video sequence defined in Section 2.1. The test generator is an application which executes in the real-time scheduling class at the highest priority on a dedicated machine. It utilizes a simple peripheral I/O device to generate an NTSC composite video signal. This device can store two video frames and allows the user to select which frame is displayed. We use this feature to avoid moving data through the system so that the generator is not limited by any bandwidth constraints. When started, the test generator downloads the pixels for the black and white-square frames into these buffers, and then enters a control loop, waiting for the presentation times of the media events. It displays video events by sending a command to the video encoder telling it which frame to display, and it displays audio events by sending two digital audio samples to the machine's standard audio output device. These samples have the maximum allowable difference in amplitude and thus create an audible click.

This produces highly accurate results since the high priority level of the process and lack of other system activity ensure that deadlines can be met. Also, since each set of media events requires only a few bytes of data to be moved, there are sufficient resources to ensure no overload exists. Further, we avoid any issues that normally arise when multiple clock domains are involved, i.e. the system, audio codec, and NTSC encoder clocks. This is because the audio/video data/commands are delivered to their respective devices under the control of the system clock and NTSC encoder clocks. While many implementations of test generators are possible, this choice represents a balanced trade-off between flexibility and performance.

3.3 Measurement System Implementation

The measurement system must be capable of measuring the media output from both the test generator and the system under test, and it must tag and timestamp any events that it detects and then pass them on for processing and display. To accomplish these goals we built a general-purpose, timestamp-generating I/O device called CHAOS (Chronological Hardware Activity Observation System). CHAOS consists of a set of input ports and a counter driven by the system clock. When a signal is detected on a port, a tag identifying the port is generated and attached to the current value of the counter. This timestamp record is then made available for processing. Since this device merely responds to signals at input ports, it is completely generic in its ability to log the times of external events. Thus, the actual display time of any type of media event can be accurately detected and used to measure synchronization quality for any of the classes mentioned in Section 1.1. In particular, we use the event records generated by CHAOS to compute the synchronization quality metrics presented above in order to obtain an accurate, quantitative measure of how well a given media delivery system performs.

For our initial experiments we utilized three inputs. The first comes from a microphone which acts as a transducer to gather audio data. When an audible click registers, a pulse is generated on an input port, causing CHAOS to create an *audio event record*. We use a photo-diode-based transducer to detect the white-square video frame and then send a pulse to a second input port. CHAOS generates a *video event record* for each frame time that the white square is displayed. The final input comes from a Global Positioning System (GPS) receiver and generates *time correction event records*, which are used to improve timestamp accuracy.

One of the most important aspects of the measuring device is the accuracy and precision of its clock, which must surpass that of the clocks used by the system under test. A precision time reference such as an atomic clock would provide an excellent timer for the device, but this is generally not practical due to the high cost and special handling requirements associated with such a device. Furthermore, the exceedingly high resolution of an atomic clock is unnecessary for measuring media synchronization, where the smallest meaningful units tend to be in the microsecond range (e.g. for stereo audio synchronization [17]). A much better approach is to use the standard quartz oscillator found in modern computers as the time base, but also have CHAOS tag and timestamp the input from a highly reliable chronometer.

An inexpensive GPS receiver can provide a precise 1Hz signal with short term error on the order of 10 parts per billion (ppb) and long term error on the order of 1 part per trillion (ppt) [2]. Given the nominal frequency of the system clock, the correct number of ticks between time correction events is known (e.g. for a 25MHz oscillator, the difference between consecutive time correction event records should be 25 million ticks). The measured value represents the true oscillator frequency and can be used to convert timestamps to real time. This frequency changes so slowly that it is sufficient to measure it once at the beginning of an experiment, and a mean computed over 60 seconds is adequate for obtaining a figure that accurately represents the true value [19]. For example, using an atomic-clock-based frequency counter, we measured the actual frequency of a 25MHz oscillator to be 25,001,109Hz. Using the GPS receiver we calibrated the same clock over a one minute interval and arrived at a frequency of 25,001,117Hz. This indicates that the clock is fast by a perceived amount of around 44μs/s.

4 Experimental Results

Using the test sequence, test generator, media player and measurement system described above, we conducted six experiments to obtain an initial assessment of the quantitative effects of some of the causes of asynchrony in modern systems. In the first five experiments we measured the test sequence generator under various conditions. Initially, the generator was run as a process in the real-time scheduling class on a stand-alone Sun SparcStation 20. No peripheral devices (except for the local disk) were attached, and no other processes (except standard system processes) were running. The output was generated using the standard speaker device and the NTSC video encoder. In the second experiment we attached the machine to the local network and repeated the test. In the next experiment we moved the test generator process into the time-sharing scheduling class, and in the fourth experiment we introduced additional load/processes by performing the test with the window system running. In the fifth experiment we rendered the video directly to the frame buffer. For each of these tests the sequence was played out of non-paged memory so that no disk effects are observed. In the final experiment we measured the performance of the media player. We used the same machine and executed the player in the time-sharing class. The same sequence was used, but the player read the data from a local disk in the format described in Section 3.1. For each experiment the system under test maintained internal state regarding the times at which it considered media elements to have been displayed (or discarded due to missed deadlines), and external measurements were made with the CHAOS device.

4.1 Internal Measurements

During each experiment the system under test gathered internal statistics by querying the system clock after the display of each media event and recording those timestamps. This is done for several reasons. First, such measures were the only indication of synchronization performance in the past, and are thus useful for comparison. Next, it provides an indication of how well the test system believes it is performing, and finally, it helps to isolate causes of poor synchronization. In the future we plan to utilize the tracing facility described in Section 3.1 to acquire more detailed information. The results of our experiments are summarized in Table 1.

intra-stream measurements show dramatic increases in the amount of observed jitter when the system under test is placed in the time-sharing class, indicating that lack of appropriate scheduling support can adversely affect synchronization quality.

Finally, there is a dramatic drop in intra-stream video and inter-stream audio/video synchronization quality in experiment five, in which the test generator displayed video on the frame buffer. This is because the test generator was originally designed to use only the NTSC encoder to produce video, and so the expected time to display a video frame is hard-coded into the application. Thus, when a display path of differing length is encountered, it cannot adjust appropriately. This emphasizes the need for adaptive display algorithms which scale automatically to account for varying display lengths.

4.2 External Measurements

In addition, to the internal measures reported above, we used the CHAOS device to gather performance information for each experiment. These data represent what is actually observed by viewers. The results are summarized in Table 2, from which several interesting observations can be made.

Type	SUT	Dest	Net	Win	Sched Class	Skew (μsecs)	Drift (μsecs/sec)	Jitter Min (μsecs)	Jitter Max (μsecs)	Std Dev	Losses (%)
A	TG	TV			RT	—	101	-70	587	30	0.004
A	TG	TV	✓		RT	—	101	-139	730	51	0.007
A	TG	TV	✓		TS	—	102	-61	867	35	0.6
A	TG	TV	✓	✓	TS	—	101	-106	728	53	0.8
A	TG	FB	✓	✓	TS	—	101	-50	723	22	0.9
A	MP	FB	✓		TS	—	150	-348425	231271	125036	0
V	TG	TV			RT	—	100	-17645	17749	9586	0.002
V	TG	TV	✓		RT	—	101	-17423	16771	9624	0.003
V	TG	TV	✓		TS	—	101	-17153	62690	9690	0.6
V	TG	TV	✓	✓	TS	—	101	-17348	66388	9610	0.8
V	TG	FB	✓	✓	TS	—	190	-247842	1027000000	426948	0.9
V	MP	FB	✓		TS	—	150	-364994	337882	136359	0.9
AV	TG	TV			RT	26095	-0.36	-17584	17812	9587	0.004
AV	TG	TV	✓		RT	25114	0.094	-17309	16667	9620	0.007
AV	TG	TV	✓		TS	25616	-0.15	-17127	62552	9689	0.6
AV	TG	TV	✓	✓	TS	24411	0.17	-17117	66326	9606	0.8
AV	TG	FB	✓	✓	TS	-13529	92	-247917	1027000000	4302378	0.9
AV	MP	FB	✓		TS	-28377	-2.0	-55798	278182	26680	0.9

Table 2. Synchronization performance as measured with the CHAOS device. See Table 1 for a description of the symbols used in this chart.

First, note that no intra-stream skew numbers are reported. This is due to the fact that the actual starting time of the experiment cannot be determined with certainty, i.e. externally, we can only determine when the first event is displayed, not when the system under test began to display it. Inter-stream skew, on the other hand, is internally measured as being relatively small (except for the media player) but is observed as being substantially larger. In fact, the value for the experiment in which the test generator displayed video on the frame buffer falls within a range that would be easily noticed by a human observer ([17]). These differences between internal and external measures can be attributed to the fact that the system under test has no means for determining how long it takes for a media element to appear

Type	SUT	Dest	Net	Win	Sched Class	Skew (μsecs)	Drift (μsecs/sec)	Jitter Min (μsecs)	Jitter Max (μsecs)	Std Dev	Losses (%)
A	TG	TV			RT	-61	0.0003	-20	610	17	0.004
A	TG	TV	✓		RT	-63	0.0012	-25	670	28	0.007
A	TG	TV	✓		TS	-46	0.0057	-54	61245	536	0.6
A	TG	TV	✓	✓	TS	-37	0.0015	-33	67266	471	0.8
A	TG	FB	✓	✓	TS	-16	0.000061	-49	64920	706	0.9
A	MP	FB			TS	0	0	0	0	0	0
V	TG	TV			RT	13	-0.0011	-13	597	22	0.002
V	TG	TV	✓		RT	14	0.00062	-19	754	37	0.003
V	TG	TV	✓		TS	27	0.006	-57	61252	536	0.6
V	TG	TV	✓	✓	TS	35	0.0016	-36	67273	471	0.8
V	TG	FB	✓	✓	TS	3342	-0.011	-586	250136	1583	0.9
V	MP	FB	✓		TS	-109329	51	-360736	464338	136877	0.9
AV	TG	TV			RT	62	0.00014	-5	11	2	0.004
AV	TG	TV	✓		RT	63	0.00019	-5	274	3	0.007
AV	TG	TV	✓		TS	74	0.00031	-15	496	10	0.6
AV	TG	TV	✓	✓	TS	72	0.00014	-14	293	4	0.8
AV	TG	FB	✓	✓	TS	3674	-0.016	-180	249852	1689	0.9
AV	MP	FB	✓		TS	-106879	51	-361860	341950	137159	0.9

Table 1. Synchronization performance as reported by the application displaying the test media sequence. Skew, drift, and jitter are the quantities described in Section 2.2, and losses refers to the percentage of media elements which were not displayed due to missed deadlines.

```
KEY:
SUT - system under test              A  - intra-stream audio synchronization    RT - real-time scheduling class
TG - test sequence generator         V  - intra-stream video synchronization    TS - time-share scheduling class
MP - SML media player                AV - inter-stream synchronization of
                                           video relative to audio
TV - video displayed on television        Net - machine connected to network
FB - video displayed on frame buffer      Win - window system running
```

It can be seen from this table that in general the players performed very well. Measured skew is insignificant in the first four experiments, and drift is negligible in the first five. Except for the media player, jitter values are within reason, and in all cases few elements were discarded since sufficient resources were available. There are, however, some interesting observations that can be made.

First, note that the media player reports that it displayed the audio data with perfect synchrony. This is because it uses the audio codec clock as a master reference and assumes that the display of audio events cannot deviate from it, i.e. it does not generate timestamps corresponding to when the audio clicks are actually played. This also helps explain the reason for the non-negligible drift values it reports for the intra-stream video and inter-stream audio/video synchronization. Since the internal time stamps for the video events are generated by querying the system clock when the audio codec clock reports that display is complete, this drift reflects the fact that the system clock is about 51μs/s slow relative to the audio clock. This drift is an artifact of the way in which internal timestamps were generated, and hence the media player itself perceives no such drift.

Next, note that even in the best case, intra-stream audio jitter is high relative to the needs of stereo synchronization ([17]). This suggests that separate control of related audio streams is not feasible with this type of approach. In addition, all

performance are insufficient. Accurate appraisals of the quality of media synchronization cannot be achieved without an external reference.

In the future we will use this methodology and test environment to evaluate different mechanisms for media synchronization, as well as the effects that changes in the system have on the provided synchronization quality. Furthermore, this tool forms the foundation for an effort to identify and quantify the various components of media players that are the major contributors of display time variation.

Acknowledgements

We would like to thank David Lee who developed the internal logic of the CHAOS board, Marc Schneider who helped construct the test setup, and Jim Hanko and Jerry Wall for many insightful discussions. This work is supported in part by Sun Laboratories, an NSF Young Investigator Award, and an NSF Fellowship.

References

1. D. P. Anderson and G. Homsy, "A Continuous Media I/O Server and Its Synchronization Mechanism," *IEEE Computer*, 24(10), October 1991, pp. 51–57.

2. Bancomm, *bc700VME GPS Satellite Receiver Operation and Technical Manual*, October 1991.

3. D. C. A. Bulterman and R. van Liere, "Multimedia Synchronization and UNIX," in *LNCS*, 614, R. Herrtwich (Ed.), Springer-Verlag, 1992.

4. J. A. Boucher, Z. Yaar, E. J. Rubin, J. D. Palmer, and T. D. C. Little, "Design and Performance of a Multi-Stream MPEG-I System Layer Encoder/Player," in *IS&T/SPIE Symposium on Electronic Imaging Science & Technology*, San Jose, CA, February 1995.

5. J. Escobar, C. Partridge, and D. Deutsch, "Flow Synchronization Protocol," *IEEE/ACM Transactions on Networking*, 2(2), April 1994, pp. 111–121.

6. D. Ferrari, "Design and Applications of a Delay Jitter Control Scheme for Packet-Switching Internetworks," *Computer Communications*, 15(6), July/August 1992, pp. 367–373.

7. K. Jeffay, D. L. Stone, and F. D. Smith, "Kernel Support for Live Digital Audio and Video," in *Computer Communications*, 15(6), July/August 1992, pp. 388–395.

8. P. Leydekkers and B. Teunissen, "Synchronization of Multimedia Data Streams in Open Distributed Systems," in *LNCS*, 614, R. Herrtwich (Ed.), Springer-Verlag, 1992, pp. 94–104.

9. T. D. C. Little and F. Kao, "An Intermedia Skew Control System for Multimedia Data Presentation," in *LNCS*, 712, V. Rangan (Ed.), Springer-Verlag, 1993.

10. C. Nicolaou, "An Architecture for Real-Time Multimedia Communication Systems," *IEEE JSAC*, 8(3), April 1990, pp. 391–400.

11. J. Nieh, J. Hanko, J. D. Northcutt, and G. Wall, "SVR4 UNIX Scheduler Unacceptable for Multimedia Applications," in *LNCS*, 846, D. Shepherd, et al. (Eds.), Springer-Verlag, 1994.

12. J. D. Northcutt and E. M. Kuerner, "System Support for Time-Critical Applications," *Computer Communications*, 16(10), Oct. 1993, pp. 619–636.

13. S. Ramanathan and P. V. Rangan, "Adaptive Feedback Techniques for Synchronized Multimedia Retrieval over Integrated Networks," *IEEE/ACM Transactions on Networking*, 1(1), February 1993.

14. L. A. Rowe and B. C. Smith, "A Continuous Media Player," in *LNCS*, 712, V. Rangan (Ed.), Springer-Verlag, 1993.

15. H. Son and N. Agarwal, "Synchronization of Temporal Constructs in Distributed Multimedia Systems with Controlled Accuracy," *International Conference on Multimedia Computing and Systems*, May 1994, pp. 550–555.

16. R. Steinmetz, "Synchronization Properties in Multimedia Systems," *IEEE JSAC*, 8(3), April 1990, pp. 401–412.

17. R. Steinmetz and C. Engler, "Human Perception of Media Synchronization," *Technical Report 43.9310*, IBM European Networking Center, Heidelberg.

18. D. L. Stone and K. Jeffay, "An Empirical Study of Delay Jitter Management Policies," To appear in *Multimedia Systems*.

19. D. B. Sullivan, D. W. Allan, D. A. Howe and F. L. Walls, "Characterization of Clocks and Oscillators," *NIST Technical Note 1337*, March 1990.

as output. Instead, it only knows when the element was last under its control, and there can clearly be a substantial time difference between those two events.

Next, since the tested systems control the display time of media elements using a single time base (either the system clock or the audio clock) and since no external reference is utilized, the internally measured values for drift were negligible (except as noted above). However, most of the external measurements exhibit a significant amount of drift. For example, in the first four experiments the test generator references only the system clock to produce its output. Hence, the measured intra-stream drift values in these cases indicate that the system clock is about 100µs/s slow relative to real-time. Additional measurements of the system clock accuracy confirmed that this was indeed the case. Similarly, the other observed drift values indicate differences between other pairs of clocks (e.g. audio clock vs. real-time, frame buffer clock vs. real-time). In addition, the intra-stream video and inter-stream audio/video drift values reported internally by the media player in the last experiment do not correspond to the externally measured values. This is because the internally reported drift is due to differences between the audio and system clocks, whereas the external drift is due to differences between the audio clock and real-time. Drift can result whenever multiple time references are used, and these observations make it clear that without an external reference, a media delivery system has no means to characterize it and will operate under the false notion that it is correctly displaying media elements.

Other interesting features can be observed by comparing the internal and external values for jitter. Most significantly, it is clear from the tables that externally observed jitter is substantially worse than jitter reported by the systems under test. In addition, when the test system is moved into the time-sharing class in the third experiment, the external measurements do not reflect the drop in jitter quality that was reported internally. This can most easily be understood by examining intra-stream video synchronization for the first four experiments, which display video using the NTSC encoder. In these cases the dispersion of the jitter is around 9.6ms about the mean. The NTSC encoder outputs video frames with a period of about 16.7ms. When a toggle command arrives at the encoder, it will be deferred until the next period. Since the period is so large relative to the internally observed jitter values, it will effectively mask the large drop in jitter quality when the time-sharing class is utilized. The lack of discontinuities in the other experimental data can be attributed to similar effects. This is significant since it suggests that accounting for the clock rates of the output devices is more important over a long interval than scheduling decisions.

5 Conclusions

This work provides a means of determining the actual effectiveness of arbitrary media synchronization schemes. First, several forms of media synchronization were defined, and then a methodology was presented for measuring the degree of media synchronization which is achieved both within and among streams of media elements. The defined approach was validated by implementing a complete test environment for measuring the audio/video synchronization performance of media delivery systems. The measurements match the expected performance of the tested systems extremely well, and thus give us confidence in our experimental design. In addition, the results clearly indicate that internal assessments of synchronization

CHAPTER TWELVE

Authoring Systems

Dick C. A. Bulterman

Oratrix Development BV, The Netherlands

THE BASIC FACILITIES for storing, fetching, transmitting, and rendering multimedia data objects discussed elsewhere in this book are only meaningful when put in the context of *multimedia presentations* that are packaged for human consumption. This chapter presents several important papers in the literature that address the issues of creating and maintaining combinations of multimedia objects into presentations for viewers/readers/listeners. This area has been historically referred to as *authoring* multimedia.

Several factors need to be considered when creating a presentation that contains multimedia objects. First, the objects themselves need to be created. These could consist of a set of images or text files (both of which are examples of *discrete* media objects), or they could consist of a set of audio or video objects (both of which are examples of *continuous* media objects). Next, assuming a presentation contains more than one object, some specification must be developed that defines the spatial and temporal relationships among the objects in the presentation. At this point, the basics of a presentation are created, but the presentation may need to be augmented with navigation information in the form of hyperlinks or action graphs. Finally, the presentation needs to be packaged for distribution to the target audience: CD-ROMs and streamed presentations via the Internet are common examples.

Although creating effective media presentations often starts with the source material, this chapter does not deal directly with the creation of media objects. Many commercial packages exist that provide extensive support for importing, editing, and modifying discrete and continuous media objects. With the advent of digital cameras and digital audio recording equipment, the creation of multimedia objects for use in computer-based presentations is becoming a commonplace activity.

I start our overview of multimedia authoring by considering the structuring of the temporal and spatial information that define a presentation. There are many ways to do this: by writing a conventional program that accesses the media objects from the computer's file system (or via a multimedia object database) or by providing a declarative specification of the presentation you wish to create. The programming-based approach often leads to highly interactive presentations that can be fine-tuned to create dramatic effects. (This is the approach taken in highly successful commercial packages such as Macromedia Director [7].) The declarative approach—in which you define what you want a presentation to do, rather than defining how to do it—typically leads to more portable presentations: presentations that can be played on more than one player, or in more than one environment.

The development of declarative specifications must anticipate the features authors will require to construct a presentation. These include basic timing and synchronization relationships between objects. A work of fundamental importance in this area is the oft-cited discussion of 13 timing relationships by Allen [1]. Note that this paper is not included in this chapter because it is not really a multimedia paper—it is a paper from the field of artificial intelligence that found wide (but unintended) applicability among multimedia language designers.

Another aspect of a presentation design must consider is the spatial placement of objects relative to each other during the presentation. The method used to define such placement can be based on absolute positioning of objects or on a constraint model, in which you define relationships among objects that must hold during the time that these objects are active.

The specification of the spatial and temporal relationships within a presentation should be viewed in terms of the overall activation sequencing of a presentation. This sequencing can be linear (as in a video or audio object) or hyper-structured, where the high-level ordering of objects is determined by the user of the presentation. Hyper-structured multimedia (or *hypermedia*) provides a significant extension to the way in which information is consumed by the user. For example, it gives viewers the flexibility to determine which stories they want to see (and when) in a newscast, rather than having to accept whatever order and duration the news producer felt was important. Unfortunately, it also burdens the runtime environment significant challenges in obtaining, scheduling, and rendering media objects (especially in streaming media presentations).

Once the designers have compiled all the information about a presentation, they must draw it together into a specification that can be processed by a multimedia player. Such a specification can be created by a text editor or a special-purpose authoring tool. The goal of an authoring tool is to provide extra value to the creative process by simplifying or structuring the authoring process, managing the assets included in the presentation or providing a layer of abstraction between the syntax of a particular low-level encoding language and the author's high-level view of the presentation. Authoring systems can also support the process by simulating the resource needs of the presentation. This is especially important for networked multimedia, where key constraints, including network bandwidth, end-user characteristics, and server loading, are not static properties known at time of authoring but dynamic properties only available at runtime.

OVERVIEW OF PAPERS

This chapter contains six papers that illustrate the approaches that have had significant impact in the general area of authoring systems.

I start with two papers on languages for describing the hypermedia structure of presentations.

The first is "The Amsterdam Hypermedia Model," by L. Hardman, D.C.A. Bulterman, and G. van Rossum. The Amsterdam Hypermedia Model was developed in response to the need for combining basic hypertext technology (as represented by the Dexter Hypertext Model [2]) and spatial and temporal layout for presentations (as represented by the CMIF environment [3]), and for combining these into a unified hypermedia model. The second article, "HDM—A model-based approach to hypertext design," by F. Gazotto, P. Paolini, and D. Schwabe, describes an alternative approach to structuring hypermedia. The main contribution of this article is the specification of a hyper-structuring model that defines links outside of the source encoding. This allows different semantic models to be associated with one syntactic information base. The work on the HDM is also significant because it was used as the basis of a wide range of practical studies, some of which are discussed in the article.

The remaining papers in this chapter define tools and techniques for addressing detailed aspects of a presentation's construction. "Automatic temporal layout mechanisms," by M. C. Buchanan and P. T. Zellweger, looks at analytical tools for sequencing objects in a presentation based on their resource requirements and the capabilities of the presentation execution environment. The historical significance of this paper is its view of presenting multimedia in the pre-Web era: It concentrates on algorithms for determining local rather than network-based resource use. This work is complimented by the paper "GRiNS: A graphical interface for creating and playing SMIL documents," by D.C.A. Bulterman and colleagues, which contains the first description of an environment for building network multimedia presentations based on the Structured Multimedia Integration Language (SMIL) [4]. This paper illustrates how the emphasis in multimedia authoring research has shifted to the user-interface aspects of presentation design.

The final two papers consider techniques for high-level and low-level document creation. "Multiviews interfaces multimedia authoring environments," by M. Jourdan, C. Roisin, and L. Tardif, shows how a presentation can be built based on a system of constraints among objects, constraints that can be analyzed via a number of separate document views. The last paper, "A multimedia system for authoring motion pictures," by R. Baecker and colleagues, gives a constructionist view of defining and combining objects for creating linear presentations.

OTHER WORKS AND FUTURE DIRECTIONS

Each of the papers selected for this section illustrates a particular aspect of presentation design, from abstract modeling to individual presentation composition. All of the papers offer insights of a lasting value for users and designers of new tools and techniques. Of course, given the constraints of a book of this type, this chapter makes no pretense of conveying every aspect of this field.

I have not included papers on scripting and programming-based approaches, since these techniques add relatively little to the development of new insights into creating and manipulating information. Readers who are interested in a survey of scripting approaches should consult the overview by Jourdan, Layaidan, and Roisin [5].

I also do not provide a detailed description of commercial authoring systems. Many of these systems make use of proprietary formats that are not extensible, or they are geared to solve a relatively narrow set of user applications. For a representative set of solutions, readers are directed to the Web sites of companies such as Adobe [6], Macromedia [7], Microsoft [8], and RealNetworks [9]. It is interesting to note that none of the dominant commercial systems has yet to capitalize on the concepts of generalized hypermedia documents as discussed in the Ansterdam Hypermedia Model or HDM. Even the extremely successful and popular HTML document architecture makes only minimal use of the concepts and facilities of generalized links and anchors, even though the intellectual framework of these facilities has been available since 1945 in the seminal work of Bush [10].

After a burst of activity in the mid-1990s, the general topic of presentation authoring has not enjoyed a great deal of attention in the research literature. This is due, in part, to the significant implementation burden of such systems, but it is also because the proliferation of the Internet has yet to result in significant use of multimedia objects, especially for complex presentations. The lack of sufficient and consistent end-to-end bandwidth has resulted in postage-stamp presentations, with little variety, quality, or excitement. It seems, however, that networked multimedia is about to enter a new era. The availability of high bandwidth DSL and cable networks, combined with the emergence of relatively low bandwidth wireless environments has created a multitier delivery environment in which the inherent complexity of presentations will increase. The low end of the bandwidth spectrum will be rich enough to allow simple slideshows or a single-stream video, but these presentations will not be compelling enough to satisfy users of higher bandwidth connections. Rather than being able to continue with a 'one size fits all' content model, authors will be forced to think about structural, logical, and semantic relationships among data objects, and how these relate to a heterogeneous presentation environment. In this context, the models, technologies, and techniques presented in the articles in this chapter provide a sound basis for the future development of (networked) multimedia.

REFERENCES

[1] J. F. Allen, "Maintaining knowledge about temporal intervals" *Communications of the ACM* 26, no. 11 (Nov 1983): 832–43.

[2] F. Halasz and M. Schwartz, "The Dexter Hypertext Reference Model," *Communications of the ACM* 37, no. 2 (1994): 30–9.

[3] D.C.A. Bulterman, "Specification and support of adaptable networked multimedia," *Multimedia Systems* 1, no. 2 (1995): 68–76.

[4] World Wide Web Consortium, Synchronized Multimedia Integration Language (SMIL) http://www.w3.org/AudioVideo/, 2000.

[5] M. Jourdan, N. Layaida, and C. Roisin, *A Survey on Authoring Techniques for Temporal Scenarios of Multimedia Documents/Handbook of Internet and Multimedia Systems and Applications, Part 1: Tools and Standards* (London: CRC Press, 1998).

[6] Adobe Systems, Inc., "An overview of scalable vector graphics," http://www.adobe.com/svg/tutorial/, 2000.

[7] Macromedia, Inc., Director 8 product information, http://www.macromedia.com/software/director/, 2000.

[8] Microsoft Corporation, Windows Media Tools product information, http://www.microsoft.com/windows/windows-media/, 2000

[9] RealNetworks, Inc., Slideshow authoring tool product information, http://www.real.com/products/slideshowplus/, 2000.

[10] V. Bush, "As we may think," *Atlantic Monthly* 176, no. 1 (July 1945): 101–08.

ADDING

Time

AND

Context

TO THE DEXTER MODEL

LYNDA HARDMAN

DICK C.A. BULTERMAN

GUIDO VAN ROSSUM

THE AMSTERDAM
HYPERMEDIA MODEL:

On the surface, hypermedia is a simple and natural extension of multimedia and hypertext: multimedia provides a richness in data types that facilitates flexibility in expressing information, while hypertext provides a control structure that supports an elegant way of navigating through this data in a content-based manner. Unfortunately, the concepts that apply to collections of static information do not all translate well to complex collections of dynamic information. What does it mean, for example, to follow a link in a hypermedia presentation when the source node consists of nonpersistent data? Does the source presentation freeze, does it go away, do parts of it go away? Similarly, how should the synchronization relationships within and among elements in a composite component be defined? Is this part of the hypermedia model or part of a data storage or data presentation model? In our view, a general hypermedia model needs to be able to specify both the conventional link-based navigation elements of hypertext and the complex timing and presentation relationships found in multimedia presentations. Such a model is presented here.

Intuitively, support for hypermedia can be defined by taking the Dexter Hypertext Reference Model [7, 8], and augmenting it with multimedia data types within its storage layer. The Dexter model provides a facility for creating links within a document, with the links being anchored inside document components. The notions of links, anchors and components are basic to hypertext systems, and since they are not tied to any particular type of implementation or to any particular type of data, integrating them into a hypermedia system would seem to be a straightforward task. (Note that this does not make the task easy: finding a general way to indicate the presence of a link in a dynamic data, or providing means of "clicking" a portion of video or audio, remain difficult and unsolved problems.) Although such a "marriage of convenience" can provide immediate results, the underlying control assumptions of the Dexter model make it unsuitable for describing and supporting generalized hypermedia documents.[1] In particular, this approach cannot adequately support

complex temporal relationships among data items, specifications that support high-level presentation semantics, or a notion of "information context" that specifies global behavior when a link is followed—all elements that are of fundamental importance in supporting hypermedia.

This article presents the Amsterdam Hypermedia Model (AHM), a general framework that can be used to describe the basic constructs and actions that are common to a wide range of hypermedia systems. We present the AHM in the context of the Dexter model's hypertext technology and terminology. We do this because hypertext is—in the time scale of information technology—a relatively mature discipline, with a well-defined model of general system behavior. The AHM is developed as an extension to the Dexter model in order to capitalize on its contributions to understanding hypertext systems. (In particular, the Dexter model allows the composition of hierarchical structures, the specification of links between components, and, through the

use of anchors, allows data-dependent information to be recorded separately from the hyperstructure.) The AHM extends the Dexter model by adding to it the notions of time, high-level presentation attributes and link context. A portion of this extension is based on the basic aspects of the CMIF multimedia document model [3, 4]. By combining the relevant aspects of the Dexter and CMIF models, we are able to take the existing notions of hypertext presentations and add to these the implementation-independent behavior model of multimedia found in CMIF.

We start our consideration of hypermedia systems with a discussion of the basic requirements for a hypermedia model. We then present the AHM, considering both the general model structure and its implementation implications. We conclude with a discussion of the current state of our hypermedia implementation experiments. (Throughout our discussion, the body of this article will refer to a running example of a hypermedia presentation; this example is described in the sidebar "A Hypermedia Example.")

Requirements for Describing Hypermedia

The use of dynamic media is not unique to multimedia systems. The inclusion of time-based information (such as audio or video data) can also be supported within conventional

---

[1]We use the following conventions throughout this article to describe hypermedia: a *document* is a complete collection of related *components*. Each component can be built recursively from other components or from primitive *data elements* of various types, also called *entities*. A *presentation* is the active form of a document. In normal use, the terms document and presentation are nearly interchangeable, as are (to a lesser extent) entity and component. Generally, context should clarify usage.

hypertext. While rudimentary support for "time" is not difficult to retrofit into existing systems, the development of a more general model for managing the elements in a presentation will be required, since more applications make use of loosely coupled collections of dynamic and static objects fetched from potentially distributed sources, all of which need to be synchronized in some nontrivial manner. To put the requirements of such a generalized model into context, a brief overview of the defining characteristics of hypertext, multimedia and hypermedia is given followed by the requirements for modeling time, links (and link context), and global presentation semantics in a hypermedia.

Hypertext, Multimedia and Hypermedia

Figure 1 provides a high-level review of the essential aspects of the hypertext, multimedia and hypermedia models. In Figure 1a, a hypertext is modeled as a network of components related through a set of links anchored in source and destination components. While various implementations of hypertext may impose different constraints on the internal structure of a component or the exact nature of a link/anchor set, all systems support the notion of "visiting" a component for a user-determined amount of time, with that visit either terminated by the end of the application or interrupted/replaced/augmented by following a link to one or more other components. Note that the meaning of visiting a component—that is, the visual effects displayed to the user in terms of pieces of text, graphics, sounds, and so forth—is usually considered an internal property of the data.

Figure 1b illustrates a generic multimedia presentation. Like Figure 1a, the presentation is made up of a collection of components. Unlike Figure 1a, the components are meant to be presented in some author-defined relative order. The existence of such an ordering relationship depends on an explicit notion of time in the model. While the user still may have control over the selection of components to be visited, the components selected and presented can change

without direct user intervention because of this notion of time. (That is, the model not only defines the components of the presentation, but it also defines an ordering relationship that specifies when the components are presented relative to one another.)

Multimedia systems typically support two types of navigation facilities that provide a user with control over the presentation. One method adjusts the current time reference in a presentation, indicated by the heavy horizontal line in Figure 1b; by using a control interface similar to that of an audiocassette or compact disc player, the user can stop/start/fast-forward/rewind (and sometimes search through) the presentation. The second—and less common—navigation type is similar to a rudimentary hypertext link, indicated by the anchor and link arrow in the figure. Here, following the link would bring the user to the time point that is indicated by the dotted line in the illustration. This is essentially equivalent to a fast-forward operation, except that the 'stop point' is defined by the document author rather than by the user.

Figure 1c gives a high-level description of one way of combining hypertext and multimedia: by having each component of the hypertext model be a self-contained multimedia presentation. This model addresses two sets of concerns: those that relate to the hyperstructured navigation through the document, and those that relate to the multimedia presentation of information. For many simple forms of hypermedia support, the sketch in Figure 1c presents an adequate model of system behavior. As we will see, however, this view limits the flexibility of the author in defining a presentation and the user in viewing one.

Temporal Information

In general, a hypermedia model should be able to specify how individual pieces of information relate to one another at any level that a document author feels appropriate. This level would depend on the way the data was stored and on the presentation/navigation abilities of the runtime systems available to users. The

specification of timing constraints within a document thus depends on the nature of the underlying data elements and on the way these can be combined for presentation. The internal structure of data will be beyond the scope of the hypermedia model, but the composition of components remains central to the model.

In conventional hypertext, time is addressed indirectly, often in terms of a presentation's behavior as it follows a hypertext link. Such an approach is unfortunate because it binds together two separate aspects of a presentation. Instead, we partition the temporal relationships among data items in two broad classes: those related to the identification of the components that are to be presented together, and those that relate to the relative order in which these components are presented. We call these classes *collection* and *synchronization*. At a coarse level, the Dexter model provides support for collection via the hierarchical definition components. As is illustrated in Figure 2, Dexter's composite components can be used to collect a set of atomic components that are to be presented together. (In terms of the Amsterdam tour example described in the sidebar "A Hypermedia Example," we could define a composite component that consisted of the various data entities that make up each screen.) Since the definition of the composite does not provide a mechanism for specifying any relative timing relationships among the entities, however, this approach is not sufficiently rich for general use. The problem to be overcome is that, once collected, the components need to be synchronized, typically both *within* and *across* components. Such synchronization can be based on structural information—that is, by manipulating data representations within components—or it can be based on the content of a component.

Consider the lower-left screen in the Amsterdam tour example. This view of street musicians can be defined as a (possibly structured) collection of files/objects/database entries that make up the components in the screen. These elements could be synchronized based on the author's

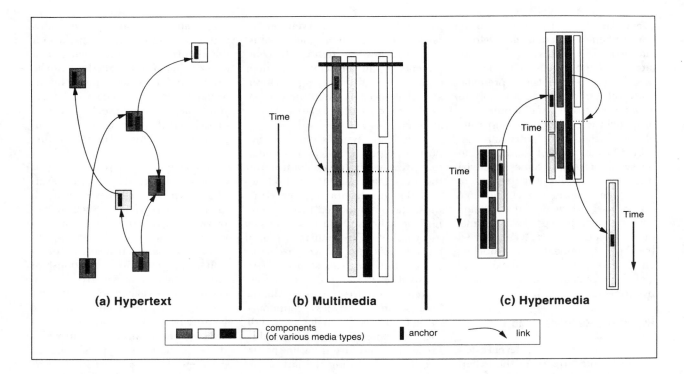

(a) Hypertext   **(b) Multimedia**   **(c) Hypermedia**

components (of various media types)   anchor   link

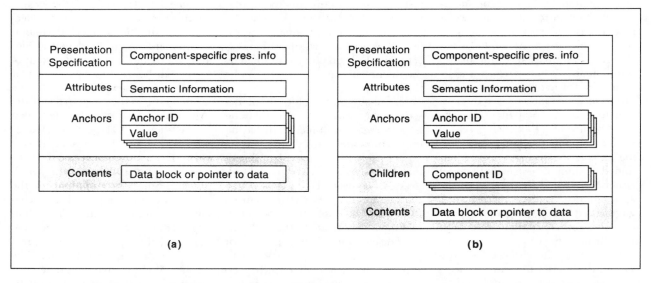

(a)   (b)

(or authoring system's) knowledge of the sample and frame rates of each item. They could also be synchronized in a content-based manner, such as specifying that the two elements needed to end at the same time, or by specifying that a cymbal crash in the soundtrack needed to be synchronized with the associated event in the video segment.

There are several ways to approach the problems of collection and synchronization within hypermedia. Three general strategies are shown in Figure 3: we call these the *hidden structure*, the *separate structure* and the *composite structure* approaches.

Hidden structure approach. The most basic (and most prevalent) way to handle time-based data in a hypertext context is to place all the data—and all the data interpretation—inside the content portion of a component. In Dexter terms, this solution pushes multimedia information into the within-component layer. Collection (in terms of defining a set of entities that are to be shown at the same time) is solved by having a sin-

Figure 1. Hypertext, multimedia and hypermedia

Figure 2. Dexter model atomic (a) and composite (b) components

A Hypermedia Example

Hypermedia presentations can take many shapes and forms. They can be models of flexibility, enabling the user to pick and choose among the data items presented, or they may be rigidly structured presentations that mimic—perhaps too closely—broadcast television, where the user has a binary interaction option: turn it on or turn it off.

One form of a multimedia presentation is depicted in Figure A. The three "screens" shown in Figure A make up part of a tour of Amsterdam. Each screen is divided into a number of regions, with each region holding a simple or composite stream of multimedia data. Some of the regions have data containing anchors (the anchors are indicated by dotted lines around the regions).

A general table-of-contents portion of the presentation containing five regions appears in the top screen: one title region at the top-left of the screen (in this case saying "Welcome to Amsterdam"), a logo-region (containing the CWI logo), a video region (shown displaying one frame of a video on a canal house in the city), a text frame displaying a set of paragraphs on the nature of the demo, and an audio track containing supplemental information. The entire logo region and a portion of the text region contain visual buttons associated with links to other portions of the presentation. Following the link from the

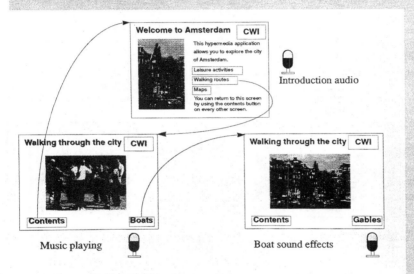

Figure A. An example hypermedia presentation

logo region, for example, will give the reader some background information on the institute where this video was created.

The lower-left screen shows a portion of the "walking tour" section of the presentation, showing a collection of street musicians entertaining commuters at the city's central railway station. This screen has a title region, a video region, an audio region and two navigation regions. One navigation button will return the user to the upper display, while the other allows a user to jump to a part of the walking tour that describes the types of boats one is likely to see in the canals. The screen at lower right is structured similarly to that at left, except that the contents of several of the regions have been changed: a new video atomic component has been used (to show boats on the canals), a new sound track is used (with boat sound effects and commentary), and a *Gables* button replaces the *Boats* button.

The presentation outlined here could have been constructed with a number of multimedia authoring systems, using a variety of underlying architectures. From a hypermedia perspective, there are a number of information structuring issues that need to be considered in describing presentations of this type. These issues, which include the logical and structural relationships of screens to one another, are discussed in the body of this article.

gle link target that uses internal techniques to define relative entity synchronization. This approach does not require a basic change in the hypertext model. It can lead to effective presentations and even a limited amount of combination of data items within a component. The disadvantage of this approach is that it does not scale well to more complex multimedia data combinations.

The structure shown in Figure 3a, for example, consists of eight pieces of information of four media types. Not all the pieces start at the same time—meaning that a sophisticated mechanism must exist to control presentation of the component. This control can be embedded in the definition of the data (such as is used in systems that take data from a single source, like a CD-ROM format [16]), or by expressing complex relationships among multimedia items that are subsequently accessed as a single entity [2]. Both of these approaches have interesting applications, but they do not extend easily to a more general case in which data is distributed over several file servers and combined at run time (or where information is stored across a collection of distributed multimedia databases). In all cases, the use of a complex composite component structure is impossible within the Dexter framework, since time is not explicitly considered in the model.

Separate structure approach. The opposite of the hidden structure approach is to define each piece of multimedia information as a separate block. Collection can be supported using a multitarget link, allowing each component to be activated when the link was followed. In terms of our Amsterdam tour example, this would mean that the top-middle picture would be made up as the target of a link containing five separate objects. When this link was selected, the run-time system would start the objects simultaneously. (Such an approach is similar to that taken by the Intermedia project [15].) While collection can be supported in this way, synchronization becomes a significant problem: in a generalized model, not all components can be expected to start at exactly the same instant. Figure 3b illustrates a combination of compo-

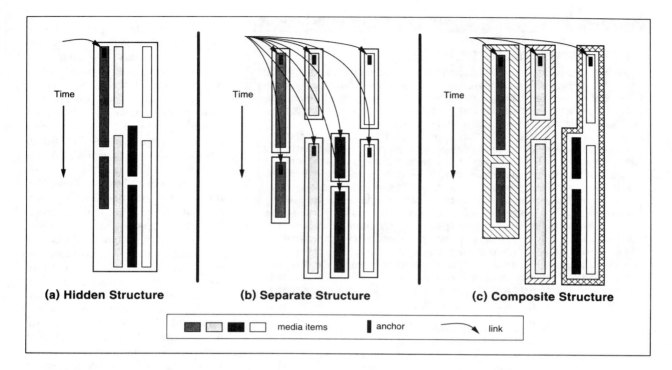

(a) Hidden Structure   **(b) Separate Structure**   **(c) Composite Structure**

media items   anchor   link

nents that all need to be activated after a link is taken, but in which the starting times are not coincident. Clearly, some method is required to state when each component should start relative to the others. One solution is to place relative timing information into the link structure, as is done in Harmony [5] and Videobook [13]. As with the Intermedia approach, this can be useful for specifying the interaction of a limited number of nodes, but it requires the author to define and maintain information in links that combine collection, synchronization and navigation control into a single construct. This increases authoring and maintenance complexity because a great number of links will need to be created and maintained by the authoring software. These approaches also have the disadvantage that the content association among components is lost, and that any user selectivity or customization of a presentation requires complex user-interface software.

Composite structure approach. A compromise solution to the problem of collecting components and synchronizing pieces is shown in Figure 3c. Here, several elements have been grouped into three composite components, one of which hides internal synchronization and collection of two

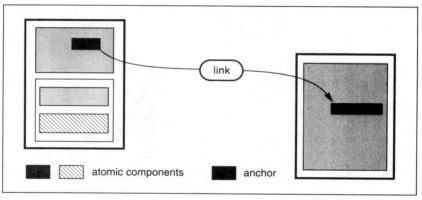

atomic components   anchor

media types and two of which manage data of a single media type. Collection is less complex than in the separate structure approach, and the synchronization problem is also reduced by internalizing any complex relationships. While direct application of such an approach may prove adequate for simple applications, it does not solve the general problem of specifying the time-based relationships within the hypertext model: it simply reduces the problem to a number of subproblems, each solved by one of the two approaches described in the two preceding paragraphs. Grouping of components is a useful way of specifying collecting structured components *if* this is accompanied by a well-developed notion of time within the general

Figure 3. Time and structuring issues

Figure 4. Dexter link components

model, as will be discussed in the following subsection.

Links in Hypermedia

Links are perhaps the most fundamental notion of hypertext systems. While links have an influence on both the order of the presentation and the components displayed simultaneously, these temporal aspects do not represent the central nature of the link. Instead, the function of the link should be to define a logical navigation mechanism in a document.

The use of links within the Dexter model is illustrated in Figure 4. Here we see a link that has its source in a composite component and its destination in an atomic component. One of the basic aspects of a link is that it defines a traversal from one component to another. The notion of a link *within* a component, however, presents a fundamental problem not considered within the Dexter model. Such a link may be used inside a long, complex component as a means of fast-forwarding through the data. (This is how it is used in Figure 1b.) Another use may be to impose a mechanism for allowing some elements of a component to persist while others change when a link is followed.

For conventional text-based systems, the use of a link as an intra-component structure is not typically considered within the context of a general model, since blocks of text can be broken into arbitrarily small collections of characters (such as books, chapters, sections, paragraphs, sentences, clauses, words, and letters). This allows new components to be created whenever a link is defined by dividing an existing component at some "convenient" boundary. (Specification of such a boundary is supported by the Dexter anchoring mechanism, which allows a general method for specifying offsets into components.) This approach works well within hypertext systems because the logical element making up the bulk of the data—the character—is closely associated with the structural element used to define the data itself, the byte. It is also aided by the relationship between two successive blocks of characters not being typically constrained by a fixed timing relationship. In multimedia systems, the association of links with and within components is considerably more complex. Data items often cannot be easily broken apart or indexed in a convenient manner. For example, dividing a video fragment into a scene-shot-frame hierarchy is possible, but the relationship of content to representation is less clean than in hypertext systems. (For films, scenes and shots are generally content-based, while frames are representation-based.) If a single video sequence is to be broken apart to support a link, a complex editing and presentation process would be necessary to ensure continuity—a process that would depend on how information is stored and accessed, as well as on the content of the data.

A second, and more fundamental problem with extending hypertext links to hypermedia is that current hypertext systems do not clearly define the notion of how much information the reader leaves when following a link. Most systems present a single hypertext node which is either replaced by the destination information, or is left on the screen while another window is created for the destination information (e.g., Intermedia [15]). There is, however, no way of choosing between these options—the choice is determined by the destination of the link. Having an either-or model is useful for text (where most readers can only focus their attention on one block of text at a time), but it is less useful for multimedia presentations, where a user can follow a link from one block to another while continuing to listen to a spoken commentary or watch a video presentation. In hypermedia, it is important that the model define a control framework so the user can specify the behavior that is appropriate to the needs of the application.

In order to address this problem, a method needs to be defined that allows portions of a component to be treated as minicomponents for linking purposes, or a new construct needs to be added to support more generalized linking behavior in hypermedia. Our solution to this problem is to introduce the notion of a *link context.*

High-Level Presentation Specification Attributes

The preceding topics have dealt with concepts that are related directly to the presentation of complex combinations of time-based and static data. Now we consider the requirements for managing the presentation of each type of data individually. We introduce the problem by way of example, once again considering the description of the Amsterdam tour presented in the sidebar "A Hypermedia Example."

Each of the screens of the Amsterdam tour uses a collection of output media, including audio, video, and several forms of text. Each screen contains unique data elements, but all screens have elements that share a common set of attributes for a particular data type used during one instance of the presentation. Consider the audio output used throughout the presentation: in each screen, different audio data sets will be used, but each screen will share attributes such as volume or tone-quality settings. Note that some of these attributes will depend on the workstation presenting the information, such as the audio quality of the local devices or the ability to support stereo/mono output. Other attributes may depend on the preferences of a particular viewer/listener to the presentation, such as the volume level of the output. Since both of these types of attributes would be defined on a per-presentation basis, not a per-screen basis, a mechanism should exist that allows their global definition.

Just as word processors allow the definition of global styles for different structures (for example, section heading or paragraph body), hypermedia documents require a higher-level way of specifying presentation information than at the per-component level. Such attributes would ensure the audio volume would not need to be reset by the user for each screen opened, or that the system's audio drivers would not need to be reinitialized for every data block sent to a device. Such global attributes would not be attached to a single component, but would instead be associated with a class of media/information types. The attribute definitions could consist of default set-

CMIFed—An AHM-Based Authoring Environment

CMIFed is an authoring and presentation environment for hypermedia documents based on the AHM [18]. CMIFed uses a hierarchy structure to represent the document; this is shown in Figure B, part (a). The use of a hierarchical document structure enables presentations to be designed where persistent objects, such as titles and logos, need to be placed only once and are retained on the screen throughout the scene (in fact, for the duration of the structure within which they are defined). This has the result that authoring work is reduced through the use of the hierarchy—items that remain for a greater part of the presentation can be defined in the higher levels of the structure.

There are two main ways of viewing a CMIF document when authoring—the hierarchy view and the channel view. The hierarchy view shows the document as a structured collection of components that are played in series or in parallel. The channel view displays the atomic components mapped onto abstract channels; it is presented in the form of a presentation time line, showing the synchronization information. A document, once created, can be presented by the CMIFed player, which maps the abstract channels to real devices based on user preference and system capabilities.

The hierarchy view. The purpose of the hierarchy view is to display and manipulate the structure of a hypermedia presentation. The hierarchical structure of the presentation is represented in the hierarchy view as an embedded block structure, shown in Figure B, part (b). Here, the rectangles enclosing the boxes represent the hierarchical structuring of the document. The outermost rectangle is the root of the tree. Components next to each other are started in parallel (unless otherwise constrained by explicit synchronization arcs), while components displayed higher in the diagram are activated before those displayed lower in the diagram.

A presentation is created by defining the structure of the presentation and assigning atomic components to the structure. Timing information is deduced from the hierarchical structure and the durations of the components within the structure. (Fine-grained timing constraints can be added in the channel view.) When a component has no explicit duration, as in a text item, it is presented for the duration of its parent. The author can navigate around the hierarchical structure and zoom in on nested structures. This not only reduces the screen space required for representing the structure, but gives a focused view on any part of the structure. Within the hierarchy view, the author can select any atomic or composite component and cut, copy or paste it, or interrogate it for more information, such as component name, data file referred to, channel used, explicit duration, comment, highlight color. An external editor can be called up to edit the data. The editing program invoked in this way depends on the media type and the choice of editor is configurable. CMIFed can read most common data formats and can be easily extended to support more.

The channel view. The channel view, Figure B, part (c), shows a transformation of the hierarchy view in terms of abstract media channels. This view is presented as a time line, with placement determined automatically by CMIFed-based on information in each component definition. The use of synchronization arcs allows fine-grained timing constraints to be specified between and among groups of components. The atomic components making up the presentation are displayed in their own channel along with their precise durations and timing relationships. If the author changes the timing in any part of the presentation, via any of the views, the channel view is updated immediately to reflect this.

The player. The CMIFed player interprets a hypermedia document and plays the presentation on the available hardware. The player allows the user to select which channels should be played, for example to select one of a number of voice-overs in different languages, as in Figure 8. The player is closely integrated with the hierarchy and channel views

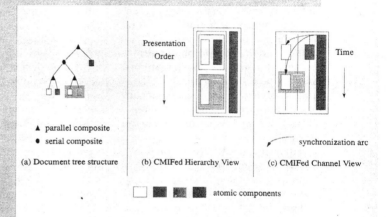

Figure B. CMIFed hierarchy and channel views

and allows the author to play a selection from the hierarchy view (atomic or composite component) or the channel view (atomic component). This facility allows the previewing of a small section of the presentation without having to start at the beginning of a long sequence.

When the system has sufficient time it looks ahead and fetches data that will be needed in the next part of the presentation. The stages of this pre-arming are shown by highlighting the atomic components in different colors in the channel view.

Implementation. CMIFed is implemented in Python [17], a high-level interpreted, extensible object-oriented prototyping language. The language has a number of practical advantages, in particular it has a good interface to the graphics facilities and user-interface toolkit on the initial target machine (the SGI Indigo workstation). Python's extensibility has been used to efficiently handle the data formats and I/O devices needed for audio, image and video processing without losing the advantages of using a very high-level language (e.g., powerful string-handling operations, shorter and clearer code, and a much faster edit-run cycle).

tings that could be overridden when necessary, or as a set of basic attributes that could be augmented on a component-by-component basis.

One motivation for providing such attributes is to support users accessing documents by allowing preference to be set once instead of at each data reference. Another is to be able to define documents having a measure of portability by abstracting presentation information that may be machine-dependent from an individual component. Although such global attributes are not considered directly in the Dexter model, they do capture some of the intent of separating presentation information for data within a component. The mechanism we use to manipulate these attributes is the CMIF *channel*, which we will consider in detail.

Amsterdam Hypermedia Model

The AHM was developed to provide a comprehensive basis for combined multimedia and hypermedia research. The model was defined by combining the Dexter hypertext model with the CMIF multimedia model and adding extensions to support those requirements of hypermedia that were left unaddressed. The AHM has been used to define the information model in CMIFed authoring/player environment (see the sidebar "CMIFed—An AHM-Based Authoring Environment"), which has been used to create several hypermedia applications.

AHM Components

Figure 5 shows the conceptual data structure for a) atomic and b) composite components. (The names and general structure of these components reflect the AHM's Dexter heritage; also see Figure 2.) The atomic component, shown in Figure 5a, contains metainformation that refers to a particular data block, while the composite component defines such information for a collection of atomic or composite blocks. Note that the composite component does not contain support for data in the composite's definition—data can only be referenced via an atomic component. This has three advantages over the Dexter approach. First, it localizes information on timing and presenta-

tion to an atomic component and concentrates information on presentation structure to the composite component; this should ease the task of document maintenance. Second, it promotes reusability of data by forcing all items to be separately maintained. Finally, it more closely models the way the bulk of multimedia information will be stored: in external databases or file systems.[2]

AHM atomic components, like their Dexter counterparts, contain presentation information, component attributes, link anchor information and a contents field. The significant addition to the atomic block is an expanded presentation information section. A portion of this expanded information is used to model time-related aspects of the block, while others are used to encode high-level presentation attributes.

The AHM composite component includes several items not found in the Dexter model. The principal change is that the composite component serves a more specific role in the AHM than in typical hypertext systems: the composite component is used to build a presentation structure rather than to simply collect related components for navigational purposes. The composite component's presentation attributes contain component-specific information but no duration value: these can be obtained from the collection of atomic components used by the composite. Instead, the presentation specification contains a collection of *synchronization arcs*, which are structures that define fine-grained relative ordering information. (Synchronization arcs are defined later.) The anchor and attribute sections of the AHM are essentially the same as those in Dexter, except for a dereferencing of anchors to a list of <Component ID, Anchor ID> pairs. The specification of the components of the composite has been expanded to include timing offsets among the children and a *composite type* attribute. The type of a composite can be either parallel or choice; parallel composite components display all of their component

parts, while choice composites will display at most one of their children. (The selection mechanism is implemented by the run-time support environment.) As noted, the composite component does not include any data directly.

Temporal Relations

The principal mechanism for supporting temporal relationships among entities is the composite component. The definition of the composite supports collection via a list of child components, each of which may be a composite or atomic component. Synchronization among components is supported in two ways: one for coarse-grained synchronization and the other for fine-grained synchronization. Coarse-grained synchronization consists of constraints defined between the children of a composite component, such as the relative starting time of each child within the composite; this information is given explicitly with the child definition. Fine-grained synchronization consists of constraints among either sibling or nonsibling (nested) children within the composite component; these constraints are specified using synchronization arcs. Note that additional synchronization is possible within the definition of an atomic component's data; this is not considered part of the hypermedia model, but is instead a characteristic of the data object.

Figure 6 summarizes the timing control within the AHM. It shows three composite components (a, b, and c), and eight atomic components. Each of the atomic and embedded composite components has a start time offset, represented by the line from the upper-left of the composite definition. (Note: the length has been exaggerated for purposes of clarity.) This offset gives the relative start time of each component. Each atomic component contains a duration attribute (or an estimate, for synthesized data); this duration is not shown in the figure. Two synchronization arcs are shown in the figure, the meanings of which are discussed in the following paragraph. Figure 6 is a crude approximation of the top screen in our Amsterdam tour example: component *a* represents the

---

[2]Individual implementations may choose to support small amounts of in-line data as an optimization; our system allows this for text blocks.

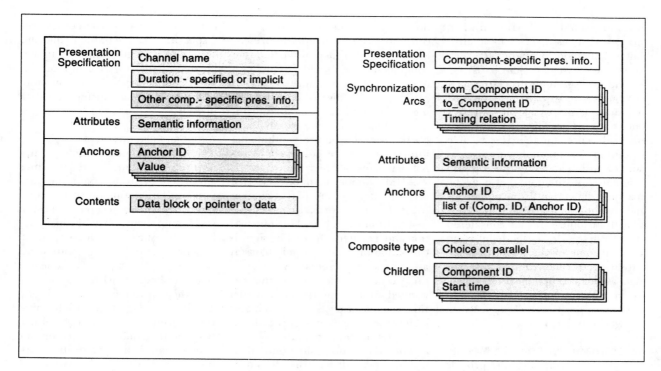

Presentation Specification	Channel name
	Duration - specified or implicit
	Other comp.- specific pres. info.
Attributes	Semantic information
Anchors	Anchor ID
	Value
Contents	Data block or pointer to data

Presentation Specification	Component-specific pres. info.
Synchronization Arcs	from_Component ID
	to_Component ID
	Timing relation
Attributes	Semantic information
Anchors	Anchor ID
	list of (Comp. ID, Anchor ID)
Composite type	Choice or parallel
Children	Component ID
	Start time

screen as seen by the user, which is made up of two top-level atomic items and one composite. The top-level atomic items of *a* represent the CWI logo and a headline text block containing "Welcome to Amsterdam." The composite *b* contains two sequential audio tracks giving an introduction to the tour, a video showing parts of the city, and a text block containing instructions and three anchors. The composite *c* contains information about our institute. (Note that the sequencing within the composite *b* depends on the ability to separately schedule events and then to constrain aspects of their run-time behavior.)

The synchronization arc (or *sync arc*) allows an author to specify fine-grained synchronization information among components [3]. It is **not** used as a navigation aid or as a type of link. It is a constraint that the run-time system should support on the behavior of two or more components. The sync arc is a construct that provides a flexible mechanism for establishing relationships in a multimedia system. Figure 7 shows the basic elements of a sync arc in detail. The end-point component IDs are given, as is the timing relation to be supported. The timing relation is given in terms of a synchronization

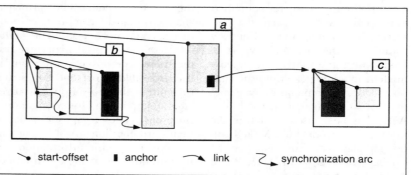

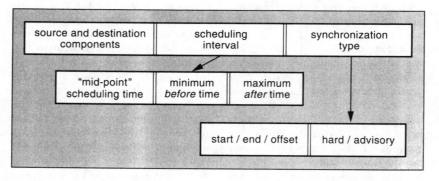

Figure 5. Amsterdam Hypermedia Model (AHM)

Figure 6. AHM components and timing relations

Figure 7. AHM synchronization

interval, containing a target time and acceptable deviations, and a synchronization type. The type consists of an indication of whether the interval is relative to the start or end of the component, or whether it is an offset from the start. The second portion of the type is an indication of whether the relationship must be met or if it is simply an advisory relationship. (If a *hard* relationship cannot be supported by the run-time system, an error condition exists; if an *advisory* relationship cannot be met, the application will keep running; the use of interval-based synchronization gives the run-time environment a measure of flexibility in supporting the relationship.) In terms of Figure 6, the intracomponent sync arc shown may define a requirement that the second audio block needs to start in time for both the audio and video components to end together, while the intercomponent sync arc can be used to ensure that two text blocks remain on the screen for an equal duration.

The primary advantage of the way that AHM specifies temporal relationships is that a clear separation is made among the collection of components that are to be shown together, the relative ordering of those objects and the detailed timing constraints that can exist during the presentation of a collection of objects.

AHM Link Context
The temporal aspects of the AHM component architecture provide a convenient method of grouping and synchronizing related objects. Composite components do not, however, provide information on how each component behaves when a link is followed out of that component or within a composite component. In order to describe this type of behavior, the AHM defines the notion of a *link context*. A context is a (typically composite) component that contains a collection of composite or atomic components affected by a linking operation. (While the Dexter model already allows the specification of composite components with a link, these are not used explicitly to define a context.) A *source context* for a link is that part of a hypermedia presentation affected by initiating a link, and

a *destination context* as that part of the presentation which is played on arriving at the destination of the link.

The context mechanism allows specific display options to be associated with each link. In particular, the source context can be retained or replaced when a link is followed. If it is replaced, the run-time environment can determine if the old resources used for the source are appropriate for the destination context. (Since the context is associated with the model, a run-time environment can perform these checks dynamically or statically.) If the source context is retained, it can be allowed to continue playing, or it can be forced to pause—with the choice left to the document author.

A benefit of specifying context is that only part of the document structure needs be affected on following a link. Components of the presentation higher in the composition hierarchy remain active and only those at the lower levels are affected. This reduces the authoring burden of repeating the same higher-level structures for different presentations. For example, when the reader activates the *Boats* anchor in the lower-left screen of our Amsterdam tour, only three of the atomic components are replaced while the others remain on the screen. (The three replaced are the illustration video, the audio track and the component specifying the next subject in the sequence, in this case the *Gables* button.) The document in the figure uses only two levels but the model imposes no restriction on the depth of the hierarchy. (Contexts are discussed in greater detail in [11].)

AHM Channels: Encoding High-Level Presentation Attributes
Both the Dexter model and the AHM allow presentation attributes to be specified for individual atomic and composite components. While these attributes are sufficient for local control, they are inadequate for specifying more global attributes of a document. Such attributes are defined in the AHM using *channels*.

Channels are abstract output devices for playing the content of a component. Associated with each channel are default presentation

characteristics for the media-type(s) displayed via that channel, such as *font* and *style* for a text channel, or *volume* for an audio channel. Channels store media-type independent specifications, such as background, foreground and highlight colors, or whether the channel is on or off; and media-type dependent characteristics such as font size and style for text, or scaling factor for graphics. The number of channels is not restricted. When a hypermedia document is played the channels are mapped onto physical output devices.

Figure 8 illustrates the allocation of abstract channels for an expanded version of our Amsterdam tour example. Two audio channels are defined, one containing commentary in Dutch and one in English. Three linking channels are defined (labeled *L0, L1* and *L2*), which are associated with the atomic components containing the text *contents, begin route over* and *next*. Two captions channels are defined (for holding Dutch and English text strings) and one screen channel is defined for the video data object. Note that the on/off channel attribute allows a user to specify which of the channels are active at run time; this allows a full presentation to be defined (for a variety of audiences), with particular instances of the presentation available on demand, customized to user preferences and to local hardware facilities on the presentation host. This feature allows the fragment shown in Figure 8 to be used to present either Dutch language audio and English language subtitles (or vice-versa), with the selection supported by the run-time environment. (While a presentation providing English and Dutch audio and English and Dutch captions would be possible—assuming enough screen "real-estate" and audio bandwidth existed—the usefulness of such a selection would depend on the nature of the user.)

The use of channels also allows the same document to be presented in different ways by respecifying the styles rather than by changing the presentation specification for every item. Just as in paper documents, this encourages consistency throughout the presentation. Flexibility is main-

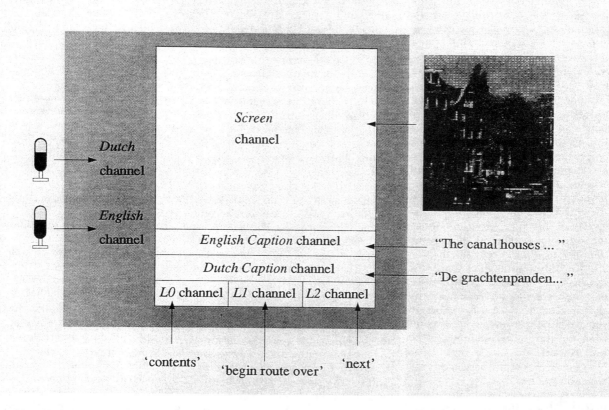

Screen channel

Dutch channel

English channel

English Caption channel

Dutch Caption channel

L0 channel | *L1* channel | *L2* channel

"The canal houses ... "

"De grachtenpanden... "

'contents'   'begin route over'   'next'

Figure 8. AHM channel architecture

tained by allowing overrides for individual components.

Current Implementation Status

The CMIFed authoring and runtime environment described in the sidebar "CMIFed—An AHM-Based Authoring Environment" is used to experiment with an implementation based on a modified version of the AHM. The most important difference in composition between the AHM and the model supported in CMIFed is that the AHM parallel component is split into two types of composition constructs—parallel and sequential. The purpose of supporting an extra type of composition in the authoring system is to allow the convenient definition of how a group of components are to be displayed during the presentation (that is, the parallel and sequential hierarchical structures are used to derive first-order timing information for the presentation). The derivation of this timing information removes the requirement for explicitly specifying timing information for each child of the composite.

Support for links and anchors in CMIFed is less general than the AHM. The source of a link in CMIFed is an anchor within an atomic component; the destination can be an anchor, or an atomic or composite component (i.e., we do not support the source of a link being a composite component). This has implications for assigning the contexts for the ends of a link. We currently derive the source and destination context from the structure around the ends of the link—the context is taken to be the child of the nearest ancestor choice component containing the end of the link (for further detail on the support for contexts see [11]).

Finally, anchors within CMIFed are of different types: normal, pausing and destination. Normal anchors define the areas which are made active for the reader. Pausing anchors are also active but require that the reader take some action (typically 'clicking') before the presentation can proceed beyond the point at which the anchor was displayed. Destination anchors are used in composite components and refer only to the complete component, removing the

requirement for an explicit value. CMIFed does not yet support composite anchors.

Conclusion

We feel that the AHM presents a flexible framework for studying hypermedia implementations. The goal of the model—the union of the basic concepts of hypertext and multimedia—has been met, at least within the limits of existing technology. Through the use of the CMIFed editor, we have been able to create a collection of hypermedia presentations that approximate the richness of the full model, and we continue to investigate new ways of providing better implementation support for hypermedia. The novelty of the CMIFed-supported approach to hypermedia is that the underlying structure can be freely manipulated, unlike many current multimedia authoring systems. This allows for quick and easy creation, copying and altering of presentations [9].

The timing constructs defined by the AHM allow a generalized specification of the behavior of a document. This behavior can be transformed for a particular instance to any SGML-like form [6], including HyTime [12, 13].

While the AHM, together with the CMIFed environment, provide a powerful way to create hypermedia presentations, it is clear that making "pleasing" presentations will remain a complex task. The gathering and editing of source materials, the definition of links in a document, and the aesthetic aspects of combining a variety of media in a useful manner remain major hurdles to the production of effective hypermedia presentations. Although we feel the AHM can provide a solid basis for encoding hypermedia documents, the artistic effort required for effective use of the media available on modern workstations should not be underestimated.

Acknowledgments

The concepts expressed in this article were developed while working with CMIFed, implemented by Guido Van Rossum, Jack Jansen and Sjoerd Mullender. The work was carried out as part of the MAGUS project, funded by the Dutch Ministry of Economic Affairs. We wish to thank the issue editors for their helpful comments on earlier versions of this article. ◨

References

1. Brown, P.J. UNIX Guide: Lessons from ten years' development. In *Proceedings of the Fourth ACM Conference on Hypertext.* D. Lucarella, J. Nanard, M. Nanard and P. Paolini, Eds. *ECHT '92* (Milano, Italy, Nov. 30–Dec. 4 1992), pp. 63–70.
2. Buchanan, M.C. and Zellweger, P.T. Specifying temporal behavior in hypermedia documents. In *Proceedings of the Fourth ACM Conference on Hypertext.* D. Lucarella, J. Nanard, M. Nanard and P. Paolini, Eds. *ECHT '92* (Milano, Italy, Nov. 30–Dec. 4 1992), pp. 262–271.
3. Bulterman, D.C.A. Specifying and support of adaptable networked multimedia, 1, 2 (1993) *Springer-Verlag/ ACM Multimedia Systems*, pp. 68–76.
4. Bulterman, D.C.A., van Rossum, G., and van Liere, R. A structure for transportable, dynamic multimedia documents. In *Proceedings of the Summer 1991 USENIX Conference*, (Nashville, Tenn., June 1991), pp. 137–155.
5. Fujikawa, K., Shimojo, S., Matsuura, T., Nishio S., and Miyahara, H. Multimedia presentation system 'Harmony' with temporal and active media. In *Proceedings of the Summer 1991 USENIX Conference* (Nashville, Tenn., June 1991), pp. 75–93.
6. Goldfarb C.F. *The SGML Handbook.* Oxford University Press, 1990.
7. Halasz, F. and Schwartz, M. The Dexter hypertext reference model. *NIST Hypertext Standardization Workshop,* (Gaithersburg, Md., Jan. 16–18 1990).
8. Halasz, F. and Schwartz, M. The Dexter hypertext reference model. K. Gronbæk and R. Trigg, Eds., *Commun. ACM 37,* 2 (Feb. 1994).
9. Hardman, L., Bulterman, D.C.A., and van Rossum, G. Structured Multimedia Authoring. In *Proceedings of the First International Conference on Multimedia* (Anaheim, Calif., Aug. 1993), pp. 283–289.
10. Hardman, L., Bulterman, D.C.A. and van Rossum, G. The Amsterdam hypermedia model: Extending hypertext to support *real* multimedia. *Hypermedia 5,* 1, (July 1993), pp. 47–69.
11. Hardman, L., Bulterman, D.C.A., and van Rossum, G., Links in hypermedia: The requirement for context. In *Proceedings of Hypertext 93* (Seattle, Wa. Nov. 93).
12. International Standards Organization, Hypermedia/Time-based structuring language, *ISO 10744,* 1992.
13. Newcomb, S.R., Kipp, N.A., and Newcomb, V.T. 'HyTime' the hypermedia/time-based document structuring language. *Commun. ACM. 34,* 11 (Nov. 1991), pp. 67–83.
14. Ogawa, R., Harada, H., and Kaneko, A. Scenario-based hypermedia: A model and a system. In *Hypertext: Concepts, Systems and Applications. Proceedings of the European Conference on Hypertext (ECHT '90).* A. Rizk, N. Streitz, and J. André, Eds. Nov. 1990, INRIA France, pp. 38–51.
15. Palaniappan M., Yankelovich N., and Sawtelle M. Linking active anchors: A stage in the evolution of hypermedia. *Hypermedia 2,* 1 (1990), pp. 47–66.
16. Ripley, G.D. Digital video interactive—A digital multimedia technology. *Commun. ACM 32,* 7 (July 1989), 154–159.
17. van Rossum, G. and de Boer, J. Interactively testing remote servers using the Python programming language. *CWIQ 4,* 4 (Dec. 1991), pp. 283–303.
18. van Rossum G., Jansen J., Mullender K.S., and Bulterman D.C.A. CMIFed: A presentation environment for portable hypermedia documents. In *Proceedings of the First ACM International Conference on Multimedia* (Anaheim, Calif., Aug. 1993), pp. 183–188.

CR Categories and Subject Descriptors: H.1.1 [**Information Systems**]: Models and Principles—*systems and information theory*; H.5.1 [**Information Systems**]: Information Interfaces and Presentation—*multimedia information systems*; H.5.2 [**Information Systems**]: Information Interfaces and Presentation—*user interfaces*; I.7.2 [**Computing Methodologies**]: Text Processing—*document preparation*

General Terms: Design, Standardization

Additional Key Words and Phrases: CMIFed, composition, context for links, editing environment, hypermedia models, multimedia, synchronization

About the Authors:

LYNDA HARDMAN is a member of the research staff within the Multimedia Kernel Systems group at CWI. Current research interests include hypertext and hypermedia systems, with a concentration on authoring systems for complex hypermedia presentations. email: lynda@cwi.nl

DICK C.A. BULTERMAN is head of the department of Computer Systems and Telematics at the Dutch National Center for Mathematics and Computer Science Research (CWI), and project leader of the Multimedia Kernel Systems project, which investigates fundamental models for supporting distributed multimedia systems. Current research interests include user-level and operating systems support for transportable and adaptable multimedia specifications. email: dcab@cwi.nl

GUIDO VAN ROSSUM is a member of the research staff within the Multimedia Kernel Systems group at CWI. Current research interests include the development of models and architectures that implement multimedia synchronization relationships. email: guido@cwi.nl

Authors' Present Address: Centrum voor Wiskunde en Informatica (CWI), PO Box 94079, 1909 GB Amsterdam, The Netherlands.

HDM — A Model-Based Approach to Hypertext Application Design

FRANCA GARZOTTO, PAOLO PAOLINI,
Politecnico di Milano
and
DANIEL SCHWABE
Pontifícia Universidade Católica do Rio de Janeiro

Hypertext development should benefit from a systematic, structured development, especially in the case of large and complex applications. A structured approach to hypertext development suggests the notion of *authoring-in-the-large*. Authoring-in-the-large allows the description of overall classes of information elements and navigational structures of complex applications without much concern with implementation details, and in a system-independent manner. The paper presents HDM (Hypertext Design Model), a first step towards defining a general purpose model for authoring-in-the-large. Some of the most innovative features of HDM are: the notion of *perspective*; the identification of different *categories of links* (structural links, application links, and *access structures*); and the possibility of easily integrating the structure of a hypertext application with its browsing semantics. HDM can be used in different manners: as a modeling device or as an implementation device. As a modeling device, it supports producing high level specifications of existing or to-be-developed applications. As an implementation device, it is the basis for designing tools that directly support application development. One of the central advantages of HDM in the design and practical construction of hypertext applications is that the definition of a significant number of links can be derived automatically from a conceptual-design level description. Examples of usage of HDM are also included.

Categories and Subject Descriptors: H.2.1 [**Database Management**]: Logical Design—*data models*; H.3.4 [**Information Storage and Retrieval**]: Systems and Software; H.4.1 [**Information Systems Applications**]: Office Automation; 1.7.; [**Text Processing**]: Miscellaneous—*hypertext*

General Terms: Design, Languages

Additional Key Words and Phrases: Derived links, HDM, Hypertext design models, Hypertext applications, Hypertext structures, models

This work was sponsored in part by the Commission of the European Communities, in the scope of the HYTEA Project (P 5252) of the ESPRIT II Program. D. Schwabe developed this work while on sabbatical leave from PUC and was partially supported by CNPq-Brasil.
Authors' addresses: F. Garzotto and P. Paolini, Department of Electronics, Politecnico di Milano, Piazza Leonardo da Vinci 32, 20133 Milano, Italy. Phone: +39-2-23993520; fax: +39-2-23993411; email: garzotto@ipmel1.polimi.it; paolini@ipmel1.polimi.it; D. Schwabe: Departamento de Informática, Pontifícia Universidade Católica do Rio de Janeiro, R. M. de S. Vicente, 225, CEP 22453, Rio de Janeiro, Brasil. Phone: +55-21-274 4449; fax: +55-21-274 4546; email: pucrjdi@inf.puc-rio.br.

1. INTRODUCTION

1.1 Background

The degree of success of a hypertext application is directly related to the author's ability to capture and organize the structure of a complex subject matter in such a way as to render it clear and accessible to a wide audience. To control the potential explosion of the number of links, a hypertext application does not really interconnect everything, but rather tries to *directly* interconnect only the most important and meaningful parts of the information so as to convey the overall meaning in a more natural way.

In a rational design approach, a hypertext application developer faces at least two different (but strongly correlated) task categories: "global" tasks, such as defining overall classes of information elements and navigational structures of applications, and "local" tasks, such as filling in contents of nodes. This is very similar to what happens when developing a highly modular software system: designing the topology and the interconnections among modules is different from writing the code for the content of the modules themselves. By analogy with software engineering, we use the following terminology: *authoring-in-the-large*, to refer to the specification and design of global and structural aspects of the hypertext application, and *authoring-in-the-small*, to refer to the development of the contents of the nodes [16, 17].

Authoring-in-the-small is very much related to the specific application area, while authoring-in-the-large has common characteristics across many different applications in a given application domain. Authoring-in-the-small is strongly dependent on the tools used for implementation and on the medium used for storing information (e.g., putting the text in a node is much different than putting an animation, or a sound, or a picture). Authoring-in-the-large can be at some extent independent from these aspects. However, authoring-in-the-large and authoring-in-the-small are typically very interwoven, and influence each other, much more than programming-in-the-large and in-the-small in the current software engineering practice.

This paper presents a model for authoring-in-the-large, named HDM—Hypertext Design Model [16, 17, 18, 36]. HDM prescribes the definition of an application *schema*, which describes overall classes of information elements in terms of their common presentation characteristics, their internal organization structure, and the types of their mutual interconnections. A schema, therefore, captures semantic and structural regularities in the representation structures for a given class of applications. Once a schema has been specified, the model also allows it to define a particular application, by providing primitives to describe a *schema instance*, i.e., actual *instances* of information classes and of connection types. In defining a schema instance, a significant number of connections can be left implicit, since they can be automatically derived from a conceptual-design level description.

HDM is mainly a modeling device. It provides ways of describing, concisely and in a system independent manner, existing or to-be-developed hypertext applications; it helps the author to conceptualize a given application without too much regard to "implementation details"; and it can be used as a communication language between designers, implementors, and users.

Additionally, HDM can be used to generate running implementations of hypertext applications [26, 36]. From this perspective, the model is a first step towards the development of application generators, in a similar way as CASE tools are used in software engineering environments. Implementation of an HDM application requires the definition of a browsing semantics, which specifies dynamic behavior and visualization properties of HDM representation structures. HDM is not closed with respect to any particular browsing semantics. So far, we have specified a *default browsing semantics*, more suitable for relatively simple card-oriented classes of systems.

1.2 Current Approaches to Hypertext Application Design

In the very closely related data base design field, models have played a crucial role in changing the data base development task from being a "hand-crafted" (and sometime inconsistent) activity into becoming a structured and rational process, based on well defined design methods [46]. Database models were born as means to define useful abstractions on large amounts of raw information ("logical" data models) and to express the intrinsic application oriented data semantics ("conceptual" and "semantic" data models [6, 21]). However, the peculiarities of hypertext (e.g., the role of links, the complexity of structures, the multimedia facility, the navigation paradigm, etc.) require the development of brand new models, specific for peculiar features of hypertext.

In the hypertext field, some approaches attempt to explicitly model the semantics of specific application domains by adopting predefined representation structures which reflect such "deep" semantics. g-IBIS [11], for example, is a hypertext tool for exploratory policy discussion. It helps capturing, storing, and retrieving the large amount of informal information which express the rationale of a system design process. g-IBIS explicitly models the semantics of its domain by assuming a well defined theory of the design process and by providing a set of specific node and link types that represent conceptual objects in the domain model. Thus g-IBIS encourages to share this model while seeking to discourage less disciplined argumentation modes.

Other works should be regarded more as "system" oriented models than as application oriented design models. They are attempts to define in an unambiguous, rigorous way some important abstractions found in a wide range of existing (and future) systems rather than of existing (and future) applications. The goal of the Dexter Hypertext Reference Model [20] is to serve as a standard against which to compare and contrast the static information structures and the functionalities of different hypertext systems. Its building blocks for defining the static aspects of a hypertext system are low level objects: nodes, links, and anchors. The Dexter model purposefully does not model the content and structure within the components of hypertext networks. It treats them, as well as their layout and visualization properties, as being outside the model per se. Garg's set-theoretical model [14] is a formalization of hypertext networks viewed as static, syntactic structures, and provides a mathematical framework to define abstraction mechanisms useful to describe or derive static syntactic properties of hypertext networks. Garg's model (as other similar ones [35]) assumes low level objects as building blocks, such as nodes (and even node components), and node-to-node links. The Trellis model [39] is mainly a "behavioral" model for hypertext. Hypertext networks are modeled as Petri nets, and various browsing semantics (that is, how information is to be visited) are discussed in terms of Petri nets computations.

Tompa [41] adopts a hypergraph formalism to model generic hypertext structures, to formalize identification of commonalities in these structures, and to directly refer to "groups of nodes" having a common link semantics. A dynamic behavior is also specified through the notion of node markings, with an end result much similar to the Trellis model.

Other, less formal, approaches emphasize preferred topological structures as building blocks to create the structure of hypertext networks. This requirement is often embodied in a concrete system implementation, and enforced by the editing tools the system provides. In Hypercard [3], for example, linear structures play a central organization role. Even if each card can be arbitrarily linked to any other card, each Hypercard node must belong to a sequence ("stack") of cards, and links to the successor node, to the first and the last node in the sequence are automatically provided by the system. Guide [7] also prescribes the extensive use of linear structures to clarify the organization of hyperdocuments. KMS [2] prescribes the extensive use of hierarchical structures to organize information, in order to encourage a top-down, step-wise design of hyperdocuments. Each KMS node (frame) belongs to a single hierarchy; however, KMS also allows "special links" that are cross-hierarchical and induce a more complex topology on the network of nodes.

Several existing approaches provide "template" facilities to help designers generate hypertext structures more easily and systematically, by allowing authors to create multiple copies of individual structures all sharing a number of common properties. HyperCard, for example, has "backgrounds" as the lay-out and linking template. The lay-out and button properties of a background are inherited and shared by all the different nodes sharing that background. NoteCards' notion of (hierarchy of) node types and link types lets writers create as many instances of a class of hypertext nodes as they require [19]. Object Lens [28] encourages a similar style of node creation, by providing an object-oriented environment which allows definition of templates corresponding to high-level abstractions in an application domain. IDE [27], an extension of NoteCards, is an interactive design and development system which assists designers with the process of creating complex hypertext material, mainly (but not only) for instruction purposes. IDE provides built-in representation primitives for describing the substance of a course and the rationale for the course design in terms of hypertext structures. IDE moreover, provides a number of domain independent mechanisms ("structure accelerators") that facilitate the rapid and accurate creation of regular network patterns in hypertext by permitting authors to create entire webs of nodes and links in a single operation. The template facility in Intermedia [38,

48] plays a similar role as IDE structure accelerators. Stotts et al. [40] introduce the notion of style templates to denote styles of structuring and browsing Trellis-based hypertext. Different style templates correspond to different translations from generic authoring notations of hypertext content elements and linkages into structured Trellis documents with a specific browsing behavior. Translations are basically mappings from string-grammars (the authoring language) to graph grammars (the abstract language for Trellis documents).

Other approaches help to organize and modularize existing hypertext material. Trigg's Guided Tours and Tabletops [29, 42], for instance, are browsing extensions of NoteCards which help designers to group and visualize existing hypertext material in a way that it is more appropriate for a particular reader, and to provide preferred paths through a hyperbase.

The remainder of the article is divided as follows: Section 2 discusses the advantages of the model-based approach to authoring in the large and presents HDM in detail; Section 3 gives an example of HDM use in hypertext application design; Section 4 draws the conclusions, by comparing HDM to other approaches, by evaluating the model's utility on the basis of a number of experiences done so far, and by outlining our future work.

2. A MODEL-BASED APPROACH TO AUTHORING-IN-THE-LARGE

2.1 Motivations

There are many advantages in having a design model for hypertext applications, which we summarize here.

Improvement of communication. A design model provides a language which can be used by an application analyst to *specify* a given application. Thus it facilitates the communication between the analyst and the end user; between the analyst and the system designer; and between the system designer and the implementor. At the very least, a basis for discussing the similarities of hypertext applications exists. To paraphrase Halasz et al. [20]: *Hypertext Application Models* can be regarded as an attempt to provide a principled basis for answering questions such as "what do hypertext applications such as Voyager's *Beethoven's 9th Symphony* [47], Harvard University's *Perseus* [30], ACM's compilation *Hypertext for Hypertext* [37], Eastgate's *Elections of 1912* [4], have in common?" "How do they differ?"

Development of design methodologies and of rhetorical styles. Design models provide a framework in which the authors of hypertext applications can develop, analyze, and compare *methodologies* and *rhetorical styles* of "hyperauthoring", at a high level of abstraction, without having to resort to looking at the detailed contents of units of information or at their particular visualizations.

Reusability. As a matter of fact, the availability of a modeling language paves the way for (partial) reuse of the back-bone structure of applications,

since model-based specifications capture the "essential semantics" of applications, and can therefore be reused when the semantics of two applications are similar enough.

Providing consistent and predictable reading environments. It is clear that tools for specifying hypertext structures can help authors to avoid structural inconsistencies and mistakes [8], and that applications developed according to a model will result in very consistent and predictable representation structures. As a consequence, navigation environments will also be predictable, thereby helping readers to master complex documents and reducing the disorientation problem [31, 33, 43].

Use by design tools. Design models are the basis for the development of *Design Tools* [45] that support a systematic, structured development process, allow the designer to work at a level of abstraction which is closer to the application domain, and provide a systematic translation process to the implementation level.

2.2 HDM Primitives

HDM is a model to describe hypertext applications. It has a number of peculiarities that make it overall different from other models, but at the same time borrows many of its detail features from existing models. From a terminological point of view, we had two extreme choices: either to create a set of brand new terms for all the features of the model, or to use only preexisting terms (and concepts), perhaps reassembled in a novel fashion. We have chosen a compromise course: some of the terms are new, others are taken from preexisting models in the database or hypertext field. Preexisting terms should be understood with the caveat that the reader should never assume that our use of the term exactly corresponds to the notion that he is already aware of.

An HDM application consists of sizeable structures of information chunks called *entities*. An entity denotes a physical or conceptual object of the domain. Entities are grouped in *entity types*. An entity is the smallest "autonomous" piece of information which can be introduced or removed from an application. In this context, "autonomous" piece of information means that its existence is not conditioned by the existence of other information objects. In HDM, only entities are autonomous, while components and units (see below) are not, as discussed in the following sections.

An entity is an hierarchy of *components*. Components are in turn made of *units*. Each unit shows the content of a component under a particular *perspective* (see proper subsection for details and examples). Entities therefore derive their information content from their components, which in turn derive it from their units. Units are the smallest chunks of information which can be visualized in an HDM application, and they have a lot in common with the standard notions of hypertext "nodes."

HDM information structures can be interconnected by *links*. HDM distinguishes among three categories of links. *Structural links* connect together

2.2.1 Entities and Entity Types.

An entity is a (relatively large) structure of information which represents some real world object of the application domain; a law (say "Law 19/8/89"), a musical Opera (say Verdi's "La Traviata"), a piece of equipment (say "electric engine") could be examples of entities.

Entities are naturally grouped in *entity types*, which correspond to classes of objects of the real world. "Law", "Musical Opera" and "Equipment" could be examples of entity types.

The notion of entity (and the related notion of entity type) is commonly recognized as a suitable notion to model information in the data base field. The most popular design model, the Entity-Relationship (E-R) model [10], and the several other related models derived from it, are based upon the notion of entity and entity class.

We should warn the reader, however, that although we have kept the term and the basic nature of the concept of Entity, in practice HDM entities are very different from E-R entities. For example, HDM entities have complex inner structures (with links inside, see Subsection 2.2.7), while E-R entities are essentially flat; HDM entities have a (default) browsing semantics associ-ated with them (see Subsection 2.4.1); HDM entities can be interwoven, via application links (see Subsection 2.2.8), in patterns much more complex than those allowed by relationships in the E-R model.

2.2.2 Components.

An HDM entity is a collection of *components* arranged in a tree-like fashion (ordered hierarchy). A component is an abstraction for a set of units (see Subsection 2.2.4), which are the actual containers of informa-tion, and derives its content from its units[1]. A component, being part of a hierarchy, in general has a *parent* (but for the root component), a number of *siblings* (which are arranged in a linear order) and a number of *children* (but for the leaf components). Components "inherit" their type from their en-tity and can only exist as part of an entity; in this sense, they are not autonomous.

Examples of components, for the entities introduced in the previous subsec-tion, could be "Article 1" (component of "Law 19/8/89", "Article 1—Subsec-tion 1.2" (child of "Article 1" component), "Ouverture" (component of "La Traviata"), "condenser" (component of "electric engine").

Many authors have observed that hierarchies are very useful to help user orientation when navigating in a hypertext [1, 7]. HDM recognizes this via the notion of entities made up of components organized into hierarchies. Hierarchies can be induced by many semantic criteria (i.e., domain relations). The "Is-part-of" relation, for example, is one of the most commonly used. HDM, however, does not acknowledge the (possibly) different semantic na-ture of different hierarchies, since it is not intended to be a semantic model. In HDM, a hierarchy is a purely syntactical device to organize information in regular building blocks within a (possibly large) application.

2.2.3 Perspectives.

In hypertext applications it is often the case that the same topic must be presented in several alternate ways. There are several different reasons why this need may arise. In multinational applications, for example, the same topic must be represented with different languages (e.g., Italian, Portuguese, English, etc.). In educational applications, it may be useful to present the same topic using different rhetorical styles (e.g., discur-sive, synthetic, schematic,...), according to different needs of the readers. In recent applications, very often different media can be used for presenting the same piece of information (text, graphics, image, video, sound, etc.).

In HDM this notion of having different presentations for the same content, is captured by the concept of *perspective*. If an entity has two possible perspectives (say "Italian" and "English", or "Score" and "Sound"), all the components belonging to it also have two possible perspectives. The set of perspectives are shared by all entities of a given entity type, and are defined at entity type level.

Perspectives are just a syntactical device to organize information. HDM does not acknowledge any predefined semantics behind this concept, and does not interpret it. The author has to decide when and how to use the notion of perspective, and what is its intended meaning. HDM only prescribes con-sistency in using the different ways for presenting information in entities of the same type.

components belonging to the same entity. *Perspective links* connect together the different units that correspond to the same component. *Application links* denote arbitrary, domain dependent relationships and connect together com-ponents and entities, of the same or different types, in arbitrary patterns set up by the author. Application links are grouped in *link types*. All perspective links, and most structural links, do not need to be defined explicitly by the author, since they can be *derived* automatically from the structure of entities. Some application links can be derived by exploiting semantic properties (e.g., symmetry and transitive closure) of the corresponding domain relationships.

As any other design model, HDM makes a clear distinction between the notion of *schema* and the notion of *instance of a schema*. A schema is a collection of type definitions that describe an application at the global level; an instance of a schema is a collection of entities, components, units, and links that satisfy the definitions of the schema. *Outlines*, i.e., access struc-tures, provide reader-oriented entry points to directly access information structures in an instance of a schema.

A *browsing semantics* has the purpose of specifying how information structures are visualized to the reader, and how he can navigate across them. HDM provides a relatively simple *default browsing semantics* as built-in; different browsing semantics however could be defined, to describe more sophisticated visualization effects for applications specified with HDM.

---

[1] For model simplicity, and also because we have verified that so far we do not need the feature, entities cannot be used as components of other entities.

2.2.4 *Units.* A *unit* corresponds to a component associated with a specific perspective. A unit is characterized by a *name* (its identifier) and a *body*. Bodies of units are the place where the actual content of an HDM application is filled in. "Ouverture/sound", "Ouverture/score" (of the entity "La Traviata"), "Article 1/Official Text", "Article 1/Annotated Text" (of the entity "Law 19/8/89"), "assembly instruction/Italian-text", "assembly instruction/English-text", "assembly instruction/Italian-graphics", "assembly instruction/English-graphics" (of the entity "Electric Engine"), are examples of units.

If the reader tries to relate HDM units to traditional hypertext notions, units, roughly speaking, may be thought as corresponding to the standard notions of "nodes". This correspondence is not completely true; for example, units can be created only in the proper context (of components and entities, under the proper perspectives), and arbitrary nodes are not allowed in HDM. Filling in a body, corresponds to *authoring-in-the-small* (in our terminology), which is purposefully outside the scope of HDM. Therefore HDM units are the border-line between authoring-in-the-large and authoring-in-the-small: identifying the units and putting them in the proper context belongs to authoring-in-the-large; filling the bodies of units with actual content is authoring-in-the-small.

In HDM, different units are allowed to share their body. This is, methodologically speaking, not encouraged in HDM; in fact, sharing of bodies implies that the same content can be accessed in different (not mutually exclusive) contexts, and this is a typical source of disorientation for the reader. Additionally, we have verified that the need for sharing of bodies arises, quite often, from a poor design of the schema and a bad use of application links (see Subsection 2.2.8). Still we have introduced the notion of body sharing since we have acknowledged that, in some applications, a good use of it can simplify the application specification for the designer (but at the possible expense of clarity for the reader).

2.2.5 *Links in General.* Links in hypertext have a twofold role: a representational role (i.e., capturing domain relations) and a navigational role (i.e., capturing navigation patterns). Sometimes these two different purposes are consistent with each other, sometimes they can be at odds. It may happen that domain relations are not suitable for navigation, i.e., they induce navigation patterns that are not relevant for an application, while, on the contrary, useful navigational links may have vague semantic meaning. Definition of links is therefore a trade-off between representational and navigational goals. However, the more the meaning of a link is made explicit and approximates a relationship of the application domain that a reader is aware of, the more the same reader will be at ease in using the hypertext, since links will evoke familiar associations.

HDM is not intended to be a semantic model. However, HDM acknowledges three categories of links: *perspective links, structural links,* and *application links.* The distinction among the three classes simplifies the job of the application designer, induces a consistent use of most links, creates more predictable navigation patterns, and finally makes it possible to introduce additional features such as derivation of links (see Subsection 2.3) and definition of a default browsing semantics (see Subsection 2.4.1).

2.2.6 *Perspective Links. Perspective links* interconnect units corresponding to the same component. Perspective links will connect, for instance, the units "assembly instruction/Italian-text" and "assembly instruction/Italian-graphics", thus allowing an Italian reader to switch from the text description of an assembly operation to the picture (in Italian) that schematizes it.

Perspective links are navigationally very simple for the reader, since activating a perspective link leaves the current topic (i.e., the reader's focus of attention) unchanged.

2.2.7 *Structural Links. Structural links* connect components belonging to the same entity. There are several different structural links, each of them corresponding to a relationship induced by the ordered tree structure of entities. Examples of structural links are *"Up"*, connecting a component to its parent, *"Down"*, connecting a component to its children, *"Down-1"*, connecting a component to its first child, *"Next-sibling"*, connecting a component to the following child of the same father, *"Root"*, connecting a component to the root of the tree, and so on.

Structural links can be used by the reader to navigate among chunks of information belonging to the same entity. Navigationally, they are a little more complex than perspective links, but they are still quite simple, since they leave the reader inside the same information context, i.e., the same entity, with limited danger of getting lost. In the worst case the "Root" link can always take the reader to a safe point (i.e., the root of the entity).

2.2.8 *Application Links and Link Types. Application links* represent the most expressive portion of any non trivial hypertext; they represent domain dependent relationships among entities, or their components. These relationships are chosen by the author as both navigationally and semantically relevant.

Application links are organized into types. An *application link type*, or *link type* for short, is specified in HDM by a *name*, a set of *source* and *target entity types*, and a *symmetry attribute*, which can assume two values—*symmetric* or *asymmetric.* Source and target entity types define what can be linked to what. Once a link type has been defined as having source entity type A and target entity type B, *instances* of this link type are allowed to connect entities or components of type A to entities or components of type B only. The *symmetry* attribute defines a semantic property of the link type—whether or not each link of that type has an inverse link. This property can be exploited for automatic derivation of application links (see Subsection 2.3).

An example of application link type is "is-author-of", whose instances connect entities or components of type "Composer" to entities or components of type "Musical Opera". Another example is "is-justified-by", whose instances connect entities or components of type of "Contract", to entities or components of type "Law".

The semantic depth or arbitrariness of an application link type can vary, and is left to the author's responsibility. If establishing the composer of an opera corresponds to expressing a purely matter-of-fact truth, deciding that a given law is particularly relevant for a (portion of) contract, may express an arbitrary and debatable judgement.

In HDM, the choice of application link types and the placement of their instances is completely left to the author. By requiring the specification of the source and target entity types in the link type definition, HDM only enforces syntactic consistency, and therefore it would not allow, for example, to establish an "is-author-of" link from a "Musical Opera" to a "Law".

From a navigational point of view, application links are typically the most troublesome, since when traversing application links the reader perceives that his information context is abruptly changed. Assume that the reader is examining a contract. While he is navigating among its different parts (following structural or perspective links), he is always within the same familiar information context. If now he follows an application link of type "is-justified-by", he will find himself looking at an article of a law and not at the clause of a contract. After having followed a number of application links, the reader might get disoriented by the different information contexts (i.e., entities of different types) he has traversed.

2.2.9 Entity Types Revisited. We can now reexamine the notion of entity type and characterize it in a more precise fashion. All the entities belonging to the same type have certain features in common: (1) the name of the their entity type; (2) the set of perspectives under which their content (i.e., the their body of their units) is presented; (3) the types of their outgoing and incoming application links.

2.2.10 HDM Schema. An HDM specification of a hypertext application consists of a *schema definition* and a set of *instances definitions*. A schema definition specifies a set of entity types and link types. Instances are allowed to be inserted in the application only if they obey the constraints specified by the schema.

The notion of schema is relatively new in the hypertext field, but it is obviously derived from the current practice in the database field. Database schemas started (in the early sixties) as simple templates, describing file structures, that allowed generic operations such as "find" or "search" to be performed, independently from structural and implementation details of files. With time these file descriptors have become more complex, incorporating more semantic features.

In the hypertext field the evolution seems to start following the same course; developers of applications, who need to perform several times the same operations on complex node/link structures, have acknowledged that "templates"—descriptors of network patterns—are useful to save effort and to ensure consistency [27, 38]. Most existing template mechanisms in hypertext, however, are defined essentially on a syntactic basis. Taking advantage of the historical experience of the Data Base field, HDM attempts to go directly to an advanced notion of Schema that is able to represent some semantic features of hypertext applications, as well as to exploit syntactical regularities.

2.2.11 Outlines. According to the HDM terminology, a hypertext application can be, roughly speaking, divided in two portions: a *hyperbase* and a set of *access structures*.

The hyperbase represents the core of the application; it consists of all the elements defined in the previous sections: entities, components, units, and links of all the categories previously discussed—structural, perspective, and application links. The reader can explore the hyperbase by traversing the links defined there.

Before he can start this navigation, however, the reader must have entry points to get a view of what the hyperbase is about, and to locate the most convenient starting point. Access structures have the purpose of allowing the reader to properly select the entry points for further navigation.

In HDM, so far, we have mainly focused our attention on modeling the hyperbase, which represents the most relevant portion of any hypertext. For access structures, at the moment, we provide a unique primitive, the *outline*, explained below. In the Conclusions (Subsection 4.4) current work for the enhancement of this part of HDM is described.

Outlines are structurally quite similar to hyperbase entities, but they have a number of restrictions and peculiarities that make them substantially different from entities. An outline is an ordered tree of components. Each component (but for leaf components) is connected to its child components, to its siblings, and to its parent (but for the root component), via structural links. Differently from entities, however, these are the *only* outgoing or incoming links for nonleaf components; additionally, leaf components *must* have a number of outgoing (untyped) links to entities or components of the hyperbase. Outlines are not typed and are not specified in the schema—they can be freely added or modified, at will, in an application, in order to provide the appropriate entry points for the reader.

An outline for applications in the legal field, for example, provides an access to "European Laws", or "National Laws" in the root component. Selecting "National Laws" corresponds to traversing a link to a component where a further choice is presented among different categories of national laws—say, for example, "Laws concerning real estate sale", "Laws concerning donation", etc. There is an outgoing link for each of the above categories of laws; each one of these links points to a leaf component, which has a number of links to specific entities of type "Law" of the selected subcategory (say, for example, "Law 10/21/87", "Law 3/5/75").

2.3 Derived Links and Derived Link Types

One of the central advantages of HDM in the design and practical construction of hypertext applications is that defining a significant number of links

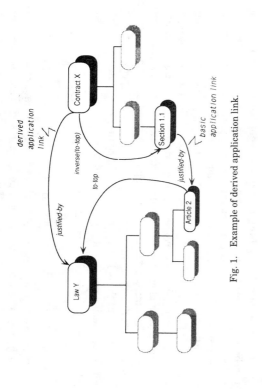

derived
application
link

inverse(to-top)

to-top

justified by

justified-by

Contract X

Section 1.1

basic
application link

Article 2

Law Y

Fig. 1. Example of derived application link.

can be left implicit—being induced from structural properties of the model—or can be defined intensionally and algorithmically derived. At the conceptual level, the author needs to provide a much smaller number of links than the number of links that will actually be present in the application; once the proper interpreter is provided, all implicit or derivable links can be generated automatically from the design level description, by using the schema definitions.

All perspective links can be left implicit and can be automatically derived from the definition of components and units. For example, if perspectives "score" and "sound" are defined for entity type "Opera", two perspective links will be generated *for each* component of an entity of this type: the first connecting the unit of the component under "score" perspective to the unit under "sound" perspective of the same component; the second being the inverse of the first.

Defining an entity is equivalent to defining a set of components plus the minimal set of "basic" structural links that are necessary to induce an ordered hierarchy relationship on the set of components: links from any (nonleaf) component to its first child, and links from any component to the next child of the same parent. A large number of other structural links can be defined intensionally, and can be computed, from the basic ones. For example: "*down(N)*" (N positive integer)—connecting a component directly to its Nth child; "*down*"—connecting a parent component to all its children; "*up*"—connecting a component to its parent; "*to-top*"—connecting a component to the root of the entity.

Derived structural link types can be defined in terms of operators such as "*inversion*", "*composition*", "*composition(N)*" (repeated composition, N times), "*transitive closure*", and "*closure*"—applied to basic structural links. All instances of derived structural link types can be automatically computed from the basic structural links, by a proper interpreter "executing" the corresponding derivation clauses.

A similar approach can be applied to application links. For example, from application link types that have been defined as "symmetric" (see Section 2.2.8), the corresponding inverse link types can be specified by using the inversion operator, and their instances can be automatically generated. As a more sophisticated case, we can specify derivation rules such as: "given an application link type, if an instance of it exists between two components of different entities, then an instance of the same link type is derived between the roots of the corresponding entities."

Assume for example that a component of an entity of type "legal document" —say "section 1.1" of a contract "X", has been connected by the author to a component of an entity of type "law"—say "Article 2" of law "Y"—by a link of type "justified-by" (see Figure 1). Then assume that the author wants to represent also the fact that, at a different level of detail, the whole contract X "is-justified" by the whole law Y. This fact can be expressed by a link between the root of contract "X" (which is intended to represent the whole entity "X") and the root of law "Y" (which is intended to represent the whole entity "Y"). This link can be derived by composing the inverse of link "to-top"—outgoing

from component "section 1.1"—with the link "is-justified-by"—outgoing from the same component—and then composing the result with the link "to-top" outgoing from component "Article 2".

2.4 Browsing Semantics

The actual use of a hypertext is largely defined by its *browsing semantics* [39], which will determine what the information objects are for "human consumption" (in HDM terms, entity types, link types, entities, outlines, components, or units), what the perceived links between these objects are, and what the behavior when links are activated is.

Given the specification of a particular browsing semantics compatible with a given target hypertext systems, it becomes possible to translate HDM application specifications into running applications, once the mapping from HDM primitives into implementation structures of the target environment has been provided. By applying different browsing semantics to the same HDM static specifications, it is possible to deliver the same HDM application under different versions, each one characterized by different visual features and dynamic behaviors, or running in different hypertext systems.

The particular browsing semantics will be closely dependent on the particular hypertext development system being used for implementation. HDM, as discussed so far, does not prescribe a priori any specific browsing semantics for hypertexts specified with it, nor does it include any high level primitive for defining browsing semantics. However, we have defined a minimal browsing semantics, compatible with plain *nodes-and-links* structures found in most hypertext systems, and we have adopted it for our experiments on automatic translation of HDM specifications into running applications (see

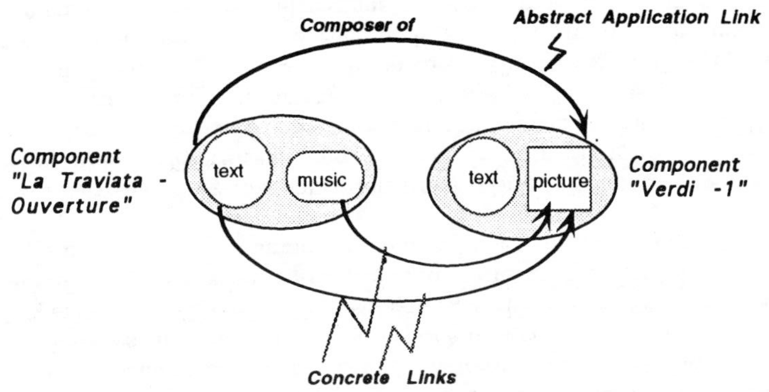

Fig. 2.   Example of translation from abstract to concrete links.

Section 4.3). For the moment, this browsing semantics is considered as the *default browsing semantics* for HDM.[2]

2.4.1 *Default Browsing Semantics.* HDM default browsing semantics assumes that only units can be perceived by the readers as standard "nodes", i.e., "loci of navigation control", and that only one node is active at any time. As a consequence, readers can perceive links only among units, and so, in the end, actual, navigable connections must be established among units.

Since in HDM only perspective links connect units, while structural and application links are established among components or/and entities, the latter must be properly translated into unit-to-unit links. We will call "abstract" the links among components and/or entities, and "concrete" the unit-to-unit links.

2.4.1.1 *From Abstract to Concrete Links.* HDM default rules for translating abstract links into concrete links are based on the idea of having a *default representative* for each abstract object (component or entity). Defining default representatives of entities and components is done by introducing a *default perspective* for each entity type, and then assuming that the default representative for a component is its unit under the default perspective and the default representative for an entity is the default representative of its root component. This corresponds to saying that the root component of an entity, in its default perspective, "stands" for that entity.

Given this notion, entity-to-entity application links translate into concrete links between their default representatives. Each component-to-component application link is translated into a *set* of concrete links connecting each unit of the source component to the default representative of the target component.

To illustrate this rule, consider the following situation occurring in a hypermedia music listening guide; "La Traviata-Ouverture" component (of entity "La Traviata" of type "Musical Work"), is linked to "Verdi-1" component (root of entity "Verdi" of type "Author"), through a "Composer of" application link. Consider furthermore that "Author" entity type has perspectives "Picture" (showing the person) and "Text" (with a textual description), while "Musical Work" has "Text" (with the music score) and "Music" perspectives. "Picture" is the default perspective for entity type "Author".

In the above case, the actual concrete links corresponding to the abstract link connecting the two components, will connect both "La Traviata-Ouverture: Text" unit and "La Traviata-Ouverture: Music" unit to "Verdi-1: Picture" unit. This is an example where one link at the abstract level corresponds to two concrete navigable links. The situation is illustrated in Figure 2.

The default rule for component-to-component *structural* links translation is the following: if a component C1 has a structural link to a component C2, then, for each perspective P, each unit of C1 having this perspective is linked to the unit of C2 having the *same* perspective. Therefore, in an entity of type T having N perspectives, N concrete links correspond to each structural link defined at the conceptual level.

2.4.1.2 *Perception of Links: Anchors and Anchor Types.* In hypertext, connections among pieces of information are usually perceived through "anchors" (or "buttons"). Anchors are link place-holders that show the existence of connection in nodes, and can be selected ("clicked") by the reader in order to get into the link target(s). An *anchor type* specifies the properties of anchors that represent links of the same type, or of a group of link types.

Consider for example, that a "Procedure" entity type has an outgoing link type "Formal-Legal-Justification" to a "Law" and an outgoing link type "Informal-Justification" to an "Informal-Regulation". The author might want to provide to certain classes of users a single reading link, simply labelled "Justification", since the distinction between formal and informal justifications might not be important for readers of that class. This can be achieved by specifying the anchor type "Justification" to be the *union of application link types* "Formal-Legal-Justification" and "Informal-Justification".

Another design requirement of the author might be to hide links of a given type for a specific application (since they might be relevant at design and specification level but not at reader level). This can be achieved by simply not assigning any anchor type to that link type. Anchor types, therefore, provide a mechanism for the author to present groups of link types together, also renaming or hiding them, as desired.

When an anchor actually refers to several possible destination nodes, the HDM default browsing semantics has the notion of *chooser*, i.e., a structure

---

[2] The default browsing semantics has been implemented in a prototype system, which uses a relational database description of HDM specifications, and generates a tabular description that can be imported into Hypercard and manipulated using Hypertalk. This prototype is described in detail in [36].

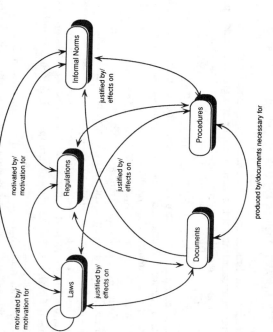

Fig. 3. Schema of entity types and application link types of the Expert Dictionary.

that is associated with an anchor and allows, via a "menus", to select one of the multiple targets of the anchor.[3]

3. EXAMPLE OF HYPERTEXT MODELING WITH HDM

This section will describe a hypertext application designed with HDM—a subset of a larger prototype application for banking environment named Expert Dictionary [15] which has been developed by ARG SpA and Politecnico di Milano within the European Esprit project SUPERDOC.

The goal of the Expert Dictionary is to provide an organized way to access to a large set of information of vastly different but interrelated nature handled by credit organizations. A credit organization manipulates *Documents* according to *Procedures*. Documents and Procedures are defined according to *Laws*, *Regulations*, and *Informal Norms*. Laws are issued by the state to discipline and control credit granting and taking activity. Most of the times laws are too broad, and must be made more specific by Regulations issued by some authority, on the basis of the text of the law. Finally, these regulations are interpreted within an organization with the addition of *Informal Norms*, which are of course valid only for that organization.

Entity types and application link types that model the above state of affairs are sketched in Figure 3. Each of these entity types has a set of *perspectives* associated with it, which are omitted for lack of space. For example: *Laws* and *Regulations* have *Structure** and *Official Text* perspectives; *Documents* have *Structure**, *Official Text*, and *Description* perspectives; *Procedures* have *Flow Diagram Structure** (*Structure** for short) and *Description* perspectives. The perspective marked with a "*" is the default. All application link types are "symmetric" (see Section 2.2.8), i.e., they represent a relation and its inverse. Thus we have drawn link types only once, but we assume that for each application link type, there is a derivable link type that corresponds to its inverse.

A fragment of an instance of the schema above is depicted in Figure 4. It shows an entity of type *Procedure* named *Mortgage Loan Procedure*, which is made up of a root component introducing the whole entity and several other components denoting subprocedures or subprocedure steps. Another entity is *Circular HyperBank 21/10/89* of type *Regulation*, which is made up of a root and four components: *Units Involved, Subject, Operational Norms in Request Verification,* and *Data Entry Rules*. These last two components represent information that respectively affect the way the procedure (sub) steps *Request Verification* and *Request Data Entry* are performed; therefore, application links of type *has-effects-on* are included. Entity *Circular HyperBank 21/10/89*, in turn, is *motivated-by* entities *Law 19/8/89* and

Administrative Council Deliberation 20/9/89. The small black rectangle on the right-hand side of the picture is an outline named *Access to Mortgage Loan Client Information*, which allows us to directly access entities describing documents needed for the compilation of a Mortgage Loan Request (in the picture, *Mortgage Loan Request Form and Notary Statement*).

The following figures show a few examples of screens (corresponding to HDM units of the appropriate components) from the Hypercard implementation of the Expert Dictionary, which was generated adopting the default browsing semantics described in Section 2.4.1. The same application, with the same browsing semantics, has been implemented also in Hyperpad.

Figure 5 shows the "Structure" perspective of a component of entity "Circular HyperBank 21/10/89" of type Regulation. Notice that all the links of type "Justified by" have been grouped under the anchor (button) "Motivations". Figure 6 shows the same component under the perspective "Official Text".

Anchors corresponding to application links ("Effects", "Motivations") and perspective links ("Description" and "Official Text" in Figure 5, and "Structure" and "Description" in Figure 6) are at the bottom of the screen. If the user is interested in seeing, for example, the effects of the regulation shown in Figures 5 and 6, he can click on the anchor "Effects". Since this in reality groups several outgoing links, a chooser is activated; from it, the user can select which of the possible destinations he wishes to go to.

---

[3] Choosers can be generated automatically from the specification of the concrete links in the hypertext application.

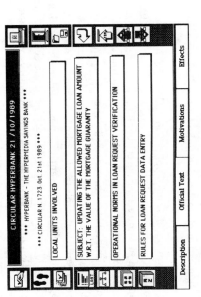

Fig. 5. "Structure" perspective of a Regulation.

Fig. 6. "Official text" perspective of the Regulation in Figure 5.

"general", oriented towards allowing the design of hypertext applications in most domains. HDM philosophy shares with IDE [27] the aim of supporting representation tasks in hypertext and of encouraging the creation of regular and consistent network structures. IDE has surely anticipated a number of concepts exploited in HDM. However, IDE is basically a development tool, while HDM is also a conceptual design device which can be useful even without an implementation of its primitives. Moreover, HDM provides richer modeling primitives—the notion of perspective, the distinction between different categories of links, the separation between hyperbase and access structures, and between authoring structures and reading structures (i.e., browsing semantics). Object Lens [28] classes resemble somewhat HDM entity types. Object Lens, however, does not impose any constraint on possi-

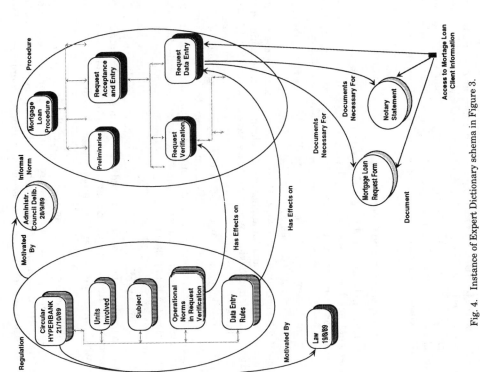

Fig. 4. Instance of Expert Dictionary schema in Figure 3.

4. CONCLUSIONS

4.1 Comparison with Other Works

HDM shares some apparent similarities with the Entity Relationship (E-R) model [10]. However, there is no E-R notion equivalent to HDM perspectives. Additionally, HDM Entities are much more structured than E-R entities, which are essentially flat and do not have structural links. Most importantly, whereas in the E-R model relations are included for representational reasons, HDM links are included also with the goal of providing navigation paths.

HDM differs from g-IBIS [11] in the fact that it does not freeze, a priori, the application domain, and therefore its representation primitives are more

ble connections between object class instances and no real discipline on actual instances creation.

With respect to other hypertext models discussed in Section 1.2, HDM differs in the fact that it is aimed at modeling applications rather than systems. HDM shares with the Trellis model [39] and Tompa's model [41] the idea of abstracting from the contents and structure of the "nodes", which are allowed to contain arbitrarily complex information structures. Differently from HDM, however, these models are more concerned with behavioral aspects of hypertext, or with operational features, rather than on representational issues.

The approach introduced in [40] shares with HDM the idea of distinguishing between authoring language, for defining hypertext structures in a system independent manner, and browsing semantics language. As far as browsing semantics is concerned, the work presented in [40] goes a step ahead with respect to HDM, by providing a graph-grammar based language for specifying patterns of visual and dynamic behaviors (style templates), and general techniques for translating generic authoring notations into systematically structured hypertext. In this sense, this work is somehow complementary to HDM, whose major focus for the moment is on static representational aspects.

4.2 Evaluation, Experiences, and Feedback

The HDM model can be used in different manners: as a modeling device or as an implementation device. As a modeling device, it allows to lay down clear and concise specifications of applications to be developed, or to describe applications already developed, in a system independent manner. Using HDM as an implementation device, means to directly support the development effort by HDM related tools, as described in Section 4.3.

A number of experiences have shown that significant gains in the quality and speed of the whole process of application development can be achieved by using HDM as modeling device. In particular, we have observed that HDM is especially suitable for applications where regularity, organization, modularization, and consistency are important factors. Typical examples of such applications are, for example, technical documentation, training and education [12, 27], auditing systems [13], and in general, large applications for corporate environments. It is therefore true that "creative" applications [5], where the author tends to follow his feelings in a somehow unpredictable way (e.g., inventing new nodes and new navigation patterns on the fly) rather than planning his exercise in advance, are not conveniently modeled by HDM. Our conjecture (not yet fully tested) is that most of the intensively used, existing or future, hypertext applications are unlikely to be of the "creative" kind, but rather they are planned, cohesive, and carefully organized.

As a modeling device, HDM has been successfully used several times. Beside the authors, several different research groups in four different countries are using HDM in a significant number of different application fields, which range from administration and technical manuals, to university class

notes, literature, philosophy encyclopaedias, art collections, and exhibitions [9, 23, 24, 25, 34]. All of them have reported that the model can be relatively easily grasped both by the users and by designers, and that a more productive cooperation can be achieved among the persons involved in the process of application development—analysts and domain experts, analysts and implementors, different implementors. Domain experts are able to discuss the design of the application in HDM terms, and to autonomously modify and improve it. This implies a tremendous gain in the efficiency and quality of knowledge and requirement analysis processes. Members of the implementation team are able to discuss the application with the analysts and to get a deep and precise understanding of the requirements of their work without the need of prototyping it. This makes it possible to split the implementation tasks among different persons, still obtaining consistent applications. Since implementors are guided by clear and precise specifications, arbitrariness is virtually eliminated.

An interesting side effect of using HDM in team work has been the fact that people who use HDM as a modeling device, tend to invest a quite extensive time in discussing "organization style" issues (e.g., the best way of organizing a set of information, the choice between establishing perspective links versus application links, etc.). These discussions are extremely effective: the overall quality of applications improves, in general, and, more interesting, groups tend to develop a common, consistent design style across different application domains.

Additionally, HDM and related tools have been shown to be quite useful in making the development of the same application in different versions easier, by "switching" from one environment to another. Target systems, so far, have been Hypercard, Supercard, Hyperpad, Toolbook, Director (the latter for animations embedded in Figure 1—Subsection 4.3).

4.3 Tools and Implementation

We have developed so far a number of elementary HDM-tools to speed up the development of our applications. For the time being, these tools perform the following operations:

—automatic suggestion of application links (out of link type descriptions in the schema);

—automatic derivation of some application links (the inverses of author-defined application links, and the root-to-root derived links based on the rule exemplified in Figure 1—Subsection 4.3);

—automatic derivation of structural and perspective links;

—maintenance of link tables (which describe the extensions corresponding to link types);

—automatic derivation of a class of outlines—those allowing to enter the hyperbase by first selecting the entity types of interest, and then choosing the desired entity within the list of all entities of the selected type;

—automatic creation of entity templates (out of entity type descriptions in the schema);

—automatic creation of visual templates for nodes, including placement of anchors and association of anchors to link instances.

For implementation purposes, HDM has not been yet tested on a sufficiently large scale; the initial results, however, are quite encouraging. Even in their rudimentary stage of development, the above tools have greatly increased the effectiveness of our development, by a ratio of four to one, and we have achieved enormous savings in the development effort. For example, in an educational application based on six entity types and eighteen link types, six hundred units ("nodes"), and four thousand link instances, all the visual templates for nodes of the different types have been automatically generated, and 80% of the link instances have been derived. It is easy to understand why this happens; just think of the effectiveness of automatic generation of visual templates, including anchors and their associations to links, and, above all, automatic generation of derived links.

4.4 Further Developments

All the above tools, although effective in their own respect, do not constitute a well defined consistent development environment. The research project HYTEA [1], within the CEC ESPRIT program, is currently aiming at the development of a full size HDM-based development environment for hypertext applications. The project involves four different companies and two research institutions, and is scheduled to be completed by March 1993. Within the HYTEA project, the modeling primitives of HDM have been "transferred" into the concrete syntax of a language, named HDL—HDM definition language [22], which has been omitted here for lack of space. HDL is more a reference language than a language which will be directly used by application designers. In the final HYTEA environment, authoring in HDM will be based on visual programming, rather than on traditional programming. Some work on defining visual objects corresponding to HDM design primitives is already in progress. A reference language is still useful, however, in order to define precisely the semantics of the interactive operations offered by the HDM authoring environment.

HDM is, obviously, an evolving model: as we gain applicative experience, new emerging needs. In particular, we will modify the model according to the relatively access structures currently provided by HDM are restricted to the relatively unsophisticated notion of outline, which has been proved to be too limited. Looking at complex corporate environments, we found out that a typical situation is to have several different categories of readers using the same hyperbase. Each category of users naturally perceives the organization of the material according to its needs. From this observation, we came to the conclusion that access structures should evolve from just providing entry points to the hyperbase to becoming something like "hypertext views", i.e., ways of presenting "fictitious" hypertext environments, specifically tailored for a class of readers. "Fictitious" means that these environments are not implemented on their own, but are rather "simulated" by a suitable mapping on the underlying hyperbase. For this purpose, the notions we are working on

are "derived entities" (i.e., entities assembled out of pieces of other, preexisting, entities), "user-derived" links (i.e., links derived only within a given reading environment), "parametric guided tours" (i.e., intensionally defined guided tours), and others of a similar kind. Another important aspect we are currently working on is multimediality. In the current version of HDM, images, animation, or video clips can be introduced as part of the authoring-in-the-small process. We have a prototype application, for example, where entities of type "history" are made of "history notes" (as their components), and each history note has two perspectives—text and animation. The reader can choose, according to his interest, either to read the textual description of an historical event or to watch the animated version of the same event. This approach works fine for simple applications, where multimedia has the limited role of presenting small chunks of information with a different perspective. In other applications, however, multimedia may have a larger role. A video showing a maintenance procedure, for example, touches different subjects; it would be artificial (and ineffective) to model it as a unit associated to a single component. We are currently working around the idea that "active" information objects such as animation or videoclips could play the role of "automated" guided tours [32, 42, 44], i.e., devices which automatically take the reader along different active information units of an underlying hyperbase, and are "synchronized" with interlinked chunks of static information. We are currently developing a large-scale application [34] around this idea. On the basis of the fourthcoming results we will introduce the proper extensions to HDM.

ACKNOWLEDGMENTS

The ideas that originated the HDM work were first developed in the context of an ESPRIT project, SUPERDOC, led by ARG—Applied Research Group SpA. We must acknowledge the technical contribution of the ARG team in general, and Cristina Borelli, SUPERDOC Project Leader, in particular. Many of the ideas described here benefited from discussions with Mark Bernstein, Norman Meyrowitz, John Mylopolous, and the members of the HYTEA Project Team, Andrea Caloini and Luca Mainetti in particular. We are grateful to the TOIS Associate Editor, Polle Zellweger, and to the TOIS anonymous reviewers for their extraordinarily helpful comments on previous versions of this paper.

REFERENCES

1. ARG-APPLIED RESEARCH GROUP SPA. HYTEA Technical Annex. Tech. Rep., ESPRIT project 5252 (HYTEA), 1990.
2. AKSCYN, R., McCRACKEN, D., AND YODER, E. KMS: A distributed hypertext system for managing knowledge in organizations. *Commun. ACM 31*, 7 (1988), 820–835.
3. ATKINSON, W. HyperCard. In *Software for Macintosh Computers.* Apple Computer Co, Cupertino, 1987.
4. BERNSTEIN, M., AND SWEENEY, E. *The Election of 1912, Hypertext for Macintosh Computers.* Eastgate Systems Inc, Watertown Mass, 1989.
5. BOLTER, J. D., AND JOYCE, M. Hypertext and creative writing. In *Proceedings ACM Hypertext '87* (Chapel Hill, N.C., Nov. 13–15, 1987), pp. 41–50.

6. BRODIE, M., MYLOPOULOS, J., AND SCHMIDT, J., EDS. On Conceptual Modelling: Perspectives from Artificial Intelligence, Databases and Programming Languages. Springer Verlag, 1984.

7. BROWN, P. J. Turning ideas into products: The Guide system. In Proceedings of the ACM Hypertext '87 (Chapel Hill, N.C., 1987), pp. 33–40.

8. BROWN, P. J. Assessing the quality of hypertext documents. In Hypertexts: Concepts, Systems and Applications (Proceedings of ECHT '90), A. Rizk, N. Streitz, and J. André, Eds., Cambridge University Press, Cambridge, 1990, pp. 1–12.

9. CALOINI, A., GARZOTTO F., AND PAOLINI, P. Hypermedia course notes: The experience of Politecnico di Milano. In Proceedings of the Italian Conference on Hypertext in Education and Research (Torino, 1991), pp. 35–42.

10. CHEN, P. The entity-relationship approach: Toward a unified view of data. ACM Trans. Database Syst. 1, 1 (1976), 9–36.

11. CONKLIN, J., AND BEGEMAN, M. L. gIBIS: A hypertext tool for exploratory policy discussion. ACM Trans. Inf. Syst. 6, 4 (1988), 303–331.

12. CRANE, G. From the old to the new: Integrating hypertext into traditional scholarship. In Proceedings of the ACM Hypertext '87 (Chapel Hill, N.C., Nov. 13–15, 1987), pp. 51–59.

13. DE YOUNG, L. Hypertext challenges in the auditing domain. In Proceedings of ACM Hypertext '89 (Pittsburgh, Pa., Nov. 5–8, 1989), pp. 169–180.

14. GARG, P. K. Abstraction mechanisms in hypertext. Commun. ACM 31, 7 (1988), 862–870.

15. GARZOTTO F., AND PAOLINI P. Expert dictionaries: Knowledge based tools for explanation and maintenance of complex application environments. In Proceedings of the 2nd ACM Conference on Industrial and Engineering Applications of AI and Expert Systems (Tullahoma, Tenn., June 6–9, 1989), pp. 157–169.

16. GARZOTTO, F., PAOLINI, P., AND SCHWABE, D. Authoring-in-the-large: Software engineering techniques for hypertext application design. In Proceedings of the 6th IEEE International Workshop on Software Specification and Design (Como, Oct. 25–26, 1991), pp. 87–98.

17. GARZOTTO P., PAOLINI P., SCHWABE, D., AND BERSTEIN, M. Tools for designer. In Hypertext/Hypermedia Handbook, E. Berk, and J. Devlin, Eds., McGraw Hill, 1991, 179–207.

18. GARZOTTO, F., PAOLINI, P., AND SCHWABE, D. HDM—A model for the design of hypertext applications. In Proceedings ACM Hypertext '91 (San Antonio, Tex, Dec. 15–18, 1991), pp. 313–328.

19. HALASZ, F. Reflections on NoteCards: Seven issues for the next generation of hypertext systems. Commun. ACM 31, 7 (1988), 836–851.

20. HALASZ, F., AND SCHWARTZ, M. The Dexter reference model. In Proceedings of the 1st Hypertext NIST Standardization Workshop (Gaithersburg, Md., Jan. 16–18, 1990), pp. 95–133.

21. HULL, P., AND KING, R. Semantic database modelling: Survey, applications, and research issues. ACM Comput. Surv. 19, 3 (1987), 201–260.

22. HYTEA PROJECT. HDL—HDM definition language. Tech. Rep. D2, ESPRIT Project 5252 (HYTEA), 1991.

23. HYTEA PROJECT. Hypermedia technical documentation for the forms processing system Siemens-SIFORM. Tech. Rep. D4.1, ESPRIT Project 5252 (HYTEA), 1992.

24. HYTEA PROJECT. Hypermedia technical documentation for IVECO-FIAT workshops. Tech. Rep. D4.2-ESPRIT Project 5252 (HYTEA), 1992.

25. HYTEA PROJECT. Hypermedia for cultural applications: Greek Modern Painting between the two world wars. Tech. Rep. D5, ESPRIT Project 5252 (HYTEA), 1992.

26. HYTEA PROJECT. Authoring/delivery HYTEA tools: Specification and design. Tech. Rep. 2, ESPRIT Project P5252 (HYTEA), 1992.

27. JORDAN, D., AND RUSSEL, D. Facilitating the development of representations in hypertext with IDE. In Proceedings ACM Hypertext '89 (Pittsburgh, Pa, Nov. 5–8, 1989), pp. 93–104.

28. LAI K. Y., MALONE, T. W., AND YU K. C. Object lens: A spreadsheet for cooperative work. ACM Trans. Inf. Syst. 6, 4 (1988), 332–353.

29. MARSHALL, C. C., AND IRISH, P. M. Guided tours and on-line presentations: How authors make existing hypertext intelligible for readers. In Proceedings ACM Hypertext '89 (Pittsburgh, Pa., Nov. 5–8, 1989), pp. 15–26.

30. MYLONAS, E., AND HEATH, S. Hypertext from the data point of view: Paths and links in the Perseus Project. In Hypertexts: Concepts, Systems and Applications (Proceedings of ECHT '90), A. Rizk, N. Streitz, and J. André, Eds., Cambridge University Press, Cambridge, 1990, pp. 324–336.

31. NIELSEN, J. The art of navigating through hypertext. Commun. ACM 33, 3 (1990), 296–310.

32. PAOLINI P., CALOINI, A., AND GARZOTTO, F. Active media and guided tours. Tech. Rep. 78-91, Dep. of Electronics, Politecnico di Milano, 1991.

33. PARUNAK, H. V. D. Hypertext topologies and user navigation. In Proceedings ACM Hypertext '87 (Chapel Hill, N.C., Nov. 13–15, 1987), pp. 43–50.

34. RAI-RADIO TELEVISIONE ITALIANA. The multimedia encyclopedia of philosophy. Tech. Rep., Dept. of Scholarship and Education, RAI, 1991.

35. RICHARD, G., AND RIZK, A. Quelques idées pour une modelization des systèmes hypertextes. Techniques et Sciences Informatiques. 9, 6 (1990), 505–514.

36. SCHWABE, D., CALOINI, A., GARZOTTO, F., AND PAOLINI, P. Hypertext development using a model-based approach. Softw. Pract. Exper. 22, 11 (1992), 937–962.

37. SHNEIDERMAN, B. (ED.) Hypertext on Hypertext. Database and Electronic Product Series, ACM Press, 1988.

38. SMITH, C. K., GARRET, L. N., AND LAUHARD, J. A. Hypermedia templates: An author's tools. In Proceedings ACM Hypertext '91 (San Antonio, Tex., 1991), pp. 147–160.

39. STOTTS, P. D., AND FURUTA, R. Petri-net-based hypertext: Document structure with browsing semantics. ACM Trans. Inf. Syst. 7, 1 (1989), 3–29.

40. STOTTS, P. D., AND FURUTA, R. Hierarchy, composition, scripting languages, and translators for a structured hypertext. In Hypertexts: Concepts, Systems and Applications (Proceedings of ECHT '90), A. Rizk, N. Streitz, and J. André, Eds., Cambridge University Press, Cambridge, 1990, pp. 180–193.

41. TOMPA, F. A data model for flexible hypertext database systems. ACM Trans. Inf. Syst. 7, 1 (1990), 85–100.

42. TRIGG, R. H. Guided tours and tabletops: Tools for communicating in hypertext environments. ACM Trans. Inf. Syst. 6, 4 (1988), 398–414.

43. UTTING, K., AND YANKELOVICH, N. Context and orientation in hypertext networks. ACM Trans. Inf. Syst. 7, 1 (1989) 58–84.

44. ZELLWEGER, P. T. Scripted documents: A hypermedia path mechanism. In Proceedings ACM Hypertext '89 (Pittsburgh, Pa., Nov. 5–8, 1989), pp. 1–14.

45. WALKER, J. H. Supporting document development with Concordia. IEEE Computer 21, 1 (1988), 48–59.

46. WIEDERHOLD, G. Database Design. McGraw Hill, 1983.

47. WINTER, R. T. Ludwig Van Beethoven Symphony Number 9. CD Companions Series, The Voyager Company, 1989.

48. YANKELOVICH, N. HAAN, B. J. MEYROWITZ, N. K., AND DRUCKER, S. M. Intermedia: The concept and construction of a seamless information environment. IEEE Computer 21, 1 (1988), 91–96.

Received January 1991; revised April 1992; accepted July 1992

Automatic Temporal Layout Mechanisms

M. Cecelia Buchanan and Polle T. Zellweger
Information Sciences and Technologies Laboratory
Xerox Palo Alto Research Center

Abstract

A traditional static document has a *spatial layout* that indicates where objects in the document appear. Because multimedia documents incorporate time, they also require a *temporal layout*, or *schedule*, that indicates when events in the document occur. This paper argues that multimedia document systems should provide mechanisms for automatically producing temporal layouts for documents. The major advantage of this approach is that it makes it easier for authors to create and modify multimedia documents.

This paper constructs a framework for understanding automatic temporal formatters and explores the basic issues surrounding them. It also describes the Firefly multimedia document system, which has been developed to test the potential of automatic temporal formatting.

Keywords: automatic temporal layout, automatic scheduling, media synchronization, multimedia document formatting, temporal constraints

1. Introduction

A traditional static document has a *spatial layout* that indicates where objects in the document appear. Before the advent of document formatting systems, such as TEX [13], a typical author manually positioned words on pages with a typewriter and positioned images on pages by drawing directly or by pasting photographs. In contrast, document formatting systems allow authors to specify the text and figures as well as formatting directives, such as justification, centering, line and paragraph leading, and figure placement. These systems use the content and the formatting directives to construct a spatial layout automatically, thus easing the creation and maintenance of formatted documents and also increasing their quality in general.

Multimedia documents increase the expressive power of documents by allowing authors to combine dynamic media segments with *predictable behavior*, such as audio, video, and animations. In addition, interactive multimedia documents can include *unpredictable behavior*, such as user interaction, reaching a particular program or document state, and programs with unpredictable execution times. Because multimedia documents incorporate time, they also require a *temporal layout*, or *schedule*, that indicates when events in the document should occur.

Authors' addresses: 3333 Coyote Hill Road, Palo Alto, CA 94304. buchanan@parc.xerox.com, zellweger@parc.xerox.com.

Most current multimedia document systems are in the "pre-document formatter" stage. They typically require authors to create temporal layouts manually by positioning media segments on a document timeline [8, 16, 18, 19], a tedious and error-prone process. Other manual methods include temporal scripting languages [9] and temporal relation trees [15, 12]. It is time for multimedia document systems to take over this task, generating the temporal layouts automatically. Analogous to automatic spatial formatting, automatic temporal formatting requires authors to specify both the media and temporal formatting directives. We expect similar advantages from automatic temporal formatting, namely easing the creation and maintenance of multimedia documents and increasing their quality in general.

The Firefly multimedia document system has been developed to explore automatic temporal formatters. Two previous papers describe how Firefly can be used to specify temporal behavior in hypermedia documents [4] and the details of its algorithm for automatic temporal formatting [5].

This paper draws from our experiences with Firefly to consider general issues and requirements in providing automatic temporal formatters. It constructs a framework for understanding automatic temporal formatters and explores the basic issues surrounding them. Given this framework, it reviews automatic temporal formatters that have been provided by other multimedia document systems. Finally, it uses the framework to describe the automatic temporal formatter provided by Firefly.

2. Issues and Requirements for Automatic Temporal Formatting

A multimedia document system that provides an effective automatic temporal formatter must satisfy three major requirements. First, it must support media segments that have a rich set of capabilities. Second, it must have a method for explicitly representing the temporal relationships among the media segments in a document. Third, it must provide a powerful temporal formatting algorithm. Table 1 in Section 3 summarizes the important aspects of these requirements; readers may wish to consult it as they read this section.

2.1 Media Segments

Media segments are the data that will be presented in documents. To permit expressive documents, a formatter must allow documents to include a rich variety of media types, such as text, images, audio, video, animations, and programs. In addition, media segments are sometimes used to represent delays [10, 12, 15]. Media segments can also be composites which support hierarchy by allowing a multimedia document to appear as a media segment in another document.

For the purposes of temporal formatting, media segments have four primary attributes: *granularity*, *duration*, *flexibility*, and *flexibility metrics*. Other characteristics of media segments, such as compression algorithms and storage devices, are considered only insofar as they impact a media segment's duration because they do not otherwise directly affect a formatter's operation.

Granularity. The granularity of a media segment deals with the amount of internal structure the media segment makes accessible to the system (and the author). *Coarse granularity* represents only the starting and ending points of a media segment's presentation. A system with *fine granularity* also represents internal points that occur during the presentation of a media segment. Fine granularity can thus permit an author to synchronize an internal point, such as the start of a lion's roar within a longer audio segment, with another media segment, such as the presentation of a picture of a lion.

Note that points in time, called *events*, can be classified as either predictable or unpredictable. *Predictable events* mark times that can be determined in advance under ideal conditions (ignoring unpredictable delays, such as excessive network load). Examples of predictable events include the time at which a specific sample in an audio recording is played. *Unpredictable events* mark times during the presentation of a media segment that cannot be determined in advance, such as when a program reaches a particular state or when a reader selects an object on the screen.

Durations. Durations provide a formatter with information on the lengths of time required to prepare and present media data. Preparing media data for presentation includes times for retrieving, compressing, transmitting, and uncompressing the data. Durations for presenting media data specify the length of time between two events in the same media segment. Durations can also be classified as predictable or unpredictable.

A *predictable duration* is one whose length can be determined in advance. Examples of media segments with predictable durations include audio, video, and animations. Typically, the length of a predictable duration is a function of the amount of data and the rate at which a unit of data is presented. Predictable media preparation times include those to spin up video playback heads or to transmit data over a network providing guaranteed throughput.

An *unpredictable duration* is one whose length cannot be determined until the media segment actually ends. Media segments with unpredictable durations include programs with unpredictable execution times, such as database search engines and simulations; and realtime communication, such as telephone conversations and live broadcasts of lectures. Unpredictable media preparation times include those to perform a graphical transformation on an image or to transmit data over a network in which resources cannot be reserved.

Some media segments, such as text and images, do not have an inherent notion of time in their specifications. These media segments can either inherit durations from other media segments, such as presenting an image while an audio media segment plays, or have either predictable or unpredictable durations imposed on them. For example, a predictable duration could be imposed on an image media segment either by presenting it for a fixed amount of time, say 10 seconds, or by presenting portions of it at a fixed rate, say highlighting 6 regions of the image for 2 minutes each for an overall duration of 12 minutes. An unpredictable duration could be imposed by allowing readers to scroll through the media segment at their own speed.

Flexibility. A media segment's flexibility specifies parameters for manipulating its duration and media type. A media segment may have no flexibility, or it may be continuously adjustable, discretely adjustable, or both.

A *continuously-adjustable* media segment specifies a *range* from which the duration can be selected. For example, a video media

segment can specify a range from 5 to 10 seconds. In addition, the system may support the specification of a *preferred duration* within that range, which is the value a formatter will initially attempt to use. For example, the above video media segment may have a preferred duration of 10 seconds. Media segments can permit continuous adjustments to their durations in several ways, including modifying the playback rate, discarding or repeating data, or performing an alternative action when there is no more data to present [20]. Unfortunately, these techniques often reduce the overall quality of their physical appearance and cannot be used indiscriminately. However, within certain ranges, the physical effects of these modifications may not noticeably reduce quality.

A *discretely-adjustable* media segment specifies distinct, alternative representations that may have different durations [2]. For example, a media segment on a technical subject might have several different representations, including an executive overview, a 5-minute overview, a conference-length talk, and a seminar-length talk. In addition, the alternative representations of a media segment may use different types of media. For example, the conference-length and seminar-length talks might be video media segments, while the executive overview might be an audio media segment and the 5-minute overview might be a text media segment.

Flexibility metrics. Media segments providing flexibility may optionally include *flexibility metrics* to provide an objective measure of the quality of a particular media segment's presentation, the expense of generating, transporting, or presenting the media segment, or both. This information can be used by a formatter to select the "best" representation for each media segment in a given situation.

2.2 Temporal Relationships

Temporal relationships describe how media segments should be combined temporally to produce a multimedia document. The temporal relationships serve both as input to a temporal formatter and as an explicit record of the author's intentions. The latter allows the temporal relationships to be retained when changes are made to the document. An analogy in spatial formatting is a table formatter that calculates column widths based on the current table content.

For the purposes of temporal formatting, temporal relationships have four primary attributes: *granularity*, *temporal relation types*, *flexibility*, and *flexibility metrics*. Of secondary importance are the temporal aspects of the document's behavior and spatial specifications.

Granularity. Granularity specifies where temporal relationships can be placed: between points in time, between temporal intervals, or both. A *point* can be a range of things: an absolute time, a relative time during the document's presentation (i.e., 10 seconds after the start of the document, halfway through a media segment); a predictable or unpredictable event in a media segment; an external event that can be passed through to the system (i.e., user interaction); or a *composite point*, which is any temporal relationship that produces a specific point in time (see below). An *interval* can be an entire media segment; a portion of a media segment (i.e., the first scene in a video); or a *composite interval*, which is any temporal relationship that produces an interval of time.

Temporal relation types. Temporal relations can be grouped into three major classes according to whether they control temporal ordering of media segments; durations of media segments; or more complex relationships, such as grouping, iteration, and conditionals.

Ordering relations are binary relations that specify the order of occurrence of points or intervals in a document. The set of allowable ordering relations are the temporal relations described by Allen [1]: before, starts (sometimes called parallel), finishes, meets (sometimes called sequential), equals, overlaps, and during. An analogy to equals in spatial formatting is justified, to starts is left justified, and to finishes is right justified. Note that different ordering relations may be allowed depending on whether the relationship is between two points, two intervals, a point and an interval, or an interval and a point. The before, overlaps, and during ordering relations may have optional parameters to specify more precise positioning. These parameters may be temporal equalities, such as 10 seconds; temporal inequalities, such as less than 10 seconds; or temporal ranges, such as between 10 seconds and 1 minute.

Duration relations specify relationships between the durations of intervals, such as requiring that the duration of two media segments be equal, that one duration be twice as long as another, or that one duration be "shorter" than another. Note that a duration relation can often be expressed as a set of ordering relations. For example, the equals duration relation is equivalent to applying both a starts and a finishes ordering relation to two intervals or to applying one equals ordering relation between their start events and another between their end events.

Finally, the more complex relations begin to provide programmatic capabilities. *Group relations* allow the author to collect temporally unrelated intervals and points together so that they can be used as a single entity in another temporal relationship. Groups thus permit a media segment to be started by the occurrence of any one of a set of events. *Iteration relations* specify that an interval be presented repeatedly a specific number of times, or until (or while) a certain condition holds. *Conditional relations* are dependent on the document or system being in a particular state, such as presenting a video media segment if the workstation has video hardware. Conditional relations could include a counting mechanism that allows the author to base relationships on the number of times a particular document or system state occurs, such as presenting a special message if the user asks for help more than five times. Note that these complex relations typically require a runtime component to maintain, monitor, and react to the states upon which they depend.

Extending temporal and duration relations from binary to n-ary can significantly reduce the number of relationships that an author must specify. Combining n-ary temporal and group relations allows a rich grouping and composition space of temporal relationships. Composite events and intervals extend this space yet further.

In the future, we hope that higher-level temporal relations, analogous to center and the like in spatial formatting, will be constructed from the basic relations described here.

Flexibility. Temporal relationships can support two forms of flexibility [6]. First, a system may permit authors to specify that a temporal relationship is either *mandatory*, meaning that this temporal relationship must be satisfied in the resulting temporal layout, or *optional*, meaning that this temporal relationship is desirable but can be ignored. Second is a *range* of times within which a temporal relationship is considered to be satisfied. For example, a finishes ordering relation between two audio media segments with a range of plus or minus one second is considered to be satisfied as long as these media segments end within one second of each other, rather than at exactly the same time. Note that some ordering relations, such as before, overlaps, and during, may have inherent flexibility.

Flexibility metrics. A system may support flexibility metrics to provide an objective basis for choosing among the flexibility options. Flexibility metrics measure the degradation in presentation quality attributable to ignoring an optional temporal relationship or to varying a temporal relationship within the specified range.

Other parameters. We now discuss behavior and spatial specifications insofar as they affect automatic temporal formatters.

Behavior specification allows authors to impose behavior on a point or an interval, much as different appearances, such as bold or italic, can be applied to characters or paragraphs in spatial document formatting systems. Authors may wish to apply behaviors to individual points, such as sending messages to other media segments; individual intervals, such as zooming in on a portion of an image; or to groups of intervals, such as setting the volume of all audio media segments to a certain level. In some cases behavior specification can affect the durations of media segments, such as when they are used to speed up or slow down the playback. As a result, a formatter must compensate for time-altering operations when producing temporal layouts.

Spatial specification allows authors to control the physical appearance of media segments, such as specifying where windows should appear, how big they should be, whether they should be visible or hidden, what font sizes and colors should be used, and so on. As with behavior specification, authors should be able to apply behaviors to individual media segments as well as to groups of media segments. Because multimedia documents introduce a temporal viewing axis, spatial positions and sizes should be able to change during the presentation of a document. For example, if the x- and y-coordinates of a window as well as its size are specified as a function of time, an author can specify that a window will initially appear in the upper right portion of the screen and will gradually grow and move to the lower left. For maximum expressiveness, it is desirable for changes in spatial states to be able to trigger events, and similarly for events to be able to trigger changes in spatial layout.

2.3 Environment Specification

In order to determine whether a document with a given temporal specification can actually be presented in a particular target environment, a temporal formatter must also consider the capabilities of the workstation and possibly the surrounding network. These capabilities are described in an environment specification.

An *environment specification* consists of two parts: workstation and network specifications [2]. *Workstation specifications* describe the capabilities of the target workstations upon which a document may be presented, such as available multimedia hardware devices and restrictions on the simultaneous utilization of these resources. *Network specifications* describe the characteristics of the networks over which media segments or multimedia documents may be transported, such as quality of service, transport costs or connection delays, and network connectivity. Environment specifications would typically be supplied by someone such as a systems or network administrator, rather than by the author of a particular document.

Differences in environment capabilities may demand different layouts. They may affect the positioning of media segments, as when media segment preparation times vary; they may affect the choice among adjustable durations or alternative media types, as when their device requirements vary; or they may show that the document cannot be presented on a workstation because there is insufficient flexibility in the media segments and the temporal relationships. In fact, the capabilities of the target environment might also alter the flexibility metrics for the temporal specification, which may in turn result in a different "best" layout.

2.4 Automatic Temporal Formatters

An automatic temporal formatter uses a *temporal specification*, which consists of media segments and the temporal relationships among them, and an environment specification to produce a temporal layout that indicates when events in a document should occur.

Abstractly, a temporal layout is a sequence of *entries*, each of which contains a time and an event. A *partial layout* is one in which some of the times have not yet been completely specified. A temporal layout is said to be *consistent* if the times satisfy the specified temporal relationships among media segments [15, 12]. Otherwise we say there are *temporal mismatches*. A temporal layout is said to be *presentable* if it is consistent and its environment requirements are satisfied.

A temporal layout is used to control a document's presentation. The resulting *presentation trace* may differ from the intended temporal layout due to media delays, which may occur for a variety of reasons, including queueing for resources or bandwidth limitations. Unpredictable behavior may be detected at runtime and fed back into the temporal formatter to affect the temporal layout.

Conceptually, an automatic temporal formatter proceeds in the following way. First, it attempts to position media segments without considering the flexibility of their durations and temporal relationships. Then, as long as the temporal layout is not consistent, it uses the flexibility to perturb the layout. Note that a given formatting algorithm may not be powerful enough to use all of the available flexibility. If a formatter also wishes to adhere to the environment specification, it substitutes "presentable" for "consistent" in the above procedure.

2.4.1 Characteristics

An automatic temporal formatter can be characterized along four primary dimensions: its *flexibility* in assigning times, the *temporal behavior* it handles, its *mismatch detection*, and *when it is run*. Secondary characteristics of an automatic temporal formatter are its efficiency and the quality of its error messages.

Flexibility. As described above, a formatter may use some or all of a temporal specification's flexibility to assign times to events, including simply positioning media segments (i.e., no flexibility), ignoring optional temporal relationships, adjusting temporal relationships or durations of media segments within the specified ranges, or selecting alternative representations. Allowing a formatter to use this flexibility increases the number of temporal specifications for which consistent temporal layouts can be created.

Temporal behavior. An automatic temporal formatter may handle different types of temporal behavior. The simplest form is predictable behavior. We can separate unpredictable behavior into three classes. *Content-based* unpredictable behavior, such as program states and user interaction with the content of the document, is actually modelled in the temporal specification. In contrast, *meta-directives*, which arise from the dynamic user control of the presentation rate, direction, and location, are not modelled in the temporal specification. The final class is *media delays*, which can arise from processor, device, or network limitations. Allowing content-based unpredictable behavior increases the expressiveness of the resulting documents, handling meta-directives increases their usability, and handling media delays, which will never become totally predictable, improves the

quality of their temporal layout.

Mismatch detection. A formatter may detect either temporal or environmental mismatches. Mismatch detection affects the quality of the resulting temporal layout and, therefore, the appearance of the resulting documents.

When it is run. A temporal formatter can be run before the document is presented (termed *compiletime*), while the document is being presented (termed *runtime*), or at both times (termed *hybrid*). This characteristic affects both the quality and the expressiveness of the presentation.

A compiletime formatter can improve the appearance of the resulting documents in two ways. First, it can take full advantage of the flexibility of the media segment durations and the temporal relationships to smooth out predeterminable temporal and environment mismatches. In contrast, a runtime formatter typically does not detect mismatches until a portion of the document has already been presented. This delay in detection limits a runtime formatter's ability to smooth out mismatches and often produces a choppy presentation. Second, a compiletime formatter can identify errors that normally would not be detected until runtime, if at all. These errors include inconsistencies in the temporal specification, such as unsatisfiable temporal relationships, and inconsistencies because of the environment in which the document is going to be displayed, such as the lack of video hardware. Furthermore, this error checking is essentially free, because the algorithm that does the error checking is the same one that produces the temporal layout.

The major advantage of a runtime formatter is its unique ability to handle unpredictable behavior, with the accompanying benefits described above.

A hybrid formatter can reap the advantages of both approaches by providing a compiletime formatter that handles the predeterminable portions of the temporal specification and a runtime formatter that handles the unpredictable portions.

2.4.2 Architectural Schema

Figure 1 shows a general architectural schema for an automatic temporal formatter.

The *runtime support system* uses a temporal layout to control a document's presentation. It maintains a document clock, which allows it to determine when to process the temporal layout entries, and it establishes a pathway for media segments to communicate with each other or the runtime support system. It may also allow the user to dynamically control the document's presentation: changing its playback rate, presenting it in reverse, or jumping to a different point in the presentation [14].

In addition, the runtime support system may monitor for the occurrence of unpredictable behavior. When unpredictable behavior is detected, the runtime support system must feed this information back to the runtime formatter, which must then adjust the temporal layout accordingly.

For temporal specifications containing only predictable behavior, either a compiletime or a runtime formatter may be used. In either case, the formatter takes temporal and environment specifications and creates a temporal layout for use by the runtime support system.

Unpredictable behavior can be handled by either a runtime or a hybrid formatter.

A runtime formatter can react to unpredictable behavior in one of two ways. In the simpler case, it has access to a manually-created partial layout in which the predictable portions have *definite* times and the unpredictable portions have *event-relative* times. The

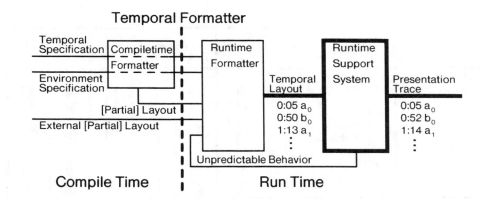

Figure 1. Temporal formatter architecture. Bold lines indicate mandatory elements; all others are optional.

runtime formatter must resolve these event-relative times to produce a temporal layout. Otherwise, it uses the temporal and environment specifications to dynamically produce a temporal layout.

A hybrid formatter can handle unpredictable behavior using methods that parallel those described above for runtime formatters. In the simpler case, a hybrid formatter uses the compiletime component to produce a partial layout in which the predictable portions are assigned definite times and the unpredictable portions are assigned event-relative times. Again, the runtime component is responsible for resolving the event-relative times. Otherwise, the compiletime component creates a partial layout in which no times are assigned to the unpredictable portions. The runtime component uses this partial layout and the temporal and environment specifications to produce a complete temporal layout.

2.4.3 Compiletime Algorithms

Determining which algorithm a compiletime formatter should use is still an open issue. Some interesting algorithms include topological sort, all-pairs-shortest-path, linear programming, dynamic programming, constraint hierarchies, and incremental algorithms. We now briefly describe these algorithms.

A formatter can position entire media segments using topological sort, a linear algorithm that cannot handle any form of flexibility.

All-pairs-shortest-path is a polynomial algorithm that supports a limited form of continuously-adjustable durations, which are specified as a minimum and maximum value [7]. This algorithm produces a range of legal times at which each event can occur. A temporal layout can be constructed by scheduling each event to occur at the earliest possible time in its legal range. Although the resulting temporal layout will be consistent, it will not be the "best" temporal layout in most cases. If the algorithm detects a negative cycle, the temporal specification is inconsistent (i.e., a temporal layout cannot be created for it). An error message for this algorithm can indicate the events in the negative cycle, but it cannot pinpoint the source of the error.

Compiletime formatters can be extended to handle continuously-adjustable durations by using linear programming [11]. In this case, the temporal specification is converted into a set of simultaneous linear equations. The linear programming algorithm solves these equations so as to minimize or maximize a linear function of the duration flexibility metrics, called *costs*. For example, it could attempt to minimize the overall cost of making continuous adjustments to the durations of media segments. This algorithm would require modifications to handle discretely-

adjustable media segments. This algorithm also cannot pinpoint the source of errors in the temporal specification.

Dynamic programming [11], such as the algorithm used in T_EX [13], and constraint hierarchies may be useful for handling discretely-adjustable media segments, because they provide a systematic way to test a variety of options.

Running a compiletime formatter incrementally while an author is creating a temporal specification may help authors locate errors by providing immediate feedback when an editing operation introduces a temporal mismatch.

Note that these algorithms could also be used in a hybrid formatter. The compiletime formatter would separate the temporal specification into a predictable portion and a set of unpredictable portions (one for each unpredictable event), and compute a partial layout. The runtime formatter would then resolve the unpredictable behavior to create a complete temporal layout.

2.4.4 Runtime Algorithms

Determining which algorithm a runtime formatter should use is also an open issue. Some interesting algorithms include interpreting a graph, using temporal data flow, merging precomputed temporal layouts to handle unpredictable behavior, prefetching data to avoid media delays, using runtime signalling to detect and correct media delays, and incrementally running a formatter to handle documents generated on-the-fly. We now briefly describe these algorithms.

In the simplest case, a temporal specification can be converted into a graph or a temporal scripting language [9], which is then processed by an interpreter that serves as a runtime formatter.

A merge approach can be used when a partial layout, with one predictable and at least one unpredictable portions, is available. This algorithm manages the individual portions of the layout, and when it detects the occurrence of unpredictable behavior, it locates the appropriate portion and merges it into the temporal layout.

Another approach uses temporal data flow representations, such as Petri nets [15], timed Petri nets [21], or temporal dependency graphs [23], in which a temporal specification is converted into a marked graph that drives a document's presentation. A node has a marker on its output arc if its temporal relationships have been satisfied. A node is permitted to proceed when all of its input arcs

Media Segments		Temporal glue	Trellis	Geneva	CMIF	MODE	Firefly
Media Segments		*Compile*	*Runtime*			*Hybrid*	
Granularity	Coarse	■	■	■	■	■	■
	Fine	■	□	■	□	■	■
Durations	Predictable	■	■	■	■	■	■
	Unpredictable	□	□	■	■	◪	■
Flexibility	Continuous	◪	□	□	□	■	■
	Discrete	□	□	□	□	■	□
	Flexibility Metrics	?	□	□	□	■	■
Temporal Specification							
Granularity	Points	■	□	■	■	■	■
	Intervals	□	■	■	■	□	□
	Composites	□	■	■	■	□	□
Relations	Ordering	■	■	■	■	■	■
	Duration [1]	□	□	□	□	□	□
	Complex	□	■	■	□	□	□
Flexibility	Mandatory/Optional	□	□	□	■	□	□
	Range	□	□	□	□	□	□
	Flexibility Metrics	□	□	□	□	□	□
Formatter							
Compiletime							
Flexibility	Position	□				□	■
	Ignore Optional	□				□	□
	Adjust	■				□	■
	Select Alternatives	□				■	■
Mismatch Detection	Temporal	■				□	
	Environment	□				■	
Runtime							
Flexibility	Position		■	■	■	□	■
	Ignore Optional		□	□	□	■	□
	Adjust		□	□	□	□	□
	Select Alternatives		□	□	□	□	□
Unpredictable Behavior	Content-Based		■	■	■	□	■
	Meta-Directives		□	□	■	■	□
	Media Delays		□	□	□	□	□

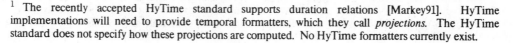

[1] The recently accepted HyTime standard supports duration relations [Markey91]. HyTime implementations will need to provide temporal formatters, which they call *projections*. The HyTime standard does not specify how these projections are computed. No HyTime formatters currently exist.

Table 1. How existing automatic temporal formatters fit into the framework of Section 2.

have markers. Temporal data flow representations have the added advantage that they inherently support a group relation that allows media segments to wait until all of a group of parallel media segments have completed. Timed Petri nets permit media segments to wait only until *any* of the preceding media segments have completed.

The algorithms described above do not handle media delays. One approach is to look ahead and prefetch media segments before they are needed [23]. However, it has the drawback that significant amounts of buffering may be needed on the target workstation, especially if temporal specifications may include unpredictable behavior. In a second approach, media segments use the runtime support system's signalling mechanism to inform each other when they reach an event [3]. Media delays can then

be handled by making media segments wait at an event until all other media segments temporally related to that event reach it. A more sophisticated approach allows media segments to make continuous adjustments to perform both a "filling" action while waiting at an event and a skipping or accelerating action to reach an event faster.

When portions of a document are generated dynamically, we call it a document generated on-the-fly. Running runtime formatters incrementally represents a promising approach to handling documents generated on-the-fly. Because it is impossible to reposition elements that have already occurred, this form of an incremental formatter is more complicated than the compiletime version described earlier.

3. Automatic Temporal Formatters Provided In Other Systems

We now apply our framework and terminology to the task of describing automatic temporal formatters provided by other systems. We can classify one system as having a compiletime formatter: temporal glue, and three as having runtime formatters: Trellis, the Geneva temporal scripting language, and CMIFed. The MODE system is closest to our Firefly system, in that it provides a hybrid formatter. Table 1 shows how existing automatic temporal formatters fit into the framework laid out in Section 2.

3.1 Compiletime Temporal Formatters

Temporal glue. Hamakawa et al. address the problem of authoring ease by allowing authors to insert special *temporal glue* media segments that represent variable-length delays at desired locations [10]. Temporal glue acts like TEX's (spatial) glue and has similar flexibility parameters controlling its stretchability and shrinkability [13]. Their system supports media segments with coarse granularity and predictable durations. Only temporal glue media segments support continuous adjustability. They do not specify what, if any, temporal relationships their system supports. They provide a compiletime formatter that produces consistent temporal layouts by positioning media segments and adjusting the durations of temporal glue. The algorithm used by this formatter is not described.

3.2 Runtime Temporal Formatters

Trellis. Trellis uses a temporal data flow representation based on timed Petri nets to describe both the structure and the browsing semantics of hypertext documents [21]. It supports only text media segments with (imposed) predictable durations. Trellis supports ordering relations among intervals and a form of group relation. The timed Petri net's release time and maximum latency provide flexibility in the temporal specification.

Geneva temporal scripting language. Researchers at the University of Geneva have developed an object-oriented temporal scripting language for composing multimedia objects [9]. This language supports media segments with fine granularity, predictable durations, continuous adjustability, and no flexibility metrics. The language includes behavior specification called temporal transformations that perform actions such as positioning an object in absolute time, scaling the duration of an object (i.e., continuous adjustment), or inverting the (temporal) direction of a media segment between "forward" and "backward". The runtime formatter for this language is its compiler/interpreter.

CMIFed. CMIFed addresses the problem of presenting multimedia documents in a heterogeneous hardware environment [6, 23]. It supports media segments, called *data blocks*, that have coarse granularity, predictable durations, no flexibility, and no flexibility parameters. It supports binary ordering relations, called *synchronization arcs*, that can only be placed between the endpoints of media segments and two n-ary ordering relations among intervals: meets, which they call *sequential*; and starts, which they call *parallel*. Although CMIFed's temporal specification supports both forms of flexible temporal relationships, they are not handled by the runtime formatter. CMIFed's runtime formatter, called the *player*, uses a temporal dependency graph traversal algorithm. Although CMIFed does not currently support media segments with unpredictable durations, it appears that the player can handle them by inserting variable length delays as needed.

3.3 Hybrid Temporal Formatters

In addition to the Firefly system discussed in the next section, one other system provides a hybrid formatter. MODE (Multimedia Objects in a Distributed Environment) was designed to address the problem of presenting multimedia documents in distributed, heterogeneous hardware environments [3].

MODE supports media segments called *objects* that have fine granularity, predictable durations, continuous adjustability, discrete adjustability, and flexibility metrics. Events are called *reference points*. Discrete adjustability, called *alternative presentations* or *presentation quality*, is specified as an attribute list consisting of the name of the attribute, a preferred value, and a value domain that describes all possible values for the attribute. Flexibility metrics, called *priorities*, may be associated with each attribute to denote its relative importance to other attributes and with each object to describe its sensitivity to media delays. MODE supports *interactive objects* that allow readers to control a document's presentation dynamically. It is not clear whether these interactive objects have unpredictable or imposed (predictable) durations.

MODE supports temporal relationships called *synchronization points* that may be placed between two or more events. A synchronization point acts like a parallel programming join operation in that the media segments cannot proceed beyond that point until all of the media segments reach it.

MODE's hybrid formatter provides a compiletime component called the *Optimizer* and a runtime component called the *Synchronizer*. The input to the formatter consists of a manually-constructed temporal layout and an environment specification. Therefore, neither the Optimizer nor the Synchronizer creates a temporal layout. The Optimizer uses the environment specification to select a presentation quality to be used for this presentation of the document. The Synchronizer handles media delays via a runtime signalling mechanism. In addition, it allows media segments to make continuous adjustments to their durations to reach the synchronization point faster. The Synchronizer also implements the meta-directives generated by the interactive objects described above, but they do not specify how this is accomplished.

In contrast to using a manually-constructed temporal layout, Firefly provides a compiletime component that automatically constructs a partial layout, as discussed in the next section.

4. Firefly's Hybrid Temporal Formatter

We have designed and implemented a multimedia document system called Firefly whose goals are to increase the expressive power of multimedia documents and to make them easier to create and maintain. A prototype of Firefly has been implemented on Sun workstations in the Cedar programming environment [22]. This section describes how Firefly fits into the framework laid out in Section 2.

4.1 Temporal Specification

In Firefly, a temporal specification consists of three parts: media segments, which we call *media items*; temporal relationships, which we call *temporal constraints*; and behavior specification, which we call *operation lists*.

Firefly supports media items with fine granularity, predictable and unpredictable durations, continuous adjustability, and flexibility metrics. The duration between any pair of temporally adjacent events in a media item is referred to as the optimum duration. Each duration can be adjusted continuously within a range specified as a minimum and maximum duration.

Flexibility metrics called *stretching and shrinking costs* may be associated with continuously-adjustable durations to provide an objective measure of the media segment's presentation-quality degredation. These costs are specified as non-negative real numbers; a stretching cost may differ from its corresponding shrinking cost.

Temporal constraints are ordering relations (with all optional parameters) that can be placed between pairs of events in one or more media items. Flexibility and flexibility metrics are not supported. Behavior specification in Firefly is handled via ordered operation lists, which can be associated with any event. Operation lists are kept separately from the media items to allow multiple documents to control shared media items differently. Although a document's spatial specification cannot be varied directly as a function of time, the behavior specification can include operations that affect window size and placement.

Figure 2 shows a temporal specification for a sample Firefly document, represented using Firefly's graph notation. Operations can be displayed in a separate window at the author's request, as shown.

To make it easier to label events within media items, we turned the timeline on its side. Thus, time runs vertically in our graphical representation, from the top of the screen to the bottom, and media items are displayed vertically. Each media item has its own timeline, based on the optimum durations between its events. Graph nodes represent events in media items: square nodes represent start and end events, and circular nodes represent internal events. Temporal constraints between events are represented as labelled, directed arcs between the source and destination events. Currently, the graphical representation does not encode operations, minimum and maximum durations, and stretching and shrinking costs.

Unpredictable behavior appears in the temporal specification in two ways. First, media items may have unpredictable durations, which are shown as dashed lines, and/or unpredictable events, which are shown as circular nodes that float above the corresponding media item's start node. Second, media items cannot be positioned relative to one another in a meaningful manner until the automatic temporal formatter computes a consistent temporal layout, and in fact, media items triggered by unpredictable events cannot be positioned until runtime. For example, to specify that two events must occur at the same time, the author places a **simultaneous with** temporal constraint between the nodes representing these events. Because the formatter, rather than the author, is responsible for generating a consistent temporal layout, the nodes representing these events typically do not line up horizontally in the graphical representation.

The sample document shown in Figure 2 describes a multimedia interface to a database on the GitaGovinda, a twelfth century Indian epic poem. It contains four media items: an image of a painting representing characters in the GitaGovinda, a GitaGovinda database, a text greeting, and an audio help message. The painting serves as a catalyst for exploring the GitaGovinda. Three unpredictable events in the image media item represent a reader using the mouse to select a "help" button, which presents the text greeting and the audio help message; a reader selecting an image of Krishna and Radha, which issues a request to the database to retrieve information on those characters; and a reader selecting the "exit" button, which terminates the presentation.

4.2 Temporal Formatting Algorithm

Firefly uses a hybrid formatter that currently handles one form of unpredictable behavior, namely content-based control of the

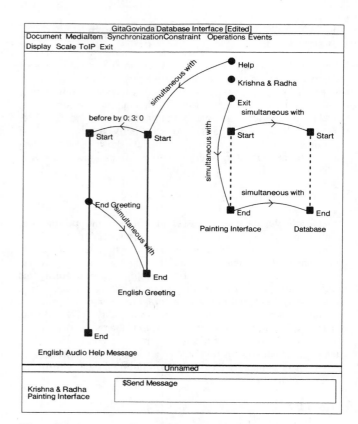

Figure 2. A sample document represented in Firefly's graph notation.

document's presentation, which we call *unpredictable events*. The compiletime component, called the *Scheduler*, constructs a partial layout consisting of a *main schedule*, which contains the entries for events in the predictable portion of the temporal specification, and zero or more *auxiliary schedules*, which contain the entries for events in the unpredictable portions. The runtime component uses this partial layout together with reports of the occurrence of unpredictable behavior to produce a temporal layout.

4.2.1 Compiletime Component

The Scheduler constructs a partial layout when a user (either author or reader) asks the system to present a document. Figure 3 shows a block diagram of the Scheduler.

The Scheduler begins by querying the media items to obtain the duration between each pair of temporally-adjacent events. Media items must adjust their durations to reflect the presence of time-altering operations, so the Scheduler supplies them with the operation list associated with each event. For each pair of temporally-adjacent events, a media item returns a minimum, optimum, and maximum allowable duration as well as a stretching and a shrinking cost.

The Scheduler then uses the durations and temporal constraints to partition a temporal specification into predictable and unpredictable portions called *connected components*. Each connected component consists of temporally-related events; no known temporal relationships exist between two different connected components.

The Scheduler processes each connected component separately. To compute the time at which each event should occur, it uses a

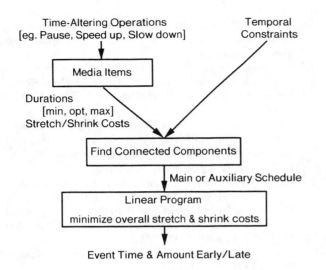

Figure 3. Firefly's compiletime formatter.

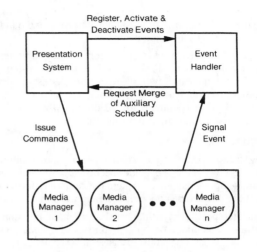

Figure 4. Firefly's runtime formatter.

linear programming algorithm that minimizes the overall cost of stretching and shrinking media item durations. The assigned times are relative to the start of the connected component. To give the Scheduler greater flexibility in assigning times, it can use the continuous adjustability of the media segment durations.

Finally, the Scheduler generates entries, called *commands*, for each connected component by visiting the events in temporal order, producing at most one command per event. Commands triggered by unpredictable events are placed in that event's auxiliary schedule; all other commands are placed in the main schedule. After commands have been generated for each connected component, the partial layout is passed to the runtime support system.

The Scheduler provides rudimentary debugging facilities. To help the author pinpoint the source of an error, it produces a list of the events for which the Scheduler could not assign times. Unfortunately, it does not report the conflicting constraints. The Scheduler also issues warnings when it discovers unimplemented operations, invalid synchronization constraints, or collapsed events, which occur when the same time is assigned to multiple events in a single media item.

4.2.2 Runtime Component

Firefly's runtime system consists of three components: the Presentation System, the Event Handler, and the media items in the document. The functionality of a hybrid formatter's runtime component and runtime support system is distributed among these components. The *Presentation System* manages a document's partial layout. This involves merging schedules into the temporal layout at the proper times, maintaining a document clock, and issuing commands from the temporal layout. The media items execute commands, which produces a desired presentation, and recognize the occurrence of unpredictable events. The *Event Handler* monitors unpredictable events. Figure 4 shows this architecture.

The Presentation System initiates the presentation of a document when it receives a partial layout from the Scheduler. At that time, the Presentation System places the commands from the main schedule into the temporal layout and starts the document clock. The document clock is incremented until the presentation of the document is completed, or until the reader explicitly pauses or

terminates the presentation of the document. For paused documents, the document time remains fixed until the reader resumes the presentation of the document. The Presentation System executes commands from the temporal layout when the document clock reaches the specified time.

For additional expressiveness, Firefly allows any event in a media item to activate or deactivate unpredictable events. When a media item detects the occurrence of an unpredictable event, it notifies the Event Handler, which maintains a list of active and inactive unpredictable events. If the unpredictable event is inactive, it is ignored. Otherwise, the Event Handler notifies the Presentation System, which merges the auxiliary schedule for that unpredictable event into the temporal layout. The Presentation System locates the auxiliary schedule triggered by the unpredictable event, converts the event-relative times in the auxiliary schedule into *absolute times* by adding the current document time, and merges that auxiliary schedule into the temporal layout by interleaving the commands in the auxiliary schedule with those in the temporal layout.

4.3 Experience with Firefly

Firefly's automatic temporal formatter has been operational for some time. We have created temporal layouts for a variety of testing and demonstration documents, including instructional documents and documents that function as multimedia user interfaces. Using these documents, we conducted a short evaluation of the compiletime formatter's performance. It takes approximately 1 second to create a schedule for a small document containing 4 media segments, 10 events, and 5 temporal constraints. For a larger document containing 45 media items, 132 events, and 80 (and 81) temporal constraints, times ranged from 40 seconds when the document was divided into 2 connected components to 90 seconds when there was only one. As the size of a connected component grows, we observed that the Scheduler spends a larger percentage of its time in the linear programming step (implemented with the simplex method). Our current simplex method implementation is straightforward and would doubtless benefit from performance tuning, such as sparse matrix techniques.

4.4 Future Work

Firefly does not yet provide all of the desired features of a hybrid formatter, namely handling media delays, meta-directives, and environment mismatches. We plan to extend Firefly to support these features. We also plan to implement group and conditional relations and composite media items.

To improve Firefly's facilities for debugging temporal specifications, we intend to experiment with running the Scheduler incrementally while an author edits a temporal specification. We hope that this approach will help authors locate errors by providing immediate feedback when an editing operation introduces a temporal mismatch.

5. Discussion

The key take-home message of this paper is that multimedia document systems should provide mechanisms for automatically producing temporal layouts. Automatic temporal formatting is important because it eases document creation and maintenance.

Automatic temporal formatting can be provided by runtime or compiletime scheduling, or by a hybrid of the two. Runtime scheduling is most important because it is crucial to handle unpredictable items, such as user interaction, program states, and unpredictable media delays. Allowing user interaction and program states increases the expressiveness of the documents, while handling unpredictable media delays, which will never become totally predictable, improves the quality of their temporal layout. However, compiletime scheduling is also important. It can also improve the quality of temporal layouts, by smoothing out predeterminable temporal and resource mismatches, and by identifying errors during the document creation phase. We thus advocate a hybrid scheduling scheme that can reap both of these advantages. Although hybrid schemes are more complicated, MODE and Firefly demonstrate that the hybrid approach is a reasonable architecture for future automatic temporal formatters.

Acknowledgements

We thank Jock Mackinlay and the anonymous reviewers for their suggestions on improving the organization and exposition of this paper.

References

1. Allen J. Maintaining knowledge about temporal intervals. *Commun. ACM* 26, 11 (Nov. 1983), 832-843.

2. Blakowski G. High level services for distributed multimedia applications based on application and environment descriptions. In *Proceedings ACSC-15: Fifteenth Australian Computer Science Conference*, Hobart, Australia, Jan. 1992. Also appears in *Australian Computer Science Communications* 14, 1, 93-109.

3. Blakowski G., Hubel J., and Langrehr, U. Tool support for the synchronization and presentation of distributed multimedia. *Computer Communications* 15, 10 (Dec. 1992), 611-618.

4. Buchanan M.C. and Zellweger P. Specifying temporal behavior in hypermedia documents. In: Lucarella D., Nanard J., Nanard M., Paolini P. (eds.), *Proceeding of the ACM Conference on Hypertext*, ACM Press, New York, Dec. 1992, 262-271.

5. Buchanan M.C. and Zellweger P. Automatically generating consistent schedules for multimedia documents. *Multimedia Systems J.*, Springer-Verlag, 1993 (to appear).

6. Bulterman D., van Rossum G., and van Liere R. A structure for transportable, dynamic multimedia documents. In *Proceedings 1991 Summer USENIX Conference*, Nashville, TN, June 1991, 137-155.

7. Dechter R., Meiri I., and Pearl J. Temporal constraint networks. In *Proceedings First International Conference on Principles of Knowledge Representation and Reasoning*, Toronto, Canada, May 1989.

8. Drapeau G. and Greenfield H. MAEstro - A distributed multimedia authoring environment. In *Proceedings 1991 Summer USENIX Conference*, Nashville, TN, June 1991, 315-328.

9. Fiume E., Tsichritzis D, and Dami L. A temporal scripting language for object-oriented animation. In *Proceedings Eurographics'87*, Elsevier Science Publishers, North-Holland Publishing Company, Amsterdam, 1987.

10. Hamakawa R., Sakagami H., and Rekimoto J. Audio and video extensions to graphical user interface toolkits. In *Proceedings Third International Workshop on Network and Operating System Support for Digital Audio and Video*, San Diego, CA, Nov. 1992, 356-361.

11. Hillier F. and Lieberman G. *Operations Research*. Holden-Day, San Francisco, 1974.

12. Kim W., Kenchammana-Hosekote D., Lim E.P., and Srivastava J. Synchronization Relation Tree: A model for temporal synchronization in multimedia presentations. Tech. Rep. 92-42, U. of Minnesota, Computer Science Dept., 1992.

13. Knuth D. and Plass M. Breaking paragraphs into lines. *Software-Practice and Experience* 11, 1119-1184.

14. Koegel J., Keskin C., and Rutledge J. Toolkits for multimedia interface design. In Proceedings *Xhibition'92*, San Jose, CA, June 1992, 275-285.

15. Little T. and Ghafoor A. Synchronization and storage models for multimedia objects. IEEE J. Selected Areas of Commun. 8, 3 (April 1990), 413-427.

16. *MacroMind Director: Overview manual*, MacroMind, Inc., March 1989.

17. Markey B. Emerging hypermedia standards - hypermedia marketplace prepares for HyTime and MHEG. In *Proceedings 1991 Summer USENIX Conference*, Nashville, TN, June 1991, 59-74.

18. Ogawa R., Harada H. and Kameko A. Scenario-based hypermedia: A model and a system. In: Rizk A., Streitz N. and Andre J. (eds.), *Hypertext: Concepts, systems, and applications*, Cambridge Univ. Press, 1990, 38-51.

19. Poole L. QuickTime in motion. *MACWORLD* (Sept. 1991), 154-159.

20. Steinmetz R. Synchronization properties in multimedia systems. *IEEE J. Selected Areas of Commun.* 8, 3 (April 1990), 401-412.

21. Stotts D. and Furuta R. Temporal hyperprogramming. *J. Visual Languages and Computing* 1, 3 (Sept. 1990), 237-253.

22. Swinehart D., Zellweger P., Beach R., and Hagmann R. A structural view of the Cedar programming environment. *ACM Trans. Prog. Languages and Syst.* 8, 4 (Oct. 1986), 419-490.

23. van Rossum G., Jansen J., Mullender K.S., and Bulterman D. CMIFed: A presentation environment for portable hypermedia documents, *Proceedings ACM Multimedia'93*, Anaheim, CA, Aug.1993, elsewhere in this proceedings.

GRiNS: A GRaphical INterface for creating and playing SMIL documents

Dick C.A. Bulterman [*,1], Lynda Hardman [1], Jack Jansen [1], K. Sjoerd Mullender [1],
Lloyd Rutledge [1]

CWI, Centrum voor Wiskunde en Informatica, Kruislaan 413, 1098 SJ Amsterdam, The Netherlands

Abstract

The W3C working group on synchronized multimedia has developed a language for Web-based Multimedia presentations called SMIL: the Synchronized Multimedia Integration Language. This paper presents GRiNS, an authoring and presentation environment that can be used to create SMIL-compliant documents and to play SMIL documents created with GRiNS or by hand. © 1998 Published by Elsevier Science B.V. All rights reserved.

Keywords: SMIL; Multimedia; Web authoring; Streaming applications

1. Introduction

While the World Wide Web is generally seen as *the* embodiment of the infrastructure of today's information age, it currently cannot handle documents containing continuous media such as audio and video very elegantly. HTML documents cannot express the synchronization primitives required to coordinate independent pieces of time-based data, and the HTTP protocol cannot provide the streamed delivery of time-based media objects required for continuous media data. The development of Java extensions to HTML, known as *Dynamic HTML* [5], provide one approach to introducing synchronization support into Web documents. This approach has the advantage that the author is given all of the control offered by a programming language in defining in-

teractions within a document; this is similar to the use of the scripting language Lingo in CD-ROM authoring packages like Director [6]. It has the disadvantage that defining even simple synchronization relationships becomes a relatively difficult task for the vast majority of Web users who have little or no programming skills.

In early 1997, SYMM — a W3C working group on SYnchronized MultiMedia — was established to study the definition of a declarative multimedia format for the Web [8,12]. In such a format, the control interactions required for multimedia applications are encoded in a text file as a structured set of object relations. A declarative specification is often easier to edit and maintain than a program-based specification, and it can potentially provide a greater degree of accessibility to the network infrastructure by reducing the amount of programming required for creating any particular presentation. The first system to propose such a format was CMIF [2–4]. Other more recent examples are MADEUS [7] and RTSL

---

* Corresponding author.
[1] E-mail: {Dick.Bulterman,Lynda.Hardman,Jack.Jansen,Sjoerd.Mullender,Lloyd.Rutledge}@cwi.nl

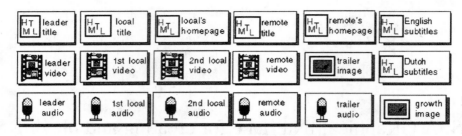

Fig. 1. Media objects for use in (part of) a Web-based newscast.

[9]. The SYMM working group ultimately developed SMIL, the Synchronized Multimedia Integration Language [13] (which is pronounced *smile*).[2] In developing SMIL, the W3C SYMM group has restricted its attention to the development of the base language, without specifying any particular playback or authoring environment functionality.

This paper presents a new authoring and runtime environment called GRiNS: a GRaphical INterface for SMIL. GRiNS consists of an authoring interface and a runtime player which can be used together (or separately) to create/play SMIL-compliant hypermedia documents. The authoring part of GRiNS can be used to encode SMIL presentations for any SMIL compliant browser or stand-alone player; the GRiNS player can take any SMIL-compliant document and render it using a stand-alone player. GRiNS is based largely on earlier experience with the CMIFed authoring system and the CMIF encoding format, both of which strongly influenced the development of SMIL.

In Section 3, we give an overview of the GRiNS authoring and playback interfaces. Section 4 then discusses the availability of the GRiNS environment as part of the CHAMELEON suite of authoring and presentation tools. We begin the paper with a review of the SMIL language and a brief discussion of typical applications and runtime environments for which SMIL was developed.

2. Declarative Web-based hypermedia

This section briefly reviews the nature of Web-based multi-/hypermedia documents and the basic

philosophy of the SMIL language. We also briefly sketch the type of runtime protocol support that is expected for processing SMIL documents.

2.1. A typical example SMIL document

In order to focus our attention on the class of applications that this paper concerns itself with, we present an example of a generic Web application: that of a network newscast.[3] The basic premise of this newscast is a story on the explosive growth of the WWW. Several media objects have been defined that together make-up such a newscast. (Note that the selection of objects is arbitrary; we have selected a moderate level of complexity to illustrate the features of GRiNS.)

Let us assume that the objects shown in Fig. 1 have been selected to make up the presentation. The newscast consists of an opening segment, a segment in which the local host gives background information, a segment in which a remote reporter gives an update, a segment in which the local host gives a wrap up, which leads into the trailing theme music. Finally, each correspondent also has a Web homepage that can be accessed from the story.

Figure 2 shows two views of the newscast example, taken at different times in the presentation. Figure 2a shows a portion of the introduction of a story on the growth of the World Wide Web. In this portion, the local host is describing how sales of authoring software are expected to rise sharply in the next six months.

Figure 2b shows a point later in the presentation, when the host is chatting with a remote correspon-

---

[2] As SMIL-V1.0 is a W3C Draft Standard, its details may change at any time up to its acceptance.

[3] In 1991, as part of the first public CMIF paper, a network newscast was also used as a prototypical example. Sometimes the electronic world moves as slowly as the real one!

(a) Early in the Story   (b) During the Remote Report

Fig. 2. Two views of the Web newscast.

Fig. 3. Augmenting information during the news.

dent in Los Angeles, who describes that many Hollywood stars are already planning their own SMIL pages on the Web.

The ability to link to various homepages makes the semantic content of the document dynamic. As shown in Fig. 3, the information content can be augmented during the story depending on the viewer's interests. Links are not restricted to homepages, of course: any addressable object or document deemed relevant by the author should be available. Such behaviour comes at a cost, however: we must be able to specify what happens to the base presentation when the link to the homepage is followed: should it pause, should it continue, or should it be replaced by the linked pages. (We discuss this in more detail below.)

A complete description of the implementation details of the Web newscast is beyond the scope of this paper. We will, however, refer to it as a running example in the sections below.

2.2. A brief SMIL overview

SMIL is a declarative language for describing Web-based multimedia documents that can be played on a wide range of SMIL browsers. Such browsers may be stand-alone presentation systems that are tailored to a particular user community or they could be integrated into general purpose browsers. In SMIL-V1.0 (the version that we will consider in this paper), language primitives have been defined that allow for early experimentation and (relatively) easy implementation; this has been done to gain experience with the language while the protocol infrastructure required to optimally support SMIL-type documents is being developed and deployed.

Architecturally, SMIL is an integrating format. That is, it does not describe the contents of any part of a hypermedia presentation, but rather describes how various components are to be combined temporally and spatially to create a presentation. (It also defines how presentation resources can be managed and it allows anchors and links to be defined within the presentation.) Note that SMIL is not a replacement for individual formats (such as HTML for text, AIFF for audio or MPEG for video); it takes information objects encoded using these formats and combines them into a presentation.

Appendix A contains a simplifed SMIL description of the newscast example sketched in Section 2.1. SMIL describes four fundamental aspects of a multimedia presentation:

- *temporal specifications:* primitives to encode the temporal structure of the application and the refinement of the (relative) start and end times of events;
- *spatial specifications:* primitives provided to support simple document layout;
- *alternative behaviour specification:* primitives to express the various optional encodings within a document based on systems or user requirements; and
- *hypermedia support:* mechanisms for linking parts of a presentation.

We describe how SMIL encodes these specifications in the following paragraphs.

2.2.1. SMIL temporal specifications

SMIL provides coarse-grain and fine-grain declarative temporal structuring of an application. These are placed between the `<body> ... </body>` tags of a document (lines 15 through 52 of Appendix A). SMIL also provides the general attribute SYNC (currently with values HARD and SOFT) that can be used over a whole document or a document part to indicate how strictly synchronization must be supported by the player. Line 1 of the example says, in effect: do your best to meet the specification, but keep going even if not all relationships can be met. Coarse grain temporal information is given in terms of two structuring elements:

- `<seq> ... </seq>`: A set of objects that occur in sequence (e.g., lines 16–51 and 31–43).
- `<par> ... </par>`: A collection of objects that occur in parallel (lines 17–24 or 36–44).

Elements defined within a `<seq>` group have the semantics that a successor is guaranteed to start after the completion of a predecessor element. Elements within a `<par>` group have the semantics that, by default, they all start at the same time. Once started, all elements are active for the time determined by their encoding or for an explicitly defined duration. Elements within a `<par>` group can also be defined to end at the same time, either based on the length of the longest or shortest component or on the end time of an explicit master element. Note that if objects within a `<par>` group are of unequal length, they will either start or end at different times, depending on the attributes of the group.

Fine grain synchronization control is specified in each of the object references through a number of timing control relationships:

- *explicit durations:* a DUR="length" attribute can be used to state the presentation time of the object (line 34);
- *absolute offsets:* the start time of an object can be given as an absolute offset from the start time of the enclosing structural element by using a BEGIN="time" attribute (line 33);
- *relative offsets*: the start time of an object can be given in terms of the start time of another sibling object using a BEGIN="object_id+time" attribute (line 41).

(Unless otherwise specified, all objects are displayed for their implicit durations — defined by the object encoding or the length of the enclosing `<par>` group.) The specification of a relative start time is a restricted version of CMIF's *sync_arcs* [4] to define fine-grain timing within a document. At present, only explicit time offsets into objects are supported, but a natural extension is to allow content markers, which provide content-based tags into a media object.

2.2.2. Layout specifications

In order to guarantee interoperability among various players, SMIL-V1.0 supports basic primitives for layout control that must be supported on all SMIL players. This structure uses an indirect format, in which each media object reference contains the name of an associated drawing area that describes where objects are to be presented. A separate layout resolution section in the SMIL `<head>` section maps these areas to output resources (screen space or audio). A example of a visible object reference is shown in line 29, which is resolved by the definition in line 6. Non-visible objects (such as audio) can also be defined (see lines 33 and 7). Each player/browser is responsible for mapping the logical output areas to physical devices. A priority attribute is being considered to aid in resolving conflicts during resource allocation. (As of this writing the name channel will probably be used as an abstract grouping mechanism [2] but the deadline for text submission came before this issue was resolved.)

2.2.3. Alternate behaviour specifications

SMIL provides two means for defining alternate behaviour within a document: via the <switch> construct and via the <channel>. The <switch> allows an author to specify a number of semantically equivalent encodings, one of which can be selected at runtime by the player/browser. This selection could take place based on profiles, user preference, or environmental characteristics. In lines 19–22 of Appendix A, a specification is given that says: play either the video or still image defined, depending on system or presentation constraints active at runtime. The <channel> statement is intended to provide a higher-level selection abstraction, in which presentation binding is delayed until runtime. It is a simplified version of the *shadow channel* concept in CMIF.

2.2.4. Hypermedia and SMIL

HTML supports hypertext linking functionality via a straight-forward process: each document has a single focus (the browser window or frame) and anchors and links can be easily placed within the document text. When the link is followed, the source text is replaced by the destination. In an SMIL presentation, the situation is much more difficult. First, the location of a given anchor may move over time as the entity associated with the anchor moves (such as following a bouncing ball in a video) — and even if it does not move, it still may be visible for only part of the object's duration. Second, since SMIL is an integrating format, conflicts may arise on ownership of anchors and the semantics of following any given link.

In SMIL-V1.0, a pragmatic approach to linking is followed. Anchors and links within media objects are followed within the context of that media object. An anchor can also be defined at the SMIL level, which affects the presentation of the whole SMIL document. This effect depends on the value of a SHOW attribute, which may have values:

- REPLACE: the presentation of the destination resource replaces the complete, current presentation (this is the default);
- NEW: the presentation of the destination resource starts in a new context (perhaps a new window) not affecting the source presentation; or
- PAUSE: the link is followed and a new context is created, but the source context is suspended.

In our example, two links are defined: one on lines 28–30 and the other on lines 37–39. If the link associated with line 29 is followed, the current presentation's audio and video streams keep going, and a new SMIL presentation containing an HTML homepage is added. If the link at line 38 is followed, the current video object pauses while the homepage is show.

General support for hypermedia is a complex task. Readers are invited to study the Amsterdam Hypermedia Model [3], which serves as the basis for the current SMIL hypermedia proposal.

3. GRiNS: authoring and presentation for SMIL

GRiNS is an authoring and presentation system for SMIL documents. It is a part of the CHAMELEON multimedia document processing suite. Where the CHAMELEON suite provides tools for the authoring of adaptive documents — that is, documents that can be converted to a variety of presentation formats based on the (dynamic) needs of the document authors — GRiNS provides dedicated tools for creating and presenting SMIL documents. Both GRiNS and CHAMELEON are based on technology developed for CWI's CMIF environment.

The GRiNS authoring tool is based on a structured approach to document creation [2]. The GRiNS presentation tool provides a flexible presentation interface that supports all of the semantics of the SMIL V1.0 specification. In the following sections, we give examples of how GRiNS can be used to create the WebNews example. We then discuss some of the issues involved in providing support for the GRiNS presenter.

3.1. The GRiNS authoring environment

The GRiNS authoring environment supports creation of a SMIL document in terms of three views:

- the *logical structure* view, where coarse-grain definition of the temporal structure takes place;
- the *virtual timeline* view, where fine-grain temporal interactions are defined; and
- the *playout view*, where layout projections are defined.

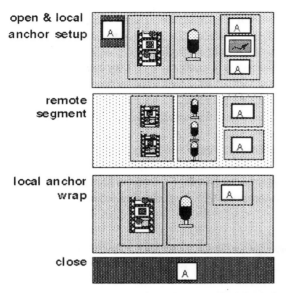

open & local
anchor setup

remote
segment

local anchor
wrap

close

Fig. 4. The structure of the Web Growth story. (Time flows from top to bottom.)

Hyperlink definition and specification of alternative data objects can occur in either the logical structure view or the virtual timeline view.

3.1.1. The logical structure view

If we were to define the Web Growth story in terms of its overall structure, we would wind up with a representation similar to that in Fig. 4. Here we see that the story starts with a opening sequence (containing a logo and a title), and ends with a closing jingle. In between is the "meat" of the story. It contains an introduction by the local host, followed by a report by the remote correspondent, and then concluded by a wrap-up by the local host. This "table of contents" view defines the basic structure of the story. It may be reusable.

The GRiNS logical structure view allows an author to construct a SMIL document in terms of a similar nested hierarchy of media objects. The interface provides a scalable view of the document being created. Note that only structure is being edited here: much of this creation takes place before (or while) actual media objects have been created.

Figure 5a shows a part of the WebNews hierarchy in terms of the logical structure view. (The green box in the middle shows two alternatives in the presentation: a video or a still image, one of which will

be selected at runtime. Figure 5b shows a typical dialog box that is used to provide details of how a particular element is to be included in the presentation. The logical structure view has facilities cutting and pasting parts of the presentation, and it allows individual or sub-structured objects to be previewed without having to play the entire application.

During design and specification, the values of object attributes — including location, default or express duration or synchronization on composite objects — can be entered by the author. In practice, duration of an object or a group will be based on the enclosing structure, will which be calculated automatically. Note that while the basic paradigm of the logical structure view is a hierarchical structure, the author can also specify loop constructs which give (sub-)parts of the presentation a cyclic character.

3.1.2. The virtual timeline view

The logical structure view is intended to represent the coarse timing relationships reflected in the <par> and <seq> constructs. While the attributes associated with an element (either an object or a composite structure definition) can be used to define more fine-grained relationships — such as DURATION or the desire to REPEAT an object during its activation period — these relationships are often difficult to visualize with only a logical structure view. For this reason, GRiNS also supports a timeline projection of an application. Unlike other timeline systems, which use a timeline as the initial view of the application, the GRiNS timeline is virtual: it displays the logical timing relationships as calculated from the logical structure view. This means that the user is not tied to a particular clock or frame rate, or to a particular architecture. (The actual timing relationships will only be known at execution time.) Note that the virtual timeline view is a generated projection, rather than a direct authoring interface. It is used as a visualization aid, since it reflects the view of the GRiNS scheduler on the behaviour of the document.

Figure 6 shows a virtual timeline of the Web Growth story. Rather than illustrating structure, this view shows each of the components and their relative start and end times. The timeline view provides an insight into the actual temporal relationships among the elements in the presentation. Not only does it

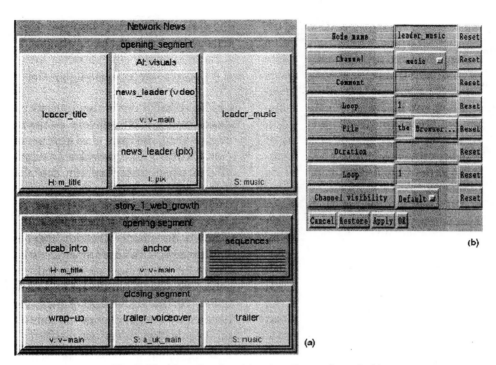

Fig. 5. The hierarchy view (a) and attributes of a node (b).

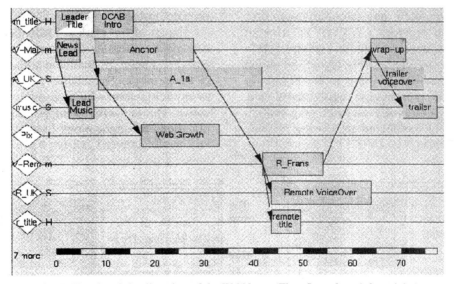

Fig. 6. The virtual timeline view of the WebNews. (Time flows from left to right.)

show the declared length and start times of objects whose duration or start offset is predefined, it also shows the derived length of objects who duration depends on the structure of the document. The timing view shows predefined durations as solid blocks and derived durations as blocks with a diagonal line.

Events on the timeline are partitioned by the various output channels defined by the user. In the figure, channels which are darkened are turned off during this (part of) the presentation. This allows the author to see the effect of various <switch> settings during the presentation.

When working with the virtual timeline view, the user can define exact start and end offsets within `<par>` groups using declarative mechanisms (the sync arc), shown as an arrow in the figure. Sync arcs are meant to provide declarative specifications of timing relationships which can be evaluated at run-time or by a scheduling pre-processor.

If changes are made to the application or to any of the attributes of the media objects, these are immediately reflected by in the virtual timeline view. As with the logical structure view, the user can select any group of objects and preview that part of the document. When the presentation view is active (see next section), the virtual timeline view also displays how the playout scheduler activates, arms and pre-fetches data during the presentation.

Note that both the logical structure and the virtual timeline views are authoring views; they are not available when a document is viewed via the playout engine only. Both views isolate the user from the syntax of the SMIL language.

3.1.3. The presentation view

The presentation view has two purposes: first, during authoring, it provides a WYSIWYG view of the document under development, and second, it provides a mechanism to interactively layout the output channels associated with the document. Figure 7a shows part of the presentation being developed, while Fig. 7b illustrates the channel map associated with the part of the document. During playout,

the values of the layout attributes can be dynamically changed if required.

3.2. The GRiNS playout engine

The GRiNS authoring interface is actually an augmented GRiNS playout engine. It is a playout engine that also provides a structure and timeline editor. GRiNS also provides a "stand-alone" playout engine which can play any compliant SMIL-V1.0 document.

The playout engine consists of a document interpreter that, guided by user interaction, steps through a SMIL document. The document interacts with a link processor (which implements the NEW, PAUSE, REPLACE semantics of the link), and a channel scheduler which builds a Petri-net based representation of the document. Actual media display is handled by a set of channel threads (or their architectural equivalent on various platforms), which interact with presentation devices. The channel scheduler and the various channel threads implement the application and media dependent parts of the RTP/RTCP protocol stacks.

As part of the general SMIL language, an author can specify alternative objects that can be scheduled based on resources available at the player, the server or the network. The GRiNS player also allows users to explicitly state which channels they wish to have active. This is useful for supporting multi-lingual applications or applications in which users are given

(a)   (b)

Fig. 7. The (a) presentation view and (b) associated channel map.

an active choice on the formats displayed. While the generic use of Channels as an adjunct to the switch for selection is still under debate, we have found it to be useful for delaying many semantic decisions to play-out time.

The GRiNS playout engine is implemented as a stand-alone application, and is not integrated directly into a full-function Web browser. This makes it suitable for separate distribution (such as on a CD-ROM), or for occasions when only limited ability to alter the presentation state of a document is required. (For example, if you are making a document to display a certain type of information, the stand-alone player can restrict the user's ability to enter random URLs and to browse other documents during presentation.) The use of a separate playout engine also allows us to experiment with new schedulers, protocols or data types much more easily than in a full-feature browser.

4. Current status and availability

The GRiNS authoring environment and playout engine have been implemented on all major presentation platforms (Windows-95/NT, Macintosh and UNIX). They are intended to provide a reference architecture for playing out SMIL documents and to integrate structured authoring concepts in SMIL document creation. While a full function description of all of the features of the environment are beyond the scope of this paper, we do have documentation available for interested parties. General information is available at GRiNS Web page (http://www.cwi.nl/Chameleon/GRiNS).

The present version of the GRiNS environment is implemented as a combination of Python-based machine independent and dependent code, and a collection of media output drivers. The quality and availability of drivers for any particular media type vary slightly across platform, but we a making a concerted effort to provide a high degree of cross-platform compatibility. (This is an on-going process.)

We feel the SMIL can play a significant role in providing a common document representation that can be interpreted by many players. Each player can make its own contribution in terms of quality of service or implementation efficiency. In this respect, we feel that our main focus will be on the development of GRiNS authoring tools that will work with anyone's playout engines. Until these engines become prevalent, we will also provide our own environment to assist in SMIL experimentation.

The GRiNS environment was developed in part within the ESPRIT-IV CHAMELEON project. Plans exist for the free or low-cost distribution of the playout environment and the authoring interface. Interested parties should refer to the GRiNS Web site for more details.

Acknowledgments

The work of the W3C's SYMM working group was coordinated by Philipp Hoschka of W3C/INRIA. A list of contributors is available at [12]. CWI's activity in the GRiNS project is funded in part through the ESPRIT-IV project CHAMELEON [1] of the European Union. Additional sources of funding have been the ACTS SEMPER [10] and the Telematics STEM [11] projects.

Appendix A. SMIL code for the Web news example

(Note: Line numbers have been added for clarity and reference from body text.)

```
1 <smil sync=nc="soft">
2  <head>
3   <layout type="text/smil-basic">
4    <channel id="matise"/>
5    <channel id="m_title" left="4%" top="4%" width="47%" height="22%"/>
6    <channel id="v-main" left="52%" top="5%" width="45%" height="42%"/>
7    <channel id="a_uk_main"/>
8    <channel id="music"/>
```

```
 9      <channel id="pix" left="5%" top="28%" width="46%" height="34%"/>
10      <channel id="v-remote" left="3%" top="44%" width="46%" height="40%"/>
11      <channel id="r_uk"/>
12      <channel id="r_title" left="52%" top="58%" width="42%" height="22%"/>
13     </layout>
14    </head>
15    <body>
16     <seq id="WebGrowth">
17      <par id="opening_segment">
18       <text id="leader_title" channel="m_title" src="the.news/html/title.html"/>
19       <switch id="news_leader">
20        <video channel="v-main" src="mpeg/logo1.mpv"/>
21        <img channel="v-main" src="images/logo.gif"/>
22       </switch>
23       <audio id="leader_music" channel="music" src="audio/logo1.aiff"/>
24      </par>
25      <seq id="story_1_web_growth">
26       <par id="node_22">
27        <text id="dcab_intro" channel="m_title" src="html/dcab_intro.html"
                dur="8.0s"/>
28        <a href="archives-dcab.smi#1" show="new">
29         <video channel="v-main" src="mpeg/dcab1.mpv"/>
30        </a>
31        <seq id="sequences">
32         <par id="background_info">
33          <audio id="a_1a" channel="a_uk_main" src="audio/uk/dcab1.aiff"
                  begin="0.9s"/>
34          <img id="web_growth" channel="pix" src="images/webgrowth.gif"
                  dur="16.0s" begin="id(a_1a)(begin)+8.6s"/>
35         </par>
36         <par id="live_link-up">
37          <a href="archives-larry.smi#1" show="pause">
38           <video id=r_larry channel="v-remote" src="mpeg/larry.mpv"/>
39          </a>
40          <text id="remote_title" channel="r_title" src="html/r_title.html"
                  dur="6.0s" begin="id(r_larry)(begin)+1.8s"/>
41          <audio id="remote_voiceover" channel="r_uk" src="audio/uk/larry1.aiff"
                  begin="id(r_larry)(begin)+1.7s"/>
42         </par>
43        </seq>
44       </par>
45       <par id="node_56">
46        <video channel="v-main" src="dcab.zout.mpv"/>
47        <audio id="trailer_voiceover" channel="a_uk_main"
                src="audio/uk/dcab3.aiff"/>
48        <audio id="trailer" channel="music" src="audio/logo2.aiff"
                begin="id(wrap-up)(begin)+6.5s"/>
49       </par>
50      </seq>
51     </seq>
52    </body>
53   </smil>
```

References

[1] CHAMELEON: An authoring environment for adaptive multimedia presentations, ESPRIT-IV Project 20597, see http://www.cwi.nl/Chameleon/; see also http://www.cwi.nl/~dcab/

[2] D.C.A. Bulterman, R. van Liere and G. van Rossum, A structure for transportable, dynamic multimedia documents, in: *Proceedings of 1991 Usenix Spring Conference on Multimedia Systems,* Nashville, TN, 1991, pp. 137–155; see also http://www.cwi.nl/~dcab/

[3] L. Hardman, D.C.A. Bulterman and G. van Rossum. The Amsterdam hypermedia model: adding time and context to the Dexter model, *Comm. ACM* 37(2): 50–62, Feb. 1994; see also http://www.cwi.nl/~dcab

[4] D.C.A. Bulterman, Synchronization of multi-sourced multimedia data for heterogeneous target systems, in: P. Venkat Rangan (Ed.), *Network and Operating Systems Support for Digital Audio and Video,* LNCS-712, Springer-Verlag, 1993, pp. 119–129; see also http://www.cwi.nl/~dcab/

[5] W3C, HTML 4.0, W3C's next version of HTML, http://www.w3.org/MarkUp/Cougar/

[6] Macromedia, Inc., Director 6.0, http://www.macromedia.com/software/director/

[7] C. Roisin, M. Jourdan, N. Layaïda and L. Sabry-Ismail, Authoring environment for interactive multimedia documents, in: *Proc. MMM'97,* Singapore; see also http://opera.inrialpes.fr/OPERA/multimedia-eng.html

[8] P. Hoschka, Towards synchronized multimedia on the Web, *World Wide Web Journal,* Spring 1997; see http://www.w3journal.com/6/s2.hoschka.html

[9] RTSL: Real-Time Streaming Language, see http://www.real.com/server/intranet/index.html

[10] SEMPER: Secure Electronic Marketplace for Europe, EU ACTS Project 0042, 1995–1998, see http://www.semper.org/

[11] STEM: Sustainable Telematics for the Environment, EU Telematics Project EN-1014, 1995–1996.

[12] W3C Synchronized Multimedia Working Group, http://www.w3.org/AudioVideo/Group/

[13] W3C SMIL Draft Specification, see http://www.w3.org/TR/WD-smil

Dick Bulterman is founder and head of the Multimedia and Human-Computer Interaction group at CWI in Amsterdam, an academic research laboratory funded by the government of The Netherlands. Prior to joining CWI, he was assistant professor of engineering at Brown University in Providence, RI. He holds Masters and Ph.D. degrees in computer science (1977, 1981) from Brown and a degree in political economics from Hope College (1973). In addition to CWI and Brown, he has held visiting positions at Delft, Utrecht and Leiden Universities in Holland, and has consulted frequently on operating systems and multimedia architectures. He is technical manager of the ES-PRIT-IV project CHAMELEON and has been involved in several European Community projects.

Lynda Hardman is a researcher at CWI, where she has worked since 1990. Prior to joining CWI, she held research and development positions at a variety of universities and companies in the United Kingdom, most recently at Office Workstations, Ltd. (OWL), where she became interested in Hypertext architectures. She holds a Ph.D. from the University of Amsterdam (1998) and undergraduate degrees from Herriot-Watt University in Scotland. She has been involved in numerous national and European research projects.

Jack Jansen joined CWI in 1985 as a member of the Amoeba distributed systems group. He studied mathematics and computer science at the Free University in Amsterdam. He is currently one of the principal implementers of the GRiNS architecture and is also responsible for development of GRiNS support for the Macintosh. He has gotten a haircut and contact lenses since this picture was taken.

Sjoerd Mullender is a research programmer at CWI, where he has worked on various projects since 1989. He received a masters degree in mathematics and computer science from the Free University in Amsterdam in 1988. Since joining CWI, he has worked on projects ranging from operating systems to user interface design. He is a principal implementer of the GRiNS system.

Lloyd Rutledge is a Post-Doc at CWI specializing in the study of hypermedia architectures. He holds a Ph.D. in computer science from the University of Massachusetts in Lowell (1996) and an undergraduate degree in computer science from the University of Massachusetts in Amherst. He has published widely on the topic of structured multimedia systems, with a special interest in HyTime and MHEG document architectures. At CWI, he has worked on the CHAMELEON project, with a particular interest in the support of adaptive projections of applications in multiple document formats.

Multiviews Interfaces for Multimedia Authoring Environments

Muriel Jourdan, Cécile Roisin and Laurent Tardif

OPERA project, INRIA Rhône-Alpes.
655 avenue de l'Europe, 38330 Montbonnot, France.
e-mail: {Firstname.Lastname}@inrialpes.fr
tel: +33 4 76 61 52 00, fax: +33 4 76 61 52 52
http://opera.inrialpes.fr/OPERA/

Abstract

This paper discusses the interface needs for the emergence of new authoring tools for the creation of multimedia documents. We think that it is possible to break down the specify-and-run process of most existing tools to have more direct editing functions close to a "wysiwyg" approach. After identifying the requirements of direct editing for multimedia documents, we describe an authoring environment based on a set of synchronized views and we illustrate its usefulness through many authoring situations.

1. Introduction

New technologies of data representation and processing allow the use of image, video and sound information in computer applications. Depending on the targeted application, these new media types can be more or less integrated into the whole information system. For example, a video/audio channel of a teleconferencing application is completely independent from other information sources. In this paper, we are interested in applications where combining pieces of information from various media types into a unique entity, called a *multimedia document*, is of high priority. Typical examples are multimedia titles on cdroms or web documents including synchronized video or audio.

A multimedia document is defined as a set of (basic) objects spatially and temporally organized and on which a navigational structure can be set. Such an entity can be rendered thanks to a presentation engine by means of the output channels of the computer (screen and speaker). The window on which a multimedia document is displayed (and on which the reader can interact) is further called the *presentation view*.

Numerous works [3], [10], [18], [11], [8] (see [9] for a survey of them) and even standards [19], [14] have been done for the definition of languages and formats of multimedia documents. They allow the specification of the temporal composition of media objects either by absolute placements [12], by event-based approaches [14], by the use of hierarchical operators [18], by constraint-based definitions [11], [3], [8] or by a combination of some of them (e. g. SMIL [19] uses both hierarchical operators and event specifications).

However, authors have often to be programmers because it is the only way for them to specify the complex synchronization of their documents (Lingo scripts in Director [12] documents for example). But it is clear that in order to increase the popularity of such multimedia applications, computer-illiterate people must have direct access to multimedia document creation. That will also drastically reduce production cost of multimedia titles.

In this paper, we would like to focus on the process of creation of multimedia documents and more precisely on what should be good user interfaces for providing real end-user authoring tools. A good authoring environment will certainly not result by simply packaging an existing programming language: not only the author has to deal with too much low level specifications, but also such authoring tools still provide slow development cycles thanks to the composition-test process (as with MhegDitor which is based on a converter tool [4]). To break down this batch approach, we can think about the experiences gained with authoring static documents: the Wysiwyg paradigm has been proven to be the right basis on which editing interfaces have been built. However, such a paradigm cannot be directly apply inside multimedia authoring applications due to the temporal dimension of multimedia documents.

Few experiences have yet tried to cope with time during the authoring process. In the Walk-Through approach [7], authors can edit the documents in the context of the presentation under construction, avoiding the use of textual notations. Editing is performed thanks to operations on timed events. The MAD system [2] aims also at providing an integrated environment for pre-producing (scripting, writing storyboards) and post-producing (assembling and storing) digital videos. Their solution is based on multiple representation of documents and easy jumps from one to the other. Hyperprop [15] is a multiview authoring tool that aims at vizualizing and editing documents structure (thanks to a fisheye function), together with their spatial and temporal organizations. However, direct editing feature is not of primary goal of the authors.

The rest of the paper aims at developing these ideas: first of all, we analyze what could mean the Wysiwyg paradigm for multimedia documents; we then state what are the main requirements for the direct editing of multimedia documents; finally, we propose an authoring environment based on a set of synchronized views and we illustrate its usefulness through many authoring situations.

2. From Wysiwyg to direct edition

Wysiwyg edition   The authoring process in a Wysiwyg environment is basically a cyclic *action -perception* process where, at each step, the author performs an action applying on the document and then the system reacts in order to apply the requested action so that the result presented to the author is the same as it will be for the reader. Typically, inserting a new character into a paragraph implies the formatting of the whole paragraph in order to compute line breaks, hyphenation and line justification. Moreover, it can also imply page formatting for updating page breaks of the document. Therefore, the author can be confident of what he sees after each editing operation: it will exactly be what the reader will get. However, we can notice that the perception step can be more complex than simply having a look at the screen: when the action implies modifications on parts of the document that are far from the chunk being displayed, the author must scroll through the document to get the whole consequences of the action.

This process fits well when the final result is a paper format document (as still most users want), but it is less and less convenient in a pure electronic communication (e. g. web documents) and when documents are multimedia. The rendering of web documents depends on the browser used, the network capacity and on the styles that are applied on client side (CSS allows the specification of cascades of styles that apply on documents). Therefore, it is not so useful for an author to compose documents with a Wysiwyg approach because many "gets" are possible from a unique document source. The case of multimedia rendering arises other difficulties as shown below.

Wysiwyg paradigm for multimedia   If we try to apply the Wysiwyg paradigm in the context of multimedia documents, we have to identify which are the basic editing operations (action step), what consequences they may produce on the document and finally what does mean the perception step for the author.

In this paper, we only consider the authoring process of multimedia documents for which the spatial and temporal composition can be expressed in a declarative and relative manner (by means of hierarchical operators like CMIFed [18]or constraints such as Allen's relations like ISIS [11] or Madeus [8] These approaches have been proved to be the most adapted for editing (easier updates are possible). In that context, a basic editing operation can be one of the following actions:

- Inserting/removing an object.

- Inserting/removing a spatial, temporal or link relation.

As a multimedia document is basically a dynamic entity, a pure Wysiwyg editing mode should allow the author to perform these operations on unstable data, which seems not to be a so good idea.

Moreover, the perception step is also concerned by the dynamic behavior of multimedia documents. Indeed, editing operations not only affect the content and the spatial organization of the document, but also its temporal dimension, i. e. the order by which the media objects are presented. The result is a dynamic document, as readers can get it. But it is very unrealistic to give the author with that resulting information after each editing operation: the whole presentation of the document should be executed.

Toward direct multimedia editing   In this attempt to apply Wysiwyg paradigm for multimedia documents, we just want to show the following: in order to provide the author with good multimedia authoring tools, i. e. close to the Wysiwyg paradigm, it is necessary to allow some way of direct manipulation of the document in the presentation view (for example for the authoring of spatial relations). However, due to the temporal dimension of documents, such a direct edition has to be completed by other features acting on the presentation process (stop/resume) or provided through new visual perception mechanisms.

This paper aims at proposing an integrating solution for direct multimedia authoring. Before that, we analyze the main requirements of such environments.

3. Requirements

Thanks to the presentation view, the author can appreciate the dynamic behavior of multimedia documents: the good balance between each object duration, the relevance of some overlapping between the presentation of two objects (from their contents point of view), the good delivering of the document message, the good use of style effects, etc. If the state of the obtained document is still not as expected, the author has to make some editing actions to reach the final goal. We analyze in the following sections the basic functionalities that must be provided in a authoring environment to help him in this task.

3.1. Global perception of the document

The author of a large textual document makes often use the table of contents to have a global view of the document. This synthetic view helps him to manage the complexity of the document. The need is the same with multimedia documents even if there is no direct equivalent to the notion of table of contents.

Another kind of needs is the global perception of the relations (spatial or temporal) between objects. Since objects are linked by relations, any action on the current state of the document can have a lot of consequences. For instance, suppose that in the current state, two objects A1 and A2 are sequentially related and that two audios B1 and B2 are respectively set in parallel with A1 and A2. The insertion of a new object A3 between A1 and A2 will also desynchronize B1 and B2. This is why the author must be as most as possible aware of each consequence of the planned action before doing it. It means that the author must have a clear representation of each relation during all the design process. This is also the only way to help the author to understand why some modifications are not possible.

Finally, a unique multimedia document specification can result in different presentations. This is due to the fact that some objects can have different presentation durations (e. g. the duration of a video can depend on the CPU load) and also that hyperlink activation differs from one execution to the other one. The authoring environment must help the author to manage these multiple possible executions.

3.2. Complex temporal access functionalities

The presentation view is a linear view of the document: except when hyperlinks are activated, documents are played from their beginning point until their end, with possibly stop and resume possibilities. This is obviously a too limited way of access for the author who needs more flexible ways to navigate in the document, such as: going faster until some important parts of the document, jumping from a relevant point to another one, etc. We can distinguish two classes of temporal access functionalities:

- Time point access by using a date (distance from the beginning of the document) or by naming an object. In the latter case, the result is the first occurrence of the object in the document.

- Different scales of fast forwarding and rewinding. In addition, to the classical VCR mechanism (Video Camera Recorder) which takes a parameterizable time

units as browsing granularity, other cases are very useful for the author:

- it should be possible to directly jump through a set of automatically computed time points. Several sets could be managed. One possibility is to use as time points the instants when an object appears or disappears on the screen, another is to use beginning and ending points of each "scene" if this notion is present in the temporal model.

- Finally, the author may want to define specific temporal points (more semantical than the previous one) for the support of VCR-navigation.

3.3. Merging instants

Suppose the author wants to spatially align two objects which are never presented at the same time on the screen; for example, to unify the spatial positions of the titles of sequences of pages or to shift forward the picture of a sequence from the previous one. Such specifications can be easily obtained by direct manipulations on the presentation view if the authoring environment provides a way to merge different time points on the screen. Moreover, to avoid screen overload, this merging functionality must be provided with some filter mechanisms that will reduce the number of objects together shown on the screen.

4. A new architecture for multimedia authoring

The basic authoring requirements being stated, it is now possible to propose an architecture for a multimedia authoring application using declarative and relative specifications. This architecture is not only based on the state of the art of multimedia authoring proposals, but also on the multimedia authoring and presentation prototype *Madeus* that is being developed in our project [8].

An editing system for multimedia documents needs to represent the different dimensions of the document (spatial, logical, temporal and hypermedia). This can be done by using multiple views, each view being the result of the application of a specific filter on the same entity, namely the document. A consequence of this architecture based on multiples views is that each editing action performs on one view is saved in the document, allowing synchronization mechanisms between views as described in section.

In the rest of this paper we mainly focus on solutions for dealing with the temporal aspects of documents and their consequences on the spatial dimension because the edition of dynamic entities has still been less addressed than spatial and hypermedia authoring needs [1].

We have identified four views as the basic architecture for the edition of multimedia documents. These views, that can be considered as the kernel environment for the construction of more elaborated tools, are the following:

1. The *presentation view*, where documents are played.

2. The *scenario view*, for the handling of the temporal specifications.

3. The *objects view*, for the access of the data entering in the composition of the document.

4. The *storyboard view*, for providing a snapshot of the document such as traditional storyboards.

All these views need to provide some common services (such as stated in section 3):

- Selection capabilities of objects or time points (to be merged for instance).

- Editing operations like editing object characteristics or inserting/deleting a (spatial or temporal) relations between two objects.

- Filtering functions on the displayed information, to simplify the display or to reduce the amount of information presented to the author.

- Navigation primitives to give the author with some perception and access facilities through the different views of the document.

These services give rise to different realizations in each view. We only describe some of them (the most relevant one) either in the description of the view itself or through the examples described in section 5 when the service involves more than one view.

4.1. Presentation view

This view (shown by Figure 1) is divided into two parts:

- The execution (or reading) space (part A of the figure): in this space, the objects are displayed as specified by the temporal scenario and the author (as a reader) can interact with the presentation by the way of the author-defined links. Moreover, this space could also be the support of selection capabilities and editing operations in order to be as close as possible to a Wysiwyg approach. Finally, the result of a merged operation between time points is shown in this space, as illustrated in section.

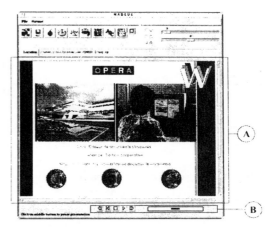

Figure 1. Presentation view

- The execution control space (part B of the figure), where the author can act on the progress of the presentation. This space supports all the temporal access functionalities defined in section 3.2. The author needs also to identify the instant being executed. This can be obtained by the way of a time indicator on a time scroll bar).

To conclude the presentation of this view, we can notice that its most important characteristic: it is both an execution and edition view, is impossible in approaches requiring a compilation step (such as in Director [12]). We do not know other authoring tools than Madeus which provides this interesting possibility.

4.2. Scenario view

The scenario view aims at giving the author with a global perception of the temporal organization of his document. It can be seen as the projection of one document presentation into the time space, in which not only temporal information of objects but also their temporal relationships are represented. Experiences with the visualization of relations graph have shown their limited benefits for authors [3]. More interesting is the visualization of the set of relations in conjunction with their effects i. e. the real temporal placement of the set of beginning and ending points in at least one possible document presentation.

This property of temporal honesty is very important to help the author to handle the complexity of temporal information in his document. Moreover, objects with unknown durations during the editing phase must be clearly distinguished from the others.

The visualization of the relations between objects depends on the underlying model. For example, in tree based approaches, the relations can be simply represented by (spatially) placing objects in sequence (with an horizontal line

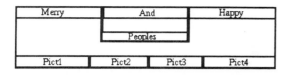

Figure 2. Scenario View

for identifying the relation) or in parallel (with a vertical line as a mark) according to the operator of the nodes. In addition, each node of the tree which constitutes a group of objects can be represented by encapsulated boxes. In CMIFed [18], the channel view is close to that idea, but the property of temporal honesty [6] is not always satisfied due to synchronization arcs. Moreover, relations between objects are not shown in this view but in another one, namely "hierarchy view". In Hyperprop [15], which is an event-based approach, the temporal view displays temporal information of a subset of objects and their synchronization links. This subset is computed relatively to a selected object by searching all the objects that are linked with it.

In constraint based approaches, in addition to the display of the relations that can be done in a similar way, it is also useful (see requirement 3.1) to show to the author the flexibility provided by the relations and the objects durations, since the scenario describes a (possibly large) set of solutions. For example, with the relation "before", the author can specify that an object is before another one without defining "how much" before it is. This flexibility has to be displayed (for example using a spring metaphor as in figure 2 or in [11]): it is a first way for helping the author in the perception of the set of solutions corresponding to a scenario. A more helpful one is to provide the author with an access of each solution by direct manipulation on the scenario view (by resizing or moving objects).

We experiment such a dynamic view in Madeus. The view provided in the ISIS environment [11] shows relations between objects but does not satisfied the temporal honesty property neither provide the author with a way to access every possible solution.

4.3. Object view

This view shows the space of the document content (i. e. the set of objects) and, for each object, the complete description of its attributes. It aims at giving to the author with a global perception of the content of the document and with easy selection/edition features on the objects themselves (although these features can be provided from the other views).

A problem raising with this view is the large amount of information that has to be displayed to the author (a multi-

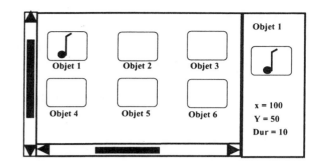

Figure 3. Object View

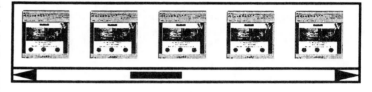

Figure 4. StoryBoard view

media document can contain several hundreds of objects). Different ways exist to reduce this problem and techniques for handling large spaces of data are well studied ([5] for instance). A solution consists in structuring and filtering the information to be displayed. In a multimedia authoring tool, this view can display the objects of a specific scene, or those involved in a given time period, and so on. It is also very important to give the author with some presentation choices such as the display order of the objects.

4.4. Intelligent storyboard view

The storyboard view is a set of screen dumps extracted from the document presentation in which a graphical representation is given to invisible objects (such as sounds). For instance, the storyboard in Director is graphical representation of the document at different time instants.

With this view, the author can survey the document and get some global information about both its spatial and temporal organization. This view can be automatically computed from the specification and the granularity of the extraction can be adjusted by the author. For instance, the author could decide that a screen dump is extracted each T time units, or each time something appears or disappears on the screen.

4.5. Views synchronization

The main interest of this four-views architecture lies both in the features provided by each view and in efficient synchronization mechanisms defined between them. As said previously, such synchronizations are possible thanks to the notion of view itself: each view is a representation of the document and each action on a view is registered in the document. As a consequence, it is possible to synchronize views from an object selection (each view can highlight the selected object).

Synchronizations between views can help the author:

- to select the current time point in the presentation view. He can use the control panel of this view but also any of the three other ones, by clicking on one screen in the storyboard view for instance.

- to understand the temporal organization of the current presentation being played, thanks to the scenario view that dynamically builds the temporal representation associated with this presentation. This is very useful since two successive presentations of the same document may be different due to objects with different durations at the presentation time.

Nevertheless, this feature is not relevant in all the situations; for example, for setting hypermedia links between two parts of the same document.

5. Illustrations through situations

In this section, we describe some authoring situations where the author wants to perform an operation on a ongoing document. Three examples have been chosen: adding an object into the scenario, adding a spatial relation and adding a temporal relation. Depending on the document and the preferences of the author, many sequences of basic actions could be performed to reach the expected result. Our main objective is to show the functions of the different views and the interest of their synchronization in such an authoring process.

5.1. Adding a new object

While running the presentation of a document, the author sees an object A appearing on the screen and decides to add a new object B which starts at the same time than A. He has no idea at that stage where to set the ending point of B. The insertion of B in the document can be done as follows:

- stop the current presentation while A is still present on the screen and select it,

- select the object B on the object view,

- add the new temporal relation between A and B on the presentation view,

- spatially adjust B on the presentation view,

- use the storyboard view to select an appropriate end point for B and jump to it,

- add a relation to decide of the end of B (e. g. when another object finishes or starts).

5.2. Spatial adjustment of two temporally disjoint objects

While running the presentation of a document, the author wants to join the left border of a picture B with the right border of a picture A. But B is displayed when A has disappeared from the screen. In order to reach this goal, the following operations can be done:

- stop the document just after B is presented,

- select the current time point corresponding to that instant in the presentation view,

- then jump backward with the control panel until A appears,

- ask to merge this time point with the selected one in the presentation view,

- and finally, spatially adjust the two objects.

5.3. Adding a new temporal relation between objects

While running the presentation of the document, the author observes that an object A follows the object B. He would like now these two objects start together. For that purpose, he can:

- look at the scenario view to understand why A and B are presented in sequence, i. e. the (set of) relation(s) which lead(s) to that synchronization,

- if needed, delete relations that are incompatible with the new synchronization,

- add the new sequential relation on the scenario view,

- check the temporal consequences on the other objects (it can be directly seen on the scenario view),

- check the spatial consequences of this modification on the storyboard view,

- finally, execute the corresponding sub-part of the document with the presentation view to verify if this editing operation gives the expected result.

6. Conclusion

In this paper, we have designed some basic principles to provide an authoring environment for multimedia documents which tend to approach the Wysiwyg paradigm. The key points of this proposal can be summerized as:

- the tight-coupling of authoring and presentation functions allowing some forms of direct edition,

- a way to allow the author to access and define each dimension of the documents through several views; moreover, views synchronization is very helpful to handle all these views.

- and the ability the let the author adapt navigation scales in the time space.

But the solution proposed goes much more further than direct editing ideas: synchronized multiviews can give powerful navigation functions not only while designing the document (i. e. for authors) but also while accessing to its content (i. e. by readers). For instance, the reader can use the storyboard view in order to see the document at a glance and then to select the part he wants to run in the presentation view.

These ideas are being implemented in Madeus, an authoring and presentation environment based on constraint specifications. Two views have been experimented:

- the presentation view, on which the execution is performed with control and navigation features [16] together with some basic editing functions (for adding/deleting relations),

- and the scenario view, on which temporal relations are displayed such as described in 4.2. We have paid a lot of attention on the ergonomic choices and on direct manipulation features to allow on that view. These choices have been evaluated through an experimentation among users (thanks to a collaboration with an ergonomics research team).

With these works, different technological problems have been identified, mainly because constraint techniques are not yet adapted to interactive and graphical environments: firstly, we have to dynamically maintain a set of solutions with real-time performances. Secondly, when adding/deleting a new constraint or object, the new displayed solution must be as "close" as possible to observe the Principle of Least Astonishment. Finally, the author needs to have some information to anticipate further manipulations. We are developing ad'hoc solutions that try to merge global techniques and local propagation techniques of constraint resolution.

References

[1] BIEBER M, WAN J., "Backtracking in a Multiple-window Hypertext Environment", *Proc. of ACM ECHT'94*, pp. 158-166, ACM press, Edinburgh, September 1994.

[2] BEACKER R., ROSENTHAL A., FRIEDLANDER N., SMITH E., COHEN a., "A Multimedia System for Authoring Motion Pictures", *Proc. of ACM Multimedia 96 Conference*, pp. 31-42, Boston, November 1996.

[3] BUCHANAN M.C., ZELLWEGER P.T., "Automatic Temporal Layout Mechanisms", *Proc. of ACM Multimedia 97 Conference*, pp. 341-350, Anaheim, August 1993.

[4] CCETT, *MhegDitor*, on line: http://www.ccett.fr/mheg/converter.htm, 1998.

[5] FURNAS G., "Generalised Fisheye views", *Proceedings of CHI'86*, vol. Human factor in Computing Systems , pp. 16-23, 1986.

[6] GRAM C.and COCKTON G., "Design Principles for interactive software", *Chapman & Hall*, vol. Chapter 5, July 1996 .

[7] HUDSON S. E., HSI C., "The Walk-Trough Approach To Authoring Multimedia Documents", *Proc. of the ACM 94 Multimedia Conference*, pp. 173-180, San Francisco, 1994.

[8] JOURDAN M., LAYAIDA N., SABRY-ISMAIL L, , ROISIN C., "An Integrated Authoring and Presentation Environment for Interactive Multimedia Documents", *Proc. of the 4th Conference on Multimedia Modelling*, World Scientific Publishing, Singapore, 18-19 November 1997.

[9] JOURDAN M., LAYAIDA N., ROISIN C., *A survey on authoring techniques for temporal scenarios of multimedia documents*, vol. to be published in Handbook of Multimedia, , CRC Press, April 1998.

[10] KHALFALLAH H., KARMOUCH A., "An architecture and a data model for integrated multimedia documents and presentation applications", *Multimedia Systems*, vol. 1995, num. 3, pp. 238-250, 1995.

[11] KIM M.Y., SONG J., "Multimedia Documents with Elastic Time", *Proc. of the ACM 95 Multimedia Conference*, pp. 143-154, San Francisco, November 1995.

[12] MACROMEDIA, *Director 6*, on line:http://www.macromedia.com/, 1998.

[13] NANARD J., NANARD M., "Hypertext Design Environments and the Hypertext Design Process", *CACM*, vol. 38, num. 8, pp. 49-56, August 1995.

[14] PRICEe R., "MHEG: An Introduction to the Future International Standard for Hypermedia Object Interchange", *Proceedings of the First ACM Conference on Multimedia*, pp. 121-128, ACM Press, Anaheim, Californie, August 1993.

[15] SAADE D. C. M., SOARES L. F. G., COSTA F. R. , SOUZA FILHO G. L., "Graphical Structured-Editing of Multimedia Documents with Temporal and Spatial Constraint", *Proc. of the 4th Conference on Multimedia Modelling*, pp. 279-295, World Scientific Publishing, Singapore, 18-19 November 1997.

[16] SABRY-ISMAIL L., ROISIN C., LAYAIDA N., "Navigation in Structured Multimedia Documents using Presentation Context", *Hypertextes et Hypermédias*, Hermès, ed., Paris, September 1997.

[17] SELCUK CANDAN K., PRABHAKARAN B., SUBRAHMANIAN V.S., "CHIMP: A Framework for Supporting Distributed Multimedia Document Authoring and Presentation", *Proc. of the ACM 96 Multimedia Conference*, pp. 329-339, Boston, November 1996.

[18] VAN ROSSUM G., JANSEN J., MULLENDER K. and BULTERMAN D., "CMIFed: a Presentation Environment for Portable Hypermedia Documents", *Proceedings of the ACM 93 Multimedia Conference*, California (USA) 1993.

[19] W3C, *Working Draft specification of SMIL (Synchronized Multimedia Integration Language)*, http://www.w3.org/TR/WD-smil, February, 1998.

A Multimedia System for Authoring Motion Pictures

Ronald Baecker, Alan J Rosenthal, Naomi Friedlander, Eric Smith, Andrew Cohen
Dynamic Graphics Project
Dept. of Computer Science, University of Toronto
10 King's College Road
Toronto ON Canada   M5S 1A4
(416) 978-6983
E-mail: rmb@dgp.toronto.edu

ABSTRACT

MAD (Movie Authoring and Design) is a novel design and authoring system that facilitates the process of creating dynamic visual presentations such as motion pictures and lecture-demonstrations. MAD supports the process by enhancing the author's ability to structure and modify a presentation and to visualize the ultimate result. It does this by allowing both top-down design and bottom-up creation with a hierarchical multimedia document representation; by supporting the flexible inclusion and combination of words, images, sounds, and video sequences; and by providing real-time playback of the best approximation to the ultimate presentation that can be produced at any stage of the design process.

MAD represents a paradigm shift from traditional methods of authoring and producing motion pictures. Its development therefore requires in-depth observation of a variety of users working on a variety of filmmaking projects. After describing the key concepts underlying MAD and the current, second-generation prototype software, we describe a number of interesting applications of MAD. In doing so, we review how we have worked with users in an iterative design process and how studies of the work of these users have informed key design issues.

Keywords

Multimedia systems, multimedia documents, multimedia authoring tools, applications of multimedia, iterative design, user-centred design.

BACKGROUND

Computer technology has been used increasingly in motion picture production over the past decade. One of the most significant uses has been in *post-production*, including the very successful digital video storage, editing, and assembly systems (e.g., Avid, [4]). *Pre-production* application systems have included word processors and specialized script writing systems, systems for the design of storyboards, project management tools and spreadsheets used for

planning and budgeting, and a variety of other authoring tools to be discussed below. Movie archiving and retrieval systems such as Media Streams (Davis, [11]) provide powerful mechanisms for describing video sequences with certain characteristics, for locating them in video archives, and for "repurposing" them. Yet there has been no system that allows the design and management of words, images, sounds, and video for visualization during the pre-production and production phases of a motion picture. As we shall see, providing design, management, and visualization support facilitates creative thought in the development of dynamic visual presentations for many kinds of applications involving many kinds of users.

Our concept (see also Rosenthal and Baecker, [37]; Rosenthal, [36]) has been influenced by precedents and ideas from other disciplines. In creating documents with word/outline processors, we can work either top-down and bottom-up, changing the approach from moment to moment, while there is always a viewable, printable document. In creating music with computers, we use systems that transact in melodies, timbres, rhythms, scores, and waveforms to define sounds, with a common underlying data representation and interchange format — MIDI (Loy, [22]). In creating software, we employ a variety of representations, both textual and graphical, at various levels of abstraction (Martin and McClure, [25]; Price, Baecker, and Small, [34]), and use these representations to support software development as a cooperative process.

As with word/outline processors, MAD supports both top-down design and bottom-up multimedia document creation. As with digital music, MAD provides a common data representation and interchange format. As with software creation, MAD incorporates a variety of visual representations in an attempt to facilitate creativity by users.

We now proceed to a discussion of MAD's design goals. We follow this with a discussion of the implementation, and a comparison of our approach to relevant research and to commercially available multimedia authoring tools. We review our iterative design process, and describe how the system has evolved in response to feedback from our users. We then present a number of novel and sometimes surprising uses of the technology. The paper concludes with a discussion of current and planned work.

ACM Multimedia 96, Boston MA USA
© 1996 ACM 0-89791-871-1/96/11   ..$3.50

KEY DESIGN GOALS

Design goals for the Movie Authoring and Design system are:

• *Idea structuring* — the ability to develop movie ideas both top-down and bottom-up and to modify the structure with ease as new ideas arise

• *Multimedia support* — the integrated handling of scripts, dialogue or narration, music, sound effects, storyboards, and video shots

• *Visualization* — the inclusion of aids to visualizing the film, as for example being able to request a real-time preview of the movie or an approximation to it at any stage in the film development process

• *Interchange representations* — the provision of mechanisms for importing, exporting, and sharing movies and their constituent elements with other software and systems to aid communication and collaboration. (This topic will be discussed in the next section, Implementation.)

Idea Structuring

Films have complex structure. In traditional filmmaking, a substantial amount of time and effort is devoted to organization. Individuals will bring different cognitive styles to the organization and authoring process. This manifests itself in two ways, in terms of film structure and in terms of the script development process.

Some moviemakers will think of their films as a linear succession of ideas, sequences, or shots. Others will articulate concepts in terms of a hierarchical structure. For example, their films may consist of acts, which may consist of scenes, which may in turn consist of shots.

Some moviemakers want to have a high-level script outline written before becoming entangled with lower-level details: a top-down approach would accommodate this thinking style. On the other hand, as the film is developed, an outline will no longer be sufficient for expressing ideas; one may then want to work bottom-up adding more and more detail in a structured manner. Other filmmakers will work bottom-up from the outset, collecting material and then looking for methods of arranging and structuring it. Thus a good movie authoring tool must allow the user to work top-down *or* bottom-up as required, and to work at whatever level of detail is desired. A hierarchical structure facilitates this goal.

Multimedia Support

In the production of motion pictures, various documents are produced, such as written scripts and the sequences of sketches known as storyboards. The properties and uses of these various items are discussed in detail by Katz [21].

Scripts implemented on modern multimedia computers such as the Apple Macintosh can include more than just text, for these machines support additional "data types" such as pictures, digitized video clips, and sounds. Thus one should be able to pick up a microphone and record the narration, and be able to include sketches representing storyboard frames. One should be able to digitize video sequences corresponding to material already shot. A good movie authoring tool will allow the user to attach these elements to the script, and manipulate all this data in a uniform and integrated fashion. MAD does all of this.

MAD also supports multiple sound tracks which may be mixed together, such as dialog, background music, and sound effects. "Commentary tracks" allow layered discussion and metadiscussion in the style of the PREP editor (Neuwirth, Kaufer, Chandhok, and Morris, [30]). Users can add commentary tracks which, for example, discuss plans for the film. However, instead of being simple text comments, these commentary tracks can use MAD's facilities to include multimedia elements such as voice annotations, and the commentary tracks retain a direct tie-in to the underlying film structure. These multiple-track mechanisms may be applied either to particular items in the hierarchy or to the entire film. An application illustrating their use appears below.

Visualization

Despite the flexibility of working at any desired level of detail there remains an overview problem. A film has a certain character: elements of the film which step outside that character may not contribute to the film. Therefore a need exists to visualize the evolving "feel" and character of the film as it is developed. A crucial aspect of this is the timing and pacing of the action, an area where amateur filmmakers often have particular difficulty.

A good movie authoring tool should contain facilities for assisting the user in maintaining both an overview of the developing film and a good sense of how it is progressing. MAD has a "play" facility which allows an approximation to the final form of the film to be viewed on the user's workstation at any time. This can help prevent the author from being surprised at aspects of the final result by being aware of the emerging character of the film during scriptwriting. It will also allow an author to present the developing script as a dynamic demonstration of ideas in process for a film that has not yet been made.

Multiple representations of multimedia documents are also aids to visualization. Movie authoring tools should provide a variety of representations beginning with those that have emerged out of traditional filmmaking practice, such as scripts, storyboards, and movie playback.

IMPLEMENTATION

The current version of MAD (version 2.4) runs on an Apple Macintosh computer with System 7.5 and QuickTime 2.0 or later.

Idea Structuring

Apart from the content of the individual items, MAD resembles most of all an outline processor, structuring a document as a hierarchy of items (Figure 1). Although MAD imposes no structure, items and subitems often represent "acts," "scenes," and "shots", and have a variety of multimedia elements attached to them. New items can be inserted into any desired position in the hierarchy. Items can be moved from place to place within the hierarchy, taking all their subitems with them. Like a text outliner, MAD allows the user to contract items to exclude lower levels of detail. Similarly, the user can zoom in on a single item, in effect hiding higher levels of abstraction in order to focus on a particular portion of the multimedia document.

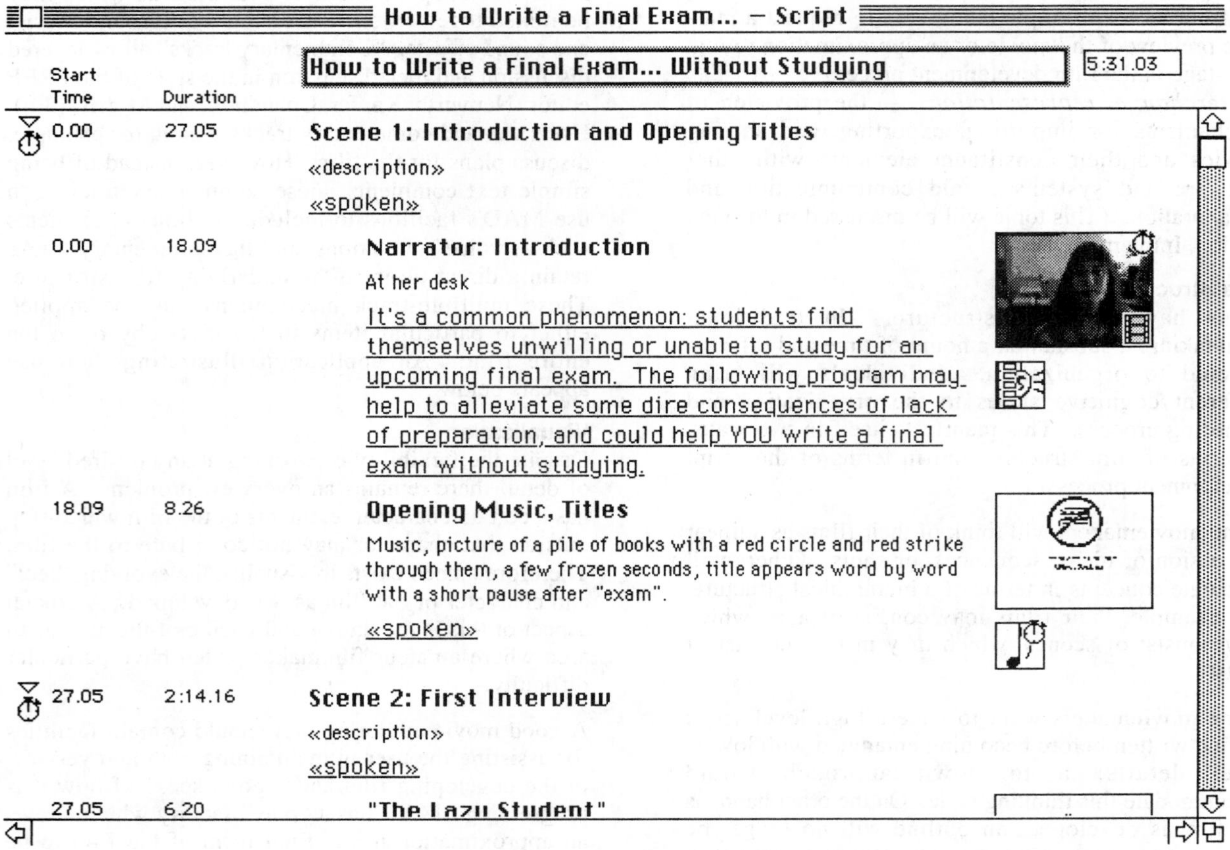

Figure 1: The script view. Hierarchical structure of items is indicated by indentation of the text. Each text item has 3 fields — title, screen directions, and narration or dialogue, and may also optionally have spoken text, music, storyboard frames, and video elements attached to it. These are noted at the right edge of the script.

The structure of the MAD document and its on-screen representation are kept separate, permitting multiple simultaneous views of the document. Currently supported view-types are Script, Storyboard, and Playback, but because of the separation between model and view, it is relatively straightforward to add new representations. The Script view is primarily intended for writing, and the items are arranged vertically, with indentation indicating their depth within the hierarchy (Figure 1). The Storyboard view hides most of the textual content of the items, replacing them with a grid-like arrangement of the graphical elements from each of the document's items (Figure 3). The Play view displays items sequentially, with each item being on screen for its indicated duration (Figure 2).

Multimedia Support

Each item can have attached to the script text various multimedia elements — still pictures; recorded narration, dialogue, commentary, music, or sound effects; and digitized video. Multimedia elements can be created in many ways. PICT and MacPaint files can be imported as storyboard frames; pictures can be drawn with MAD's rudimentary sketch editor. QuickTime movies can be imported with or without sound, and can be excerpted within MAD. Sound can be recorded, and narrative or descriptive text can be entered. Timing for the items can be based on their attached multimedia elements, or can be specified explicitly, when imported video or audio is not present or is not representative of the plans for the final film.

Visualization

MAD's multiple views are tools for visualization. Since each is parameterized, there are actually entire families of Script, Storyboard, and Play views. For example, only including the titles in the script view allows us to see a compact representation of the outline of the film. Other examples include varying the size of the frames in the storyboard view, and specifying whether dialog and director's notes are to be visible in the playback view.

The system also keeps track of timing information. Time is represented using hours, minutes, seconds, and frames as in SMPTE time code. Each item has associated with it two times: a start time and a duration. The start time is simply based on the duration of all preceding items in the movie. The duration for an item can be calculated in a number of different ways. If the item has an attached sound or video element, its duration can be used to determine the item's duration. If the item has subitems, the duration can be calculated from the duration of those subitems. Finally, the user can explicitly enter an item's desired duration. This is particularly useful in the early stages of a document's evolution, when an author may have planned lengths for the various

scenes, but as yet have little or no material. In version 1 of MAD, each item had an actual duration and a planned duration, but this feature was difficult to explain to users, and in version 2 only the actual duration is included. Examples of how durations are used in planning and visualization are presented below.

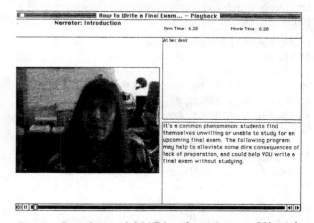

Figure 2: One of MAD's play views. Visuals, narration or dialogue, and screen directions appear in separate screen areas.

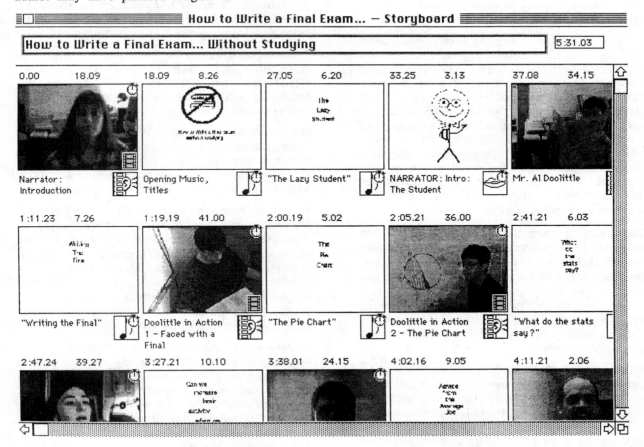

Figure 3: A storyboard view. All MAD views are parameterized. In this case we have specified the size of the storyboard frames and the additional details to be included in this view of a film by Naomi Friedlander.

MAD also supports varieties of playback which have different affordances for movie authors. For example, one very useful feature allows a viewer to see part of an item, then skip forward to the next item, which in turn can be viewed in its entirety or interrupted to skip forward to the following item. Use of this capability feels very much like flipping through the chapters of a multimedia book.

Interchange Representations

MAD documents are stored in files, and this alone provides an interchange representation of an author's ideas for a film. Two users can therefore collaborate on a film by exchanging MAD files. Furthermore, since MAD movies are represented as standard QuickTime (Apple Computer, [3]) files, they can be played back on a variety of non-Macintosh platforms. This also makes it possible for MAD movies to be viewed by other applications, integrated into World Wide Web pages, and played back by Web browsers.

COMPARISON TO OTHER WORK

Systems that support the entry and editing of textual or graphical representations of documents in some application domain are generally known as document editors, computer-aided design systems, or authoring tools. There is some relevant research from the academic literature.

Woolsey [42] suggests ways to develop multimedia based on precedents from "print, audiovisuals, speeches, activities, materials, and expression." Davenport, Smith, and Pincever [10] propose the use of film terminology and concepts for the organizing of video clips. Pea [31] describes a multimedia authoring toolkit consisting of programs for multimedia database access, storyboarding, and video-clip editing. Mills, Cohen, and Wong [29] propose an innovative Hierarchical Video Magnifier which allows users to view linear storyboards of fine levels of film detail while still seeing storyboards that provide an awareness of temporal context.

Ueda et al. [39] report on the use of computer vision techniques for the automatic computation of video structure, such as by cut detection and object tracking. Hardman, van Rossum, and Bulterman [18] and Hardman, van Rossum, Jansen, and Mullender [19] describe a system for structured multimedia authoring that employs both a hierarchy view of components and subcomponents and a channel view of what is happening over time.

Hudson and Hsi [20] present a kind of "multimedia through demonstration" system in which presentations are defined by "walking through" a screen presentation. McKay and Pagani [28] propose a novel system that incorporates scanning paper storyboards and coupling them to an interactive video editing subsystem. Geissler [15] report on browsers, maps, history lists, and tours as aids to navigation and visualization of movie-only hyperdocuments.

We have also recently completed a study of commercial multimedia authoring tools. These cluster into eight categories:

Script Writing Software

Script writing software (see, e.g., BC Software, [8]) is specialized to the task of facilitating the writing, editing, formatting, and printing of movie and television scripts.

Storyboard Design Software

Storyboard design software (see, e.g., PowerProduction Software, [33]) aids users in creating pictorial representations of a movie or presentation. Digitized graphics can be created, rearranged or removed in order to aid in creating and visualizing a concept.

Personal/Home Graphics Software

Personal/home graphics software (see, e.g. Delrina, [12]) provides children and adults with tools to create and maintain personal multimedia documents, such as journals, photo albums movies, and animation (see, e.g., Halgren, Fernandes, and Thomas, [17]).

Desktop Video Software

Desktop video software tools allow users to convert recorded video to a digitized form or digitally record live footage. Digitized film editing tools (see, e.g., Adobe, [1]) allow scenes to be cut, copied, pasted, faded in, faded out, merged, and modified.

Presentation Graphics Software

Presentation graphics software tools (see, e.g., Adobe, [2]) provide users with methods of organizing and exhibiting slide shows which can incorporate multimedia elements.

Multimedia Authoring Tools Without Scripting

Multimedia authoring tools without scripting languages (see, e.g., Pierian Spring, [32]) allow users to create non-interactive or interactive multimedia presentations without requiring or allowing the use of programming.

Multimedia Authoring Software With Scripting

Multimedia authoring tools with scripting languages allow users significant flexibility in tailoring all sorts of presentations, including interactive ones. An example is Director (MacroMedia, [23]), which employs a theatrical metaphor in a low-level visual scripting environment in which the behaviour of graphical elements known as cast members is arranged with respect to a timeline, or score.

Professional Multimedia Authoring Software

Professional multimedia authoring software allows users to create intricate and diverse presentations, either interactive or non-interactive. The previous two categories accomplish these tasks as well; however, this category was added to represent a more expensive class of tools which have more extensive functionality (see, e.g., MacroMedia, [24]).

Interpretation

MAD draws upon much of this prior art. For example, we heed the advice of Woolsey, Davenport et al., and Pea in drawing upon the traditions and terminology of film and other precedent disciplines. We share with Hardman et al. a commitment to the authoring of structured multimedia documents using a variety of metaphors and views. We share with Mills et al. and with Geissler an interest in novel representations of video content.

Yet MAD differs significantly from other existing filmmaking and multimedia systems. Unlike current script and storyboard tools used in film pre-production, it provides integrated multimedia support and real-time visualization capabilities. Unlike current desktop video software and presentation software, it incorporates a full motion picture metaphor. and is designed for use in pre-production and production. Unlike existing multimedia authoring tools, it facilitates and encourages a strong concern for narrative and dialogue structure. And, although the current implementation is only a start in this regard, MAD incorporates a rich and expanding set of visual representations of motion pictures designed to aid in imagining and visualizing film concepts. The system that is closest to the spirit of MAD is a low-end commercial digital movie creation system called QuickFLIX (Radius, [35]), which lacks a script view but does have a storyboard view and a timeline view.

OUR ITERATIVE DESIGN PROCESS

Although we have studied traditional filmmaking processes and achieved useful insights, especially about the roles of visualization and collaboration in the authoring process (Venkatacharya, [40]), we explicitly did *not* want to replicate traditional filming processes, especially the typical separation between pre-production and production.

MAD introduces a paradigm shift in the making of motion pictures. It allows the easy intermingling of pre-production and production. It allows film concepts to be made tangible, demonstrable, and accessible in a way not possible with traditional technologies. It encourages tight artistic control by an "author" over all aspects of a production — words, images, and music. It also encourages the interaction by members of a creative team through an artifact representing the planned production in a way not possible with traditional technologies, in which words, music, still images, and moving pictures appear in separate media.

We therefore felt we had to build and refine a working and functional (not "smoke and mirrors") prototype in order to convey the concept before we could make the best use of domain expertise and user feedback. From the outset, we adopted a user testing methodology (McGrath, [26]) that eschewed the internal validity of standardized designed tasks in favour of the external validity of free form exploration by users seeking to make real films of their own devising. We have employed a variety of interview and observational techniques to study and learn from our users' experiences. Both adults and children have worked with MAD on over twenty-five 2- to 10-minute movie making projects, seven of which we describe below in the context of a discussion of applications of MAD.

The first project to be described (and actually the first executed) was a plausibility argument to show that we were on the right track. We used MAD ourselves in designing an 8-minute movie, and learned much about what we had done right and how much we still had to do. The second project was an extended study in which we videotaped 3 film-makers working on 2 films over 16 hours, and analyzed their work process both quantitatively and qualitatively. Based on insights derived in these two major uses of the system and several minor uses, as well as some screen design prototyping exercises, we planned and carried out a reimplementation of much of the system's interface and internals.

The third project was our use of MAD to plan and write a lecture-demonstration of MAD. The fourth project consisted of participant observation of the creation of short films by an 11-year-old and a 12-year-old. The fifth project involved video taping a small group of novice filmmakers working for 3 hours on the high-level structure of a film they were about to make.

The sixth and seventh projects are still ongoing or being analyzed. The former project involved 24 seventh-graders learning to make short movies using MAD and other multimedia tools during a 2-week summer camp under our guidance as participant-observers. In the seventh project, we were also participant-observers, but here school children and their teacher were using MAD to help them think about and discuss how they learn. Qualitative and occasionally quantitative analysis have yielded design insights which we shall discuss below.

APPLICATIONS OF MAD

MAD is a versatile tool that can be used for many different purposes including:
• Sketching, designing, thinking about, blueprinting, authoring motion pictures
• Developing, presenting, and selling film, video, advertising, and multimedia concepts
• Brainstorming, planning, structuring, and executing lecture-demonstrations and multimedia presentations
• Teaching filmmaking to novices; novices learning filmmaking
• Kids making films
• Encouraging and facilitating reflection on and dialogue about classroom practices by students and teachers
• User interface prototyping
• Usability testing of new technologies
• Multimedia messaging over the Internet.
Let us now look at each of these uses in turn. Most of the uses will be illustrated with a real example.

Authoring Motion Pictures

In September 1993 MAD was used to design a movie (Baecker, Glass, Mitchell, and Posner, [5]) to demonstrate the SASSE collaborative writing system we were developing (Baecker, Nastos, Posner, and Mawby, [6]). The senior author had previously produced a number of short films.

First a very top-level outline of the film was defined, a listing of the acts of the production. Next, shots for the first few acts were proposed. We then took each of the acts in turn and began to draft suitable narration for the script. The narration was recorded so that times could be estimated and judgments made about film flow, timing, and pacing.

The material required three kinds of shots. Shots of the narrator were indicated in metatext describing the shot and also in "storyboard frames" containing text only. Longer descriptive metatext was entered as shooting instructions for the camera crew that would later film user interactions with the SASSE system. Finally, where suitable video clips existed, we imported them into MAD and viewed them in the context of the emerging production.

Playback of the movie was of course incomplete, but display of the script, reading of the narration, display of the storyboard, and screening of the video clips in correct order and with correct timing sufficed to convey a good sense of the whole and to guide the authoring process.

We used MAD for roughly 6-8 hours in this way. Because the film crew was coming the following day, and MAD at this point didn't deal with hard copy or still images very well, two members of the team switched to a traditional word processor and markups of paper printouts to produce a final script and shooting instructions for the director and film crew. After filming was completed, a traditional computer-based editing console was used for title generation and post production.

Despite the flaws of the early prototype, MAD allowed us very efficiently to develop and refine a concept for the movie, write and edit the script, revise the script after hearing how it sounded and how it flowed, and preview likely video sequences for inclusion in the film in the context of a playback of a very rough but continually improving approximation to what the final film would be like.

On the other hand, there was clearly much room for improvement. For example, we could see the utility of allowing audio and video tracks belonging to one item to start at different times, a serious complication to our very simple item model which we still have not undertaken.

An example of another MAD motion picture is illustrated in Figure 4. Requirements for its production caused us to generalize our model of audio tracks so that they could be attached to items located anywhere within the movie hierarchy.

Figure 4. A partial storyboard for Alexandra Mazalek's rollerblading film. This was developed in MAD primarily with pre-existing footage.

Pitching Film Proposals

In the summer of 1994, three undergraduate students (two who had never made movies before and one moderately experienced film-maker) entered a user interface design competition for which they had to create a variety of materials documenting their research, designs, and user testing. One of these materials was to be an ten- to fifteen-minute interactive presentation of their interface design in MacroMedia Director, and another was to be a ten-minute video describing the design and testing process.

MAD assist the students very effectively with their authoring process. In 16 hours with MAD, and additional work off-line, they created a fairly complete script and production plan for the video and to some extent for the interactive presentation (Figure 5).

The students were videotaped with 4 cameras while they were working with MAD. We analyzed the tapes for MAD feature use and took supplementary notes using MacSHAPA (Sanderson et al, [38]), an application program for the Macintosh that controls a VCR and facilitates notetaking about a tape's interesting events.

The test proved to be a rich source of information, confirming the usefulness of some features, identifying serious problems with others, and also suggesting that some future directions we had in mind were likely to be of value. Of particular interest was the use these individuals made of multimedia presentations of film concepts for purposes of communicating and "selling" ideas among themselves. This suggests that the "play" feature may be effective for "pitching" ideas for films, videos, and multimedia presentations to collaborators, managers, clients, and potential sponsors.

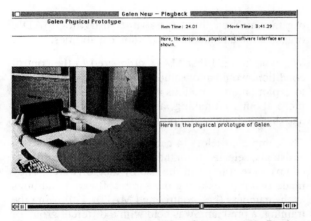

Figure 5. Image from a film documenting Project Galen. This project submitted a prototype of a hand-held, Internet-connected device for patient medical education to an international design competition.

Planning Lecture-Demonstrations

In April 1996 we were planning a demonstration of MAD (Friedlander, Baecker, Rosenthal, and Smith, [14]) for the SIGCHI Conference. Our 30 minute presentation was intended to contain lecture and demonstration, high-level concepts and low-level detail, creation in real-time of a MAD movie as well as review of already completed motion pictures.

We used MAD to aid in the brainstorming, planning, outlining, and writing of the script for the lecture-demonstration. The evolving script represented the working model for our talk. Because it was tangible and printable, we were able to print it, review it, and conceptualize it. Because it was editable, we were able to modify and evolve our concept with ease.

Of particular utility was the ability to record narration or dialogue and insert it into the script. We used this to ad lib portions of the talk and then review how they felt in the context of the evolving whole.

Kids Making Films

In August 1995 an 11 year old girl (Aha) and a 12 year old boy (Ethan) separately created movies using MAD.

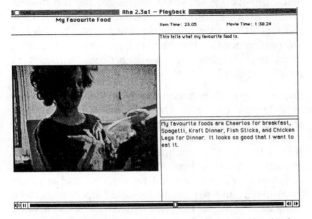

Figure 6: Image from Aha's movie This playback view shows narration and director's notes.

In her first hour with MAD, including being introduced to the system, Aha wrote a rough script for a 2 minute film, "A Movie About Me," based on a template we had created which provided a rough outline for an autobiographical movie and ideas for possible scenes. She recorded visual placeholders for all scenes on video, and thus had completed a "draft" of her movie. She then went out and did the location shooting implied by her script. Finally, she returned to the lab to digitize various video shots and still photos and assembled the result into a final movie (Figure 6). Total time expended was roughly 8 hours.

Ethan used MAD during 3 sessions totaling approximately 9 hours, creating a movie about Arab Mythology based on material from a book. He had decided to organize scenes using roughly the same outline as found in the book. Short introductions to the material were included among narrated passages from the book. After considering visuals to accompany these passages and how to include sound effects, Ethan drew some pictures, recorded some sound effects, and shot some more video. The result was an interesting movie (Figure 7) that allowed him to explore the use of a variety of multimedia resources.

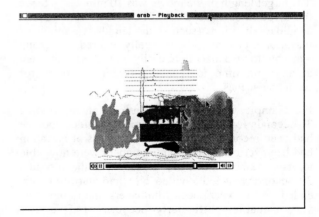

Figure 7: Image from Ethan's movie. Here we see the more movie-centred playback view in which only images are shown.

In these projects MAD accommodated two radically different approaches: Aha's film was organized hierarchically, and was composed predominantly of video footage, much of this shot on location, as well as some scanned photographs. Ethan's movie was organized linearly, and was composed predominantly of recorded narration over still drawings, with some video footage and sound effects.

As always, these users forced us to challenge assumptions we had made. We had viewed MAD as a design, authoring, and visualization tool, not as a production tool, so we had not implemented the ability to output the final result to videotape. Our young users insisted upon having copies they could take home, so we happily added this feature.

Teaching and Learning Filmmaking

In May 1995 another group of students at the University of Toronto were selected to present a novel interface design at an international competition. None of the participants had any filming experience. The group used MAD to help design a video presentation during 2 work sessions totaling approximately 6 hours in length, about 3 of which were solely dedicated to using MAD.

The analysis of videotapes made of the sessions showed that MAD helped the group with its idea development. Initially, they had no script for their video and no concept of what should be included in the final product. After working with MAD for 40 minutes they had outlined their film in terms of 6 scenes and had given each a title, brief written descriptions of what would be shot and what would be said, some improvised spoken narration, and a sketch or digitized image as a visual reference. For the first time, they were starting to see how they might organize the film and what the final product could look like.

The target length of the movie was 10 minutes. Since the duration of a scene could be chosen from various candidate durations (such as the length of a movie or narration attachment) or manually entered, the group was able to visualize more easily how close they were at any one time to reaching target durations for particular scenes.

For example, when working on a scene intended to be 30 seconds long, where 10 seconds of video footage had been recorded and where 20 seconds of narration had been scripted, the group members were now able to visualize how much time remained of the allocated 30 seconds once the video clip and narration had ended. As inexperienced filmmakers, they found this very valuable, particularly because MAD allows visualization of the timing of multiple media streams in parallel, in this case video and narration, and also of the timing of items *in context*, that is, with respect to their inclusion in a sequence of items.

Following up both on this experience and on the work of Aha and Ethan, we decided to carry out a more significant test of our hypotheses that MAD provides an excellent environment for teaching principles of filmmaking and multimedia creation, and that it can be quickly learned and effectively used by school children. Thus in July of 1996 we used MAD in a multimedia summer camp held in Toronto.

The camp was designed to test MAD in a classroom-like setting where groups of students would work together to learn new technologies and use their creativity to produce movies. We compared MAD to a control condition consisting of a word processor and a digital movie editor. The editor allows a computerized "cut" and "paste" of digital video and easy creation of digital movies but does not provide MAD's organization and media integration capabilities.

We hypothesized that MAD, compared to the control condition, would allow students to make movies faster, to explore more variations within their movies, to learn more about filmmaking, and to make better movies, and that students would prefer MAD.

The camp counselors (4 camp counselors, and 3 camp assistants, selected from the high school that hosted the camp) were trained in the use of the software. They made two movies using the same software conditions as the campers (i.e., control and MAD). Following the training, a pre-camp was held with a different group of campers. This pilot study enabled us to refine our methodology and data collection methods and also served to give the counselors valuable experience.

For the actual camp, a total of 24 campers were randomly picked from among interested grade 7 students from a local school district. The camp was run for a two week period with twelve students attending each week. The students were divided into four groups of three. Assignment was controlled to ensure that students were from different schools and that the computer experience across groups was balanced. Each group made two movies, one in each software condition. Half of the groups were randomly assigned to each of the two orders of working with MAD and the control software.

A wide variety of experimental instruments were used. These include raw video footage, digital records of movies at various stages, paper artifacts, several questionnaires, discussions with campers and counselors, paper logs and audio journals, and video records of some of the students' interactions and work.

The camp was a success. The children learned how to make movies, produced two interesting pieces of work in each group, and enjoyed the experience. As expected, MAD proved useful and usable for the task. Initial analysis of the campers' questionnaires indicates that campers found MAD easier to use for movie-making than the control software (t=1.64, 21; p<.059), and that 91% of the campers preferred MAD (9% had no preference). Further analysis of this study, including insights into work process, appears in Baecker et al. [7].

Supporting Reflection on Classroom Process

In February of 1996, Dr. Andrew Cohen, a post-doctoral researcher spending part of his time with our group, began an innovative application of MAD in the Nashville Public Schools. MAD's multimedia authoring tools allow the process of classroom activities to be (a) captured by students and teachers themselves, and (b) easily reflected upon and voice annotated by the viewer. Annotated videos can also be the object of inquiry by teachers.

Groups of two or three 11- and 12-year old school children and their teacher record on videotape seven to ten minutes of their own collaborative mathematics problem solving process. They enter this sequence into a MAD movie, and then review it, producing a meta-movie in which each student overlays as an additional audio track his or her interpretation of what was going on. The result becomes a tangible, shareable, discussible artifact embodying the collaborative learning process. As it evolves, it engages student and teacher alike in reflection on and enhanced understanding of that process (Cohen et al, [9]).

Dr. Cohen's approach builds on other attempts to use video as an aid for reflecting on classroom practice. For example, viewing videos of one's own and a peer's teaching practice has been shown to be effective in motivating change in classroom practice (e.g. Fredrickson, [13]), while viewing videos of expert teaching practice has been shown to facilitate 'noticing' relations between theory and practice (Michael et al., [27]). However, MAD allows students and teachers to take over the process of reflection and allows the documents to be archived and reviewed with annotations for continual professional development as opposed to short duration workshops. Cohen plans further studies of this kind involving groups of teachers as well as groups of students.

User Interface Prototyping

User interface designers often produce animated or video scenarios in the early stage of conceiving and prototyping new systems and interfaces (Vertelney, [41]). Because MAD encourages a thoughtful, structured development of an audio-visual presentation, it affords significant advantages for uses of this kind.

Usability Testing of New Technologies

Imagine you are making a film called "X". To do so in MAD, you open a window called X and engage in various activities such as writing dialog, recording sounds, and digitizing video. MAD allows you to work on several movies concurrently, so you also create a film called "The Making of X." In this meta-film, you enter various remarks about your ideas and thought processes in designing X. You can also enter screen snapshots that represent stages in the development of X's script, and can even record video depicting your work on X. Furthermore, you can also document problems in the process, whether these are conceptual issues in the design of the film, features desired but currently lacking in MAD, or bugs in MAD. We have used MAD in this way to good effect. Since MAD can be so used in conjunction with applications other than MAD itself, MAD is a useful general tool for usability testing.

Multimedia Messaging Over the Internet

Finally, our newest endeavor is to explore high-bandwidth multimedia collaborative environments. The goal here is to investigate the affordances of "multimedia mail" for communication and collaboration. Here we are attempting to link together a multimedia representation of the knowledge about and the problems collaborators are working on, with their discourse (textual, audio and video) about that problem. This work capitalizes on the fact that MAD stores films as QuickTime files. Therefore, MAD movies can be played back by standard QuickTime players including those incorporated in other applications such as Netscape. This makes MAD the "messaging" tool for constructing and refining multimedia messages to be transmitted over the Internet.

As an example of an investigation in progress, consider the work described above with teachers and students using MAD to produce and reflect upon their mathematics problem solving in the classroom. Our goal is to establish communities of teachers and students in geographically distributed regions discoursing about teaching and learning. Using MAD, however, the teachers and students would not only be able to talk about what their doing, but they would be able to make the process of teaching and learning visible to the community as a conceptual anchor for their discussion. Rather that have that discussion solely in a written mode, teachers and students could make use of the additional rich communicative affordances of multimedia formats.

SUMMARY AND CONCLUSIONS

We have completed a prototype of MAD, observed its use in over twenty-five short productions, redesigned the user interface based on these experiences, and re-engineered it for greater reliability and flexibility. MAD has proved useful, usable, and robust for small filming projects. It has been used successfully and enthusiastically and with only minutes of training time by amateur filmmakers as young as 11 years old who have never made a movie before. Careful observation and study of individuals working on these projects has yielded significant insights into system functionality and user interface and into ways of thinking and working while using MAD, which in turn has enabled us to improve MAD through an iterative design process grounded in realistic user experiences.

FUTURE RESEARCH

Our major current goals are:
• to explore further the use of MAD both by novice and professional filmmakers
• to extend the uses of MAD to allow the creation and annotation of informal video documents
• to extend the mechanisms by which such statements and records can be transmitted via Internet transmission and viewed via remote playback
• to enhance MAD's capability to manage libraries of video sequences and to represent alternate "takes" when the filmmaker is not sure how best to express an idea.

• to extend MAD's metaphors and representations to support the creation of dynamic visual sequences with mechanisms other than scripts and storyboards
• to investigate collaboration in the process of designing movies with MAD (see, for example, Gidney, Chandler, and McFarlane, [16]).

One major stream of research deals with process and representation. We have to date identified four major approaches to authoring motion pictures:
• a script-based approach, typically used by the screenwriter
• a storyboard-based approach, typically used by the production designer
• an available shot-based approach, used by directors and editors
• a flow- and timing-based approach, used by directors and cinematographers.

Each approach requires different visual representations of the movie and different interface mechanisms. Our hypothesis is that a system that supports these four points of view will support different cognitive styles as well as collaboration among different supporting disciplines. We anticipate that supporting a greater variety of working styles will enhance creativity by allowing filmmakers to switch modes of work as is suitable for authoring different portions of the film. For example, film sequences can be entered and edited using the storyboard view as well as with the script view.

We have identified many professional uses for MAD, in the creation of dramatic, documentary and training films and video, in the design of animated films, in the planning of radio shows and museum exhibits, and, ultimately, in the creation of interactive multimedia. MAD can be used both in production and in pre-production, for sketching concepts ("dynamic film treatments"), selling concepts, developing concepts ("animated scripts"), and executing concepts ("rushes in context").

Yet lately we have begun to believe that the major impact of MAD may be in working with amateur authors, storytellers, filmmakers, and communicators. We anticipate children working on video scrapbooks and diaries, messages to parents and politicians, documentation of what and how they have learned, and statements about themselves and the world in which they live. They will then be able to write their creations to video tape, and, increasingly, be able to ship them as video mail over the Internet to friends, electronic penpals, and other children located elsewhere in the world.

We shall investigate in the next 2 years if students can go beyond the basic use of the tool to a more sophisticated discipline which involves the careful crafting of various media representations such as script or storyboard, which may involve collaborative work by multiple contributors bringing different skills to the endeavor, and which must involve thoughtful critiquing and iteration upon the result in order to produce the best possible product. If we can achieve this, we believe that tools such as MAD supported with reasonably straightforward learning materials can enable a powerful and compelling new classroom literacy for telling stories, exploring concepts, and expressing ideas.

ACKNOWLEDGMENTS

We are grateful for assistance to collaborators John Bertram, Diba Bot, Jason Chang, Alexandra Mazalek, Ferdie Poblete, Steve Poplar, Ilona Posner, Jesse Reiter, Patanjali Venkatacharya, and Vanessa Williams, and for past financial support to the CulTech Collaborative Research Centre, the Natural Sciences and Engineering Research Council of Canada, and the Information Technology Research Centre of Ontario, and now also the Networks of Centres of Excellence on Telelearning of Canada.

REFERENCES

1. Adobe Systems, 1994. Premiere 4.0, Mountain View, CA.

2. Adobe Systems, 1995. Persuasion 3.0, Mountain View, CA.

3. Apple Computer, Inc., 1993. *Inside Macintosh: QuickTime.* Addison-Wesley.

4. Avid Technology, Inc., 1993. *Media Composer Version 4.5.* Tewksbury, MA.

5. Baecker, R., Glass, G., Mitchell, A., and Posner, I., 1994. SASSE the Collaborative Editor. CHI '94 Video Proc., *ACM SIGGRAPH Video Review* 97.

6. Baecker, R., Nastos, D., Posner, I., and Mawby, K., 1993. The User-Centred Iterative Design of Collaborative Writing Software. *Proc. INTERCHI '93*, 399-405, 541.

7. Baecker, R., Posner, I., Jevans, I., Homer, B., Cohen, A., and Poplar, S., 1996. A Study of Children Learning to Create Motion Pictures, submitted for review.

8. BC Software, 1992. Final Draft Professional Screenwriting Software, Santa Monica, CA.

9. Cohen, A., Friedlander, N., Baecker, R., and Rosenthal, A. (1996, in press). MAD: A Movie Authoring and Design System — Making Classroom Process Visible. *Proceedings of ICLS 96 International Conference on the Learning Sciences.*

10. Davenport, G., Aguierre Smith, T., and Pincever, N., 1991. Cinematic Primitives for Multimedia. *Computer. Graphics & Applications* 11(4), 67-74.

11. Davis, M., 1995. Media Streams: An Iconic Visual Language for Video Representation. In Baecker, R.M., Grudin, J., Buxton, W., and Greenberg, S.,

Readings in Human Computer Interaction: Toward the Year 2000, Morgan Kaufmann, 854-866.

12. Delrina Corp., 1995. Echo Lake, Toronto, Canada.

13. Fredrickson, C. (1992). Presentation at the Cognitive Studies and Educational Program of the Annual Meeting of the McDonnell Foundation, Stanford, CA.

14. Friedlander, N., Baecker, R., Rosenthal, A., and Smith, E., 1996. MAD: A Movie Authoring and Design System. Demonstration at CHI'96.

15. Geissler, J., 1995. Surfing the Movie Space: Advanced Navigation in Movie-only Hypermedia. *Proc. ACM Multimedia 95,* 391-400.

16. Gidney E., Chandler, A., and McFarlane, G. 1994. CSCW for Film and TV Preproduction, *IEEE Multimedia* 1(2), Summer 1994, 16-26.

17. Halgren, S., Fernandes, T., and Thomas, D., 1995. Amazing Animation: Movie Making for Kids Design Briefing. *Proc. CHI '95,* 519-524.

18. Hardman, L., van Rossum, G., and Bulterman, R., 1993. Structured Multimedia Authoring. *Proc. ACM Multimedia 93,* 283-289.

19. Hardman, L. van Rossum, G., Jansen, J., and Mullender, S., 1994. CMIFed: A Transportable Hypermedia Authoring System. *Video Proc. ACM Multimedia 94.*

20. Hudson, S. and Hsi, C., 1994. The Walk-Through Approach to Authoring Multimedia Documents. *Proc. ACM Multimedia 94,* 173-180.

21. Katz, S., 1991. *Film Directing Shot by Shot: Visualizing from Concept to Screen.* Michael Wiese Productions, Studio City, CA.

22. Loy, G., 1985. Musicians Make a Standard: The MIDI Phenomenon. *Computer Music Journal* 9(4), 8-26.

23. MacroMedia, Inc., 1993. Director 3.1, San Francisco CA.

24. MacroMedia, Inc., 1995. Authorware 3.0, San Francisco CA.

25. Martin, J. and McClure, C., 1985. *Diagramming Techniques for Analysts and Programmers.* Prentice-Hall.

26. McGrath, J., 1995. Methodology Matters: Doing Research in the Behavioral and Social Sciences. In Baecker, R.M., Grudin, J., Buxton, W., and Greenberg, S., *Readings in Human Computer Interaction: Toward the Year 2000,* Morgan Kaufmann, 152-169.

27. Michael, A., L., Klee, T., Bransford, John D., Warren, Steven F. (1993). The Transition from Theory to Therapy: Test of Two Instructional Methods. *Applied Cognitive Psychology* 7, 139-154.

28. McKay. W. and Pagani, D., 1994. Video Mosaic: Laying Out Time in a Physical Space. *Proc. ACM Multimedia 94,* 165-172.

29. Mills, M. Cohen, J., and Wong , Y.Y. (1992). A Magnifier Tool for Video Data. *Proc. CHI '92,* 93-98.

30. Neuwirth, C.M., Kaufer, D.S., Chandhok, R., and Morris, J.H. Issues in the Design of Computer Support for Co-authoring and Commenting. *Proc. CSCW'90.* ACM, 183-195.

31. Pea, R., 1991. Learning through Multimedia. *Comp. Graphics and Applications* 11(4), 58-66.

32. Pierian Spring, 1994. Digital Chisel 1.2, Portland, Oregon.

33. PowerProduction Software, 1993. Storyboard Quick.

34. Price, B., Baecker, R., and Small, I., 1993. A Principled Taxonomy of Software Visualization. Journal of Visual Languages and Computing 4, 211-266.

35. Radius, 1996. QuickFLIX.

36. Rosenthal, A., 1995. Computer Support for Authoring Motion Pictures. M.Sc. Thesis, University of Toronto.

37. Rosenthal, A. and Baecker, R., 1994. Multimedia for Authoring Motion Pictures. *Proc. Graphics Interface '94,* 133-140.

38. Sanderson, P., Scott, J., Johnston, T., Mainzer, J., Watanabe, L., and James, J., 1994. MacSHAPA and the Enterprise of Exploratory Sequential Data Analysis (ESDA). *International Journal of Human-Computer Studies* 41(5), 633-681.

39. Ueda, H., Miyatake, T., Sumino, S., and Nagasaka, A., 1993. Automatic Structure Visualization for Video Editing. *Proc. INTERCHI '93,* 137-141.

40. Venkatacharya, P., 1995. Visualization and Collaboration in the Authoring of Motion Pictures. B.Sc. Thesis, University of Toronto.

41. Vertelney, L., 1989. Using Video to Prototype User Interfaces. In Baecker, R.M., Grudin, J., Buxton, W., and Greenberg, S., *Readings in Human Computer Interaction: Toward the Year 2000,* Morgan Kaufmann, 142-146.

42. Woolsey, K. Hooper, 1991. Multimedia Scouting. *Computer Graphics and Applications* 11(4), 26-38.

Author Index

Subject Index

About the Authors

PHILIPPE AIGRAIN heads the Software Technologies sector of the Technologies and Engineering for Software, Systems and Services unit of the European Commission Information Society Technologies R&D Programme. Trained as a mathematician and theoretical computer scientist, he holds a doctorate and the Habilitation à Diriger les Recherches from Universitè Paris 7. From 1972 to 1981, he worked in software engineering research labs of software companies. In 1982, Mr. Aigrain was a research fellow at University of California, Berkeley. Prior to joining the European Commission in 1996, he headed research teams in computer processing, indexing, retrieval and interaction for audiovisual media (video, music, and still images). He is the author of more than 60 technical papers, as well as papers on the economy and sociology of information exchanges.

DICK BULTERMAN is founder and CEO of Oratrix Development in Amsterdam, a company providing authoring solutions for streaming media on the Web. Prior to starting Oratrix, he was head of Multimedia and Human Computer Interaction at CWI, the Dutch national center for mathematics and computer science in Amsterdam. Mr. Bulterman's interests include authoring and operating system support for networked multimedia and providing for adaptive, accessible information regardless of location or physical situation/constraints of the user. He received his Ph.D. in computer science from Brown University and has held faculty appointments at Brown University, Delft University, and the University of Utrecht. He currently lives in Amsterdam with his wife and two children.

KEVIN JEFFAY is the S. Shepard Jones Professor of Computer Science at the University of North Carolina, Chapel Hill. He received his Ph.D. from the University of Washington in 1989. Professor Jeffay has published widely in the areas of multimedia networking, operating systems, and real-time systems

and currently serves as the editor-in-chief of the ACM/Springer-Verlag journal on multimedia systems. He was the program co-chair of ACM Multimedia '99 (with HongJiang Zhang), program chair of both NOSSDAV 2000 (the International Workshop on Network and Operating Systems Support for Digital Audio and Video), and the 2000 IEEE Real-Time Systems Symposium.

KETAN MAYER-PATEL is an assistant professor of computer science at the University of North Carolina, Chapel Hill. He received his Ph.D. in 1999 from the University of California, Berkeley. At U.C. Berkeley he wrote the widely used public domain MPEG-1 decoder "mpeg_play." His thesis work involved building a parallel software-only video effects processing system. Mr. Mayer-Patel's current research interests include multimedia systems, multicast applications, networking, and video compression. He is a member of IEEE and ACM and has serve on the program committees of ACM Multimedia, NOSSDAV, and Multimedia Computing and Networking.

Klara Nahrstedt is an assistant professor in the computer science department at the University of Illinois, Urbana-Champaign. Her research interests are directed towards reconfigurable multimedia services, multimedia protocols, multimedia security, middleware systems, quality of service (QoS) provision, QoS routing, and QoS-aware resource management in distributed multimedia systems. She coauthored the widely used multimedia book *Multimedia: Computing, Communications and Applications* published by Prentice Hall and received the Early NSF Career Award, the Junior Xerox Award, Lucent Award, and IEEE Communication Society Leonard Abraham Award for Research Achievements. In 1984 and 1985, Dr. Nahrstedt received her B.A. in mathematics and her M.Sc. in numerical analysis from Humboldt University, Berlin. She was a research scientist at the Institute for Informatik in Berlin until 1990. In 1995,

861

she received her Ph.D. in computer and information science from the University of Pennsylvania.

LAWRENCE A. ROWE is a professor of electrical engineering and computer science at the University of California, Berkeley. He received his Ph.D. from the University of California, Irvine, in 1976. Professor Rowe has published extensively in the areas of multimedia systems and applications, programming and database systems, and computer networks. His research group has produced many widely used software packages, including the Berkeley MPEG-1 Video Tools and the Open Mash Multimedia Toolkit. His current research interests include Internet webcasting, distributed collaboration, and educational technologies for teaching and learning. Professor Rowe is an ACM Fellow, chair of the ACM Special Interest Group on Multimedia, and a member of the editorial board of the *ACM/Springer Multimedia Systems Journal*. He has organized and chaired many conferences and served on numerous program committees. Professor Rowe was a cofounder of Ingres Corporation and served on the board of directors until the company was sold in 1990. He currently serves on the board of directors for iCAN Corporation, nCast Corporation, and Siemens Technology-to-Business Corporation.

PRASHANT SHENOY received his Ph.D. in computer sciences from the University of Texas, Austin, in 1998. He is currently an assistant professor in the Department of Computer Science at the University of Massachusetts, Amherst. His research interests are multimedia systems, operating systems, computer networks, and distributed systems. He has been a recipient of several awards including the National Science Foundation CAREER Award, IBM Faculty Partnership Award, and the Best Doctoral Dissertation Award from the Computer Sciences Department, University of Texas. He is a member of the ACM and the IEEE.

HARRICK VIN is an associate professor and Faculty Fellow of Computer Sciences, and director of the Distributed Multimedia Computing Laboratory at the University of Texas, Austin. His research interests are in the areas of multimedia systems, high-speed networking, mobile computing, and large-scale distributed systems. Professor Vin received his Ph.D. in computer science from University of California, San Diego, in 1993. He

has coauthored more than 75 papers in leading leading journals and conferences in the area of multimedia systems. He is currently an editor of *ACM Multimedia Systems* journal, *IEEE Transactions on Multimedia*, and *IEEE Multimedia* magazine. He has served as the program chair, the program co-chair, and a program committee member of several conferences (including the ACM Multimedia conference, the IEEE Multimedia Systems conference, and Multimedia Computing and Networking, among others). He has also been on several NSF panels as well as serving as a reviewer for numerous conferences and journals. Professor Vin has been a recipient of several awards, including the Faculty Fellow in Computer Sciences, Dean's Fellowship, IBM Austin CAS Fellow, National Science Foundation CAREER Award, IBM Faculty Development Award, AT&T Foundation Award, National Science Foundation Research Initiation Award, IBM Doctoral Fellowship, NCR Innovation Award, and San Diego Supercomputer Center Creative Computing Award.

BING ZENG is an associate professor at the Department of Electrical and Electronic Engineering of the Hong Kong University of Science and Technology (HKUST). In 1983 and 1986, he received his B.Eng. and M.Eng. in electrical engineering from the University of Electronic Science and Technology of China, Chengdu. In 1991, he received his Ph.D. in the same field from Tampere University of Technology in Finland. From 1991 to 1992, he worked as a postdoctoral fellow at the University of Toronto and Concordia University. He joined the Department of Electrical and Electronic Engineering of HKUST in January 1993. In 2000, he was on sabbatical at Microsoft Research, China. His research interests include digital signal and image processing, linear and nonlinear filter design, neural networks, and image/video coding and transmission. His most recent research focus is on arbitrarily shaped video coding and various solutions for real-time video streaming applications over Internet and wireless networks. Professor Zeng has published over 100 refereed papers in various journals and conference proceedings. He was an associate editor for the *IEEE Transactions on Circuits and Systems for Video Technology* from 1995 to 1999.

AIDONG ZHANG received her Ph.D. in computer

science from Purdue University in 1994. She is an associate professor in the Department of Computer Science and Engineering at State University of New York, Buffalo, where she has taught since 1994. Her research interests include content-based image retrieval, geographical information systems, distributed database systems, multimedia database systems, digital libraries, and data mining. She serves on the editorial boards of the *International Journal of Multimedia Tools and Applications*, *International Journal of Distributed and Parallel Databases*, and *ACM SIGMOD DiSC* (Digital Symposium Collection). She has also served on various conference program committees. Dr. Zhang is a recipient of the National Science Foundation CAREER Award.

HAO ZHANG received his master's degree from Harbin Shipping Engineering College in 1995, during which time he archived the research project on Chinese speech synthesis. In 1999, Dr. Zhang received his doctorate in electronic engineering from TsingHua University, China. As an assistant researcher in the university's microwave and digital communication key national laboratory, he worked extensively in digital signal processing and information source encoding. His thesis, in which he proposed the FWI and SELP algorithms, focused on high-quality, low-rate speech encoding, especially in wireless channels. He joined Microsoft Research, China, in 1999, where he works in the field of audio signal processing.

HONGJIANG ZHANG received his Ph.D. in electrical engineering from the Technical University of Denmark in 1991. From 1992 to 1995, he was with the Institute of Systems Science, National University of Singapore. He joined Hewlett-Packard Laboratories in October 1995 and was a research manager until he joined Microsoft Research, China, where he currently works in multimedia research as a senior researcher and assistant managing director. He has published over 150 peer-reviewed research papers and book chapters and is a coauthor of *Image and Video Processing in Multimedia Systems*, the first book addressing content-based image and video retrieval. He was the program co-chair for ACM Multimedia '99 and also served on committees of over 40 other conferences on multimedia and image processing. He is a member of editorial boards of four international journals and a senior member of IEEE and a member of ACM.